D1502375

Defense and Diplomacy

DEFENSE AND DIPLOMACY

THE SOLDIER AND THE

CONDUCT OF FOREIGN RELATIONS

by Alfred Vagts

KING'S CROWN PRESS, NEW YORK 1956

THE MEMORIAL LIBRARY
UNIVERSITY of DELAWARE

KING'S CROWN PRESS
is an imprint established by Columbia University Press for the purpose of making certain scholarly material available at minimum cost. Toward that end, the publishers have used standardized formats incorporating every reasonable economy that does not interfere with legibility. The author has assumed complete responsibility for editorial style and for proofreading.

341
V126d

Library of Congress Catalog Card Number: 56-11216

© Columbia University Press 1956

Published in Great Britain, Canada, India, and Pakistan
by Geoffrey Cumberlege, Oxford University Press
London, Toronto, Bombay, and Karachi

Manufactured in the United States of America

THE MEMORIAL LIBRARY
UNIVERSITY OF DELAWARE

11/22/57

Foreword

Defense and Diplomacy is the first of the "Topical Studies in International Relations" to be published. The series has been planned to show the contributions that the various social sciences can make to the systematic study of international relations. Dr. Grayson Kirk, now President of Columbia University, organized the series and invited experts in the various fields to prepare the individual studies.[1]

A grant by the Carnegie Corporation to Columbia University has made the Topical Studies series possible. Neither the Foundation nor the University, of course, assumes responsibility for the findings in this study by Dr. Alfred Vagts or in those that are to follow. The opinions expressed are those of the authors alone, and to them properly belongs the credit as well as the responsibility.

Among the fields of knowledge that can contribute greatly to the understanding of international relations is military history, and more particularly the history of military policy in its relation to foreign policy. Dr. Vagts' analysis of the soldier's role in the formulation and conduct of foreign relations is therefore eminently suited to introduce this new Topical Studies series. The present study, however, differs in certain respects from those that will follow. A word of explanation is necessary.

Military history, or at least certain aspects of it, as Dr. Vagts emphasizes in his preface (p. vii), was for so long neglected that a massive amount of spade work proved unavoidable. It was not possible simply to report on research already completed which would be of interest to students of international relations. The present work is therefore narrower in scope and greater in length than those dealing with less neglected fields.

Dr. Vagts has deliberately let his materials speak for themselves, and his conclusions remain largely implicit. Much of his illustrative material is drawn from the experience of Continental armed forces before World War I. This is natural, since archival materials for this earlier period are more accessible and the important memoirs all written. As a consequence, the "normal" civil-military relationship and the "normal" behavior of soldiers when working with politicians, diplomats, and other bureaucrats may appear to be the pre-1914 Continental pattern. Whether it is also the post-1914 Anglo-American, constitutional-democratic pattern will surely be a matter for debate; and the debate, one may hope, will prove a stimulus to the type of research that the Topical Studies program has been designed to encourage.

The original manuscript of Defense and Diplomacy was completed in 1952-53. It has been somewhat compressed in order to bring the materials within the limits of size dictated by 1955 publishing costs. Dr. Vagts' material on military attachés was particularly voluminous. To permit its later publication as a separate monograph, we reluctantly decided to omit these chapters almost in their entirety. In acceding to this major excision and to other less extensive bits of surgery on his manuscript, Dr. Vagts has been generous, patient, and sympathetic.

When President Kirk assumed major administrative responsibilities at Columbia—as Provost, Acting Head, and finally as President—he found it desirable to have a collaborator in the supervision of the Topical Studies series. I have worked with him in this capacity since 1951. I must emphasize, however, that the burden of detailed editing of this very large work has fallen on Dr. Kenneth N. Waltz, my colleague in the Institute of War and Peace Studies and Instructor in Government in Columbia College. It would have been easy to mistake the forest for the trees, but he has kept the whole in view throughout. Finally, Miss Lisa Hendrian of the Institute staff has called freely on her multiple skills in the social sciences and in foreign languages in preparing the final typescript for publication.

William T. R. Fox

Institute of War and Peace Studies
Columbia University
New York City
January 15, 1956

1. These are described in a research note by Grayson Kirk, "Materials for the Study of International Relations," World Politics, I (April, 1949), 426-430.

195126

Preface

War weariness and the preponderance of non-military interests among nineteenth-century Liberals resulted in a far-reaching neglect of military problems at the hands of historiography during large parts of the nineteenth and twentieth centuries. In many places the historiography of war slipped into official hands. This disregard approached an eclipse in the treatment accorded the vital boundary zones where diplomatic and military questions meet and interpenetrate. In this neglect of a highly problematical field "normative" political science went easily as far as, if not further than, descriptive historiography.

As though taking their mot d'ordre from above, these sciences merely followed the well-established lines of separation that the bureaucratic administrators—rather than the constitutions—of most Powers had themselves established. While this separatism looked like division of labor, it was only too often the outcome of a fierce, sometimes vicious, struggle for supremacy between civilian and military officials, a struggle presided over, sometimes effectually, sometimes feebly, by monarchs, presidents, commanders-in-chief, prime ministers, and other actual or supposed directors of national policy. They were, or were supposed to be, the radiating center of a polygon, its sides representing the several departments of government which often proved imperfectly joined, so that the impulses of governmental policy would only imperfectly circulate, throwing off instead the ominous or dangerous sparks of inter-departmental conflicts.

Much of the preparation and conduct of the wars between 1815 and 1918 suffered from this departmentalism. It was those "terrible simplifiers" and forceful coordinators, the totalitarian governors and makers of total wars who brought about a close, though not necessarily more efficient, unification of policies. In the contemplation and in the conduct of total war, military men had to learn of the inevitable connections between foreign policy and war, while the diplomat more than ever had to recognize the military implications of diplomacy. The exigencies of total wars forced a closer coordination upon the agencies of government and administration in non-totalitarian states as well. This reunion, while perhaps reminiscent of the close-knit arrangement of the absolute monarchs, was made infinitely more difficult by the complexities of modern problems, including the number of friends and ex-friends, foes and ex-foes, to be taken into consideration. Along with the size and intricacies of modern armaments and the ever wider extension of the open and hidden battle lines of total and "cold" wars went an increase in size and complication of the administration of foreign affairs, now more than at any other time since the downfall of the First Napoleon confronted by defense problems and their implications.

Since they started upon their separate establishments, diplomats and military men have frequently clashed. Their basic outlooks have only too often been antagonistic, even when both were members of the same "ruling class." Their views on whether, when, and how to undertake a war have differed many times, and most acutely over the question of undertaking a preventive war, an enterprise more often proposed from a military than from a diplomatic point of view. The usually temporary entrance of military personnel into diplomatic employment, often as ambassadors or service attachés,[1] created problems of subordination and competency, as did the various other appearances of armed forces personnel in the international sphere, such as on military missions. Many of the latter resulted in international incidents and many more gave occasion for disputes among the home authorities concerned.

Diplomatic history—including the "History of Diplomacy" produced by the Bolshevists[2]—and the more general literature of international relations have given these phenomena scant and on the whole unsystematic consideration. It has seemed imperative, therefore, to attempt a re-balancing of diplomatic and military historiography by providing, in historical outline, a description of the ties between diplomacy and strategy, between diplomats and military men and their offices, their ideas, problems and practices, their unity and disunity. The attempt at re-ballasting may easily produce an overemphasis of the oft-neglected military factors. One can, however, hope that instruction and information about these problems will aid in establishing new and more correct accents on some of the constituent elements of international relations.

A word in explanation of the organization adopted is perhaps necessary. It was found convenient to order the varied materials relevant to a study of Defense and Diplomacy according to a historically generalized

---

1. The author hopes to publish a separate monograph dealing with the service attachés, treating a subject too large for inclusion in the present work.
2. Histoire de la diplomatie. Publiée sous la direction de Vladimir Potiemkine. 3 vols. Paris, 1946-47.

war-peace cycle. The use of a cyclical pattern is not intended to imply the inevitability of its continuation but merely reflects the historical alternation of periods of war and periods of peace, a pattern distinct at times, as in the years following 1815, less so at others, as during the so-called Hundred Years' War, in the period 1792 to 1815, and again since 1945. Besides being a mechanical convenience, this scheme helps bring the roles of soldiers and diplomats into the context of the varying expectations of the states for which they labored and facilitates as well a weighing of the relative significance for the conduct of foreign and military policy of internal constitution and external situation.

Alfred Vagts

January, 1956

Table of Contents

Soldiers and Diplomats

Of all the conflicts among officials inside the ruling and administering circles, those between military and naval men on the one hand and diplomats on the other have been the most acute and the most significant. These conflicts and antagonisms are at least as old as specialization and professionalism in governing and warring. In fact, even before the professions of governing and fighting had fully emerged, the pen-wielders and the sword-bearers had begun to compete. Which was mightier, which more useful, which more honorable—the pen or the sword? For long periods of warfare it seemed sheer presumption to recall that the word could also do wonders in war, to remind anyone that even such a warrior-king as Pyrrhus, before he had conquered himself to death, admitted that "Cineas had taken more towns with his words than he with his arms."[1]

To the soldier and the sailor, the word was only given to command—as the word that allows no equivocation—and to speak the truth, if bluntly; to the diplomat, to hide his thought.[2] Soldiers and sailors take pride in their professional integrity and truthfulness, which they claim is altogether foreign to the diplomats.[3] The latter often discover that when they meet in the political sphere, the soldier or sailor will be found hiding his thoughts as often as they and their like, particularly when service interest seems to demand it.[4] Sometimes accused of mendacity, the soldier at other times has been accused of deficiency in the arts of dissimulation: an inability, for example, to conceal from the foreigner his own estimate of the situation where state policy deems it inadvisable that this information be divulged.[5]

Lying or not, both groups will compete for the ear and the favor of the final political authority in their countries, whether this final authority be the head of the state or the masses. Both groups are habitually at a considerable social distance from the latter, due to a double remoteness: they are aristoi and they are keepers of secrets which they share with the head of state as far as he cares or is able, in the midst of other concerns, to share them.[6] While the upper ranks of diplomacy and the armed forces have more or less ready access to the heads of the state, the latter have more often relied on intermediaries such as politicians, publicists, and other propagandists to influence the masses. However, even outside the American democracy, which somewhat unmercifully forces its military men and diplomats to orate though they may be plainly

ungifted for it, there have been speakers and writers who have presented their services' views directly to the people. Moltke, though he "knew how to be silent in seven languages," was nevertheless a member of the Reichstag after 1867, representing a district in which he did not have to go on the hustings. But the greatest publicist of them all was Alfred Thayer Mahan of the United States Navy.

In the traditions of Western and Westernized society, neither diplomats nor military officers have been eager friends of democratic institutions, and both have often shown very little appreciation of the potentiel de guerre which they may possess. They have tended to consider irksome and obnoxious the parliamentary bodies concerned with approving the declaration of war, with approving the budgets for the particular services, and with examining their organization and performance. They have, of course, been particularly opposed to publicists and others eager to extend their control or condominium over secret diplomacy and armaments. Against such attempts at democratic control, which were nowhere completely successful, there was a strong common interest to be defended by both diplomats and military officers. Thus in 1869, Bismark, acting as their common spokesman, told the Reichstag:

> In Prussia, the Army would never tolerate for long being commanded from a scribe's room or from a hall of discussion. The necessary discipline and Prussian tradition are opposed to being dependent in any truly military manner on anyone but the warlord. Military organization, Army strength and its composition cannot be discussed in Parliament and cannot be made dependent on its favor. The resolutions of the Government in this matter, besides, derive more or less from foreign policy which is more or less a closed book to them and from the knowledge which the Government has about the political plans and the military measures of foreign States which are not communicable [to Parliament].[7]

CONFLICTING HONOR CONCEPTS

In their claim to being the world's oldest male profession, the military, as knights and the heirs of knighthood, have expressed through the ages the demand to be recognized as the most honorable of all estates. The warrior is inclined to identify his concept of honor with the honor of the state and to rank it, in the extreme case,

even above the national interest.[8] At first
sight, the military concept of honor seems to involve considerable self-negation, but, upon
closer inspection, this concept of honor will
often be found to cover a conservatism reluctant to participate in technological and other
progress, or it may reveal itself as the sacred egotism of an estate loath to have the underlying national interest examined to determine whether
or not the version of honor and interest provided
by the service coincides with broader interpre-
tations of the requirements of national interest.
Thus, while the Reichstag was sold on the famous
"Risiko" theory of the new German navy, the
German diplomats were not. The navy argued, to
use the words of the Naval Bill of 1900, that what
Germany wanted was not "a peace at any price but
a peace with honor taking care of our justified
needs."[9]

The true diplomat, though far more reluctant
to pronounce the word "honor" in negotiation,
serves the best interest of his country, including
its security, while trying at the same time to
preserve its honor in peace treaties, and in other
treaties. "Peace with honor" is demanded of him
and his work, though many if not most treaties
have been declared dishonorable by at least some
protesting individual or group, and though some
may have sacrificed honor for more material state
reasoning.[10] His experiences with those who
clamor for honor, the warriors in particular and,
more recently, the masses, have made many a
diplomat cynical. This is expressed in Comines'
statement: "He who has success has honor," and
in Talleyrand's: "Honor in our age of corruption
has been invented in order to make vanity do the
work of virtue."[11] It may be disagreeable for
the diplomat to advise the soldier, on grounds
of prudence, not to stress the point of honor; but
if he is possessed of any courage, he will do it.
"Rather pocket three more slaps in the face than
march before you are ready," the Saxon diplomat
Count Beust advised an Austrian general before
the war of 1866.[12]

While the diplomat will endeavor to save his
country's interests even if "full honor" cannot
be salvaged,[13] the military extremist will
proclaim his readiness to defend his country's
honor even if the national interest would obviously
suffer thereby.[14] In the defense of honor he is
willing to lay down his life, a readiness, genuine
or not, on which he greatly prides himself. It is
the sword-bearer's instinctive reaction that has
involved him in so many international incidents
and the diplomat's reluctance to invoke the national honor that has kept him out of such.[15]
In the final balance, if it were possible to strike
it, it would appear that the national interest has
suffered from the emphasis on honor more often

than national honor has suffered from the safeguarding of the national interest. Expressed in
different words, there have been fewer soldiers
(or sailors) with diplomatic talent than occasion
has called for. One sound argument against the
employment of more military men in purely diplomatic posts has been their readiness, if not
eagerness, to see their own and their country's
honor involved on the slightest provocation.

Not a little of the claim to greater honor by the
soldier is founded on the greater dangers that he
goes through in the exercise of his profession.
"A scar nobly got is a good livery of honor"
(Shakespeare). Had not the men of courage shown
fearlessness and bled and died on the battlefields
while the diplomats were sitting safely at home
or far behind the battle lines? Such sacrifices
should entitle them to fight and finish the war as
they see fit and then be heard at the peace conference. At least by the age of general conscription that claim had become fairly hollow. Courage
on the battlefield was now very common, while by
comparison civilian courage, the kind of courage
needed to oppose and brave the military in matters of state policy, was far too often lacking.[16]
This was particularly true in Germany, as Bismarck remarked at the outset of his political
career. The medieval-minded warrior might not
care how many enemies his country had, or made,
if honor forced him to incur hostility. "Many
enemies, much honor" might be his motto or,
still worse "the more enemies, the more honor."
For the diplomat, "the more enemies, the less
honor" is the maxim; the more friends he can
make for his country, the more glory he gets, and
the better it is for his country and its security.

Courage apart, who was better suited to settle
the fate of nations, diplomats or soldiers? Who
should decide when war ought to be made or when
it ought to be avoided, or at least postponed? Who
should decide to what lengths it ought to be carried and what the terms of the peace should
be?[17] Who was more ignorant as to the conditions and difficulties under which the other had
to labor? Who, in the age of specialization, has
been more able or ready to pass judgment on or
assume the other's business?[18] Who has fared
better by the judgment of historiography?[19]
Or, differently put, whose task has been the more
rewarding one?[20] Who was to rank higher at
courts and in society generally?[21] More often
than not the soldier was considered "the first
man in the whole State."[22]

GENERAL RECRIMINATIONS

Mutual low opinions were formed, from experience or prejudice, and pronounced: one side
maintains that the other is trespassing upon its

field. Diplomats say that soldiers and sailors are endangering the peace; soldiers and sailors, that diplomats are endangering victory; diplomats may point out to soldiers that, in spite of their assurances, they are unable to win the war undertaken on their promise of victory; soldiers maintain that diplomats overlook their timely warnings against dangerous hostile armaments and cause the government to neglect armaments when they are necessary; soldiers maintain, moreover, that diplomats are usually ready to sign away what arms have won in the field, and are inclined to interfere with the conduct of wars that ought to be pursued in accordance with the rules of strategy.

The diplomats demand, or at least wish, that the soldier and sailor not endanger peace by warlike acts and gestures; the soldier often regrets that the diplomats are so exclusively concerned with preserving the peace. Thus, after he had lost the Marne battle in 1914, the younger Moltke sighed:

It would have been better for us if in more recent years we had looked the coming event, war...firmly in the eye, and had prepared ourselves for it, in the diplomatic way as well. The highest art of diplomacy in my opinion does not consist in preserving the peace under all circumstances but in shaping the political situation of the State continually in such a manner that it is in a position to enter the war under favorable circumstances. That is the undying glory of Bismarck before the wars of 1866 and 1870.[23]

A soldier is not easily inclined to repent or even to remember the relevant circumstances: Moltke neither recalled that undying glory had crowned his uncle because his plans had suited Bismarck's policies, nor that the plans of his own General Staff had exercised a dictatorship over German policy in the last days of peace because policy and strategy preparation had gone their separate ways in the Reich, ever since the dismissal of Bismarck and Caprivi, nor that he had failed to make use of the power that his office of director of the senior service gave him by demanding that the vast expenditure for naval purposes be applied to the army instead.

The younger Moltke's complaints and oversights point to intra-departmental conflict, which becomes triangular in nature in the age of air power.[24] Which branch of the armed services was typically or from time to time closer to its country's diplomacy—army, navy or air force? Or did the forces prefer to form a common front against the diplomats? Who best understood and appreciated diplomatic considerations most readily? In addition, one might ask: Which of the various services was favored by the diplomats?

While in Japan there may have been a definite long-lasting affinity between foreign office and navy, no over-all answer can or should be given. A triangular opposition between army, navy and foreign office was most obvious in the final stages of the Second Reich. The Wilhelmstrasse found no reason to favor the big Tirpitz Navy, which would give Germany at least one and perhaps two additional enemies, Great Britain and the United States. The Army, however, never officially sought to use foreign office backing against the Navy, perhaps because, as Tirpitz could justly maintain, the demands of the Navy had never stood in the way of Army requests for funds in the Reichstag. Never did the self-satisfied Army veto the Navy's demands. Instead, when occasion so demanded, it stood in a common front with Tirpitz against the Wilhelmstrasse in a struggle over which William II presided more as supreme warlord than ever on a battlefield.[25] And only in September 1914 did Falkenhayn, Moltke's successor, tell Tirpitz to his face: "If we did not have the Navy, we would have had two extra Army Corps and would not have lost the Marne battle."[26]

Throughout history another set of mutual recriminations has revolved around the preventive war doctrine. Military men, convinced that war is inevitable in the long run, have on occasion urged that it be started at the moment that will maximize the chances of victory. The diplomat is inclined to reply that the promising war advocated by the military will almost inevitably lead to an incalculable general war. The military will countercomplain that they will eventually be invited or forced to fight when their forces are no longer ready or have lost their comparative advantage. Politicos are apt to forget, the soldiers will complain, that forces for modern war cannot be improvised, that they must be built up over periods of years. As Conrad argued with the Austrian minister in 1907, when he, and not they, wanted preventive war: "Treaties can be concluded overnight; but an Army ready to strike needs years for its formation; it cannot be improvised on the first day of mobilization; its development must therefore never be allowed to be disturbed by diplomatic considerations."[27] Proposals of preventive war by military officials have not been restricted to semi-absolutist Powers such as Austria-Hungary. Even in the French Republic, the General Staff suggested to the Government toward the end of 1912, when the diplomatic situation appeared highly critical, that France proceed to a bold offensive, for technical reasons, without waiting for that declaration of war which constitutionally required the Chamber's approval.[28]

Soldiers are inclined to believe that war, at

least war rightly exploited, will produce a "decision," to the same degree that battle—leaving
the many indecisive battles aside—is decisive;
that once war is won, the victor can unilaterally
proceed to such settlements as "unconditional
surrender."[29] When the politician or the diplomat is not carried away by war and victory sentiment, he will think of peace by agreement, a
peace that may be more lasting, the more it is
based on agreement. "The soldier thinks in decisions, the politician in developments. The latter
is considered by the other as a weakling looking
for compromises, while conversely the soldier, in
the eyes of the other, is merely an unintellectual
gallant blade. They live in two worlds."[30]

Neither side has understood or appreciated the
other profession's principles, tasks, and methods
very fully, and, even where they seem to have
understood, they have been unable or unwilling to
formulate the basic differences. It was a rare
practitioner, such as Ambassador Paul Cambon,
who, long after his own violent run-in with one of
the most dangerous political generals, Boulanger,
endeavored to formulate them. We can do no better than to conclude this introduction by quoting
from Cambon's correspondence the section that
begins with his appraisal of Talleyrand as

> blessed with the prompt and sure coup d'oeil
> which discerns amidst the most difficult cir-
> cumstances the position to take, as one who
> knows, after having taken it, how to let it oper-
> ate while waiting for the consequences with
> composure.
>
> That...is the whole art of diplomacy. I know
> very well that it is not given to everyone to
> have that coup d'oeil. Many of those with whom
> we have been associated at the Quai d'Orsay
> were absolutely devoid of it; but one also
> knows of men who, though provided with the
> coup d'oeil, good sense and intelligence do not
> know how to allow the force of things to oper-
> ate by itself once a position has been taken.
> They become restless, they want to acceler-
> ate events, they discount the success and they
> spoil their business.
>
> This denotes the profound difference between
> the qualities necessary for a diplomat and for
> a military man. The military man is in need
> of promptitude and precision, of the glance
> necessary to discern the dominant position,
> but once in that position, it is rare that he can
> allow events to operate by themselves. Most
> often he must act, and act quickly. Or else
> a general is nothing but a professor of a mil-
> itary school, inadequate on the battlefield.[31]

A Short History of Diplomatic-Military Conflict Since Absolutism

A rapid sketch of the historical relations of
diplomats and soldiers, a subject never yet
treated in detail, may serve to highlight their
disagreements (at the risk of overstating their
conflicts rather than their understandings).

The rationalist monarchy of the age of Absolutism was at its best when dealing with problems of
administration. One such problem was how to
clarify the division of labor between soldiers and
sailors and civilians. The importance of this
problem was recognized during the last third of
the seventeenth century, dating roughly from the
death of Mazarin and the assumption of government by Louis XIV (1661). The relentless, cruel
rationality of bourgeois principles of administration was introduced into army affairs by Louvois.
As adviser to the King he won out over such generals as the Maréchal de Luxembourg or Turenne,
who used to say he had more dangerous enemies
at home than among the Austrian generals.[32]
Louvois, winning out over the proposals of diplomats and generals alike, created the first big
standing army and largely determined how it
should be used. Such frightfulness as the devastation of the Palatinate in 1689 was a measure of
warfare which for tactical reasons he did not
recommend, but which he undertook with the intention of destroying forever the war potential of
the enemy. Louvois displayed to the world a combination of diplomacy and warfare as directed
from the office of the war minister.[33] Others
found his rationality too frightful and inhumane,
and, in the end, France herself found it too expensive; for, as the continual aggressor, she
found herself isolated. What remained forever
after was the standing army, the brain-child of
the new Rationalism, the instrument, if not always of the most pliable nature, of policy and
diplomacy, and also the nourisher of the impoverished nobility.

Most of the monarchs of Absolutism preferred
to be or behave as soldier-kings, which meant,
among other things, a readiness to put the diplomats in their decidedly lower place. Before he
had seen much of war and before he had made
any himself, Frederick II told his department of
foreign affairs that "when the civilian ministers
reason about negotiations, they are capable people; but when they speak of war, that is like having an Iroquois talk of astronomy."[34] In the
same way, Napoleon I and his marshals and generals were full of militaristic contempt for the
civilians, and especially for the diplomats. Only

rarely were the latter able to strike back at their detractors, for to do so required the talents of a Talleyrand. The latter had once invited General Dersenne Le Paige, commander of the Foot Grenadiers of the Guards, to dinner. The General was late and excused himself rather cavalierly: he had been detained by a damned pékin. "General," asked the Prince, "may I ask you what a pékin is?" — "We are in the habit of calling pékin all that is not military." — "Very good, that. Just as we call military all that is not civil."[35]

The powerful position of the military in the affairs of Prussia, a state which the military believed had been built by the sword alone, could not have been more drastically demonstrated than by the doings of the half-mad Field Marshal Blücher during the Wars of Liberation, who, incidentally, expressed his scorn for the diplomats as pen-pushers by using the most atrocious spelling. When in the early spring of 1813 Prussia's break with Napoleon was being prepared with due caution, he wrote to Scharnhorst:

> I cannot sit quiet all the while and keep my mouth shut when the fatherland and liberation are concerned. Let the lousy and...pack of diplomats go to all the devils. Why should not everyone mount and start against the French like holy thunder? Those who propose to the King to still hesitate and keep peace with Bonaparte are traitors to him and the whole German fatherland and deserve to be shot to death.[36]

And when the Allies halted along the Rhine at the end of 1813 in the hope of coming to peace terms with Napoleon, the Prussian generals grumbled and cursed: this halt would allow the Emperor to regain his strength. The allied diplomats countered with remarks on the Prussians' mad and drunken race for Paris, in which they exposed themselves to an occasional lick by the paw of Napoleon. "Blücher, by no means chastened by the lesson of Brienne," Metternich wrote to one of his lieutenants in Vienna,

> has thrown himself forward towards Paris... Providence, incidentally, has never given a better hint than it did a fortnight ago [at Brienne] that only reason and straight sense, far above prejudice and passion, make one suited for victory. Blücher and all the brave fools will fall into desuetude and our bold courageous resolutions, our sobriety, will appear in a light without arguments which shall persuade even the maddest of our age — only complete fools excepted — that we [the diplomats] are right in war and in peace.[37]

Napoleon's return from Elba, however, only proved to the soldiers how poor the peace was that the diplomats were making at Vienna. "If only you gentlemen of the pen would once get under a really sharp fire in order to learn what it means to repair your mistakes," Blücher said to the Prussian Premier.[38]

Knowing well his popularity not only at home but in England, Blücher at one point considered resigning with éclat from the Prussian supreme command in order to demonstrate that he had no intention "to submit outright to the despotism of the diplomats."[39] Not only the foreign and allied diplomats were horrified at Blücher's insubordination; Prussia's own diplomats shared the horror about the army's presumptions, which put a continuous strain on the country's limited resources. Even the foremost statesman of the Prussian Reform, Baron von Stein, complained after the close of the Wars of Liberation (when there was "not at present anything to fear from France"), that Prussia had "an army much too numerous and expensive" and "a precious General Staff, a club of military metaphysicians who cannot see the forest for the trees."[40]

The struggle for supremacy between civilians and soldiers continued endlessly in Prussia. Prime Minister Hardenberg confessed to a British diplomat in Paris in November 1815 that he felt as if surrounded by Pretorian bands when he was forced to tell Blücher that it was he alone who would judge the political situation and that the Field Marshal might now leave France for home. Before Blücher departed, the ambitious military "Reformers" made him write to King Frederick William "in the Army's interest" about the soldiers' disagreeable relations with the always undecided diplomats. These relations, he wrote, made him "feel deeply how sad and disadvantageous it is to be dependent on Prime Ministers and how destructive it would be for the Army if this influence should continue and Your Majesty not retain the supreme command in the future."[41] Until the end of the monarchy there was constant struggle between soldiers and civilian governors in Prussia for the soul of the supreme warlord, a struggle that gave Prussia a reputation of being caught in the clutches of what later came to be called militarism.[42]

Conflicts between soldiers and diplomats continued in many places throughout the century that began in 1815, sometimes conducted behind the scenes so as not to endanger the façade of the governing set-up, sometimes conducted more openly when one or both sides endeavored to win over public opinion. Again in Prussia and, later, in Germany, these conflicts took a clear and notable form. His background and political convictions made Bismarck, "the greatest of all Junkers" (Max Weber), forever a "friend of the Army." This did not save him, early or late in his career, from numerous and quite bitter conflicts with the military: with "honest but thickheaded adjutant generals" and their traditionally great influence at the Prussian court, [43] with Army commanders who like Wrangel would advise the King that diplomats who interfered with the conduct of the war deserved the gallows, with military plenipotentiaries and attachés, and finally with the new "demi-gods," the engineers of Prussian victories from 1864 to 1871, the Great General Staff, originally an experts' office which now raised political claims on the strength of the always easily convertible credit of military success.[44] Bismarck's conflicts with them were most acute at the beginning and end of his diplomatic career. At the Bundestag in Frankfurt, he had to battle not only with Austrian diplomacy but also, and not quite successfully, with the military plenipotentiary of his own government.[45] Towards the end of his chancellorship, officers of the General Staff were most active among those who endangered the peace he wanted to keep.[46] In the end it was they who pulled him out of the saddle.

In the defense of peace Bismarck moved on various occasions into a supra-national front with foreign, even enemy, diplomats against the peace-endangering soldiers. When a new seven-year Army budget was being prepared in Berlin early in 1880, he agreed with the French ambassador's fear that Moltke might go too far in his speeches and "evoke the war of revanche and the French peril." He promised to make a pressing appeal to Moltke's prudence "and ask him to restrict himself as far as possible to the technical, purely military side of the project and look less in the direction of the Vosges and rather more in that of the Vistula, if he thinks it necessary to touch on the chapter of foreign perils." Apparently Bismarck's appeals to Moltke's prudence were fairly effective.[47] In dealing with an ally, Bismarck's understandings with foreign diplomats naturally went still further. Thus Bismarck assured Kalnoky during a war panic that "we have no military party, at the most only individual officers who must speak on occasion of their readiness for war," as they did in most other countries as well. But, he added, they have no influence on general policy—if they did have, "all large European countries would constantly stand close to war, for the majority of military men everywhere love to rattle the sabre, even if they often do so in the certainty that the peace will not be broken."[48]

Publicly, Bismarck had remained on good terms with the generals from Moltke down, saying at one time in the Reichstag, while pointing in the Field Marshal's direction: "There sits the gentleman to whom we owe German unity, next to His Majesty the Emperor, not to me. Without the Army, no Germany; neither could it have been created nor can it be preserved."[49] However, Waldersee noted in 1889, "the world does not suspect how little the two men harmonized."[50] The world, least of all the German people, knew little of the meaning of the grinding noises which the rouages du gouvernement produced occasionally in Berlin; they were rare enough, not because the gears meshed smoothly but because they did not mesh at all—"the Army henceforth proceeded along its own way."[51]

Then William II was moved into Bismarck's stead by a parallelogram of forces in which the military predominated. His gesticulating, often under military prompting, soon made Bismarck say ruefully: "I have helped the monarchical rider into the saddle; perhaps, in the heat of battle, my assistance has been too lively."[52] The position that Bismarck had given the Emperor-King, enabling him to exercise his "personal regiment," was used by the military for their own ends, not merely for continued armaments, which Bismarck himself would not have minded, but also for the militarization of the restless mind of William II. After Waldersee had left Berlin, the military influences upon the monarch became those of a whole entourage of officers who turned their low joking against the diplomats:

The King of Prussia must put an end to the trading of these pen-pushers, pedants of formality who have forgotten what an order from the King is. These people who confuse and distract the simplest things must be commanded from the saddle. A simple military order, a clear, indubitable word brings order as quickly even into so-called diplomatic difficulties as does the order to a squadron on the Bornstedt training ground near Potsdam.

By 1894, William II had acquired the habit "of making policy with everyone and his aunt," as the Wilhelmstrasse people sighed, something not always compatible with the orderly conduct of business. Only occasionally could the standpoint of Chancellor Hohenlohe or the Wilhelmstrasse be presented and made acceptable, and then only by a diplomat like Eulenburg, who was also the scion of an old Prussian family and who had at one time been an officer of the Guards. Germany's foreign affairs became "the battlefield of bitter struggles between the Foreign Office on the one hand and the high military offices on the other," not to mention the Kaiser's private diplomacy from sovereign to sovereign, "and thus came about inevitably the circumstances that made the Prussian Army a political factor." And, continued Eulenburg, "it also came to pass, logically, that, considering the faulty education for and experience in political activity, the best Army pursued the worst policy."[53]

The Wilhelmstrasse diplomats, with Holstein as their hidden spokesman, if his paradoxical position might be thus described, lost out in their attempt to restore civilian control and orderly "parliamentary-bureaucratic concepts" of government. They remained in the nadir of influence and respect with him while army and, increasingly, naval officers filled the imperial mind with notions as to the superiority of military men in all possible offices, whether inside the Reich or abroad. Thus William let it be known that he would prefer an admiral as director of Russian foreign affairs, rather than "a stinking bureaucrat and inkslinger out of a chancellory" like Lamsdorff. At least an admiral would know to what extent it was useful, or imperative, for Russia to be on good or on bad terms with Germany for military reasons.[54] Bülow, the man of the Kaiser's own generation, as Secretary of State and Chancellor, sided with "Old Prussian royalism" (as he said to his friend Eulenburg) which, because it had the strongest battalions, would be strongest also in home affairs.[55] Even so, he attracted and bore the contempt of the generals and admirals for a long time, until he bowed out before the power of Tirpitz. The latter, together with his attachés, fought the "unmanly" diplomats.[56] They were to have no other tasks than to persuade the British that the German Navy was not directed against them, although its creator had actually expressed the hope that it would some day outstrip the British Navy.[57] Bülow bowed as well before the power of generals like von Einem or that type of military primitive in politics represented by Hindenburg who authorized the ghost-writers of his memoirs to confess his "dislike of everything diplomatic...."[58]

There has been no change in sentiment on the soldier's part, only a progress in spelling since Blücher's day; and on the side of the diplomats, the same bitterness. "I am an opponent of Tirpitz," wrote Secretary of State Kiderlen in February 1912, in a private letter, "because I fear that his policy will bring us into war with England. I think he is the greatest swine that Berlin pavement supports."[59] Under military influence German diplomats could neither be nor appear as peaceful as they would have liked. They were captives, rather than directors, of a system. Their only consoling thought was that Germany's armed forces might procure victory in the war they were unable to avert. Only when defeat, instead of the oft-promised and long-expected victory, stared

them in the face did they realize that the strategists of the Königsplatz had not only thought exclusively in divisions and cannons but had also thought wrongly in these terms. Defeat demonstrated to German diplomats not only the purely military errors of a "miserable general" like Ludendorff who had "taken it upon himself to direct our policies" during the war, but also that this general was "in point of character a canaille of the worst kind, intriguing and despotic; an excellent organizer in the military field, mediocre as strategist, a zero on the political terrain. And this blackguard was our dictator!"[60]

So far as modern monarchs have had any free choice left, they have been attracted more by military than by civil institutions, not only because of the anti-revolutionary support that bayonets can give but also because military successes can give the crown more glory than almost any success in the diplomatic field.[61] Only Austria's defeats of 1859 and 1866, largely due to military advice, inclined Francis Joseph towards civilian-diplomatic rather than military counsel, at least until Aehrenthal's death in 1912. Under the pressure of the Pan-Slav front of the military and the bourgeoisie, the last Tsar sided most often with military advisers and shared their outlook and judgments, especially on diplomacy and diplomats. To the last, Nicholas II "always mistrusted politicians and diplomats generally speaking." In the Russian GHQ in 1916, the Chief of Staff told a British liaison officer in the Tsar's presence that the diplomats "might, perhaps, be allowed to have a say when the enemy was vanquished." The Tsar commented: "They must not be allowed to draw up the terms of peace, as then it would be 'sure to be a bad peace.'"[62]

While the Tsar was completely the prisoner of the Stavka, in spite of the prolonged series of Russian defeats, the diplomatic bureau with the field army was as if emancipated by the absence of victory. Presuming on his "grand seigneurial" rank in the nobility and on the failure of the military to deliver victory, Prince Kudashev, the head of this office, applied civilian courage and criticism to the strategy of the Stavka in his reports to the Foreign Ministry.

While similar conflicts and recriminations, often even more intense, were common in the Russian and Austro-Hungarian Empires, the societal and governmental structure of the Western Powers produced far fewer conflicts between diplomats and military officers. Although conflict occurred, civilian power and civilian arguments remained in the ascendency, although this result was not obtained in France without the Boulanger and Dreyfus crises and in Britain without the Curragh mutiny of 1914 when Henry Wilson "engineered an attempt at a military overlordship."[63] Grey, during the

July-August 1914 crisis, "did not overlook," as he admitted to the German Ambassador, "the difficulty of keeping the military on either side in inactivity," among whom would have to be included Henry Wilson.[64]

The French governors before 1914 could not consider their country fully ready for war until the violent civilian-military clashes had been ended. At home, civilian prefects and commanding generals had often come into conflict; abroad, conflict was centered in regions undergoing French penetration by the "cooperation" of civilian administrators and military power, as in Tunis and Morocco. Thus while Minister-Resident Paul Cambon was installing the French protectorate in Tunis (1882-86), he clashed violently with the commander of the French occupation forces, General Boulanger, who disregarded orders from Paris to consider Cambon his superior.[65] Until the fall of Jules Ferry in 1885, civilian supremacy had been respected by the General; but following that crucial change of government, and almost of governing principles, he took the military part of the occupation into his own hands and instructed the troops under his command to make use of arms should foreigners—which meant Italians—become offensive. Various foreign governments protested against these outrageous orders which, as it seemed to Cambon, threatened to interfere with peaceful and undisturbed pénétration. Both Cambon and Boulanger traveled to Paris to obtain from cowardly politicians and officials the removal of the other. Instead, both were catapulted upward towards higher echelons in the service of France. Though Cambon came off with the "greater honors," French politicians and the nation generally emerged from the clash without taking due notice of Boulanger's mischief-making powers.

There have been moments since that time when the military element has been resentful and has grumbled at the domination of the "frocks," as at some of the immediate post-war conferences. Though the "frocks" thought they had done good work at the San Remo conference of 1920, "we soldiers," Henry Wilson said, considered them "all rotters. Nothing is decided...." When, on a later occasion, the British Cabinet turned down some military advice, Wilson called them "a miserable crowd. My contempt for their brains, knowledge, pluck, and character deepens every day. They will ruin England and the Empire." And, standing before the London Cenotaph on a ceremonial occasion, when some other thought might well have been entertained, Wilson was pleased to hear Pershing whispering to him: "This is my first happy moment. No frocks here."[66]

Like most other diplomatic conferences, the Paris Peace Conference meant a lowering of the exalted war-time position of the military commanders and staffs. But unlike former peace conferences, Paris called upon the military as "experts." How much good they did will in all probability remain controversial. They proffered advice, and they were prepared to back it up with pressure tactics. At one time, Foch, buoyed up by the Khaki election sentiment in France and Britain, threatened to resign ostentatiously in protest against the civilians' dictate, as Blücher had done in 1815. But generals are almost as loath as politicians to resign. Foch, even if with a wry face, swallowed it when Woodrow Wilson asked him "affectionately" on one occasion "to act more as a diplomat than as soldier," or when Lloyd George declared that some of Foch's political directives for the French Army on the Rhine were confounding policy and strategy.[67]

The peace the civilians made with the soldiers' help at Paris provided the latter with enough insurance against unemployment, as was realized by some at the time. "Be without uneasiness as regards your military career," Clemenceau told French soldiers in July 1919, "the peace we have made guarantees you ten years of conflict in Central Europe." And Pétain consoled them: "You will still have occasion to fire your cannon."[68]

CONCLUSION

The long-continued conflict between soldiers and diplomats has been one of professions and competing ethos, rather than a product of competition for office among different social strata. This has been particularly true in Europe and Japan. Conflict became irrepressible in various places despite the essential homogeneity of the social origin of diplomatic and officer bodies, though there was nearly everywhere a more plutocratic element among the former. During the larger parts of their history both parties were conservative, the diplomats favoring conservation through peace and peace-making, the soldiers through war and war-making; the former believing that territorial and other gains for their countries, if necessary at all, could be made by negotiations; the latter, that for such purposes war, long and constantly prepared, was indispensable and in the final resort profitable and in the best national interest. As individuals, diplomats seek their triumphs through peace-keeping and peace-making, soldiers through martial deeds in war.[69]

When the Schlieffen Plan was conceived, however, the military already realized that war might no longer be conservative. That plan was based on the most undiplomatic opening of the war in order to make a quick victory possible, for a short war was the only kind of conserving war left. After that war, a war much different from the one the military had planned, the historical conflict of the diplomatic and the military outlook assumed new acuteness. And this result derived from a number of factors: (1) through the rising influence of younger officer-politicos who either deposed the traditional gerontocracy of higher rank or used them for their own, largely imperialist, purposes [70]; (2) through the admission of new, rawer strata to the officer corps of the armed forces, notably in Japan, in Germany and, less observably, in Soviet Russia; (3) through the appearance of the Soviet system on the international scene, a system whose directors consider that a state of war with the capitalist world underlies all relations and who denied, except in tactical terms, the possibility or advisability of the peaceful co-existence of the two systems.

Since our object in the present chapter is to provide a perspective for recent history rather than a summary of it, our search for examples of military-diplomatic conflicts can appropriately end on the threshold of this new era.

FOOTNOTES

1. Plutarch, Pyrrhus.
2. During the French expedition to Syria in 1860, General Ducrot wrote that the British Ambassador Lord Dufferin supports Fuad Pasha "hotly and maintains principles completely opposite to those he had stated to me. That does not surprise me, the word being given to the diplomat in order to hide his thought." Ducrot, Vie militaire, p. 432.
3. When General von Stosch served under Field Marshal E. H. von Manteuffel, a court general often used on diplomatic missions, he found him "even relatively truthful, though through and through a diplomat." Stosch, Denkwürdigkeiten, p. 256.
4. From their discussions of the Reichswehr budget with the officers, the Reich Ministry of Finance officials drew the sad conclusion that "the Navy is always lying, and the Army speaks the truth but rarely." Trials of War Criminals, XII, 560.
5. In February 1908, the Russian War Minister told the German military plenipotentiary that Turkish armaments and her challenging attitude could only be explained by German backing, something the Germans could justly deny. Isvolski told the German ambassador that he had reproached his colleague, whose statements were not those of the government, for using such language, but that the latter had answered:

"What do you want? I am no diplomat. As a soldier I have said what I think...." G. P., XXV, 8723, 8730.
6. One of the tricks used by Waldersee and his friends in their endeavor to undermine Bismarck's position with William II was to accuse him of having withheld some consular reports about Russian armaments from the Kaiser, who considered them important and new when actually they were neither. Ibid., VI, 1360 ff.
7. Bismarck, Gesammelte Werke, VII, 294.
8. "In Gneisenau's memoranda [during Prussia's Reform period] this [idea of national honor] often assumes a specifically military shading, that is to say, it appears as the naïve transference of the particular estate honor of the Prussian officer to the field of grand policy where it does not belong because the power competition of the nations cannot be regulated along the lines of chivalric duelling." Ritter, "Gneisenau und die deutsche Freiheitsidee," Lebendige Vergangenheit, p. 202.
9. Scheer, Vom Segelschiff zum U-Boot, p. 216. Against this stressing of the point d'honneur Count Wolff-Metternich asked, as the diplomat: "What was there that was humiliating in our relations with Britain at the time when we had not yet tied ourselves to a Naval law challenging Britain, when we could rely on her good will in many respects? Every nation depends in a number of respects on the good will of other peoples, unless, as in the case of the later Roman Empire, one rules over all others." Europäische Gespräche, IV, 61.
10. "It is true, there were conditions contained in that treaty [with Spain in 1513 after the Battle of the Spurs] which were not honorable for such a prince as the King [of France] but necessity knows no law when it comes to saving a province." Mémoires de Martin du Bellay, I, 137.
11. Lacour-Gayet, Talleyrand, III, 311.
12. Mémoires du Comte de Beust, I, 290. Compare this view with that expressed in 1867 by General Ducrot: "As between folly and cowardice, I do not hesitate. Whether a people or an individual is concerned, cowardice always dishonors, that is to say, morally kills." Ducrot, Vie militaire, II, 290.
13. The last Foreign Secretary of the Second Reich, von Hintze, a former naval officer, had to tell the officers of GHQ in the autumn of 1918 that "the German people was far from wanting to fight for its honor to the point of destruction; it wanted to live, even at the price of territorial cessions, if not of political

and economic servitude." Foerster, Der Feldherr Ludendorff im Unglück. This book was circulated in typewritten form among the general staff officers of the OKW in the autumn of 1943.

14. When German acceptance of the Versailles Treaty with its defamatory terms was under discussion in Weimar, Seeckt wrote: "Have we the right to rank the question of military honor above the public weal?" as some extremists were demanding. Rabenau, Seeckt, II, 186.

15. When, during the Anglo-Russian conflict over Merv (1885), the Russian military plenipotentiary in Berlin told Waldersee that the British could not swallow the shamefulness of their position forever, the German was not at all convinced: "...in England commercial calculating is predominant; and they tell one another there that disgrace is easier to take than a long war for which they are not prepared." Waldersee, Denkwürdigkeiten, I, 259.

16. 1847. Keudell, Fürst und Fürstin Bismarck, p. 8. Cf. Juvenal: "It is easier to find false witness against the civilian than anyone willing to speak the truth against the interest and honor of the soldier." Satires, XVI, 128.

17. Salisbury wrote to Evelyn Cromer in Egypt on March 28, 1890: "When once you have permitted a military advance, the extent of that military advance scarcely remains within your own discretion. It is always open to the military authorities to discover in the immediate vicinity of the area to which your order confines them, some danger against which it is absolutely necessary to guard, some strategic position whose invaluable qualities will repay ten times any risk or cost that its occupation may involve. You have no means of arguing against them. They are upon their own territory and can set down their opposition to civilian ignorance." Cecil, Life of Salisbury, IV, 327.

18. "In diplomatic circles there was often the opinion that foreign policy represented an untouchable esoteric art not to be disclosed by diplomacy to anyone, but that the army was a requisite which one would pull out if some conflict should arise, without ever considering which means and forces might be needed in order to be prepared for all incidents and that it took years to make all the preparations for one definite casus belli." Conrad, Aus meiner Dienstzeit, I, 40 f.

19. For the diplomat's complaint about historical injustice done to his profession, see Jules Cambon's grievance: "Generally speaking, diplomats are not, like the military, the spoiled children of the historians. Hardly do the latter even mention their names, and that secret of negotiations over which their contemporaries often contend with them remains largely theirs, thanks to the silence preserved by posterity." J. Cambon, Le diplomate, p. 37.

20. Talleyrand called diplomacy the "unthankful art, because the public saw on the whole only the defeats and not the successes." Mackay, Die moderne Diplomatie, p. 59. By comparison, military success is more spectacular at most times and in most places, but so is military failure.

21. When, in a quarrel of precedence between a secretary of legation and an ensign, Frederick the Great decided in favor of the latter, the diplomat left the civil service and became an ensign. Borchardt, Die Randbemerkungen Friedrichs des Grossen, I, 33; II, 28.

22. Cf. the German ditty: "Der Soldate ist der erste Mann im ganzen Staate." Moltke, Erinnerungen, Briefe, Dokumente, pp. 11 f.

24. In the Third Reich, the Nazis, from Hitler down, called the Army "reactionary," the Navy imperialist or "Christian," and considered the Luftwaffe alone to be politically reliable, thanks to Goering. Herzfeld, Das Problem des deutschen Heeres, p. 18.

25. See Bernhardi's naïve remarks about this: "In the true spirit of statesmanship, the Emperor has powerfully aided and extended the evolution of our fleet without being under the stress of any political necessiaty." F. von Bernhardi, Germany and the Next War, p. 126.

26. For a detailed survey see Vagts, "Land and Sea Power in the Second German Reich," Military Affairs, III, 210 ff.

27. Since the number of Austria-Hungary's enemies—Russia, Rumania, Serbia, Montenegro, and Italy—was so great and their combined strength so overwhelming, and since they would have to be fought eventually, all of them, Conrad's recipe was to fight them singly and consecutively, beginning perhaps with Italy in 1907. Conrad, Aus meiner Dienstzeit, I, 40.

28. G. P., XXXIII, 12471.

29. For a modern soldier's doubts about dictated peace, see Wedemeyer's testimony, Military Situation in the Far East, p. 2440.

30. Schmitthenner, Politik und Kriegführung, p. 224.

31. Cambon's example of a professor-general is Trochu. Paul Cambon, Correspondance, II, 160 f.

32. Rousset, Louvois, I, 327.

33. The War Ministry (Secretariat de la guerre) had been set up in France by Richelieu, after he had become first minister in 1624, replac-

ing the older geographic principle for sub-dividing business by the professional one. Weygand, Histoire de l'armée française, p. 133.

34. July 16, 1740. Politische Correspondenz Friedrichs des Grossen, I, 7.
35. Lacour-Gayet, Talleyrand, III, 429.
36. Scherr, Blücher, III, 48.
37. Fournier, Der Congress von Chatillon, pp. 256 f.
38. Unger, Blücher, II, 324.
39. Ibid., II, 322, 325.
40. Botzenhardt, Freiherr vom Stein, VI, 150.
41. Srbik, Metternich, I, 726; Conrady, Grolman, II, 367.
42. Not long before he resigned from the government, Wilhelm von Humboldt, one of the Prussian negotiators at Vienna, pointed out the bad reputation into which Prussia was being brought "by careless over-bearing talk of individuals, by the strange rumors and gossip about the independence of the Army, and fermentation among the people." Gebhardt, Wilhelm von Humboldt als Staatsmann, II, 208.
43. Bismarck, Gedanken und Erinnerungen, I, 301, 308.
44. Bismarck wrote to his wife on November 22, 1870: "The plot, if it exists at all, is located in the General Staff which, apart from the good and wise old Moltke, does not please me at all; success has gone to their heads, megalomaniacally, and I am often afraid that we shall yet be punished for this haughty presumption; others hide behind Moltke's name, who himself has grown old and lets go what goes. It is the regiments that pull us through, not the generals." Rehlen, Bismarck, pp. 149 f.
45. For details, see Meyer, Bismarck's Kampf mit Oesterreich am Bundestag, pp. 394, 473 ff., 582.
46. During the Berlin Congress, Moltke made the rounds of the foreign diplomats just when the Congress seemed in danger of blowing up. At least to French diplomats, it seemed that people in Berlin "were urging Austria more and more to participate in the partition of Turkey. Moltke," they reported, "has pressed Karolyi to make his Government act in that sense, telling him: 'Go to Salonika, and we shall approve and back you up.'" Doc. dipl. fr., Ist series, II, 286 f.
47. Ibid., III, 23, 43.
48. 1887. G. P., VI, 1256.
49. January 10, 1885. Bethcke, Politische Generäle, p. 41.
50. Waldersee, Denkwürdigkeiten, II, 44.
51. Ziekursch, Politische Geschichte des neuen deutschen Kaiserreichs, III, 19.
52. 1891. Cited by Hegemann in Entlarvte Geschichte, p. 160.
53. Hohenlohe, Denkwürdigkeiten, III, 15; Haller, Eulenburg, pp. 386 f.
54. G. P., XVIII, 5413 (1902).
55. According to Holstein, Bülow's speeches of January 8 and 10, 1902, in which he defended the Prussian Army and its behavior in the war of 1870-71 against criticism by J. Chamberlain, an exchange of speeches which added greatly to Anglo-German estrangement, had been delivered against Bülow's own better judgment. "But he had to speak that way; the Army demanded it from him," Bülow said in his own defense. For Holstein, this was tantamount to a historical switch-setting and "gradually brought us close to war with England. Only the English cabinet change [1905-06] reopens peaceful perspectives." Brauer, Im Dienste Bismarcks, p. 411.
56. In 1912, when Anglo-German negotiations about a partition of the Portuguese colonies were beginning, the naval attaché wrote to Tirpitz: "As we know from experience, making concessions starts as soon as the ink-diplomats want to achieve results...We will have to be on our guard that no conditions are raised and accepted by our diplomats which we [the Imperial Navy] cannot accept." Tirpitz, Politische Dokumente. Der Aufbau der deutschen Weltmacht, pp. 355 f.
57. "I have heard with my own ears how Tirpitz in confidential circles before Reichstag members openly and without reserve expressed his hope of outdoing the British Navy [during the late 1890's]. The basic fault of the Tirpitz outlook was that he, as easily happens to us Germans, considers arms an end in themselves and forgets that policy is the essential thing, that arms, whether those of the land Army or the Navy, are only means to an end and that fixing the armed strength must be sovereignly decided by policy." Kühlmann, Erinnerungen, pp. 292 f.
58. Hindenburg, Aus meinem Leben, pp. 44 f.
59. Jäckh, Kiderlen-Wächter, II, 155.
60. December 8, 1918. Monts, Erinnerungen und Gedanken, p. 296 and passim.
61. Elevated to the throne by a military conspiracy, Alexander I at times screamed at his civilian ministers: "I hate civilians; I am a soldier; I only like soldiers." Nicolson, Congress of Vienna, p. 18.
62. Waters, "Secret and Confidential", pp. 328, 333 f.
63. Lloyd George, War Memoirs, V, 134.
64. B. D., III, No. 596.
65. The following is based on Paul Cambon's Correspondance, I, 245 ff.

66. Callwell, <u>Sir Henry Wilson</u>, II, 163-235. 258, 275, 310, etc.
67. Vagts, <u>Militarism</u>, pp. 311 ff.
68. Percin, <u>Les erreurs du Haut Commandement</u>, p. 137.
69. On the eve of Jena, Clausewitz wrote to his bride (whom he could not marry for another four years): "My country needs war and—clearly put—war alone can lead me to a fortunate end. In whichever manner I would tie my life to the rest of the world, my road always leads across a large battlefield; without treading on such a field, there is no permanent happiness for me." Schwartz, <u>Leben des Generals von Clausewitz</u>, I, 219.
70. For Japanese conditions, see Kase, <u>Journey to the "Missouri"</u>, p. 88.

Soldiers in Diplomatic Posts

Until Napoleon I there was, in general, no primacy of the military in the counsels of great governments, not even in Prussia. Soldiers and sailors were subordinated to the primacy of civilians in government who were often greatly concerned as to whether it was at all "safe" to employ the available arms-bearers. It was only gradually that the latter "came into their own," to use an ambiguous but portentous phrase, a development paralleled by the soldier becoming literate, or acquiring administrative gifts, or showing diplomatic talents that many believed to be innately foreign to him.

Like all modern political institutions, diplomacy on the one hand and the armed forces on the other underwent the process of division of labor and of specialization, with this curious difference: once it had taken place, a military man could still become a diplomat, but a diplomat could no longer turn to soldiering, except in subordinate positions. In the case of naval personnel, the separation between fighting forces and diplomatic services became even more complete. Or, putting it differently, many more military officers have changed over to diplomatic employment, temporarily or permanently, than have naval officers. Ships and fleets kept their officers busier—on the waters, away from the courts—even in peacetime, than did the contemporary armies. Army officers, always underemployed in peace periods, had time to spare for diplomatic service or for party politics. In Great Britain during the eighteenth and nineteenth centuries, for example, many more army officers sat in Parliament than did naval officers. Also, the naval officer as a courtier remained a comparatively rare figure, rarer because the naval officer was less often a nobleman than the military officer who was admitted to court by virtue of his nobility.[1]

THE SOLDIER-NEGOTIATOR OF ABSOLUTISM

By the end of the Ludovican wars, a new type of ambassador seemed to have emerged, as the theoreticians of diplomacy thought—the soldier as negotiator with absolutist princes. With respect to one large part of the regular duties of the ambassador, no one seemed more suitable, for the ambassador was to instruct himself "about the state of the forces of the Prince near whom he is stationed, land as well as naval forces, the number of his fortified places, and whether they are well provided and well fortified, the state of his harbors, the number of troops he can put in the field, cavalry as well as infantry, without stripping bare his places and frontiers, and the annual expenditure for the maintenance of his troops." In order to maintain good and intimate relations between the sovereigns of Absolutism, who had no interest closer to their hearts than their soldiers, it appeared best to choose generals en mission. They seemed "more in keeping with the inclinations and the way of living of kings and princes, seemed to have more occasion to entertain them about things which were their principal occupation; they were also more fit to insinuate themselves with the ladies who as a rule enjoyed credit in the majority of the courts." It was thought most fitting to send a soldier-diplomat to courts that were at war. "A good general could, in effect, serve with success as ambassador in a country that had to sustain a war because he could give useful advice to the Prince or State to whom he was sent about all that regarded his profession; this would enable him to gain credit in the country where he was negotiating, if that country should be a friend of his master's, and he would be in a better position than anyone else to render good account of the forces of the country where he resided, of the quality of the troops, the experience of the generals, the state of the fortified places, the arsenals and magazines."[2]

The seventeenth and eighteenth-century wars of coalition, prepared by diplomatic negotiations that had only poorly laid the ground for the disagreeable eventualities of such wars, called for the application of considerable talent of a combined military and diplomatic nature in order to keep the often incongruous partners united in the war effort. Marlborough, while in command of the combined English and Dutch forces in the Spanish war of Succession, was constantly forced to exert himself in this field of endeavor during the campaigns. In the season between campaigns, he used to travel from one friendly court to another in order to keep well inclined and to arrange new subsidy payments. His pupil and assistant was William, first earl of Cadogan (1675-1726) who had first come to the Duke's attention when, in 1701, he assisted effectively as a staff officer in the task of making an army out of the heterogeneous contingents furnished by the various partners of the coalition against Louis XIV. Marlborough soon made him something like his chief of staff and

quartermaster general. His manifold business included the negotiation of truces with the French.[3]
An amply tested man, he passed the severest
trial of pride and discipline: when, on an inspection of the lines around besieged Menin in 1709,
the Duke purposely dropped his glove and told
Cadogan to pick it up, the latter obeyed without
a word. After their return to the camp, when the
Duke ordered a battery to be placed on the now
historic spot, Cadogan informed him that orders
to that effect had already been given—an occurrence that, even if only invented, illustrates the
ideal relation between the general and his chief
of staff. Remaining loyal to Marlborough in spite
of such tests and in spite of the temptation that
Tory pamphleteers offered when they wrote that
the Duke's success was "all owing to Cadogan's
advice,"[4] he shared the Duke's disgrace, losing
position, rank and pay. He was reinstated by
George I, whose succession he as well as his old
master had been ready to secure through their influence over British troops.[5] He was employed
again in the military as well as the diplomatic
field.[6] On one of his diplomatic missions he
went to Berlin, but was unable to persuade Frederick William I, the "soldier-king," to make more
warlike use of his well-drilled force by "selling"
it to Britain in return for subsidies.

Another soldier-diplomat of Marlborough's
school was his one-time aide-de-camp, John, second
earl of Stair (1678-1747), field marshal and ambassador. He was the first after the accession of
George I to be sent to Paris (1715-20), where his
diplomatic talents won Voltaire's admiration. In
1742, he was commander-in-chief of the British
forces on the continent.[7] He was leader in the
battle of Dettingen, if that battle had any leadership; and also a wastrel, gambler and inveterate
stock exchange speculator who seems on occasion
to have found diplomatic information of help in
his financial speculations.[8]

The Powers of the eighteenth century, relatively
untouched by nationalism, employed numerous
foreigners on nearly all levels in their army,
navy, and diplomatic services. While England was
most exclusive in this respect, the countries with a
scarcity of such experts—Russia, Austria, Prussia, and Spain—all drew heavily on this freely
mobile element. In most cases, a patent of nobility heightened acceptability; in others, as in Spain,
a co-religionist was most welcome. Generally
speaking, the soldiers and the officers who, in
return for pay and the chance of a career, were
willing to shed their blood on the battlefields of the
the employer-countries were most readily received. In diplomacy, there was more selectivity
as regards the employment of foreigners, while
the employment of a foreign-born general as
diplomat remained distinctly rare.

The case of the foreign-born general-diplomat
may be illustrated by the life and services of
General Richard Wall (1694-1778), Irish-born
soldier, diplomat and cabinet minister in the service of Spain. Excluded from all offices at home,
he, like so many Irishmen since Cromwell's day,
entered the military service of Spain. He obtained
a diplomatic post in 1727, being well qualified by
a knowledge of languages, a ready wit, and a
gift of repartee for service in the midst of
"touchy" grandees. He inspired such confidence
among his employers that he was even sent on a
mission to Spanish America, usually the reservation kept by Spain for Spaniards. He took part in
the negotiations of the Peace of Aachen (1747)
and went as minister to London the following year,
where he stayed until 1752. In London he was very
popular as the advocate of the peaceful policy that
was in the interest of both countries, a policy he
continued to pursue after his recall to Madrid,
where he became foreign minister. His endeavors
to maintain peace with England, which proved successful until 1761, when the depredations of English privateers in Spanish waters became unbearable to Spanish pride, seem in no small part due
to his true military judgment of Spain's irreparable weakness, a kind of knowledge not usually
included among the qualifications of the soldier-
diplomat.

The first condition—first in time, at least—
for the success of a diplomatic mission, namely,
that the ambassador must be persona gratissima
to the government of the country to which he is
sent, meant that he had to be particularly welcome
to the sovereign himself in the absolutistic age. When
the receiving monarch was absorbed in military
affairs above all else, one could think of no better
diplomatic representative than a general or other
high officer. He could reckon upon a welcome by
the prince and he might be the best judge of the
latter's main concern, the army.[9] Lieutenant-
General Frederick Henry, Count of Seckendorff
(1673-1763) was sent in 1726 to Frederick William,
predecessor of Frederick the Great, as Austrian
ambassador. He stayed for eight strenuous years
in order to keep the soldier-king in line with
Austrian policies, little as they may have been in
line with the Prussian interests. In order to please
the King and win him over to the Austrian side—
"which of course must be done in a natural and
unaffected way," as his instructions told him—he
had to hide from him that he was reading books
or that he did not smoke when he participated in
the King's Tobacco College, the circle of the
King's intimates to which he was admitted. He
made him presents of tall recruits from the Austrian possessions to serve in the Potsdam Giant
Guards. "I could achieve more with such a present than with the most powerful argument," he wrote

to Vienna, not long before the conclusion of a secret treaty favorable to Austria alone. Like later military ambassadors, Seckendorff made full use of his admission to the King's military entourage, even though the pace of the soldier-king was at times too much for the gentleman from Vienna. His military status made approaching the autocrat much easier and less conspicuous, for a civilian representative would have to apply for audiences and seek other more formal occasions to meet the King. However, Seckendorff, neither very efficient nor successful as a general in the field, remained unable to penetrate Prussia's greatest secret. About the Crown Prince he reported to Vienna: "He told me that he is a poet and can write one hundred lines in two hours. He could also be a musician, a philosopher, a physicist, or a mechanic. What he will never be is a general or a warrior."[10]

The large majority of the French diplomatic representatives at the Berlin court from 1684 to 1789 were former military men, several of whom returned to army service after their Berlin tour of duty, having learned in Berlin something worth the attention of the home army. According to his instructions, this was expected of Comte, later Duc de Guines, who held the rank of brigadier general in the Army and who was sent to Berlin at the end of 1768. He had been sent to Berlin before, as observer of the great annual maneuvers that were considered the high school of eighteenth-century tactics. King Louis XV expected the Count to perfect his previously acquired knowledge in this field during his stay,

in a country which, in several respects, can pass as an excellent school in this genre. It is, however, important to warn him that he must carefully avoid divulging his views in this respect and that it is proper to keep his researches secret; a marked curiosity would certainly displease the King of Prussia who always effects to cover with a veil of secrecy his simplest operations of this kind.

The minister was expected to submit his findings to the King in memoranda on all military subjects that might strike his attention.[11]

The interchange between the two institutions was, as has been remarked, largely from one side to the other, from military to diplomatic service, a changeover which the grand seigneur could most easily undertake and perform.[12] In an age of ceremonial birth it might well have better prepared him for such a position than previous military experience. But the clerks, the more or less permanent personnel in the foreign offices at home, did not think very highly of the diplomatic talents of the grand seigneur. As one

of the commis of the French foreign ministry under the ancien régime wrote:

The majority of the grands seigneurs are more fit for a ceremonial embassy than for negotiations. On an embassy for merely listening, where a borrowed orator is the spokesman on the occasion of a baptism or a wedding, on the occasion of a death or a birth, or for the purpose of watching the observance of a treaty sworn to, there is where they triumph. They are only born for compliments and allow themselves neither time nor trouble to prepare themselves for business.[13]

But as the lights of the absolutistic age and of still later times were distributed, the clerks always worked in the dark, and the ambassadors acted at least part of the time in the sunshine emanating from the thrones before which they had to seem "highly representative." They had to be physically impressive in uniform, and possibly out of it as well.

The first Duc de Broglie (1671-1745), maréchal de France, was employed on various diplomatic missions, including the ambassadorship to London (1724), in the periods between the wars he fought. One of his sons, Charles François, Comte de Broglie (1719-81), after some years of army service, became the foremost member of Louis XV's private diplomatic service, the Secret du Roi, which employed other officers like Dumouriez on somewhat adventurous military-diplomatic missions.[14] Serving inter-changeably, first in military and then in diplomatic positions, were the brothers Belle-Isle, the Duke and Marshal (1684-1761) and the Chevalier and lieutenant-general (1693-1746), the grandsons of the financier Nicholas Fouquet. Both started in military service, the best way then as in other ages to clear the family of the disgrace in which it found itself. As a diplomat, the elder of the two prepared the way for the War of the Austrian Succession. In the same war he commanded the first army France put into the field. His brother served under him in the diplomatic missions preceding this war, and both were captured on another mission by the Anglo-Hanoverians, through whose territory they traveled. The duke was able to make good his escape from beleaguered Prague by a heroic winter march (1741-42) with the remains of his troops. He was again commander in the field in the campaign of 1746 and was also able to retrieve his position in the court. Louis XV made him minister of war (1757-61). In this office he carried out several reforms, but not enough of them to prepare the French army adequately for the Seven Years' War. His contemporary, the Maréchal de Noailles, the loser at Dettingen, went into retirement by accepting a mission to Madrid in 1746. There he did nothing, or almost nothing, except to busy himself with military operations and the working out of plans against the possessions of the King of Sardinia, which he made the Spaniards accept.[15]

THE NAPOLEONIC ERA

> "Ma mission a bien plutôt la guerre
> pour objet que la paix."[16]

Leaving aside the group of generals whom Louis XIV sent out as ambassadors between the Treaty of Ryswick and the outbreak of the Spanish War of Succession—with the intention, or at least the effect, of bringing about the latter rather than preserving the former—the first considerable spate of general-diplomats to be loosed upon a peace-desiring world was sent out by Napoleon Bonaparte. The Directoire (1795-99) had sent out such "soldats ambassadeurs."[17] Of all the generals, Bernadotte was and remained most in need of being sent abroad. He had remained aloof on the Eighteenth Brumaire. When, after the Peace of Campo Formio, he demanded a command au loin, he was offered the government of the Ionian Islands. He preferred, however, the less distant command of the Italian Army, where he hoped to preserve enough visibility to carry on his rivalry with Bonaparte. Instead, without having asked for the post, he was appointed ambassador to Vienna (January 11, 1798). His embassy personnel were military rather than diplomatic, comprising a considerable number of aides-de-camp and only two diplomatic secretaries, whose job it was to be "au courant des formes." The French embassy's behavior in old-aristocratic Vienna was thoroughly Jacobin and led to the famous flag incident of April 13, 1798, one of the first of these incidents provoked by modern nationalism. War with Austria was resumed soon after.

Since he had not appointed Bernadotte himself, Napoleon found it easy enough in later years to term the mission unfortunate. Said he at Saint-Helena: "This choice was not good; a general cannot be agreeable to a nation that had been so constantly beaten; one ought to have sent a person of civilian status; but the Directoire had few of these at its disposal; they were either too obscure or had been sent away. Whatever is said, Bernadotte, at that time of a highly excitable character, committed grave errors during his ambassadorship," including that of abruptly hoisting the tricolore over the embassy building.[18] When Napoleon recalled this unfortunate experience, he preferred not to consider his own repeated use of the military diplomat. He was, in fact, the true transformer of generals into diplomats, and back again. His original purpose in sending them to foreign courts was to keep the peace at home rather than abroad. Following the Treaty of Lunéville, the majority of the army leaders returned to Paris. They were far from "unpolitical" in their views and in their relations with the First Consul, and promptly betrayed resistance to the policies of their camarade Bonaparte. In order to remove them from Paris, they were dispatched on distant missions, a form of exile not unknown in the history of diplomacy. Practically all of them, except Moreau, accepted. Bernadotte went to command the Army of the West (Vendée). Later, in 1802, it was planned to send him still farther West, as governor of Louisiana or as minister to the United States. He was on his way to the port of embarkation when an incident delayed him and finally postponed forever his trip across the Atlantic.[19] Lannes was at first made commander and inspector of the Garde consulaire; but he accepted an ambassadorship to Lisbon after peculations from the funds of these Guards to the amount of 200,000 francs had been uncovered.[20] Lisbon was one of the best places to restore the finances of Napoleonic generals, such as the extravagant Junot, who made his entry there twice, as ambassador (1804-05) and as military conqueror (1807). When the war of 1805 began, Napoleon recalled him to his headquarters in order to give him a chance to distinguish himself in either the military or the diplomatic field. Following Austerlitz, he was sent on a mission to Alexander I who had, however, departed for St. Petersburg when Junot arrived in the camp. Not thinking that "he should run after him," Junot returned with his mission unaccomplished. Savary and others felt that had he dared to follow the Tsar to St. Petersburg, "peace would have been made that very year," instead of two years later.[21]

Duroc went to Berlin, Macdonald to Copenhagen, Brune to Constantinople, each of them for a few years, while practically the whole of the politically-suspect Army of the Rhine was exiled to Santo Domingo to die. Bonaparte sent his chief of staff, Berthier, to Madrid (August 1800) without diplomatic title in order to negotiate the retrocession of Louisiana to France, the borrowing of a number of Spanish men-of-war, the setting up of an Italian principality for one of the infantes, and a Spanish attack on Portugal, England's old ally. His experiences as chief of staff were to be helpful to the Spaniards in devising the war plans against Portugal. Berthier was to inspect Spain's naval establishments and their resources for the case of war as well as for the provisioning of French-held Malta. Even though some of the purposes of his mission became known through the press, the negotiations were brought to a successful close, a success that earned Berthier the appointment as minister of war.[22]

In later years, after he had become not only war minister and chief of staff but also the first dignitary of the Empire with various ceremonial duties, Berthier had to witness such great occasions as the exchange of the ratifications of the Rhine Confederation Act. This took place in Munich in July 1806, whence, less ceremoniously, he proceeded to the military occupation of various German Imperial cities that had preserved their independence until then. And it was he who in 1810 proceeded to Vienna, after the civilian diplomats had arranged everything, to apply in the name of Napoleon for the hand of Marie Louise and thus seal the Anschluss of the upstart Corsican to the old House of Hapsburg.[23]

One of Berthier's successors in Madrid was Gouvion Saint-Cyr, sent there in February 1801 to replace Lucien Bonaparte as ambassador and to head a French division and possibly all the other forces to be used in case of a war of Spain and France with Portugal. A still later general-ambassador to Madrid was de Beurnonville, who had earlier served in Berlin. He aroused the protests of the Spanish Government by large-scale smuggling through the misuse of his diplomatic immunity. But Bonaparte backed up his general-ambassador to the hilt.[24]

After the Treaty of Amiens, Bonaparte considered General Andréossy, a deserving man who had shown his mettle not only on the battlefield but also on the Eighteenth Brumaire, for the post of ambassador to London. Talleyrand, foreign minister at the time, was determined to thwart the appointment—he wanted to keep the peace with Britain and thought an artillery general was not the right person for the job. One day, Bonaparte brought up the name of his candidate. Talleyrand pretended not to understand:

> Vous voulez nommer André aussi? Quel est donc cet André?...Je ne vous parle d'un André, je vous parle d'un Andréossy. Est-ce que vous ne le connaissez pas? Pardieu! Andréossy, général d'artillerie. ....Andréossy! Ah! oui, oui, c'est vrai, Andréossy. Je n'y pensais pas; je cherchais dans la diplomatie, et je ne l'y trouvais pas. C'est vrai; oui, oui, c'est vrai; il est dans l'artillerie.[25]

He was appointed over Talleyrand's ironical opposition and proved more peaceful than the archdiplomat had expected an artillery general to be, far more peaceful than the other artillery general, Bonaparte himself. He served again as ambassador, from 1808-09, in Vienna, where he showed much more hostility to the country of residence than Napoleon seems to have expected of him. Following the war he had helped to bring on rather than avert, he was made military

governor of Vienna, turning to use the knowledge of local conditions he had gained as ambassador. From 1812 to 1814 he served as ambassador to Constantinople, the last in the line of Napoleonic soldier-ambassadors on the Bosporus. He arrived too late, however, to keep the Turks from concluding peace with the Russians, who were able to free an army in time to use it against Napoleon.[26]

Another soldier-ambassador serving Napoleon was Sébastiani, a fellow-Corsican and Bonapartist. He served as ambassador to the Porte in 1802 and again after the close of the war of 1805. As well as being ambassador, he was head of a military mission composed of a considerable number of French officers serving under him as instructors of the militarily-backward Turks. He persuaded the Turks, probably contrary to their better interest at the moment, to declare war on Russia and helped them to put the Straits into a more defensible condition. Guided by him, the Turks, turning down a British ultimatum to send Sébastiani home, forced a squadron under Admiral Duckworth to retire rather ignominiously. In 1808 the fall of Sultan Selim II found Sébastiani quite unprepared, but he planned at once to remove the usurper. He resumed contact with the deposed Sultan and assembled Turkish troops for a march on the capital. Before they had arrived, the usurper had strangled the fallen Sultan (his uncle) with his own hands. The army nevertheless put the usurper aside and proclaimed a new Sultan, Mahmud III. Unfortunately, the reforming army had left the Danube provinces unprotected, and these provinces thereupon fell all the more easily to the Russians. The bloody episode put an end to Sebastiani's usefulness at the Porte, and he was recalled in April 1808.[27]

Sebastiani possessed a considerable flair for politics, diplomacy and social life. During the Hundred Days he took Napoleon's part. In 1819, however, he entered the Chamber of Deputies, later became Minister of Marine, and then Minister of Foreign Affairs under the July Monarchy. In 1833 he was sent as ambassador to Naples, and from 1835 to 1845 served as ambassador to Britain. It was in vain that he warned Louis-Philippe against the coming of the February Revolution. As blind as his predecessor had been eighteen years earlier, the King told his mentor: "You are on your way down, marshal, definitely, you are slipping."[28]

An even closer amalgam of ambassador and military instructor was intended by Napoleon for Claude Matthieu, Count Gardane (1766-1818). In addition to his diplomatic mission, he headed one of the first modern so-called military missions sent by a great and advanced Power to a backward one at the behest of the latter. In the spring of 1807, at the request of distant Persia, then also at war with Russia, Napoleon sent Gardane to Teheran where he was to support the war against Russia and against England in India. [29]

Several of these generals en mission were proconsuls of the First Consul and Emperor. They were under his orders to turn the countries to which they were accredited into satellites of the Republic and Empire. General Jourdan, "minister extraordinary" to the Provisional Government of Piedmont after Marengo, was to see that King Charles Emanuel vacated the throne. This was the first step in the annexation of Piedmont to France. Similar procedures, presided over by General Dejean, "minister extraordinary" there since Marengo, put an end to the independence of Genoa. General Clarke, as minister to Florence, supervised the new and ephemeral Kingdom of Etruria (1801-03). He submitted proposals to extend French control over Lucca where "everything was anarchy, dilapidation, corruption, low intrigue, spirit of vengeance." This condition made her ripe for annexation by France, or rather for a new ruler, such as Napoleon's sister and brother-in-law, the Baciochi, who were installed in 1805.[30]

The belief in the versatility of the soldier and his consequent employment in the most diverse offices, from post-masterships to the direction of theaters, might well be called a characteristic of militarism. By this definition, Napoleon was decidedly a militarist. He was strongly convinced of the fitness and usefulness of the officer in non-military fields. The ones he employed as diplomats might be classed in two groups—those occasionally used on missions who afterwards reverted to command or staff duties, and those leaving military service altogether. The missions carried out by the former were mostly fatal to peace, as they were probably intended to be.[31] Those performed by the latter group were more sincerely in the interest of peace, on the Emperor's own terms.

Such a diplomat with an early officer career was Nicolas-Auguste-Marie Rousseau, Baron, later Comte, de Saint-Aignan (1770-1815). He left the army with the rank of chief of battalion in order to become, as a protégé of his brother-in-law Caulaincourt, first a court official and then, at the end of 1811, minister at the court of Weimar with the special task of supervising the goings-on among the lesser German princes. The allies of 1813 made him prisoner of war during their advance and sent him back to France in the autumn of that year in order to persuade Napoleon to enter upon peace negotiations on what seemed to them fair conditions. Savary and Caulaincourt, both tainted in the eyes of their contemporaries

by their connection with the judicial murder of the Duc d'Enghien, served on the highest plane of Napoleonic diplomacy. Both had their greatest task in the attempt to keep Tsar Alexander on France's side. And both remained as faithful to the Emperor as any of his soldiers. This was due, at least in part, to the particular nature of their employments under the Emperor, which made the change to another regime rather difficult unless one possessed the dexterity and the sense of timing shown by Talleyrand and Fouché.

Savary, Duke of Rovigo (1774-1833), had won Napoleon's confidence as a commander of a body of gendarmes who were to guard the First Consul, and later through his dark role in the Enghien case. Prior to Austerlitz, he was the carrier of a proposal for an armistice to Alexander I, who promptly fell for the ruse and rushed into battle instead of postponing it. Later Savary served on a similar mission, again with satisfactory results. Believing that Savary had made himself persona gratissima with Alexander, Napoleon sent him to St. Petersburg after the Peace of Tilsit in order to strengthen the uneasy harmony arranged on the Memel float. To become more acceptable to St. Petersburg high society, which called him one of the murderers of Enghien, Savary surrounded himself with a suite of young officers, men with great names or good looks, a Montesquieu-Fezensac, a Fedoas de Barbazon, a Leborgne d'Ideville. Their old titles or social talents assured them of a better reception than did their chief's earlier activities.[32] Either because he could not break down this resistance or, more likely, because Napoleon considered him eminently suited for new business at hand, Savary was recalled before a year was over and sent on the particularly louche business of removing the Spanish Bourbons from their throne. After the fall of Fouché, he became Minister of Police. While Fouché had somewhat civilized this institution, Savary made it more military, more brutal and more inquisitive, though hardly more efficient. In the end he became himself the much ridiculed victim of the conspiracy of General Malet. It may be a moot point in employee psychology whether such "discreet" services induce more loyalty or disloyalty in the servitor. In Savary's case, they produced one of the most faithful of the faithful. It was through no fault or lack of eagerness on his part that he was excluded from the group of those who followed Napoleon to Saint Helena.[33]

Caulaincourt, "ambassadeur-général-duc-grand écuyer," was the âme damnée of Napoleon to only a slightly lesser degree than Savary. He came from the non-emigrating nobility, reached the rank of colonel and received his first diplomatic task after the Treaty of Lunéville. In 1801 he was sent to Russia in order to re-establish diplomatic relations with that country. The fact that he was an officer and a member of the old nobility seemed to provide a basic element for the restoration of peaceful relations abroad. Though also implicated in the affair of Ettenheim, an accusation which he always protested, he was made Savary's successor in St. Petersburg. His aristocratic background helped him to overcome some of the repugnance on the part of St. Petersburg society, and his undoubted diplomatic talents helped him to preserve the partnership of Tilsit for some uneasy years. He realized only too well the dangers of Napoleon's plan for a Russian expedition and added his own warnings to those of Alexander, which he submitted to Napoleon after his recall in 1811. "We shall let...our winter wage the war for us," Alexander had said.

The military judgment of the ambassador, strengthened by his four years in Russia, proved sounder than that of the Emperor's suite on the march to Moscow. He and other dignitaries had hoped that Napoleon would stop at Witebsk. After their arrival at Moscow and the seeming victory, the Emperor wanted him to negotiate a peace with Alexander; but Caulaincourt declined the hopeless task. The Emperor then sent Lauriston, Caulaincourt's successor in the St. Petersburg embassy, to Kutuzov to start negotiations, saying: "He will have the honor to have concluded the peace and to have saved the crown of your friend Alexander." When, on the march back, Napoleon suddenly left the Grand Army, Caulaincourt was his closest companion and subsequently his last negotiator: at the armistice of Poischwitz in the summer of 1813, at the congresses of Prague (August 1813) and at Chatillon (February 1814). At Chatillon neither he nor Metternich was able to avert the consequences of Napoleonic hubris. As foreign minister of the Hundred Days, Caulcaincourt, was unable to convince Europe that the intentions of the returned Emperor were peaceful; and only the intercession of "his friend Alexander" kept his name from the list of the proscrits.[34]

The large-scale employment of military diplomats and the constant renewal of war by Napoleon drove the other continental Powers to similar measures. England's governors, however, withstood the urge to imitation that came from certain quarters within, no less than outside, the state. C. M. Pasley, perhaps the best English writer of his time on questions of military policy, suggested that in their wide-flung struggle with Napoleon "the Government perhaps would do better if they more frequently appointed military men as their agents," particularly in such unpacified regions' as Greece; that a return to the Roman system, when soldiers were negotiators and negotiators soldiers and when politics were necessarily mixed with war, was advisable and that "a vigorous

martial policy insures success in diplomacy." He added that "The nation which acts upon the most vigorous system of martial policy, will always have the most successful, if not the most accomplished diplomatic agents: so that if we choose to adopt, in our national councils, the determined and persevering spirit of the Romans, without their arrogance, which is not to be commended, we shall seldom or never fail of carrying our point in our foreign negotiations."[35] But the governors of England tried as much as possible to keep politics and the services unmixed. That seemed the safer thing, more apt to insure their conservative system against the revolution that might be furthered by almost any imitation of Napoleonic measures.[36]

On the Continent, such a determination against imitating the most successful man seemed less feasible. Napoleon set the fashion for a diplomacy that was military in personnel, outlook and methods, as against that of the arch-civilians, such as Talleyrand, Metternich, Hardenberg, and Castlereagh. In some cases the European Powers that had to deal with Napoleon diplomatically might have used military personnel in imitation of his own habits as flattery. In other cases, they had to do so practically at his behest. At their first meeting on the Memel float at Tilsit, Napoleon told the Prussian king that he would not treat with his minister Hardenberg—"He has offended me, me and the French nation." But, he added, he would welcome as negotiator field marshal Count von Kalckreuth (1737-1818), a man in whom neither Prussian nor any other historians can find much to praise. He had long been an intriguer and enemy of the Reformers, one of the reasons why the Emperor's choice might have fallen on him. Having been denied a front-line command, he had failed to lend the support of the reserve corps he commanded at Jena, though he was only a quarter of a mile away from the battlefield. He had, however, defended Danzig with great energy against a French siege. He concluded the armistice after Friedland, the last battle of the 1806-07 campaign, accepting conditions that were more onerous than the military situation of Prussia, bad as it was, seemed to demand. He was the inspirer of the singular idea of having Queen Louise meet Napoleon and plead with him for a better treatment of Prussia, saying to the King: "Even though Napoleon was not accustomed to wend his way in the society of women of high upbringing, one must do him justice and admit that in such society he behaves like a polished and well brought up man." (The Emperor himself, after the interview, wrote to Josephine that Louise had made no impression on him. "I was like an oilcloth from which all this slides off.") Kalckreuth's signature under the Convention of July 12, 1807, settling the details of the execution of the Franco-Prussian Peace, gave the French an instrument on the strength of which they could prolong the military occupation of Prussia almost indefinitely. This dupe of French trickery, hated by Reformers whose aims he considered chimerical, remained convinced well into the year of liberation that a rising against the then shattered power of the Corsican was hopeless.[37]

The deception of the new diplomacy, style _militaire_, did not last; and in the end it was Napoleon who was cheated and misled by the soldier-diplomats whom his adversaries sent into his court and camps. Their list included Count Peter Tolstoi, a Russian soldier-ambassador in Paris after Tilsit, through whom the Tsar began to give Napoleon hints, friendly as yet, that "the circle of iron" was forming around him;[38] and, after the Peace of Vienna of 1809, Prince Charles Philipp zu Schwarzenberg (1771-1820), one of Austria's best generals, whose reputation had remained quite untarnished in her defeats, and who was a member of one of the few families of Austria's high nobility that had not become ineffective. He had been sent to St. Petersburg on the eve of the foreseen war of 1809 in order to obtain either active help or a benevolent neutrality from Napoleon's ally. After the defeat of 1809 he negotiated the marriage of Napoleon and the archduchess, like a Theseus, failing in his first attempt against the Minotaur, now preparing an innocent sacrifice for the monster. He led Napoleon and his foreign minister Maret, Duc de Bassano, to believe that marriage and other alliances with Austria were solid and reliable.

> The manners of the ambassador of Austria were of a nature to confirm this opinion; never has one seen more assiduous, more minute attention being paid than by the Prince zu Schwarzenberg....He succeeded in inspiring such confidence that Napoleon put great emphasis on his receiving the command of the Austrian auxiliary corps [in the war of 1812]; he believed that he would thus obtain the best guarantee of a sincere execution of the treaty of alliance.[39]

In that war, Schwarzenberg led the troops under him like a diplomat, avoiding large battles, and thus qualified himself for his subsequent post as commander-in-chief of the Allies' Grand Army in 1813-14, an army which, according to some generals, he again led far too much in the diplomatic style.

Napoleon's adversaries fought the war with a strict division of labor between their civilian-diplomatic and military components, partly be-cause their mass armies with their new cadres could not spare officers for non-military employment. As a war of coalition it had its inter-allied frictions, but liaison was on the whole good and crowned the last battle, that of Waterloo, with success. Only at the close of the first War of Liberation did one of the victorious generals change to the role and post of diplomat. Wellington accepted the post of first post-war ambassador to Paris, doing so with due modesty—"Much obliged and flattered by your thinking of me for a situation for which I should never have thought myself qualified...ready to serve in any situation in which it may be thought that I can be of any service."[40] He proved definitely the most diplomatic and the least militaristic general, helping the returned Bourbons in their struggle for recognition at home and abroad. As a diplomatic observer, however, he did not grasp the psychological preparations among the French people, and above all among the military, for the return from Elba. And at the time of Napoleon's landing, Wellington thought he would be destroyed by Louis XVIII "without difficulty and in a short time." His Government showed their appreciation by sending him to Vienna as Castelreagh's successor in January 1815, where he found the work of the Congress mostly done. There he was the only military man among the chief delegates, but, like the others, a conservative statesman in or out of uniform, with his blind spots, particularly regarding the newer mass movements and sentiments. For example, he insisted at the time of the second Restoration, for which Louis XVIII had to thank him almost alone, that the French _tricolore_ be eliminated as "a symbol of rebellion." He was again the conservative statesman in uniform when, following the Second Peace of Paris, he became commander of the inter-allied forces occupying France. This occupation was to last for five years, but, unlike other military occupants, he pressed for an earlier evacuation. The Allies agreed to this at the Aachen Congress of 1818, turning down a Prussian proposal to maintain an army of observation in the Netherlands.

While French diplomacy sought to break the ring kept for a time around its country by the ex-enemies of the Wars of Liberation, who relented on the whole much faster than other ex-enemy groups, some circles of the ex-allies tried to preserve or revive embers of the sentiments that had animated their wartime alliances. These brotherhood-in-arms sentiments were to form part of the stock-in-trade of diplomacy by generals. And it often proved to be a powerful mass sentiment. When Blücher visited England after the close of the war in 1814, the people gave him an enthusiastic welcome. In Prusso-Russian relations the memory of the battles that the two allied armies had fought from 1807 to 1814 was appealed to as long as their relations remained cordial. France remained an outsider to this world of feelings. Only after the Crimean War did she gain her opportunity of invoking a recent brotherhood-in-arms.

GENERAL-DIPLOMATS DURING THE "HALT IN THE MUD"

Court service became a training school for military diplomats from the beginning of the nineteenth century when the heads of the military monarchies began to surround themselves with an increasing number of adjutant-generals and aides-de-camp (Flügeladjutanten, in Prussia and Russia). Or, one might prefer to say, the armies from then on began to militarize the courts, a process to which Napoleon greatly contributed. Tsar Alexander I, who inherited four adjutant-generals from his murdered father, added forty-five new ones, including several of his father's murderers, and appointed no less than 113 Flügel-adjutanten.[41] The last of the tsars had eighty-nine adjutant generals and some fifty aides of lesser rank.[42] Both groups were to furnish diplomats, the former on the ambassadorial level, the latter often as military attachés. In spite of their comparatively low rank the attachés were, as former members of their sovereign's maison militaire, privileged in such countries as Prussia to address themselves directly to the monarch. This privilege of "immediacy," as it was called, was rather fatal to the supremacy of civilians as well as to the unified conduct of diplomatic business.

The immediate post-Napoleonic period gave the military little employment in wars and little opportunity of achieving military progress, which the conservative Powers shunned rather than sought. The officers of the armies of the great Powers, on all levels of rank, were men of leisure during the long periods of peace that occurred from 1815 up to and well beyond the middle of the nineteenth century. The "work ethos" of the industrial century was late in catching up with them. While they waited for the wars, their duties on most days took but a few hours.[43] Leisure increased with rank, and generals in considerable numbers were always en disponibilité for all kinds of honorable work, including diplomacy. This availability, coupled in nations like Prussia and Russia with the firm conviction on the part of the governors in the all-around abilities of the soldier, led not only to the frequent change of officers into diplomatic employ but also to the often repeated use of officers, usually generals, in ad hoc diplomatic missions. When their mission was not of a ceremonial character, it was most often

in the interest of reaction—rather than conservatism—or of war preparation, or both.

In Prussia and Russia particularly, officers were employed to cultivate the reactionary intimacy between St. Petersburg and Berlin. But in France as well, the "halt in the mud," as the standstill following the Napoleonic wars was called by the military, led the many supernumeraries of military life into politics, for and against the Bourbon government. Sébastiani took an active hand in the organization of the French Philhellenes (Société Philanthropique) in 1825. Its emissary on the spot in Greece, General Roche, promptly proposed an Orleans prince for the throne in preparation. Other politicizing generals joined the cry for the Rhine frontier. General Dessolles was foreign minister under Decazes (1818-19) and went into retirement when the Duke proposed a new and more reactionary electoral law. General de Latour-Maubourg was recalled from the London Embassy in order to become successor to war minister Saint-Cyr, who had resigned in protest together with Dessolles. General de Guilleminot, chief of staff of the French army of intervention in Spain in 1825, became afterwards (until 1831) ambassador to Constantinople.[44] General Maison, one of those faithful to Louis XVIII during the Hundred Days but not to Charles X in July 1830, became after that year ambassador to Vienna and later to St. Petersburg, and finally war minister in 1835.

More than one of these posts of honor and emolument was given as a reward for political services. While the character of such missions by generals was still not devoid of some military éclat, care was taken that they should not have too much. The ordinance of 1819 on the organization of the French General Staff provided, for example, that general officers employed outside the Army would not be provided with aides-de-camp, which meant not only a diminution of military pomp but also of potential "honorable spies."[45]

Poorer nations like Prussia made provision for deserving generals by appointing them to court and diplomatic posts, for not all of them could receive landed estates as rewards for their services. In 1860, Leopold von Gerlach, a court general, noted that immediately "following the war of 1814 nearly all the important Prussian legations were filled with generals; now, there is hardly one among our generals who could be used on an important mission."[46] This meant that, on the eve of Prussia's three wars, they were once more nothing but generals, competent ones, as the outcome of these wars was to show. One of Moltke's predecessors, Field Marshal von Müffling (1775-1851), almost became Prussian minister to London instead of becoming Chief of the Great General Staff. Müffling had been liaison officer on Wellington's staff in 1815 and again when the latter was commander of the inter-allied army of occupation. In the winter of 1818-19, he negotiated with the King of the Netherlands the question of furnishing a Prussian auxiliary corps in case France should invade Belgium. From 1821 to 1829 he was Chief of Staff and in 1829 helped to re-establish peace between the Tsar and the Sultan, one of the first Prussian military men employed near the Porte to save her with the help of army reforms.[47]

In order to participate to a minimum extent—never more—in the military and naval progress of the West, the Turks had for centuries employed foreigners as experts and commanders. And they received additional advice, hardly ever altruistic, from the foreign ambassadors to the Porte, among whom were probably included more generals than could be found at any other post.

But the holding of such offices by generals had more significance than merely as an honor and as a reward. It pointed to problems of close cooperation between diplomacy and the armed forces and to the broader problem of the "primacy of foreign affairs." The latter problem was to trouble the governments, parliaments, peoples, and politicians very much during the century from 1815 to 1914. In the countries more or less governed by parliamentary systems, unity in foreign policy was sought in civilian dominance. That is to say, civilians headed the defense department as well as the other departments. In the more absolutist countries, where the military exercised great political influence, the irreducible minimum of regularized military influence was the tenancy of the ministries of defense by generals and admirals or, rarely, by officers of lesser rank. They invariably headed these ministries in France (to 1871), in Russia (to 1917), in Prussia and the German federal states (to 1918), in Austria (to 1918), in Japan (to 1945), and also in Italy. In France under the Third Republic there was a frequent changing of these portfolios from military to civilian hands and back again. In the Anglo-Saxon countries, on the contrary, a practically complete civilian supremacy existed until far into the twentieth century. While the American Republic has elected a relatively large number of generals and men of lesser military rank to the presidential office, it has not preferred the army general for offices like the Secretaryship of State until lately. In the smaller and particularly the so-called backward countries—Spain, Serbia, the Latin-American countries—this distribution of offices, depending largely on the victories and successes or defeats of the middle class, was highly irregular; the

part that officers played in their politics was in strict proportion to the absence or the weakness of the middle class.

One way of achieving the unity of foreign and military policies was, or seemed to be, the appointment of a military man to the office of either prime minister, as the supreme arbiter between departments, or minister of foreign affairs. The French after the Bourbon Restoration, and even after the July Revolution, tried generals in the direction of foreign affairs—Dessolles and Sébastiani—with unconvincing results. The Russians never tried the experiment; the Prussians tried, but with doubtful success. General Frederick William von Brandenburg (1792-1850), a Hohenzollern bastard, headed a ministry after November 1848 that imposed a reactionary constitution on the country. In 1850 he had to bow to the Tsar in the conflict with Austria for predominance in the German Bund. The saying at the time, that this diplomatic defeat, in lieu of a military one, "broke his heart," is only one indication of his failure and meant in effect that he had allowed his foreign minister, General von Radowitz, to bring Prussia into a position where a war threatened for which, according to the minister of war, the army was not ready.

Not until 1845, considerably later than France, did Prussia draw her first foreign minister from the army and also from one of the old Prussian families. He was Karl Wilhelm Ernst, Freiherr von Canitz, who had served with Yorck in 1812-13, had been aide-de-camp to one of the royal princes, observer of political and military events in and around Constantinople in 1828, and had served afterwards, without quitting the army, as minister to Cassel, Hanover and Vienna. He was so utterly subservient to Russia, where he had been "military chargé d'affaires" in 1842[48] that he used to read to the Russian minister at Berlin the instructions he was about to send out and would ask for his advice when his own diplomats abroad did not agree with him. All of this confirmed the haughty Russian in his conviction that these people, the Prussians, "must not be allowed to make grosse Politik, because they know nothing about it."[49] Canitz was swept out of office by the Revolution of 1848, by which time he was far less Russophile.

OFFICER-DIPLOMATS IN THE SERVICE OF POLITICAL REACTION

In the politics of the first half of the nineteenth century a few military officers had taken a liberal line, such as the Dekabrists in Russia (1825), General von Boyen in Prussia, Colonel Fabvier in France, and Sir Robert Thomas Wilson (1777-1849) in Britain.[50] The vast majority of European officers after the fall of Napoleon were, however, conservative if not reactionary. And many of them suffered something like an "interior Jena," a temporary defeatism and loss of nerve, when the revolutions of 1848 swept away existing governments, and fighters on the barricades appeared victorious over the regular soldiers in many lands west of Russia.

A Prussian colonel, regaining his nerve a little sooner than many around him, wrote in the title of his counter-revolutionary pamphlet: "Gegen Demokraten helfen nur Soldaten" (Against Democrats, only soldiers are effective). Generals everywhere on the continent helped to bring about the second European restoration of the nineteenth century, in civil wars and in wars of intervention in favor of reaction, in cabinets, in the police ministries of countries like Austria, on diplomatic missions, and in diplomatic posts. Metternich was beaten twice in succession, first as a reactionary by the masses and then as the asserter of civilian supremacy by the soldiers. Military politics and the assumptions underlying them made the Tsar bold enough to say, in the summer of 1848, that in case of war with Prussia, declared by her civilian Liberal ministers, he would ride all alone before the Prussian Army and would ask his old comrades: "Is it possible that you want to march against me? No, I cannot believe that."[51] Another period of Russian domination in Prussian affairs had begun, which only Bismarck could terminate, during which it was said in Berlin:

"Erst kommt der Zar, der Herr aller Reussen,
Dann kommt das offizielle Preussen."
(Th. Fontane)

The Tsar considered his own army as a police force for Europe, designed "to encourage on the one hand the powers that had fought against a revolutionary force...and on the other hand to spread terror amongst the revolted inhabitants of those States in which, according to him, authority had not been sufficiently restored."[52]

The "mad March" was hardly over when the "non-political soldiers" had taken their posts against the Revolution. In May, the Prussian Government sent General von Pfuel, who like Clausewitz and other Prussian officers had served against Napoleon in the Russian Army, to Tsar Nicholas in order to calm him about Prussia's policies in Schleswig-Holstein and Posen. Pfuel was one of the out-and-out reactionaries, whose hour had not quite arrived again in Prussian politics. In October of 1848, however, Pfuel, who had briefly served as Prime Minister, was replaced by General Count von Brandenburg, the King's half-brother, "the Bastard of Prussia." In December his ministry sent General von Willisen to Paris in order to ascertain whether

the election of Louis Bonaparte to the Presidency meant peace or war, revolution or counter-revolution. Incidentally, the temporary removal of Willisen from Berlin meant that Liberal influences around the King were further reduced and that the Reaction could take him still more firmly in hand.[53]

At St. Petersburg, Prussia—and no less, if not more, Russia—was served by General Theodor von Rochow (1796-1854), an Old Prussian reactionary. In order to please the Tsar (and himself), he called the far from revolutionary constitution of his country "abominable." When he was a lieutenant-colonel, he had changed from a military to a diplomatic career. In 1835 he became Prussian minister to "anarchic" Switzerland, that "detestable country" which gave asylum to political refugees, and in 1848 he became minister to St. Petersburg. Never, prior to the years following the Second World War, was there a period in which Prussia was more the vassal of Russia. Von Rochow took leave from St. Petersburg for a few months in 1851 to become minister to the Bundestag at Frankfurt where he introduced Bismarck, the novice in diplomacy, to this business and excelled as "crawler" before the other power of reaction, Austria.[54] Despite his subservience, von Rochow was not always able to explain the policies of his own Government in ways that would please the Russians. He had to compete for their favor with General Oxholm, whom Denmark had dispatched following Pfuel's mission to explain the Danish side in the Schleswig-Holstein question.[55]

In Vienna, the old high aristocracy once more took over direct control of things, through Windischgrätz and Schwarzenberg. The grands seigneurs again demonstrated their easy mobility from one high office to another. Prince Felix zu Schwarzenberg (1800-52) had entered Austrian diplomatic service after six years of military service, on the advice of Metternich himself, whom he came to embarrass, though only temporarily, by his close association with one of the Dekabrists while serving in St. Petersburg. His reactionary opinions did not blind him to the essential fact that absolutism, if it were to continue to exist, needed to apply at least some of the administrative progress achieved outside Austria. In 1848 he returned once more to army service, against Piedmont and the Revolution in Vienna. As prime minister (from November 1848) he became convinced that only the military arm could conquer and hold down the Revolution, and since the Austrian army proved insufficient, he did not hesitate to call on the Russians for help against the Hungarians, who had declared their independence from Vienna. Following the defeat of the Hungarians, he once more established Austria's predominance in Germany. He forced Prussia to give up her reform plans for the German Bund and, under the threat of Austrian mobilization and Russian displeasure, to sign the convention of Olmütz (November 29,1850). Schwarzenberg liked to rub in the "humiliation" it brought to Prussia, for he wanted to see Prussia humiliated first and afterwards destroyed. This set off the final determination of Prussia's governors to reorganize the Army and seek a showdown with Austria.

The head of the defeated war party in Berlin at the time of Olmütz was General Joseph von Radowitz (1797-1853), Prussian Foreign Minister for a short time, who had demanded war with Austria. He, unlike the war minister, thought the country and army were ready. To support his demand he produced what were, according to Bismarck, altogether unlikely figures of Austria's mobilized strength. Following his capitulation on the question, Radowitz resigned from the office to which he had risen from such services as that of Prussian military plenipotentiary at the Bundestag and leader of the extreme right in the Frankfurt Parliament of 1848-49. In all, he was (according to Queen Victoria's brother-in-law in Coburg) "a figure as though taken from the Middle Ages, a political general as though coming from the days of Frundsberg and Schärtlin [two sixteenth-century German condottieri:] and at the same time a bishop in armor, a man of great knowledge and wide reading."[56] But according to Bismarck's gruffer judgment he was merely "the dexterous master of wardrobes for the medieval fantasies of the King."[57] The Tsar could not suffer his politics, though King Frederick William IV had recommended him as "the most determined reactionary."[58]

While political parties and their strengths may be judged by their programs and the votes they obtain, the political influence of the military must be traced by the extra-military positions they hold at various times. Hence the importance of tracking down such employments. Thanks to the military, Reaction had never been so powerful; never had it formed more of an Internationale, truly the first Internationale of the nineteenth century, with Tsar Nicholas as its head both before and after 1848. Diplomats whispered to one another in St. Petersburg that the Tsar had said in March 1848: "J'ai le sang russe pour souffrir que les ouvriers gouvernent l'Europe."[59]

To that seat of reactionary power the troubled countries sent their emissaries in order to obtain military, diplomatic, and even financial support. To make them more acceptable to the autocrat, several of them were generals. Prussia kept General von Rochow, Bismarck's predecessor, at his court as minister. Cavaignac, a

general with Republican traditions whose services to the sake of order in the Paris street battles of June 1848 were nevertheless appreciated by the Tsar, sent his friend General Le Flô to St. Petersburg as the representative of the as yet unrecognized Republic. And the Tsar received with outspoken benevolence the representative of the man thanks to whom, in the original formulation of Sebastiani, "order reigned in Paris." "General," he told him cordially, "I receive you first of all as a soldier...I shall recognize the French Republic, and the hand which I stretch out to you is the firm assurance of that. However, the habits of this Empire prescribe that I should wait with that until your Government is completely constituted; after that I shall receive you as minister. In the meantime, count on our lively and sincere sympathies for France" (September 26, 1848). Apparently Le Flô's "somewhat brusque frankness" and his military openness did not displease the sovereign. Beginning with their first contact, the General, carried away by his military impetuousness, spoke of an alliance. The Tsar, far from resisting, acquiesced: "No one can move and do anything in Europe as long as France and Russia are united and hold one another's hand." Still, the French Republic remained unrecognized. The rise of Louis Napoleon, a name of bad augury in Russia, displeased the Tsar so much that he could no longer carry on even such completely unobligating conversations. After Le Flô, general followed upon general in the French legation in St. Petersburg. His first successor, Ferrière, reported in January 1849 that "while the Emperor did prefer the new form of our Government to the July Monarchy, there was neither at the Court nor in society much liking for the Republic. After all, that liking would be singular enough on the part of an Emperor who has not been accustomed to look for power beneath the throne, and it would not be less so in the case of Nesselrode who is one of the authors of the Holy Alliance. The legitimate monarchy, that is today as always the subject of the innermost predilection of the Emperor of Russia and of the Chancellor."[60]

Tocqueville, during his short ministry (June-November 1849), sent to St. Petersburg his friend Lamoricière, general and deputy, who, like his predecessors, was received by Nicholas "with that noblesse mixed with benevolence which gave value to the most unimportant words"—so a partisan of the later Franco-Russian alliance writes admiringly of "its beginnings" in 1849. Both Tsar and general found the basis of an initial understanding in a strong dislike of German unity, if not also in common dislike of Louis Napoleon.[61] But such sympathies remained ineffective; Nicholas' first concern was still the Revolution and its suppression wherever it survived. Modest French remonstrances in favor of conquered Hungary, which it was hoped would not be treated too rigorously, were coolly received by the Tsar, who told Lamoricière in September 1849: "General, the cause for which we fought is the same for which you yourself fought in June 1848. It is against anarchy and demagogy that we have battled. I am sure that France will understand it thus, and as far as we march in accord, the peace of Europe is assured."[62] After a period of probation, the French Republic was at last recognized, on the strength of its good behavior at home and its peacefulness and moderation abroad, as Lamoricière was told.

When Tocqueville resigned and General Lahitte became his successor as foreign minister, Lamoricière also resigned and entered the ranks of the opponents of Louis Napoleon, becoming one of his bitterest enemies.[63] His immediate successor was General de Castelbajac. Von Meyendorff, Russian ambassador at Berlin and one of the sharpest watchdogs of the Reaction, described him as follows:

...old white moustache, honest and martial face, simple and loyal language, going to Russia merely in order not to refuse his support to the cause of order and because as a passionate admirer of the Emperor he is happy to be accredited near him. His suite is equally comme il faut; ancient names, good sentiments, they bring us no communist ideas; and our young people, when hearing them speak of the dangers which the social order is hatching, may well reflect on the consequences of that faultfinding and doubting spirit to which they surrender so easily out of levity and laziness.[64]

While the continued services of Castelbajac helped to make Napoleon III somewhat more acceptable to the Tsar as a co-sovereign and to obtain for him the latter's recognition, the diplomatic amateur allowed himself to be overwhelmed by Nicholas' favors and engaging manners. All this was booked and reported to the Tuileries as evidence of diplomatic success. The general-ambassador was, however, the last to penetrate the Russian intentions against Turkey.[65] And it was only befitting that when Castelbajac had to announce the breaking off of diplomatic relations at the beginning of the Crimean War, Nicholas conferred on him, and Castelbajac accepted, a high Russian decoration, a rather exceptional occurrence in the annals of diplomacy.[66]

Prussia's delicate position during the Crimean War was effectively served by one of her most adroit, and at the same time most reactionary military diplomats, Edwin von Manteuffel (1809-

85). His double career had from an early date included aide-de-camp services with royalty—a stay of several months in St. Petersburg in 1847 where he entered into the good graces of Nicholas I. His vigorous anti-revolutionary attitude during 1848-49 qualified him for various diplomatic missions to reactionary courts. In June 1854 he was once more near the Tsar, this time in order to persuade the Russians to evacuate the Danube principalities, since Prussia would otherwise be forced to help Austria, who demanded this evacuation, under an assistance pact. He was in Vienna from December 1854 to March 1855, trying to persuade the Austrians to preserve their neutrality in the Crimean War by not joining the Western Powers. He was less successful in the Neufchatel affair, a territorial diminutio of Prussia in which the generals employed as diplomats showed nothing but bad grace and failure. From 1857 to 1865 he headed the all powerful Prussian Military Cabinet—"a fatal man in a fatal position," as one of the leaders of the Progressives called him. During the same period he served repeatedly on missions to places like Dresden, Hanover, and Vienna, where his reputation as a staunch reactionary would serve Prussian purposes in connection with the coalition war problems of 1864. At last he became so powerful and so dangerous to Bismarck's own position that the latter had him removed from Berlin and King William I, whom he served as general aide-de-camp. During the war of 1866 he negotiated the capitulation of the Hanoverian Army more tactfully than his superior wished. The war had tumbled so many thrones inside Germany that Manteuffel, when he stood before the Tsar once more, was told: "The complete dethronement of whole dynasties frightens me." Manteuffel had to explain to him why these changes were essentially non-revolutionary and why cordial Prusso-Russian relations could safely continue, in the preservation of which Manteuffel was to do still further service.[67]

After various military diplomats had done or attempted to do their duties in the service of "order" in mid-century Europe, they obeyed still other orders in the diplomatic field in the interest of the next war. Late in February 1853, Tsar Nicholas sent Prince Mentchikov, "soldier and sailor more than negotiator," on an inspection tour among the Russian land and sea forces on the Black Sea. Immediately afterwards, so that the demonstrative character would not be missed, he was designated as ambassador extraordinary to the Porte, bringing with him a large military retinue.[68] Castelbajac's sympathies with Mentchikov went a good deal further than the diplomacy of his master would allow. He compared him to "one of our grands seigneurs at the Court of Louis XV, fond of women, play, horses, good and bad company," but also a man of probity and independent character, sparing none in his witty and caustic remarks. The Prince displayed in full the haughtiness of bygone ages and threw the procrastinating Turks into a panic, even forcing their foreign minister to resign by ignoring him. His actions caused the chargés of the Western Powers to telegraph for squadrons of their navies to appear at the Straits. Stiffened in his resistance by the Western Powers, the Porte turned down Mentchikov's demands and the ultimatum that had threatened Turkey's independence, if not its further existence.[69]

Peace, as yet precariously maintained, was not helped in any respect when Napoleon III in the autumn of 1853 appointed one of his loyal serviteurs among the generals, Baraguay d'Hilliers, to the ambassadorship at the Porte, a "wrongheaded (brise-raison) and troublesome bedfellow, bound to embroil himself with everybody and with Lord Stratford first" as an Austrian ambassador characterized him. Promptly Stratford found in him "the very quintessence of French vanity and recklessness."[70] His stay was not a long one, but while he was at Constantinople he quarreled with nearly everyone—Stratford, the ranking British and French admirals, and finally the Turkish officials. He clashed so violently with the latter during the first months of the war that he wanted to break off diplomatic relations with France's Turkish ally, and at one time ordered the French naval commander to get up steam and carry the embassy personnel away. The cool-headedness of Benedetti, the embassy councillor, quieted things down; but the report of this ridiculous incident brought the General his repeal and the new job of commander of the military component in the expedition of the Western allies into the Baltic, where he gained his baton. The Emperor appointed no immediate successor at the Porte, realizing fully all the reasons that spoke against the appointment of General Saint-Arnaud, who entertained hopes that he would play the double role of ambassador and military commander of the French armed forces, and would earn laurels on the diplomatic terrain as well as on the battlefield and draw the double salary.[71]

As the Crimean war continued on its wasteful way, the military men before Sebastopol—Raglan, Canrobert, Saint-Arnaud, Pelissier—became fairly good coalition partners, while the governments drifted apart, the England of Palmerston preserving its ardor for war longer than Napoleonic France. In order to make some diplomatic capital out of the scanty military successes, Canrobert, at one time commander in the Crimea, was sent to the courts of Sweden and Denmark on a special mission in order to persuade them to join the war against the colossus of the North and

reopen the war in the Baltic. In spite of an outwardly splendid reception, the General's mission remained without tangible results.[72] The military successes of the Allies had remained far less convincing than the continuance of Russian power. While the small Northern Powers would gladly have seen this military power reduced and pressed back from "the window open to the west," the military inefficiency and the appalling amount of time, money and lives they had seen wasted before Sebastopol did not convince them that Russia could be more easily or more permanently defeated in the North, even with their help. A general could dispute these sound military conclusions as little as a regular diplomat.

One might have thought that the older conviction about the usefulness of the division of labor between the civilian and the military branches of government would have been strengthened by bourgeois disappointment over this military performance and would have excluded the military from participating in the negotiation of the Peace of Paris. Yet Palmerston, who probably knew the mass mind better than his colleagues, had to be persuaded that Admiral Lyons, one of the very few admiral-ambassadors of the century, was not a suitable First British Delegate, judging by his record.[73] The new Tsar had no bourgeois views to consider in choosing his representative. He sent as his First Plenipotentiary Count Alexej Orlov (1787-1861), a bastard offspring of the Orlov who had had a hand in the murder of Paul. He had been in turn cavalry general, chief of the police, diplomat on occasional rather than permanent missions, and for a long time in the most intimate confidence of the late Nicholas I. He who had stormed Montmartre in 1814 now took the hearts of the war-weary Parisians by storm with more subtle means, including that deceptive "military candor" which is the usual stock-in-trade of soldier-diplomats. The close understanding established from the outset between him and Napoleon and their common front behind scenes in opposing the British demands helped this negotiator equally as much as "his manners full of dignity." Neither his own concepts of honor and dignity nor those of the times kept him from attending a French victory parade celebrating the home-coming of Pelissier's troops from the Crimea. "Yesterday against you, tomorrow with you." Many of his contemporaries (and also the author of the Bolshevist History of Diplomacy) saw in him one of the most accomplished Russian negotiators of all times.

In the years following the Crimean War, military men on either side of the Prusso-Russian frontier were among the preservers, active and passive, of good relations between the two countries. They were also foremost among those who prepared Russia to shake off what they considered Bismarck's "yoke" and the ties of the written and unwritten alliances between Berlin and St. Petersburg. In the latter group belonged men like General Count Ignatiev, Russian ambassador to the Porte on the eve of the Russo-Turkish War of 1877-78, a man with an early love for Paris rather than Berlin.[74] This man, the "father of the lie," as the Turks called him, was not greatly restrained by the concepts of honor that are usually identified with soldiers.[75] Ignatiev, a protagonist of the renewed forward policy of Russia in the Balkans, provoked the war that began in 1877, and negotiated the Peace of San Stefano in which Russian Pan-Slavism overshot its mark. When Giers (and not Ignatiev, as many expected) became Russian foreign minister in 1882, Bismarck was greatly relieved and gladly accepted congratulations from his faithful.[76]

However, other enemies of a solid Berlin-St. Petersburg axis came closer to the top of the Russian hierarchy, among them soldiers like War Minister Miljutin or General Skobelev, an early and eager advocate of the alliance with France. Only temporarily did the pro-German orientation maintain an unfirm upper hand. The German orientation was represented by Count Paul Shuvalov, typical of an older Russia in which a member of the high aristocracy could freely move from high military to high diplomatic to high administrative posts, spared from the limitations under which the lower-born struggled, having to pay for their lower birth with the restriction to the one service for which they had prepared themselves by hard work and special examinations. This gave rise to group, or class, conflict in which the older group lost out to the rising Pan-Slav, military, pro-French group. The supposedly autocratic Tsar and the majority of the grand-dukes eventually passed over to the latter group. Resentment on the part of the military-bureaucratic group, mixed with admiration for dash and versatility, comes out clearly in the remarks made about Shuvalov by the later War Minister Suchomlinov, who had served under him in 1874. At that time, Shuvalov was chief of staff to the Supreme Commander of the St. Petersburg Military District and wore the uniform of the General Staff without having passed through the General Staff Academy. Like all other General Staff officers, Shuvalov was a confidant of the Tsar, and, to Suchomlinov, a man who was "in his whole bearing and inclinations nothing but a grand seigneur." "In the person of the Count," writes Suchomlinov, "we were often made conscious of the deep chasm that separated the great mass of the officer body of all ranks from the actually governing thin upper stratum."[77] These remarks furnish an excellent sketch of the Russian governmental set-up until about 1890—the high aristocracy in actual power without doing the necessary work itself, served by experts, military, diplomatic and administrative, many of foreign (and particularly German) descent. Bismarck himself might have been among them had he accepted the Tsar's offer of 1862 to remain in St. Petersburg and change over to Russian service.[78] As it was then arranged, this system, supported by German loans and German banking connections, favored so-called good German-Russian relations. Resentment rather than reason came to undermine it, resentment that found expression in the Pan-Slavist bourgeoisie, in the bureaucracy with its xenophobic measures, in the works of literati like Dostoievski, and, finally, in the group of professional soldiers inside Russia who were the pioneers of the French alliance.

On the Berlin end of this axis, the enemies of the Russian alliance were to be found in the General Staff, with Waldersee, Moltke's quartermaster-general and successor (1888-91), at their head and, less actively hostile, the epigoni of Bismarck in the Wilhelmstrasse who did not trust their own ability to carry on the Chancellor's complicated diplomacy. Included in the latter category was Bismarck's Reinsurance Treaty with Russia, which Shuvalov, ambassador in Berlin from 1885, endeavored to renew, provided (as he let the Bismarcks and the Kaiser know) the Chancellor was kept in office. The new Chancellor, Caprivi, a military man, let lapse the treaty designed to assure Russian neutrality in case of a war with France. He, rather honestly, preferred to prepare for the two-front war that he considered equally as inevitable as the Russo-French military alliance. Further, he thought that if the two-front war should come, it could still be won by the Central Powers, provided England remained neutral, an expectation likely enough during his term of office.

French diplomacy had long and often attempted, particularly since Sadowa (Austria's military and Napoleon's diplomatic defeat), to undermine the intimacy between Berlin and St. Petersburg. Generals as ambassadors seemed most suitable to perform this task, which primarily involved reaching the ear of the Tsar with argumentation and insinuation. It was only later, after 1888, that argument came to be supported by the more tangible persuasion of French capital steered by the Paris government in the direction of St. Petersburg. The directors of French diplomacy told themselves that "an ambassador obtains action in Petersburg only if he carries the epaulette and rides horseback; only in this way does he have the facilities to approach and hold conversation with the Tsar. And this was the reason why the Emperor, in order to counterbalance the influence

of Prussia in Russia, had chosen a general as his
representative."[79] The general chosen was Count
Fleury, a close companion of Napoleon III in their
parallel rise from adventurer to high, if still somewhat dubious, respectability. Fleury had been the
Emperor's military chief of personnel, keeper of
an office that was singularly similar to the Prussian Military Cabinet and that was invaluable for
a regime that still had to fight doubters and favor
followers. Fleury, who was also Napoleon's grand
écuyer, had been on several missions before, short
and occasional ones since the Emperor could not
spare him for long.[80] But the Russian mission,
beginning in 1869, seemed important enough to
warrant prolonged separation. And to have him
away from Paris proved quite desirable to the
more reactionary Rouher Ministry, which considered Fleury a representative of the Liberal
sentiment just then struggling for the upper hand
in the Emperor's unsteady mind. In order to preserve some of his old intimacy with Napoleon,
Fleury managed to maintain so-called immediacy
in his relations with the Emperor, that is to say,
he wrote to him directly.

Fleury's instructions were innocuous and as
vague as Napoleon's diplomacy at the time. While
Alexander gave him ample opportunity to approach
him, Fleury could make but little use of his
chances, for Paris sent him no instructions. "They
did not know at Paris what they wanted. And how
could he tell that to the Tsar? However, a little
blinded by his personal successes, he believed
that friendship had been regained and he persuaded
the Emperor of that."[81] But the latter could
hardly mistake the signs of continued Prusso-
Russian intimacy. Old King William had at first
been puzzled by Fleury's mission to his nephew,
as the latter told Fleury. But soon the men in
power at Berlin took a calmer view. "Fleury has
always been, and still is, a fanfaron," War Minister Roon wrote to Bismarck. The Russo-Prussian
family alliance was repeatedly celebrated, much
to the chagrin of the French, by invoking memories
of 1814. In order to combat these, Fleury's later
instructions told him to emphasize in St. Petersburg "the progresses of the Germanic idea" (later
called Pan-Germanism), which might come to be directed against Kurland-Livonia as much as against
Alsace. But the Russians did not find that bogey
very believable at that time.[82] The more willing
partner of a French anti-Prussian policy, Beust,
and his assistants in Vienna were deeply disappointed with Fleury's efforts. "He has allowed
himself to be soft-soaped in St. Petersburg,"
Beust wrote to Metternich in the Paris embassy
after war had broken out in 1870. "We know now
above all doubt that Russia is more than ever
allied with Prussia and will go at once into action
if we take up arms."[83]

The double set of Prussian diplomats at the
Tsar's court had of course observed Fleury's
activity sharply, though without alarm, reporting
him as "in the highest degree irritated and trying
everything to rouse sentiment against Prussia."
They were informed by the Tsar himself about
Fleury's last pre-war audience: He had spoken of the
échec France had suffered due to the Prussian
victories of 1866, and of the slurs that French
self-respect had received then and later. To this
the Tsar had replied that he could see no such
échec and that the general should not always speak
of French self-respect and forget that the Germans also had their self-respect. Later in the war,
when Germany proved victorious beyond Russian
expectations, it had to be reported to Berlin that
some of Fleury's insinuations, such as mention of
the threats that would be posed to Russia's Baltic
provinces by a stronger Germany, were finding
credence now in St. Petersburg.[84]

The essence and the trappings of Tsarist governance during the half century and more after
1815 seemed to call so imperatively for the general
en mission that even a representative of the
United States became convinced on the eve of the
Crimean War that

> a Minister from the United States, particularly
> at this time, ought to be a military man. I mean
> a man that has seen actual service, and who
> would be able to maintain his pretensions. This
> is not suggested for the mere vain show of
> wearing a uniform, but because the Government
> of Russia is a military government...There is
> no question but that a Minister of respectable
> military attainments and reputation would have
> much more might than a civilian. The ordinary
> reasons for such an appointment are, in my
> judgment, enhanced by the present position and
> prospects of Russia. Its influence over the rest
> of Europe is irresistible, particularly with the
> German states. Its vast military power and
> military spirit are the secrets of this ascend-
> ancy, aided by a system of diplomacy which has
> perhaps no equal. In short I mean that Russia is
> such a power that it is important to conciliate
> her by all honorable means, and of these the
> proper accomplishments of a Minister would
> certainly be the cheapest to our Government.[85]

In Austria, possibly even more than in Prussia,
the Reaction was run by the military, one of whom
was heading the police. The military entourage of
Francis Joseph, headed by the all-powerful aide-
de-camp-general Count Grünne in 1859, took on
the challenge offered by Italy with France behind
her, and presented those two countries with a
diplomatic excuse for war at the very time when
Cavour was engaged in "the search for this cause
of war so very difficult to find."[86] The foreign

minister Graf Buol had been somewhat hesitant about, if not, as he afterwards maintained, opposed to the war. But, as he added: "All our generals said that we were invincible. Could I keep them from undertaking it?"[87]

It might well be one of the characteristics of generals to take on missions that a career diplomat would decline as hopeless. From the outset this seemed to be the fate of Field Marshal Prince Windischgrätz's mission to Berlin during the war of 1859. When the Prussian statesmen could not make up their minds as to who was to be their friend and who their enemy, Austria dispatched this arch-reactionary to them. His unwritten accréditif was that it was he who had confirmed the death sentence that an Austrian court martial had pronounced against the Democrat Robert Blum, member of the Frankfurt Parliament of 1848. But even that proved insufficient to bring Austria into Prussia's camp.[88]

The Austrian foreign minister next defeated after Buol was also a former soldier, Count Mensdorff, who had reached the high rank of field marshal-lieutenant.[89] The documentary record tends to prove that after the war of 1866 he was more doubtful of his qualifications for that office than he had been before. In September 1865, he wrote to a ministerial colleague that Prussia betrayed her grasping tendencies with ever greater clarity and that he was dissatisfied with being pushed out of one position after another by her. "From what I say you will find that I do not possess the patience which is necessary for a diplomat— that I have known for a long time and I only regret that my official activity falls into just such a period when a more active proceeding, which is probably more in keeping with my temperament, appears impossible."[90]

In spite of his military background, he had done little to prepare for the coming war on the military side. He had, for example, neglected such measures as the concluding of military conventions with possible allies among the German middle states. When an emissary of the General Staff urged this, Mensdorff, with the almost operetta-like superciliousness of the Austrian aristocrat, answered him: "You know something of strategy, and I understand it too; of diplomacy you have no trace of an understanding, that is only understood by statesmen like myself." Despite all this self-infatuation, he felt so little qualified to represent Austria in the European congress proposed to avert war, where he, neither a powerful speaker nor a debater, would have to meet Bismarck face to face, that he turned the proposal down, even though Vienna ought to have accepted it, at least in the hope of gaining time for armaments in which she was very backward as compared with Prussia. After the lost war Mensdorff confessed: "I knew

nothing at all of politics, have told the Emperor this repeatedly."[91]

MILITARY APPRENTICESHIP OF DIPLOMATS

Up until this point our attention has been concentrated on military men who have engaged in diplomacy without thereby forsaking their military careers. Another type of soldier-diplomat made his appearance in nineteenth-century diplomacy—the man who had served as officer in his country's armed forces in his earlier years and then, dissatisfied or with changed ambitions, turned to a career in politics and diplomacy. The type was represented by men like Cavour, who had passed through cadet school and a few years of service in the Piedmontese army, or Lamartine who went through a similar career, or Count Walewski (1810-68). Walewski, the first Napoleon's bastard son, had, like most military politicos in mid-century France, at one time served in Algiers, where continuous war offered the occasion to officers of being turned into military heroes by that new power, journalism. Walewski gained a hero's reputation before he began to write for the press and the stage himself. Employed on some distant missions by Foreign Minister Thiers, he rose higher after Louis Napoleon had come to power. Among the various officers and ex-officers employed by the latter was Count Daru, nearly the last in the series of his foreign ministers. Daru was a graduate of the Ecole Polytechnique and an artillery officer for a few of his earlier years. Having accepted ministerial office early in 1870, he introduced himself to the Prussian representative by saying that "he was not a diplomat at all but a former military man and that he did not know how to hide his thoughts"[92]—the typical "disarming" gesture on the part of the military man in diplomacy.

A modicum of military service, often including war, gave the diplomats and ministers some military experience and judgment—still "quite insufficient," in the eyes of most military professionals—which they might consider and apply in their subsequent civilian careers. It often made them quite critical of the military and their views on politics, as well as their intrusion into the political-diplomatic field. Quite a few of the German ambassadors who were critical of the last Emperor's military and naval politics began their public service and acquired the basis for their criticism in army service. Prince Philipp zu Eulenburg (1847-1921) entered the army in order to participate in the war of 1866, but left it after a few years, "embittered by the tortures on the part of unjust, narrow-minded and uncouth superiors." He next studied law, served again in the war of 1870-71, and then, under the powerful

aegis of the Bismarck family, entered the new
Reich's diplomatic service. As ambassador and
representative of the Wilhelmstrasse in the traveling Kaiser's largely military entourage, he had to
combat the military influence and the Kaiser's
view "that military men are more reliable than
civilians." This at least was his assignment as
Holstein outlined it for him during a feud between
the Wilhelmstrasse and the Chief of Staff, Waldersee, in 1890. His struggles with the military resulted in Eulenburg's late-in-life conviction that,
in the case of Germany, "the best army made the
worst politics."[93]

Two ambassadors to Washington, Baron Speck
von Sternburg (1903-08) and Count Bernstorff
(1908-17), were what Bismarck called horses
from the "stables of diplomacy." Both had changed
uniform after a few years of cavalry service,
Bernstorff at the suggestion of Herbert Bismarck,
who had been on the lookout for diplomatic remounts. Sternburg, whose nobility was still recent, became the trusted friend and military
counsellor of Theodore Roosevelt on such questions as army discipline and the formidable qualities of the Japanese army. Sternburg had observed the Japanese army and reported on it to his
American friend as early as 1894-95. In 1907, during a period of high American-Japanese tension,
Roosevelt wrote to "Speckie" that his was "the
best advice the country received."[94] Another
high-ranking diplomat chosen by the Bismarcks,
and falling into our present category, was
Count Friedrich Pourtalès (1853-1928), at first
an army officer. In 1879 he was attached to the
Vienna embassy; in 1881 he changed over altogether to the diplomatic service and finally rose
to the ambassadorship at St. Petersburg (1907-14).
Prince Karl Max von Lichnowsky (1860-1928) also
falls into the present category. Beginning as a
cavalry officer, he entered diplomatic service in
1889, left it in 1904, but returned in 1912 in order
to become ambassador to London with the impossible task of maintaining British-German harmony
in spite of naval rivalries. Baron Hermann von
Eckardstein (1864-1939) was also selected by Bismarck and his son Herbert, who had heard of the
drinking prowess which he combined with the
stature and good looks of cuirassier. The old
Chancellor examined the young lieutenant himself,
who was not aware he was being examined, and
passed him, offering him an opening in the diplomatic service. Eckardstein had not thought of such
a career himself but accepted, though one of his
superiors, Count Haeseler, advised against the
change. "What do you want to do among those
scribifaxes in the Foreign Office? You won't make
your fortune among those brethren. You ought to
remain a soldier, go to the War Academy and then
try to get into the Great General Staff."[95] With-

out reaching the very highest post Eckardstein
nevertheless came to play an important role in
Anglo-German relations, the increasing dis-
harmonies of which he did his best to dissolve.

The diplomatic beginnings of Count Ulrich von
Brockdorff-Rantzau (1869-1928) were post-Bis-
marckian. He made the change from cavalry to
diplomacy in 1894, became in due time minister
to Copenhagen, Foreign Secretary at the time of
the "dictation" of Versailles, and, still later, ambassador to Moscow. Another diplomat marking
the enjambement in diplomacy from the military
Reich to the peace-intending Republic was Gerhard von Mutius, who served as an army officer
until 1902, married into the Bethmann Hollweg
family, and changed to the foreign service to become in due time minister to Oslo, Copenhagen
(1923) and Bucharest (1924), as well as head of
the German Peace Delegation in Paris in 1920.
He was also the author of various philosophic
writings.

A roster of names and vitae of pre-1914 German diplomats would reveal some military
service, active or reserve, in the majority of
cases. Most of these had originally entertained
military ambitions; others merely acquired reserve commissions. Here we are dealing only with
the former group. Still, there is not one in the
top rank who could be called an outspoken
militarist. They all shared the Bismarckian
view that Germany, in her geographic-diplomatic
situation, needed to keep her Army as strong as
possible with the available "good" officer material; but several of them had misgivings about the
necessity of a strong Navy for Germany.

Practically all of the higher-ranking diplomats
were bearers of great names, as a rule greater
than the majority of those reaching the highest
military posts, while the names in the Imperial
Navy were still newer and of lower standing.
The rule that "no knight ever went to sea" was
only slowly abandoned under William II.[96] The
names in the case of the diplomats indicated that
they were bound to represent and preserve an
older and more conservative interest than those
of the military officers. The fighting services
could, among other things, serve to create new
reputations and new names and also to refurbish
the escutcheons of old families that had fallen
into disrepute or poverty, like the Hindenburg and
von der Goltz families. For them the wars that
many diplomats strove to avert could still be productive.

Superior to these men in diplomatic talents,
though scarcely as regards character and independence, was the later Chancellor Bernhard von
Bülow. Like many of them, he began as a cavalry
lieutenant (1870-72), leaving that service in order
to pass his law examinations and take up diplo-

macy under the prompting of his father, then Secretary of State, who was convinced that while his
son might in due time become a good cavalry
colonel, his best talents lay in the diplomatic
field. Bismarck kindly brushed aside the elder
Bülow's scruple that there were already three of
the very large Bülow family in the service, saying that he could not have too many of the good
breed.[97] This took place immediately after the
war of 1870-71, when the sons of Prussia's first
families were not eager to enter the diplomatic
service but preferred the military service, at
that time both higher in prestige and less exacting in its entrance requirements. The dearth of
candidates of the desirable kind went so far that
Bismarck had to call on the Army to send him
some qualified officers, who were always of the
nobility, to be tried in the foreign service. Not all
of them proved successful in their new field.

British governing society during the nineteenth
and twentieth centuries did not generally allow
that easy mobility with which members of other
aristocracies moved from military to diplomatic
posts, and possibly back again. There are, however,
a number of notable exceptions. After a distinguished career under Wellington in the Peninsula,
Lord William Russell changed from Army to diplomatic service, becoming minister to Berlin in
the 1830's. "He much preferred the sword to the
pen, although he was a keen and able diplomatist."[98] His successor in that military capital
was another ex-soldier, Lord Burgersh, afterwards Earl of Westmoreland, who had served before at Florence and still earlier as British Military Commissioner in Schwarzenberg's headquarters in 1813-14.[99] Field Marshal Hugh
Henry Rose, First Baron Strathnairn (1801-85),
the son of another British minister to Berlin,
entered the Army at nineteen. In 1840 he served
"under the orders of the Foreign Office" with a
British detachment in Syria that was to cooperate
with a British naval force and Turkish troops for
the purpose of ousting Mehmet Ali's French-
backed forces from that province. He displayed
such diplomatic talents in services as liaison
officer with the Turk that he was appointed British
consul-general for Syria in 1841. He served there
for seven years as a peace-maker among the
warring tribes and factions of Maronites and
Druses. In 1851 he was made secretary of embassy at Constantinople, where he was acting as
chargé in 1852, during the absence of Stratford
Canning, when the trouble over the "Holy Places"
started developments leading to the Crimean War.
During that war he served in a very acceptable
manner as British Commissioner at French
headquarters. Still later, he returned to exclusively military service, commanding in India during
the Mutiny and after.

General Stanton is among the still later trans-
fers from military to diplomatic service in
Britain. He was consul-general in Cairo at the
time his country acquired the majority of the
Suez Canal stock, and a careful opponent of the
French influence in Egypt that was exerted
through the employment of French capital.[100]
To this list one might also add Evelyn Baring,
First Earl Cromer, who began his career as
British imperialist in the Royal Artillery and
became a pro-consul rather than a diplomatist;
Edgar Vincent, First Viscount d'Abernon, youngest son of Sir Frederick Vincent, whose public
services began in the Army and ended in the
British embassy at Berlin (1920-26); and Sir
Claude Macdonald, Minister to Peking during
the Boxer Rebellion when he, as director of the
armed resistance of the foreign legations, could
apply the military experiences he had gained
during some earlier years of service in a High-
land regiment.[101] British foreign service during the last two centuries has included a number
of former officers as consuls and consuls-gene-
ral: Colonel Hodges, who reported from Hamburg on the Schleswig-Holstein question after
1848; Colonel Trotter, Consul-General at Galatz
at the beginning of the twentieth century; and
finally, a number of officers whom Salisbury
appointed as consuls to various Turkish cities,
from where they were to watch Russian expansion into Asia during the 1870's and 1880's.[102]

Other Powers took army and navy officers
into their diplomatic services, though nowhere in
considerable numbers. We note the Austrian
cases of Baron Giesl von Gieslingen, military
attaché and last Austro-Hungarian minister in
Belgrade; Prince Franz zu Hohenlohe, military
attaché in St. Petersburg and later ambassador
in Berlin. And there are the American cases of
John B. Jackson, a former naval officer and
attaché, before and after 1900 chargé at Berlin,
later minister plenipotentiary to various Balkan
capitals;[103] and Gilchrist B. Stockton, retired
rear admiral, Democratic politician and United
States Minister to Austria (1930-33) and appointee
to various other naval and diplomatic posts.[104]
The Swedish Minister to Berlin during the
Weimar Republic years, Af Wirsen, had come to
his post from Constantinople, where he had been
military attaché and had won the friendship of
General von Seeckt.[105] The service most
strictly civilian in composition, though not necessarily in outlook, was that of the French
Third Republic, especially in its later years.

LATE NINETEENTH-CENTURY SOLDIER-
DIPLOMATS

In his mastery over the diplomats, Bismarck
had to contend from the outset with considerable

self-will and independence on the part of some of Prussia's ambassadors. Diplomats were brought under strict control, sometimes ruthlessly, as in the case of Count Harry Arnim, ambassador to Paris. They were taken on, beyond the stock quota from the governing families, regardless of rank and regardless of whether their background was civilian or military.

One of Bismarck's under-cover agents with a military background of a sort was Theodor von Bernhardi, a writer of military and historical works of some distinction. Though a civilian, he was made a military attaché, the only case of its kind on record, which is but one more indication of the unconventionality of Bismarck's diplomacy before 1871. A few years later Bernhardi was active in Spain, where he spent Prussian money in the interest of the Hohenzollern candidature. If successful, the Great General Staff considered that the candidature would keep at least one French army corps stationed along the Spanish border and thus away from any fighting on the Eastern front of France.

Bernhardi's co-agent in Spain was Major (later General) von Versen, qualified for the task by his good Spanish and his earlier experience as military observer for Prussia in the war between Brazil and Paraguay. Versen's orders of April 1870 were to travel secretly to Madrid (where his incognito did not remain totally unpenetrated) and study there the chances of the Hohenzollern candidature from the political and military points of view. He thought the chances excellent, particularly regarding the essential approval of the army. He was back in Berlin in May to report to Bismarck who, however, would not see him. Instead of receiving thanks, he was ordered back to garrison duty, which he resumed after a last attempt on his own to persuade the candidate's father not to cancel the original permission for his son's candidacy.[106]

The employment of military diplomats by Cavour and his successors was somewhat in the style of Bismarck's diplomacy. His first visit to Napoleon in 1856 disappointed Cavour in his hopes for a war alliance against Austria. He left a double set of negotiators behind to carry on in Paris, his own secretary Nigra as minister and Count Vimercati as military attaché. The latter, an intimate of Victor Emmanuel with a somewhat stormy past, including a term of service with the French Spahis in North Africa, was to be the secret direct intermediary between Napoleon and Cavour and the King. When the two Governments became estranged over the Roman question following the War of 1859, Vimercati served again in his old role between the two monarchs, both of whom liked to by-pass their regular ministers.[107] Out of Cavour's school came General Giuseppe

Govone (1825-70), liaison officer with the various Western Powers during the Crimean War and participant in the Zürich peace negotiations of 1859. Thus prepared, he was sent in March 1866 to Berlin, where he had once served as military attaché, in order to negotiate the alliance that led Prussia to Sadowa and Italy once more to Custozza.[108] The diplomatic reaction to Sadowa, the never-quite-completed alliance of France, Austria and Italy, was first started by a general of the European irregulars, General Türr, once a commander in Kossuth's army, who carried his grand design between Paris, Vienna and Florence beginning early in the year 1868. He found Victor Emmanuel eager, while Francis Joseph, who did not say no, wanted to wait until the Austrian Army was more nearly ready for another war.[109] Soon the regular diplomats and military men took the strands of the web into their hands. Finally, among the later Italian soldier-diplomats, one must mention General Menabrea, ambassador to Paris (1882-91) during the period of sharp French-Italian conflicts that made Italy join the Central Powers in the Triplice.

For many years, both before and after 1848, military men were the most decided adherents of a Holy Alliance, the old one or a new one, between Vienna, St. Petersburg and Berlin, an utterly reactionary formation in the eyes of the bourgeoisie of the three monarchies. The military closely surrounded the three monarchs, whose absolutism they tried either to maintain or to restore. The entourage of most nineteenth-century monarchs was far more military than that of the majority of their ancestors. And, as representatives of specific interests, these soldiers were as determined as any parliamentary representatives then or later and had in hand mandates as fixed as those of any parliamentarian. The aides-de-camp generals were, as a rule, nearest to the monarchs. They were the most political and the most courtier-like of all generals, whether in the entourage of the tsars, the Hohenzollern, Francis Joseph or Napoleon III.

From the illustrious circle of the Berlin Nebenregierung came such ad hoc military diplomats as von der Gröben, Gustav von Alvensleben and Edwin von Manteuffel. Before 1871, when he became a conservative in diplomatic technique, Bismarck was always ready to employ unconventional agents on foreign business. He went so far as to make use of Karl Blind, the father of the young man who had fired at him, after the attempt on his life.[110] Blind began his practical work with the hurried mission of Alvensleben to St. Petersburg for the purpose of concluding a convention providing for common measures, in-

cluding military ones, against the Polish Insurrection of 1863. The General was a reactionary
of the purest water, ready "to fight the Revolution
everywhere," so eager in fact that he rather exceeded his instructions and caused some subsequent embarrassments to Bismarck's diplomacy.
After all, a Prussian foreign minister had to be
more aware of Prussia's in-between situation than
an army man readily opting for the East, as did
so many of his kind before and after him.[111]

Manteuffel was almost a diplomatic-military
commis voyageur, later to become a field marshal.[112]   As a commanding general in the war of
1870-71, Manteuffel, when in the exclusive company of officers, found it "a shame that such a
politician as Bismarck should have more influence
than army leaders and generals."[113] In spite of
their constant bickerings and Manteuffel's growing
desire to become Bismarck's successor,[114] the
Chancellor had to suffer him in such high military-
political offices as commander of the German
troops in France after the Treaty of Frankfurt and
as Statthalter of Alsace-Lorraine (1879-85). In
the last position his governing gifts proved of a
nature to win many non-Prussian hearts and
minds. Even French testimony paid tribute to "the
rare qualities which gave the Marshal distinction,
his military firmness, his moral authority joined
to an eminently supple mind, his ability to handle
men, his originality full of seduction, the infinite
resources of his familiar eloquence, his ardent
proselytism of a Teutonic knight, tempered by
the tact and the fine graces of a man of the world."
These talents could endanger the French grip on
the protesting minds of the Alsace-Lorrainers.[115]
Coming from one who as diplomat and Frenchman
was doubly opposed to Manteuffel, this was high
praise indeed, and considerably more than Bismarck would have been willing to concede him.
Bismarck's own later experiences with Manteuffel
on diplomatic missions largely served to convince
him that generals, whatever their usefulness before 1870, were not fit and suitable instruments
for the diplomacy of the new Reich.

In August 1876, German aloofness from the Balkan problems had put the Russian governors out of
humor. Ambassador Schweinitz was on leave, and
thus the regular channels for the enlightenment of
the Tsar were temporarily broken. Under these
circumstances, no one seemed more suitable than
Manteuffel to calm the Tsar and interpret German
diplomacy and its intention of proving to him "the
same friendly tendency (Gesinnung) that he has
shown us in 1864, 1860 and 1870." Asked by the
Prussian military plenipotentiary whether he would
be welcome, the Tsar replied by inviting him to
Warsaw, where they would meet at the forthcoming
maneuvers. Manteuffel was the bearer of a message from William I to his nephew the Tsar, assuring the latter that "the memory of your attitude

towards me and my country from 1864 to 1870-
71 shall guide my policy towards Russia, no matter what happens."[116]

The assurance that Germany would stand by
Russia "no matter what happens" was delivered
by Manteuffel with great aplomb and with the full
appreciation of the military man for the mobilization of 300,000 Russian soldiers along the Austrian frontier during the recent war. In fact,
Manteuffel accomplished his task with more feeling and soldierly sentimentality as to the past
than Bismarck, with an eye on the future, thought
necessary.[117] It was a direct outcome of the
Warsaw concerto as played by Manteuffel that the
Tsar, through another Prussian soldier-diplomat,
General von Werder, submitted to Berlin some
weeks later the trying question as to whether, in
the case of an Austrian-Russian war, his uncle
would act in the same manner as he, the Tsar,
had done in 1870.[118]

In 1879, while Bismarck prepared his fateful
option for the Austrian alliance, Manteuffel
arranged a personal meeting of uncle and nephew,
which took place at the frontier station of Alex-
androwo. Bismarck wanted to prevent the meeting
but could not. Manteuffel tried to confirm the
old Emperor in his traditional Russophilia, which
Bismarck believed outdated and which, he threatened, could only be maintained by his own retirement in favor of Manteuffel. Thus intimidated,
the Emperor agreed reluctantly to the Austrian
alliance.[119]

With this case, the usefulness of generals on
ad hoc missions came practically to an end, as
far as Bismarck's diplomacy was concerned.

After 1871, Bismarck's diplomacy became
rather more conventional in the methods and persons employed. A few military men were still
used on occasion, provided he found them faithful
to himself rather than to old army loyalties. In
private talk at this time he did not hesitate to express the opinion that military men had on the
whole fallen in his estimation:

Of all the marshals, Moltke and Manteuffel are
really outstanding men [he confided to a
trusted interlocutor]. Steinmetz was a reckless
waster, a butcher of men, Herwarth owed his
career to his guardsman's physique. Manteuffel
is made of noble metal, for him the State interest far surpasses the personal; he would always subordinate himself when the former
enters the case. I have offered him the post
of ambassador to Paris, the highest post next
to that of Chancellor. He turned it down with
the words: "Should the case of a Federal execution in Bavaria arise or should the Revolution have to be thrown down in Prussia, that
would be my case." [These last, rather indis-

creet remarks the Chancellor spoke in English in order not to be overheard by the rest of the company present.] [120]

Bismarck's conflicts with the Army in the conduct of foreign affairs during his last three wars and on several later occasions, increasing again toward the end of his regime, made him hesitant about the further diplomatic usefulness of officers. The conflicts were fairly typical ones: the fashioners of victory are as apt to fall out as thieves over such matters as the allocation of credit, the recipes to which the successes are to be ascribed, and the recipes that will apply most appropriately to the future. Bismarck found the military esprit de corps too strong for their complete absorption into the diplomatic corps. "Once a general, always a general" was an attitude generally reflected among them.[121] During his last twenty years in office, Bismarck, although always remaining "a friend of the army," used officers who remained officers sparingly on diplomatic work. In 1871, during the transition from military occupancy to the resumption of full diplomatic relations with France, he made Count Waldersee, then a young colonel but later Chief of Staff and foremost helper in the Chancellor's downfall, chargé d'affaires in Paris, where later none but civilians came to be employed as ambassadors. Only in his dealings with Russia was Bismarck unable to dispense with the diplomatic services of generals. And even in this direction, their services, their outlook, and their methods did not always prove satisfactory to him.

And it was hardly better or more convenient to receive than to send military diplomats, as Bismarck came to conclude in his last years, and as his successors felt even more strongly. Even such a sympathetic man as Prince Paul Shuvalov, Russian ambassador to Berlin from 1885 to 1894, an honest supporter of the Three Emperors' League and the Reinsurance arrangements, a Russian grand seigneur to whom the term professionalism hardly even applied, so versatile was he in his employments, was hard to bear. This the Chancellor once confided to another civilian, the French Ambassador Herbette. Shuvalov was, he complained, not enough of a diplomat to avoid raising certain questions. "There is something inconvenient," he continued, "in these kinds of questions. If they are embarrassing, one does not answer them, or one answers them with lies. Now it is always bad to put someone under the necessity of committing an impertinence or of lying." This, he indicated, occasionally happened with regard to Shuvalov, "who puts questions on all occasions by saying: 'Excuse me, I am a soldier, and not a diplomat.' That reduces one to give some kind of an answer."[122] That is to say: generals as diplomats, in their false or genuine naïvete, insist on obtaining answers to questions that should never have been raised.

When Ambassador General von Schweinitz confessed to Bismarck in 1879 that his personal relation with Alexander II "made it directly impossible" for him to answer a question of the Tsar with an untruth, Bismarck, somewhat chagrined, said: "Then you cannot be ambassador at all"; and when Schweinitz sighed that he had a great desire to retire for a while, the Prince grumbled: "One should never again send a general to Petersburg."[123] However, the master-diplomat, knowing well that honesty is a means of diplomacy no less than the lie, kept Schweinitz at his post. When his ambassadorship came to a close in 1892, Schweinitz himself advised against another general in the embassy; his successor must be a professional diplomat, a born Prussian, for there remained still closer ties between Prussia and Russia than between Russia and the Reich. In the case of a violent conflict, the Reich might go to pieces but a Prusso-Russian alliance might survive. Also, he specified, the next ambassador should be a personality inspiring confidence rather than awe. On a still later occasion, around 1900, he again advised Bülow not to employ any more generals at St. Petersburg: "That which was formerly so useful, the frequent meetings with the Tsar, is gone; a phenomenon like Werder and myself sitting at the dinner table at Tsarkoie Selo when Emperor Alexander II drank a toast with me to St. Privat and had the Paris Entry March played in the presence of General Chanzy, would be now, when the Marseillaise is being played, a spooky anachronism. An admiral might almost be more suitable than a general."[124]

While the military attachés acting beyond their assigned sphere gave Bismarck increasing concern, he nevertheless used an opportunity to reward one among them who limited himself to his duties and in addition seemed of promising diplomatic talent. As a very exceptional thing in diplomatic routine, he had Count Carl von Wedel, the military plenipotentiary at Vienna from 1878 to 1888, serve repeatedly as chargé d'affaires during the absence of the ambassador. Somewhat handicapped as a "creature of Bismarck," as Waldersee described him, and also held up by the civilian clique of Holstein-Eulenburg in the diplomatic race, the long promised prize of the Vienna embassy was withheld from Wedel for some ten years, until 1903, during which time he served as minister to Stockholm, ambassador to Italy and in military-ceremonial jobs in Berlin. A Russian military attaché who was simultaneously stationed in Vienna admiringly confirmed from his observations the favorable judgment of Bismarck on the then

all powerful General Count Wedel. He was a
man of tall stature, penetrating eye, imperious,
full of dignity, knowing to perfection the maze
of Austrian affairs and informing himself in
Vienna as in his own home. He had at the same
time assurance and authority, strength and
suppleness, character and wit. His prestige
was hypnotic. In plain terms, they were a bit
afraid of him in Vienna and considered him an
all-powerful representative, tacitly aggressive
and easily conquering, imposed on Austria by the
victor of Königgrätz. Still, even he could not
quite adapt himself to the resistance which
Aehrenthal cunningly opposed to the hegemony of
Prussia at Vienna.[125]

While the Wilhelmstrasse after Bismarck did not
preserve the predominance of civilian reasoning in
matters of state policy, it was at least able to make
the foreign service a civilian preserve, for better
or for worse. After 1890, the services of generals
on ad hoc missions remained restricted to a few
occasions of a ceremonial nature, and only seldom
were they mixed with a diplomatic task.[126] Almost everywhere the number of general-diplomats
was materially diminished on the eve of the First
World War. None of the great embassies were held
by any of them; the civilians were everywhere in
the ascendancy in diplomacy; and only a few minor
embassies and legations were held by former military men of high rank. The reasons for this can
partly be found in the spread of professionalism and
departmentalization in the governments, which tended to exclude the soldier from diplomatic service
unless he entered it at an early stage. And also we
must look to the trend among civilian high officials
not to interfere with or even inform themselves
thoroughly of the implications of the military obligations of their countries or of the intended war
plans. The latter trend is exemplified most fatally
by Bethmann Hollweg and Edward Grey. The exclusion of military men was also due to the tendency
of the various foreign offices in both camps to reserve, as they thought, all decision about the casus
foederis and not have it prematurely admitted by
any general-diplomat for reasons of temperament
or outlook on the inevitability of war or judgment
on the fitness of the hour for launching the war. The
point came to be of particular importance in a system which, under the influence of English morality
and indecision, placed great importance on innocence from war guilt.

Aside from all this, there had come about, by way
of an inter-office truce, a more or less clear-cut
division between the foreign offices and the general
staffs. By this truce, most clearly seen in the case
of the Central Powers, least so in the case of France,
the detailed arrangements for military cooperation
in the case of war were left to the military staffs.
Bismarck had still supervised these staff conversa-

tions, even though the staffs in Berlin and Vienna
found this irksome. When he went, both German
and Austrian staffs breathed a great sigh of
relief. "Thank God that we are rid of the whole
family," wrote Archduke Albrecht, the designated
commander-in-chief of the Austro-Hungarian
army, to his Chief of Staff. Both Albrecht and his
Chief of Staff had long resented Bismarck's
"cajoling" of Russia during periods of "war
danger." In order to obtain closer military ties
with Berlin, the Vienna General Staff henceforth
considered sending a cavalry general as ambassador to William II, whom they expected would
himself take the government in hand. Unfortunately
for their scheme, this candidate died suddenly,
and the candidacy of still another general had to
be dropped. However, as they could console themselves, "the fall of Bismarck had certainly eased
the intercourse of the general staffs."[127] How
much, and how much too much, 1914 was to show.

GENERALS IN THE PREPARATION OF THE
FRANCO-RUSSIAN ALLIANCE

The bloody suppression of the Commune had re-
established the credit of the French generals and
the belief in their versatility, despite such
grumblers as Flaubert, who had hoped that France
was now forever rid of "messieurs les militaires,
lesquels se connaissent à tout, sauf à faire la
guerre."[128] The French Republicans now tried
to compete with Berlin for the ear of the Tsar by
sending him some of their generals as ambassadors. One of the first war ministers of the Republic, General Le Flô, served from 1871 to 1879 in
St. Petersburg, with the standing instruction to
make it "always our first interest not to allow
Berlin to again become the pivot of Russian
policy."[129] He let it be known to Russian society
that he was an Orleanist rather than a Republican
and that he served his country rather than "ces
messieurs de Paris." The latter, however, allowed
him to act as he pleased, in the safe supposition
that a general of monarchistic politics would win a
better position at the Russian court than a staunch
Republican. This expectation, according to German observation, proved to be quite correct: the
old trooper of low origin, in spite or because of
his unceremonious manner, became the darling
of St. Petersburg society.[130] Both he and his
successor, General Chanzy (1879-81), leader of the
French Loire Army of 1870-71, were more apolo-
getic than enthusiastic in their defense of French
politics.[131] And French ambassadors could always agree with the Tsar in condemning the post-
Commune "revolutionaries," even if handicapped
in their striving for the Tsar's favors by the unwillingness of the Paris authorities to grant the
Russian demands for extraditing Nihilists, a legal-
ism which, as Chanzy pointed out, only played into

Bismarck's hands.[132] When Chanzy left St. Petersburg in order to assume command of the Sixth French Army corps, the corps de révanche, he once more expressed regret that the problem of extradition "could not receive the solution one had hoped for here. For the new [Gambetta] Government this would be the best means of asserting itself in the eyes of the rest of the world and of reserving for France the place that the elevation of her ideas has always assured her."[133] That is to say, the denial of asylum and extradition of political criminals would be the higher idea.

As Chanzy's successor the directors of French diplomacy, as if at a loss for generals, selected an admiral, one of the few admiral-ambassadors of the century, Jaurès, uncle of the later Socialist leader. (Another admiral was the French ambassador to London in 1879, Admiral Pothuau.) The elder Jaurès had begun the diplomatic interlude in his life as ambassador to Madrid in 1880.[134] The Germans at St. Petersburg found his selection for the Russian post very much to their own interest. "A more peculiar representative of the French Republic could not have been chosen...Should there really be intentions and desires for an alliance between Russia and France, no one is less suited to promote it than this ambassador who is not at all being taken seriously." After less than a year's service, the Tsar informed the Prussian plenipotentiary that Jaurès had been recalled. "It was rather a pity," said the Tsar, "for one could never know whether the successor would not be much worse. Nearly all persons who serve that Government are canailles."[135] Even a member of the French embassy had to admit that the choice of Jaurès was unfortunate. "Each diplomatic post demands certain special aptitudes, and the admiral soon gave the impression that he was not endowed with all the necessary qualities to render all the services expected of him at a court like St. Petersburg."[136]

Chanzy's second successor was General Appert (1883-86), for whom Alexander had great sympathy, as he told the Germans. At the same time, however, and as late as 1887, he assured them that he would never do business with the French Republicans.[37] Appert, one of the military leaders in the suppression of the Commune, was no ardent Republican. He even allowed the Tsar to express to him, within hearing of the German ambassador, the hope that "you [the Army] will chase away that ignoble Republican Government."[138] When he fell, it was as a victim of his loyalty to the Tsar rather than to French institutions. In order to please the Tsar, Appert tried to persuade his Government not to discharge Prince Kropotkin, the anarchist, from

jail and not to include him in a general amnesty for political prisoners. The Paris Government, in the absence of legal means, had to decline the proposals; when the General still insisted, he was recalled. He did not hide the reasons for his retirement from Alexander, who had informed the French Government of his desire to see Appert remain and who attributed the recall to Appert's former and present stand against the Commune and Communards. It was an indication, he said to the departing General, "of the march which your Republic is pursuing towards the extreme Left. That's why, with you gone, I find it absolutely useless that your country be represented near me and I near them." Greatly infuriated by what he called "a political act disobliging to my person," he ordered his own ambassador in Paris away on a prolonged leave and declined to receive another French ambassador for the time being. He turned down General Billot, a former war minister who was represented to the Tsar as a Leftish politician, for whom the French, rather abjectly, sought the agrément.[139]

After he had been refused, it was long discussed at Paris whether it was more advisable to send a general or a civilian to St. Petersburg. On the one hand, "relations were more direct and more frequent between the Emperor and a military ambassador. At every moment parades and reviews and other solemnities of the same nature give a general the occasion to approach the monarch and to be invited to the imperial table, privileges rarely accorded to a civilian." Since Appert's recall, only General von Schweinitz and the Danish Minister, General Kjoer, were in this enviable position. But the French chargé at St. Petersburg still warned against sending yet another general: "Considering the well-known temperament of Alexander III and his brusque manifestations of bad humor, one asks oneself whether the too frequent opportunities of approach are really desirable." While things had gone off well enough with Appert, Le Flô, and Chanzy, it still seemed more useful to carry on business in the future through a civilian ambassador and through a prudent, conciliatory, temporizing minister such as Giers, who on his part had always tried to avoid, or at least to soften, the occasionally violent sallies of the Tsar. Giers had even hinted that, while the Tsar was still inclined to see another general as France's ambassador, he himself would prefer a civilian.[140] In the autumn of 1886, the Russians mentioned the name of an admiral and of a general who would be quite agreeable to them. The French, however, begged that St. Petersburg not insist again on a general-ambassador—it would too severely injure the feelings of General

Billot, whom the Tsar had thrice declined. Alexander agreed: "Tant mieux, if the new French ambassador is not a military man, I see him just that much less often."[141] Thenceforth France sent civilians as ambassadors to St. Petersburg for the most part, career men rather than politicians, who obtained and preserved the military alliance for which the general-diplomats had striven in vain. As Ambassador, de Laboulaye, under whose aegis the first military pourparlers in connection with the military convention took place, remarked, not without some self-satisfaction:

> It is a rather singular accident that this useful result has been obtained during the course of a civilian embassy to St. Petersburg. The partisans of a military embassy ought to see that one must not be too absolute in this respect and that our officers always know how to fulfill their task, whatever it may be, by remaining within their competency. Who knows whether it has not been essential, under these circumstances, that the Ambassador of the Republic clung, on his part, to his role and was not directly concerned with an act of fairness (acte de bonne guerre) which, coming from him, might have had the appearance of a diplomatic intrigue and might have given rise to the most lively polemics.[142]

The French, in June 1893, following the appointment in the preceding November of General von Werder as German ambassador, offered to replace the incumbent of their embassy with a new man, leaving to the Russians the choice between a general, Boisdeffre, the negotiator of the Franco-Russian military convention, and a civilian. The Tsar declined the offer of another general: Boisdeffre received a flattering eulogy, but, the Tsar added, "he is not a diplomat...though it is true that Werder is not one either." He wanted no change.[143] When some years later Boisdeffre pressed his own candidacy and seemed bent on pushing the civilian ambassador aside, Foreign Minister Muraviev much preferred the old ambassador to "a general who was not suitable as a diplomat,"[144] generically speaking. By the end of the century, a civilian foreign minister had determined, even in a capital like St. Petersburg, that a civilian was preferable to a general as ambassador. And there was a kind of international craft unionist agreement on that point among career diplomats.

Only once more did France see fit to make use of a military, or rather naval man as ambassador to St. Petersburg, which, after the failure of the Douma experiment, had again become the foremost citadel of European reaction. This seemed called for during the ministry of George

Clemenceau in 1907-08. The Russians believed that he had remained "faithful to his revolutionary antecedents," that he sympathized with the opposition in the Douma, and that he had allowed the French ambassador Bompard "to lose the sympathies of Petersburg upper class society and finally surround himself with none but Cadets and Social-Revolutionaries." At the time, and later in his memoirs, Bompard himself vigorously denied the latter accusation as something impolitic if not indecent. In order to save the alliance, which could not be based on the sympathies of a fast-weakening Douma, it was thought necessary to replace Bompard rather unceremoniously by Vice-Admiral Touchard, former chief of staff of the French Navy and commander of the Mediterranean squadron at the time of the appointment. The thought of again sending a general was given up in Paris, since it might allow unfriendly elements "to impute to the French Government ulterior motives of a bellicose nature." Strangely enough, an admiral seemed less open to such a charge. Clemenceau pleasantly remarked that "a sailor stood midway between a civilian and a soldier anyway."[145] In St. Petersburg

> the choice of this general officer was received with satisfaction. One appreciates the return to the French tradition, inaugurated in 1870 and interrupted only by the missions of Messrs. de Montebello and Bompard, that is to say, to select from the military element, which is a stranger to the party battles, the representative of the French Republic with the Tsar.[146]

The admiral, though well received by St. Petersburg society, including the German ambassador who called him "the old loyal and noble admiral," lasted only fourteen months. Then he was recalled, without knowing why. There had been doubt from the outset in the Russian capital as to whether he might not be "as republican as M. Bompard." This suspicion seems never to have vanished altogether after he had introduced himself to the newspapers with the statement that "in a country where the sovereign is the supreme chief of all the military and naval forces, a military man can count on a more intimate reception than a civilian," and at the same time had stated that "republican ideas" stood in the way of pursuing and extraditing political criminals as the Russians desired.[147] He was followed by two civilian ambassadors, Georges Louis (1909-13) and Maurice Paléologue (1913-17), whose earlier careers closely identified them with the Quai d'Orsay itself and who, as "strangers to the party battles," could be relied upon.

. . . .

An ambassador is not only a man charged with affairs of state, but he is also a symbolic figure, at times intentionally so, at times contrary to the intentions of his own government. A military ambassador in particular may easily "mean too much": it may seem as if he were sent more in contemplation of war than of peace, as if he were sent not merely from government to government but from army to army as well, a friendly chivalrous messenger when the two countries are friendly or allied, an ominous one when they are not. His mission may raise the impression that military subjects have been, are, or are to be the supreme consideration in the dealings between his own country and the one in which he is residing. His appearance can easily be over-emphatic and over-demonstrative, and his government has to consider whether that is in keeping with its own intentions of the moment, whether they are as warlike as the appearance of a general tends to make them. The question came before the Reich Government in the spring of 1891, the year of Kronstadt, when French révanche gestures were more vigorous than usual. The Kaiser's immediate military entourage, including a former military attaché in Paris, were alarming him and themselves with talk of an impending French attack. And yet neither the ambassador in Paris nor his military attaché raised an alarm corresponding to the excitement in the Kaiser's mind. In order to punish them for their carelessness, the Monarch resolved to recall both the very conciliatory ambassador Count Münster and his unalarmed attaché, and replace the former by one of his own aide-de-camp generals, General (and former military attaché) Count Carl von Wedel. The Wilhelmstrasse at once set its dissuasion apparatus to work, arguing that there were really no recent indications of French aggressive intentions, that for Germany to make a preventive war was absolutely out of the question. A Russian loan of five hundred million francs had just failed in the Paris market, with the approval of the French Government, certainly a sign that they did not count on the immediate military help of Russia. The Wilhelmstrasse continued:

> The appointment of a German general as ambassador is nothing unusual in itself. In Paris this has not happened for a long time; and the argument of not putting the negotiation of numerous delicate questions into the hands of a representative of the victorious army had without doubt contributed to this. (We have even found it troublesome when filling consular vacancies in France, that candidates had carried the title of officer up to then.) Should conditions become more acute with a military man in the office of ambassador, the sharper tone resulting will be interpreted

in a manner undesirable for us. The very appointment itself will be interpreted everywhere as a sign that we intend to talk more seriously with France. One will say, "We have started," and that is the very thing to avoid.[148]

War rumors soon calmed down, as did the Emperor, and Count Münster stayed in Paris for another nine years, finally to be succeeded by another civilian. In such attempts to demilitarize Wilhelminic diplomacy, not always as successful as on this occasion, the Wilhelmstrasse sometimes had allies, whether it knew it or not.[149] It best suited Salisbury's diplomatic aim of a loose understanding with the Triple Alliance to keep British-German diplomacy underemphatic in its terms and outward gestures. Meanwhile, military contacts of some intimacy were maintained between London and Berlin, but a military ambassador would decidedly have been de trop for England either to send or to receive. In 1895, when the question of replacing the British ambassador came up, the Queen herself had hinted at sending Field Marshal Lord Wolseley to Berlin, "which William jumped at." The latter was at the time fairly anxious "to increase and not to diminish" British military power and was eager to send advice to London to this end. Salisbury promised to find out at once whether the Queen's candidate was inclined to accept, but the Foreign Secretary himself was clearly determined to avert the mission. No better way seemed open than offering the passionate soldier the post as commander-in-chief of the British Army, even though, or because, this would eliminate the Queen's own candidate for that post, the Duke of Connaught. When the War Secretary informed the Queen of the proposed change in command, she insisted that Wolseley be told how eager her grandson was to have him at Berlin and how disappointed William would be, should he not come. But Wolseley still preferred the supreme army post.[150]

British unwillingness to employ military men in diplomatic posts, stiffening into principle rather than relenting as time went on, occasionally ran up against a situation in which the military interests and temperament of a sovereign or head of state seemed to make it advisable to approach him through a military man. William II was not the only militaristic sovereign in his time; by many signs Theodore Roosevelt was hardly a lesser one. It was generally believed that the President's military interests caused him to include the German ambassador, Speck von Sternburg, a former army man, in the circle of his intimates, from which the British ambassadors remained excluded. Roosevelt's other European friend, Cecil Spring Rice, was therefore "so glad" that Count

Edward Gleichen, British military attaché at the Kaiser's court, was transferred to Washington in early 1906. As he wrote to Lord Knollys, Edward VII's private secretary, "I am sure that a military attaché is the very man to get at him." He then proceeded to tell Grey the same thing: "The best person to keep in touch with the President is the military attaché, and as Gleichen has been shot in the stomach and the back, he is quite certain to meet with a favorable reception... Gleichen would certainly get on there, although he is rather apt to be scandalized by the unexpected," which one had to expect around Roosevelt.[151] Although possessing these somewhat curious qualifications for obtaining a diplomatic-military agrément from Roosevelt, Gleichen seems to have been called upon very rarely for diplomatic business by either the President or Grey. Only once, in the autumn of 1907, did Roosevelt send a message by Gleichen to Edward VII.[152]

The Americans had long shared the British reluctance to use military men as ambassadors and ministers. It was somewhat bewildering or perhaps misleading to foreigners to see the United States begin to use generals in diplomatic posts early in the twentieth century. Did this have a military significance? Early in 1906, during a somewhat critical state of affairs in the Far East, Roosevelt appointed the Governor of the Philippines, General James C. Smith, as ambassador to Tokyo. The German ambassador at Washington found it "in any case striking" that Roosevelt at this juncture "chose a man who is considered one of the men most familiar with conditions in the Philippines." "The President," he continued, "has assured me several times that he would evacuate the Philippines without delay if he should be able to get rid of them in an honest way. That the President clearly realizes the dangers that are threatening the island due to the growth of Japanese power, I have reported before."[153] Another general-ambassador, Horace Porter, had begun as a professional soldier and West Point graduate, serving in the Civil War, toward the end on Grant's staff and afterwards as the latter's private secretary. Still later, Porter had made a fortune in the railway business. This allowed him to accept and to fill with the necessary dignity the appointment to the Paris embassy, (1897-1907) though without donning either a military or a diplomatic uniform. But all these were citizen-generals, having spent more or less long years in retirement. Under a law of 1870, military officers on active duty were prohibited from holding civilian posts except with the permission of Congress.[154]

MILITARY DIPLOMACY IN THE BALKANS

While it remains a matter for speculation as to whether the compartmental system in the conduct of foreign affairs as established by the Great Powers on the eve of 1914 contributed to the dangers of war or lessened them, the strong intermixture of the military in Balkan politics and diplomacy was to prove definitely harmful to the maintenance of peace. The incomplete development of either a high aristocracy or a strong middle class in the Balkan countries left the door wide open to officers' politics. And military interference in politics was further encouraged by the readiness customary in such countries to proceed rapidly to the political application of violence.

While the Great Powers reduced the number of generals used as ambassadors or as cabinet ministers, the Balkan States continued to employ them on an ample scale. To highlight the situation by some examples: in Berlin, Turkey was represented from 1897 to 1908 by General Tewfik Pasha; Bulgaria, from 1904 to 1910, by Major-General Nikyphorov, who was afterwards (1911-13) minister of war. When General Pendezec, Chief of the French General Staff, visited St. Petersburg for one of the periodic staffs talks, he found that the Turkish ambassador was an old comrade from the days when they both had graduated from the French Staff School.[155] In order to normalize diplomatic relations with Montenegro, which had been interrupted for a time, Serbia, in July 1901, appointed Colonel Vasa Antonich, then military attaché to Vienna, as minister to Cetinje. This was to please the patron of Pan-Slavism, Russia, and was to signify to the Balkan public that, despite the dynastic conflicts between the Petrovitch and the Obrenovitch, there was still unity among the Balkan peoples. [156] In Montenegro, where trouble-making and ambition always stood in inverse relation to her size, generals were repeatedly made prime ministers and, at times, as in 1912 and 1914, combined that office with the war or the foreign ministry, or both. The Bulgarian Lieutenant General Paprikov filled such posts as foreign minister (1908-10), minister to St. Petersburg (1912-13), and member of the Bulgarian-Rumanian Boundary Commission after the close of the Balkan Wars. In November 1911, the hard-pressed Turks sent a mission, headed by the Marine Minister General Mukhtar Pasha, to Livadia in the Crimea, where the Russian Court was residing, in order to obtain Russian help against Italy in return for the eased or even altogether free passage of Russian warships through the Straits. But the Russian assurances went no further than a vague promise of non-aggression.[157] A colonel and adjutant-general of Ferdinand of Bulgaria was one of the two military members of a special mission to St. Petersburg in May 1912, which, after obtaining the patron's moral and material support, was to announce the conclusion of the Bulgarian-Serbian alliance, the basic instrument in preparation for the Balkan wars.

The sword-bearers in the Balkan capital were apt to be opposites in diplomatic business one day and opposites in the field the next. The Turkish chargé at Cetinje in 1912, Colonel Ali Riza Bey, changed from his peace-time post, in which he had learned to despise the Montenegrins and they to hate him, to the command of Scutari, a place that he defended heroically against the same people almost to the close of the Balkan wars.[158]

In contrast to the habits of the Balkan states themselves, the Great Power representatives in the Balkan capitals were nearly always civilian career diplomats, with a few notable exceptions among the Austrians. The specifically Austrian conceit exhibited in dealing with Balkan people might not have reached its peak of haughtiness without the military contribution to that traditional attitude. Count Bernstorff, who spent part of his diplomatic apprenticeship at Belgrade in the early 1890's, found there an old fieldmarshal-lieutenant, Baron von Thömmel, as Austro-Hungarian Minister. In Bernstorff's words:

> There could hardly have been a more unsuitable person for the post. He was typical of the spirit that provoked the war. Overbearing in manner and irresolute in act. He is alleged to have once said to the Serbian Premier: "I have served in Persia and in Montenegro, where the people are notoriously the biggest swindlers in the world, but in comparison with you they are honest men." He had indeed made not one single friend in Serbia, having undoubtedly taken the view from the outset that to make any was impossible.[159]

One of von Thömmel's successors at Belgrade was Baron Giesl-Gieslingen who, after sixteen years of service as military attaché in Constantinople, had changed over to the diplomatic service and had become minister to Cetinje (1909-13) and Belgrade (1913 to July 1914). It was he who delivered the Austrian ultimatum of July 23, 1914. Trembling with his tragic importance, he assured Vienna, which had ordered that the delivery of the ultimatum be postponed for a few hours, that he "would exert himself to the utmost in order not to perform his démarche before six o'clock." Five years of purely diplomatic employment had not given him a diplomatic temper. When the Serbian answer to the

forty-eight-hours ultimatum came, Giesl hardly even read it. When William II later came to study it, he thought that on the strength of it Giesl "could have quietly remained in Belgrade."[160] Giesl instead sent off the note prepared in anticipation of Serbian non-compliance, in which he announced the breaking-off of relations. Thirty-five minutes after the receipt of the Serbian note he was on the express train to Vienna, as if fleeing from the last chance of preserving peace.

The military took a hand in the preparation of the Balkan wars of both the nineteenth and twentieth centuries.[161] Among the four signers of the first of the twentieth-century treaties that prepared a robbers' coalition for the "liquidation" of Turkey, the Bulgarian-Serbian Treaty of Alliance of April 1904, were one general, who was the Serbian premier at the time, and one general staff colonel, the then Bulgarian chargé at Belgrade. At the same time the prime minister at Sofia was a general. Again, when the indignation over the annexation of Bosnia-Herzegovina by Austria once more brought the disappointed Balkan nations together for negotiations, it was the military men who attempted an alliance between Belgrade and Cetinje and had ideas of including Constantinople in a common front against Austria and Bulgaria.

While the negotiators of the treaties that actually prepared the First Balkan War were mostly civilians, the military drew up the military conventions implementing them. And it was the military part of the understandings that made Poincaré welcome them "as a factor in favor of the strengthening of the Balkan States." At the same time, he considered their treaty to have "a more aggressive than defensive character, since complications in the Balkan peninsula are possible at any moment."[162]

Once the Balkan Wars had been unleashed by soldiers and civilians in close cooperation and had been won by some and lost by others of the war-makers, the generals came forth to prepare the peace—and also new wars, including wars of révanche. After General Savov, as commander-in-chief, had lost the war for Bulgaria, he became a delegate to the two peace conferences at Constantinople and Bucharest. In the latter place he was succeeded by General Fitchev, former chief of staff, who had opposed the second Balkan War, saying that it was started by the aggression of his own country. Fitchev had concluded earlier than others that the Bulgarian position was hopeless and had urged her to conclude the Peace of Bucharest.[163] These Bulgarians promptly began negotiations for a secret military convention with the other loser, Turkey. They did not at once come to a definite agreement and the final consummation, Anschluss of both with the Central Powers, took still more time and preparation. One of the preparations was the practical exiling of the extremely Russophile General Radko Dimitriev, whom King Ferdinand considered "more Russian than Bulgarian," to the post of Bulgarian minister to St. Petersburg (September 1913). "Cette canaille," as his sovereign called him after the outbreak of war in 1914, returned once more to service with the Russian Army, did valuable service as army commander and was finally murdered by the Bolshevists, a victim of military Pan-Slavism before the Bolshevists came to renew it thirty years later.[164]

In spite of the strong military component in the Young Turks Party, military men in Turkey claimed only a moderate number of diplomatic posts. Among the posts claimed was that of the Berlin ambassadorship, held by General Mahmud Mukhtar Pasha (1913-15).[165] Though he drifted into disagreement with the Young Turks, Mukhtar could still not be removed by them since he was a friend of William II himself, both having served in the same regiment in their younger years.[166] Nearer to home, the rapprochement of the two losing parties in the Balkan Wars was still being pursued. For this purpose the Turks stationed Fethi Bey, a young hero of the Tripolitan War, as minister in Sofia (1913-19).[167] Mustapha Kemal Pasha, even younger, served under him as military attaché. At the time when the Russian Minister in Sofia reported that "one must suppose that his mission is principally a military one" (March 16, 1914), a secret Bulgarian-Turkish military convention had actually been concluded seven weeks earlier.[168]

In preparation for the Balkan and the First World Wars, the most aggressive group among the Balkan politicos, the Serbian officers, preferred terrorist to diplomatic action, awaiting the international results with some complacency and sang-froid. Russia, the patron of the original Balkan alliance, had not stopped the course plotted in 1912, even though she was well enough informed throughout. The Russian military attaché at Cetinje knew beforehand when the first aggressor would declare war. Why then, in 1914, should a cease-and-desist order be expected from the clients of military Pan-Slavism in the Balkans? And, in terms of broader speculation, they could rely on the Balkanization of Europe, still latent but bound to reveal itself more and more from that time on. The murder at Serajevo was, after all, promptly followed by the assassination of Jaurès, a crime never even punished. A supposedly civilian primacy in diplomacy was no longer able to cope with such an act, even if its will to do so was genuine, as it hardly was any longer in July 1914. By then, the two power-groups of

Europe had taken the several Balkan nations as valuable military allies.[169]

THE TWO WORLD WARS

The problem of the post-war employment of its military heroes has bothered American democracy and its governors and politicos from time to time. Electing them to the highest offices in the land has not proved uniformly satisfactory, nor would their frequent employment on diplomatic tasks be fitting. The Army's Chief of Staff during the First World War, General March, did what he could to relieve Pershing of everything even bordering on work of a diplomatic nature. For such work, March said, Pershing "had about as few qualifications as any man I knew," being as unfitted for it "as the average army officer." Pershing did not agree with this judgment, considering himself the equal of "the frocks"; and when they attempted to "coerce" him, he even did a little "desk thumping" himself. After his experiences as head of the American Expeditionary Force in a war of coalition, those who knew him well, like March, no friend of Pershing, thought that his "failure in diplomacy at Tacna-Arica might have been predicted, and that the subsequent solution of that matter by our diplomatic representative in Peru...under the direction of the State Department, only showed the truth of the old adage, 'Let the shoemaker stick to his last.'"[170]

In this period, as so often before, the use of military personnel in non-military assignments went well beyond the ceremonial. The demands of the two World Wars, as wars of coalition on both sides, were served by a multitude of liaison officers and missions, sometimes to the satisfaction and, perhaps more often, to the dissatisfaction of the senders and the recipients of such missions. The milites missi applied as much diplomatic persuasion as they possessed to their business, which was military, even if in some cases the diplomatic purposes may have surpassed the military ones. This was the case, for example, with Joffre's mission to the United States in 1917. The Marshal was packed off with the words of Prime Minister Ribot that "the prestige which he enjoyed in the United States was considerable" and that his presence there would set off a current of opinion very favorable to French interests. Joffre himself was convinced that "on the day of the peace negotiations, when France would be exhausted, American aid would be of inestimable value."[171] In his first task—to arrive in the United States ahead of a British mission which was also to apply for American help—Joffre was overtaken by the faster-traveling British. However, in the military

arrangements for the detailed shape in which
American aid was to be given, he showed distinctly better judgment than his home government.

The First World War brought in its train the
far-reaching subservience of diplomacy to the
military. It seemed supererogation on Austria's
part to appoint a former officer and military
attaché to St. Petersburg, Prince Gottfried
Hohenlohe, as war-time ambassador to Berlin.[172] It was merely a crossing of the t's and
dotting of the i's on the part of Ludendorff's
military dictatorship to replace Foreign Secretary von Kühlmann, the last defender of the independence of diplomacy, by von Hintze, a former naval officer, naval attaché, military plenipotentiary, and minister to minor courts. Tirpitz
and other naval officers had long wanted Hintze
at the head of the Foreign Office to replace an
inefficient civilian like von Jagow. In July of 1914,
they had thought of Hintze for the role of bearing
a last-hour message from Kaiser to Tsar in order
to avert the war that would profit none but the
Navy's own enemy, England. But alas! Hintze
was then in far-away Mexico. They proposed to the
Emperor on August 2, 1914, that he be called
home from overseas. He returned, making his
way through the Allied blockade in disguise. But
when he appeared in GHQ during the battle of
the Marne, the Wilhelmstrasse managed to send
him away again, halfway around the world, to
Peking. He was, after all, a dangerous man who
had expressed the view as early as September
1914 that "the governing class," by allowing the
war to come, had betrayed such deficiency in
leadership that its position was lost forever,
thus making it necessary that Social Democrats
be admitted at once to a share in the power and
that a democratic franchise be granted in Prussia.[173] When the aged Count Hertling was at
last appointed Chancellor, he wrote to Hindenburg
and Ludendorff, the dictatorial dioscuri in German politics, that "a great difficulty for Hintz
will be the fact that he is considered a kind of
foreign body in the diplomatic service and therefore will meet with distrust on the part of the
Auswärtiges Amt, the reorganization of which the
Emperor will hand to him as his special task."[174]
This was the moment of hubris, a month before
the beginning of the defeat in the field of German
militarism.

For some time after the close of the war, the
victorious marshals and generals showed themselves on visits to the countries of their late
Allies and Associates. They then went, for the
most part, into dignified retirement, from which
they might on occasion be recalled for a ceremonial mission to an ally or ex-ally inclined to tire
of the old union sacrée. The generals and lesser
officers on the losing side went in for conspira-

torial politics of various kinds, some bursting
out prematurely, as in the Kapp putsch of 1920,
others ripening more slowly but in still more
deadly fashion. The peaceful people, with the
exception of the Russians, were more grateful to
their generals, whether they had led them to victory or defeat, than they were to their wartime
politicians. Still, generals in diplomatic posts
did not seem the proper harbingers of peace. The
people, craving peace, wanted diplomacy to be demilitarized.

But already the first of the wars against the order of the Paris treaties brought forth the first
general-ambassador. He was General Pellé,
French military attaché to Berlin before 1914
and Joffre's chief of staff in the early days of the
war. In 1921 he was sent to Constantinople as
High Commissioner (practically speaking, as
ambassador), where he died soon after. There the
first of the peace treaties, the fragil one of Sèvres,
went to pieces over a profound British-French
disagreement. A farewell visit that Pellé paid to
Sir Henry Wilson, who since before 1914 was the
most devoted Francophile in the British War
Office, apparently did nothing to prevent this parting of British and French ways in the Near and
Middle East.[175]

In general, the political role of the officer assumed an importance in direct ratio to the increase
in disturbances in the various countries of Europe.
They helped to bring more violence into the governing of certain countries. In Hungary, Turkey,
Poland and other countries on the fringe of the
Occident, generals and their cliques held power
for long periods of time. In Germany, the
Reichswehr refrained from the thorough-going,
or at least from the open use of the near-monopoly
of power it sometimes held. In return for this
the Reichswehr gained the parties' tolerance of
rearmament, clandestine and extra-legal, at
home and in Soviet Russia, and the granting of
ample military budgets. And officer politics
were involved in the coming to power of Fascism
in Italy, Hungary, Bulgaria, and Poland.

The Polish variety of Fascism was characterized by the strongest militocracy, the government
of the colonels around Pilsudski. For example,
Pilsudski made Josef Beck foreign minister in
1932, quite undeterred by the cloud of scandals
hanging over Beck's head since his service as
military attaché to Prague and Paris, where he
was said to have spied and traded secrets in a
manner that led the French war minister to cause
his recall in 1923.[176] Pilsudski and Beck, however, reserved the great embassies of Poland for
career diplomats. Despite the vaunted versatility of
the colonels, they generally remained restricted to
home affairs. Nevertheless, an occasional colonel
appeared in the foreign service, such as Colonel

Ryzanek, at one time member of the circle of colonels around Pilsudski. In October 1936, he was appointed Polish consul-general at Hamburg.[177]

The militarization of politics and diplomacy that Fascism implied—as did Bolshevism in a way, with the class war concept projected into the international field—brought at first only a slight increase in the number of soldier-diplomats (leaving aside the increasingly important service attachés). The expansion of the services both before and after the failure of the disarmament negotiations furnished ample and on the whole more congenial employment for the true military temperament. The army men of the Fascist countries could usually trust the miltarized minds of the Ciano and Ribbentrop type, the one an admiral's son, the other a reserve officer of the war, to keep military interests and war preparations well in the forefront of their concerns. Since this seemed assured, Mussolini employed only a few ex-officers in diplomatic posts. His most trusted agent in Latin America in the later 1930's was General Italo Campenni, a participant in the March on Rome, Minister to Panama and the other Central American republics, and organizer of the Italians living in those regions. Campenni stepped into the spotlight of the press for a moment when he arrived as an "observer" at the Pan-American Conference at Lima at the end of 1938.[178] The earlier stationing of Badoglio in the Rio de Janeiro embassy was less directly in the service of Fascism, being in the nature of an exile of a general not wanted at home.

German diplomacy in the Weimar Republic had found very little use for the thousands of professional officers whom the disarmament provisions of the Versailles Treaty had put among the unemployed and the unemployable.[179] Of the 4,360 former naval officers whose subsequent employment was ascertained at the end of the 1920's, about one third remained without work, that is to say, drew their pensions and were thus provided with the material basis for an indulgence in politics. Many of these found their way into the National Socialist Party.[180] The Wilhelmstrasse did not even welcome the services of the most prominent Reichswehr general, Hans von Seeckt. When the politicians around Stresemann had finally engineered his fall from power in the autumn of 1926 and Reich President von Hindenburg had promised him re-employment within the very near future, it was thought that he should either direct all the disarmament negotiations for the Republic or else receive an embassy. He was still hopeful for such a post in May 1927, but the Wilhelmstrasse proved totally uninclined.[181]

After 1933, party membership, in addition perhaps to some other qualifications, earned some foreign service posts for a still limited number of German ex-officers. By 1938, the resistance of the Wilhelmstrasse to outsiders was sufficiently broken to permit the admission of some Party-and-military men. The gatekeeper, the man to admit old comrades from Army and civil war services to the Wilhelmstrasse building, was Hermann Kriebel (1876-1941). Kriebel's was a checkered career. In the First World War he had been a captain in the General Staff. As a member of the German Armstice Commission he had bidden farewell to his opposites on the Allied side with the words: "See you again in twenty years." He was a participant in the Munich beer hall putsch of 1923, spent a jail term along with Hitler, was a member of the German military mission to Chiang Kai-shek (1929) and after, and served as Consul-General at Shanghai.[182] Finally he advanced to the important post of Chief of Personnel in the Auswärtiges Amt. One of the earliest admitted from among the new recruits was a retired frigate captain and Ph.D., Nolda, who was appointed Reich consul at Le Havre early in 1937. Due to an earlier connection with officers of the counter-espionage section of the Reichsmarineamt, it was suspected from the outset that he was charged with spying as much as with routine consular business. A former U-boat commander, Baron Edgar von Spiegel, was made Reich consul-general at New Orleans. His antecedents do not seem to have helped in making him persona grata with the population of his district or in rendering his statements discreet. When, during the first year of the Second World War, he declared ("informally and not for publication" as he insisted when the press printed it) that Germany "would not forget that the United States was giving aid to her enemies," threats were phoned to the Consulate, which requested police protection. A Louisiana legislator proposed his recall because he was "a dangerous man to have in the United States."[183]

A corporal has not often had the opportunity of rewarding his captain with high office. Hitler proceeded to do that after he came to power with regard to his one-time company leader, Captain Wiedemann, who was retired and not a Party member at the time. He made Wiedemann his personal aide, as his manners were sufficiently good among the upstarts of the transition period to be sent around the dining circles of the diplomats. The "adjutant" in diplomacy once more made his appearance in Berlin when Hitler, in July 1938, sent Wiedemann to Lord Halifax with a personal message and the assurance that the German Government desired a peaceful solution of the Czech problem. (Hence the Runciman mission.) Actually,

as he declared in his own Reichstag speech in
January 1939, he had given orders on May 28 to
prepare the military invasion of Czechoslovakia
for the 2nd of October. How much the "honest
soldier" bearing of the emissary contributed
to the British will to believe is as hard to judge
as the "adjutant's" own belief in the Corporal's
honesty. In any case, an incompatibility of the
two "Führers" arose, nourished by Ribbentrop's
jealousy, and led to the exile of Wiedemann as
far away as the San Francisco consulate-general.
According to well-informed gossip, the post was
offered him by Ribbentrop with the remark that
he hoped to spare the Captain further conflicts
between his own views and those of the
Führer.[184] Wiedemann accepted with some
alacrity, arriving on the Pacific coast in March
1939. After the outbreak of war with America,
he sailed for another post, the Reich Consulate General at Tientsin, where he was arrested
as a "war criminal" by the Americans in
1945.[185]

Wiedemann's predecessor in the San Francisco
office had been Manfred von Killinger, participant
in the Kapp putsch, whose share in the murder of
Foreign Minister Rathenau had helped considerably
to introduce the word "kill" into German usage.
He became S. A. leader and prime minister of
Saxony, and was then sent to the Golden Gate,
whence he was recalled after decided blundering
in office. This did not disqualify him for the post
of minister to countries much less independent
than the United States, such as Slovakia and Rumania (from 1940 on). As these states were being
brought down to the status of satrapies, the office
of the diplomat changed to one of proconsul. Two
years later, the satrapy of Slovakia was ruled over
by Reich Ambassador Ludin, one of the officers
of the Ulm Reichswehr case, a case in which some
young Reichswehr officers had been dealt with
very leniently, though they had betrayed their
Nazi sympathies a trifle prematurely. Ludin
showed the new style of diplomacy of the Greater
Reich by speeches to the German minority in
which he slighted the nominal heads of the Slovak
Government. Still another war-time proconsul of
the Reich was Harold Turner, officer of the
Kaiser's Army, a civil servant in the Prussian
administration, an early NSDAP member, SS
Sturmbannführer (with rank of lieutenant general),
president of a Regierungsbezirk, and, from 1941,
Minister to Croatia.[186] Still later, he was chief
of the military administration of Serbia.

All the great embassies, however, were
reserved for careermen, even when the Wilhelmstrasse was under Ribbentrop. None of these—except von Neurath, and he was appointed against
his own will[187]—accepted that higher SS rank
by which the Party tried to tie high officialdom to
itself, much as the Wilhelminic regime had done

by either ennobling a man or promoting him in
the reserve or Landwehr officer corps. The one
high post evacuated by a career man in favor of
a soldier rather than of a Party man was the
Tokyo embassy. There the then military attaché,
Major General Eugene Ott, succeeded Ambassador von Dirksen (March 31, 1938) on the
occasion of that great and fatal shift that gave
Ribbentrop the post of Foreign Secretary. It was
remarked that this was "the first time that Germany had sent a general to Japan as ambassador."
In more than one way, the appointment, which was
due to the personal initiative of Hitler, was intended to win over the militaristic groups then
governing Japan and striving to cement their
power.[188] German-Japanese diplomatic ties at
the time included exchanges between the two
Home Offices of information on "State-endanger-
ing" elements about which they might possess information, such as the Korean "agitators," living
quite undisturbed in Germany up to that time.
This arrangement was based on the pattern that
had prevailed in the period of the closest Prusso-
Russian intimacy in the nineteenth century. Ott's
ambassadorship also marked the end of the older
pro-China line of the Wilhelmstrasse, as it had
been exemplified by the military mission to Chiang
Kai-shek. Hitler, Ribbentrop, Ott, and the school
headed by retired General Professor Haushofer,
one-time instruction officer with the Japanese
Army, all favored close ties with the "Prussians,
or Aryans, of the Far East." While still in London,
Ribbentrop, together with Oshima, the Japanese
military attaché at Berlin, was preparing the anti-
Comintern Pact of November 25, 1936.[189]
If one omits Ribbentrop, the surmise of one of the
ambassadors in Tokyo at the time that "the
negotiations had been conducted entirely through
military channels" is largely correct.[190]

"That we are now making ambassadors out of
military attachés is probably in accordance with
the spirit of the times," Secretary of State von
Weizsäcker wrote to the ambassador in China.
Thinking of his own past as a one-time naval
attaché, he did not criticize this new trend, though
the ruthless writing off of the German interest in
China seems to have grated somewhat even on
him. But, he rationalized, that was a heritage of
Weimar times. Now "the connection between the
War Ministry and the Foreign Ministry is closer
than ever and I believe there is a very good reason for this. As long as we were only a pawn of
foreign policy and by no means in a position to
defend ourselves, this connection was perhaps not
too important. Our thoughts now move in new
channels, however." The first phase of German rearmament was safely over. The new
power was being transmuted into a new diplomacy. "The pace here is getting faster and
faster."[191]

In the prolonged fight between the peace and the war parties for supremacy in Japanese affairs, the fatal ascendancy of the military found its expression in the missions of generals and admirals to such "war-important" countries as Manchukuo (following its declaration of independence), Germany, Russia and the United States. In some of the capitals, notably in Berlin, these soldier-diplomats "freely indulged in unauthorized activities, often completely disregarding instructions from the home government," according to a career-diplomat and spokesman of civilian supremacy.[192]

For certain periods of time, the Berlin-Tokyo "axis" was most symmetrically adjusted, insofar as the former military attachés were serving as ambassadors in both capitals—General Ott in Tokyo, whence he returned to service at the front in 1942, and Major-General Hiroshi Oshima in Berlin, from 1938 to 1939, and again from 1940 to 1945. Oshima represented the military, anti-American and, as special nuance, the anti-Soviet line. This introduced double aim and double agencies in Japanese foreign affairs, as in the days of Louis XV and his Secret du Roi, with the difference that the weak Mikado controlled neither of the two currents of policy dividing his counsellors.

German-Japanese intimacy was deep even before the outbreak of the war, and extended to fields that could stand publicity even less than traditional secret diplomacy. At the end of January 1939, in one of their confidential exchanges of opinion and information, Himmler, as the head of all German police, learned from Oshima that the latter, together with German counter-espionage, was undertaking long-range "decomposition" work inside Russia via the Caucasus and the Ukraine. The organization was to become effective in time of war, but already at that time he maintained a staff of six Russians to write and print leaflets that were sent off by balloon from Poland whenever the winds were blowing towards Russia. They were arriving there, he had learned, and were being eagerly circulated among the people. An attempt to carry propaganda leaflets from Rumania by motorboat across the Black Sea to the Crimea had failed in the fall of 1938, but was repeated in the summer of 1939. According to his own tale, Oshima had even succeeded in bringing ten Russians across the Caucasian border. They were supplied with bombs and had orders to assassinate Stalin. Some other Russians whom he had sent across in the same region had been shot near the border. A Japanese officer whom he had set to work among the Moslems in Afghanistan had been expelled because he had aroused the suspicion that he wanted to overturn the government there. At this, Himmler confessed that he also maintained an officer of the police in that country

and that if the Japanese should replace their man, he and his own man could very well cooperate.[193]

When the same Ribbentrop who had concluded the anti-Comintern Pact signed the German-Russian Non-aggression Treaty of August 23, 1939, there was naturally consternation among the militarists of Japan. The cabinet in power at the time resigned almost at once, and Oshima, from whom his "friend" Ribbentrop had withheld all advance information about the negotiations with Moscow, promptly asked for and obtained his recall. But he was considered by the Germans as too valuable a connecting link to be allowed a sulking retirement. Emissaries, including Ott's successor Stahmer, and events, like Japan's full adhesion to the Axis pact (September 27, 1940), brought Oshima, who had helped to bring this about at the Tokyo end, back to the Berlin embassy once more. At their first reunion (February 27, 1941), Ribbentrop volubly assured Oshima that the latter's policy of close connections with Germany had at last won out over the many doubters in Japan, a policy fully justified now by Germany's victories on the Western front.

[He] regretted that the alliance between Germany and Japan, on which he himself together with the ambassador had worked for years, had been arrived at only after many detours, but sentiment in Japan had not been ripe for it before.

Germany's treaty with Russia of August 1939 was necessary

in order to avoid making a war on two fronts. Perhaps this moment had been a difficult one for Japan. But a German-Russian agreement had also been in the Japanese interest, for Imperial Japan was interested in the quickest possible victory of Japan which was assured by the arrangement with Russia. As for the rest, he, Ribbentrop, had at once clearly stated to Stalin and publicly that the agreement with Russia was in no way affecting German-Japanese relations. Now, the German-Japanese pact had been concluded at last. Ambassador Oshima was the man who carried the credit for this on the Japanese side. After the conclusion of the Alliance its further fashioning was coming to the foreground.

Oshima on his part declared that at the time of the triple pact diverse opinions had still prevailed in Japan. But at this point an imperial edict had taken effect. However, it must be stated that under the impression of the German victory in the West sentiment among the Japanese people had changed altogether in favor of the Triple Pact...Japan was resolved to maintain its imperial rank...New times needed new concepts. The concept of the sup-pressed and of colonies must be abolished. His statements referred to the Dutch Indies, Burma and Africa...[194]

Far more than in the Third Reich, the conflicts of the opposing Japanese schools of peace and war were mirrored in the diplomatic field. There were three main groups: the army, the navy, and the civilians. The Navy was partly opposed to the Army and partly opposed to the civilians, partly for war and partly against war. And among the civilians there was also a strong war party. The successes of Japan's warlike generals found expression in the manning of the offices of prime and foreign minister and some of the foreign di-plomatic posts by either military or naval men, while setbacks suffered by the generals brought civilians to such positions. The changes in these posts were somewhat like the forward and back-ward movements of weather-box figures. Admiral Yonai, who formed a short-lived cabinet early in 1940, had succeeded in putting "the blocks to a military alliance with Germany" in the spring of 1939, an endeavor he continued during half a year in the office of prime minister. He was followed by the Konoye cabinet, the mouthpiece of "popular and especially military demand, giving every in-dication of going hell-bent toward the Axis."[195] When the break with America came, General Hideki Tojo was prime minister, while the am-bassador at Washington, Admiral (retired) Kichisaburo Nomura—himself foreign minister from September, 1939, to January, 1940—had been maintained there because of the reputation of peacefulness that he enjoyed. The last hope of the peace party was that he might save American-Japanese relations "from disastrous deteriora-tion."[196] He had indeed set out from Japan with a brave little speech before a mixed American-Japanese audience:

> I am a plain sailor, brought up amidst masts and sails, unaccustomed to elegant society and not meant for an Ambassador. I accept the Washington post in the heroic spirit of the com-mon sailor called to the colors. Sink or swim, survive or perish, I don't care. I am only anxious to serve the cause of better under-standing between our two nations. I believe that the isles of the Pacific are God-ordained to serve not as hostile bases but as stepping-stones to goodwill. The light has gone out in Europe where nations have been thrown into the fearful vortex of war. Let us guard the peace of the Pacific, the only bright light of hope now left to mankind.[197]

That was almost the ideal speech and metaphor for a peace-minded admiral in diplomacy, peace-

ful enough to make Mussolini regret, as he said to Ribbentrop in May of 1941, "that the discus-sions with Roosevelt were conducted through Nomura, for Nomura was in his heart rather close to the Anglo-Saxons," peaceful enough also to serve as a screen for the plans of the war party in Tokyo.[198]

Even at that time, there were definite limita-tions put on Nomura and his conciliatory inten-tions. For one thing, according to his antagonist Cordell Hull, he was not a very good diplomat and did not always grasp the meaning of American proposals. Besides, he had two non-diplomatic advisors by his side, like guardian angels, one black and one not quite white, one "representing the Japanese Army," as Hull defined the extra-diplomatic status of Colonel Hideo Iwakuro, while the other, Tadao Wikawa, a banker, was "close to the most influential civilian group in the Japanese Government." Iwakuro had, according to Hull, "all the virtues and shortcomings of a Japanese army officer, a very fine type, honest, calmly poised, very sure of himself without being annoy-ingly self-confident," who would, "of course, see only his Army's point of view, not ours or the real interest of Japan." He proved considerably more eager than Nomura to declare what did or did not befit Japan's dignity as a Great Power, making it clearer than Nomura from the outset of the negotiations that the Japanese Army was determined to remain in China, whatever settle-ment should be proposed by the Americans. He was not a participant in the more immediate pre-Pearl Harbor negotiations, having left Washington together with Wikawa in July.[199]

Even the Tokyo militarists in power before and after Pearl Harbor, who had chosen America rather than Russia as Enemy Number One, a choice that shows in the final analysis that im-perialist considerations ranked above strategic ones in their minds, did not care to have all possible conflicts at once. They liked a war on two fronts as little as did their German counter-parts, who tried to draw them into just such a war after Pearl Harbor and Stalingrad. But while Oshima listened sympathetically at Berlin and reported German entreaties to enter the war against Russia, while he showed himself "very enthusiastic about the idea" and expressed the hope that the two allied armies would eventually meet in India,[200] the home authorities would not extend the war and thus further scatter Japan's forces, at least not for some time. In the interest of the strategic idea, General Yoshitsugu Tatekawa, who had been Army Chief of Staff for a time and had also represented Japan and the Army interest in some Geneva negotiations, was sent to Moscow as ambassador in October 1940 (to 1942) in order to avert or at least postpone the war with Russia.

In fact, by 1944 even Oshima was advising Hitler to break off the Russian war, though such advice was not listened to.[201]

It has been remarked by various old China-and-Japan hands, Orientals included, that the minimum of international contacts a Japanese naval officer was bound to encounter in the course of his duties made him a better diplomat than the army officer who in most cases was a stay-at-home. While the latter had almost no occasion to obtain even glimpses of the possible military competitor, the naval man, if he kept his eyes open, could observe very real aspects of the foreign nations' power for war. The measurable and comparable technological components in naval strength—tonnage, number and caliber of guns—could give the sailor a clearer view of the odds facing him. To such considerations the more tradition-bound soldier would shut his eyes—"the more enemies the more honor." The greater isolation in thought and knowledge of those Army cliques who strove for and came to power in the early 1930's was also due to their background: they came from less aristocratic strata, were often sons of farmers and had little to fall back on but much to look forward to; and their career prospects were made brighter by war. As Viscount Makoto Saito, at one time admiral and later prime minister, told a Western interviewer not long before his assassination in February 1936: "Always remember that those whose careers depend upon war always want war."—"Do you mean the Navy, Your Excellency?"—"Oh no, no, no. The Navy is all right; but the Army knows very little about the world."[202]

The Navy might know the world better, but it could not summon up the resolute courage to oppose the Army in its drive toward war. After sitting on the fence for a long time, it agreed to war, at least if the war were one in which the Navy would "also serve" and earn laurels, namely one in the Pacific rather than in Siberia.

Once a career including a modest but safe salary and tenure of office is guaranteed, unworldliness, including remoteness from the larger material interests making up the national economy, can easily become determinant in the modern soldier's outlook. The soldier today is more remote from property and the respect for private property than his forebears were. This was shown during the Second World War by the return to looting, probably on a greater scale than at any time since the Thirty Years' War. This aloofness may be ascribed to a variety of causes, such as the disappearance of old family fortunes, the afflux of new strata to the officers' career with ambitions that cannot be satisfied by a slow peacetime promotion, and also the general weakening of respect for capitalistic concepts. Where

this type of soldier held sway, as in Germany and Japan, material interests, even those of the nation itself, became endangered and had to suffer "absolute" war and actual destruction, which even with Clausewitz had been a mere metaphor. The war-starting Fascist governors were Nihilists enough not to shrink from this prospect, while the "appeasers" realized only too well that their socio-economic systems might be shaken beyond repair, even in the case of victory. "With us the making of resolutions [for war] is easy," Hitler told the German Army leaders on August 22, 1939. "We have nothing to lose, only to gain. Our economic situation in consequence of our stinting is such that we can see it through only a a few years longer. There is nothing else left for us; we must act. Our opponents risk much and can gain only very little."[203]

This war-preparing Nihilism called for the services of diplomats who were either ignorant of their masters' true intentions and could therefore be used as camouflage, or else those who, out of ambition or despair, had become Nihilists themselves. Except in German-Japanese relations, where the military represented themselves, even the war-planning Powers still employed mostly civilian and career diplomats, who were now merely relics of a past in which the maintenance of peace, or at least of property, had been the task to which they had been dedicated by a never clearly formulated hippocratic oath.

In Germany's nearest East, Austria, another military diplomat was chosen to serve Nazi imperialism, Franz von Papen. Von Papen was a man with the worst possible antecedents as far as indiscretion and bad luck went. During the First World War he had been military attaché in Washington until he was declared persona non grata at the end of 1915, after some of his sabotage attempts became known. The Weimar Republic, which denied even the smallest diplomatic post to the ex-major, fully realized his unsuitability. After he had barely escaped murder in the "purge" of 1934, he accepted the murderers' mandate to go as minister, later as ambassador, to Vienna, "charged with the mission," as he told his American colleague "in the baldest and most cynical manner," of facilitating German economic and political control over all Southeastern Europe and with getting command of Austria as the first step. He was the negotiator of a Concordat with the Vatican (July 20, 1933), and declared that he intended to make capital out of the reputation of himself and his wife as devout Catholics in order to overcome the fear of Austrian Catholics with regard to the fate of their Church after the perfection of the Anschluss.[204] He was less outspoken about his intentions to win over Austrian officers, men like von Glaise-Horstenau, Krauss and others, to whom the idea of a Grossdeutschland appealed as strongly as a larger business concern does to the ambitious employee of a lesser concern on the eve of the merger. Through his military attaché, von Papen "maintained good relations with the Army circles which were inclined towards National Socialism."[205]

With his subsequent appointment to Ankara (April, 1939), von Papen returned once more to an earlier scene of activity—where, when serving in Palestine, he had lost another part of his incriminating papers to the British—and to intercourse with a Turkish officialdom that was still heavily sprinkled with military men. He proved unable to stop the drift of Turkey toward the Western Powers and toward neutrality, though his efforts were valiant enough to cause an attempt on his life by Russian assassins in February 1942, and to prevent Turkey from breaking off relations with the Reich until August 1, 1944. By then it had become obvious that Germany would not win the war.

A militarist regime like that of the Third Reich naturally attracted the sympathies of other militarist nations, especially among the "have-not" Powers. Several of these chose to be represented at Berlin by military men as diplomats, in addition to the military attachés. Hungary, as early as 1935, sent as minister a lieutenant-field marshal who had served there before as military attaché (1928-32).[206] He prepared the terrain well enough for the visit of Regent Horthy and the Hungarian prime, foreign and home ministers in August 1938. As Jodl described it, they came "with the idea that in a great war within a few years the Old Hungary will be restored with the help of German troops. They go with the knowledge that as far as they are concerned we have neither wishes nor demands, that Germany, however, will not tolerate a second provocation on the part of Czechia, even if that should take place tomorrow. Whether they want to participate, then, or not, is up to them. However, Germany would not assume an arbiter's role between them and the Poles." Less than two weeks later, the Hungarian Chief of Staff arrived in Berlin for conversations with his counterpart, Halder, in order to discuss Hungarian participation in the rape of Czechoslovakia.[207]

The officer serving on military missions of instruction has usually been gifted with energies for which home conditions would not supply a full outlet, rather than the diplomatic talents that such posts may also require. From this category came General Faupel, who later rose to a Nazi ambassadorship and in whom the Nazi governors recognized a useful combination of military en-

ergy with diplomatic and linguistic gifts. He had been a Freikorps leader in 1919-20, adviser to the Argentine Army, and organizer of the Peruvian Army, which for long periods in the past had been a nursling of French instructors. In these parts, he had come to know South America well. In and after 1933, when a number of the research institutions founded by the Weimar Republic were Nazified and militarized, Faupel took over the directorship of three Ibero-American Institutes and turned them far more completely than before into propaganda centers. He propagandized for Franco as soon as the caudillo had started his insurrection. He was made Hitler's first ambassador to Salamanca, the seat of the Franco Junta (1936-37), with the special task of receiving and transmitting the detailed demands for military assistance and materiel to Berlin and presenting Germany's early counter-claims for services rendered. Addressing himself to his old soldier-comrades in South America, he told them (March 9, 1937) that a Franco victory would aid Fascism's effort to save Ibero-America from domination by the United States.[208]

It was a sorry and obvious imitation when democratic France later sent her then most distinguished general, Marshal Pétain, to Franco in the hope of undoing the work of the emissaries of Berlin and Rome, whose activities reminded people of the strategy of the Hohenzollern candidature of 1870. While the Fascist states were clearly contemplating war, Petain's mission to Franco (from March, 1939) was one for peace with victorious Fascism, even implying a measure of homage.[209] The somewhat childish explanation for this mission was that the "savior of Verdun" could be expected to win the favor of Franco, his one-time pupil at the French War College (Ecole des Hautes Etudes Militaires) and lure him away from the Axis powers that had installed him.

It was not the Marshal's first diplomatic charge. The first two had been ceremonial, on special embassies in 1935 to the funerals of King Alexander of Yugoslavia and of Pilsudski. Not all ceremonial missions are meant to remain unpolitical. While Pétain's mission to Warsaw did nothing to strengthen the shaky alliance with Poland, it did bring him together with Laval, who on this funereal occasion first suggested to him his qualifications for a MacMahon-Hindenburg role in French politics. At Warsaw, Pétain had also assiduously sought the acquaintance of Marshal Göring, Germany's chief mourner.

"The regulars of the Quai d'Orsay had not preconized this choice of Pétain for Madrid. The designation of a marshal of France for the embassy of Madrid seemed to them excessive and, by that very fact, contrary to the right psychological attitude regarding the Franco Government.

Under the circumstances it was perhaps not bad to have recourse to a soldier, to some undoubted worthy conservative." But, then, why did they not choose the mentally much more alert Weygand? The answer was simply that his candidature might have been attacked in parliament, whereas Pétain's would be welcomed there and by the French public and would be helpful in furthering that union nationale which Daladier tried to form after the Stavisky scandals and other deep-cutting divergences in French politics.

The reception on Franco's part was glacial, but, insisted Pétain with the stubborn vanity of senility: "I have felt in Franco's handshake that he regretted he could not treat me better," which is more than most diplomats have been able to feel in another man's handshake. As a marshal, he was entitled to a military staff of his own. This he took along to Burgos and Madrid, but in order to keep the officers from taking the Marshal in hand, the Foreign Ministry sent with him one of its most active career men. He was to guide the Marshal and prod him into resistance to Franco's more disagreeable demands. These Pétain tried to evade, saying: "I am here to create a good atmosphere." The old man attempted to rid himself of this watchdog, while his military staff sought control of affairs. And French nationalists of the Action française groomed Pétain for the (to them) inevitable case of France following the example of Spain. Meanwhile the war had come, and while French politicians of one sort wanted Pétain to play a role for them in home politics, others, like Daladier, tried equally hard to keep him away. By spring 1940, tired with Franco's tergiversations, Pétain was back in France, ready for the sorry role that the hero of Verdun was to play from the summer of 1940 on.[210]

A survey of diplomatic personnel just prior to the beginning of the Second World War (still leaving aside the increased number of service attachés) would include only a very limited number of soldier-diplomats. At that time not more than two of the ambassadors of the Great Powers were military or naval men, while a few of the lesser Powers still employed them, notably in such places as Berlin and Tokyo. The diplomatic corps in Berlin included more than a sprinkling of them from 1932 to 1941. In addition to Major General Ambassador Ott, there were generals from China, Siam, Mexico, Manchukuo and Holland serving as ministers at various times. Among the ambassadors and envoys from and to London at the beginning of 1941, only Nepal sent and received a military man, and among those sent by Washington, Admiral Leahy, ambassador to Vichy, was the single case for the time being.

President Roosevelt and Secretary Hull had taken as their first choice for this post General Pershing, the liberator of France at the head of the AEF in 1917-18, a role he was expected to resume on a different plane. They had already invoked his authority once before, by having him advocate the granting of the fifty over-age destroyers to Britain, the basis of the Lend-Lease deal.[211] They "agreed that the appointee should be one who could talk to Petain on the highest and the most personal level. Preferably, he should have high military or naval rank, and thus be better able to approach the Marshal. Either Pershing or Leahy could have fulfilled these requirements, but Pershing's doctors refused to let him accept."[212]

"In his place," (writes Langer) the President "named Admiral William D. Leahy, whose long naval career and varied experience in special assignments were guarantees of his qualifications. As an admiral, he would, in addition, be able to talk with Darlan as one sailor to another." As an admiral associating with high officers of the French Navy, he was to persuade them never to allow their fleet or naval bases to come under German control, or else they would forfeit American friendship and goodwill.[213] Whether Leahy's own declaration, made on arriving in New York, from Puerto Rico, that France's island possession of Martinique "would make a perfectly splendid base—if we had it," helped him greatly in talks with French naval men who clung tenaciously to France's outlying possessions is certainly open to question.[214]

The Senate agreed to Leahy's appointment despite its unusual, tradition-breaking character. This made the Admiral (as he was well aware) "the first person who has held military rank to be selected as ambassador to a European country." Four weeks later Leahy sailed for France, "the first U.S. ambassador to be sent to his post in a warship," it was claimed, although probably incorrectly.[215]

Pétain and Darlan proved rather impervious to the admiral-ambassador's persuasions. Hitler's thumb, under which they found themselves, was too near and Washington's too far to exert much influence. His patience also proved not quite up to the expectations that Roosevelt had entertained. By February 1942 he called for demonstrations against the Vichy French in order to show them that "we were not bluffing." Soon after, it was proposed that Leahy be recalled. After he had proved "a tower of strength to Pétain on desperate occasions of pressure," as Hull put it in a public eulogy of Leahy's mission, the Admiral was called home "for consultation" in mid-April 1942. Due to the advent to power of Laval, open collaboration with Germany replaced the less than half-hearted secret attempts at collaboration with Washington.[216]

After his return, Admiral Leahy moved from one unconventional post to another, including that of Chief of Staff to the Commander-in-Chief, an always-at-the-elbow post reminiscent of posts surrounding European "warlords." In this new capacity Leahy was also Presiding Officer of the Joint Chiefs of Staff organization.

In his person the breakthrough of the heretofore preserved if not jealously guarded walls of separation between civilian and military functions had taken place in America. At first, this penetration merely seemed to give military counsel the weight due it in time of war, and to allow a process of osmosis (largely one way) to function freely, by which military consideration could penetrate everywhere in total war. Incidentally, it was also a process calling for inter-departmental talents. The presence and absence of such talents could be observed in war-time Washington, as when Admiral Leahy, as presiding officer in the meetings of various war-making agencies,[217] grew easily impatient with civilians who were among the least qualified of Washington war-makers. He seemed painfully right on most matter-of-fact things on such occasions and painfully wrong on the diplomatic side of handling people new to war and its means and ends.[218]

SOLDIER-DIPLOMATS IN THE COLD WAR

It is widely believed that both President Roosevelt and President Truman showed great openness to advice of all kinds from admirals and soldiers. The actual decisions made by them, presumably guided by the latter's advice, contradict such a view to a considerable extent. It is hard to discover in the Rooseveltian diplomacy, as it is in the thoughts of the military, any early consideration of a strategy conducive to American security in the future vis-à-vis Russia. For example, the arrangements for the joint occupation of Berlin put American forces in a most advanced position without that regard for rearward connections that even a platoon commander would not have overlooked. Must one conclude that the elementary military facts of this situation were never pointed out to Roosevelt by competent military authorities?[219] or that they were swept aside? or rather that the "unconditional surrender" sentiment had swamped the American military mind so thoroughly that it eschewed even elementary caution? In any case, Berlin proved one of the worst oversights in an essentially improvised and over-confident diplomacy, and, in diplomacy, improvisations arising out of over-confidence are apt to turn out worse than those based on distrust.

Only after months of unending Russian expansion, after the irretrievable hour of American victory had gone by, did advice that it was necessary to contain Russia have any effect. One can only guess whether this came first and most emphatically from the military side or from such civilian advisers as Harriman and Forrestal. The idea that the political outlook had to be "remilitarized," had to be strategical again so soon after the end of hostilities, received strong outward expression by the subsequent extensive and, for America, quite unprecedented employment of military men in diplomatic posts, from Secretary of State down to minister plenipotentiary to countries of not even minor strategic importance. The "cold war" was on, with its various armed demonstrations, with the continuance or resumption of armaments, of officers in diplomatic posts, military alliances and coalitions, a war with the ever-unobtainable aim of recapturing the hour of victory. But was the wide use of officers in the supra-military posts due to their own early advice, their special fitness, or merely to the circumstance once pointed out by Truman, that no other men were available at the time for posts that had to be filled?

It was the early denigration of the American contribution to victory by Russia, the coalition partner who was supposed to have good reasons for gratefulness toward America, that brought into the open the first signs of dissension between Moscow and Washington. When Admiral William H. Standley, an old friend of Roosevelt and his eager supporter in the discussions about aid to the Allies before Pearl Harbor, was appointed early in 1942, the President told Molotov that he was chosen "because he was direct, frank and simple." Molotov agreed that "these were among the Admiral's conspicuous qualities." In March 1943, Standley caused a minor diplomatic scandal by publicly charging that the Kremlin purposely kept the Russian people in the dark about the actual extent of Lend-Lease from America and made them believe that they were fighting unaided. With this "outburst," his usefulness was over, as was noted at the White House[220] and as the Admiral himself realized when he "finally resigned because he didn't like the way our relations were being handled."[221]

The administration of the occupied countries and the zones of Japan, Germany, Austria and Korea by Generals MacArthur, Clay, Keyes and others, much prolonged beyond the traditional duration of military government, made these generals the up-builders of American defenses at the outer perimeter. Whether much military diplomacy was or is applied in these zones seems questionable. For such generals are, above all, holders and supervisors of territories of high strategic importance for the United States, somewhat like Panama had been for a longer period.

Whatever the employment of military officers might have signified in earlier periods of diplomatic history—and some of the older features of this usage survive, such as the appeal to the recent comradeship-in-arms—it has come to mean since the eve of the Second World War and again after its close, that between the nations that send or exchange them, defense and military considerations have become predominant. Following the Second World War, military considerations reached such pre-eminence that it was thought that the regularly-employed service attachés, with their limited authority and outlook, could no longer adequately represent and take care of them. It was thought, indeed, that the weightiness of military considerations demanded or at least justified putting high military officers in charge of them by installing them in the post of chief of mission. Measured by the number of such appointments (in which must be included those of the missions of Generals Marshall and Wedemeyer to China), the United States has become the foremost user of this style of diplomacy. While some may see indications of militarism in these ambassadorships, others will interpret the phenomenon as a sign of the enhanced position of military considerations in the complex of America's foreign interests, of the vast changes in her strategic and power position, which no civilian diplomat seemed able to judge rightly. There was, in the earlier part of Truman's tenure, a definite diminution in the American civilians' traditional self-confidence in matters of defense.

When Lieutenant-General W. Bedell Smith, Eisenhower's war-time chief of staff, was appointed U.S. Ambassador to Moscow, retaining his military rank while on diplomatic duty by express permission of Congress[223], another dividing line drawn between civilian and military activities in the American system of politics was rubbed out. Why was this necessary? Largely because the after-glow of victory had faded much sooner after the Second World War than in earlier peace periods. Actually, not many war coalitions went to pieces so quickly as that of 1941-45. Although Smith and Eisenhower had tried to make the peace as severe as they could in their treatment of the Germans, they did not receive Russian thanks for their pains. America, the class enemy in Russian eyes, had reverted to its old status as Russia's primary enemy. The two sides were measuring and comparing strengths again, if indeed Russia had ever given up such an attitude even during the coalition phase. Marshal Stalin openly referred to this comparing of strength and positions by telling Ambassador-General Smith: "We do not want war any more than the West

does, but we are less interested in peace than the West, and therein lies the strength of our position."[224]

The hope and belief "that a soldier in the Moscow job actually would be an advantage, because Generalissimo Stalin had, on a number of occasions, indicated a certain distrust of career diplomats, and shown some preference for military men" faded soon after Truman and Byrnes had picked General Smith. The expectation that a soldier-diplomat, clothed in the prestige of recent success in the field, the field of a coalition war, would be permitted to get on good or intimate terms with the Russian military leaders, who had been "almost deified during the war," and who were now expected to exert a strong and conciliatory influence on Soviet policies, proved equally erroneous. The comradeship-in-arms, whether it had been genuine or not, was not permitted to continue. Whatever his civilian superiors might have expected to gain by surrendering the traditional civilian supremacy in diplomacy, the military ambassador remained as unsuccessful in Moscow as a mere civilian.[225]

Post-1945 arrangements in Russia around the Red Tsar proved not at all similar to those at the court of the Romanovs, where military ambassadors had been selected because their military character made it possible to approach the autocrat often and directly. When General Smith resigned, after a three years' tour of duty, the newspapers recounted that he had met Marshal Stalin only five times in all.[226] The preference Smith gave to a command position at home over a semi-diplomatic one like the successorship to General Clay in Germany[227] would indicate, as do his Moscow memoirs, a certain disappointment with diplomatic experience on the part of one whom the Moscow Literary Gazette had called "a member of the military clique that has taken over the U.S. State Department."[228] His successor, Admiral Alan G. Kirk (retired), the second admiral in the Moscow embassy, seemed undismayed by his own previous diplomatic experience or that of others on the spot. He had been ambassador to Belgium since 1946 and earlier naval attaché to London (1939-41), Director of Naval Intelligence during the months before Pearl Habor, and still later commander of various American naval units in European waters. He arrived in Moscow at the end of June 1949, without, it was emphasized, the personal letter or message from the President to Marshal Stalin of which his predecessors had been carriers.[229]

In warfare, one side endeavors at least to imitate if not to surpass the means of warfare introduced by the other. The so-called cold war is not without that imitative-competitive aspect, and in their conduct the Russians and Americans have imitated and countered each other in the use of military diplomats. In the occupied territories of Europe and Asia they have placed generals in positions analogous to those held by the Western Powers. They have put military ambassadors in the posts that are to them of supreme military importance or interest: Helsinki and Athens, Washington, Chiang Kai-shek's (later Mao's) capital, and the capital of North Korea. Their ambassador to the United States (since the end of 1947), Alexander S. Paniushkin, graduate of the Military Academy, rose in a military career to the command of a division, and entered the foreign service in 1939.[230]

In the cold war, Athens is or was an observation point behind the enemy's line, well behind the actual battle line along the burning Greek border, where the two perimeters of Western and Russian influence touch and throw off dangerous sparks. While Britain and the United States, in addition to their regular legations, maintained military missions with the Greek Army, Russia was represented in Athens after November 1945 by an admiral, Konstantine Rodianov, whose diplomatic services had earlier included membership in the Russian delegation to the San Francisco Conference. He was twice recalled by Moscow, once for a prolonged vacation in August 1946, on the eve of the plebescite that was to bring back the exiled monarch, and again in April 1947. The second time he did not return, much as if the anticipated Russian expansion into the Mediterranean, which the appointment of an admiral seemed to presage, had been put off.[231]

The first Soviet embassy post filled by a soldier-diplomat was that to Chiang Kai-shek. When Ivan Luganets-Orelsky arrived as the new ambassador to the Generalissimo in December 1943, foreign diplomats at Hankow (the temporary capital) saw in the arrival of this new man, only thirty-eight years old, "indications that closer military relations between China and Russia were in prospect." They also noticed that on his journey by plane from Moscow he had spent weeks in Soviet-protected Outer Mongolia and at Urumchi, capital of Chinese Turkestan, where the new ambassador had gained his only previous diplomatic experience as vice-counsul. At a time when coalition sentiment was still in flower, it was anticipated that military help would come along this route.[232] The help that came to the Chinese Reds from Moscow would have to travel along this route as well, in so far as it did not come from the materiel and men surrendered by the Japanese to the Russians in 1945. The first Russian Ambassador to the Chinese Reds in Peiping was also a general, N. V. Roschin.[233]

In adjacent Korea, General Terenty Shtykov (a Russian name meaning "Bayonet man") represented Russia and its military interest as delegate on the joint U.S.-USSR Commission, whose work consolidated the split along the 38th parallel. By the time of the Red invasion of South Korea, Shtykov was the Soviet ambassador in Pyongyang and presumably the supervisor of the army built up in North Korea for the aggression unleashed by Moscow.[234]

How far the appointment of Major General Patrick Hurley as ambassador to China in November 1944—following the removal of General Stilwell—was an American counter-move in the diplomatic struggle for China, and how far it signified merely an attempt to make the American support of Chiang Kai-shek more effective in the war against Japan cannot yet be said. At any rate, Hurley might be considered one of the most militarized of the "temporary gentlemen" of the U.S. Army, having served in the First World War as officer at the front, as Hoover's Secretary of War (1929-33), returning to active duty as brigadier-general in April 1942, and serving as observer with the Russian armies in the field for some months.[235]

President Truman continued the practices of Roosevelt, who had not only sent Leahy to Vichy, but also Admiral Standley to Moscow and General Thomas Holcomb, former Commandant of the Marine Corps, to South Africa (1944-48). Truman and Congress, accepting the "cold war" as a fact, became convinced of the high suitability of officers—military rather than naval ones—for this kind of war as fought from the vantage point of either military or diplomatic posts. Admiral Leahy preserved his war-time position and functions around the President until long after the close of the fighting, and General George C. Marshall accepted the office of Secretary of State in January 1947, bringing a number of military men with him to the State Department as his assistants. "Ten of the twenty ranking executives in the State Department are military men," exclaimed a Congressional critic of the personnel set-up of mid-1948.[236] The list included the following as Assistant Secretaries: Brigadier General Marshal S. Carter, John Peurifoy, a West Point graduate, and General John H. Hilldring, the latter in charge of occupied areas. In September 1947, Hilldring was succeeded by Charles E. Saltzman, Vice President of the New York Stock Exchange, born into a military family, himself a graduate of West Point, an engineer officer until 1930, and Brigadier general in the Second World War.[237] The U.S. representative at the United Nations from 1946, former Senator Warren R. Austin, while in Congress a member of the Military Affairs Committee and always an "Army friend," had as his understudy Frederick Osborn, former major-general in the U.S. Army, also deputy U.S. representative on the U.N. Atomic Energy Commission.

Following World War II, the diplomatic scene was again almost Napoleonic in its prolonged warlike setting. Countries were kept occupied long after the fighting had ended, under directives (such as the famous JCS-1067) that had been laid down for generals (who were supposed to serve as democratizers of the "occupees") by the Joint Chiefs of Staff. An essential part of the diplomatic personnel, at home and abroad, was military. The great man was missing, it is true, but things had become too complicated for one all-director. Much that characterized Napoleon's diplomatic regime, the readiness for war as the supreme consideration, the strong military influence on the formulation, direction, and execution of diplomacy, the application of means militarily conceived, such as demonstrating through movements, has re-appeared unexpectedly on the American scene. It is hardly recognized that the Marshall Plan, for example, represents quite clearly a return to the policy of paying subsidies to financially weaker allies. The means, to be sure, are far more Napoleonic than the ends. But, with the prolonged application of the means, can the end remain forever un-Napoleonic?

CONCLUSION

A century ago, at the mid-point of the French bourgeois kingdom, Auguste Comte, his memory still fresh with the revolutionary and Napoleonic wars, in viewing the progress achieved since 1815, came to the positive conclusion that war was at last losing out to peace, and military men to diplomats. Already during the eighteenth century, he thought, military activities had essentially become subordinated to commerical interests. The French Revolution, "a great warlike aberration," and what followed immediately afterwards, had only interrupted this trend towards commercialism. Since then, a last essential transformation had taken place, making for the "inevitable final decadence" of militarism, while at the same time the importance of industry promised to become more and more preponderant.

In his belief in progress towards civilian governance Comte ascribed, as few historians or sociologists have done before or after him, the gradual gains of the civilian part and the "radical disorganization of the military regime" to the activity of

a new class, not very numerous but quite remarkable, the diplomatic class... Undoubt-

edly, there has been no class in Europe, during the course of the last three centuries, no class so completely emancipated from all political and perhaps even philosophical prejudices, by virtue of the natural superiority of its habitual point of view. In any case, it is clear that this eminently civilian class, born and grown conjointly with the ministerial power, properly speaking, of which it forms a sort of natural appendix, has everywhere tended directly to rob the military more and more of their political attributions, in order to reduce them to the simple status of more or less passive instruments of designs conceived and directed by the civil power whose final ascendency has been so much supported by diplomacy... There is no doubt, then, that the diplomatic class has directly contributed, and with a special efficacy, to the continued decline of the military regime and spirit, in taking away, irrevocably, from the generals such a precious part of their original functions; all of which explains easily the instinctive antipathy which has always existed in modern times between the higher ranks of the two classes.[238]

As a vision of peace-creating diplomacy, this could not be surpassed; as a version of the history of diplomacy and its relation to the military power or as an interpretation of the tendencies at the moment of writing, nothing could have been more erroneous.[239]

Actually, before and since the days of Comte, the employment of military men as diplomats has been on the increase, periodically if not generally speaking. The reasons for this have been various and have acted singly or in combinations:

a) Defense considerations have at times obtained priority in the foreign relations of one country or within a state system; military judgment seemed therefore to be required; master diplomats like Bismarck would draw officers, preferably young ones, into the diplomatic service in order to have diplomats with some understanding of military affairs.

b) Strong military influence in the sending or receiving country tended to invite or to impose the sending of generals on diplomatic missions.

c) On occasion, the absence or weakness of the non-military strata that usually furnished diplomats has forced government to recruit diplomats from military ranks.

d) The ceremonial talents of military men, suitable for moments when ceremony counts for as much as or for more than words, have sometimes proved useful.

e) Honorific motives have been important, that is, military members have been appointed to diplomatic posts to honor the receiving country or to reward the military man or the service he represents.

f) Diplomatic appointments for the military have at times served to give employment and remuneration to generals, who reach retirement age earlier in the military than in the diplomatic service.[240]

g) Diplomatic appointment has sometimes been a convenient means of exiling a "dangerous" general from the home scene into the splendid exile of a foreign capital.

h) Public or governmental dissatisfaction with the negotiations of civilian diplomats may lead to their replacement by military personnel.

i) Governing circles may think that their own people will believe more strongly in the firmness of their policies toward a certain country if a general, and not a civilian diplomat, is sent to that country. The popular expectation in this case will be: he will not surrender, and the governmental expectation: even if he is forced to make concessions, they will not appear as such. The government sending him on a mission intends either not to surrender, but to let matters come to an honorable break, or to make concessions and hide by the military uniform the unavoidable actual surrender or concession. Concession, considered weakness in the civilian diplomat, is not expected from a soldier and is therefore not easily recognized as such. That a general on diplomatic mission may be forced to crawl is not excluded from the diplomatic record.[241]

Much of the soldier-diplomat's success will depend on whether he is met abroad with the spirit of chivalrousness in which he supposedly wants to negotiate. It was a mixed reception that met Marshal Soult coming on an extraordinary mission to London in 1838 for the coronation of Victoria. While Wellington gave orders to keep back for the time being the volume of his Despatches dealing with the battle of Toulouse and Soult's role in it because it would possibly annoy the guest, the editor of the Quarterly, "the ill-conditioned dog," though begged by the Duke to postpone an offensive article on Soult, would not do so. However, the British public gave the old soldier a generous reception and proved, for no apparent reason, "desperately fond of him"—a somewhat typical case of misreading a general's character.[242] For while Soult's military career was quite creditable, his political line had been

far less so. It was said of him that he had character only in the face of the enemy, while proving a true weather-vane in all other positions. American attempts to revive the brotherhood-in-arms of the Second World War by sending generals and admirals to Moscow fell singularly flat: there is no chivalrousness in class-warfare, national or international.

Whatever chances for success the military envoy may find in his reception abroad as persona grata to the governing circles, one great risk is incurred by his home government—the soldier's inclination to be disobedient in political assignments. The sense of subordination, almost typically weakening with the approach to the top of the military hierarchy, is likely to be still further relaxed when a military man comes to serve under or with civilians, whom he is inclined to consider his merely temporary superiors and colleagues, and whose instruction or advice he may disobey, transgress or disregard.[243] In many societies, it is notoriously difficult to call a military man to order. Such are the hazards inherent to his diplomatic employment. This is not to say that civilian diplomats have always filled their positions well. Their deficiencies have in fact often proved greatest when military judgment and understanding have been required of them. To be anointed with a drop of military knowledge should have been and ought to be among diplomatic qualifications. How much the relatively, perhaps surprising large, employment of military men in diplomatic posts has contributed to the waging of unnecessary wars is yet another matter worth new and broader study.

FOOTNOTES

1. "Young noblemen and gentlemen" in the seventeenth century and later would not "think of going to sea, as being as honorable service as land war." June 4, 1661. Pepys, Diary, II, 49.
2. F. de Callières, De la manière de négocier avec les souverains, pp. 153 ff., 335, 339.
3. Trevelyan, England under Queen Anne, Vol. III, The Peace and the Protestant Succession, p. 18.
4. Ibid., Vol. II, Ramillies and the Union with Scotland, p. 120.
5. Ibid., Vol. III, The Peace, pp. 272, 301.
6. For a mission to Vienna in 1719, see American Historical Review, LVII, 59.
7. Evan Charteris says that he "well knew the difficulty of persuading the Dutch to put off their inveterate habit of delay and of inducing them to cooperate either in military operations or in diplomatic negotiations." William Augustus, Duke of Cumberland, p. 116.
8. For details, see Graham, Annals of the Earls of Stair, II, 59 ff., 98 f., 151 f.

9. Always provided the prince was not a
    Frederick the Great. Frederick had little
    use for officers as diplomats and would
    neither send nor receive them in any con-
    siderable numbers, except as visitors cur-
    ious to see his army on its maneuvers.
10. For American readers, the most convenient
    treatment of Seckendorff's embassy is in
    Ergang, The Potsdam Führer.
11. Recueil des instructions données aux ambas-
    sadeurs de France, XVI (Prusse), 480.
12. Provided he did not belong to any fronde.
    Under Louis XIII, practically no grands
    seigneurs were employed on diplomatic mis-
    sions of any length. Vicomte d'Avenel,
    Richelieu et la monarchie absolue, I, 288-89.
13. Cited by J. Cambon in Le diplomate, p. 65.
14. For the Broglies, see the various books by
    their descendant, Jacques Victor Albert, Duc
    de Broglie, such as Le sécret du Roi and
    Frédéric II et Louis XV.
15. Flassan, Histoire générale et raisonée de la
    diplomatie française, IV, 340.
16. Sébastiani on his mission to Constantinople.
    Cited by Bertrand, Lettres inédites de
    Talleyrand à Napoléon, p. 333.
17. Fleury, Soldats et ambassadeurs sous le
    Directoire; A. Sorel, L'Europe et la Révolu-
    tion française, V, 306-07; Vivenot, Zur
    Geschichte des Rastadter Congresses, pp.
    xxviii ff.
18. Las Cases, Mémorial de Sainte-Hélène, IV,
    147-48.
19. Guillon, Les complots militaires sous le
    Consulat et l'Empire, II, 1244.
20. Mémoires de Caulaincourt, II, 331.
21. Mémoires du Duc de Rovigo, II, 95.
22. Derrécagaix, Le Maréchal Berthier, I, 452 ff.
23. Ibid., II, 115, 361.
24. Browning (ed.), England and Napoleon in 1803,
    p. 104.
25. Lacour-Gayet, Talleyrand, II, 65.
26. Mémoires du Duc de Rovigo, III, 85 f.
27. Ibid., II, 242 f.; Driault, La politique orientale
    de Napoléon: Sébastiani et Gardane (for details).
28. Guichen, Les grandes questions européennes.
    I, 52.
29. For details, see Driault, La politique orient-
    ale de Napoléon.
30. For this, see Fugier, Napoléon et l'Italie, pp.
    56, 58 f., 63 ff., 79, 132, 170, 178 f.; also,
    Houdard, "Les généraux Bonaparte et Clarke,"
    Revue des études napoléoniennes (1932).
31. Sorel, L'Europe et la Révolution française,
    VI, 255. The names of Decaen and Lauriston
    as general-ambassadors might be added.
32. Waliszewski, Le règne d'Alexandre Ier, I,
    243.
33. For Savary, see Mémoires du Duc de Rovigo.
34. Mémoires de Caulaincourt, II, 47.
35. Pasley, Essay on the Military Policy and
    Institutions of the British Empire, I, 186,
    294 ff.
36. One of the few British admiral-ambassadors
    during the Napoleonic age (1801 and after)
    was Sir John Warren who served in St. Peters-
    burg, where his fears of Russia's eastward
    expansion made British-Russian understand-
    ing against France more difficult. Bryant,
    Years of Victory, p. 90. Typical members of
    the British aristocracy, serving alternately
    in the Army and diplomacy, were the First
    Earl of Cathcart (1778-1843), Sir Charles
    Stewart (1778-1854), Castlereagh's half-
    brother, and Lord William Bentinck (1774-
    1839).
37. For Kalckreuth, see the article in ADB;
    Revue des études napoléoniennes, IV, 198 ff.
38. Waliszewski, Le règne d'Alexandre Ier, I,
    244. Tolstoi, "more soldier than diplomat,
    often engaged in war discussions with the
    generals in Paris who were no more diplo-
    mats than he was, but also good soldiers;
    nothing but inconvenience could result from
    that when the generals reported as words of
    an oracle all that the ambassador of Russia
    had told them." He was replaced in 1808 at
    the time of the Erfurt Congress (marking the
    last and already insincere agreement be-
    tween Tsar and Emperor) by a civilian, Prince
    Kurakin. Mémoires du Duc de Rovigo, III,
    12 f.
39. Mémoires du Chancelier Pasquier, I, 523 f.
40. Wellington, Dispatches, XI, 668.
41. Waliszewski, Le règne d'Alexandre Ier, I,
    49 f.; II, 479 f.
42. Waters, "Secret and Confidential", p. 264.
43. General von Stosch wrote, with reference
    to the Prussian service in the 1830's: "The
    time of a lieutenant was very little called
    upon, considering the very primitive drill of
    the infantry man at that period, particularly
    since there were so many of us officers.
    There were often weeks when no other duties
    were incumbent on the officer except to
    appear in Wednesday and Sunday parades."
    Stosch, Denkwürdigkeiten, p. 9.
44. Some details about his activities at the
    Porte are given in Seton-Watson, Britain in
    Europe, p. 144.
45. Beauvais, Attachés militaires, p. 14.
46. Denkwürdigkeiten aus dem Leben Leopold von
    Gerlach's, II, 734.
47. Article on Müffling in ADB.
48. This was then the title of the later so-called
    Militärbevollmächtigten.
49. Valentin, Geschichte der deutschen Revolu-
    tion von 1848-49, I, 100.

50. Wilson's liberalism, however, balked at the Reform Bill.

51. Austrian minister to Berlin, Trautmanns-dorf, to Wessenberg, June 20, 1848. Guichen, Les grandes questions européennes, I, 150.

52. Bavarian minister to St. Petersburg to his British colleague, April-May 1850. Ibid., II, 85.

53. Hoetzsch, Peter von Meyendorff, II, 128 f. The Prussian soldiers never afterwards cared to have Willisen in military jobs. In 1862, the King asked Bismarck to take him over into the diplomatic service. He was sent to Turin as minister. Kohl (ed.), Kaiser Wilhelm I und Bismarck, p. 35.

54. Bismarck, Gedanken und Erinnerungen, I, 97 ff.; Kelchner and Mendelssohn Bartholdy (eds.), Briefe des Generals Theodor H. R. von Rochow (1873); Meyer, Bismarcks Kampf mit Oesterreich am Bundestag, pp. 26 ff.

55. Guichen, Les grandes questions européennes, I, 128 f.

56. Ernst II, Aus meinem Leben und aus meiner Zeit, I, 142.

57. Bismarck, Gedanken und Erinnerungen, I, 84.

58. Guichen, Les grandes questions européennes, II, 358.

59. Valentin, Geschichte der deutschen Revolution, I, 547.

60. Pinon, Histoire diplomatique, 1515-1928, pp. 485 f.; Guichen, Les grandes questions européennes, I, 190, 257, 321.

61. Pinon, Histoire diplomatique, p. 486; Guichen, Les grandes questions européennes, I, 415

62. Guichen, Les grandes questions européennes, I, 412.

63. Tocqueville had been very satisfied with Lamoricière's services. "He acted with a prudence and a moderation which surprised those who did not know him, but did not astound me. I knew that his temperament was impetuous, but that his mind, formed in the school of Arab diplomacy, the most skilful of all diplomacies, was circumspect and refined to the degree of cunningness,"--that is to say, Lamoricière had learned diplomacy in the colonial wars in Algiers. Fernandez, Itinéraire français, p. 343.

64. January 16, 1850. Hoetzsch, Meyendorff, II, 251.

65. de La Gorce, Histoire du Second Empire, I, 138, 150, 158 ff.

66. Binkley, Realism and Nationalism, p. 176.

67. See article on Manteuffel in ADB by Poten.

68. Mentchikov's mission had been preceded quite closely by that of the Austrian General Prince Leiningen to the Porte, for the purpose of obtaining the recall of an objection-able Turkish general commanding in Montenegro. The Russians found enough precedent in this for their own mission. Martin, Triumph of Lord Palmerston, p. 31.

69. Seton-Watson, Britain in Europe, p. 308.

70. Ibid., p. 337.

71. Bapst, Le maréchal Canrobert, II, 114 ff., 122.

72. Ibid., III, 16 ff.; Fleury, Souvenirs, I, 306-07.

73. Seton-Watson, Britain in Europe, p. 348. Admiral Baron Edmund Lyons (1790-1856), who was believed to be an illegitimate son of Nelson, had served from 1840 to 1853 in such diplomatic posts as Athens, Berne (a rather bizarre spot for an admiral), and Stockholm, and had proved the best British admiral in the Black Sea after he had been recalled to active duty during the Crimean War. His son, First Earl Lyons (1817-87), minister to Washington during the Civil War and to Paris from 1867 to 1887, the better diplomat of the two, had begun his career by a few years service in the Royal Navy. Eardley-Wilmot, Life of Lord Lyons.

74. G. P., II, 273.

75. During the Constantinople conference of the plenipotentiaries of the Powers in December 1876, Ignatiev, as senior ambassador, was in charge of the map on which certain conference decisions were officially recorded. On one occasion, Salisbury discovered that a frontier line accepted at a previous meeting had in the meantime been redrawn by the Russians. Cecil, Life of Salisbury, II, 110.

76. Bismarck, Gesammelte Werke, VIII, 445.

77. Suchomlinow, Erinnerungen, p. 76.

78. Bismarck, Gedanken und Erinnerungen, I, 338.

79. Ollivier, L'Empire liberal, XII, 278 ff.

80. For these, see Fleury, Souvenirs, II, 110-11, 225, 272 ff., 290 ff.

81. Ollivier, L'Empire libéral, XII, 283.

82. de La Gorce, Histoire du Second Empire, VI, 162.

83. Oncken, Rheinpolitik, III, 275-76, 465.

84. Reports of Prussian military plenipotentiary von Werder to William I, July 13, 1870, and February 21, 1871. Berliner Monatshefte, September 1939.

85. Cited by Walter Bedell Smith in My Three Years in Moscow, p. 13.

86. Seton-Watson, Britain in Europe, p. 381.

87. Beust, Mémoires, II, 343.

88. Eyck, Bismarck, I, 328 f.

89. His predecessor, Schmerling, had confessed to Julius Froebel: "I have no real interest in politics and have come to play this political role against my intention. I hate this continued

restlessness...The political gentlemen are in a continual excitement. Always something must happen...." Schmerling, Ein Lebenslauf, II, 303.

90. Srbik (ed.), Quellen zur deutschen Politik Oesterreichs, V[1], 59.

91. Friedjung, Der Kampf um die Vorherrschaft, I, 227; Beust, Mémoires, I, 290 ff.

92. Oncken, Rheinpolitik, III, 296 f.

93. Philipp zu Eulenburg-Hertefeld, Aus fünfzig Jahren: Erinnerungen, Tagebücher und Briefe; Haller, Eulenburg, pp. 80, 386-87.

94. G. P., XXV, 8550.

95. Eckardstein, Lebenserinnerungen, I, 95.

96. For details, see Vagts, "Land and Sea Power in the Second German Reich," Military Affairs, III, 216 ff.

97. Bülow, Denkwürdigkeiten, IV, 272 ff., 288.

98. Tauchnitz (ed.), The Diplomatic Reminiscences of Lord Augustus Loftus, I, 28.

99. Ibid., I, 75.

100. Monypenny and Buckle, Disraeli, II, 781 ff.; Doc. dipl. fr., 1st series, II, 21 ff.

101. Keyes, Adventures Ashore and Afloat, p. 294.

102. Cecil, Life of Salisbury, II, 316, 321 f.

103. See article on Jackson in ADB.

104. N. Y. Times, June 26, 1951.

105. Rabenau, Seeckt, I, 72.

106. Werthern (ed.), General von Versen; de La Gorce, Histoire du Second Empire, VI, 204 ff.

107. Fleury, Souvenirs, I, 355 f.; II, 230.

108. Brandenburg, Die Reichsgründung, II, 127 ff.; Govone, Il Generale Giuseppe Govone; Eyck, Bismarck, II, 131.

109. Ollivier, L'Empire libéral, XI, 205 f.

110. Eyck, Bismarck, II, 496.

111. Ibid., I, 466; Zechlin, Bismarck und die Gründlegung der deutschen Grossmacht, pp. 436 ff.

112. For his earlier career, see above, Chapter II, p. 25.

113. October 31, 1870. Stosch, Denkwürdigkeiten, p. 204.

114. Ibid., p. 262.

115. Report of the French Ambassador to Berlin, de Courcel, July 10, 1885. Doc. dipl. fr., 1st series, VI, No. 44.

116. G. P., II, 229-31.

117. Ibid., 234 f.; Eyck, Bismarck, III, 246 f.

118. G. P., II, 239.

119. Ibid., III, 447 f., 453, 460, 467, 478; Dehio, "Edwin von Manteuffel und der Kaiser," Deutsche Rundschau, Vol. 206 (1926).

120. To Lucius, November 28, 1874; Bismarck, Gesammelte Werke, VIII, 127.

121. General Marquis de Gallifet, when minister of war, received a visitor who called him "Mr. Minister"; he told the latter not to use that term, "only general. Minister I am for a few days. General I shall remain all my life long." Combarieu, Sept ans à l'Elysée, p. 54.

122. Doc. dipl. fr., 1st series, VI, 496 (1887).

123. Schweinitz, Denkwürdigkeiten, II, 81.

124. Bülow, Denkwürdigkeiten, I, 407 f. Among the very few diplomats from the naval service employed by the Second Reich were Eisendecher, who was stationed at Washington (1882-85) and other second-rank places; von Hintze, military plenipotentiary in St. Petersburg (1908-11), subsequently counter-admiral and minister to Mexico (1911-15), Peking (1915), Oslo (1917-18) and secretary of state for foreign affairs in 1918; Corvette Captain Zembsch, Consul General in Samoa and Tonga (1879 and after) and later in South American stations.

125. Martchenko, La catastrophe austro-hongroise, pp. 59 f. Part of Wedel's memoirs are in Wedel (ed.), Zwischen Kaiser und Kanzler.

126. During the visit of General Boisdeffre to Russia for the coronation of Nicholas II, he arranged the latter's forthcoming visit to France, which was to offset the participation of French and Russian naval units at the opening of the Kiel Canal and the Tsar's visit to Queen Victoria. Doc. dipl. fr., 1st series, XII, 603 ff.

127. Glaise-Horstenau, Franz Josephs Weggefährte, p. 340.

128. Halévy, La République des ducs, p. 408.

129. Doc. dipl. fr., 1st series, II, 121.

130. Brauer, Im Dienste Bismarcks, pp. 62 f. Le Flô was always eager to point out an "important success" he had achieved to the home authorities. Doc. dipl. fr., 1st series, II, 4.

131. Ibid., II, 45 f.

132. Ibid., III, 54, 62.

133. Chanzy to Gambetta, December 9, 1881. Ibid., IV, 193.

134. G. P., III, 665.

135. Berliner Monatshefte, September 1939, pp. 775 f.

136. Toutain, Alexandre III, p. 14.

137. G. P., V, p. 326.

138. Ibid., VI, p. 114.

139. Ibid., VI, p. 94; Doc. dipl. fr., 1st series, VI, 177, 206 f., 211, 233, 242 f., 248; Toutain, Alexandre III, pp. 74 ff.; d'Ormesson, Enfances diplomatiques, pp. 12 f. The French had already in 1883 tried to make the Russians accept Billot as eminently

qualified, possessing social talents, wealth, a beautiful wife, a great German-hater, designated as commander in case of war. Koerlin, Zur Vorgeschichte des russisch-französischen Bündnisses, p. 85. Toutain, Alexandre III, pp. 130 ff.; Doc. dipl. fr., 1st series, VI, 330 ff.

141. G. P., VI, 1209.

142. To Ribot, August 24, 1890. Documents diplomatiques, l'Alliance franco-russe, No. 1.

143. Doc. dipl. fr., 1st series, X, 387.

144. Hohenlohe, Denkwürdigkeiten, III, 377.

145. Bompard, Mon ambassade en Russie, pp. 285 ff.; Doc. dipl. fr., 2nd series, XI, 544 ff.

146. Zur europäischen Politik 1897-1914 (Belgian Documents), III, No. 6.

147. G. P., XXVII, p. 733.

148. Ibid., VII, 1565-66.

149. When Ambassador Marschall died in 1912, after only a few weeks' service in London, the Kaiser thought of making Admiral von Eisendecher, Prussian Minister at Karlsruhe, his successor, but Eisendecher cautiously declined the impossible job. Kühlmann, Erinnerungen, pp. 374 f.

150. The Letters of Queen Victoria, 3rd series, II, 544 ff.; Maurice and Arthur, Life of Lord Wolseley, pp. 276 ff.; Waters, "Secret and Confidential," pp. 161 f.; Newton, Lord Lansdowne, pp. 130 ff.

151. The Letters and Friendships of Sir Cecil Spring Rice, I, 23, 25.

152. Gleichen, A Guardsman's Memories, p. 282.

153. Sternburg to Auswärtiges Amt, January 21, 1906. Archives of Auswärtiges Amt.

154. The question arose when President Truman nominated General Mark W. Clark as first American ambassador to the Vatican in October 1951, and the general declined to retire from army service. Before Congress could act on the nomination, it was withdrawn by the administration. N. Y. Times, October 22, 1951 and later.

155. Doc. dipl. fr., 2nd series, I, 133.

156. Ibid., I, 372.

157. Oesterreich-Ungarns Aussenpolitik, III, 3027.

158. Hubka, "Kritische Tage in Montenegro," Berliner Monatshefte, IX (1931), 27 ff.

159. Memoirs of Count Bernstorff, pp. 40 f.

160. Deutsche Dokumente zum Kriegsausbruch, I, 271.

161. This was least so in Rumania, where an upper class set of politicos, partly large landowners, partly an office-holding intelligentsia, preserved for itself the conduct of diplomatic affairs.

162. Stieve, Schriftwechsel Iswolskis, II, 223.

163. Oesterreich-Ungarns Aussenpolitik, VII, 8204, 8794.

164. Dimitriev was in St. Petersburg in the spring of 1913 in order to obtain Russian approval for a Bulgarian march on Constantinople and Russian pressure on Rumania in order to make the latter accept the Bulgarian offer of only part of the Dobrudja, without Silistria, the loss of which would make the rest of the Dobrudja indefensible. He was unsuccessful on this occasion. When he left, he expressed in a public statement his hope that Slavism would become increasingly conscious of its strength. G. P., XXXVI, p. 750. Should it ever again become necessary for Bulgaria to seek Russia's favor, Dimitriev would still be a useful intermediary. Oesterreich-Ungarns Aussenpolitik, V, 6269; VII, 9279, 9499.

165. For Mukhtar, see his memoirs, Die Türkei, Deutschland und Europa (also in French).

166. Oesterreich-Ungarns Aussenpolitik, VII, 9577.

167. Ibid. VII, 9349, 9391 for his doings and methods.

168. Die internationalen Beziehungen, 1st series, II, 18 f.

169. Oesterreich-Ungarns Aussenpolitik, IV, 4465, 4479, 4496 f., 4517, 4627, 4698, 4719.

170. March, The Nation at War, pp. 193 ff.

171. Fabry, Joffre et son destin, p. 236 and passim.

172. One of Hohenlohe's main achievements was to help the opposition against Bülow's return to power, which would have meant a more determined attempt to buy off Italy at the price of the Trentino and other Austrian territory. Bülow in turn calls the Prince one of "those Austrian aristocrats who through thoughtlessness and incompetence have contributed much to the downfall of the Hapsburg Empire." Bülow, Denkwürdigkeiten, III, 115, 217, 241, 221.

173. Tirpitz, Erinnerungen, pp. 237, 239, 245, 379, 404, 411, 473.

174. July 8, 1918. Hertling, Ein Jahr in der Reichskanzlei, p. 132.

175. Callwell, Sir Henry Wilson, II, 277.

176. Pertinax, Les Fossoyeurs, II, 93; Potiemkine, Histoire de la diplomatie, III, 668.

177. Frankfurter Zeitung, October 4, 1936.

178. N. Y. Times, December 15, 1938.

179. Among those who applied for a transfer from military to diplomatic service was the later military attaché to London, Geyr von Schweppenburg, whose application, although backed by Neurath, was turned down. Geyr von Schweppenburg, Erinnerungen, p. 7.

180. Gässler, Offizier und Offizierkorps der Alten Armee in Deutschland als Voraussetzung einer Untersuchung über die Transformation der militärischen Hierarchie (Dissertation). The next largest outlet for former naval officers was "industry" (25.5%). This furnished a connecting link between the services as buyers of industrial output and what is called by some "monopoly capitalism," which the critics of later capitalism have not usually taken into consideration.

181. Rabenau, Seeckt, II, 548.

182. N. Y. Times, February 18, 1941.

183. Ibid., June 17, 1940.

184. The von Hassel Diaries, p. 33; Schwarz, Ribbentrop, pp. 9 ff.; Feiling, Neville Chamberlain, pp. 341, 356, 390.

185. For Wiedemann's activities, see also Wheeler-Bennett, Munich, pp. 50 f., 340; and Tansill, Back Door to War, pp. 348, 401.

186. N. Y. Staatszeitung, August 27, 1941.

187. Trial of the Major War Criminals, XXXI, 423.

188. Documents on German Foreign Policy, 1918-1945, Series D, I, 851.

189. Schwarz, Ribbentrop, pp. 172 ff.

190. Grew, Ten Years in Japan, p. 191.

191. Letter of May 30, 1938. Documents on German Foreign Policy, 1918-1945, Series D, I, 864.

192. Kase, Journey to the "Missouri," pp. 17 f., 38.

193. Trial of the Major War Criminals, XXIX, 327-28.

194. Notes on the meeting of Ribbentrop and Oshima at Fuschl on February 23, 1941. Ibid., XXVIII, 554 ff.

195. Grew, Ten Years in Japan, pp. 312, 324.

196. Ibid., p. 357.

197. N. Y. Times, December 20, 1940.

198. Trial of the Major War Criminals, XXIX, 38. For Nomura's post-war statements on his mission, see N. Y. Times, September 17, 1951. For his unwillingness (in early November 1941) to continue what he called "this hypocritical existence, deceiving other people," see Langer and Gleason, The Undeclared War, p. 849.

199. Hull, Memoirs, II, 1003 ff., 1009, 1014, 1030, 1097.

200. Trial of the Major War Criminals, XXIX, 280, 320, 394.

201. Kase, Journey to the "Missouri," p. 165.

202. Grew, Ten Years in Japan, p. 102.

203. Trial of the Major War Criminals, XXVI, 340.

204. Affidavit of George S. Messersmith, U. S. Minister to Vienna, 1934-37. Ibid., XXVIII, 272 ff., 291.

205. Nazi Conspiracy and Aggression, II, 943.

206. Frankfurter Zeitung, December 12, 1935. This gentleman, by the name of Sztojay, originally Stoyakovic, a name given up around 1933 as being too Serbo-Croatian, was subsequently Hungarian Prime Minister (March-August 1944). He was tried by a war crimes court, sentenced to death, and executed in August 1946.

207. Diary of General Jodl. Trial of the Major War Criminals, XXVIII, 374-75.

208. Schuman, Night over Europe, pp. 52, 54.

209. Hitler noted with particular satisfaction that Pétain "during the German-French War (1939-40) always made it a point to greet our ambassador and again and again advised his government to come to terms with Germany." Hitler's Tischgespräche, p. 84.

210. This is based on Pertinax, Les Fossoyeurs, II, chap. ii. As the longest surviving case of Fascism, Franco-Spain sent Admiral Moreno as ambassador to Buenos Aires at the time when Peron came to power, who gave the Argentine government a more and more Fascist turn. Not long before Pétain died, Franco offered him asylum in Spain "where, until passions die down, he could spend the last years of his life, loved and respected." N. Y. Times, February 25, 1951.

211. Pershing's radio address of August 4, 1940.

212. Hull, Memoirs, I, 883.

213. Langer, Our Vichy Gamble, p. 118. At the time of his appointment, Leahy was Governor of Puerto Rico and had, before retirement, held such posts as that of Chief, Bureau of Ordinance, Admiral commanding Battle Force, and Chief of Naval Operations. It is hard to say which post might have brought the most diplomatic experience.

214. N. Y. Times, December 3, 1940.

215. Britannica Book of the Year, 1941, p. 16.

216. Langer, Our Vichy Gamble, pp. 161, 236, and passim. Leahy, I Was There, chaps. ii-vii.

217. The Board of Economic Warfare, with which the present writer served, was one of these.

218. Langer, Our Vichy Gamble, pp. 266 ff.

219. At present, the late John G. Winant, wartime ambassador to London, is considered by the fable convenu to be largely responsible for this oversight.

220. Sherwood, Roosevelt and Hopkins, pp. 496, 561, 705 f., 733.

221. Leahy, I Was There, p. 124.
222. When General Walter Bedell Smith was appointed to Moscow, the New York Times wrote that it was "Washington's conviction that the Russians understand best and deal most cooperatively with our military men. If this is true, perhaps it is because our military forces are a constant reminder to the Russian people of the recent comrade-ship-in-arms which smashed the Axis. It may also be because military men have a tradition of blunt realistic talk—a kind of talk which the Russians themselves use and admire, in others. The Soviet leaders have little patience with the polished clichés of the professional diplomat." It was General Smith's belief "that his new job won't be very different from the old one. He concedes, however, that in one particular there will be a major change. 'You see,' he recalled, 'I've been in a way a kind of ambassador for General Eisenhower's headquarters. But when I talked for the General, I had 4,000,-000 men and 15,000 heavy bombers behind me. Now—'" N. Y. Times, March 17, 1946.
223. Ibid., March 12, 1940.
224. Time, June 13, 1949, quoting a statement made by Smith after his final return from Moscow.
225. Smith, My Three Years in Moscow, pp. 14, 31, 104 and passim.
226. N. Y. Times, June 12, 1949.
227. Ibid., March 15, 1948.
228. Ibid., June 13, 1948.
229. Ibid., June 29, 1949.
230. Ibid., December 16, 1947.
231. Ibid., August 28, 1946, and April 3, 1947.
232. A. P. Dispatch from Hankow, December 27, 1943.
233. N. Y. Times, May 26, 1951.
234. Time, July 17, 1950.
235. N. Y. Times, November 28, 1944. Plans to make General Wedemeyer (later Army Deputy Chief of Staff) Hurley's successor were dropped because of his anti-Communism, considered too outspoken in 1946. Military Situation in the Far East, pp. 2296 f., 2309 ff.
236. Congressman Blatnik of Minnesota, in the House, June 15, 1948. Congressional Record, p. 8463.
237. N. Y. Times, June 20, 1947. For a discussion of the military influence in Washington, see Hanson Baldwin, "The Military Move In," Harper's, December 1947 and in N. Y. Times, January 12, 1947.
238. Comte, Cours de philosophie positive, V, 440 ff. The parts quoted here were written early in 1841.
239. It might have been statements such as these that moved Guizot, at first fascinated by Comte's proposal of establishing for him a chair of the general history of science, to deny him such a chair. As an historian and practicing statesman, he may have felt he could not do otherwise in the face of such irrealism.
240. A relatively poor country like Italy employed numerous generals as diplomats, at least down to the end of the nineteenth century.
241. Pétain in Franco-Spain. See above, pp. 48-49.
242. Wilson (ed.), The Greville Diary, I, 72.
243. For the case of a French general who went well beyond his instructions on a ceremonial mission to Italy in 1893, see Doc. dipl. fr., 1st series, X, 377.

Diplomacy, Military Intelligence, and Espionage

"Intelligence about the enemy is the
basis of all ideas and actions in war."
Clausewitz

Both the war-maker and the diplomat, in order to be well prepared for their tasks, are in constant need of information about their opponents, if not also about their friends. The military, since the late sixteenth century, have come to call this information "intelligence," a usage that has of late been spreading to other governmental departments, notably in America since the outbreak of the "cold war." Some of the information gathered will be of use and interest to various departments of government; some of it, such as operational intelligence, only to one of them.

All intelligence gathered and evaluated must be, or is silently presumed to be, relevant to the competition between states as it exists from time to time. While the degree of hostility in the opponent's intentions will be of equal concern to civilian and military departments, they will ascertain it, prove, or disprove it by their own special methods of observing and evaluating enemy behavior. A degree of concurrence as to the estimate of other countries' intentions is taken for granted as part of orderly modern government, as is the availability of one department's intelligence to the others. The application of scientific methods to the problem of intelligence is presumed to guarantee that departmentalism and its ancient vices will be overcome. At the same time, its slowness, inevitable or not, may impede resolution, decision and action, something that unscientific absolutisms have scorned.[1]

INTELLIGENCE: SOURCES AND EVALUATION

Information and intelligence are obtained in various ways, openly or secretly, honorably or less so, with or without the help of spies. Once it is collected, it must be processed, which includes analysis, evaluation and distribution to the interested parties.[2]

Without processing or "sifting," information cannot be of maximum usefulness and reliability.[3] Instead it may become dangerously misleading or remain puzzlingly incoherent. Whether or not the gathering, coordinating and evaluating of military information is done with full objectivity, free from preconceived ideas and political bias on the part of the directors and evaluators

at the center of intelligence, may well be doubted.[4] One recalls, for example, the case of Admiral Sir Barry Domville, one-time Director of British Naval Intelligence and Assistant-Secretary of the Committee of Imperial Defence. Following his retirement in 1936, he became one of the most enthusiastic pro-Hitlerites in Britain and Chairman of "The Link," a hands-across-the-North-Sea organization. Whether he knew it or not—and one can well interpret the "appeaser's" policies as an attempt not to repeat the "errors" of British policy in and before 1914—he was reversing the tendency of the pre-1914 Intelligence Section of the War Office. At that time Grierson and Robertson had deduced (from their preconceptions rather than from any tangible German war preparations against Britain) that Germany must be Britain's enemy.[5] And Domville may also have been influenced by the fact that Admiral Canaris, Chief of the Abwehr, and several of his assistants were political opponents of Hitler.

The directors of policy, to whom the most important intelligence must inevitably be communicated in "processed" form, will come to their conclusions on the strength of such information. But can or must they trust it implicitly? If not, are they in a position to verify it themselves, technically speaking? Clearly, Bismarck relied heavily on counter-espionage reports when, at the end of 1873, he told the British ambassador in Berlin that the French Army was back to its old hostility. The French were, he said, sending "military agents in plain clothes into Germany to study the ground with a view to a future campaign... That did not look like peaceful intentions, and if they intended revenge, he would greatly prefer to fight it out at once and declare war tomorrow than wait until they were prepared to attack."[6] The violent reaction in European diplomacy during the "war in sight" crisis of 1875 showed Bismarck that other states did not believe in French warlike intentions and that he had given too much credibility to the preventive war ideas of the Great General Staff, ideas which were supported by meager intelligence.

If German Intelligence had been over-belligerent in the 1870's, the British service was over-pacific when it misinformed the Cabinet about the strength of the Luftwaffe. Relying on its reports,

Baldwin declared in November 1934, that, while the RAF had 560 first line planes, the Germans had only 260, so that "Germany's real strength has not even reached fifty-per-cent of that which we have in Europe alone." Within a year, he said, British superiority would be as 760:520. On June 29, 1936, however, the Prime Minister had to confess to the Commons: "In my estimates I was mistaken. I was thoroughly mistaken on that point. I freely acknowledge it before the House: thoroughly mistaken, I repeat."

Earlier intelligence endeavored to get at the heart of the enemy's secrets, often buying them from corrupted members of a bureaucracy that had not reached its later more complete integrity.[7] Modern intelligence is forced to form its picture of the enemy's intentions and strength from mosaic pieces of information. The indiscreet press proved a great source of information for the whole nineteenth century. Consequently Bonaparte, at the very outset of his regime, ordered the Ministry of Police to tell the journalists not to print anything on troop and ship movements. Five years later, in preparation for Austerlitz, he ordered the papers to be absolutely silent about the Army of the Rhine, as if it did not exist. At the same time, he instructed his chief of staff to make an index-card system of all Austrian regiments, to note their movements and to draw on German gazettes, which were echoing with the names and movements of these formations. Meanwhile, Napoleon kept away from his camp all those "factious ones who would sell their country in order to augment the numbers of their subscribers."[8]

While wartime censorship was often designed to cover up military inefficiency and errors, contined indiscretions on the part of the press also provided a great deal of military justification for it. From the French newspapers, for example, the Germans were able to construct, on July 24, 1870, an order of battle of the French Army which proved completely correct. After the close of the war, a German general paid them the dubious if exaggerated compliment that they "had done us as much service as two army corps."[9] The two World Wars restricted the freedom of the press far more than all the wars since 1815, that is until the height of restriction was reached during the "cold war." Intelligence has become so scientific in character that science, rather than the daily press, has become the great source and processor of intelligence.

The spy, in his long evolution as provider of intelligence, has become a scientist. Spies have been used from time immemorial by governments and armed forces who have more often trusted them and their abilities too much rather than too little. "There is a good deal of <u>charlatanism</u> in

what is called procuring intelligence," Wellington warned his superiors at home just before Waterloo.[10] And a Bavarian duke instructed his son in 1428, on the eve of an expedition that he was to head: "Whosoever wants to wage war well, must look out for good intelligence, much of it, and of varied kind; but you must not trust them [the spies] and not tell them what you intend to do on the strength of their findings."[17] For doing so would easily become an invitation to one's own spy to become the opponent's spy as well. Too much reliance on such reports has repeatedly proved dangerous to the user and occasionally to the spy who has furnished them.[12]

Although often highly paid by their employers, most spies consider themselves underpaid. Hence the temptation to serve two masters at the same time. Their rewards come from the employing country's secret service funds, the larger part of which are expended by the diplomatic and military offices. In a few places, such as Austria before 1914, these funds were administered by the foreign ministry, presumably the seat of greater discretion. In most other countries each service had or has its own secret funds, varying from almost zero at certain periods of American history to forty per cent, the largest single item in the budget of the Tokyo Foreign Ministry for 1930.[13]

The amount and value of intelligence data furnished by spies has been vastly over-estimated and over-valued, at least by outsiders, often contrary to the voice of common sense.[14] Actually what they have contributed is relatively little in quantity and not too important in quality. This has become especially true with the introduction of modern intelligence sections. It has been estimated that, under modern conditions, only about one per cent of peacetime intelligence is derived from secret agents and confidants, while ninety-five per cent of the data used is taken from open sources. Another four per cent is furnished by service attachés.[15]

The paymasters of spies, usually the general staffs, have habitually given little attention to the effects and consequences that the work of such agents, if discovered or suspected, might have on the general relations with the countries spied upon. They have left it to the diplomats to smooth things over should protests be made. That each new discovery might thicken the international atmosphere of suspicion and fear was of less concern to them than to the diplomats. In the autumn of 1908, when the case of a wide-spread French spy-net, in which a number of German non-com's was involved, was about to break, the Kaiser begged the French military attaché in Berlin to recommend to the Paris General Staff that an end be put to such practices. Franco-German relations were so strained that "it was very unfortunate to have this incident arise at this very moment—when Germany and France could show one another signs of goodwill and lend one another support in the Orient—for it was of a nature to excite public sentiment in Germany." The Colonel answered, "naturally, that the French Great General Staff had nothing to do with these doings."[16] Such a reply was even less convincing than most other so-called diplomatic replies.

ANCIEN RÉGIME DIPLOMACY AND MILITARY INTELLIGENCE

Until well into the eighteenth century, diplomacy did not observe a strict division of labor. Thanks to that social mobility which membership in the aristocracy conferred, the diplomat was frequently able to change from diplomatic employment to military service and back again. On occasion, he also served as spy in military things, as far as the decorum of his estate allowed him or personal inclination drove him to do so.[17]

The war-makers of the ancien régimes seem not to have rated such ambassadorial reports very highly, finding them neither sufficiently complete nor up-to-date. Instead, they employed generals and war-preparers, in the diplomatic as well as the military field, such as the Duc de Belle-Isle (1684-1761) and his brother, who prepared and fought the War of the Austrian Succession, or the Prussian General von Winterfeldt (1707-57). The latter was, of all Frederick's generals, the one to whom he allowed the greatest insight into his political intentions and the most influence thereon. After the close of the first two Silesian Wars, Winterfeldt was convinced that Vienna would never give up the hope of regaining Silesia. He closely followed all its moves pointing in that direction

and continued in the midst of peace to consider Austria a definite enemy. Therefore, every Prussian officer who happened to travel to that country received secret orders from Winterfeldt to reconnoitre the country and its establishments and was instructed to take different routes for the going and returning. He had spies posted in Vienna and Dresden who reported to him all that happened there and could be espied; bribery had to open the way to the most hidden secrets...The systematic combination of all these threads made them really useful, and the whole network, the cost of which the always so parsimonious King granted willingly, remained under the direction of Winterfeldt, who did not even spare his own money and who in his zeal went ahead the more vivaciously the more the conviction grew in him that Prussia was in danger. He was thus forced into

the boldest undertakings which, it must be said, opened up for him a career of ambition and glory to the highest degree.

One of Winterfeldt's agents learned about the diplomatic dispatches arriving in Dresden, full of information about the anti-Prussian negotiations between Vienna and St. Petersburg. These were bought from a Saxon official. Winterfeldt was also able to persuade the King to give up his old preference for France, whose unreadiness for war his agents had reported, and change over to an alliance with Britain, which Winterfeldt himself helped to conclude. In the summer of 1756, already fully armed for war, Frederick sent Winterfeldt to the Bohemian spas, ostensibly for his health,

in reality for a close inspection in order to find out where and how strongly the Austrian troops had been assembled, what difficulties and what aid the Prussian troops could expect on the war into Bohemia, which regions and which roads seemed preferable. He travelled through the mountains in several directions, made sketches secretly in various places...and returned with rich results, which to his joy irrevocably decided the King to march into the field at once.[18]

The unity of war-preparers and war-makers in the various fields of politics, diplomacy, intelligence and staff work could not have been more concentrated than in such a servitor of Absolutism.

Except in times of immediate preparation for war against a specific country, the ambassadorial reports on military questions were apt to be soon forgotten, largely because there was no agency where they were continually evaluated and remembered until the time when they might become useful. There was no central intelligence, to use modern language. To cite an example: Complete success of the French campaign against Holland in 1672 depended on obtaining the possession of Muiden, the center of the inundation system. A small French detachment had succeeded in entering the place for a moment but, unaware of its importance, had allowed itself to be thrown out again. Apparently no one in France was aware of the military importance of the system of sluices except the former ambassador to the Hague, Count d'Estrades, then governor of Wesel. At the time the French troops entered Muiden, he wrote a letter to Louis XIV urging him to take Utrecht and Muiden, "where the sluices are." But the letter arrived too late, the waters had begun to rise and these places were beyond French control. Who was to blame? D'Estrades, possessor of such a vital secret, should have told it in time.

The army leadership, in an age when there was so much emphasis on "key" positions, ought to have made timely inquiries about the system of sluices and about inundations. The point is a fine one that need not be decided in the diplomat's disfavor, as the historian of War Minister Louvois has done.[19]

THE NAPOLEONIC AGE: DIPLOMACY AS AN INTELLIGENCE SERVICE

Eighteenth-century diplomacy, moderate in its conquests and expectations, withdrew somewhat from the business of military spying. Napoleon knew no such restraint. He used his generals and marshals as diplomats and his diplomats as spies. He put an occasional spy into the diplomatic service and even made organizational arrangements to evaluate such reports in the modern fashion by means of a filing system.[20] Eventually his example proved contagious and corruptive among his adversaries. For example, Lord Whitworth, the British Ambassador to Paris after the peace of Amiens, was instructed to do his utmost to acquire militarily useful information for his home government.[21] His instructions looked to the resumption of war rather than to the long continuation of peace, a decision usually more in the hands of Napoleon than in those of his enemies.

The outbreak of the war of 1812 against Russia was preceded by what the Emperor was pleased to call a scandal, the discovery in Paris of a vast Russian espionage system headed by Count Tchernitchev, an aide of Tsar Alexander. The Emperor had his foreign minister write a strong letter to the Russian ambassador expressing his pained surprise at the conduct of a gentleman whom he had always treated well, who had resided in Paris not as a political agent but as an aide-de-camp of the Emperor of Russia. "H. M. The Emperor is complaining," the letter continued, "that under a title which conferred trust, spies should have been placed around him, moreover in time of peace, something which is only permissible to an enemy and in time of war, that the spies should have been chosen not from the lowest class of society but from among the men whom their position places so closely to the sovereign." On the higher or political level, Nesselrode, the future Chancellor, carried out espionage from within the Russian embassy by entering upon close relations with Talleyrand and other Frenchmen who had come to oppose Napoleon's overweening ambitions.[22]

NINETEENTH-CENTURY DIPLOMACY—ALOOFNESS FROM MILITARY INTELLIGENCE

The freeing of the regular diplomats from the often uncongenial duties of spying was part of the strong post-1815 reaction against the militarization of diplomacy that had occurred under the influence of Napoleon. How much of what was useful to them the war offices could still learn through the reports of their countries' diplomacies is not determined. According to one of its regular members, the British Intelligence Service, toward the end of the nineteenth century, entertained regular contacts with the Foreign Office, "all of whose 'blue-prints' and despatches on any questions affecting military or strategic affairs all over the world were put at our disposal."[23]

The diplomat's concepts of professional honor made him shun spying.[24] Spying, even successful spying, could not earn much credit from either superiors or colleagues, and detection or even suspicion was likely to make later stationing in most foreign capitals nearly impossible. In general, diplomats agreed among themselves that no officials, not even police officials or service attachés, "ought to be pressed into performing this kind of business."[25] As the German Chancellor Prince Hohenlohe, one-time ambassador to Paris, confided to Herbette, the French Ambassador in Berlin, early in 1895: "I have never been a partisan of the institution of military attachés, which is difficult to keep under control because of the attachés' desire to distinguish themselves by the importance of their information and of the more or less tempting offers made to them. When I was in Paris, I had only 12,000 francs secret funds and at any moment I received offers which were sometimes ridiculous, sometimes rather tempting." In an age of nationalism the Frenchman could not but remark that things were no different in Berlin, where similar treasonable offers were made.[26]

Diplomats of this era were loath to admit that spies were actually being used by their own governments, an admission that painful discoveries forced on them from time to time. There was, in fact, ample occasion to regret the lack of discretion on the part of such agencies and on the part of the spies themselves.[27] The diplomats in their discretion wished that spies would never be used, or at least would never be apprehended. They wished, moreover, that they would never talk, which was expecting too much, for spies were not gentlemen, not even the gentlemen-spies.[28]

How far the more lowly consular services of the Powers shared the honor concepts of the diplomats and their aversion against spying cannot be said with certainty. Down to 1914 and still later, their military services were, on the whole, considered minor, even though some of them did make military matters subjects for reporting.[29] When war approached or after it had arrived, the consuls of the belligerents, on orders or without them, multiplied such reports. The United States' Consul General in Havana in 1897-98, General Fitzhugh Lee, a veteran of the Confederacy, received the tribute of the commander of the Maine for his considerable spying activities.[30] Occasionally their reports might have proved quite valuable if only the military had accepted them, instead of giving preference to their own reports.[31]

The history of diplomacy has not yet turned to this question: How far has the breaking off of diplomatic relations among belligerents been due to the desire to end the opponent's chances of spying from within the embassy? In its readiness to resume negotiations as soon as possible, eighteenth-century diplomacy occasionally refrained from dismissing the enemy's ambassador. A British minister, for example, remained at St. Petersburg during the Seven Years' War.[32] In later centuries, the break has been made more hastily and more completely, presumably under the pressure of those popular passions that lead to the inclination to smash embassy windows at the outbreak of war. In 1914, the new German embassy building in St. Petersburg was set on fire. Among the lower classes the belief in the foreigner's spy mission has never died, and this destruction of his habitat is popularly thought of as punishment for spying in the past and the means of preventing it in the future. After handing departing ambassadors and embassy personnel their passports, belligerents have sometimes delayed their departure from the country, as if to keep them from taking home the latest information from behind the enemy's lines. And they have often adopted the precaution of fixing their departure along routes where there was little or nothing of military importance to see. [33] During the First World War, one or the other Power left personnel behind in the embassy buildings in order to take care of installations and archives and, as in the case of the caretaker of the Russian embassy in Constantinople, to do some spying and reporting from behind enemy lines.

Following the severance of diplomatic relations between belligerents, neutral countries assume great importance as centers of observation and espionage and also as peace feelers. According to one of the foremost military writers of the late nineteenth-century, "a great deal of information reached the theater of war by way of neutral neighboring countries" during the war of 1870-71. "Legations and agencies abroad can thus render their country great services," and, one might add, some disservice as well.[34]

While there was a certain exchange of information between diplomatic and military offices before 1914, there is good reason to assume that what the military learned from the diplomats' ob-

servations abroad contributed very little to what is called military intelligence. The value and amount of information exchanged was limited both by the soldier's traditional low opinion of the diplomat's military abilities and by the actual ignorance of the diplomats in military matters. Without a central intelligence service to overcome the prevailing departmentalism, exhaustive utilization of information for intelligence purposes was impossible.

On the basis of available documentary material, it would seem certain that interdepartmental cooperation for the purposes of military intelligence was closer in Paris than in any other capital. Together the relevant offices would make inquiries and render reports on such problems as the German preparations for a march through Belgium. The most obvious manifestations of the Schlieffen Plan were German railway and other constructions, and these were almost more carefully observed by the French than by the Belgians.[35]

Generally speaking, however, nineteenth-century diplomats left it to the military to obtain the wanted information about foreign forces in their own ways. They admitted service attachés to their embassies and legations, though sometimes unwillingly. They closed their eyes to the latter's activities and assumed a Pilate's attitude towards spying. Only a few foreign offices, such as the pre-1914 Austrian one, retained political spies or secret agents. The reports of these Konfidenten seldom agreed with those of the General Staff agents. Those paid by the General Staff were usually more pessimistic as to the outlook for peace, a view not always justified by the facts or subsequent developments. It was, however, quite in keeping with Conrad's attempts to bring Austria into the war.[36] Even humble agents know what their paymasters want to hear.

In a field where the recruiting of agents must most often rely on the "corrupting of members of the lower classes," as Napoleon thought, or, more actually, of individuals from all classes, it is impossible to define groups that for various reasons, not always materialistic, will prove ready to do espionage work for a foreign government. There is one exception—decided, if not desperate, political opponents of the government in their country. During the century since 1815, the various irredentas have furnished spies in considerable numbers, notably against Austria-Hungary,[37] but also against Germany[38] and against Tsarist Russia. The suppressed minorities of the latter supplied espionage agents until the Internationale, more spying than spied against, created in various individuals that sense of class irredenta that prepared them for work as spies on behalf of "the homeland of Socialism." If some of this

spying was clothed as "cultural," that was only
a reversion to the "civilizing mission" undertaken to the westward by the homeland of nineteenth-century reaction.

OFFICERS' SPYING: AN INTERNATIONAL PROBLEM

There were several pre-1914 armies that did
not altogether discourage their officers from
acting as spies. A number of such spies were detected, notably in Germany, arrested and sent to
an honorable jail, usually to be pardoned after
serving short sentences, sometimes in order to
improve so-called bad relations between the two
countries concerned. More indirect and refined
spying, or reconnoitring, was done by officers
travelling abroad, who were sometimes provided
with specific orders to spy out foreign fortresses.
[39] Even officers of higher ranks, including
prospective commanders in wars to come, travelled abroad in order to study battle fields of
the past and the future. This was done most
notoriously and most habitually by generals of
the Second French Empire. Following long map
studies of Northern Italy during 1857-58, Napoleon III sent General MacMahon, who had voted
in the Senate against a measure favored by the
Emperor and was therefore in need of rehabilitation, on a somewhat perilous mission to Venice
in order to study a prospective landing beach in
the Adriatic. In order to appear more like a
tourist, the general took his family along. En
route he visited the Austrian military commander
in Upper Italy, General Gyulay, who received him
kindly but also put two police agents on his track
whom he could shake off only occasionally. He did
manage a boat-ride to Pola, which enabled him
to observe the coastline. On his return to Paris,
he reported to the Emperor that a landing would
be easy. In the meantime Napoleon had met
Cavour at Plombiéres, and they had agreed that
the French troops that were to help Piedmont
were to land at Genoa and that only a naval diver-
sion was to be undertaken in the Adriatic.[40]

By far the most zealous and most indiscreet
information-gatherer among the soldiers of the
Second Empire was General Ducrot. Appointed to
the command of a division in and around Strasbourg in September 1865, he at once proceeded
to direct reconnaissance work on both sides of the
Rhine. His officers studied the Rhine crossing on
the French and the non-French sides, the routes
through the Black Forest, and the highways in
the direction of Würzburg. He himself crossed the
Rhine incognito on various occasions, studying
the fortified places of Mainz, Landau, Germersheim, and Rastatt. He also crossed over into the
political field in order to negotiate with the rabidly

anti-Prussian Grand Duke of Hesse and his minister Dalwigk, promising them parts of pro-
Prussian Baden if they would cede the Hessian
trans-Rhine districts to France. The information he gathered on the violent separatism of the
Hessian governors only served to strengthen
mistaken French beliefs that the German States—
righters would not march with Prussia in case
of a war with France. By June 1868 at the latest,
Ducrot's activities were known in Germany
and openly discussed in the press on both sides
of the Rhine. The German Punch, Kladderadatsch,
even published caricatures of the General as spy,
a destruction of the secret that could go no further. Still, he defended himself naïvely: "But I
have acted with the greatest prudence and with an
extreme reserve. In this manner I have visited
the principal passages through the Black Forest,
the regions of Heidelberg, Darmstadt, Mainz...
but so discreetly that I have not left a trace of
my movements." In August 1868, Ducrot, after
having received praise for his work, was ordered
to refrain from further missions abroad without
express permission from the capital. His transfer away from Strasbourg was under discussion.
Nevertheless, he went on pressing for a more
systematic infomation service, "which would put
at our disposal a number of agents charged with
keeping us informed about the smallest incident...
and who, on the day war should break out, would
render us incalculable services. The moment
when relations are broken off is not the one for
organizing such a service; it calls for time
and much ingenuity to organize it conveniently."[41]

Napoleon's improvisation and Ducrot's indiscretion were no substitutes for an intelligence
center. In 1867, when General Jarras took over
the directorship of the dépôt de la guerre, the
information-gathering office in the War Ministry,
he found it badly in need of reorganization. New
data had to be gathered from all over Europe, and
especially from Germany, the most likely enemy
in the most likely war and, as was confidently assumed, also the theater of that war. But information that had been wanting in 1854-56 and 1859 was
still unavailable. When Jarras asked the War
Minister, Marshal Niel, to which parts of Germany his labors should be first dedicated, he
learned to his stupefaction that the Marshal saw
no reason to occupy oneself with one region more
than with others. There was no plan of operation
in existence, even though the recent Luxemburg
affair had led close to war. Niel explained this by
saying that he was not one of those who wanted
the war with North Germany at any price, knowing full well the numerical superiority of that
country's army over the French and the excellence
of its organization. While that war had to be pre-

pared, care must be taken, he added, that France would not have to fight it alone. The alliance with Austria seemed natural and probable. Niel held these convictions until his death in 1869.

From these vague hints, Jarras concluded that it would be best to study first Prussia and then Rhenish Bavaria. With this in mind, a considerable number of officers were set to work and information assembled, in part by studies on the spot. In 1869, a study of the whole German railway system was undertaken. The officers entrusted with these tasks inside Germany were too numerous to receive an official character in every case, and it was feared that they would attract the attention of local authorities, in spite of the urgent injunction to these officers to proceed with the greatest circumspection. However, only one officer was arrested and forced to return posthaste to France. The Prussians refrained from protesting vigorously since they themselves had numerous officers reconnoitring inside France whose activities had not remained unobserved. Prussia apparently proceeded on the assumption that their officers would learn more of value in France than French officers would in Germany and that the war to come would be fought on French soil. Eventually, the number of officers on such duties was reduced by France and limited to those who were accredited through diplomatic channels. These officers had occasion to observe the German troops in garrisons and on maneuvers. On the whole, their observations supported the alarming reports submitted by the military attaché in Berlin, Colonel Stoffel. The data procured included a fairly correct order of battle of the German armies, their war strength—twice as great as that of France—their artillery equipment, and the mobilization time-table. This was information that ought to have been a warning not to undertake the war light-heartedly and to prepare more immediate and concrete counter-measures than were actually taken in France.[42]

The Prussian agents observed by the French in their frontier districts since the end of 1866 seemed to extend their studies to the sentiment of the population. The Prussians also evidenced a desire to influence the Protestants in Alsace, some of whom General Ducrot thought "are much less French than is generally believed." Prussian activity in Alsace was, he thought, "a fact well worth noting for it might be considered with good reason as reconnoitring for the campaign plans of the enemy. The Prussians proceeded in the same manner in Bohemia and Silesia three months before the outbreak of hostilities against Austria."[43] Some of these remarks on Prussian officer-spying are true enough. What they fail to indicate is the systematic nature of the

reconnaissance and its evaluation in Berlin.

The Great General Staff at this time was no more fastidious in the choice of its ways to obtain information. One of its members was caught in Bohemia shortly before the outbreak of the war of 1866 where he had been sent at the last hour to remedy some of the failings in the reports of the regular military attaché in Vienna, who happened to be against this war. In Vienna, information was bought which included the reports of the Austrian military attaché in Paris. Some of these reports were sent to his German colleague in that capital, Count Waldersee, who thought that, judging by these reports "replete with Prussophobia... a more perfidious and malignant character could not easily be found." Waldersee and his predecessor were on good terms with the directrice of a Paris fashion shop, who was the maîtresse of General Lebrun and who had offered to obtain the French operation plans for them. Another of Waldersee's spies was a former Austrian officer "who had served us well in 1866." Before his departure from Paris at the outbreak of the war in 1870, Waldersee had arranged for a system of agents that would last well into the war, if not beyond. When he returned to Paris once more in 1871, as the first chargé after the resumption of diplomatic relations, he had two Frenchmen in his pay. He prided himself, however, on having no "personal relations with them." Instead he had them write to him or see Holstein, the later eminence grise of the Wilhelmstrasse who was at that time in the Paris embassy doing the "dirty work." "One of them," according to Waldersee, "was of a good family and had several relatives in the National Assembly. He repeatedly wrote quite good reports. That one has to employ riff-raff is a weak side of diplomatic positions. According to my firm conviction one cannot get along without such people in Paris; he who tries to do without them does not serve his cause as well as he might."[44] Not all diplomats would have agreed with Waldersee, who was only a temporary diplomat, though a future chief of staff.

The lively mutual spying that had preceded the war of 1870-71 left a bad heritage of suspicions on either side of the Vosges, suspicions not in every case unjustified.[45] During the 1880's, as part of Boulangisme and the Schnaebele affair, both the French and the Reich Governments put severe legislative and administrative restrictions on visiting officers. The Reich administrators practically excluded French officers from visiting Alsace and Lorraine, where they had been renting hunting preserves. The rent moneys were being refunded by the French War Ministry, as the Great General Staff learned.[46] The restrictive measures would have a twofold effect,

Bismarck opined. For one thing, the reconnoitring and spying on the part of French officers inside Germany, quite as lively as at the time of Napoleon III, would be stopped or at least made more difficult. In addition, the French "would receive at the hands of Talion a demonstration of the inadequacy of their hospitality," which had resulted in various insults to visiting German officers.[47] Occasionally a gentleman spy, an officer in retirement or on leave, was caught by the police. His fate would set the diplomats to work. Although they would not intercede in favor of the hired spy, they would obtain a pardon for officer spies, as when William II released two French Army officers in 1894 after they had served a short term in an honorable and comfortable prison.[48]

The diplomats' continued attempts to have restrictions on travel and residence removed, as incompatible with the age's ideas of free movements, ran up against the opposition of the German General Staff and repeated waves of "smelling spies." The Dreyfus affair was, for example, further complicated by the arrest of two German ex-officers for spying in France. As Anglo-German relations became worse, the popular espionage neurosis spread to both countries on the North Sea, catching the hitherto sheltered British even more than the Germans.[49] The Germans were apparently unaware that Sir Henry Wilson of the British General Staff repeatedly (seventeen times by his own count) visited the battlefields of the future war, which he placed in the vicinity of Metz.[50] Occasionally at least, an officer travelling abroad would protest, if his rank or nobility allowed him to do so, against the standing or ad hoc orders of his superiors to do a little spying.[51] The later Governor of the Kremlin, Prince Odoevsky-Maslov, visited British India during the 1890's in the entourage of the later Tsar Nicolai II. He was much troubled, as he later told Sir Samuel Hoare, by "the wish of army officials in Russia that he should send them reports about the British Army in India. 'How could a gentleman send reports about friends whose hospitality he was actually receiving?'"[52] Many officers would not have felt such qualms.

Such officers' voyages were considered indispensable by the intelligence sections of various general staffs, partly because they were to control the regular spies by checking their reports on the spot. It was, as Conrad wrote from his Austrian experience, "such a painful and difficult service, calling for great dexterity, calmness of nerves, presence of mind and good luck, that it could not cause surprise that from time to time an officer entrusted with this task was detected. This would then result in diplomatic discussions, highly unwelcome to the Minister of Foreign

Affairs." The latter was sometimes unwilling to intercede in favor of such gentlemen-spies and rather inclined in case of detection to leave them to their fate and to insist that "it is absolutely self-understood that the officer travelling abroad must not undertake espionage, for by that he gets into conflict with the laws of the foreign country and has no longer any claim to the protection they confer." This question occasioned several controversies between Conrad, who wanted his officers protected in case of the occasionally unavoidable detection, and Aehrenthal. In November 1909, the latter obtained the Emperor's order that such officers' trips were to be henceforth prohibited. This dealt "a sharp blow" to Conrad. "From then on," he wrote, "we were in many respects, militarily speaking, blind and reduced to the observations of the military attachés and the uncontrollable sources of Konfidenten." As long as Aehrenthal lived, Conrad could not even obtain permission for a military attaché to be placed in Cetinje. Only Berchtold would agree to man that Balkan lookout.[53]

To Conrad such officers' trips seemed the more indispensable as they allowed the economizing of the secret service funds that were under the control of the Ballhausplatz. In 1910, Conrad demanded that the annual funds at his disposal, 150,000 Kronen, be raised by 50,000 in order to enable him to buy more expensive Konfidenten to make up for the fact that the Foreign Ministry would not have travelling officers. He was turned down by the diplomats, who, he thought, bent over backwards in their endeavor to avoid complications.[54] In 1910, when these civilians allowed an Itallian officer and "explorer" to make a so-called scientific voyage through Austria's Adriatic possessions, Conrad protested energetically: "To admit this internationally known spy is to thwart all the measures of precaution that it is our bounden military duty to arrange. I regret exceedingly," he wrote Aehrenthal, "that Your Excellency has not consulted me in this matter that touches counter-espionage so eminently."[55] The complete stopping of officers' leaves for travel in certain countries, notably Serbia, put Austria at a great disadvantage, Conrad thought. This was even more true since her enemies, Italy and Serbia, easily found helpers for their espionage among the Italians and South Slavs inside the Double Monarchy.[56]

Thanks to Aehrenthal's ultra-caution, Conrad's Evidenzbureau was greatly handicapped, so much so that during the three years to September 1911, thirty-four spies—thirteen for Italy, twenty-one for Russia—were arrested inside Austria-Hungary, while only four Austrian agents were caught in Italy and three in Russia.[57] In Serbia, four Austrian spies were arrested and sentenced in the spring of 1909. At that time Serbia had at her disposal a whole system of confidence men among the South Slavs inside the Empire. Considering these statistics, which he interpreted as proof of the inferiority of Austrian espionage, Conrad was exasperated to read, in reports that Aehrenthal received from the Austrian ambassador in Rome, views like these: "I must leave it to Your Excellency to judge whether the present forebearance on the part of the Italian Government in the face of the increasing number of espionage cases can be expected to continue and whether our official friendly relations and our alliance with Italy can support such a test of strength much longer."[58]

On the eve of 1914, no Great Power indulged in more direct officer spying, through its service attachés, than Russia. The Central Powers treated these discoveries in a somewhat routine manner. However, a smaller Power intending to remain neutral in the impending holocaust, such as Sweden, reacted violently against the activities of the Russian military attaché in Stockholm, Colonel Assanovitch, who was uncovered in November 1913. Sweden took this final proof of the "Russian danger" so seriously that French diplomacy feared the Swedes would finally be driven into the German camp. A popular movement for increased armaments got under way, backed up by a march of the peasantry on Stockholm, and whipped up by violent Germanophiles like Sven Hedin. "Never before had Russian diplomatic representation in Stockholm been in such a painful position," according to the last Tsarist minister there. On his return from St. Petersburg in July 1914, Poincaré made it a point to visit the Swedish capital in order to bring reassuring explanations from the Tsar and "certify that the Assanovitch incident had not the importance attached to it by public opinion in Sweden."[59]

DIPLOMACY AND ESPIONAGE IN THE TOTALITARIAN AGE

While an aristocracy of birth and wealth filled the highest diplomatic positions before 1914, the soldiers and sailors in the directing posts were, on the whole, lower born and poorer. Nothing is more striking than the almost complete retirement of the higher European aristocracy from the military field. With few notable exceptions, however, the aristocracy of diplomats were oblivious to the threat that any war would pose to their group position. They attempted almost nothing to mitigate the acuteness of military competition, except occasionally to inveigh against the chauvinistic oratory of some officers

or their overt spying. The diplomats conceded much to the soldiers, perhaps too much; for in the three empires at least they practically put the casus belli into their hands. They expected, however, that the latter would refrain from acts, such as spying, that would make their peace-pretending business more difficult than it already was. There survived from an earlier day only a little of the irenic ethos or of the supranational class-consciousness (or class-subconsciousness) which had established and maintained the order of the Congress of Vienna. The military, once part of this system, had allied themselves with nationalism and hyper-nationalism, with Pan-Slavism, and, inside the Central Powers, with Pan-Germanism.[60] Against them the civilian courage of a Bismarck was no longer evident in the twentieth century. Plutocratic diplomacy was singularly uncourageous—there is often surprisingly little actual kratos in plutocracy.[61]

Very little of the international class-consciousness of monopoly capitalism, which the Bolshevists assumed, actually existed, least so against them and their new government. The Bolshevists themselves, however, introduced class-consciousness and class warfare into the practice of international relations. After their advent to power, military and other international competition took on a new acuteness, with fewer and fewer holds barred. Soviet embassies and legations and other agencies became the seats of subversive propaganda and espionage. "The recent examination by the police of the premises of Arcos, Ltd., and of the Russian Trade Delegation has conclusively proved that both military espionage and subversive activities throughout the British Empire were directed and carried out from 49 Morgate": so read the British Government's note of May 27, 1927, in which relations with Moscow were broken off. Quite mechanically, the same accusation of military (aggravated by economic) espionage was raised by the Russians against the British Trade Mission in Moscow, with economic espionage a new gravamen under Soviet law. This could be extended to cover any kind of economic information, which bourgeois countries and governments had not hitherto considered an object of espionage.[62]

As the Bolshevist regime continued to survive, despite all the dangers it suspected, there was a definite attempt, or pretence, to divest the work of the official embassies of all suspicious activities such as propaganda and spying.[63] Other organizations at the command of the Kremlin—such as local Communists, or Amtorg, or the Red Army Intelligence Service[64]—took over such tasks. These, if detected, could more easily be disavowed and all official connection denied.

The other totalitarian Powers followed the Russian example to varying degrees.[65] For a number of reasons, the demands on German diplomacy to aid in intelligence work seem to have been minor or infrequent. They did include, however, such demands as making it impossible for post-Munich Czechoslovakia to entertain an intelligence service of her own directed against Germany, or to tolerate on her soil intelligence activities directed by third Powers against the Reich. The diplomats were to see to it that the "Protectorate" prevented that.[66] Hitler's contempt for the diplomats made him think rather poorly of their contributions to useful intelligence. What information they might furnish was to go directly to him, not to the General Staff, which in turn was bidden not to communicate reports to the Wilhelmstrasse. And when Admiral Doenitz on one occasion wanted the Führer's permission to see some Foreign Office reports on enemies, it was given with the proviso that this was "exclusively for the personal information of the Commander-in-Chief, Navy."[67] The Führer wanted to be at the switchboard himself where the various reports were to be connected or to remain unconnected, as he might prefer. He wanted to extend the "divide and rule" principle of dictatorship to intelligence work when, under modern conditions, the highest usefulness of such work had become dependent on keeping clear lines of connection with all sections of government.

On the eve of the German invasion of Denmark in 1940, "secret reconnaissance still had to be carried out in Denmark itself, in order to check and complete the material on hand." The chief of staff of the landing corps, after discussing matters with Wilhelmstrasse officials, departed for Copenhagen in the guise of a civil servant, with his uniform in the diplomatic valise he carried. In this guise, accompanied by the air attaché, he used the day before the scheduled landing for last-minute reconnoitring. Only after this had been done was the Minister himself informed about the forthcoming military events. He then, according to the soldiers' testimony, "fitted himself into his difficult task quickly and in excellent manner."[68]

From such as yet sparse indications, it would seem that from 1939 on, if not earlier, most diplomatic and consular services had come to pay greater attention to the supply of information that would interest military intelligence services.[69] While keeping its diplomatic service out of "this dirty business," generally speaking, the Japanese maintained a consular establishment of some two hundred persons in Honolulu, near the main American naval base in the Pacific, which, under guidance from the Japanese Navy, provided ample and correct information on American ship movements before Pearl Harbor. Afterwards, it seemed "a matter of great imprudence for the State and War Department" to have permitted such an aggregation of spies at such a point.[70] Unlike the Western Powers, who allowed the foreign consulates to continue in their various activities on a basis of reciprocity, the Soviet Union, judging either from her own espionage methods or other confirmation of her suspicions, closely supervised all foreign bureaus and individuals inside the Union. In the later 1930's, she shut down more and more foreign consulates and restricted the movements of diplomats. The Wehrmacht, for one, felt deprived of some of its "last remaining sources of information, though the consuls had become more and more inadequate" of late. The German representative in Moscow begged the Wilhelmstrasse to at least continue the courier service between Berlin and Moscow on the old scale, "for what the couriers saw on the way and would then report to him was in the present situation actually the last remaining source of information outside of Moscow."[71]

The foremost American observation post in Europe after 1940 was the embassy in Vichy, a town "full of spies," while a vastly expanded consular service in French North Africa helped from an early date to prepare the invasion of that continent.[72] According to Ambassador Admiral Leahy,

> our attachés had excellent contacts and kept me completely informed of what they were doing. An Ambassador may choose to "forget" some of the things he is told. Intelligence is not a subject to be discussed freely at any time. No mention of this important activity was made in my conversations with the President when we discussed the Vichy appointment, or in his letter of instructions. Many times we had no idea as to the value of the information we were passing on. It would have to be weighed and measured against other intelligence by those in Washington responsible for this work.[73]

American studies of efficiency extending to this field have not yet estimated how much worthwhile war intelligence came from diplomats' observations. It was definitely not enough to satisfy the war-makers who eventually set up the military-civilian Office of Strategic Services, with a military man—a reservist—in command. The O.S.S. was fully removed from State Department and Foreign Service control, whose installations they might use on occasion.

So much has been revealed about the espionage work of Russian embassies and legations during war-time that it is safe to assume that even Ribbentrop spoke the truth when he charged that a number of Russian offices, including those in the Berlin embassy, had not shrunk "from unscrupulous abuse of the rights of extraterritoriality for espionage purposes."[74] The hints he gave about the organization of this work, as directed by a seemingly subordinate member of the embassy, are quite in keeping with the more detailed descriptions given by ex-members of the Russian foreign service who have since broken with the Soviet regime.[75] Soviet war-time espionage against partners within the anti-Axis coalition indicated clearly that during the seeming moratorium on international class warfare the basic antagonism against the capitalist Allies remained virulent, leading to systematic spying against them from whatever vantage point was available.[76] According to Kravchenko's testimony, Soviet diplomacy was "indivisible" from espionage activities, every Soviet diplomat having undergone extensive training for espionage work before going abroad. In order not to make scandal too great in case of discovery, or merely for the sake of the best division of labor, the ambassador himself might be exempted from espionage duties. When the Canadians uncovered the war-time spying within the Ottawa embassy, they exempted the ambassador himself, Zarubin, indicating that the directors of spying on the spot and in Moscow had agreed not to have him participate in their doings. This clearance allowed him to continue his career as ambassador to London.

While denying practically all charges of espionage brought against any or all of its agents, the Soviet Government and the obedient and imitative satellites went over to the counter-offensive and accused various members of the Western embassies in their capitals—usually satellite capitals—of espionage and subversive actions against the Communist regimes.[77] In that chain reaction which carries on the genealogy of an evil, Tito followed his break with the Cominform with the arrest of some thirty Soviet citizens charged with espionage, sabotage, counter-revolutionary activities, and collaboration with the Germans during the occupation from 1941-44. At the same time he accused the Soviet Embassy in Belgrade of being the center of all these nefarious activities "that have nothing in common with the work of diplomatic missions of a Socialist country in another Socialist country."[78] (Was that to mean that such activities are among the duties of a Socialist embassy in a non-Socialist country?)

The "cold war" brought with it in many quarters an almost psychotic suspicion of total espionage. Wolf hunts, archeological researches, mountain climbing in regions adjacent to the Soviet Union: all were denounced as signs of the activities of the "intelligence agents of the Anglo-American military bloc."[79] One Russian spokesman declared that the blockade of Berlin was due to the fact that "spies from the British and U.S. zones were coming en masse to Berlin and the Soviet zone."[80] The morbid obsession of the masses about spying made Russian propaganda indulge in constant accusations against Western diplomats, not excluding the highest ranking ones such as W. Averell Harriman and Alan Kirk. Such a barrage was unleashed once more in late 1951 when the appointment of George F. Kennan to the Moscow ambassadorship was impending.[81] A little later, the Soviet Government gave its agrément, which they would certainly have denied had they believed their own accusations. But a spy scare is, in the Soviet system of home affairs, too valuable a means of government to let go. It served to strengthen the conviction that Stalin and the police had to protect and were protecting the homeland of socialism against foreign enemies.

AMERICAN INTELLIGENCE IN THE "COLD WAR"

Espionage cases in American and British courts have resulted in the conviction of Soviet sympathizers from among a new irredenta—not strictly proletarian, as might have been expected, but rather from among the psychotic fringe of white-collar employees. These cases have proved to the American public how deep into their midst the tentacles of Soviet spying have reached. The accusations of Senator McCarthy hint that they reach still higher and deeper into the offices of government. As the American nation was comparatively late to experience such scares, it was also late, by comparison, in setting up its first central intelligence offices.[82] The National Intelligence Authority was established in January of 1946 and, superseding it, the Central Intelligence Agency (CIA) in 1947. The CIA is, under the National Security Act of 1947, a Federal office with its own appropriations.[83] Though headed by a succession of military officers, with General Walter Bedell Smith, Eisenhower's Chief of Staff during the War and later an ambassador to Moscow, and Allen Dulles, brother of the Secretary of State, as its latest directors, it is nevertheless a civilian agency. It is charged with these major duties:

(1) To advise the National Security Council as

to intelligence activities of governmental departments and agencies as related to national security;

(2) To make recommendations to the Council for the coordination of such intelligence activities;

(3) To correlate and evaluate intelligence relative to national security and disseminate it through the various interested branches of Government, which are to continue in their own earlier arranged ways of collecting, evaluating, correlating, and disseminating intelligence;

(4) To perform, for the benefit of the existing intelligence agencies, such additional services of common concern as the Council determines can be more efficiently accomplished if centrally organized.[84]

There was no thought, then, on the part of the law-givers, of making the CIA a substitute for all hitherto existing agencies concerned with intelligence.[85] But even as a coordinator of intelligence, it can not possibly pick up, examine and evaluate all the threads that run so thickly over the war-suspecting world.[86] Which agency is to supply which other agency with necessary intelligence? This will remain a baffling inter-departmental problem, one that is further complicated by the conditions prevailing during a time of cold war. Which among these departments is to draw what kind of conclusions from the intelligence data gathered by itself and/or submitted by the CIA? How far are the data submitted by the latter to be evaluated by the CIA itself? Such questions first presented themselves in connection with the Berlin blockade. Did the blockade point to Russian war intentions in the near future? General Clay, in March 1948, submitted to the Director of Army Intelligence his "feeling" (rather than "data, or outward evidence") that, while up to then he had considered war unlikely for at least ten years to come, now "it may come with dramatic suddenness." While nothing is known of an exact evaluation of this danger signal by CIA, it had considerable political shock effect in Washington, where a new attempt was made to push Universal Military Training through an unwilling or unconvinced Congress.[87] The problems multiplied following the North Korean aggression, which came as a great surprise to most Americans in and out of offices.[88] Had the CIA given timely warning? It turned out that CIA had known of heavy military concentrations north of the 38th parallel and had passed on the information to the Departments concerned—State, Defense, etc.—without itself forming an estimate as to the meaning of the information. Did it, or did it not, Time asked, go far enough in its duty "to correlate and evaluate intelligence relating to the national security?"[89]

Another problem of competency arose during the U.N.-U.S. intervention in favor of the South Koreans: must counter-intervention by the Communist Chinese be expected and who can be relied upon to signal it first? When it came, it was unexpected by the U.N.-U.S. side. There was great disappointment with "the quality of intelligence regarding Korea." General MacArthur had expressed himself with great confidence as to the outcome of his push to the Yalu River. It was held against him and his field intelligence that they had not foreseen the intervention. As General Bradley put it, "a lot of that intelligence should have come from his own field command."[90] MacArthur and his staff countered by maintaining that such a finding "was basically a political one, involving decisions made in Peiping and quite beyond the reach of General MacArthur's field intelligence," that CIA in Washington and its representatives in the field had not been equal to their tasks.[91] While the secret of Peiping-Moscow counsels might well be termed impenetrable,[92] it is still hard to see why field intelligence ought not to have extended at least far enough to cover Chinese troop movements north of the Yalu, preparatory to their intervention in Korea. It is also difficult to understand why there should have been "disposition in the military services at one time not to cooperate with the CIA." This was, according to ex-Secretary of Defense Louis Johnson, the prevailing attitude at one time.[93] Cold war, like hot war, does not allow the departmentalization of intelligence.

Spying aimed at foreign Powers might be considered a constant on the international scene, due to the needs of the war-envisaging military. At times the military have drawn the diplomats into their service, while at other times the latter have refused such servitude. So far as espionage is concerned, our age is characterized by the actual and suspected involvement of outward-directed espionage with inward spying. Ever since the Kremlin again became the seat of Russian governing its political architecture has included a Dionysius' ear, the tyrant's listening-in device on the prison that is Russia today. While Liberals in their several shadings abhor spying on principle, though not as strictly in practice, absolutists in their many incarnations take it for granted. Since the rise of totalitarianism, spying has become far more inhumane and the reservations against it much weaker.

FOOTNOTES

1. It took the Central Intelligence Agency ten days—much too long as some in Washington thought—during the March 1948 crisis over

Berlin to submit to President Truman "a brief combined estimate by State, Army, Navy and Air Force saying that war was not probable within sixty days." Two weeks later, the CIA felt that the no-war forecast could be extended beyond this sixty-day period, an estimate in which the Air Force would not concur. Forrestal Diaries, pp. 395, 409.

2. "The function of Naval Intelligence is to 'collect, coordinate, interpret, and disseminate' all information of military significance. The most difficult step is the last." Admiral Halsey's Story, pp. 47 f.

3. In his eagerness to give England permanent safety by building a coastal fortification system against France, Palmerston at the end of 1859 made use of a report by the military attaché in Paris, according to which peasants in the vicinity of Chalons had declined the Government's offer of lending them horses, for the reason that these animals would soon be taken from them for the purpose of the impending war with Britain. While the majority of the Cabinet backed Palmerston and the Secretary of War in their far-reaching conclusions based on this scrap of information, Gladstone protested vigorously: "Surely such a statement, put into so prominent a place, was well worth verifying and testing. For if this was the real ground of the proceeding, the farmers about Chalons must be very extraordinary farmers...My meaning is that the evidence is unsifted evidence...and such evidence, until sifted, should not be used nor reported as part of the foundation for the proceedings of a Government—proceedings which, by multiplying preparations for war, have in the present state of men's minds no small tendency to bring it about. If you ask me what I would do with the evidence, I answer at once, Sift it; appoint men; use your multitude of agents abroad, and your ample means, to examine every one of these stories, which may be mountains or may be molehills, and let us have, with the utmost degree of particularity that can be reached, the whole attainable evidence on such a vital matter" (to Secretary of War, November 28, 1859). Stanmore, Sidney Herbert, II, 229; Morley, Gladstone, II, 43 ff.

4. For the political errors of Admiral Hillenkoetter, former head of the U.S. Central Intelligence Agency, see Forrestal Diaries, p. 512.

5. Robertson, From Private to Field-Marshal, ch. ix. When Robertson remarked to a cabinet minister in 1912 that war with Germany was inevitable, he received the gentle rebuke: "No, General, I would not say inevitable, but conceivable." Ibid., p. 139.

6. Taffs, Ambassador to Bismarck, p. 66.

7. In 1674, when William of Orange was preparing his plans, including an invasion of France, Louvois "was fully acquainted with all these projects; he entertained correspondence with one of the most intimate servitors of the Prince, by the name of Launoy." Rousset, Histoire de Louvois, II, 38.

8. Ollivier, L'Empire libéral, XV, 27 f.

9. Ibid., XV, 69.

10. Wellington, Dispatches, XII, 416, 524.

11. Jähns, Kriegswissenschaften, p. 321.

12. Following a set-back in Eastern Prussia in February 1807, Berthier wrote the commander of the Army corps most severely hit: "The Emperor is chagrined that you have not stopped the corps of General Essen...The first thing to do is to shoot the spy who seems obviously to have misled you." Derrécagaix, Le Maréchal Berthier, II, 203.

13. Takeuchi, War and Diplomacy in the Japanese Empire, pp. 80 f.

14. An article in The Spectator cautioned against the spy: "He can have no great ties of honor, or checks of conscience...He will be more industrious to carry that which is grateful, than that which is true...." The Spectator, July 24, 1712.

15. Zacharias, Secret Missions, the Story of an Intelligence Officer, pp. 117 f. See also "Open Sources Give U.S. Data on Soviet" in New York Times, December 26, 1951.

16. Doc. dipl. fr., 2nd series, XI, 851 f.

17. For a set of typical instructions, see Recueil des instructions données aux ambassadeurs de France, XIII (Danemark), pp. 11 f., 64.

18. Varnhagen, Leben Winterfeldts, pp. 103 ff., 116 f.

19. Rousset, Histoire de Louvois, I, 367 ff.

20. See, for example, Correspondence de Napoleon Ier, XII, 9919. For Napoleon's agents who at the same time did intelligence work, stirred up revolutionary sentiments, collected statistics, and carried on diplomatic negotiations, see Bryant, Years of Victory, pp. 26, 33, 38, 41.

21. Browning (ed.), England and Napoleon in 1803, pp. 2, 4.

22. Mémoires du Duc de Rovigo, III, 34 ff.; Mémoires du Chancellier Pasquier, I, 518 f.; Waliszewski, Le règne d'Alexandre Ier, I, 128 f., II, 5; Hauser, Tchernychev et l'agence russe d'espionage.

23. Gleichen, A Guardsman's Memories, p. 143.

24. In 1867, the Hessian Minister Resident in Paris learned part of the secret of the French miracle gun, the mitrailleuse, which he at once handed over to the Prussian ambassador for submission to Berlin. When he reported

this to his superior, Minister Dalwigk, a violent Prussophobe, the latter expressed his "deep regret" that the diplomat had allowed himself to be used in such business; and when the latter defended himself by saying that these guns would eventually be used against Germany, Dalwigk corrected him: there was no question of a war between France and Germany but only between France and Prussia; he preferred to leave it to Prussia to find out the secret of France's arms herself. "In any case, business of this kind was not worthy of a minister." Die Tagebücher Dalwigks, p. 337.

25. During the Schnaebele affair of 1887. Doc. dipl. fr., 1st series, VI, 530.

26. Ibid., XI, 267.

27. Three months before the First World War, a Russian vice-consul in Urmia urged that the military use more caution when sending agents into his consular district, that they entrust such work to older instead of careless junior officers, that they inform consuls beforehand and not start on intelligence work without their foreknowledge, either in Turkey or Persia. Obviously, even a consul could teach the soldiers discretion. Die internationalen Beziehungen im Zeitalter des Imperialismus, 1st series, II, 307.

28. The United States naval attaché in Berlin during and after the Spanish-American War was indignant that an amateur spy who had worked for him in Spain during the war promptly revealed his adventures to the readers of The Cosmopolitan (December 1898). "I had no idea that so discreet a spy could be so indiscreet afterwards as a sensation writer. Everybody seems to want to tell about themselves during the war in the U.S. magazines now." Barber to Navy Department, December 8, 1898. National Archives.

29. From reading thousands of consular reports in the archives of Berlin and Washington referring to the period 1890-96, the author concludes that their military interest was slight as compared with the commercial aspects.

For the famous reports of the German consul in Kiev of March 1890 (which Bismarck was accused of having withheld from the Kaiser in spite of their alarming allusions to Russian concentrations) see G.P., VI, 1360 ff. For a military report by the French consul-general in Budapest during the Bosnian annexation crisis, see Doc. dipl. fr., 2nd series, XI, 787.

30. Report of Captain Sigsbee to Navy Department, February 1, 1898, communicated to State Department on February 7, 1898. Archives of State Department.

31. A telegram of the Austrian Consul General in Iassy of August 14, 1914, reported quite correctly the composition and strength of the two Russian armies opposite Eastern Galicia. But the Austrian GHQ gave more credit to its own reports as to Russian strength in the region in question, the more so since they happened to coincide with deductions from peace-time intelligence. The consequence was a fatal neglect in the protection of the Austrian right wing and the pushing of the offensive farther to the north, exposing the weakened wing to a successful Russian offensive. Oesterreiches Bundes-Ministerium für Heereswesen, Oesterreich-Ungarns letzter Krieg, I, 326 f. When Hull handed to the Russians the warning given the U.S. commercial attaché in Berlin in January 1941 by a member of the Hitler opposition about the Führer's intention of attacking Russia, it made only a slight impression in Moscow. Hull, Memoirs, I, 967 f.

32. von der Goltz, Volk in Waffen, p. 129.

33. For French complaints about the treatment of the Berlin embassy by the Germans in August 1914, see Doc. dipl. fr., 3rd series, XI, 571 ff.

34. von der Goltz, Volk in Waffen, p. 193. For false information from the French legation in Bern about the arrival of an Austrian army corps on the Rhine on August 8, 1914, see Doc. dipl. fr., 3rd series, XI, 578 f.

35. For the 1896 inquiries and reports, see Doc. dipl. fr., 1st series, XII, 708 ff.; for later developments, see Ibid., 2nd series, I, 456 f.; X, 638 ff., 797 f.; XI, 101 ff., 218 ff., 990 f.

36. Auffenberg-Komarow, Aus Oesterreichs Hoehe und Niedergang, p. 208; G. P., XXXIII, pp. 428, 473.

37. The chief of the Piedmontese intelligence service, Colonel Govone, the later negotiator of the treaty with Prussia against Austria in 1866, was the inventor of the carrier pigeon system, by way of which his agents among the Italian population behind the Austrian lines sent him valuable information in the war of 1859. Bapst, Le Maréchal Canrobert, III, 242.

38. G. P., VI, p. 202. The French High Command learned about the German intentions on the eve of the Second Marne Battle through "an Alsatian officer who had agreed to serve in the German Army in order to keep us informed." Gamelin, Servir, II, 195.

39. Napoleon III was particularly interested in the Austrian fortifications at Verona. A captain was sent there in 1853 to make a croquis of various forts; he was caught by the Austrian police, but his drawings were saved. They provided the basis for the French maps of the place, finished in 1858. Still nearer to the war of 1859, a major disguised as a tourist visited Verona, bribed the sexton of the church with the highest steeple, and studied the outlying forts from its height; he escaped the police, took a train to Venice and handed his notes and drawings to the French consul there, who was already gathering information about the Austrian Army. Bapst, Le Maréchal Canrobert, III, 203, 209 f.

40. Ibid., III, 199.

41. For this, see Ducrot, Vie militaire, II, 121 ff., 176 ff., 222 ff., 255 f., 299; Dalwigk's Tagebücher, passim; Oncken, Rheinpolitik, III, 98; La Gorce, Histoire du Second Empire, VI, 136 ff.

42. This is based on Souvenirs du General Jarras.

43. Ducrot, Vie militaire, p. 147.

44. Waldersee, Denkwürdigkeiten, I, 53 f., 65, 158.

45. As one of the military reformers in France, General Trochu proposed to have added to the regular intelligence service which France acquired after 1871 a group of officers to be formed from among those who spoke foreign languages and who would assemble military information on trips abroad. In addition, he proposed a special intelligence service to work along the French frontiers. Unfortunately for the scheme, too few Frenchmen were travelling abroad or spoke foreign languages. Trochu, Oeuvres posthumes, II, 253 ff.

46. Waldersee, Denkwürdigkeiten, II, 404; Hohenlohe, Denkwürdigkeiten, II, 404, 425 ff.

47. G. P., VI, 1284 ff.

48. Doc. dipl. fr., 1st series, VI, 393, 397; G. P., VII, 1605 f. According to Waldersee, "many people were shortsighted enough to believe that in this way an improvement of our relations with France could be brought about." Waldersee, Denkwürdigkeiten, II, 315.

49. See, for 1908, G. P., XXIV, 8215.

50. Callwell, Sir Henry Wilson, I, 127.

51. For the successful protest of a Prussian general against a mission he considered to be dishonorable, see Die Auswärtige Politik Preussens, II¹, 139 f.

52. Hoare, The Fourth Seal, p. 272.

53. Conrad, Aus meiner Dienstzeit, I, 450 f.; II, 240.

54. Ibid., II, 230 f.

55. Ibid., II, 18.

56. The minorities problem also worked against the effectiveness of Russian espionage. As Sir Samuel Hoare observed in Russia during the First World War, the Russians neglected the services of Finns, Balts and Poles because they could not trust them. Hoare, The Fourth Seal, p. 53. He might have added the Jews, whose services the Germans found extremely helpful before, during, and after 1914.

57. From 1907 to 1914, the German police uncovered eighty French and forty-one Russian espionage attempts. Görlitz, Generalstab, p. 205. (Corresponding statistics do not seem to be available). This led to a new and much stricter German law dealing with the betrayal of military secrets, passed on June 3, 1914. For details, see Zwehl, Falkenhayn, pp. 38 ff.

58. Conrad, Aus meiner Dienstzeit, II, 230 f., 239 ff.

59. Nekludoff, Diplomatic Reminiscences, pp. 265, 275 f., 293; Die internationalen Beziehungen im Zeitalter des Imperialismus, I, 346, 467.

60. The breaking away of the Prussian Army from the old system dated from Olmütz. At the time of that conflict, the Tsar informed the Prussian Prime Minister that he would side with Austria in case of an Austro-Prussian war. After the Tsar's threats had forced Prussia to demobilize, the old unwritten alliance with Russia became "utterly hateful" to the Army. Aus dem Leben Theodor von Bernhardis, II, 59, 70, 83, 297.

61. It was not only American diplomacy that was so often recruited from wealth before and after 1914. The 1913 Yearbook of the Millionaires of Berlin, where most of the German diplomats were taxed, included over a dozen of the highest-ranking diplomatic personnel, for example Chancellor Bülow (with a fortune of six-and-a-half million marks), Schoen, Bernstorff, von der Lancken. Most of these inclined towards understanding and against war. Martin, Jahrbuch der Millionäre in Berlin. An outstanding feature of Prussian-Russian estrangement was Russian legislation against foreigners, partly due to military initiative; it deprived Chancellor Hohenlohe of vast land holdings in the Russian frontier zones.

62. The Slavonic Review, VI, 211 f., 445, 685 ff. In its answer, the Soviet Government passed over "with contempt the insinuations of British Ministers regarding espionage by the Trade Delegation and considered it beneath its dignity to reply to them."

63. Potiemkine, Histoire de la diplomatie, III, 815 f.
64. The Red Army Intelligence Service got hold of the Polish plans for assembly in 1931 and promptly informed the Reichswehr of them. Görlitz, Generalstab, p. 377.
65. Emulation was apparently very slight among the Japanese, where aristocratic concepts of diplomatic business prevailed to the extent that soldiers were kept out of it as far as possible.
66. Documents on German Foreign Policy, Series D, IV, 168.
67. July 8. Führer Naval Conferences, 1943.
68. Trials of War Criminals, XII, 1142 ff.
69. For French diplomatic and consular reports on war and anti-war sentiment inside Germany during the summer of 1939, plus other subjects of military interest, see Gamelin, Servir, II, 451 ff.
70. Pearl Harbor Hearings, passim; 79th Congress, 2nd Session, Senate Document 244, pp. 514 ff.
71. Documents on German Foreign Policy, Series D, I, 915.
72. "In the preparations for the landing in North Africa the State Department had nothing to do with the military angles, although the consuls and vice consuls we had stationed in North Africa by virtue of our economic accord with General Weygand...rendered invaluable assistance in this field. [One wonders which other field they should have served.] They collected and sent information which was used by the War Department and maintained secret contact with the local French underground groups." Hull, Memoirs, II, 1185.
73. Leahy, I Was There, pp. 22, 57, 69 ff.
74. N. Y. Times, June 23, 1941.
75. In addition to Victor Kravchenko's testimony in I Chose Freedom (New York, 1946), see the testimony of a former commercial attaché of the Soviet Embassy in Mexico before the Senate Judiciary Committee, or Kravchenko's testimony before the House Committee on Un-American Activities. N. Y. Times, May 13, 1949 and March 8, 1950, respectively.
76. In May 1945, American Naval Intelligence ascertained that the Russians had "established an elaborate system of espionage in South America with headquarters in Mexico City." Forrestal Diaries, p. 58. Cf. statement by Lt. Gen. Leslie R. Groves, former head of the Manhattan Project: "Within a few months after I took over the Project I realized we had little to fear from German es-

pionage but a great deal to fear from Russia [which was maintaining] a far-flung organization under direct control of the Russian embassy in the U. S." N. Y. Times, May 7, 1947 and September 28, 1948.
77. Regarding the Fuchs case, Tass, the Russian news agency, was authorized to state that the British accusation that Fuchs had given away atomic secrets "to agents of the Soviet Union [was] a gross fabrication since Fuchs is unknown to the Soviet Government and no 'agents' of the Soviet Union had any connection with Fuchs." N. Y. Times, March 8, 1950. See also, Walter Bedell Smith, My Three Years in Moscow, passim; also N. Y. Times, December 22, 1947, February 4, 1948, April 24 and December 4, 1949, and June 5, 1948.
78. N. Y. Times, August 1, 1949.
79. Ibid., April 13 and 28, 1949.
80. Ibid., April 3, 1948.
81. Ibid., December 9, 1951.
82. For the early ideas about such an agency, which was to collect "both internal and external" intelligence, and for the misgivings about it, see Forrestal Diaries, p. 37 (March 29, 1945).
83. An act of June 20, 1949, in a fuller realization of the facts of cold war, authorized the CIA to admit one hundred aliens per year who had been helpful in intelligence work. It was also authorized to spend funds for espionage purposes without accounting for them in detail.
84. For discussions and criticisms of CIA's tasks, see Fletcher Pratt, "How Not to Run a Spy System," Harper's, September 1947; a series of articles by Hanson Baldwin in the N. Y. Times, July 20, 22, 23, 24, 25, 1948; Kent, Strategic Intelligence for American World Policy; The Army Almanac, p. 7; McCamy, Administration of American Foreign Affairs, ch. xiii; Roger Hilsman, "Intelligence and Policy-making in Foreign Affairs," World Politics, October 1952, pp. 1-45.
85. "The State Department has only one direct way of getting intelligence, and that is through its own missions abroad. However, through the CIA the intelligence which comes to the other branches of the Government is put together and that is made available to all branches of the Government so that there is a pool of information and intelligence on various subjects which is made up of some that comes to the State Department, some that comes to the various armed services or to any other branch of the Government." Ache-

son testifying in Military Situation in the Far East, p. 1832.

86. Truman claims the founding of the CIA as "one of the basic things I did...Strange as it may seem, the President up to that time was not completely informed as to what was taking place in the world...The CIA now coordinates all the information that is available to the State Department, the Department of Defense, and the individual offices of the Army, Navy, Air Force, the Department of Commerce and the Treasury. In this way I am able to get a concentrated survey of everything that takes place." Cited in Hillman (ed.), Mr. President, p. 14.

87. Forrestal Diaries, pp. 387 ff., 454.

88. The State Department took some pride that the ambassador in Seoul had given better warning about the continued threat of North Korean aggression than the military offices. Military Situation in the Far East, pp. 1052 f.

89. Time, August 28, 1950.

90. Military Situation in the Far East, p. 1036. Cf. the following statement: "Whenever there is a failure of information about the enemy the more literate military men, outside of G-2's, bitterly quote a passage from Shakespeare...King John: 'O, where hath our intelligence been drunk? Where hath it slept?' The gibe was justified. MacArthur's intelligence had...failed to find out what it should have found out about the enemy." Time, December 11, 1950.

91. Statement by Major General Courtney Whitney, N. Y. Times, April 24, 1951. According to MacArthur, the CIA had considered as late as November 1950 that "there was little chance of any major intervention on the part of the Chinese forces." And while front-line intelligence had realized that there was a stiffening of North Korean resistance due to the influx of some forty to sixty thousand Chinese south of the Yalu, more extensive findings were not within MacArthur's competency: "The intelligence that a nation is going to launch war is not an intelligence that is available to a commander, limited to a small area of combat." Military Situation in the Far East, pp. 18 f., 84-86.

92. Before starting on his CIA assignment, General Smith commented: "America's people expect you to be on a communing level with God and Joe Stalin, and I am not sure they are so much interested in God. They expect you to be able to say that a war will start next Tuesday at 5:32 p.m." Time, August 28, 1950. Cf. MacArthur's statement before the Senate Committee on Far Eastern Affairs on May 9, 1951: "There is a pretty definite limit to which intelligence can be gathered. The difficulties of first ascertaining the facts, and then of making conclusions from those facts, I don't think the normal public quite understands. It is not as though you had captured an enemy order and there it was all laid out there. Even if you know troops are being concentrated in a certain area, it doesn't follow that you make the correct conclusion whether they are there for defensive purposes, aggressive purposes; whether they are put there as a blind or as a bluff or caution or not...About all the local command could do is to tell you what is going on on its immediate front. There has to be an evaluation made in the highest governmental level of all the information that flows in from the chancelleries of the world to make the predictions. I don't see how it would have been humanly possible for any men or group of men to predict such an attack as that, any more than you could predict such an attack as took place at Pearl Harbor. There is nothing, no means, or methods...if you can get somebody to betray the enemy's higher circles, that can get such information as that. It is guarded with a secrecy that you cannot overestimate. Not even, probably, the commanding officers of the units, military units, concerned knew what was going on until they got the order to march." Military Situation in the Far East, pp. 293 f.; see also pp. 350, 436, 640, 1832 f., 1990 f.

93. Ibid., p. 2630.

Foreign Offices and General Staffs[1]

IN TIME OF PEACE

Since problems of foreign policy and diplomacy often have military implications, and since
defense problems have their actual or potential
diplomatic consequences, no two departments
ought to be in closer and more continued correspondence than foreign offices and general staffs.
The closeness of coordination will, as a rule, be
vastly greater in times of war or of immediate
war preparation.[2] In such times, defense departments only too readily assume the role of coordinator for war planning, sometimes to such
an extent that the directive role passes over to
them. At other times, cooperation and coordination may fall below a wholesome minimum,
notably in time of "deep peace" when, due to the
faults or weaknesses of the supreme constitutional coordinator, the vices of departmentalism,
disguised as division of labor, generally spread.
Where true "primacy of foreign affairs" is established, general staffs are permeated by it
even in time of war and thus avoid anything like
l'art pour l'art in war, which has tempted many
a general to go after war laurels when, for political reasons, armed action on his part might
well have been held to a stricter minimum.[3]

As a matter of theory, the military side readily admit that "the political questions are the
premises of military decisions," to use one of
Moltke's formulations. But at times the necessary preliminary agreement on policy, obtained
with or without early military participation, is
lacking. This was the case, for instance, in Berlin on the eve of the war of 1859 between France
and Austria, when the order of mobilization to
the Prussian Army was nothing but an expression
of political indecision.

IN THE CONTINENTAL MONARCHIES

In his resolution to make Prussia great by a
"waffenmässige Grossmachtspolitik,"[4] Bismarck, as prime minister and minister of foreign affairs, never left the military in doubt as
to what his policy was and that he meant it to be
supreme in peace or war. He believed, on the
whole rightly, that he knew enough of the military considerations in Prussian-German affairs
never to ignore them. He derived his information
from his friend Roon, the war minister. Roon was
closer to him than Moltke and his assistants,
those "demigods, of whom only very few had the

makings of a full god," and who had to be
forced into compliance with his policies.[5]

The wars from 1864 to 1871 gave the military
an increased prestige and power that even the
Chancellor often found hard to overcome. Never
particularly appreciative of the great services
that he rendered them in the Reichstag, they considered it part of their duty to advocate preventive war against France or Russia, not only, as
would have been correct, in direct communications from office to office, but outside the walls
of the Red House as well. When Gortchakov
arrived in Berlin in May 1875, in order to preserve the peace during the "war in sight" crisis,
Bismarck told him that "certain statements on
Moltke's part had been given unjustified importance; the Field Marshal was considering only
the military and strategic side of the question,
but did not also consider it from the political
viewpoint." And he added humorously: "In fact,
Field Marshal Count Moltke is a child in
politics."[6] While the thought of a preventive war against rapidly rearming France
was not altogether foreign to his own thought
at the time, Bismarck was always ready to
assure the diplomats that he was at one with
them in maintaining the peace regardless of military advice—"even the most circumspect
soldiers might be at times mistaken about their
premises."[7]

The alliances concluded by Bismarck remained
under his supervision even when they received
their military implementation. Direct talks between the general staffs were kept at a strict
minimum and subject to his permission. Following the arrival of Waldersee as Moltke's adlatus
in the General Staff (1882), the inclination of the
military to enter upon direct understandings with
Vienna increased. Bismarck told Waldersee to
refrain from exerting direct influence on representatives of foreign governments for he, the
Chancellor, could not carry on business if exposed to such interference on the part of the
military. At the same time Bismarck reminded
Austria that Waldersee was not politically responsible for his statements to them, could not
speak with authority about the political situation,
and did not even always express Moltke's views.[8]
All was not harmony between himself and the
occupants of the Red House, who were left as
little in doubt about this as were the foreign
governments concerned.[9]

Was the military sector of Reich affairs to be freed from the Chancellor's overall control? Around this problem revolved the prolonged conflict between the chief of staff in spe and Bismarck. When he asked Moltke in February 1888, whether Waldersee, with his string of journalists harping on "the danger of war," was really the right man for his job, Bismarck received no help from the nonagenarian strategist. The crown prince of the General Staff won the support of the other Crown Prince, the future William II, who promised Waldersee that he would never permit the Bismarcks to interfere in Army affairs. William II was anxious to keep Waldersee "out of the grip of the Bismarck family." Bismarck's attempt to remove Waldersee from Berlin during the "hundred days" of 1888 failed because Moltke threatened to resign should he lose his adlatus—the old man's revenge for the defeat on the interior front in 1871. Instead, Waldersee became Moltke's successor in August of 1888. Soon Waldersee seemed slated to become Chancellor. The anti-Bismarck party was convinced that there must be war with Russia soon. From this it followed that the policy-maker must prepare this war better than was being done by Bismarck who, they reasoned, had grown old, wanted peace at any price, was the captive of his ancient preference for the Russians, was wrong in his belief that better relations with them could be restored, and was letting the most favorable military moment slip by unused. In May 1889, Waldersee believed the moment for the war would arrive around April 1 of the next year; the war minister, also anti-Bismarck, preferred the autumn of the same year. In the meantime, they wanted to make use of the Chancellor's "great talent and prestige in the world," until the moment they would pick for war—"together with the Chancellor; but when things become serious, without him, even against him, if necessary." William II seemed won over. He told one of the Reich ambassadors, home on leave: "If Bismarck doesn't want to come along against the Russians, our ways must part."[10] In preparation, Russia was to be denied further access to the Berlin capital market which until then (1887) had not only strengthened Russian arms but had also provided a golden tie between the two countries. While one part of the Berlin press, guided by the General Staff, attacked these loans, the Bismarck press, invoking Clausewitz on the supreme role of policy, pilloried those who advocated "war for war's sake." These out-front battles reflected the behind-scenes cabals in which the Waldersee group of generals won out. These generals made much of the accusation that Bismarck did not keep the Emperor correctly in-

formed of the alarming state of Russian military preparations.[11]

Waldersee never quite reached the position of major domo of the Hohenzollern that he wanted for himself and the General Staff. The Bismarckian constitution left the monarch in a position where he, surrounded by a mutiplicity of major domos, proved unable to unite them to one purpose. He could merely molest and disturb them in the pursuit of their various activities, until the chiefs of staff forced him to stop being a nuisance. The directors of foreign affairs never obtained such a state of nonmolestation for themselves. There was no one-field policy during his reign. Everyone of those in "immediate" relations with him ploughed his own field, great or small, but in any case carefully fenced off.

Only on a few occasions, during such diplomatic crises as those over China in 1900 and Morocco in 1905-06 and 1911, was the General Staff asked by the Wilhelmstrasse what the military implication of these crises might be or what military meaning the Anglo-French entente of 1904 or the war in the Far East of 1904-05 might have.[12] Occasionally, as during the Balkan crises of 1912-13, the younger Moltke, apparently on his own initiative, informed the Wilhelmstrasse of recently gathered and evaluated military intelligence regarding changes in France and Russia, in the same manner as army corps commands in the frontier districts were kept informed.[13] But he did not tell them, and they did not ask him, what kind of arrangements had been made with Austria for the case of war. There were none. This was the Great General Staff's very own secret, and the reason for that was a secret too: the fear that the secret of its own plans might not be kept either in Vienna or in the Wilhelmstrasse.

Contacts of a similar nature between the Wilhelmstrasse and the naval offices were even more sporadic. The diplomats did not seek to change the situation. Tirpitz was regarded in the higher brackets of German civilian bureaucracy as a mauvais coucheur, someone hard to get along with. He had a marked tendency "towards sacrificing other, also important and worthwhile interests to his own purposes"; and among these purposes his hankering for naval stations proved particularly irksome to the diplomats.[14] As it was, German naval policy was full of unwanted surprises. During the first of the Anglo-German war scares in November-December 1904, an admiral appeared in the Wilhelmstrasse to tell the diplomats that the Emperor and the Navy expected a British attack in the spring of 1905. There were discussions. Should Marines and cruisers at foreign stations be called home or should they be left where they were in order not to arouse British suspicions and precipitate the attack in which Holstein now believed for the first time? The sedative was for once supplied by the military attaché in London, who advised that, in spite of the confirmed Germanophobia of Britain, immediate aggression need not be feared.[15] On the next occasion, during the second Moroccan crisis, Foreign Secretary Kiderlen asked the Naval Staff for "proof" of the alleged British preparations for an attack on Germany. What they submitted seemed to the diplomats proof rather of an English fear of being attacked by Germany during the railway strike of 1911.[16]

In their preparation for war, the Berlin military offices took certain steps without first considering the possible diplomatic implications. The Liman von Sanders Mission was arranged at the suggestion of the General Staff and on orders of the Kaiser through the latter's Military Cabinet, as if it had been a matter of giving an officer leave to spend a few years abroad. There was no thought that "this command might have political implications"; there was no previous consultation with the Wilhelmstrasse and the Chancellor. The protesting Russians, who ought to have been familiar from their own practices with this way of doing business, gained the impression "qu'un grand désordre règne dans les sphères dirigéantes de Berlin" when they were told of the genesis of the Mission by the harried Chancellor. He promised that the Wilhelmstrasse would take care that such incidents should not occur again.[17]

The Great General Staff considered its own war preparations so completely adequate to meet any contingency that no new or renewed specific understandings with the Wilhelmstrasse seemed necessary. Other general staffs might be filled with similar convictions, but in most other countries they remained under somewhat more stringent controls. These were weak in places, notably in Vienna. Conrad, contemplating his own responsibility for "timely operative readiness," came to the conclusion at the outset of his first term of office that, in case of a war or diplomatic crisis,

the chief of staff is under the obligation to prepare everything...for the eventuality that the appeal to arms may become inevitable. No state is able to be ready for war completely and at all times. Each is in need of certain complementary measures before concentration begins, which takes considerable time itself...Postponing it even by a day may become fatal if a diligent opponent acts more unscrupulously or more resolutely. It is only natural that in such situations the minister of foreign affairs and the chief of staff clash temporarily; but it is inconceivable how such a

duty-bound precautionary action on the part of the responsible military offices can be described as illegal interference with the prerogatives of the minister of foreign affairs, as disturbing his policy, as a provocation of foreign governments harmful to his policy. Yet Baron Aehrenthal did habitually, even in case of the slightest military measure.[18]

When Conrad took up the duties of Chief of Staff in 1906, he considered it "the first and most important thing...to establish harmony with the Minister of Foreign Affairs, because I considered most essential the intimate connection between foreign affairs and the labors of preparing for war, which are the duties of the Chief of Staff." Thus far, his conception of the duty to cooperate did not seem exceptional, particularly when Conrad promised that he by no means "claimed interference with the directorship of policy." He added, however, that, considering the intimate connection between war-preparation and foreign policy, he could not exclude the consideration of the latter from his own field of thoughts. "Policy does not reach over into the field of the assembly and concentration of the armies only, but also into various questions of the organization of our forces. I cannot approve of the standpoint that the Army is a strictly separate organism, independently evolved, on which one calls in case of need, at the very last moment." Hence the need for constant direct contacts with the foreign office.[19]

Unfortunately, however, later developments, for which he never admitted his own responsibility, "gradually produced many a divergence of views, other momenta contributing, so that harmony was not established in all questions which I would have considered absolutely necessary."[20] For one thing, Conrad complained, he learned little about the actual negotiations, nothing beyond what Aehrenthal saw fit to let him know. Only during the Annexation crisis of 1908-09 did inter-office relations become lively, and then only because there was a possibility of war. Not even the text of the Triple Alliance was communicated to him, and from the outset there was deep-seated divergence in outlook on Italy. For Conrad, Italy was always one of Austria's enemies, who must be beaten sooner or later, while Aehrenthal, as well as most of the German diplomats, and quite a few German generals still considered Italy as an ally of some military value. It was one of the signs of their disparateness that there never was a down-to-earth discussion between the foreign offices and the general staffs of the Central Powers as to the actual "alliance value" of Italy. In 1908, Francis Joseph decided that the Chief of Staff could deal directly with the Foreign Ministry on certain questions without having the War Minister act as intermediary. Even so, Aehrenthal failed to respond to Conrad's proposals or queries. Which of Austria's enemies, for instance, was to be struck first with the maximum of force? According to Conrad, that must be Italy.[21] According to the diplomats, Italy must come last, if ever.

The strong inner contradictions of Tsarist imperialism were due to the fact that the soldiers and, since the 1890's, the sailors were providing the main driving force for an expansion that could not add to, and in some respects would detract from Russian security, both internal and external. The traditionally ruling grand seigneurial aristocracy had retained control over diplomacy and had terminated the Crimean War, which the military had been unable to win. The diplomats, however, did not realize until too late that the expansion overland, resumed after the Crimean War, was incidental to the reform work undertaken by War Minister Miliutine (1861-81). These reforms relied on certain quasi-democratic features, on nationalism and on territorial expansion. In their endeavor to get rid of Miliutine, the aristocracy called into its service the poison pen of General Fadejev. Fadejev was "the real creator, or at least codifier, of Russian General Staff chauvinism," and the originator of the slogan: "The road to Constantinople goes by way of Vienna."[22] The upshot was an alliance between the Devil and Beelzebub—between the General Staff and the Russian bourgeoisie. The General Staff assumed a greater independence under Miliutine's successor, who "committed the serious error of giving the General Staff under General Obrutchev a much too independent position" (Schweinitz). And the Russian bourgeoisie had some new instruments of power, notably the press. Against this alliance the Foreign Ministry nearly always proved powerless. A man like Giers, foreign minister since 1882, was, as the German ambassador put it, "in his relations with Miliutine like the earthenware pot by the side of the iron one."[23] This made it advisable for Giers to stay out of Miliutine's way as much as possible. Consequently, the delimitation of the fields of these two offices was (as it had been earlier in Germany) one of power rather than of competence.

At most times the two ministers carried on their business without much understanding or conflict. This is clearly indicated in War Minister Suchomlinov's description of his relations with Sasonov: "I never had differences with the Foreign Minister...There were between us no constant points of contact, since I did not care much for diplomacy and Sasonov did not have an interest in military questions. His landing plans in the direction of the Bosporus showed me how little he

understood military things."[24] The problem of the Straits brought the various office holders in St. Petersburg together from time to time, all of them equally eager to complete Russia's "historic mission." On these occasions, as 1914 approached, the military were compelled to tell the diplomats that Russia would have to rely on the help of the allies in the conquest of Constantinople, even though there was danger that these allies might deny her possession.[25]

NAVAL BASES: AN EXAMPLE OF MILITARY DEMANDS AND DIPLOMATIC EMBARRASSMENT

Military peace-time demands on diplomacy, even if not as radically perverse as those made by Conrad, are apt to be painful or highly inconvenient to the diplomats. The inconvenience may derive from the very logic of such demands: If other navies possess and acquire naval stations, why not one's own navy as well? Besides, if the navy considered the acquisition of stations as absolutely necessary, how could the foreign office protest and argue? Under existing conditions they were precluded from passing judgment on a desire declared imperative by the professionals. This demand for stations and bases abroad plagued diplomats at various times before and after 1900: first when various navies, under the impact of Mahan's teachings, demanded them; and again from 1945 on.

When presented with demands for bases, the diplomats became instantly aware of the difficulties in the way of acquiring them. There was the reaction of other states to worry about, and there was also doubt in the diplomat's mind as to whether the security interest of his country really required their possession. By the end of the century there was, however, not much of the civilian courage of the Bismarck-Salisbury generation left that could nip such service desires in the bud. When British forces in 1892, in the name of Egypt, held and wanted to keep certain points occupied on the northern shore of the Red Sea, Salisbury warned Britain's pro-consul in Cairo not "to be too impressed by what the soldiers tell you about the strategic importance of those plans. If they were allowed full scope, they would insist on the importance of garrisoning the moon in order to protect us from Mars."[26]

A less bold generation of diplomats did not presume to pass an equally independent judgment as to the actual value and need of naval and other stations.[27] When caught between the pressure of the services for stations and the accusation by foreign Powers of an immoderate imperialism, they would "go through the motions" of attempting the acquisitions, and in the end would tell the sailors that for many accumulated reasons all or most of them were unobtainable. A few stations were acquired by Germany around 1900, at the cost of considerable diplomatic labor and political irritation.[28] Certainly more labor was expended and more irritation provoked than the meager strategic advantages warranted.

Such desires for stations, justified in the name of national security, are usually mixed with imperialistic urges. It is the latter that, in an imperialist age, make it even more difficult for diplomats, who are almost as often imperialist-minded themselves, to oppose such acquisitions. When there is no such imperialist infection, the question arises as to whether and how far the political direction must bow to the strategic demands of the military and naval and air offices. These may represent, or seem to represent, the essence of military considerations. No civilian could lightly contradict them—except by pointing out political consequences, which in their turn eventually become strategic concerns.

In 1914-15 the Japanese Foreign Office and elder statesmen felt constrained to bow to the Twenty-One Demands that were presented to them by the armed forces before they were presented to the hapless Chinese. As instructions from the Japanese General Staff to the service attachés in Peking clearly betrayed, this forward policy was not originally welcomed by the Foreign Office, more aware than the services of its far-reaching consequences. In fact, the General Staff itself doubted that the violent measures against China which they had resolved upon "would have a beneficial influence on our foreign policy. But following careful consideration we are convinced that for the sake of our national defense it is necessary to obtain effective power in China." There the Navy hoped to neutralize the American naval base in the Philippines by getting control over the Santuao region in Fukien province. The Army demands were aimed more against Russia and her Siberian Railway, the military usefulness of which diminished as Army plans matured during the next ten years. These plans were declared to be of life-and-death importance to Japan's destiny, for which reason "we have always pressed the members of the Government to push ahead this forward-directed policy." For their part, the service attachés were to pursue this on the spot in China.[29]

The military experience with stations in the two World Wars was largely adverse. This was true of Kiaochow, of Singapore, the Philippines, and the stronghold that Japan had built up as a mandatory in the former German islands in the Pacific. Their indefensibility proved greatest in proportion to their distance from homegrounds. These experiences, however, had no great deterring

effect on the aspirations of the services for more foreign stations. Among these, air bases assumed a new significance during the Second World War. While the Lend-Lease arrangements of the United States tended to keep the imperialistic features of holding such stations at a strict minimum, the Russians, resuming their partly traditional search for final frontiers and warmer waters, made such stations the focal points of imperialist penetration. This was notably the case in the Baltic countries, where control and conquest began with the demand for stations.[30] The Americans and British were at first either not suspicious of Russian aspirations or felt themselves in no position to protest against them. Only when they realized at last that Russian aspirations were reaching over into spheres of their own security interest—into Greece, the Straits, the Far East, and Czechoslovakia—did the active opposition of the Western Powers begin or the American determination to evacuate Lend-Lease positions reverse itself. Only then did the original strong aversion of the State Department against the services' desires for stations abroad diminish. Only then did most of the diplomats' anti-imperialist hesitancies vanish.

Other matters that create peace-time problems between foreign offices and defense offices are: service attachés and other military personnel stationed or travelling abroad;[31] military missions of instruction or ceremony; military instructors or Salisbury's hybrids, "the military consuls";[32] the selling[33] or buying abroad of military arms and other equipment; ship movements, demonstrative or not;[34] information and intelligence about foreign lands. These subjects are later dealt with separately.

PRIMACY OF FOREIGN POLICY AND CIVILIAN PRIMACY—AMERICA AND BRITAIN

The ties between general staffs and foreign offices in time of peace involve two basic governmental problems: (1) that of establishing and maintaining a mutuality and consonance of policy, resulting in a diplomacy that does not go beyond feasible military implementation,[35] and military measures that stay within diplomatic intentions, and (2) that of preserving civilian control, or, in other words, of avoiding undue military influence. Civilian control was most wanted and best realized in the Anglo-Saxon countries, with France holding an intermediate position since 1871. The intention of preserving civilian control delayed the development of general staffs in the Anglo-Saxon countries just as long as this could safely be done under the prevailing conditions of military competition. The civilian governors there wanted to see as few ties as possible established between bureaucracies as difficult to control as foreign offices and general staffs. Presidents and Prime Ministers wanted these ties to be supervised by the ministers concerned, the foreign and defense ministers, who were presumed to keep these connections under the cognizance of the cabinets.

Actual developments did not conform with such expectations on the Continent. The general staffs soon escaped from the original control by the war ministers, even where these were military men. Instead of the original channels, by way of the war minister and the supreme war lord and/or chancellor or premier, a double set of wires between foreign offices and general staffs was strung— one direct, between the two offices, and one indirect, by way of the supreme war lord. This resulted in a maximum of independence on the part of the war planning office, an independence, its directors insisted, necessitated by the secret nature of war preparations. Once a secret was shared by civilian governors—as in the old Austrian Hofkriegsrat where a civilian would begin the first draft of such a plan by starting (logically, as it seemed then) from the political premises—, it came in various countries to be shared by none of these.[36] Neither William II nor the Wilhelmstrasse knew before August 1914 the great secret that there was only one German mobilization plan.

Under the impact of total war things did not turn out fundamentally differently in the Anglo-Saxon countries. The civilian constitutional commanders-in-chief, the American President and the British Prime Minister, took counsel with the chiefs of staff and determined and shared their secrets—Roosevelt allowing them to guess his obvious secret, the intention of getting the United States into the war against the Axis. However, they conceded their countries' diplomatic offices relatively little knowledge, not to mention influences, distinctly less on the part of Roosevelt than of Churchill. The existing direct wires between the diplomatic offices and the separate or joint staffs were clearly not overloaded with significant communications, at least not until the time of the "cold war."[37]

CONCLUSION

In some former ages, peace—as the main objective of diplomacy and foremost determinant of its methods—projected its light into war, to a certain extent limiting its excesses and its logical consequence, "absolute war." Total war now throws its shadow farther over peace than have other types of war. In keeping with this change, which has taken place less abruptly than is commonly presumed, a shift in the relative positions of foreign offices and general staffs has come

about. While the role of the former has been considerably reduced, the general staffs have moved from a merely technical advisory position into one of co-determination of, or even domination over, policy. Their locus standi is now near the commander-in-chief, the ultimate arbiter between diplomatic and military advisers. While some of the earlier motivations behind these shifts of position might be called militaristic, to others must be conceded a definite amount of objective necessity. This is notably true in time of threatening total war, which necessitates the contemplation of the unprecedented number and variety of military implications and consequences of diplomatic moves, as well as the diplomatic consequences of military measures. Plans and measures of both must remain flexible, despite the massiveness of the organizations and popular psyches involved.

It may be impossible or futile to say whether "cold war" is more peace or more war. As yet, neither diplomatic nor military means have been able to finish it. And it is not likely to be finished by anything that can be called outright victory for either diplomacy or armed forces. With no likely hope for victory by either exclusively military or diplomatic methods, as far as the West is concerned, an altogether remarkable situation of non-competition between foreign offices and general staffs has come about on this side of the "iron curtain." MacArthur's proposals for the ending of the Korean war by old-fashioned military victory furnished indication of how unprecedented this new relation was, one of a new approximation, if not yet integration, of civilian and military offices and objectives.

FOOTNOTES

1. For the problem in general, see Mowat, Diplomacy and Peace, ch. viii.
2. According to Holstein, Schlieffen would come to his office, usually once a week "in livelier periods," to read the latest diplomatic dispatches. Rogge, Friedrich von Holstein, p. 187.
3. The occupation of Bosnia-Herzegovina in 1878 was so staged by the Austrian military command that the inhabitants had time to organize their armed resistance. From the outset, Philippovic, the commanding general, and his staff wanted no simple peaceful occupation but rather one that would earn them laurels. When a local commander was ready to take Serajevo, he was told to wait for the arrival of Philippovic, himself a Croat and thus an enemy of the Moslems, who were up in arms, whereas Andrassy, the foreign minister and a Hungarian, wanted to win the Moslems over to the Double Monarchy from the outset. At

Andrassy's suggestion, Philippovic was transferred to Prague just when he was approaching the high point of his glory. Wertheimer, Andrassy, II, 154 f., 162. Other military actions beyond the necessary ones were staged by Waldersee in China in 1900-01, and by American and British ship commanders intervening in Samoa in 1899. Vagts, Deutschland und die Vereinigten Staaten, p. 936.

4. December 24, 1863. Bismarck, Gedanken und Erinnerungen, II, 20.

5. For details, see Bethcke, Politische Generäle, pp. 1 ff.

6. Ibid., pp. 30 f. Bismarck told another Russian diplomat: "We have a General Staff that is continually making war against our three neighbors, Austria not excepted. In 1875, the military went too far, they found that France was recuperating too fast. I had an explanation about that from the French Government. I knew where I would stop; the military never know that." Lavisse, Histoire de la France contemporaine, VII, 419.

7. A message for Gambetta. Bethcke, Politische Generäle, p. 31.

8. Waldersee, Denkwürdigkeiten, I, 340 ff., 419 ff.

9. A present from the General Staff for Bismarck's seventieth birthday (1885) could not be delivered because the Chancellor did not want it. Keim, Erlebtes und Erstrebtes.

10. Holborn (ed.), Aufzeichnungen und Erinnerungen aus dem Leben des Botschafters Joseph Maria von Radowitz, II, 295 ff.

11. Waldersee, Denkwürdigkeiten, II, 48, 60, 89 and passim; Bethcke, Politische Generäle, pp. 127 ff.

12. G. P., XVI, 4585; XXI, 6942 ff., 7226; XXXIII, 12412, 12433.

13. Ibid., XIX, 6031 f., 6194 f.

14. Bülow, Denkwürdigkeiten, I, 109; II, 245.

15. G. P., XIX, 6150-54.

16. Ibid., XXIX, 10664 f., 10671, 10673.

17. Schmidt-Bückeburg, Militärkabinett, pp. 226 f.

18. Conrad, Aus meiner Dienstzeit, I, 101.

19. To Aehrenthal, November 1, 1907. Ibid., I, 517.

20. Ibid., I, 39.

21. Ibid., I, 81, 582 f.

22. Schweinitz, Denkwürdigkeiten, II, 435.

23. Ibid., II, 103, 292.

24. Suchomlinow, Erinnerungen, p. 375. Suchomlinow was War Minister from 1909 to 1915.

25. Die internationalen Beziehungen im Zeitalter des Imperialismus, 2nd series, I, 283 ff.

26. Cecil, Life of Salisbury, III, 218. For the British Cabinet discussions prior to the acquisition of Cyprus as a "fresh place of arms" and the protest of the Foreign Secretary, see Monypenny and Buckle, Disraeli, II, 1123 ff., 1143.

27. For the Wilhelmstrasse's most extreme program for acquiring naval stations in the late 1890's, see Ziekursch, Politische Geschichte des neuen deutschen Kaiserreichs, III, 117 f.

28. For the poisoning effect of the competition for naval stations on American-German relations, see Vagts, Deutschland und die Vereinigten Staaten, ch. xiv.

29. Instructions of April 3, 1915, communicated by the Chinese to the Russian embassy in Peking. Die internationalen Beziehungen im Zeitalter des Imperialismus, 2nd series, VII, 683 f.

30. Nazi-Soviet Relations, pp. 103 f., 117 and passim.

31. Prior to 1914, military officers in Germany were often used as diplomatic couriers, especially the so-called Feldjäger, members of the Reitende Feldjägerkorps. This consisted of candidates for the higher forestry career who were also reserve officers; their employment dated back to Frederick the Great. In order to express his contempt for the divine right-ism of the Elector of Hessia, who did not want to resume diplomatic relations with Prussia, Bismarck sent a simple Feldjäger to Kassel in 1862 to present the Elector with a note from him. Eyck, Bismarck, I, 444.

32. For some details, see Nicolson, Portrait of a Diplomatist, pp. 21, 23.

33. For the opposition of relatively subordinate officers in the U.S. Navy Department to State Department-approved dealings of American shipyards with Russia in 1937, see U. S. Foreign Relations: The Soviet Union, 1933-1939, pp. 481 ff.

34. For the State Department's reaction to a proposal by the Navy Department to have a cruising vessel visit Leningrad in the summer of 1934, see Ibid., pp. 112 ff.

35. During a visit to Berlin in the summer of 1952, when asked what he would do if the East Germans should try to take over West Berlin and cut off its communications with the West altogether, Secretary Acheson replied "that his first action would be to listen to the advice of the military, presumably the Joint Chiefs of Staff. He said the counter-measures would depend on their advice but he would not speculate on the nature of such measures." N. Y. Times, June 30, 1952.

36. For the old Austrian practice, see Jähns, Kriegswissenschaften, pp. 2289 f.

37. Hull's statement that he was "in constant
    contact" with the two chiefs of staff before

Pearl Harbor is never really substantiated.
Hull, Memoirs, II, 1071.

Military Conventions and General Staff Conversations

The use of military conventions dates from the early eighteenth century. They are generally defined as international agreements not in need of ratification.[1] At times, however, they have been negotiated with a view to subsequent ratification. Some military conventions have proved to be of the greatest historical importance, an early example being the Westminster Convention of January 1756, signed on the eve of the Seven Years' War, which brought in its wake a complete upsetting of the European alliance system. The negotiators of military conventions are military officers equipped with only a minimum of diplomatic powers, in addition to the actual and obvious powers which their rank, position, and command confer on them.

Military conventions are concluded either between hostile parties at war (armistice, capitulation, and other suspension or cessation of hostilities) or between friendly parties, most often in contemplation of war. Military conventions may stand in lieu of political alliances, or they may implement political alliances by fixing the specific military obligations and other military arrangements deriving from them. The Franco-Russian convention of 1892-1893, which was designed to by-pass French parliamentary ratification, is an example of the first type. The military convention of March 18, 1778, by which Saxony put her 22,000-man army at Frederick's disposal and thus sealed Prussian-Saxon opposition to the Emperor in the War of the Bavarian Succession, is an example of the second.[2]

MILITARY CONVENTIONS AND PEACE-MAKING: 1796-1815

The often very considerable power of military negotiators has usually reached its fullest extent in the commander's privilege of arranging the conditions of a truce, armistice or capitulation without interference from the home government or its representatives. Bonaparte entered upon his first conflicts with the civil power when, as general in command of the Army of Italy in 1796, he insisted that the power of concluding armistices must remain with him, even though the Directoire had assigned this function to civilian representatives. After he had concluded a few armistices unaided, however, he was forced to admit the civilian representatives of the French government to the negotiations with the remaining Italian principalities. He soon accused them of mismanaging these and of exacting conditions neither

favorable nor severe enough. The armistice of Leoben in the following year was again all of his own making.[3]

Wellington and his contemporaries called the armistices that he concluded with the Napoleonic marshals in 1814 and 1815, conventions. The first was made on April 8, 1814, with Marmont and Suchet in Southern France; the second with Davout on July 3, 1815. The first of these conventions was strictly military in nature. It provided for the suspension of hostilities between the forces under their command, laid down a line of demarcation, provided for the treatment of wounded and ill, for the free passage of couriers, and even for the mutual exchange of deserters should this be demanded.[4] The 1815 convention did not escape political interpretation, despite Wellington's early explanation that it "decides all the military questions of this moment, and touches nothing political." It was negotiated by the aides of the three marshals and ratified by the commander. It provided for the termination of hostilities, evacuation of Paris by the French forces within three days, recognition of the existing French authorities, respect for public and private property, and also for the provisioning of the Paris population. According to Wellington's early understanding, "the convention binds nobody excepting the parties to it; viz., the French army on one side and the allied armies on the other and...cannot be considered, and never was intended, to bind any other persons or authorities whatever." Differences of interpretation arose when the Allies demanded the return of the art treasures that Napoleon had gathered from their countries and when the defenders of Marshal Ney maintained that the convention guaranteed his life. By reference to the armistice negotiations, Wellington denied both claims.[5]

MILITARY CONVENTIONS AND PREPARATIONS FOR WAR: 1811-1814

While these conventions terminated wars, others of the same period had prepared for them. In 1811, when the Emperor's march into Russia was being prepared, Prussia was hard pressed both by Napoleon's "reparations" policy and by his occupation measures. She tried desperately to ease her lot either by obtaining an alliance with him, which would make her more nearly an equal partner, or by coming to a secret agreement with Russia. Scharnhorst, head of the military Reformers, was sent to St. Petersburg in July 1811 to explain the Prussian king's position to Tsar Alexander. Prussia, he explained, was forced to maintain the appearance of a good understanding with France but would take no other side than that of Russia in a Russian-French war. That is, she would side with Russia if Russia would approach the common frontier with enough forces to bring effective help to Prussia. Scharnhorst brought back a military convention, which he had signed on October 17. He had obtained the promise that the Tsar's forces would march out, but only in the case of clear French aggression or of the massing of considerable French forces along the Vistula, not the Elbe! The results of this mission were discouraging, as were the attempts to persuade Vienna and Metternich to join in active resistance against Napoleon. The Emperor forced both German Powers to serve him in his expedition against Russia. By a convention of March 5, 1812, Prussia promised an auxiliary army of 20,000 men and sixty guns to serve in all of Napoleon's wars except in Spain, Italy and Turkey. She also promised to open her provinces to his march against Russia and to the cruel exactions of his soldiery. Many of the military Reformers left the Prussian service in disgust and entered that of Russia.[6] They were to be instrumental in leading Prussia out of the French camp.

The Prusso-Russian Convention of Tauroggen (December 30, 1812) was the instrument by which the Prussian auxiliary corps under General von Yorck was pried away from Napoleon's overlordship and brought closer to the Russian side. The contracting parties were Yorck and General von Diebitsch, commanding the Russian forces opposite him. There were no instructions from above and no full powers on either side. The six signatories and the two ratifiers were all Germans, even on the Russian side, among whom was Clausewitz, who was temporarily serving the Tsar. To Pan-Slavists with French sympathies, this was very shocking. Even a century later, Waliszewski wrote of the event: "There is a mutual agreement among Germans for the purpose of disposing of Russia, and on this structure of falsehoods and impostures they treat and they sign."[7] It was, indeed, a revolutionary move. Metternich, who recognized the like when he saw one, spoke of it to a British agent as of "a kind of revolution." The arch-diplomat who "in general appears incapable of any emotion, really seemed to be greatly agitated" by what he called the capitulation (which it was not) of the Prussian contingent.[8]

It was actually more of a neutrality convention, not an armistice, though whether Yorck himself was quite clear about this seems doubtful. It was concluded by the Prussian general in a situation which was not, militarily speaking, hopeless; for Yorck definitely had local military superiority. He negotiated without authorization from Berlin and without any knowledge on his part of either the momentary or ultimate intentions of his King and his home government: both were continually in flux and neither was marked by courage or determination. Berlin was far less convinced of the impending ruin of Napoleon's armed power than the general in the field. Swayed by his entourage, Yorck signed an agreement providing for the neutrality of his corps until the necessary orders from the King had arrived. Should these orders express disapproval of a further understanding with the Russians, the Prussians would be at liberty to march off in accordance with the royal orders. Considering circumstances and the royal character of timidity, Yorck risked being disavowed by King and Government, if he did not in fact risk his own head. "If the step which I had taken should have proved disadvantageous to our policy," he asked, "was not then everything in such a state that with the falling of my head the Minister of Foreign Affairs would have regained a free hand?" While grumbling, the King was, however, at least satisfied that "Yorck's corps had been preserved and was beyond the influence of French army leaders." Publicly, Yorck was disavowed, but only until King and Government had departed from Berlin, where they were still under French pressure and control, to the safety of Breslau. Driven onward by Yorck's bold step, they soon concluded an alliance with Russia (Treaty of Kalisch, February 28, 1813), which provided the nucleus of the anti-Napoleonic coalition in the Wars of Liberation.[9]

Still another subsequent desertion from Napoleon was sealed by a military convention—the defection of Murat, King of Naples. The evening of the first day of the Battle of Nations found him ready to negotiate with Metternich, who promised him a guarantee of his Italian throne if he would leave the Emperor and keep further Italian reinforcements from reaching the latter. Soon after Leipzig, Murat departed, coming to new agreements with Austria and Britain early in 1814. The agreement with Britain took the form of a military convention with "the person exercizing the government of Naples." The main interest of the two Powers was to withhold and withdraw aid from Napoleon. Both determined to get rid of Murat later on, and he facilitated their game by his recklessness.[10]

MILITARY CONVENTIONS AS INSTRUMENTS OF HEGEMONY

In the life of the majority of states the moment arrives, usually recognized only very reluctantly and sometimes too late to save even a relative independence, when the armed forces they maintain, partly for internal reasons, no longer serve an efficient purpose unless combined with the forces of other states of comparable or superior strength. This relative, or absolute, shrinking of military strength has led to the various power combinations of history, from the amphictyonic arrangements among the Greek city states to the Soviet satellite system and the North Atlantic Treaty Organization of the 1940's and 1950's. Like other agreements between unequal parties, military conventions have tended to establish the hegemony of the superior partner, temporarily, as in arrangements for the supreme command, or permanently.

The relations of Austria and Prussia with the many small states of Germany, and especially the processes by which Prussia unified them, offer many instructive lessons in the uses to which military conventions can be put in establishing the dominance of larger over smaller states. The position of hegemony which Prussia gained fairly promptly in the Zollverein was acquired much more slowly in the military field, where she met more determined resistance from the parties and institutions to be absorbed. Her endeavors, as old as the Austro-Prussian conflict for predominance in the old Reich and in the German Bund, were aimed at military leadership in the non-Austrian areas and at the long-overdue reform of the motley soldiery raised in the many small principalities.[11] The legal instruments on which Prussia's predominance came to be based were military conventions with the various North, Central and South German states. A few of these were concluded before 1866 with states like Saxe-Coburg, stipulating uniformities and standardization with regard to equipment and training, exchange of officers, and strength of the contingent in case of war. They did not, however, call for having the small states unconditionally follow Prussia into war.

Those few and small North German states that had sided with Prussia in 1866 concluded military conventions with her. By these conventions they put their little armies at her disposal and thus created the nucleus of the North German Bund. Under the typical arrangements inside this interim federation (1866-71), the members surrendered most of their military states' rights in favor of Prussia, enabling the latter to create a homogenous, up-to-date force under the King of Prussia as federal commander-in-chief

(Bundesfeldherr). By the end of 1869, only two North German States, Brunswick and Mecklenburg-Strelitz, had not yet concluded such conventions. In order to make the officers of these miniature armies prod their governments, they were pointedly reminded from Berlin that this obstruction on the part of their governments denied them chances for further promotion and education that would be open to them within the framework of the larger army of the North German Bund.[12] Nor did Bismarck make the German states conquered in 1866 go to their Appomatox for the unconditional surrender of their military states' rights. In addition to the defensive and offensive alliances which he concluded with them immediately after victory, military conventions were successively concluded by Prussia, through her military negotiators, with Saxony, Hesse-Darmstadt, Baden, Württemberg and Bavaria. These conventions somewhat impaired the "independent international existence" of the small states but at the same time left them a large number of traditional military rights. The German army until 1919—in some respects even until Hitler's day—was actually an army composed of state contingents, based on the conventions concluded between Prussia and the other federal states.

In places like Munich, the spokesmen of extreme states' rights saw in the alliances and conventions "sheer vassalage" and "the source from which the misfortune of militarism had poured over the once so happy countries of Southern Germany."[13] For some time, however, Moltke would not even admit that they had brought much help to Prussia. At the end of 1868 he expressed his conviction that "we are superior to France unless she is supported by a coalition. There was little to expect from the South German States. Not that they would commit treason openly in case of a conflict; on the contrary, they would exhibit the best of goodwill, but would be hesitant and arrange things in such a manner that they would be too late." They might postpone the opening of operations by as much as a fortnight, the very fortnight during which the decision must fall. Should it go against Prussia, the South Germans might even join the winning side.[14] Even as late as the beginning of 1870, Prussian generals from Moltke down were in favor of counselling and replacing the existing treaties. They still did not seem to provide sufficiently for the defense of the whole of Germany; this only a unified army under Prussian direction, reaching from the Baltic to the Alps, could do.[15] By the time of the outbreak of the war of 1870, however, the arrangements for military cooperation, mobilization and command were so far perfected and the casus belli so skilfully handled by Bismarck that no political or military hesitation interfered with military operations.

His own experiences as constitutional commander-in-chief and his relations with the "Allied" princes of the Reich might well have inspired Emperor William II with what he called his recipe for the solution of the Serbian problem—a military convention between the Double Monarchy and its troublesome neighbor. As he developed his bold notion to Berchtold in the autumn of 1913, he thought that Serbia would be ready to put her army at Austria's disposal and under her command in return for Austrian protection against foreign encroachments. If necessary, force, including a bombardment of Belgrade, could be used to persuade her. "And," said William, "you may be certain that I shall stand behind you, ready to draw the sabre when your steps should make this necessary." While pleased by this assurance of the Ally's support, Berchtold could not quite conceal his doubts about the feasibility of the Emperor's notions.[16] Still, the idea found favor, if not with Berchtold then with some of his ministerial colleagues. On July 14, 1914, they discussed the demands to be presented to Serbia following Sarajevo. Count Stürgkh, the Prime Minister, pointed out that even if Austria-Hungary were to make a self-denying declaration as to territorial acquisitions at the expense of Serbia, it would still be possible to bring that Kingdom into a relation of dependency by such measures as the deposition of her dynasty and by concluding a military convention with her. None of those present protested, though the suggestion was not made a part of the ministerial resolutions.[17]

The age of nationalism, with officer nationalism a particularly strong variant, did not easily support the often grating forms of military hegemony established on the basis of military conventions. Germany after 1866 was the exception. There, ambition or a higher than local patriotism often favored the amalgamation of the local force with a larger one.[18] The same was true in Austria before and after the Anschluss.

The story in the Balkans was a much different one. Rumania, for example, concluded a convention with Russia on the eve of the Russo-Turkish War of 1877-78, by which she granted Russian troops free passage through her territory. The Rumanians, however, then proceeded to declare their independence from Turkey and open hostilities against them on their own, even though the Tsar-Liberator had originally declined the military assistance they had offered. This seemed to them the safest way to preserve their independence and avert Russian hegemony. Elsewhere in the Balkan nations Russia attempted to use Pan-Slavism as the medium for making Russian military overlordship palatable. But even a miniature state like Montenegro at times attempted to shake off Russia's military tutelage, even though sweetened by ruble payments and deliveries of military materiel.

The Balkan nations that were liberated in 1918-19 gained a maximum of military independence. Only the weakest among them, Albania, gradually succumbed to Great Power tutelage when, after 1926, she accepted loans from and protective treaties and collaboration with Fascist Italy. The arrangements included the mission of an Italian general as military adviser, who equipped and drilled the Albanians in the Italian manner, which finally led to a "personal union" of the two states. In 1939, Victor Emmanuel assumed the crown of Albania in addition to that of Ethiopia.[19] The latest creation of nationalism in Europe, Slovakia, was taken under German protection at its founding. On the strength of a twenty-five year treaty of protection, Germany assumed the right to military occupation. This was in addition to the political and military Gleichschaltung by which the small Slovak forces were to be organized in "close cooperation" with the Wehrmacht. During the German war in the East, Slovakia served as a springboard for the aggressor, in the same way that Albania served Italian aggression against Greece. In a new manner (and at the same time very old) both totalitarian Powers made the territories and soldiers of their "satellites" serve in their wars, an example that Russia was to follow after 1944.

Military conventions, though they seldom fall in the category of "open covenants openly arrived at," are still, in a sense, an expression of the "capitalist" respect for treaty and contract and even of equal partnership, though the equality may find its existence only in the power of the weaker party to sign away its sovereign prerogatives. The Communist concept of treaties is basically different. When dealing with capitalist states, Moscow has always been eager to seal a favorable status quo by treaties and other agreements. This has been true from Rapallo to Yalta and Potsdam. At the same time, the Soviet Union has considered treaties with other Communist states to be as superfluous as they are presumed to be "among friends." Treaties and conventions, as far as one knows, are largely, though not altogether,[20] dispensed with in the process of Sovietizing satellite armies. "Russian hegemony, the right to command other nations, the right to create Soviet provinces out of free nations, the right to produce Soviet marshals for export and the right to shape the destiny of civilization," to quote a Titoist protest, is a formidable but not in all respects a formalized process that remains on the whole "unconventional."[21]

Coeval with this new enslavement, an emancipation process of freeing certain colonial regions of the earth from "imperialism" was taking place. In a world increasingly dominated by military considerations, this process could be least complete in the military field. Britain completely gave up the overlordship claims she had acquired in Ethiopia during World War II, partly "to silence [American?] charges of prolonged occupation."[22] But to a large extent she retained her position of hegemony in tiny Transjordan. A new treaty of 1948 reduced her military privileges in Transjordan, but other ties remained, such as an annual subsidy of two million pounds and a British military mission.[23] In December 1950, France and Vietnam signed a military convention for the purpose of setting up a Vietnamese national army with French assistance and with a permanent French-Vietnamese committee of general staff officers to take care of liaison and work out a joint defense plan.[24] The treaties of the NATO Powers with Western Germany of May 1952, while they granted Bonn a definite increase in sovereignty, at the same time imposed much of the servitude inherent in military hegemony. They raise once more the question as to whether a member treated as inferior can ever be expected to perform military services with conviction. That the answer must almost certainly be "no" France seems to forget in the case of Indo-China, as in the case of Germany.

THE THREE EMPERORS' LEAGUE

The original instrument as well as the spirit of the Three Emperors' league of 1873 was that of a military convention. As far as the Germans and Russians were concerned, it was a resumption of the tradition and formality of the Alvensleben Convention of 1863.[25] Following the two disappointing wars of 1866 and 1870-71, Austria sought, or at least accepted, a rapprochement with Germany. The two Emperors had their first interview in 1871 on Austrian soil, and Francis Joseph was to return the visit in the autumn of 1872. Not wishing to be left out, Tsar Alexander elicited a German invitation to make the event a meeting à trois. The Tsar hoped that this spectacular event would help to keep the peace in Europe, that it would discourage subversive elements everywhere and would even open the way towards a general reduction of armaments. Russia, with her backward economy, always found armaments particularly burdensome until, after the Franco-Russian alliance, French capital came to her assistance. The hope

for a measure of disarmament was fervently expressed by those Russian military circles of the older generation who were often bearers of German names, such as old Field Marshal von Berg. They were particularly opposed to the anti-conservative Pan-Slavism that was seizing the army and making it expansive and warlike. The Tsar, already afraid of army Pan-Slavism, was reported as whispering to visiting German generals late in 1871: "You don't know how much I love you, but I am not allowed to show it to you."[26]

Initial oral agreements were arrived at during the Berlin visit of the Emperors in September 1872. The year after, the Russians, speaking not through Gortchakov, whom the Tsar kept aloof, but through Berg, returned to the idea of a more definite and formal defensive triple alliance. As Berg, who was ready to push the somewhat timid Tsar ahead, saw it, "a military convention was to be concluded by the three Sovereigns, consisting of just a few articles, without engaging the diplomatic chancelleries. Each of the sovereigns would promise to support with 200,000 men the one whose territory was attacked, without any indemnification beyond the feeding of the men and horses of the auxiliary force while on the soil of the assisted power." It would be first agreed upon between the Tsar and Emperor William. Afterwards, since Bismarck insisted that the convention should never become valid without Austria's accession, Francis Joseph would be invited to accede. Such an agreement would effectively stifle Polonism, Pan-Slavism and Pan-Germanism. At the same time, it would enable the three contracting Powers to reduce their army budgets considerably—"for what would be the reason," asked Berg, "to keep 200,000 men under arms if one could be certain of getting these from an ally in case of need?" (Still, "one's own are safer to have," Bismarck remarked.)

The Russian-proposed military convention was agreed upon, largely as outlined by Berg, during a visit of Emperor William to St. Petersburg. It was signed by the two field marshals, Berg and Moltke, and ratified at once by the two emperors (May 6, 1873).[27] Bismarck, who was along on the visit, would not put his signature to it because, as a matter of principle, he did not believe in signing conventions "in circumstances where there was as yet no positive object in view." (William I reminded Bismarck of this when the Chancellor pressed him for his approval of the Austro-German Alliance of 1879.)[28] Austria joined on June 6, 1873, during a visit of the Tsar to Vienna. Since both Francis Joseph and Andrassy took strong exception to the form of a military convention, an engagement between the sovereigns was agreed upon. The Tsar took German approval for granted and also assumed that the original German-Russian convention would still stand. This it could not, according to Bismarck, who wanted no agreement with the Russians alone. The instrument of the Three Emperors' League consisted, therefore, of the Austro-Russian agreement of June 6 plus German accession, through the signature of William I, on October 22, 1873.[29]

The instrument signed by elderly soldiers came to be discarded by younger, more imperialistic, more sharply competing soldiers who no longer believed that conservatism might still be in the best interest of their three countries. The new competition had left far behind a conservatism that, even well into the twentieth century, vaguely dreamed of the Three Emperors' Alliance as "the high rock, light-surrounded, on which the tidal wave of our days is breaking, above it rising the far shining sign of the Cross."[30] Later attempts to restore the Holy Alliance, which had lived on in these arrangements, were made at Bjoerkoe and, even more in the ancient style, during Aehrenthal's first years at the Ballplatz. Then, in 1908, Bosnian annexation cut off the last remaining threads between Vienna and St. Petersburg and sent Isvolski reeling back into the arms of French diplomacy.[31]

BERLIN-VIENNA GENERAL STAFF CONVERSATIONS AND CONTACTS[32]

Bismarck's conception of the Austro-German alliance of 1879 was both military and conservative. He intended to use it for the defense of the status quo of 1871 through arrangements that must do nothing either in their diplomatic or their military aspects to upset the status quo and bring war closer. Of all possible alliances for Germany, the one with Austria-Hungary still seemed the best, mostly because Austrian policies, unlike Russian ones, were, or at least ought to have been, peaceful and non-expansionist. Germany alone might have been able to face the combination of Austria, Italy, and France, but that of France and Russia was considerably more dangerous. In all of this Bismarck considered Italy insignificant. "He did not attach great importance to that country since the Army was bad and policy unreliable."[33] The alliance with Austria, the only valuable part of the Triplice, procured "a strategic position which was advisable in view of the dangers threatening at the time of its conclusion." But, Bismarck realized, it must not be considered an unalterable

foundation freeing German statesmen from being toujours en vedette!

The civilian governors held the controlling lever in their hands. It was given to them by Bismarck's formula on which the casus foederis rested—assistance only in the case of "unprovoked attack." He wished to reserve the decision as to what constituted "unprovoked attack" for the civilian heads of government. It must not be decided by the military judges of "military necessity." "The shifting of politics to the general staffs" must be avoided by all means; the question "who is the aggressor," he laid down, "will be honestly taken under consideration by our Emperor, should the case arise."[34]

The alliance of 1879 was not at once implemented by military arrangements between the two general staffs. Bismarck was not anxious for these, and the Vienna General Staff in the 1880 revision of its war plans against Russia did not even envisage German cooperation. Two years later, however, military conversations did get under way. They were first suggested by the Austrians in March 1882.[35] The proposal was eagerly accepted as a piece of military progress by the new man in the Berlin General Staff, Count Waldersee, Quartermaster-General and Moltke's successor-designate. The soldiers met, with Bismarck's permission, in August of that year during maneuvers. Bismarck insisted, however, that the occasion be made as secret and unalarming as possible. The military representatives of the two states, always duly aware of the Chancellor's frown, discussed possible joint measures for the case of war with Russia. When General Beck, the Austrian Chief of Staff, reminded Moltke that Bismarck did not want the direct intercourse of the two General Staffs through military attachés, old Moltke flared up: "My position is such that I do not depend on the Foreign Office."[36] But such anger did not prevent him from accepting and following Bismarck's directives in the end. They were that no binding agreements were to take place on this occasion. The international scene was peaceful, and the labors of the two General Staffs seemed mere peace-time exercises for which the younger generation was pressing and in which they might for once be allowed to indulge.

The exchange of ideas between Moltke-Waldersee and Beck resulted in a basic understanding about "the first stages of the operations, usually so difficult to obtain between allies"—so Archduke Albrecht, mindful no doubt of his own negotiations with the French in 1869-70 and also of the still backward Austro-Hungarian mobilization, wrote to Emperor Francis Joseph. The understanding was in keeping with Moltke's most recent plan of operations for the war on two fronts. Immediately after 1870-71, this war was to be opened by an offensive in the West, with delaying action in the East. After 1879-80, the offensive was to begin in the East, while action in the West was to be delayed.[37] Twenty out of the thirty-seven German divisions were to be employed in the East at the outset, together with the Austrians, in a joint envelopment movement against the Russian forces. Many, probably too many, of the total Russian forces had been garrisoned forward of the Vistula in recent years under the westward urge of Miliutin, Skobelev et al. While the Germans were to attack from the North, the Austrians were to advance from the South on the Eastern bank of the Vistula. The pincers would close behind Warsaw. While the Germans would cross the frontier on the twentieth day of mobilization with 400,000 men, Austria would not be ready until the forty-fifth. But despite the slowness of Austrian mobilization, the joint operations of the Central Powers could still be based on their superior speed and readiness as compared with Russia. For this reason the soldiers always insisted, or at least wished, that Russia not be allowed to gain time through diplomatic negotiations for preparing her armaments.

The generals decided that it would not be necessary to establish a supreme joint command, at least not until after the two armies had joined hands behind the Vistula. In the meantime, all necessary arrangements could be made by telegraph. The Austrians were offered the use of the Prussian railways in Silesia for their concentration movements. This was of considerable help, since their own important line of Oswiecim-Cracow was exposed to Russian cavalry raids. To Waldersee's question as to what Austrian intentions were with regard to Poland, Beck answered that that must be left to the diplomats. As far as he knew, Austria did not intend to revolutionize Congress Poland—after all, one could not entirely forget that in the Polish question the question of peace with Russia was also involved.

At Waldersee's suggestion the Austrians gladly agreed that all further exchanges of information and views be made through their respective military attachés. As Archduke Albrecht reported to Francis Joseph: "The very deepest secret about the operations and hence the smallest possible number of persons in the secret is the prime condition of their success." Bismarck was not the proper person to share it. His "inconsiderate, often curiously open-hearted character, his conflicts in this respect with Moltke during the last two wars as well as the officious, meddlesome nature of the Ambassador Prince Reuss justify all the more this wish on

the part of the two Prussian generals [Moltke and Waldersee] which I on my part must altogether respect." The fateful direct wire between the two general staffs, their understanding without, if not against, Bismarck became established in this manner, during a momentary relaxation of the Chancellor's control and at a time of international peacefulness rather than of tension. Whatever the soldiers had agreed upon in case the next period of tension were to result in war remained apparently unknown to the Chancellor.

The seat of the deepest secret remained in the Red House in Berlin, hidden from the Chancellor as well as from the ally. Austria could never be quite certain as to how the Germans would divide their forces between East and West. When Crown Prince Rudolf came to Berlin in March 1887, he placed numerous questions before Waldersee regarding the joint war against Russia. Above all, he wanted to know how many German army corps were to be employed in the East. Less now than before? Waldersee tried to extricate himself by generalities. Absolutely rigid plans were impossible. They did not know in Berlin whether they would have to do with France alone at first or with both France and Russia from the outset.[38] Such explanations, and Bismarck's reserve, left the Austrians in an uncertainty which they thought made it impossible for them to plan consistently. Above all, the Austrians would like to have had the casus foederis defined in militarily precise terms. "Our two General Staffs cooperate diligently and in a spirit of unity, and that is a true consolation at the present time," Francis Joseph told the German military attaché. "As to the rest, we are at present treated badly at Berlin, very badly. It is absolutely necessary that we should know when and for which eventualities we can count on your help; if not, we are without any foundation for our military preparations."[39]

The next tense period in Europe resulted from Boulangisme. The danger from France should not be taken lightly, Bismarck told the Austrians in December 1886; "the French Army is at present stronger than our own. In order to defend ourselves safely, we shall need practically our full strength on the Rhine and shall be only too glad if that should prove sufficient. We consider the French war as rather imminent and have therefore the wish to avoid if possible a war with Russia," a war in which Austrian policy in the Bulgarian question threatened to implicate Germany.[40] Ignoring, or pretending to ignore that the bulk of the German forces had been pledged to the war in the East initially, the Wilhelmstrasse officials spoke to the Austrians of circumstances under which the whole German army might have to be used against France, with hardly anything to spare for the Austrians. The Austrians would then be thrown back on their own strength, unless they should find other allies, such as England. Was the disagreement between the Berlin Foreign Office and the Great General Staff seeming or real? Did Bismarck merely use a seeming disagreement in order to keep the Austrians unwarlike and make them strengthen their own defenses, which he was always eager to see improved? In any case, the Berlin soldiers assured the Austrian ambassador of their continued conviction that "in case of war with Russia you as well as we must proceed to the offensive." The Austrians, however, were not quite certain what this meant. Had nothing changed since 1879, and must the Chancellor's recent statements about Germany's disinterest in the Eastern question be considered as never spoken? There was in Berlin, they thought, an increasing tendency in both military and civilian circles to goad France into war. A complete German victory over France would, however, only be favorable to Austria if afterwards she were strongly assisted against Russia by her ally.[41] Less optimistic, the Vienna military suspected that the German preoccupation with France meant shifting the whole burden of Russia's threat to Austria's shoulders.

Actually, Bismarck was at this time inclined towards seeking the decision in the West first, while remaining relatively passive in the East— or, in keeping with the Reinsurance Treaty, in a state of armed neutrality. However the diplomats might have talked, Moltke's dispositions had always left considerable forces reserved for use in the East. He continued to cling to the idea of a prompt offensive against Russia in order to seek the decision there. Not the least of his reasons was that Austria alone could not have borne the Russian onslaught and would have been exposed to the risk of a crushing defeat.

The difference in strategic views between the two German leaders reduces itself to the contrary views about the military strength of the Double Monarchy and Russia at the time and in years to come. The Chancellor, probably comparing the Russian performance in the Crimean War and Austrian valor in the wars since 1859, in all of which both had been losers, ranked Austria higher than did the General Staff, whose reports were up-to-date and not altogether favorable. Austria was falling behind Russia in relative strength. And the long-term trend in the development of military potential made Waldersee and the younger element in the Great General Staff, who at times could win Moltke over to their view, favor the idea of an early preventive war against Russia and the closest possible

Anschluss with Austria. A favorable occasion, from the military point of view, arose in the autumn of 1887. Russia, alarmingly at first but unwisely in the final analysis, massed very considerable forces in the region between East Prussia and Galicia. The situation was more dangerous for Russia than for Germany and Austria, because it exposed the Russian troops to the swift double-envelopment movement of German-Austrian forces.

The drive of the soldiers in Berlin and Vienna for a preventive war, in the diplomatic staging of which they would have needed all the arts of the Chancellor, met with the latter's strong opposition. His opposition was most decided when the Austrians proposed that the casus foederis be changed in such a manner as to allow the starting of a preventive war in the spring of 1888. In a way, the Austrians were also trying to insure themselves against the consequences of the fundamental conflict between Bismarck's and Moltke's strategic views about the conduct of the war on two fronts. Whatever this difference of views, Moltke still conceded the claim to civilian control and supremacy:

> The question when war is to come is exclusively a matter for the cabinets to decide; simultaneous mobilization and as far as possible simultaneous invasion of enemy territory are, however, necessarily required from a military point of view. A plan for joint operations can be outlined in advance only in great strokes. Considering the great distance between the two armies, they will at first operate separately and in line with their own interest. While both try above everything else to seek out the enemy, they render one another the most weighty services. Only after battles on either side are won can direct cooperation take place.

Whether or not these ideas of the foremost strategist of the age about the conduct of a coalition war represent the best that could be envisaged at the time in point of organization, the prevailing military aspects of sovereignty would hardly have allowed greater unity and subordination, except perhaps at the price of a military convention.[42] The latter could have been concluded only at the price of surrendering the diplomatic arbitrium liberum which Bismarck would never forego. The passing of the war danger, seeming or real, in 1887-88, allowed Bismarck's diplomacy to by-pass these fundamental decisions.

Once Waldersee had become Moltke's successor (1888-91), the Austrians found him much less accommodating. This led them to believe that Bismarck, for whose downfall Waldersee had worked, kept even him under his broad thumb. Considering the German attitude, the Austrians found it necessary to demand greater funds for armaments at home, to which the Foreign and Finance Ministers strongly objected. Waldersee backed up these demands in a letter to Beck, emphasizing how important the granting of them was for the strengthening of the Double Monarchy as a military ally. Since the war dangers felt during the three winters prior to 1889 resulted at last in better Austrian armaments, the Berlin authorities were well satisfied with the outcome of the crises. They served at least to accomplish the disagreeable task of bringing an ally to spend more funds on his armaments.

Whatever Bismarck's reservations, the German soldiers continued their assurances of "Nibelungen loyalty." On a visit to Berlin in August 1889, Beck was told by Waldersee and the Prussian War Minister Verdy du Vernois that "Germany, should Austria march (losgehen), must in any case 'come along'...Your mobilization is for us the signal to come in with everything we have." They expressed the hope, however, that the year 1890 would pass peacefully in order to make possible the complete rearmament of the German army then under way. After a momentary uncertainty, Waldersee had adhered to the view that Russia was the main opponent. Twenty-two infantry and five cavalry divisions would form the Eastern army, which would push with its strong left wing against the lower Narev and Grodno. Waldersee would even be willing to pay the price of temporarily evacuating Lorraine in order to knock out the Russians more quickly. Moltke, now emeritus, thought the continued massing of Russian troops in the West an insufferable threat; in the event of war the Russians must be attacked first and with the most forces. And in the presence of Francis Joseph the new Emperor told Beck: "For whichever reason you mobilize, whether for Bulgaria or for other reasons, the day of your mobilization is also the mobilization day for our Army, whatever the Chancellors say." In saying this he evidently had in mind the fact that for Bismarck Bulgaria was not sufficient grounds for war.

The visiting Chief of Staff could not have been more satisfied: Bismarck's definition of the defensive war, he believed, was now to be filed away. It seemed almost necessary to calm the various Berlin personalities rather than push them ahead. Archduke Albrecht thought that, considering the cooling-off of German-Russian friendship and the increased nervous irritation between William II and Alexander III, the outbreak of war had come closer and must be expected in the spring of 1891. "In Berlin as well

as in Vienna the question must be faced whether the Russians can be allowed more time to quietly strengthen themselves for war and determine on their part when it is to start, whereas the preparations on the part of the Allies and their strength can hardly be pitched any higher." Bismarck's dismissal cheered none more than the Austrian military. "Let us thank God that we are rid of the whole family," Albrecht rejoiced. Henceforth, the closest possible relations between the two General Staffs seemed guaranteed. But the shifts in the higher offices of Berlin did not end there; within a few months Beck's closest friends, Verdy and Waldersee, were also removed from their positions.

Both Bismarck's and Waldersee's successors disappointed the Austrians. Caprivi was the new Chancellor; Schlieffen, the new Chief of Staff. During a visit of various German dignitaries to the Austrian maneuvers of 1891, the Austrians proposed that an Austro-German council of war should take place in order to discuss a possible future campaign against Russia. Both Caprivi and Schlieffen thought the idea "exceedingly undesirable." As no one could know under which conditions the next war would start, all commitments to formulated plans, Caprivi explained to the Austrian ambassador, were highly precarious; and such discussions as were proposed could only narrow the freedom of action that Germany preserved under the treaty of 1879. Besides, "while people in Austria are accustomed to such councils of war since ancient times, it is not in the Prussian habit to apply this medium which so easily shifts responsibility and paralyzes action. If only the plans for concentration of both parties are to be discussed, this is best done by the two Chiefs of the General Staffs alone; all other participants are too little informed of the relevant details to be able to pass a well-founded judgment." Thus Austrian hopes to extract more detailed German commitments for cooperation in any and all wars were foiled. Caprivi, like Bismarck, could still hope that Austria would never start a frivolous war, "because she can use such a war less than any other empire."[43]

The new man in the Red House, Count Schlieffen, had assured the Austrians, shortly after taking up the reins, that, in keeping with Moltke's advice, no fundamental changes in the present plan of operations would be undertaken. And thus, he said, "everything that has been arranged for the joint conduct of the war on the part of both States would be preserved" in Berlin and, he hoped, in Vienna as well. Caprivi had allowed the Reinsurance Treaty with Russia to lapse. The growing Franco-Russian intimacy forced upon him and upon Schlieffen the conviction that a war on both fronts would have to be envisaged in any case. Russia would try to protract the decision. This she indicated by a rearward regrouping of her forces along the Njemen and the line Rovno-Proskurov-Kamieniec, beginning in 1892. The Russian regrouping led necessarily to the discarding of Moltke's latest plans and to the application of Germany's main strength along the Western front. The new plan called for only eighteen infantry divisions in the East at the outbreak of the war. Four infantry divisions and one cavalry division would remain in East Prussia, while the main body would push forward from Silesia against the Vistula in the direction of Zavichost-Annopol and join with the Austrian forces advancing on the Eastern bank of the river. While the Austrians regretted that Schlieffen had dropped the grand design of the double envelopment maneuver, they had to admit that the possible temporary sacrifice of East Prussia was justified. They themselves strengthened their position by building more lines for concentration in Galicia, fifty per cent more as measured by railway mileage, and by a further speeding up of their mobilization and concentration schedules.

As compared with Waldersee, Schlieffen was strongly inclined to minimize inter-staff relations, which moved the Austrians to complain about his reticence. In February 1894, when their military attaché inquired about certain details of the German concentration, Schlieffen intimated that he could not be as communicative as his predecessor had been. He could only act in close agreement with Chancellor Caprivi who, as he reminded the Austrian, had obtained Waldersee's removal because of his tendencies to act on his own. But he kept Vienna fully informed of the ups-and-downs in the promises of Italian help. (For 1894, Italy promised a 250,000 rifle strength against Russia, which made the outlook for the Central Powers quite hopeful.) Schlieffen also informed Vienna of his willingness to shift the spearhead of the German offensive out of the Upper Silesian corner in order to give better flanking protection to the Austrian concentration in Galicia.

The political effects of Schlieffen's reticence were definitely wholesome. Towards the end of 1895, Beck counselled against any reopening of the Balkan and Straits questions on Austria's part. That would lead to war with Russia, which Austria had reason to fear unless Germany and Italy came along. But German support seemed uncertain, even if Austria should have more definite British assistance in opposing a Russian march on Constantinople. Beck would have liked a clear statement from Schlieffen: at what point could German military support be expected? The vague assurance that it would come whenever Austria's further existence was threatened did

not seem sufficient. What kind of Russian action in the Balkans or what sort of arrangement among the Balkan States would, according to German judgment, seem to endanger this existence? Besides, Beck wanted clarity in case it should prove necessary to hold back the Vienna diplomats from incurring obligations towards Britain, Russia's other opponent. But Berlin again refused to define the concrete cases in which the casus foederis would arise or to allow discussions of the two chiefs of staff to take place at the time.[44]

Thoughts and fears of war receded in Vienna as Russia's military efforts became centered on the Far East. By 1906 when Schlieffen and Beck, both septuagenarians, left office, little remained of the earlier intimacy between the two staffs. Austria had been informed that in a two-front war the decision would be sought first against France. Beyond that it would not have occurred to Schlieffen to confide his plans for the war in the West to Germany's ally. Under their successors, the younger Moltke and Conrad, inter-staff relations remained at first as before, aloof on the whole, unmoved by any individual or common anxiety, kept somewhat apart, in fact, by their divergent views of Italy as an ally. Moltke thought Conrad saw things in too dark a light and would not himself believe in the possibility of Italy's default. Conrad, in view of the constant increase of Italy's military activity in the direction of the Austrian border, was convinced that the Italians were continuing the discussions of troop transport through the Tyrol merely in order to spy on the Austrian transport system.[45]

The Bosnian crisis of 1908, precipitated by Austrian policy, brought the first serious "war danger" in twenty years to the Central Powers. Even though the Austrians had not informed Germany of their action beforehand, they at once received an extravagant endorsement from William II, an endorsement that Bismarck would never have given. The Emperor reminded them of his assurance of 1895 that, since their Emperor was a Prussian field marshal, he had only to give orders and the whole Prussian Army would be at his command. This, he said, was still his standpoint; and while he was convinced that no warlike complications would ensue, he still wanted to emphasize that if war were to come, he would fulfill his alliance obligations, as he understood them, "with true passion."[46]

On previous occasions Conrad had suggested to Aehrenthal, Austrian Foreign Minister, that discussions should be held with the Prussian General Staff. By December 1908, the general political situation seemed dangerous enough to require renewing the suggestion. This time the Foreign Minister, caught like the sorcerer's apprentice in the hostile floods he had conjured up and could not assuage, almost certain that Italy could not be trusted to live up to her obligations and would at best remain neutral, agreed to arrange for such conversations. He wrote Bülow, the German Chancellor, that "it might perhaps not be super-fluous" if, during the coming winter, Moltke and Conrad would enter upon a written exchange of ideas, including among their hypotheses the possibility of Italian neutrality. Should Bülow consent, he would, after obtaining the Emperor's authorization, arrange to put Conrad in contact with his Berlin colleague. Bülow readily agreed. Aehrenthal's views as to the expected neutrality of Italy agreed with his own, and he had dis-cussed the matter with Moltke, who would be at Conrad's disposal.[47] After having played match-maker to the soldiers' reunion, the civilian heads of government left them alone and did not attempt to control or limit the arrangements they eventually made. Civilian supremacy bowed out before military expertise, even though Bülow and Aehrenthal were only too familiar with Conrad's drive for a preventive war.[48] Divi-sion of labor had progressed far beyond Bis-marck's day. Bismarck had never hesitated to say that he also understood what the soldiers maintained they alone knew.

For Conrad, the military head of the weaker partner, this alliance was "the fixed point in the fluctuations of the political relations among the European states. The landpower represented by this alliance will always remain a determining factor. To maintain it by mutual, loyal guarding of the interests on both sides and by conciliatory peaceful settlement of possible conflicts, is the best possible policy from the military point of view as well." As compared with Austria, Ger-many was to be envied: she was working "with rich funds, steady consistency and conscious purpose towards the development of her armed forces, particularly with the aim of preparing her land forces for the war on two fronts, al-ways resolved not merely to sharpen her instru-ment for war but also, if necessary, to apply it." He opened his correspondence with Moltke by stating that he sought discussions in view of the possible warlike developments in the Balkans and also with regard to Russia and Italy, whom he particularly distrusted. In conflicts with these nations, Austria was looking forward to having Germany by her side, in keeping with the casus foederis. While assuring Conrad that Ger-many would protect Austria's rear should Italy enter the war against her, Moltke still thought that Italy would be unable to undetake a war be-fore another two or three years.[49]

Altogether unlike Schlieffen, the younger Moltke opened up to Conrad about the possibilities and probabilities of war. Serbia might be driven

by her economic crisis into a desperate war with Austria, and the moment could be foreseen when the latter's forbearance would end, with hardly anything else left for her to do but to march into Serbia. "I believe that only an invasion of Serbia by Austria-Hungary could release possible active interference on Russia's part. With this, the casus foederis for Germany would be given." Interference from Italy need not be feared since she was not and would not be ready for war. As for France, the general impression was that she did not want war. But whether that country, dis-posing of an army almost equal to the German army, would be able to bear having a mobilized Germany on her flank without mobilizing herself appeared highly dubious. And "two mobilized armies such as the German and French will not be able to stand face to face without a passage at arms." Although he had no detailed knowledge of France's obligations to help Russia in case of a German-Russian conflict, Moltke took them for granted:

> Generally speaking, Europe of today seems so much criss-crossed and permeated by alli-ances and ententes that hardly any one of the European great powers can draw the sword without forcing all of the continental states to attack each other. I believe, therefore, that Germany, if she should mobilize against Rus-sia, must also reckon with a war against France. France's decision is likely to occur as early as the mobilization period, a welcome thing since that would create clarity as early as possible. The conditions thus indicated are familiar enough to the whole European diplo-macy, and in that fact lies the guarantee that none of the Great Powers will lighten the torch of war on account of Serbian ambitions, which could put the fire to the roof of all Europe. That, therefore, Russia for these same reasons will keep quiet in a warlike Austro-Serbian conflict appears to me not improbable (sic!)...But should it come to a war between Austria and Russia in spite of everything, Germany will stand at the side of Austria-Hungary in keeping with the treaty of 1879.

Naturally, Conrad could feel nothing but "sin-cere satisfaction over the clear and conclusive words" with which Moltke had promised "the full warlike commitment of Germany in casus foederis."[50]

From this correspondence, Conrad also learned about the latest assignment of the Ger-man forces for the case of a war with Russia and France. A small army of twelve or thirteen divisions in East Prussia plus a weak Landwehr corps in Silesia was all that was to remain in the East. Austria would have to support the opening battle with Russia until Germany had finished with France. After that, about thirty-six to forty days after mobilization, mass transports of German forces would be thrown eastward and would seek the decision there hand in hand with the Austrians.[51] With this exchange of information and views between the two chiefs of staff during January 1909, the war preparations of the two empires came to rest. Their understanding, although it transformed the original defensive treaty of 1879 into an offensive agreement,[52] cannot by any accepted definition of the term be called a military convention. There was no rigid arrangement for the case of war, only an exchange of information as to the intended employment of the respective armies in the case of war. There were no automatic obligations as in the Franco-Russian arrangements and none as to the minimum strength to be put in the field by either party. There was, however, at that time as well as later, a serious lack of supervision on the part of the civilian diplomats as to what the soldiers conversing with one another meant and said about the casus foederis which, as the younger Moltke had formulated it, gave Austrian policy towards Serbia most dangerous encouragement.

The two chiefs of staff continued their exchange of ideas (in writing and occasionally orally), usually preceding the annual revision of their mobilization plans.[53] Their plans, however, never became unified. Moltke always remained apprehensive that Austria would commit too much of her strength against Serbia, and Conrad always remained fearful that Germany would spare too little strength for the opening of the war in the East. They considered the various cases of war, including what they thought in 1910 the most difficult one, war by Germany-Austria-Rumania against the coalition of Italy-Serbia-Montenegro-France-Russia. While it did not seem a hopeless case, Conrad still thought that it was up to the diplomacy of the Central Powers to prevent such a constellation. Moltke believed that such a life-and-death struggle could be won, provided it was clear who were the enemies from the moment of mobilization. To obtain this certainty was the task of diplomacy.[54] The very worst of all combinations, the actual one of the First World War—a war against England as well, and without Rumanian help—did not enter into their considerations.[55] Not even when they met for the last time before the war, in May 1914 at the Austrian spa of Karlsbad, to discuss such problems as the defection of Rumania and the employment of Italian troops north of the Brenner, did this contingency occur to them. Conrad once more expressed his hope that Moltke would spare larger forces for the war in the East and thus re-

lieve the Austrians from the expected Russian pressure in the direction of Galicia. He obtained no promise.[56]

At the outset of the July 1914 crisis, the Berlin General Staff relied calmly on its time-table preparedness. Moltke's deputy, First Quartermaster General Count Waldersee—the two names indicating how hereditary high military offices had become—wrote to the head of the foreign office that "we of the General Staff are ready; for the time being there is really nothing to order."[57] After his return from a prolonged leave, Moltke at first went along with German diplomacy in its endeavor to preserve peace, or at least not to incur the imputation of war guilt. He objected "mildly, very mildly" when, in the night of July 29-30, the Chancellor told the soldiers that Russia's partial mobilization did not produce the casus foederis for Germany and that no German mobilization was as yet called for.[58] On the morning of July 30, Moltke had the aide Conrad had sent to him in Berlin wire his chief that "Russia's mobilization is as yet no cause for mobilization [meaning Germany's mobilization, not Austria's, as Conrad seems to have understood it]...In contrast to mobilization and demobilization, which have been customary in Russia, Germany's mobilization would unconditionally lead to war. Don't declare war on Russia, but await Russia's aggression."[59] Even the soldier realized that it was important to make Russia appear as the aggressor.

But in the afternoon of that day, after receiving more information about Russian mobilization measures, Moltke began to regard the situation as more critical. He informed the Austrian military attaché of this opinion and added that the danger would be particularly great if Austria "does not mobilize immediately against Russia." In a message for Conrad, he urged the following:

> The declaration Russia has made concerning mobilization ordered by her makes countermeasures on the part of Austria-Hungary necessary, something that would also have to be cited in the public explanation. Thereby the casus foederis for Germany would arise. Effect honest agreement with Italy by assurance of compensations in order to keep Italy actively with the Triplice; by no means leave one man on Italian frontier. Turn down renewed British measure for preservation of peace. Sticking to European war last ways and means for salvation of Austria-Hungary. Germany will go along unconditionally.[60]

This was a message from one wrought-up soldier to another. It is accounted for mainly by Moltke's fear that, with a backward Austrian mobilization, or one directed against Serbia rather than against Russia, Germany might have to bear more of the brunt of the Russian attack than assumed by the plans. The actions of the military at this stage of the crisis constituted what Bismarck had always dreaded, a "shifting of policy to the general staffs," who were arrogating to themselves an opinion, if not a decision, on the casus foederis. This was a decision that should have remained within the prerogative of the civilian governors. Besides, the Berlin Chief of Staff infringed on the civilian direction of policy by presuming to give advice to Vienna that was contrary to Bethmann's in regard to Britain's peace-making role. Since the political direction in Vienna was weak, weaker even than in Berlin, this military advice coming from Berlin—where a less monolithic order existed than was assumed in Vienna— proved particularly effective. "Who is governing: Moltke or Bethmann?" Berchtold cried out. He became convinced that Germany would not back down, that he had "now from the most authoritative military side the most reassuring declaration," and that this reassurance justified issuing the order for general mobilization in Austria.[61] For a weakling like Berchtold, the military formed "the most authoritative side" in Berlin and it seemed to favor war.

Previous plans for military cooperation between the two allies did not justify—if indeed it can ever justify—military influence on political resolution and irresolution in Berlin and Vienna. Actually, the military plans were very sketchy. As Falkenhayn put it, very discreetly sparing his predecessor: "The question of the conduct of war of coalition had not been settled between Germany and Austria, either before the war or following its outbreak. The reasons why this had been neglected, in spite of earlier coalition wars, are not known."[62] The reasons are of course known, and Ludendorff once blurted them out: "It was an error not to have included among our war preparations a joint German-Austrian plan of operations. The German General Staff was afraid that the secret would not be preserved in Vienna." If, instead of exerting influence on the political directors, the soldiers in Berlin and Vienna had applied their political urges to the notably thorny problems of arranging for a coalition war plan, things would have been better for the Central Powers.[63]

THE TRIPLE ALLIANCE AND MILITARY AND NAVAL CONVENTIONS

The treaties on which Bismarck's alliance system was built did not provide for separate peace treaties in joint wars and envisaged, under given circumstances, full military support to the contracting parties. The treaties were, however, essentially diplomatic in their nature: they reserved for Bismarck or for his successors the decision as to whether or not the casus foederis had arisen. Bismarck was always reluctant to have the military staffs discuss in advance the measures to be taken should the casus arise. But such talks seemed necessary to the military, if they were to be properly prepared for the emergencies envisaged by the diplomats. Nevertheless, Bismarck shunned accessory or complementary military conventions, a reluctance which was, at least at the outset, shared by one or the other of his partners. Prince Karol of Rumania, unable to forget the loss of Bessarabia to Russia, suggested to Andrassy in October 1879 that his country accede to the Austro-German alliance. The Austrian minister dissuaded him. He pointed out that at the very moment when the danger of Russian aggression had been banned by the alliance, an accession amounting to the "preventive enrollment" of a third state could easily be interpreted by Russia as an offensive threat. This was something that neither Vienna nor Berlin wanted. Should the possibility of Russian aggression appear closer, he added, negotiations could be resumed "and a military convention would then come automatically."[64] In October 1883, when Rumania did join the Triple Alliance, it did not take the form of a military convention, though such an implementation had been contemplated.[65] There were, however, understandings between the Vienna and Bucharest general staffs for the case of war with Russia or Bulgaria.

Military conventions were obligations that the older Bismarck shunned, for they were apt to take the interpretation of the casus foederis out of his hands. They would enhance the "military necessity" argument and tend to bring military measures into play earlier than he might wish. The Triple Alliance Treaty of 1882 consequently contained no military stipulations beyond saying that the Allies, should danger arise, would in due season agree about the measures required for joint operations (Article 5). That arrangement remained in all subsequent Triplice treaties. From time to time Austria or Italy endeavored to take the decision on the casus foederis out of his hands and bind the Reich by more specific instruments and conventions, to replace the diplomatic liberum arbitrium by automatic arrangements and definitions of what constituted aggression. The most persistent attempt of the Austrians in this direction was made during the diplomatic crisis of 1887-88. They even prepared a military convention to be signed by the two chiefs of staff, Moltke and Beck, for the approval of the two governments and ultimately of the two sovereigns. The drafts provided for two alternatives—either a convention defining the casus foederis or another laying down details for a war of aggression to be undertaken in the spring of 1888. The latter was to include arrangements for the distribution of the allied forces, with at least one third of the German army to remain in the East. Both allies were to start the war simultaneously on a prearranged date; no separate peace was to be made. These proposals of the Austrian soldiers went too far for Kalnoky, who could not agree to a timetable starting of war. They also went too far for Moltke, who emphasized that the decision as to when war should come was for the cabinets to settle.[66] It seems that Bismarck never saw this draft. If he had seen it, he might not even have allowed the representatives of the two General Staffs to discuss measures of cooperation in case of war. It was during such discussions that Moltke explained to the Austrians "the difficulties of winning the Chancellor over to the idea of an aggressive war."[67]

Bismarck was somewhat more inclined to give in to the importunities of the weaker ally, Italy, if only for the reason that they would prove to be less onerous and less dangerous.[68] He was always inclined to consider her positive contribution to the defense of the two German powers as slight. "It was merely important for us to relieve allied Austria of the concern about covering the Italian frontier in case of war," he remarked at the conclusion of the first Triple Alliance.[69] Crispi, the most Francophobe of the Italian statesmen, was content to leave military obligations unspecified. On his spectacular visit to the Chancellor in October 1887, however, he expressed his hope that France's active opposition to Italian aims in the Mediterranean and the Red Sea might be checked by implementing the still incomplete treaties of 1882 and 1887. His argument, typical of arguments in favor of military conventions, ran as follows:

> One envisaged the possibility of mutual aid of the two powers in case of war but one did not think of concluding a military convention which is absolutely required. No one can know when and how the war will break out. It may suddenly become a fact. But we will not wait at first but agree beforehand about the tasks which will fall to each of us in the common defense. It is necessary to lay down as quickly as possible a plan of defense and attack which envisages all possibilities in order that if war once breaks out each of us knows what he has to do. With one word: a military agreement is the necessary implementation of our treaties.

Crispi had earlier proposed to Lord Salisbury that such a convention be concluded by the Powers of the Mediterranean entente. Salisbury would hear nothing of it; despite the suspicions of the Liberal opposition, he would not bind Britain's Army or Navy to those of any foreign Power. Bismarck, when presented with the same kind of proposal, agreed that the suggestion was reasonable. He accepted it, provided Emperor William would agree. William did, and he even suggested extending the staff conversations to the two navies.[70] The Great General Staff was informed that Crispi's visit had resulted in a firm union with Italy for the case of a war with France, which case, in accordance with Crispi's wishes, was to be discussed at once by the soldiers. "The French and the Russians were quite beside themselves about Crispi's visit," the Chancellor's son told Waldersee. Waldersee, however, thought that these two Powers were hardly strong enough as yet to attempt the fight. "Unfortunately, we do not want to provoke it either at the present moment."[71]

When the conversations among the general staff representatives got under way, not all concerned were enthusiastic. The German military attaché in Rome thought political conditions and the views of Italian politicians and generals were too changeable to permit hard and fast agreements. The Great General Staff considered it advisable to invite the Italians to Berlin, thus avoiding travel by their own outstanding members, which might arouse speculation. The conversations centered on Italy's military role in a joint war with France. The latter had the Alpine frontier so strongly fortified that, by 1886, Italy had given up all hopes of undertaking a successful offensive in the Maritime Alps. There she could only hope to tie down two French army corps and two reserve divisions at the most. This was the military gain for Germany from the Italian alliance, unless the numerous though untried Italian forces were employed elsewhere in the common cause. It was agreed that these forces, six army corps and three cavalry divisions, a whole third army, should be employed on the German left wing, north of the Alps. They were to be brought there via Austrian and German railroads. An Italian suggestion that this might be done by violating Swiss neutrality was ignored by the Germans. Fortification of the St. Gotthardt Pass put an end to such Italian dreams, which may have had their origin in a hankering for the Italian-speaking cantons. Austrian officers were called in for consultation. Kalnoky thought it advisable to have Italy participate in a war fought by Austria and Germany, if only because at the end of such a war a neutral Italy would have her army intact, while her allies would have exhausted themselves.

The existence of a German-Italian military convention was taken for granted in Berlin and elsewhere; modern war seemed hardly feasible without such understandings of a technical nature, referring to the mobilization of enormous masses of men by ways and means practically scientific in nature. The high-speed concentration of troops might decide the fate of a campaign before the first shot had been fired. Given such conditions, a military convention that settled all the details of performance could alone render an alliance truly efficacious. It was generally assumed that the authors of the German-Italian alliance had given it this necessary implementation.[72] And whatever their own surmises did not tell the French about the existence of such a convention was betrayed to them in Rome.[73]

The promised Italian help to Germany north of the Alps always had a make-believe character. "The agreements existed actually only on paper and nobody really believed in their serious character," either in Rome or in Berlin.[74] For it seemed dubious whether Italian public opinion could really be convinced, as the statesmen and soldiers were, or pretended to be, that Italy's fate would or should be decided on the Rhine, and not on her home soil. The Third Italian Army did not figure in the German plans for the concentration and opening moves. It was, however, welcomed each time its coming was promised. In 1891, the Italian General Staff offered to send the Third Army even earlier and faster than contemplated in 1888, provided Germany would put a sufficient number of locomotives at Italy's disposal. The reasons for this acceleration were political, foreign as well as domestic. In fact, the offer was likely to be made whenever Franco-Italian tensions increased. That of 1891 was made, according to the Italian General Staff, because it seemed highly advisable to confront public opinion in Italy with an accomplished fact immediately after the outbreak of war. The German Government was ready to loan locomotives, as it had been ready to help out in the case of other Italian deficits.[75]

Chronic financial embarrassments and, later, the defeat at Adua reduced the eagerness and the ability of the Italians to help out in a war north of the Alps. Through these difficulties and the vicissitudes of cabinet changes, the Italian General Staff remained for many years the most convinced protagonist of the Triplice, far more so than the Italian masses. The new King, Victor Emmanuel (since 1900), was, however, so afraid of internal revolution, as the Chief of Staff informed the Germans, that in 1901 Germany released Italy from her earlier unconditional obligation. Schlieffen's scepticism regarding the fighting value of the Italian Army made this relinquishment easier. Italy's membership in the Triple Alliance was, militarily speaking, nothing but an arrangement for "keeping her from biting Austria in the heel," as Bismarck had once put it, an advantage that was not to be underestimated.[76] However, even that slight advantage was soon no longer to be counted on. The Franco-Italian agreement of 1902 ensured Italian neutrality in practically all wars in which France might be involved. In the same year, the building of Italian fortifications along the Austrian frontier began. The Italian release from the obligation of sending the Third Army northward enabled Prime Minister Prinetti to declare in the Chamber (May 22, 1903) that there were no conventions or secret protocols in existence among the Triplice partners.[77] At the same time the Italian General Staff, perhaps as ignorant of the Franco-Italian agreement as the French General Staff was, acted as if the protocols were in force. During the Algéciras Conference, they approached the Germans once more to ask whether the agreements for the case of a war in the West were still considered to be in force. The procedure, in its false naïveté, struck the Germans somewhat like the action of one whose conscience is not quite clear, who fears that he may be distrusted and therefore protests innocence before he is accused. They decided to consider the old agreements as still in force and kept the time-tables for the transports of the Third Italian Army up-to-date in the annually revised and re-examined mobilization schedules. At the same time, the Germans fully realized that "the center of gravity of Italian military interest quite gradually but surely was shifting from the Western to the Eastern frontier." They assumed, correctly, that Italy no longer reckoned with the possibility of war with France and rather preferred to take all measures in order to be ready for the war with Austria that was expected sooner or later.

The transport of the Third Army became "legendary," as they called it in Berlin, and a piece of camouflage for the concentration against Austria, which was only slowed up by Italy's recurrent financial embarrassments. France, now the capital-supplier, had to relieve these embarrassments instead of Germany. Italian public sentiment favored all anti-Austrian measures. The German ambassador in Rome, Count Monts, was without illusions as to the value of the alliance with Italy and doubted whether "in view of the reality of things it was still in keeping with the dignity of our General Staff to dedicate more hours of serious work to the so-called Third Army and fictitious eventualities of concentration via the Brenner." The German and Austrian General Staffs, however, once more agreed, in May 1907, to hold conversations among the chiefs of the railway sections of all three staffs such as the

Italians had proposed. The initiative, Conrad thought, was merely due to Italy's continued military weakness, which made her wish to postpone the planned war against Austria, and to her hopes of finding out about Austria's railway and entrainment arrangements for the case of mobilization.[78]

The situation remained highly equivocal, not to say treacherous, though it is hard to say who was betraying whom. The French were informed of the older plans and assured that they had been given up. They concluded that by 1908 there would be no Italian forces on their right wing, in Alsace or the Alps. They and their partners were assured by the civilian ministers in Rome that, in case of war, even war provoked by France, Italy would remain neutral. No government could bring the country into war against France. They were told that the obligation of bringing Italian troops to the German left wing in the West no longer existed, that as things stood in 1908 Italy would not (because, given the state of her preparations, she could not) attack Austria, but that things might be different three years hence, following the reorganization of her military forces. This state of affairs was considered highly advantageous by the majority of the statesmen of the Triple Entente. The British Foreign Office had hoped almost from the beginning of the Anglo-French Entente that Italy would remain inside the Triple Alliance for the sake of appearances. In London, Italy was considered "a source of weakness for Germany and Austria." According to a French official in London, "one fears above all to be embarrassed by her the day when, following our counsel, she should abandon her two allies. Italy is an exacting client who serves herself better by her friends than she serves them; England knows it."[79]

Italy's I.O.U. to Germany and Austria still stood on paper when, in 1912, the new Italian Chief of Staff, General Pollio, pointing to Italy's engagements in Tripoli and elsewhere, once more gave notice that it could not be honored. He assured the Triplice partners, however, that if the casus foederis should arise, Italy would mobilize and attempt an offensive across the Franco-Italian frontier. This announcement followed the renewal of the Triple Alliance in December 1912. The younger Moltke, who was less pessimistic than Conrad, would not allow the Italian thread to break altogether. In January 1913, he sent his quartermaster-general, Count Waldersee, to Rome for further negotiations with the General Staff. The Wilhelmstrasse was not informed of this mission beforehand and was given no opportunity to make its suggestions. The ambassador in Rome learned of it merely because he happened to be a friend of Waldersee. The emissary found the terrain well prepared by the military attaché

and carried away a strong impression of continued Italian loyalty. It was agreed that close cooperation between the naval units of the Triplice partners in the Mediterranean against the French and British navies would be arranged in the near future. Pollio, whom Waldersee considered a friend of the Triplice, even promised to send whatever Italian troops he could spare to the German Western front, though the main Italian endeavor was to be directed against France along Italy's own frontier. The most important thing for the German General Staff was to get Italy actually engaged in the coming war—very much like Joffre, who wanted one British soldier in order thus to engage the whole British people. On his way back from Rome, Waldersee discussed these arrangements with Conrad and others and induced them, in spite of the ineradicable distrust of Italy, to agree to naval staff conversations, which were to take place in April and May 1913.

During the German Imperial maneuvers of 1913, the three chiefs of staff had an exchange of views. Pollio was persuaded to send at least two army corps through the Brenner Pass in case of war. He promised to obtain the King's approval of this arrangement. Urged by Conrad, who wanted firmer agreements with the Italians and larger Italian masses north of the Brenner, Waldersee traveled once more to Rome. His instructions read as follows: "Present-day conditions demand that the decision must come quickly; the peoples can hardly be expected to support long wars. But even if one wants to reckon with a relatively long duration of the war, circumstances force the Triple Alliance to seek at once the decision against France in the case of war. As yet, Russia is getting under way rather slowly. France must be fought down before the other can interfere effectively. It might even come about that, following a serious defeat on the part of her ally, Russia might be forced to come to an arrangement," that is to say, a separate peace. Waldersee and the authorities in Vienna, where he reported on his return, considered his mission quite successful. The feeling was reinforced when, in February 1914, Pollio informed Moltke that Italy was now ready to send three army corps northward. A general who was to command the Italian Third Army came to Berlin and settled the necessary transportation details. These general staff conversations took place without the participation and also largely without the fore- or after-knowledge of the German Foreign Office. About the Italian foreign office one does not know.[80]

The common interest of Italy and Austria in an independent Albania and their opposition to the Slavic pressure towards the Adriatic brought not only a diplomatic rapprochement but also a renewal of the Italian promise for an army on the upper Rhine. Renewed military arrangements in combination with the existing Naval Convention seemed to provide for the military functioning of the Triplice in case of war.

The negotiations for a Triplice Naval Convention also go back to Crispi's time. Nearly a year after a German-Italian Railway Convention concerning the transport of Italian troops north to the Western front had been signed, the Italian naval authorities proposed to the German naval authorities that the same close contact be established between the navies of the three Powers as already existed between the armies. An exchange of technical information was brought under way by the stationing of naval attachés in Berlin and Rome. On strong German advice, Italy sought conversations in Vienna with a view to obtaining Austrian naval support in case of a war with France. She was also urged to find out with greater certainty about the help she could expect from Britain in the case of such a war. Germany could render little help, since her still small navy could not make its appearance in the Mediterranean. Bismarck was inclined to see in this bustle merely "a pose" useful to Crispi.[81] The latter proposed a naval convention to Austria. Kalnoky turned down the proposal, considering the maritime interests of the two Powers too different and divergent for such a convention. While Austria's interests were in the East, those of Italy were in the West, against France. Without England's help, which Italy must first obtain, little could be done.[82]

A naval convention among the Triplice Powers was not agreed upon until December 5, 1900. The initiative for this "understanding among the Triple Alliance Powers regarding the measures to be taken in a joint war" was Italian, resulting, after prolonged conferences of admiralty officers, in an "Agreement between the Admiralty Staff of the Imperial German Navy, the Royal Italian Naval Ministry and the Naval Section of the Austro-Hungarian Imperial War Ministry." The content was slight: in case of war, each navy was to act on its own. The contemplated operations remained uncoordinated. The Wilhelmstrasse, which did not even receive a text of the agreement, knew or cared little about it.[83] The agreement never gained any importance and was replaced by a new one in 1913. The initiative this time was German, not Italian, as the Austrians thought. Italian naval officers approached the Austrian naval attaché in Rome. Their foreign minister, they said, was somewhat slow in his resolutions. Why not give him the necessary impulse from without? Was it not time to make arrangements for the case of war similar to those in existence among the three general staffs? The Italians were very anxious to have the navies arrive directly at the

necessary understandings. The Austrian attaché was properly distrustful. The Italian partners, he reasoned, were disloyal. They had recently renewed the Triple Alliance only because they still needed six years to ready themselves on land and sea, during which time the Alliance insured them against an attack by Austria. He warned against a naval convention "which might reveal to them much that they don't know."[84]

The negotiations were conducted at Vienna, with a bare minimum of information given or asked by the diplomats. They resulted in a new convention for the case of a war involving all three members of the Alliance.[85] Instead of assigning distinct and separate zones of operation to each of the three navies, as in the agreement of 1900, all naval forces in the Mediterranean were, in case of war, to unite under one command for the purpose of gaining naval control. The interception of French military transports from Africa to metropolitan France was the supreme objective, at least in the minds of the Germans. Plans for joint operations were to be prepared in peacetime by the three admiralty staffs and were to be laid down in a supplementary convention, subject to the approval of the three sovereigns. Naval units outside the Mediterranean were to be instructed by their home authorities to cooperate following the outbreak of a joint war, when they would be informed of the existence of the convention. In addition, the convention covered questions of a supreme command, closer communication among the Allies, signalling, the preparation of operation plans, the exchange of intelligence, the reciprocal assignment of naval officers to the respective headquarters, the reciprocal assignment of merchant vessels for purposes of warfare, and the reciprocal use of harbors. To some of the German and Austrian participants the negotiations brought a pleasant surprise, revealing "a state of mind that represents a complete novelty in the annals of our alliance relations."[86]

After such pleasant experiences with military and naval conventions, the military who had negotiated and nourished them were rather more surprised and shocked by the default of Italy in 1914 than were the diplomats of the Central Powers. Several of the diplomats, Count Monts for example, had long written off the Italian partnership, and regretted that the governments had continued to assure their peoples that it still held good. The parliaments were thereby misled, and the Austro-Hungarian delegations were dissuaded from granting larger funds for the defense of the southern border. The Berlin General Staff, far more than the Viennese, had maintained the belief in Italian support north of the Brenner.[87] In a conversation with Monts in the autumn of

1914, Moltke asked whether the ex-ambassador had expected the Italian betrayal. When Monts said that it was inconceivable that one could have based any expectations on such uncertain, slippery fellows, Moltke pointed to the well-intentioned Pollio. The Great General Staff was inclined to ascribe his untimely death in July 1914 to political assassination by pro-Entente elements.[88] The devious procedures of Italian diplomacy had used the Italian General Staff as a screen. In other countries the military might not have lent itself so readily to such camouflaging purposes. The usual question in such situations, "Who is the dupe in the case?" reduces itself to the question as to whether the Italian chiefs of staff were included among the dupes or not.

CONVENTION TURNED INTO ALLIANCE: FRANCO-RUSSIAN UNDERSTANDINGS AND STAFF CONVERSATIONS

On the Russian side, military rather than diplomatic conditions, influences and personalities prepared the way for the Franco-Russian alliance. A military convention was its instrumental mainstay. Politico-generals like Skobelev, Ignatiev, and Gurko, who were foremost among the military Pan-Slavs, men like Obrutchev and Vannovsky, who were war minister and chief of staff respectively before and after 1890, and some of the military grand dukes had proposed such an alliance ever since the 1870's. They had agitated in its favor publicly and behind the scenes. Had not Russia and France one and the same enemy, Germany?[89]

Autocracy, seemingly above such agitation, was actually forced to listen to it and at times to compete with it. Pobiédonostsev, Grand Procurator of the Holy Synod, warned his pupil Alexander III not to treat the unruly Skobelev too coldly. People of his kind, possessed of great will-power, intellect, and ability to act, were rare in Russia. In times of excitement the Tsar might be forced to put them to use. Even if Skobelev were a person without morality, that had been true of many great army leaders of the past, and this shortcoming must needs be overlooked. A Skobelev could still be the carrier of a great moral power and exert great moral influence over the masses—people believed in him and were ready to follow him.[90] Speaking "as Russian to Russian," many high Government officials agreed that Bismarck was the root of Russia's misfortunes, that he had put her hors de combat without firing a shot. "Germany could, if she wanted to," wrote Pobiédonostsev, "throw herself on France and wipe her out. But then, due to a bold step undertaken by Skobelev, Russia and France discover for themselves that they have interests in common, to the great stupefaction

and fear of Bismarck. From that day on, France or Russia are no longer isolated. Skobelev died as the victim of his convictions: that not a single true Russian can doubt."[91]

Russia's weak economy and backward technology greatly retarded her military progress. A large part of her capital supply had to come from abroad to pay for the railway equipment and army supplies provided by foreign industry. Until the later 1880's, Germany had been the largest supplier of capital and goods of this character. By this time, however, the tendency of Russian armaments had become so obviously directed against the Central Powers that Bismarck, only five months after the conclusion of the Reinsurance Treaty, took steps to restrict the flow of German capital to Russia.[92] From then on, despite some relaxation of the German restrictions, the larger part of Russia's foreign capital supply was to come from the French market. The price that France was to pay for twenty-five years of alliance finally amounted to more than four billion gold dollars.

The junctim of foreign loans and military armaments in the Russian economy, which was to lead to repeated Russian suggestions for armament limitation, was obvious enough to French diplomacy well before the conclusion of the alliance. The German press, on hints from the Great General Staff, cried out that an attack on Germany and Austria was being planned and that a Russian loan projected in the autumn of 1888 ought not to be admitted to the German market. At the same time, the French foreign minister wrote to the ambassador at St. Petersburg that "the measures taken by the Russian Government in order to strengthen its strategic situation in Poland have an importance that has not escaped my attention. As regards the large share reserved for France in the projected emission and Russia's determination to emancipate herself from the financial tutelage of certain European markets, I believe, as you do, that in this we have a new fact, the import of which is not purely economic." This Russian "emancipation" loan, three times over-subscribed in Paris, was greeted in Russia as the liberation from the German financial yoke of the last twenty years. In spite of Waldersee's warnings, the German banks, over which the Government exercised much less control than was the case in France, still took seventy-five million of the five-hundred million total. With the help of this new money supply, Russian armaments were increased, "designed to face the Triple Alliance," as French diplomacy noted with great satisfaction.[93]

The country that supplied capital was also obliged, in the logic of things, to supply the weapons and munitions for the Russian soldier.

Krupp and other German manufacturers were supplanted by French firms, a shift engineered by such dignitaries as Grandduke Vladimir, who came to Paris late in 1888.[94] As Freycinet, the determined revanchard, tells the story, the Grandduke was so fascinated by the new French infantry rifle, still a secret, that the French cabinet voted to let him have a sample piece as part of the endeavor to establish "more intimate contacts with Russia." Russian orders were placed for artillery material and for the manufacture of 500,000 rifles. The latter order was accepted by the French on formal Russian assurance "that these rifles would never fire against us." In this spirit of accommodation the French military authorities greatly facilitated the studies of Russian engineers in France, prior to the building of new powder mills in Russia based on French models and experiences. Russian thanks were emphatic. In May 1890, one of the granddukes went so far as to assure Prime Minister Freycinet that, if he had any say in the matter, "our two armies will form one in time of war. And that fact, once well known, will avert war. For no one would care to face France and Russia arm in arm. That's what I repeat within my family...France has a friend in me."[95]

Once Bismarck's successor had allowed his Reinsurance Treaty to lapse, thus weakening the resistance of Russian diplomats who were the really conservative force against French overtures at the time, the diverse military pacemakers of the Franco-Russian alliance had the way cleared for them. The Tsar was encouraged to invite General Boisdeffre, deputy-chief of the General Staff, former military attaché in St. Petersburg and well-remembered in Russian military circles, as his guest to the August maneuvers of 1890—a gesture the Germans took as a warning. Boisdeffre was instructed by Freycinet to find out what the Russians would do if war were declared against France and to what extent she could count on their support. He had long conversations with Vannovsky and Obrutchev, both friends of an alliance with France. He was told that, if war threatened, Germany would be informed by Russia that French existence and French strength must not be touched, both being indispensable to the European balance of power. Boisdeffre tried to dispel Russian doubts about France's readiness for war by offering them a military convention centered on the point of simultaneous mobilization. But the Russians shied away from written agreements, as well as from the obligation the French were to urge constantly in the years to come—that Germany must be considered the foremost enemy, even by the Russians, whose main endeavor must be directed against her, and not against Austria. Austria

was, of course, the preferred enemy of the soldiers and the Pan-Slavs.[96]

Even at this early date Russian autocracy foreshadowed its claims on French constitutional government. Following Boisdeffre's departure, the French ambassador emphasized that in subsequent negotiations "we have an interest in not revealing a fault inherent in our constitution which, out of fear of an executive altogether too strong, has taken away from him the essential prerogative of concluding treaties, and consequently has robbed our policy of the advantages of secrecy. However, there remains the military field." These approaches could be made, and the way was prepared by the friendly gestures of France in facilitating the rearmament of the Russian infantry. Boisdeffre's visit had been the first step in that direction. Thanks to his conversations, there was henceforth contact between the two general staffs. The second-level officials proved ready to make far-reaching secret arrangements before their superiors were. This was true of men like the Russian military attaché in Paris, Baron Fredericks, who could discover no obstacles to an understanding between the two war ministries, assuming the Tsar would approve, covering such measures as the peace-time disposition of troops and the wartime cooperation of the armies, notably in case Germany should undertake war. In his opinion, "a military convention if kept absolutely secret... could be useful even without a formal alliance existing between the two countries...The present entente, based on a community of interests and dangers, is equal to a written alliance" (March 25, 1891).[97]

For a time yet, the French offers appeared a medication still too strong for the condition of Russian isolation. But this condition grew worse, due to the seeming approach of the Triplice and Britain, that is to say, of the combination of land power with the strongest naval power. That combination, the greatest power array of its time, the peaceful military Chancellor Caprivi saw as the answer to the war on two fronts threatening Germany. It was not his fault that the Anglo-Triplice flirtation did not develop into a marriage tie, as the Russian counter-flirtation did.

While Pan-Slavism and Germanophobia provided the political motivation and the strategic direction of the Russian military, it was the seeming accession of Britain to the Triplice that drove the Russian diplomats closer to the side of France and made them suggest to the long-waiting French that "a further step might be made along the road of the entente." The first direct stimulus of the Franco-Russian Alliance was provided by the almost frantic welcome given to the French squadron visiting Kronstadt in July and August 1891. While the French ships were on their way, the representatives of the two general staffs, Boisdeffre and Vannovsky, discussed once more, this time in Paris, the question of inter-staff agreements. The Frenchman, under instructions from Freycinet, declared that a general understanding (entente) would be insufficient. It would leave the Tsar himself altogether uncommitted. And it was disturbing that the Tsar remained so strangely silent while William II loudly proclaimed the Triple and the Quadruple Alliance. "When I report that you will march together with us and mobilize simultaneously," Boisdeffre urged upon Vannovsky, "I shall be asked why, if that is the case, we, instead of leaving everything vague, do not sign an official convention which puts an end to the uncertainties, ambiguities and insecurity, a convention that might simply say that if France or Russia is attacked by Germany, they oblige themselves to start general mobilization simultaneously and as promptly as possible." The Russian was somewhat doubtful. In case of such a war, might not France be bought off by the offer of Alsace-Lorraine? Impossible, said Boisdeffre. Nevertheless, Vannosky felt that simply to state that both Powers would mobilize at once in case of German aggression would be altogether insufficient. France and Russia had a diversity of interests all over the world that might lead them into war. Certain questions of honor and dignity, as in the Schnaebele affair, could not well bring Russia into war, while she herself was more likely to become involved through one of the many Oriental problems. What would France do if Russia should get into a war with only one of the Triple Alliance Powers? What would Russia do should France be attacked by Italy alone? It was agreed in these conversations that, in the face of aggression from any direction, there must be immediate mobilization and war must be begun the first day of mobilization. In that case, Russia would at once send out all the cavalry she had ready to destroy railroads, etc. From the standpoint of military necessity, the two generals considered an absolute defensive alliance imperative, regardless of the adversary, with an exception made only for Powers like China. They then discussed war aims. Russia must have Galicia, which would put an end to the Polish problem forever, and the control of the Straits. France must have Alsace-Lorraine and, if military success would allow it, the line of the Rhine, which was always the design of the general staff. However, said Boisdeffre, "Let's begin by beating the Germans; with that the most difficult thing will be done."

The Frenchman argued that the Germans must be considered Enemy Number One in every respect. They must be attacked first and by both Powers. Once they had been defeated, everything would crumble. For this reason Russia must not seek cheap successes against Austria-Hungary, as she was inclined to do. Her inclination was dictated more by Pan-Slavism than by exclusively military considerations. Speaking as a soldier, the Russian was willing to agree, and in general betrayed more readiness to come to terms than he had the year previous. He was willing to sign a convention if the French would conclude a defensive alliance that would put France in the field at the moment Russia entered the war against any of four Powers, Germany, Austria, Italy, or Britain. And Russia would do the same for France. The convention would also stipulate the price that would be demanded in case of victory.[98]

Meanwhile, what was going on in St. Petersburg? Was Giers thinking of a military convention which would bring the two general staffs into contact and thereby avoid a waste of forces in the case of an attack, asked the French Ambassador? Why not an accord between the two Governments, asked Giers? At this point the questioning ended. Instructions from Paris were needed.[99] These went out as the French squadron was arriving at Kronstadt. They suggested concerted action on all questions that might endanger the peace in Europe, where the Franco-Russian understanding would restore the balance and provide for automatic, instantaneous mobilization without the necessity of any further previous understanding whenever one of the Triplice Powers should mobilize its forces. Britain was not mentioned. If the French were to have their way, one more step toward the automatism of mobilizations in Europe would be taken. Giers proved reluctant. Britain must also be considered an enemy, perhaps even the main enemy from a diplomatic point of view. For him at least, the diplomatic enemy and the military enemy were not identical, and there were dangers to peace outside as well as inside Europe. For the French, little else counted in comparison with the enmity focussed on Germany. The French hoped to keep Britain neutral in a conflict with the Triplice. The Russians, on the other hand, even among the military, had not fully resolved that Germany was necessarily a future enemy. If Russia were at war with Austria while Germany was fighting France, might Germany then be willing to sacrifice Austria in order to avoid a two-front war? In the French view, the dangers of the situation could perhaps be lessened by obliging Russia, through a military convention or similar instrument, to commit a definite number of army corps against Germany. This would be the less satisfactory substitute for an agreement to regard Germany as the principal enemy and the first to be attacked.[100]

The French governors at the time felt no desire to become engaged in a war on account of Afghanistan or even the Balkans. Neither were they of "the party of the immediate revanche," as they dubbed Deroulède and his consorts, but rather of the eventual one. "We must not lose sight for a moment of the war that we shall have to sustain one day against Germany and which will decide the fate of Europe for a long time to come," Foreign Minister Ribot wrote to Prime Minister Freycinet. "What is most important in our eyes is to get a military arrangement with Russia concluded. In this way we shall oblige her to reveal her views and tell us clearly whether we can count on her in case of a war with Germany."[101] But as yet Giers shrank from the automatic commitment of both armies in case all or one of the Triplice Powers were to mobilize. He considered it "very undesirable to bind ourselves prematurely by any positive engagements whatsoever in the military way and thus interfere with our freedom of action" (to the Tsar, early September 1891). This attitude was very disappointing to the French.

The highly critical condition of the Russian economy during the winter of 1891-92 kept diplomatic negotiations from going beyond the informal entente state. A transfusion of capital from France failed.[102] The banks, it turned out, could not make the French public buy a large Russian loan; the Kronstadt enthusiasm had not swept the investors off their feet. This failure made Giers still less amenable to the continued French argument in favor of making more definite military arrangements in order to be prepared for any abrupt declaration of war against either or both parties. Under pressure from the French, however, he agreed that the military might enter upon conversations once more, provided these did not become public, in order to further prepare the terrain. In Russia's present state of mind it seemed advisable to make the project of a military convention appear not as a menace to, but rather as a guarantee of, peace.[103]

A note composed by the French Chief of Staff, General Miribel, and revised by Freycinet, outlined the situation on which a military convention had to be based. France and Russia, the note stated, were equally filled with a desire for keeping the peace and need therefore consider only the case of a defensive war provoked by aggression—left undefined, now as later—on the part of the Triplice Powers against one or both of them. Reciprocity of support was to be complete: in case of an attack against one Power the other would bring all forces to its support. Since rapidity was more than ever the essential condition of success, both countries would begin to prepare as soon as the danger was known. The simultaneous mobilization of France and Russia would follow within a

few hours the initiative on the part of the Triplice, the only possible enemy. The military commitment of Russia, as proposed by the French, was new in Russian military and political diplomacy. It was, however, only the logical outcome of the ever-closer posting of the Russian Army along the Western frontier. Their being in an exposed position made the Russian soldiers look to the alliance with France. The military had gone out on a limb, for the support of which they were eager to have France as an ally. The military reason for alliance was more obvious than the diplomatic. The military commitment, if she were inclined to honor it, would serve to bind Russia diplomatically. The military commitment to instantaneous war would make diplomatic exertion in favor of peace very difficult, if not impossible. Russia's semi-isolation would be gone.

Miribel's note put the military strength of the Triple Alliance states at 137 infantry divisions, nineteen independent cavalry divisions, 6,432 cannon, and 2,810,000 men. On the French-Russian side, he listed 141 infantry divisions, sixteen independent cavalry divisions plus 80,000 cossacks, 7,160 cannon, and 3,150,000 men. The slightly superior numerical strength on the latter side, which would just about be cancelled if Rumania should enter the war on the side of the Triplice, was balanced by the greater speed of concentration on the Triplice side. In such a situation it seemed essential to the French General Staff to make the destruction of the principal enemy, Germany, the supreme aim; Austria's and Italy's defeat would follow inevitably. On the basis of this reasoning, France had dedicated over five-sixths of her mobilized strength to the German front. Russia was invited to follow this example, although not quite to the same extent, and concentrate at least half her forces against the enemy, whose plans were based on the expectation of beating France first and then turning around to tackle Russia. In order to accomplish this, Russia must speed up her mobilization and concentration against Germany and seek merely to contain "the secondary enemy," Austria.[104]

The French deductions and proposals did not please Giers and his diplomatic assistants. The French were going too far and too fast. They had already succeeded in restoring balance in Europe. Why try to go beyond this? "We need," thought Giers, "peace and tranquility in view of the disasters of the famine, the incompleteness of our armaments, the desperate state of our railroads and finally the renewed agitation in the camp of the Nihilists"—there could be nothing better for Russia than an understanding with Germany. Besides, it was difficult to treat with the French. The Freycinet cabinet had fallen, and there were always new faces. The diplomats were hesitant

to go ahead on the road that might prove dangerous to Tsarism. However, the Tsar was won over
by the military to the view that, for military reasons if for no other, Germany was to be the
principal enemy in case of war with the Triplice.
"We must indeed come to an agreement with the
French," he decreed, "and in case of war between
France and Germany we must immediately hurl
ourselves upon the Germans in order not to give
them time to crush France first and then turn
upon us. We must correct the mistakes of the
past and crush Germany at the first opportunity.
When Germany breaks up, Austria will not dare
anything."

The Tsar-Liberator complex had once more taken
hold of Alexander. He believed, as Giers
confided to his assistant Lamsdorff, that "once
he has downed Germany he will be the ruler of
the world, have the Balkans in his pockets, etc."
When Giers asked the monarch what Russia would
gain by helping France defeat Germany, Alexander
answered that a defeated Germany would fall to
pieces. The pieces presumably would be picked up
by Russian-related princelings. Giers, dubbed
"the German" in the Bolshevist History of Diplomacy, held that any threat to German unity would
only unite Germany still more firmly and that a
successful France would soon turn away from
Russia, whose help she would no longer need.
Could she, with her notoriously unstable governments, be trusted with such a compromising document as a military convention?[105]

All that Giers could obtain was a postponement
of the general staff conversations on the proposed
military convention until July 1892. The French
were given assurances that the Russians agreed
in principle to mutual assistance and simultaneous
mobilization. The French were also informed by
their military friends in St. Petersburg, while
Giers retired to a sick-bed, that they were already
working on the text of a convention. The technical
part of it would be arranged between the soldiers;
the foreign offices would do the rest—a division of
labor in which War Minister Vannovsky, as Giers
complained, did not entirely remain within his own
field in his desire to make "everything precise and
lucid." Giers did not share Ribot's conviction that
"the signature on the military convention will put
the seal on our political accord."[106]

The French were hopeful that the Tsar would
follow the lead of the War Minister and Chief of
Staff, rather than the timorous hesitations of the
Foreign Minister. They prepared the way for
Boisdeffre's visit to Russia by various means.
They invited Russian officers to maneuvers
where no other foreign officers were to be admitted; they inspired newspaper articles presenting the alternative between "alliance and flirtation." As they envisaged the military convention,

it need not contain every technical point of agreement. Such questions could properly be made the
object of a subsequent exchange of notes between
the two general staffs with the approval of the two
war ministries. The civilian ambassador was told
not to enter upon questions of detail outside his
own competency. The civilian abdication was far-
reaching: "We can," said Ribot, "only lay down
principles and then leave to the military the task
of working out the plans of concentration accordingly. The simpler and shorter the convention on
which joint action will be based, the better...But,
of course, such a convention is, above all, a political act and ought to be signed, if not by the
heads of state, at least by the two foreign ministers, in the name of the Emperor on the one
hand and that of the President of the Republic on
the other."[107]

Giers' feeble attempts to bring Britain into
consideration as a possible enemy were carefully
pushed aside. Such a discussion would only com-
plicate matters. The French diplomats, in close
cooperation with the Russian Chief of Staff and
War Minister, sought to remove all obstacles
standing in the way of the great desire of the two
general staffs "to get out of this period of waiting
which already lasts too long." Actually, the diplomatic situation was less threatening for Russia
than it had been for a long time. Salisbury had
been replaced by the much less Russophobe Gladstone. But still French diplomacy in St. Petersburg succeeded in establishing a "perfect community of ideas" with the Russian soldiers, always
pointing to the danger of war breaking out before
a military convention had been signed. The French
found a ready ear with the chief of staff, who
proved even more talkative and indiscreet than the
war minister. He assured the French that he was
taking measures as if war would break out within
a few months.[108]

All augured well for the French, except the continued inclination of even the partisans of "a military entente with France" to be unduly concerned
with Austria as an enemy. To make the intimacy
complete, the military servitors of the Tsar informed the French beforehand of the arguments
they would use with the Tsar in favor of the French
entente. They even confessed that they had perhaps more reason than the French to be ready for
warlike eventualities. These were confidences that
diplomatic negotiators would not easily have made.
They strengthened Boisdeffre's negotiating position still further and allowed the French to proceed at times almost by way of ultimatum, insisting that everything be finished by the end of
September. Boisdeffre, on the eve of his departure,
brought up the question of the duration of the convention. In order to mark the new arrangement as
purely defensive, it should last only as long as the

Triple Alliance. Since the Triplice was also purely defensive, the competition as to which side would appear more innocent was thus begun.

Such provisions would meet less resistance than the French demand that France and Russia both mobilize, even in case Germany alone were to mobilize.[109] The French proposals for the convention provided: (1) that the armed forces of both parties should mobilize immediately and completely if either the forces of the Triplice or of Germany alone should mobilize; (2) that the direction of all the forces of both parties to the convention that are not absolutely required at other points should be put against Germany, thus forcing her to fight a two-front war; (3) that the forces to be put into the field at the opening of the war should be specified; (4) that no separate peace treaty should be made; (5) that the two general staffs should arrange the implementation of the preceding points; (6) that the duration of the convention should be determined.[110]

The French expectations went considerably further than the Russian soldiers were ready to concede when they committed themselves to paper. Written agreements would come under the eyes of the Tsar or the diplomats. If the latter, as the representatives of an older Russia, were not yet fully aware of the importance and consequences of modern mobilization, Obrutchev left them little occasion for doubt. "Beginning of mobilization," he stated, "cannot now be regarded as a peaceful act; on the contrary it is the most decisive act of war." For this supreme military reason the two allied Powers ought to mobilize simultaneously. At this point, diplomatic action would cease, and the chances of localizing war would be minimal. Whatever the diplomatic situation, it would be a mistake to deal with the problem of mobilizing against any single enemy rather than the whole of the Triplice. The specific terms of his analysis are indicated in the following quotation:

The French regard Germany almost exclusively as their immediate enemy; to Italy they attach secondary importance, while for Austria they cherish certain sympathies, continuing to regard her as the historic antagonist of Germany. Hence the French would like, if possible, to conclude with us a convention solely for the event of war with Germany. To a certain extent this condition is mutually profitable. But one cannot help noticing that it is considerably more profitable for France than for us. Having secured a guarantee against her most dangerous enemy, France might, in case of war by Russia against Austria, even though it broke out at Germany's command, remain inactive and wait for developments, which might prove fatal to us...Hence it is scarcely convenient for us to conclude a convention exclusively for the event of a war with Germany. We are faced by a Triple Alliance closely cemented in military matters; in no case can we imagine separate action against us by Germany or Austria; hence, in the convention it is necessary for us to base the simultaneous mobilization of the armies of France and Russia on the idea of an attack, not by Germany, but by any Power of the Triple Alliance.

The readiness of the soldier to be committed to war was as complete as the French could expect. Obrutchev, however, wanted to preserve absolute freedom of action on questions of where to strike and in what force.[111] Military sovereignty wanted no obligation as to how the war of coalition was to be fought, only as to how it was to be brought on.

Still afraid that his chief of staff might commit Russia too deeply, the Tsar refused to give him any formal full powers for dealing with Boisdeffre.[112] Signalled by the Paris press and closely observed by the diplomats and military attachés of the Triple Alliance, Boisdeffre arrived on August 1, 1892. He plunged at once into visits and negotiations. He found less encouragement for the French standpoint than he had been led to expect by his military opposites. The chief of staff proved considerably more accommodating than the war minister. The latter seemed suddenly to remember that he was, after all, a political official and not merely a soldier-technician. The Russians even expressed doubts as to whether a formal agreement was required at all, whether a gentlemen's agreement would not suffice. In any case, an agreement was not constitutional until ratified by the French Chamber. And an agreement of this type could not be submitted to the parliament, since the Tsar insisted on keeping it absolutely secret. Military conventions signed in advance, they argued without giving examples, were never executed. Understandings founded on the word of honor of honest men were the ones adhered to. The Tsar was not in a mood for exchanging signatures, and he was determined to make the divulging of the convention a cause for nullifying it. One reason advanced for secrecy was the fear that publication would set off another arms race in which Russia could not at the time afford to indulge. In any case, was France, in view of her domestic politics, a suitable signatory? There were other Russian reasons against a tight convention. Would not the French, as soon as they had it in their hands, precipitate things and bring on a war? Or would not the Germans, once they learned about it, bring on the war for which Russia would not be ready for another two years at least? Such questions Boisdeffre answered with peaceful assurances. To him a military convention was still the best form for a Franco-Russian entente because it preserved, better than a political treaty could, the condition of absolute secrecy. (This assumes that a secret is better preserved by soldiers than by politicians.) The general existence of the entente need not be denied. In fact it was, as Boisdeffre told the Tsar, an article of faith with the whole French nation.

"The delicate point of defining the casus foederis" was settled to French satisfaction. It was agreed that there should be simultaneous mobilization by both parties to the convention—mobilization that was tantamount to a "declaration of war," as Boisdeffre emphasized when he was received by the Tsar at the close of negotiations. The Tsar added that he understood it to be so—even if Germany alone should mobilize—but that France would also mobilize, should Austria alone mobilize against Russia. This was in Article II, whereas Article I bound France to bring active assistance only if Russia should be attacked by Germany or by Austria supported by Germany. Russia's obligations were of a similarly contradictory character. The contradictions were the outcome of the struggle "between French nervousness and Russian laziness, between clarté and cunning," as it has been characterized by Eugen Fischer. In order to save the convention, both sides gave up their original objection to becoming involved in either a one-sided German-French or a one-sided Austro-Russian dispute. They did this at the price of clarity as to their engagements and with some mental reservations which the hybrid character of the political-military convention invited. Both parties agreed to the article on immediate and simultaneous mobilization, and each hoped to have to apply it only under certain desirable conditions. Each side thought this obligation most rewarding, the French probably more so than the Russians, for they were inclined to value Russian help early in the war higher than in the later stages.[113]

In the remaining articles were stipulated such matters as the forces to be put in the field against Germany—1,330,000 men on France's part, 700,000 to 800,000 on Russia's. These forces were to begin "full action" speedily, in order to force Germany to fight the war on two fronts as early as possible.

The Convention bore only the signatures of the French and Russian Chiefs of Staff, making it "a convention of the two general staffs."[114] The Tsar accepted it in principle, saying that "it gave him full satisfaction." The instrument was, therefore, still incomplete and could not be considered as fully binding upon the two governments. In France, it was to hang fire for months. The Freycinet Government pressed for ratification. It

might fall from power, and there was danger that the next government would divulge the secret. The Freycinet government tried to get Russian approval for submitting the political part of the agreement to the Chamber for ratification, while its military part would remain secret. Their argument was that

> if the convention were purely military, there would be no difficulty because it is in the nature of these kinds of arrangements never to be communicated to the Chambers. It is with regard to the political part of the convention that the President of the Republic would feel scruples about engaging himself in secret and under terms that would seem to exclude the control of the Chambers.

There were some proposals to escape the dilemma by announcing the existence of the Convention not in the near future but only at the moment when it was to be executed, immediately before mobilization. In fact, Viviani carried a copy of the Convention with him on August 4, 1914, when he asked the deputies for the war credits. He was ready to read it if that should be called for. Since no parliamentarian was curious enough about the character of France's obligations, it remained unread and unknown to the public until 1918.[115]

The Russians could not at once be brought to ratify the Convention. The Panama scandals discredited France in the eyes of the Tsar to the extent that negotiations could not be thought of for months. The Tsar had feared that German armament would be spurred if the Franco-Russian Convention became known. This happened even without the secret being divulged. In 1893, a German army bill introduced the two-years' term of service, which meant a much-improved preparation for a two-front war. In justifying this measure, the existence of Franco-Russian understandings was taken for granted. At the same time, the French told their Russian friends that the German measure made prompt ratification of their instrument necessary. It would counter the strengthening of the Triple Alliance, the partners of which would be even more firmly tied to Germany in the future, due to the attraction always exercised by the strongest partner.[116]

The visit of a Russian squadron to Toulon, in October 1893, furnished the French people with the occasion to ratify a convention, the contents of which they would not know for twenty-five years, and for which they would pay the price of an estimated four billion dollars in loans, not to mention the blood-letting to which France exposed herself by the alliance with Russia. The Tsar, probably swayed once more by the military, responded at the end of the year with the declaration that the Convention was now "definitely adopted."[117]

The declaration was contained in a letter from Giers to the French ambassador, dated December 27, 1893. The French reply of January 4, 1894, likewise considered the Convention, which the ambassador thought gave France "absolute security," "as executory henceforth." And he added: "In consequence of this agreement, the two staffs shall have power immediately to deliberate at any time and to communicate all the information possibly useful to them."[118]

By diplomatic standards the Convention was a singularly weak instrument. An escape from its obligations could easily have been engineered. This was one more reason for the French governors not to draw on it too heavily for purely diplomatic purposes, but rather to spare it for the supreme contingency of the war with Germany. No primacy of diplomacy was ever re-established in Tsarist Russia, once Giers had allowed it to slip from his weakening hands. The military retained their ascendancy. Tsarism, shaken to its foundations by the movements of discontent and revolution, thought the Army represented the truly conserving force in the land. It was the Army that established and tightened the foreign ties in which Russia was entangling herself. It was the Army that took Russia out of her isolation, which was more military than political before 1892, just as, in a sense, American navalists after 1890 took the United States out of isolation. If pre-1914 military alignments were on the whole political in origin, this was not true for Russia whose soldiers sought and largely concluded the alliance with France—unless one sees them as the Pan-Slav politicians they were. The Pan-Slav motivation, affecting military planning, persisted for a long time after 1892. As French military attachés later found, through inspections on the spot, Obrutchev "by fooling (leurrant) General de Boisdeffre with nice words, prepared himself far more for the war on the Austrian than on the German front, along which he prepared only the strictest defensive."[119]

It took considerable urging on the part of the French to move the Russians out of this attitude. Their heart was in the war against Austria, the foe of the Slavs, against whom easy and brilliant victories were to be won. To align them against the Germans continued to be difficult. German military power was formidable. A war against her would require a greatly accelerated mobilization and a greater ability to concentrate rapidly, neither of which could be easily achieved by Russia. In nearly every one of the staff conversations after 1894, the mechanical connections with France were tightened and made more automatic. A chance for preserving peace had once rested in Russia's geographic aloofness and in the slowness of her mobilization and concentration. That chance was rapidly disappearing. Diplomatic figures such as Sasonov, Grey and Bethmann were mediocrities. The war-abettors, like Poincaré and Isvolski, were powerful and decisive personalities. The monarchs were weak; their title "supreme warlord" had become more than ironical. Under such conditions, the mechanism of military preparation, so up-to-date and complex that the diplomats did not dare interfere with it, became supreme. The military time-tables were so highly regarded that the question of where they might lead was not carefully considered. The firmness in the Franco-Russian alliance—as also in the Franco-British and Austro-German arrangements for the case of war—came to rest in the soldiers, who kept these ties up-to-date. True to their concepts of honor and true to the plans they had made, the soldiers proved more powerful than the supreme warlords and the cabinets who, on all sides in 1914, happened not to be strongly averse to war, or at least lacked the courage to resist it.

The immediate usefulness of the Franco-Russian Convention was not great. The Fashoda crisis showed France that in such conflicts little or no Russian support could be expected. France herself denied support to Russia's "historic mission" in the direction of the Straits. In 1895, Russia asked France what help she could expect, should the initiative of a third Power force her to intervene militarily in the Near East. France declared that "only a great national interest, such as a new settlement of the question which since 1870 divides Germany and France so profoundly, would be considerable enough to justify in the eyes of the French people engagements implying military action into which the Great Powers might find themselves drawn and in which consequently our effort ought to be carried to its highest point of intensity." In other words, the French Government was ready for a general war for the sake of regaining Alsace-Lorraine, a war aim that Poincaré repeated to the Russians in 1912.[120] But France did not specify the Russian cause for which she would be willing to make a war general in character.

The French-Russian-German Far Eastern alliance of 1895 was, by the standards of imperialism, a very profitable one. Russia toyed with the idea of turning it to still larger purposes. This increased the tendency of the Russian governors to shrink from the specter of a settlement of the Alsace-Lorraine problem through war. Russia turned to the one-sided pursuit of her Far Eastern venture, still certain that the French would not deny her their support. To the French, this seemed a thoroughly one-sided bargain. They felt that they had helped the Russians greatly without receiving anything tangible in return. Because the Russians had insisted, France had, with some humiliation, sent a delegation to the ceremonies of the Kiel

Canal opening. French politicians were bombarded by the opposition at home with demands for explanations of the usefulness of the arrangements with Russia. Under these conditions, on June 10, 1895, the word "alliance" was first used by them to describe the ties with Russia. Filled with the sentiments of a bad debtor, to whom a new loan was coming soon, the Russians, from the young Tsar down, allowed this public characterization to stand while the military convention remained secret.[121] While French diplomacy found the majority of Russian diplomats still hostile to close ties with Republican France, Russia's soldiers continued to pledge their loyalty. When General Boisdeffre came once more to visit Russia, in the summer of 1896, Obrutchev gave a toast at an intimate military dinner, saying: "Often in war one does not act and excuses oneself by saying that there were no orders. We shall not take cover behind similar pretexts. Let France give her orders, and we shall march! If she has trouble along her frontier, we shall not even wait for her appeal; and she can rely on it that we shall march forward on our own."[122]

In order to strengthen the existing though little used ties with Russia, Delcassé, during a visit to St. Petersburg in 1899, obtained a formal renewal of the agreement of 1892-93. The demise of Francis Joseph was expected in the near future, and vast changes in Central Europe in favor of Germany were thought likely after his death. An exchange of notes of August 9 declared that the Franco-Russian alliance aimed not only at the maintenance of world peace, as had been stated originally, but also at the preservation of the European balance of power. The military convention was to last as long as the political alliance rather than for the duration of the Triple Alliance, which might break up with the death of Francis Joseph. In addition, Delcassé obtained a Russian promise that part of the next loan to be placed in France would be applied to the construction of Russian strategic railway lines.[123] This diplomatic tightening-up was followed by the closer military cooperation envisaged in the original convention. Conversations between the two chiefs of staff took place in Paris in 1900. The French Chief of Staff, General Pendezec, came to St. Petersburg in February 1901 for conversations with his Russian colleague. The discussions concerned the details of mobilization and concentration and led to the Russian promise to cross the German frontier on the eighteenth day of mobilization. Also taken up was the question of a military convention to be directed against England, which had already been discussed in 1900. The construction of the Orenburg-Tashkent railroad was necessary in order to be able to make forceful military demonstration in the direction of India.

Since this would not be finished for another three years, further discussion of this convention was put off, never to be resumed.

The chiefs of staff compared their estimates, which were nearly identical, of the German war strength and its expected distribution. The Frenchman again urged the Russians to detract the Germans from the Western front and thus give the French a better chance to win the opening battle, which might begin about the fourteenth day of mobilization. Should this battle go against them, they hoped for good news from the Eastern front in order to offset the bad effects on public opinion and army morale. The Russians, however, could promise nothing before the eighteenth day. Not for another two years would Russia's strategic railroad construction make possible the speed the French so much desired. Experiments with dirigibles and wireless were to be undertaken with a view to bridging the great distance separating the two countries whose telegraphic communications were rather tenuous. In other respects, there was less harmony between the two armies at that time. The Russians thought the French Army reforms under the Dreyfusard War Minister General André, which seemed to approach a militia system, dangerous, because democratic. They did not even shrink from attacking him through the Paris press. The most promising outcome of the exchange was the Russian pledge to build the purely strategic railroad Bologoy-Sielce, which Witte, representing the economic point of view, did not want but had to grant if his next loan in Paris was to be successful. (Since it was not a success, Witte in the end denied the military this road.) To the Germans, who had watched the Franco-Russian discussions as closely as they could, "the occurrence proved that France for the first time has succeeded in profiting from Russia's economic situation in order to obtain a far-going political concession."[124]

This and other bargains evoked criticism of the Alliance from some groups in both France and Russia. The Radical and Socialist elements in France, somewhat more influential in the early years of the twentieth century than later, distrusted Russia, according to War Minister Kuropatkin, "because the autocratic regime is hateful to them." And he thought that they must not be allowed to come to an understanding with Germany because that "would altogether detract from the weight of our treaty with France."[125] That is, in the judgment of the war minister and presumably other highly placed Russian officers, a certain hostility must be kept up in order not to weaken the military alliance.

Much to the regret of the French Right, the Russian gaze was not steadfastly fixed on the Vistula or on Berlin. The adventure in the Far

East was a highly undesirable deviation from preparations for a war of <u>revanche</u>, the only war worth preparing. The French chief of staff, who, together with the ambassadors, was one of the more permanent fixtures in the relations between Paris and St. Petersburg, went to Russia again in 1903. In part, his purpose was to complain of the neglect into which strategic railway building in the westward direction had fallen. This, the German Emperor thought, was a somewhat hopeless task, for "the Russian Army had only Japan in mind; the 'West' is not being considered an enemy at the present."[126] General Pendezec was still so favorably impressed by what he had seen of the Russian Army that Ambassador Bompard thought it necessary to warn him that the Russian nation, the nation behind the Army, might, under the strain of a great war, fail the Army and France. It had failed the Army once before, during the Crimean War, when the power of the Tsar had been greatly and permanently shaken. "Nicholas II might well, in such a case, find himself faced by the same dilemma as his grandfather, forced to divert his arms from the foreign to the domestic danger."[127]

In French eyes, the war in Manchuria was a completely wasted military effort. Strong Russian support was lacking in the Moroccan question, an occasion that offered the Germans their best chance to fight and win the war on two fronts. After 1905, the Russians would remain <u>hors de combat</u> for years to come. Worse still, the French found them at first loath to liquidate the Asiatic adventure and to give up the English as enemies. They were also loath to restore the military situation along their European frontiers, where Germany had rendered some anti-revolutionary help, somewhat as if the Alvensleben Convention were still alive.[128] There were even French fears that the revolutionary movement of 1905 might change the control of the Russian Government over Poland and thus upset the old plans for the concentration. For military reasons, the French were hoping that the Polish movement for autonomy would not succeed and that Russia would remain "one and indivisible."[129]

As early as April 1904, the French General Staff and the French Foreign Ministry found the military value of the alliance "obviously greatly diminished by the colossal task facing our ally in the East." Again and again they concluded that, "while the Russians are at grips with the Japanese, French diplomacy must carefully avoid quarrels, <u>a fortiori</u> a war with Germany." The French General Staff had just then gotten hold of Germany's new war plan, the Schlieffen Plan. It provided for a covering force of only five German army corps in the East, as against thirty-six army corps, including reserve

formations, to be employed in the West. At that time the French would have been utterly unable to resist an attack in such force. "We would be overrun at once," Pendezec told the diplomats, even with the transfer of 40,000 men from the Italian front to the Vosges. On the strength of the secret agreements with Italy of 1902, the French war plans of November 1904 envisaged such a transfer. The Italians, as the Quai d'Orsay assured the Chief of Staff, would not remain neutral in a general European war but would attack Austria. This would partially compensate for the depreciation of the Russian alliance. However, no changes in planning were made to meet the threat of the Schlieffen Plan, since the Generalissimo, Brugère, and others in authority could not bring themselves to believe in the authenticity of the documents sold to the French intelligence service. The Moroccan crisis found the French Army, by its own admission, hopelessly unable to fight. As Pendezec exclaimed:

> A sudden attack by Germany! We couldn't resist it! It would be worse than 1870! Our defeat would be even more rapid and complete! ...Not a vestige of help from Russia! What would we have with which to meet the 1,500,000 men of the German Army? 900,000 men at the outside—of which 100,000, possibly 200,000 would refuse to take the field...We'll fight if we have to fight. But what a ghastly risk... France may easily perish altogether...Except for Verdun, not one of our fortresses is in a state to resist them.

In June 1905, when the Moroccan crisis reached its most acute stage, the question of asking for Russian help in an immediate war was considered in Paris. "Is it not time to remind our allies of the heavy obligations towards France which the agreement of 1894 imposes upon her?" The Russians were told at the time that France was "compelled to envisage an attack by Germany." What would they do in such an eventuality? If they could render no military help, they could at least make the Tsar try to influence the Kaiser in favor of peace. The French soldiers thought that although Russia might still be able to concentrate 350,000 men along her Western frontier, that would not prove very useful. Neither would, in the opinion of Pendezec, "the help from England at the present time be of any value to us. I put it at nil. I should prefer an alliance with Switzerland."[130]

Military-political conditions changed considerably between the two meetings of the chiefs of staff in 1903 and 1906. The much-feared <u>Anschluss</u> of the German provinces in Austria appeared less imminent.[131] The French entente with Britain, which made first for a restoration of the military balance, and finally for an over-balance, made all discussion of an anti-British convention superfluous. On the other hand, the Russian Chief of Staff, General Palitsine, was, at least for a time, in favor of the Bjoerkoe policy; and, shocking as it was to the French, he was not absolutely convinced that the Germans must be faced from the outset of war by a distribution of allied strength that would force Germany to fight the two-front war at once. It was painfully obvious that the Russians would be unable to furnish help with the strength once promised for at least three years. Still, it was important not to do anything that might shake the de jure value of the old commitment. French savings must again be offered to the Russians, but only on their promise to build at last the necessary strategic railway lines to the West.

The April 1906 meeting of the chiefs of staff, following the close of the Algéciras Conference, dealt with such problems as the contribution Russia would be able to make in case of war during the prolonged state of her military weakness, how many combattants she would be able to place on her Western frontiers, whether she would remain on the defensive, and how the Russian forces would be reconstituted during the ensuing years.[132] The disclosures made by the Russians about the condition of their home affairs could not have been very reassuring to the French. The Russians did promise, however, that they would, like the French, at once mobilize all their forces on receipt of the first news of a German mobilization.[133] There was no promise as to the day following mobilization on which they would invade Germany. The French Chief of Staff was rightfully discouraged, at least in 1906 and 1907. Following a visit of General Palitsine to Paris, Ambassador Bompard found him "in a state of mind rather peculiar in a chief of staff of the army: the war did not enter into his expectations"; he could not foresee, he said, that "some day, some day soon perhaps, his labors would find their practical application in the field."[134]

The meetings of the chiefs of staff in 1906, 1907, and 1908 revealed not only Russia's military weaknesses but also the hesitations of the new foreign minister, Isvolski. To the French, it looked as though a new flirtation with the old Three Emperors' Alliance idea was in the offing. Isvolski declined to give his written consent, as the French Government had already done, to the understanding arrived at by the Chiefs of Staff at their April 1906 meeting, even though he substantially approved of them. "It did not seem permissible to him to let the Chiefs of Staff, who no doubt did not know better, to act contrary to a formal accord concluded by their two Governments." At the meetings, he was highly

unwilling to pledge an offensive against Germany at the very beginning of the war, because he considered his army to be still lacking in the coherence or the tactical instruction required of a good instrument for an offensive. Even the first condition for such an offensive was still missing— an absolute superiority over Austria. Could not Italy be brought to take an attitude ambiguous enough to force the Austrians to leave at least twelve divisions on the Italian front? And was the French Army, during the change from a three-year to a two-year term, in the best condition to undertake the promised offensive against Germany? (This democratic measure, as well as various mutinies in French regiments during the summer of 1907, gave the Rightists in Russia reason to wonder whether their country should not look for another political constellation.) In the talks of 1908, Isvolski even made reservations regarding the article of the original convention which provided for simultaneous mobilization in the face of a German mobilization. He wanted to provide that a German mobilization exclusively directed against Britain would not automatically cause French and Russian mobilization. In 1908, the French General Staff had not yet obtained what it had been dreaming of for sixteen years, namely, hard and fast provisions against Germany.[135] In the train of events set off by the Bosnian annexation, the French General Staff came much closer to obtaining such provisions. This affair ended Isvolski's vague hankering for the revival of the Three Emperors' Alliance. Although the Russian Army was still too weak for "the practical application" of the convention, French observers saw an improvement. They reported that

the Tsarist Empire had profited from the lesson of the Russo-Japanese war, which besides took place at a 9,000 kilometers' distance under extremely unfavorable circumstances; the materiel is rapidly being restored; the officers are reforming and shedding their habits of laziness and debauchery; and as to the Russian private, disciplined, frugal, tough, inured to fatigue and suffering, it is impossible to find a better one....

The meetings of the chiefs of staff were put on an annual basis from 1910 on when, in keeping with the more activist Delcassé-Poincaré-Isvolski policies, General Dubail went to meet his counterpart in order to again urge him to give the Russian plans a more offensive character. But as yet no promise beyond that of crossing the German frontier on the twentieth day of mobilization (as against the eighteenth, envisaged in 1900 and 1901) could be elicited. It was, however, agreed that "the defeat of the German armies remains, whatever the circumstances, the first and principal objective of the allied armies."[136]

Faced by the second Moroccan crisis, it seemed to the French that, in case of the ever more likely war, their own army would still have to bear an inordinate part of the German onslaught. "In order to block the German intentions, to re-establish the balance of forces in favor of the Triple Entente, to allow us to free ourselves from a purely defensive attitude, the safest way was to obtain a more intensive effort from our Russian ally." On his visit to St. Petersburg in August 1911, General Dubail was promised that mobilization and concentration would be acceler-ated. From the childish Tsar he received the as-surance that "Germany must be struck at her heart, the common objective must be Berlin."[137] Such intentions reflected the offensive à outrance theories of the French, rather than the special genius of the Russian army. The two chiefs of staff agreed that the words "defensive war" in the Convention did not mean a war fought in a defen-sive manner, but rather that it was absolutely necessary that the two allied armies undertake a powerful offensive, simultaneously if possible, in order to achieve the supreme and primary ob-jective, the defeat of the German army. The French at this time were again hopeful that a war pro-voked by Germany would find her alone, deserted by her two allies. But the Russians knew better and could not share the optimism with regard to Austria. "Pour encourager les autres," Dubail assured the Russians that the concentration of the French army would take place as rapidly as that of the Germans and that, beginning on the twelfth day of mobilization, France, with the help of the British Army on the left wing, would be in a posi-tion to take the offensive. The Russians could not promise more than to go into action on the six-teenth day, a promise still valid in 1914. Russian reorganization was still so incomplete that she could not undertake the war against Germany "with the certainty of success" for another two years. As they had done in 1910, the two chiefs reached far over into the political domain and agreed that Article 5 of the Convention bound the parties not only to make no separate peace but also not to cease operations or conclude a separ-ate armistice. (A few years later, this was to serve as text for the French attacks on Brest-Litovsk.) The exchange of information between the two general staffs was to be made still more com-plete and continuous. And in order to make the understandings still more binding, it was agreed that the protocol of the conversations was to be submitted to their two governments, to be signed by either the two war ministers or the prime ministers. Thus governmental support would be obtained for the improvements the military de-clared desirable. At least since 1906 the French

had wanted a maximum of signatures on the pro-tocol. The Russians, more autocratically, con-sidered that of the war ministers sufficient. Their standpoint prevailed.[138]

In all these matters the feeling of urgency or-iginated on the side of the French. They were finally forced to realize that certain desirable improvements in the alliance remained unobtain-able and that some of them should remain un-attempted. When the Russians suggested that the Convention be re-negotiated, the French replied that, despite its faults, it would be better to leave it alone. Such negotiations would only pro-voke unwelcome rumors, the French Chief of Staff told the Russian military attaché early in 1912. The political horizon was dark enough as it was; his intelligence reports were very disquiet-ing and he was ready for war in the spring. "We work as if we had war." Both Triple Entente and Triple Alliance had a defensive character, and diplomatic wisdom dictated that one should not appear as the aggressor. The Russian agreed: a change in the military convention could take place "only during a complete calm."[139]

The French chief of staff found the Russian Army still unready in 1911, with the exception of the spectacular cavalry. Uniforms and much materiel for most of the reserve formations were still lacking. A new model shell was in short supply. Part of the reserve divisions were with-out artillery, the heavy artillery outdated, the army corps artillery seriously incomplete as re-gards howitzers, and heavy army artillery very scarce.[140] These and other shortcomings were due to Russian under-industrialization, a situation on which German plans could safely be predicated in 1914 and after.

At the July 1912 meeting of the chiefs of staff, Joffre emphasized that the German war plans were still predicated on destroying France first, that this was indicated by recent railway instal-lations, such as unloading ramps, but that France was countering this by her own railway arrange-ments, which would speed up the concentration by one or two days and give her an advantage over Germany within a year. But he demanded that the Russians do still more in the field of railroad con-struction. He submitted a costly itemized construc-tion program that was to enable them to assem-ble on the Vistula the troops destined to attack the German armies in the direction of Allenstein or Thorn-Posen-Berlin. He brought also the promise of French loans for this purpose. They would be more readily available now since Poin-caré—contrary to Caillaux's principle that the financial soundness of all foreign loans must be considered before they were admitted to the Paris cote—was placing the national interest above financial considerations.[141] This means that Poincaré, the patriot, was more willing than the financier to have the French investor, rather than the French Government, pay out of his pocket what in earlier times had been called "subsidies" and what came to be called "Marshall Plan" later on. The French investor was induced to invest by the high interest rates for the Russian railway loans.[142] When the French tried to veto the building of Russian railroads against Austria, the Russian Chief of Staff pointed to that country's recent military strengthening as by no means negligible. Russia could not afford to risk a defeat at the hands of Austria because of the moral effect it would have. That is to say, the impression it would make on Slavs and Pan-Slavs would be fatal. Russia must therefore continue to direct a considerable part of her force against that country and must also envisage Sweden's entry into the war on Germany's side. Hence Poincaré's visit to Sweden in the summer of 1914.[143]

The 1912 meeting of the soldiers was complemented, for the first time, by deliberations of the naval chiefs of staff. The original initiative for these was Russian, going back to 1911 when Italy's temporary blocking of the Dardanelles had touched a neuralgic spot in the Russian nerve system. The meetings were also a sign of the rebirth of a Russian fleet, which, since 1908, had had for the first time an admiralty staff, responsible for the strategic preparation of war. Isvolski had suggested early in 1911 that, since the relations among the three Entente navies were as yet rather incomplete, and immediate contact between the French and Russian naval staffs still lacking, a start toward cooperation might be made by Franco-Russian naval talks. In this way Russia might at least learn the totality of French plans for the case of a European war.[144] While there was practically no military-technical reason for Isvolski's proposal, diplomatic-political considerations spoke in its favor.

The Russian fleet, in order to rationalize the diplomatic proposals, declared itself greatly in need of French support if it were to retain naval domination in the Black Sea, where Austrian and Italian naval units must not be allowed to penetrate. They must be stopped on their way, if necessary, by the French fleet which was to open its base at Bizerta to Russian ships on the way from the Baltic to the Black Sea, if ever the Straits were to be opened for them. While the practical importance of naval agreements with Russia would clearly remain slight for a number of years to come, Delcassé, minister of marine at the time, and Poincaré were eager to meet the Russian wishes that the relation as it existed between the two armies be also established between the two navies.[145] If it could not contribute much

to the common war endeavor, it could still pledge another group of Russian governors to the Franco-Russian alliance.

With Paléologue, Political Director of the French Foreign Ministry, at their elbows, the two naval chiefs of staff—whose signatures were subsequently ratified by the two naval and the two foreign ministers—agreed that Russia must retain naval supremacy in the Black Sea and that she must be helped by French pressure on the Austrian and, possibly, the German and Italian navies in case of war. For this reason France was to concentrate her naval forces farther to the East, at Bizerta. While the eventualities contemplated did not look very likely, the Russian negotiator considered the obtaining of this French promise quite a success, the more so since it did not call for any Russian quid pro quo.[146] The main articles of the convention provided that the two allied naval forces would cooperate "in all the eventualities where the alliance foresees and stipulates the combined action of the land forces." Their cooperation would be prepared in time of peace, and to this end the two naval staff chiefs were henceforth authorized to correspond directly, exchange information, study all war hypotheses, concert all strategic programs, and meet for conferences at regular intervals.[147]

Immediately following its conclusion, the new convention was discussed by the political authorities during Poincaré's visit to St. Petersburg in August 1912. Prime Minister Kokovtzov saw no reason against confirming it by a diplomatic accord. It might be a good thing to supervise the conventions of their chiefs of staff. "These gentlemen would be capable of engaging us a bit light-heartedly. They talk and talk and do not bother about the financial possibilities or even the diplomatic considerations. This time they have occupied themselves with Turkey, with Sweden. What do I know? They will lead us a little too far in the end." Poincaré does not say whether he shared these fears of Kokovtzov, who was soon removed because of his unwanted peacefulness. It is most likely that he did not, for he clearly considered the ties between the various armed forces of the entente as reinforcements or substitutes for treaties of alliance. Terming the Franco-Russian alliance "a thing not discussed, not discussable," the Tsar was agreeable to Poincaré's proposal that this new convention be made a diplomatic accord by an exchange of letters between himself and Sasonov. This was done on August 15 and 16, 1912. Poincaré also suggested that the naval forces of all the Triple Entente partners be brought into closer cooperation. Under the seal of absolute secrecy he confided to Sasonov that, in the absence of any treaty, close contacts had been established between the Army and Navy Staffs of France and Britain, which assured France of Britain's military and naval support in case of a German attack. He proposed that the Russians should seek for themselves a naval agreement with Britain, which they subsequently did.

The existence of the naval convention was revealed by Le Temps early in August, before any ratification had taken place. While the Quai d'Orsay pretended that the disclosure was very harmful to it, Russian diplomats were suspicious.[148] Perhaps the leak had been arranged by the Foreign Office itself. It seemed altogether in keeping with Poincaré's policies to reassure the French public by such signs that strong friends had been tied to France by still newer instruments, and, on the other hand, that such recent interviews as that of Tsar and Kaiser in Baltischport did not need to be taken very seriously. This kind of assurance dispelled any doubts as to what new obligations the new ties might involve.

The Central Powers were not greatly alarmed: for at least five years to come the convention would have "merely a Platonic character." It seemed superfluous, except for making good weather for a new gigantic Russian loan in Paris. What other sense could a convention between an existing and a non-existing navy have?[149] Their representatives were told by Paléologue that France remained attached to the traditional principle of her policy, the maintenance of the European equilibrium, and that certain problems that forced themselves on the attention of the chancelleries involved strategic corollaries with which the General Staffs of the allied armies and navies had necessarily to occupy themselves.[150]

The Balkan wars, plus new large German and French Army bills—the propaganda for the latter being aided by Russian funds paid to the French press—gave the military staff conversations of August 1913 their urgent character.[151] Joffre pressed still harder for more strategic railroad building, in order to accelerate Russian concentration and achieve that initial success in war which seemed so imperative to the war planners before 1914. His suggestion that the troops of the Warsaw district should, even in peace time, be massed in such a manner as to represent a direct threat to Germany, was a more doubtful proposal.[152] If the Germans reduced their forces destined for the West, as Joffre must have hoped, this advanced Russian force would be exposed to German-Austrian encirclement. The automatism of mobilization was made still more mechanical. The old understanding that German mobilization bound Russia and France to mobilize their forces completely and at once was extended to cover the case of any hostile act committed by German forces against any of the allies.

As in most of the staff conversations, the French partner was again pressing, if not importunate, and the Russian yielding. "France expressed her wishes, Russia considered the feasibility and the means of satisfying them, a situation which was to restrict the free disposition of our forces during the first period of the war," the Russian First Quartermaster-General Danilov later wrote. On the whole, the Russians promised more than they could give and more than they intended to give, if only in order to calm the impetuous ally and money-provider. The "energetic offensive" the French wanted was not really envisaged in the plans of the Russian General Staff at the time. There is hardly any doubt that they were actually driven too far out of their original defensive attitude. The primary concern of the French was to have the Russians in the war from the outset. "On les engage, et alors on voit," to rephrase a Napoleonic formula. The discussions hardly ever went beyond that; they did not extend to plans for a joint war, not to mention unity of command.[153]

The agreement that the protocol of the 1913 conversations was to be submitted to the two governments concerned was partly designed to enable the chiefs of staff of the allied armies to base themselves firmly on this document in interdepartmental discussions of their demands for desirable improvements. It also indicated that, to a certain extent at least and to a somewhat greater extent than in the Berlin-Vienna staff conversations, the governments insisted on being informed about the talks of their staffs. While Joffre found the actual Russian governors "strictly oriented towards France," there were still counter-influences in the entourage of the Tsar. War Minister Suchomlinov, for example, regretted the French "orientation," which seemed to him more of a Westernization than the preservation of Tsardom would allow.[154] Others were asking whether Russia was not contributing the larger or more valuable assets to the pool of allied strength. Not everyone in Russia considered French loans for Russian railroad construction as an equivalent French contribution. It was on such reasoning that the Russians insisted, without "wanting to interfere in France's internal affairs," that the three-years' army service, which the French Left wanted to revoke, be continued.[155] Suchomlinov went so far as to bring about the publication of an article which, under the title of "Russia is ready, France must also be ready," interfered publicly in that battle of French politics. "Russia," it was argued in the article, "did everything she was bound to do by the alliance with France; she expects that her ally do her duty as well." This meant that France should produce the 770,000 men that only the three-years' service term could furnish.

Russia at the same time provided a peacetime strength of 2,300,000 men, with four annual contingents serving, whose term had only recently been prolonged by six months.[156]

Certain French circles were bold enough—or impudent enough, as was thought in the Russian General Staff—to consider the alliance as one essentially ruled by business considerations, with France furnishing the money and Russia the war strength, a business arrangement which, it was thought, entitled France to raise the military demands whenever Russia demanded more money, as she did at the turn of the year 1913. Such sentiments, combatted by Isvolski with the help of his press funds, did not escape attention in Russian military-political circles. They must not be allowed to spread and thus cool the French ardor for the alliance and the revanche sentiments against Germany. In these rested, after all, the Russian soldiers' guarantee of a continued supply of capital. Fortunately, the deep and blind belief of the French people in Russia's military power still strongly persisted, fortified by the creditor's interest. The French were strangely incurious about the forms which this support would take and the consequences it might have. With minor exceptions, neither the public nor the parliament took any considerable or continuous interest in this problem.[157] Democratic control of foreign, including military, affairs went no farther in France before 1914 than elsewhere in Europe. The masses and most of their chosen representatives remained unaware of such dangerous convictions prevailing among the soldiers and diplomats.

The staff conversations of August 1913 were the last. Their resumption in 1914 was suggested by the French, as "part of a happy tradition," and also for the reason that a new Russian chief of staff had been appointed in March 1914.[158] Henceforth, liaison between the staffs had to take more indirect ways. From July 27 on, Joffre's "first thought was to tighten up communications with our allies." He and War Minister Messimy were not relying on past promises and understandings. At least until August 6 they feared that the Russians would follow their penchant, attack the Austrians, and remain on the defensive against the Germans. Again and again they urged the Russians to undertake an offensive in the direction of Eastern Prussia and treat Austria, in spite of all Pan-Slavist desires, as a secondary consideration in the fighting of the war.[159] Soon the French went to the length of demanding Russian soldiers for the Western front, an eventuality as little discussed in peacetime as such problems as providing Russia with war materials.

If, in the individual general staff preparations for war, much of the character of the coming war had been misjudged or unforeseen, this was even more true with regard to the joint endeavor of the allied general staffs. The hybrid nature of their discussions took its revenge. There had been too much diplomacy in them. It had always seemed that once the problem of insuring Russia's entry into the war was settled, little else mattered. There was little understanding among the French people that at the outbreak of a war Russian help must necessarily be slow, much slower than popularly expected. Only occasionally before August 1914 was the question raised—and left unanswered—as to whether there should be an attempt to acquaint the French people with this fact of military and political life. As far as one can learn from the protocols, the problem of how to enable Russia to stay in the war, as the old regime had promised in Article 5 of the Convention, the problems of Russia's war supplies from abroad, and of a war industry, were never discussed by the chiefs of staff. The Russian war minister demanded, some time before August 1914, that such problems be considered. The Prime Minister, together with Grand Duke Sergei and Russian and French diplomats, opposed him.[160] They won out in the council of ministers, before the Tsar, and in the Duma.[161] The absence of a domestic war industry commensurate with the demands of this unforeseen kind of war, the shortcomings in Allied munitions shipments, the absence for a long time of a railway line from the accessible ports of the White Sea to the metropolis—one line the French had never demanded—gave cause and reason to the Russian defection of 1917-18. One more military convention was added to the long list of those that could not be kept. As War Minister Obrutchev had said to Boisdeffre in August of 1892: "Mais pourquoi vouloir signer une convention militaire? Les conventions signées d'avance n'ont jamais été exécutées."[162]

THE BRITISH-FRENCH ENTENTE AND MILITARY AND NAVAL STAFF CONVERSATIONS[163]

British opposition to secret treaties and similar understandings was to a large extent based on the strategic fact of Britain's geographic aloofness and relative unassailability, which allowed the postponement of technical arrangements for actual participation in Continental wars until after their outbreak. "Military necessity," however, already during the conservative regimes of Disraeli and Salisbury, seemed to call for Britain's earlier and more careful preparation for entry into such wars, though the temptation would pass. As the end of the Russo-Japanese War drew nearer, upsetting the military equilibrium on the Continent, in which Russia would play a much diminished role for a number of years to come, Britain's balancing position in relation to the Continent appeared greatly endangered. The new power situation was impressed on the Balfour-Lansdowne Conservative Government when the Germans provoked the Moroccan crisis of 1905, seeking, in the most foolish manner, to profit by the changed power situation.

So sudden and so far-reaching was the British break with tradition that Lansdowne seemed at first to offer the French almost more than they could safely take. Following the Kaiser's visit to Tangiers, Lansdowne wanted to enter upon negotiations that might result in staff talks or a military convention. This involved support stronger than the mere diplomatic kind promised to France under the Entente of 1904. "What are we to reply if he suggests that, in view of the formidable possibilities, the chiefs of staff of our navies should meet? This is the sort of proposal we shall get if we accept the idea of a general discussion too readily," Cambon wrote to Delcassé from London (June 1). "Your Cabinet colleagues and public opinion certainly would not follow you and you would be accused of bringing war down on us. So I think it is wiser to reply in terms cordial enough not to throw cold water on Lord Lansdowne's good intentions but vague enough to discourage any suggestion of immediate cooperation." The French Chief of Staff considered the military help immediately obtainable from Britain as almost without value, worth much less, for example, than an alliance with a much smaller country such as Switzerland (June 24). That was also the valuation that the French Cabinet put on the expected British offer when they decided to get rid of Delcassé, who was inclined to rank it much higher and even risk war with its help. That war, according to Premier Rouvier, could bring only "defeat and the Commune."[164]

Late in August, when the immediate danger of war with Germany seemed well past, a new French chief of staff discussed with the permanent officials of the Quai d'Orsay "the practical form and real value of an alliance with England." He had ordered the military attaché in London, Huguet, to study the whole problem very quietly, and estimated that Britain could land 150,000 men between the fifteenth and twentieth day of mobilization on the Continent, where they could be used on the French left wing. "But from a diplomatic point of view, do you think that we shall really see this English alliance an accomplished fact some day?" he asked the diplomats.[165]

Did the French actually receive British offers of military help in the summer of 1905, as has long been assumed? While there may have been orders to the British fleet to be "in readiness to make a descent on the German coast at short notice,"[166] it is now certain that no such offers were made at this time. Contrary to misleading memories, such as Grey's and Lansdowne's of 1925-26, experts from both sides of the Channel did not meet in that summer "as was their business" and talk "indiscreetly, as they always will do" (Lansdowne).[167]

It was left to the incoming Liberals, traditional opponents of secret treaties and naval and military conventions, to arrive at highly informal understandings with France, which grew into the most binding kind of obligation.[168] Although they gave both partners a very uneven sense of obligation and assurance, they committed Britain as effectively as any more formal instrument. Military progress, and the possibility of quick decision on the battle field that was expected by Schlieffen, Foch, and Sir Henry Wilson alike, together with a change in the military balance of forces, seemed to justify, if not to prescribe this change in diplomatic method to the governors of Britain. There was no thorough examination of this situation. Re-examination took place later, partly as a result of the re-growth of Russia's military strength and imperialism, which were never well observed nor appreciated by British military and diplomatic officials of the Liberal regime. Besides, German naval construction later beclouded the issue and helped to make British policy the firm captive of the course it had taken in 1905-06. The reorientation of British policy originated with the fear of war and unpreparedness, and helped so greatly to ready Britain for war that war was less feared and even sought by British sailors and soldiers like Fisher and Wilson. Some of these soldiers and sailors were the bearers of a new tradition which seemed threatened by the change in Government from Conservatives to Liberals. In December 1905, Admiral Fisher, who had earlier sent encouraging messages to Delcassé, told Colonel Repington, military correspondent of The Times, that he was prepared (then? or earlier?) "on his own responsibility, to order our fleet to go wherever they might be required...that he had seen on paper Lord Lansdowne's assurances to M. Cambon, and that they were quite distinct in their tenor. He had shown them to Sir Edward Grey and declared that they were part of the engagements taken over from the last government and would hold good until denounced."[169] Actually, no such assurances had been given, except possibly by Fisher himself to Delcassé.

That such notorious alarmists as Fisher and Repington should try to take care of the enjambement from the Conservative to the Liberal Government in this delicate matter gave the new Foreign Secretary no pause. Naval and military talks with the French seemed to him "sheer precaution."[170] The permanent officials of the Foreign Office did not dissuade him from listening to these outsiders during the December-January interregnum, when the Liberal Party had yet to win the general elections, and the French, with the Algéciras Conference to open in mid-January, had yet to win assurances of continued support in their Moroccan policy from the Liberal Government. That they expected no such declaration before the elections was indicated by Paul Cambon's absence from London at the year's end. This was also in keeping with the peaceful attitude of German diplomacy on the eve of Algéciras.

But this diplomatic interregnum, like a political vacuum, attracted the political soldiers who, not having to win elections, were always à la vedette. Repington started off on December 27 by publishing an alarming article in The Times. Since there was no other disquieting feature in the political and military scene, he attacked the "detestable" inclination of some Britishers to talk about an understanding with Germany. This the colonel wanted to stop, since it would only add to military unpreparedness. While he did not think highly of the military deductions of the article, the French military attaché, Major Huguet, went to congratulate the military correspondent for it. He assured Colonel Repington that it would make an excellent impression. Repington then began to expiate on British politics. He reassured the Frenchman, who was somewhat disturbed about the seemingly greater reserve of the Liberal Government, that they actually were as Francophile as their predecessors, that in this respect Grey shared Lansdowne's views. It was only because he was new in office that he not yet opened himself to the French diplomats. He was equally reassuring about British public opinion. The French must avoid just one thing in their war plans, the violation of Belgium neutrality, which would greatly estrange public opinion.[171]

The French soldier reported the conversation to his superiors, the war minister and the temporary head of the embassy. Repington reported it to Grey who was absent from London, electioneering and fishing, and who answered the newspaperman promptly (December 30): "I can only say that I have not receded from anything Lord Lansdowne said to the French, and have no hesitation in affirming it."[172] How far Grey had actually informed himself about Lansdowne's offer to the French during the few days he had spent in Downing Street, or whether the Foreign Office officials, or perhaps Admiral Fisher, had advised him in his answer, is not known. That a foreign secretary would put such a statement into the hands of a newspaperman showed either high confidence in that man (and, incidentally, in

his military judgment) or indicated that the secretary's novitiate in diplomacy had not progressed very far.

As a Times correspondent and as an ex-officer, Repington had full entrée to practically all of the officials to whom Britain's defense affairs were entrusted at the time: Lord Esher, Sir John Fisher, Sir George Clarke (civilian secretary of the Imperial Defence Committee), General Grierson (head of the Operations Bureau, and the chief of the intelligence section of the War Office). From them he learned the details of British military plans for intervention in case Germany should violate Belgian neutrality.[173] Grierson told him that two divisions could be put into Namur by the thirteenth day of mobilization and the field army as a whole into Antwerp by the thirty-second day. Together with the men just named, Repington worked out a questionnaire, directed at the French General Staff, about Franco-British cooperation in the case of a Franco-German war. He handed it to Huguet with the remark that he "had been sent from the War Office." Huguet hurried at once to Paris to obtain the answers of the French General Staff. On January 12 he showed them to Repington, who then retired, somewhat to Grey's relief, from the negotiations which were to be carried on by the officials, notably Grierson and Huguet. These questions and answers were as follows: (1) Had the French General Staff considered the question of Franco-British cooperation in the case of a Franco-German war? Answer: Yes, they had and hoped for a maximum of British divisions on their own left wing. (2) Could it be assumed that France would not violate Belgian neutrality unless forced to do so by a previous violation on Germany's part? Answer: Yes. (3) What plan of joint operations was suggested? Answer: Without previous knowledge of the ally's strength, etc., it was impossible to make suggestions.

In the meantime, the French naval attaché had had a long conversation with Fisher, whom he considered "the uncontested master of the English Navy thanks to his official position as well as to his personal influence." Fisher initiated his visitor into the naval precautions taken in England for the case of conflict with Germany, as well as into his own views on peace and war on the eve of Algéciras. With the Conservatives, he said, France had been certain of Britain's effective assistance.

That was a thing agreed upon: our naval and military forces were to join yours in case of war with Germany. As regards the new Liberal Government, without being quite as affirmative, I am convinced that nothing will be changed. I know Sir Edward Grey well, I see him often and am advised of his sentiments. He is firmly decided to continue the policy of the late Government as regards France. Public opinion is, besides, so strongly in your favor that it would be impossible not to lend you effective support in case of a conflict. I have, therefore, every reason to believe that we shall march together. While I am thinking and hoping that the war will not break out, I have taken all my dispositions so that the English Navy will be ready for any eventuality...I suppose that you in France have taken your own precautions.

Fisher then proceeded to give the French sailor the dispositions he had made for the case of war with Germany. He expected her to open the war by a brusque attack preceding any declaration of war, like the Japanese attack on Port Arthur. He believed so firmly in this danger—which seems based far more on a sailor's interpretation of German diplomacy than on a study of German naval strategy—that he was presently to mobilize and concentrate all available torpedo boats and submarines at Dover. A British squadron, then near Vigo, could easily join the French at Brest. Should Britain take part in a war against Germany, that country would soon find itself without one ship or one colony.[174] While Fisher revealed what Britain would do in case of a war with Germany, he did not (at least on this occasion) propose the ways in which she and France would, could, or should jointly meet this contingency. He apparently assumed that Britain, as the stronger naval partner, would, after the outbreak of war, lay down and communicate the details, prepared in advance, to the weaker partner and expect him, as in most coalition wars, to accept them without protest or reservations.

While the soldiers and sailors conversed, the civilians in London campaigned for election. Grey and Campbell-Bannerman, a little more apprehensive at the time than the Foreign Secretary that the military conversations might create an obligation or at least an "honorable understanding," controlled the situation less than a Salisbury would have under similar conditions.[175] They allowed themselves to be rushed by all those who had been in office longer than they had been. Cambon returned from his leave in haste in order to make use of the reportedly favorable sentiments of the Liberals. On January 10, he told Grey that, while the eventuality of war had not been discussed between Lansdowne and the French Government in 1905, it now (when actually the war danger was definitely less) seemed desirable that this eventuality should also be considered.[176] None of the actors in this situation was so much the student of history and carrier of diplomatic tradition as Paul Cambon. He, if any one, must have realized that France's alliance with Russia had grown out

of an alarming military situation, that soldiers had initiated it, that they had found the monarch on their side. There was much in the situation of 1906 to remind one of the origins of negotiations with Russia. Soldiers and sailors in Britain were as anti-German as the Russians had been and therefore as ready to seek and give military assistance; Edward VII was as pro-French as Alexander III had been; and British diplomacy seemed far more ready for negotiations than Giers and his assistants had been in the 1890's. It was worth trying to tie the British down more firmly than they had been by the Entente of 1904. That arrangement, as Grey soon realized, since it does not bind the British "hand and foot to the French, makes the latter nervous and suspicious."[177]

Through the French ambassador (and not through Fisher himself?) Grey learned that the French naval attaché had been in communication with the Admiral, "unofficially and in a noncommittal way, as to what help we could give in a war between Germany and France." He thought it advisable to inform the civilian head of the Admiralty about Fisher's initiative. Although Grey emphasized that "we haven't promised any help," he added that "it is quite right that our Naval and Military Authorities should discuss the question in this way with the French and be prepared to give an answer when they are asked, or rather, if they are asked."[178] Fisher had not been asked.

The Liberal Government postponed answering the question as to the help France could expect if attacked by Germany until after the elections, hoping meantime for "a pacific issue favorable to France."[179] Grey, however, did not protest Cambon's suggestion that a break over Morocco would constitute the casus foederis. Nor did he protest Cambon's proposal that "unofficial communications" between the British Admiralty and War Office and the two French attachés should take place "as to what action might advantageously be taken in case the two countries found themselves in alliance in such a war." Such communications had already taken place, either before his taking office or before his approval. They might now be continued with official sanction.

Cambon remarked that the recent fears of war, little founded as they were, had "imposed upon the military and naval administrations of the two countries the duty of studying certain measures and of exchanging semi-officially (officieusement), outside the Governments and by safe intermediaries, certain confidential information." This set Lord Sanderson to making inquiries. As Permanent Under-Secretary of State for Foreign Affairs (1894-1906), Sanderson was the embodiment of Foreign Office tradition and more bent on preserving diplomatic primacy than his successors Hardinge and Nicolson. He asked Grierson what kind of communications had taken place between himself and Huguet. Nothing much, was the answer, beyond mentioning the possibility of the British fighting Germany in Belgium, a problem that Grierson had worked out as a strategical exercise in the spring of 1905. On his own, Grierson suggested to Sanderson that

> if there is even a chance of our having to give armed assistance on land to France or to take the field on her side in Belgium in consequence of a violation of Belgian territory by the Germans, we should have as soon as possible informal communication between the military authorities of France and/or Belgium and the General Staff. There are a great many points which we must settle before we can make our plans for the despatch of a force to join either the French or the Belgian armies, and these we cannot settle without information which the staffs of these armies alone can give us. Then there are arrangements to be made as to the utilization of railways, harbours, billets, transport, and supplies, which would be quite different in a friendly country from those we should have to make "on our own" in a hostile country, and these greatly influence our establishments and consequently the numbers we can put in the field. All these take a great deal of time, and it is exactly that factor which will be wanting on the outbreak of war. To make our help effective we must come at once with every available man. First successes are everything, and if the French could gain those, they would "get their tails up" and all would go well....

Such were the reasons for staff conversations with possible war-allies from a soldier's point of view. Grierson, like the civilians, thought they could be held on the express understanding that they committed the Government to nothing![180]

Grey, having obtained Haldane's agreement with regard to the War Office, and taking Fisher's forwardness for granted, approved the continuance of inter-military and inter-naval conversations. The civilian heads of the Liberal Government were only now catching up with their subordinates, who were authorized to study the matter of armed support "academically," "without prejudice," on a "solely provisional and noncommittal" basis, with the understanding that "we were in no way committed by the fact of having entered into communications." In addition, and as a new thing, the British military attaché at Brussels was to discuss with the Belgian military authorities how British assistance was to be rendered for the defense of Belgium's neutrality in case of war.[181]

By this time, Grey's colleague at the War Office, Haldane, had also come back from electioneering to take part in the conversations that had started without him and, according to the available documentation, had continued largely without him. By his own account, he "at once went to London, summoned the heads of the British General Staff, and saw the French military attaché." He became aware at once "that there was a new army problem. It was how to mobilize and concentrate at a place of assembly opposite the Belgian frontier, a force calculated as adequate (with the assistance of the Russian pressure in the East) to make up for the inadequacy of the French armies in their great task of defending the entire French frontier from Dunkirk down to Belfort, or even farther south, if Italy should join the Triple Alliance in an attack." Consequently, he undertook what he called "a complete revolution in the organization of the British Army," a task which he considered completed by the end of 1910.[182] In the meantime, he more than any other British Liberal leader was, because of his presumed Germanophilia, best suited to misguide the Germans about British-French military understandings. They, like some others, had become suspicious about these arrangements. A French senator asked Clemenceau in November 1906 whether such a convention did exist. He received the famous answer from Clemenceau that he did not know for certain, for he had not yet studied all the treaties of the Quai d'Orsay.[183] As the German ambassador remarked to Haldane, this was a question too indiscreet for a British M.P. to have raised. Haldane replied

> most definitely that a military convention between France and England did not exist, and had not existed; and also that no preparations had been made for the conclusion of one. Whether non-committal conversations between English and French military persons had taken place or not, he did not know. (Kaiser: "Impudence! He, the minister of a parliamentary country, not supposed to know that! He lies!")....It was possible that a General Staff Officer of one country might have expressed himself to the General Staff of another country as to war-like eventualities. He, the Minister of War, however, knew nothing of this. (Kaiser: "Magnificent lies!").

More credulous than his sovereign, the ambassador remonstrated that he had never yet caught Lord Lansdowne or Mr. Haldane in a lie; "they have to start sometime," the Kaiser thought.[184]

Once the Liberal Government had received the overwhelming endorsement of the electorate, Cambon returned on the 31st of January with his question; what British support could France expect in case of a German aggression? Grey thought that a good deal of progress had been made since their previous interview: the military and naval authorities had been in communication and he assumed—

there is no record that he had been kept au cour-ant—that "all preparations were ready, so that, if a crisis arose, no time would have been lost for want of a formal agreement." Cambon was in-formed that the Germans had again been given to understand that, in case of a German attack aris-ing out of the Franco-British Morocco agreements, public feeling in Britain would not allow the Gov-ernment to remain neutral. Cambon was also told that the British people would not be prepared to fight "in order to put France in possession of Morocco." More than ever, Grey felt (or so he said) bound to listen to the popular mandate, even when Cambon reminded him that the conditions of modern war did not allow waiting for the manifes-tation of British public opinion.[185] Only on a popular issue would the British people go to war —Belgium, not Morocco. This was clear enough and need not be put in words; it was better not to have it on the record of diplomacy.

The inter-staff "conversations," as Grey pre-ferred to call them, had not actually gone as far and fast as he had assumed. They were concerned with the expeditionary forces that Britain could offer in case of war, their strength, their mobili-zation schedules (which were accelerated), em-barkation and debarkation; the dove-tailing of French preparations for their reception, quarter-ing, transporting, and supplying; British bases and communications in France, liaison and inter-preters, press, maps, etc.[186] They could only get under way once the conflict between Fisher and the War Office as to the destination of the BEF had been settled in favor of France-Belgium. The Admiral, and even Sir John French, the lead-er-designate of the force, would have preferred to land it on the German coast.[187]

After the tension, the staff conversations seem-ed to lose their urgency in the minds of at least some British leaders. Grey, however, remained under the influence of this experience forever after (as under the influence of an astrological constellation under which his secretaryship had been started). The schemata arrived at in 1906 were kept up-to-date. When they were revised and submitted to him in 1907, Grey approved and the French military attaché was informed of his approval. At the same time, it was made quite clear to the French that "the paper must only be regarded as an expression of the view of the Brit-ish General Staff as to what might be done, under certain circumstances, and that it was not binding on the Government."[188] Whether the schedules were also submitted to Prime Minister Campbell-Bannerman is not apparent. He had from the out-set disliked "the stress laid upon joint prepara-tions. It comes," he pointed out, "very close to an honorable understanding, and it will be known on both sides of the Rhine."[189] He seems to have entertained hopes that things would "blow over" and that all occasion for rendering armed help would be removed. With this expectation in mind, he never, during the few remaining years of his life, informed the Cabinet of the extent of British obligations, and Grey never urged him to do so. Only when composing his memoirs under the public opinion-conscious guidance of Mr. Spen-der did Grey come to see things differently. "I have," he wrote, "always regretted that the mili-tary conversations were not brought before the Cabinet at once; this would have avoided unneces-sary suspicion."[190]

This was not done until 1912, long after Campbell-Bannerman's death in 1908. Grey and Haldane, and later Asquith and Churchill, the imperialist Liber-als, considered the staff conversations as inevitab-le features of imperialist competition and indispens-able parts of an efficient preparation for the war into which Britain might be drawn. However, much distrust of the entangling effects of the doings of general staffs, all general staffs, survived in Campbell-Bannerman, who had not wanted this institution in Britain during his premiership. In April 1907, Clemenceau had proposed that Britain, like France, should introduce conscription in or-der to fully live up to her Continental obligations. Campbell-Bannerman replied that British public opinion, while willing to see the Navy intervene with full force, was much opposed to a military expedition to the Continent.[191] This kind of warning, which Grey never issued, scared the French considerably. Did his people intend a change in their policy? they asked the Franco-phile ambassador, Bertie. Was the Premier per-haps ignorant of the staff conversations of 1906, when the dispatch of some 115,000 British troops had been promised, to be used in Belgium in sup-port of France? Would only maritime support be forthcoming? Grey reassured the French. The chief of the Liberal Government had not pronounc-ed himself against intervention generally. British public opinion would support entering a war only very hesitantly, but once in the war, there would be no limitation on the use of British force.[192]

There had been some reason for Campbell-Bannerman and other Little Englanders to distrust the moves of the General Staff, had they but known how much of the initiative came from that quarter. From October 1906 on under Grierson's successor, Major General Ewart, and with General Nicholson as Chief of Staff (1908-1912), contacts with the French languished, much to Huguet's chagrin. Soldiers such as Ewart and Nicholson still seemed able to restrict themselves to the technical tasks be-fore them. But after Sir Henry Wilson took over the office of Director of Military Operations in August 1910, Anglo-French staff cooperation in the preparation for possible—to most of the military, inevitable—intervention became far more intimate and became much more than technical. In the dedication of his book on Britain's military intervention in 1914, Huguet terms Wilson the "initiator and preparer" of this intervention. This he had taught at the Staff College and this he propagated behind the scenes of British politics, among Cabinet members and leaders of the opposition.[193]

Such convictions, freely and volubly expressed, removed all or most of the reserve in the numerous conversations Wilson had with the French military leaders, notably Foch. Foch was then head of the École Supérieure de la Guerre. Wilson introduced him to Sir Arthur Nicolson at the Foreign Office, thus extending the firm network of top-level permanent officials who felt they were making better preparations for war than their temporary political superiors. At times they were scornful of the attempts of politicians to preserve the traditional British habits of constitutional government and civilian and parliamentary supremacy.[194] Why should not a British-French alliance be concluded? Had not the British-Japanese alliance also been signed without previously informing Parliament, Foch asked Wilson? Firmer understandings between the two governments were necessary regarding their joint action in case of a war between France and Germany. The British must realize that France could not very well reserve so much rolling stock and whole railway lines for the British expeditionary force without previous assurance that she could absolutely count on the arrival of the British contingent.[195] The fact that such convictions were expressed in staff officers' conversations was not the kind of information to be brought to the attention of the Radicals in the Cabinet. Grey ordered that the report of this talk be shown only to Asquith, Morley and Haldane.

In the talks that Wilson had with French officers, more details for cooperation in case of war were agreed upon. The support of practically the whole British Army was pledged, and mobilization was to be accelerated so that the landing of these forces in French ports would be completed by the twelfth day of mobilization. Another political crisis confirmed and tightened these understandings. During the Agadir crisis, on July 20, 1911, the day before Lloyd George's Mansion House speech, Wilson and the French Chief of Staff, General Dubail, signed a report concerning "the new conditions for the participation of an English army in the operations of the French armies in the North East in case of a war with Germany."[196] Although it was called merely a "memorandum of meeting," it represents the nearest approach ever made to a Franco-British military convention. It was agreed that further studies were to be undertaken, including those on the terrain of the likely battlefields over which Wilson and other British officers repeatedly travelled. This agreement provided the technical basis for British cooperation in 1914. The politicians might still believe that there was nothing to bind England. Nevertheless, this "memorandum" went much further than the Franco-Russian convention in technical detail, even envisaging, though in a somewhat veiled form, the placing of the British expeditionary forces under French supreme command.[197]

In his restless activity, including numerous trips to France, Wilson was never hampered or controlled or called to order by "the frocks," as he called the civilians. "He was deeply in the secrets of the French General Staff," writes Winston Churchill. [198] Actually, Wilson was not informed of the French concepts concerning the totality of planned operations.[199] Nor was Wilson always certain whether the French had finally given up all ideas of a preventive offensive against the Germans through Belgium, in spite of his repeated warnings that this would estrange public sentiment in Britain.

The authorization he received for the conversations of 1911 came from the Asquith-Grey-Haldane triumvirate. Only to the Premier did they seem "rather dangerous; especially the part that refers to possible British assistance. The French ought not to be encouraged, in present circumstances, to make their plans on any assumptions of this kind." It does not appear that they were warned by Grey, who answered Asquith that "it would create consternation if we forebade our military experts to converse with the French. No doubt, these conversations and our speeches have given an expectation of support. I do not see how this can be helped."[200] One of these speechmakers was Lloyd George. In 1911, apparently following his Mansion House speech, which seemed to indicate his crossing from the Radical to the Imperialist group of the Cabinet, Lloyd George was informed of the Franco-British military arrangements. The rest of the Cabinet was not initiated until 1912.[201]

With all his ebullience, Fisher, who to the French was "the veritable chief of the British Navy," did not allow his conversations about the role of the British Navy in case of a Franco-German war to reach as great an intimacy as had the military. Definite plans for cooperation resulted neither from the 1906 conversations nor from their resumption at the end of 1908, at the time of the Bosnian crisis. The conversations of August 1911, during the Agadir crisis, led to a verbal agreement about the apportionment of squadrons and commands, organization of forces in the Dover Straits, etc.[202] The failure of Haldane's mission to Berlin in the spring of 1912 was greeted with great relief by the French soldiers. They no longer had to fear that Germany would increase army expenditures at the expense of her navy.[203] The British Government was moved by the mission's failure to bring more ships to the home stations from the Mediterranean in order to oppose the growing threat across the North Sea. The Mediterranean was left in the care of the French Navy.

"The time has arrived for the Staffs to talk matters over and to reach some sort of convention," Winston Churchill told the French naval attaché. The British offers did not at first satisfy the French, since they were based on preserving the liberty of action of both parties in the case of war. As the French saw it, their own concentration of naval forces in the Mediterranean and the consequent denuding of their Channel coast called for a more binding quid pro quo, even though they could not have covered both regions adequately with their own forces. The basis on which an agreement was reached was consultation and concerting as to action to be taken if war should threaten. This, the British wanted to believe, did not "allow the naval arrangements to bind us in any political sense."[204] The agreement was put into final written form in February 1913. It provided for Franco-British naval cooperation and the division of naval labor in the Mediterranean, the Western Channel, the Dover Straits and the Far East.[205]

Before this agreement was concluded, the Imperialist group in the Asquith cabinet though it advisable to take the pacifist-radical majority into their confidence and obtain their approval for the subsequent conversations, if not also for the earlier talks. The revelations left the majority "aghast." Grey allayed the apprehensions of these colleagues to some extent by "emphatic assurances that these military arrangements left us quite free, in the event of war, to decide whether we should or should not participate in the conflict"; this was all part of Grey's habitual concealing of his secret diplomacy from the Cabinet majority, who received no more than "hush-hush allusions to our relations with France, Russia and Germany," while much essential information was "deliberately withheld" from them.[206] They approved an exchange of letters between Grey and Cambon (November 22 and 23, 1912), reiterating that the various consultations among French and British military and naval experts in recent years did not restrict "the freedom of either Government to decide at any future time whether or not to assist the other by armed force"; that they did not "and ought not to be regarded as an engagement that commits either Government to action in a contingency that has not arisen and may never arise. The disposition, for instance, of the French and British fleets respectively at the present moment is not based upon an engagement to cooperate in war." Cambon had pointed out, however, that "if either Government had grave reason to expect an unprovoked attack by a third

Power, it might become essential to know whether it could in that event depend upon the armed assistance of the other." Grey agreed that with such expectation, or in case of a threat to general peace, either Government "should immediately discuss with the other whether both Governments should act together to prevent aggression and to preserve peace, and, if so, what measures they would be prepared to take in common. If these measures involved action, the plans of the General Staffs would at once be taken into consideration, and the Governments would then decide what effect should be given to them."[207]

From this point on, the British Cabinet was informed about the experts' conversations, though still incompletely and only in general terms. The pacifist-radicals did not learn as much as they might have, and that was partly their own fault. There is no record that they demanded or even that they wanted to be better informed. Instead, they refrained from what Grey might have resented as interference with the business of his office. The bureaucratic division of labor had gone so far and was so much respected that the co-determination of British foreign policy, for which the Cabinet was the chosen organ, was lost by default. The various French cabinets, incidentally, also were not well-informed about the cross-Channel negotiations, except for the Prime Minister and the war and naval ministers.[208]

The sense of commitment created by the diplomatic and military-naval conversations varied a great deal from group to group as well as from time to time. Expectation of military assistance to France ran highest in the military circles on both sides of the Channel, and next among the diplomats concerned. Eyre Crowe was to remind Grey, on July 31, 1914, of the "moral bond" implied by the distribution of the two navies.[209] As early as October 1911, Lord Esher of the Imperial Defence Committee told Asquith,[210] who asserted after the war that "there were neither military nor naval compacts," that in his view "the mere fact of the War Office plan having been worked in detail with the French General Staff (which is the case) has certainly committed us to fight, whether the Cabinet likes it or not... It is certainly an extraordinary thing that our officers should have been permitted to arrange all the details, trains, landing, concentration, etc., when the Cabinet had never been consulted."[211] In the mind of the civil servant, the information given the Cabinet in 1912 could only serve to deepen British obligations. This conviction was not shared, at least not by those Cabinet members who resigned in 1914 rather than approve of the war into which the now leading group in the Liberal Cabinet was able to carry the majority in Parliament and in the country by making Germany's action appear as the carefully undefined "unprovoked attack by a third power" referred to in the exchange of November 1912. That the Germans and not the French had violated Belgian neutrality created a sense of liability in many Britishers, since the French had abstained from making this same move, though it seemed highly advantageous to them, too; and in the minds of many Frenchmen, a claim was staked on British help because they had refrained from the march into Belgium.[212]

In the July-August crisis of 1914, British defense officials felt most definitely obligated to come to the help of the French. The French military attaché wrote from London that the British were "thinking of proceeding with the first measures of mobilization" without waiting for the final decision of their Government,[213] while the Cabinet majority still favored neutrality. Grey's assistants, Nicolson and Crowe, reminded him of the consequences of the whole Entente policy. More explicitly than ever before,they warned him that the expectations that England had built up in France forced England to stand by her friends in a just quarrel. "This honorable expectation has been raised. We cannot repudiate it without exposing our good name to grave criticism."[214] The more secret the diplomacy, the stronger the feeling that the pledged word, though never spoken and covered by many reservations, must be redeemed.

As a soldier, Sir Henry Wilson felt such an obligation as strongly as the Foreign Office officials. He thought war unavoidable from July 30th on and began his own activities on the 31st in favor of Britain's entry. He first visited the French military attaché to advise him that Cambon should tell Grey that France would break off relations with Britain unless she rendered the assistance expected from her. The next day, Wilson found the ambassador very bitter, saying that the only question was whether the word "honor" was to be expunged from the British dictionary.[215] But to Wilson personally he was very gracious, as he had every reason to be. Before he and his colleagues could mobilize the army, he proceeded, on the 1st and 2nd of August, to mobilize the Conservative leaders for war. Their sense of British honor moved them to assure Asquith of their Party's unhesitating support. This assurance moved the Government to promise Cambon that Britain would protect France's Atlantic coasts, subject to Parliament's approval.[216] According to Lloyd George, no one wanted war in 1914 but simply skidded into it. If so, Wilson was the one who put more grease on the skids.

During his term in the Foreign Office, Grey communed far more intimately with the members of Britain's permanent officialdom than with the politicians of the Commons. He shared the views of the former with regard to the obligations and honor debts that they, above all others, had incurred. "Grey was a high-minded man, a sincere patriot, a perfectly honorable Gentleman in his dealings with those whom he regarded as equals." But "his belief in honorable dealing did not extend to the House of Commons, since he held the aristocratic opinion that ordinary mortals could not understand foreign politics."[217] On August 3, he told the Commons for the first time of the military and naval arrangements with France, in consequence of which the French Navy was now in the Mediterranean, leaving their Atlantic coasts "absolutely undefended." His own feeling, developed over the years, was that "if a foreign fleet engaged in war with France which France had not sought, and in which she had not been the aggressor," England could not passively stand aside. This assurance had been given the French the day before. This commitment alone, unless disavowed by the Commons, prevented Britain from proclaiming unconditional neutrality. And this was quite apart from the long expected violation of Belgian neutrality and Britain's precarious position in the then likely event of German victory.

AN ANGLO-RUSSIAN NAVAL CONVENTION: SUBSTITUTE FOR AN ALLIANCE

While there was some military justification for the British-French staff conversations (whether or not they were worth the diplomatic entanglement arising from them), there was practically none for the negotiations concerning an Anglo-Russian naval convention. These took place from 1912 on and were initiated by the French and the Russians in order to entangle the British. They were agreed to by the British in lieu of political arrangements, which were not feasible. A naval convention was to stand for the diplomatic instrument that could not be concluded publicly between Liberal Britain and re-autocratized Russia. The utter disparity of the two political systems, little as it meant to sailors and diplomats, could be brought into agreement only by the most secret of instruments, a military or naval convention.[218]

The Russians were informed by the French diplomats and soldiers that Britain had been deeply committed by their staff conversations and that a Franco-British military convention had been in existence since 1912, providing for every detail of cooperation in war and as exhaustive as the Franco-Russian one, with the only difference "that the former bore only the signatures of the chiefs of the two general staffs and was not therefore, so to speak, binding on the government."[219] Even with such limitations, it seemed worthwhile for St. Petersburg to obtain a similar bond. Poincaré recommended this to the Russians. He told them, under the seal of the most absolute secrecy, about Britain's readiness to aid France with her military and naval forces in case of an attack by Germany. Since a military convention between London and St. Petersburg had no foreseeable basis in strategic reality, the Frenchman proposed that Sasonov discuss an Anglo-Russian naval convention on his forthcoming visit to England. This would serve to complete the naval cooperation of all Triple Entente Powers against Germany[220]—an encirclement on water to complement the one on land.

The deduction drawn by the Russian military attaché in Paris from the cross-Channel arrangements was that they brought military superiority to the British-French side, even if Spain should join the Germans. During his visit to Britain in September 1912, Sasonov broached to Grey the proposal of an Anglo-Russian naval convention. The recently concluded Franco-Russian naval convention would give Russia support on her southern flank. Could not Britain do the same in the North and keep the German fleet out of the Baltic? Grey was informed enough to deny this kind of help—which Fisher always thought feasible—because a British fleet might be caught in that sea as in a mouse-trap, should the Germans lay hands on Denmark. Britain would have to confine her operations to the North Sea where she could deal German naval power the most crippling blows. However, Grey informed him of other British assistance in case of war. This was based on the Anglo-French agreement "under which in the event of war with Germany, Great Britain has accepted the obligation of bringing assistance to France, not only on the sea but on land as well, by landing troops on the Continent." He was too polite to suggest that Russia had as yet no navy to give or even to receive the mutual help usually provided for in such conventions. Nor did he, as Fisher and a few other Britishers had done, advise the Russians not to rebuild their navy but to concentrate on their army instead.[221]

Before their naval rebuilding program had gone very far, the Russians approached Grey once more with the proposal of a naval convention. The attitude of the British seemed a bit more promising by the beginning of 1914. Their sailors had even come to a little deal with the usually backward Russians. Would the Russian Government allow them to obtain certain information about a Sikorski airplane and allow talks to take place between a representative of the British Admiralty and the Sikorski people? While emphasizing that the plane in question involved a very important military secret, the Russians, desiring to show their friendly sentiments, were willing to grant the request. At the same time they expressed the hope that the

British would in turn help them to acquire some Chilean warships, then under construction in British naval yards and reputedly for sale. Unfortunately, the Chileans would not sell under any conditions. But, thought the British, this misadventure should not keep the Russians from arranging for the meeting of the Admiralty expert and the Sikorski management.[222]

The Russians chose a state visit of the English royal couple to Paris in April 1914 (the only time Grey ever visited the Continent officially) to review their suggestions, formulated and transmitted with French help, for a "closer agreement" between their two countries, for a better order of the whole Entente system. The best way to do this, they thought, would be by means of a naval convention.

The French Foreign Minister, Doumergue, rather than Isvolski, who was kept out of the way, served as the middle-man. He suggested an Anglo-Russian naval convention in his conversations with Grey, mentioning that Russia was now a better partner on the sea and that in two years she expected to have a strong Dreadnought squadron in the Baltic. Grey pointed to the difficulties he would have to expect from the Russophobes inside the Liberal cabinet and party. In any case, he thought that only a naval convention would be feasible, since all British land forces had already been covered by the Franco-British understandings and Anglo-Russian military cooperation was hard to imagine in any case. While Doumergue would have liked a tripartite agreement, Grey thought such a thing feasible only in the more distant future.[223]

When he returned to London, Grey obtained Asquith's and the Cabinet's approval for Anglo-Russian naval conversations, about which, he says, he never afterwards inquired at the Admiralty, much as if that ostrich attitude could obliterate all the political consequences of such talks. The Russian diplomats were highly gratified by this willingness on the part of the British. The main thing to them was "to replace the up-to-now altogether too theoretical and peaceful basic idea of the Entente by something tangible." The Russian ambassador in London doubted, however, "whether a stronger guarantee for joint military operations in the case of war could be found than in the spirit of the Entente as it is being exhibited now, strengthened by the existing military arrangements." An open alliance with England was inadvisable because of the likely opposition it would meet in England. "Even the Englishman who is firmly convinced that a conflict with Germany is sooner or later unavoidable will shrink from the thought of tying England down by definite alliance treaties, which would impose upon him obligations, the conditions and consequences of which could not yet be foreseen." Sasonov who considered the arrangements desirable from a military point of view, emphasized their general political aspect: "We see in the conclusion of such an agreement an important step in bringing about a closer Anschluss of England to the Franco-Russian alliance."[224]

The Russians had several projects for the London conversations. One hope of the Russian Navy was that England would draw a maximum of German forces away from the Baltic, possibly to the extent of enabling Russia to land troops on the coast of Pomerania. This promising enterprise, a pet project of Fisher, who had been along during King Edward's visit to Reval in 1908, was, however, much handicapped by the lack of transports in the Baltic. The suggestion that the British Government should send a definite number of transports into the Baltic in order to make up for this shortcoming showed how little the Russians understood the difficulties of British war-making. A more definite preponderance of the Entente over the Austro-Italian naval forces was to be sought after in the Mediterranean. If the talks of the sailors were to touch upon the Straits question, all political aspects were to be shunned and only the operational ones considered. The remaining matters to be considered were technical in nature, such as signalling and the periodic exchange of views between the naval staff chiefs.[225]

The Russian naval attaché, thus instructed, found that the British were in no hurry to proceed with the business, that in fact all pressure in favor of it had originated with the French.[226] There was good reason to hesitate at the outset. The negotiations had become known to the Germans through their agent in the Russian embassy in London, and the Germans made press revelations about them in the Berliner Tageblatt of May 19 and later, with the rather peaceful intention, at the time, of giving the British pause on their way into deeper Continental entanglement. The Liberal Government and the British press tried at first to avoid discussion by keeping silent. Then the independent Manchester-Guardian, which best preserved the Cobden-Bright traditions, called for explanations to be given in Parliament before it adjourned. It was, the Guardian pointed out, difficult to imagine an agreement having been reached with Russia during the Paris visit that was not sinister in its nature. When at last the question was put in Parliament as to whether Britain and Russia had entered into a naval agreement and whether negotiations concerning it were pending, Grey gave an evasive answer. What he said was true, but he did not answer the question put to him. He later amplified in his memoirs by stating as a principle that: "Parliament has an unqualified right to know of any agreements or arrangements that bind the country to action or re-

strain its freedom. But it cannot be told of military and naval measures to meet possible contingencies."[227] Even when writing his memoirs, Grey still indicated (or feigned) unawareness of the possibility that these very same military and naval measures might "bind the country to action or restrain its freedom." In fact, Grey limited parliamentary control over the military part of foreign dealings quite as narrowly as any Continental statesman of his day, and the "mother of parliaments" did not seem discontented with the arrangement. Nearly everywhere, before 1914 and after, Liberalism shrank from claiming control over or even cognizance of matters on the secrecy of which military success must depend—or so at least it was argued by those in power.

In St. Petersburg, Sasonov was very disappointed by the slow progress towards the conclusion of a "convention," as the French and Russians always called it. The British tendency to put it off disturbed Sasonov. For example, he would find it difficult to obtain the Tsar's approval of concessions to the British in Tibet without a convention. But his ambassador in London soothed him. Grey only wanted to wait until calm had returned to the international scene. People in Berlin were quite wrought up. They had sent Ballin, the shipping magnate, to London to find out whether an Anglo-Russian naval convention did exist. Grey denied it, and added that it was not England's intention to agree to such a thing.[228] It was a little hard to give démentis and negotiate at the same time, as Grey was forced to do by the Germans, as well as by part of his own Party and part of the British press. But, the ambassador continued, there could be no doubt that the British Government wanted to see the arrangement that had been started in April carried through. Negotiations would probably be resumed during the forthcoming visit to St. Petersburg of Admiral Prince Louis of Battenberg, who filled Fisher's old post.[229]

Viewed from a military-technical rather than a moralistic point of view, the Anglo-French as well as the other pre-1914 agreements for the case of war marked only a slight progress towards an effectively prepared division of labor. The armed forces of the Entente, as well as those of the Central Powers, were still largely conceived of and shaped in the light of the individual needs and ideas of the component states, or even by the ideas of the individual services of the five great European Powers. The German Navy was the outstanding example of rampant service egotism. In general, the soldiers and sailors had only a hazy concept of the requirements of a coalition war. Surprisingly enough, it was Grey, generally an ignoramus in military questions, who as early as 1910, came to view the component parts on either side of the Channel as a military whole, as a pool of strength to which Britain would contribute a navy of maximum strength and France an army also of maximum strength. These views clearly indicate how much Grey had, even at that early date, surrendered the diplomatic liberum arbitrium in favor of military efficiency in the preparation for war. While Grey shrank from the contemplation of "moral obligations" from which "embarrassing questions" might later arise, he instructed the ambassador in Paris that he much preferred that France spend all she could on her army, rather than too much on her navy.[230] Yet it was this military division of labor that increased the moral obligations of each partner to the other.

MILITARY CONVENTIONS OF THE FIRST WORLD WAR

During the transition from Bismarck and Salisbury to Bethmann Hollweg and Grey, the absolute primacy of diplomacy over military considerations was lost on both sides of the North Sea. The soldiers were allowed to hold staff conversations and make "purely technical," supposedly non-binding arrangements with alliance and entente partners for the case of war, arrangements which, if executed, promised victory in war to their own side and which could not be interfered with lest victory be endangered. Without any great effort, the soldiers were able to make the civilians believe that the arrangements they had made were a guarantee of victory in war. No statesman would have resolved upon war in July-August 1914 without such promise and hope. Thus war was undertaken for victory's sake—the military ideal—rather than for the national interest which, rightly or wrongly, Bismarck in his wars and Salisbury even in the Boer War had before their eyes in the shape of tangible aims. In 1914, however, both Germany and Britain, as contrasted with France and Russia who knew what they wanted, were singularly devoid of such specific war aims. Organizational progress in making coalition war, highly incomplete as it remained, swept the statesmen from the firm ground of national interest.[231]

That the war on either side was "marked by a complete absence of coherence," as Joffre has concluded,[232] does not speak in favor of the various military conventions and kindred arrangements concluded before as well as after August 1914 as bases for coalition warfare. The earliest such instrument was a German-Turkish one, providing for "factual supreme direction" of the Turkish forces by the German military mission.[233] It was followed by the Austro-German-Bulgarian Convention of September 6, 1915, arranging for Bulgaria's entry into the war on the side of the Central Powers. As a convention, it was poorly observed from the outset.

Due to setbacks in Volhynia and Galicia, Austria was unable to furnish more than two divisions, and Germany had to substitute for her. Austrian prestige was greatly diminished in the Balkans due to the failure of the 1914 campaign in Serbia. Conrad, although agreeing to actual German command under Mackensen, still demanded a formal Austrian supreme command. The Bulgarians, viewing Austria as little more than another Balkan Power, would not hear of this. They preferred German command as presumably more disinterested. The patched-up compromises for supreme command did not work out very satisfactorily. Contrary to the Convention, the Austrians, at the close of the Serbian campaign, proceeded to the conquest of Montenegro. Driven by the desire to regain prestige, they went ahead without a previous understanding with Falkenhayn, Chief of Staff of the German Field Army, and without consideration of a more rational use of coalition forces. The consequences were disastrous, and they might have been worse if Mackensen had not been such a suitable commander of coalition forces. There was never again any mutual trust between Conrad and Falkenhayn.

Falkenhayn failed in his attempts to establish more effective arrangements for a coordinated direction of the war. These were considerably improved, however, when, in September 1916, his successors in the OHL, Hindenburg and Ludendorff, signed a convention with the three other chiefs of staff of the Central Powers. According to Ludendorff, it gave the OHL "a certain authority which proved useful," notably when the OHL was appealed to by the three other commands in cases of conflicts among themselves.[234]

Italy descended from the auction block of her neutrality by an instrument similar to the Austro-German-Bulgarian convention of 1915, although her terms were considerably more detailed and usurious. Her negotiations with the Entente Powers during March-April 1915 resulted in the London Agreement of April 26. This agreement included the historic assurance, kept by no one more poorly in the past than by Italy, that no separate peace or armistice would be concluded by any of the four contracting parties. It promised her vast territorial gains, largely at the expense of Austria and "the Slavs." A proviso referred to military and naval conventions, which were to be concluded at once by the four general staffs, fixing the minimum strength that Italy was to put in the field against Austria and Turkey and the troop strength that Russia would direct against Austria in order to keep the latter from concentrating her main strength against Italy.[235] The convention was also to settle the problem of the future armistice, which was to be within the competence of the several high commands. The navies of Britain and France were to lend Italy their active and constant help until the Austro-Hungarian fleet had been destroyed or until peace had been concluded.

The negotiations among the military and naval representatives began in Paris on May 1 under the chairmanship of Millerand, the French War Minister, who emphasized especially the need for establishing direct connections among the allied armies and—as an expression of a haunting fear— the need for another proviso against the conclusion of a separate armistice. The main endeavor of the Western Powers was aimed at getting Italy into the shooting war as promptly as possible. The Italian military declared, however, that they could not be ready before the end of May since they had to move considerable forces up from the south of the peninsula and since the roads in the Alps would not be free of snow before May. Due to the unfavorable military situation of the Entente at the time, the War Office and Admiralty in Britain had pressed for granting a maximum of concessions to Italy. On May 21 the British-French-Italian-Russian Military Convention was signed in the Russian GHQ, where the moral stiffening promised by the Italian accession was particularly welcome after the defeats inflicted by the Central Powers' offensive, begun at Gorlice-Tarnov on May 2.

Article I laid down the duty of all signatories to unite for the ultimate aim, victory over the common enemy. The Allies were to act in harmony as far as possible with regard to both their objectives and their operations. By Article II, the Italian Army bound itself to open hostilities not later than May 26. (The actual declaration of war against Austria was made on May 23.) Its offensive intervention was to be supported by the operations of the three other armies, who promised on their part to undertake all possible military measures to keep the enemy from concentrating overwhelming forces against Italy. Article III obliged the three original belligerents to proceed against the Central Powers should they try to interfere with Italy's concentration by a preventive attack. And Article IV envisaged a joint offensive on the part of the two arch-enemies of Austria, Serbia and Italy, in the direction of Laibach. Italian-Serb disunity prevented this contemplated operation from taking place.

The British-French-Italian Naval Convention of May 4 was concluded in the ominous shadow of the Dardanelles enterprise. Under it the three Allies promised to cooperate with the utmost harmony. Their cooperation was to include the formation of an allied fleet in the Adriatic under an Italian admiral. To be the arbiter Adriae was a main preoccuation of the Italians, who insisted that there must always be Allied superiority in these waters,

an imperialist obsession about a mare nostro that was not always conducive to the best common interest.[236]

The Balkan-Latin nation of Rumania followed the example of her sister Italy in many respects by putting herself up for auction between the two camps of the belligerents. Until 1916, there were sound reasons for her hesitation, political as well as military. Among the latter, the question of munitions and other military supplies loomed particularly large. She finally decided to side with the Entente, at a price that Austria was to pay. A treaty of August 17, 1916, settled the political side of the accession and a military convention of the same date the military side. Both were followed ten days later by Rumania's declaration of war on Austria. A special Rumanian-Russian military convention bound Russia to unite with Rumanian forces, once they had entered Transsylvania, and then to march hand in hand on Budapest. Russia was also to send troops into the Dobrudja in order to help Rumania keep Bulgaria in check. The prompt offensive of the Central Powers upset these plans completely and sent Rumania clamoring for Russian help in order to restore a stable front after most of the country had been lost.

The three original Entente Powers had solidified their agreements into a war alliance by the London Treaty of September 5, 1914. By this alliance they undertook not to make a separate peace, and to come to an understanding among themselves about the peace conditions prior to any negotiations with the enemy. These and other war-time diplomatic accords were comparatively easy to establish, since the enemy was to furnish the rewards of victory. The military agreements for the purpose of victory offered far more difficulties. With their heavy initial casualties as the motivating factor, the French high command became the driving force in the endeavor to unify Allied warfare on land. In good French style, they sought to obtain the agreement of the partners in writing. During a meeting of representatives of the Allied Armies at Chantilly in December 1915, Joffre proposed to organize a true battle of coalition for the year 1916, to be directed by himself. He submitted his conclusions in writing to the meeting, which accepted them, with the exception of the Salonika proposals. Nearly a year later, a "plan of action on the part of the coalition, a plan that has for its aim to give to the campaigns of 1917 a decisive character," was again signed by the representatives of the Allied Armies assembled at Chantilly.[237]

The "association" of the United States with the Entente Powers was arranged during the then deposed Joffre's visit to Washington in May 1917. The "association" never took an absolutely binding form—Wilson and his adlatus, House, could on occasion threaten to leave the association and make a separate peace with the Central Powers.[238] However, in conversations with Secretary of War Baker and Generals Kuhn and Bliss of the General Staff, the intentions of the American Government as to the conduct of war and the American share in it were defined and put into writing, altogether as Joffre had proposed it. A "note" submitted by him "was entirely approved of" by Baker on May 14. Joffre informed him that he would communicate it in this form to his own Government. "It constitutes therefore a kind of convention," Joffre thought, "which the American Government has bound itself to execute." In the text it was stated that "with a view to represent as soon as possible the American colors on the French front, the United States will send an expeditionary corps of the effective strength of one division." At the conclusion of the conversations, General Kuhn read the "note," sentence for sentence, English and French. After each sentence Baker (for the Americans) and Joffre's aide (for France) said, "I accept." The session ended with Baker's final declaration: "I approve entirely of the tenor of this note," and Joffre's: "I shall deliver this to the French Government." No signatures were affixed, in accordance with American traditional phobia, "but the contract thus endorsed was scrupulously executed."[239]

Did the understanding constitute a new thing in international military understandings, at least in point of form? Or was it also covered by Wilson's condemnation of "private understandings of any kind" and military alliances in particular? Did this arrangement mar the opening of the new diplomatic era of "open covenants openly arrived at"? Or was the occasion simply one to remind the idealists that military understandings even less than others could be arrived at openly and made known?

MILITARY CONVENTIONS AND STAFF CONVERSATIONS, 1919-1939

The First World War counted treaties and conventions no less than human beings among its many casualties. The German treaties and agreements that were intended for post-war contingencies became dead letters, whether they had been actually signed, as with Turkey, or still under discussion in 1918, as with Austria. Russia's withdrawal from the war in 1917-18, following the Bolshevist Revolution, indicated that military conventions were no more binding to the new regime than any other Tsarist-imperialist obligation. The French ex-partner viewed this default as particularly heinous and as sufficient, or additional, justification for the military intervention against the Soviets. Nothing survived, after Chanak,

of British-French military agreements. They fell into great discredit in the Anglo-Saxon world, due largely to the civilian disappointment with the war's results, the post-war disclosures about staff conversations and the absence of civilian control over them. French policy continued to consider such arrangements indispensable, though improvable.[240] In wide circles, military conventions continued to be held in utter disrepute.[241] To some, they seemed almost responsible for the war. When the need for new military understandings arose, they could not at once be established, due to pacifist opposition and abhorrence. Hitler banked on this in order to get safely through the danger zone of German rearmament. On March 26, 1936, Lloyd George spoke in the Commons against such new entanglements. On March 31, Hitler told a fearfully listening world that "there was great danger that from a general entanglement with military alliances a condition might arise similar to the one to which the world owed in the first place the outbreak of its most terrible and senseless war."[242]

The re-examination of pre-1914 diplomacy and the 1914-1918 experiences with coalition warfare led at first to a reassertion of military sovereignty among the Realpolitiker, including the vast majority of the soldiers. On the part of the "idealists," it led to the idea of doing away with exclusive alliances and conventions by the institution of the League of Nations. The League was to be the great solvent of conflicts, and of exclusive alliances and conventions as the perpetuators of conflict. Seen through French eyes, the League was to be the substitute for the old alliances and military conventions. It was to have at its disposal either an international force of its own or forces of member states acting under a mandate from the League Council against peace-breakers. Few or none of these ideas entered the realm of reality. Instead, new military conventions, usually more onerous and precise than before 1914 and just as secret, were concluded.[243] Such was the Franco-Polish convention of 1921, with its stipulation of the minimum peace-time effectives and reserves that Poland would have to maintain, in return for which she would receive specified French aid. But they remained unequal by far to the exigencies of the total war that the Western Powers allowed to assume its fearful reality.

Belgium: Retirement from Military Convention into Neutrality

Belgium's post-war mood remained at first that of the shocked victim of German aggression, grateful to France rather than to Britain for having saved her. It was in this mood that she gave up her neutrality and entered upon a military convention with France in 1921. This convention, signed by Marshal Foch and the Belgian chief of staff, ranged her squarely by the side of France in case of a new aggression. The concentration of the French Army's left wing was to extend into Belgian territory. Whether further details were elaborated appears doubtful. In February 1929, a Dutch paper published what purported to be an English-French-Belgian staff agreement about the joint concentration of the three armies. The Germans tried for a number of years thereafter to ascertain whether the document was false, or genuine, as the Dutch authorities firmly believed. They had come into the possession of British diplomatic papers that seemed to confirm their suspicion that the so-called protocol might be genuine. Included in the dossier were proposals of the British ambassador in Brussels, made in December 1925, that an agreement with the Belgians should be reached as to landing ports for the BEF, railway transports, minimum strength of forces to be employed, etc. These followed soon after the Locarno pacts, with which they could not easily be squared. Proof was never obtained as to whether the publication in the Utrechtsch Dagblad was a falsification or not. The Germans, however, concluded that its contents were in keeping with realities.[244]

No known changes in the joint French-Belgian plans were effected after the Locarno pacts or the evacuation of the Rhineland in 1930. The Maginot Line strategy of the French made it increasingly likely that Belgium, rather than France herself, would be the theatre of the future war to the eastward. As early as 1926-27, the French had concluded that, for various reasons, a Maginot Line along their Northern frontier was not feasible and that its defense would either have to take place forward, on Belgian soil, or farther to the rear. The best line of defense for France and Belgium as a whole would be formed by a prolongation of the Maginot Line northward on the Belgian-German border, and it seemed only fair to many of the French officials and politicians concerned with defense problems that France should help Belgium build such a defense system by granting her a substantial "loan." But Pétain and other partisans of a mobile defense on Belgian territory, unhampered by a fortified line, won out. Some of them were determined to enter Belgium in case of war, even against her own will. We must, they argued, "carry ourselves into Belgian territory in order to ensure the defense of our Northern region" (1932).

The feeling of having become a mere object of French strategic considerations finally made Belgium such an unwilling partner that by 1936,

the time of the remilitarization of the Rhineland, she felt more aggrieved by French proposals to consider counter-measures by way of an attack across her soil in the direction of the Ruhr than endangered by a renewal of the German threat. As late as May 1936, the Belgian General Staff agreed to plans for the entry of a French army into Belgium to operate north of Namur. However, the horror of having their country serve once more as the battlefield of the giants proved overwhelming to the civilian governors, including young King Leopold, and made them once again seek Belgium's neutrality as the best way of "keeping war away from our territory." In a joint note, France and Britain recognized and guaranteed the new neutrality (April 24, 1937). Belgium, also released from her Locarno obligations, was determined to defend this neutrality against threats from all sides, including France, which seemed at times so dangerously allied with Red Russia. All French warnings of the likelihood of a German surprise attack through Belgium proved in vain. Such an attack would make it a hopeless task for France to come to her aid. Assistance could be made effective only if called in "preventively." Nothing but a vague understanding between the two general staffs remained. Gamelin assured the Belgian chief that his sentiments towards the Belgian Army had not changed in the least and that the French Army would carry out the plan of support and would in any case do all that was possible for its allies of the last war.[245]

The Little Entente

While the Western nations struggled with their conscience over the nature of their military ties and pondered whether they were more useful or more dangerous,[246] a whole new network of alliances and conventions sprang up in the Balkans. The Little Entente (so-called derisively or defiantly) was the system intended for the preservation of the status quo established at Paris in 1919. Now largely "saturated," the partners established their system for the defense of the Treaty of St. Germain as readily as they had established their pre-1914 conventions de guerre. They were still anti-Hapsburg and, as was felt in London, also anti-British, in so far as they contributed to the establishment of a French hegemony upon the Continent. Lord Curzon regarded them "almost as a personal affront," if not also as an affront to British notions of a Continental balance of power.[247]

France, the original patrona of the "succession states," had for a while seemed disappointed with the new order as established at St. Germain. By the time the first anniversary of that treaty approached, she was almost willing to see a Hapsburg restoration come about and to allow Hungary a certain amount of "revisionism." On August 14, 1920, therefore, Czechoslovakia and Yugoslavia assured one another of mutual assistance in the case of an unprovoked attack by Hungary, and agreed to refrain from concluding any alliance with a third Power without the consent of both signatories. The treaty was to last for twenty years. A military convention settled the modalities of armed assistance.[248] From Belgrade, where this agreement had been signed, Beneš, the most active creator of the Little Entente, proceeded to Bucharest where, on September 17, he negotiated another entente. Rumania entered into obligations similar to those established between Czechoslovakia and Yugoslavia.

The first test of this grouping took place following the putsch of ex-Emperor Karl on Easter, 1921. The three governments presented Hungary with an ultimatum either to force the Emperor to leave the country by a certain date or to take necessary measures to settle the Hapsburg question. Under the impact of this restoration attempt, Rumania concluded alliance treaties with Czechoslovakia (April 23, 1921) and, later in the year, with Yugoslavia (June 7), both accompanied by military conventions. The treaties were made public; the conventions were not.[249] This marked the final establishment of the Little Entente. A second restoration attempt in Hungary in October 1921 also failed. Both attempts failed, according to Beneš, "only because they met with the combined armed resistance of Czechoslovakia, Yugoslavia and Rumania," a resistance which included partial mobilization in the three countries.

The following year brought a further strengthening of the tripartite alliance for the purpose of maintaining the status quo in East Central Europe. The foreign ministers of the three original partners met at Marienbad. Poland was also represented, but she declined to join the new pact. The question of Teschen kept her forever at loggerheads with the Czechs. The quarrel was one that no amount of French conciliation efforts could remove, then or later.[250] However, Poland entered on somewhat looser agreements with the Little Entente members. They would be bound to render armed help if Poland were attacked by one or more Powers. In the case of an attack on any of the Entente Powers, Poland, already bound to Rumania by a military convention aimed at Russia, would either declare a friendly neutrality or would intervene actively in favor of the Little Entente. At the Bucharest meeting of November 1925, another attempt to draw Poland closer to their triangle came to naught when the Czechs insisted on a more cautious treatment of the casus belli with Russia.

The military center-piece of the Little Entente was the secret tripartite military convention signed by Czechoslovakia, Yugoslavia and Rumania on September 14, 1923. This replaced all previous understandings directed against Hungary. It stipulated that, in case of an attack by "revisionist" Hungary against one of the signatories, the other two would start their mobilization within forty-eight hours and complete it within twenty days. It also laid down the zones of concentration of the three armies and the minimum number of divisions that each would have to mobilize.[251]

Hungary was not a serious enough enemy to keep the Triplice firmly together. Some of the members had more dangerous enemies to fear. Rumania, the not always happy possessor of Bessarabia, had to view Russia as her enemy. So did Poland. From an early date, these two states allied themselves against the successors of the Tsars. Neither Czechoslovakia nor Yugoslavia, for political or for geographic reasons, would consider Russia as a likely potential enemy. At the same time, the Czechs and Rumanians could not share Yugoslav enmity for Italy, and the Czechs remained foreign or aloof to the antagonisms between "revisionist" Bulgaria and her immediate neighbors. From beginning to end these were "the inner contradictions" of the Little Entente.

Beginning in 1923, the instruments on which the Little Entente was based provided for annual meetings of the three foreign ministers "in order to discuss additions and changes of the existing agreement or its unchanged continuation." Meetings of the chiefs of staff were also provided for, although little is known about them. When they met at Belgrade in November 1935, they did so, according to an official announcement, for the purpose of "exchanging views regarding the recent autumn maneuvers." They could, however, hardly have avoided discussing the implications of the recently concluded Czech-Russian military agreements.[252] All three were sensitive to the advent of National Socialism to power and to the renewed revisionist agitation in Hungary. In February 1933, at a meeting in Geneva, the three Little Entente members arranged for a Pact of Organization with a standing council and a permanent secretariat to carry out closer co-ordination of policies and to provide for economic collaboration. Military collaboration was not specially mentioned among the purposes, probably in deference to the Western Powers, who frowned upon military preparations made too openly at a time when disarmament negotiations, though hopeless, had not yet come to a final close.

By the Treaty of St. Germain, the Eastern states were founded on the design of keeping Germany weak, rather than making the succession states strong and defensible and able sooner or later to replace Russia, the one-time military ally of France in the East.[253] Shortly after the war, France, overcoming some temporary aloofness, became the tutelary deity of the small Eastern nations. Poland appeared as the strongest military entity among all the states between the Baltic and Black Seas. She received assistance from France that contributed to the victory over the Red Army in 1920. And France concluded with her a political alliance and a secret military convention. The latter was signed by Foch and the Polish minister of war on February 19, 1921. It was the civilian heads of the French Government at the time—Millerand was President, Briand Premier and Barthou War Minister, all three of them ministrables of pre-1914 vintage—who had rushed into these treaties. It was they, rather than the soldiers, who wanted to "reconstitute 'a barrier in the East' and make Franco-Polish collaboration against Bolshevist Russia and Germany an essential element of European stability." These civilians secreted themselves with Pilsudski during the latter's visit to France and worked out the instruments, while Foch and the other generals cooled their heels before the closed doors of Millerand's cabinet. Their categorical objections against France's commitments as "far too extensive" were overruled. They bowed before civilian supremacy.

The commitments included mutual "efficacious and rapid," though not quite automatic, assistance. The sanction of the French Parliament would be required. "Constant consultations as to the necessary means and preparations" for fulfilling the obligation were provided for in the Convention, which envisaged a German attack on either country as well as the case of war between Poland and the USSR. In the case of such wars, France was to act on land and sea in order to assure Poland's security vis-à-vis Germany. She was also to assist her in defense against the Red Army. The two general staffs were to maintain "constant understanding as to the preparations and the means required for the execution of the decisions based on the convention and for the maintenance of the communication lines between the two countries." France promised Poland materiel and financial help, as well as technical personnel, but she would not promise the expedition of French units in case of a war. Poland was to maintain, in time of peace, nine cavalry brigades, thirty or more infantry divisions, and the necessary reserves.

The Locarno pacts guaranteed the status quo of Germany's Western frontiers far more securely than those in the East. This made French and Polish mobilization and assistance dependent on Article 16 of the League Covenant. In Polish eyes, this seriously weakened French support. A persistent slackening of the ties between the Seine and the Vistula followed, although France and Poland had cautiously agreed at Locarno to lend one another immediate aid and assistance in case failure on Germany's part to fulfill her pact obligations should lead to an unprovoked armed conflict. A secret protocol of March 22-April 13, 1926, settled in detail the cooperation of the French and Polish intelligence services in the pursuit of their tasks vis-à-vis Germany and the USSR. In June-July 1928, staff conversations concerning a revision of the Convention of 1921 took place in Paris. Each party tried either to introduce changes or to preserve obligations that favored itself. France endeavored to make Poland standardize her equipment along French lines and to persuade Poland to release her from the now unrealistic obligation of keeping the sea lanes open. The Poles wanted to make France deposit considerable supplies in their country in time of peace, which would remain French property but would be turned over to Poland in case of war. They also wanted to retain the explicit naming of Germany and Russia as possible aggressors. No agreement on these points was reached, then or later. During the remainder of Pilsudski's regime, the convention became largely a dead-letter agreement, with only the exchange of information of the intelligence departments still operative. The French military mission in Warsaw lost its importance at an early date and was recalled.[254]

The Maginot Line became a military expression of the Locarno pacts. Both were signs of that purely defensive spirit that was unlikely to undertake the offensive deep into Germany, although only such an offensive could bring military aid to the Eastern allies of France. Nevertheless, France preserved her old political and military arrangements with them or proceeded to negotiate new ones. Relations with Rumania, not a Locarno partner, were based on a series of accords of June 10, 1926. There were few formal military ties between France and Yugoslavia. The French sought them even less than did the Yugoslavs, who were suspicious of French understandings with their arch-foes, the Italians. In 1928, when Belgrade hinted that it would like to see regular general staff conversations take place with a view to fixing the terms of eventual military cooperation, the French were not encouraging. Such conversations did not seem opportune. No extensive study was undertaken until at least 1930[255]—it could serve no good purpose as long as France could hope for a continued military understanding with Italy. When these hopes came to an end, it was not France but Italy, acting together with Germany, who drew the Yugoslav governors near her.[256]

Czechoslovakia's value to France was, or seemed, infinitely greater than Yugoslavia's. From the

beginning of her independence she had been a fos-
ter-child of France, which maintained a military
mission in Prague to the last. The treaty of alliance, signed on January 25, 1924, followed rather
than preceded the military ties. The two states
bound themselves to come to an understanding on
those matters of foreign policy likely to endanger
their security, as well as on measures suitable to
safeguard their common interests in case they
should be threatened. A secret exchange of notes
on January 26 and 31, 1924, provided that the two
general staffs were to continue their collaboration
"as regards the establishing of concerted plans for
the purpose of parrying an aggression directed
against one of the two countries by a common enemy [a euphemism for Germany] as well as regards the study of the means of mutual resistance
in case the common interests should be threatened."
Collaboration was never very active, except through
the French military mission in Prague. A first
meeting of the two general staffs, held in January
1924, was never followed by a second.[257]

Czechoslovakia's utterly exposed and encircled
position and her vast minorities, from whom the
Czech governors could not fairly expect more
loyalty as citizens and soldiers than they themselves had rendered the Double Monarchy, made
her a most faithful satellite of France. The advent of National Socialism and the accentua-
tion of the Sudeten German problem could only
serve to increase this dependency. At first the
French declined to be greatly alarmed by the military consequences of Nazism. France "must do
everything together with her allies, and nothing
without them," Daladier told the Czechs in 1933.
Responsible Frenchmen predicted that, for at
least three years to come, France would have the
superiority in effectives, and for ten years in
point of materiel.[258] In 1935, when Hitler denounced the disarmament provisions of the Versailles Treaty and reintroduced conscription,
Beneš declined to take too tragic a view of the
event. Although very serious and fraught with
consequences for the future of Europe, it might
yet serve to clarify the diplomatic situation:

Aside from the great disadvantage, the introduction of conscription in Germany has the
advantage that we now leave behind the earlier
fictitious and paper superiority of the French
bloc and come to a state of reality in which
everyone sees where he stands, in which Italy
and Britain are clearly forced to go together
with France and in which the bloc of the great
powers vis-à-vis Germany must move into
a common front and henceforth must conduct
something at least of a common policy. Czechoslovakia will proceed together with the bloc
of the great powers and strictly continue her
present policy. In addition to France, Italy and
Russia, and eventually England as well, will
from now on take a larger interest in Czechoslovakia. The diplomatic position of Czechoslovakia is growing ever more important. Our
ministers plenipotentiary from now on must
point out systematically the importance of
our geographic position and our military, political and diplomatic importance generally.[259]

Russia had been attentive to the dangers much
earlier. In November 1933, she had initiated negotiations for a Franco-Russian alliance. This resulted in the pact of May 2, 1935. This was a mutual aid pact for the case of an unprovoked aggression and not an old-style military alliance, something in bad repute with Britain, whom France was
not willing to estrange, even for such a price.
"From the outset," Foreign Minister Flandin declared during the discussion about ratification,
"the concept of an alliance analogous to the pre-
war kind had been resolutely put aside."[260]
Subsequent Russian attempts, as in 1937, to arrive
at closer military relations with France remained in vain for a variety of reasons.[261]
These included an over-estimation of the military
value of the smaller East European Slav states
and an under-estimation of Russia's power. By
the time of the first German-Czech crisis in
March 1938, the French had come to doubt the
strength of the Red Army. The military experts
in Paris were divided and the civilian politicians
generally in doubt as to the value of the Russian
assistance to be expected under the Treaty. According to German observation in Paris, "even if
the active assistance that may be expected from
Russia is not too highly assessed, the military
are nevertheless in favor of keeping the Treaty
in force because it will keep Russia, that vast
reservoir of raw materials, closed to Germany
and because in the event of a war a part of the
German Army will be tied down by the Soviet
Union."[262]

On May 16, 1935, closely following the moves
of French policy, Czechoslovakia complemented
the Franco-Russian pact with a Russian mutual
aid pact of her own. The pact bound Russia to
come to her aid, provided France did so too.
Although conservative Czechs, notably the officers, put little trust in the arrangements, they
received more military implementation than the
Franco-Russian pact ever did.[263] By means
of an air convention, Bolshevism received bases
in the heart of Europe (as German propaganda
put it), while it appeared highly doubtful whether
Rumania would even allow Russian planes to fly
over her territory. From the outset, Polish and
Rumanian fears of Russia and of Bolshevism
threatened to make all hopes of bringing Russian

help to Czechoslovakia illusory. Realizing this all too well, Beneš, following Pilsudski's death, when some reasonableness seemed to return to Polish policies, attempted once more to bring about better Czech-Polish relations. He sought the help of the soldiers—the chief of the French military mission in Prague, Gamelin, and Smigly-Rydz—in this endeavor, which could only contribute to the better security of all three states concerned. He assured the Poles, and incidentally the French, that he had always wanted to come to better terms with them, that he had tried three times since 1933 to establish a treaty of friendship with Poland, that he had scrupulously avoided accepting any guarantee from Russia that might seem to be directed against Poland. He had never received an answer to his propositions from Poland. In the summer of 1936, when Beneš' proposals were handed to Smigly-Rydz by Gamelin, acting as the honest broker, the successor to Pilsudski gave assurances that Poland would never take part in operations against Czechoslovakia. In case of an attack on her, Poland would be faithful to her obligations under the League of Nations and the Czechs need not waste their money on extending their fortification lines eastward along the frontiers with Poland. Polish morgue never gave a more direct answer—until 1938, when Polish troops crossed the frontier that Czechoslovakia had left unfortified.[264]

At the outset of the 1938 crisis, the French declared that they were resolved to go along with Czechoslovakia, should she be attacked by Germany and threatened in her independence. While the French General Staff affirmed its belief in the strength of Czech fortifications, the Quai d'Orsay expected the English to stand by France in the support of Czechoslovakia and assured Prague that French aid would be prompt, faster even than they expected.[265] Foreign Minister Delbos informed the British of France's decision to consider any aggression against Czechoslovakia as one directed against herself and asked them to consider how German intentions vis-à-vis Czechoslovakia could be thwarted. But subsequent Anglo-French talks (in London, April 27-29) produced no British promise of aid—for one reason because it appeared impossible to render Czechoslovakia any military help. From the military point of view, Secretary of War Hore-Belisha told American diplomats, the fate of Czechoslovakia was sealed.[266] And finally Poland proved utterly unhelpful in the crisis. He did not understand her policy, the French foreign minister told the Polish ambassador after his return from London, least of all her policy regarding Czechoslovakia, toward whom France had obligations with which Polish policy seemed

to want to interfere. Rather Poland should consider whether, in the case of German aggression against Czechoslovakia and the latter's defeat, France would still be in a position to render military assistance to Poland.[267] Czechoslovakia's Little Entente partners, while not as hostile as Poland, proved no more helpful. Rumania informed her, and Berlin, that she would not permit the passage of Russian troops through her territory. The Yugoslav Premier told the Germans that he intended to bring the matter up at the summer 1938 meeting of the Little Entente and there to support the Rumanian stand.[268]

Franco-Polish Military Ties

"Internal contradiction," the favorite Russo-Marxist expression, could be applied most appropriately to the military-political system in the European East, which France patronized. France was forever unable to bring Poland to reason, or so she thought. And according to the Czechs, Poland was never a sincere friend of military cooperation with France and even less of a one with Czechoslovakia.[269] Poland's policy of the free hand had no basis in any superior condition of the Polish Army. The Army suffered greatly from the economic depression of the early 1930's and almost as much from neglect at the hands of the "colonels" who were running the country and who allowed the Army to rest on the doubtful laurels of the battle of Warsaw. At the time, Poland seemed utterly lost to France. In fact, people at the Quai d'Orsay wondered whether there was not, in addition to the Polish-German non-aggression pact of 1934, a secret one, which, in the case of a European war, would have placed Poland on Germany's side, possibly for the dismemberment of Czechoslovakia.

According to Noël, the French ambassador to Warsaw, the Franco-Polish alliance, as a measure for war-preparation, represented backwardness rather than progress when compared with the pre-1914 arrangements of France. Although "essentially a military alliance," he pointed out, "relations between the two armies had practically ceased for some time...The Military Convention of 1921 settled no details...It was a political rather than a technical agreement...Strange as it may seem, never in the course of the fourteen years [to 1935] had the two General Staffs tried to fix things in concrete terms." (This is somewhat too sweeping, since there had been military conversations in 1924-25.) Both as soldier and as diplomat, Beck agreed that the state of things was unsatisfactory. He told Noël repeatedly during 1935: "We have no illusions, we know that our alliance with you is unilateral; if you were attacked by Germany, Poland would march because it would be to her interest; but the opposite does not hold; we do not forget the press campaigns in France with the slogan: 'We shan't fight for the Corridor.'"[270]

Following Pilsudski's death in May 1935, a new rapprochement between Poland and France and their armies was tried. But the French refusal to follow Poland's renewed suggestion that Hitler be stopped by a preventive war, on the occasion of the Rhineland re-militarization, threw relations between Colonel Beck and the Quai d'Orsay back into the old jarring groove. Shortly after the rise of the front populaire, the Smigly-Rydz regime tried to place a rearmament loan in France. It seemed unobtainable below an interest of eleven per cent. The enemies of the "colonels" at home, such as General Sikorski, were also partisans of an understanding with Prague. They advised the French not to grant the loan without definite political assurances, including the removal of Colonel Beck. Otherwise no reliable change in the course of Polish policy could be expected.[271]

Neglecting the opportunity for imposing such conditions, the front populaire Government decided that Poland's vast military potential— thirty-five million inhabitants, with only one half of the military manpower receiving training— must not be neglected any longer and that the backward army must be modernized. Here, at least one cause of Russia's inability to serve France effectively in 1914-17 came under consideration: Should Poland be encouraged and given the funds to build up a better, more self-sufficing war industry? For the time being, the Czech Skoda Works were the arms producers for the Little Entente, including even Poland. And hopes were still entertained that some day Poland would come to terms with Czechoslovakia, perhaps under the threat of a German-Russian rapprochement along Bismarckian lines. "It would not hurt," the Czech and French representatives in Warsaw agreed in April 1937, "if the Poles became aware that a possible agreement between the Germans and the Russians would be at their expense."[272] But only after the Skoda works had fallen under German control and were producing for the Germans and the Russians did Gamelin, in May 1939, urge the Poles to develop their own war industries and locate them in a more secure locality than Upper Silesia.

Gamelin's first trip to Warsaw, in August 1936, reminded him of the regular eastward journeys of his predecessors in the office of Chief of the General Staff before 1914. He soon realized that it was even more difficult to come to a "convention about operations" with the Poles or the Red Russians than it had been with the Tsarist Russians.

He tried to explore the ideas of Poland's soldiers as to military collaboration against Germany, together with France, Czechoslovakia, and Russia. The military situation had changed considerably and was still changing for the worse, as Gamelin unrolled it to them. A simple knockout blow against Germany was no longer feasible, as it had been in 1933 and even early in 1936. France must henceforth think of the use of her forces not only in the opening stages of a war, but for the later stages as well. Consequently, Gamelin urged the Poles to place themselves "in a position to resist an initial German attack." The best way to do that would be to build fortified lines along part of their frontiers, and above all on the two wings, opposite East Prussia and Silesia— Maginot everywhere! The Czechs would cooperate at the left wing, Gamelin suggested. He offered his mediation once more, but the Poles would not hear of "those so-called Slav brethren." The still bigger brother, Russia, was even more odious to them. They would concede nothing beyond temporary landing fields for Russian planes on Polish soil. When Gamelin suggested a Russian movement in case of war with Germany to be directed through Lithuania against East Prussia, the Poles declined such help on their right wing as well. Their argument was that, once the Bolshevists entered Lithuania or Poland itself, they would never leave again.[273]

French pessimism as to Poland's ability to fight a war of the kind that had henceforth to be envisaged was obvious enough, except to the Poles themselves and a number of civilian politicians. At times, the French were not even certain whether the seeming intimacy between Germans and Poles would not grow into an alliance against Russia. French diplomats and soldiers wanted to avoid such an eventuality under any circumstances. This accounts in part for the hesitation about implementing the Franco-Russian Pact. They feared to make it appear as directed, even in the slightest, against Poland.[274] Other hesitations arose, either from the distrust of Russia's military value as an ally or of her role as the active center of Communism. With these fears in mind, Laval told the Cabinet on the eve of the ratification of the Soviet Pact that he had taken the most dangerous features out of that instrument. And he added: "All the same, I distrust them. I do not want them to drag France into a war...The French always congratulate themselves on account of pacts, but they don't see the counterpart." Much better to live in peace with Germany![275]

Soon after Gamelin's visit to Warsaw, Smigly-Rydz, together with the chief of staff, came to visit Paris and the French army. Rearmament credits up to two billion francs were opened to Poland, with practically no strings attached--not even the promise to remove the fatal Beck or to become reconciled with Czechoslovakia. "Even on the purely technical plane our generals completely failed to take advantage of the occasion," said Noël afterward. The military strengthening of the Polish alliance partner by French loans was proportionately as much below similar past help to Russia as the franc of 1936-38 was depreciated below that of 1900. Instead of forming a common front together with Czechoslovakia, a logical though no longer a very hopeful military move, Poland allowed Hitler to take Czechoslovakia. Poland played the jackal. She massed and shot across the Czech border the troops that she had previously withdrawn from the German frontier. The acquisition of Teschen in no way strengthened her for the coming conflict with Germany, whose talon now began to point to Danzig and the Corridor, or a corridor through the Corridor. With Czechoslovakia, her most loyal follower, lost, with Russia aloof and scornful of France's failure in the Munich crisis, what remained in the Franco-Polish alliance that was of real military value to France? Were not her governors told again and again by Ribbentrop that her "military alliances in the East were clearly an atavistic remnant of the Versailles Treaty and of the Versailles mentality? A strong Germany would never have tolerated such military alliances, but a weak Germany was obliged to acquiesce in them. But at the moment of the revival of her power, it was clear that this kind of policy of encirclement must sooner or later be shaken off as an intolerable state of affairs, whether by means of negotiations or by some other means."[276]

Shortly after Munich, France's diplomatic and military representatives at Warsaw re-examined the situation and "the full bearing" of her commitments. They concluded that they "should be allowed to stand only to the extent to which we have the means and the will to face, if need be, the obligations devolving from them." Since March 1938, the danger to Poland from Germany had grown so much that the casus foederis had to be contemplated as something that would arise suddenly from Germany's unprovoked aggression. The French obligations for this case could not have been "more precise or more extensive." The occasion for them would arrive with the German demand for Danzig and the Corridor, something that French public opinion showed little readiness to fight for. The unequal give-and-take in the alliance—the typical problem for the Great Power when confronted with the alternative of either fighting for the subsidy-recipient or allowing it to perish—led Ambassador Noël to propose that it be re-fashioned. Obligations should be re-defined and the risks, "which are too vague and too wide," limited. It seemed preferable to reduce the alliance to a mere treaty of friendship and consulta-

tion, with the "automatism" of instant military help removed. The never concretely defined joint military dispositions should be agreed upon. The seventeen-year period of evasion, during which the Poles and also the French had constantly tried to leave the actual commitments undiscussed and untranslated into concrete military detail, should be ended.

On a visit to Paris in November 1938, Noël found the military chiefs of France, Weygand and Gamelin, in agreement with his views. They wanted less automatism in the assistance to Poland, and also wanted to reconsider whether the recent supplying of Poland with modern equipment was to continue, to the detriment of France's own requirements. The civilian heads of government were not persuaded that this was necessary. Foreign Minister Bonnet proved to the Ambassador that legalistically "our agreements with Poland contain enough fissures under all circumstances to keep our country protected against war (à l'abri de la guerre)." Eventually succumbing to a still more complete dependency on British policy, the French ministers agreed to reinforce rather than reduce the commitments to Poland. They were, according to Noël, inwardly reassured by the thought "that if our rich collection of pacts did not deter Hitler from a general war, they would at the last moment, by some ingenious formula, manage to elude our most precise and most formal agreements."

Britain's rather desperate determination to help Poland contributed very little to the improvement of the atmosphere in which further Franco-Polish attempts to clarify the obligations under the Military Convention took place. Gamelin wished to avoid precise conversations with the Poles before matters had been discussed and clarified with the Russians. Without their support, "a prolonged Polish resistance was unthinkable." However, while Bonnet was negotiating a new political agreement in conformance with the British guarantees, the Polish War Minister, General Kasprzycki, thought it appropriate to appear rather suddenly at Paris, to the annoyance of Gamelin, in order to negotiate a military protocol. The French generals showed a complete lack of curiosity about Polish war plans. They limited their conversations to such generalities that the Polish officer, though authorized to disclose his country's war plans, refrained from bringing the matter up. The Frenchman explained that his own plans "had to be very flexible," since many unknown factors were apt to enter into the calculation. His idea was that whichever of the two partners, France or Poland, was not faced by Germany's main forces should try to tie down a maximum of these on its own front. Kasprzycki showed the better knowledge of German war plans when he argued that the initial German effort would fall on his own country in the form of a surprise attack by motorized forces. Gamelin was willing to forego the demand for a decisive effort on Poland's part in case France was attacked first, since that might exhaust her ally prematurely. When the discussions proceeded to naval and aviation problems, the representative of the French air forces, much against Gamelin's intentions, committed himself well beyond what seemed reasonable by saying that "the French Air Force can from the outset act vigorously with a view to relieving Poland." This promise went considerably beyond what the French air forces were actually in a condition to deliver. The Poles, conscious of their own shortcomings in the air, were greatly encouraged by this promise, which was then put into an "unprecise formula." This "kept the future open," as Gamelin put it.

When they came to discuss the likely distribution of the German forces against themselves, the Poles' guess was again better. They estimated the force to be directed against their frontier at seventy to eighty divisions, with only twenty deployed against the French at the outset and eighteen to twenty placed along the frontiers of the neutrals. France, Gamelin insisted, would face many more divisions on her border. Would the mass of the French forces be able to undertake an offensive within less than a fortnight, the Poles asked? A fortnight was more or less the period envisaged, said Gamelin. If the main German endeavor were to be directed against Poland, would these forces be expected to cross the frontier and undertake an offensive against Germany? They would, Gamelin assured the visitors. The sixteenth day of mobilization was laid down in the Protocol as the starting date of the major French operations which, Gamelin thought, the Poles themselves did not expect to be directed against the Siegfried Line. (Against what, then, did he expect them to be directed? Against Belgium?)

The Poles submitted the draft of a "final Protocol," saying in the preamble that "in case of German aggression against Poland, or of a threat to Danzig that would lead to armed action on her part, the French Army will automatically go into action with its various armed forces." Gamelin insisted that this must be preceded by a declaration that "the French and Polish High Commands were acting within the framework of decisions taken by the two Governments." The text of the Protocol, agreed upon on May 17, said: "As soon as a part of the French forces shall be ready (about the third day after the initial day of the French general mobilization), France will unleash progressively offensive actions with limited objectives. As soon as the principal German effort is clearly seen as directed against Poland, France will unleash an offensive action against Germany with the gros of her forces (beginning the fifteenth day following the initial day of French general mobilization)."[277]

Before this was signed, Gamelin expected that the political agreement under negotiation would be ready. Bonnet, who had learned by accident that the military protocol was being discussed, insisted that the military understanding had to depend on this political agreement. Until this was done, Gamelin did not consider the Protocol as binding. Of this he was rather glad, "especially because of the Air Force clause," and more subconsciously because of his own feeling of helplessness in view of the more than likely German onslaught on Poland. The Franco-Polish political agreement was not signed until September 4, and the technical Protocol remained a dead letter. Between May and September it was not implemented or confirmed by any conversations or exchange of ideas between the two general staffs regarding their operational plans.[278]

Anti-Nazi Staff Conversations

The rise of the National Socialists had early occasioned various military understandings and staff conversations among some of the status quo Powers. The Anschluss agitation in Austria and the murder of Dollfuss in 1934 produced more than a momentary rapprochement between Italy and France. Not only did Italy move several divisions to the Brenner at the time, making Hitler pause in his onward sweep, but she also entered, or re-entered, upon "general staff contacts" with France. The Stresa front found its military implementation in plans that included the sending of a French army corps into Italy to serve as a combination of liaison and buffer between the Italians and the Yugoslavs. The three were then to march together in the direction of Vienna, there to uphold the independence of the Austrian Government and to join with the Czechs. The Italian army was to dispatch a corps across the Alps to fight on the French right wing, near Belfort. These contacts survived the assassination of Barthou, who had entertained and promoted hopes for a French-Italian Balkan understanding and, at the far end of this road, an encirclement of Germany.

Deceptively enough, the understanding of the two general staffs was largely based on the close personal relations of Gamelin and Badoglio. Both were strong believers in the need for a "Latin" community of interests, as well as alliance, with Germany as the prime enemy. Mussolini tolerated their agreements for a time. Gamelin's visit to Rome, in June 1935, was made the occasion to disclose to Hitler and to others that the visit was part of an understanding between the two Governments and that staff conversations had taken place with a view to the military cooperation of the two countries. Actually, a protocol had been signed amounting to "a real military alliance" as Laval termed it, as well as an air convention. During the French maneuvers in the autumn of 1935, Gamelin informed the three chiefs of staff of the Little Entente of the great plan he had concerted with Badoglio, which "would be of such great consequence for their own possible action." The Yugoslavs showed considerable reticence. While the presence of a French corps between their own forces and the Italians would be only too welcome, the idea of possibly serving under Badoglio as the commander of the joint forces was utterly repugnant to them.[279]

This intimacy was based on, or at least resulted in, the French army's very high opinion of the Italian army. In the summer of 1935, Gamelin abolished the Italian section of the intelligence service in his own General Staff, something that is usually done only with respect to trusted allies.[280] But the Stresa front, of which these Franco-Italian intimacies were a part, was never very solid. The first thing to disrupt it, soon after the Stresa meeting, was the Anglo-German Naval Convention of June 18, 1935, concluded behind France's back. The next thing was the Little Entente's opposition to Italian proposals that Austria and Hungary be allowed to rearm.[281] Soon after that, Mussolini took Italy out of the front of the status quo Powers and indulged in the war against Ethiopia. No soldiers regretted this change of fronts more than Gamelin and Badoglio.

British policy rather rudely detached the French (as represented by the General Staff no less than by Laval) from the side of Italy, where the interests of military security as well as pro-Fascist sympathies had placed them. Disavowing the Hoare-Laval attempt to buy off Italy, the British picked up a thread that had remained broken ever since Chanak. Early in October 1935, they queried the French as to whether, considering the Mediterranean situation and the possibility of League sanctions, British-French military cooperation ought not to be resumed. Laval could not very well help giving "his political imprimatur ...to the undertaking which binds not the General Staffs but the Government[s?]." Technical conversations, at first between the naval staffs, began immediately afterwards. Military talks started early in December after Gamelin had received a delegation of the British high command, who approached him somewhat cap in hand: "In August 1914 it was France that asked Britain to stand by her side against Germany. We responded to your appeal. Today it is we who, in the name of our comradeship in the war, come to seek your support." By all considerations, Britain was an ally so much superior to Italy that the Stresa front, of which the British General Staff had thought so little that it had declined to participate in its military implementations,[282] and the Gamelin-Badoglio military accords were instantly dropped. On the twentieth of December, the Italians were informed of these decisions, as well as of the fact that British-French staff conversations had taken place and were limited to the case of hostilities directed against "our fundamental allies."[283]

British post-1933 policy with regard to Germany was strongly historicized. They acted as if the actual or seeming errors committed before and in 1914, such as exclusive alliances and ententes, encirclement of Germany, staff conversations and naval conventions for the case of war, must on no account be repeated. Happily, the naval agreement concluded with Hitler seemed to indicate that he too was determined not to repeat the errors of his predecessor, who had never agreed to mutual limitations. Men like Eden had to struggle against such inhibitions in the English political psyche for their contention that the great new military changes, like the remilitarization of the Rhineland, called once more for staff conversations with France and with Belgium. The cabinet majority was antagonistic at the outset, and the public mood distinctly unfavorable. Lloyd George's recently published War Memoirs had been outspoken in condemnation of the pre-1914 practices. According to an American observer, the average member of Commons at the time was "more suspicious in such matters now than he was before 1914."[284] As late as the week of Hitler's march across the Rhine, the Chamberlain Government declared to Commons that Britain had not entered upon military conversations and that it did not intend to do so. "We are still assuming that the nations are going to behave in a civilized manner."[285]

The German assurances regarding the limitation of forces in the Rhineland proved unconvincing even to the Chamberlain Cabinet, although it could not bring itself to believe that public opinion would support sanctions of any kind against Germany.[286] Foreign Secretary Eden, however, obtained authorization for Belgian-British-French General Staff conversations to start without delay. Still mindful of the pre-1914 conversations and the ill repute into which they had fallen, the participating governments decided that the soldiers were to be under strict civilian control in their talks. They were to be held in London, and the political authorities of the three countries were to draw up the agenda in advance. Such conditions made the military conversations altogether untraditional. They were openly announced and intended as demonstrations to impress the Germans with a show of unity that was more apparent than real. Or, to put it in Churchill's words: "Usually such conversations do not play any part as diplomatic counters and take place secretly or even informally. Now they were the only practical outcome of three weeks' parleyings and protestations, and the only Allied reply to Hitler's solid gain of the Rhineland."[287]

The detailed results of these conversations are not known. They seemed compromising enough to the Belgians to cause them to decide, "in a spirit of detachment," as Churchill put it, that they would no longer continue the staff talks with Britain and France and would instead maintain a strict neutrality.[288]

The British were aroused by the breach of the Locarno pacts, which since 1925 had been the guideposts of the British General Staff's outlook on the Continent. The more peaceful-minded elements of the Wehrmacht, serving with some misgivings as paravent for the wilder Nazi elements, tried, with little hope of success, to dissuade the British from talks with the French. They warned that the latter would get more out of the deal than the British could hope for. The dangerous understandings between Sir Henry Wilson and the French General Staff before 1914 should caution everyone against a repetition. The renewal of staff talks would signify that Britain was entering the front of Germany's enemies once more, in spite of Chamberlain's public assurance that Germany, if she intended to remain peaceful, had nothing to fear from such conversations. Besides, understandings with Britain, added to those that France already had with Russia and the Little Entente, would make Paris totally disinclined to seek the understanding with Germany that the British had hoped for in the interest of a pacification of Western Europe. They would make pacification less likely than ever because a man like Hitler would act in his own perhaps not so peaceful way.

The British soldiers replied that only "preliminary" or "temporary" understandings were intended, which might even result in loosening up the Franco-Russian pact. Moreover, they added that the shock of the Rhineland occupation had shattered all hopes of the General Staff, hopes that had outlasted the patience of the politicians in the Foreign Office and elsewhere, of coming to a durable understanding with Hitler's Germany by giving her fair and just treatment. Fair and just treatment here meant the moderate rearmament the Reichswehr had sought, which the French, rather than the British, had denied her for years. [289] They gave the German soldiers to understand that it was highly disagreeable to the British General Staff to resume military agreements with France. They feared the day when the conversations would have to be extended to the Russians, who could not be forever excluded. And that would bring the danger of a general European war ever closer, with the spread of Communism over all Europe, only the British Isles excepted, as the likely outcome.[290] For soldiers who were also genuine conservatives, the outlook could not be more frightful.

The British considered the mere fact of the military conversations to be already a great concession on their part. They would not agree to any commitments going beyond those that already existed under the Locarno pacts. The French argued that all conciliation attempts with Germany had failed and that firmer ties across the Channel were required. But not even an air pact resulted.[291] The staff talks continued for a long time. As the most useful part of their labors, they seem to have settled the arrangements for the landing of the British forces, their liaison with French units, their subordination under the French command of General Gamelin—though he had never inspired great confidence in the British[292]—and plans for the British-French Supreme Council as the top organization for the conduct of the coalition war.

Russia had been strangly left out of consideration in all of these conversations. Neither military nor political judgment in the West ranked her as high as she had stood in Tsarist days. In November 1937 Gamelin rated "even Rumania a better asset than the Russian army."[293] The Franco-Russian Mutual Assistance Pact of May 2, 1935, proved abortive. According to the Russian view, it "remained without real efficacy because it was not strengthened by a military accord between France and the Soviet Union."[294] As early as 1933-34, the French military had recommended to Paul-Boncour and Barthou that some way be found for cooperating with the Soviets. They at least sought to cut off supplies from the Reichswehr, to relieve France's Eastern allies from the nightmare of Russian hostility, to assure them of the war supplies which France might prove unable to bring to them by way of Italy, and to draw Turkey, a sort of Russian ward since Kemal's days, into the ring of the Western military world.[295] Subsequently the French military lost most of their belief in Russia's strength.

Various talks between French and Russian general staff officers took place in 1935-1936. Two of Gamelin's sous-chefs, accompanied by a former military attaché to Moscow, traveled through Russia, inspecting arms plants and other military installations. They returned favorably impressed by what they had seen. But the "purges," which reached the high military commands, further undermined Western belief in the value of the Red Army. "That's a gendarmerie that cannot leave Soviet territory," said Weygand and Gamelin. "That's the ancient Russian Army, this time provided with materiel. But what can one expect from it after generals and higher officers have been put to death by the thousands?"[296] During the final Czech crisis of 1938, the French, both civilians and military men, could not persuade themselves that the Russians would bring the promised help to Czechoslovakia.[297] During that crisis, the Labour Party urged Chamberlain to take a firm stand, together with France and Soviet Russia, against Hitler. On March 25, 1939, he told their delegates that, quite apart from Britain's military unpreparedness, France could not be counted upon, partly for the reason that she did not trust Russia's willingness or ability to take action. He himself felt "the most profound distrust of Russia, had no belief whatever in her ability to maintain an effective offensive, even if she wanted to...."[298]

The waning belief in Russian military strength shared by the various civilian and military "appeasers" did not make more convincing the attempts of the Western Powers to persuade Russia's immediate neighbors to allow Russia to carry military aid to the westward, to grant her bases and the right of marching through and flying over their territory. They feared that Russia as occupant would never release her grip and would turn the military hold into political control. No people were more unbending on this point than the Poles, whose own military strength and self-reliance was by none more overrated than by the Poles themselves and, next to them, by Chamberlain and his friends. His Government rushed into the alliance with Poland as if it alone could stop Hitler, who, with all appeasement ended, must now be stopped. The alliance of April 6, 1939, included a guarantee of Danzig, military assistance, and an armaments loan. When Beck had come to London to obtain this assistance, Chamberlain found him "very anxious not to be tied up with Russia, not only because Poles don't like Russians, but because of the effect on German opinion and policy. He thought such an association might lead Hitler to make an attack, which otherwise he hoped it might still be possible to avoid." And Chamberlain very much agreed with him, for, he said, "I regard Russia a very unreliable friend ...with an enormous irritative power on others."[299]

Both Beck and Chamberlain relied for a time on the political effect of their alliance on Hitler, rather than on the military strength it might represent. The military and financial negotiations that were to give Poland strength got under way only belatedly. On July 19, General Ironside—who had commanded the British forces at Archangelsk against the Bolshevists, a fact that did not assuage Russian misgivings—arrived at Warsaw to open talks with Smigly-Rydz and Beck. He had little to offer beyond assurances of a political rather than a military nature, and he hardly knew what to ask for. What would the Polish reaction be if the Anschluss of Danzig were proclaimed without military action on Germany's part? Answer: Poland would favor a joint démarche by Britain, France, and herself in Berlin. Should Reichswehr units enter Danzig, the Polish General Staff would send officers there to demand explanation. What did they think about the present military activities of the Germans? Answer: they seemed aimed at intimidation, rather than at an imminent conflict.

The agreement for an eight-million-pound loan to finance Polish arms purchases in Britain was not signed until August 2.[300] As the Germans were given to understand by certain London circles, there was "still doubt regarding Poland's military value, which finds expression in financial reservedness." Many people in the City and Government circles would have preferred to grant Germany a very large "disarmament loan" rather than the armament loan to Poland. And Ironside's report on his mission to Warsaw was "likewise said not to have been excessively favorable."[301]

The belated and partial recognition of Poland's military weakness did little or nothing to accelerate the negotiations opened by the British and French with the Russians for a triple alliance. In order to make the projected pact an "organic politico-military whole," the Russians, at an early stage in the negotiations, suggested consultations among the three general staffs. Very much as if soldiers should not be allowed to cut through diplomatic red tape, this Soviet invitation was not accepted in London and Paris until July 25. Traveling by slow boat, instead of airplane, the missions did not arrive in Moscow until August 10. And they were composed of relatively subordinate officers, not equipped with full powers to conclude the military part of any pact. By that time, the German-Russian talks that led to the pact of August 23 were well under way. After a few perfunctory meetings with the Russians, the military missions departed on August 25. They had not agreed, explained Voroshilov, on the fundamentals of the situation as the Russians saw it:

> The Soviet military mission considered that the USSR, not having any common frontier with the aggressor, could not lend assistance to France, Britain and Poland except under the condition of being enabled to march its troops through Polish territory, for there are no other ways for Soviet troops to get into contact with the aggressor. Just as the English and American troops could not collaborate militarily with the armed forces of France during the last World War unless they could operate on French soil, Soviet forces could not collaborate militarily with the armed forces of France and Britain unless they were given permission to cross the territory of Poland. In spite of the obvious justness of this position the French and British military missions did not declare their agreement with the position taken by the Soviet mission, and the Polish Government insisted openly that it was not in need of military aid on the part of the USSR and would not accept it. This circumstance made military collaboration between the USSR and these countries impossible.[302]

Ostensibly, the Russians' thesis was that those who could be helped by them in a military way would not allow such help to be rendered. Therefore they must wash their hands of them and conclude the neutrality pact with Hitler. This reasoning did not persuade the intended recipients of such help, convinced as they were that Soviet aid would only result in the complete and irretrievable loss of their independence. The French and British largely shared this view. With their high respect for the small nations, whose military importance was fast shrinking and who could no longer be efficient war-makers in their own right, but only as integrated members of a strategic bloc, the British and French could not connive at the destruction of these states as the Germans so readily did when they negotiated and signed the Molotov-Ribbentrop pact.

Staff Conversations of the Axis Powers

The military implementation of the Anti-Comintern Pact and its "reinforcement," the Pact of Steel of 1939, always remained below Italian expectations, below German promise, and below the vague hopes of the Japanese military. The discussions for the latter Pact started in 1938, after Munich. They originated in a Japanese suggestion and in Hitler's own view "that an armed conflict with the Western democracies must be regarded as being within the bounds of possibility in four to five years time." For the purposes of such a conflict "Britain and France had concluded detailed military agreements with each other." The Axis partners would have to counter this by a new pact of their own, an initial version of which was given to the Italians at Munich. On the basis of the pact, "all technical, military, economic, and other agreements would then be reached in further separate negotiations." Ribbentrop promised this much to the Italians late in October 1938, when they were pressing for military conventions.

When the Wehrmacht at last agreed to such conversations, they insisted from the outset that all understandings with regard to war were to be based on the principle of "no local joint warfare under unified command." Instead, there was to be "allocation of special tasks and theaters of war for each state, within which areas it will act independently." They did not want any German forces to be placed under Italian command and had almost the same feeling about having Italians under German command. The contemplated joint war was to be the one against Britain and France, the latter to be knocked out first. The German plans imparted to the Italians, which were not the true ones even at that time, envisaged strict observation of Dutch and Belgian neutrality and suggested instead an attack against the Maginot Line which, the Germans explained, could be broken through. Close cooperation was welcomed as to the exchange of intelligence, propaganda and economic warfare. But the OKW had "no intention of giving the other side a full insight into our operational intentions."[303]

Despite such reticences, there was a great deal of intimacy between the German and Japanese armies and navies. During the tension of Munich, the Japanese Navy had even promised to protect German ships against British or French attacks in all waters where Japanese vessels were present. And the armed forces in Japan remained the strongest supporters of the anti-Comintern policy. However, as their commitments in China increased, they felt in no position "to cooperate actively against a third Power, despite the best of intentions." By January 1939, army circles still "anticipated a military alliance between Germany, Italy and Japan...officially directed against Russia," though it was also to include secret protocols aimed at other Powers. But they were held back by the fears, mainly voiced by the civilians, of such "other Powers." Japan's dependence, economically speaking, on the Anglo-Saxon countries was a predicament for which the German ambassador in Tokyo, General Ott, showed great understanding: "Her task on the mainland weakens Japan temporarily as a partner but may later make her into a more valuable ally, if the danger of her becoming exhausted is counteracted. This is the duty of the partners of the Anti-Comintern Pact." A military pact would help, for it "would be primarily in Japan's favor and would stimulate morale, whereas active support for Germany and Italy, amounting to more than a tying-down of forces on the spot, could not be expected for the time being" (March 15, 1939).[304]

The Japanese military did not obtain their country's signature on the so-called "Pact of Steel." On May 22, 1939, when this merely bilateral act was signed, nothing so concrete as a military convention had been agreed upon. There was only the vague though sweeping promise that each partner would go to the other's assistance "with all his military forces on land, sea, and in the air" in the event of hostilities. The OKW was hanging back. More historical-minded than the Nazi leaders, it entertained memories of the Italians that went back to 1914 and before. The OKW merely agreed to a secret additional protocol, laying down in outline how the various military and economic negotiators were to proceed, and how cooperation in the field of press activities and propaganda was to be established. No hard and fast military conventions were in existence when Hitler began the war in September 1939, and none were created by the German-Italian-Japanese Treaty of September 27, 1940.[305] With the possible exception of the Italians, the military of the Axis Powers much preferred an alliance of a general nature to a specific military convention with its inherent threat to national, including military, sovereignty.

As far as the preparation of a global strategy by detailed and continued understandings among military partners constitutes true military progress, the Axis members proved strangely backward. They were as nationalistic and as egotistical as the partners of the old-fashioned coalition wars. Each was obsessed by the belief in his own superiority, his own timing, his own aims. They might term their wars "parallel" wars, but, strategically speaking, the Axis was not an axis of symmetry. The much-vaunted oneness of totalitarian Weltanschauung did not produce a one-field strategy. Nor did an instrument such as the German-Italian-Japanese Military Convention on the joint conduct of war, concluded on January 18, 1942, six weeks after Pearl Harbor, produce such a strategy.

AMERICAN PARTICIPATION IN STAFF CONVERSATIONS—THE MILITARY END OF ISOLATIONISM

From the time of the Hitler-Stalin pact on, war was imminent—thus concluded another commander-in-chief, Franklin D. Roosevelt. He was convinced that in all likelihood America would have to enter the war "if the democratic way of life were to be saved."[306] This view logically led to another: the United States must be better prepared for this contingency than it had been in 1917.

In order to make American assistance for Britain and other democratic "associates" as effective as possible—both before the United States entered the war and at the moment it should do so—technical discussions with the prospective associates ahead of war seemed imperative to the President. Such convictions, possibly going back to Roosevelt's own experiences in the Navy Department in World War I, found their first expression when, following his "Quarantine" speech of October 1937, he sent the chief of the Navy's War Planning Division to London for exploratory talks. The talks led to an "agreed record" of January 12, 1938, on the modalities of opening the waters of Britain and the United States to one another's naval vessels in case both states should become involved in war with Japan. A good deal about the mission became known and was used by isolationist elements in the opposition to the large naval bills sponsored by Roosevelt.[307] This did not quite stop American-British peace-time naval talks. In May 1939, a member of the Admiralty's Planning Staff discussed in Washington the disposition of the two fleets in the case of war with the Axis. The Amer-

ican Chief of Naval Operations, Admiral Leahy, gave his "personal" view that, in case of both nations' involvement in such a war, the United States Navy would take over control of the Pacific and would share that of the Atlantic and Mediterranean with the British.[308] But the isolationist protest against such staff talks was still well-remembered by Roosevelt and Hull when, in June 1940 with the fall of France impending, the British Ambassador Lord Lothian submitted to them Churchill's suggestion that "staff conferences be held between naval officials of our two Governments with regard to fleet movements in both the Atlantic and Pacific." A special committee of the Admiralty began at once to discuss what form American aid ought to take, how theaters of war were to be divided between the two navies, and what information was to be exchanged.[309]

Two days after the Franco-German armistice of Compiègne, Lothian returned with the suggestion for staff conferences of the two navies. They would, he said, be highly important in the event that his government should be forced to evacuate to Canada following Hitler's expected onslaught on the British isles. He proposed that at least a senior American admiral, like Sims in 1917, be sent to London for discussions. Hull thought an exchange of information through diplomatic channels more desirable at the time, more likely to avoid publicity and "leaks" that might bring down on the Administration the accusation that "the President was planning to get the United States into the War."[310]

What both Roosevelt and Hull considered as more immediately feasible, even in an election year, were discussions about matters of joint defense with Canada. Such discussions began early in July 1940, negotiated by high-ranking army and navy officers on both sides. They resulted in the Ogdensburg Joint-Defense agreement of August 8, 1940, under which a Permanent Joint Board of Defense was set up.[311] This organization might have served to a certain extent as a transmitter between London and Washington. When the time came, however, it was considered more appropriate to transfer the fifty American destroyers directly to Britain rather than use Canada as the middleman. The subterfuge would have seemed too obvious, even at home.[312]

Roosevelt's hesitations, due to the domestic situation, did not last long. A navy, an army, and an air force officer were sent on a supposedly "secret mission" to London. While they were on the high seas, their mission became publicly known. Joined by the service attachés, the three Americans, beginning in mid-August, met for weeks "on a purely exploratory basis" with British naval, military and air officers of the highest rank, including Sir John Dill, Chief of the Imperial General Staff. The meetings of this so-called "Anglo-American Standardization of Arms Committee," while restricted to mere discussions and recommendations, still met with British expectations of "continued economic and industrial cooperation of the United States in ever-increasing volume."[313] They practically agreed on a joint strategy for (1) the time when America was still a neutral, so-called, and (2) for the case of her open entry into the war. While these discussions were still going on, the German-Italian-Japanese agreement of September 27, largely aimed at the United States, was signed. Thereupon Hull and other advisers urged Roosevelt to give the London talks a "more formal and constructive character." But Roosevelt, fully aware of the dangerous odium still clinging to such negotiations, declined to do so before the elections.

With the elections out of the way, elections during which both candidates had promised that no American would be sent abroad to fight, American strategic planning in its more politically dangerous aspects could be resumed. In mid-November, Admiral Stark, Chief of Naval Operations, submitted his ideas on "our national objectives" to Navy Secretary Knox. These included not only the defense of the Western hemisphere but also the "prevention of the disruption of the British Empire, with all that such a consummation implies." He foresaw America's eventual entry into the war, the need for sending "large air and land forces to Europe or Africa, or both, and to participate strongly in this land offensive." These were soldiers' views, expressed by an admiral who did not share the sailors' major obsession with the Pacific as the main theater of a future war. As a "preliminary to possible entry of the United States into the conflict" he recommended that American sailors and soldiers enter at once on secret staff talks regarding technical matters with the British, the Canadians, and the Dutch, in order "to reach agreement and lay down plans for promoting unity of allied effort should the United States find it necessary to enter the war."[314]

In the meantime, Ambassador Lothian had returned from London for the diplomatic season, which reopened after the elections. He proposed to Hull that, considering the visible deterioration of the Far Eastern situation and the likelihood of an early Japanese attack on Singapore, "there should be conferences between naval experts of our two Governments with respect to what each would or might do in case of military outbreaks on the part of Japan." The British authorities had tried to get such conversations under way through the American naval attaché in London. The latter, however, "consistently declined to discuss possible future plans on the ground that

he had absolutely no authority." Hull answered that "of course, there could be no agreements entered into in this respect, but that there should undoubtedly be collaboration with the view of making known to each other any and all information practicable in regard to what both might have in mind to do, and when and where, in case of a military movement by Japan in the South or in some other direction." But he declined to discuss anything further, such as the value of Singapore for the United States Navy. This was "a matter for experts to pass on." Lothian expressed his hope that "there would be discussion between his and our high naval officials with respect to all phases of the Pacific situation."[315]

While the Lend-Lease bill was getting under way, American-British staff talks were held in Washington from the end of January to the end of March 1941. The visitors were in mufti and were said to be "technical advisors to the British Purchasing Commission." The conversations were to be "technical discussions on a staff level." They were "non-political" in their nature and did not commit the United States.[316] So argue the Roosevelt apologists who will not see or will not admit the unavoidably entangling nature of such talks.[317] Like the pre-1914 conversations inside the Entente, these conversations, deliberately kept below the highest echelons, remained neither "purely technical" nor completely secret. The Axis Governments got wind of the talks and broadcast news of them in order to strengthen the opponents of Lend-Lease. Still later, through intentional leaks in the American press, the Japanese were given to understand that there was an American-British "naval alliance" against them.[318] By December 3, 1941, some of them expected that American-British joint military action, with or without declaration of war, was certain in case of a Japanese occupation of Thailand.[319]

The Washington conversations were, in the language of official war history, "a rational development in the drift of the U.S. toward active participation in World War II."[320] They resulted in agreements, signed by nine American and five British officers, on such questions as the exchange of scientific information for war; the pooling of military intelligence; close cooperation between FBI and British security services;[321] the stationing of American specialists in Britain to instruct in the use of American equipment and to study British war experience, greater concentration of American warships in the Atlantic to guard the sea lanes there and relieve the British in anti-U-boat activities; planning for the occupation by American forces of Greenland, Iceland, the Azores, and Martinique; repairs of damaged British warships in U.S. harbors; training of British airmen in the United States, and continued American-British staff talks. The staff talks were, in official American terms, to determine "the best methods by which the armed forces of the United States and the British Commonwealth, with its present allies, could defeat Germany and the Powers allied with her, should the United States be compelled to resort to war." A United States-British Commonwealth Joint Basic War Plan, the so-called ABC-1 plan, for the grand strategy of such a war was laid down in very great detail. The plan contemplated both Germany and Japan as prospective enemies. The Germans were considered Enemy Number One, while only a containing war would be undertaken against Japan, pending Germany's defeat. The report read as follows:

The Staff Conference assumes that when the United States becomes involved in war with Germany, it will at the same time engage in war with Italy. In those circumstances, the possibility of a state of war arising between Japan and an association of the United States, the British Commonwealth and its Allies, including the Netherlands East Indies, must be taken into account...Since Germany is the predominant partner of the Axis Powers, the Atlantic and European area is considered to be the decisive theatre. The principal U.S. Military effort will be exerted in that theatre, and operations of U.S. forces in other theatres will be conducted in such a manner as to facilitate that effort.[322]

It can be assumed that the British found it easy enough to fall in with the indicated line of American strategic thought on which Marshall and Stark had agreed for some months. The Americans hardly needed to invoke the primacy usually conceded the stronger partner in such arrangements for a coalition war. Both Stimson and Knox approved of the report and so did the President, although not "officially." According to Stark's testimony, Roosevelt "was not willing to do it officially until we got into the war."

The war plan, drawn up jointly by the U.S. Army and Navy "had its basis in an international agreement with the British Army, Navy and Air Force." These were the terms of Admiral Turner, War Plans Officer for the Chief of Naval Operations, who was a participant in the staff conversations. "It was," he said, "a world-wide agreement, covering all areas, land, sea and air, of the entire world in which it was conceived that the British Commonwealth and the United States might be jointly engaged in action against any enemy." They were predicated on a major effort "on the part of both the principal associated Powers against Germany, initially," as the most dangerous enemy. Should war come in such a way that only Japan was America's enemy and Ger-

many remained uninvolved, the United States Navy Department determined that "the United States would, if possible, initiate efforts to bring Germany into the war against us in order that we would be enabled to give strong support to the United Kingdom in Europe."[323] The possibility that American policy might be made the prisoner or servant of the agreed American-British strategy was happily averted by Hitler's declaration of war against the United States following Pearl Harbor.

The staff conversations in Washington were promptly followed by American-British-Dutch conversations held in Singapore in April 1941, with twenty-six representatives from the United States, Dutch, British, Australian, New Zealand and Indian forces participating. They met to prepare plans for the conduct of regional military operations. While they agreed that "no political commitment is implied," the report proved so political in parts that Stark and Marshall could not fully and formally approve of it. They accepted and jointly recommended to the President, however, one of the main Singapore proposals, which seemed to them strategic rather than political in nature: that joint military counter-action against Japan should be undertaken in case she should attack or directly threaten the territory (including mandated territory) of the United States, Britain, or the Netherlands or should move forces into Thailand west of 100° east or south of 10° north, Portuguese Timor, New Caledonia, or the Loyalty Islands.[324]

All the American and British chiefs of staff participated in the Atlantic Conference of August 1941. But their direct discussions, contrary to British expectations, produced nothing beyond the tentative agreements already reached, except that America gave assurances of more convoying in the Atlantic. Roosevelt would not empower his officers to take up British proposals that new staff talks to discuss the joint defense of the South West Pacific be held at Singapore.[325] Nor were the Navy and War Departments willing to be drawn too far into technical arrangements ahead of war.

In spite of some polite rebuffs, the British considered the pre-Pearl Harbor understandings to be filled with promises of ultimate American all-out help.[326] Considering their predicament, it would have been a miracle if they had not. They drew from the staff conversations the same somewhat uncertain certainty of ultimate American support that the French had derived from their staff talks with the British before August 1914. By December 5, 1941, various high-ranking British officers considered that their Government had "assurance of American armed support" in such cases as Japanese landings on the Kra Isthmus,

or the invasion of Siam or the Dutch East Indies.[327] And Roosevelt's War Cabinet, at a
meeting of November 27, 1941, feeling itself under such obligation, agreed that "if the Japanese
got into the Isthmus of Kra, the British would
fight; and, if the British fought, we would have to
fight."[328]

The last objections to the report of the American-Dutch-British conversations held in Singapore[329] were being smoothed out when discussion was begun by the American and British
naval commanders in the Far East in November
1941. They completed arrangements for the initial American and British fleet dispositions to
meet the expected Japanese moves in Far Eastern
waters. Their report was before the Chief of Naval
Operations in Washington on December 6 and was
put into effect by him on the 7th, following the
Pearl Harbor attack.[330] Other war plans that
had resulted from many months of Anglo-American
staff conferences, plans giving priority to the
operations against Germany, were also put into
effect.[331] This meant, incidentally, that war
plans against Germany were put into effect four
days ahead of her declaration of war against
America and the latter's declaration of a state of
war. Consequently, due to two years of American
inter-staff work and more than a year's conversations with British staffs, the United States was
far from unprepared for war. As Sherwood has
written: "These staff talks provided the highest
degree of strategic preparedness that the United
States or probably any other non-aggressor nation has ever had before entry into the war."[332]
The pre-war staff conversations and political
understandings between Americans and British
prepared for the close cooperation of the two
Powers from the outset of the war, arrangements
which culminated in the establishment of the
Combined Chiefs of Staff.[333] This was undoubtedly the best organization ever achieved for
the conduct of a coalition war. The waste of effort
and time that has marked the opening, if not the
whole duration, of most wars of coalition was
avoided. It was an achievement that required discarding a long-cherished Liberal tradition, or
prejudice, as it seemed now, against peace-time
military understandings.

In acting as he did, the President and his advisers found his powers as commander-in-chief
and subsequently his authority under the war
power elastic enough for him to "enter into military agreements in the nature of staff agreements
with the commander-in-chief of a third power
as to military action and policy." But would each
of these powers by itself be sufficient? "The
binding quality of staff agreements has never been
fully ascertained under our practice," wrote
Assistant Secretary of State Adolf Berle, in-

voked as an authority on constitutional law and
practice in March 1943, "but it is fairly arguable
that agreements of this sort, so far as they are
related to military policy, are binding to a large
extent even on a successor, since a commander-
in-chief having the power to lay and carry out
campaigns must be deemed to have the power
necessary to make agreements reasonably appropriate to carry out such campaigns."[334]

The heritage of Liberalism includes strong distrust, if not abhorrence, of staff conversations
and military conventions. The most recent
governors of the United States have repudiated
this tradition in favor of a great deal of executive
absolutism. They have thereby acted in defense
of other concepts and interests of Liberalism that
they consider more vital. The guarding and preservation of such interests have come to rest
more immediately than ever before in armaments
and the best preparation for war. The exigencies
of mid-twentieth-century warfare, as presented
by soldiers and sailors, have brought on the
fateful repudiation of the earlier inhibitions in
the American customs of governing and to a large
extent in the political psyche of America.[335]
Quite a few of them survived, however. For example, after the war's end, the United States
allowed the Combined Chiefs of Staff Committee
to lapse, while the British would have liked to
continue it into peace-time.[336] Still, American-
British staff conversations were never completely
broken off.[337]

WESTERN UNION

The ways in which the Russians fought the war
of coalition and garnered an inordinate share of
gain from it at first taught their Western associates nothing about the safeguarding of their own
post-war interests. Their one-sided belief that
the alchemistic marriage of "lion and lily" would
and could take place, and would hold in "the luke-
warm bath" of the United Nations Charter, was
shattered within a few years after the close of
hostilities. In more official language: "The expectation that the cooperation among the great
powers pledged during the war and reflected in
the Charter would be continued, has not been
realized."[338]

Western errors of judgment allowed the Russians, meeting with little interference except
from Greece and Turkey, to resume international
class warfare to the West, the South and the East.
Communist parties served as instruments for
turning weak democracies into states subservient
to Russia. These states were tied to her by mutual
assistance treaties, the instruments of Russian
military hegemony. Each one declared that it was
primarily directed against the renewal of German

or, in the case of China, Japanese aggression.[339] The U.N. Charter received a certain amount of lip service in these instruments when they stated, as did the Russo-Bulgarian Treaty of March 18, 1948, that they would be "implemented in accordance with the principles of the Charter of the U.N. organization." In military actuality, the Russian arrangements forced on the satellites went far beyond most earlier forms of military domination.[340] They displayed a Gleichschaltung tendency which surpassed that of the Third Reich in its relations with military subsidiaries and approached Old Oriental satrapism to such an extent that the most military of the satellites, Yugoslavia, finally revolted against it. By Yugoslavia's own declarations, this was a revolt of military communism against communist militarism.

By count of the Quai d'Orsay, Russia concluded twenty-three mutual assistance pacts with her satellites and other states under her patronage. These produced "manifest disequilibrium of force between the now disarmed Western Europe and what must be called the Eastern Bloc formed by the twenty-three treaties made long before there was any question of any military pact among the Western nations."[341] In the long run, this disparity of forces proved to be a stronger psychological fact than the common memory of German aggression on which the Russians had based their treaties, not only with the satellites but also with Britain in 1942 and with France in 1944. This psychological capital was practically used up by the time the Russians chose to base their protests against the Atlantic Pact on the memory of the recent struggles of coalition. The Pact, they argued, as well as violating the U.N. Charter, "absolutely ignores the possibility of a repetition of German aggression, not having consequently as its aim the prevention of a new German aggression."[342]

The more or less immediate realignment of the friends and foes of a recent war is a phenomenon as old as states and state systems. Again and again statesmen have been forced to learn this and to relearn how to handle the problem. Metternich, Castlereagh and Talleyrand engineered the re-admission of the ex-enemy to friendship and alliance during the Congress of Vienna, before there was even a signed peace. The Balkan belligerents of 1912-13 behaved similarly. The thoroughly propagandized democratic mind is, however, inclined to resent such rapid transition and re-orientation as immoral. Its own willingness to discard and accept alliances is slow-going. The state of Western public opinion immediately after 1945 was that of molasses, sticky, sweet and opaque, unwilling even to be stirred by considerations of its own security. It

was in a trusting mood that the United States Congress, for example, surrendered—not necessarily irrevocably—some of its war-making powers upon America's entry into the United Nations. The Congress voted that "the President shall not be deemed to require the authorization of the Congress to make available to the Security Council the armed forces, facilities or assistance" that might possibly be requested under the Charter.

At last the facts of Communist aggression became too obvious to be overlooked any longer. In February 1948, Czechoslovakia fell to Communism. Winston Churchill's comment was that, in Czechoslovakia, "Stalin had perpetrated exactly the same aggression in 1948 as Hitler did when he marched into Prague in 1939."[343] Russia's strategic reaching beyond Finland into Norway was particularly alarming to Britain.[344] The pressures built up by such events resulted in the Brussels Pact of March 17, 1948, among Britain, France, and the Benelux countries, with the United States as godfather.[345]

The military purposes of the states adhering to the Brussels Pact were "to afford assistance to each other, in accordance with the Charter of the United Nations, in maintaining international peace and security and in resisting any policy of aggression; to take such steps as may be held necessary in the event of a renewal by Germany of a policy of aggression." The Pact further provided that "if any of the high contracting parties should be the object of an armed attack in Europe, the other parties will, in accordance with the provisions of Article 51 of the U.N. Charter, afford the party so attacked all military and other aid and assistance in their power." There was thus full commitment for a period of fifty years. In this way, tribute was paid to the popular tendency to believe in lasting friendship rather than to historical evidence of their usual duration.

The Pact was preceded by staff conversations among the signatories, apparently under way since the summer of 1947, and by other exchanges, such as the lending of a British aircraft carrier to France, the stationing of an RAF mission of instruction in France in order to introduce the French to British plane types and radar, and by other British assistance of a military nature to the Continental partners.[346] The Pact itself was altogether unprecedented in its provisions for the conduct of a war of coalition well ahead of war itself.

Whereas old-style military agreements purposely had little or no public character, the new ones of 1948 and 1949 were given just that accent in order to win broad popular support for the military part of the alliances and, it was hoped, to impress the Russians. The strength that these treaties envisioned would have first to be created in each state by perpetuating conscription, by lengthening terms of service, and by large expenditures of resources. Then the union of the various states could be expected to present an impressive and effective force. As compared with earlier military alliances, the partners would have to put up capital for the amalgamation, and this would mean transferring it from other national uses. The organization for these united forces preceded rather than followed their actual availability. This was another complete reversal of the old experience with coalition warfare. Usually forces had been available, but not the organization.

Conferences of the defense ministers of the five countries and continued deliberations of representatives of their general staffs, constituted as a Permanent Military Committee and sitting in London since May 5, 1948, followed the signing of the Brussels Pact. While the military's own urges in the direction of immediate unification did not at first appear strong, the prolonged Russian blockade of Berlin gave the problem new urgency in their eyes. And it appears that at this and at other times it was the military in the United States who interpreted Russia's moves as having military meaning and insisted on their being met by strategical preparations, despite the obstacles of the presidential race going on at the time.[347] Although always informed by the Brussels Powers and aware of their expectation that American help would be needed to keep the Russians from overrunning all Europe west of the Elbe or the Rhine, the Truman Administration was at first inclined to postpone specific pact arrangements with the Western Union until the latter's military arrangements were more nearly perfected.

Meanwhile, the American staffs had carried on conversations with British staff representatives concerning European security and American participation in it. Britain and Canada preferred a grand alliance by means of a formal treaty. In the United States, isolationist sentiment, even more to be respected in an election year, seemed at first to require formal aloofness—no treaty, but instead willingness to take steps in the direction of a regional agreement under Article 51 of the U.N. Charter. It was hoped that action would be initiated by the Republican Party, something duly agreed upon between Lovett, the main architect of NATO, and Senator Vandenberg.[348]

The Vandenberg Resolution of June 11, 1948 (S.R. 239), announcing that as a matter of high national policy the United States would give military aid to defensive alliances among the free nations of the world, allowed the Administration to go

further and faster.[349] From July 1948 on, a group of American officers, headed by Major General Lyman L. Lemnitzer, participated in the London staff conferences of the Brussels Pact members as "observers," as did Canadian officers. American soldiers thus took the share in the preparation of the defense of Atlantica that seemed incumbent on them from military considerations of the hour and of the years to come. The concepts of security and stability that they urged upon the European partners tended strongly towards European unification, economic, military, and technological. Much of the material would clearly have to come from the United States, "the arsenal of democracy" in the cold war as it had been in the hot war.[350]

The deliberations of the soldiers led, at the end of September 1948, to the creation of a permanent defense organization of the five Western European powers. This was a combined general staff for planning, not for command. It was to relate local strategic considerations to the wider ones that had to be envisaged along the European fronts of military Communism. This scheme had the tacit approval of the American Government which would not, however, go to the extent of providing a general—welcome as a quasi-neutral would have been to several of the member states—to fill the top office of the super-staff. The appointment of an American would have avoided the dilemma of choosing between a British and a French general for the chairmanship and would have avoided the necessity, as the French saw it, of choosing between an essentially British and an essentially Continental strategic conception. The French feared that England would be too readily inclined to evacuate the Continent once more, as in 1940, and then attempt to reconquer the Continent from the vantage point of the British Isles. The French hoped that American strategists might be persuaded to agree to a defense of the Continent, preferably along the line of the Rhine.[351] Continued British reluctance to join in the political and economic unions of Europe proposed by the French seemed to have a military counterpart in this British island-based strategy. The British view was, however, only too understandable, considering the existing discrepancy of forces, particularly infantry, on the Continent, a discrepancy not likely to be overcome for a number of years. In spite of French misgivings, the chairmanship went to Field Marshal Montgomery.

Political compromise was combined with military considerations in the filling of the other high appointments to the Western Union defense organization. These were announced on October 4: French General Jean de Lattre de Tassigny was to be commander-in-chief of the Union's ground forces (Uni-Terre),[352] British Air Marshal Sir James Robb was to be in command of the air forces (Uni-Air), and French Vice-Admiral Robert Jaujard was to be flag officer of the combined naval forces (Uni-Mer). High-ranking officers of the forces of the lesser Powers were to serve on the various "Uni" staffs. In order to demonstrate to the French that they were committed to the defense of the continent, the British agreed that Montgomery's staff ("Uni-Lion") would have its forward headquarters in the heart of France, at historic Fontainebleau castle, while a rear headquarters would be set up at Dover House in London, near the Horse Guards.

Never before had national armed forces been put, in peacetime, within such an organization.[353] In many respects the new organization transcended war-time integration—now one man would do one job, whereas on an American-British wartime staff a Briton and an American each did a parallel job. National sovereignty was to be abrogated to a large extent, an impairment much attacked by traditionalists, such as the de Gaullists in France.[354] Montgomery, however, proclaimed that he was an international soldier belonging "not to Britain but to Western Europe." Speaking about his early experiences with an international peacetime military organization, he assured interviewers that

We are all working together very well. Countries have sent me some excellent officers. The really necessary thing is for every officer to understand that he is an international and not a national person. Although by accident of birth he happens to be British, for instance, he must be concerned just as much for the defense of France, Belgium and Holland as for the defense of England. I am an international soldier; so must they be. It is not always easy to make people understand that. If I allowed national feelings to rule, I would never get anything done at all. We try to see all the nations of the Western Union linked together in one show. We are all one team and we sink or swim together.

But the strength to be considered by such a staff would still be national, furnished by the member nations. "National armies, national navies, national air forces will remain and fight on that basis." They and the nations behind them still gave rise to "frictions." Cooperation was as yet less effective outside his staff than within it. "My biggest single problem," he said, "is how to get five nations, all willing to cooperate, actually to do so in peacetime. I have come to the conclusion it is very difficult to get real cooperation without some small loss of sovereignty. This

might become necessary to make a complete success of our work."[355]

While it became Communist tactics to fragmentize opposition by emphasizing traditional concepts of sovereignty, soldiers like Montgomery and, following him, Bradley, were ready to advocate partial renunciation of national sovereignty in the interest of a more efficient defense of the West. The planning of such a defense still suffered from many nationalistic disagreements.[356] It was hoped that with America's accession most of them would be smoothed out.[357] General Bradley, for one, looked hopefully towards the achievement of unity of plan and purpose. He told the United States Senate:

On the battlefields, responsibilities are great, tempers are short, and differences of opinion are quickly magnified to become wounds not easily healed. But here in the North Atlantic Treaty defense planning, and in the arms-assistance program, you are giving us the opportunity to achieve, in peacetime, a unity of will and understanding of each other that will be invaluable should an aggressor precipitate another war.[358]

On the political level, the Brussels Pact nations provided for a Consultative Council, composed of the five foreign ministers, and a Permanent Commission, in the nature of a secretariat general, which was to consist of the four London envoys of the Continental members plus a British assistant foreign secretary. The five defense ministers were to meet every three months in order to transmute the political decisions of the Consultative Council into commensurate defense measures. The highest military stratum was formed by the chiefs of staff. Thirteen senior officers were to meet every other month to plan over-all strategy, deciding—together, as far as possible—size, disposition, and commanders of their combined forces. Their deputies were to sit as a Permanent Military Committee.

The Military Supply Board was concerned with the output of war materials by the Western Powers themselves and with procurements from the outside, notably from the United States. A Financial and Economic Committee was to meet in London to deliberate what the five national budgets could afford for defense purposes then and in the future. The five finance ministers were to meet when necessary to settle the extra-national aspects of the defense program's financing. The Permanent Military Committee was to supply the chiefs of staff with military inventories, plan future war production and stockpiles, and settle standardization problems. In addition, there were subcommittees to handle special tasks. "Uni-

Force," only a shadow force, was under the chiefs of staff. American military observers came to sit on many of these committees and staffs. They or their superiors emphasized from time to time that these observers had entered upon no commitments and that this remained "far above the Army's responsibility and must be decided in high political areas." But, they added, they would be remiss in their duty if they did not constantly study such possibilities as, for example, the integration of the American forces stationed in Europe with those of the Brussels Pact nations in case of war or other sudden emergency in Europe.[359] Even if there were no legal obligations incurred, the psychological commitment resulting from such participation can hardly be doubted. The soldier's concept of obligation had not changed since 1914.

NORTH ATLANTIC TREATY ORGANIZATION (NATO)

The European nations found the United States more willing to be associated "with such regional and other collective arrangements as are based on continuous and effective self-help and mutual aid," to use the terms of the Vandenberg Resolution. Negotiations for a North Atlantic pact got under way in Washington in July 1948, recessed in September, and started again in December. Representatives of the five Brussels Powers, the United States, and Canada participated.[360] They set out and proceeded in the awareness of the lesson taught by two world wars, "that their security is inextricably linked together and that an attack on any of them is in effect an attack on them all." The developments in Europe since 1945 had demonstrated time and again "the need for joint defense on a continuing and intimate basis."[361]

During the negotiations, the Americans expressed the optimistic hope that "if we can make it sufficiently clear in advance that any armed attack affecting our national security would be met with overwhelming force, the armed attack might never occur."[362] Pessimistic expectations were, however, embodied in the military arrangements for the use of forces then and later available for use against the one and only aggressor thinkable. In preparing against this eventuality, the "danger zone" of an early preventive aggression might have to be crossed.

The Scandinavian countries were closest to the Russian menace and most remote from American aid. Seeing one of their members, Finland, firmly in the military grip of Russia—from which a Scandinavian League might have saved it in the autumn of 1939—they came to consider, at least from the spring of 1948 on, how they could cooperate for their joint defense. In a meeting of the three Scandinavian foreign ministers, it was agreed that their soldiers should discuss joint staff planning for defense—rather than a military pact.[363] At an early stage, the diplomacy of the Western Powers, notably the United States, attempted to persuade Norway, Sweden and Denmark to come into a wider Atlantic pact. It was pointed out to them that help in the form of American arms deliveries could go only to close associates and not, within a foreseeable time, to those who were solely members of an inter-Scandinavian pact, in the military strength of which the Americans do not seem to have put much confidence. Norway seemed to agree with this American appraisal. By mid-January of 1949, she informed Sweden that she would accept an invitation to join the Atlantic Pact, to which all of her political parties, with the exception of the Communists, had agreed.[364] Sweden, who was determined to adhere to her unconditional neutrality of one hundred and thirty-five years' standing, and who was also afraid of provoking the ire of the Soviets, had offered Norway and Denmark a ten-year inter-Scandinavian military pact. When Sweden would not consider Norway's coincident membership in both a Scandinavian and an Atlantic pact, negotiations for a Scandinavian pact came to an end.[365]

A Northern regional pact had appeared altogether innocuous to the Soviet Government. They protested, however, as soon as Norway indicated her willingness to join either the Western Union or the Atlantic Pact. In Russian eyes, both of these were designed for aggression against Russia and for Anglo-American world domination by force. When Norway replied that the pact she intended to join was aimed at averting aggression, something which the United Nations, contrary to earlier hopes, was not able to do, the Russians declared themselves unable to share this opinion. Would not Norway be better off with a Russian-Norwegian non-aggression pact, they asked? But Norway had hardly forgotten the non-aggression pact that Denmark had concluded with the Nazis early in 1939. And what about air and naval bases on her soil under an Atlantic pact? No such establishments would be permitted, Norway replied, unless she were attacked or threatened by attack. She would not permit the use of her territory in the interest of a policy with aggressive aims. The answer was still unsatisfactory to Moscow:

This statement means that any provocative rumors or hastily concocted falsifications about a threat of attack against Norway would suffice to make Norway grant Norwegian territory for military bases and armed forces of foreign countries at any time, including the

present peace time...It is known that the drawing of small countries into this [Atlantic] union
has precisely the aim of using their territories
for the establishment of such military bases,
which in this case is of particular significance
for the Soviet Union since Norway and the
USSR are neighbors with a common frontier.[366]

Any suggestion that a threat of attack could eman-
ate from the Soviet Union was "void of any foundation," Moscow maintained, in view of the always
friendly attitude adopted by the Soviet Union with
regard to Norway.[367] Unmoved by such blandish-
ment, Norway sent her foreign minister to Washington for discussions early in February 1949.
This led to her joining the discussions of the North
Atlantic Treaty in their latest stages, not without
misgivings that her security might be endangered
by Russia before the Atlantic treaty was signed,
ratified, and implemented.[368]

The North Atlantic Treaty was published on
March 18, 1949, signed on April 4 in Washington
by the seven original negotiators plus five ac-
cessories (Norway, Denmark, Iceland, Italy and
Portugal), and ratified by the American Senate by
a vote of eighty-two to thirteen on July 21. It
went into effect on August 24, after all signatories
had deposited their ratifications.

By the military provisions of the Treaty, the
signatories bound themselves for twenty years,
"separately and jointly, by means of continuous
and effective self-help and mutual aid," to maintain and develop their individual and collective
capacity to resist armed attack (Article 3). That
is to say, the participants were bound to arm to
the extent of their own capacity, and beyond that
with the help of the United States. As Secretary
Acheson said, American help was indispensable
if security in the North Atlantic area were to be
established.[369] "There are no free rides," the
U.S. Senate Foreign Relations Committee warned
in its report on the Treaty. United States aid was
not to be considered unlimited. The limitations
were, in part, spelled out by the Committee in
geographical terms: "A definite obligation is undertaken by each party to contribute, individually and
collectively, to the defense of the North Atlantic
area," but not outside it. The non-Atlantic overseas possessions of the contracting countries
were not covered. The Committee also attempted
to make the Treaty appear as unlike a military
alliance as possible. "There is no specific obligation as to the timing, nature and extent of assistance to be given by any party," the Committee
stated.

Consultation, and nothing more for the time
being, was to take place—or was to be permitted,
as the Committee report preferred it—as soon
as the territorial integrity, political independence

or security of any of the parties was threatened
in the opinion of any signatory (Article 4). With
a last show of isolationist reluctance, the Committee assured their colleagues that consultation
"could be requested only when the element of
threat is present." They expressed the hope that
this limitation would be strictly observed. The
provision for consultation was designed to end the
hope, or miscalculation, of any potential aggressor that he might succeed in overcoming the isolated Powers one by one while the United States
remained neutral, as she had done in the late
1930's. No more of Hitler's "artichoke" tactics!

What would happen if the political independence
of one of the signatories should be threatened
from within? Secretary Acheson replied that if, in
such a situation, the signatory in question "wanted
to confer about it, undoubtedly you would have a
conference." He did not consider that the Treaty
created either a right or an obligation of intervention, such as the Holy Alliance powers had
once claimed. His own view of the matter was
that "purely internal revolutionary activity would
not be regarded as an armed attack; a revolutionary activity inspired, armed, directed from
the outside, was a different matter." Greece furnished the example of the threat of a foreign-sup-
ported revolution.[370] When French Communists
professed to see in Article 4 a plan to put down
internal uprisings, French Foreign Minister
Schuman declared that this did not cover occurrences like strikes, such as had recently taken
place under Communist direction in Italy, but
referred only to violent threats through foreign
interference in internal affairs.[371] Gromyko,
however, told the U.N. Assembly on April 13,
1949, that

the signatories to the treaty also act as strang-
lers of democracy and they do not conceal
that one of the aims of the treaty is interference
in the internal affairs of other countries, which
goes as far as armed intervention under the
pretext of the struggle for the maintenance in
certain countries of regimes which please them.
They take care, of course, to support reactionary Fascist regimes, to support all kinds
of measures to stifle the movement for national
liberation in colonies and dependent countries.

Article 5 was "the heart of the Treaty." In it
the parties agreed, on the strength of the experience of two world wars, that an armed attack
against one or more of them would be considered
"an attack against them all." An armed attack on
one or more of the signatories is defined (Article
6) as an attack on the territory of any of the member states in Europe, North America, French
Algiers (with Tunis and Morocco added in early
1952), their Atlantic island possessions north of

the Tropic of Cancer (which would include the Gulf of Mexico, but not the Caribbeans), the occupation forces maintained by any party in Europe, or on their vessels and aircraft in this area. In the exercise of the right of individual or collective self-defense, the parties agreed to assist the attacked party or parties "forthwith, individually and in concert with the other parties" by action deemed necessary, including the use of armed force. According to official American commentary, this does not mean that the United States "would be automatically at war if one of the nations covered by the pact is subjected to armed attack. Under our Constitution, the Congress alone has the power to declare war."[372] To a Senator's query as to whether Article 5 bound Congress "in effect to take the same steps as it would take if our own territory were attacked, and to proceed in the same way," the main American architect of the Treaty, former Under Secretary of State Lovett, answered that he did not consider Article 5 as giving the assurance "that the line of action we take must be identical with the line we would take in case of an attack at home."[373] This became the Senate's own interpretation: the attack "against them all" has not the same effect on all as it would presumably have on the party first attacked. In spite of such reservations, which withheld automatic American assistance, a powerful deterrent effect on any would-be aggressor as well as an encouraging effect on the European partners was hoped for.

Before American armed assistance would be rendered it had to be ascertained whether an armed attack had in fact occurred—ascertained, that is, by consultation, but in the final effect by every participant himself. What constitutes "armed attack" came no nearer to a final definition when the United States Senate spoke of it as "ordinarily self-evident," as the attack of one state upon another, but as not including incidents created by irresponsible groups of individuals or by purely internal disorders or revolutions. In the defense of its own prerogative, the Senate emphasized that the measures deemed necessary to restore and maintain the security of the North Atlantic area did not commit the parties as to the declaration of war. A threatening situation might well lend itself to the application of means short of war, "from a diplomatic protest to the most severe forms of pressure." On these measures as well the members to the Treaty would preserve their freedom of action and decision.[374]

While the processes of the United States Constitution allow for the immediate automatic application of force in the event of an armed attack upon any state of the Union, the same automatic action would not result in the case of an attack upon a member country under the North Atlantic Treaty. In such a case the other partners would carry out their obligations "in accordance with their respective constitutional processes" (Article 11). What action the President and the Congress "within their sphere of assigned constitutional responsibility" would take and could be expected to take the Senate left undefined, particularly the authority of the President, as Commander-in-Chief of the armed forces, to use these forces.

According to the State Department's White Paper:

> ...this constitutional question does not present a real obstacle to the Pact. The United States certainly can obligate itself in advance to take such action, including the [belligerent or non-belligerent?] use of armed force, as it deems necessary to meet armed attack affecting its national security...While the North Atlantic pact does not expressly commit the United States to furnish military assistance to the other parties of the pact, the decision to do so by the United States would be one way in which this nation could logically contribute to the mutual aid consent, expressed in Article 3.

The Congressional debates were curiously one-sided in their concentration on the legalistic-constitutional aspect of the Treaty. There was little reference to past experience with military staff talks, their entanglements, and the often so-called moral obligations stemming from them; to the differences and similarities between this new military alliance and earlier ones; to the question of what constitutes aggression and what mere defensive action.[375] There was an occasional early reminder that "agreements on a lend-lease arms program, secret ones on joint strategy and the co-ordinated use of troops, etc., would, in fact, bind us even more firmly to the fate of Western Europe than would the legal terminology of a treaty."[376] But the Senate passed over that foreseeable contingency with a silence that must have been imposed by strategic considerations of the moment rather than by historical ignorance. To all appearances, the Senate majority was too firmly persuaded of the strategic necessities of the hour to evoke reminiscences which might still speak in favor of American isolationism or warn against the risk of entanglements through the negotiations of soldiers. For the legislative majority, as for the soldiers, the United States had entered upon a stage where military allies, however weak, however distant, were to be welcomed. It was realized that "solitary armed might is little better than unarmed isolation."[377]

While it is doubtful that every Russian move since 1945 has been militarily conceived, there is still great plausibility in this military interpretation, which has brought the greatest peace-time cycle of armament competition the world has yet witnessed. Such an interpretation meant that the threat centered in Moscow had to be met in an increasingly military manner. With the fatal concept of class conflict as essentially warlike, no clear distinction between political as non-military, and military as non-political, was any longer possible. As a matter of historical sequence the soldiers and soldier-statesmen of the Western nations, such as General George C. Marshall, first viewed this conflict as fundamentally military in its nature and persuaded the sometimes reluctant civilian politicos to embrace this outlook and prepare more energetically for the eventuality of the cold war turning into a hot one. According to Field Marshal Montgomery, the nations of the West were already at war with Communism as the anti-Christian religion challenging Western civilization.

> As a Christian soldier I declare myself an enemy of Communism and all it stands for. It is my view that the nations of the West are today at war with Communism. It is often called a "cold war" but is nonetheless war. It is possible that this struggle between communism and democracy might eventually lead us into a "hot" or shooting war. This would be disastrous for the whole world. Therefore it must be prevented [by organizing the Western nations' united strength].[378]

After the American monopoly of the atomic bomb had ended, American framers of strategy were forced to re-examine the strength of Western Europe as a defensible base or beachhead. This re-examination, as of 1948, found the West lamentably weak as compared with Russian landpower. The number of soldiers of the monolithically-organized Soviet bloc was estimated by Washington at 5,200,000 in the autumn of 1948, as against a military strength of 4,400,000 in the non-united anti-Communist countries. And the latter figure included such dubious elements as Greece, Turkey, Portugal, Spain, Switzerland, and the several hundred thousand French and Dutch soldiers who were on colonial duty in the Far East.[379] It must have appeared highly doubtful at that time whether the European foothold could be defended successfully on the Rhine or whether the American frontier would not have to be held along the Pyrenées instead (with troops, incidentally, who had never shown any particular talent for mountain warfare). This would, however, amount to a strategic sacrifice of terrain that by any political consideration was intolerable.

The will on America's part to defend the line of the Rhine was the underlying strategic idea of the North Atlantic Treaty. It rested on the determination to establish a common defensive frontier "in the heart of Europe," to defend Western Europe against an aggressor at the outset of aggression and not to liberate it from aggression for a second or third time. The American soldiers, in their language of deference to the constitutional authorities, expected to receive orders to move quickly in the case of an invasion of the guaranteed area covered by the North Atlantic Treaty.[380] This assurance was necessary in order to meet European expectations, notably those of the French. To them it was of supreme importance that France and Western Europe be spared the invasion that an Anglo-Saxon concept of "fluid" strategy might permit, on the principle of reculer pour mieux sauter. The French Premier Henri Queuille told an American reporter:

> We know that once Western Europe was occupied, America would again come to our aid and eventually we would again be liberated. But the process would be terrible. The next time you probably would be liberating a corpse ...The real frontier of Western Europe which must be defended must be moved well beyond the actual frontiers, because once the geographic frontiers of these countries are crossed it will be too late for America to save very much. Even fifteen days after the invasion will be too late.[381]

Political sentiments still impeded strategic considerations. French fears and American phobias at first forbade the rearmament of Western Germany, which, because of its great military potential, American and British soldiers were the first to advocate.[382] But that seemed a long time off, marked by a Western slowness that tended to deny the seriousness of the Bolshevist menace.

In order to build up a Western force of even modest proportions before a Russian aggression might move westward, a great deal of American aid had to be given, in the form of arms and men. Arms aid, freely given, not lent, was required to equip the Pact nations' armed forces and make of them "sturdy, self-reliant" partners across the sea.[383] In an exchange of notes of April 5, 1949, the Brussels Powers applied for material assistance from the American Government as essential to their program of collective self-defense. They were hopeful that the defense program would not interfere with their economic recovery program, also American-aided. The United States Government promised to recommend to Congress that such assistance be rendered.[384] This material assistance program was actually "conceived and developed slightly in advance of the North Atlantic treaty."[385]

The Truman Administration consequently asked Congress for $1,145,000,000 for the fiscal year 1949-50 to cover military equipment to be delivered over the ensuing two years, with one billion dollars-worth earmarked for the Atlantic nations.[386] The Administration argued that without such aid there would be nothing on which to base the general strategic plan of defense to be developed among the Treaty partners.[387] Even if the transfer of arms, to be taken partly from reserve stocks, should temporarily weaken the American forces, that, Secretary Johnson said, would still be no loss, for "any temporary impact on our own forces will be more than outweighed by the resultant strengthening of our allies." And in this way we would provide, General Bradley told the economy-minded Congress, "at a minimum expense, additional measures for our own security." With the help of these American supplies, at least a beginning was to be made towards restoring Western European strength. Within five years perhaps, attainment of the ultimate goal of thirty to fifty fully-equipped divisions might enable Western Europe to resist the Russian steam-roller. Or, differently put, we might thus succeed in compensating for the relative decrease in American atomic power.

An opposition move in favor of economy was also the expression of a hope that the Atlantic Treaty would prove effective by its mere existence on paper. In the end, the move for cutting down the Administration's arms aid bill was overcome. The Mutual Defense Assistance Act of October 6, 1949, was voted in the proposed amount (223 to 109 in the House and 55 to 24 in the Senate), subject only to the proviso introduced in the Senate that the larger part of the material would not go abroad until the President had approved of an "integrated" European defense plan prepared by the Common Defense Council envisaged under the North Atlantic Treaty.

Unter the Act, bilateral agreements were to be made by the giver and by those asking for aid, which is to say, all signatories with the exception of Portugal, Iceland and Canada. These agreements were to cover the use of the arms and the purposes to which they might and might not be applied. This provided the United States with yet another lever to press for the integration of the recipient national forces into one organized whole, in the hands of which American arms would find their most effective use. American missions were to be permitted to inspect and observe the uses to which such aid was put. As a partial quid pro quo, the United States expected to receive assistance from the partners for its own stockpiling of strategic materials. The recipients bound

themselves not to use the American supplies for any other than Pact purposes, not to use them outside the North Atlantic sphere, and not to export any of the materiel supplied without prior agreement of the United States. The recipients were further required not to pass on any information on any secret weapon supplied by the United States.[388] These restrictions were agreed to by the recipients. Agreement came less easily and less fully on American attempts to form a common export policy with regard to Soviet Russia and its satellites.[389] United States demands, including the forming of a permanent consultative committee to supervise exports to the Communist countries, met with concerted opposition on the part of the European nations, whose economy could not easily dispense with a considerable amount of East-West trade.[390]

In an age of still-increasing obstacles to the free movement of civilians, the North Atlantic Powers in their bilateral agreements assured free movement to the military and other personnel discharging responsibilities under these agreements. Such personnel would operate as part of their home country's embassy under the direction and control of the civilian head of the mission and would enjoy the usual diplomatic privileges and immunities. Their strength was assumed to run from twenty-five military men for the smaller countries to a much higher number for the large ones.[391]

Accords between the United States and the eight active members of the North Atlantic Treaty embodying these provisions and tied in with the Economic Cooperation agreements with the countries in question but designed to outlast the latter, were signed on January 27, 1950. They were to meet the specific conditions prescribed in the Mutual Defense Assistance Act, requiring certainty that the resources to be made available would be used with maximum efficiency and would not be used to develop separate and unrelated defenses.[392] After such guarantees had been given, arms shipments to the European partners, including the transfer of American naval vessels, began on a small scale. Their arrival and the arrival of supervisors of the arms aid program—dubbed "American military controllers" by the Communists—were greeted by Communist demonstrations, including some longshoremen's strikes in France and Italy.[393]

The development of the North Atlantic Treaty Organization was not a simple thing to achieve. After the passing of the Mutual Defense Assistance Act, Secretary of Defense Johnson stated that no less than 15,000 individuals on the American end alone would be required to administer the program.[394] The organization would have to cover the purely military side of staff cooperation and ultimately unified command, as well as the political, financial-economic and war-industrial fields. After the middle of 1949, an International Working Group, largely identical with the one that had drafted the Treaty itself, began to work out an organizational schema "under the leadership of the Department of State" and with full participation of the Office of the Secretary of Defense, assisted by the Joint Chiefs of Staff and the Munitions Board.[395]

In the interest of furthering these organizational labors, the American Joint Chiefs of Staff undertook a trip to the European countries in August 1949 and entered upon an exchange of ideas with the military representatives of the other Treaty Powers. They discussed problems such as these: Should the Fontainebleau set-up, which was still without an operating staff and had not progressed beyond strategic studies, be absorbed by an overall organization? Should an executive committee of three or four members of the larger Powers be formed? (This proposal was favored neither by the smaller Powers nor by France if she were to be excluded from it.) How should the members contribute to the pool of strength? Should each nation provide its share of each military element? Or should each nation's contribution be made according to its special abilities, such as the American ability in the field of strategic bombing? Must the members give up any conception of their own forces as "balanced" in themselves? How was the national inclination towards having a balanced force to be reconciled with the supra-national interest for which duplication was apt to prove a waste? How many regional defense groups, subordinate to the Atlantic Defense Committee, should be formed, four or five? And in the background remained the all-transcending question of unified command, which was urged by some Congressional spokesmen who demanded that it be set up in advance of any armed aggression.[396] An organizational pattern, which took all or most of these problems into consideration, was approved by the North Atlantic Council at its first meeting on September 17, 1949.

The first meeting of the Defense Committee, which was composed of the defense ministers of the twelve nations, was held in Washington on October 5, 1949, under the chairmanship, for a year, of Secretary Johnson. The tasks before it were largely organizational: to prepare, approve, or change the machinery for the coordination of the military, naval and air plans of the signatories and to give the green light for the soldiers to go ahead with their specific arrangements. They also set up a Military Committee, headed by General Bradley, and other subordinate groups, which were "to translate their basic directions into concrete steps" and to commence planning for the in-

tegrated defense of the North Atlantic area. The whole tenor of announcements was one of profound respect for civilian supremacy, thus satisfying the requirements of the Mutual Defense Assistance Act.[397] Civilian supremacy was also provided for in the personnel set-up of the various committees, as well as in the transfer of much of the powers and authority vested in the President by the Mutual Defense Assistance Act to the Secretary of State. He was to have "responsibility and authority for the direction of the programs authorized by the Act" and was to be coordinator of the operations of such programs, while advising and consulting with the Secretary of Defense and the Administrator for Economic Cooperation in order to assure the coordination of the mutual-defense-assistance activities with the national defense and the Economic Recovery programs.[398] A civilian-diplomatic supervisor was to be added to each American embassy or legation in the North Atlantic area to head the operation of the military aid program in the country in question, together with a military staff that would help to ascertain what military equipment was required, assist in training, inspection, etc. Their activities were to be centered in the Washington office of the director of the Mutual Defense Assistance Program, of which the first incumbent was James Bruce.

The forming of a Financial and Economic Committee was publicly announced in mid-November 1949. It was to keep military costs of the mutual assistance program in line with the economies and recovery programs of the member nations. And, if found desirable and appropriate, it was to prepare plans for economic mobilization in case of emergency. A Military Production and Supply Board was to function somewhat on the model of the American Munitions Board, with the United States Department of Defense reviewing and if necessary modifying materiel demands presented by the Military Committee. And it was to consider problems such as production, exchange, and standardization of weapons. Both the Financial and Economic Committee and the Production and Supply Board were to have permanent working staffs located in London. Meetings of the full memberships would rotate among the capitals of the treaty nations.[399]

The continual military conversations about a joint strategy for the North Atlantic area resulted in a "strategic concept for the integrated defense" of the area. This was announced at the second meeting of the Defense Committee in Paris on December 1, 1949. This meeting completed "the organizational phase of the Treaty" and could now be followed up with more detailed defense plans.[400] The "strategic concept" had been worked out by the Military Committee, under

Bradley's chairmanship, and by its standing committee, following the first meeting in Washington. The objective was "adequate military strength accompanied by the economy of resources and manpower."[401] This over-all concept was to absorb the concepts and plans formulated earlier in the year by the Brussels Pact nations in the presence of American and Canadian observers, "the first peace-time plan of the sort in modern European history and the biggest allied battle plan since D-day."[402] This mutual defense plan was formally approved by the Council of the North Atlantic Treaty Organization, meeting for the third time in Washington on January 6, 1950. The diplomatic representatives on the spot acted for their foreign ministers and also maintained final civilian supremacy even in questions of strategy, at least in a formal sense. The question of supreme command, though mooted, was left for future consideration. It was not considered a necessary pre-condition to the release of supplies and funds authorized in the Mutual Defense Assistance Act by the United States President.

The functioning of the highly important Military Committee was another question that remained open. It meets in full every three months, while a Standing Group of soldiers (American-British-French) sits almost continuously in Washington and reports to the Military Committee. The British have had experience in the past with such spark-plugs among civil servants in defense activities as Lord Esher, who "for years thought daily of war—both by land and sea," Sir Maurice Hankey and others. In the British view, the office of secretary-general seemed necessary in order to maintain the communication lines among the military groups and the Defense Committee. The Defense Committee would have final responsibility for military decisions, for which the usual war minister's parliamentary and other political preoccupations might not always allow the necessary time and concentration. The Americans were said not to favor this idea, which appeared somewhat foreign to their own much shorter bureaucratic traditions. They were afraid of conferring such great powers on a seemingly irresponsible personage and preferred merely to have a glorified filing clerk in the position.[403]

The Standing Group was to form the keystone of the military structure of the North Atlantic area. It was to unify the plans of the five regional groups—North European, Western European, Southern European-Western Mediterranean, North Atlantic Ocean, and Canadian-United States. The activities and achievements of these groups have been reported as greatly varied.[404] In the case of each group, American membership was requested, even where there was no geographic proximity on America's part. And America acceded

each time in order to participate actively in defense planning. It was also hoped that American participation would serve as a harmonizing factor.

The staff conversations at the top level were occasionally illuminated by joint peacetime maneuvers of various sub-groups of the Atlantic allies, something from which pre-world war allies had always abstained as too provocative.[405] As compared with the more polite usages prevailing in the earlier periods, there was never any doubt about "the enemy" against whom they combined for action. In exercises held by British and Belgian groups near Aachen in October 1948, the theme was that "strong invading forces reached the Rhine and are attempting to cross it."[406] A Canadian army unit of some one hundred men joined an American regiment of Marines for the American naval exercises in the Caribbean in March 1949. The exercises included landing maneuvers that were to furnish the guests with the latest amphibious warfare experiences, as demonstrated in an attack on one of the islands in the Caribbean Sea.[407] Combined exercises of the Brussels Pact navies were held off the British coast early in July 1949, under the general command of French Admiral Jaujard, "Flag Officer, Western Europe." The standardization and unification of signalling were said to have been the principal object of these naval games, in which some sixty British, French and Dutch warships participated.[408] Even before the ratification of the North Atlantic Treaty by the United States Senate, American air forces joined Western European airmen in exercises that were to bring out tactical lessons in connection with the use of high-speed jet planes.[409] Small units of various Powers joined in the September 1949 maneuvers held on German soil by the occupying forces. The British Pacific Fleet combined in exercises with the United States air forces stationed in Japan in 1948 and again in July 1949. On the latter occasion, the purpose was to ascertain whether ships and planes based on Japan would be able to detect and destroy an enemy force of aircraft and surface vessels during its approach to Tokyo Bay.[410] In March 1950, the U.S. Navy for the first time held maneuvers in the Western hemisphere in which not only forces of Canada but also British and Dutch units participated.[411] In July 1950, British, Norwegian, and Danish troops undertook joint exercises on the Luneburg Heath, just west of the Russian zone, carefully sealing off the area against observers from behind the Iron Curtain.[412] The following month, British and Italian naval units carried out joint maneuvers designed "to familiarize the former enemy with British anti-submarine tactics."[413]

A review of first achievements and persisting deficiencies was held at the third meeting of the

Defense Committee, convened at The Hague on April 1 and 2, 1950. The contributions of the various member nations came under discussion: Could Britain, hard-pressed to maintain her recovery plans, contribute still more in arms productions, notably jet planes, to the re-equipment of the Continentals? Could the desire of each member to have a military force balanced within itself be at all reconciled with the need for specific assignments in accordance with specific military tasks and functions in the event of war? Under a system of apportionment, the United States would still shoulder responsibility for strategic bombing, Britain and France for tactical bombing. The American and British navies, supported by French, Italian and Dutch units, would maintain supremacy on the seas, while the Continental nations would provide most of the ground forces, at least at the outbreak of a war. It was agreed that certain weaknesses had to be accepted by all Treaty nations "so far as a balanced structure is concerned, in order to achieve a greater collective capability."[414] Imbalance within the forces participating in the Treaty was, General Bradley declared, part of an agreement by which

> a small bit of sovereignty is relinquished. But when I think that national pride and sovereignty are often paid for with the life and blood of soldiers, I feel that we must accept the more difficult alternative which comes with this joining of hands in collective defense...In future years we must consider most carefully what our friends can best contribute before we decide what the American dollar should buy for the collective defense. If necessary, in future years we can identify our armed forces so closely with those of our allies that we can achieve a collective force for security. This is in keeping with the principle that each nation must provide that for which its resources and its geographical location are best suited.[415]

The imbalance would, in the case of America, lead to the strengthening of naval and air force at the expense of the ground forces. And it would oblige the French to furnish most of the first and most expendable infantry against an onslaught in Europe. (This was exploited a good deal by Communist propaganda.) It would, however, also tend to keep the partnership from breaking apart, since no partner could expect to fight without the others. It would also make the partnership more peaceful. No partner would dare to undertake a war alone, since as a lone belligerent he would find himself without the required components of strength.

The fourth meeting of the Council of the North Atlantic Treaty in London in May 1950 endorsed the conclusion to which the military men had come, not without reluctance. The difficulties of pooling manpower and economic power appeared nearly insuperable, unless it could be convincingly demonstrated that to agree to a national imbalance of forces, and thus to avoid duplication, might prove to be the way to avoid the bankruptcy of the various national economies or the lowering of their living standards. For these consequences would unfailingly result, should there be insistence on the traditional balanced national force of infantry-artillery-air force-navy. The horns of the dilemma were labelled aggression and depression. In the attempt to meet the first danger, the second must not be overlooked. The Council therefore unanimously agreed that

> if adequate military defense of the member countries is to be achieved it must be along the lines of the most economical and effective utilization of the forces and materials at the disposal of the North Atlantic countries. They accordingly urged their governments to concentrate on the creation of balanced collective forces in the progressive build-up of the defense of the North Atlantic area, taking at the same time fully into consideration the requirements for national forces which arise out of commitments external to the North Atlantic area.[416]

In its infrequent meetings, the Council was unable to cope with the scope and constancy of the problems coming before it. The Council thereupon decided to set up a sort of North Atlantic high command "in order to improve the functioning of the North Atlantic Treaty Organization and to guide its future work." This was formed by their own deputies, sitting in perpetuity, who were to give direction to the work of the Treaty organization. It sat in London with an American chairman, Charles M. Spofford, as the principal coordinator of all defense matters. The deputies were given the following tasks: (1) To coordinate the various planning activities related to defense; (2) To recommend the measures necessary to carry out these plans; (3) To consider common political problems related to the objectives of the treaty; (4) To promote and coordinate public information on treaty questions; (5) To consider the development of political and economic cooperation as contemplated in Article 2 of the treaty."[417]

The Permanent Committee of Deputies had its constituent meeting in London on July 25, 1950, in the shadow of Communist aggression in Korea. As far as the published part of their deliberations showed, the Committee continued to shun the problem of assigning a role in the defense of the West to Western Germany. It set out, however, to re-

vise earlier plans for the defense of Western Europe
by aiming at a complete defense set-up for the
area within three, or possibly two years, instead
of five. Russian tolerance was no longer taken for
granted as extending over the five-year period.
They also aimed at raising the originally contemplated strength of thirty ground force divisions to thirty-six as the required minimum—
the immediate lesson of the Korean War being
to re-emphasize the infantry-tanks combination.
Another impact was registered in the shift of
emphasis from economic reconstruction and stability to security. The deputies agreed, as one of
their communiqués stated, "that if economic recovery and social welfare are to be assured, adequate security based on the establishment of an
effective system of integrated defense is more
than ever essential."[418] They proposed that the
several governments boost their defense expenditure and lengthen the term of service for their
conscripts, as they subsequently did; and they discussed the organization of a North Atlantic
command headquarters in Europe with full American participation. Supreme strategic direction
would continue to come from Washington.

In order to further the "balanced" defense of
the North Atlantic area, the Truman Administration proposed continued material assistance to the
European partners, who were only beginning to receive arms shipments. In June 1950, Truman suggested another billion-dollar appropriation bill
for this purpose to Congress. It was passed in
August 1950. Nevertheless the partners had
unprecedented arms budgets to carry—8.2% of
the national income in the case of France, with
an 18% rise in the 1951 budget over the original
1950 budget. France, rather than be forced back
into a war economy, sought additional assistance
from the United States. The latter tried to set a
standard of spending at 10% of the national income,
a rate to which Britain was willing to lift her
outlay from the previous rate of 8%.[419] (Meanwhile the Soviet Union continued defense expenditure at a rate of approximately 30% of the
national income.)[420] These demands, akin to
those that had arisen among partners to earlier
military coalitions, were burdens not specified
in the Pact itself. They were even imposed on
non-members. In November 1950, well ahead of
any Pact membership, the West Germans were
told that their contribution to the defense of Europe which, in the form of payments for the cost
of military occupation, amounted to less than 5%
of their national income at the time, would have
to be raised nearer to 10%. The American per-
centage at the time was fifteen.[421]

The soldiers of the Western nations, among the
earliest to become disillusioned over the outcome of the coalition war against the Axis, soon

conceived of the mounting conflict between the
expanding East and the shrinking West as primarily, or ultimately, military in character. Still,
the Marshall Plan, bearing the name of a distinguished soldier, was an attempt to avoid or postpone the full military interpretation of the conflict
and to meet Communism in the socio-economic
field. Then the experience of the coup in Czechoslovakia and the Berlin blockade convinced the
Western civilian governors of the unavoidability
of military counter-measures. The soldiers of
the West remembered their own recent experience with coalition warfare and thought of combined staffs as the organizational minimum for
fighting such a war. They observed the tight control that the Russian Army had extended over
the armies of the Communist satrapies. They
were fully aware that in the democratic world
all long-term agreements of a military nature
had to be freely and openly arrived at—as openly
as their military character would permit. They
in turn agreed to and even advocated a far-reaching, though still far from complete, renunciation
of military sovereignty and national planning for
the case of war. The actual exercise of supreme
command, however, would be postponed until a
state of war should arrive or approach still more
closely. These military arrangements made the
anti-Bolshevist front not only capitalist-democra-
tic, as the Russians dogmatically expected, but
also military—a set of coalescent factors that
was not extant when Red Army and Reichswehr
cooperated against the victors of Versailles.
The fronts became more than ever those of two
"uni-forces" in the world, with only a few independent local fronts left, as in the Middle East.
Understandings of a military nature, and more
or less permanent agencies set up for military
purposes, ranged all over the world.[422] They
were approved and sought after by the civilian
governments and occasionally attempted over
their heads.[423] By 1949, the predominant content and purpose of alliances and pacts had become
military, even if they were no longer called
"military conventions."

THE EUROPEAN DEFENSE COMMUNITY

At the Brussels meeting in December 1950, the
year of Korea, the various NATO representatives
were full of promises that they would increase
their forces and give greater priority to defense
expenditure, while trying at the same time to
safeguard economic recovery and standards of
living. They received the promise of assistance
towards these ends from the United States. Once
more the American officials directly and indirectly concerned with defense questions had examined America's position in the world vis-à-vis

the Soviet Union. Once more they had come to the conclusion that retirement into isolation, for which there was political rather than military temptation, could only mean giving the Russians a strategic opportunity that would be catastrophic for the United States.[424] Germany must not only be kept out of Russian control but must also be drawn into active participation in the defense of the West. The Truman Administration had been thoroughly, if hurriedly, persuaded of this need by its soldiers.[425] The most outstanding of these soldiers was to take supreme command of the NATO forces.

On April 1, 1951, General Eisenhower assumed command of NATO and held it until June 1, 1952. To the Supreme Headquarters [Allied Powers in Europe (SHAPE)] were transferred the staff organization already existing at Fontainebleau and other groups of the Western Union, which itself remained in force juristically speaking. Its provisions for automatic military assistance to any member attacked contained an automatism still stricter than that provided for in the North Atlantic Treaty. Greater unity and acceleration in the production of materiel was to be attempted through a Defense Production Board of the twelve countries sitting in London and responsible to the Defense Committee composed of the defense ministers. This Board was to overcome the persistent inclination of each member state to produce as far as possible its own forces' equipment for the case of war, instead of having them produced where it was most economical and safest to manufacture them. However, it could hardly ever reach an integration of European-American defense production as complete as that of the military forces under Eisenhower's command. National economies would not as easily surrender their sovereignty as soldiers now were ready, or even anxious, to do.

Organizational changes are usually not made for managerial reasons alone. Political motives also enter in, sometimes pushing an organization well ahead of mass sentiment and conviction which, it is hoped, will later give it sanction and substance. While the original Council of Ministers —foreign, defense, and finance—was to continue in its policy-making role, its Lisbon meeting (February 1952) decided to set up a Permanent Council of NATO. The Permanent Council was to sit in or near Paris, close to SHAPE, with members of ministerial rank continually representing the home ministries having to do with defense affairs. This Council was to have a Secretary General, a post that went begging for a long time until filled by retired General Lord Ismay. Ismay, Secretary for Commonwealth Affairs in the Churchill Cabinet at the time, was a life-long soldier "with vast experience in military

planning, strategy and administration." This Secretary of NATO was to be "the chief of an international secretariat for the civilian side of the Treaty organization," a civilian pendant to General Eisenhower. He was also to be vice-chairman of the Permanent North Atlantic Council.[426] Whatever else his appointment signified, it indicated general unreadiness on the part of civilian politicians to assume a task in the interest of supra-national defense. Other organizational changes were indicative of the difficulties encountered in the operation of a peace-time coalition without precedent. These difficulties, political, psychological, and economic, meant that the goals set from time to time for NATO forces were never reached.

Security and interest, still too nationally conceived, and considered in short terms, interfered on numerous occasions with supra-national strategic considerations. When the problem of stationing additional American ground forces in Europe arose, Congress hesitated to see such a large part of American force invested in what was essentially a very exposed position. Reluctance was put aside when Congress was told that without such new divisions, four in addition to the two already stationed in Germany, the European allies would succumb to "a mood of neutralism which is, for them and for all of us, a shortcut to suicide." Without them, it was argued, the supreme aim of American strategy, "to prevent an attack against Europe," could not be achieved; whereas their arrival would spark additional European endeavors and would double their contribution within a year's time.[427]

The cold war produced nearly all the old problems of coalition wars, and some new ones as well. Subsidies, although no longer so-called, were expected or demanded. And they were granted by the strongest Power in the coalition for direct or indirect military purposes.[428] An American pay office, the Mutual Security Assistance Agency headed by W. Averell Harriman, was to coordinate these matters. The appointments to unified command in several of the local theaters, such as the North Atlantic and the Mediterranean, provoked traditional nationalistic protests. British conservatives, inside and outside the Royal Navy, took exception to the appointments of Americans that had been made by the twelve defense ministers. The protests resulted in political compromises at the expense of clear lines of command.[429]

Repeated British suggestions that the well-tested wartime joint and bilateral staff arrangements be revived met with ill-concealed protests, especially from France. The Washington Standing Group, staffed by American, French and British officers, remained the highest military echelon.

American criticism of British reluctance to participate more closely in the various Western European bodies for unification was deeply resented in Britain.[430]

Political strife within the member states reacted continually, and most often unfavorably, on the initiation and functioning of the various NATO plans, interfering with what seemed to the military exclusively military considerations and necessities. The Dutch Government dismissed a chief of staff in 1951 because he had publicly warned against the neglect of alliance duties, something which General Eisenhower had indicated more tactfully.[431] Party politics and ideology interfered with the close cooperation of new allies with considerable military potential, such as Western Germany, Spain, and Yugoslavia.[432] Whenever the threat from Communism seemed to abate, if only slightly, the protest against alliance with these states, who to some were hereditary enemies, grew in strength. This exasperated the soldiers and the by now most strategic-minded of all diplomatic offices, the United States Department of State. The Department's difficulties grew with every new alliance, such as the ones with the nations in and around the Pacific (with the Philippines, of August 30, 1951, with Australia and New Zealand of September 1, 1951, and to a certain extent the treaties with Japan of September 8, 1951). The drawing of Greece and Turkey closer to NATO and finally into actual membership fortunately provoked less trouble among the partners, even though Greece expressed reservations about having her forces serve under an Italian commander.

As far as Franco-German relations were concerned, the French recalled the "hereditary enemy" tradition somewhat more often than the Germans. This proved to be the greatest obstacle to the building up of a Western force of the size deemed necessary by the soldiers, French soldiers not excepted. German rearmament was finally agreed to at the Lisbon meeting in February 1952. It had been publicly proposed by the Americans, soldiers first and then civilians, during the NATO Council meeting in September 1950. Rearmament was accepted by the Adenauer Government, despite the various limitations imposed by the Allies on German Wehrhoheit, or military sovereignty. The occupation of German territory continued, though under a new title, and Bonn was denied membership in NATO itself. This second-rate status was compensated for by the NATO Powers' assurance that an attack on any part of Germany, including Berlin, would be regarded in the same way as an attack against the territory of any member state.

The German contribution to the defense of the West proved to be a military prescription that large parts of the peoples and the politicos of the NATO group could not swallow or, having swallowed, could not digest. Despite much matter-of-fact American suasion, historical memories, not always taught à propos or rightly applied, proved stronger than military necessity as understood by the soldiers.[433] Liberalism and Labor seemed unable to bring forth the political ideology required for a re-understanding with Germany, something which older ages and societies had known how to produce and apply even with grace and dignity. Seldom has a bare-faced necessity remained so utterly devoid of ideological wrappings. The civilian fear and suspicion of Germany, Spain, and Yugoslavia proved, intermittently if not basically, stronger in many places than fear or suspicion of Russia. It was the soldiers who had to furnish not only the military advice but also the better part of the political-internationalist argument.[434] As General Eisenhower told the North Atlantic Council sitting in Rome on November 30, 1951:

> We need German assistance both in geography and military strength if these can be obtained with justice and respect to them and to ourselves...Gaining German strength without creating a menace to any others and in such a way that the Germans could cooperate with self-respect, our goals will become much more readily obtainable. Here I must say one word about the Germans. We cannot have mere hirelings and expect them to operate efficiently. The North Atlantic Treaty Organization has no use for soldiers representing second-rate morale or a second-rate country. German help will be enormously important if it is freely given and it can be given, I believe, through a European Defense Force.

In this statement, a warning to politicians, one sees the awareness of a modern general that using Germans as mere barbarian auxiliaries, Old Roman-style, is impossible. At the same time, endorsement, perhaps half-hearted, was given to the French attempt at military alchemy, the so-called European force as the solvent that, by keeping German units at a minimum size, would render harmless any German contribution to the defense of the West. Originally, France, almost as if she could not forget her own Foreign Legion and the continued German blood contribution to it, had striven for regiment-size units, then for 6,000-man units. Finally she was convinced by the soldiers that, considering language and other difficulties, units below division-size, perhaps 13,000 strong, were unfeasible. To what came to be called the European Defense Community Germany was to contribute—possibly by April 1954—twelve divisions, France herself fourteen, Italy eleven, and the Benelux countries three.

Without the shock of Korea, felt even by the French, not even such a limited readmission of German Wehrhoheit would have been possible. The actual performance of the NATO members in the field of rearmament still remained uneven and undecided. While comparisons of military burdens and exertions are not easily established, the following survey roughly indicates the varying contributions that members were making to the pool after one year.[435]

of militant Communistic expansion. This pattern of events, which points so surely to ultimate disaster, can be changed if only the peoples of the West have the wisdom to make a complete break with many things of the past and show a willingness to do something new and challenging. NATO itself is a significant step to meet both the present danger of aggression and the tragic struggles and dissensions that have divided our peoples in

	% age of nat'l budget for defense	% age of nat'l income for defense purposes	Mil. service term (months)	Armed forces [436] strength
U.S.	68	31.4	21	3,462,000
U.K.	33	9.7	24	608,100
France	34	13.	18	359,000
Canada	52	7.		62,000
Italy	30. 7 (or 32)	7.7	15	382,000
Netherlands	23.8	7.	16	200,000
Belgium	16.2	5.[437]	24	88,484
Luxemburg	10.1		12	2,600
Portugal	26		16	44,700
Denmark	28		10-12	15,000
Norway	18		12	
Turkey	36.71			
Greece	50 (1951)			

From 1949 to early 1952, in terms of measurable improvement, the European members of NATO doubled their arms budgets and their peacetime strengths. Adding perhaps half a million armed men, they quadrupled their output of defense goods and lengthened the service term for their conscripts by a varying number of months. [438] With the exception of Iceland and Portugal, all of them received American economic assistance. Only Canada among the full-size members could or in fact would do without it. The "Pas de monnaie pas de Suisses" attitude of ancient allies and mercenaries was not always absent, although the helper tried conscientiously not to notice.[439]

For a century and a half, the military had been the embodiment and occasional spokesmen of extreme nationalism.[440] Now it was they who had to set the civilians, notably the French politicians, and electorates straight. They provided not only the experts' purely military considerations for a defense of the West but also the ideology and historical argument for Western unity. Because the urgency was so great, this uncongenial task had to be shouldered in addition to others. Looking back over the first bloody half of the twentieth century, it seemed to General Eisenhower

almost as if the nations of the West have been, for decades, blindly enacting parts in a drama that could have been written by Lenin, prophet

the past. But NATO's development is not automatic: action is the test. To advance this great effort, unified action is required, not only among but within our nations. Yet, it has seemed more than once within our countries that political factions hold their own immediate gain higher than the fate of their nation or even that of civilization itself.[441]

For the greater effectiveness of his mission, General Eisenhower hoped to establish the unity he sought as a soldier among the free nations in better ways than prevailed in the Communist camp. For this purpose he expected more support from the politicians in Europe who, he indicated, sometimes did not do "too good a job" towards achieving unity.[442] Nearly the worst obstructionist in the field, little worse than the Communists, was another general, Charles de Gaulle, once a military anti-traditionalist himself. He protested against the European Army plan— national armies in both France and Germany seemed far preferable to him. He also protested against Eisenhower's "foreign command that apparently decides how and where French forces will be used, which of our territories will be defended or not, how our generals shall be employed."[443]

In the competition for the soul of Western man, the Soviet Government appealed to the recent frightful experience of German militarism. They warned the peoples that the negotiations of their own governments with Bonn were "legalizing the re-establishment of a German army headed by Nazi generals" and thereby paving "the way for a resurgence of aggressive Western militarism." "All this," they continued, "indicates that the revanchist ruling quarters of Western Germany and the North Atlantic group of powers are making a deal. This deal can only be founded on support of the revanchist aspirations of the Bonn Adenauer Government, which is preparing to unleash a new war in Europe."[444]

Undeterred by such appeals over their heads, the Big Three of the West signed a peace treaty—or contract, as they preferred to call it—with Western Germany at Bonn, on May 26, 1952. They thereby admitted her "to the community of free nations as an equal partner" with equal obligations, if not quite with equal rights. The next day, the Treaty establishing the European Defense Community was signed at Paris. While the United States Senate promptly ratified the Bonn contract, (on July 1, 1952, by a vote of 77 to 5) the two instruments have been awaiting the ratification of most other states ever since. They were held up by sharp opposition and conflicts in French and German internal politics and by the temporary absence of American urging, due to preoccupation with a presidential campaign and the transition from a Democratic to a Republican regime. Meanwhile, the precarious state of the various national economies kept rearmament at a much lower level than had been hoped for.

**　　　　**　　　　**

Of all democratic policies, those concerning national defense have least often originated in a genuine mass sentiment. In the development of the North Atlantic Treaty system, the very considerable unity of governmental and military leadership proved, outside the United States, considerably in advance of mass sentiment and understanding. At various times, this caused (notably in France) the disavowal of governments accused or suspected of having neglected the national interest to undertake onerous military obligations. The United States received very little credit for her surrender of isolationism.[445] At the same time, resentment at her prodding hindered the acceptance of American policies, suggestions, and military and material help.

FOOTNOTES

1. Herre (ed.), Politisches Handwörterbuch, I, 1027.
2. Jany, Geschichte der preussischen Armee, III, 110.
3. Fugier, Napoléon et Italie, pp. 53 f.
4. Wellington, Dispatches, XI, 653 ff.
5. Ibid., XII, 541 ff., 557, 643, 694.
6. Berner, Geschichte des preussischen Staates, pp. 530 ff.
7. Waliszewski, Le règne d'Alexandre Ier, II, 158 f.
8. Webster, The Foreign Policy of Castlereagh, 1812-1815, p. 114.
9. The literature on Tauroggen is ample. A good summary can be found in Voss, Die Konvention von Tauroggen.
10. Bernhardi, Geschichte Russlands und der europäischen Politik in den Jahren 1814 bis 1831, I, 163.
11. Triepel, Die Hegemonie. Ein Buch von führenden Staaten, pp. 547 ff.
12. Stoffel, Rapports militaires, pp. 354 ff.
13. Oncken, Rheinpolitik, III, 431; Eyck, Bismarck, II, 421.
14. Bernhardi, Geschichte Russlands, VIII, 373 f. For the details of the arguments with Bavaria, see Leyh, Die bayerische Heeresreform unter König Ludwig II; for those with Baden, see Oncken (ed.), Grossherzog Friedrich I von Baden und die deutsche Politik von 1854-1871, Vol. II.
15. Oncken, Rheinpolitik, III, 306, 309 f.
16. Oesterreich-Ungarns Aussenpolitik, VII, 8934.
17. Ibid., VIII, 10393; Republik Oesterreich, Diplomatische Aktenstücke zur Vorgeschichte des Krieges 1914, I, 67.
18. After 1866, the Chief of Staff of the Army, Colonel Suckow, was also the leader of the Unionist party in Württemberg. Gregorovius, Roman Journals, p. 337.
19. For details of this Italian military penetration in its earlier stages, see an article by Hamilton Fish Armstrong in Foreign Affairs, January 1928, pp. 191 ff.
20. The Russo-Chinese agreement of February 14, 1950, provides that Port Arthur may be jointly used as a naval base.
21. Omladina (Bèlgrade), quoted in the N.Y. Times, October 25, 1950.
22. N. Y. Times, December 20, 1944.
23. Ibid., March 18, 1948.
24. Frankfurter Allgemeine Zeitung, December 9, 1950.
25. The Alvensleben Convention was a Russo-Prussian instrument negotiated by soldiers, which provided for common measures against the Polish Insurrection.
26. Tirpitz, Erinnerungen, p. 26.
27. G. P., I, 120 ff.
28. Busch, Bismarck. Some Secret Pages, III, 264 ff.
29. G. P., I, 128 ff.
30. Deutsches Adelsblatt, November 15, 1903, cited by Eisner in Der Geheimbund des Zaren, p. 5.

31. Doc. dipl. fr., 2nd series, XI, 126 f., 174, 678.
32. For the following discussion, see Rudolf Kissling, "Die militärischen Beziehungen und Bindungen zwischen Oesterreich-Ungarn und dem Deutschen Reiche vor dem Weltkriege," Berliner Monatshefte, November 1926; Georg Graf Waldersee, "Uber die Beziehungen des deutschen zum oesterreich-ungarischen Generalstabe vor dem Weltkrieg," Ibid., February 1930; Eduard Heller, "Bismarcks Stellung zur Führung des Zweifrontenkrieges," Archiv für Politik und Geschichte, VII (1926), 677 ff.; and Seyfert, Die militärischen Beziehungen und Vereinbarungen zwischen dem deutschen und dem oesterreichischen Generalstab vor und bei Beginn des Weltkriegs.
33. March 1875. Hohenlohe, Denkwürdigkeiten, II, 152.
34. Bismarck, Gedanken und Erinnerungen, II, 287; G. P., VI, 1190, 1193.
35. Waldersee, Denkwürdigkeiten, I, 219.
36. Glaise-Horstenau, Franz Josephs Weggefährte, p. 289.
37. Kuhl, Der deutsche Generalstab in Vorbereitung und Durchführung des Weltkriegs, pp. 154 ff.
38. Waldersee, Denkwürdigkeiten, I, 319.
39. Ibid., I, 354 f.
40. G. P., VI, 1237.
41. Heller, "Bismarcks Stellung," Archiv für Politik und Geschichte, pp. 681 f.
42. Perhaps the most cogent military criticism of the German-Austrian alliance is by General Marx in Militärwochenblatt, October 15, 1937.
43. Caprivi to Ambassador Prince Reuss, August 25, 1891 and the latter's answer of August 27, 1891. G. P., VII, 1433 ff.
44. Ibid., XI, 2670 ff.
45. Conrad, Aus meiner Dienstzeit, I, 68 f.
46. October 22, 1908. Oesterreich-Ungarns Aussenpolitik, I, 362.
47. G. P., XXVI, 9145; Oesterreich-Ungarns Aussenpolitik, I, 703, 751 f.
48. Bülow, Denkwürdigkeiten, II, 404 f.
49. Conrad, Aus meiner Dienstzeit, I, 142, 269, 631 ff.
50. Ibid., I, 379 ff.
51. In January 1910, when Moltke informed Conrad that Germany intended, should she be forced to go to war with Russia, to clarify France's attitude by a short-termed summons in order to obtain complete certainty as to who was an enemy and who was not, Conrad proposed that a similar measure be prepared with regard to Italy. While Aehrenthal thought this appropriate, he still believed that Italy would remain neutral and that Russia would not be able to go to war for a number of years to come. He thus put him off. Ibid., II, 11, 16; Oesterreich-Ungarns Aussenpolitik, II, 1987, 2002.
52. This is the thesis of Heinrich Kanner in Der Schlüssel zur Kriegschuldfrage (1926).
53. Conrad, Aus meiner Dienstzeit, II, 102 ff.
54. Ibid., II, 57, 60.
55. In February-March 1911, Conrad proposed that he should be authorized to discuss with Moltke the case of an Anglo-French attack upon Germany, something not contemplated in the original Triplice. What should Austria do under the circumstances, particularly if Italy and Russia were to remain neutral? If Germany was to receive Austrian military support, this must be prepared and planned for well ahead of the contingency. Francis Joseph and Aehrenthal thought the Germans could not very well be approached in this matter and indicated that Conrad's officiousness went rather too far. Oesterreich-Ungarns Aussenpolitik, III, 2475, 2480, 2543, 2549.

    As for Rumania, her defection from the Triplice had become obvious, at least since 1913 when old King Carol frankly told the Germans that in a coming war his people would not fight on the side of Austria-Hungary. The Rumanian officers, particularly the younger ones, were highly wrought up against her, demanding Transylvania, where the Hungarians were maltreating the Rumanian minority. Rumanian mobilization plans for 1914 for the first time included the case of war with the Double Monarchy. Still, the certain defection of Rumania, estimated by Conrad in July 1914 at the equivalent of twenty divisions or 400,000 men should she remain neutral, or at forty divisions should she join the Entente, did nothing to deter Berchtold in his Serbian policy. Ibid., VII, 9056, 9457, 9463, 9544; VIII, 9995, 10879; D. D., I, no. 19.
56. Conrad, Aus meiner Dienstzeit, III, 667 ff.
57. July 17, 1914. D. D., I, no. 74.
58. Zwehl, Erich von Falkenhayn, p. 57.
59. Conrad, Aus meiner Dienstzeit, IV, 151 f.
60. Ibid., IV, 152.
61. Ibid., IV, 152 f.
62. Falkenhayn, Die Oberste Heeresleitung 1914-1916 in ihren wichtigsten Entschliessungen.
63. For a critique, see General Debeney, La guerre et les hommes, pp. 321 ff.
64. Wertheimer, Andrassy, III, 314.
65. The second Treaty of Alliance of Rumania with Austria, Germany and Italy of July 25, 1892, stipulated (in Article Three): "If one of the contracting parties finds itself threatened by an aggression...the Governments shall put themselves in agreement as to the measures to be taken with a view to the cooperation

of their armies. The military questions, especially that of unity of operations and of passage through their respective territories, shall be regulated by a military convention." Pribam, The Secret Treaties of Austria-Hungary, I, 166. For the belief in the existence of an Austrian-Rumanian military convention, see Doc. dipl. fr., 2nd series, XI, 496, 510, 650 f. (1908).

66. Heller, "Bismarck's Stellung," Archiv für Politik und Geschichte, VII, 687 f.
67. Glaise-Horstenau, Franz Joseph's Weggefährte, pp. 312 ff.
68. For German-Italian military collaboration, see André Fribourg, L'Italie et nous.
69. G. P., III, 572.
70. Palamenghi-Crispi (ed.), Die Memoiren Francesco Crispis, pp. 193 ff.; Bismarck, Gesammelte Werke, VIII, 574; G. P., VI, 1291 f.
71. Waldersee, Denkwürdigkeiten, I, 330 f.
72. Report of French embassy in Berlin. Doc. dipl. fr., 1st series, VII, 503.
73. G. P., XVIII, 5919.
74. Ibid., XVIII, 5817.
75. Ibid., VII, 1431, 1437, 1439.
76. Ibid., XVIII, ch. 124.
77. Ibid., XVIII, 5826; Doc. dipl. fr., 2nd series, II, 316, 318, 348.
78. G. P., XXI, ch. 154.
79. Doc. dipl. fr., 2nd series, XI, 860 ff., 939, 975, 977, 999.
80. This is based on Graf Waldersee's article "Von Deutschlands militärpolitischen Beziehungen zu Italien," Berliner Monatshefte, VII (1929), 636 ff.; G. P., XXX, 11284 ff.; Conrad, Aus meiner Dienstzeit, II, 393 f.; III, 38 f., 87 ff.
81. G. P., VI, 1318-27.
82. Pribam, The Secret Treaties of Austria-Hungary, II, 85 f.
83. Ibid., I, 241; G. P., XVIII, p. 691.
84. Oesterreich-Ungarns Aussenpolitik, V, 5696, 6366.
85. The convention was signed on June 26, revised on August 2, and came into force on November 1, 1913.
86. Oesterreich-Ungarns Aussenpolitik, VII, 8245, 8384, 8833; Pribam, The Secret Treaties of Austria-Hungary, I, 282 ff.
87. Monts, Erinnerungen und Gedanken, pp. 223, 252 f.; Waldersee in Berliner Monatshefte, VII (1929), 661.
88. Eckardstein tried to explain to Moltke in a conversation of June 1, 1914, why help from Italy in case of war could not be expected. The General indicated that he knew better. Eckardstein, Lebenserinnerungen und politische Denkwürdigkeiten, III, 185.

89. Doc. dipl. fr., 1st series, VII, 577 f.; VIII, 705 ff.
90. Pobiédonostsev, Mémoires politiques, pp. 200 ff.
91. Ibid., pp. 424 ff. Actually, Skobelev died in a Moscow bordello in 1882.
92. G. P., V, 1137 ff.
93. Doc. dipl. fr., 1st series, VII, 285, 294, 296, 575.
94. Menne, Krupp, pp. 134 ff.
95. Freycinet, Souvenirs 1878-1893 (9th ed.), pp. 415 ff., 441 f.; Doc. dipl. fr., 1st series, VIII, 439 ff.
96. Doc. dipl. fr., 1st series, VIII, 234 ff.
97. Ibid., VIII, 440 f.
98. Ibid., VIII, 576 ff.
99. Ibid., VIII, 582, 589 ff.
100. Ibid., VIII, 593 f., 599, 641 f.
101. August 11, 1891. Ibid., VIII, 646 ff.
102. Many at the time believed France to be, actually or potentially, the strongest military power, stronger than Germany; for being the richer nation she could arm herself better. Ibid., 1st series, IX, 25.
103. Ibid., IX, 113, 163, 200.
104. Ibid., IX, 263 ff., 317 ff.
105. Langer, Imperialism, I, 32.
106. Doc. dipl. fr., 1st series, IX, 341, 428, 434 f., 453, 499, 523.
107. Ibid., IX, 523 ff.
108. Ibid., IX, 575 f., 584.
109. Ibid., IX, 601, 604 f.
110. Ibid., IX, 614 ff.
111. Langer, Imperialism, I, 34 f.
112. Bompard, Mon ambassade en Russie, p. xii.
113. Boisdeffre told President Casimir-Périer: "We must get an assurance from our ally that she will go all out from the very start of hostilities. History shows that Russia is at her strongest only at the outset of a war. The vices of her administration and the instability of public opinion confuse and discourage her very quickly." Paléologue, The Turning Point, pp. 44 f.
114. The Convention was dated August 17, 1892.
115. Doc. dipl. fr., 3rd series, XI, 524.
116. Ibid., 1st series, X, 13, 17, 60, 139, 141 ff., 155, 359, 396 ff., 485 f.
117. For an account of pro-French demonstrations in the Russian Army at about this time, see G. P., VII, 1534.
118. Doc. dipl. fr., 1st series, X, 711 f. This is based (in addition to the documents contained in Doc. dipl. fr., 1st series, Vols. VII-X) on Langer, The Franco-Russian Alliance, 1890-94; the same author's Diplomacy of Imperialism, chaps. i and ii; Fischer, "Der Sinn der russisch-französischen Militärkonvention," Preussische Jahrbücher, April 1923; and

Renouvin, "Les engagements de l'Alliance Franco-Russe," Revue d'Histoire de la Guerre mondiale, October 1934.

119. Doc. dipl. fr., 1st series, VIII, 705 ff.; 2nd series, X, 492.

120. Ibid., 3rd series, II, 199.

121. When the French ambassador reminded the Tsar that the word "alliance" had been pronounced in the French parliament for the first time, the monarch answered: "And why not? Isn't that alliance a fact? What reason is there to hide it? What we should not state, that is the form of that alliance, the existence of a military convention, which ought to remain secret." Ibid., 1st series, XII, 100.

122. This is based on Ibid., 1st series, XII, 77 f. 101 f., 410 f., 435 f., 556, 561, 619, 761, 766.

123. French Yellow Book. L'Alliance Franco-russe, pp. 200 ff.

124. This is based on Doc. dipl. fr., 2nd series, I, 131 ff., 158; and G. P., XVIII, 5891 ff.

125. From Kuropatkin's diaries, quoted in Suchomlinow's Erinnerungen, pp. 229 f.

126. G. P., XVIII, 5914, 5919.

127. Bompard, Mon ambassade en Russie, p. 38.

128. For these police measures, see Eisner, Der Geheimbund des Zaren.

129. Doc. dipl. fr., 2nd series, VIII, 116, 176 ff., 231 f.

130. This is based on Paléologue, The Turning Point, pp. 62 ff., 105 f., 128, 143, 192 f., 210 f., 240, 277, 279, 281. See also Paléologue's Un prélude à l'invasion de la Belgique; le plan Schlieffen.

131. The early concern of the military with this eventuality helps to show why it was stopped twenty and thirty years later.

132. Doc. dipl. fr., 2nd series, IX, 117 ff., 273 f., 407 f.

133. Stieve, Schriftwechsel Iswolskis, II, 29 f., 368 f.

134. Bompard, Mon ambassade en Russie, p. 276; G. P., XXII, 7381.

135. This is based on Doc. dipl. fr., 2nd series, X, 152, 183 ff.; XI, 95 ff., 118 ff., 727 f., 764 ff., 787 ff.

136. Messimy, Mes Souvenirs, p. 408.

137. Joffre, Mémoires, I, 26 f.

138. Berliner Monatshefte, VII (1929), 931.

139. Ibid., 932; Doc. dipl. fr., 2nd series, no. 383; II, no. 3, 90; Stieve, Schriftwechsel Iswolskis, I, 137 ff.; Livre Noir, I, 182 f.

140. Messimy, Mes Souvenirs, p. 180.

141. Stieve, Schriftwechsel Iswolskis, II, 37, 181 ff.; Doc. dipl. fr., 2nd series, X, 28 f.

142. The rates for these loans were from seven to eleven per cent. In June 1913, France declared her readiness to allow Russia to place loans of 400-500 million francs annually on the Paris market for a number of years to come, provided the construction of the strategic railways was begun at once and the peace-time strength of the Russian Army considerably raised. Suchomlinow, Erinnerungen, pp. 243 f.

143. Text of the protocol of 1912 in Süddeutsche Monatshefte, July 1922.

144. Stieve, Schriftwechsel Iswolskis, I, 30 f.

145. Doc. dipl. fr., 3rd series, I, no. 618; II, no. 20, 24, and p. 309.

146. Stieve, Schriftwechsel Iswolskis, II, 194 ff.; Livre Noir, I, 296 ff.

147. Text in Yellow Book, L'Alliance franco-russe, pp. 210 f.; Livre Noir, I, 299.

148. Livre Noir, I, 302 ff.

149. Oesterreich-Ungarns Aussenpolitik, IV, 3667, 3685, 3704, 3711; G. P., XXXI, 11543, 11579 ff.

150. This is based on Poincaré, Au service de la France, II, 83 ff., 112 f., 131, 136; Stieve, Schriftwechsel Iswolskis, II, 204 ff.; Fay, The Origins of the World War, I, 326 f.

151. Stieve, Schriftwechsel Iswolskis, III, 178 f.

152. Ibid., III, 272 ff.

153. For details, see Frantz, Russlands Eintritt in den Weltkrieg, pp. 52 ff., 86; and Danilov, La Russie dans la guerre mondiale (1914-1917), pp. 113 ff.

154. Joffre, Mémoires, I, 131.

155. Die Internationalen Beziehungen im Zeitalter des Imperialismus, 1st series, III, 199 ff., 226, 267, 384.

156. Suchomlinow, Erinnerungen, pp. 246 ff.

157. Report of Russian military attaché in Paris, Nostiz, January 22, 1914. Die Internationalen Beziehungen, 1st series, I, 65 ff.

158. Suchomlinow, Erinnerungen, pp. 241 ff.

159. Joffre, Mémoires, I, 211; Messimy, Mes Souvenirs, pp. 186 ff.

160. Sergei, director of munitions supply, was notoriously connected with French manufacturing interests.

161. Suchomlinow, Erinnerungen, p. 243.

162. Doc. dipl. fr., 1st series, IX, 651.

163. For the problem in general, see George Ashton, "The Entente Cordiale and the Military Conversations," Quarterly Review, CCLVIII (1932), 363 ff.; Ernst Kabisch, "Die Militär- und Marinekonventionen der Triple-Entente vor dem Ausbruch des Weltkriegs," Berliner Monatshefte, V (1927), 282 ff.; J. D. Hargreaves, "The Origin of the Anglo-French Military Conversations in 1905," History, October 1951; Mary E. Thomas, "Anglo-Belgian Military Conversations of 1906," Florida State University Studies, IV (1951).

164. Paléologue, The Turning Point, pp. 261 f., 281; Doc. dipl. fr., 2nd series, VIII, 560

165. Paléologue, The Turning Point, p. 298.
166. Anderson, The First Moroccan Crisis, pp. 228 ff.
167. See Hargreaves, "The Origin of the Anglo-French Military Conversations in 1905," History, October 1951.
168. "Alliances, especially continental alliances are not in accordance with our traditions. My opinion is that if France is let in for war with Germany arising out of our agreement with her about Morocco, we cannot stand aside, but must take part with France...If we give any promise of armed assistance it must be conditional." Grey to Bertie, January 15, 1906. B. D., III, 177 f. Speaking in the House of Commons on August 8, 1918, Lloyd George at first called the understanding with France a "compact," but retracted that term and called it an "obligation of honor."
169. Repington, First World War, pp. 4 f.
170. January 15, 1906. B. D., III, 178.
171. Doc. dipl. fr., 2nd series, VIII, 410 ff.; Repington, First World War, pp. 10 ff.
172. B. D., III, 169.
173. British plans were as yet unconnected with French plans for this or any other case.
174. Doc. dipl. fr., 2nd series, VIII, 423 ff.
175. Spender, Life of Sir Henry Campbell-Bannerman, II, 257; Grey, Twenty-Five Years, I, 83.
176. Grey, Twenty-Five Years, I, 70.
177. B. D., III, 389.
178. Grey to Tweedmouth, January 16, 1906. Ibid., III, 203.
179. The intricacies of the aggression question, usually left undefined in pre-1914 discussions, were brought out by Cambon on this occasion when he said that there might be aggression on Germany's part "in consequence of some necessary action on the part of France, for the protection of her Algerian frontier or on some other ground which justified such action." Grey did not protest against the supposition that Britain might be committed for such a trivial thing as a frontier incident. Ibid., III, 175.
180. Ibid., III, 172 f. A comparison of Grierson's letter to Sanderson and Huguet's report on his talks with Grierson brings out that the British soldier revealed more to the French soldier about British war plans than to the British diplomat. Doc. dipl. fr., 2nd series, VIII, 256.
181. January 13-16, 1906. B. D., III, 174, 177, 179.
182. Haldane, Before the War, pp. 30, 32.
183. G. P., XXI, 7226; Doc. dipl. fr., 2nd series, X, 483 ff.
184. G. P., XXI, 7205 (Fay's translation).
185. B. D., III, 182 ff.; Doc. dipl. fr., 2nd series, IX, 149 ff.
186. Doc. dipl. fr., 2nd series, X, 66 ff.
187. Ibid., IX, 52 ff., 103 ff., 438; B. D., III, 186.
188. B. D., II, 187. Cf. Grey's letter to Asquith of April 16, 1911: "[What the military experts] settled, I never knew—the position being that the Government was quite free, but that the military people knew what to do if the word were given." Grey, Twenty-Five Years, I, 92; Doc. dipl. fr., 2nd series, XI, 167 f.
189. To Lord Ripon, February 2, 1906. Spender, Life of Campbell-Bannerman, II, 257; Haldane, Before the War, p. 162.
190. Grey, Twenty-Five Years, I, 84, 96.
191. During a conversation with Edward VII at Marienbad in August 1908, Clemenceau referred three times to the need for conscription in Britain: "It was all very well for Britain to build warships, but that whole labor would be in vain and the results of the French-British alliance null, unless she created a continental army able to cut a figure on the great battle fields." In the end, the Tiger had the satisfaction of seeing that the King attributed as much importance as he himself to the matter and promised to go to work on the problem, and that he had already made a start by breaking with his friend General Gallifet, who had told him that it was not in the interest of Britain to put the entente cordiale with France to a practical application. Doc. dipl. fr., 2nd series, XI, 751 f.
192. B. D., VI, 22 ff.; Doc. dipl. fr., 2nd series, X, 707 f.
193. For the innumerable details, see Callwell, Sir Henry Wilson.
194. When Haldane's successor, Seely, was bold enough to come out against the agitation for conscription and implied that the General Staff agreed with him that the territorial army was equal to all demands, Wilson and Sir John French forced this weak-kneed Liberal to take back his statement. Repington applauded in The Times (April 19, 1913): the soldiers had justified their existence. Callwell, Sir Henry Wilson, I, 125.
195. Foch to British military attaché in Paris (Colonel Fairholme) on April 8, 1913. B. D., VI, 618 ff.
196. Even though the protocol stated once again that these "conversations, devoid of all official character, cannot bind either Government in any way," General Dubail at once told his Russian opposite that he could now count on having the British Army on the French left wing.

197. Texts in <u>Doc. dipl. fr.</u>, 3rd series, II, 257 ff.; <u>B. D.</u>, VII, no. 640. Cf. Iswolski (December 5, 1912): "At the present moment, the Anglo-French military convention has a character as absolute and complete as the Franco-Russian convention." <u>Livre Noir</u>, I, 367.

198. Churchill, <u>World Crisis</u>, p. 50; <u>G. P.</u>, XXIX, 10642, 10652.

199. Renouvin, "Les engagements de l'Alliance Franco-Russe," <u>Revue d'Histoire de la Guerre mondiale</u>, October 1934, p. 163.

200. September 1911. Grey, <u>Twenty-five Years</u>, I, 92 f.

201. Lloyd George, <u>War Memoirs</u>, I, 46.

202. <u>Doc. dipl. fr.</u>, 3rd series, II, No. 336.

203. Stieve, <u>Schriftwechsel Iswolskis</u>, II, 48 f.

204. Churchill, <u>World Crisis</u>, p. 116.

205. <u>Doc. dipl. fr.</u>, 3rd series, II, No. 332; III, No. 50, 189, 207, 420, 446; IV, No. 15, 398; V, 397 (text); VI, 198. At the outbreak of war in 1914, two French armored cruisers and two Russian light cruisers in the Far East were placed under British command, "thus sensibly increasing our predominance." Churchill, <u>World Crisis</u>, p. 314.

206. Lloyd George, <u>War Memoirs</u>, I, 47 f.

207. <u>B. D.</u>, X, 448; Grey, <u>Twenty-five Years</u>, I, 94 f.

208. Renouvin, "Les engagements de l'Alliance Franco-Russe," <u>Revue d'Histoire de la guerre mondiale</u>, Oct. 1934, p. 167.

209. <u>B. D.</u>, XI, No. 369.

210. Asquith, <u>Genesis of the War</u>, p. 83.

211. Brett, (ed.), <u>Journal and Letters of Reginald, Viscount Esher</u>, III, 61.

212. Renouvin, "Les engagements de l'Alliance Franco-Russe," <u>Revue d'Histoire</u>, October 1934, p. 170.

213. Renouvin adds: "How far they actually contemplated this plan is a secret which neither the documents nor the evidence available have hitherto [1934] disclosed." <u>Ibid.</u>, p. 173.

214. Crowe, July 31, 1914. <u>B. D.</u>, XI, 369.

215. Lloyd George, <u>War Memoirs</u>, I, 47.

216. Callwell, <u>Sir Henry Wilson</u>, I, 152 ff.

217. Russell, <u>Freedom versus Organization</u>, p. 444.

218. For this problem, see Hans Rothfels' article on the Convention in <u>Berliner Monatshefte</u>, May 1934.

219. December 5, 1912. Stieve, <u>Schriftwechsel Iswolskis</u>, II, 377 f.

220. <u>Livre noir</u>, II, 339.

221. Sasonov, Isvolski, and other pseudo-Liberals were inclined to obtain larger funds for the navy and thereby neglect the army, as War Minister Suchomlinov thought, in order to make Russia a somewhat more equal partner of Britain on the seas and enable her to exert an influence on the <u>dominium maris Baltici</u>. Suchomlinow, <u>Erinnerungen</u>, pp. 281 f.

222. April 1914. <u>Die internationalen Beziehungen</u>, 1st series, II, 130, 208, 330.

223. <u>Ibid.</u>, IV, 95 ff.; Grey, <u>Twenty-five Years</u>, I, 273 ff.

224. Stieve, <u>Schriftwechsel Iswolskis</u>, IV, 111 ff., 117 f.

225. <u>Ibid.</u>, IV, 122 f.

226. <u>Die internationalen Beziehungen</u>, 1st series, III, 160.

227. Grey, <u>Twenty-five Years</u>, I, 279. Grey's denial at the time, or the subsequent one formulated and published by his friend Spender that there was "no naval agreement and no negotiations for a naval agreement between Great Britain and Russia" was hardly even technically truthful. <u>Westminster Gazette</u>, June 13, 1914.

228. <u>G. P.</u>, XXXIX, 15889.

229. Siebert, <u>Diplomatische Aktenstücke</u>, pp. 826 f.

230. <u>B. D.</u>, VI, Nos. 331-334. See, in addition to the literature cited, <u>G. P.</u>, XXXIX, 15873 ff.; Wolff, <u>The Eve of 1914</u>, pp. 379 ff.; A. Bach "Die englisch-russischen Verhandlungen über den Abschluss einer Marinekonvention," <u>Preussische Jahrbücher</u>, Vol. 197.

231. In fact, the pre-1914 military conventions did more for the diplomatic than for the military preparation for war. According to Quartermaster-General Danilov, during the particularly intimate Franco-Russian conversations between the chiefs of staff "they never raised the question of working out in common a plan for a joint war. They did not even discuss the proper means of coordinating the operations of the two armies in the possible war." Cited in <u>Revue d'histoire de la guerre mondiale</u>, XIII (1935), 226.

232. Joffre, <u>Mémoires</u>, II, 95.

233. <u>D. D.</u>, Nos. 320, 517, 733.

234. Cron, <u>Die deutschen Heere im Weltkriege</u>, pp. 6 f. Texts with discussion by Curt Liebmann in <u>Wissen und Wehr</u>, VIII, pp. 34 ff., 68.

235. This last provision would become important if Russia should decide to turn her main endeavor against Germany.

236. This is based on Russian documents in <u>Die internationalen Beziehungen</u>, 2nd series, VII. See also Danilov, <u>Le premier généralissime des armées russes: le grand-duc Nicolas</u>.

237. Fabry, <u>Joffre et son destin</u>, pp. 35 ff., 109 ff.

238. Seymour, <u>House Papers</u>, IV, 165.

239. Fabry, <u>Joffre et son destin</u>, pp. 260 ff.

240. According to Tardieu, speaking in the Chambre on September 2, 1919, the old conventions with Britain had revealed themselves as much below the actual needs. The new assistance pacts with her and the United States would serve France far better.

241. A Cobdenite like William Harbutt Dawson concluded that "treaties by which military or naval alliances are concluded...should be rigidly prohibited as contrary to the comity of nations." This was written in 1926. Dawson, Richard Cobden and Foreign Policy, p. 271.

242. Following the rumors of new British-French staff conversations in February 1936, a Wilhelmstrasse official, speaking to an American diplomat, said he thought that denials were as valueless as those of 1913 and 1914 had proved to be. Tansill, Back Door to War, p. 308.

243. Louis Marin, a Rightist, asked the Chambre as early as September 14, 1919, for "military and economic conventions with our immediate neighbors, Belgium, Luxemburg and Italy," which ought to have been concluded at the same time as the Peace Treaty, La France de demain, 25e année, No. 215, 51.

244. Geyr, Erinnerungen eines Militärattachés, pp. 128 ff. Gamelin does not refer to the Utrecht publication in his memoirs, although it made quite a stir at the time.

245. This is based on Gamelin, Servir, II, 25, 68 ff., 239; and William E. Lingelbach, "Neutrality versus Alliances. Belgium and the Revolution in International Politics," Proceedings of the American Philosophical Society, Vol. 79 (1938), 607 ff. The French military attaché in Brussels, who had been unable to avert the Belgian withdrawal from the French system of security, was recalled and retired. Geyr, Erinnerungen eines Militärattachés, p. 140. See also Miller, Belgian Foreign Policy between Two Wars.

246. The non-open covenants, such as the French-Belgian agreements, were never registered at Geneva.

247. Nicolson, Lord Curzon, p. 213.

248. In the article "Little Entente," which Beneš contributed to the thirteenth edition of the Encyclopedia Britannica, the military conventions are not even mentioned, one may surmise out of deference to Anglo-Saxon opinion.

249. Repington, After the War, 1920-1922, p. 297.

250. Much to the chagrin of the French, it proved forever impossible to establish a military understanding between Prague and Warsaw, even in the face of the re-emerging German threat. During 1928, the Quai d'Orsay suggested that both satellites should enter upon separate studies of their respective military situation, which should then be exchanged through the good services of the French General Staff. The Chief of Staff at the time was willing to play the role of peace harbinger but reminded the diplomats that they would first have to obtain the agreement of the two none too friendly Slav brethren as to the purpose and limits of such studies. After that, the suggestion was dropped. Gamelin, Servir, II, 471.

251. A secret Yugoslav-Rumanian military convention, aimed at Bulgaria, was first signed on June 7, 1921, renewed in January 1922, and probably thereafter. The French, while well-informed about most others, received no precise details about this pact. Ibid., II, 473.

252. N. Y. Times, November 25, 1935.

253. For details, see Hölzle, Der Osten im ersten Weltkrieg, pp. 85, 140, 193 ff., and passim.

254. Noël, L'Agression allemande contre la Pologne; Namier, Diplomatic Prelude, pp. 434 ff.; Gamelin, Servir, II, 224 ff., 466 f.

255. Gamelin, Servir, II, 413, 469.

256. On the eve of a visit to Belgrade in January 1939, Ciano exclaimed that "his object, to disintegrate the Little Entente, had been achieved." Documents on German Foreign Policy, Series D, IV, 560.

257. Gamelin, Servir, II, 468 f.

258. Europäische Politik 1933-1938 im Spiegel der Prager Akten, p. 23. In April 1934, Gamelin was convinced that in the armaments race France "would retain an immense superiority. You will see how long it will take Germany to catch up with the twenty billions we have spent on armaments." François-Poncet, The Fateful Years, p. 127.

259. Circular dispatch of March 21, 1935. Europäische Politik, p. 46.

260. Wolfers, Britain and France between Two Wars, pp. 136 ff.

261. Gamelin, Servir, II, 285 f.

262. Documents on German Foreign Policy, 1918-1945, Series D, I, 1070 ff.

263. The Czech Army's Inspector-General, Syrovy, who had fought the Bolshevists in 1918, told a Britisher: "We shall fight the Germans, either alone, or with you and the French, but we don't want the Russians in here. We should never get them out." Wheeler-Bennett, Munich, pp. 81 f.

264. Gamelin, Servir, II, 225 ff.

265. Europäische Politik, pp. 89 f. See the report of a Czech agent, following conversations with Léger on March 11 and 12, who answered Bullitt's query as to how French help would get to the Czechs by saying that French

troops "would pass through Rumania and Yugoslavia." Tansill, Back Door to War, pp. 328 f.

266. Europäische Politik, pp. 94, 104.
267. Ibid., pp. 105 f.
268. Documents relating to the Eve of the Second World War, I, 139 ff.
269. In March 1935, the Poles invited the Czech General Staff to send representatives to Warsaw "in order to discuss, as was the habit, the military cooperation of both armies." Beneš decided that as long as Czech-Polish relations remained unclarified, the invitation could not be accepted. Czechoslovakia could not afford to estrange Russia by associating too closely with the Poles and their adventurous Ukrainian policy. Europäische Politik, pp. 47 f.
270. Noël, cited by Namier in Diplomatic Prelude, p. 440.
271. Europäische Politik, pp. 63 f.
272. Ibid., pp. 70 f.
273. Gamelin, Servir, II, 227 ff. Cf. also Beck's statement to Bullitt in November 1937 that "under no circumstances would Poland become involved in protecting French satellites in Central Europe, especially Czechoslovakia." Tansill, Back Door to War, p. 360.
274. Gamelin, Servir, II, 166.
275. Ibid., II, 178 ff.
276. Documents on German Foreign Policy, Series D, IV, 473.
277. Gamelin subsequently argued that le gros of the French forces merely meant the main body following up the avant-gardes in the opening operations, and not the gros of the whole French Army. But he could not explain away the obligation to make some move.
278. This is largely based on Namier, Diplomatic Prelude, pp. 434 ff. and Gamelin, Servir, II, 233 ff., 413 ff.
279. Gamelin, Servir, II, 162 ff; Churchill, The Second World War, I, 105. According to a disclosure in Le Matin in June 1935, Badoglio had worked out a joint plan of action for the two armies as early as 1924, which had been communicated to the Paris Government. Frankfurter Zeitung, June 20, 1935. (An interesting parallel might be drawn between Pollio in 1914 and Badoglio in 1935.)
280. Pertinax, Les Fossoyeurs, I, 18.
281. Feiling, The Life of Neville Chamberlain, pp. 257, 259.
282. Geyr, Erinnerungen eines Militärattachés, p. 81.

283. The Diary of Pierre Laval, pp. 13 f.; Gamelin, Servir, II, 176.
284. Ferdinand Kuhn, Jr., in N. Y. Times, March 13, 1936.
285. Alfred Duff Cooper, Secretary of State for War, in Commons on March 12, 1936.
286. Feiling, The Life of Neville Chamberlain, pp. 279 f.
287. Churchill, The Second World War, I, 203.
288. Ibid., I, 381.
289. François-Poncet, The Fateful Years, pp. 31 ff.
290. Geyr, Erinnerungen eines Militärattachés, pp. 92 ff.
291. Feiling, The Life of Neville Chamberlain, pp. 280, 353.
292. Ibid., pp. 370, 425.
293. Ibid., p. 334.
294. Potiemkine, Histoire de la diplomatie, III, 704.
295. France subsequently came to terms with Turkey directly, ceding to her the sanjak of Alexandrette. For the treaty arrangements, which included a military convention (July 3, 1938), see Toynbee, Survey of International Affairs 1938, I, 486 ff.; Potiemkine, Histoire de la diplomatie, III, 706.
296. Pertinax, Les Fossoyeurs, I, 15 f.
297. On September 21, 1938, Litvinov declared before the League Assembly that he had assured the French Government, inquiring about Russian intentions regarding Czechoslovakia, as follows: "We intend to fulfill our obligations under the Pact, and together with France to afford assistance to Czechoslovakia by the ways open to us. Our War Department is ready immediately to participate in a conference with representatives of the French and Czech War Departments in order to discuss the measures appropriate to the moment." Churchill, The Second World War, I, 304 f.
298. Feiling, The Life of Neville Chamberlain, pp. 369, 403.
299. Ibid., pp. 407 f.
300. Namier, Diplomatic Prelude, pp. 245 f.
301. German Embassy report of August 1. Documents relating to the Eve of the Second World War, II, 103. For the highly erroneous views as to Poland's ability to resist a German attack, which Ironside had gained in Warsaw, see Tansill, Back Door to War, p. 554.
302. Interview in Pravda, August 27, 1939. Potiemkine, Histoire de la diplomatie, III, 708; cf. also Tansill, Back Door to War, pp. 532, 539.

303. <u>Documents on German Foreign Policy</u>, Series D, IV, 515 ff., 521 f., 524, 539 ff., 544 f., 584 f., 587 ff.

304. <u>Ibid.</u>, 680, 688 f., 698, 703 f., 711.

305. Kordt, <u>Wahn und Wirklichkeit</u>, pp. 149, 258; Nevins, <u>The New Deal and World Affairs</u>, p. 221.

306. See Beard, <u>President Roosevelt and the Coming of the War</u>, pp. 414 f.

307. <u>Ibid.</u>, pp. 444 f.; Watson, <u>Chief of Staff</u>, pp. 92 f.; Tansill, <u>Back Door to War</u>, pp. 491 f.

308. Watson, <u>Chief of Staff</u>, pp. 99 f.

309. <u>Ibid.</u>, p. 107.

310. Hull, <u>Memoirs</u>, I, 796 f.

311. <u>Ibid.</u>, I, 834; for the defense plans elaborated by the Joint Board, see <u>Pearl Harbor Hearings</u>, Part 15, 1585 ff.

312. Stimson and Bundy, <u>On Active Service</u>, pp. 357 f.; these memoirs are silent about staff talks.

313. Watson, <u>Chief of Staff</u>, pp. 113 f.

314. <u>Ibid.</u>, pp. 118 ff.; see also Harrison, <u>Cross-Channel Attack</u>, pp. 1 ff.

315. <u>Pearl Harbor Hearings</u>, Part 20, 4072 ff.

316. In the directives for the discussion, as worked out by the American military planners, their purpose was stated as being to determine "the best methods by which the armed forces of the U.S. and the British Commonwealth can defeat Germany and the powers allied with her, should the U.S. desire to resort to war." The war-guilt-minded President changed that to "should the U.S. be compelled to resort to war." Watson, <u>Chief of Staff</u>, pp. 372 f.

317. Sherwood wrote: "They could have been altered or renounced at any time 'in the light of subsequent events.'" Sherwood, <u>Roosevelt and Hopkins</u>, p. 274.

318. <u>Ibid.</u>, p. 272; Beard, <u>Roosevelt and the Coming of the War</u>, pp. 450 f.

319. <u>Pearl Harbor Hearings</u>, Part 39, 446.

320. Watson, <u>Chief of Staff</u>, p. 367.

321. This was by Roosevelt's order, despite the reluctance of the State Department, and amounted to a further Europeanization of American diplomacy, which had hitherto refrained from such policy tie-ups.

322. The report of the staff conversations is in <u>Pearl Harbor Hearings</u>, Part 15, 1485 ff.; Sherwood, <u>Roosevelt and Hopkins</u>, pp. 270 f.; Beard, <u>Roosevelt and the Coming of the War</u>, pp. 445 f.; Watson, <u>Chief of Staff</u>, pp. 367 ff.

323. Testimony of Admiral R. K. Turner, <u>Pearl Harbor Hearings</u>, Part 26, 264 f.

324. The report of the American-Dutch-British conversations is in <u>Pearl Harbor Hearings</u>, Part 15, 1551 ff.; Beard, <u>Roosevelt and the Coming of the War</u>, pp. 443, 447; Watson, <u>Chief of Staff</u>, pp. 391 ff.

325. Sherwood, <u>Roosevelt and Hopkins</u>, pp. 349 ff., 358; Watson, <u>Chief of Staff</u>, pp. 400 ff.

326. As late as September 1941, there was strong conviction among the American war planners that, as yet, "contrary to the British idea that American entry into the war would help, the U.S. would be of more assistance as a neutral able to supply munitions in large quantities, the nation's potential combat strength not being sufficiently developed to permit more than a moral effect in land or air operations, and the Navy being still incapable of offensive operations against Germany." Watson, <u>Chief of Staff</u>, p. 407.

327. Beard, <u>Roosevelt and the Coming of the War</u>, pp. 537 ff.

328. Statement of Secretary of War Stimson, <u>N. Y. Times</u>, March 22, 1946.

329. For these see <u>Pearl Harbor Hearings</u>, Part 15, 1677 ff.

330. Beard, <u>Roosevelt and the Coming of the War</u>, pp. 449 f.; <u>Pearl Harbor Hearings</u>, Report of the Joint Committee, 70th Congress, 2nd session, Senate Document No. 244, p. 170.

331. Sherwood, <u>Roosevelt and Hopkins</u>, p. 445.

332. <u>Ibid.</u>, p. 273.

333. Cf. General Marshall's judgment, reported to the Secretary of War: "[It provided] the most complete unification of military effort ever achieved by two allied nations. Strategic direction of all the forces of both nations, the allocation of manpower and munitions, the coordination of communications, the control of military intelligence and the administration of captured areas all were accepted as joint responsibilities." <u>Biennial Report of the Chief of Staff of the U.S. Army</u>, (July 1, 1943, to June 30, 1945,) p. 8.

334. Sherwood, <u>Roosevelt and Hopkins</u>, pp. 719 f.

335. See for instance the Navy Court of Inquiry report on Pearl Harbor: "In time of peace it is a difficult and complicated matter for the U.S. to prevent an attack by another nation because of the constitutional requirement that, prior to a declaration of war by Congress, no blow may be struck until after a hostile attack has been delivered. This is a military consideration which gives to a dishonorable potential enemy the advantage of the initiative, deprives the U.S. of an opportunity to employ the offensive as a means of defense...." <u>Pearl Harbor Hearings</u>, Part 39, 298. See also the discussion in Beard, <u>Roosevelt and the Coming of the War</u>, pp. 580 ff.

336. Cf. the complaints of various speakers, in-

cluding Churchill, in the House of Commons, November 30, 1950, that "at the American suggestion and under American pressure," this organization, "the keystone of our arch of victory," had been dropped. There were various proposals, in the face of Korean events, that it be reconstituted, that another Sir John Dill be sent to Washington. Parliamentary Debates, 5th series, Vol. 481, 1337 f., 1370, etc. There is still a British Joint Services Mission in Washington, D.C.

337. For meetings of the American Joint Chiefs of Staff with British Army and Navy planners in August-September 1946, see Forrestal Diaries, p. 198. They discussed concerted measures such as an evacuation of American occupation troops from Germany, presumably in case of a Russian aggression. As suggested by the British, the meetings were to remain secret and informal.

338. State Department, White Paper on the Atlantic Pact, March 19, 1949.

339. For a list of the Soviet alliances and inter-satellite pacts, see Hoskins, The Atlantic Pact, pp. 92 f.

340. This had begun with the Russian treaties with the three Baltic States of September and October 1939, which made the small nations dependent on Russia by way of the military supplies they were to receive from her "on favored terms," not to mention the dependency established through the garrisoning of Red Army troops in the "leased" naval, air and other bases on their territory.

341. French Foreign Minister Schuman, N. Y. Times, March 19, 1949.

342. Soviet Government memorandum on the Atlantic Pact, March 31, 1949.

343. Churchill, speech of October 9, 1948. A. P. dispatch from Llandudno.

344. March 12, 1948. Forrestal Diaries, p. 392.

345. Cf. Truman's message to Congress on March 17, 1948: "I am confident that the U.S. will, by appropriate means, extend to the free nations the support which the situation requires...that the determination of the free countries of Europe to protect themselves will be matched by an equal determination on our part to help them do so." In the second half of April, the State Department began to consider some form of military lend-lease to the Brussels Pact nations. Statement of Secretary of State Marshall, N. Y. Times, April 29, 1948.

346. See N.Y. Times, March 19, 1948.

347. See the criticism by Sumner Welles of "the growing control of our foreign policy by those who speak primarily for the armed services." N.Y. Times, December 4, 1948.

348. Forrestal Diaries, pp. 422 ff., 434.

349. See p. 151.

350. Under the pressure of military necessity, an Anglo-American agreement was concluded in the autumn of 1948, following fifty years of negotiations, whereby common standards for universally used nuts and bolts were set up. N.Y. Times, October 1, 1948. This was part of the general agreement, arrived at during Forrestal's visit to London in November 1948, that "there should be planning now by the U.S.-U.K. agencies for combined production problems in the event of war." Forrestal Diaries, p. 524.

351. Cf. de Gaulle's statement at the time: "Europe must be defended in Europe...I simply say that England is an island. I can't do anything about that, neither can she. And I say to you that Europe is not an island but a continent...The natural center of a defense plan is France. But for the present, France is hardly present. The problem of European defense will have to be reconsidered when France has a real government," (that is to say, one headed by de Gaulle). Time, October 11, 1948.

352. This choice was not greatly liked by some Americans, as de Lattre was said to have refused to obey orders from General Eisenhower during the war. Congressman Fulton, quoted in N.Y. Times, July 30, 1949.

353. A faint precedent might be found in the command of Field Marshal Count Waldersee over international contingents in China in 1900-01, when there had been war actions without a declaration of war. An international staff was set up at the time, but compliance with Waldersee's "suggestions" was never good.

354. N.Y. Times, December 28, 1948.

355. Ibid., July 13, 1948. See also Montgomery's address before the English-Speaking Union in New York on November 29, 1949: "I found myself transformed into an international servant of five governments...." Ibid., November 30, 1949.

356. See items like "De Lattre denies Montgomery rift"; "Atlantic Pact rift"; "British Military peeved at French"; "British irk French by attack on Army. French deny their military forces are the weak link in European defenses." N.Y. Times, August 9, September 11, October 29 and November 5, 1949.

357. Ibid., November 7, 1949.

358. Ibid., October 22, 1949.

359. Statement of General J. Lawton Collins,

Vice Chief of Staff of the U.S. Army, on his return from Europe, where he had conferred with Montgomery. Ibid., December 28, 1948.

360. For the latter two, the defense agreement of 1940 was still in effect. It was activated by various measures such as the exchange of officers. For details, see Ibid., April 5, 1949.

361. U.S. White Paper on Atlantic Alliance, March 19, 1949.

362. President Truman's inaugural address, January 20, 1949.

363. N. Y. Times, September 10 and October 3, 1948; for earlier inter-Scandinavian discussions, see Ibid., April 7, May 7 and June 7, 1948.

364. Ibid., January 14, 19, 23, 31, and February 10, 1949.

365. Ibid., December 3, 1948; January 30, February 13 and 15, 1949.

366. This "neighborhood" was due to Russian annexations at the expense of Finland.

367. N. Y. Times, February 2 and 7, 1949.

368. Ibid., February 8, 11 and 22, 1949.

369. Secretary of State Acheson, broadcast talk of March 18, 1949.

370. N.Y. Times, March 19, 1949.

371. Ibid., March 19, 1949.

372. Acheson broadcast of March 18, 1949.

373. N.Y. Times, May 3, 1949.

374. "Action short of the use of armed force might suffice, or total war with all our resources might be necessary. Obviously, Article Five carries with it an important and far-reaching commitment for the United States; what we may do to carry out that commitment, however, will depend upon our independent decision in each particular instance reached in accordance with our own constitutional processes." Senate Foreign Relations Committee Report on North Atlantic Treaty.

375. According to Senator George's view, the Treaty did not add anything to the President's powers. "He can act defensively, but to implement Article Five he must await Congressional approval and the pact cannot act automatically...It is my interpretation that in the event of an armed attack we agree to take certain action, and that it is Congress instead of the Chief Executive who determines what action." N.Y. Times, June 5, 1949.

376. Hanson Baldwin in N.Y. Times, December 5, 1948.

377. Address of General Bradley, Chief of Staff, April 5, 1949.

378. Address before Netherlands Society, at The Hague. N.Y. Times, July 16, 1949.

379. Ibid., October 7, 1948.

380. General Bradley's address of April 5, 1949, and his statement before Senate Foreign Relations Committee, May 3, 1949.

381. N.Y. Times, March 3, 1949.

382. Montgomery told selective American audiences in the autumn of 1949 that Western Europe could be made defensible only by rearming the Germans. Warburg, Faith, Purpose and Power, p. 65.

383. The dangerously underequipped French forces had already been recipients of American aid in the form of arms when they were loaned American equipment worth five million dollars from stocks maintained in Germany. N.Y. Times, November 5, 1948.

384. See texts, Ibid., April 9, 1949.

385. Statement of Secretary of Defense Louis Johnson, July 29, 1949, before House Foreign Affairs Committee.

386. Message of President Truman to Congress on July 25, 1949 and "Act to promote the foreign policy and provide for the defense and general welfare of the U.S. by furnishing military assistance to foreign nations."

387. Statement of Secretary Acheson before the House Foreign Affairs Committee, July 28, 1949.

388. For measures taken or contemplated in order to safeguard confidential military information, see N.Y. Times, May 13, 1948.

389. On October 21, 1949, Secretary Johnson assured a Senate committee that information about the military assistance program would be withheld from any Communist, even if he were a Cabinet member of a participating nation; in such an event he would at once consult with Congress as to the possible stopping of military aid to the country in question.

390. N.Y. Times, April 25, October 1, December 11 and 16, 1949; February 1, 1950.

391. Ibid., December 22, 1949. The five Brussels Pact governments signed an agreement, applying to peacetime only, whereby soldiers stationed in each other's territory were given the right to move freely, be exempt from passport and visa regulations and alien control and registration. In crossing frontiers, such troops must wear uniforms and carry identity cards. While on foreign soil, they were to be subject to local ordinances regarding the wearing of uniforms and the carrying of weapons. During their sojourn, such troops must abstain from political activities and respect the laws

of the country of their stationing, failing
which the offended nation may try them in
their courts.

392. Statement of President Truman, January
27, 1950; full text of the U.S.-British Accord in N.Y. Times, January 28, 1950.
393. Ibid., January 30, 1950, for example.
394. Ibid., October 22, 1949.
395. Department of Defense, Semiannual Report
of the Secretary of Defense, July 1 to December 31, 1949, p. 13.
396. Congressman Judd, N.Y. Times, August 1,
1949.
397. "Diplomats to run arms aid abroad; U.S.
names civilians as supervisors who will
each have a staff of military experts."
N.Y. Times, November 9, 1949.
398. Executive Order of President Truman,
January 27, 1950; text in Ibid., January 28,
1950.
399. For details, see Ibid., November 18, 1949.
400. Department of Defense, Semiannual Report,
July 1 to December 31, 1949, p. 14.
401. N.Y. Times, November 24, December 2,
3, and 4, 1949.
402. U.P. dispatch from The Hague, April 8, 1949.
403. N.Y. Times, December 24, 1949, dispatch
from London.
404. For details of the North European group
planning, see Ibid., October 28 and 31, and
December 18, 1949. As to another group,
see these headlines: "The defense relationship between France and Italy is at present
confused...Headquarters of this group is
divided because of national rivalry...between
Paris and Italy. Yet, at the same time, the
defense of France as part of the Western
European group is being planned in London."
Ibid., April 11, 1950.
405. Following the Napoleonic wars, the period
of their greatest politico-military intimacy,
Russia and Prussia occasionally held joint
peace-time maneuvers, in 1835 for example.
Berner, Geschichte des preussischen
Staates, p. 609.
406. Time, October 11, 1948.
407. N.Y. Times, February 10, May 8, 1949.
Similar exercises were held in 1950.
408. Time, July 18, 1949; N.Y. Times, May 8,
1949.
409. N.Y. Times, June 26, 1949.
410. Ibid., July 15, 1949.
411. Ibid., March 23, 1950.
412. Ibid., July 25, 1950.
413. Ibid., September 4, 1950. Similar maneuvers took place in 1951 and 1952.
414. Report of Secretary Johnson on the Department of Defense, January 30, 1950. Ibid.,
January 31, 1950.

415. Address of General Bradley in Chicago.
Ibid., April 15, 1950.
416. Secretary of State Acheson before Informal
Joint Session of Congress, May 30, 1950.
Ibid., June 1, 1950. In June 1950, the Council
asked the French and Dutch Governments to
build up their ground forces and tactical air
strength, instead of assigning defense funds
to the building of warships, which the U.S.
would furnish them instead.
417. Ibid., June 1, 1950, plus communiqués of
the Council of May 18, 1950, including the
announcement of the creation of a North
Atlantic Planning Board for ocean shipping.
418. N.Y. Times, June 29, 1950.
419. See text of a British memorandum on defense expenditure of August 3 and of a similar French one of August 7 in Ibid., August
4 and 8, 1950.
420. Estimate by the U.S. Army, in report to
Senate Appropriations Committee, August
1, 1950. Ibid., September 13, 1950.
421. Statement by a spokesman for the American High Commissioner in Germany, Han-
noversche Allgemeine Zeitung, November
3, 1950. He put West German national income at the time at one hundred billion
marks, the Germans themselves at only
sixty-seventy billions.
422. As of 1948, the United States was a partner
to these international military agencies:
Permanent Joint Board on Defense, U.S.
and Canada; Combined Chiefs of Staff, U.S.
and Great Britain; Joint Brazil-U.S. Defense Commission; Joint Mexican-U.S. Defense Commission; and the Inter-American
Defense Board. McCamy, Administration of
American Foreign Affairs, p. 132.
423. When General MacArthur visited Chiang
Kai-shek in Formosa at the end of July 1950
in order to discuss the island's defense
against the Chinese Communists, the American declared, clearly ultra vires, that it
was his "responsibility and firm purpose"
to defend the island. Chiang stated that an
agreement as to joint defense of Formosa
and for Sino-American military cooperation
had been reached. Newspapers spoke of a
"pact." N.Y. Times, August 2, 1950.
424. Acheson at press conference, December 22,
1950. Ibid., December 23, 1950.
425. On June 5, 1950, twenty days before the outbreak of the war in Korea, Acheson had told
the House Committee on Foreign Affairs:
"The policy of all the Governments, the
Russian, our own, France and Britain, is
that Germany is to be demilitarized (and
not remilitarized)...We are proceeding on
that basis. There is no discussion of doing

anything else." Two and a half months later, Acheson explained to another Congressional committee that "a program for Western Europe which does not include the productive resources of all the countries of Western Europe—Germany as well as France—and the military manpower of all of Western Europe—Western Germany as well as France—will not be effective." Ibid., February 20, 1952.

426. Ibid., March 13, 1952.
427. Acheson and Bradley on troops-for-Europe issue before Senate Committees, February 17, 1951. For the discussions, see U.S. Senate, 82nd Congress, 1st Session, Assignment of Ground Forces of the U.S. in the European Area, and Senate Report No. 175, March 14, 1951.
428. In a message to Congress on May 24, 1951, President Truman proposed an outlay of $6,250,000,000 for military assistance to all free nations, of which $5.3 billions was to go to the NATO group. At the same time, $1,650,000,000 in economic aid was proposed for the same countries. This group, he said, must not fall under Soviet control since this would result "in a tremendous shift of world power and would compel us to convert the United States into an isolated garrison state."
429. A British labor union paper came out in favor of an American admiral as commander of the North Atlantic naval forces because British admirals were too strict and snobbish, accustomed to "very tight, autocratic lines" and a set-up based on "the most rigid class distinctions." Hence they could not "win the mixture of affection and respect essential to successful command from the sailors of nations used to a more liberal view of naval life." U. P. dispatch from London, March 8, 1951.
430. Anthony Eden at Columbia University, January 11, 1952.
431. N. Y. Times, January 12 and 24, 1951.
432. E.g. London dispatch in N.Y. Times, July 20, 1951: "British friends of U.S. feel Spain talks offend public—Fear moral position of West is weakened in 'cold war'—Washington held inept."
433. When British Defense Minister Shinwell left for the United States in September 1950 to participate in discussions relating to German participation in Western defense, the Foreign Office gave him for reading matter J.H. Morgan's "Assize of Arms," a virulent discussion of Germany's evasion of the disarmament obligations after 1919. Ibid., September 21, 1950.
434. For a French contribution, see General E.

de Larminat, L'Armée européenne. Larminat arrives at the conclusion that coalition armies have always fallen apart and disagreed; that European unification should start with unified armed forces; that from a technical standpoint such an army is superior to a coalition, more efficient and more economical; that an EDC force is the best way of liquidating a regrettable past; that only admission to equal status for Germany will produce an adequate German contribution to EDC if the latter is to be more than a mere "community of defiance."

435. N.Y. Times, February 12, 1951; data as calculated are for the year 1950. For more details, see Blair Bolles and Francis O. Wilcox, The Armed Road to Peace, pp. 25 ff.
436. In the Allied European countries in 1951, there were, per 1,000 population, twenty-five men in the armed forces or reservists subject to recall, of which thirteen per thousand were on active duty. The latter figure breaks down as follows: 17.8 in France, 15.2 in the United Kingdom, 14.5 in Belgium, 10.7 in Portugal, 10.4 in Norway, 9.8 in the Netherlands, 7 in Luxemburg, 6.3 in Italy, and 5.2 in Denmark. Iceland has no army. Bolles and Wilcox, The Armed Road to Peace, p. 28.
437. In a public speech in Brussels, U.S. Ambassador Robert Murphy told the Belgians that "there was quite frankly doubt that Belgium is making a contribution to Atlantic defense proportionate to its wealth and resources." Time, April 30, 1951.
438. N.Y. Times, March 2, 1952.
439. During the discussion of the French defense budget for 1953, the Minister of Defense told the National Assembly that France would not increase her forces in Europe and North Africa (420,000 men) unless she received more foreign, that is, American aid. Should she get $85,000,000 more of such help, she would add 30,000 men to the army and 9,000 to the air force. N.Y. Herald-Tribune, January 26, 1953.
440. Military internationalism might be traced from the Prince de Ligne's eighteenth-century proposal for an international military academy, via General Max Hoffmann's propaganda for an anti-Bolshevist crusade during the 1920's, to the NATO's Defense College in Paris, set up in 1951.
441. N.Y. Times, April 2, 1952. It was reported that Lord Ismay "urgently favors a strong campaign to convince the peoples of the United Nations of the necessity of Western unity either to enforce peace by strong diplomatic action or to ensure adequate defense

in case of war...He feels this simple fact
must be stressed to the point of redundancy."
Ibid., May 3, 1952.

442. *Ibid.*, September 20, 1951.

443. *Ibid.*, November 27, 1951.

444. Soviet note to U.S. Government on German
problem, May 24, 1952.

445. British isolationism, which stood forever in
the way of European unification, was based
on the obligations the U.K had towards the
Commonwealth. However, no demands on
the part of Commonwealth members that
England must not join in European unity
plans have been put on the record.

Military Missions and Instructors

In diplomatic usage, a mission is a group of persons provided with a diplomatic character and sent abroad for a specified purpose. Military missions are ordinarily of the following types: (1) ceremonial ad hoc missions; (2) missions sent for the purpose of establishing and maintaining liaison with allies and coalition partners; (3) missions for observing the execution of treaties and other international agreements in their military aspects. These include missions in the service of international organizations such as the League of Nations, the United Nations, or the Organization of the American States; (4) missions sent and received for the purpose of instructing foreign armies, navies and air forces and imparting to the more backward nation the military progress achieved by the dispatching Power.

DEFINITIONS AND CONDITIONS OF EMPLOYMENT

We shall deal here with missions of instruction, many of which have served as instruments of military policy, if not also as the tools of national diplomacy,[1] of imperialism, and of certain elements within the national economy, thus further sharpening the competition among the Great Powers. To avoid these entanglements as much as possible, many employing governments have preferred to engage individual instructors, even if in fairly large numbers. An organized mission is much harder to keep in its place. The German reformers in Turkey, for example, were not organized as a mission until 1912-13. As a rule, however, the more systematically a mission is organized the more effective its labors will be.

In the majority of cases military missions were intended, on the part of the sender and the recipient alike, to strengthen a backward military Power against penetration, peaceful or warlike, by another imperialist Power with whom the dispatching Power might be in more or less open competition.[2] To lessen the resentment that inevitably arose, the aid obtained through foreign assistants remained, as a rule, restricted to peace-time employ or, in time of war, to non-combat activity. Certain contracts for the services of foreign advisers provided that the services were to end should the employing Power become involved in war. It would be expecting too much to see this neutrality always punctiliously observed by the foreign instructor, who would be eager to observe in action the troops he had trained, if not to share the fight with them. The instructor might even resign altogether from his own country's forces and fully enter the foreign service. The Soviet Government is reported to have solved such conflicts of dual allegiance by giving dual citizenship to the appropriate Russian generals.

In order to preclude the possibility of imperialist penetration, certain recipient states have preferred to draw foreign reforming talent from the armed forces of smaller, non-imperialist Powers. Before 1914, Persia employed Swedish officers to reform and even to command her gendarmerie. Ethiopia preferred Swiss, Swedish and other small-nation officers, although she also employed officers from France as a Power less threatening to her sovereignty than Italy or Britain. In the war with Fascist Italy, the Swiss instructors proved more cautious than the Swedes and retired from the scene, while the Swedes remained a good while longer with the practically forsaken Emperor. The Emperor gratefully re-engaged Swedish instructors following the Second World War.

In order to participate in still another way in the military progress achieved by the various Great Powers, the backward nations have at times sent military missions of their own to visit and to watch the superior Powers and to study military institutions, training, and materiel on the spot. Often they have arranged for such study by having individuals serve with the foreign army or study in their service schools. Admission to service aboard foreign ships has remained the rarest arrangement for such apprentices.

Before the nineteenth century, however, the carrier of military progress from the advanced military Power to backward ones was most often the unattached individual soldier. Driven out by conflicts with the society at home or attracted by the opportunity for adventure or higher pay, the foreign soldier would go abroad and offer his services to an employer in need of the latest in the military arts. In the eighteenth century the greatest international mobility was allowed for the military employment-seeker. When Turkey was falling back into the military competition of the Powers, she accepted foreign soldiers and sailors to impart at least a modicum of Western military progress to her rapidly-decaying forces; without such services from the Giaour, Turkey could hardly have survived, even as precariously as she did. To make his services acceptable and effective, the foreigner had to undergo conversion, a condition that was more often waived as the nineteenth century advanced. Turkey most needed such assistance against Russian expansion. And Russia in turn could hardly spare the services of the Western officer, who was allowed his religious and other freedoms. He could leave after he had fulfilled his contract or stay and be assimilated into Russian society. The struggle of the American colonies, North and South, could not have been fought and won without the services of foreign officers, who came with encouragement on the part of interested foreign governments, or sometimes against their wishes.

MILITARY MISSIONS IN NAPOLEON'S TIME

Not every feature of Napoleon I's imperialism was without precedent. In 1796, the Directoire had attempted to revive French Turkophilia by sending a military embassy headed by General Aubert-Dubayet to the Porte. After his oriental adventure in Egypt and Palestine, Napoleon resumed the ties with the Porte. Following an invitation from the Sultan, who was anxious to learn the secret of the brilliant military victories won by the French, the Emperor sent General Sebastiani to Constantinople in the summer of 1806 as ambassador and military instructor. He was accompanied by a suite of officers who were to give expert help in making the Turkish Army into an army on the Western model. Under Sebastiani's influence, the Sultan challenged Russia. A Russo-Turk war was contrary to all British interests. On January 25, 1807, British diplomacy, backed by a naval squadron, demanded that Sebastiani and his officers be dismissed and that an alliance be concluded with Britain and Russia. The ultimatum was rejected. When a British squadron sailed up the Dardanelles to enforce it, the Turks, guided by Sebastiani, protracted the negotiations until the French artillery and engineering officers had fortified the capital and the Straits. They then forced the British admiral, who was without the landing troops that would have further strengthened the ultimatum, to retire rather ignominiously through the badly-firing Turkish artillery.[3]

The orientalism of Napoleon's imperialism, the dream of India, accounts for the eager response of the French to a Persian invitation to send a military mission to Teheran in order to train a Western-style army for the Shah. A treaty of alliance was concluded. It provided for a mission of French officers, who were to train Persian troops in accordance with European discipline. France was also to furnish specially qualified workmen and arms, and Persia in return promised to declare war against Britain and prepare the invasion of India. The mission was headed by General Gardane, who was at the same time ambassador, and

counted among its members Colonel Fabvier, who had been in Constantinople with Sebastiani and was later to prove a stormy petrel in Restoration politics. Its members were also to strengthen the Persian forces vis-à-vis Russia, Persia's worst despoiler, and to undertake reconnoitering in order to ascertain what kind of obstacles there were to a march to India by way of Persia. They were to impart to their hosts a knowledge of the progress of the military arts in Europe and to assist them in the construction of new fortifications. They were to inform the Emperor about "the geography, topography of the country and its environs, population, finances, the state of military affairs in all its details."[4]

The achievements of the Gardane mission fell far short of the fantastic expectations entertained by Napoleon and his entourage. Although his family had Levantine connections, Gardane felt out of place in Persia. His frugality and simplicity proved unimpressive to the Orientals. Besides, Persia, freed from the Russian danger by the friendship between Napoleon and Alexander, had no desire to go to war against Britain in India. Gardane believed that such a war could be successfully accomplished by an expeditionary force composed of Frenchmen, Afghans, and Persians. Considering the new Franco-Russian friendship, a prolonged stay in Teheran seemed fruitless to Gardane. He took it upon himself to return to Paris in 1809 without being recalled, not long before this friendship was approaching its end.[5] He thus robbed the Emperor, who was not altogether satisfied with the general's return, of the means of bringing Persia into the coming war against Russia.[6]

The British posted military missions to Teheran at various times from the late 1790's on. By the end of Gardane's mission, they had begun to work at replacing French influence there. Only a few days after the Frenchman's departure, a British diplomatic mission arrived and started to negotiate. It was followed by an Indo-British mission in 1810, which included two British army captains who were to assist the Shah in his wars and direct some guns which the British had furnished him. When war between Russia and Persia could no longer be averted by British mediation, the two instruction officers disregarded their recall and chose to stay with the Persian Army to fight against the Russians in 1812 and 1813. Though one of them died at the head of a brigade, they were unable to stem the Persian rout.

In his employment of Western European confederates, Napoleon used the military forces supplied by them largely as they had been processed by the confederated governments themselves. He paid at least enough respect to military nationalism not to insist on a thorough standardization on the French model, or on constant French supervision. The British would fain have done the same, as they had to in their irritating relations with the Spanish forces in the Peninsular campaigns. But they were constrained to take the reshaping of one allied army into their own hands. Beginning in February 1809, Major General William Carr Beresford took over command of the Portuguese Army and re-disciplined and reorganized it through the instrumentality of British officer-instructors. This was achieved in a relatively short time and with such good effect that the Portuguese Army came to serve Wellington very well until 1814.

After the close of the war, Beresford, who had been running Portugal with an iron hand, stayed behind as commander-in-chief of the Portuguese Army. Numerous British officers remained. They formed the general staff and were stationed as supervisors with various regiments. In 1817, they had to suppress a military pronunciamento which had been directed largely against the often-humiliating xenocracy of Beresford and his assistants. The leader, a Portuguese general, was executed. The incident might well be considered the first of its kind, the outcome of the resentment of military nationalism against foreign military commanders and instructors. A second pronunciamento, in 1820, proved more successful. Beresford had gone to Brazil in order to urge the King, absent since 1809, to return to the homeland, and incidentally to stop the drain of money to the colony which had kept the metropolitan army constantly underpaid. The insurrection took place during his absence, having as its first result the enforced embarkment of all British officers. When Beresford returned from America, he was forbidden to land and was obliged to return to England, where he entered politics as a follower of his old chief Wellington.

MILITARY MISSIONS AND NINETEENTH-CENTURY DIPLOMACY IN THE NEAR EAST

The strong reaction against Napoleonism, including the new primacy which diplomacy had achieved and would not lightly surrender, at first restricted military progress and kept competition among the Powers within certain bounds. The smaller Powers, after 1815, were even less inclined to arm or rearm and to fight.

(a) The Moslem States: Turkey and Egypt

Incurably unmodern, Turkey lost the first of her new series of wars against Russia with but little assistance from Western reformers. Only slowly did she revert to her old inclination of looking for aid from England. Palmerston was eager to preserve Turkish integrity and independence, encourage financial reform, and supply British-manufac-

tured muskets for the Turkish army. To make their effective use more certain, a group of British officers went out in 1836 to study the army and to suggest necessary military reforms. The Turks decided in the end that these reforms should be entrusted to a group of Prussian officers instead, perhaps because they believed that Prussian reformers (among whom was Helmuth von Moltke, the later Chief of Staff)[7] would be suffered somewhat more gladly by Russia. With the permission of their home government, Moltke and five other Prussians entered Turkish service for a number of years.[8] Moltke himself acted for a time as adviser to a general commanding an army corps against Mehmed Ali of Egypt, but his advice, the best available at the time, proved less acceptable to the commander than the prophecies of the mullahs. Moltke resigned his staff position and took charge of the artillery, which, in the battle of Nisib (1839), was the last unit of the Turkish forces to take flight. The reality of war, usually more unrestrained along the frontiers of civilization than near its center, taught Moltke infinitely more than he was able to teach the Turks.

The dynamics of industrial progress, extending into the field of armaments production, broke down much of the restraint that diplomacy had sought to maintain since 1815. Setting the pace for competition, the Great Powers underwent constant rearming. The smaller Powers, including even those far from the European center of competition, were forced to follow their example. In Egypt, Mehmed Ali was helped in his resistance against the sultan-suzerain by French officers and other Frenchmen who, having the interests of French industry close to their hearts, made the Viceroy spend the profits from his cotton plantations on arms. At the same time, the English interest in preserving the status quo in Turkey was demonstrated in the person of a British admiral who was head of the rotting Turkish Navy.[9]

In some cases the services of these officers were of the relatively disinterested nature of the mercenary. More often they took up foreign service in order to serve their home country's interest in the country of their new and usually temporary residence. The foreign instructor, putting loyalty to his native land above that to his temporary employer, "remained essentially French,"[10] or British or German. He became even more a tool of his country's diplomacy, armed forces, and economic interests.

Countries in need of assistance were either considered as objects of imperialist penetration or as allies with a certain deterrent value for European war-makers. In October 1853, when Bismarck sketched the image of a European war originating from British-French antagonism, he proposed that

Russia concentrate her forces against Britain in India, where British power could be broken; a Persian army, disciplined by Russian and French officers, was to be used in this Alexanderzug, pushing to Herat and beyond, while Prussia and France would take care of Austria.[11]

(b) The Christian States: Rumania, Bulgaria, Greece

Military prestige exercised a strong influence over the choice of foreign instructors by those in need of them. Following 1866 and 1870-71, Prussian officers replaced French instructors in such countries as Japan and Rumania. Following independence, the latter's original military organization had been guided by a French mission. French influence was, however, gradually eliminated, once Prince Karol I had taken a Prussian colonel as his principal military adviser. Prussia proved very helpful by letting him have 15,000 needle guns at a time when she could hardly spare them herself. In 1869, the French mission was sent home. "Thus," to quote the Emperor's last Premier, "in spite of the nice words that were still lavished on Napoleon III, friendship with France was definitely broken and identification with Prussia brought about," which was to last until the eve of 1914.[12] Prussian support did not prove protective enough to save Bessarabia for Rumania in the Peace of San Stefano, but it at least spared her the utter dependency on Russia to which newly-liberated Bulgaria succumbed for the first years of her still-far-from-complete independence.

In the case of Bulgaria, officers and officials provided by the Tsar-Liberator arrived to run the country after 1878. The first three war ministers were Russian generals. A young Russian general and nephew of the Tsar, Alexander von Battenberg, was Bulgaria's first prince. Two-thirds of the officers training and commanding the new army were Russian, and Russian was the language of command. The administrators, corrupt and domineering, proved to be the worst that Russian officialdom could furnish.[13] They aroused the protests of the liberated, who particularly resented the high salaries the helpers were drawing.[14] A Russian colonel who had entered the nascent Bulgarian Army told young Alexander: "Highness, do not take all this too seriously. No Russian officer sees in you the supreme warlord. We stand here on an outpost and fight for Russian interests only. Your displeasure is the best recommendation for me at home."[15] At last, a Bulgarian-Russian military convention brought the insubordinate Russian officers under Alexander's authority. He then began to make Bulgarians officers.

Bulgaria was systematically prepared to serve as a zone for the initial assembly of the Russian Army whenever it should resume the offensive in the direction of the Straits. Contrary to the Act of the Berlin Congress, the Russians would not give priority to the railway line from the Serbian frontier to Constantinople via Sofia-Philippopol, a line that might prove helpful to the Austrians in blocking a new Russian advance on the Straits. They wanted first to construct the line from Sistowo, where they had crossed the Danube in 1877, to Sofia, a line that would enable them to by-pass the difficult Balkan range. Exasperated by this kind of help, Alexander and his Bulgarian counsellors tried to move out of the orbit of Russian domination. They found Russia quite unwilling to relax her grip. In 1885, under pressure from Bulgarian nationalism, Alexander was impelled to put himself at the head of a rising in Eastern Rumelia. Rumelia, still a Turkish province nominally, aimed at a more intimate union with Bulgaria. The Russians, contrary to their original policy of letting the Bulgarians have Rumelia, denied all help in order to make Alexander's position among his people untenable. Maddened by Bulgaria's striving for independence from Russia, the Tsar, in the midst of Bulgarian mobilization, recalled all 170 Russian officers and the Russian officials employed in Bulgaria and Rumelia in the hope that Alexander's regime would not survive the withdrawal of these props of administration and command.[16]

As good neighbors, Serbia and Greece considered the moment propitious to restore the balance of power on the Balkan peninsula, which they considered upset through the events in Rumelia, by attacking Bulgaria. Greece was restrained by the appearance of a British squadron. Austria, then Serbia's protector, felt unable to keep her protegé in leash in spite of Bismarck's warning that "no permanent alliance with the Balkan powers was possible. You will experience the same ingratitude from Serbia and the same bitter disappointment that Russia suffered in Bulgaria and Rumania."[17] Contrary to most expectations and many hopes, the Bulgarians won the war which the Serbs had started. The credit for the victory that was so unwelcome to them was still claimed by the Russians. The Tsar, in an order of the day, insisted that the brilliant successes were due to the conscientious and useful labor of the Russian officers who had been in charge of the formation and instruction of the Bulgarian troops. That proclamation, Foreign Minister Giers explained to the diplomats, represented "a purely military act," without any political second thought. Still, while the Tsar kept his violent hatred for Alexander alive, the Russian Army was willing to forgive him his "revolutionary prank." Alexander appealed to this sentiment when, in an order to his army following the armistice, he "recognized gratefully that it was indebted for its successes to the constant solicitude which the Tsar had shown it and the exemplary activity of the Russian instructors."[18]

The Tsar, however, was not to be reconciled. In August 1886 a band of Russian-inspired Bulgarian officers, "traitors debauched by foreign gold," as Salisbury called them publicly, forced Alexander to sign his abdication under the revolver held by Captain Radko Dimitriev, and leave the country. Strong national resentment, directed by the peasant-politician Stambulov, who jailed the military conspirators, brought Alexander back in triumph. But under the continued frown of the Tsar-Liberator, Alexander's nerves failed him. He abdicated once more and this time definitively.

Fondly believing that the Bulgarians would now return to the proper attitude of thankfulness, the Tsar sent General Kaulbars, brother of one of the former Russo-Bulgarian war ministers, to Sofia in order to bring them back into dependence. He was to obtain liberty for the imprisoned military conspirators (most of whom later emigrated to Russia and entered military service there), to organize a Russophile party and make it elect as their regent a minion of the Tsar. The stupid and crude methods of Kaulbars proved altogether unsuccessful. The Stambulovists could not be brought to postpone Sobranie elections for even the few weeks Kaulbars thought necessary to build up a Russophile party. The national assembly convened and at once elected a Danish prince, brother-in-law of the Tsar and close relative of the British royal family. He cautiously declined the doubtful honor. The Kaulbars mission departed, completely unsuccessful, and Russia was temporarily without influence in the Balkans. Austrian policy was nearly everywhere in the ascendency. In July 1887, the Stambulovists elected Prince Ferdinand of Saxe-Coburg, who was at first denied recognition by all the Powers, out of deference to the Tsar's wounded amour propre. Russian hostility kept his position precarious for years. In 1890, an army conspiracy against Ferdinand, Stambulov, and other ministers, headed by a Russian partisan, was discovered. A courtmartial found the participants guilty and Russian agents deeply implicated.[19]

Only after a prolonged exile and after Ferdinand's regime had been stabilized were the conspirators of 1890, with Radko Dimitriev as their spokesman, allowed to return and ultimately to serve in the Balkan wars. Their return did not contribute to harmony within the Bulgarian Army. Severe conflicts arose between those who had had their schooling in Russia and those who had been trained elsewhere. Austrophiles and Russophiles fought one another well into the First World War, at which time the memory of Kaulbars was still alive in Bulgaria.[20] In the language of a later day, the episode provided an early case of "Titoism."

Bulgaria's Russian experience kept most of the Balkan states from using military missions as the vehicle of military progress. On the whole, they preferred to have considerable numbers of their younger officers study with the armies of the great military powers, Germany, France, Russia, and Italy. Following their break with Austria, the Serbs sent their student-officers to either Russia or France. When, in 1909, they sought permission for a number of them to serve with German units, the Reich Government declined the compliment which the proposal implied.[21]

Only Montenegro, poor and small, continued to receive a military mission from Russia, her military protector and provider almost from the beginning. The mission, headed by the military attaché in Cetinje, supervised the use of funds and supplies that Russia had sent. This arrangement was in force on the eve of the First Balkan War, when, as even French diplomats reasoned, it would have been impossible to prepare for war without the foreknowledge of the Russian military mission and its home government.[22] When Montenegro began the Balkan Wars, the Russian minister at Cetinje was a little more mindful of the duties of neutrals than were the soldiers. He advised the chief of the military mission either to depart for Russia or to stay in the capital and abstain strictly from all activity in connection with the Montenegrine field army. But the general could not be bound for long by such advice. He soon followed the field army to Scutari, "in order to function there at least as an adviser," if not as the actual commander. In vain did Prince Nikita try to conceal this helpfulness by complaining to the non-Russian diplomats that the Russian general "was too neutral." Later, during the Balkan Wars, when the wily gospodar fell into disfavor with Tsardom, he approached the Austrians with the proposal that they take Russia's place and provide him henceforth with military instructors and administrative advisers and possibly a monetary subvention as well. But they considered his soul forever sold to military Pan-Slavism.[23]

Ever since her war for independence, Greece had been beset by the problem of obtaining the outside military assistance necessary for independence and self-government. Earlier she had received the help of such military Philhellenes as Cochrane, Sir Richard Church, and Colonel Fabvier. Her first King Otto brought along civilian and military advisers and commanding officers from his native Bavaria. Their autocratic ways kept Greek politicians and soldiers out of higher positions and influence. A military revolt in 1843 forced the King to dismiss his Bavarians and grant a constitution. Thenceforth the factions of the politicians grouped themselves as English, French, and Russian parties, while their King endeavored to evade the restrictions imposed upon him as constitutional ruler.

THE MEMORIAL LIBRARY
UNIVERSITY OF DELAWARE

After twenty years of juggling between parties and powers, another military insurrection sent him home to Bavaria (1862). A new ruler of foreign extraction was chosen, soon to be confronted with the problem of how to use the royal prerogatives in the face of the violent party strife, and whom to use from among the outside helpers. It signified a victory of the democratic principle when, in 1884, Trikoupis, for many years party leader and prime minister, arranged with France that she send a military mission to Athens for the reorganization of the Greek army. Since the enemy in all imaginable wars was Turkey and Turkey was employing German officers, the choice of French helpers seemed logical. However, the convention on this mission cautiously provided that it would be terminated whenever Greece should declare war. Several times during the 1880's and 1890's the turbulence of Greek politics led close to war, and the French Government on occasion reminded the mission's chief and the Greek Government about this stipulation.[24]

The Turkish victories of 1897 resulted in greater prestige for the German military teachers of the Turk and brought discredit upon the intermittently-employed French instructors in Greece. The vicious system of Greek politics in which officers took a lively part, some of them as members or candidates for parliament, did not provide very good working conditions for a foreign mission. In 1906, when officers were made ineligible for parliament, no real de-politization was effected. The "Military League" practically dominated Greek politics from 1908 to 1910, nominating ministers and endangering the crown. Finally the League lost its power when the army and navy fell out.

The question of again inviting foreign military or naval missions in order to direct and supervise necessary reforms was repeatedly an issue in Greek politics. For some time a constitutional amendment, brought forward in the officers' interest, excluded foreign officers from Greek service. Besides, foreign creditors represented by the commissioners of a Dette sitting in Athens frowned upon the extravagance of military reforms. However, in April 1908, the party in power voted to call in a foreign naval mission, preferably French. The year before, a French admiral had worked out "a naval plan which contains, for Greece, the revelation of a maritime power, the possibility of which she had not known," provided France was willing to lend the necessary material support. The proposed navy would "give Greece the maritime and political influence to which she can pretend, thanks to her exceptionally favorable geographic position in the Eastern basin of the Mediterranean and her racial qualities." In conjuring up this mirage, the French negotiators in Athens,

among whom were agents of Schneider-Creusot, went much beyond what their home government considered feasible, for London was hesitant, Greece's creditors had to be considered, and Greek offers to join the newly-concluded Mediterranean accords would simply be de trop.[25]

The international controllers of Greek finances, with a French-British-Italian majority, gave their permission for reorganization on a moderate scale. But in 1908, when King George brought in a French admiral for the purposes of naval reform, the naval officers, their "racial" vanity wounded, protested violently and effectively.[26] The King and his faction were inclined to learn from the Germans rather than the French in the military field, an inclination which the latter resented as ingratitude. In 1901, when the King's fourth son was to be sent abroad to complete his military education, French diplomacy regretted that he would go to Germany for that purpose. "Our own democratic regime does not allow the presence of foreign princes in the ranks of our Army," the French Minister at Athens thought. But the Prince ought to have done service in the army of Russia, the orthodox homeland of his mother, instead of undergoing Germanization like his older brother Constantine.[27] French diplomacy gave the Greeks to understand that they had never ceased to take an interest in the Hellenic Army. In 1905, the Prime Minister at the time assured them that this was not forgotten and that the German marriage of the Crown Prince would not alter that. But Greek public opinion had been made hesitant by the Franco-Russian alliance in which it did not want to get entangled and, still more recently, by the much too lively interest that the French had shown in Bulgaria.[28]

Nothing could be done until the constitutional reforms, inaugurated by Venizelos early in 1911, opened the way for the employment of foreign missions. Three missions were then invited—a French one under General Eydoux for the Army, an Italian one for the gendarmerie, and a British one under Admiral Mark Edward Kerr for the Navy. All three Powers accepted with alacrity. The work of the naval mission drew little attention until late in 1913 when Greek-Turkish tension over the disposal of the Aegean islands produced the threat that Turkey, by buying one or two Dreadnoughts, might transfer the dominion of the Aegean Sea to the Porte.

The French mission caused conflict and concern almost immediately. Within little more than a year, before its work could have taken great effect, the first Balkan War broke out. Credit for the Greek successes was promptly claimed as being due to the work of the French officers and the Schneider-Creusot artillery,[29] whereas the Turkish defeats were ascribed to faulty German methods and Krupp guns. No one was less inclined to admit the justness

THE MEMORIAL LIBRARY
UNIVERSITY OF DELAWARE

of such claims than Crown Prince Constantine, the commander of the Greek field army who had served in the army of William II. Questioned by a German observer during the first Balkan War as to the performance of the Eydoux mission, Constantine replied: "You can put that briefly—their performance equals zero." Their work on the mobilization plans had never been finished; mobilization and concentration had taken place on the strength of his own earlier plans; only the supply system had been reorganized by the French, and that with little success. The German observer himself found that the French officers had worked diligently and cleverly. Above all they had striven to obtain political influence and in so doing had suited Greek political psychology, something for which he thought his own fellow-countrymen were not gifted.[30]

As King from March 1913 on, Constantine grew no fonder of the French mission. He would gladly have rid himself of it, not the least since they continued to ascribe most of the Greek successes in the war to their own work rather than to his. He saw in its members "nothing but political agents and intriguers" against his own policies. According to Austrian and German reports, the French minister at Athens was forced to assemble them from time to time and lecture to them on political behavior and tactfulness.[31] At least one member of the mission later admitted that his Chief was not above errors in his treatment of Constantine. They would not have parted ways in such a deplorable manner if Eydoux had not made an enemy out of Minister Dousmanis and "above all, if the exaggerations of our press had not hurt royal susceptibilities during the Balkan Wars in making it appear that we had been the inspiration of the commander-in-chief of the Hellenic armies."[32]

But the King writhed helplessly under these insults. The continuance of the mission was a prerequisite to the placing of further badly needed Greek loans in the Paris market.[33] They were not obtainable elsewhere, at least not in Berlin where "Tino," visiting in September 1913, received nothing but the embarrassing encomium of his brother-in-law. William publicly reminded him of his earlier statement that, next to divine help and the bravery of the Greek troops, his successes were due to the time-tested principles of war that he and the officers of his staff had learned in Berlin. The Hellenic King obliged his hosts by paying them such compliments that French vanity was in turn deeply hurt. When Constantine arrived in Paris, an exchange of toasts was arranged in which the King duly praised the French mission, but the French attitude towards him was a cold one thereafter.[34]

The painful dependency of Greece on French capital handicapped Constantine in his inclinations towards the Triplice and in his dealings with the

military mission, whose claims to influence were still increasing. According to the King, Eydoux demanded a position tantamount to that of a commander-in-chief and control over the General Staff as well. The King was willing to give him the command of the Athenian army corps, but no more. "The officers were really nothing but French agents."[35] They were agents more directly and fully than many another military mission. In that respect the mission, and in particular Eydoux's own position, furnished the precedents for the Liman von Sanders Mission to Turkey, although the Entente Powers were unwilling to recognize or admit this.[36]

At the outbreak of the war in 1914, the French mission left Greece in order to resume service in the home army. They were little thanked by the King but excessively praised by Venizelos, who told them on their departure: "Having served our country before and after the Balkan Wars like a second homeland, you have undeniably contributed towards the formation of Greater Greece. I express to you in the name of the nation its gratefulness." The members, if not their Government, came to regret the hasty recall. After the battle of the Marne, with the great increase it had brought to French prestige, they could have kept Greece in the Entente camp and might have persuaded her to take a different stand on the Dardanelles enterprise.[37]

The British Naval Mission stayed behind at Athens in 1914 and endeavored to help Venizelos to oppose the King's neutrality policy and to bring Greece into the war on the Allied side. Trusting some pro-Entente declarations by Venizelos, the British government ordered Admiral Kerr, in August or September 1914, to arrange plans with the Greek naval staff for a possible occupation of Gallipoli. The King told Kerr, to his surprise, that he would not declare war against Turkey unless first attacked.[38] The King and a strong majority of the General Staff, mostly German-trained, continued to oppose Venizelos' policies of non-neutrality or preventive war. About one half of the army and navy officers were anti-Venizelos and anti-Entente and hostile to the foreign military and naval missions, while some of the Greek officers with whom the French had made friends went over to the Allies after they had landed in Salonika and there joined the Venizelist Junta or Committee of Public Welfare.[39] Only forceful intervention by the French and British could have overcome the King's and the officers' policy of neutrality: one whole army corps preferred internment in Germany to the alliance with the Entente.

MILITARY MISSIONS TO THE EXOTICS

Other countries or areas, such as Egypt, Persia, and South America, are fertile fields for historical investigations similar to the ones that follow. The three states dealt with in this section indicate the patterns of relations that have prevailed generally in the "exotic" regions of the world. In the sections immediately following, Turkey provides a more extended example.

(a) Japan

In the modernization of Japan, Western salesmanship and native militarism and navalism clasped hands eagerly. As early as the mid-1850's, the Japanese received a training ship as a gift from the government of the Netherlands. This set Japanese navalism off on its career, as it had set off that of Tsarist Russia one hundred and fifty years earlier. The Japanese bought additional warships from the Dutch in 1857-58, and sent their young officers to Holland to receive instruction in navigation. This nascent navalism was further aided by the present of a small naval vessel from Queen Victoria. This was like handing presents to one of Barnum's midgets, just as thoughtless and far more dangerous. These gifts, the nucleus of the modern Japanese Navy, proved as powerful as any gift of seeds. A little later, in 1868, the last of the Shoguns began remodeling the army along French lines and engaged British naval officers to help in the building of a Western-style navy. And in the same year, the first year of the Meiji era, the Emperor's powers were restored. He vowed that "knowledge shall be sought after throughout the world, so that the welfare of the empire may be promoted."[40]

The foreign influences that accrued from this search for knowledge were properly divided and carefully balanced. In 1872, twenty-three French military and thirty British naval instructors, the latter organized as a naval mission under Admiral Archibald Douglas, were engaged. Their home countries received most of the armament orders placed abroad and at least temporarily replaced Krupp, who had been an early provider.[41] In the 1880's, several German officers were engaged as teachers of military science at the War Academy.[42] They formed another group of foreigners who felt entitled to ascribe to their work a good deal of the credit for the victories on land and sea during the war of 1894-95. Prior to this war, a French naval engineer, Louis Emile Bertin, had organized Japan's naval yards and arsenals.[43] In the war, the British naval constructor Sir William White "was represented by two ships on either side," ships that fired at one another in the battle of the Yalu estuary. He did not say which were the better, but did insist that the German-built vessels proved unsatisfactory.[44] The Japanese were polite enough to concede all the teacher-nations a share in the success. Prime Minister Marquis Ito told the Germans, even after their intervention against the Treaty of Shimonoseki, that the Japanese Army "owed its organization and hence its victories to Germany, whose general staff officers had worked for years with well-known results in the training of the Army and the officer body in particular." He might also have mentioned the conservative German influence on Japan's constitution and the revival of the monarchical principle, which had happily averted the influence of American ideas to which young Japan had been so dangerously exposed for a time. In German Army circles, the Japanese military successes were hailed "for the simple reason that they were considered as indirect victories of German military science."[45] German influence on army thought remained strong until the war of 1904-05,[46] which proved a still greater teacher than all the foreigners put together. The war brought final emancipation from foreign teaching, an independence that went along with independence from foreign armament industries. By the time of the Second World War, Japanese Army men were advanced to the point where they could give their German Axis partners a few pointers on landing operations, which they had evolved in the Far Eastern fighting, should the Germans want to tackle the invasion of England.[47]

(b) The Chinese, who would not or could not be helped

Although certainly as much in need of foreign military and naval instruction as Japan, the governors of China were much less ready to accept the proffered services of Westerners. Following the employment of Western mercenaries in the Taiping War, the Chinese, haughty and slothful, slumped back into the exclusivism that then and always made employment conditions difficult for foreigners. A group of British naval officers on half-pay had started to build up an Anglo-Chinese flotilla. Almost immediately they threw up their appointment. The mandarins would not accept their demand to receive orders from the Peking central government, to the exclusion of the local bureaucrats. This refusal indicated Chinese unwillingness to admit the measure of centralism on which modern military administration must rest. It led to the break-up of the flotilla in 1863.[48]

The British willingness to help was at least partly due to Russian expansion from the North. In 1863, to meet this danger, the Commander-in-Chief of the British Army proposed not only that British forces in China be strengthened but also that the Chinese be assisted "by every means in our power as regards officers and non-coms to drill their troops."[49] Nothing was achieved. The Chinese were almost incurably slow in recognizing Russia's boundless ambitions in China.

His country's political disinterestedness and his own personal ambition combined to make an American officer offer military aid to China. Colonel Emory Upton was one of the few outward-looking American officers in the period following the Civil War. He hit on China as a field in which his individual professional labors and interest might be combined with the national interests of his country, in the development of China's military resources. As suggested by him, Secretary of State Seward proposed to Peking in 1871 that Americans ought to organize them "on the principles of modern science and economy" through the services of "some competent military man to be taken from the West." Upton, he mentioned, had offered his services for five years, during which he would be given leave by his Government and would receive a sum of $150,000 as down payment, plus a yearly salary. The United States Minister in Peking replied that the time and opportunity for such services had not yet arrived. Besides, Army affairs were in the hands of the provincial governors, and not in those of the Imperial Government.

Upton visited China in 1870 while on a governmental round-the-world trip. He was "still open to propositions from the Celestials," but unwilling to accept anything that "did not promise a fortune." He discussed his proposals with American consuls in the Treaty ports and others who were to bring to the attention of Chinese officials his plans for founding a Chinese West Point. His argument was simple: "In view of the powerful and encroaching nations of Russia in the North and England in the West, also of Japanese ambitions in the East, the great want of China is an army of not less than 150,000 men, organized and equipped like the armies of America and Europe, and, above all, commanded by officers thoroughly trained in discipline and the art of war." Within a ten-year period, such an institution would prove a success, provided its direction were entrusted to American directorship for the first six years, slowly passing into Chinese hands during the ensuing four years.[50]

Chinese officialdom could not, then or for many years to come, be persuaded to make any fundamental changes in the military organization. Nor would they trust the few foreign advisers employed. Such advisers as often seemed to be pacemakers of foreign imperialism as helpers against it.[51]

Upton's efforts are a reminder of the sociological fact that the officer who is eager to seek or accept employment as a military instructor in foreign and usually distant countries is of the more venturesome type, or someone held up in his career by conflicts with superiors or comrades or society in general, or someone threatened by debts and poverty. Upton himself was possessed of a neurotic drive and finally ended in suicide. In Germany the military career was always more difficult for non-noble officers, who consequently provided by far the larger number of instruction officers abroad. One of the relatively rare noble officers to serve as instructor was Erich von Falkenhayn, the later Prussian War Minister and Chief of Staff (1915-17). His was always "a problematical nature."[52] A summary of his career reads almost like fiction. He was an excellent officer, but also a gambler crushed by debts. Practically on the verge of being expelled from the army, he was obliged to accept employment in China. Finally reclaimed by Field Marshall Waldersee, he was returned to grace and thereafter rose rapidly in his career.

He had some predecessors in China, notably General (Chinese rank) Constantin von Hanneken (1854-1925) who had left Prussian army service and since 1880 had served Viceroy Li Hungchang as instructor of his provincial army. He was military adviser to the commanding Chinese admiral in the Yalu River battle, where he was seriously wounded. After the war he was given the task of reorganizing the Chinese Army as a whole, which he soon gave up as hopeless.[53] In this as in other fields, it was practically impossible to work on a businesslike footing with the Chinese governors.

In 1896, German diplomacy had been given the task by its imperial master to see to it "that China orders as many ships, etc., from us as possible, and that we get the military reform into our hands through the medium of German officers."[54] But German diplomats and military personnel found it as difficult as Anglo-Americans before them to come to any definite arrangements with the Tsungli-Yamen about the services of co-national instructors. Concessions were retracted by the Chinese almost as soon as they had been made. Even in questions of vital interest for China, such as the reform of her army with the help of German instructors, the Chinese Government did not act in a manner that inspired great desires in German diplomacy to make further attempts. Secretary of State Marschall told Li Hungchang during his visit to Berlin in 1896 that if China wanted to employ military instructors, they must be given a position enabling them to really do something. The Chinese ought not to beg for instructors one day and then, after months of discussion, break off negotiations on frivolous pretenses. It was, he added, so much easier to deal with the Japanese.[55]

Chinese procrastination in the negotiations with

Berlin were at least in part due to colonial aspirations pursued by the Reich in the Far East,
following its earlier disinterestedness. In the end,
Berlin officialdom was able to persuade Li to
engage a whole German mission of some fifty
officers. The mission was headed by Colonel
Liebert, who was very much the "colonial"
and "politico" type of officer. The road was to
be smoothed by the German members of the
Chinese Customs Service, including Hanneken.
The members of the mission, which included
Captain von Falkenhayn, were picked and ready
to go when the Russian Government, informed
by an indiscretion of the Chinese minister in
Berlin, began to protest. Russian imperialism
did not wish to see the strengthening of China in
a military or in any other sense. They had made
the Chinese central government promise in a
secret treaty that in the Northern provinces
(Manchuria, Tchili, and Chinese Turkestan) no
non-Russian military instructors would be employed. Foreigners active there were to be dismissed, including some Germans who, the Reich
insisted, had severed connections with the German Army and were employed under private contract. Least of all did the Russians want a man
like Liebert in China, "fearing," according to
Waldersee, "that he might endanger their influence
in that country." In the end, Germany proved willing to agree to Russian wishes if in turn her wish
for the acquisition of Kiautschou were supported.[56] The full fifty-man mission never
departed; only a few went, including Falkenhayn,
whose coming was urged by the energetic viceroy of the Yangtse provinces.

Falkenhayn, stationed at Hankow, got little
satisfaction from his activity. There was no
building in which to house the military school
he was to run and no money for it. And as a
constant obstacle to all success, as he wrote
home, there was "the indescribable inward
hauteur of each member of this nation which stood
in curious opposition to their outward politeness,
or even subservience, and which practically ex-
cludes the taking over by them of the achievements of the thinking of other human groups. In
addition, the lack of logical thinking combined
with the complete neglect of strengthening physi-
cal powers—both of these things a consequence of
the altogether rotten method of education."
The opposition of militarism and Mandarinism
could not have been more succinctly stated, nor
the fundamental reason for the failure of Western
military reformers in China, continuing until
nearly this day, more clearly elucidated. The
German minister in Peking at the turn of the
century stated a generally arrived-at conclusion of occidental officials when he wrote that
"the experiences...with military instructors furnish new proof that the Chinese cannot be helped
since they resist being helped." Falkenhayn
stayed in Chinese service until 1899 and then
switched over to the staff of the German expeditionary force sent out to combat the Boxers.[57]

In a completely unsystematic way, China continued to engage individual officers from abroad
until the Revolution of 1911. The experiences of
these instructors were no more satisfactory or
effective. Sir Robert Hart, head of the Chinese
Maritime Customs, strove on his part to extend
the modernization of China to her backward
armed forces and to create at least the nucleus
of a modern force with the help of foreign instructors. The strongest opposition came, as
usual, from Russia. Russia was seconded by
her ally France and, after the conclusion of the
Entente, even by Britain. When Hart pursued his
plans during the Russo-Japanese War, Jules
Cambon complained to Edward VII that Hart was
strengthening the "yellow peril": it was the duty
of the Powers not only to keep China neutral but
also, in their own interest, not to help China in
the development of her military strength. The
King more or less agreed: Hart had long since
become more Chinese than English. Cambon added
that it was the duty of all Europeans not to provide the Yellow Race with arms that might eventually fire back at them, seemingly oblivious of
the fact that the British were still the allies of
Japan.[58] The "Yellow Peril," as a military
danger, seemed to grow after the war of 1904-05.
The outcome of the war portended a growth of
Asiatic prestige. The Chinese governors, for example, came to prefer Japanese instructors,
though never quite without hesitancy.[59] Chiang
Kai-shek was one of the officers who visited a
Japanese military academy.

Nearly every one of the foreign instructors
seemed to the Chinese to be merely a tool of his
home government's imperialism. The element of
distrust, however justified, only impeded their
usefulness as instructors. By the end of 1907,
the general understanding among the Entente
Powers as to spheres of interest and zones of
future acquisition was extended to China. Germany
and the United States were both to be frozen out.
They thereupon posed as the last defenders of the
"open door." It was proposed to the Chinese governors that, for the purpose of increasing China's
military strength, they dismiss the Japanese instructors and replace them with Germans and
Americans. "Chinese pride must not be underestimated," thought William II, who had trampled
on it severely in earlier years, "and if the reorganization of their army would be somewhat supported and influenced by us, that would be all to
the good."[60] Nothing tangible or useful for China
came out of these discussions; they merely

sharpened the competition of the Powers at the expense of China. Every foreign instructor was now doubly distrusted, by the Chinese and by the other foreigners.

The issue came to the fore again when the question arose as to whether the Chinese Revolution of 1911 would ultimately strengthen or still further weaken China.[61] The relatively disinterested German policy in China was greatly resented by the more aggressive Russian and Japanese imperialists for the very reason that German activity was bound to help the Chinese to help themselves. And this was against the immediate interests of Japan and Russia, with the latter using the institution of the instruction officer as an instrument of penetration in Mongolia.[62] On the eve of the First World War, Russian diplomacy considered German policy in China as consistently anti-Russian. As the latest proof of this, the legation in Peking reported from a French source that the German adviser to the Chinese War Ministry had lectured the Chinese on plans for an attack by Chinese troops on Russian forces in Northern Manchuria. In doing so, the German reportedly was not acting on his own initiative. He was missing no chance to remind the Chinese that in the case of a general war in Europe they must find an opportunity of taking back from Russia her most recent acquisitions in China. The French thought that these suggestions—which the Chinese followed after 1914—were due to the German desire to draw Russian forces away from her Western frontier, the thing in which the French were mainly interested.[63] This was a piece of the military aspect of world policy as it looked through the trouée des Vosges.

(c) Morocco

Like other overseas states, such as China and Abyssinia, Morocco attempted at various times to save itself from colonialism, imperialism and Christian civilization by isolationism, by having as little intercourse as possible with foreigners. This proved more and more impossible as time went by. The French succeeded in foisting a military mission on them in the 1870's. Later, Spain, Britain and Italy concluded similar arrangements with the Sultan. The Sultan, when he detected ulterior French intentions, endeavored to rid himself of the French mission. The French promptly ascribed this to hostile British or German influence.[64]

The best-known anti-French military adviser of the Sultan was Kaid Sir Harry Maclean, a former British officer who arrived in the late 1870's. According to the common belief among diplomats, he, "though a Moroccan official, re-

mained of course an Englishman and looked after the interest of British policy."[65] Into the first years of the twentieth century, the British were still far from disinterested in Morocco. French diplomacy, eager to enter upon the Moroccan heritage, considered the British, and at other times the Germans, as most likely to interfere with the process of making Morocco dependent. When the negotiations leading to the British-French entente got under way, they began at once to complain about Maclean. The Sultan had made him commander-in-chief of the Sherifian army, which he was reorganizing and re-equipping. That, the British explained, was perfectly natural: the employment of Maclean and other British advisers was due to the Sultan's alarm over French activity along the Algerian border. The Sultan in his perplexity had sought and received British advice of the soundest description, directed mainly against the extravagant borrowing habits of the Sultan, which the French had encouraged.[66] Another measure of self-defense, applied by the Maghzen, was the boycotting of the French military mission. The French ascribed this "very vexatious situation" to the steadily-increasing influence of Britishers in the immediate surrounding of the Sultan. Boycott could not rid Morocco of the mission. But it still seemed advisable to French diplomats to stop the activities on its part that aroused the greatest suspicions among the Moroccans. For example, they stopped the cartographic work that French officers were carrying on in the most remote and unsafe parts of the country as too "graphic" an indication of the penetration under way, even for the non-picture-minded Moslem. Instead, the diplomats thought, the members of the mission should restrict themselves to the work for which they had been engaged, the instruction of troops.[67]

Despite all French invitations to the Maghzen "to address itself by preference to the great neighborly and friendly nation" that France was, the Moroccans continued to hesitate.[68] Only after a particularly serious and costly tribal upheaval did they make use of the proffered Paris money market for a loan, the proceeds of which were to be used to once more reorganize the army. "Tunisification" of Morocco had advanced one step further.

The British-French entente of April 8, 1904, removed the main obstacle in the way of French predominance in the Sultanate. Britain recognized that "it appertains to France" to preserve order in Morocco and "to provide assistance for the purpose of all administrative, financial and military reforms which it may require." In December 1904, the Maghzen, anxious to avert this fate of absorption through reforms, proposed to the Powers that all foreign advisers be forthwith withdrawn. This included the French military mission which, in 1903, had taken over the reorganization of the Moroccan troops along the Algerian border, the British military instructors, Italian personnel in the arsenal, and the German engineer who was heading the public works and was also the Krupp agent in the country. Instead, they intended to call in "Eastern," that is, Turkish advisers. The French were properly resentful: such a move towards independence must be punished by the Power "which is to be henceforth the predominant one in Morocco."[69] And the Maghzen's vent de folie was promptly ascribed to foreign, that is to say, German influence. Delcassé would not hear of the recall of the French military mission. He put funds at the disposal of the minister at Tangiers for bribing the ulemas, the public opinion-making clergy. The minister was just then readying himself to proceed to the Sherifian court at Fez in order to arrange for the modalities of Moroccan dependency.[70] Such a protectorate was to include, as a vehicle of imperialist penetration, the instruction of all Moroccan troops by none but French officers. This was a more or less typical feature of "protectorate treaties." Financial control and control of foreign relations were also included.[71] The miserable Sultan protested to the Powers and obtained a hearing in Berlin. On March 31, 1905, William II visited Tangiers, demonstratively, and in July German diplomacy forced the French to accept an international conference on Morocco. They hoped to preserve the "open door" in the Sultanate.

Even while these dangerous negotiations between Berlin and Paris were under way, the French stuck doggedly to the maintenance of their military mission in Morocco.[72] The Germans, before and during the Algeciras Conference, hoped that a Moroccan police force, to be organized under non-French direction, would form a counter-influence. This would keep a foot in the door that France was so obviously trying to shut by obtaining an international sanction from the Conference for a general policing mandate for Morocco, exclusively or together with Spain. The exclusive employment of French and Spanish officers, the German Government surmised, "would eventually bring the Sultan into a dependence on France and Spain. For the officers, as a matter of course, would be active in the interest of their Governments and could not avoid considering their task as national rather than international... The whole institution would be tantamount to a French-Spanish double mandate, that is to say, the preponderance of France to the exclusion of the other nations."[73]

Whether under the conditions of imperialist competition any representative or ressortissant of a Great Power can act in a disinterested way—the belief or pretence underlying the mandate idea, which goes back before 1919—is doubtful. This was the general opinion at the time of the Algeciras Conference. British diplomacy, in strong support of the French entente partner, protested that an international police force would do no good. The Germans, with much more justice, maintained that "whosoever had the police power had Morocco, and the principle of equal opportunity was then broken." The French held out and threatened to let the Conference break up on this point rather than give in. All that the Germans obtained was a nominal general-inspectorship of the police force to be held by a neutral, Dutch or Swiss, with very limited powers. Needless to say, the French military mission stayed on, more than ever inclined to expand its activities.[74]

The arrangements made at Algeciras cut France somewhat short of a complete Tunisification of Morocco. The control of the Sultan came to extend less and less to those troops which the French trained and directed.[75] The Sultan was still nominally free to regulate his military affairs in the interior, outside the harbor towns where the police were stationed. He tried to dodge French pacific (cum military) penetration by hiring a small number of foreign ex-officers, including two Germans, as drill masters of the small units which he endeavored to keep under his own control. Even these attempts at playing with soldiers disquieted the French out of all proportion.[76] So did the presence of Spanish troops in Morocco in 1908. They had come to intervene, together with French troops, but the two forces cooperated so badly that in the end they were firing at one another.

France's "special interest to see that order and tranquillity should reign in Morocco" led her officials in Morocco and the officers of the military mission to support various factions hostile to the weak central power of the Sultan. Later, his rival, Mulay Hafid, won over the larger part of the country, which in turn led to armed intervention by French troops. When they finally resolved to give their backing to the old Sultan, who seemed more pliable than Mulay Hafid, the military mission took him fully in hand. According to a German report from Tangiers in the summer of 1908, he and his ministers "were surrounded by a ring of French officers in whose hands lies already the administration of this country. The Sultan receives his instructions as well as the money for the expeditions which he dispatches from the hands of the chief of the French military mission, Colonel Fariau, who even counter-signs the checks which Abdul Asiz draws on his account in the State

Bank. Should the Sultan or the Maghzen ever attempt to oppose one French directive, Regnault [the French Minister at Tangiers] would order Colonel Fariau to hang the bread basket higher."[77] Nominally still Sultan, Abdul Asiz amused himself with military trifles and with the card tricks he was learning from a German instruction officer. He willingly abdicated in 1908 in favor of the successful pretender Mulay Hafid, who represented a crude nationalism. French intervention had been unable to stop his progress.[78]

The second Moroccan crisis in Franco-German relations had its starting point in the Moroccan disorders and the French intervention measures of 1911. These disorders were provoked by the application of new disciplinary rules dictated by the chief of the French military mission in Fez, Major (later General) Mangin. Under these rules, two Moroccan soldiers had been sentenced for desertion and shot to death publicly. According to German observation, "the indignation of the whole Moslem population about the death penalty against believers on the basis of a ruling originating with a French officer could at once be felt...His title of 'Kumandar' (commandant) became instantly a word of unbelievable agitating force." A wave of unrest developed. French officers on detached duty were murdered. The fact that they were leading Moslem troops against Moslem insurrectionists added new fuel to the tribal opposition. The military mission at Fez became the focus of hostility. Since it could not easily be removed from the capital without a loss of face, the French Government proposed a march of French troops to Fez where no lives seemed threatened, except possibly that of the mission members. The situation seemed favorable to Kiderlen, the originator of the second Moroccan crisis, to embark on talks with France. A German warship was anchored off Agadir to indicate German willingness to trade her stake in Morocco, poor as it had become, for French concession elsewhere.

Was Morocco, run more or less like a protectorate since 1912 by General Lyautey, a military liability or an asset for France? In the present and near future, it seemed the former. But there were potentialities in Morocco as a recruiting ground for France which both the Foreign Office and General Staff in Berlin took into consideration. By 1910 the military concluded that "in a German-French war, France would certainly employ Moroccan troops on European soil, though only an employment of masses can count for something. But the whole question is one of the more remote future since the first condition for the forming of such Moroccan units would be taking possession of Morocco."[79] The diplomats thought that the military utilization of Morocco would come about

sooner, for France and Spain had already begun to take "goums" into their service. But the process had certain setbacks. According to General Weygand, "the Sherifian army, taken in charge by France in 1911, had been developed too fast, with the help of doubtful elements insufficiently taken in hand by the instructors. This carelessness was dearly paid for during the days of April 1912 in Fez when sixty-eight Europeans, including sixteen instructors and forty other soldiers, fell victim to the doings of the rebels. Ruthless suppression promptly re-established order."[80] With such setbacks, often due to French misunderstanding of native psychology,[81] Morocco proved still more of a liability to France during the First World War. To soldiers like Lyautey, however, it remained a fertile field for colonial action, "not merely for its own sake but because he thought that France, 'swaying between the Utopianisms of one party and the snobism of the other,' had unconsciously need of a 'team of men of action' as a stimulus to national endeavor."[82]

TURKEY--Prelude to World War: Military Reform vs. "Peaceful Destruction"

Sociologically and diplomatically, the military penetration of Morocco had many features in common with the military reform attempted in Turkey before 1914. Two basic similarities were the difficulty of making foreign instruction effective against Moslem inertia and corruption and religious-nationalistic xenophobia, and the diplomatic conflicts over the question of which Power or Powers were to furnish assistance. There was, however, one essential difference: it was tacitly agreed that Russia, who considered herself the main heir-expectant, was not to furnish such assistance. On Russia's part, there was a fundamental unwillingness to allow such help to ever become effective and thus give the "sick man" another lease on life.

From time to time, the "sick man" received various blood transfusions from the Western world. The failure of the revolutions of 1830 and 1848-49 in such countries as Poland and Hungary drove many of the officers on the losing side to take service in Turkey. There they could still serve against the counter-revolution and its leader, Russia, as they did in the Crimean War. Following that war, the Porte chose her two principal allies, France and Britain, as models for her army and her navy respectively. French was taught in the military and English in the naval schools. Imitation of the French system was so close and so blind that not even the disasters of 1870-71 gave the Turks warning that their old model had failed and that imitation might fail even more than the original, as it did in the war of 1877-78.[83]

The Turkish Navy received enough British

assistance to survive the peaceful interlude from 1856 to 1877 in fighting trim. It was headed by a former British naval officer, Hobart Pasha, who, after a successful career as a blockade-runner in the American Civil War, had entered Turkish service in 1867. He performed such great services in the suppression of an insurrection in Crete that he was made pasha. At the demand of Greece, which in 1869 had been forced to bow to a demonstration by a Turkish squadron under his command, he was stricken from the British Navy list, but restored to it in 1874. Re-entering the Turkish service at the outbreak of the Russo-Turkish war, he was able to keep the Black Sea under full control of the Turkish fleet.[84]

The Turkish Army that was to fight this war had sunk into a much worse condition than the Navy. Nor was it easy for the friends of Turkey to help her. First the British ambassador had to rid the Sultan "of all the Ministers who were jealous of foreigners and so deprived him of the services of many distinguished English officers."[85] Then some of the help, such as that of Valentine Baker Pasha, could be made effective. Baker, holding the rank of major-general in the Turkish Army, was employed at the outbreak of the war in organizing a Turkish gendarmerie. Since the autumn of 1877 he had served with the field army as adviser and commander of a brigade which he had built up with the help of several other British officers, an activity much resented by the Russians. Both Baker and Hobart were thoroughly convinced of the unavoidability of Anglo-Russian conflict over Turkey, India and Central Asia. They tried to prepare, if not also to bring about, British intervention after the Treaty of San Stefano.[86]

Kept from returning home by a scandal that had ruined his career in the British Army, Baker continued in the Turkish service. At first he was employed as inspector-general of reforms in Asia Minor, where Salisbury had initiated a system of British colonel-consuls to observe Turkish reforms and Russian progress in the direction of India. But he was soon divested of all executive functions. Hopes of the British Government to obtain a high military post for him in Kurdistan, close to the Russian route to India, were foiled. "There are too many great Powers who have an interest in baulking any scheme of general employment of Englishmen in the Administration to leave us the slightest hope that such an issue will ever be reached," Salisbury wrote in 1879 to one of the military consuls in Asia Minor.[87] Baker left Turkey in 1882 for Egypt, where he had been offered the command of the army to be formed. On arrival, however, he found that his services to Victorian Britain in Turkey had not erased the scandal of his earlier career. Instead, he was merely given command of the police, which he proceeded to train as a reserve force of the army. He led this force in the Sudan war, but it failed him in the face of the Mahdist forces.

The next set of military helpers was called in by the Porte after 1878, during the period of the rather irksome execution of the Treaty of Berlin. In the early 1880's she applied to the German Government for a group of officers who were to direct the modernization of the army. She also requested administrative personnel to serve as reformers of her civil service.[88] The diplomatic situation was just then darkening. Turkey proved obstreperous in the final settlement of her frontiers with Greece and Montenegro (Dulcigno), and the other Congress Powers believed she was trying to obtain Bismarck's good will by this somewhat flattering invitation. Clearly it meant a diplomatic maneuver rather than any serious intention of reforming. So far as the recent Greek-Turkish tension was concerned, the French were convinced that their own mission "was merely a question of such good offices as we have rendered so often to either of these two countries." But to send a German or any other military mission to Turkey at this juncture would hardly appear neutral. Under these circumstances, the old Emperor and his son hesitated to give their approval. Bismarck, as he informed the Crown Prince, was quite willing to accept the Turkish invitation.

Several of Germany's more permanent motives for taking an interest in Turkey's army were already visible at this time.[89] Bismarck was even reported to have said that "since the last attempted run for Constantinople had induced the Powers most interested in it to take up their posts of observation for the future at Sofia, Novibazar, and Cyprus, the next race would probably bring them all still nearer to the winning post, when a comfortable seat, secured beforehand, in the grandstand, might better enable Germany to judge of their respective chances and make her book accordingly." However, despite the paraphrases on his often played theme qui parle Europe a tort, Bismarck recognized as justified the suggestions of the other Powers that German officers should not depart for Turkey at the moment of the crisis of 1880 or for some time thereafter. First the problem of the frontiers had to be settled. While he reserved the right for such officers to go later, he turned down a Greek invitation to have some German officers help in the instruction of their army.

The Turks went on begging in Berlin. They declared that Germany was the only disinterested Power in Europe that could lend the necessary officers and officials for seeing the reforms through. Bismarck told them that he was willing to send civil servants "but would not lend them any officers to serve in their army, first because they had plenty of excellent officers of almost every nation in Europe who could drill their troops, and secondly because the best German officers would not consent to serve in Turkey and bad ones would be of no use to them." To this the Turkish emissaries modestly replied that the worst German officers would still be better than the best Turkish officers, a compliment which greatly pleased the Chancellor. But he still advised them to seek this sort of help from Britain, traditionally Turkey's best friend.[90]

When Bismarck finally gave permission for a number of German officers to enter Turkish services, most of them reserving the rights of seniority and of returning to German services at the end of their engagement, none of the other Powers protested further, though the Pan-Slavists grumbled. Ignatiev, the pre-San Stefano ambassador to the Porte, thought it desirable

> that the material interests of Germany should not be too deeply engaged in the Orient, something which the Turks would like to see in the hope of thereby attaining that Power's efficacious protection. Considerable orders for Krupp cannons by the Porte, the presence of Prussian instructors in the Ottoman Army, the considerable augmentation of German engineers employed in the construction of railroads—they are already ties which bind Turkey to the Germanic Empire and which the latter could exploit the day it should wish to play an active role in Turkey. Considering the dispositions of the Sultan, the dignitaries of the Porte and even the populations, it would be easy for Germany to acquire a preponderant influence in Turkey against which it would be much more difficult for us to fight than against the other occidental powers.

All such help, including railroad construction, would only serve to hinder Russia in her work of "the peaceful destruction of Turkey."[91]

Among the officers who entered Turkish service in 1882-83 was Colonel Colmar von der Goltz. At that time he was a poor man, a prolific writer for military publications and fiction publishing houses, and a man possessed of energies and ambitions that could find no adequate outlet in the German peacetime army. Von der Goltz organized the territorial distribution of forces, prepared mobilization and concentration plans, and organized the general staff and the military schools. Three other German pashas directed the training of the infantry, the cavalry and the artillery. They found their employment beset by many difficulties, the greatest of which was Sultan Abdul Hamid's (1876-1909) instinctive rather than conscious fear of the power a good army would wield. He wanted only an army that

would impress the various heirs-expectant to his dominions, an army that merely looked like a fighting instrument.[92] He considered the army his most dangerous enemy, more immediately dangerous than Russians, Bulgarians, and British together, and was always obsessed by the fear of conspiracies and pronunciamentos. Every assembly of troops, every independent act on the part of some military commander excited in him the suspicion of plots. This morbid fear undermined the army and made it unable to prepare for war. Differences among the reformers before the days of the Germans did not improve matters. The officers from the several European military Powers merely served the purpose of helping the Sultan to bluff Europe and make it believe that in a little while, after a new set of reformers had been hired, there would again be a Turkish army to reckon with. "To watch that, to have ever growing decay continually before one's eyes, is no joy for a military man," Goltz wrote home. "I have a little bit of a free hand, but not much, and above all, since we have no executive powers, no real leverage. Everything must be done through intermediaries and thus time and energy get lost." That is to say, the Turks conferred no command on foreign instructors. That would have been contrary not only to their concepts of sovereignty but also to the religious notion that Christians must not have such power over Moslems.

Some of the most vital defense installations along the Straits fell into disrepair before they had even been finished. Goltz had persuaded the Porte to construct a road in the direction of the Black Sea from Constantinople. After a few miles had been built, the work was given up and the projected fortifications, which were to protect the Bosporus against a Russian landing from the Black Sea, were never even started. For the time being, Goltz concluded, in case of war not the Turks but the Power that acted with the greatest speed and energy and appeared first off Constantinople would be master of the Straits. Quite in keeping with the policy of "the new course," this judgment was communicated to London in the hope of energizing the British for the defense of the Straits.[93] Goltz and his colleagues became so disgusted at various times with Turkish procrastination that they wanted to resign, but always they were told by Berlin that they must stick it out.[94]

Soon the ever-recurring problem in this kind of employment arose: what role were the instructors to play in case of Turkish involvement in war? The British-Russian conflict in the spring of 1885 over the Pendjeh seemed to lead to the brink of war. This brought up the question of Turkey's obligations to block the Dardanelles against either Power's fleet. The Turks themselves were doing nothing to prepare such blocking measures which, in the nature of things, would be directed only against the British fleet. The German ambassador to the Porte recommended that the instructors stir the Turkish officials into doing the things that Turkey's military interest demanded. But Bismarck frowned on this. He thought it went too far and that the officers ought to abstain.[95] He would not suffer the remotely connected agents of German diplomacy to implicate Germany in Balkan affairs.

This was to change under William II, at least temporarily. The German ambassador to the Porte was von Radowitz, a left-over from the Bismarck era. Finding out through tales of the instruction officers at Constantinople that he was losing ground to French and Russian influences, William II transferred him to the quieter post of Madrid.[96] It appears that the true failing of the Ambassador had been his lack of exertion in the competition between Krupp and Schneider-Creusot along the Golden Horn. During the most recent phase of that historical competition, the diverse agents of Krupp had imperilled their own good position, as Goltz thought, by their high-riding pride, developed during the time when the Sultan had been completely in their hands. While they lost ground somewhat to their French competitor on this occasion, the instructors were able to persuade their pupils to introduce the Mauser rifle, the product of the L. Loewe arms factories in Berlin. Gratefully the company offered Goltz a block of their shares, but he declined—a Prussian officer could not accept pourboires.[97]

Unlike some of his colleagues, such as Kamphoevener Pasha, who, having risen to the rank of Turkish marshal and aide-de-camp general of the Sultan, remained in Turkish services for over twenty-five years, Goltz had always wanted to return to the Prussian army service. After various renewals of his contract, under pressure from the Sultan, he resumed home service in 1895. But for the personal dislike of William II for this uncourtier-lîke general who wrote so much and wore glasses, Goltz might have risen to the head of the Great General Staff, repeating Moltke's career, who had also served in Turkey.[98]

At times, probably at most times, the work of the foreign reformers seemed to the serious and honest ones among them quite hopeless and futile. Turkey's financial situation remained consistently bad and curtailed the army budget. The soldier material was basically sound and sufficiently numerous, but Abdul Hamid's insane distrust would not allow a thorough organization of the available potentialities, whether of the recruits or of such non-Moslem elements within the Empire as the Armenians.[99] Moslem dissatisfaction against the latter was unleashed in the Armenian massacres of 1896. The massacres were allowed in the hope that this "liberty" would regain popularity for the Sultan among his Moslem subjects. Army and police failed completely in their task of maintaining law and order on this occasion. Seemingly giving way to the protests of the Powers and the foreign press, the Sultan ordered an investigating commission of high military officers. The commission included four foreign generals in the Turkish service—an Englishman, a Frenchman and an Austrian, in addition to Kamphoevener. The Sultan wished them to serve as a white-washing instrument before the eyes of indignant Europe. Only the German and the Frenchman declined to obey the political orders of the Sultan and his favorites as incompatible with their concepts of officers' honor, and they resigned from membership in the commission.[100] Abdul Hamid's true intentions in employing reformers was to have them form part of the make-believe of his regime, but this fooled none but the European newspaper readers and the Greek army politicians.

The Greeks started the war of 1897 in the belief that Turkish corruption had gone far enough to assure them victory. The opening moves of the Turks were under the direction of Grumkow Pasha, one of Goltz' colleagues, who led them as far as Larissa in Thessaly. At that point he was recalled to Constantinople because William II would not allow a German officer to fight and beat his brother-in-law, the Greek Crown Prince Constantine.[101] Constantine, who was commanding on the opposite side, had learned his craft among the Berlin Guards. And his wife sent imploring telegrams to her brother William to save "Tino" from disgrace. The dynastic complications made it a little awkward to accept the credit that the modest victories seemed to confer upon the reformers. Most of this credit was ascribed to Goltz by the Turks and others. "The Turkish officer corps knows and acknowledges that they have won the recent war only through the activity of this man and the younger members of the General Staff schooled by him; they only regret that the supreme command in this war was not pervaded by the spirit of this school," reported the German ambassador Marschall from Constantinople.[102] Almost everywhere, except in France and Russia, the Turkish victory was acknowledged as a success of the German reformers. The victory redounded to the prestige of the German Army and strengthened the German position in Constantinople. A German court official visiting in England in the summer of 1897 heard it said that "at present Germany is the predominating power."[103]

This was indeed the aim of Marschall's policy in Turkey, at times at least as much self-directed as it was guided by the Wilhelmstrasse. Marschall was just then beginning to build up his long and powerful control over the situation along the Bosporus and beyond. The means employed were those of twentieth-century imperialism in combination:

loans, railway concessions, armament orders, instruction officers, service of Turkish officers in
the German Army. The Sultan permitted the latter
only with the greatest reluctance. He feared that
in spite of "his admiration for the Germany Army
as the bulwark of authority against radicalism and
revolution," they might become infected by Socialism while abroad.[104] Germany rejected Bismarck's view that Balkan affairs were not worth
the bones of a single Pomeranian grenadier.[105]
Nevertheless German aims in Turkey remained
limited: to do business for her business interests
and "to give the brave Turk a lift and develop and
strengthen him so that at a later time he can defend himself alone."[106] Such a policy, which had
British approval at the outset, was diametrically
opposed to the traditional Russian policy of keeping Turkey, as the long-intended victim of her imperialism, weak and backward. Whenever the Porte
was about to order new war materials, the Russians would raise the still unsettled question of the
war debts incurred in 1878. They must be paid
first, but actually never were. Such Russian demands did not keep the Porte from placing orders
for 200 million cartridges in Germany at that moment and 250,000 new Mauser rifles later.[107]
Russian diplomacy endeavored to keep the route
of the Baghdad Railway from following strategic
lines, to keep the Black Sea mouth of the Bosporus
unfortified, to supply the most restless Balkan
peoples, such as the Montenegrines, with arms.
The Russians were frank enough—"colossally cynical" thought William II—to tell the Germans that
"a Turkey strengthened by foreign powers and
foreign capital was not in keeping with Russian
interests," and that visits of German officers in
such zones of special Russian interest as the Turkish side of the Caucasus must be avoided.[108]
By the end of the century, the Russians declared
themselves "very much preoccupied" by German
activities in Turkey.

Various regimes have considered either the
military or the naval branch of their armed forces
as the more revolutionary one. Abdul Hamid suspected both equally of conspiring against him. He
allowed his navy, third in rank among the European fleets in 1874 and supreme in the Black Sea
during the war of 1877-78, to rot and rust until
the Greek War of 1897. Then it was sufficiently
reconditioned to steam inside the Dardanelles,
where the ships were allowed to continue in their
decay. At the turn of the century, the Sultan decided that he must have a fleet again, or something
that looked like one. He ordered some torpedo
boats in Germany and a cruiser each from Great
Britain and the United States. Payment for these
vessels was to come out of the indemnity he had
been forced to pay for losses suffered by the Armenian subjects of these Powers during the massacres of 1896. Along with the American-built
vessel arrived an American naval officer, Admiral
Bucknam Pasha, who had been in the service of
Messrs. Cramp, the Philadelphia shipbuilders. He
and another American naval officer, though able to
eliminate some of the graft in the Navy, could do
very little for the training of officers and crews.
The suspicious Sultan would not even allow the new
ships to steam out to sea.

All these years the Straits had been only diplomatically secured; they were not secured militarily. When the Russian cruiser Potemkine was on the
loose in the Black Sea in July 1905, its revolutionary
crew could have set off the whole Straits problem
in a manner not contemplated by any diplomat. The
Russian ambassador demanded that the Porte prepare measures to keep the vessel from steaming
through the Straits. The Turks were utterly at a
loss as to how to do so and were only spared further embarrassment by the cruiser's internment
in a Rumanian port.[109] Later, the Turks considered the acquisition of submariens for the Turkish
Navy. The use of submarines was urged upon them
by the salesmen of Krupp and other firms, and there
were rumors that the necessary Turkish officers
were to be trained in the German Navy. This eventuality made it seem advisable to the British naval
attaché in Constantinople "to endeavor to place the
orders for submarines in England or America, and
to offer to train the officers in the British or
American Navy, if anywhere."[110]

What was practically the last fairly general
agreement of the six Powers on Turkey was based
on the Austro-Russian agreement of Meurzsteg in
1903, to which the other Powers more or less
whole-heartedly acceded. It was occasioned by a
particularly violent outbreak of Bulgarian Komitadji
activity in Macedonia. It was thought that a repetition of this could best be averted by a reorganization of the Turkish gendarmerie in the Macedonia vilayets
with the help of foreign officers. Since Italy still
seemed fairly neutral in Turkish affairs, an Italian
general was appointed chief of this force with numerous officers of other nationalities under him.
German participation was kept at a minimum; there
seemed to be enough Germans active in Turkey already. From the German point of view, it seemed
more profitable not to make the Sultan feel that
Germany fully approved of this measure of international control, which was derogatory to his utterly irresponsible sovereignty. Since Russia was
soon preoccupied in the Far East, Austria became
the Power most active in the gendarmerie question.
She tried to block any Italian advance in the Balkans,
and to block Serbian attempts to expand by the use of
armed bands.[111] Hoping for the best from the
Young Turks' reforms, the Powers withdrew their
gendarmerie officers in the summer of 1908.

This revolution fully confirmed Abdul Hamid's

suspicions. Many officers of both army and navy declared against him. As a member of the British embassy put it, the Sultan found his "Wat Tyler in the shape of the military and Young Turks."[112] Several of the ringleaders were army officers who had studied in foreign armies, like Enver Pasha and his friends. Less of the revolutionary infection seems to have been derived from the foreign instructors. Their teaching, however, must have made all Turkish backwardness irksome to the more ambitious officer-pupils. At first, the various representatives of the Western wing of the Entente were jubilant. A British diplomat wrote home from Constantinople: "As for us, we have the ball at our feet, to the great chagrin of our German friends, who pivoted their policy on the Sultan and his camarilla." This same diplomat mentioned, among wholesome changes, that two of the German instructors had left Turkish services and had not been replaced by other Germans.[113] The German chargé himself, Kiderlen, the later Secretary of State, thought the days of the Reformers were over and was rather glad of it. They had often made trouble for the Embassy members, going directly to the Emperor with their complaints and denunciations.[114] Soon the Young Turks went to the foremost constitutional power, Britain, and begged her for technical advice about their armed forces. The Navy, headed by an old crypto-liberal, requested the loan of an officer of elevated rank to be adviser to the Minister of Marine. This led to a contract with Rear Admiral Gamble for a three-year period, beginning in February 1909. Actually, he resigned a year later. A number of junior Turkish officers were invited to sail on board a visiting American squadron on its voyage home to America. The Turks were duly thankful for the gestures from the constitutional Powers. Their gratitude would find expression in orders for ships to be built in English shipyards, once the money was available.[115]

The Russians were unenthusiastic from the outset. They told Grey that the constitutional movement would not last. There was nothing behind it but young officers who did not receive their pay and who were not allowed to speculate, as nearly everyone else in the government service did.[116] After they had recovered from their first shock of surprise, the Germans also realized that the movement was largely one of officers of the better class who had become estranged from the Sultan because he had seen in the Army nothing but an "enemy threatening him in his own corrupting power." This view is reflected in the description written by Ambassador Marschall for the eyes of William II:

Over a hundred officers, in part excellent ones, have served for several years in the German Army. There they have not only perfected their military knowledge but have also absorbed that spirit which has made the German Army the first in the world—the spirit of loyalty to the king, of discipline, of honor, and when these officers returned to their country, in the hope of turning to use in their own army what they had learned, the most bitter disappointment awaited them. The Sultan, whose distrust and fear were nourished systematically by an unconscionable entourage, largely put aside these officers who might have rendered his army the greatest services. Full of resentment, they were forced to look on as the Turkish Army went from bad to worse. And when the Revolution came, the revolutionary committee called upon those "German" officers at once and entrusted them with the foremost military position in the country.

William II could not then foresee his own fate of 1918, when he left the officers and the officers left him, despite their oath. But he became at once aware that Britain, however sympathetic to Turkish attempts at constitutionalism, would never be allowed by her entente partner, Russia, to let Turkey become strong. At the same time, the Young Turks realized that the Reval interview of Tsar Nicholas and King Edward signified a close British-Russian understanding at the expense of Turkey.[117] England was no longer Turkey's best friend. In common with the German ambassador, the officer-politicians were convinced that Turkey could only be saved by a thorough reorganization of the Army. The Army was at least semi-modern, which was more than could be said of administration and justice. Before and after the counter-revolutionary attempt of April 1909, it was the most important factor in Turkey's political life.[118] "If Turkey is to be preserved at all," the Austrian Ambassador thought, "she will have to become again what she always was, a military state. Only the Army is able to maintain the domination of the Turks—inside the Ottoman Empire—and all depends on whether it will be possible to make out of the Army a solid support for the Turkish state."[119] Even a Liberal like Edward Grey concluded that the best men on the Turkish scene in 1909 were Army men. However, largely due to the influence of the German-trained officers, their sympathies had completely swung back to Germany as their hope and model.[120] Reorganization of the army was brought under way at once.

When the first hints of a re-engagement of Goltz reached Berlin, Bülow hesitated. He thought that the Turks should engage first, or at least at the same time, an outstanding Frenchman for the reorganization of the finances and an Englishman or Italian for the reorganization of the navy "and thus prevent us from doing a solo dance with our colonel-general."[121] Immediately following the failure of the putsch of April 1909, the Turkish Government approached Berlin with a request for the services of Goltz, who had already made an unofficial visit to Turkey in the summer of 1908, and who was now to be given leave for one or more months every year to supervise the reorganization of the Turkish army. While the Wilhelmstrasse was a little hesitant, the Emperor and the Chancellor saw no objection. Goltz, they said, (although he must not compromise himself), will "improve the Turks for us militarily, politically, and economically, and chain them to us." Goltz knew Turkey too well to promise an early execution of such a tall order. He made arrangements with the Porte which seemed least likely to involve too deeply his country's policy and himself. Possible English protests could easily be answered by pointing out that a British admiral was already at the disposal of the Turks. Goltz did not find the situation too hopeless. On several visits in 1909 and 1910, he worked out various organization plans, such as separation of general staff and war ministry, schools for non-coms and for musketry, a system of pensions and of reserve officers. More generally, he tried to instill confidence in the officers, to strengthen the feeling for military authority and discipline, and to take the officers' interest away from politics. The number of German instructors was raised from four to twelve, representing all arms categories, including supply and medical services.[122]

Several of the younger German and Austrian diplomats and officers began to place great hopes in a Turkey freed of Abdul Hamid, whom they thought of as the incubus of backwardness. Within a few years Turkey might become a worthwhile alliance partner, might join the Triplice and even replace, as some Austrians thought, that thoroughly unreliable partner, Italy.[123] The military-diplomatic constellation of the First World War was here foreshadowed. It was developing out of the relation between the sender and the recipient of military instructors. Less realized was the danger that Italy, the Balkan States, or Russia might strike rather than wait for Turkey to grow strong. On this road to a rebuilt Turkey, German diplomacy hoped to keep on fair terms with Britain by an understanding about the Baghdad Railway and other interests and by leaving to her and her naval officers the task of reorganizing the Turkish Navy.[124]

Work on the Navy, begun in the fervor of constitutionalism, had soon run into difficulties. A nationalist-professional reaction had set in against the British influence. Turkish naval officers called for a new minister, who was to be more master in his own house. Admiral Gamble, who had demanded that all ships be bought in Britain and that twenty more British naval officers be engaged, was to be reduced to the role of instructor. In February 1910, however, he resigned for "reasons of health." In order to obtain an instant strengthening of their fleet against such likely enemies as the Greeks, the Turks shopped around for immediately available warships. They found the German Navy ready to sell one of its modern cruisers at cost price, but on condition that, in order to preserve the secrets of German ship construction, a connection similar to that between the two armies be established between the navies. Before that ambitious and entangling plan had gone very far, another British admiral was engaged. He was not to hold command, however, since the officer-chauvinists would not tolerate it. In order to keep the Greeks from beginning a war over Crete, the Turks stayed in the market for second-hand warships. Two ships, sufficient to neutralize the Greek strength, were sold to them by the Germans in August 1910.[125] The Entente Powers were highly displeased. Russia, disturbed in her traditional policy of "patronizing and exploiting a weak and languishing Turkey," pretended to be threatened in the Black Sea.[126]

Military Failure of the Young Turks—and of German Instruction?

The slow process of changing the Turkish army from the make-believe force of Abdul Hamid's days into a true fighting force had not gone far when first Italy and then the Balkan States decided to strike before Turkey became strong through reorganization. The Turkish defeats at Kirk-Kilisse and Luele Burgas were widely considered as German defeats, especially in France, but also inside Germany. In Constantinople, Schadenfreude on the part of the French and Russians was particularly great, less so on the part of the British. The Germans complained to each other: "Each Turkish defeat takes on the character of a German échec, political as well as military. All our dear friends tell the Turk: 'That's what German friendship does for you. What use is German drill, German guns and ships?'" The German reformers, none of whom had gone with the field army, were removed from all army committees, and one of them was told by a high Turkish dignitary: "For this we have Goltz to thank."[127]

Did these defeats signify more than the inevitable loss of prestige of a Power that had only begun to shift from the role of window-dresser to that of a true reorganizer? Were they truly a defeat of German methods and materiel? The French above all had no doubt on this point. Their press was convinced that Turkish military leaders, as schooled by the Germans, had proved to be below their task and that the French guns with which the Balkan armies were equipped had proved superior to the products of Krupp used by the Turks. The most chauvinistic papers saw a promise even of French victory over Germany in the Turkish defeat: "It is the breath of France which swells the victorious folds of the banners of Greece, Serbia and Bulgaria ...It is we who have educated a part of the victorious officers; the irresistible cannon, we have furnished them; the troops attacking the Turkish Empire, it is we who have in part instructed and disciplined them...The new star rising on the European firmament therefore throws a definite light on our dearest hopes and desires."[128]

French diplomacy everywhere endeavored to stress the defeat of German-trained commanders and Krupp artillery. They looked upon the Balkans as "nothing but a dueling ground between the French and the German art of war,"[129] somewhat ad nauseam as other neutrals thought, who also claimed a bit of credit for the unexpected victories of the Balkan nations. Italy put in her claim: such Bulgarian army leaders as Dimitriev and Fitchev had graduated from the Turin War Academy. Italy was particularly gratified in ascribing the defeat to Goltz, who had sharply criticized the Italian campaign in Tripolis.[130] As for Bulgaria, the Belgian minister at Sofia would grant scarcely any justification to the French claims: whatever the Paris journals maintained, the Bulgarian officers had not studied in France, but mostly in Russia, with a few in Italy and, last but not least, in Belgium. It was true that Schneider-Creusot had furnished the artillery. But this was due to the francophilia of King Ferdinand, despite the opposition of the general staff, as well as to diplomatic pressuring on the part of the French who had made the orders for Schneider the condition for a Bulgarian loan in the Paris market. "The result of the battles does not allow drawing conclusions as to the ballistic inferiority of the Krupp gun; it proves only one thing: the superiority of the Bulgarian gun layer; if he had been made to go to field equipped with German pieces, his success would have been the same."[131]

The German diplomats and soldiers themselves found many causes for the Turks' defeats—above all, the complete failure of the food and ammunition supply which had literally starved the stoic Turkish soldiers to death. Nevertheless they were greatly downcast. Goltz did not want to see anyone, although, as Marschall's successor thought, he had no particular reason to be depressed. The Turkish rank and file, in whom he had always trusted, were by no means the true cause of the cataclysm. Ambassador, military attaché and reformers tried their best to inspire the Turks with new courage and move them, after the defeats in Macedonia, to take a stand in the Tchadalja lines. William II thought his officials had no

business doing so. He himself had given up all hopes of a Turkish survival in Europe. Bulgaria seemed "the nation of the future" in the autumn and winter of 1912.[132] Others in the Reich were less ready to write off the German investment in Turkey or even swallow, without reparation, the loss of military prestige suffered there. Before the end of 1912, it could be observed that a turn in favor of Turkey was taking place in German circles, that they entertained "hopes to make up for the moral defeat suffered in the person of Goltz, the German instructors and the Krupp gun, and restore the credit of Turkish arms."[133]

The new military factors revealed by the Balkan Wars made a new German Army Bill imperative. In introducing it to the Reichstag, Chancellor Bethmann Hollweg pointed to the racial antagonism between German and Slav, sharpened more recently by the outcome of these wars. Germany would have to take this factor into account in considering the military future. In addition, he pointed out that French confidence had increased. With their lively temperament, the French claimed victories of French instructors over their German counterparts in the battles of Kirk-Killisse and Luele Burgas. The Reich would have to provide against the upshot of such convictions.[134]

Turkey's reorganization, begun at the close of the Balkan Wars and even earlier, covered nearly all fields of administration. They started with the Navy. It was entrusted to the care of British Admiral Limpus in June 1912. The fact that this mission was quite small was probably the reason why Russia did not protest against it from the outset. Whether any definite assurances were given her that it would never amount to anything worth Russian disquietude is not apparent. On the whole, such assurances must be taken for granted within the context of alliance diplomacy. At any rate, the Turks suspected such understandings among the Entente Powers. Competition within the Central Powers also seemed bound to impede the effectiveness of the reform work. Djemal Pasha, subsequently grand vizir, once exposed the false naïveté with which some of the competitors, in supplying reformers, urged their own services while denigrating those of their competitors. The French in Constantinople expostulated with him about the Liman von Sanders mission. The Turk argued that the three branches of the armed forces had been distributed among the British, the Germans, and the French. "Why now the quarrel?" he asked. "Do you want us to entrust the reorganization to the Russians? And now consider this: The Russians say that if the German officers take over the command of the First Army Corps, the defensive strength of the Straits would be raised. This means that if we should entrust the same mission under the same conditions to the French and British, the

Russians would have to raise the same protest, for I cannot conceive of the French or British officers combining with the taking over of the command the purpose of possibly opening the Straits to Russia. Your protests necessarily lead us to believe that you harbor no friendly intentions towards us." While not denying the Turk's logic, they answered: "What do you want? First, the Russians are our allies, and we are forced therefore to support all their demands, and second, the Germans are our enemies and we are forced to think of the dangers to us which are inherent in all of their enterprises. And even if there were no danger, we consider it our patriotic duty to tell ourselves: since this is something which the Germans claim for themselves, we must oppose it."[135]

While German diplomacy regretted somewhat that the British naval mission directed the orders for ships to British naval yards, they were still content to see Britain engaged, to a certain extent, through naval and other instructors, against Russian expansionism. They hoped that Turkey might in time furnish the starting point for an Anglo-German understanding. This hope was strengthened rather than weakened when, in November 1913, a large-scale contract with Vickers and Armstrong was concluded, envisaging a reorganization of Turkish wharfs, docks and arsenals on the Golden Horn.[136] But if the Germans and the Turks and later historiography[137] had expected that this would move Edward Grey and his assistants to back Russian demands less fully, they were in for disappointment.

The powers conferred on Admiral Limpus were quite extensive. Although called "instructor" in his contract, he was in effect given power of command. The Turkish public referred to him as the "accessory sultan for the navy." When asked by the British ambassador, a new-comer on the Bosporus, how he conceived of his position, the Admiral was honest enough to reply that he was actually the commander-in-chief of the Turkish Navy and as such had a jurisdiction which went beyond that of Liman von Sanders. He added that he could not understand just exactly how England could take exception to the German mission.[138] The Turks never obtained the help they wanted from their old friend Britain. When the Director of Military Operations, Sir Henry Wilson, was visiting Constantinople in October 1913, Djemal Pasha asked him point-blank why Britain hesitated to lend Turkey more officers for the gendarmerie and the services of men like Milner. Djemal said he understood that "England was afraid of offending Russia. What business was it of Russia? He would prefer going to hell in his own way rather than to Paradise under the tutelage of Russia... A strong Turkey in Asia would be good for England."

He wanted the assistance of England, of "men who could administer, execute, and command. The Turks could not now change their military teachers [Germans], but in all else, in finance, administration, navy, they wished to be under English guidance." Wilson, the soldier, was at a loss as to how he should answer.[139]

The British continued in their slightly embarrassed way in Turkey. The Russians found it very regrettable that the Limpus mission remained and provided the Germans with an argument in favor of the Liman mission which was hard to contradict. While they could be certain of one hundred per cent French participation in case of a war with Germany, British readiness, they concluded from the experience in Turkey, could only be put at fifty per cent.[140] After the Porte had bought two second-rate Dreadnoughts, negotiations began for the engagement of fifty British non-coms who were to serve the big guns on those ships. While there was still some haggling over their salaries, the Greek naval attaché in Constantinople—his ominous name was Krisis—warned the Russians that the services of such gunners must not be underrated. Such guns as these had been responsible for the satisfactory performance of the Greek cruiser "Averov." Since these Dreadnoughts and other British-built ships would upset the balance of sea power in the Black and Aegean Seas, the Russians indicated to London their wish that the ships should not be delivered promptly. The corresponding units in Russia's own fleet would not be ready until 1915. The engagement of the fifty gunners and mechanics also seemed to them highly undesirable. In any case, the Liberal Government, duly afraid of Parliament, could not provide them. With new engagements, however, the British naval mission reached a strength of seventy-two, including ten electro-technicians and twenty gunners. They worked with "ever increasing energy" since Djemal Pasha, naval minister at the time, truly wanted a serviceable fleet and in all things followed Limpus' advice. Everything was readied for the arrival of the first Dreadnought scheduled for September 1914, with the second to follow in December.

The Russian ambassador Giers and Captain Krisis were equally interested in preventing the arrival of these battleships. The former said he would not be sorry if they never reached the Straits. The Greek Government, however, had to take into consideration that the British Government might take it amiss if a dreadnaught should be intercepted en route, as the attaché had proposed. In the face of this threatening growth of Turkish naval strength, Sasonov indicated to Grey that Russia would be very grateful if "Admiral Limpus could be influenced to act in a manner desirable to Russia, and to slow down the reorganization." If there were to be a true rapprochement between Russia and Britain, the latter must prove "by the deed that she is ready to respect our vital interests." (This was in May 1914.) For an imperialist like Grey, there was no ethical problem involved, no conflict between keeping the entente with Russia and yet providing the Turks with an efficient fleet. If his Government had thought that the development of the Turkish fleet would become a threat to Russia, he told her diplomats, they would not have given British officers permission to enter that service. It had been granted at the insistence of the Turkish Government in order to enable it to reorganize the Navy sufficiently to help in the maintenance of Turkey's independence. Anything going beyond that purpose would be disapproved by the Government. If they had denied the Turks such services, Germany would have supplied them, something contrary to both the British and Russian interest. The Government could not legally interfere with the construction of Turkish vessels in British shipyards.

During the July 1914 crisis, Sasonov reiterated his hope that Britain would not allow the first Dreadnought to depart, as was about to happen. Urged by the naval minister, he emphasized to Downing Street "what tremendous importance this question has for us." Nicolson assured the Russians on August 1 that the case had been considered. The first Dreadnought was ready to sail but had not yet done so. Convenient interpretation of its war powers made it possible for the British Government to prevent the departure and to take over Turkey's Dreadnoughts for the British fleet long before Turkey's entry into the war.[141]

The Liman von Sanders Mission

German army circles continued to search for the true causes of Turkish defeat. They thought these causes were not to be found in the failings of the Turkish soldiers or the Krupp guns, but rather in the faulty system through which German instruction had been imparted. The group of instructors had been only loosely held together by the military attaché in Constantinople, and they had had no particular plan to go by. German military teaching could only become truly effective through a mission of selected officers under the unifying direction of an outstanding general who would serve as mission chief.[142] This military view coincided with a similar one that had arisen among the Turks themselves, and so it is difficult to clearly ascertain where the initiative for the Liman von Sanders mission lay. Some believe the originator was the German ambassador at the Porte, von Wangenheim; others believe it was the German military attaché, Major von Strempell, an ardent sales agent for Krupp.[143] In any case, reorganization with German help seemed to the Turks the only way of salvation. This was all the

more true since no substantial help could be expected from Britain. The latter now seemed almost as ready to agree to the partition of Turkey as she had been in the case of Persia.

The military results of the Balkan Wars had revealed considerable weaknesses in the armor of the Central Powers. The Balkan States, tied to the Entente by military Pan-Slavism, and in other ways as well, would now have to be reckoned with as military factors worth several German and still more Austrian army corps. To the German military authorities, the necessary corps seemed unavailable inside the Reich. When the General Staff demanded three additional army corps in 1913, the conservative war ministry decided that the necessary officers were not available "without reaching out into circles little suited for the supplying of the officers corps, which would thereby be exposed to democratization."[144] Austria-Hungary's military evolution was at a similar impasse. Her governors likewise did not dare to draw on circles "unsuitable" for the recruiting of additional officers. The military reorganization of Turkey was in a way to provide for an _Ersatz_ for the three army corps unobtainable at home. The conservation of Turkey was part and parcel not so much of German land-hungry imperialism as of German military conservatism. This conservatism had its active center less in the General Staff that had called for the three extra army corps from the available home resources than in the Prussian Ministry of War and the Emperor's Military Cabinet. Besides, a strengthened Turkey could open a second front against Russia. Germany seemed on the verge of developing the same kind of military satellite that Russia had built up over the years in the Balkans. The Russians found it also very alarming that while the earlier instructors had, as they thought, come from among the worst elements in the German Army, the new mission would be selected from among the best.[145]

The German documents tell the following story of the beginning of the Liman mission. Very early in 1913, during the armistice following the First Balkan War, a Young Turk politico broached the question of a German military mission. He asked Ambassador Wangenheim about the details of the obviously exemplary position of General Eydoux as head of the French military mission to Greece. What were the conditions under which he had been engaged? What was his position in regard to the Greek Army? There seemed a recipe for victory in that arrangement. He continued: the Government of the Young Turks wanted to know about Eydoux's powers "because it considers applying for a German general as commander-in-chief in time of peace, particularly for the purpose of putting the Army out of politics." They would also like a German admiral at the head of the Navy, but were afraid that that would bring on a conflict with Britain, which must be avoided as long as possible. The Turks had concluded that the time for half-measures, as represented by the old arrangement with instructors here and there, was over. A full-sized military mission had to come and take one army corps completely in hand, which would serve as a model for the rest. They must also reorganize the war ministry, the general staff, the military schools and the arsenals.

Late in March 1913, following these first exploratory queries, the Turks begged William II to put an officer at their disposal as soon as peace was restored in order to direct the re-fortification of Constantinople. The request was made through the attaché, von Strempell. Either Strempell or the Turks themselves, both of whom knew very well of the Emperor's eagerness to obtain orders for Krupp, added that the officer should be in a position "to direct considerable orders in the direction of Germany." Wangenheim, with the Junker's cunning pretence of appearing up-to-date in the pursuit of trade and the favor of public opinion, asked the Wilhelmstrasse a little later: "What would our public opinion and Krupp say if the instruction of the army should suddenly be lost to France? And what of our trade which is progressing pari passu with our influence?" [146] The Wilhelmstrasse saw no political objections to the proposed undertaking.

The next step was taken when the grand vizir approached the Emperor, through Strempell, with the request for a general to head a German military mission. He was to have functions similar to those of Eydoux in Athens. He was to head all other military reformers, prepare mobilization and concentration plans, and reshape the general staff. Such a mission, Wangenheim was convinced, would give Germany the strongest position inside Turkey and would restore the old balance of influence which had been somewhat upset by the calling in of so many British administrative reformers.[147]

A month later, with peace restored through the Treaty of Bucharest, a general had been found who seemed qualified for the task and was willing to undertake it. He was Liman von Sanders, commander of an infantry division, "of elegant military appearance—something which Goltz never pretended to--accomplished manners, many-sided in his military experience." For long years in the past he had been a member of the Great General Staff and successfully active in the most varied army positions. In this way the Military Cabinet described his qualifications to the Foreign Office.[148] During prolonged negotiations, largely carried on among the soldiers, the modalities of his office were arranged. As

the Emperor had insisted from the outset, Liman was made the direct superior of all German officers to be employed—forty-two in all, it was proposed. He was entitled to inspect everywhere, and no foreign officer was to be engaged for the Osman Army without his agreement. The whole system of military education, including gunnery schools and training camps, was to be under his supervision. He was to be made a member of the Supreme War Council and was to have a definite say in the promotion of officers, including generals. The fact that his contract was to run for five years—instead of two as in the contract with the British naval reformers—and that transfers and dismissals of the higher Turkish officers were made subject to his approval would guarantee to the work of the German reformers the continuity that had been denied to earlier reform work.[149]

While these terms were being settled, Liman prepared himself for his work and got acquainted with conditions in Turkey, where he had never been, by reading the reports of Goltz and other predecessors. They could not have proved very encouraging. But his energies were equal to it. While he never forgot that he would have to act amongst a people utterly foreign to him and to German standards, he at times grew quite impatient with Oriental procrastination. Above all he was determined to keep himself and all officers under his command out of politics. The work of the mission was to be strictly military, as laid down by the terms of the contract. In a farewell audience at the end of November, William II told him: "You must not care in the least who is in power—the Young Turks or the Old Turks. Drive politics out of the Turkish officer corps. Their greatest mistake is dabbling in politics... Be on good terms with the head of the British naval mission... He works for the Navy and you for the Army, each of you in his own separate field."[150]

Ever hopeful to unite British with German influence against Russia, the Porte had informed the British Government about the project in May 1913. And William II spoke about it to King George and the Tsar during their visit to Berlin in May. The King found it "quite natural that they should turn to you for officers to reorganize their army while we were asked to send people to reorganize their police and gendarmerie which we shall do." The Tsar thought it necessary to strengthen the Tchadalja lines in order to keep the Bulgarians away from Constantinople.[151] The Wilhelmstrasse had taken very little interest in the matter, and the Chancellor even less. The negotiations were carried on in well-preserved secrecy by competent military officers, including the military attaché in Constantinople, and with the cooperation of the Berlin War Ministry and the Military Cabinet.[152] In the division of labor among the Berlin offices—which was also a désarroi of authority, as even the Russians recognized—this seemed the business of the military, an assumption that was very easy to make in Berlin, especially when the restoration of Army prestige, the obtaining of armaments orders, or the preparation of a possible military ally were involved. So alien did the Wilhelmstrasse remain to these negotiations that it did not receive a copy of Liman's contract until January 1914.[153] The diplomats were not certain that Turkey could be saved by means of a military mission. If Turkey were to be partitioned, Germany must not come out of it empty-handed. "It would mean a second Morocco for us," Secretary of State Jagow opined, while others remained a little more hopeful for Turkey. And Wangenheim thought that in case of disintegration, Germany would be in control of "an Anatolian colonial army" on the spot.[154]

In October 1913 Sasonov passed through Berlin on his way to Paris and had a friendly conversation with Bethmann. Neither mentioned the Liman mission—Bethmann perhaps because he did not consider it important in German-Russian relations, Sasonov either because the Tsar had not informed him about the Kaiser's communication in May or because the situation had not been pointed out to him as alarming by his soldiers or diplomats.

During the first days of November, Giers learned of the forthcoming German mission and that it was to be in the pattern of the Eydoux mission.[155] He also learned that Liman was to hold command of the First Army Corps, an arrangement made at the suggestion of the Turks and not yet known in the Wilhelmstrasse. This struck a neuralgic spot in the system of Russian imperialism, for the First Corps was in Constantinople, along the Straits. While the Russians would not object to a German command in some parts of Turkey, they would not suffer it in the capital or in certain other sensitive regions. With Liman in command in Constantinople, the Russians argued that their ambassador "would be protected, so to speak, by a German army corps." Turkey had been Russia's enemy for centuries. It had never pleased Russia to have Germans reorganize the Turkish Army. (Actually, the German instructors had always operated in and from the capital.) Holding command of the Constantinople army corps would be virtually handing over "the key of the Straits" to the Germans. If the Russian Government were to permit that, it would not long be able to maintain itself against the storm that would be raised by the military and Pan-Slavist elements.[156]

This internal pressure made the Russian pro-

tests forceful and threatening, though hardly logical in argumentation. The Russian embassy was even more "protected" by the Turkish ships under British command. Given the nature of the sea arm, the reorganization of the Turkish fleet would become effective far more rapidly than that of the army. There was no immediate military threat to Russia in such a command. But what the Russians were truly afraid of was, as put bluntly by William II, "the strengthening of Turkey by us and an increase of her military resistance power or her usefulness to us in case Russia should attack us. Russia wants to keep Turkey a-dying and receive Stambul as an easy piece of booty. England would not like that. Russia in her land-hunger bags Manchuria, Mongolia, and Northern Persia without our blinking an eye. But when we send officers to Turkey, then Russian 'public opinion' is excited!! Should we give way to Russian wishes, our prestige in the Moslem world would be done with."[157] Prestige was pitted against prestige, always a very dangerous situation in international relations.

When Sasonov sought support for Russian policy in Paris and London, the diplomats there felt bound more by alliance duties than by the strength of Russian argumentation. Only very late in the crisis did Grey realize that there was too much analogy between the position of Liman and that of British Admiral Limpus[158] to expect full backing from his own party for Sasonov's demand for British support.[159]

From Bethmann Hollweg's point of view, the Liman affair was not worth the trouble it caused in foreign relations. It was, however, so popular at home—three hundred officers volunteered for service in the mission—that he could not drop the project. Bethmann, whom the German military had brought into this dilemma, finally worked out a peaceful, timorous, face-saving solution. By promotion in the Prussian Army, Liman automatically acquired a rank in the Turkish Army that kept him from continuing in command of the Constantinople army corps. He retained the post of inspector-general and director of military schools but held no command, as the British admiral continued to do. The Constantinople army corps was given to a Turkish general, while a German officer took over the command of the Adrianople corps.

The occasion provided a severe test of the strength of the two parts of the alliance system. Throughout, France gave encouragement and approval to Russian diplomacy and expressed her willingness to stick with Russia "to the bitter end."[160] Britain backed out of an overly advanced position, thereby leading the Germans to misjudge England's devotion to the Entente. Austria considered the German compromise a full-sized defeat, showing once more how unreliable or over-cautious Berlin was apt to be in Balkan questions. It would have to be taken in hand by Vienna.[161]

Inside the Tsarist Government, the episode of the Liman mission had occasioned a sort of diplomatic-military test mobilization. On January 13, 1914, when the settlement of the crisis was in sight, a conference of Prime, Foreign, War, and Navy Ministers, together with the Chief of Staff, considered what "measures of constraint" might be applied against Turkey if Liman's command in Constantinople were not rescinded. Seizure of certain Black Sea ports, such as Trapezunt, was envisaged, to be accompanied by the declaration that Russia would hold the port until her demands had been granted. If that should lead to a European war, as it well might, the support of France, which seemed above doubt, and of Britain, which was more uncertain, should be solicited beforehand. The Prime Minister asked if "war with Germany is desirable and could Russia undertake it?" The War Minister and Chief of Staff declared "categorically the full readiness of Russia for a dual combat with Germany, not to speak of a dual combat with Austria."[162] What this meant in terms of material and psychological readiness for war no one outside Russia knew better than Poincaré. In March 1914, he stated that although the Liman incident had been settled, "badly settled, incidentally," and Russia had accepted the solution, nevertheless "her patience is at an end. Whatever conflict, great or small, may arise between Russia and Germany in the future, it will not come out as the last one did."[163] Though few contemporary eyes saw it, the Liman von Sanders affair demonstrated the strong militarization of European diplomacy on the eve of 1914. Military considerations had provoked the crisis and had sharpened it. The soldiers had got the diplomats effectively under their broad thumb. The diplomats either proved badly informed about the obligations the soldiers and sailors had entered upon or they became militaristic in their proposals for a settlement and thus bad negotiators.[164] For example, Bompard, the French ambassador to the Porte, proposed that Russia re-enact Agadir by having an armored cruiser anchor in the Bosporus and then declare that it would not be moved until the contract for Liman had undergone the changes Russia wanted.[165]

It was the soldiers who had begun to consider Turkey as a military factor, some with a mind to building up her strength, others to prevent this from coming about. Not all soldiers were convinced that Turkey could be reformed, even by means of a German military mission. General Radko Dimitriev, the Russo-Bulgarian soldier who had commanded in the Bulgarian Army during the Balkan Wars and was afterwards minister to St. Petersburg, was one of the skeptics. In St. Petersburg he told the Austrians that Liman would fare no better than Goltz, for he could not change the basic weakness in the Turkish army, which was in its officers. In the recent wars, they had always been the first to give the signal for flight. Other experts on war expected that a basic reform would once more make Turkey a factor in the military situation. The inspector-general of the Turkish gendarmerie, a French general, was one such expert. He confessed to the Austrian military attaché that the Triple Entente had very weighty reasons for demanding Liman's recall: "Considering that the great European settlement of accounts was not very far off, it was not a matter of indifference to France whether or not half a million Russians should be tied down by the Turkish Army under German command. Under these circumstances France could not lend any more money to Turkey."[166]

Russian officers were equally frank with the prospective enemy. "One day we shall settle accounts with Turkey," general staff officers told the German military attaché in St. Petersburg. "At that time, we want to find her weak. She will become strong, militarily speaking, through German reforming labor in its present form. We would have had nothing to protest against a largely advisory activity of German officers, it would have been as ineffective as the earlier attempts. Now, however, an organization has been effected which promises success. It is for this reason that we don't want the German generals to have direct commanding powers." These men of the General Staff were also convinced that Russian diplomacy had chosen the wrong address for their protest. They should have threatened the Turks directly, in the manner of the Austrian ultimatum blocking the Serbian desires for an outlet to the Adriatic.[167]

Liman's position was, in his own opinion, neither very satisfactory nor very promising. He himself proved, the diplomats thought, "a very impetuous gentleman, who approached his task with great consciousness, but also with enthusiasm and an idealism based on ignorance of Turkey and therefore uninclined towards very far-reaching concessions." The compromise worked out by the diplomats seemed to him nothing less than backing down on the part of the Wilhelmstrasse. When Enver Bey took charge of the War Ministry, Liman's relations with the Turks became very difficult and at times hopeless.[168] But when Enver was willing to let dissatisfied German officers resign, Liman told him that they all had orders from Berlin to stay. For the Russians, that was further proof of Germany's intention to exploit Turkey and keep up friction between her and Russia.[169] Turkey's finances kept all reform work within narrow bounds. The Army could not even be clad; it went away from the capital in rags.[170] The French were making use of the leverage which their capital supply for Turkey gave them by insisting that orders for Turkish field artillery go to Schneider-Creusot, which "was obviously intended as a stroke against the prestige of our military mission," Attaché von Strempell thought.[171] He considered the mission a mission in the interest of Krupp, not because he was an agent for Krupp but because Krupp must find non-German orders for its products in peace-time in order to be the better ready for Germany's own war. This was essential for the pre-1914 "stand-by" arrangement for industrial mobilization of the German general and other staffs.

When the war of 1914 broke out, the French military mission promptly departed from neutral Greece, but the Liman and the Limpus missions stayed on. The action of the Entente partners in the conflict over the Liman mission had filled the Turks with grave suspicions of their ultimate intentions regarding Turkey. The Turks feared Russia and her aim of getting possession of the Bosporus. Therefore, from the bottom of their hearts, they wished success to Russia's enemies, as Russian ambassador Giers reported on the first day of war. "This feeling is strongly supported by the officers of the German mission who apparently are remaining in Turkey. They form a highly undesirable element which no doubt incites the Turks against us." The Russian military attaché believed that the Turkish Army did not as yet represent any danger to Russia. It was clear to the Russians, however, that the Germans were bent on drawing Turkey into the war and thus to "tie down at least part of our forces and divert attention from our western frontier."[172] Wouldn't Turkey send the Germans packing? the French ambassador asked the Grand Vizir. Their stay, he pointed out, was incompatible with Turkey's neutrality. In reply, he was told that there was no reason at this juncture to dismiss the mission, which was very useful to Turkey.

Before the end of July, the accession of Turkey to the Central Powers was already being negotiated. Ambassador Wangenheim had doubts about her alliance value at that time. He was told to dismiss his doubts, which he did more readily after Liman told him that the military value of the Turkish Army could be trebled if it were commanded by German officers. There were sixty of them employed at the time. Five army corps could be put in the field at once. German command would make it possible to force Tur-

key to fulfill her engagements in case of war. The German-Turkish Treaty of August 2 provided that "in case of war Germany will put her military mission at the disposal of Turkey," which assured the mission an effective influence on the general leadership of the Army, along lines arranged between Enver and Liman. In effect, this guaranteed supreme command to the German mission, perhaps more than was wise to take on.[173] With this step, the pro-German Turks won out over the pro-Ententists. The Entente group had lost much ground when Britain took over Turkey's dream-ships, the Dreadnoughts, and Germany sold her the Goeben and the Breslau. The Russians had, in vain, made last-minute desperate endeavors to strike against the Germans by trying to persuade the Turks to dismiss them. For, as the Russian military attaché in Constantinople reported, "the dismissal of the German officers from the Turkish Army by itself would destroy their prestige completely and forever put an abyss between Turkey and Germany."[174]

The acquisition of the Goeben and Breslau, which could hardly be deemed unneutral (as Grey admitted after England had cheated Turkey of her Dreadnoughts), would not greatly strengthen the Porte. Nicolson tried to impress this fact upon the Russians, who found themselves outranked in sea power in the Black Sea since the British had allowed the Goeben to escape. Britain would recall the Limpus mission eventually, and without it the Turkish fleet could not function. Entente diplomacy tried to persuade the Turks to send home the German crews of the Goeben and Breslau. As Isvolski put it: "In Turkish hands these ships will be completely harmless." But they also stayed.[175] "The curious position of a British admiral being in theoretical command of two Turkish cruisers manned by German officers and men"[176] could not last for very long. The Limpus mission was recalled on September 13, 1914. Much to the regret of the Russians, they went directly home instead of sending at least a few members to Russia to inform her Navy about conditions in Turkey.[177] Following the Goeben's attack on Odessa on October 29, the Entente representatives again asked the Porte to dismiss all German instruction officers, military and naval. When the request was turned down without much hesitation, the Entente representatives demanded their passports and left, despite the entreaties of the pro-Entente group.[178]

Liman von Sanders and his mission remained in Turkey throughout the war. A new contract was signed in October 1917, followed by a German-Turkish military convention designed to regulate military relations in postwar times, when Liman was to be replaced by another officer, possibly Seeckt. This brilliant though "difficult" staff officer was transferred to Turkish services at the end of 1917, as Chief of Staff of the Turkish army. Did this make him a member of the military mission? Nominally only, said Seeckt; Liman, who considered Seeckt his subordinate, maintained the contrary. Their relation was never clarified and led to numerous conflicts and recriminations. Liman ascribed the responsibility for his defeat in Palestine to Seeckt. Seeckt accused Liman of having ruined the Turkish Army while saving the Dardanelles. In the end, Seeckt came to have grave doubts about the work of the mission under the conditions which Turkish military nationalism imposed upon it. At the close of the war, he summed up his conclusions in the following way:

The two allied supreme commands have worked in full agreement, the Turkish partner has remained loyal to the very end. In spite of that, we are confronted at the close of the war with a military failure of German activity in Turkey. It is perhaps to the Germans' credit that Turkey could conduct the war for four years along the various fronts, but German influence in the end proved powerless against corruption... German activity was heavily mortgaged by the institution of the German Military Mission, pet child of the Prussian Ministry of War, created at a time when Turkey was calling for help and was receptive to conditions of any sort. It is doubtful whether von der Goltz' advice was sought when the contract was drafted; it is hardly likely that he would have agreed to arrangements impossible to execute, as is obvious to anyone who knows the Turk. The contract put practically the whole organization of the Army into German hands and enabled the chief of the Mission to interfere in practically all military affairs. No doubt the Mission achieved much during the spring time of Enver's reforms. But the contract ought to have been cancelled at the outbreak of the war and the German-Turkish alliance put on a simpler, more decent basis, instead of allowing Enver to practically disregard it. From then on, the Mission...only impeded German work in wartime Turkey.[179]

The Powers that considered themselves victors over Turkey intended to make her a military non-entity. By the terms of the Treaty of Sevrès, they reduced the army to 15,000 men, under the supervision of an Interallied Control Mission, and staffed the gendarmerie of 35,000 men with foreign officers. But Kemalist Turkey shook off this yoke of foreign control before it was fashioned. While still eager to participate in foreign military progress as far as its slender means would allow, Turkey did not return to the system of the old-style foreign military missions and instructorships.

The memory of the Liman von Sanders mission, the strong impression that, despite all its failures, it had been able to turn backward Turks into a fighting force of considerable strength, was fresh in the minds of the Allies when they came to contemplate and make peace. At that time, the potentialities of future German military missions working in the revolutionary East of Europe seemed terrifying enough. Should defeated Germany throw herself into the arms of Bolshevism, as was feared, then all Eastern Europe might follow. Within a year, reorganized by German instructors, commanded by German generals, and equipped with German guns, it might line up as a gigantic Red Army ready for a new attack on Western Europe. It was the Welsh imagination of Lloyd George that foresaw this future possibility.[180] He wanted to avert it by a moderate peace with Germany, while Foch and the French "frocks" looked forward to the forming of anti-German and anti-Bolshevist armies in the buffer states under the guidance of French military advisers. All agreed in the Versailles Treaty (Article 179)[181] that Germany herself must not again be allowed to send military missions abroad. But should France replace her and become the new imperialist Power, working through military missions?[182] Many if not most Anglo-American statesmen and soldiers felt that the war had not been fought for that end.

MISSIONS BETWEEN THE TWO WORLD WARS

The various military and naval missions sent and received by the belligerents of the First World War served to maintain liaison in a war of coalitions. In some cases, they formed the media for the communication of certain military advances achieved by one partner and more or less urgently needed by the other. The greatest technical backwardness was found among the Arabs, whom T.E. Lawrence was to organize, pay, and lead. Aside from this case, the most typical function of the modern military mission, to raise or reform a foreign military force that had either fallen behind or had to be created from nearly zero, was not called for again until 1919. At that time, the British, French and Italians maintained military missions with the various White Russian armies, such as Denikin's, in order to help organize the struggle against the Bolshevists. The three missions did not coordinate their activities very well. In October 1919, the Great Power representatives in Paris were forced to consider how coordination could be improved.[183]

While Article 179 of the Versailles Treaty forbad the sending of military missions, the victorious Powers continued to send missions to their allies, friends and satellites. Among some of the now independent Arab states, notably Transjordania, British officers like Glubb Pasha carried on the traditions of T. E. Lawrence well beyond the Second World War. Missions were sent to old states like Portugal, to new ones like Poland and Czechoslovakia, and across the Atlantic to South America. The Brazilians asked for a French military mission early in 1919. Joffre nominated and the French Government proposed Gamelin, later Chief of Staff of the French forces, to head it. His mission lasted until 1925. It proved highly satisfactory to the General himself, and, as he thought, was also in the interests of both France and Brazil. His successors continued the work until the eve of the Second World War, during which they were to find a Brazilian expeditionary force fighting side by side with French units in Italy.[184]

The most intensive and extensive use of military missions was made in servicing the military part of the Franco-Czech alliance. The new Czech Army was organized strictly along French lines, a tendency which was further strengthened by the fact that numerous Czech officers were studying in the military schools of France.[185] The first heads of the French mission in Prague were Generals Pellé (1919) and Mittelhauser (1919-26). The latter's successor was General Faucher, an original member of the mission who remained until the end of Czech independence. Mittelhauser subsequently headed the Central European section of the French General Staff and in 1939 he reactivated a French military mission to Warsaw.[186]

These several French missions (plus loans) were essential parts of the French alliance system, which also provided arms where necessary or, as in the case of the original Polish fleet, vessels built in French shipyards. In 1919, 1920, 1921, before Poland's petulant emancipation from French tutelage, various missions were sent by Paris to contribute to the building up of the Polish Army. These missions were headed by distinguished war leaders, such as Weygand, who arrived during the Russo-Polish war. Whether the French were adequately thanked for their labors, or whether there was ever reason to thank them, became one of the poisoning problems in Franco-Polish relations. The more Pilsudski's power grew, the less use he and his colonels had for the French mission, the continuance of which had been stipulated by a military convention of 1921. Its role was constantly reduced and it was at last recalled, years before Pilsudski's death.[187] Everything was done to spare Polish pride. The French officers were merely "technical counsellors of the Polish military authorities, with whom they were placed. The did not receive orders from Polish officers and gave them none."[188]

Franco-Czech military relations were far less spasmodic and much more harmonious, even though they ended in a deep disappointment that lasted beyond the Second World War. During the May 1938 crisis—when the Czechs mobilized and the Germans did not—General Faucher was "in the best of spirits and declared he felt twenty years younger." He expressed his confidence that in the event of an international conflict his own country would march at once. The Sudeten German leaders considered him a "thorough intriguer." He showed and imparted equal confidence to the Prague General Staff during the September crisis. Both General Staff and Mission asked the French Government whether the casus foederis had not arisen, and they received a preliminary answer that seemed encouraging to them. When no confirmation came, Faucher resigned as mission chief and put his services at the disposal of the Czechs, hoping perhaps that they would choose to fight alone.[189]

Ending Franco-Polish estrangement on the very eve of the Second World War, a French military mission headed by General Faury appeared once again in Warsaw. Sent "with the intention of securing the full effectiveness of the Franco-Polish alliance," it never successfully arranged the details of the military part of it, such as the coordinating of French action with the expected German attack on Poland. Though considered a sincere friend of Poland, Faury merely proved to be an instrument of the weak Bonnet policies. On August 25 he recommended that the Poles refrain from rash action in connection with the frontier incidents which the Germans were staging in ever increasing numbers.[190]

Only at first sight does it seem curious that the losers in the First World War were in greater demand than the winners as providers of military instructors. There were various reasons; for example, their employers, if not they themselves, were convinced that defeat had taught them more than victory had taught the victors, plus the view, justified in the beginning, that instructors from these nations were more above the suspicion of imperialism than others. China, profoundly disappointed with the work of earlier instructors, freed herself from the military bondage that the Japanese had tried to fasten on her through the Sino-Japanese military pact of 1918 (cancelled January 28, 1921).[191] The China of Sun Yat-sen called upon temporarily non-imperialist Russia to provide her with instructors. "We no longer look to the Western Powers. Our faces are turned towards Russia," Sun declared in December 1923, the Russia who had turned her back on "force and utilitarianism," the bane of the Occident. She would help China to develop her tools and improve her means of defense.[192] And when the First National Congress of the Kuomintang met at Nanking in January 1924, a manifesto composed by Sun ascribed the country's woes to militarism, imperialism, and the unequal treaties.[193] The Russians had forsworn all these (or so it seemed) at the time when they had sent Borodin as political adviser and General Galen-Bluecher as head of a group of one hundred or more instruction officers. They were to undertake, "under the control of Dr. Sun, the modification of the internal organization of the Kuomintang and of the Cantonese Army."[194]

One of the first steps to be taken was the founding of a revolutionary military school, the Whampoa Academy in Canton. It was opened in June 1924 by Sun with such hopeful words as these:

> The value of the revolutionary soldier surpasses one hundredfold that of a simple soldier. We must organize a solid revolutionary army. The School will furnish you the means and will show the most suitable way of working for the triumph of your cause... The Russian Army has not been formed in one year. It needed no less than six. We shall profit by the Russian example and create a revolutionary army as strong as hers. Only if we pay this price will our country become powerful and strong.

The School was headed by Chiang Kai-shek, at that time called "the yellow Bonaparte." He soon proved to be one of the stumbling blocks in the way of Galen-Bluecher, who complained (after three years of labor): "I know what the Russian Revolution is. I hesitate to define the Chinese Revolution." Such a phenomenon as the plague of the twentieth-century condottieri that overran China was a thing hard to fit into a Russian scheme of revolution. Galen, the true military leader, had brought Chiang in triumph to the North.[195] Chiang then gave him to understand that Chinese military nationalism would no longer tolerate either him or Communism, which were synonymous with the destruction of China. "Applied to China, Communism would have the same effect as an error in treatment would have on a sick person." Borodin and the other advisers were thrown out of China, Galen being the last to go. "Had she a Communist Party like ours, she would astonish the world," were his parting words. The next stage of his strange career was command in the war against the China of Chiang Kai-shek in 1929-30. This was followed by his holding the office of supreme commander in the Russian Far East until he disappeared in the "purge" of 1937.[196]

His successor as adviser to Chiang Kai-shek, after Seeckt had declined the offer for the time being,[197] was Colonel Max Bauer. During the war, Bauer had been one of Ludendorff's trusted assistants. He was an artillery expert but also an inveterate officer-politician. He was a leading member of the post-war overseas emigration of German officers who had been made unemployed, though not unpensioned, by the reduction of the Reichswehr to a strength of 100,000 men. The German ex-officers entered foreign services individually, as advisers and instructors. They were men of venturesome nature, participants in free corps, putsches and other activities directed against the Weimar Republic. Whether the Government could have kept them from departing, as the Versailles Treaty seemed to demand, appears doubtful. In any case, in the eyes of the Weimar Republicans they were "better out of the country." While the Reichswehr seems to have known about their engagements, it did not serve as a placement agency. After Locarno, the Versailles Powers informed Germany that their jurists had concluded that Article 179 of the Peace Treaty was not intended to keep her from sending military attachés abroad, that it merely referred to "military missions of instruction." This left the way open for individual instructors to leave Germany.[198]

Their destination was either China or South America. Lieutenant-Colonel Hans Kundt, who was considered to be one of the most gifted and cleverest of the general staff officers, returned to Bolivia in 1920, where he had served from 1911-14. Under his guidance, and finally command, which seems to have extended far into the political field, Bolivia undertook the bloody and unfortunate Chaco War.[199] Colonel Faupel served in Argentina and later became inspector-general and chief of staff of the Peruvian army. Reinecke and von Kiesling found employ in Peru, and Roehm in Bolivia. Roehm had left Germany and German politics after a break with Hitler, to whom he had given early support, including Reichswehr funds. He was making progress in La Paz when Hitler, shortly after the Nazis' great successes in the Reichstag elections in October 1930, recalled him to Germany to shoulder a more fatal military mission—to become Chief of Staff of the S.A. and S.S., the Party's military formations. He returned at once to take over the position which he had long craved.

Whether the conditions under which these officers had been engaged or were working warrant the use of the term "military mission" appears fairly doubtful, except possibly in the case of China. Still, their activities were included in the indictment, ordered by President Roosevelt in October 1943, for the numerous breaches of the Versailles Treaty. They were said to have maintained, at one time or another, military missions in China—where they served the side that America also favored—Argentina, Colombia and El Salvador, and, in addition, an aviation mission to Argentina.[200] When drawing up the indictment, it escaped the American prosecutors that there might have been other additional breaches. German naval personnel, at best only temporarily retired, had worked closely with various foreign navies[201] and shipyards as counsellors and as agents of the post-war Reich Navy. The Navy was as much interested in keeping submarine construction alive as the Reichswehr was in experiments with tanks and airplanes. The latter were equally prohibited by the Versailles Treaty, but could be tested on Russian soil. After long negotiations, Argentina twice declined to build U-boats according to German plans. However, Finland (since 1924) and Spain (since 1927) were found willing to have such vessels constructed in their shipyards. Some of the boats were sold to Turkey, while others served to train German personnel for the rebirth of the submarine arm in the post-1933 German Navy.[202]

The services of German officers in Nationalist China most closely approached those of a traditional military mission, not only with regard to organization but also with regard to the diplomatic complications into which it finally ran. Following the death of Colonel Bauer in Shanghai in 1929, the "Advisory Staff Nanking," as the group came to be called, was headed by General Wetzell, another Ludendorff man and an excellent organizer. All the members were retired from German army service and were under long-term and financially generous contracts with the Chinese Government. There were forty-three officers employed in October 1935, thirty in August 1937, and twenty-four in April 1938. Their activities extended to all military fields. Progress was very slow. Again and again, the model infantry brigade they endeavored to build up was taken from their hands and used up as a stop-gap in the civil war. However, relations with the Gimmo, who believed strongly in German military knowledge and ability, were fairly harmonious, if at times difficult. They were strengthened when the old problem of Chinese arms supply was at least partly solved by a Chinese-German trade agreement of 1933 under which an exchange of raw materials and military equipment was arranged. In the following years, fifty to eighty per cent of Chinese arms imports came from Germany, with Italy next in importance.[203]

In the autumn of 1932, Chiang invited Seeckt to come to China and advise him, after a prolonged study, as to further reorganization. Seeckt arrived in Shanghai in May 1933. His recommendations to the Marshal and Madame Chiang[204] were as much based on his German experiences as on his Chinese observations; first of all, obtain peace if only to reform your armies, something impossible in time of war (including civil war); strive for ten excellent divisions rather than twenty mediocre ones; continue the model brigade; have the war minister subordinate to the commander-in-chief; rationalize promotion and employment of officers through a central personnel office. In the final analysis, Chiang would have to be his own principle helper. Recipes could not be bought abroad. Still, Seeckt's and his successor's advice was good enough to guide the Gimmo in his anti-communist campaign of 1934-35, which drove them on their "long march" to seek refuge in the Northwest.[205]

In 1934, at Chinese insistence, Seeckt returned once more to China. This time he came not privately but officially, as "general counsellor" of the Marshal and superior of all the German officers in his employ. Much to Seeckt's regret, Wetzell would not accept a position under him and left China in 1934, to be succeeded by General von Falkenhausen. Seeckt's mission had the approval of the Hitler Government, which had not yet established its intimacy with the Japanese, the Wilhelmstrasse, and German industry. Seeckt's second stay resulted in his stressing proposals for Chinese industrialization, if only for military purposes. Seeckt left China in March 1935 because of illness. Nominally he remained Chiang's general adviser. His own ideas were well represented and continued through Falkenhausen.[206]

Chinese-German intimacy was growing, and in part it was genuine. Chiang received what he considered sound advice and help from the soldiers and diplomats of Germany, who had disinterested herself in the Far East. Because of his own Fascist sympathies, Chiang welcomed the Germans and the Italians, who were also among his advisers. German industry, through its bartering system which was largely independent from the monetary payments that were beyond China's power, provided him with most of his war materials. The Germans believed that they had given Chiang some power of resistance when the Japanese became openly aggressive in China. Japanese victory in China was far from certain, Falkenhausen informed Blomberg in Berlin in July 1937. "The morale of the Chinese Army was good. It would fight desperately, and a war would turn into a death struggle." The Anti-Comintern Pact partners soon came to feel and resent the German help given Chiang, "private" as it was in character, and not unneutral, since no war was declared. An officer from the Tokyo War Ministry told the German military attaché that German activity on behalf of China "was seriously prejudicing the sentiments of the Japanese officers corps towards Germany. The Japanese Army Command could raise no legal objections against the military advisers, but its policy of German-Japanese collaboration was gravely jeopardized by Germany's conduct, since opposition already present in individual officers' groups threatened to spread throughout the forces." When the Japanese tried to represent their action in China as dictated by the Anti-Comintern Pact, the Wilhelmstrasse, unwilling to evacuate the position it held in China, would not accept this interpretation. Besides, recalling the German advisers would only lead to their replacement by Russians, "an undesirable result for the Japanese as well." That the Italian advisers to Chiang were soon trying to curry favor with the Japanese by recommending a peaceful settlement to the Gimmo did not help German diplomacy.

For the time being, the Wilhelmstrasse would do nothing beyond reminding the advisers, who were planning the Chinese operations, of their obligation to abstain from an active part in them. Japanese diplomats at first agreed that the presence of German advisers was more agreeable to Japan than that of "nationals of another Power." But they soon succumbed to what their military men demanded—the recall of the advisers. They would not accept the German excuse that the Reich Government had no authority over these privately-employed officers, hinting that it would also be well to recall the ambassador, Dr. Trautmann, from Nanking. He was considered, and rightly so, to be pro-Chinese. The coming of Ribbentrop was like a break in the well-kept dike of diplomatic argumentation. He informed Keitel in October 1937 of the Führer's decision that "in the Japanese-Chinese conflict the Wehrmacht was to avoid anything which might in any way hinder or obstruct Japanese aims." The Japanese had actually threatened to renounce the Anti-Comintern Pact, should German support of the Chinese continue in its present form, which included the sale of arms by German firms. Long-term contracts with the Chinese had to be cancelled overnight. The upstart powers of the Third Reich rode roughshod over the foreign office and the army, even though the latter reminded Hitler and Goering that Falkenhausen's recall would mean a Soviet general in Nanking. Hitler curtly told Blomberg that the War Ministry must rid itself of the reputation of being pro-Chinese. As the new and ever obsequious man in the OKW, Keitel assured Ribbentrop that he had given up all direct contact with the advisers.

At the suggestion of the German ambassador in Tokyo, the Germans in Nanking were then (early in 1938) made the bearers of a Japanese peace offer to Chiang. However, it proved much too onerous to be acceptable. Falkenhausen thought the Chinese could hold out another six months, provided the right military measures were taken, domestic morale restored, and sufficient ammunitions provided. But the mission had come under fire from inside China. In their bitter defeatist mood, Chinese agitators spread word that the German advisers had betrayed operation plans to the Japanese at the same time that they were accused by the Japanese of directing the Chinese in their plans. The ambassador in Tokyo, naturally interested in preserving German-Japanese harmony, pointed out that the continued Chinese defeats would in the long run be blamed on their German advisers, "not only by the parties to the conflict but also by third countries interested in lowering German prestige in the Far East...The advisers will in the long run have to share the responsibility for the Chinese defeats." The argument of the German China merchants that the advisers were pioneers and trail blazers for a considerable part of German exports to China proved less and less valid as Japanese occupation of Chinese territory increased. Ambassador Trautmann, however, contradicted the arguments of his Tokyo colleague: his solicitude for the reputation of the advisers was quite unnecessary, for their position was never so good as now. The true Bolshevizers of the Far East were the Japanese, etc., etc..

The Nazi element in Berlin made short shrift of these arguments. In April 1938, all further war materiel deliveries to the Chinese were forbidden and the advisers were told to come home. These measures, "highly appreciated" by the Japanese, deeply shocked the Chinese. The advisers were reluctant to throw up their jobs and share in what they considered their home government's disloyalty to China and to themselves. The brutal Ribbentrop informed them that the Reich Government "expects its request for their return to be complied with as speedily as possible." Should any individual officer refuse to comply, he would be liable to heavy punishment, such as loss of Reich citizenship and confiscation of property. This was the Führer's express order. He would not hear of Chiang's last-minute attempts to retain the services of at least a few advisers. Chiang had suggested that Falkenhausen be appointed military attaché to Nanking.[207]

Their departure was greatly regretted by the Gimmo. The Germans' immediate successors in China were Russians, so-called "volunteers," who came to serve with the Chinese armies as pilots, instructors and technical advisers. "But not being men of high rank and long military experience, the Russian advisers offered no adequate substitute for the German staff officers whom their Government had recalled." Japanese protests against their services and against Russian arms deliveries remained unheard in Moscow. Russia's greatest service to China at the time, however, consisted in drawing considerable Japanese forces to the Siberian frontier, where various clashes occurred.[208]

The recall of the German advisers from Nanking was merely the sacrifice of a pawn carved with some care by an earlier, less war-like regime in the interests of the bigger game the Nazis were playing. The only pre-war military mission originating with the Nazis went to the Franco forces in Spain. There it encountered no similar group

from the democracies but only one from Red Russia, in which "Tito" Broz, a refugee from Yugoslavia, was included. The operational activities
of these milites missi of the Revolution and the
Counter-Revolution are too inexactly known to be
treated at length. They themselves considered
the battlefield of the Spanish Civil War largely as
a testing ground for their latest weapons and
tactics.

Under the pretence of safeguarding Germany's
"purely economic" interests in Rumania, German
military units and a military mission were sent
there in October 1940. As the measure was explained to the suspicious Russians, Rumania herself had requested such a mission for the better
training of her army. Contrary to British propaganda, there was no anti-Russian intent behind
the measure. It was designed to train the Rumanians, to help maintain order and quiet in the Balkans and to protect German oil and grain interests
against British interference with these supplies.
Molotov, who inquired about the strength of these
units without receiving an answer, thought that
this danger was not really very great. Considering the German-supported re-annexation of Bessarabia, the Russians could not protest too much.
They were assured, as on Molotov's visit to Berlin in November 1940, that these troops would be
withdrawn as soon as peaceful conditions again
prevailed.

While their alleged task was to show allied Rumania how to organize and train its armed forces,
the real purpose of the mission was to protect the
oil fields against third Powers and to make Rumania's armed forces capable of carrying out
tasks devised for them by German plans and in
the German interest, including war against Russia, to be carried forward from Rumanian soil.
Members of the mission were to be subordinate
to the German minister in Bucharest, from whom
the chief of the mission was to receive "the political directives and instructions which are necessary as a basis for his military task." By the
time of the attack on Russia, nearly 700,000 Germans had been transferred to Rumania.[209]

THE U. S. AS A MISSIONARY POWER

The United States is a late-comer to military
competition. It is one feature of this lateness that
for long periods she did not send or receive military missions. The question whether she was
more unwilling to apply for or to send out such
missions cannot be easily answered. Until well
into the twentieth century, the Monroe Doctrine
and Pan-Americanism[210] found little military
implementation in the form of military and naval
missions from the United States to the other countries of the Western hemisphere. Not until the

intervention and temporary occupation of some of
the Republics around the Caribbean Sea, notably
Haiti (1914-34), Santo Domingo (1916-24) and Nicaragua (1926-33), did "missionary" tasks confront
the United States military forces. Before American occupation was terminated, the Marines were
sent to provide these countries with reorganized
native forces. Legislative sanction for such missions was given by Congress under "An act to authorize officers of the naval service to accept offices with compensation and emoluments from
Governments of the Republics of South America"
(June 5, 1920). The act permitted the detailing of
naval officers to assist the South American governments that might desire and ask for help in
organizing and instructing their navies. How much
this was a piece of ad hoc legislation due to proposals from the south, or how far it represented
an outward urge of the Navy is not ascertainable.
The first requests considered under the act came
from Peru, Haiti, and, with more far-reaching
effects, from Brazil.[211]

In March 1922, the Rio de Janeiro Government
announced publicly that it would shortly invite an
American or British naval mission. The naval
mission would hold a position analogous to the
French military mission under General Gamelin.
Privately, the Brazilian President indicated his
wish that Captain Carl T. Vogelgesang, U.S.N.,
who had headed a United States war-time naval
mission to Brazil in 1918, should have this mission under his direction. The American ambassador, naval attaché and other naval officers detailed
to Rio supported this proposal and urged the State
Department to arrange for such a mission. The
State and Navy Departments were quite willing to
send such an officer "in special recognition of the
close relation between the two countries." To
make the candidate for the post still more suitable,
Captain Vogelgesang was promoted to rear-admiral.
Brazil expected the mission to start at the earliest
possible date. Vogelgesang was to serve on the
General Staff of the Brazilian fleet as technical
assistant, and he was also to superintend all the
duties entrusted to the mission. The mission was
to include nine officers, holding the rank of captain
or lieutenant-commander. They were to be assigned
technical tasks in naval yards, depots, and in the
aviation service. Vogelgesang travelled to Rio as a
member of Secretary Hughes' Special Mission of
Friendship, during the centenary celebration of
Brazil's independence in September 1922, and began the arrangements for the organization and
personnel of the mission.

The mission itself and the emphatic character
conferred on it by the pomp of the Friendship mission aroused great resentment in Argentina, traditionally Brazil's closest competitor in armaments.
Since the American officers had not been engaged

by private contracts, her Marine Minister thought it might even indicate an American-Brazilian alliance. What would its position be in time of war? Was not the very aim of Pan-Americanism defeated if one country was singled out for American favors? The Marine Minister detected in this action an expression of ill-will towards Argentina who had the less deserved this unkindness since she had of late placed most of her orders for Dreadnoughts and other naval armaments in the United States. The United States ambassador in Buenos Aires suggested that his Government make it a point to convince the Argentines that the naval mission had no political significance and was "not different from similar ones that England, France and Germany have often furnished to smaller countries in past years." In the light of a little bit of history, this might not prove too convincing! Still, Secretary Hughes tried his best. He pointed out that, under the Act of 1920, any South American government could obtain a similar mission if it wished to. He argued that the mission to Brazil was merely technical, not political. The terms of the contract provided that the officers were not to take any part in the operations of the Brazilian Navy in either foreign or civil war. Should hostilities between Brazil and another state appear imminent, the United States Government would at once notify the Brazilians of its intention to terminate the contract. The mission in no way indicated any change in the desire of the Government to maintain Pan-American solidarity and closer relations with each and every one of the American Republics.[212]

Whether this allayed Argentine fears altogether appears doubtful. On the whole, Argentina leaned on European Powers for military advice and arms supply, while Brazil continued to lean heavily on the United States. She followed the United States promptly in entering the European war and even in the active preparation for it. When diplomatic relations with Argentina came to a break early in 1944, Hull and Roosevelt agreed, reacting almost automatically, to provide Brazil with more arms in order to impress "the present military gang in control of Argentina." According to Hull, the President thought it essential "that we make a move at once to build up Brazil's strength. This should cover American arms and munitions and possibly more Army instructors, so as to give Brazil an effective fighting force near the Argentine border, such as two or three divisions of motorized regiments."[213]

As a reaction to European rearmament for war, Pan-Americanism took on stronger military aspects, somewhat contrary to its original character. The United States offered assistance to those republics willing to actively support her anti-Fascist policies. Alarmed, perhaps unduly, by State De-

partment reports that Nazi and Fascist agents were offering military training personnel to certain Latin American governments, the War and State Departments agreed in January 1938 to underbid the Axis and offer such governments American assistance in the form of missions "at low cost."[214] In May-June 1939, a United States military mission visited Brazil. It was a non-resident mission led by General Marshall, the future chief-of-staff. With the approach of America's entry into the war, Washington intensified military negotiations with Latin America. American attempts in 1940 to obtain naval and air bases in addition to those arranged for under Lend-Lease were not successful except in Brazil. Argentina and strong elements in Uruguay protested against plans for a naval base at Punta del Este on the Uruguayan coast.[215]

Under the war powers granted the President to assign military missions to the other American republics and the Philippines, a series of agreements were signed providing for the dispatch of military, naval and/or air missions. Congress authorized that twenty regular students per year from the Latin American republics be enrolled in the United States Military Academy, with no more than three at a time to come from any single country. In 1948, this welcome was extended to Canada. The training of up to five hundred Latin American nationals as aviation pilots and technicians on American airfields was offered by the United States Government in October 1941.[216]

More momentous were the labors of General MacArthur as Military Adviser to the Philippine Government since 1935. Following his retirement from the American Army, he attempted to build up a Philippine army as a concomitant of independence, scheduled for 1946. His work had not gone very far, as judged by the American regulars stationed in the islands, when he offered the services of himself and the Philippine forces in February 1941. Five months later the general returned to active status with the United States Army as commanding general of all Army forces in the Far East, including the 75,000-man Philippine Army.[217]

With the return of the peace, most of the American missions south of the Rio Grande were recalled. Where they stayed behind, as in Brazil, they furnished the Communists with the slogan that the armed forces in question were "ruled by Yankee generals."[218] While Brazil remained "the fair-haired hemispheric boy of U. S. military planning" and the United States showed no inclination to abandon such a strategically-located friend, it was still considered advisable not to estrange Peronist Argentina to any great extent. There was also a desire to preserve her as a market for United States armaments, provided she could pay for them. Congress had blocked further militarization of Pan-

Americanism somewhat by pigeon-holing the Truman Administration's Inter-American Military Cooperation Bill, which would have authorized the Administration to sell arms to the Latin American republics at bargain prices.[219]

The exigencies of coalition warfare called for the sending or exchange of numerous military missions during the Second World War. Their use was practically restricted to the United Nations side. The Axis preferred more "monolithic," unicephalous forms of liaison, instruction, or persuasion. Even as a "neutral," and as early as July 1940, Roosevelt sent a naval and military mission to Britain for "exploratory conversations." Out of this grew the secret Anglo-American staff discussions (begun in January 1941) that were to frame "a combined world strategy." Great Britain kept a mission of suasion in Ankara in the hope of bringing Turkey into the war on the Allied side. When the negotiations stalled in February 1944, she proposed that the mission's chief be withdrawn in a demonstrative manner and shipments of military supplies, including those from America, suspended. The United States agreed.[220] What Turkey really needed was greater certainty about Germany's ultimate defeat.

There was more inter-Allied jealousy and friction in the case of the missions which Russia and the Western Powers sent into Yugoslavia after resistance there had revived,[221] and between Britain and the United States in Saudi Arabia. In the wake of the development of vast co-national oil interests, an American military mission was sent to Saudi Arabia at the end of 1943. It had been invited by Ibn Saud in order to survey his military requirements. A small United States army training mission was to arrive in the spring of 1944. "That puts us potentially into the power politics of a warlike nation whose neighbor, Iraq, has some very tempting valleys," an American journal somewhat woefully commented on this occasion. It marked a close skirting of the imperialistic entanglements likely to be connected with military missions.[222]

The British would not at once surrender their tutelage over the Arab world; they demanded and obtained American approval for their suggestion that a joint American-British military mission, headed by a Britisher, be sent to the desert king. The State and War Departments agreed that "the primary responsibility in the Near East was British." Considering the preponderance of American economic interest in the country, however, it was specified that an American should head any economic or financial mission that might go there in the future. Despite some hedging, the British agreed.[223]

The first American military mission to China preceded the entry of the United States into the war.[224] It combined the traditional function of the instructor with the new one implied in Lend-Lease, for which form of assistance China was declared eligible on May 6, 1941. Under this American arrangement for the giving of materiel in return for a lease of time in which the United States was to prepare itself for war, the old-style combination of military instruction and the sale of arms came to an end. The German mission in Chiang's China was nearly the last of its kind. As Roosevelt's public announcement of the American mission put it:

> [Its function] will be to study, in collaboration with the Chinese and other authorities, the military situation in China, the need of the Chinese Government for materiel and materials; to formulate recommendations regarding types and quantities of items needed; to assist in the procurement in this country and in delivery in China of such materiel and materials; to instruct in the use and maintenance of articles thus provided, and to give advice and suggestions of appropriate character toward making lend-lease assistance to China as effective as possible in the interest of the United States, of China, and of the world effort in resistance to movements of conquest by force. The sending of this mission is in keeping with and is on parallel lines to the sending of a similar mission to the Soviet Union. The purpose of the two missions are identical.

Its head was General John Magruder, who had served twice as military attaché in China. He was to be accompanied by an adequate staff of thoroughly qualified officers.[225]

The mission arrived in China in November 1941, having been preceded by an American Air Mission, sent in May. The air mission had returned with such recommendations as a training program for Chinese pilots and mechanics. A Chinese-American Composite Wing of the Chinese Air Force was formed out of these trainees plus American aviators. It never found adequate combat usage, least so against the Communists, who were themselves without an air force for the longest time.

Magruder and Lieutenant-General Joseph C. Stilwell after him, as heads of America's military missions in China, found their tasks beyond their country's strength. They found their own powers of endurance insufficient to meet the needs posed by Chinese inertia, corruption, and inefficiency, and by Chiang's stubbornness. All the urgency of war, foreign and civil, proved insufficient to overcome the obstacles that obstructed fundamental military reorganization and the fullest use by the Chinese Nationalists of the foreign aid given them.

Under American direction, training centers for

Chinese troops were set up in India. They turned out some of the best fighting units used in Northern Burma and elsewhere in 1943. The opposition of Chiang and his clique to similar training centers within China was never fully overcome. They were more ready to agree to American-run officers' training camps in China, but American-trained rank-and-file seemed too dangerous an innovation. They would be spoiled for such commanders as the Whampoa clique preferred. With the exception of Stilwell's command in India, no foreigner exercised command functions, even during the darkest hours of the war. The Nationalists were nationalist enough to want to avoid the "loss of face" involved. Such transfer of authority was finally offered the Americans only a few months before the fall of Chiang.

American disappointment with the Gimmo, who often would not listen to the soundest and most obvious military advice,[226] was so great that for a time his cause was nearly disregarded. It seemed that help for China, which America was still ready to provide, must go to some more worthy recipient. To make post-war military help available to China, Congress authorized, in 1946, the establishment of American training centers in China, military as well as naval, to be directed by the Joint United States Military Advisory Group in China (JUSMAG). This group reached a maximum strength of 1,000 officers and men. Under it there was organized a Military Advisory Group in China (MAGIC) of 750 men and smaller naval and air groups. Eventually MAGIC attained a strength of 1,200 to 1,300 officers and men,[227] the largest group of its kind to that date.

Beginning in 1946, General George C. Marshall endeavored to arrange a shot-gun wedding between the Nationalists and the opposition, including the Communists. The shot-gun, made in America, proved unimpressive. The basic conflict inside China could not be bridged. The United States wanted unity; Russia did not. She considered that American intentions were aimed towards a protectorate over China, to be exercised through the Kuomintang.[228] The original idea of sending a number of American instructors and weapons to Kalgan, the Communists' capital at the time, in order to train Communist officers prior to the expected unification of the forces of both parties, was discarded. MAGIC's activity was limited to helping the Nationalists. Its work was to be mainly restricted to organizational reforms, particularly in the Ministry of National Defense, and to the schooling of Chinese military instructors who were later to apply American methods throughout the forces. A training period of five years, not long by Chinese standards, was expected to bear fruit at last. Advice given was not to extend directly to field operations in the re-opened civil

war. It would be given to Chiang "on a personal and confidential basis," not involving American responsibility. Its work was "strictly divorced" from the conduct of hostilities, Secretary Marshall told Congress in June 1947.[229] For example, American advisers working on an air field would give the Chinese assistance in the organizing of personnel, records, repair work, but would abstain from briefing crews for flights against the Communists. The War Department promised that "every effort will be made to minimize publicity to the effect that this action constitutes direct U. S. participation in the Civil War."[230] A certain amount of help was doubtless derived from this all too neutral advice, but definitely less than might have been given. And Communist propaganda could easily disregard this fine distinction. It attacked American policy in China on such points as the presence of MAGIC and of United States naval forces, "sale" of $800 million worth of surplus property to the Chinese Government, and the transfer to it of several hundred small craft to be manned by American-trained personnel.[231]

For a general's mission, the one undertaken by George C. Marshall in China, lasting for thirteen months, was singularly devoid of military character. It also achieved nothing for peace, which it was believed possible to obtain through "the assumption of leadership by the liberals in the Government and in the minority parties" (not including the Communists) under Chiang's guidance. The Nationalists could derive no strength from such American hopes for their conduct of the Civil War. The withdrawal of the American occupation forces of some 12,000 men, which had already come under deliberate attack by the Communists, began in January 1947. This withdrew another prop, if only a moral one, from the Nationalists' defenses. The Americans remaining in China found it hard, even impossible to get along with the Gimmo. He would not heed their advice, and he would not discard his old comrades of Whampoa in spite of their obvious corruption and incompetence. After prolonged bickering with Chiang, Major General John P. Lucas was replaced as head of MAGIC by Major General David G. Barr. Like his predecessor, Barr was authorized to give advice of a strategic nature to Chiang, but not to assume, for himself or his country, "responsibility for the strategic direction of the war." For, as Marshall advised him, "implications of our accepting that responsibility is in logic inseparable from the authority to make it effective. Whatever the Generalissimo may feel moved to say with respect to his willingness to delegate necessary powers to Americans, I know from my own experience that advice is always listened to very politely but not infrequently ignored when deemed impalatable." For such reasons the United States refrained from assuming responsibility for the strategic direction of the war against the Communists. In the Eightieth Congress, the House voted to authorize military aid on the Greek model, but the Senate successfully opposed this. While recognizing that military aid was necessary in order to make economic aid effective, Senator Vandenberg, for example, held that "as a matter of elementary prudence this process must be completely clear of any implication that we are underwriting the military campaign of the Nationalist Government."[232]

Whatever others had come to think of Chiang, Lieutenant General Wedemeyer, sent as an observer to China in the summer of 1947, still saw in him the only anti-Communist leader in China worthy of further support with American funds and arms. But if he was to hold out against the Red flood, he must have "military support" from the United States over at least a five-year period. That is to say, military supplies, including weapons and ammunition and competent officers to advise as to their best use, would have to be sent. Military advice and supervision would have to be extended to the field forces. In short, the United States would have to go about as far in China as she had in Greece. This, however, was not done.[233]

During 1948, the Nationalists' military position deteriorated rapidly. The deterioration was ascribed by Chiang to Soviet help rendered the Communists, though little of this could actually be observed by the Americans.[234] He now suggested that American officers should assume actual command of Chinese Army units, "under the pretence of acting as advisers." It was a sign of the hopelessness of the situation when the uniformed personnel of MAGIC were ordered to leave Nanking and China by mid-November 1948.[235] By that time, all senior American military personnel had come to the conclusion that there was no longer any step the United States or China could take to retrieve the military situation.[236] The United States Mission had not fulfilled its task. Was this due to lack of support? The head of the Advisory Group reported to Congress that the loss of battles by the Nationalists was not due to lack of American arms. And, he added, with the loss of battles went another loss--the great bulk of American arms found its way to the Communists. With their thrifty nature, "the Chinese seemed inherently unable to destroy anything of value." They preferred rather to equip the enemy. He also pointed to an ingrained Nationalist resentment "against killing Chinese Communists who had no air support."[237]

The socio-economics of Chinese decay proved as impervious to the organizing endeavors of American military missions as they had to the efforts of earlier missions. This experience made proposals of late 1949 and early 1950 to send still another mission to Chiang, now retired to Formosa, appear rather hopeless, more so to the State Department than to the Joint Chiefs of Staff.[238] Acheson feared that "this could not be successful and that only the interposition of armed forces of the United States could save the island." Anything else would do "further damage to our prestige and to our whole position in the Far East." However, the soldiers' view prevailed. They first kept an enlarged group of attachés in Taiwan, in lieu of a mission, in order to gather impressions of Chiang's force. They were then authorized to send a new complete assistance and advisory group of some three hundred men to the island. They started their work about May 1, 1951. Their orders were "to supervise the distribution of supplies," which Formosa was to receive on equal priority with European countries, and to supervise training.[239]

Developments in Korea and the firming of the American system of bases in the Pacific provided Chiang with a new lease on life. Russian assistance to North Korea, including the services of Russian-trained Korean soldiers, some of whom had fought at Stalingrad, had preceded American military assistance to the South Koreans. Early warnings, such as General Wedemeyer's, that the situation in Korea was "potentially dangerous to United States strategic interests," had not made a deep impression on Washington. However, a Military Advisory Group of some five hundred officers and men, headed by General Roberts, began to work with the South Korean forces in 1947. They had to start almost from zero. There were only a small number of native officers available, who had undergone apprenticeship in the Chinese and Japanese armies. The group worked under severe handicaps, which were not at all lessened by the usual cautious arrangement that its members were to hold no command in the South Korean Army. They formed no part of MacArthur's Far Eastern proconsulship, but "functioned under the Ambassador, under the State Department," as the General put it.[240] Constantly harried by raids from the Russian-supported North, the Southern forces did not acquire the military stamina and combat readiness which so often has been developed along the frontiers of civilization by the forces defending civilization. They were overrun when the Russians unleashed North Korean aggression.[241]

During the Korean war, various arrangements for the training of South Korean troops and their amalgamation with American forces were made by the American commanders of the United Nations forces. General MacArthur, hard-pressed for ready-at-hand troops once the Chinese Reds had openly intervened in Korea, proposed to Washington the use of the almost written-off Chinese Nationalists on the Asiatic mainland. However, Washington either valued these forces less than the theater commander, or thought it more important that they should be used to "neutralize" Formosa to keep it from falling into the hands of the Communists. Even for that purpose the services of an American military mission were needed.

In May 1951, the number of American missions abroad reached eighteen, of which twelve were in Latin America. In deference to nationalist sentiment on the part of the recipients, they had come to be called military advisory groups rather than missions. In any case, they were, according to their superiors at home, all moving "steadily forward in the accomplishment of their mission—to provide to the armies of the nations concerned concrete assistance and advice in military organization, training, and the use of modern military equipment."[242] At the same time, personnel from the eighteen nations included in the Mutual Defence Assistance Program were given training at schools in the United States and at United States Army installations abroad. The number of men receiving such training reached nearly two thousand during the twenty-one months to the end of 1951.[243] These are the channels of military progress today, including, as it does once more, the financing of this progress by subsidies from the foremost capitalistic Power. Half the world has come to rely on United States income and "know-how", while the other half is made to pay tribute, in many guises and long before war, to the center of the world's other half.

MILITARY MISSIONS IN THE COLD WAR

The end of the "hot war" left only the United States and the Soviet Union strong enough in either power, prestige, materiel, or transferable money to give military assistance and advice to other countries. Britain, though greatly exhausted, did maintain a few such missions: one in Greece, in addition to a military force, where it was to be relieved by the United States; another in Transjordania, where it dated back to mandate days and continued until full independence was achieved in 1946. That country's Arab Legion is still advised and commanded by forty-eight "seconded" British officers and equipped by British arms and supplies, including an eight-million-dollar annual subsidy.[244] The Legion's chief of staff is Brigadier General John Bagot Glubb Pasha, in person and office a representative of the Lawrence tradition in Britain's Arab policy. Since 1939 Glubb has been in the immediate service of King Abdullah, thus being no longer visibly or formally connected with the British Army. The imperial conveniences of this arrangement were nearly outweighed by its inconveniences. The support given to the Legion and its employment before and after Britain's retreat from the Palestine mandate exposed British policy to violent attacks from the Zionists and

their friends. This was particularly the case when the Legion succeeded in preventing the Israeli from gaining all of Jerusalem in 1948-49. Its success was the only one scored by the Arab side in the conflict, and it was promptly, probably properly, ascribed to British assistance and leadership. The British personnel involved were divided into a training and organizing group, active only inside Transjordania,[245] and a number of individuals who had resigned from the British Army altogether and were serving with the Legion as individuals, inside and outside Transjordania.[246]

Ethiopia was at first, at the time of the joint victory over the Italians, eager to grant Britain a near-monopoly in providing outside assistance, including the furnishing of military advisers.[247] By the end of 1942, this welcome had considerably diminished, partly due to British unwillingness to support to the hilt the shadowy Ethiopian claims to all ex-Italian territory. A new treaty concluded at that time still provided for a military mission from Britain, "which shall be a unit of the military forces of H. M. the King under the command of the Head of Mission." The latter was to be responsible to the war minister of Ethiopia "for the organization, training and administration" of her army. The agreement could be terminated by either side within the comparatively short time of three months, following receipt of notice of cancellation. The British mission spared neither sweat nor blood in their labors. Some of the members were killed when they helped in the suppression of an insurrection dangerous to Haile Selassie's regime. Nevertheless they found working conditions so trying and unrewarding that by the end of 1944 nearly all British advisers, military and civilian, had left. Some of their places were taken over by military missions or instructors from such small Powers as Belgium and Sweden.

The United States did not shoulder the burdens involved in giving post-war military aid in its various forms either gladly or willingly. To the isolationists, this seemed the final reversal of the traditional no-foreign-entanglement policy,[248] and to the friends of Soviet Russia such measures amounted to putting the United States "on the road to ruthless imperialism."[249] American institutions of military education and training, such as West Point and the Army Command and General Staff College at Leavenworth, attracted a considerable number of foreign officers, as the Ecole Supérieure de Guerre and the Berlin Kriegsakademie had done in their day. At the beginning of 1949, Leavenworth included among its students, in addition to 365 U. S. Army officers, no less than fifty-two officers from twenty-six foreign lands.[250]

The constitutional authority for the granting of foreign military aid was largely found in the extensive war powers of the President, which reached over into the period of the "cold war." They were deemed sufficient to send and maintain a number of military missions to countries dangerously close to the fringe of Soviet expansion, such as China, Greece, Turkey, Iran, Korea, and still later to the countries with membership in the North Atlantic Pact. Case by case, Congress granted the funds necessary to furnish the military supplies that went along with or followed the missions. In 1947, with the demise of the Presidential war powers in sight, the State, War, and Navy Departments went before Congress with the proposal that it grant permanent discretionary authority to the President to send such missions as are "consonant with American interests"—as interpreted by the Executive. The President already had powers to assign military missions to the American Republics and the Philippines. General Marshall, then Secretary of State, testified in favor of the bill. He told Congress that if the United States did not send such missions, then "some other country would." Present missions, such as those in Iran and China, would have to be recalled, once the state of war had ended. He considered their recall detrimental to the interests of the United States in view of the increasing "strategic importance of the Near, Middle and Far East," where countries were just then emerging "from a state of semi-subjection and needed educational and technical assistance." He continued:

> Article 78 of the Charter of the U.N. states that relations between members "shall be based on respect for the principle of sovereign equality." This objective could hardly be achieved in the case of any nation in which there is serious danger of internal disorder.
>
> Lack of authority to send military and naval missions to assist friendly foreign governments, when requested by them to do so, deprives the President of the use of one of the tools which should be at his disposal, we think, if this Government is to implement its avowed policies of interest in the conditions of peace throughout the world and of full participation in world affairs commensurate with its new responsibility as a world power.[251]

But Congress remained reluctant to grant the Executive such extensive powers to involve the United States by use of military missions.[252]

The United States relieved war-weary Britain in Turkey and Greece. Britain, the traditional opponent of Russia's "historic mission," was tired, and Russia's mission was now being resumed.[253] After Britain had kept the "iron curtain" from encompassing Greece, the Communist guerillas had taken to the mountains, supported from bases in the adjoining Communist countries. The State Department declared flatly that "foreign complicity in the guerrilla movement" went well beyond the giving of military advice and other aid to the Greek rebel forces.[254] That is to say, Russia supplied arms. As the head of the Joint U.S. Military Advisory and Planning group in Greece, Lieutenant-General James Alward Van Fleet saw the situation as "a first-class war of international communism." "It is," he said, "a war of annihilation with no respect for the rules."[255] In Communist eyes, the battle situation was as follows: with Greek bourgeois leaders vying for greater "subjugation of the country to foreigners," Greek life was now determined by American-British imperialist intervention, which nourishes monarcho-fascism, keeps the country in economic backwardness, and throws the people into unprecedented misery, while at the same time turning Greece into a springboard for moves against rehabilitation and the progress of peace in the Balkans and the whole of Europe.[256]

In May 1947, Congress authorized funds to implement the Truman Doctrine. A considerable strengthening of the American mission to Greece in point of members and authority had taken place by early 1948. General Van Fleet was appointed in February. While heretofore American advice had been limited to matters of supply and logistics, with organization and training of the Greek forces in the hands of a British mission, American officers were now to sit "at the elbow" of Greek unit commanders in the attempt to finally wipe out the guerillas. The Greeks did not always consider their methods to be the most suitable ones for a war against guerillas. The usual mandate for such American missions, to remain aloof from advising on or conducting operations, could not be observed in Greece. Communist aggression had gone too far to permit semi-neutrality. Van Fleet's predecessor and his British counterpart had merely participated as observers in the deliberations of the Greek National Defence Council. The new man was made a member of it in order to give him more power, including power over the appointment and removal of high commanders with which Greek party politics was apt to play havoc.[257]

The military mission formed part of the American Mission for Aid to Greece, headed by Dwight P. Griswold, which was to help in the rehabilitation of Greek economy. The economic task was equally urgent but had to take second place. The armed forces program absorbed the larger half of the $300 million assigned for the year ending June 30, 1948. However it was all to one purpose, to save Greece from "totalitarian domination from the North." As Griswold told Congress when he was pleading for continued help in May 1948: "We went there to keep Greece from falling under the domination of a foreign country, and we have accomplished that goal."[258]

As soon as American aid got under way, guerilla

activity was stepped up, in accordance with previous threats,[259] with help from Communist-controlled countries.[260] One season of American military aid proved insufficient. It was thought necessary to continue the aid for another two years. To make it more effective, more intervention in Greek army affairs would also be necessary. Such measures, taken at the "Temple of Knowledge" as the American HQs were called, were not always particularly to the liking of Greek officers.[261] The Greeks were as inclined to blame the American mission for the severe setbacks in the autumn of 1948 as the Americans were to criticize the Greeks. In October 1948, Secretary Marshall was obliged to go from Paris to Greece to talk with the United States mission and the Greek politicos, uniformed and ununiformed. Some Greeks had begun to question American aid and advice. Inside the mission, which now counted nearly seven hundred men, there was also some difference of opinion as to whether military matters and security should still rank above economic and political questions. Like any schoolmaster, the American soldiers found that their pupils sat at their feet only with great reluctance. When Van Fleet arranged schools for the training of junior officers, of whom there was a shortage, the students at first did not show up. Their divisional commanders thought that these men needed no further training.[262]

The next campaign, in the summer of 1949, was under a new commander-in-chief, Field Marshal Papagos. Papagos was the hero of the Greek successes over Italy in 1940, and Van Fleet had helped to get him into the saddle. This campaign was infinitely more successful. Tito's departure from the Cominform helped more than a little. In the autumn, guerilla hostilities came practically to an end. Moscow must have given the signal to halt. Britain proceeded to withdraw the 3,000 men she had on Greek soil.[263] The American advisers had to consider how far the Greek forces, which had reached a strength of 260,000 men, could safely be reduced. But the day for their own withdrawal seemed distant. Still, at least a temporary barrier against Communist arms in the hands of irregulars had been put up by the time Van Fleet departed from Greece in July 1950. He left behind him a re-trained Greek Army, which he considered "the finest in this part of the world" at that time.[264]

American aid to Turkey also came under the Truman Doctrine and the same strategy of containment. The difference was that help to Turkey could be more largely confined to the military field.[265] A Turkish-American army group (TUSAG) was to supervise and instruct in the use of materiel and train the Turkish Army in the latest methods of warfare. TUSAG was part of the so-called Joint American Military Mission for Aid to Turkey (JAMMAT), headed by Major General Horace McBride.[266] A reorganization of the general staff, command, and supply system was instituted during the first two years of this aid. Instruction centers were opened for ground forces, as well as two for the Navy along the shores of the Sea of Marmora. In courses lasting from three to six months, four hundred officers and 3,000 men were to be trained at one time. They were to return to their units and instruct in turn. By the end of 1949, 10,000 Turks of various rank had completed such courses of instruction under American direction.

The Turkish Army, which had previously tried to make up by numbers for its shortcomings in equipment, could be reduced by twenty per cent from its strength of half a million without any apparent loss of combat effectiveness by the end of 1949. The British continued in their instruction activities, kept on a more moderate scale than the American work. Both Americans and British encountered the troubles and vexations that were inevitable among a force in which eighty per cent were peasant soldiers: slowness of progress, carelessness in the handling of modern equipment by the trainees, language difficulties as obstacles in the way of understanding, doubts of the trainee whether he was always receiving the best and latest equipment.[267] Still, General McBride could say by the autumn of 1949: "They have improved."[268]

In the public language of the State Department, Turkey was "holding the fort" against Soviet Russia in the Eastern Mediterranean area. Therefore she deserved continued American help. Pleading for funds for Turkey for the year 1948-49 and beyond, if necessary, Secretary of State Marshall told Congress in March 1948 that that country, during the last year, had experienced "intensification of Communist pressure." In her twofold strategic position, in the Eastern Mediterranean Area and in the resistance against the spread of Communism, Turkey must remain strong. She could not do this "on her own meager resources," but only with continued American help.[269]

Iran was and is a much weaker obstacle in the way of Russian-Communist expansion, so weak that Russia, to the surprise of some, evacuated it after the war, if only as a position which she, rather than any other Power, could always easily re-occupy. Iran's own weaknesses kept American assistance to her relatively small. It amounted to only some $10 million-worth of military equipment, given under the Foreign Arms Aid bill, as compared with the several hundred million dollars given to Greece and Turkey. To a Russian eye, American interest and activity might appear to be a resumption of the older British policy of keeping Persia intact, whereas a naïve American might be inclined to see it as the resumption of the altogether disinterested activity of Mr. Morgan Shuster in that country in 1911-12.[270]

The close of the Second World War found Russia in control in the North of Iran. The Russians supervised the forces of the Azerbaidjan provisional government, set up under Russian auspices, and supplied them with Soviet uniforms and equipment. They offered military advisers to the Central Government as well. But the latter definitely preferred personnel from far-away America for such purposes. Beginning in 1943, the United States maintained two small-sized missions in Iran. One, under Colonel Norman Schwarzkopf, former head of the New Jersey State Police, was to advise and reorganize the national gendarmerie. The other, a twenty-six-man military mission, was to advise the Iranian army general staff. Their presence never went quite unchallenged by the partisans of Russia inside Iran or by those who were merely afraid that the Americans would bring down Russian wrath on the still very weak Iran. When the usual xenophobia was added to these factors, the result was a demand—from the Persian left rather than from the right—for the removal of all foreigners from the country.[271]

The demand was renewed after a new contract, revising that of 1943, had been concluded in June 1947. The new contract stipulated "cooperation with the Iranian War Ministry and Iranian Army for the purpose of increasing the fighting capacity of the Iranians."[272] For the duration of the American missions, no officers of other Powers were to be employed in the Iranian forces, except with American consent. The two missions at that time consisted of some forty Americans. Seven officers and six non-coms advised in the reorganization of the gendarmerie and also held actual command in it. Eighteen officers and eight non-coms, under Major General Robert W. Grow, advised the Iranian War Department and General Staff on matters of organization, administration and training methods. Grow's group was specifically enjoined to refrain from even helping to formulate strategic and tactical plans for operations against foreign enemies or from taking on command or staff responsibilities. In connection with these missions, a credit was opened to Iran for the buying of American surplus war materiel.

While the agreement was awaiting ratification by the Teheran Parliament, a movement got under way to throw it out and thereby "clear up present misunderstandings between Russia and Iran."[273] At the same time, the Soviet Government began public and diplomatic protests in Washington and Teheran against American activities in the Near East, extending from Italy, where

American warships were visiting in a somewhat demonstrative way, and from Tripoli-Cyrenaica, where the American Air Transport Command used airfields, to Iran. A Russian note of January 28, 1948, accused the United States of militarizing Iran by training the Iranian Army, equipping it with American arms identical with the type used in the rearming of Turkey, building up a war industry capable of turning out and repairing American-type weapons, building airfields much beyond the need of Iran herself, arranging for underground fuel storage facilities, and helping to fortify the frontier against the Soviets. Iran, they said, was being turned into an American "strategic base" that "can create danger" to Russia's southern frontier. These allegations were promptly denied or corrected by the State Department, with a reminder to Russia that the agreements with Iran had been publicly reached and communicated to the United Nations.[274]

The Iranians likewise rejected the Russian protests. In their answer, they included the charge that Russia was permitting Iranian refugees to form military units on her soil. While the contract was still before the Iranian Parliament, which ratified it on February 17, 1948, the exchange of notes between Moscow and Teheran continued. Russia declared herself unconvinced by Iran's denials that American personnel were in dominant positions, asserting that "the American military advisers' role is one of leadership of the Iranian Army." Iran's charges that Russia was forming Iranian refugee units were, on the other hand, nothing but "provocative fabrications," hardly compatible with the good-neighborly relations envisaged by the Iranian-Russian treaty of friendship of 1921. This very same treaty, the Iranians countered, excluded any Russian protests against Iran's making "decisions that would benefit the country or improve" its internal affairs. One Russian diplomat asked: "Why should there be American advisers and not Russian? We are your neighbors and the Americans are far away."[275] Could Russians seriously mean to overlook the basic tendency of the smaller Powers to obtain so-called advice from the far-away great Power rather than from the dangerously near-by one?

A new American ambassador, John Cooper Wiley, arrived in Teheran in April 1948 to further support the military aid program under which Iran was to receive $60 millions-worth of "non-aggressive weapons." These included tanks, guns, and fighter planes from American surplus stock and were to be paid for over a fifteen-year period with an interest of two-and-three-eighths per cent. As it was explained to Congress by the head of the State Department's division of Greek-Turkish-Iranian affairs, this aid was designed to "maintain the international security of Iran."[276]

The first shipments were delivered in March 1948 via Persian Gulf ports, despite continued Russian criticism. As the result of a six-week visit of the Shah to the United States in November-December 1949, Iran was again assured of American aid, through the Truman Point Four program and through military assistance. In an agreement signed on May 23, 1950, details of American arms shipments to Iran, probably to the amount of $10,000,000, were stipulated.[277] In March-April 1950, following an inspection tour of the Near and Middle East, J. Lawton Collins, United States Army Chief of Staff, stated publicly how much better off he had found Greece, Turkey and Iran, militarily and otherwise. He attributed this to self-help as well as to American professional guidance and technical equipment. Their strategic position, it was conceded, remained precarious— none of these nations could defend itself against serious attack by "a major power."[278] However, tangible proof of the military valor of at least one of these American-trained armies was furnished by the Turkish brigade fighting as part of the United Nations forces in Korea.

The military mission has become an instrument of American anti-Communist policies, an agency to supply and, wherever necessary, to direct, in the immediate military way, American aid against the spread of Communism. In the first instance, this aid had to be of a military nature, because other help could not become effective unless militarily protected. "We must have military support and protection of our economic investments— such as under the Marshall and Truman plans— wherever forces threaten what we hold dear," Lieutenant General Wedemeyer, the Army's Director of Plans and Operations at the time, told Congress in March 1948. Further aid to China was then being considered. "I don't think that dollars alone will stop Communism," Wedemeyer continued. "Help must include military aid, the providing of military supplies, and competent officers to advise as to their use."[279] Such help came too late or was not made effective in China, while it arrived in the nick of time to save Greece.

Still later missions, now usually called "advisory groups," were sent to the North Atlantic Pact nations. They provided a minimum of American personnel to assist in the use of American materials. Late in 1949, the United States Government prepared to send abroad some two hundred military aid experts to the eight Pact nations, ahead of the actual shipments of arms and other supplies which got under way in March 1950. More permanent missions, headed by generals and admirals, were attached to the United States embassies in Belgium, the Netherlands, Norway, Denmark, Italy, France (including Indochina), and Britain.[280] They were to instruct the armed

forces of these countries in the use of the American arms they were to receive. Some of the governments to which they were to be accredited, notably Denmark and Norway, begged that these missions be kept small in size in order to avoid criticism from the local Communist parties and the Soviet Union.[281]

Military missions abroad are apt to run into difficulties with local national sentiment and interests, which may be inclined to underestimate the urgency of the dangers to be met or to overestimate the difficulties in the way of necessary reforms. But these obstacles are not insuperable, provided tact and efficiency operate on one side and receptive military minds on the other. If experience gained in German military history is acceptable as an example, the unification of the armies of the federal states after 1866 offers a good one. At that time, military conventions were concluded between Prussia on the one hand and the South and Central German States on the other. Prussian generals were sent to the several capitals to work out the modalities of unification, as far as it was to go. There remained enough reservations to reconcile the States-Righters. The principles of organization and the personalities of the generals entrusted with the work proved so felicitous that even the bitterest opponents of the unification, the French, were forced to admit its success.[282] The present role of the United States is, in this matter, not so radically different from Prussia's in the 1860's.

SOVIET RUSSIANS ON MILITARY MISSIONS

In many of the Communist putsches attempted outside Russia since 1918, the directing or supporting hand of Moscow agents has been detected or suspected. More closely inspected, this hand, as a rule, turned out to be that of civilians rather than of military men. As time went by, the Kremlin maintained a stricter separation of Russian diplomatic and military agents, whose actions and responsibilities were hard to disavow, and Comintern agents, for whom the Kremlin could not be made directly responsible. In the selection of Comintern agents, the emphasis was on non-Russians who might have undergone training for the military side of the worldwide class warfare in such Moscow institutions as the Eastern Toilers' Institute. There Chu Teh, commander-in-chief of the Chinese Red Army since 1931, studied in the 1920's, as did General Kim Li Sung, for some fifteen years a leader of Korean guerillas and since 1945 Secretary of the Communist Party in Northern Korea.[283] Before the Second World War, Russian military men en mission were only observed in those revolutionary situations where the military side was assuming supreme importance—in China in the 1920's, in Spain from 1936, or in the earliest of the satellite states, Mongolia, from the mid-1920's.

The Russian military mission in its traditional aspects and usages, including imperialist control, came into its own as the Second World War neared its end. Russian intentions of controlling the military forces of the reconstituted eastern states, Poland, Czechoslovakia, Yugoslavia and others, were clearly indicated by the early actions of the liberator-occupant of these countries.[284] The Czechs, whose gratefulness for the liberation from Hitler knew no bounds, not even the bounds of caution, agreed as early as May 1945 that Russia was to train and equip their army. A Russian military mission would proceed to Prague to direct training, while Czech officers would study in the various Soviet military schools.[285] Thus Czechoslovakia made herself a satellite state even before she was Communist-governed. Once the Communists gained complete control in Prague, they tried to eliminate the remnants of military recalcitrance. Perhaps a thousand Russian "advisers" were sent to the Czech Army, headed, it was rumored, by Marshal Ivan S. Konev or else by the Soviet military attaché in Prague, Colonel General N. I. Gusev. The Gleichschaltung comprised not only Soviet tactics and weapons but also, to make it symbolically complete, the uniform.[286] Moscow was military governor in Czechoslovakia.

Arrangements of a similar kind were made with all the Russian satrapies from the Adriatic to the Yellow Sea.[287] In Outer Mongolia, Soviet advisers were attached to every unit of the army and Soviet officers participated in the operations of the army of that state, whose political independence and territorial integrity Russia had once promised to respect.[288] In Korea, the Russians believed their side so superior that they unleashed the attack on the American-trained Koreans in the summer of 1950. The build-up of the North Korean People's Army had taken place under the guidance of a Russian military mission of some 3,500 to 4,500 persons, as was estimated in Washington, working down to company level. The mission was headed by the Russian ambassador to Pyongyang, General Terenti Shtykov. "Our people's armed forces have learned the art of war from the Soviet Union," boasted the North Korean radio shortly before the attack on South Korea.[289] Russian officers continued to act as advisers to the North Koreans following the opening of hostilities, and they manned certain advanced types of aircraft. They were, however, careful not to be caught, alive or dead, by the United Nations forces and thus to be offered up as testimony of Russian participation in the North Korean aggression.[290] How much immediate Russian guidance there was with the Chinese forces that intervened in Korea, United Nations intelligence has not been able to ascertain. Inside China proper, "Soviet military influence is primarily exercised through Marshal Kyril A. Meretskov, adviser to the Peiping Government. The Soviet Ambassador is also a military man, Major General Nikolai V. Roshchin."[291]

In the West, Albania's dependence on Russia was about as complete as that of Montenegro had been in Tsarist days. In some respects it was also, as Montenegro had been at various times, a sub-satrapy of Yugoslavia. In this backward and poverty-stricken country, tied to Yugoslavia by long-term trade agreements and a customs-union, instructors from Belgrade advised an army largely provided with Yugoslav equipment. In this revival of military Pan-Slavism, there was more than one General Kaulbars stalking the Balkan countries again. In Bulgaria, General Atanasov, a native son subsequently naturalized in Russia, was made Deputy Minister of War in the spring of 1951. He supervised the introduction of Russian materiel and organization, while a Russian inspector-general directed the training of the Hungarian army from Budapest, where a Soviet Danube flotilla was based. In Bucharest, the Russian military attaché with the high rank of general, assisted by a number of other high-ranking officers, supervised the Gleichschaltung of the Rumanian forces on land and on the Black Sea.[292]

Even before the West had discovered the essential and painful parallels between the 1880's and the later 1940's, one satellite revolted against the Russian satrapy system, Tito's Yugoslavia. The visible break between Belgrade and Moscow began with the abrupt withdrawal of all Russian military personnel from Yugoslavia in March 1948 on the ground that they had found themselves in "hostile surroundings." It had its deeper roots in the Yugoslav disappointment over ineffectual Russian support in the Trieste question which, as the Russians told them, was at such an impasse that it could only be solved by war with the Anglo-Americans. The story of this mission has to be pieced together out of accusations and counter-accusations. The mission had come to Yugoslavia, the Kremlin reminded Tito, at his own request, something which was probably only formally true. It had come to his assistance at a time of grave crisis in the National Liberation movement. It had liberated Yugoslavia and "created conditions for the Communist Party to come to power." Instead of gratefulness, the Russians soon found themselves confronted by hostility on the part of Yugoslav officials, who proposed that the number of advisers be reduced by sixty per cent, who hinted that the advisers' pay was too high,[293] and who hinted that the Yugoslavs were not in need of the benefits of Soviet Army experiences. Yugoslav military leaders became insulting. The security police, just as in bourgeois states, controlled and supervised the visiting Soviet representatives.

When accused of breaching the law of Communist hospitality, Tito, "terribly surprised by the tone and content" of the letters from Moscow, replied that the Yugoslav attitude toward the visitors had been more than good; it had been brotherly. However, the Government had found it necessary to stop lesser authorities from giving important information directly to the inquisitive guests. They ought to apply to the higher echelons for such enlightenment. While some Yugoslavs might possibly have made untimely remarks to or about the Soviet military experts, some of the latter had also not always behaved as they should. Obviously the hosts expected better manners from experts whose wages, as was rather plaintively stated, "were three times higher than the wages of our cabinet ministers." This was "one of the reasons which led us to request the reduction in number of the Soviet military experts." Besides, "we feel it inconvenient for the Soviet Intelligence Service to recruit our citizens in our country for their service." In so doing they cast doubts upon the credit and reputation of the Party leaders in Yugoslavia. "Even though we love the USSR, we cannot love our own country less": this became the basic formula of what was promptly called Titoism.[294]

What seemed at the outset of the quarrel to be soldiers' nationalism, a very hardy perennial in Yugoslavia, led, in the language of the Cominform, to a broad "retreat from Marxism-Leninism." In June 1948, the Cominform expelled Yugoslavia.

While it is impossible to evaluate the backing that Tito received from the Yugoslav masses, the officer element—by a curious sort of "movement for higher wages" not contemplated by Marxism—backed him completely. This was true of those officers who were studying at the time in the three highest Soviet military academies, the Lenin Military and Political Academy, the Frunze Military Academy and the Voroshilov Cavalry Academy. Undaunted, they sent messages home praising "the manly and honorable answer given by our glorious Central Committee" to the Cominform charges.[295] Such at least were the messages as published in Belgrade, though one does not see how they could have passed over the Russian wires.

Russia's attempts to undermine Tito's hold resulted in no less than six hundred and fifty-two "anti-Yugoslav frontier incidents perpetrated by troops of the Cominform States" between June 28, 1948 and December 1, 1949. "Increased foreign intervention brings about increased resistance on the part of the people," Tito's Foreign Minister Edward Kardelj warned from the platform of the UN General Assembly in September 1948, "for it is a well-known fact that nations do not approve of armed foreign missionaries in their country." He applied his comments to Greece, he said, and to his own country as well.[296] To strengthen his hold, Tito revealed to the army that, prior to the break in 1948, Russia had suggested that "it was no longer necessary for Belgrade to maintain a large standing army or rebuild the armament industry... Yugoslavia could rely on military assistance from her Eastern allies in case of attack and could therefore dispense with a large army and big supply facilities."[297] No proposals could make a mission that was supposedly sent to strengthen a friendly army more unpopular than such a military unemployment program.

Some of the satellite governments admonished their peoples and their armies not to fall into the errors of Titoism. They should continue to look to the Soviet Army, "our best friend and ally," and to continue "hand in hand with the soldiers of the brotherly Soviet Union and other Slav allies."[298] Nevertheless, Soviet officers took over directly in Albania, where the government had promptly and unilaterally cancelled all existing agreements with Yugoslavia and expelled all Yugoslav military and civilian advisers. In that strategic position, poised against Yugoslavia and the Mediterranean Powers, the Russian mission promptly grew from a mere three hundred to 3000 men, officers and civilians.[299] The arrival in Albania of an additional contingent of four hundred and eighty Soviet Army officers and political and economic experts was observed and reported from Belgrade in September 1950. They were obviously intended to further strengthen this outpost in the cold war against the West and against Tito. In 1950, when the latter's position was seriously endangered by crop failures and troubled by incidents along the frontiers, the United States proceeded to shore up the Belgrade regime with large-scale food shipments and other measures of assistance.[300] The military part of the aid was administered through an American military aid mission of twenty-eight members.[301] The United States appeared at times almost like the heir to Austria, both in its involvement in Balkan politics and in its ancient civilizing mission, which was never too well understood in Anglo-Saxon countries.[302]

Titoism was clearly a source of danger neither envisaged nor discussed by Marxism-Leninism-Stalinism. Armies seemed to be its best breeding ground. The "fanatical devotion" of officers would not readily turn from the traditional devotion to their country's interests and security, as interpreted and understood by them. Nor would army traditions easily give way to obedience to Moscow. After Tito had escaped, new means had to be devised to put satellite armies under more direct Russian control.

The Polish army, estimated at 250,000 men, seemed most exposed to the Titoist infection. Despite all the cruel Russian purges of the ten years previous, including the Katyn murders, too many officers survived from the days of Polish independence. In order to keep them under control, an estimated seventy-five per cent of the Polish high commands, inspectorates, and chief of staff positions were filled by Russians in the first year of Titoism. While Polish conscripts provided the military mass, Russian units had been entrenched in strategic locations all over Poland ever since the days of "liberation." The military arrangements closely paralleled those of the British Raj in India before India obtained dominion status. To make Russian control more effective,[303] and the parallel with British imperialism still closer, the Polish Government "applied to the Soviet Government" for the services of Soviet Marshal Konstantin K. Rokossovsky in the fall of 1949. He was to be Polish Minister of Defence and Marshal of the Polish Army—"in view of the fact that Marshal Rokossovsky is a Pole and is very popular with the Polish nation." The Kremlin proved obliging and the Polish-Soviet officer took over on November 7 with an order of the day calling on the Polish forces to consolidate their bonds with the powerful Russian army and to intensify political work and military training. The choice of the man was more than symbolic: he was the commander of the Russian forces who had denied all help to the insurrection in Warsaw against the Germans. His functions were clear—those of the "pro-consul," as the State Department defined them; of a Russian Gauleiter, as the Titoists called him; of a satrap, as the despotic semi-orientalism of the case would suggest.[304]

Whether the same arrangement would be applied to the other satellite armies remained to be seen. Meanwhile, zealous Communists admonished the officers that "loyalty to the people's democratic fatherland, the Soviet, is the first requisite for all military commanders."[305] Bulgaria seemed slated for closer military ties. After an inspector-general's visit by Marshal Bulganin of the Polit-bureau, the Chief of Staff and the political commissar of the Army were relieved of their duties and a minister sharply rebuked for his "refusal to take Soviet expert advice."[306]

Only part of the arrangements for Soviet control through "the export of Soviet marshals," military missions, and political commissars assumed formality. And few came under observation by the West, whose representatives found their range of reconnaissance constantly narrowed by Soviet-imposed measures. Where there is diplomatic reason to cover up such relations, as in the Korean War, the secret has proved almost impenetrable. American intelligence services in the Far East, repeatedly in error or default, were never fully able to expose Russian military participation in the direction of the North Korean and subsequent Chinese aggression.[307]

****

To modern nationalism, foreign advice in military affairs is and seems likely to remain vexatious.[308] Even under conditions of abject political subservience, protests arise. By tradition and upbringing the officer is ready to die for his country, but for his country alone. He can hardly be expected to rise above the concept of the nation and its sovereignty. Consequently, the nationalism of military officers, above that of all other groups, is ready to revolt against national subservience to a foreign Power. The suspicion that the small and comparatively backward nation is being put into the service of another bigger nation has impeded the work of many military missions. The sense of disproportion of power between the giver of instruction—nowadays nearly always one of the two or three Great Powers—and its recipient may also interfere with the acceptability of instruction. The attempt to teach military progress is often enough made still more unacceptable and unavailing by the easy reversion of the teacher to the language and attitude of the giver of orders. For many reasons, then, the officer-nationalism of the lesser Powers is apt to clash with the officer-nationalism of the greater Power.

In part, the great competition in arms between East and West is one between the persuasive talents of military missions. Never before in peacetime have so many military personnel appeared on the international scene. Military talents, perhaps more so than diplomatic talents, are pitted against each other on both sides of the line from the Baltic to Trieste and along a corresponding line in the Far East. The much-celebrated "Soviet Nationalism" has not proved a better article of export in the 1940's than Tsarist Nationalism did in the 1880's, even if both are disguised as Pan-Slav brotherhood-in-arms.[309] Nor have all military missionaries from the United States been accepted eagerly or proved themselves full of tact.[310]

FOOTNOTES

1. Cf. Italian Foreign Minister San Guiliano to the German ambassador: "He knew that people in Berlin were inclined to make further concessions in favor of the Greeks and were indulging in the hope of detaching Greece from

the Triple Entente. This, however, was an il-
lusion. In particular, the French influence
was on the increase due to the clever procedures of the head of the French military mission." Report of April 22, 1913, by General
Eydoux, G. P., XXXIV, 13192.

2. For example, during the period when the
French were endeavoring to force their protectorate on Madagascar (1886-94), the Mala-
gassies, in order to better resist them, engaged individual British officers to train bodies of native soldiers, who put up a strong
fight before the island was finally penetrated
and conquered. Encyclopedia Britannica (11th
ed.), XVII, 278.

3. E. Driault, "Sébastiani à Constantinople," Revue des études napoléoniennes, IV, 402 ff.

4. Correspondance de Napoléon, No. 12363.

5. At the height of their anti-British friendship,
Napoleon had lent the Tsar the services of an
outstanding French engineer, Deponthon, who
was to direct the fortification work at Kronstadt. By 1808, he came to the conclusion that
this officer showed far too much zeal in
strengthening the Russian works. "Too many
accidents could intervene to change the existing friendship between the two countries into
a state of war." Waliszewski, Le règne d'Alexandre Ier, I, 248, 259.

6. Mémoires du Duc de Rovigo, II, 213; III, 165;
Driault, La politique orientale de Napoléon;
Gardane, Mission du Général Gardane en
Perse.

7. Seton-Watson, Britain in Europe, p. 193.

8. Moltke, "poor as a church mouse" when he
went to Turkey as adviser in 1835, saved
some 10,000 Thalers, which he invested in
shares of the Hamburg-Berlin Railway, combining his material interest with his interest
in the new instrument of warfare. Article on
"Moltke" in ADB.

9. See Slade, Records of Travels in Turkey and
Greece.

10. The French ambassador to the Porte in 1881
reported, with regard to a French engineer in
Turkish services, that "this honorable offical,
while preserving all the reserve which his
present position as an Ottoman delegate imposes upon him, has remained essentially
French," amenable to any possible hints
from the Quai d'Orsay. Doc. dipl. fr., 1st series, III, No. 343.

11. Zechlin, Bismarck und die Grundlegung der
deutschen Grossmacht, p. 119.

12. Ollivier, L'Empire libéral, XI, 141 f., 154.

13. For details, see Hallgarten, Imperialismus
vor 1914, I, 214.

14. In the late 1940's, when a new edition of the
old Russia sent instructional officers abroad,
the wages that the receiving nations had to
pay, at Russia's insistence, were so high that
they aroused resentment and envy among
Yugoslav officers and politicians. This was
apparently a factor in provoking Titoism.
See Russian-Yugoslav exchange of letters
and notes of 1948. Time, August 23, 1948.

15. Corti, Alexander von Battenberg, pp. 83 f.,
89 and passim.

16. A convenient description of the Bulgarian
Army in the 1880's is in Hermann Vogt,
Die europäischen Heere der Gegenwart,
pp. 306 ff.

17. Corti, Alexander von Battenberg, p. 204.

18. Doc. dipl. fr., 1st series, VI, 137, 153 f.,
164.

19. G. P., IX, 2075.

20. Oesterreich-Ungarns Aussenpolitik, VII,
9476. In 1915, the same Kaulbars was entrusted with the task of preparing an expedition in the direction of the Straits. The diplomats strongly advised against his holding
command, for he was still unforgotten in
Bulgaria, which could not be brought into the
camp of the Entente should Kaulbars be in
command. Die internationalen Beziehungen im
Zeitalter des Imperialismus, 2nd series,
VIII, 212 f.

21. Oesterreich-Ungarns Aussenpolitik, II, 1915.

22. Helmreich, Diplomacy of the Balkan Wars,
p. 139.

23. Oesterreich-Ungarns Aussenpolitik, IV,
4148, 4191; VII, 8548.

24. Doc. dipl. fr., 1st series, VI, 144.

25. Ibid., 2nd series, XI, 105 f., 110 ff., 129, 136,
325, 358; B. D., VIII, 45 ff.

26. Giesl, Zwei Jahrzehnte im Nahen Orient, p.
173.

27. Doc. dipl. fr., 2nd series, I, 312.

28. Ibid., VIII, 418 ff.

29. Stieve, Schriftwechsel Iswolskis, III, 234.

30. Gleich, Vom Balkan nach Bagdad, pp. 32 f.,
61.

31. Oesterreich-Ungarns Aussenpolitik, VII,
8175, 8955; G. P., XXXVI, 13972.

32. Herbillon, Du général en chef au gouvernement, I, 140 f.

33. G. P., XXXIV, 13192.

34. Ibid., XXXVI, 13918.

35. Ibid., XXXVI, 13972.

36. Ibid., XXXVIII, 15450.

37. Herbillon, Du général en chef au gouvernement, I, 7 ff., 141.

38. Encyclopedia Britannica (12th ed.), XXXI,
305; Grey, Twenty-Five Years, II, 182.

39. Herbillon, Du général en chef au gouvernement, I, 335.

40. Encyclopedia Britannica (11th ed.), XV, 273.

41. Europäische Gespräche, IX, 290.

42. One of these was Major General Klemens Wilhelm Jakob Meckel (1842-1906). He was a member of the Great General Staff and a well-known military writer when called to Japan in 1885, where he taught in the War Academy. For details, see Roemer, in Haushofer (ed.), Deutsche Kulturpolitik im indopazifischen Raum, p. 271.

43. Togari, Louis-Emile Bertin. Togari was Japanese naval attaché in Paris.

44. Manning, The Life of Sir William White, pp. 159 ff., 342 f.

45. G. P., IX, 2306; XIV, 3663.

46. It still seems rather far-fetched for Winston Churchill to ascribe the Japanese naval men's greater discretion and less violent imperialism to the fact that the Army had been trained by German instructors and the Navy by British instructors during the nineteenth century. "This," he argues, "left lasting differences of mentality which were emphasized by the conditions of Service life." Such a conclusion would ascribe a vast and long-lasting influence to a very few German individuals, teachers of tactics and strategy, and not enough to the autonomous growth of Japanese army politics. Churchill, The Second World War, III, 581.

47. Trial of the Major War Criminals, XXVI, 392 f.

48. Wrottesley, Life and Correspondence of Sir John Burgoyne, II, 445.

49. Verner, The Military Life of George, Duke of Cambridge, I, 362 f.

50. Michie, The Life and Letters of Emory Upton, pp. 284 ff., 291, 309.

51. Take the case of the Futchow arsenal: It had been built with the assistance of French engineers in 1866, then shot to pieces in 1884 by French warships, with the help of maps furnished by the French builders of the arsenal. In 1896, when Li Hungchang came to Europe, the French Government persuaded him to have the arsenal rebuilt under the supervision of French naval engineers. The French Minister at Peking was happy to report that "China did not bear us a grudge" on account of the earlier destruction. Vagts, Deutschland und die Vereinigten Staaten, pp. 892 f.

52. Bülow, Denkwürdigkeiten, III, 186; Beyens, Deux Années à Berlin, II, 75, and Das alte Heer (Von einem Stabsoffizier), pp. 38, 69 f. This anonymous officer observes that "our position in Eastern Asia has largely been created by ex-officers to whom Germany had become too narrow and too boring."

53. For his life story, see Roemer, in Haushofer (ed.), Deutsche Kulturpolitik im indopazifischen Raum, p. 265. For his activity in China in favor of Krupp and other interests, see Hallgarten, Imperialismus vor 1914, I, 351, 357.

54. Heyking, Tagebücher aus vier Weltteilen, p. 174.

55. G. P., XIV, 3663.

56. Ibid., XIV, 3743-46; Hohenlohe, Denkwürdigkeiten, III, 280 f.; Waldersee, Denkwürdigkeiten, II, 384.

57. Zwehl, Erich von Falkenhayn, pp. 18 ff. For Admiral Lord Charles Beresford's proposals of 1898-99 to the Chinese to replace the German instructors by British officers, see Hallgarten, Imperialismus vor 1914, I, 389.

58. Doc. dipl. fr., 2nd series, V, 307.

59. In March 1907, William II spoke to the French chargé in Berlin as follows: "And while that goes on in Europe, the triumphant Yellow ones carry on their work of rapprochement. The Japanese, to whom their successes have given an insolent confidence, no longer know any bounds to their ambitions. They have artfully invaded China, their instructors replace the European instructors everywhere, they obtain openly or by infiltration the employments most favorable to their designs." Doc. dipl. fr., 2nd series, X, 706.

60. G. P., XXV, 8556 f.

61. Ibid., XXXII, 12018.

62. Early in 1914, the Russians advised the Mongolian puppet Government not to arm the whole population in order to continue their fight for independence from China because that would in the end prove dangerous for the central government, but rather to make better use of the existing brigade under Russian instructors. Mongolia was financially unable to maintain a force as strong as Russia had proposed; the local Russian agent believed that not more could be done than have a body of Russian officers and non-coms drill three hundred men at a time, for three or six months. Die internationalen Beziehungen, 1st series, I, 124; II, 262.

63. Ibid., 2nd series, II, 107 f.

64. Doc. dipl. fr., 1st series, VII, 457 (1889).

65. Eckardstein, Lebenserinnerungen, II, 363. For his relations with the British legation in Tangiers (embarrassing in the end), see Nicolson, Portrait of a Diplomatist, pp. 82 ff., 102 ff. See also A. J. P. Taylor, "British Policy in Morocco, 1886-1902," English Historical Review, July 1951.

66. B. D., II, 263, 269, 272 f., 295.

67. Doc. dipl. fr., 2nd series, I, 379 f. (1901).

68. Ibid., I, 405.

69. B. D., III, 55.

70. Doc. dipl. fr., 2nd series, V, 580 f., 597, 612 ff.

71. G. P., XX, 6538, 6545.

72. B. D., III, 55.
73. G. P., XXI, 6922, 6927, 7009.
74. Ibid., XXI, 7018 ff., 7134.
75. Ibid., XXI, 7315, 7331, 7332, 7334.
76. Doc. dipl. fr., 2nd series, XI, 1048.
77. G. P., XXIV, 8343, 8355.
78. A German consul found that in Mulay Hafid "the national religious aims of the Khalifate are only weakly accentuated. The Moroccan idea outweighs it by far. But the ideal state, in which it is to become real, is still that of the enlightened absolutism of an Islamitic prince of the church." Ibid., XXIV, 8457.
79. Ibid., XXIX, 10509, 10549; B. D., III, 147 f.
80. Weygand, Histoire de l'armée francaise, p. 350.
81. The conspiracy inside the Sherifian army in 1912 was attributed to the introduction of the French type of knapsack, which proved hateful to the native conception of the "free man's back." Stieve, Schriftwechsel Iswolskis, II, 82.
82. W. L. Middleton in The Fortnightly, November 1925, p. 637.
83. Baker Pasha, War in Bulgaria, II, 350.
84. See Hobart Pasha's autobiography, Sketches from My Life.
85. Disraeli to Lady Bradford, September 6, 1877. Monypenny and Buckle, Disraeli, II, 1051.
86. G. P., II, 403.
87. Cecil, Life of Salisbury, II, 322; Seton-Watson, Britain in Europe, p. 543.
88. See Hajo Holborn, Deutschland und die Türkei, 1878-1890.
89. For details, see Hohenlohe, Denkwürdigkeiten, II, 302.
90. This is based on Doc. dipl. fr., 1st series, III, 176 f., 183, 195, 201, 255; Taffs, Ambassador to Bismarck, pp. 326 ff.
91. B. H. Sumner, "Ignatiev at Constantinople," Slavonic Review, April 1933, p. 564.
92. Giesl, Zwei Jahrzehnte im Nahen Orient, pp. 41 ff.
93. Schmiterloew, Von der Goltz, pp. 108 f.; G. P., IX, 2074, 2094 ff. Goltz enjoyed a high reputation among British soldiers.
94. Giesl, Zwei Jahrzehnte im Nahen Orient, p. 47.
95. G. P., IV, 767.
96. Doc. dipl. fr., 1st series, IX, 595.
97. Schmiterloew, Von der Goltz, p. 116.
98. One of the candidates for his successorship was Friedrich von Bernhardi, an equally prolific writer. He wanted to complete Goltz' work because he foresaw that in a European war, which would come about sooner or later, "Turkey would be our ally." Bernhardi, Denkwürdigkeiten, p. 135.
99. Statements of Kamphoevener to Chancellor Hohenlohe, June 1896. G. P., XII, 2892.
100. Ibid., XII, 2904 ff. See Ibid., XXXIV, 12873, for the difficulties of introducing honor concepts among the Turkish officers.
101. Giesl, Zwei Jahrzehnte im Nahen Orient, p. 95.
102. G. P., XII, 3339.
103. Hohenlohe, Denkwürdigkeiten, III, 368.
104. G. P., XII, 3341 f.
105. Ibid., XXII, 7385 f. That saying, according to Marschall, was now outdated as far as the Straits were concerned.
106. William II in 1898. Ibid., XII, 3339, 3350.
107. Ibid., XII, 3340; XIV, 3988.
108. Ibid., XIV, 3990, 4022 ff.; XV, 4225.
109. Giesl, Zwei Jahrzehnte im Nahen Orient, p. 52.
110. B. D., V, 40 ff.
111. G. P., XVIII, 5611, 5616; Berliner Monatshefte, VII (1929), 199 ff.
112. B. D., V, 269, 275.
113. Ibid., V, 269, 282.
114. Jäckh, Kiderlen-Wächter, I, 287.
115. B. D., V, 283.
116. Ibid., V, 308.
117. G. P., XXV, 8906; B. D., V, 208, 311.
118. The German reformers tried to resign during this putsch, saying they could no longer belong to an army in which all discipline had ended. But Marschall told them— as did the Emperor himself—that they must wait. To resign at that moment would cut all ties with the Turkish Army. In the higher interest of German policy, they must hold out in their posts. G. P., XXVII, 9576.
119. Oesterreich-Ungarns Aussenpolitik, I, 600.
120. Ibid., II, 757; B. D., V, 320.
121. G. P., XXVI, 8937.
122. Ibid., XXVII, 9798 ff., 9964; Schmiterloew, Von der Goltz, pp. 155 ff.
123. G. P., XXVII, 9635, 9789.
124. Ibid., XXVII, 9964.
125. Ibid., XXVII, 9804 ff.
126. Report of the Austrian military attaché in Constantinople, October 1910. Conrad, Aus meiner Dienstzeit, II, 30. The Russian Ambassador Tcharikov had endeavored to draw Turkey into the Russian orbit while allowing her to reform, but his Government would have none of this; it could not believe "that the existence of a strong Turkey, even if subordinate [to Russia], could be useful to her." Zur europäischen Politik, IV, 54.
127. G. P., XXXIII, 12364.
128. Cited in Ibid., XXXIII, 12303, 12331.
129. Ibid., XXXIV, 13500.
130. Oesterreich-Ungarns Aussenpolitik, IV, 4525.
131. Zur europäischen Politik, IV, 131 f.

132. G. P., XXXIII, 12364, 12379 f.

133. Report of Russian minister to Sofia, November 25, 1912. Stieve, Schriftwechsel Iswolskis, II, 359.

134. Speech of April 7, 1913. Cf. Poincaré, Au service de la France, III, 192 f.

135. Djemal Pasha, Erinnerungen eines türkischen Staatsmannes, pp. 71 ff.

136. G. P., XXXVIII, 15439, 15462.

137. "It might well appear strange that the Power which had accepted the task of reforming the Turkish Navy should support Russia's protest against Turkey's invitation to Germany to reform the Army. But British policy in the Near East was to follow Russia whenever possible." Cambridge History of British Foreign Policy, III, 474 f.

138. G. P., XXXVIII, 15468 f., 15479, 15481 f.

139. Callwell, The Life of Sir Henry Wilson, I, 128 f.

140. Pokrowski, Drei Konferenzen, pp. 10, 39.

141. This is based on Die internationale Beziehungen, 1st series, I, 369, 379, 411, 301 ff.; II, 381 f.; III, 207; V, 195.

142. In Berlin military circles, it was only dimly realized, if at all, that such an organization, which threatened to make Turkish force at last effective, was bound to arouse the protest of the Entente Powers.

143. There is considerable literature on this point. In addition to that cited by Fay in The Origins of the World War, I, 498 ff., the following titles should be mentioned: Hallgarten, "La portée politique et economique de la mission Liman von Sanders," Revue d'histoire de la guerre mondiale, 1935, pp. 17 ff.; C. Mühlmann, Deutschland und die Türkei 1913-14, as well as his article, "Die deutsche Militärmission in der Türkei," Wissen und Wehr, 1938, pp. 847 ff.; Herzfeld, "Die Liman-Krise," Berliner Monatshefte, XI (1933), 837 ff., 973 ff. The fullest treatment is by Kerner in Slavonic Review, VI, 12 ff., 344 ff., 543 ff. I disagree with his conclusions.

144. Herzfeld, Die deutsche Rüstungspolitik vor dem Weltkriege, p. 63.

145. Pokrowski, Drei Konferenzen, p. 37.

146. G. P., XXXVIII, 15376.

147. Ibid., XXXVIII, 15436 ff., 15440.

148. Ibid., XXXVIII, 15441.

149. Ibid., XXXVIII, 15444; September 19, 1913.

150. Liman von Sanders, Fünf Jahre Türkei, pp. 9 ff.; Oesterreich-Ungarns Aussenpolitik, VIII, 8984. See also the biographical sketch of Liman by Mühlmann in Deutsches Biographisches Jahrbuch, XI (1929).

151. G. P., XXXVIII, 15451 f., 15461.

152. Schmidt-Bückeburg, Das Militärkabinett der preussischen Könige, pp. 226 f.

153. G. P., XXXVIII, p. 213.

154. Ibid., XXXVIII, 15371; Oesterreich-Ungarns Aussenpolitik, VII, 8951, 9068.

155. None of the monographic treatments of the Liman mission have bothered to compare in detail the powers of these two missions. According to German reports, Eydoux's were greater. G. P., XXXVIII, 15449.

156. Ibid., XXXVIII, 15445 ff.; Fay, The Origins of the World War, I, 509 ff. "The British Government were disconcerted by the importance attached by M. Sasonov and by M. Delcassé to an incident which they felt was not intended to be provocative. M. Sasonov, however, insisted that 'this question must be the test of the value of the Triple Entente.'" Nicolson, for once, was not inclined to adopt the Russian point of view. Nicolson, Portrait of a Diplomatist, p. 293.

157. G. P. XXXVIII, 15452.

158. Limpus was personally convinced that his powers exceeded those contemplated for Liman. G. P., XXXVIII, 15479, 15481, 15484.

159. Colonel Repington, military correspondent of The Times, told the Russian military attaché in London that British public opinion had only belatedly been brought to take an interest in the Liman mission and to realize that it was disadvantageous not only to Russia but to Britain as well, because she was importing a considerable part of her food. The Liman mission, so to speak, brought England's food supply into the hands of a German general who, in case of war, would be able to expose Britain to the danger of famine. In addition, this mission strengthened Germany's position in Asia Minor and thus threatened the road to India. The Times did not favor the British naval mission to Turkey; still it was better to have the Turkish fleet under British rather than under German control. Die internationale Beziehungen, 1st series, I, 14.

160. Isvolski to Sasonov. Die internationale Beziehungen, 1st series, I, 129.

161. Oesterreich-Ungarns Aussenpolitik, VII, 9175, 9573. "The attempt to make Turkey, cut up as it was into spheres of interest, livable once more by way of the Liman mission found an inglorious end when, in the face of Russian protest, Turkey was left in the lurch by Germany. Thus the German position in Turkey was evacuated, as it had been evacuated in Persia and in the Balkans." Report of Austrian ambassador in St. Petersburg, May 8, 1914. Ibid., VIII, 9656.

162. Pokrowski, Drei Konferenzen, pp. 32 ff. For the most recent Russian historiography, post-Pokrowski, "the Liman von Sanders affair was a new provocation on the part of German imperialism," leading exactly a year later to the world conflict. Potiemkine, Histoire de la diplomatie, II, 252 f.

163. Judet, George Louis, p. 233; cf. Poincaré, Au service de la France, III, 327.

164. For Grey's ignorance as to the terms of the contract for Limpus, see G. P., XXXVIII, 15476. Grey said at the time this contract was being negotiated that he had merely emphasized that British instructors must under no circumstances become involved in warlike actions. He supposed that this was also true with regard to the German instructors. According to William II, this was not so. The Russians were under the impression that, in the case of Greek-Turkish war over the Aegean islands, which threatened in the early summer of 1914, British officers would command the Turkish fleet. Oesterreich-Ungarns Aussenpolitik, VIII, 9655.

165. Stieve, Schriftwechsel Iswolskis, IV, 10; Suchomlinow, Erinnerungen, pp. 249 ff.

166. Oesterreich-Ungarns Aussenpolitik, VII, 9211, 9314.

167. G. P., XXXVIII, p. 299.

168. Ibid., XXXVIII, 15493, 15515.

169. August 3, 1914. Die internationale Beziehungen, 1st series, V, 304.

170. Oesterreich-Ungarns Aussenpolitik, VII, 9505.

171. G. P., XXXVII, p. 596.

172. Die internationale Beziehungen, 1st series, V, 291 f., 324.

173. Deutsche Dokumente zum Kriegsausbruch, I, 117, 256; II, 411; III, 517, 733; Oesterreich-Ungarns Aussenpolitik, VIII, 1134.

174. August 11, 1914. Die internationale Beziehungen, 2nd series, VI, 47.

175. Ibid., VI, 53, 61.

176. Puleston, High Command in the World War, p. 112.

177. Die internationale Beziehungen, 2nd series, VI, 197.

178. Bompard, Mon ambassade en Russie, pp. 325 ff.

179. Rabenau, Seeckt, II, 13 f., 86, 89, 98, 105, 111 f.

180. Memorandum of March 25, 1919. Baker, Woodrow Wilson and World Settlement, III, Document 65.

181. "Germany...agrees not to accredit nor to send to any foreign country any military, naval, or air missions nor to allow any such mission to leave her territory and... to take appropriate measures to prevent German nationals from leaving her territory to become enrolled in the Army, Navy or Air service of any foreign Power or to be attached to such Army, Navy or Air service for the purpose of assisting in the military, etc., instruction in any foreign country." At the same time the signatories agreed not to employ such German instructors, except that France was free to use Germans in the service of her Foreign Legion.

182. Cf. confidential report of Maj. Gen. F. J. Kernan, chief American representative on the Inter-Allied Mission to Poland, April 11, 1919; "In Central Europe, the French uniform is everywhere in evidence...There is a concerted, distinct effort being made by these agents to foster the military spirit in Poland, Czechoslovakia and...Rumania. The imperialist idea has seized upon the French, like a kind of madness, and the obvious effort is to create a chain of states, highly militarized, organized as far as possible under French guidance and intended to be future allies of France...Under the guidance of the French, a strong military combination is being built up capable, perhaps, of dominating Europe." Baker, Woodrow Wilson and World Settlement, III, 218 ff.

183. Documents on British Foreign Policy, 1919-1939, 1st series, II, 67.

184. Gamelin, Servir, II, v ff. According to American reports, Gamelin and his mission "enjoyed a considerable degree of authority and received suitable remuneration," something which it was hoped American members of a naval mission which was under consideration would also receive. Foreign Relations of the United States (1922), I, 651.

185. Anders, An Army in Exile, p. 7.

186. See obituary in N. Y. Times, December 22, 1949. Pertinax, Les Fossoyeurs, II, 52.

187. Gamelin, Servir, II, 226.

188. Bartel, Le Maréchal Pilsudski, p. 207; "Les armées alliées de l'est," Revue de Paris, tome 50 (September 1931), 69 ff.

189. Documents on German Foreign Policy, 1918-1945, Series D, II, 329, 355; Wheeler-Bennett, Munich, p. 154. This mission was withdrawn in December and received a fervent accolade from the embittered Czech press. N. Y. Times, December 14, 1938.

190. Namier, Diplomatic Prelude, p. 317.

191. Foreign Relations of the United States (1922), I, 636 f.

192. Speech on Pan-Asiatism, delivered at Yokohama, November 28, 1924, N. Y. Nation, March 2, 1927.

193. Current History, November 1928, p. 280.
194. Lytton Report, p. 20. One of the instruction officers was the later General Chuikov, commandant of Berlin, described by his Western opposites as "probably the roughest and almost certainly the rudest officer in the Soviet Army." Newsweek, April 11, 1949.
195. For some of the Russian methods of instructorship, see McNair, China in Revolution. "One or more Russians held strategic positions for military or propaganda purposes" in each of Chiang's army corps. Their advance was preceded by "plain-clothes propagandists who preached to peasants and townsmen the principles of Dr. Sun and Lenin; scattered vast quantities of placards, etc.; organized the people, willing and unwilling, into peasants' and workers' unions; and set up Soviet local governments."
196. Goul, Les grands chefs de l'armée sovietique, pp. 77 ff.
197. Rabenau, Seeckt, II, 271.
198. Beauvais, Attachés militaires, p. 39.
199. Hoffmann, Aufzeichnungen, II, 22; Pearson and Brown, The American Diplomatic Game, pp. 201 ff.; Roemer, in Haushofer (ed.), Deutsche Kulturpolitik im indopazifischen Raum, p. 270.
200. Foreign Relations of the United States (Paris Peace Conference, 1919), XIII, 333.
201. Argentina, Finland, Spain, Turkey, Japan.
202. For details, see Trial of the Major War Criminals, XXXIV.
203. Toynbee, Survey of International Affairs 1938, I, 570. The Chinese Communists also had a German military adviser, called Li Teh, whose counselling did not always prove to be the best. Payne, Mao Tsetsung. Ruler of Red China, pp. 131 and passim.
204. Seeckt found her "deeply interested in politics, and political means military with her, she is surprisingly well-informed and in spite of may aversion towards women who want to have a say in things political and military, I soon gave up my initial reserve."
205. United States Relations with China (Department of State Publication 3573), p. 45.
206. This is based on Rabenau, Seeckt, II, 677 ff.
207. This is based on Documents on German Foreign Policy 1918-1945, Series D, I, 736 ff. Cf. also Tansill, Back Door to War, pp. 481 ff.
208. Toynbee, Survey of International Affairs 1938, I, 568 f.
209. This is based on Nazi-Soviet Relations, pp. 206 f., 211, 232, 253, 266 ff., and Trials of War Criminals, XII, 1250 ff. The OKW wanted the service attachés in Bucharest included in the Mission, but the Wilhelmstrasse protested, unsuccessfully it would seem, pointing out that they were "members of the diplomatic corps with all the privileges but also all restrictions that arise therefrom."
210. For the Pan-Americanism of the U.S. Navy in 1897, see Vagts, Deutschland und die Vereinigten Staaten, p. 1638.
211. Foreign Relations of the United States (1920), III, 367 ff.
212. Ibid., (1922), I, 651 ff.
213. Hull, Memoirs, II, 1390 ff.
214. Watson, Chief of Staff, pp. 89, 91.
215. Britannia Yearbook, 1941, p. 342.
216. Hull, Memoirs, II, 1139 f.; N. Y. Times, May 19, 1948; Aikman, The All-American Front.
217. Watson, Chief of Staff, pp. 426, 434 ff.
218. Time, December 19, 1949.
219. Ibid., May 31, 1948.
220. Hull, Memoirs, II, 1371.
221. For some of the details, see Markham, Tito's Imperial Communism, pp. 155 ff.
222. Fortune, September 1944, p. 266.
223. Hull, Memoirs, II, 1513 f.
224. The following is based on the ample documentation in United States Relations with China, the so-called "China White Book."
225. N. Y. Times, August 28, 1941.
226. See Military Situation in the Far East, pp. 3238 ff. for Wedemeyer's counselling.
227. Ibid., p. 2815.
228. The Moscow New Times, July 1, 1946, as proof of the American intentions towards a protectorate, cited the N. Y. Herald Tribune as saying: "American representatives seem to be determined to extend the rule of the Kuomintang government over the present Communist areas, regardless of how many supporters of the Reds must be killed by American weapons in the process."
229. Before House Armed Services Committee, N. Y. Times, June 4, 1947. And, General Barr added later, our ambassador was "the overriding agency in China of the U.S." Barr's relations with the embassy were on the whole harmonious: "I was an agency of the Joint Chiefs of Staff, with the Ambassador exercising supervisory control over me and my keeping no secrets from the Ambassador." Military Situation in the Far East, p. 3031.
230. U.S. Relations with China, p. 349.
231. Dispatch of Henry R. Lieberman from Nanking, N. Y. Times, September 30, 1946;

D. B. Copland, "U.S. Policy in China," Pacific Affairs, December 1948.

232. Military Situation in the Far East, pp. 1854 f.

233. Testimony of Wedemeyer before House Foreign Affairs Committee, N. Y. Times, March 5, 1948; U.S. Relations with China, pp. 255 ff. When Congressman Judd asked Secretary Marshall to apply the directive covering Greece to the mission in China (to "advise and train at all levels"), he refused. Time, August 20, 1951; Military Situation in the Far East, pp. 558 f., 1854 f., 2413 ff., 2963.

234. U.S. Relations with China, p. 895.

235. Ibid., p. 288; N. Y. Times, November 17, 1948. Barr left China at the end of January, 1949.

236. U. S. Relations with China, p. 894. Bradley commented: "Undoubtedly he [Chiang] did not make very effective use of the equipment we gave him." Military Situation in the Far East, p. 1126. General Barr commented in mid-November 1948: "The military situation has deteriorated to the point where only the active participation of U.S. troops could effect a remedy...Their military débacles can all be attributed to the world's worst leadership." Ibid., p. 1856. For Barr's final report, see Ibid., pp. 2069 ff.

237. General Barr, cited in letter to the editor by John K. Fairbanks, N. Y. Times, July 30, 1949; U.S. Relations with China, p. 320; Military Situation in the Far East, pp. 2959, 2070.

238. N. Y. Times, November 17, 1949; Time, January 2, 1950.

239. Military Situation in the Far East, pp. 23 f., 56, 106, 1078, 1674; N. Y. Times, April 25, 1951 and November 11, 1951.

240. Military Situation in the Far East, pp. 37, 1987 ff., 2011 f.

241. Cf. the following dialogue between Senator Lodge and General Bradley, May 24, 1951: (L) "Looking back on it, hindsight, certainly it would have been an excellent thing if we had started in 1946 developing officer material in not only Korea but in a great many other places where there is available military manpower which could be effectively used if the leadership had been developed, isn't that true?"(B) "Yes, sir, that is a very important preparedness program." (L) "... and the Soviets...have never overlooked an opportunity to train satellite armies not only in the Orient but in Eastern Europe and every other place. The result is that they fight us without using their own troops, and we have to use our troops because we have not trained these natives." (B) "We haven't trained them and we haven't equipped them sufficiently." (L) "Doesn't that argue then as a future policy we certainly ought to go ahead and train young officers in all of these anti-Communist countries?" (B) "Yes, sir, we should...." (L) "Because we have manpower shortage in this country and we can't possibly carry the full load of combat for the free world by ourselves...." Military Situation in the Far East, p. 1114.

242. Semi-annual Report of the Secretary of Defense (January 1 through June 30, 1950), p. 78.

243. N. Y. Times, January 1, 1952 (Army News Features).

244. To "second" in British military parlance is to put an officer into temporary retirement with a view to staff or other extra-regimental appointment.

245. This group retired from Palestine after the outbreak of hostilities there. Cf. statement of Sir Alexander Cadogan to UN Security Council, May 27, 1948: "UK Government are making immediate arrangements to insure that the twenty-one seconded officers shall not serve with the Arab Legion in Palestine." N. Y. Times, November 5, 1948.

246. Statements of Foreign Secretary Bevin in House of Commons on May 26 and November 4, 1948.

247. Perham, The Government of Ethiopia, pp. 92 ff., 358, 418 ff., 430 ff.

248. Voiced, for example, by Representative Dewey Short in House Armed Services Committee, N. Y. Times, June 4, 1947.

249. Henry Wallace, statement of April 27, 1947, criticizing plan of aid to Greece and Turkey.

250. Hanson Baldwin in N. Y. Times, January 17, 1949.

251. N. Y. Times, June 4, 1947.

252. In December 1948, Secretary of Defense Forrestal pleaded with Congress for legislation "to permit such missions to be sent, in the discretion of the President, to countries which request advisory missions to assist them in their military planning." Ibid., December 30, 1948.

253. Stalin to Ambassador-General Smith: "But Turkey is weak, and the Soviet Union is very conscious of the danger of foreign control of the Straits, which Turkey is not strong enough to protect. The Turkish Government is unfriendly to us. That is why the Soviet Union has demanded a base in the Dardanelles. It is a matter of our own security." Smith, My Three Years in Moscow, p. 53.

254. Speech of Loy W. Henderson, Louisville, Kentucky, on February 18, 1948. N. Y. Times, February 19, 1948.
255. Time, May 23, 1949.
256. N. Y. Times, July 13, 1947.
257. Ibid., January 9 and February 15, 1948.
258. Ibid., May 29, 1948.
259. "If America continues to interfere in Greek affairs, the end may become very bad," the Yugoslav ambassador to Turkey, Colonel Bojin Sunitch, declared in an interview. Did he mean war? "Yes, but this will not mean Yugoslavia only. How would Mexico like troops on her frontier? Naturally, we do not want foreign soldiers near ours." AP dispatch from Istanbul, January 19, 1948.
260. Statement of Secretary Marshall. N. Y. Times, March 4, 1948.
261. Ibid., August 3, 1948; Time, October 25, 1948.
262. Time, May 23, 1949.
263. N. Y. Times, December 25, 1953, and January 9, 1954.
264. Time, July 24, 1950.
265. U.S.-Turkish agreement of July 2, 1947. N. Y. Times, July 13, 1947.
266. By mid-1951, JAMMAT was the largest military advisory group the United States maintained abroad, counting 1,250 officers, enlisted men, and civilians.
267. N. Y. Times, June 21, July 5 and 6, August 10, September 26, 1948; January 4, 1950. Some ancient problems of military linguistics have been solved by Russia by making Russian the language of command in such satellite armies as the Hungarian one.
268. Time, October 24, 1949.
269. N. Y. Times, March 4 and 16, 1948.
270. The Soviet-Persian Treaty of 1921 had laid down that "if a third party should desire to use Persian territory as a base of operations against Russia, Russia shall have the right to advance her troops inside Persia." There were ominous references to this clause in Russian protests against American activity in Iran.
271. AP dispatch from Teheran, April 29, 1946.
272. According to text quoted by the Russians, UP dispatch from Teheran, March 28, 1948.
273. AP dispatch from Teheran, January 1, 1948.
274. N. Y. Times, February 3, 1948.
275. Ibid., April 17, 1948.
276. Ibid., May 29, 1948.
277. Ibid., May 24, 1950, with a statement by Acting Secretary of State, James E. Webb. By that time, the U.S. Military Mission counted seventy-seven members, whose activity had stirred Iran's "new power"
and was giving "the nation on Russia's border tough confidence." Ibid., May 7, 1950.
278. Ibid., April 11, 1950.
279. Ibid., March 5, 1948.
280. For the U.S. Military Advisory Group in Saigon, see Ibid., September 5, 1951.
281. AP dispatches from Copenhagen, December 17, 1949, and from Washington, December 25, 1949, and February 2, 1950.
282. Ollivier, L'Empire libéral, X, 4 ff.
283. Time, February 7, 1949; N. Y. Times, January 27, 1946.
284. For details, see Vagts, "The Foreigner as Soldier in the Second World War," Journal of Politics, IX, 398 ff.
285. Announcement by the Czech Chief of Staff, General Bocek, N. Y. Times, May 21, 1945.
286. Ibid., January 9 and 10, 1951; Frankfurter Allgemeine Zeitung, February 9, 1951.
287. Soviet influence in the "native military forces in Manchuria" was supreme by the end of 1949. "Chinese Communists have openly admitted this Soviet participation." Military control extended beyond the armed forces to the secret police, air service, and war-potential industries. "Background material issued by State Department to support its charges that Russia was absorbing areas of Northern China." AP dispatch from Washington, January 25, 1950. For reports on a joint Soviet-Chinese-North Korean staff headquarters in Manchuria at the end of 1950, see N. Y. Times, December 14, 1950.
288. The Chinese delegate, Dr. T. F. Tsiang, before Political and Security Committee of the UN General Assembly, November 25, 1949. N. Y. Times, November 26, 1949; Just, Militärmacht Sowjetunion, pp. 69 f.
289. N. Y. Times, June 26, 1950. Speaking before the UN on October 24, 1952, Dean Acheson gave a detailed description of the building of the North Korean Army, "a large army, raised, trained and heavily equipped and tactically and strategically advised by the Soviet Government."
290. N. Y. Times, June 28 and July 19, 1950.
291. C. L. Sulzberger in dispatch from Tokyo. Ibid., May 24, 1950.
292. C. L. Sulzberger in Ibid., July 24, 1951.
293. In Bulgaria in the 1880's, "these Russian officers preserved their rank in the Army of the Tsar and their Russian emoluments, were therefore not only in a much better pecuniary position than the officers of Bulgarian nationality but were convinced

that in their character as Russians they possessed the necessary immunity for all sorts of disobedience to lawful authority." Vogt, Die europäischen Heere der Gegenwart, p. 310.

294. Excerpts from the Kremlin-Tito correspondence of April-May 1948. Time, August 23, 1948.

295. N. Y. Times, July 11, 1948.

296. Ibid., September 30, 1948.

297. Speech of Lt. Gen. Otmar Kreatitch, head of the political department of the Yugoslav Army, on the eighth anniversary of the founding of the present Yugoslav Army. Ibid., December 22, 1949.

298. Czech President Gottwald to Czech soldiers, AP dispatch from Prague, July 8, 1948.

299. These are Belgrade statistics. See N. Y. Times, July 4, 9 and 10, 1948; April 5, November 18, 19 and 20, 1949; March 27, September 24, November 19, 1950; March 25, 1952.

300. Ibid., September 24, and October 25, 1950.

301. For some details of its progress and troubles, see statement by its chief, Brig. Gen. John Harmony in UP dispatch from Belgrade, April 10, 1952. It was remarked on the occasion that "the normal starting complement for military-assistance missions is seventy-three men, but in this case it was cut down because of Yugoslav misgivings."

302. For a positive appreciation see Disraeli's speech of July 25, 1850: "I hold the maintenance of the Austrian Empire necessary to the independence, the civilization and even to the liberties of Europe."

303. A Soviet citizen, General Korzycycz, was made Polish chief of staff immediately after the close of the war, and Russian officers came to direct Polish economy, turning it into a war economy. In 1951, Soviet General Lomonossov directed the Economic Coordination Office, Soviet Colonel Tchermakov the employment of Polish labor, Soviet Major Stojanov the distribution of Polish coal. For details, see Die Zeit, (Hamburg), August 16, 1951.

304. N. Y. Times, November 8, 9, 15, 21, 1948; Time, November 21, 1948.

305. Rudolph Stransky, Secretary-General of the Czechoslovak CP, at the opening of a new military school for higher officers. Ibid., November 23, 1949.

306. Ibid., November 23, 1949.

307. For reports of a joint staff headquarters consisting of Soviet, Chinese and North Korean military representatives in Manchuria, see Ibid., December 14, 1950.

308. Problems of this nature have arisen in such "young" national states as Indonesia, Burma, Nepal. Under strong nationalistic pressure, supported by Communist "fronts," the departure of the Dutch military mission of about 1000 officers and men was speeded up in Jakarta, even though high-ranking officers of the Indonesian Army regretted this haste, since they still felt in need of technical assistance. Such assistance was unobtainable from other places such as Western Germany, where an application was turned down on the grounds that such a German mission would be regarded as "a hostile act" by the Dutch. N. Y. Times, February 17 and March 26, 1953. For the Burmese wishes to terminate or change the labors of a British military mission in their country, see Ibid., January 8, 1952. For Nepalese protests against the presence of an Indian military mission resulting in conflicts between the Nepal people and those of "the huge southern neighbor," see Ibid., March 15, 1953.

309. The simplest way for the Communist parties to combat officers' nationalism in the satellite countries is to accuse them of treasonable connections with Western spies. Hence the great number of spy trials in Poland and Czechoslovakia in 1949 and later.

310. "All has not been as smooth between JAMMAT and the Turks as would be desired or has generally been reported. Basic troubles have been blustering lack of tact and feeling by certain Americans dealing with proud and sensitive Turks; and on the other side, the Turk's distrust of any foreigner." Time, October 15, 1951.

Armed Demonstrations

Often the purpose of political demonstrations is to express in unmistakable form, by a display of force, previously disregarded, misunderstood, or misconstrued intentions of a nation or government, party or other group. In some political demonstrations, however, the effort is not to convey to other states the real condition and intentions of the demonstrating state, but instead to create a misleading impression of these. Political demonstrations are usually intended to stop short of war and revolution, although they have not always stayed within such bounds. In contradistinction to other political acts, they are meant to be of a highly spectacular and resounding nature.

Some demonstrations closely approach or go over to violence. This happened in the Boston Tea Party, in "bleeding Kansas," and in the storming of the Bastille. Others keep within the bounds of symbolic gesturing, such as the Wartburg Festival of 1817, when German students solemnly burned the symbols of oppressive government. The pre-1914 Socialist parties and the post-1917 Communist parties liked to remind the world, and themselves as well, of the class war concept of their movement by mass demonstrations, as when they "marched for" or "struck for" international solidarity and understanding, or against the "war mongering" of capitalist governments. The Fascist parties demonstrated themselves into power by street parades, the next step beyond propaganda and agitation. These parades moved steadily in the direction of violence, which was hinted at by uniforming the demonstrators.[1] There is undeniably a certain stylistic unity underlying such internal demonstrations and the armed demonstrations of nineteenth- and twentieth-century governments.[2]

Since the seventeenth century, governments have not maintained armies and navies merely for the purposes of making war and maintaining order at home. The existence of armed forces in peacetime was also designed to have a continuous or occasional diplomatic effect. They provided governments and their diplomacy with arguments a fortiori.[3] As bodies charged with potential violence, a number of their actions could be made highly demonstrative, pointing to an application of the force presented, with more to come if necessary.

A certain suddenness is almost imperative in order to make armed demonstrations impressive. The unprepared medieval armies would not have been suited for such purposes. It was the standing army, such as that of Louis XIV, that brought on the custom of armed demonstration. His policy of the conquering peace, or the peaceful conquest, kept all Europe in a state of alarm. It did not, however, always succeed in its ulterior intentions. In 1679, for example, the French failed in their attempt to force the Dutch into an alliance. The vast camp which Louis set up in Alsace in 1683, during the struggle of the Emperor and much of the rest of Christianity with the Turk, was designed to keep Austria alarmed. Some of her troops were forced to stay on the Rhine, instead of relieving besieged Vienna. The Christian protest, in pamphlet and other form, left Louis cold. As he pointed out, camps for training purposes were nothing new in the military practice of France, and the King was only using his sovereign prerogative in exercising his troops and visiting and inspecting them. This he did in June-July 1683, suddenly leading them in the direction of the Spanish Netherlands in order to enforce his demands upon Spain by a "peaceful occupation."[4]

Where a country's navy was more nearly in a state of permanent readiness than the army, as was usually the case in England, it too could be used for demonstrative purposes. At the beginning of 1688, when Louis XIV invited James II to join him in the intended war against the Dutch, the Stuart King could not be brought to go that far, partly for the reason that the battle fleet then in process of reconstruction, under the administration of Secretary Pepys, was not yet prepared for naval battle. "The most he would agree to was to fit out a small squadron in the spring to make a joint, though pacific demonstration with the French fleet. This would serve as a warning to the Dutch, who had angered him both by opposing English commercial claims in the East Indies and by delaying the return of certain English regiments which he had lent his son-in-law." The preparations actually undertaken "were soon magnified in Holland, where they were quickly followed by retaliatory and far more warlike measures. The Dutch burghers were seriously alarmed. For the first time, William of Orange saw a possibility of enlisting the aid of his fearful and jealous countrymen in a crusade of armed intervention in England to secure his wife's inheritance."[5] The foolish James may be said, then, to have started the last phase of his downfall by an armed demonstration that never got under way.

In drawing on the language of international law, such armed demonstrations may be defined "as the state or condition of one government contending by the threat of force," usually after other ways of diplomacy have been tried in vain. Hence the widely accepted French expression of "persuasion en rade," which follows attempts of persuasion in camera and cabinet. They are among measures short of war. If the original intention of not applying but merely threatening force can be adhered to, they even fall short of measures of forcible redress—retortion, reprisal, embargo, pacific blockade—although any of the measures named are apt to result, should mere demonstration remain ineffective.

To be demonstrative in character, the actions of armed forces must be clearly visible, pointing in a definite direction for a definite purpose. There is often the possibility of misunderstanding; a measure may be interpreted as demonstrative when not intended that way. Again, a demonstration may not be understood as such, at home or abroad, perhaps because it was badly staged. During the agitation over the "Bulgarian atrocities" in 1876, Disraeli insisted that "we must be careful about 'demonstrations' [at the address of the Porte]. Nothing of that kind will do, which is not very effective. Unless it hits the nail on the head, it will be looked on as weak and hysterical."[6]

Demonstrative actions on the part of land forces include calling reservists to the colors, retaining conscripts whose term of service has normally come to an end, provisioning of fortresses as for a siege, movement of troops in the direction of or army maneuvers in the vicinity of the indicated frontiers, recalling military commanders from leave or sending them to deliberate with an ally. In the naval forces, they include movement of ships and squadrons in the direction of the party to be impressed,[7] anchoring in the port of such a nation or off its coast and making ready for action, possibly in connection with an ultimatum to be delivered at the same time. Often the diplomatic representative of the demonstrating Power leaves the capital and goes on board the demonstrating vessels, to return and resume his functions only if and when the ultimatum is accepted. The threat of farther-reaching violence is always involved and must be contemplated beforehand by the Power that demonstrates in the direction of another less strong.

An echec, a failure in a demonstrative action, is bound to lead either to war or to a loss of prestige for the Power attempting it. Such a resounding failure was suffered by a British squadron under Admiral Duckworth before Constantinople early in 1807. Turkey had behaved in a rather challenging manner towards Russia, Britain's ally. Britain wanted to see all of the Tsarist forces directed against Napoleon without the distraction of a war with Turkey. The Porte was encouraged by

Sebastiani, one of Napoleon's general-diplomats, to resist British demands, which were finally presented in the form of an ultimatum with the threat of bombardment by a British squadron lying ready at Tenedos. When the ultimatum was rejected, the British ambassador went on board the squadron. It then sailed up the Dardanelles, burned the Turkish ships found in the Sea of Marmora and appeared before Constantinople on February 21, 1807. Acting according to the advice of Sebastiani, the Turks protracted the negotiations and, with the help of French officers in Sebastiani's suite, strengthened and manned the fortifications along the Straits, through which the British were forced to retire with some losses and without having attained their ends.

Armed demonstrations are the most visible and spectacular acts of secret diplomacy. Occasionally they are tantamount to a public declaration of despair after more peaceful means of persuasion have failed. They spring with seeming abruptness from the darkness of cabinets to the lime-lighted international scene.[8] While they may appear to be spontaneous in character, they seldom are so. In fact, their modalities and their effect, abroad and at home, are as a rule very carefully considered and calculated beforehand by the diplomats, acting alone or in consultation with the army or navy representatives that are to supply the demonstration forces. The latter must be asked what is possible —the units available, the likely effect of material force, the most suitable vehicle, the best locality and season for it. The effect on public opinion has to be considered without giving it much opportunity to be heard beforehand. It will usually find itself deeply committed by the first fait accompli of such a demonstration. Its subsequent criticism will often be limited by national sentiment or by considerations of class politics. The most consistent criticism of armed demonstration as power diplomacy has come from the Cobden-Bright-Gladstone school in Britain, isolationists in America, and Social Democrats in Germany.

In diplomatic practice, armed demonstrations are usually undertaken with the general aim and purpose of posing a threat of war in order to avoid war. The expected effect is that of pars pro toto, the hope that the appearance of a fraction of power will have the desired effect, will inspire the belief that the limited show of force will be followed by more if necessary.

In most cases demonstration forces have been limited to token character. The gunboat Panther, chosen for the demonstration at Agadir in 1911, was one of the smallest boats in the German navy. One measure that went far beyond such a strength was the Roosevelt-staged round-the-world cruise of the United States Navy in 1907-09, which included no less than sixteen armored battleships. Its purpose was manifold, technical no less than diplomatic. While it did not stop the Entente, notably Japan, from continuing in the partition of China, it did serve to make, or keep, the Navy popular with the people at home.

Armed demonstrations are undertaken (1) on the part of a single great Power in order to intimidate a lesser Power; (2) on the part of a combination of Powers, such as the "concert of Europe," or on the part of a more restricted group brought together by common interests against one of the lesser Powers; (3) on the part of one state or group of states roughly equal in power; (4) on the part of one state in order to demonstrate its steadfastness to an alliance already in existence or as part of the preparation of closer ties between Powers not yet allied.[9]

If the demonstration is directed against a weak state, that state will usually give in. It may, however, try to resist with armed force and thus compel the demonstrating Power either to back down or to apply force as threatened and possibly go to war. Should the party demonstrated against be or feel sufficiently strong, it may stage counter-demonstrations.

Ever since a concert of the European Powers came into being in all its infirmity, armed demonstrations, usually by naval contingents, have been used for the purpose of remonstrating with recalcitrant states and to prove to them that there was unanimity of purpose among the great Powers. On certain occasions, as against Turkey towards the end of the nineteenth century or against the Cretan insurgents, all the Powers were represented by ships of their own in order to strengthen the appearance of a firm and unified front. On other occasions, ships of the foremost naval powers acted as the mandatories of the concert. In conformity with the genuine desire of the Congress of Vienna to see the ancient sea plague of the Barbary pirates suppressed at last, Britain and France, and on another occasion Britain and the Netherlands, demonstrated against Algeria and Tunis. Although their demonstration included bombardment of the pirates' lairs, the effect was not a very lasting one.

It was a more fractional concert of the Powers that intervened in the Greek struggle for independence. What was intended as mere demonstration led to unforeseen and far-reaching results. Before the battle of Navarino (October 20, 1827), the British, French, and Russian Governments had agreed to impose an armistice on the belligerents. This was at the very moment when the Turks were resolved to deal the Greek insurgents one final blow, with the help of the Egyptian forces just arrived under the command of Ibrahim Pasha, Mehmet Ali's son. While the Allies' squadrons in the Aegean were able to enforce an armistice on the sea, Ibrahim continued the land war within sight of the Allies. In order to protest more effectively, the fleet sailed into Navarino Bay where his ships were anchored. A shot fired by the enraged Turks led to the historic battle in which the Turkish-Egyptian fleet was destroyed and freedom for Greece determined. This went beyond the original intention of the Allies. Their companionship-in-arms did not long outlast the glorious event.

An unwritten code of international behavior has resulted in certain distinctions as to the application of armed demonstrations. Among the great Powers, demonstrating by means of mobilization measures was found to be rather dangerous, very apt to arouse hostility, and in any case very expensive. It was therefore largely discarded by diplomacy. If measures in that direction were thought to be necessary for military reasons, ostentation was to be avoided rather than sought. The last pre-1914 mobilization measures directed by two great Powers against each other were those made by Austria and Russia during the Balkan crisis of 1913, which were limited to a number of army corps. Mobilization as a gesture became highly inadvisable once certain Powers like Germany, whose initial advantage in war was based on the superior speed of her mobilization, had come to consider it as practically the equivalent of war. Under the prevailing conditions of nationalism, it also had a deep effect on the people that was not easy to terminate or revoke. Mobilization measures aimed as a threat against a smaller Power also became much rarer, often because such a Power happened to be part of the clientèle of a great Power, which was likely to intervene in its favor. Russia, still exhausted from the war of 1904-05, had been unable to do this when Austria brought Serbia, protesting against the annexation of Bosnia, "back to reason" by the deployment of land forces and the appearance of the Danube flotilla before Belgrade.[10]

Some demonstrations by the great Powers, ostensibly directed against Powers unable to resist, were, under the conditions of imperialist competition, actually aimed at a competing great Power or Powers. The Agadir affair in 1911 is an example. As 1914 approached, however, persuasion by the brandishing of armed force became restricted to the Balkan States, so far as Europe was concerned. In extra-European waters it had a much wider sway. Great Powers like the United States and Japan from the end of the nineteenth century were exempted as a matter of course, but few other overseas nations were, unless they proved either good debtors or moderate revolutionaries and as such avoided giving occasion for such intervention. The Drago Doctrine, evolved by the overseas debtors, expressed their protest against the forcible settlement of public debts. Even in the days before it attained the status of a Great Power, the United States was rarely the object of armed demonstrations of hostile intent. Among the few might be included the strengthening by the British of their forces in Canada following the Trent incident. Oftener the demonstrations were friendly, such as the much over-estimated visit of a Russian squadron to American ports during the Civil War.

If armed demonstrations are to give effect to diplomatic threats, they must follow closely on the heels of the latter. The cause-effect connection must be obvious. Armed forces must be available to follow up if not to accompany diplomatic moves in their final stages. This combination first became possible with the establishment of standing forces in Europe, on sea as well as on land. In the application of such forces for demonstrative purposes, the power urges and gesticulations of princely absolutism were united with the rising bourgeoisie's satisfaction at seeing such burdensome and costly forces being made useful in time of peace and without going to war.

The power demonstrations of the pre-steam age, such as military parading and an occasional firing of shipboard guns against land fortifications, had only a superficial effect at best. As yet there was too little calculability in the application of sea power for demonstrative purposes. Wind, weather, the long distances and the difficulties of transporting and maintaining troops, beyond the marines regularly carried by warships, interfered too strongly with demonstrative intentions. In order to be impressive, demonstrations must be not unlike the ceremonial of the courts of the time—planned, studied in effect, stunning to the uninitiated. In addition, the inland effect of demonstrative sea power was very limited. Other ways of convincing overseas nations of the superiority of European power without going to war, such as preaching the gospel or demonstrating technological superiority, did not always prove impressive either. In 1792-93 when the British, working through the Macartney Mission, attempted to open regular diplomatic and trade relations with China, they hoped to demonstrate their superiority quite peacefully by bringing gifts of a scientific nature. They thought to use them, rather than cannon, as door-openers; but the governing intelligentsia in China remained haughty and unimpressed.[11]

Steam fleets and steam locomotives vastly extended the range of power and made it more calculable. They made possible the execution of demonstrations according to plans, lifted above the opposition and deterrence of winds, weather, current and space. The steam locomotive could throw thousands of soldiers in the direction of frontiers where demonstration or counter-demonstration was to take place. The elements could no longer interfere with the timing and dignity which a demonstration needs so much that they are practically

preconditions of its success. The majesty of the machine served as had the symbols of government in earlier times, only now the symbol was also the weapon to impose the sovereign will. Gone were the days when a demonstration was endangered by such hazards of weather and locality as had hung over the initial steps of the French conquest of Algeria. At that time, the French Navy, prior to the landing of troops, had blockaded the ports for two years without making much impression on the Dey, at a cost of seven million francs per year. The enterprise was described as "more dangerous to the squadron than harmful to the State against which it was directed."[12]

The century following 1815 was an era of unprecedented intervention. The interventions often began with an armed demonstration. Whatever the psycho-political urges behind interventionism—and they ranged from humanitarian to economic and power urges—the armed forces now lent themselves much better to such purposes, thanks to their increasing mobility. Armies could be more quickly mobilized, almost as readily as money. (The term 'mobilization' was itself borrowed from the original financial usage.) Mobilization, though costly and at times ruinous, could now be used to strengthen diplomatic moves. While armies did not always prove as ready as their leaders boasted, large parts of the navies always were.

Technical progress furnished diplomacy with new media. The danger lay in the fact that they were often uncontrollable. Armed demonstrations might be carried beyond original diplomatic plans by so-called "military necessity." Since ship and other movements of armed forces might be interpreted in unwelcome ways, the diplomats had on occasion to advise the navies that certain proposed movements, even if technically required, be omitted or postponed. At the time of the opening of the Algeciras Conference, "the mood of the German Emperor was said to be pacific and the tone of German diplomacy was quiet and not aggressive." The same could not be said of the mood of Lord Fisher. Grey begged the civilian head of the British Navy to remember that

> any movements of our ships which could be interpreted as a threat to Germany would be very undesirable at this moment and most unfortunate so long as there is a prospect or even a chance that things may go smoothly at the Morocco Conference which meets today. I hope therefore that the Admiralty won't plan any special cruises or visits to foreign ports or unusual movements of squadrons without consulting the Foreign Office as to the possible political effect. I assume that the present disposition of the Fleet is satisfactory as regards

possibilities between Germany and France; if so, the quieter we keep for the present the better."[13]

Similarly, naval movements of certain Powers in waters touching on zones of imperialist intention are apt to arouse alarms and fears in the people or government of the Power that has been preparing expansion. The presence of a British squadron in Moroccan waters early in 1889 aroused Spanish and French fears that Britain, alone or together with Germany, might aspire to a preponderant position in the Sultanate.[14] It was feared that a German naval demonstration against Morocco in 1895, following the unpunished murder of a German merchant, indicated ulterior motives, much too similar for comfort to those of France herself, against the status quo in the Sultanate.[15] The closer the French grip on Morocco became, the more French sensibilities were provoked when other Powers continued to treat the Sultan as a sovereign and to honor him as such. In such zones of imperialist expansion and susceptibility, naval demonstration, or what was interpreted as such, provoked counter-demonstrations. After the British Channel squadron had steamed by within view of Tangiers, in the spring of 1901, the French minister there thought it appropriate "to eventually have our flag appear under analogous conditions on the coasts of Morocco." Approached by the Quai d'Orsay, the Marine Minister promised such a demonstration for July 1901. At that time a French squadron visited Tangiers for three days, greatly impressing the natives, while the Russian representative helped his French colleague to make the visit still more memorable by demonstrating the firmness of the Franco-Russian alliance in that rathole.[16]

For technical no less than psycho-political reasons, naval forces lend themselves better than military forces to the purposes of demonstration. For one thing, they are practically always more ready for war than land forces and can set out at very short notice. Their movements can more readily be changed from a peaceful to a hostile character—by diverse announcements—and back again, from routine visits and "showing the flag" as the sign of constant readiness to protect national interests abroad to active interference with guns and landing forces. Their movements can be stopped on short notice and their meaning can thus be quickly re-interpreted. Their actions can be easily disavowed as due to the initiative of local or subordinate commanders. As a rule, their action does not seem to engage the demonstrating Power quite as deeply or irrevocably as the similar use of military forces. Nor does their presence leave quite such a deep impression on the collective memory as military enterprises of similar intent

—it seems to vanish like the tracks ships draw in the water, unless there should be a cumulative application, as in nineteenth-century Greece.

Considering the dangerous and potentially far-reaching character of the demonstrative use of armed forces, home governments have usually reserved for themselves the decision as to when and how to apply this weapon. Before the development of means of communication gave them full control over the movements of armed forces even at the most remote points of the globe, they managed to entrust the decision to local representatives, diplomatic, consular, and possibly even naval.[17] The readiness of local officials to invoke armed force in demonstrative and other ways had unfortunately often grown in inverse ratio to the narrowness of their political horizon. A furor consularis, of which Bismarck spoke with reference to Samoan affairs, sometimes combined with that of naval officers, could lead to bombardments and landing operations.

Undeterred by experiences in which the United States had participated in Samoa, the McKinley Administration dispatched the U.S.S. Maine to Key West. The Administration was peacefully inclined but it was driven by public opinion "to do something" in Cuban affairs, and it was subject to incessant appeals from the consul-general in Havana, Fitzhugh Lee. In Key West, the ship was put at the disposal of Lee, to be called upon when necessary for the protection of American lives and property. "Thus, at a time when the whole policy of Mr. McKinley and his administration was still officially directed toward peace, a machine of the most incendiary character had been prepared, ready to be sprung at a touch of the finger by a minor diplomatic official who had given ample evidence of a bellicose temperament."[18] When called in by Consul Lee, the Maine steamed into zones of fearful expectations. According to diplomatic reports, "the movements of North American naval forces in Cuban naval waters and elsewhere seemed fit to make the Spanish Government seriously concerned about the intentions of the Washington Cabinet."[19] But McKinley wanted neither Cuba nor the war. And, with all its bellicosity, the Navy Department would have liked to remove the new and valuable Maine from the doubly unhealthy waters of Cuba. The Spanish Ministry was afraid its presence might lead "through some incident or other to conflict." But the local American powers would not let the ship go: "Ship or ships should be kept here all the time now. We should not relinquish position of peaceful control of situation," Lee telegraphed.[20] And the commander of the Maine suggested that the commanding position given the United States by the arrival of the Maine must not be lessened by replacing her at once by a vessel of less power.[21] The (still unexplained)

destruction of the Maine took the intended "peaceful control of the situation" out of McKinley's
hands.

HISTORICAL ABRÉGÉ

As the use and form of demonstrations are related to the technology of an age, so also are they
related to its social structure and governing forms.
In the nineteenth century, the bourgeoisie surrendered more readily to the modern media of warlike power, steam and electricity, when it was
persuaded that the feeling behind the demonstration of force was ancient. That was tempting to a
society in which the ancient and the new competed
for the dominance of the soul. One of the numerous irritants of the pre-1914 world was provided
by the German gun-boat Panther: it had made
people "jumpy" long before 1911. It had participated, always in a "smart" way, in the blockade
of Venezuela and had sunk a Haitian rebel ship in
1902. This performance was greeted by a telegraphic "Bravo, Panther!" from the Kaiser, which
drove the commander into a frenzy of "smartness"
in South American waters. As a result, the German ambassador had to warn that, in the United
States, "her name alone works like a red rag."
The commander's scant regard for Brazilian sovereignty smashed so much precious diplomatic
porcelain that the Wilhelmstrasse, against much
opposition on the navy's part, caused his recall.
The vessel's wild reputation remained, and, in
1905, the Washington Reich embassy insisted for
that reason that she be kept away from American
ports.[22] Still, it was the same Panther that was
placed before Agadir in 1911.

The limited rationalism or pseudo-rationalism
of nineteenth- and twentieth-century politics found
in armed demonstrations an occasion for the useful—because limited—application of the military
power that the taxpayers supported for such long
periods without visible profit to themselves. As
short-of-war measures, demonstrations could
serve to maintain or restore order in the most
distant parts of the world, teach "the natives"
manners and the rules of international intercourse,
teach them to cut short revolutions harmful to
world trade and to become better customers or
debtors. In 1902 the Haitians were undergoing
another revolution and German traders asked for
a visit by a Reich warship. The German consul
emphasized that "the Negroes are quite particularly receptive to a demonstratio ad oculos"; since
the appearance of German warships three years
ago, "they are much in awe of us. It would be regrettable if this should vanish in the present
stormy period, particularly since we shall probably be most prominently concerned in the later
negotiations about claims."[23]

The naval services have usually proved ready
and willing to render such services to trade and
investment, ranging from demonstrative visits in
foreign ports to serving as a modern silver fleet,
as when British men-of-war carried away Mexican
silver bullion belonging to foreign creditors. Such
services were apt to be remembered when the next
annual naval bill was discussed in the parliaments.
It was then considered practical to have a navy.

How convincing the immediate pay-off resulting
from a mere demonstrative use of men-of-war
could be is shown by the emphasis that the German
burgher put on the action of his ships in distant
waters. This was perhaps the most "rational" factor in the agitation of 1897-98 preceding the passage of the first big naval bill of the Wilhelminic
Empire. Again and again the miserable Lüders
affair in Haiti was taken to show, according to one's
view, either that a navy demonstrating in favor of
German traders paid for itself or that there were
not enough ships available as yet to do this demonstrating properly. "Power that was not made visible could not be believed in," so the argument ran.
Another put it this way: "A German war ship in a
foreign port demonstrates ad oculos the best sides
and qualities of our national character—obedience,
orderliness, discipline, conscientiousness, good
comradeship. The worse the caricatures of German life our enemies and begrudgers know how to
spread abroad, the more usefully a German war
ship demonstrates, now here, now there, an exem-
plar of German kind and German strength." The
traditional argument that to have a navy was good
for trade was still strong. British history was taken
as proof—"more naval protection, more trade; more
trade; more exports." Only advanced business
men, like the elder Rathenau, realized that the
modern navy needed trade even more than trade
needed the navy, that "nowadays only a rich nation
is strong."[24]

The rationale of armed demonstration lies in the
promise that, through it, small means will achieve
much at little additional cost, that power, even if
designed ultimately for war, may well be employed
to help trade. But this kitchen use of power, this
seeming economy has not always turned out well.
Diplomatic and other complications have, for example, followed the show of force off the coast.
Countries with capitals far inland, like Morocco,
Madagascar, and Mexico, have remained unimpressed by mere naval demonstrations. And after
a long and outwardly successful series of interventions in favor of claimants and creditors, the European bourgeoisie came to realize that dangers of a
non-military character might be inherent in armed
demonstrations. They might well prove upsetting to
stock exchanges and aggravate economic crises. As
1914 approached, capitalist demands for intervention by armed demonstration were fewer than they

had been in the balmy days of Palmerstonism. Mere newspaper reports that Italy, unable to bring the war in Tripoli to a good end, had arranged with Russia that the latter would make a naval demonstration in the direction of the Bosporus while Italy would start operations against the Dardanelles, was sufficient to depress all values on the Paris Exchange, including the Russian. Isvolsky thought a Russian démenti was called for, and it was promptly given.[25] When the Italian fleet finally bombarded the Dardanelles, the European press was more or less agreed that nothing pointed to an intention of forcing the passage "and that it had restricted itself to a simple demonstration."[26] As such it left the Turks unimpressed. What it did to the Balkan governments by way of chain reaction is still another matter.

The fact that naval estimates might also depend on the vote of clerical parties or other churchly interests made the navies relatively eager defenders of the co-national missionary interest abroad. The murder of German Catholic missionaries in Shantung made the Catholic Center Party more eager to endorse the Reich Navy's plans for the acquisition of Kiachow. In France, the separation of Church and State deprived French diplomacy and the French Navy of various opportunities to render such protection.[27] This was a task in which newcomers, such as the Germans and Italians, threatened to—and did—replace them.

While persuasion en rade was something relatively unmistakable in intent to those to whom it was addressed, other armed demonstrations—marches, reinforcements, etc.—remained often less unequivocal, notably military movements along the as yet undetermined frontiers of civilization, and expansion by great Powers. When, between the Jameson Raid and the outbreak of the Boer War, the question of reinforcing the British garrison in South Africa was under consideration in the Cabinet, the question centered on "how we are to intimidate Kruger without provoking him," while the effect upon British opinion at home and in the Colonies had also to be taken into account.[28]. The Russians and the British would alarm one another from time to time by their military measures along, if not beyond, their military frontier zones in Central Asia. The "meaning" of such moves would be variously interpreted by the soldiers, the diplomats, and the press. In one of his most mischievous moods, during the tense Doggerbank episode, William II would advise "Nicky" to make some military demonstration along the Perso-Afghan frontier "where the British think you powerless to appear with troops during the war."

Even should the forces at your disposal not suffice for a real attack on India itself, they would do for Persia—which has no army—and a pressure on the Indian frontier from Persia will do wonders in England, and have remarkably quieting influence upon the hot-headed jingoes in London. For I am aware and informed that this is the only thing they are afraid of, and that the fear of your entry into India from Turkestan and into Afghanistan from Persia was the real and only cause that the guns of Gibraltar and of the British fleet remained silent three weeks ago. India's loss is the deathstroke to Great Britain.[29]

DEMONSTRATION POLITICS IN THE MEDITERRANEAN: PALMERSTON TO GLADSTONE

The blustering diplomacy of Palmerston found its characteristic medium in the demonstrative use of British men-of-war. In its appeal to British pride and even humanitarianism, the civis Romanus sum cry was happily combined with that of the real, or apparent, utilitarianism in the peace-time employment of British vessels. The British trader and usurer could be confident, as Palmerston put it, that "the watchful eye and the strong arm of England will protect him against injustice and wrong." It was the Don Pacifico case of 1849 that occasioned Palmerston's civis Romanus sum speech. It did not greatly jar the man in the street if it turned out that British warships occasionally, as in this case, intervened in favor of a Portuguese Jew under British protection and in favor of a claim that proved vastly—one hundred and forty per cent— exaggerated when finally examined by British commissioners. To quote the politico-lawyer's understatement: "Obviously the right of reprisal was in this case exercized by Great Britain with excessive rigor."[30]

Greece was repeatedly the address of the demonstrative use of British men-of-war. They blockaded the Piraeus in 1847 in order to force her to pay the interest on a debt contracted under very onerous conditions after the end of the war of independence. A joint British-French naval demonstration during the Crimean War was designed to keep pro-Russian sympathies in Greece from becoming active in Thessaly. The Piraeus was occupied during the greater part of the war for no good reason and under conditions humiliating enough to arouse nationalistic discontent against the foreign-born King Otto.

Next to Greece, Turkey was most often the target of naval demonstrations on the part of some or all of the great Powers. In order to protect her from Russian and Austrian demands to surrender Kossuth and the other Revolutionary refugees in and around Constantinople, the British and French governments kept squadrons near, and at last inside, the Straits. These were at the disposal of their ambassadors to the Porte. Palmerston wanted to have them recalled late in 1849.

They were inside the Dardanelles, contrary to the Treaty of 1841, and he did not want to give the Russians any reason to base any action on their part on treaty infraction by the Western Powers. For a time, the prayers of the Western ambassadors to leave the ships at their disposal prevailed, but in January 1850 the French vessels and, a little later, the British vessels were recalled. The British public fondly believed that the two Emperors had backed down when faced by the two Western fleets at the Straits. In Britain, this became a very firm and enduring article of faith.

Whether we call the Crimean War "a just but unnecessary war" or "an unjust but [above all psychologically] necessary war," it originated, as far as the various publics were concerned, with a number of demonstrative acts. Prince Menchikov, a Russian general and admiral, was sent to Constantinople on a special diplomatic mission. In order to give added weight to the Russian grievances against the Porte, he was carried there by a squadron, which remained anchored off the Bosporus while the negotiations proceeded (February-March 1853). On March 19, a French cabinet council, presided over by Napoleon III, resolved to send a squadron into the Eastern Mediterranean. This decision was announced in the Moniteur the following day, and the fleet left Toulon on the 23rd, headed for the Aegean Sea. A corresponding move on Britain's part followed early in June 1853. The Government, however, was still hesitant to grant the disposal of the fleet to the ambassador to the Porte, a "fearful power to place in the hands of any Minister, involving, as it does, the question of peace and war,"[31] as Lord Aberdeen, the most peaceful of the ministers, put it. As yet, the violent Turkophile Ambassador Stratford Canning was denied the "discretionary authority" that he wanted to call the fleet inside the Straits, though it seemed to one of the ministers "the least measure that will satisfy public opinion and save the Government from shame hereafter, if, as I firmly believe, the Russian hordes will pour into Turkey from every side." Such an intention seemed indicated by the movements of Russian troops into the Danube Principalities. Thus the two sides became deeply engaged. It was their psychological readiness for war that brought on military measures, and not vice versa. The movements of armed forces negated the efforts of diplomats to avert war. The bellicose British public wanted their armed forces close to the center of the conflict and not in the military camp at Cobham or on the roadstead of Spithead, where Army and Navy were paraded in the summer of 1853. These were mere displays "arranged to avoid honest aid to Turkey," as the bellicose Daily News cried out.[32]

When news of public disturbances in Constantinople reached London in September, Stratford Canning was authorized to call the fleet inside the Straits for the protection of the Sultan and the lives and property of British subjects. To the Russians, the measure was defended as justified by their march into the Danube Principalities. "We passed the Rubicon when we first took part with Turkey and sent our squadron to her support,"[33] wrote Palmerston in retrospect. Napoleon's foreign minister denied that this "demonstration was aggressive. We do not invite the Porte to start hostilities against Russia who is in peace with us; we come to protect her in a European interest against sudden attacks."[34] The sight of the squadrons greatly encouraged the Turks, who, on the refusal of the Russians to evacuate the Principalities, declared war on them. Thus they hoped to obtain more help from the Western Powers than the diplomats had given them reason to expect.

The final plunge into war, which the Western diplomats had come to consider "unavoidable," was due to the action of the armed forces. As was clearly foreseen in London by the Queen, the Prince-Consort, and the Prime Minister, the Turks were courting armed conflict. Contrary to the strong advice of the Allied diplomats, they sent their fleet cruising in the Black Sea. A superior Russian squadron caught up with it and destroyed it at Sinope, with the British squadron only a few miles away. Was this challenge to the protectress of the seas, whose guardianship extended even to the barbarian Turk, to go unanswered? The British press emphatically declared No, and the Government echoed a feebler No.

Whereas the mere demonstration of sea and land power had had a very precipitating effect, the action of the land and sea forces during the war proved slow in effecting a settlement. One of the demonstrative acts during the war, Austria's threat to Russia, expressed by her army mobilization, forced Russia to evacuate the Principalities. This proved to have the longest and strongest after-effect. Russia accused Austria of ungratefulness for the help rendered her against the Revolution in 1849, and later favored Prussia against the Double Monarchy in 1866 and 1870. Prussia had bound herself to an agreement with Austria to place an army along the Russian frontier, should certain eventualities arise. But when Austria one day declared that these had arisen, Prussia denied that they had. King Frederick William IV called Bismarck from Frankfurt for consultation. "Mobilize an army, not along the Polish frontier but rather around Oppeln [in Silesia], then You can dictate the peace to Europe," he told the King. Frederick's nervous system was not equal to such bold proposals, which put more trust in the Prussian Army than did the King himself.

Besides, he thought that Prussia "had not enough money for demonstrations."[35] Demonstration by mobilization could indeed be costly. Such demonstrations proved ruinous to Austria's finances during and after the Crimean War.

Neither the depressing experience of the Crimean War, which had originated in demonstrations, nor its disappointing results cured the British governors and people of their penchant for demonstrative politics. John Bright called this habit "the monstrous insolence and guilt of British agents abroad who so readily have recourse to violence on the smallest pretext." When a hostile, anti-interventionist parliamentary combination defeated Palmerston over the issue of the flag-insult to the Arrow lorcha—a vessel as doubtful in her true British character as Don Pacifico—he dissolved the Parliament. The electorate returned him and his like rather than the Manchester Radicals. The first British minister to Peking, Bruce, brought on another war with China by his insistence on taking the river route of the Peiho to the capital, "the road of honor," rather than the overland road, as the Chinese had suggested. Bent on forcing open the "road of honor," he called in a small British squadron. But its passage was heavily opposed and it was forced to retire with a heavy loss of men and face (January 1860). While Bright and his friends tried to avoid a full-fledged war, Lord John Russell was inclined to back up the Minister from the outset. He "thought the nation would have complained if the Fleet had left the Peiho without an attempt to go up the river."[36]

These incidents were part and parcel of the power politics of nineteenth-century British Liberalism, whose leaders, quite as much as an enlightened Tory like the later Lord Salisbury, were aware "that whatever folly or madness an English Government may commit, the appeal to the civis Romanus sum doctrine is rarely without its effect upon an English audience."[37] Palmerston's "roaring like a lion in the southern and eastern seas" was quite in keeping with "his lamb-like bleating at home," Salisbury wrote after the Navy had burned down a Japanese village in retaliation for the murder of an Englishman by unidentified brigands in another part of the island. A fleet was dispatched to Brazil in 1862-63 and, without allowing further opportunity for inquiry and explanation, seized Brazilian merchant ships. Under the threat of bombarding Rio de Janeiro, they exacted humiliating apologies and the promise to punish innocent officials, "all on account of what turned out to have been a purely imaginary insult said to have been offered to three half-tipsy British sailors."[38]

Palmerston's bluff was called by the German land forces, who disregarded his threats of 1863-64 to send the British fleet into the Baltic and thereby stop their war against little Denmark. Bismarck would not be intimidated and thus British prestige was dealt one of its worst blows. "The European dictatorship which England was arrogating to herself, particularly with regard to Germany, and which was reminiscent of Louis XIV and the first Napoleon, was no longer to be suffered," Bismarck told the Austrian ally, who was still inclined to be impressed.[39] Even as early as this, Bismarck proved highly sceptical of mere armed demonstrations, and Napoleon III knew him well enough to doubt that these would have any effect on him. After Sadowa, when Austria sent Beust to Paris in order to move the Emperor to intervene, he found him a very sick man and little inclined to make a move. "He kept on stammering: 'I am not ready for war!'" And he could not be brought even to stage the armed demonstration that Beust proposed to him: "I do not demand, Sire, that you make war; I am in spite of everything too good a German to wish for that; but that is not the question. You have 100,000 men at Chalons; send them in the direction of the frontier; let a squadron depart for the Northern Seas; that is all that is necessary. The line of operations of the Prussian Army is already so far drawn out that it would be forced to come to a halt thereby."[40] But Napoleon would not move, and the military experts at Bismarck's elbow were certain he could not very well do so.[41]

Disraeli was plainly the successor of Palmerston in supplying the flamboyance and exaltation which the sober-minded British at times need so much. While the soot settled on Manchester, he brought British imperialist imagination along the road to India, an imperialist-military conception in the creation of which literati like Laurence Oliphant and Disraeli himself played as large a role as the diverse material interests. The striking acts of this imperialism were the creation of the Empress of India (1876-77), the acquisition of control of the Suez Canal, and the support of the Turk. Disraeli, "a Prime Minister of Oriental extraction and imagination," as his biographer called him, was much more inclined to see Turkey as a going concern than were statesmen of the Continental Powers. In his most oratorical flights, Constantinople was "the key of India, and not Egypt and the Suez Canal."[42]

Britain's modest though highly self-righteous role in the "war in sight" episode of 1875 made Disraeli believe that "since Pam we have never been so energetic, and in a year's time we shall be more."[43] A new Eastern crisis was in the making. At first, British "masterly inactivity" did nothing to alleviate the growing crisis in and around Turkey. Then the sending of a British fleet to Besica Bay in May 1876 brought the fever up several degrees. The Porte greeted this "as a harbinger of a British alliance such as twenty years ago led to the Crimean War," as The Times reported from Constantinople.[44] The same memory haunted the Queen, who objected to the demonstration. But Disraeli told her that the fleet had "not been ordered to the Mediterranean to protect Christians or Turks [the excuse before public opinion], but to uphold Your Majesty's Empire. Had Your Majesty sanctioned the Berlin Memorandum, Constantinople would at this moment have been garrisoned by Russia and the Turkish fleet placed under Russian protection."[45]

The assertion was preposterous. Russian intentions were as yet far from anything so extreme. In fact, they stuck more closely to a European concert in the reopened Oriental question than did the British government. In October, following the Serbian attack on Turkey, which Russia brought to a stop by imposing an armistice, the Tsar proposed that the Powers send their navies inside the Straits in order to dominate the situation. An honest proposal, the German ambassador in St. Petersburg thought. The Tsar rightly saw "in a great joint maritime demonstration beneath the Sultan's windows a way to force him to back down, to protect him against the ire of his own people and avert a land war." Even Bismarck, who never liked joint naval demonstrations, was willing to agree, provided all the Powers participated, especially England, without whose entry the naval contingents of the Powers in the Levant could effect nothing.[46]

While attempts were still being made to settle—or postpone—the Turkish question by conference diplomacy, Disraeli thought that Constantinople was greatly threatened by a Russian military attack and, almost worse, Britain threatened by a most serious loss of prestige: "Constantinople occupied by the Russians while the British fleet was in Besica Bay, would be the most humiliating event that has occurred to England since the surrenders of Burgoyne and Cornwallis, but infinitely more important and disastrous."[47] The Turks were supplied with military advice from the British, but not with much more, though the moving of the fleet inside the Straits in case of a Russian attack on them was contemplated as early as October 1876. While the Russo-Turkish War went through its first year, Disraeli's policy was one of demonstrations against Russian military successes, such as the strengthening of British garrisons in the Mediterranean by bringing Indian troops into that sea. The British military thought that this was merely wasteful. Only a large-size military expedition could promise relief to the Turks and would not deceive foreign diplomacies. Such movements were in tune with the music-hall ditty of the day—"We don't want

to fight, but by Jingo, if we do...,"—while Gladstone's Turkophobia represented "the other England." England was divided, her trade depressed. This condition made some more bold, some more cautious. It made the Queen wish she were a man and could give the Russians a beating. And it made demonstrations such as the intended sending of the Fleet up the Dardanelles in January 1878 more unconvincing than ever. Even the Turks begged that it be put off for a while, as it would merely offer the Russians a pretext for seizing their capital. Gladstone denounced the measure as "an act of war, a breach of European law."

Russia's closer approach to the Straits changed British indecision to panic. The fleet was ordered to go inside the Straits. The Tsar stormed. He would not quietly suffer this insult.[48] And the Russian commander-in-chief warned that in this case his troops would occupy Constantinople, as they were in a position to do. But this time neither the Russian threat nor the wish of the Sultan to postpone the measure were of any avail. Britain would make herself "utterly ridiculous and lose all weight in Europe" should she agree to postponement, as even Salisbury, the least Turkophile in Disraeli's cabinet, insisted.[49] On February 13, the Fleet sailed up the Dardanelles and anchored in the Marmora Sea. The Russian commander-in-chief, knowing his army to be exhausted, acted on his own discretion. He cut himself off the wire to his brother, the Tsar, and thus worked for peace far better than Disraeli and the Cabinet or the Queen. But Britain could not avert the exacting Peace of San Stefano at the time. Before it could be softened in its terms by the Congress of Berlin, Bismarck's mediation had to disengage the Russian Army and the British Fleet from their "Platonic war" and arrange for their removal from the Straits to points equidistant from Constantinople. Anything else would have been unbearable to the British state of mind. On the other hand, care had to be taken that the Russian Army not be obliged to retire before the British Navy, which, as the later-comer, had to retreat first.[50]

The decisions laid down by the Congress of Berlin were not executed without some obstruction on the part of the Turks. They refused to evacuate the small port of Dulcigno, assigned to Montenegro, and made difficulties over the boundary settlement with Greece. In their resistance they relied on dissensions among the Powers, in the main those of Austria and Russia, about Balkan politics. While the Tsar was anxious to let Montenegro have Dulcigno, Austria cared little to see the Balkan Slavs gain better access to the Adriatic. Bismarck, whose favor the Porte had sought in the summer of 1880 by applying for German military and other instructors, was reluctant to take a hand in the enforcement of the Congress mandate, lest he incur the dissatisfaction of either Russia or Austria, or both. Besides, he did not believe in the effectiveness of armed demonstration such as the Gladstone Government came to propose in the autumn of 1880. To him it seemed that "Dulcigno was a nonsense. Since Tsar Alexander has pledged his word that Montenegro must have Dulcigno, the town is first turned into a heap of debris," all because "Gladstone was a crazy professor."[51] The French Government was equally reluctant. Like Germany and Austria, she was unwilling to proceed beyond a naval demonstration. And this would be ineffective, "an impotent measure which will not avoid hostilities being carried on inland while the Allied navies are cruising off the coast." France would not even spare the few battalions that might then become necessary, because every one was needed for the ever-threatening war with Germany.[52]

The driving force of Gladstone, newly returned to power, brought the Powers to dispatch ships, which assembled at Gravosa in mid-September. Under the chairmanship of the British admiral, the naval commanders deliberated ways and means to help Montenegro get what was by rights hers. The first step was to be the evacuation of the Europeans from the town, the next a summons to the Turkish local authorities to hand over the place within a given period. But should they decline to do that, what then? Should force be applied? Canons à mer against rocky shores did not seem very promising. Besides, the French admiral was instructed to act in such a way that he would not be bound to participate in any coercive measure, while at the same time he was to avoid the appearance of disagreeing with the other admirals. "The concert of Europe became instantly what Mr. Gladstone called a farce, for Austria and Germany made known that under no circumstances would they fire a shot" (Morley). Gladstone and his people were placed in a certain dilemma. There was at most only a moral interest of Britain involved. The only Great Power truly interested in the transfer of Dulcigno was Russia, whom Gladstone's policy of principle thus came to serve.

The problem of action, should the Turk prove obdurate (as he did), had not been considered beforehand in the British Cabinet. They now conceived the idea of shifting the scene of coercive activity to Smyrna in order to lay hands on the receipts of the customs house there, which the Porte could not well afford to lose. Only Russia and Italy were ready to go along. Bismarck, the concert master of Europe, would not even confer a mandate on them: "No, we abstain, but as well-wishers, should be glad if there is success, but doubt this, hence give no mandate."[53] Learn-

ing of the British proposal, but unaware of the unwillingness of the three Powers to participate, the Sultan thought better and pledged evacuation. In order to make the decision stick, the British now proposed that the intervention squadron be kept together for some time to come; but the French, and Bismarck, who was anxious to get out of this uncomfortable company, did not favor the continuance of "a combination that would expose us, on a new or larger scale, to the perils and the expense of the naval demonstration."[54] No new complications arose, and on November 30 Montenegro could thank the Powers for their intervention on her behalf. The effect was entirely due, as Gladstone testified on his own behalf, "not to a threat of coercion from Europe but to the knowledge that Great Britain had asked Europe to coerce."[55] Bismarck, however, spoke of the episode as "a pitiful adventure." He bitterly reproached Gladstone, partly because he had improvised an enterprise which ought to have been thought through to the last detail, partly because of quite different concepts of the uses of power.[56] Bismarck could hardly bring himself to believe in the possibility of applying force in the name of Europe—qui parle Europe a tort. Gladstone was over-ready to see power (and British power alone if the others would not join) justified in the name of Europe, and preferably in favor of such a small Christian principality as Montenegro. His political eye was altogether blind to her powers for mischief-making.[57]

The fixing in detail of the Greek-Turkish frontier again raised the question of applying the force of the Concert against the two parties immediately concerned. While Bismarck was ready to agree to a settlement by way of arbitration, he insisted that there must be agreement beforehand as to the practical execution of a judgment. In his view, the other Powers were too ready to rely on the prestige of the Concert. He told the British that "public opinion and the political situation in Germany make it absolutely prohibitive for the Government to claim the country's resources for warlike enterprises in which our own interests are not engaged." The diplomacy he directed induced the two governments at Athens and Constantinople to accept the decision of Europe even without the threat of force.[58] But in 1886, when the boundaries had been drawn by officers of the Powers, public opinion in Greece would not agree to them or to the status quo in the Balkans. Once more, the Powers had to consider the applicability of a naval demonstration "with moral effect in order to weigh on the Government and give it strength to resist the currents of public opinion." Britain, with all her Philhellenism, was the driving force in the attempt to "bring Greece to reason" by maritime pressure. The other Powers, even Russia, were agreeable. France, however, proved unwilling to coerce a nation for whose emancipation she had done so much in years gone by and whose army a French military mission was just then trying to reorganize. She was even willing to allow the war between Greece and Turkey for which Greece was preparing. Germany and Britain, "exasperated at this fresh threat of disturbance," wanted no dangerous complications in the Balkans that might arise in connection with Bulgarian events. They remained determined to keep the peace, which was endangered by recent Greek threats of a descent on the Turkish coast. A blockading squadron of the Powers, minus France, arrived at the Piraeus in February 1886 with instructions to declare a blockade of Greek ports and to sequester and if necessary destroy Greek merchant ships. The ministers, with the exception of the French, left Athens after their ultimatum that armaments be stopped had received an unsatisfactory answer. On French advice, Greece stopped further land armaments. The Powers, utterly fed up with Greek procrastination, remained unsatisfied. In May they proclaimed a blockade that lasted into June and served to keep the country out of the war that Serbia had undertaken against Bulgaria.[59]

Europe, i.e., (in Gladstone's phrase) "the united Powers of Europe who in such a case represent the civilized world,"[60] had two mandatories in Egypt—Britain and France. Before 1919, the mandate "system" was informal, unwritten, and very fluid. The Arabi movement of 1881, anti-European as well as anti-Turk in character, soon posed the problem of intervention for the reluctant Powers. As the Gladstone Government fixed the moment of imperilment for European interest, intervention should take place once a state of anarchy had been reached. Who was to intervene at that moment? According to the French representative on the spot, the consul-general in Cairo, France must in any case be first, in order to maintain her old prestige. Accordingly, he proposed in August 1881 that a squadron be assembled in the Piraeus in order to steam to Alexandria at the first signal. "Should the Malta fleet arrive ahead of us, the consequences would be disastrous for us."[61]

Later in the year, it was agreed between Britain and France that they would be the sole interveners. France strongly resisted British attempts to have other Powers participate with demonstration ships. She also denied the use of French military forces, should the landing of troops become necessary. Somewhat against her original intentions, Britain was more and more pressed in the direction of unilateral intervention. Since May 1882 a British and a French squadron had been lying in the harbor of Alexandria. The question raised by the British beforehand, whether their mere presence would have any effect in Cairo, was soon answered in the negative. Egyptian nationalism was as unimpressed by persuasion en rade as most other inland-nationalisms. This confirmed Bismarck's pessimistic forecasts: "Nothing can be done with the fleet without a landing force, and this is not at hand, and so it will be merely a repetition of the demonstration before Dulcigno. There the rocks were in the way, here the warehouses with European merchandise; without that, they would probably have been bombarded already... So there they are, with their ships, in a blind alley."[62] When Arabi's land forces threw up fortifications against the demonstrating seapower, the British admiral was instructed to warn them to stop, and to open fire against the earth works, should his warning prove ineffective. Gladstone attempted to remain firm "against extravagant proposals generated in the atmosphere of the services." Nevertheless, "the eagerness of War and Navy Departments to organize forces and ships for 'operations' in Egypt," as John Bright saw it, led to the bombardment of Alexandria (July 11, 1882).[63] The French ships had steamed away. They declined to share in this "act of war." They could not participate without the consent of the Chambre and the majority there were still fascinated by the traditional conviction that France's civilizing mission in Egypt was incompatible with gun-fire. Furthermore, the dread of Germany made it impossible to spare troops beyond those already employed in "Tunisification." It was in vain that the ambassador in London warned that Britain, if left alone, would make herself "the mandatory of Europe."[64] For Gladstone, "a situation of force had been created which could only be met by force." In this way he defended the action to John Bright, who was inclined to consider all use of military force as approximating unlawfulness.[65] The British followed up the action of the fleet by landing an expeditionary force and taking over military control of the Suez Canal. France declined to enter the still waiting bus headed in the direction of condominium and thus came to miss it. In vain did she afterwards maintain that "the success of the British arms in Egypt could not modify, in point of law, the situation of that country."[66] In point of fact, it did.

NAVAL DEMONSTRATIONS OF THE THIRD REPUBLIC

The fear of Germany and certain concepts of her own mission civilisatrice occasionally hampered Republican French governments in the demonstrative use of her armed forces. Although they proved "gun-shy" under the pressure of public opinion in Greece and Egypt, there was no hesitation when it came to using force in the more clearly colonial ventures, in Tonking, Madagascar, and North Africa. Control over Tunis was acquired and carried through by a combined application of French land and sea forces, largely demonstrative in nature, at least in the initial stages.

Wrought up by the acquisition of a Tunisian railway line by rival Italian interests, the French Government stationed three armored ships before Tunis in August 1880 and instructed its diplomatic representative to make use of their presence to obtain certain concessions for France. At the same time, the Governor-General of Algiers was informed by Foreign Minister Freycinet that "we have a great interest in having an important and loud (bruyant) demonstration of troops taking place along the frontier of Tunisia and at the earliest possible moment." There was, however, to be no crossing of the frontier. That would come later, when depredations of Tunisian troops would give the welcome pretext for French troops to march into the Bey's possessions. The Bey was duly impressed by the warships. In fact, he gave the chargé rather more than the Government had wanted. France owed her success "not only to the energetic language and demonstrations on the part of our Government but also to the pretensions and the unheard-of clumsiness of the Italians which in the end exasperated the Bey." The Bey was assured by the chargé that the presence of French warships was sanction of the "guarantee which I had given His Highness against any danger" and was sanction against all the indemnity demands of the Italians. When Freycinet ordered that the demonstrative presence of the ships be cut short, the chargé begged that they be left in Tunis until Italy had calmed down. Her extreme irritation might still disquiet the Bey. This was granted for a time, though it still took Italy many years to recover her calm and agree to French control.[67]

"Tunisification" was much less rapidly achieved outside of Tunis. When the tidal wave of imperialism struck the shores of Madagascar in the early 1880's, the Malagasy proved opposed to the march of civilization. "Back in Paris they had imagined that a naval demonstration would suffice to bring about the submission of Madagascar," as one of the minister-residents in that island admitted. After the island-queen had turned down an ultimatum demanding immediate and complete compliance with French demands, Tamatave was bombarded and some companies of marines landed. But "the Malagasy Government fortified itself by passive resistance which could not be overcome. It became necessary to enter upon negotiations."[68] A treaty was concluded in 1886

which put the conduct of Madagascar's foreign relations into French hands and established a French agent in the capital. This gave the French more than the Malagasy thought they had surrendered, but it did postpone the far from peaceful penetration for a number of years.

The fall of Ferry in 1885 turned the French gaze back to the trouée des Vosges and put off the execution of further plans against Madagascar and Siam. By 1891, the French coloniaux resumed their aggression against Siam, which had been strengthened in its resistance, morally rather than militarily, by Britain. French warships appeared off the Siamese coast in 1893. They were followed by British vessels, whose appearance rather stiffened Siamese resistance. The French naval commander on the spot made a diplomatic understanding more difficult by ignoring a message from the French minister there and proceeding to Bangkok. He made ready to bombard that capital the following day, until he was dissuaded by the Minister, who himself presented the Siamese with far-reaching demands. These were backed up by a "pacific blockade," very harmful to British trading interests and to British sensibilities. Britain accused France of misusing her power by oppressing a small people. Nothing so "cynically vile" was on record, Rosebery wrote to the Queen. Franco-British tension led close to war, which was averted by concessions at the expense of Siam and incidentally at the expense of the prestige of British sea power.[69] As one German general wrote to another at the time: "The attitude of the British Government in the Siamese question exposes it to the ridicule of the whole world. The famous English Navy showing a fair pair of heels to the French admiral is an occurrence unprecedented in history. That's the kind of people arm in arm with whom we are supposed to impress Europe."[70] Within a week of the Siamese crisis, the Russians, equally impressed by the British failure in the conflict, yielded to French "importunities" and promised the visit to Toulon that took place with considerable éclat in October 1893. This was another demonstration of the fact that the two Powers had found their way together, and against Britain first.

Kronstadt and Toulon

Toulon, and the Kronstadt episode before that, opened and characterized a new era in the style of diplomacy, that of the demonstrative alliance. The alliance was initiated and maintained in the open by naval demonstrations on the part of two distant Powers who were to fight a common war on land, though the war against Britain was at first uppermost in Russian thought. Since the two could not fight side by side, they demonstrated

together. Only by movements of their ships could
Russia and France come into visible contact and
show their peoples that the meeting of the twain
was feasible. Demonstration by the navies and, to
a far lesser extent, by the armies served to bring
together and keep united two peoples who had
little in common except their enemies and who had
to cover up the dissimilarity between bourgeois
republic and Tsarist autocracy. Through these
demonstrations the peoples of the two countries
were given a kind of pseudo-participation in and
a pseudo-democratic control over the alliance
for war.

The style-setter in this novelty, as in so many
other fashions, was bourgeois France. It was
she who grasped for the hand of the alliance partner, both by secret diplomacy and by public
gesturing. In August 1890, the ambassador at St.
Petersburg was asked by his home office whether
the visit of a French squadron in the Baltic and
at Kronstadt late in the month seemed opportune.
He advised that it was not. It would coincide with
a meeting of German, British and Austrian naval
units off Alsen, to be followed shortly by a visit
of William II to St. Petersburg. After some more
inquiries, the Tsar indicated that a French
squadron would be welcome in the month of July
1891. The announcement of counter-demonstrations by Germany and England followed in due
course. William II was to visit England and a
British squadron was to visit Venice—both events
scheduled for July. They hinted at a closer British approach to the Triplice, which had just been
renewed. However, as if to efface the appearance
of belonging to such an exclusive alliance, the
British Government invited the French squadron
to visit Portsmouth on its return from the Baltic.
On their outbound voyage, the French paid a
visit to Copenhagen where mixed sentiments—a
Nordic feeling of revanche for 1864, sympathiz-
ing with France, and dynastic ties with Britain—
made for an awkward reception. But at least there
was a bourgeoisie in Denmark to welcome the
bourgeois French mariners. This element, the
French ambassador in St. Petersburg warned his
Government, would be missing in the Russian
port. Would the police allow "the people" to assemble and greet the visitors? If it did, this
would practically mean that Russia favored the
ties with France.

The reception given the sailors in Kronstadt-
Petersburg was frenetic. Three hours of hurrahs
without an interruption, the French ambassador
reported to his Government, was proof that "the
French and Russian souls beat in concord." And
the Court stood up while the Marseillaise was
played. But must the French visit England immediately afterward? France was not "very constant in her amours," the public voice would say.

However, the ministers agreed, "we must not
get into trouble with Britain. That's why we go to
Portsmouth, in spite of the indignant outcry of
some journals." State visits were as primitively
motivated as private ones, if not more so. Before
the fleet reached Portsmouth, however, it had to
be arranged that Victoria's grandson, Prince
Henry of Prussia, who was on a family visit to
Osborne, not be present at the review. The French
ambassador told Downing Street officials that
"our sailors come to Portsmouth in order to be
reviewed by the Queen, and not by a Prussian
prince." This, at any rate, was in his report,
which might have been bolder than the fact.

The visit went off without any unpleasant incident. The Marseillaise was listened to by the
Court standing up, but the temperature in which
the exchange of politenesses took place was distinctly lower than in Russia. Only three hundred
French sailors were given land leave, only the
best elements, no drunkards. "The junior officers mixed little with the English," so the official
French description reads; "the memory of their
reception in Russia was still intact and their
sympathies are exclusively Russian. Following
the kind of adoration which the Russian population
had lavished on them, they could not help finding
the English reception rather cool."[71] On the
English side "the invitation appeared [and no doubt
was intended to appear] as an assertion of England's resolved detachment from the enmities of
her friends." And when the moderate shouting
was over, Salisbury wrote the Queen: "Though in
the present state of Europe our interests lie on
the side of the Triple Alliance, it is most important to persuade the French, if we can, that England
has no antipathy to France, or any partisanship
against her."[72]

The French found it quite beyond their power
to believe this. They continued to woo Russia by
way of secret diplomacy and public demonstration. In the latter might be included the showing
of the Kronstadt interviews in the Paris waxworks,
in pre-movie days the most popular medium of
political optics.[73] Would not the Russians like
their Mediterranean squadron to meet the French
squadron in the Piraeus in February or March of
1892? They obliged, and French diplomacy was
convinced that the meeting made a good impression on Greece and probably also on Italy and
Britain, the other contestants for the dominium
maris in that sea. The Russians, however, were
slow to repay the French visit to Kronstadt. For
one thing, the Russians did not quite trust the
effect of such fraternization on their sailors. A
revolutionary germ might be imparted. While
waiting for them to come, the French continued
their diplomacy by demonstration, from army to
army, from navy to navy. A French squadron

greeted the Italian King in Genoa in September 1892, during the Columbus centenary. It was feted by the Italian Francophiles, without putting Berlin and Vienna too much out of humor, as French diplomacy thought.[74] Little did they reckon with the painful counter-arrangement for the next year. The Italian Crown Prince was to be present at the German maneuvers that took place in the lost provinces of Alsace-Lorraine. In this way he underwrote, so to speak, the annexation.

At long last the promised Russian counter-visit was obtained. In order to make this entree more striking, it was agreed that the visitors would visit only in France and nowhere else.[75] Public announcement of the forthcoming visit to Toulon was made at the moment when the Kaiser and his Italian guest made a triumphal entry into Metz.[76] It was answered at once by the announcement of a British naval visit to Italian ports, on Italian invitation. And this in turn was answered by an ostentatious visit of the Tsar, who was staying with Danish relatives, to a visiting French squadron.[77]

The visit to Toulon in October 1893, and of a large part of the crews to Paris, marked the high point of diplomacy by naval demonstration. It meant many and various things: to the peoples of the Central Powers it was a proof of encirclement; to the British, a challenge to her just then rather uncertain naval supremacy in the Mediterranean, which had been threatened since 1888 by the concentration of naval power at Toulon;[78] while to the French people, who threw themselves at the visitors in an almost bacchanalian frenzy, it proved that they were "no longer alone"; the Times thought it "perhaps the most remarkable outburst of international feeling ever witnessed." That the events helped directly towards the conclusion of the written instrument that the French Government truly wanted is less certain—public enthusiasm was not a thing to move Alexander III in the desired direction.[79]

The scheduled British naval visit was eagerly expected by the Italians. They would consider a postponement of the visit for reasons of public health as something that would be "interpreted throughout Europe as a severe slap in the face of Italy which she did not deserve after her loyal support of British foreign policy." The visit was also urged by the Foreign Office, "most desirous (a) not to offend the Italians who had taken up the visit with great good will, (b) to produce some counter-blast to the Toulon demonstration."[80] Instead, the British temperament took Toulon as a cue for a naval scare at home. The British naval visits to Taranto and La Spezia in October were marked by an absence of enthusiasm, due

more to a fault of the British than of the Italian temperament.

Once the French had obtained the secret Russian signature (January 4, 1894), it had to be celebrated over and over again in public. The solemn opening of the Kiel Canal took place in the summer of 1895, to which deputations came from all the Powers. The French visit to Kiel was forced upon them by the Russians, who entertained hopes that the Far Eastern "alliance" formed on the occasion of the Treaty of Shimonoseki could be continued. At the insistence of Foreign Minister Hanotaux, the French and Russian squadrons met in Danish waters and steamed together, "arm in arm," into the harbor of Kiel. In order to out-demonstrate the Kiel ceremony, Hanotaux arranged that the Tsar send the French President the highest Russian order on the very day the Kiel festivities opened. He also announced publicly, and without asking the Russians beforehand, that there was in existence an "alliance" between their two countries.[81] It was the extreme sensitiveness of French pre-1914 public opinion to armed demonstrations of practically any kind, a curious form of "democratic control" of foreign affairs, that forced these portentous moves upon the governors. Le Temps celebrated the Franco-Russian alliance on the day of the formal opening of the Canal by a publicistic quod erat demonstrandum: "Truly, one cannot very well see what more undeniable proof of the conclusion of an alliance two Governments penetrated by their responsibilities could have given. There is a determined ostentation in this démarche. The very locality where this manifestation has taken place is well chosen for emphasizing its importance. It is in view of the German coast, in the waters of Denmark that the two squadrons have joined their ranks and have combined for the march."[82]

French and Russian warships had still further occasion to demonstrate the alliance of their two countries and their common hostility towards third Powers. In March 1901, during the diplomatic struggle over the control of Manchuria, a Russian admiral appeared with three of his best ships in Yokohama, where none had been shown for two years. According to the French naval attaché in Tokyo, the diplomatic aim of this visit was unmistakable: "During the numerous receptions which followed one another, the commander of the Russian squadron in the Far East endeavored to advertise before the eyes of the Japanese the ties which unite the Empire of the Tsars with our Republic."[83] This tie, impressive as it was made at the time, was not one to keep the Japanese from making war in 1904. They were certain that France would not participate in such a war.

Nor could such gestures as the placing of an American gun-boat for the winter of 1901-02 in the Manchurian port of Newchang, on which the Russians had laid their heavy hand, stop the Russians from closing the door in that region. But while the only obvious results of the stay were sailors' quarrels with local Russian officialdom,[84] it still served to indicate where American sympathies and bets would be placed in the forthcoming war.

NAVAL GREETINGS, BEFORE 1914

Naval (rather than military) demonstrations became the outward manifestation and confirmation of the diplomatic understandings in Europe and were thus an essential part of the pre-1914 alliances and ententes. The visit of an Italian squadron to Toulon in April 1898 and a counter-visit of the French in Sardinian ports to salute the royal couple a year later marked the beginning of Franco-Italian rapprochement. Other such visits in 1901, the first fruits of Barrère's diplomacy, confirmed it. The Germans covered up a situation that was hardly even ambiguous by saying that Italy's cordial relations with France, underlined as they were by "maritime fraternization festivals" at the very time when the Italian and German General Staffs were still discussing the modalities of military cooperation against France, were not incompatible with her membership in the Triplice.[85]

The sailors of the navies concerned loved these demonstrations, which invariably led to a "shower of orders and medals," and perhaps also preferred the political constellations they were to point up. The admiral of the Russian squadron in the Mediterranean at the time of the Italian visit to Toulon would have dearly loved to be among the celebrants. He appeared at Toulon a few days before the Italians, but the diplomats decided that that was too much and asked that his Government order him away.[86]

Due respect for British seapower kept Italian inclinations towards France within certain bounds. Once the British-French entente was concluded, the bounds could be disregarded. A very elaborate demonstration visit of the French President and Navy to Rome and Naples occurred in April 1904, returning a visit of the royal couple to Paris in October 1903. This forced Bülow to tell the Italian ministers that "assurances and declarations made to us under four eyes could no longer efface public demonstration." Italian promises to curtail the program to a certain extent and keep the toasts within the bounds of "soberness" were only partly kept.[87] According to Barrère, the principal arranger of the visit, it completed the inward break of the Triplice. "Popular collaboration with the political action" had been overwhelming. "All Italy, from the Alps to the Gulf of Otranto, has participated in it, spontaneously with heart and mind," furnishing proof that the Italian nation "was convinced by it as by a tangible and symbolic fact...By general admission, whether from partisan, indifferent or hostile side," he concluded, "Italy ceases being a military force in the employ of the Germanic powers. Should the battle between Germany and France break out tomorrow, even if the latter should be the aggressor, no Government would have the strength, even should it prepare to do so, to force Italy to join her forces with those of our enemies. That is one of the unavoidable facts against which the will of statesmen and of international parties can do nothing."[88]

The increase of traveling comfort and safety during the steam-and-neurosis-driven nineteenth century and the boredom of governing at home led to the increasingly frequent journeying around and visiting abroad of the heads of states. Napoleon III, probably inaugurating the custom, went on state visits to Victoria in London and she and Albert to Paris in 1855. William II became the "Reisekaiser," the traveling monarch, an imperator in medieval style, seeming at times to be almost without fixed residence. Unlike their predecessors, American presidents like Theodore Roosevelt and Wilson left their country during their terms of administration for state visits abroad. "Our time has introduced in a heretofore unknown measure the decorative factor into politics," a German ambassador observed near the turn of the century. "This would include the visiting trips of heads of states. Even if these are undertaken for purposes of pleasure and recreation, they are never without a political by-taste. On the other hand, it would be wrong to overestimate such visits in their after-effects. As a rule, they are merely the attendant phenomena or upshots of political constellations."[89] Whether or not "decorative" is the right word to characterize the role of the visiting head of state may be doubted. "Demonstrative" would describe it more correctly. For they were in most cases to demonstrate to the peoples concerned, in a manner that would be quite unmistakable, the existing or planned alliances. More equivocally they sought to demonstrate the seeming continuance of traditional ties, such as between Britain and Germany, long after the inward break had come about. A visiting head of state could demonstrate existing harmonies until even the man in the street understood. On rarer occasions, the people demonstrated against the visitor to express existing grievances against his country.

The King of Spain was gravely insulted while passing through Paris after a visit to Germany in October 1883, where he had accepted the honorary rank of colonel of a regiment stationed in Strasburg. Invited by the Spanish Government to make a joint protest against this insult, Bismarck had to decline the invitation. The incident offered no legitimate grievance for Germany. But Bismarck's press violently attacked the kind of hospitality offered by France. And when the German Crown Prince paid a return visit to Madrid, his route of travel was laid out in such a manner that French territory was ostentatiously avoided,[90] a manner of demonstration that was imitated twenty-six years later when the Tsar ostentatiously and awkwardly avoided crossing Austrian territory while going to Italy, in protest against Aehrenthal's "doing in" of Isvolski the year before. No sense of chivalry kept French revanchards from insulting the mother of William II and daughter of Victoria when she visited Paris half-incognito in 1891.

The demonstrative or theatrical character of state visits was heightened by the use of armed forces in the ceremonies. Military personnel provided a large and most visible part of the entourages. It was a rather unfortunate innovation when naval units, small ones at first, later larger ones, came to accompany the visiting heads of state. The bellicosity and suspicions of naval personnel were on the whole strengthened during such visits, which offered occasions for friction and incidental inspection, if not spying. British-German naval rivalry was made only more acute by the exchange of visits to Kiel and Portsmouth, whatever contrary beliefs Edward VII or some diplomats might have held. Somewhat too melodramatically for true history, Tirpitz dates the British alarm over the German naval constructions from Edward VII's visit to Kiel in 1904. "At that time, against my wish, Edward VII was shown all that we had of ships and the Emperor celebrated in his toast 'the regrowing naval power of the newly-created German Empire.' King Edward answered coolly and during the inspection of our ships exchanged meaningful glances and words with the First Lord of the Admiralty Selbourne which impressed me as unpleasant."[91] When Edward politely invited a German squadron on a counter-visit to English ports, and they appeared in full force, the majority of the British press "saw in them nothing but a threat to England. At the same time, a whole series of voices was heard openly pronouncing that the remarkably frequent visits of German ships in British waters could have no other purpose except to obtain information about the installations of the British Navy and the English coastal fortifications which the German admiralty might want. The sight of the German fleet in Plymouth reminded Great Britain that she must be sufficiently prepared in order to maintain her naval superiority in any

case."[92] The sight of the growing German fleet was least suited to restore a modicum of Anglo-German harmony, the diplomats concluded. It would be a good thing, Count Bernstorff wrote from London late in 1904, "to treat our Navy like a hidden, though indispensable treasure and to let the British see and hear of it as little as possible." William II remarked that this was of course impossible.[93]

In order to reassure the French, with their almost morbid impressionability about these things, that such an Anglo-German exchange of visits meant no threat to the Entente, a British fleet visited Brest in July 1905. This was followed by the meeting of Kaiser and Tsar at Bjoerkoe, which in turn was followed by a stay of French ships in British ports in August. The British-French exchange took on greater meaning as a joint demonstration against the German Moroccan policy, which British public opinion interpreted as an attempt to break up the recently concluded Entente.[94] In fact, the exchange was arranged as an answer to the Kaiser's visit to Tangiers (March 31, 1905), which had already been given a counter-demonstrative answer before the event. On March 29, the Queen of England passed through the Straits of Gibraltar, where she was ceremoniously greeted by the British and French diplomatic representatives at Tangiers. According to the French press, this event gave the world to understand "that the British Government wanted to express publicly its determination to remain in close accord with France and to actively apply the Entente policy inaugurated by the arrangement of April 8, 1904."[95] According to another version, "all England cheered its Queen when she left Gibraltar...as soon as William—on the way to Tangiers—approached, and was escorted home by a French warship."[96] In the collective memory, never a very reliable one, only the German demonstration stuck, and not the counter-demonstration.

The Kaiser's carefully contemplated and laid-out visit to Tangiers—where he arrived not on board a warship or his yacht but in a Hapag liner—took the place of a German naval demonstration against Morocco. A naval demonstration had been considered the year before as a means of forcing the Sultan to settle German claims and, following the Entente of April 1904, of showing the French and the British that Morocco was not yet recognized as French. But the Kaiser would not agree to it: control over a port on the West coast, even temporary occupation of a place like Agadir, would only move the British closer to supporting French policy. It was he, above all other Berlin governors, who pronounced himself against all German measures of a military nature in Morocco during 1904.[97] In the German Moroccan policy

of 1905, so widely considered as essentially Wilhelminic, the Kaiser was actually a passive actor,
pushed from behind by the stage-directing set
of Bülow and Holstein. He finally stumbled onto the
shabby stage of Tangiers. He had intended to land
like a tourist in a town mentioned by Baedeker,
but he was made to promise the Sultan support
of his independence. Bülow and Holstein would
not let him stay in the coulisses, as he would
have preferred. If he did so, they argued, "the
awe of the intrepid energy of Your Majesty in
which the world lives today, the awe which was
up to now a main factor in the peaceful preservation of Germany's position of power" would be
gone.

This "demonstration voyage," the success of
which seemed dubious from the outset to the
German Social Democrats (who, as leaders of
a mass party, were also experts on demonstrations), touched off the first Moroccan crisis.[98]
There was no other visible victory for German
policy in it, except the fall of Delcassé. When he
proposed to send some "good armored frigates to
Tangiers in order to bring the Sultan to reason,"
and also to call the Germans' bluff, his colleagues
in the Ministry promptly removed him.[99]

Before his departure from the Quai d'Orsay,
however, Delcassé had the satisfaction, which
raised him "to the clouds" as his assistant
Paléologue put it, of receiving the British proposal that an exchange of naval visits take place
shortly. While such visits would have had no
political significance under ordinary circumstances, "it is different this time," Paléologue
noted. "On the suggestion of Edward VII the British Government has—for Germany's benefit—
deliberately given us a proof of its friendship, a
demonstration to the whole world of the entente
cordiale between the two nations. It is understood
in that sense in Berlin."[100]

The diplomatic annus mirabilis of 1905 was to
see yet another demonstration or counter-demonstration, as emphatic in character as any sensation paper could wish it. After a long absence
from the Baltic, the British Navy announced that
the Channel squadron would cruise there in 1905.
The announcement preceded diplomatic notification in Berlin and elsewhere, long enough to give
rise to a new press polemic. The vaunted tactfulness of the British was conspicuously absent on
this occasion. The squadron in question was the
same one which the First Lord of the Admiralty
Lee had declared, earlier in the year, would
strike the first blow in the coming war in the
North Sea; the separation of the two Scandinavian
Kingdoms and the question of a king for Norway
were under discussion; the Bjoerkoe meeting of
Kaiser and Tsar was just over; and there was
no more Russian Baltic fleet in existence, a fact

which the Russians thought need not be emphasized by a showing of British naval strength just
then. It was largely in vain that Lansdowne protested that the voyage had not the least demonstrative meaning.[101] The press, particularly the
pro-navy sector, drifted into such a violent campaign that the German Social Democrats implored
the British and German proletariat to put an end
to the dark schemes of statesmen and diplomats.
"As we raised our voice a month ago in the direction of our French comrades, we today address
ourselves to our comrades in Britain."[102]
William II conceived the most childish schemes,
such as having the British fleet "shadowed" by
his own Navy, sending his aides-de-camp to the
ports where the British would stop to observe
their doings, etc., from all of which Bülow had
to dissuade him.[103] In periods of tension, practically any movement of even the smallest naval
or military unit unfortunately took on political
meaning.[104]

The British Navy wanted to repeat the cruise
in the Baltic in 1906. According to the French
minister in Copenhagen, the powerful squadron
had left an impression there that German diplomacy could not easily efface. Asked whether such
a visit would be welcomed by them, the Russians
accepted with good grace, though it was actually
far from convenient. British-Russian rapprochement had not gone far enough to justify such a
demonstration. Furthermore, the visit was considered by many as a sort of fraternal greeting
to Russian Liberalism, with which Tsardom was
then contending. After the Liberal leader Campbell-Bannerman had made his famous remark
before the Interparliamentary Union, "La Douma
est morte, vive la Douma," Grey arranged with
Isvolski to cancel the visit for 1906.[105]

Demonstrative acts in connection with the
further building of the Anglo-Russian Entente
of September 24, 1907, were kept at a minimum.
A small Russian squadron, all that could be
shown after Tsushima, visited Portsmouth in
March 1907, and a deputation of sailors was feted
in London by a vaudeville show. The visit of a
British squadron in the Baltic that same year
was postponed as still inopportune.[106] It was
the visit of Edward VII to Reval in June 1908,
prepared by a much-discussed voyage of General
Sir John French to Russia in October 1907, that
put the ratifying stamp of resounding demonstration on the Entente. Additional celebration of this
Entente was planned in later years, including a
meeting of a British and a Russian squadron in
Danish waters scheduled for the summer of 1912.
The hardly mistakable intention to stage a demonstration against Germany, or the unavoidable
impression that this was intended, moved the
Danish Government to beg the two powerful

friends not to meet and celebrate in their territorial waters. When the fleets did come, they came at different times.[107]

Royalty, traveling on state visits in uniform and in the midst of military pomp, was capable of arousing more than curiosity among the European and to a certain extent among the American masses. There was no fundamental difference between democracies and more or less autocratic monarchies as far as the fascination exercised by such foreign state visitors went. None were more eager than the French politicians to parade august guests, and themselves, before the French people, even if not much of the vaunted "burghers' pride before royal thrones" was preserved in the cringing solicitation of such visits.

In April 1901, Delcassé returned from a second visit to St. Petersburg, where the Alliance had been confirmed by the Russian promise to build more strategic railways against Germany and the French promise to permit another loan in Paris. Delcassé, who even to his best friends seemed at times "a bit carried away by and inclined to consider personal attentions as national profits," disappointed the government by not obtaining the promise of the Tsar to visit France in the autumn. This would have been more in the interest of France than all the personal favors garnered by Delcassé. Instead, it became known that the Tsar had accepted the Kaiser's invitation to be present at the German naval maneuvers. In the Elysée they were convinced that "public opinion in France will be profoundly affected by it and will turn its dissatisfaction against the Government and the Alliance." The ambassador at St. Petersburg was inclined to minimize the affair, but not Loubet and Delcassé. The ambassador was soon replaced for his neglect. Loubet and Delcassé informed St. Petersburg that "the only way to attenuate the effect of that news on our public spirit which is greatly in need of being treated kindly" would be the presence of the Tsar by the side of the French President at the French Army maneuvers. The St. Petersburg diplomats answered that the Tsar was doing only the minimum of what courtesy demanded of him, though Foreign Minister Lamsdorff admitted that France was entitled to a compensation. It came in the form of a visit of the Tsar to France later in the year.

Tsar and Tsarina, immediately following her recent confinement, had to give way to the impetuosities of the French Republicans. They had told their electors what interest and significance the visit would have— "to show off the worth of the French Army and Navy and to manifest before the eyes of the world the solid character of the Alliance, pledge and guarantee of the peace." In September 1901 the Russians arrived hours late at Dunkirk after a most excruciating voyage, in the midst of a heavy storm that played havoc with the program. "Neptune was certainly hostile to the Alliance or the Republic," they whispered in the entourage of President Loubet.[108]

ARMED DEMONSTRATIONS AT TURKEY'S ADDRESS

The necessary "as if" in armed demonstrations —the convincing show that the Powers involved would in extremis apply the forces with which they were demonstrating—was only barely maintained in the forceful measures of the "concert of Europe" against Abdul Hamid's Ottoman Empire. The Porte was the address of various actual or contemplated shows of force, some of them joint enterprises, more often exhibits of single Powers, but all carefully watched by the rest of the Powers. In spite of the strategic strength of the Straits, which was never really tested, these demonstrations were successful. The Sultan's abject fears of efficient home forces was still greater than his dread of the threat expressed by the guns of foreign warships. This obvious weakness in turn exasperated Turkish religious nationalists, who turned against the government and against the Christian minorities. The more enlightened elements in Turkey would at times have liked to see "Europe's armored fleets...placed before the Sultan's Yildiz Palace in order to lay down the conditions for a more just government or to replace him by a new Sultan." At times of greater exasperation, at least some of the foreign ambassadors believed that the appearance of such ships in the Marmora Sea would help to remove the tyrant.[109]

In practically all cases the Powers proceeded with great reluctance to the resolution for joint interventions. They were moved far less by their common Christianity, as in the case of the Bulgarian or Armenian massacres, than by the fear that one Power alone might intervene if the Concert did not. Abdul Hamid could rely far too often on the disunity of the ambassadors and their conferences and their home governments. In 1893, it was rumored that the British intended to stress their predominant role in Egypt, where the Sultan's suzerainty still survived, by having the Khedive escorted on a trip to Constantinople by a British naval division. The Sultan begged the French to protest against this proposal which was damaging to his sovereignty by joining French units to the escort and thus "counterbalance if need be the effect of the English demonstration." Ambassador Paul Cambon reported the request with the observation that "we have a great interest in convincing the Sultan of the efficiency of our support against the English."[110]

At other times, Russia and Austria were the antagonists, even during the period of the Mürzsteg arrangements, or again, Austria and Italy. In the spring of 1903, renewed activity of the Bulgarian-Macedonian bands led to dynamiting and other violence in and near places like Salonika, where there was an Austrian colony of some 20,000. An Austrian naval division was dispatched to the scene. An Italian contingent also showed up promptly in order to remind the Powers that Italy's advice and help had been neglected in the Macedonian reforms. This measure aroused fears in the Porte, but the Austrians gave assurances that no demonstration at the address of the Government was intended. In St. Petersburg, there was resentment to the fact that these vessels had been dispatched without previous announcement.[111] However, the resentment was not strong enough to break the temporary Austro-Russian entente. The murder of a Russian consul in Monastir led to a unilateral Russian naval demonstration in August 1903, which took place at Inadia Bay, astride the Turkish-Bulgarian frontier. It had a Pan-Slavist cause—to please the Pan-Slavists at home—and a Pan-Slavist effect—to further encourage the Bulgarian comitadjis.[112]

As a measure of quasi-permanent intervention, each of the Powers, from the 1890's on, kept one "stationary" ship, usually of small size, at the disposal of the ambassadors in the vicinity of Constantinople. Whenever more protection of their co-nationals seemed called for, the ambassadors would propose that their governments, in keeping with the Straits Convention of 1856, send in additional "stationaries." The Armenian massacres of 1895 raised anew the question of sending more of these ships and of armed intervention or demonstration. Starting with an Austrian proposal to demonstrate, the Triplice, with the agreement of Salisbury, who personally believed that nothing short of the Sultan's deposition would ever help, arranged to send more ships. If the Austrians sent some, the Italians would not fail to do the same, the Kaiser remarked. But where should they go to do some good? What would the French and Russians do? Would they demonstrate as a separate group? If the French were to land troops in the long ear-marked region of Smyrna, Italy wanted to disembark troops in her future possession of Tripoli. Germany, urged by her partners to take a full share with more naval units, was most unwilling to participate. But Germany warned the Sultan, "the Emperor's friend," that she might be forced to join unless he pursued a policy that would inspire more confidence in Europe. Only if he changed to such a policy would he be able to maintain himself, "since Europe was today mightier than the Sultan." It was a ratio of power of which very little use was ever made. Russia proved highly reluctant to agree even to the sending of a second "stationary," fearing a partition

policy on Salisbury's part. These states, in their careful ways, were hampered rather than helped by Italy's greedy eagerness to side with British policy. Her eagerness was indicated by her joining naval units to the British ones in Turkish waters outside the Dardanelles. No agreement was reached by the Powers, even after the British, reacting under humanitarian impulses, had made some initial fleet movements.[113]

The failure on the part of the Powers to agree and act on this and similar occasions encouraged the Turks in their repressive measures against the Christian minorities and discouraged subsequent attempts to agree on intervention. Warships of the Powers, except Germany, arrived at that always-troubled island, Crete, in May 1896. They came partly to protect, partly to demonstrate—to Greece with the warning not to support the insurrection any longer, to Turkey with the warning not to repeat the Armenian massacres, which would do more to endanger the survival of the Ottoman Empire than almost anything else. A maritime demonstration in Athens by all six Powers, in order to make the Greeks stop sending supplies to the Cretan insurrectionists, was proposed by Austria. This time, British phil-Hellenism provided the obstacle to unanimity in the proposed power pantomime. Instead, the Sultan, under pressure and persuasion from the ambassadors, granted the Cretans certain reforms in September 1896. A new outbreak occurred in January 1897, bringing with it the Greek-Turkish war.[114]

The new insurrection in Crete stirred up a wave of Pan-Hellenism. An Anschluss movement in Greece put the Athens Government under severe pressure to help the insurgents by sending ships and supplies. The Powers, set against the "intolerable aspirations" of the Greeks, strengthened their forces around Crete in order to cut off this support. Even Germany, the only great Power "with no façade on the Mediterranean," joined with a cruiser and was equally determined, along with the others, to avert war between Turkey and Greece, a war that might become a general Balkan war. Blockading the Piraeus seemed to some of the governments to be the only way of "impressing the Greek action party." The Kaiser considered diplomatic "declaration and disapproval useless; guns before the Piraeus is the right answer." It seemed doubtful that "Europe in its present grouping would prove able to protect the European peace even against little Greece." The Concert could do no more for peace than keep the war restricted to Greece and Turkey and restore order in Crete, where the Greeks had landed some 1,500 regulars in open defiance of the Concert. Marines were landed from the twenty-six warships of the six Powers in February 1897. The Greeks were sent home and the island was taken "in deposit" by the

Powers, with the British attempting to keep their participation as unemphatic as possible. Their philanthropic pretences seemed to the Continental Powers to endanger the general peace and the Concert of Europe. The long hesitation on the part of the Powers, induced by Salisbury's cunctatory methods, helped to bring on the war between Turkey and Greece, which might have been averted if early and unmistakable pressure had been brought to bear on Greek Government and royalty, helpless in the face of the agitation from Pan-Hellenism and the officers.[115] Without admitting any British responsibility, Queen Victoria thought that the Concert had become "contemptible and very useless, to say the least."[116]

Russia's Drang nach Osten and Britain's Drang nach Süden brought a let-up in the pressure zone of the Straits. Could British sea power alone still defend Turkey against Russian land power? While Salisbury considered the task hopeless, a demonstration of the continued will and ability to do so was staged. At the very moment of the outbreak of the Boer War, a strong British naval squadron was anchored in the Turkish port of Salonika. It was clearly meant to say to Russia: Hands off the Straits while Britain is busy elsewhere.[117] And they were kept off because Russia was also engaged in other regions.

Italy's Drang for il mare nostro had long resulted in resentment over the third or fourth place accorded her among the sea Powers in the Mediterranean. Her gradual shift to the camp of the Entente was slowed up whenever French notions about un lac français found new expression. According to Barrère, the chief engineer of Italy's desertion from the Triplice, Italian opinion with regard to the Mediterranean consisted "principally in the conviction that if a Power undertakes an action of some kind, Italy is despoiled and dishonored unless she does the same thing. Among the victims of this state of mind, the most ambitious designs are attributed to France." Italian suspicions were raised once more when two not overly equitable French claims—the so-called Lorando and Tubini claims—were presented to the Porte by way of an ultimatum in 1901. This was at nearly the same time that Britain, placing warships at the possible terminal of the Baghdad Railway, diminished the realm of the Sultan along its shadowy rim by forcing him to cede the suzerainty over Kuwait. Did France, who broke diplomatic relations with the Porte, have further ambitions, such as the acquisition of Tripoli, an Aegean island, the recognition of a special zone of interest in Syria? Was she proceeding, hand in hand with Russia, towards a partition of Turkey?

The Porte protracted settlement of the claims for months. With the approach of the parliamentary season, the French Government decided to send a naval squadron in order to enforce payment by occupying the customs house of Mytilene. The announcement proved highly irritating to Italy. The Foreign Minister, Prinetti, told the German ambassador that it would raise a storm: "Public opinion was excessively ticklish in all Mediterranean questions and the Government must pay respect to such a movement. Temporary occupation was apt to become permanent. What would the Triplice allies do to support Italian claims for compensation in case the French should lay hands on Turkish territory?" An Italian squadron was ordered to cruise in the Aegean, like a Nimrod who follows another hunter into a contested zone where neither, under the conditions of imperialist competition, have a right. In the Chambre, Delcassé declared that in occupying the Mytilene customs house France was not pursuing additional objects. But no one should ignore "that France, through this effort, wants to obtain respect for its rights regarding the whole of French labor in Turkey," such as schools, charities, and religious institutions. The days of claims à la Don Pacifico were over and French nationalism craved to be told that the naval action was not intended merely to enforce some dubious claims, such as were represented at one time by the Premier Waldeck-Rousseau himself. Action was justified only if designed to support France's prestige and her civilizing work in the Orient, which even anti-clerical governments could not afford to neglect. Consequently the Chambre voted its confidence, three hundred against sixty Socialists, that the Government would cause "the honor and rights of France" to be respected (November 4).

After a three-days' stay of the French squadron in Mytilene, the Porte gave in on all points. The ships retired, steaming off slowly through the Archipelago, ready to seize the pawn again at any moment. The Turks did not understand why such a "banker's affair" should have raised so much dust. They swore never to forgive the French for their violent procedures. Only later did they come to regret that they had not applied a truly defensive measure at the time, boycotting the goods of the interventionist Power, the weapon which the Asiatic peoples were bringing slowly into use.

In the first years of the new century, there was a definite recrudescence of xenophobia against foreigners and Christians from one end of Asia to the other. To French ministers, the most suitable means for the reassertion of French civilizing superiority seemed to be the demonstrative appearance of French warships in the Eastern Mediterranean. Here Russian, German, and even American influences seemed to threaten the old French supremacy. A German warship was paying regular visits in Haifa; French units must be stationed there for a while in order to counter German influence. As the carrier of France's civilizing mission the admiral of a French squadron would soon report from Haifa: "Our still privileged position is the object of the interested envy on the part of most other nations and all their efforts tend to supplant us in the minds and hearts of the Christians in the Orient."[118]

One-sided pressure on Turkey to make her reform her ways alternated with collective measures of the Powers. These collective measures were always difficult to concert, but for a time they were made a little more feasible by the Austrian-Russian agreements of Mürzsteg on reforms in Macedonia (1902). How far should the Powers go? Should the "financial sovereignty" of the Sultan be further curtailed and international financial control established in Macedonia? The Powers approved; the Turks put up obstructions. In order to break them, the Ambassadors' Conference in Constantinople in 1905 recommended a joint naval demonstration in Turkish waters. The ships were to assemble at the Piraeus. (This feature of assembling at the capital of an enemy like Greece was especially injurious to Moslem pride.) After three days of waiting, the fleet was to proceed to Mytilene, rather than to the coasts of European or Anatolian Turkey "where their appearance might be interpreted in different ways by the population and might become either an encouragement towards insurrection or an excitation to fanaticism."

Germany, as Turkey's best friend, was most reluctant to join. The Kaiser warned the Tsar that a demonstration at that time might lead to the most unexpected consequences, should the amour propre of the Islamic world resent the pressure brought to bear upon its master.[119] He held that, for such an enterprise, his "war flag was too good! Either to be employed in bitter seriousness or not shown at all! For masquerades like this it is not available! All such demonstrations are simply ridiculous disgrace. Considering the present so highly tense conditions, when we are practically alone in the face of the great coalition forming against us, Islam and the Moslem world is our last trump card. To arouse it against us and madden it by participating in this absolutely miserable and ridiculous comedy, that I absolutely refuse to do." He wanted the Wilhelmstrasse to reply that, while the invitation was accepted, no German ships would be available for the demonstration, since the Reich kept no ships in the Mediterranean. This decision was much regretted in Vienna. It was feared that Germany's abstention from the naval demonstration, while participating in the diplomatic one, would only encourage the Sultan in his stubbornness. The Sultan was beginning to consider whether he would give in under the distant pressure of a demonstration fleet, or whether it

would prove more convincing to his Moslem subjects if the fleet were allowed to approach nearer to Constantinople. The Sultan's nerves for once withstood the shock of mere demonstration. No one seemed much impressed. The more intelligent Turks smiled ironically at the dispatch of twelve armored vessels belonging to the Powers to conquer the miserable customs office of a small island. The worst thing of all was that Europe herself, preoccupied with other political problems, would not take the whole affair very seriously and thus did not make it serious. The "blow-up," the magnifying function of the press, was curiously wanting. The dispute was settled, not on the original terms of the ambassadorial conference, but by a compromise.[120]

At one time or another in the years preceding the Young Turk Revolution, all the Powers, with the single exception of Germany, threatened the Porte with naval demonstrations. Great Britain made a boundary dispute in the Sinai Peninsula the occasion of such a demonstration in favor of her tutelary, Egypt (1906). Since "there was no longer any doubt that the Ottoman Government was trifling with His Majesty's Government," an ultimatum was presented with the demand that the Turkish troops withdraw within ten days from the territory in dispute "and the Mediterranean fleet [move] to the Piraeus." Under this threat, and strongly advised to give in by the French and Russian ambassadors, the Porte surrendered its claims. This served to confirm Britain's actual suzerainty over Egypt while it further undermined Turkey's formal one.[121] Even more abject, if possible, was the surrender of the Sultan in the face of an Italian threat. A quarrel over the Italian post offices in Turkey led to the dispatch of three Italian naval divisions in the direction of Turkish waters. By the time they reached Crete, the Porte had complied (April 1908).[122]

This last case of "helpless submissiveness" before a threat by the weakest of the six Powers caused particularly bad feeling and resentment against the Government among the Young Turk officers in Macedonia. It was among them that the Revolution of 1908 began. While the Revolutionaries as constitutionalists at first turned away from Germany as "the friend of the Sultan," they did so less as nationalists. "There will be an end now to naval demonstrations and reform actions in the face of suddenly awakened national consciousness," the German chargé foretold in July 1908. "And that strikes others more than us." Germany could prepare her return to influence by pointing out that "a constitutional Turkey would have a stronger backbone against those who up to now had interfered with her internal affairs with or without naval demonstrations."[123]

The Powers paid the constitutionalists the

compliment of indefinitely postponing their reform demands, in the hope that the Young Turks would now proceed to reforms on their own initiative. Such kindness did not make the Turks forget and forgive the earlier humiliations to which ambassadors like Constant, who had represented the Tubini-Lorando claims, had exposed their country. A member of the Young Turk Committee told a Frenchman who was disappointed with the scant Francophilia shown by the new Turks: "As long as you are represented by Constant in Constantinople, the situation can't be changed. We do not forget the occupation of Mytilene and the pressure put on Turkey in favor of the onerous claims of those usurers, Tubini and Lorando. What a pity we did not think of a boycott at the time."[124]

Constitutionalism and nationalism could not save Turkey's territory, as the patriots had hoped. The fear that they might do so aroused the greed of the heirs who were threatened with disappointment, Italy and the Balkan nations. Late in 1910, Turkey's relations with Italy, who was bent on war, grew more strained. The Turkish foreign minister was convinced that "under present-day conditions naval demonstrations and the like could no longer have the same effect on Turkey as in earlier times." His hope, however, that, if Italy should press the issue further, the problem would become a European one and the Powers would interfere in favor of Turkey, was doomed to disappointment.[125] They allowed Italy to undertake the war at the expense of Turkey.

NAVAL DEMONSTRATION IN THE BALKAN WARS

The Great Powers before 1914 had refrained from aiming demonstrations directly at one another. The ostensible address of a German display with regard to French ambitions in Morocco was not France but still the miserable Sultan. A somewhat similar case is provided by British-French rivalry over Muscat in 1899. In Europe proper, persuasion en rade became restricted to the Balkan States as addressees. Before the disruption of the Concert of Europe had allowed the war of 1912 to break out, a joint naval demonstration had been suggested as a means of averting it. The proposal had originated in Paris in September 1912. There it was thought that the three Entente Powers, "equally concerned to save the peace and to maintain the status quo in the Balkan peninsula," should agree that only collective action by the great Powers could alleviate the grave events threatening the tranquillity and the equilibrium of the European Orient. They proposed, in Berlin and Vienna, a joint démarche at the address of the Balkan States with a view to maintaining peace and the status quo, while Turkey was to be advised to undertake necessary reforms. This was to be supported possibly by military or naval demonstrations. Since the Balkan Governments were no longer accessible to good advice, pressure by warships against Greece, even against Bulgaria (at Varna), following the passage of warships through the Straits, was to be arranged. Paléologue, who talked of this to the Germans and Austrians, was called "a poet" by them for these suggestions. Sasonov, and particularly Grey, objected to anything like naval or military demonstration, which seemed to be in great discredit at the time.[126]

The joint naval demonstration having been laid aside as an instrument for the prevention of war, one wonders what kind of military demonstration the French authors of the proposal might have had in mind. Naval demonstration was considered again early in 1913 by the London Ambassadors Conference that was to restore peace following the first Balkan War. Since Turkey was unwilling to admit her defeat and pay the price for it, including the cession of Adrianople and the Aegean islands, Paul Cambon proposed that an international naval detachment be sent to bring Turkey around. Grey, in a fit of British gun-shyness, did not favor the proposal, but was willing to send ships into Besica Bay where they were to arrive simultaneously and from where they might intervene, should Bulgaria resume the march on Constantinople. In that case, it would be "no longer a naval demonstration but a measure of precaution in the case of perilous events." The Germans, thinking Cambon's proposal through from a military point of view, found it impractical. It was up to the diplomats, as their Chief of Naval Staff put it, to think up other ways to restore peace. The Austrians, with their relatively small navy, would not send any units so far away. The war might spread, and Conrad, recently returned to his old office, thought that "now more than ever one must keep one's powder dry and one's forces concentrated since no one knew what the next weeks might bring." The plan of concentrating warships in Besica Bay found equally little favor in Berlin, though more in Vienna and Rome. Some vessels, not including German ones, were stationed there. They were there in anticipation of the worst of developments inside Constantinople rather than for purposes of demonstration.[127]

Such half-hearted use of the diplomatic weapon of armed demonstration could only serve to debase it. It remained for the smallest and most reckless of the Balkan belligerents, Montenegro, to utterly discredit it and the so-called Concert of Europe. When told by the members of the Concert, jointly and also individually, to desist from the siege of Scutari, Montenegro refused. She still hoped to acquire Scutari as the "future capital of the future State," even though it had been assigned to Albania (March 1913). Austria, the not too saintly patron of Albania, threatened to proceed independently, something quite dangerous in the light of Pan-Slavist inflammation. Rather than allow this, Grey, to the relief of the Powers, proposed a joint naval demonstration. When Montenegro persisted in open defiance of the London Ambassadors Conference, Grey and the five ambassadors recommended that their Governments send ships into the Adriatic. English vessels started at once for Corfu. Austria had a squadron ready near the scene, at Antivari. But Russia begged to be excused. She had no ships in the Mediterranean at the time. This was also a relief, considering the Pan-Slavist aversion for having anything done against its spoiled child, King Nikita. Under the pretext of keeping the sides even, Germany would also have preferred to remain unrepresented. Urged strongly by London and Vienna, the Wilhelmstrasse agreed to contribute a cruiser, the Breslau, but not the bigger Goeben. The Goeben had an admiral on board whom Germany did not want to see in command of the demonstration fleet. The Kaiser found occasion to gloat over the outlook: Britain demonstrating side by side with the Triplice against Slavdom. The French would not participate unless they were first given a clear mandate, one that could be shown publicly, from their ally Russia. For this Sasonov did not have the courage. He begged the French to associate themselves with the demonstration but, as Poincaré put it, "he was so much afraid of the commentaries of the Slavic world that he would not authorize us to make known that we were acting in accordance with him." Sasonov also begged the British not to abstain. But they, "out of loyalty and délicatesse," would not cooperate with the Triplice Powers alone, since that might indicate "rapprochement between England and the Triple Alliance, or at least a divergence of views among the Entente Powers." Should the Triplice Powers proceed alone, with a clear mandate from all the Powers? At last Sasonov lost patience with Nikita who was ready, as Sasonov told him, "to start the conflagration of a world war in order to cook his omelette on it."[128] He told Nikita to submit to "the will of Europe" as shown by an "imposing display of naval forces" and give up the siege of Scutari, for the sake of which no Russian blood would be spilled. He announced publicly that he wished France, which could now no longer be "more Slavophile than official Russia," and Britain to participate in the joint naval action.

The ships of the five Western Powers, six Austrian, two Italian, one German, one French, one British, with the British admiral in over-all command, appeared in seeming unison before Antivari. But Montenegro would not give up the siege of Scutari, now on the verge of surrender. Montenegro expressed regret at the presence of the squadron in her waters and termed its action a breach of neutrality. She even threatened to fire should the Powers land troops, an idea which they gave up in view of the dangers to which such troops might be exposed. Montenegro was not afraid of the blockade. She was ready to live off native mutton and what a ship loaded with gifts from Russia had brought in just ahead of the blockade. In defiance of the will of the Powers, she forced —or bought—the surrender of Scutari on April 23, 1913. The Powers could only resolve to dislodge her by the application of military power. The Russian and the French diplomats, who pretended to be most under the pressure of public opinion, dreaded this step the most. This Offenbachiade, as the Kaiser termed the faintheartedness of the Powers, betrayed a weakness of the Concert of Europe. It also betrayed a weakness of the individual nations when faced by a challenge to peace brought on by the weakest of all the sovereign states of Europe. The world knows what this weakness led to in 1914. The lack of responsibility on Europe's part in 1913 encouraged an Austrian threat to proceed with forceful measures against Montenegro and drive her out of Scutari. Grey compelled the governments of the Entente, though not their public opinions, to approve of this threat. It seemed real enough to convince the Montenegrins to submit. On May 14 they left, and landing troops of the Powers took over Scutari in trust.[129]

"I do not see Europe." In 1913—and even less in 1914—there was no common will in a common interest left. There was hardly even the determination to preserve peace against the drift towards Balkanization that took hold of the Powers and kept them from arranging and imposing an order for the Peninsula. Austria was trying to keep Serbia away from the Adriatic. Nor did Italy want her there; Italy did not care to see Greece enlarge at the expense of Albania. Germany was trying to salvage Turkey, at whose expense the Entente backed up Greece. Russia wanted to keep Bulgaria out of Constantinople by putting her Black Sea fleet before the Bosporus if necessary. France would not let her ally Russia touch off the whole Straits problem and thereby estrange Britain, her other ally. France felt that if there was to be a naval demonstration to bring Turkey and Bulgaria to terms, it must be a demonstration by all the Powers. However, before that could be arranged, an armistice was concluded by direct negotiations between the two (April 1913).[130]

The new outbreak of war in the Balkans in June-July 1913 found the Powers still disunited and therefore helpless. Would any of the decisions of the London Ambassadors Conference be allowed to stand? Would Turkey, re-entering the war, now pay the price demanded from her on the basis of her defeat in the First Balkan War? No collective démarche of the Powers or even the threat of a naval demonstration seemed to promise success in making her do so, in making her recognize the frontier line of Enos-Midia laid down in London, which she had now crossed to and beyond Adrianople. And no intervention by Russia, as mandatory of Europe, was desirable, even, or perhaps one should say least so, to the French ally. The Porte declared that it was beyond its power to recall the army. Eventually Turkey was left in possession of Adrianople. Serbia was dislodged from Albania by the threat of Austrian force and not by any warning of the concerted Powers, who thought her action quite as inexcusable but could not agree on a removal action. Afterwards, the Russians assured the Serbs that "similar action dare not be repeated" on Austria's part, whereas Germany's governors gave the energetic Austrians something like a blank check to be used against Pan-Slavism.[131] The question of the Aegean islands remained. How were the Powers to enforce their own solution? By a naval demonstration against Turkey?

The Wilhelmstrasse was at least honest enough to at once restate its well-known opposition to the application of such measures "of a not purely diplomatic nature." Since even the demonstration against tiny Montenegro had exposed deep-running dissensions, the much greater interests of all the Powers in Turkey could only result in still greater disunity. And in so far as a naval demonstration was to keep Turkey from reconquering islands like Chios and Mytilene, it was unnecessary. Superior Greek naval forces could hinder that. Turkey could do nothing at sea until the arrival of her newly acquired Dreadnoughts, expected during the second half of 1914. Early in 1914, it seemed far more likely that Turkey would commence a land war against Greece, perhaps in alliance with Bulgaria. How would the Powers intervene in such a war? They would find themselves in the absurd position of guarding islands with their ships while the fate of those islands was being decided elsewhere. Would Grey then turn the ships against Constantinople? The outcome of an action in that direction might so easily carry much further than intended. These embarrassing problems were posed by German diplomacy.[132] They were still unsolved in July 1914. By that time, shock treatment by way of armed demonstration had become so thoroughly ineffective and discredited that there was no thought of such a display during the July crisis.

ARMED DEMONSTRATIONS DURING AND AFTER THE WORLD WARS

In time of war, armed demonstration reverts to a nearly exclusively military character—"threatening a certain point in order to mislead the enemy and move him to disperse his forces." The parties to the First World War refrained for the most part from demonstrations, largely because no military forces could be spared at most times of the war. Where the forces were available, diplomatic offices succeeded in averting such steps, which were likely to be misconstrued by other Powers.[133] Certain measures that might appear demonstrative but were intended to be simple measures of security, such as the assembly of German or Russian troops along some neutral borders, were kept as undemonstrative as possible.

The principal addressee of armed demonstrations during the First World War was Greece. There, half of the politicos, including the King, expected the victory of the Central Powers. They wanted to remain neutral. The rest, led by Venizelos, would have preferred to enter the war on the Entente side. In the autumn of 1915, Greece threatened to proceed against the uninvited Serb, French and British troops on her soil, possibly to disarm and intern them. For Joffre, there was "only one solution: Force. The French Government understood it, that of London after a short hesitation fell in." A note was presented in Athens demanding observation of the benevolent neutrality that Greece had promised the Entente at various times. "An Allied squadron, concentrated at Milo under a French vice-admiral, was ready to support this demand." Greece gave in at once. "The attitude of Greece was thus settled in extremis."[134]

On the eve of Bulgaria's entry into the war, Venizelos tried once again to bring Greece into the Entente camp. In order to break the King's resistance, the French proposed the application of force, but the British, restrained by monarchist solidarity, at first wanted to go no further than staging a naval demonstration. The French thought the landing of troops was the only way "to restore order in the country."[135] French intransigeance won out. On September 1, 1916, a strong demonstration squadron of the two Powers appeared in the Piraeus. The British Minister on the spot believed that "with a little tact" Greece might yet be brought to declare war against Bulgaria. The French minister and the inter-Allied military commander in Salonika, General Sarrail, proceeded on very different views. By their demands, including the surrender of the Greek fleet which was still under the command of a British admiral, and the landing of troops, they precipitated an armed conflict in which two hundred and twelve French and British men were killed or wounded. Rather than winning over large elements of the Greek people, the Allies here only succeeded in estranging them. As Sir Frederick Maurice put it: "We had made the independence and rights of small nations one of the main causes for which we were fighting and were now being dragged into open violation of our principles with but slender justification on the ground of military necessity."[136] This is a British post mortem of an armed demonstration and its consequences. Under the conditions of coalition warfare, the British could not very well protest against French impetuosity and ruthlessness, the ruthlessness of those bled white at the time.

The forces released by war worked a deep change in the style of diplomacy. So also did the fact, soon to become evident, that the states at which armed demonstrations had been directed before the war had greatly changed. Their largely revolutionary governments and peoples were no longer impressed by the appearance of warships of great Powers on their coasts. Such appearance had lost nearly all its penetrating effect. A new psychological armor-plating had taken place. The so-called nominal equality of all member nations under the League of Nations Covenant ruled out the old armed demonstration by the Great Powers as part of the order of accepted things. Endless negotiation, litigation, and more or less open armed resistance (Poles in Vilna, Syrians, Egyptians) obstructed the "dictate" of the disunited Concert, which lost all chances of becoming united when the United States repudiated the League.

In China, the presence of foreign warships was largely disregarded. The landing of Greek troops at Smyrna in May 1919 was carried out in the presence of American, British and French war vessels. The demonstrative gestures of the latter were directed alike at Italy, which had temporarily withdrawn from the Paris Conference and had landed troops in Adalia, the zone assigned to her in the secret partition treaty of St. Jean de Maurienne (1917), and also against Turkey. Neither was greatly impressed. The Greek action led to massacres of civilian populations in Asia Minor and a war with the Turkish nationalists. This was disastrous to Greece and fatal to Anglo-French unity, with Chanak the gesture that marked the end of the entente.

It was not application of force short-of-war that went out of fashion from 1919 on—there was ample use of it, notably by the French—but demonstration with the use of armed force. The use of military power changed in style from the desire and hope to impress others to the urge to express oneself. Semblance of power was no longer enough, either for the exhibitor or for the threatened party.

The few attempts to make armed demonstration effective were unconvincing. During the phase of the Polish-Russian War of 1920 that was favorable to the Russians, British diplomacy tried to intervene in Poland's favor and urge the Soviets to halt their offensive. Krassine, their representative, was called in by Lloyd George and Bonar Law to be told that the Soviets must stop their alarming advance towards the West. If a satisfactory answer were not received, the British fleet would be ready to go to sea within three days, the blockade of the Soviet Union would start again, and reinforcements would be disembarked at Danzig. "This ultimatum was underlined by a naval demonstration: the fleet left the British ports and gained the high seas." The Soviets, however, were undaunted by Lloyd George's threat: "I shall order the British fleet into the Baltic." The Soviets answered within twenty-four hours that they were willing to negotiate directly with the Poles on the basis of the recognition of Polish independence, but that the offensive as a purely military move could not be halted.[137] The ineffectiveness of British sea power as compared with the spectacular role played by the French Army contributed greatly to the diminution of British credit in Central and Eastern Europe. Weygand actually or seemingly turned defeat into victory within a few weeks at the gates of Warsaw.

As a matter of power expressionism or exhibitionism, Mussolini proceeded almost at once from ultimatum to bombardment in the Corfu episode of 1923. There were only four days between the incident—the murder of an Italian general on Greek soil by unknown parties—and the bombardment and occupation of Corfu, "a peaceful measure for the purpose of insuring Italian prestige," as Italian diplomacy put it. It was high time, the Duce told a British interviewer, "that the small Balkan States should learn at last that Italy is not a small State, but a great power conscious of its strength."[138] The incident was one of those applications of force that the League of Nations was supposed to prevent. Others were the taking of Vilna (1920), the Japanese actions in Manchuria and China, Fascist and Communist intervention in Spain. In Spain, the Germans proceeded to bombard Almeria without further ado in reprisal for a Loyalist bombing of one of their warships. On these and on other occasions, it was French diplomacy above all that allowed these blows against the League's credit. The French conceived the League only as a potential alliance against Germany. Demonstrativeness had gone out of French diplomacy—"between the prestige of the League of Nations and the interest of peace, no possible hesitation: peace above everything."[139] There was never an armed demonstration on the part of the League, although such a demonstration could have added to its credit with the masses by proving that a concert of Europe, and more-than-Europe, was in existence. Peace-disrupting events led merely to diplomatic remonstrations on the part of the status quo Powers.

The show of arms after 1919 was largely reserved for the fait accompli of conquest or intervention. The Fascist governments, after a rare demonstration such as Mussolini's setting a number of divisions in march in the direction of the

Brenner Pass following the murder of Dolfuss, which proved quite effective, came to consider mere armed demonstrations as an almost frivolous misuse of armies and navies, a not uncommon view among soldiers and sailors as well. The Soviet Government, for its own reasons, shared this reluctance about the demonstrative application of military power, except for the annual May Day parade on the Red Square. "Shamming military action," the spreading of "false but creditable information" about one's own military preparations, as in the Nazis' arrangements for the conquest of Austria in 1938, was not a diplomatic move but a military ruse.[140] In the end, the Fascist states were so deeply in war before it was declared that the difference between armed demonstration and warlike action was imperceptible. Armed demonstration became part of war: a German training ship arrived in Danzig during the last August days of 1939 on a visit agreed to by the Polish Government. This drove the Danzigers into a frenetic welcoming of the "liberators."

During the war, armed demonstrations more nearly assumed the strictly military character of ruses and stratagems. Still, some of them may have possessed a political meaning. Norway and Sweden had denied the Western Powers permission to carry aid to Finland across their territories. Churchill proposed to a meeting of the Sub-Committee of the Allied Supreme War Council that a naval demonstration be staged off Narvik. This might yet induce Norway to grant permission for the passage of men and materiel. The crumbling of Finnish resistance came before more open threats directed at the Scandinavians could be formulated.

In the same period, President Roosevelt, siding with the State Department, had upsetting ideas about the use of naval units during the period of the "undeclared war," ideas that according to the Chief of Naval Operations were "nothing less than childish." In March-April 1941, while Foreign Minister Matsuoka was on his momentous voyage to Berlin and Moscow, Roosevelt dispatched ships to the Anzacs on several different occasions. "I just want them popping up here and there, and keep the Japs guessing," he explained to Admiral Stark. The latter was much opposed to having his ships used "for popping up purposes in aid of diplomacy," thus dispersing them while the war was coming closer all the time.[141]

Much of the pre-1939 blurring of the line between war and peace reappeared in the so-called cold war. There is no place here to state in detail how far this conflict between East and West is war and how far it is not. It is not war insofar as the conflict is fought with basically different arms and tactics, for in true war, military

necessity forces both sides to use approximately the same weapons, tactics, and strategy, whatever the deviation from the ideal line may be under the influence of socio-economic circumstances. In its more spectacular part, this cold war is carried on by demonstration, of which there is far more on one side than on the other. The West, in democratic style, tries to bring at least certain features into the open and to have its masses participate in the conflict and the moving about of land, sea, and air forces. In order to appear the lesser provocateur, the Russians on the whole have preferred to make the movements of their forces inconspicuous if not secret. They seldom announce them, and one learns about them after the military intelligence services of the West have ascertained and publicized some of them and have proceeded to react with counter-moves of their own.[142] These tactics give the Russians a psychological advantage in making it appear that not they but their opponents make most of the "peace-endangering," "war-mongering" moves, a suggestion that takes on great significance for the fellow-traveling element in the West. The total appearance is that of a game of chess in which only the Western side is played in full view. In addition, it is a game in which certain moves seem less dictated by military considerations than by the pressure of the observers and taxpayers who insist on seeing something done with the magnificent forces for which they have provided.

Much if not most of Western demonstrativeness is inward, rather than outward. It is directed towards their own citizenry, rather than at the address of the Russians, about whose impressionability they know far less than was known about the effect of demonstrations before 1914. The time of the most "outspoken" American demonstrations in the cold war was in 1948 (a presidential campaign year, incidentally). One weekend in July, sixty B-29's landed in Britain for a prolonged stay. To demonstrate what? "The Russians would note their arrival. If they were wise, the Russians would also note the ease with which this air armada was accommodated at British fields and fitted into British air operations. The RAF and the USAF are, in fact, essentially one air force. The war-born union is the forerunner of an Atlantic system of military security."[143] The following year an American jet-fighter unit of seventy-five planes was transferred from the Panama Canal Zone in order "to bolster the United States in Germany" and to double the size of the American fighter force in Europe. In further explanation, it was stated by the United States Air Force that "across the zonal border the Russians reportedly operate a constantly growing fleet of jet fighters and some jet-

powered bombers," that in spite of the reinforcements, the American fighter force in Europe was
"still far short of the strength that Russia could
muster in a matter of hours."[144] In this grim
play, the Berlin Air Lift, involving over 276,000
flights by American and British craft, was the
most gigantic move. It broke a blockade, or
siege, which had lasted for 462 days. It was, in
the words of the American Secretary of Defense
"another demonstration of how military power
can be a power for peace."[145]

This demonstrativeness had originated with the
United States Navy and its Secretary, James
Forrestal, early in 1946. Persuaded that appeasement with regard to Russia had become futile,
he asked for and obtained Secretary Byrnes'
approval of the plan to place a task force in the
Mediterranean. He also obtained the approbation
of elder statesman Winston Churchill, who
warned him "that a gesture of power not fully
implemented was almost less effective than no
gesture at all, that to make the gesture effective
the entire task force should sail into the Sea of
Marmora." Since the task force was not at once
available, the more casual-looking visit of American cruisers in Mediterranean ports was arranged. Byrnes again agreed, and he ascribed
"most satisfactory results" to the recent ceremonial visit of the battleship Missouri to Turkey.
Others in the State Department seemed more
"unaware of the very great influence that the
Navy particularly can exercise in Europe" while
"its prestige was high, the record of its accomplishments in the Pacific widely known and its
personnel in general disciplined and of good
conduct." Navy men thought that the presence
of American warships in European waters "would
be a tremendously helpful and stabilizing influence." Shortly after the dismissal from the Government of Henry Wallace as the last remnant
of Russophilia, the general public was made acquainted with the meaning of the more or less
continuous presence of American warships in
the Mediterranean by a Navy Department statement, "cleared" with White House and State Department. It "formally linked naval operations
with American foreign policy for the first time."
So a New York paper noted the significance,
though less correctly the newness, of the measure.[146]

Ship movements were linked with those of
planes: one United States Very Heavy Bomber
squadron was stationed in Southern Bavaria, from
where it could take off on occasion "to simulate
a bomb attack on the Suez Canal, demonstrating
in theory the necessity for control of Central
European air bases by the Western Powers if
they are to keep Mediterranean communications
lines secure in emergency."[147] As was explained to the citizenry at home, America's
"restless Mediterranean fleet, by 'showing the
flag,' did what it could to help keep the peace in
various parts of the world."

Foreigners realize that the full strength of
America might well not be used unless there
has been a previous political catastrophe.
However, they have a different impression of
ships which are capable of landing marines
to spike local troubles. They apprehend the
punitive possibilities of a ship which can pin-
point a target without sounding the signal for
another world war. In backing up our diplomacy, the Navy, with its possibilities for local
precise action, can break up small incidents
before they mushroom into catastrophic
size.[148]

What could this mean but the intention of blocking the spread of Communism deeper into the
Mediterranean, where it would be pacemaker for
the budding Russian Navy and prepare bases for
it? This much was hardly mistakable, although
other moves in the cold war invited misinterpreta-
tion. A Russian fleet of trawlers, changing from
fishing grounds in the Baltic to others in the Black
Sea, assembled at Falmouth "for orders" for
several days. This occurred at the very time when
naval maneuvers of the Brussels Pact Powers
were about to start. The Russians were suspected
by the press of intending to have a peep at these
exercises. The head of the British Military Mission to war-time Moscow suggested that the visit
to Britain's coastal waters "might be for reconnaissance for some operations planned for the
future and for the purpose of accustoming the
officers to British waters." But official Britain
attached no special significance to their arrival
and short stay.[149]

REDUCED EFFECT OF DEMONSTRATIONS

Looking back over the short history of armed
demonstration, one cannot help but wonder whether
a fundamental change has taken place in this instrument of diplomacy during the last thirty
years. The main purpose of demonstrations
seems nearly outdated. And this is the case even
when the strongest weapons in the armory of
modern warfare are employed, as in the experiments at Bikini and elsewhere, bringing the scientific semantics of demonstration over into
politics. While they produced a traumatic impact
on the impressionable and at the same time observable section of mankind, that is to say, the
West, the effect on the other half of mankind is
largely hidden. The Soviets deny the demonstrators on this side of the curtain nearly all occasion to observe the impression their demonstra-

tions may make on the other side, whether on the governors themselves or on the masses. Meanwhile, they move their own forces as undemonstrably, but with as much finality, as possible.

Most of the traditional effect of armed demonstrations is gone, together with the older state system among whose long-standing fictions was once the belief that the demonstrating Power was nearing the end of its patience and was contemplating serious measures. The Soviets declined to share this view, or fiction. From all external appearances, they refuse to be impressed by short-of-war moves and gestures, because they are persuaded that their adversaries are not going to war even if they demonstrate, or are least ready to go to war when they demonstrate. Such unreceptiveness limits the effect of armed demonstration. The principal effect of Western demonstrations is on the people of the Western world, proving to them that their forces are attentive, and are moving with actual or symbolic strength into positions which may carry them from demonstration to what the Germans call the Ernstfall, the case of extreme gravity, war.

FOOTNOTES

1. Strausz-Hupé and Possony, International Relations, p. 388.
2. Cf. G. Sorel, Réflexions sur la violence (6th ed.), pp. 249 and passim.
3. For example, President Poincaré insisted that "a great number of troops be sent to Syria where one must not give an impression of weakness" (December 30, 1918). Au service de la France, X, 459.
4. Rousset, Histoire de Louvois, III, 5 ff., 235 ff., 242 f.
5. Bryant, Samuel Pepys. The Savior of the Navy, pp. 237 f.
6. Monypenny and Buckle, Disraeli, II, 923.
7. As early as 1931, "Japanese statesmen regarded American naval maneuvers in Hawaiian waters as a covert threat to their position in the Far East." Tansill, Back Door to War, p. 145.
8. There is naturally not much objectivity to be found in reports about the effects of such demonstrations. Those staged by one's own country are usually called effective, those by the opposite party, particularly if intended as counter-demonstrations, as failures. For those on Tangiers in 1905, see Vagts, Deutschland und die Vereinigten Staaten, pp. 1840 f.
9. German-Japanese Axis intimacy might be dated from the good-will visit of a Japanese squadron to German ports in the summer of 1934. Tansill, Back Door to War, p. 139.

10. G. P., XXVI, 9105, 9109.
11. Barrow, Some Account of the Public Life of the Earl of Macartney, I, 348 f.
12. Pasquier, Mémoires, VI, 201.
13. B. D., III, 203.
14. Doc. dipl. fr., 1st series, VII, 368 f.
15. G. P., IX, 2361.
16. Doc. dipl. fr., 2nd series, I, 264, 373.
17. For example, during the Austro-Russian pressure on the Porte to surrender Kossuth and other Hungarian refugees in Turkey, Stratford Canning considered it indispensable to have a part of the British fleet at his disposal and have it appear in a demonstrative way in the Archipelagos. Guichen, Les grandes questions européennes, I, 447.
18. Millis, The Martial Spirit, p. 93.
19. G. P., XV, 4123.
20. Millis, The Martial Spirit, p. 97.
21. Vagts, Deutschland und die Vereinigten Staaten, p. 1285.
22. Ibid., pp. 1758 ff., 1794 f., 1941.
23. Ibid., p. 1794.
24. Die Ergebnisse der von der Allgemeinen Zeitung veranstalteten Flotten-Umfrage.
25. Stieve, Schriftwechsel Iswolskis, II, 88, 96.
26. Journal des Débats, April 19, 1912; Gauvain, L'Europe au jour le jour, III, 407.
27. For a relevant case of 1907, see Doc. dipl. fr., 2nd series, XI, 57 ff.
28. Newton, Lord Lansdowne, p. 242.
29. Willy-Nicky Correspondence, letter of November 17, 1904.
30. Smith, International Law (5th ed.), p. 178.
31. Martin, The Triumph of Lord Palmerston, pp. 34, 114 ff.
32. Ibid., p. 145.
33. Ashley, Life of Palmerston, II, 45.
34. Bapst, Le Maréchal Canrobert, II, 79 f.
35. Bismarck, Gesammelte Werke, VII, 221.
36. Diaries of John Bright, pp. 223, 246.
37. Salisbury, in Commons, March 1863.
38. Cecil, Life of Salisbury, I, 312 ff.
39. Die auswärtige Politik Preussens 1858-1871, V, 236.
40. Beust, Mémoires, II, 12 f.
41. Cf. the French answer to a British proposal for a naval demonstration on behalf of Denmark: "The first gun shot of a naval demonstration would bring on a war on the seas and on land. We would not be at liberty as Britain would be to undertake our operations as we should like. Despite our efforts to localize the war, we would hardly succeed in preventing its outbreak along our land frontiers...Would Britain, in the face of such an eventuality, be ready to grant us unrestricted support?...Lord Russell seems to believe that a naval demonstration could

take place without a conflict arising from it and that threats would suffice to beat down the demands of Germany. However, could not this calculation in which national self-esteem is engaged to such a high degree go wrong?" Seton-Watson, Britain in Europe, pp. 445 f.

42. Monypenny and Buckle, Disraeli, II, 749, 956.
43. Ibid., II, 764.
44. Seton-Watson, Britain in Europe, p. 517.
45. Letters of Queen Victoria, 2nd series, II, 455.
46. October 4, 1876. G. P., II, 242.
47. Monypenny and Buckle, Disraeli, II, 971.
48. Wertheimer, Andrassy, III, 88 f.
49. Cecil, Life of Salisbury, II, 197 f.
50. G. P., II, 388 ff.
51. Bismarck, Gesammelte Werke, VIII, 379.
52. Taffs, Ambassador to Bismarck, p. 283.
53. G. P., IV, p. 17.
54. Hohenlohe, Denkwürdigkeiten, II, 306; Doc. dipl. fr., 1st series, III, 214 ff., 221, 225, 230, 240, 263.
55. Morley, Gladstone, III, 10.
56. Ibid., III, 260.
57. Ibid., III, 527. Throughout his tenure, Bismarck was very reluctant to proceed to armed demonstrations, alone or in combinations. Still, there were a few to which he agreed, aside from those connected with his colonial policy. In 1877, diplomatic relations with Nicaragua were broken because of a murderous attack on a German consul, for which the Government declined to punish the guilty parties. A small squadron was dispatched in 1878. Its presence moved Nicaragua to give satisfaction. Following the murder of the German and French consuls in Salonika by a fanatic mob, warships of the two nations appeared on the spot and enforced punishment (1875).
58. G. P., IV, 719 ff.
59. Doc. dipl. fr., 1st series, VI, 106, 186, 189, 239, 249; Cecil, Life of Salisbury, III, 255; Schweinitz, Denkwürdigkeiten, II, 332.
60. Gladstone to John Bright, July 14, 1882. Morley, Gladstone, III, 84.
61. Doc. dipl. fr., 1st series, IV, 102.
62. Busch, Bismarck. Some Secret Pages, III, 51 ff.
63. Diaries of John Bright, p. 485.
64. Doc. dipl. fr., 1st series, IV, 307.
65. Morley, Gladstone, III, 84.
66. Doc. dipl. fr., 1st series, IV, 553.
67. Ibid., III, 201 f., 204 ff.
68. Bompard, Mon ambassade en Russie, p. 306.
69. Lafuze, Great Britain, France, and the Siamese Question; Vagts, "William II and the Siam Episode," American Historical Review, XLV, 834 ff.; Doc. dipl. fr., 1st series, X, passim.
70. Waldersee, Denkwürdigkeiten, II, 454 f.
71. Doc. dipl. fr., 1st series, VIII, 209, 228, 433, 550 ff., 596, 600, 607 f., 610 ff., 620, 625, 646, 659 f., 696, 704, 709.
72. Cecil, Life of Salisbury, IV, 395.
73. G. P., VII, 1517.
74. Doc. dipl. fr., 1st series, X, 35 f., 44.
75. Ibid., X, 476.
76. Langer, Franco-Russian Alliance, p. 342.
77. Doc. dipl. fr., 1st series, X, 556, 567, 584.
78. Marder, Anatomy of British Sea Power, p. 145.
79. Langer, Franco-Russian Alliance, p. 350.
80. Marder, Anatomy of British Sea Power, p. 178.
81. This is based on Doc. dipl. fr., 1st series, XII, 42 f., 51, 64, 72, 99, 100 f.
82. G. P., IX, p. 356.
83. Doc. dipl. fr., 2nd series, I, 171, 177.
84. Vagts, Deutschland und die Vereinigten Staaten, p. 1127.
85. G. P., XVIII, 5830 ff.
86. Doc. dipl. fr., 1st series, X, 182 f.; Combarieu, Sept ans à l'Elysée, pp. 125 f.
87. G. P., XX, 6388 ff.
88. Doc. dipl. fr., 2nd series, V, 132 ff; Combarieu, Sept ans à l'Elysée, p. 276.
89. Monts, April 25, 1904. G. P., XX, 6404.
90. Taffs, Ambassador to Bismarck, p. 360.
91. Tirpitz, Erinnerungen, p. 172.
92. G. P., XIX, 6042.
93. Ibid., XIX, 6052.
94. Ibid., XIX, 6218; XX, 6840 f.
95. Ibid., XX, 6838.
96. Eyck, Das persönliche Regiment Wilhelms II, p. 395, citing A. Melvil, De la paix de Francfort, p. 216.
97. G. P., XX, 6514 ff., 6520, 6529, 6531 ff.
98. This is based on Vagts, Deutschland und die Vereinigten Staaten, pp. 1838 ff.
99. G. P., XX, 6685.
100. Paléologue, The Turning Point, pp. 210, 292.
101. G. P., XIX, 6228; XX, 6868 ff.
102. Doc. dipl. fr., 2nd series, VII, 328 f.
103. Bülow, Denkwürdigkeiten, II, 152 ff.
104. During the Cowes regatta in 1905, the London sensational press, such as the Daily Mail and the Daily Express, reported that the Emperor's yacht Meteor with the German ambassador aboard had turned tail during a race, in order, it was said, to avoid greeting the admiral's flag of an approaching French squadron. G. P., XX, 6870.
105. For details see Poltz, Die anglo-russische Entente, 1903-1907, pp. 105 ff.; Doc. dipl. fr., 2nd series, X, 234, 238, 269.
106. G. P., XXI, 7169; XXV, 8526, 8528.

107. Ibid., XXXI, 11597; XXXIII, 12256.
108. For the details—partly grotesque—see Combarieu, Sept Ans à l'Elysée, pp. 150 ff.
109. G. P., XII, 3073.
110. Doc. dipl. fr., 1st series, X, 410, 415 f.
111. G. P., XVIII, 5544, 5548.
112. Ibid., XVIII, 5577, 5580 ff., 5585.
113. Ibid., X, 2505 ff., 2551, 2564, 2572.
114. Ibid., XII, 3026, 3031, 3033, 3039, 3043, 3048.
115. Ibid., XII, 3145, 3168, etc.; Langer, Diplomacy of Imperialism, chap. xi.
116. Letters of Queen Victoria, 2nd series, III, 148 ff.
117. G. P., XVIII, 5640 ff.
118. The French documentation is in Doc. dipl. fr., 2nd series, Vol. 1; G. P., XVIII, 5668 ff.
119. G. P., XIX, 6256.
120. B. D., V, 80 ff.; Doc. dipl. fr., 2nd series, VIII, 121 f.; G. P., XXII, 7566 ff., 7585, 7587, 7594.
121. B. D., V, 189 ff.
122. G. P., XXV, p. 568.
123. Ibid., XXV, 8881, 8886.
124. Oesterreich-Ungarns Aussenpolitik, I, 922.
125. Ibid., III, 2371.
126. Doc. dipl. fr., 3rd series, III, No. 451; Poincaré, Au service de la France, II, 213 f.; Oesterreich-Ungarne Aussenpolitik, IV, 3864; Helmreich, Diplomacy of the Balkan Wars, p. 123.
127. Helmreich, Diplomacy of the Balkan Wars, pp. 260 f.; Oesterreich-Ungarns Aussenpolitik, V, 5341, 5348, 5368, 5371, 5390, 5410; G. P., XXXIV, 12684.
128. Potiemkine, Histoire de la diplomatie, II, 245.
129. Helmreich, Diplomacy of the Balkan Wars, pp. 310 ff.; Durham, Struggle for Scutari.
130. G. P., XXXIV, 13140, 13149 f., 13164, 13178.
131. Helmreich, Diplomacy of the Balkan Wars, pp. 427 f.
132. G. P., XXXVI, 14278.
133. For example, in March 1915, the underemployed Japanese Army proposed to back the demands on China by a large-scale military demonstration. Takeuchi, War and Diplomacy in the Japanese Empire, p. 191.
134. Joffre, Mémoires, II, 137 f.
135. Herbillon, Du général en chef au gouvernement, I, 335.
136. Maurice, Lessons of Allied Cooperation: Naval, Military and Air, 1914-1918, pp. 66 ff. The official British version is in Official History of the War (Naval Operations), IV, 140 ff.
137. Potiemkine, Histoire de la diplomatie, III, 93 f.; Callwell, Sir Henry Wilson, II, 225.
138. Europäische Gespräche, I, 317, 321.
139. Henry de Jouvenel, French delegate to League Assembly during Corfu crisis. Wolfers, Britain and France between two Wars, p. 193.
140. Nazi Conspiracy and Aggression, IV, 357, 361.
141. Pearl Harbor Hearings, Part 16, pp. 2163 f.
142. Following large-style maneuvers of the Russian occupation forces in Germany in June 1949, American troops staged their largest training exercises since Armistice Day only fifty miles away from where the Russians had held theirs. AP dispatch from Frankfurt, June 22, 1949.
143. Time, July 26, 1948.
144. N. Y. Times, June 19, 1949.
145. Semi-annual Report of the Secretary of Defense, July to December 31, 1949, p. 23.
146. See Forrestal Diaries, pp. 141, 144 f., 171, 184, 196, 211; N. Y. Herald-Tribune, October 1, 1946. Early attempts of 1949 on the part of the U.S. Navy to demonstrate that Spain belonged to the NATO system by a visit of some vessels to a Spanish port met vigorous opposition from the State Department, though not for long. Military Situation in the Far East, p. 2695. For an earlier instance, compare Truman's ordering the Mediterranean Fleet into the Adriatic and three divisions into Northern Italy when "the Government of Yugoslavia decided to take Trieste." "There was no march on Trieste," he pointed out seven years later when reporting the incident at a news conference. N. Y. Times, April 25, 1952.
147. C. L. Sulzberger in N. Y. Times, May 5, 1948.
148. Vice-Admiral Radford, Vice Chief of Naval Operations, before a Chatauqua assembly. Ibid., July 11, 1948.
149. Ibid., May 21, 1950, and after.

Preventive War

The problem of preventive war is, simply put, the problem of whether a war considered inevitable in the long run is to be fought now, rather than later when the advantages may lie with the opposite camp. Wars are called preventive when they are undertaken in order to keep an enemy, who is preparing or suspected of preparing an attack, from striking the first blow at a later date, which threatens to be more unfavorable to one's own side.[1] Before certain inhibitions had been formed, it could be stated frankly and axiomatically that "men do not only defend themselves against a superior when he has attacked them, but also strike the first blow, to prevent his attacking them."[2] The opponent's intention to attack eventually is readily taken for granted in such a situation, even if proof of this intention must largely be furnished by history.

Generally speaking, the argument in favor of preventive war has been brought forward and stressed by military men rather than by civilians. The military are the closest, most expert, and often the most suspecting observers of dangers threatening their country from an enemy growing superior. In judging the danger that a preventive war is to meet, military opinion will often if not typically insist that such a danger must not be underestimated, that it will keep on growing rather than decrease. Civilian judgment and policy will more often incline towards thinking and arguing that this danger must not be overestimated, that it may decrease in due time with the help of diplomacy and counter-alliances and additional armaments on one's own part, that too much additional armament may even unleash a preventive war by the opponent in his determination to prevent an overbalancing. This was part of the argument of the British Liberals against the introduction of conscription before the war of 1914.[3] The civilian skeptic might even go so far as to say that too much foresight in this field could become positively dangerous and bring on rather than avert misfortune. In his "gay science," the Abbé Galiani (1728-87), an advocate of laissez faire not only in economics, maintained at least half seriously that "the misfortunes of mankind derive from foresight,...the actual cause of wars. Because one foresees that the House of Hapsburg will increase, because the French, a hundred years from now, will do such a thing, we begin to cut one another's throats right now."[4]

In deference to such Christian-bourgeois sentiments, preventive war intentions and motivations of governments had to be increasingly veiled. Since at least the eighteenth century, they had been forced to exercise great care not to admit preventive motivations when going to war, a discretion that the blunter military spokesmen might consider altogether dishonest. A Woodrow Wilson, perhaps subjectively honest in this respect, would never explain or justify America's entrance into the war in 1917 as due to the fear of an eventual German victory. This thought, however, was foremost in the minds of many American politicos, some of whom were very close to Wilson. Only militarists and revolutionaries failed to pay deference to the Christian-bourgeois abhorrence of preventive war, as the kind of war that seemed most preventable. Throughout the more recent history of the idea of preventive war, German soldiers and political authors have been far more outspoken in their discussion and advocacy of such warfare than Anglo-Saxon or Latin spokesmen, true in this frankness to their historical penchant for "stating that which is."[5]

The soldier who is merely technical-minded may consider it his plain duty to state the facts and arguments about preventive war, but he will leave it to the political governors to decide whether other factors and considerations add to or deduct from the weight of his counsel. Even at Nuremberg, some of the generals were frank enough to admit the necessity of prevention in one or the other of Hitler's wars. Colonel-General Halder, for example, stated that "preventive war is ultimately a question for political decision, and for a soldier, as a military operation, it is no different from any other military action. The thought of preventive war is not unfamiliar to military men... Now, if you imagine that—and this is a political opinion—the conflict with Russia was inevitable, then the military men knew that the issue of this conflict must not be postponed to such a point of time in which, for instance, the Western Powers would be ready to strike." Halder was asked: "What possibility existed for military leaders to check and examine" whether Hitler's statements to them on the need for such a war against Russia were correct or not? He answered: "Possibilities existed insofar that one could—militarily speaking—obtain a picture of the steadily increasing Russian military strength facing our front. That was in favor of the ideas expressed by Hitler. To examine and check up political information, no possibility was given to us."[6]

The doubtful point in governance over peace and war is reached when politically-minded military men try to determine political action, either through their strong influence inside a government or by advocating specific preventive war measures through the channels of propaganda available to them. The problem of the separation of powers as conducive either to peace or war has been much neglected. Where political and military responsibility have not been clearly separated, the great makers of preventive war—Louis XIV, Frederick the Great, Napoleon I, Hitler—have been able to hold sway. Hitler was even able to disregard the most expert military pronouncement against his schemes, not to mention the warnings of diplomats, whose nadir of influence is usually reached under the rule of "great men."

The urge to preventive war often derives from a dangerous geographic situation-encirclement by enemies, as in the case of the pre-1918 Central Powers—although this does not explain propensities for preventive war in the island empires of Japan or Britain. It is also true that analogy, which is, even today, of greater persuasiveness in politics than it ought to be, often works in favor of preventive war suggestions. "Prevention is better than cure." Preventive action is advocated in numerous fields of government and administration other than war. Thus the governors of Massachusetts Colony, considering the religious strife in Central Europe since the reign of Anabaptism in Münster, resorted to preventive measures to avert a similar plague on their distant shores. When they banished dissenters in 1637, they declared:

> Whereas the opinions and revelations of Mr. Wheelwright and Mrs. Hutchinson have seduced and led into dangerous errors many of the people heare in New England, inso much as there is just cause of suspicion that they, as others in Germany, in former times, may, upon some revelation, make some suddaine irruption upon those that differ from them in judgment: for prevention thereof it is ordered, that all those whose names are underwritten shall... before the 20th day of this month of November deliver...all such guns, pistols, swords, shot and match as they shall be owners of.[7]

The bloody terrorism of a number of revolutions from the French to the Russian has been explained and justified by its perpetrators as a measure of "general prevention," brutal perhaps, yet necessary. While it might strike numbers of innocents, they were after all only class or racial opponents and hence enemies of the new "totality" which did well to "liquidate" them preventively by <u>noyades</u>, or work camps, concentration camps, or gas chambers. Transfer-

ence of this basic conviction, usually filled with neurotic anxiety and anticipation of the worst, to the foreign scene prepares the shift from civil to foreign war on the part of revolutionary governors.[8]

IDEOLOGICAL OPPONENTS OF PREVENTIVE WAR

The strongest and most outspoken opposition to preventive war has come from the Christian churches, international lawyers (though not all of them), and diplomats. To the typical opponents of the idea also belong certain enemies of the social evils of the day, such as Liberals, Socialists, anarchists,[9] latter-day psychoanalysts, and perhaps the plain, unenlightened people.[10]

Generally speaking, the Christian churches, as peace-seekers, strongly disapprove of preventive war as perhaps the worst kind of the generally condemnable wars of aggression. They are more united on this point today than in the past. In some of the old religious wars, members of the Catholic clergy participated in such preventively-intended strokes as the St. Bartholomew massacre.[11] Whatever wars the Roman Catholic Church may have backed in past periods of militancy, the Papal See can no longer expect any salvation of the Church by means of war.[12] Defensive wars are still considered justified and participation in them a duty of the Christian citizen; but this does not include participation in wars of aggression, even if they are designed to free the Church in Communist-controlled countries. During the post-1945 period, when the idea of preventive war against Russia appealed to many people in the Western world, including numbers of Catholics,[13] a French bishop formulated a set of theses on this particular kind of war which emphatically set forth the stand of the Church:

> I know that there are in America and even in France a certain number of followers of the preventive war idea...He who starts a preventive war is always a war criminal...He who really wants or wishes that the Americans start a preventive war against Communist Russia, is in a state of sin. He has committed a deadly sin against the Fifth Commandment: Thou shalt not kill...Every offensive war is a sin and a crime.
>
> Invasion for the purpose of liberation is a war undertaken in order to free a people from the injustice with which it is burdened. It is, therefore, no defensive war, it is an offensive one. The liberating invasion is therefore as much a war crime as a preventive war. Should the United States start a war in order to free the nations of Central Europe from the Soviet yoke, they would be war criminals...A treaty

of alliance which draws one into a war of prevention is null and void...Assuming that France is bound to the United States by a military pact, what would one have to do in France should the United States start a preventive war against Russia? There can be only one answer: the pact would automatically become null and void. It would no longer be valid. A pact becomes null and void if contrary to moral law. Not only would France not be bound by such a treaty, she would not even have the right of marching side by side with the United States. If, out of loyalty to this treaty, she allowed herself to be drawn into preventive war, she would become a war criminal...One has no right to obey a government which might intend to draw its nation into a preventive war...What ought one to do, personally, if France should follow the United States into a preventive war? There can be only one answer: One has no right to obey. One would have to refuse to fight!...A government must know that it will find no obedience if it starts a preventive war.[14]

In other words it is the duty of a Christian to oppose a preventive war. This at once raises the question of how to recognize a war as preventive in character. Often such a judgment has only been possible long after the particular war, if at all. How will the adviser of the Christian conscience be able to know at once, at the outbreak of a war, whether or not that war is preventive? Is he not in danger of falling victim to the propaganda of the side which proclaims most vociferously that the war was started by the opponent, with preventive intention? Or is he not likely to be torn between the two sides if they should accuse one another of preventive intentions? Is he not apt to fall victim to "peace" propaganda that never mentions preventive war as a possible motivation, except to accuse the "war-mongering" opponent of planning just such an attack?

To ascribe preventive war intentions to the opponent is indeed part of the propagandistic tactics of the non-Christian camp centered in Moscow. Before 1939, and after 1945, the political and military position of the Soviet State allowed it to leave the idea of preventive war out of all public discussion, though the little war against Finland in 1939-40 was in actuality, and even by admission, a preventive war.[15] Otherwise, Russia's position of military weakness in the period up to 1941 made it advisable for her governors to remain on the defensive and to postpone the actual outbreak of the conflict with the Western capitalist and Fascist Powers, which they considered inevitable. The latter, from all theoretical declarations of the Communists, could still expect that Russia would intervene abroad, and even attack in the interest of world revolution,[16] once she was able to do so. In other words, the Communist expectation is that, at the last moment before the Russian-Communist superiority becomes obvious to them, the remaining capitalist Powers will undertake a preventive war against Russia in order to block the final victory of Socialism. Moscow might do well to avert or postpone or in other ways make such a war difficult by draining away the strength accumulated by the non-Communist world for this Armageddon. From this point of view, the small wars along the frontiers where capitalist civilization and Red expansion meet (such as in Korea, or in Indochina) are essentially wars of prevention.

Psychoanalysis shares one role with the Church, that of the confessor. Both make therapeutic use of this method, though in rather diverse ways. The confession of a patient who "believes so firmly that someone has evil intentions on his life that he protects himself by forestalling him and carrying out a prophylactic murder must remind one of the so-called 'preventive wars' and opens up the question of the original source of the aggressive intentions" on the part of a nation or its leaders against another nation, according to an outstanding analyst of the Anglo-Saxon world, Ernest Jones. It is fear that leads to acts of aggression, the aggressor being possibly "also afraid of external aggression conceived by his conscience as retaliation or punishment for his own aggressive impulses. Moreover, he often projects these on to the outer world and responds with fear to what may in that case be a largely imaginary danger. This is a typical paranoid reaction. Much more important than all these, however, are the purely internal sources of anxiety ..."[17] While it will be worthwhile to keep in mind the psychotic character of some advocates of preventive war, it ought also to be remembered that the psychoanalyzable data on them is scanty. The generalizations proceeding from the case of one or a few patients under psychoanalytic observation to that of a mass may easily amount to that over-generalization which is the besetting sin of psychoanalysis when trying to describe and evaluate mass phenomena.

Preventive war, its contemplation, undertaking, and justification, marks the utmost conflict of Law and Power. According to its advocates, international law and treaties must be broken and disregarded when the prevailing power situation makes the application of available power superiority most advisable.[18] To those who hold that international relations belong under the regimen of Law or to diplomats who consider the prevention of war, and not merely the veiling of war intention, as the highest purpose of their profession, preventive war is the least justifiable kind of war.

Waging preventive war requires a complete disregard for war-guilt accusations. A few of the war-makers even admitted, as Prussian Colonel von Tiedemann did during the 1870's, that "the most unjust way of preparing the war is, in a military way, the best."

Most listings of "just wars" have excluded preventive war. But a few international lawyers, whom we shall meet in our subsequent short history of the idea of preventive war, have included them. Francis Lieber's list of just wars, reflecting the views of his time no less than of his own personal experience, included "wars of insurrection," wars of independence on the part of colonies ripe for self-government, wars to quell armed factions, wars to unite distracted states of the same nation, and wars of defense against invasion or conquest. "A war may be essentially defensive," he wrote, "and yet we may begin it, for instance, if we must prevent an invasion which is under preparation."[19] From the point in time from which this author wrote, this might have meant that if Britain were preparing a war on Canadian soil, which could only be directed against the United States, the latter would be justified in proceeding to preventive measures, including war.[20] Such a conviction as Lieber's as to what is right and permissible for the United States was then and still is at the bottom of the Monroe Doctrine. For a century, practically all threats that actually or seemingly endangered that doctrine and American security were not immediate military threats but only threats existing in a more or less remote future. At many times in American history there has been a great readiness to anticipate the growth of dangers arising from the actions, even innocent ones, of a potentia tremenda, and to proceed to anticipatory and preventive action, diplomatic or military. Hence the demonstrative concentration of troops in the direction of Napoleon's soldiers in Mexico. Hence the entry into two world wars in anticipation of the German danger, although this remains, in the practice of American politics, among the undeclared motivations.

THE MILITARY ARGUMENT: MOST WARS ARE PREVENTIVE OR PREVENTABLE

Behind the various pacifist concepts lies the idea that war and peace are utterly different and separate. Bellicists, however, have usually viewed peace as a state very close to war and preventive action against the unwary enemy as the supreme imperative, whether in war or in peace.[21]

> "But while he stood with helm unlaced,
> Guichardo eager, with preventive haste,
> Th'encounter dared....."
>
> (Orlando Furioso)[22]

Many soldiers have considered themselves as essentially praeventores.[23] Napoleon, for example, was more concerned with winning battles than with avoiding the onus of the epithet "aggressor." In fact he could scarcely conceive of "circumstances where any consideration should balance the advantage of anticipating (prévenir) the enemy and of attacking first."[24] Some military authors, impatient with the civilian pretence that war has been "forced upon them," have gone so far as to declare that essentially all wars are "what is commonly understood as preventive war, or, better put, there are no preventive wars, for every war could have been avoided." Thus wrote the retired Austrian General Alfred Krauss, a protagonist of the Anschluss, in his Theory and Practice in the Art of War. Krauss was clearly an heir and perpetuator of the Conrad school of thought on preventive war-making. According to him, preventive war is one

which one brings about in the supposition that it will not be possible to avoid it...because the other party gives no peace and works itself in the direction of war. Consequently, the wars of 1864, 1866, and 1870, that is to say, all the wars brought about by Bismarck, were "preventive wars" because all of them could have been avoided or put off. Every war would be avoidable, if the side politically attacked were yielding, yielding to the will of the adversary who is acting politically aggressive, as Bismarck did with respect to France in 1867. He might have yielded again in 1870, and much easier than in 1867, because in 1870 no vital right of Prussia was involved but merely the turning down of an insolent demand. It would have been better in any case for Prussia and the South German States if the war with France would have broken out as early as 1867, even if under the stigma of preventive war—they would have found France altogether unready.

A Bismarckian policy true to that name would certainly have brought on the unavoidable war with France—France's war of revanche—as early as the year 1904 or 1905, at the risk of having been accused of undertaking a preventive war...But the successors of Bismarck, imitating only the most unessential part of his diplomacy, have had the fatal concept of preventive war before their eyes, have shied from it, or rather by appealing to the authority of Bismarck have refrained from wholehearted resolution and have consequently missed the good opportunity of striking down France when she was alone, and finishing her off; they have incurred serious guilt before the German people and were instead pushed into the World War, for which they were not prepared, by enemies much less scrupulous than they themselves.[25]

Another Austrian, the "little corporal" from Braunau, entertained a similar war doctrine. He began his wars for the admitted reason of prevention. To the end, he justified them as imperative for this very reason and protested that it was impossible to act too preventively. As he told the divisional commanders who were to fight the Battle of the Bulge:

> The objection that we acted too preventively has to be rejected at once. All successful wars of mankind, gentlemen, have been preventive wars. He who recognizes that a war is inevitable and does not make use of the moment which appears favorable to him commits a sin against his own people...We had for once the great luck to have established, by a gigantic endeavor, a complete superiority where none had existed in most fields of arming. But it was obvious that this superiority could be only of a transitory nature.[26]

Most advocates of preventive war-making have concerned themselves very little with the odium of war-guilt that attaches itself to the aggressor. The risk of incurring this odium has, however, stood in the way of many if not most proposals in favor of preventive war and has kept their numbers small. Proposed wars of prevention have largely remained unfought wars, far more often advocated, notably by soldiers and sailors, than actually undertaken by their countries.

A SHORT HISTORY OF THE IDEA AND PRACTICE OF PREVENTIVE WAR

1. Greece and Rome

The problem of justifying a war, either before its opening, as a measure of policy, or following its close, as a matter of history, is practically as old as written history. While it did not arise where war was undertaken for motives of simple loot-gathering, among nomads or Vikings or inside the old despotisms, it presented itself irrepressibly in deliberative commonwealths, such as in the Greek city-states, which were less and less willing to spend money on war as wars became expensive rather than remunerative for the upper classes. In the great oratorical duel between the reckless duce, Alcibiades, and the cautious Nicias, the spokesman of Athenian wealth, on the eve of the Sicilian expedition of 415, it was Alcibiades, eager for the supreme command in the coming venture, who brought forth the argument for preventive action. He, the unprincipled

demagogue, played the role of the far-sighted statesman. The dangers that might menace Athens, were she to refrain from supporting her allies in Sicily, were clearly as remote as Syracuse was from Attica. Nicias, advocating non-intervention, reminded the people of this. Yet Alcibiades won out with his arguments in favor of empire and security and rich spoils, to be secured by preventive action: The Athenians had concluded leagues with some of the Sicilian cities, he argued,

> not that they might come here to help us in their turn, but that by annoying our enemies there they might prevent their coming here to attack us...Men do not only defend themselves against a superior when he has attacked them, but also strike the first blow, to prevent his attacking them. And it is not possible for us to portion out exactly how far we wish to hold dominion; but since we are in our present situation, we must form designs against some, and not give up others; because we should be subjected to the rule of another party, if we did not ourselves rule over others. (Thucydides, VI, 18).

The frightful outcome of the Sicilian expedition should have robbed the preventive war argument of its strength among the Athenians for a long time to come. Still Demosthenes, the last of the Greek statesmen of stature, could safely appeal to the preventive motive in his anti-Philippian policy. He warned Athenian democracy that, while it was succumbing to a peace-at-any-price sentiment, Philip was encircling it like a piece of game in the nets of a hunter (First Philippic, §351). In the first of his Olynthian orations (§349) he favored sending Athenian forces, one to help the Olynthians defend themselves against the engulfing Macedonian, one to attack him outright. "Better now than later" is the Leitmotif of this oration, better to stop Philip outside Greece proper than have him come inside and play on the basic disunity of the Greeks.[27] Olynthus and the league of cities around it were destroyed before the Athenians were ready to render effective help. Now it was the turn of the war party in aroused Athens to demand a full-sized preventive war against Philip, while Demosthenes had to advise his people not to become more bellicose than the state of their armaments would allow.

To the extent that the Romans were more military than the Greeks, the soldiers' argument in favor of preventive war found acclaim among them more readily than among the citizenry of the Greek polis. It was the argument by which Caesar justified the successful campaign undertaken by him, without any mandate from the Senate, against the Helvetii in 58 B.C. This tribe, the bravest people of Gaul according to Caesar, were hard-pressed by the Germans at their back. They wanted to leave Lake Geneva and migrate to Western Gaul. This resettlement, Caesar thought, would bring that war-like tribe much too close to the Roman province in Gaul to afford peace and security. While the Helvetii refrained from acts of aggression on their march and offered Caesar no lawful pretext for war, the latter attacked them for preventive reasons. Mommsen, in terms of nineteenth-century Bismarckian state-reasoning, defends this step: "To prohibit their march, the Romans had no basis in law; however, other and higher interests were involved for them than the question of the formal integrity of Roman territory..."[28]

At home, Caesar's preventive wars were at first thought to have been undertaken on slight or no provocation and were considered unjust and dangerous. These convictions led to such proposals as Cato's that Caesar be delivered up to the foreign enemies in order to expiate his breach of faith, which ought to have been observed, even with barbarians. But the magnitude of his successes overcame the humanitarian ideas of the younger Cato and of Cicero.[29]

2. Early Christianity

The problem of the just war that troubled some non-militarized Romans was occasionally raised and most incisively discussed by the early Christian Church, and above all by Saint Augustine (354-430). He made the sharp distinction between wars of aggression and wars of defense. Of the two, only the latter are just, even with regard to pagans. "It was Augustine who introduced 'war guilt' into Christian history."[30] He does not seem to have contemplated preventive war; but insofar as it is the most aggressive kind of war, he would logically have considered it the most unjust form.

The practice of the Christian soldier was at first largely in keeping with the theologians' condemnation of aggressive war. The pagans were on the offensive everywhere, the Moslems in the East,[31] the Hungarians and Avars against Central Europe, and the Normans against the West of Christianized Europe. Christians were forced to be on the defensive. In Byzantium, Christian war theory, permitting only defensive war, coincided fairly well with military necessity.[32] The result was to exclude preventive war, even when, in the opinion of Edward Gibbon, occasion seemed to call for it.[33] As Carl Erdmann has put it, "one still kept so closely to the defensive character of the just war that even as regards the pagans only the truly defensive war was recognized" by the Christian Church. In medieval Western Europe, however, the secular princes showed less

hesitation in undertaking preventive wars, judging by the reports of the chroniclers. Some of the military leaders along the frontiers of Christianity even thought preventive assassination advisable and justifiable. Odo, first of the Capetian kings (elected 887) had a banner-bearer named Ingo, who had won battles for him against the Normans. When the Normans' leader later underwent baptism, Ingo killed him in the baptistery, thinking that this converted heathen was best prevented from making further mischief by an early death. The King and magnates approved of this thoroughly preventive measure, which had the additional advantage of carrying off the new Christian in a state of freshly acquired innocence.[34]

The Christian nations were going over to the offensive along most frontiers during the tenth century, backed and blessed by a slowly developing crusading theology. Leo IX (1049-54) was the first pope to justify the Christian wars of his time by the tenets of religion. He harmonized war with the doctrines of the Church, permeated the warlike spirit of knighthood with the Churchly spirit, and made the Church militant in war. During the First Crusade, the concept of the miles Christi or miles Dei was formed, replacing the earlier martyr or ascetic spirit of sainthood.[35] The theology of conquest was now more or less complete. At various times it could even cover a preventive war.

In Thomas Fuller's Historie of the Holy Warre (Cambridge 1639) the "arguments for the lawfulnesse of the Holy warre" (and also against it) are fully assembled, though not too strictly in accordance with historical principles. However, in an outline history of preventive war, his ideas must serve as a shortcut from the medieval to the Renaissance view of that special kind of war. Fuller, a Puritan divine, found it "stiffly canvassed betwixt learned men" whether crusades were lawful of not, the reasons for the affirmative being taken either from "pietie or policie." Among the latter was the need for preventive action against the Saracens.[36]

A preventive warre grounded on a just fear of an invasion is lawfull: But such was this Holy warre. And because most stresse is laid on this argument, as the main supporter of the cause, we will examine and prove the parts thereof.

Though umbrages and light jealousies created by cowardly fansies be too narrow to build a fair quarrel on; yet the lawfulnesse of a preventive warre founded on a just fear, is warranted by reason and the practice of all wise nations. In such a case it is folly to do as country-fellows in a fense-school, never ward a blow till it be past; but it is best to be before-hand with the enemie, lest the medicine come too late for the maladie. In such dangers to play an after-game, is rather a shift than a policie: especially seeing warre is a tragedy which alwayes destroyeth the stage whereon it is acted: it is the most advised way, not to wait for the enemie but to seek him out in his own countrey.

Now that the Mahometans...were justly to be feared, cannot be denied. So vast was the appetite of their sword, that it had alreadie devoured Asia, and now reserved Grecia for the second course. The Bosporus was too narrow a ditch, and the Empire of Grecia too low an hedge to fence the Pagans out of West-Christendom: yea, the Saracens had lately wasted Italy, pillaged and burned many churches near Rome itself, conquered Spain, etc....The case therefore standeth thus, this Holy warre was both lawfull and necessary: which like unto a sharpe pike in the bosse of a buckler, though it had a mixture of offending, yet it was chiefly of a defensive nature to which all preventive warres are justly reduced.[37]

3. Preventive War Ideas of the Renaissance

In most periods of history, the argument in favor of preventive action has been basically aristocratic. It has been proposed by aristocratic elements, considered in secret councils, and rarely brought forward in public discussion. It might well be called a typically Renaissance motif, in politics and historiography.

In Machiavelli's History of Florence (written 1521-25) it is related that, before the war with Filippo Maria Visconti of 1424, the parties in Florence were at first divided as to the advisability of war. The upper classes in 1422 thought it wise to arm and prepare to thwart the plans ascribed to Visconti. Others, however, either from envy of the party in power or from fear of war, believed that there was insufficient ground to suspect Visconti, who was still nominally an ally of Florence. The peace party accused those in power of implicating the state in unnecessary war in order to keep the people in subjection. They urged waiting for an open attack by Filippo, rather than appearing, arms in hand, as the aggressors. But the war party, still the strongest among the popolo grasso, insisted that "it would be better to seek the enemy out in his house than wait for him in one's own; Fortune was favoring the attack rather the defensive; if not also at less expense, it was at least with less damage to carry war into foreign territory." This view at last carried the day, but the Florentines were beaten by Visconti, with unfortunate reactions against the war-making party at home. They were hard put to defend the war as "necessary" and had to shoulder a heavy levy on their property (Book IV).

Feeling that they alone could not resist Visconti's superior power, the Florentines appealed to Venice for help in order to maintain the threatened balance of power in Italy. Allies were sought with the argument that a common enemy—such as Milan under Visconti—must be met before it grew too powerful.[38] The Venetians at first proved difficult because of their basic dislike of land warfare. However, Francesco Carmagnola, an outstanding condottiere, brought them around. He had fled from the service of Visconti, who, he told the Venetians, "once he had conquered the Florentines, would promptly attack them since he was aspiring for the dignity of king over Italy; Visconti was beginning with the weaker of his opponents in order to be able to measure up and become superior to the more powerful ones, once he himself had become more powerful through the victory over the weak ones." Florentine diplomacy pleaded in the same vein: "Why do you hesitate? If we succumb to Filippo, we shall make him king of Italy; and you as well as the Emperor will be conquered." Moved by such representations, the Venetians entered the war on the side of the Florentines "without ire," as Aeneas Silvius puts it. That is to say, they acted not rashly but only after considering the advisability of war in order to prevent the eventual overgrowth of Filippo's power.[39]

Renaissance governors were expected to act beforehand with their enemies, at home and abroad, in diplomacy and war, if they wanted to remain in power. In fact, the age prided itself greatly on preventive action. Machiavelli in his Arte della guerra and his Discorsi dedicates whole chapters to discussing and justifying the application of deception and preventive action in international or civil warfare.[40] The Renaissance prince, he argues, must be prompt to apply preventive action in moments of crisis, if not earlier. Hesitation may prove fatal. "You do not want to be subjugated? Then promptly proceed to subjugate the neighbor as long as his weakness offers you the occasion; for if you let it pass, fugitive opportunity will move over into the enemy's camp; and he will subjugate you."[41]

For the sixteenth-century legists and moralists persevering in the Christian tradition of Augustine and Thomas Aquinas, men like Erasmus, Luther and Vitoria, there was no just cause for war, except the violation of a right, if that.[42] That such judgments could be shrugged off as extramundane and impractical was due to the disintegration of the Christian world into balancing states. Being sovereign, they were less subject to Christian morality and used religion as a State servant more than before.

The balance of power, as the divisor of the Christian world, came to call for war as a guarantee of its preservation, acting in anticipation if possible. This practice of states was "legalized," that is, accepted and systematized into law and legal argument by the international lawyers of the later Renaissance, notably Alberico Gentili (1552-1608), Francis Bacon (1561-1626), and, to a markedly lesser degree, Hugo Grotius. The former two taught these "non-theological" concepts of law from the political vantage point of Elizabethan England. The international law of all three bore a deep imprint of the political systems they served and adhered to. The Italian Protestant-exile Gentili, a fugitive from the Inquisition, was the importer and systematizer of the teachings of Roman law and Italian statecraft, as examplified by Lorenzo de' Medici, who was constantly concerned "that the balance of power...be maintained among the princes of Italy." "Is not this even today our problem," Gentili asks, "that one may not have supreme power and that all Europe may not submit to the domination of a single man? Unless there is something which can resist Spain, Europe will surely fall." Since it is lawful to anticipate a wrong—praevenire licet—this very great evil of a Spanish or other dominatus can lawfully be met by war, including an anticipatory war. "I call it a defence dictated by expediency, when we make war through fear that we may ourselves be attacked. No one is more quickly laid low than one who has no fear, and a sense of security is the most common cause of disaster...Then, we ought not to wait for violence to be offered to us if it is safer to meet it halfway."

With great erudition, Gentili discovers the superiority of the preventive everywhere in the history of politics and warfare. The necessity of prevention makes it "lawful for me to attack a man who is making ready to attack me," a maxim laid down "for the benefit of humanity and confirmed in the courts...No one ought to expose himself to danger. No one ought to wait to be struck, unless he is a fool. One ought to provide not only against an offence which is being committed, but also against one which may possibly be committed. Force must be repelled and kept aloof by force." However, there are necessary doubts as to the point where "it is necessary to resort to that expedient defence. A just cause for fear is demanded; suspicion is not enough. Now a just fear is defined as the fear of a greater evil, a fear which might properly be felt even by a man of great courage." There are limits to comparison and analogy: while private persons have ways of obtaining reparation through the courts of law, that is not possible for great empires. For Gentili, the world of states is a world full of fear. States have a right to their fears, which are more subjectively certain than objectively ascertainable and of which there is usually more than one justifiable cause, "and no general rule can be laid down. We will merely say this: namely, that we should oppose powerful and ambitious chiefs. For they are content with no bounds, and end by attacking the fortunes of all." In his own time Gentili considered the Spanish and the Turks to be such Powers.

We must, therefore, oppose them; and it is better to provide that men should not acquire too great power, than to be obliged to seek a remedy later, when they have already become too powerful...We must unite in opposing the common danger..."It is not enough to be able to do harm. Destroy in advance whatever can harm others" (Ovid, Fasti).

But to conclude, a defence is just which anticipates dangers that are already meditated and prepared...and those which are not meditated but are probable and possible. This last word, however, is not to be taken literally, for in that case my statement would be that it is just to resort to a war of this kind as soon as any one becomes too powerful, which I do not maintain. For what if a prince should have his power increased by succession and elections? Will you assail him in war because his power may possibly be dangerous to you? Some other reason must be added for justice's sake. We shall add this reason to others which have some justice.[43]

In spite of such hedging, preventive war received a goodly measure of legal approval from Gentili, who was also aware of the great psychological motivation in it—fear and anxiety in the governors.

Still more blunt and apodictic was the endorsement given to preventive action by Francis Bacon. He considered that in the relations of neighboring states, where so many variables enter in, no general rule, other than that of keeping the balance of power, was possible. "Standing counsel," a higher bureaucracy to whose membership Bacon had aspired and to the vices and corruption of which he himself succumbed, were to foresee and hinder any overgrowth of power. The hindering was to be through alliances or wars, which the counselors were to recommend to their prince. In this matter, the views of medieval "schoolmen" were no longer to be accepted when they said "that war can not be justly made, except upon a precedent injury or provocation; for there is no question, but a just fear of an imminent danger, though there be no blow given, is a lawful cause of a war."[44]

In Holland a fighting burgherdom had experienced enough of the wilfulness and unreliability of princes, as enemies or allies, to become wary of their motives, to be wary even of the princes who were their own military leaders, and to be sceptical about the balance of power as a principle in international relations. Such experiences, added to strong theological views, were among the formative influences on Hugo Grotius and his Law of War and Peace (1625).

He finds that in "private wars," where a person is attacked without expecting it, a right prevails to defend oneself and one's goods. This is a right, however, that lasts only briefly and ends when the regular organs of justice again prevail. In a public war, on the contrary, where no party recognizes a common judge, the right of self-defense is of longer duration. While the private war is directed only towards simple defense, the Powers entering upon a public war have in addition the right of vengeance and the right to punish for injuries they have received. From this it follows that they are permitted to prevent an insult that seems to threaten them, even from afar. But in conceding this, Grotius will not agree with Gentili and Bacon that it is legitimate and part of the law of nations to take up arms in order to weaken a state whose power is increasing daily, out of fear that if it is allowed to grow too great, it may reach a position of being able to do one harm when occasion arises. Grotius is willing to admit that, should the question of war come to be deliberated, this circumstance should be taken into consideration to some extent, in an accessory way, not as a justifying reason but as a "motive of interest." The view that "one should have the right to attack some one for this reason alone that he is in a position to do us harm, that is a thing contrary to all rules of equity. Such is the condition of human life that in it one never finds oneself in perfect security. It is not to the ways of force but to the protection of Providence and innocent precautions that one ought to look for resources against an uncertain fear"(§16). That is to say: the life of states is so dangerous already that they should not go to war for the reason of a threat to the existing balance of power. Prevention is in the hands of Providence.

And now for a look at the practice of states and governments. Princely absolutism and the forces behind it, including those composing the Counter-Reformation, were on the offensive nearly everywhere during the seventeenth century. The forces of absolutism put the parliaments, estates, and other self-governing institutions on the defensive in diplomacy and war. Venice and the other surviving city-states shut themselves away behind their fortifications. Within the Evangelical Union, on the eve of the Thirty Years' War, the city members were generally inclined to a strict defensive, whereas the princely members, particularly those of the Reformed religion, were far more ready for energetic and active resistance to the Counter-Reformation. At last European Protestantism regained the initiative when Gustavus Adolphus landed on German soil on July 4, 1630. In his manifesto he told his Swedes, all honest Germans, and Christianity in general, why, after exercising so much patience, he had finally undertaken "the just war expedition." The measures of the Imperialists

had at last reached the point where preventive measures on his own part were called for. His opponents, as they approached the Baltic, were looking for war against him. They planned to set up an armada by which they would vomit their poison over the Baltic. This aim they had clearly revealed "by transferring such tremendous, unheard-of titles as General over the Oceanic and Baltic Seas" to Wallenstein, and by the siege of Stralsund, from which place they had hoped to undertake their future piracy and spread their power over the sea. "For such reasons, His Majesty has been forced to meet such calamity beforehand..., the more so since the Kings of Sweden from time immemorial had possessed the right of the defence of the Baltic Sea." Putting the claim to the dominium maris Baltici on a share-holding basis, the King invited all states with whom Sweden was connected by ties of neighborhood, common religion, and commerce to oppose the Imperialists with him.[45]

He was soon to have a stronger ally, Richelieu's France, a power of different religion but equally anti-Hapsburg in political sentiment. French diplomacy had helped to free Gustavus for his enterprise "of preventing the oppression of the princes of the Empire," of helping France against Austria and Spain. "Is there prudence and justice which allows one to wait until the others are devoured, merely to be the last one oneself?" the Cardinal cried out against those Catholics who wanted no war with Catholic Hapsburgs.[46] In the public legacy of his politics, the Testament politique, Richelieu defends his dealings with Sweden as above all designed to prevent possible prejudice to the Catholic religion by obligating the Swedes not to disturb it in the regions of their future conquests. The literate, devout, but politically weak French bourgeoisie craved this reassurance of care for the old religion, but also wanted proof of its own government's prudence. Richelieu himself was conducting the business of government in the manner in which the bourgeoisie was itself accustomed to provide for the contingencies of the future—by habitual business prudence and foresight, and by occasional bold speculation. He took care to let them know this, occasionally in his lifetime, more systematically in his Political Testament. Prévenir, with God's help, was the first principle of his government, in peace and in war. Wars, he wrote, sometimes become necessary for states "in order to guarantee allies against oppression, to halt in its course the pride of a conqueror, to prevent the evils by which one is obviously menaced and from which one cannot in any other way exempt oneself."[47]

Under Absolutism, the prince and military commander were often one and the same person. An even more common arrangement was the two-sided counselling between prince and war minister, as between Louis XIV and Louvois from 1661 to 1691, instead of the King-in-Council arrangement in which all or many ministers participated. The latter arrangement brought military considerations to bear on proposed military measures. The former was on the whole favorable to the practice of preventive war. And, at the same time, civilian voices favoring preventive war were never quite wanting. One of the mouthpieces of seventeenth-century merchant militancy as organized in the East India Company, Sir Dudley Digges (1538-1639), defended, even if as a paradox, the view "that warre is sometimes less hurtful, and more to be wisht in a well governed State than peace." Such a useful war draws off bad humors, while the wish for eternal peace remains a hopeless speculation. Considering this, was it not safer and more honorable to threaten others than wait until they attacked? Was it not more reasonable to hold neighbors down at the point of the sword than allow them time to prepare a war?[48]

The soldier becoming literate used his pen to express his sentiments in favor of preventive war. Being as much of a professional soldier as the conditions of English politics in his time allowed, Monk, during an enforced period of leisure in the Tower from 1644 to 1646, wrote his Observations upon Military and Political Affairs. Monk advises the prince "to invade an enemy in his own country, rather than to attend him at home. He proceeds to call it "an excellent property of a good and wise Prince to use war, as he doth Physick, carefully, unwillingly, and seasonably; either to prevent approaching dangers, or to correct a present mischief, or to recover a former loss. He that declineth Physick till he is accosted with the danger, or weakened with the disease, is bold too long, and wise too late. That peace is too precise, that limiteth the justness of a war to a sword drawn, or a blow given..."[49]

But British opinion was never fully agreed as to the justness and advisability of preventive war. In 1650, when war with Scotland had become once more imminent, the Council of State "determined to anticipate the expected attack of the Scots by an invasion of Scotland." Commander-in-chief Thomas Fairfax, however, would not command the army unless the Scots invaded England once more and made themselves the aggressors. "Human probabilities," he said, "are not sufficient grounds to make war upon a neighbor nation, especially our brethren of Scotland, to whom we are engaged in a solemn league and Covenant." Such conscientious scruples did not bother Cromwell, who accepted the post of "captain-general and commander-in-chief of all the forces raised or to be raised by authority of parliament" and who then invaded Scotland.[50] From there he was soon to report that "on the Lord's day, hear-

ing that the Scottish Army meant to meet us at Gladsmoor, we laboured to possess the Moor before them and beat our drums very early in the morning."[51]

The structure of Restoration politics made it difficult for Charles II to justify his wars against the Dutch as preventive in nature. Instead, he tried to maneuver Parliament into starting the war, "to make them in honor begin a war which he cannot in honor declare first, for fear they should not second him with money," as Pepys noted well ahead of the outbreak of the Second Dutch War.[52] The King succeeded in this endeavor to the extent that both Houses soon petitioned him to take measures for redressing the harm done by the Dutch to English trade, "and for prevention of the like in the future."[53] By that time, the end of April 1664, sentiment in London was much in favor of this war. "We all seem to desire it, as thinking ourselves to have advantages at present over them," Pepys noted. Knowing the unprepared state of the Navy, Pepys himself dreaded the war,[54] with good reason, as the outcome was to show. Only a courtier-poet like Dryden thought it justified afterwards as a preventive measure:

"What peace can be, where both to one [trade] pretend?
(But they more diligent, and we more strong).
Or if a peace, it soon must have an end,
For they would grow too powerful were it too long."

(Annus mirabilis. 1666)

On the other hand, one of the parliamentary critics declared that preventive wars are nothing "but ne moriare mori, and for fear of being conquered by a foreigner, we put ourselves in a condition almost as bad."[55] The strong and often-used formula against preventive war, that it is tantamount to suicide in fear of death, seems to have emerged first as a piece of oligarchical political wisdom. While the oligarchies of England and of the Dutch Republic were much too similar in their aspirations for trade to allow lengthy peace between them, as Dryden and others thought, their attitudes towards war were basically similar and resulted in the tendency to postpone it as long as possible. As Grand Pensioneer Jan de Witt wrote to Grotius in 1670: "The character of the Dutch is such that, unless the danger is right under their eyes, they are not disposed to take on themselves the burdens of their own defence."[56] Preventive action was impeded by the deliberative processes of Dutch government. When Louis XIV openly prepared war against the Dutch during 1671 and 1672, he and Louvois feared that the Republicans would forestall them and destroy the French magazines built up along the lower

Rhine. After he tried in vain to avert the war, Jan de Witt had indeed proposed such action against the French to the States General. They, however, did not want to incur the odium of aggression, even for the obvious military advantage that such a coup seemed to promise.[57]

4. Absolutism and Prevention

All the wars of Louis XIV, including the last one, the War of the Spanish Succession, were by declaration or admission of their author wars of prevention. While neither the King nor his war minister Louvois were soldiers by upbringing or temperament, they were always at least as ready as the marshals and generals to make use of the superior preparedness of French armies to attack prospective enemies, regardless of the latters' true intentions or their military abilities to realize them. Justification of these wars was based on the claim of the absolutistic prince to greater foresight and superior penetration of hostile diplomatic designs against France.[58] Justification was also based on the claim of exemption from the rules of law and justice that prevailed among private individuals, as clerics and even philosophers such as Descartes came to admit.[59] The great philosopher's approval of French and other Absolutisms and their wars is indicative of the long-continued willingness of the French bourgeoisie to believe in the justice and advisability of their Kings' wars, including their preventive actions. The pseudo-rationalism of absolute government, progressive indeed, but only by comparison to feudalism, fascinated bourgeois-capitalistic thought of the seventeenth century to such a degree that it blinded them to the unproductiveness of even the so-called "trade wars," and to the vicious morality of the governors and the governing system.

Preventive war intentions figured in Ludovican diplomatic procedures in the opening of wars and was announced as such in some of the King's war manifestos. In 1664-65, Louis heard of some new Spanish armaments, which were actually not, nor could be, of a serious character, considering the financial embarrassments of Spain. He heard also of a supposed understanding between Madrid and Vienna. He thereupon informed his ambassador in Madrid that "since both of these two designs, whichever may be the true one, are equally prejudicial to me, I am resolved not to allow myself to be forestalled in such a way as to remain with my arms crossed while they prepare a business of that nature, which would grow irremediable as time goes on."[60] The first of his wars followed these threats by some two years.

The military beliefs of the age—often sheer superstitions—emphasized the value of the "key position," the holding or gaining of a point that might decide a war or campaign at the outset or guarantee security and peace. Thinking in terms of the "key position" led many a monarch to attempt to wrest such a point from the control of an opponent. Louis XIV learned in 1674 that the Palatine Elector was to hand over the small town of Germersheim to the Emperor. Occupation of the poorly fortified little town was considered a threat to the French-held fortress of Philipsburg, as well as a menace to Alsace and Lorraine. In terms of conventional historiography, "there was not a moment to lose. After he had vainly tried...diplomatic means, Louis made his troops occupy Germersheim. This coup de main against the State of a prince who, however close to giving up neutrality, had not yet crossed the borderline, threw great alarm into the Empire." It was futile for Louis to send the text of the treaty between the Palatinate and the Emperor to all the German courts—his aggression was generally considered as unjustified and only served to accelerate the declaration of war against him by the Regensburg Diet.[61]

The war against Holland (begun in 1672) was prepared by diplomatic isolation of the States-General and several coups of a preventive nature. In the summer of 1671, the French ambassador explained to the Swedes that the measures against the Dutch were part of the King's "prudence in order to precede his enemies, whose bad intentions would grow the more dangerous the more they were allowed time to hide them...; that therefore His Majesty had resolved to repel these diverse offenses with arms."[62] A potential ally of Holland was eliminated two years before the attack. When Louis learned that the Duke of Lorraine was negotiating with the Emperor and Holland for the loan of a force of 13,000 men in case of a war, he at once marched French troops into Lorraine "in order to make it impossible for the Duke of Lorraine to do me any harm."[63] While these obvious war preparations were going on, Jan de Witt still could not induce the States-General to proceed to energetic preventive measures. The unpreparedness of Holland, revealed by the overwhelming initial military successes of the French, cost the de Witts their lives and the oligarchs their power, which slipped into the hands of the Orangemen and their party, who had advocated more armament than the oligarchy had been willing to grant.

The repeated shock of Louis' preventive wars greatly helped to bring his opponents together in the League of Augsburg of 1686. An envoy of William of Orange met with a group of the ministers of the North German princes in August 1688. William was then planning his expedition to England, for which he sought the princes' aid. His

envoy told the assembly that James II would
convoke a Parliament in the autumn, which would
certainly vote as James wished and would grant
an army and navy. France would also have a navy
the coming spring. "Hence it would be better to
act beforehand." Recalling the war experience of
1672, the States-General granted William the funds
for his expedition in September. As the historian
of the "fall of the House of Stuart" put it: "It is a
wonderful example never heard of before, that
peaceful burghers, merchants above all, resolved
on an attack which, however, appears as a preventive defensive in their eyes, against a King
who indeed, if he had really striven for unity
among his own subjects, would have been more
powerful than all these opponents."[64] Still,
their enterprise could hardly be termed preventive war, or at least they would not have called
it so.

At Versailles, Louvois again pressed for war:
unless the peaceful policies of Colbert were reversed, "we shall pay dearly for the repose
which we have enjoyed these five or six years."[65]
France seemed to him to be in danger of falling
back into the competition of states, unless she
put to an active use her superior military readiness, Louvois' own achievement. Military potential was then but little contemplated by the war-
makers, but a subconscious awareness lay at
the bottom of the proposal. Brought up in the
school of Ludovican war diplomacy, the French
minister at the Hague advised attacking the Dutch on
the Rhine, thus keeping them from aiding William
in his enterprise against James II. Louis agreed
that this would give the Dutch a wholesome fright.
"But the necessity of preceding the wicked intentions of the Vienna court [of which there were no
immediate indications, though the Emperor had
achieved notable successes over the Turk] has
left us no other choice than the one I prefer,"
in the direction of the upper Rhine. He tried to
justify his aggression défensive by a manifesto,
"Memoire of the reasons which have forced the
King of France to take up arms once more"
(Versailles, September 24, 1688):

> Those who will examine without passion and
> without any other interest than that of public
> welfare the conduct of His Majesty from the
> beginning of the war in Hungary until now will
> have good reason to be astonished that, having
> been well informed of the design to attack
> France long harbored by the Emperor, as soon
> as peace with the Turks had been concluded,
> he should have deferred until this hour in or-
> der to advance on him and that, far from mak-
> ing use of the pretexts which the rules of good
> policy might have suggested to him in order to
> prevent the aggrandizement of that Prince, he

> should even have been willing to sacrifice in
> favor of peace the just causes, with which he
> has been so often provided, in order to make
> use of the forces which God has put into his
> hands, as much for the purpose of taking from
> the court of Vienna the means of hurting him
> as well as to avert the course of the unjust and
> violent usurpations of the Palatine Elector.[66]

There was at first a genuine desire on the part
of most Powers to avert a war over the Spanish
succession. William III expressed his desire
"to contribute all that depended upon me to prevent a war and to preserve the tranquillity of
Europe."[67] But the foreign King's foresight,
his timely measures taken to avert future
dangers, had little appeal for nearly one half of
the English people. Tory isolationism and anti-
militarism continually forced him to reduce the
peace-time army, which they considered a standing threat to English liberties. In the ensuing war
of pamphlets, Daniel Defoe took up the pen,
anonymously, for Whiggism. To him the standing
army in England was a preventive of war. "The
prudentest course is to prevent the trial" by having a sufficient force available to keep the
treaties intact.[68] While William's policy of the
Partition Treaties failed to settle the Spanish
succession, a strong current of opinion favored
abstention from entanglements on the Continent,
regardless of the threat of French domination
that was certain to arise unless England intervened. As the most agile defender of the King's
policy, Defoe published another pamphlet, "The
Two Great Questions considered. I. What the
French King will do, with respect to the Spanish
Monarchy. II. What measures the English ought
to take" (November 1700). In this pamphlet, he
pointed out to his countrymen that French rule
over Spain would upset that just balance of power,
arrived at after so much bloodshed through the
Ryswick Treaty, which was the life of peace. It
would not be easy to deter the French, thanks
to those sham patriots who had robbed the King
of the standing army that could be put into the
field at once. Not only the power situation, but
also a more immediate interest might force
England into war with France. Something perhaps
alien to the country gentlemen, England's future
trade, was the interest most immediately endangered.

> What is England without its trade, without its
> Plantation trade, Turkey and Spanish trade,
> and where will that be when a French garrison
> is planted at Cadiz, and the French fleet brings
> home the plate from Havana? What will the
> Virginia colony be worth when the French have
> a free commerce from Quebec to Mexico be-

hind ye, what will our northern trade be worth in a war, when the ports of Ostend and Nieuport are as full of pirates as Dunkirk and St. Malo?

A more lofty interest, the Protestant religion, would likewise be threatened by French domination of the Continent. This was the last argument from the pamphleteer's quiver, bound to strike home where the other arguments might have failed.[69] In the theology of war, as a clever pamphleteer like Defoe must have well known, approval of preventive war for crusading purposes was a sentiment as yet available in some strength.

The exhaustion of Europe by the Ludovican wars produced great scepticism towards the princes' and governors' claim to foresight and prescience. It came to be treated with a great deal of irony by the bourgeois writers of the eighteenth century, such as Voltaire or Chamfort. The former, in his satiric tale Zadig (1748), had a hermit throw the nephew of a harridan into the river, because "ce jeune homme aurait assassiné sa tante dans un an."[70] Had not using the foresight of evils as a justification for wars proved to be the cause of evils even greater than those foreseen or foretold? Jean Rousset, a French refugee writing and publishing among the Dutch, put the conclusion into more religious terms:

> Providence which disposes in a sovereign way of events, often deceives what is called human prudence, and that is also a reason to be surprised that men torment themselves with preventive dispositions which they imagine to be all to their glory or in their interest. Out of that are born so many wars....[71]

The thinking bourgeoisie wanted more reasonableness in war-making and treaty-keeping. It formed, therefore, an archetype of treaty, the social contract, under which rulers hold their powers only conditionally, not absolutely: "Whoever has the supreme power of any commonwealth, is bound to govern by established standing laws...and to employ the force of community at home only in the execution of such laws, or abroad to prevent or redress foreign injuries and secure the community from inroad and invasion."[72] This rule for governors stops short of the discussion of the more factual problem of whether or not they should undertake preventive wars if need be.

The question posed itself anew to the new generation of jurists: Is a war lawful that is undertaken in order to avert a threatening danger, including an impending attack? The ensuing wars of the eighteenth-century repeatedly raised this question. In October 1733, the French army occupied Lorraine under the pretext that the enemy might seize it if it were left to itself. The whole procedure struck the Paris bourgeoisie as one to which it had become too thoroughly accustomed by the grandfather of Louis XV. "That is what happens in all the wars with Germany," noted Barbier, a citizen of Paris, in his journal.[73] But was what one could expect from absolutistic governors also legal? The bourgeoisie was inclined to ask this question.[74] The answers provided by the university teachers of law and politics and by publicists could hardly be satisfying, for their public character put nearly all of them under the control, or made them integral parts, of the bureaucracy of Absolutism.

One of the crudest and bluntest of the German university teachers of political science during the first half of the eighteenth century was Nikolaus Hieronymus Gundling. Frankly, and in the mixed learned language of the day, he told his students that "everyone reasons in accordance with his interests; as long as they are happy, no one reasons about justice." According to him, a jus praeventionis could not be exercised in vita civili. However, "great lords can do it in statu naturalis; it then forms part of their defense; hence a princeps can, on occasion, do away with dexterity those a quibus ipsi pericula imminet...One calls this coups d'état, according to Naudé...And thus Wallenstein was diligently removed, and if no one had done it, the Emperor would have lost the Kingdom of Bohemia." In statu naturali "there is no judex, hence I obtain remedy as well as I can. Here there is no time left for waiting lest I should perish...It would be like waiting for a mine to blow up...He who is expecting mathematical demonstration is apt to deceive himself very much...Those people are least fit for politics who have a morale outrée and would insist on plenty of mathematical demonstration..."

"Since I may play the praevenire and may attack, re, actu, corpore at a time when you do not attack me as yet, but are about to do it, the question arises: Whether I may attack someone propter metum crescentis potentiae. He who increases in such a measure or disrupts the balance, as one nowadays puts it, and still does not attack anyone, makes it very dubious whether in such a case a sword may be drawn." Still Gundling is inclined to answer in the affirmative. Since the praevenire may be played, "it is hard to determine quis sit aggressor." That is to say, when preventive war is considered permissible, the war-guilt question can hardly be raised.[75]

Open protest against the practice and "ideology" of preventive war was slow to form. Montesquieu helped to hinder rather than promote it. When dealing with "laws in the relation they bear to offensive force" (Esprit des Lois, Book X, chap. ii), he appears only slightly less crude than Gundling. He considered power competition inevitable and to a certain extent desirable and the position of being the greatest Power, such as France in his own time, a happy one. Her governors, he wrote, seemed to have reached the stage where their prudence would confine the state within bounds (Ibid., Book IX, chap vi). But such a belief in the at least temporary goodness of one's own country is not always shared by others, who continue to view foreign power as potentia tremenda. An international lawyer with sufficient diplomatic practice to make him doubt the goodness of power, Emeric de Vattel (1714-67), Swiss-born and in the service of minor German courts, found it

> unfortunate (malheureux) that one can nearly always presuppose the will to oppress where there is the power to oppress. Shall one wait to avert ruination until it has become inevitable? If an unknown man aims at me in the midst of a forest, I cannot as yet be certain that he wants to shoot—what to do to assure myself about his design? It is perhaps without precedent that a state receives some notable accretion of power without giving others just reason for complaint. Hostile intention is always presumed: all those are enemies who are not either friends or allies.[76]

For Vattel, as for other publicists of the eighteenth century, the balance of power, whether a preventive defense should be considered its prime cause or its consequence, calls for prevention, including war, whenever a relative increase on the part of one Power becomes dangerous to another Power or group of Powers. This would make diplomacy's main task one of preparing alliances for war, except in the short post-war periods when its preventive activity would be required to avert the recurrence of war.[77]

The balance of power was often a preoccupation of statesmen. However, wars were as often undertaken to disrupt as to preserve it. It may have been invoked more often against than in favor of the aggressor, whose main argument was the fait accompli of success. Inside the secret du roi, one of his counselors, the Comte de Broglie, advised Louis XV that "a great power that has a great design, begins by executing it in spite of all clamors. It settles later with the neighbors, and the settlement of the accounts will always be in its own favor."[78] Crown Prince Frederick of Prussia was evolving such maxims, common to the governors of the age, for his own conduct and that of his future government. "It is a matter of wisdom to know everything in order to be able to judge everything and to prevent everything... A politician must never say: I did not believe

that such and such a thing would come about; his business is to foresee everything and to be prepared for everything."[79] This claim to foresight as a statesman's virtue, if not also as a prince's gift, was first conceded by the secularizing flattery of Renaissance authors and never fully revoked. It was renewed in Frederick's favor by Voltaire.[80] Frederick added also the hindsight of the historian by claiming that "the policy of great monarchies has always been the same. Their fundamental principle has been to attack everything continually in order to aggrandize themselves without end, and their wisdom has consisted in being beforehand against the artifices of their enemies and playing the finest game" (1738).[81] Frederick found various wars of the past justified, including offensive wars for the maintenance of the balance of power in Europe, as well as "wars of precaution when the excessive grandeur of the strongest power in Europe threatens to overflow and swallow up the universe." Much better praevenire than praeveniri. Great men have always fared well if and when they have employed their power before their enemies were in a position to tie their hands. Preventive war against an impending supremacy seemed to Frederick to belong among the "good wars" that made for a "good peace." To him this was as justifiable as war to repel an aggressor, as an attack provoked by the denial of just claims, and as war in fulfillment of one's obligations as an ally (Antimachiavelli, 1739).[82]

When he "flew to his first rendezvous with fame" in the First Silesian War, Frederick's public claims for Silesia were based more on the conventional, historical-hereditary rights of Prussia. Hardly had the first victory been won at Mollwitz when he began to wonder whether, since Saxony still could not decide whether to enter the anti-Austrian camp or join the Anglo-Hanoverian-Austrian group, "it might not be the best thing to play the praevenire and break loose on Saxony, before she could make a conjunction with the Hanoverians." However, his ministers dissuaded him, and he gave in: "Bon. On ne commencera la guerre."[83] Breaking his alliance treaties, he gave up the war against Austria in 1742. But he thought it advisable to reenter the field less than two years later for the Second Silesian War,

> since the ill-will of the Queen of Hungary as regards my person unveils itself more and more, and since I am advised from more than one quarter that all demonstrations by which that Queen assures me that she intends to observe religiously the peace she has concluded with me, are only intended to lull me into sleep until she has finished her war with France and

that then she will with one swoop fall on me in order to overwhelm me...In order to put myself into a state of defense against said Queen and even to be beforehand with her, if possible, as regards her evil intentions and also in order to save the Empire from the enslavement with which it is being threatened, I have resolved to oppose the torrents of misfortunes which are threatening me... Hence there remains for me no other solution than to ally myself with those whose interest it is to reduce the House of Austria.[84]

Frederick maintained that the plots prepared against him were fully matured, the batteries brought into position, and his opponents only waiting for the time to attack, once they had their hands free. They must be prevented from doing this. He was forced to go to war in order to oppose the quite obvious designs of his enemies. Even if he was not then in the best thinkable position for undertaking an aggressive war, his position was still steadily deteriorating. It was necessary to make a virtue out of necessity and crown the work of the acquisition of Silesia by consolidating and securing that province. "I preferred," he said later, "to make things still worse rather than allow myself to be subjugated by my enemies: I chose war, risking to go down in it, even though with honor."[85]

The boldness and initial successes of Frederick's preventive wars were not unique in his day. Various other governors undertook or contemplated similar preventive actions. The destruction of the Spanish fleet off Sicily in 1719, without a declaration of war, went back to the fears of the British Admiralty, the traditional seat of the "Copenhagening" ideas that were older than the Copenhagen coup itself. The Admiralty was stirred by the regrowth of Spain's navy under Alberoni's administration and the memory of having once before, under Charles II, allowed a foreign navy to grow into a menace to Britain's supremacy of the seas.[86] Britain opened the Seven Years' War not with a declaration of war but with what many people, even in London, considered to be actions contrary to the law of nations—Boscawen's attempt of June 1755 to intercept the French transports that were taking the new governor and a considerable force to Canada, and Hawke's orders of late July 1755 to proceed against and seize French merchant ships.[87] The measures were afterwards defended as designed to keep France from making new usurpations.[88]

These British coups made the ally Frederick wonder whether it was at all expedient to start a war which would be restricted to the defensive, to his mind the most laborious and dangerous manner of fighting, as he told a French ambassador early in 1756. It was impossible to remain inactive, if convinced of one's own moral strength, and to allow the enemies to make war preparations at their discretion. The quicker the interference with their plans, the more certain a happy issue. The history of wars offered proof of this: "When Louis XIV attacked the Dutch in 1672, he overran them at once and thus achieved the greatest successes; enterprises of this kind must be started with impetuosity; they fail if the enemy is left time for counteraction."[89] These general strategic-political views of Frederick's younger years and his easy successes in his first two wars led him the more readily into taking a pessimistic view of the unavoidability of war against the slowly forming coalition of the enemies of Prussia. They were preparing, as he learned when some of their secrets were betrayed to him, a highly precarious future for her. Considering Maria Theresa's ultimate intentions, he "had no nose to receive fillips on," as he told the British minister at his court. "That lady wants the war. She shall have it. My troops are ready; it is necessary to break up the conspiracy before it becomes too strong."[90] By the middle of 1756, he came to consider war inevitable and was resolved "to play the praevenire" against the attack that he believed his opponents were planning for the spring of 1757. "Il ne me reste plus que prevenire quam preveniri" (July 23).[91]

The group of Berlin generals in favor of preventive war was part of a Rococo youth movement, with the King himself, now forty-four years of age, and General von Winterfeldt (forty-nine) as the main and almost only proponents of war in 1755-56. The latter, according to his biographer, went "the more determinedly ahead, the more the conviction grew in him that Prussia was in danger and forced into the boldest enterprises in which, it must be admitted, the path of ambition and glory opened for himself in the greatest splendor." The older generals, notably Schwerin (seventy-two), the victor of Mollwitz, and the Royal princes remained opposed to such a war and in favor of continued diplomatic negotiations.[92]

Frederick asked one last question of the Viennese Government: Were their large-scale military preparations directed against Prussia? Would they promise the King not to attack Prussia during 1756 and 1757? The answer was given in "oracle style," designed either to force Frederick "to take upon himself the onus of aggressor or to continue carrying the concern about the future upon his heart."[93] Unwilling, as he put it, to base the future of his State on the beneficium temporis—the usual diplomatic argument against preventive war—Frederick marched into Saxony on August 28, 1756. He satisfied Maria Theresa and Kaunitz by starting hostilities in this manner, for he was undoubtedly the aggressor now, and France and Russia could no longer shirk their obligations to Austria.[94]

Frederick's action was, then, somewhat like the 1914 German violation of Belgian neutrality, expected rather than unexpected by his contemporaries. Moral indignation was greatest where it had been counted on most, in Austria! Propagandists made the most of the issue. However, as so often in the face of martial success obtained by whatever means, and seduced by Prussian heroics and Frederick's generalship, histrionics, and economies, bourgeois judgment in Europe came to favor the side that proved successful against so many odds. It made Frederick its hero, in spite of all he did that was contrary to its own concept of lawfulness. The long-continued admiration of the preventive war-maker, inside Germany as well as in France and England, did not extend to all of the British policy-makers of Frederick's day. They balked at the application of preventive measures against nations with whom they were at peace. While Pitt believed he had irrefutable evidence (in September 1761) that Spain would shortly join France in the war against England and hence proposed to his colleagues in the Ministry that immediate action be taken against her instead of waiting for her to strike, they could not be persuaded. A preventive blow seemed inadvisable to them, even from a military point of view, on which Pitt's amateur strategy so often prided itself. In the last of the decisive councils, Pitt's colleague Granville declared: "I would be behind-hand in nothing but the actual striking of the blow... But consider your strength. My opinion is to give no hostile answer to Spain; for what hostilities can you begin with advantage?" Thereupon Pitt resigned with his famous, rather too pompous declaration: "I will go on no longer, since my advice is not taken. Being responsible I will direct, and will be responsible for nothing that I do not direct."[95]

The long war gave birth to a general weariness—weariness with the offensive, of which the preventive war was the maximal form, and weariness resulting from experiences with the great strength of fortified camps in the later years of the war. The Seven Years' War induced a new appreciation of the defensive, which even Frederick came to share. In military thought there was a shift in emphasis from Vernichtungsstrategie to Ermattungsstrategie, from annihilation to exhaustion. In military literature, writings dealing with "reasons for preventing an enemy"[96] were followed by Montalembert's L'art défensif

supérieur à l'art offensif (1784), the century's greatest work on fortification. Count Wilhelm of Schaumburg, a noble if eccentric representative of enlightened absolutism and teacher of the military sciences in his tiny principality, argued in his Mémoires pour servir à l'art militaire défensif (1785) that "to lead the war in the way of the offensive means serving the wicked passions; to dedicate oneself to the defensive means dedicating oneself to the welfare of mankind."[97]

In this climate of thought, participants in Frederick's Seven Years' War, such as Berenhorst and the King's long-surviving brother Henry, came to highly critical conclusions about the aggressive opening move of 1756—not for having incurred the onus of aggressor but for having been "duped and pushed into war" by false counselors such as General von Winterfeldt and Frederick himself. "The treaties which he [Frederick] calls threats to the safety of Prussia were defensive only. He says himself that no one planned to attack him that year. He should have waited. It was his ambition and Winterfeldt's which provoked an unnecessary war...My brother always wanted to give battle, that was his whole art of war."[98]

Desire for revenge after the Seven Years' War in Europe and "the Indies" led to French intervention in favor of the American Revolutionaries. Entry into the Revolution was defended partly in terms of the world balance of power—Britain must be reduced in power through at least the loss of her American colonies—and partly in terms of prevention. Intervention, however, must not take place too early, not until Britain was irrevocably involved in the war. Bourbon policy must not venture too close to war before really ready for war, so as not to offer the British occasion for such dangerous preventive measures as the capture of the Spanish silver fleet. French reverses in the last war had been caused principally by the fact that the British had seized the initiative (in 1775), and that there had been no French plans to meet them. It was hardly doubtful, argued Vergennes, that Britain was preparing the war against France and Spain by summer 1777:

> It is an axiom acknowledged in politics as it is in war that it is better to be beforehand than to be overtaken. The two Crowns are in the happy situation that they can decide to take the side that their wisdom, their glory, and the protection they owe their subjects may counsel. They need only a few months more to complete preparations and their understandings.

The next year France, more ready for war, concluded treaties of alliance and commerce with the Americans. Thereafter she found herself "in the position of being forced either to make war or to receive it." Prevention had changed from a consideration of diplomacy to one of war.[99]

Convictions in favor of the military defensive were so strong after the wars of the second half of the century that they pervaded even the thought of the early revolutionary soldiers in France, such as the bourgeois-born engineer Carnot. To him, from the beginning to the end of his career, defensive war was "the only legitimate war," and the offensive defensive, as in the defense of fortified places, the preferred form of strategy (De la défense des places fortifiées, 1810). In a memoir of 1789, he called war "preeminently the art of conserving; the art of destroying is the abuse thereof. Every just war, every war that merits this name is essentially defensive and the right of the weaker part." Carnot's subsequent political and military life was to be in keeping with the principles of his strategy. On the eve of Napoleon's departure for the army on June 12, 1815, Carnot, then minister of interior, advised the Emperor not to attack the Anglo-Prussian army. He pointed out the dangers of losing a decisive battle on home grounds. "I want to prevent the enemies," Napoleon replied. "I ought to have attacked them earlier, if I could only have done so." Carnot still thought there was no need for hurry. Wellington could not expect any reinforcements before the end of July. But the Emperor proceeded to get a headstart on him.[100]

REVOLUTIONARIES AND COUNTER-REVOLUTIONARIES AND PREVENTIVE WAR

On its perilous zig-zagging way towards the somewhat separate goals of greater safety for life and property and more political liberty, the Western bourgeoisie could never ignore the problem of war for any great length of time. It could not always indulge its predilection for the absolute defense behind walls and inundations or at long and safe distances from the seats of power that would be most in keeping with its own military ignorance. Little of the warfare preceding the American and French Revolutions was in its direct interest, and the endless preparations for further conflict created burdens that it was forced to shoulder.[101] Or so the bourgeoisie believed, conveniently overlooking the greater burdens imposed upon the peasantry and the city proletariat. Still, it was reluctant to forego possible benefits of war and hence was willing to consider certain kinds of war as just, even including preventive war under certain circumstances. For Kant, not only "active injury," that is to say being attacked, conferred per-

mission to undertake war, but also actual threat through preparations on the part of another Power. Even the mere "tremendously increasing power (through territorial acquisition)" of another Power conferred a preventive right to make war against such a Power.[102]

Much less remote from the practical politics of the hour in which he wrote and infinitely bolder in deed and expression than the Königsberg professor, Mirabeau in his Monarchie prussienne (1788) asserted that Frederick's war of 1756 was thoroughly justified: "The King of Prussia felt that there was nothing to save him from danger but danger itself, and he, great man, resolved to prevent his enemies. Never, one must admit, was there a more just war" (Tome I, chap. i).

Often an historical figure is declared a genius in order that this figure be acceptable to the later generation as a model, serving as a justification for deeds that might not be in keeping with generally accepted mores. Frederick II, an absolutistic prince in his political convictions and war actions, was brought nearer to the French by Mirabeau's writing. His preventive war of 1756 was invoked by the bellicose Gironde in the summer of 1791, when they advocated war against Austria, nominally still France's ally by treaty. "The rupture of this alliance is a resolution as necessary for Europe as was the demolition of the Bastille for France...Attack, as long as everything promises you a happy success. If, in his war in Saxony, Frederick had temporized, his successor today would probably be a mere marquis of Brandenburg." Thus spoke the Gironde through the mouth of Vergniaud. He declared "that if France waits to declare war, she will perish ingloriously and will bury with her own liberty the hope for freedom in the world."[103]

From July 1791 on, Brissot, a most determined warhound, propagated the idea of a revolutionary crusade, a "crusade of universal liberty." He told the hesitant Jacobins that foreign Powers had reason to fear the war, but not France. The Powers might attempt to frighten her, but would never make good on their threats. "It would be worthy of us to anticipate them. The French Revolution will be the hearth from which will arise the spark to set ablaze the nations whose masters should dare to draw near it." For Roederer, still another Girondist, speaking on December 18, 1791, there was no longer peace, only class warfare:

It is not we who have begun the war. We are attacked, shall we defend ourselves? We are at war. It is the war of the nobility against the people, of all the tyrannies against

Liberty...To attack, that is to defend ourselves, and to make war is to will the peace. Will you wait until our villages are pillaged and our women and children strangled?

Brissot was not above secretly proposing that some French soldiers be disguised as Austrian Uhlans and sent to attack a French village on the frontier—the recipe for Adolf Hitler's opening move against Poland in 1939. Thus the Assembly at long last would be forced into a declaration of war. Brissot did not want to lose any more time through diplomatic negotiations. They would only favor the enemy and

lose for us precious time for outright war, the good war...It is much better for a free people which wants to preserve its independence, to ensure success by means of arms than through diplomatic finesses...It is in fact necessary to be beforehand with our enemies, time only improves their position and makes ours deteriorate...I have only one fear, and that is that we may have no war. The war is a blessing... overthrows the aristocracy, consummates the Revolution, cements our independence, re-establishes credit and prosperity.[104]

Frederick provided the precedents for the Girondists' justification of war. They had no hesitation about borrowing them from Absolutism to use against Absolutism. "Examples would not be wanted to prove the justice of this attack," Brissot argued. "Remember in the last instance the famous campaign in Saxony by the celebrated Frederick... Four powers threatened the storm against them. And, certainly, our cause is more just than his...Circumstances make this attack a law for us, as they did for Frederick" (January 17, 1792).[105]

The dangers imagined from the side of the dubious Pillnitz alliance, which the Gironde wanted to avert by timely war, were even less real than those threatening Frederick in 1756. While Frederick's dilemma was largely due to outside pressure, that of the Gironde was thoroughly endogenous and bourgeois; the fear of the huts, as felt in the bourgeois homes, unleashed the war against the palaces.[106] In an instruction of April 1792 designed to enlighten London, General Dumouriez, foreign minister at the time, explained: "We carry the war into the states of the House of Austria in order to avoid our own ruin by wreaking hers." But "it is contrary to the principles of our constitution to conquer."[107]

Danton had stood out against war until the middle of December 1791. Then he gave in before the general pressure: "If the question were to know whether in the long run we shall have war, I should say: yes, the trumpets of war will sound, yes, the exterminating angel of liberty will cast down the satellites of despotism." Almost alone Robespierre held out against war. Wars, he argued, are wanted by governments that crave more than they already have. During wars the executive power, assuming a sort of dictatorship, wins out at the expense of nascent liberty. The people neglect the deliberative processes, get interested only in external events, in victorious generals rather than legislators, and thus acquire the habit of passive obedience. The danger to the new liberties was to be found not at Coblentz, the center of the émigrés, but at home. "Aren't you," Robespierre asked, "like a man who hastens to put on fire the house of his enemy at the very moment when the fire catches his own?" Before the Revolution is carried abroad, where its armed missionaries are certain to be disliked, it must be consolidated at home. Otherwise it will merely favor the counter-revolution and the military dictator, whose coming haunted Robespierre as long as he lived.[108]

Following the declaration of war against Austria, a manifesto was composed to give the reasons for this step. Condorcet was its principal author. His task was to explain to the world, to paraphrase his words, the progress in history through preventive war making: The war had been forced on the French from without, was in its nature a preventive war against the unjust aggression that was being prepared against France. The National Assembly had long persisted in its will for peace. It was at last forced to prefer war to a patience that had become dangerous to Liberty:

for it does not mean aggression if we deny our enemy the time to exhaust our own resources in prolonged preparations, to get all his traps ready, to collect all his strength, to tie more firmly his original alliances and seek new ones, to buy understandings in our own midst, to multiply in our provinces conspiracies and secret plots. Does one deserve the name of aggressor if one, threatened, challenged by an unjust and dishonest enemy, takes away from the latter the advantage of striking the first blows?...[109]

There was probably no period of history with so much open demand for war as during the Girondist phase of the French Revolution. There was certainly none, earlier or later, where there was as much oratory and politics in favor of preventive war, more commonly the subject matter for cabinet deliberations.

The next quarter century was to unlearn the sharp distinctions once made between war and peace. If there was peace, war was never away for very long in Europe. Usually warfare was reopened with a preventive intention on the part of one, if not both, sides. Beginning with Dumouriez, the diplomatic and military director of the first phase of the revolutionary war, generals were more often than before policy-makers. As he confessed unrepentingly during his exile, the resolution for war in 1792 had seemed to him the only dignified and appropriate step. He would have thought it cowardly and unworthy of her new liberty if France had suffered any longer the disdain and animosities offered her by the Viennese court. "In the last resort, this was only anticipating that court and making the stormcloud burst instead of letting it grow...It was wise to make Belgium the first theater of war in order to anticipate the House of Austria which did not spare us any longer."[110] For the later Dumouriez, busy giving advice on how to make war against France, the undertaking of preventive war was a royal virtue! "To maintain order in the interior of the State, repel attacks from without, even anticipate them if necessary—such are the duties which the Crown imposes, such the true bounty of kings." He addressed this advice to all anti-revolutionary kings.[111]

The majority of the preventive actions of this era were admittedly on the French side. The invasion of Switzerland in 1798 was declared to be a measure of prevention by the French revolutionary governors.[112] By mid-August 1805, Napoleon realized that his landing plans against Britain had failed. He was ready to attack Austria and the Austrian-Russian coalition unless Vienna reduced its armaments. "I have come to my conclusion," he wrote Talleyrand. "I shall attack Austria and be in Vienna before November in order to face the Russians...One must not allow oneself to be anticipated." Thereupon Talleyrand told the Austrian ambassador that "the Emperor is not so insane as to give the Russians time to arrive." Since no satisfactory Austrian assurances were forthcoming, Napoleon left the camp of Boulogne and the futile invasion plans behind in order to meet the Austrians before they were joined by the Russians.[113]

Prussia avoided membership in the coalition of 1805. In 1806, she found herself alone facing Napoleon, without allies and without subsidies. "The enemy with whom she had to deal would not allow her time to obtain all those supports. He did not belong to those who allow themselves to be anticipated and he did not hesitate to take the offensive. His army, with precision and speed, meeting with fewer difficulties than in the campaign of Austerlitz, found itself transported to the Saale in a moment. There the hostilities began." Thus one of Napoleon's, and later the Bourbons', outstanding civil servants expressed his admiration of preventive war.[114] Doubts of the French civilians were as dormant as those of the soldiers

until the days of Napoleon's defeats began. The naïve soldiers' belief was still unshaken on the eve of the war of 1812. "As soon as the Emperor realized that it was impossible for him to avoid the war, he resolved to hasten the moment in order to prevent the junction of the Russian forces," one of his generals writes in his reminiscences.[115] And the Emperor himself perorated on St. Helena: "I was not in the habit of allowing myself to be anticipated; I could march into Russia at the head of the rest of Europe."[116] When the rest of Europe combined against him, there was little occasion left for Napoleon's preventive strokes. And perhaps Waterloo was lost because he struck preventively and prematurely.

The preventive procedures undertaken or advocated by the Revolution and by Napoleon upset convictions in the unjustness of preventive war that may have prevailed in non-French lands. George Heinrich von Berenhorst had been a Prussian participant in the Seven Years' War who had thereafter left the Prussian service and who had studied Kant. He had thought that Frederick's war might safely have been put off, as might the war which France had started in 1792. Now, early in 1796, he thought that the saying that it was better praevenire quam praeveniri deserved reinterpretation. What both Prussia in 1756 and France in 1792 considered immediate threats were

mere nebular shapes arising on the horizon, intrigues, incitements towards a coalition when none of the kings, empresses and premiers chasing after political phantasmagorias had any desire to make a start. Quite different if the powerful neighbor is an autocrat, a conqueror, having his main interest directed towards his army. If, then, the most irrefutable political prognosis points to war, and we see clearly that by suffering and concessions the desire for war is only enhanced, then the saying becomes a golden rule, becomes the duty of self-preservation.[117]

Convictions of this kind underlay the formation of the Second Coalition against France (by the Treaty of December 24, 1798). Could countries like Austria ever hope to live in permanent peace with France? As soon as France had achieved her present objectives, Cobenzl reasoned, she would certainly attack Austria. "It is beyond doubt that the Austrian monarchy must expect a call to arms much more dangerous than the war which would take place at the present moment."[118] The military effectiveness of the Second Coalition was not great enough to cope with the generalship of Bonaparte returning from his first defeat in Egypt, and neither was that of the Third Coalition of 1805. Its formation had been urged in Vienna and other capitals by inarticulate

resentment, no less than by the persuasive voice
of Friedrich Gentz. In order to restore the
thoroughly upset balance of power in Europe,
Gentz argued, there must sooner or later be a
preventive war against the usurper.[119]

It remained impossible for the enemies of
Napoleon to forestall him in the military or political field until he had overreached himself in
Russia. He had forced Britain to reverse, at least
temporarily, her laissez faire tendencies in foreign, military and economic policies. For her
preventive war measures at sea, however, she
was hardly in need of the examples furnished by
the Revolutionaries and by Bonaparte. She could
draw on precedents of her own, such as those of
1755, which had their main repository in the
Navy. "It was the fiery Nelson who began the
offensive, reflecting the new belief of his country
that aggression was justified where it anticipated
a ruthless foe," when he persuaded the hapless
Neapolitan court to attack the French occupation
forces in the Pontifical States in 1798.[120] In
1801, Madeira, a possession of neutral Portugal,
was taken over without previous communication
with the Government in Lisbon "for fear it should
fall into the hands of the French." Canning afterwards thought this measure "justifiable upon the
grounds of probable necessity."[121] While Britain
was still negotiating with Spain, her Navy intercepted the Spanish silver fleet in October 1804,
with the subsequent explanation that this precaution seemed indispensably necessary. It was
taken in order to prevent Spain, who had often
before prolonged discussions until she got her
galleons safely into a port before declaring war,
from repeating this stratagem and thus strengthening her armaments if not those of France as
well.[122]

The most outspoken anti-French group in Britain centered around Wyndham, who at various
times was secretary of war. They pressed for
the resumption of war after the peace of Amiens
with the argument that it was better to prevent
than parry the blow that must be expected from
France. They obtained their wish and war was
reopened. The seizure of French merchant ships
preceded the official declaration of war.[123]
The far from inconsiderable parliamentary and
other opposition protested the illegal nature of
these preventive measures of British policy,
complaining that "at the very time we were most
vehement in condemning the atrocity of France,
we went far beyond it," as in the Copenhagen
expedition of 1807.[124] Canning, speaking for the
Government, declared that they could not refrain
from measures "which prudence and policy dictated, in order to meet and avert those calamities that threatened our security and existence,
because if we sunk under the pressure, we should

have the consolation of having the authority of
Pufendorf to plead." Under the dictates of such
considerations, Britain proceeded to attack
groups and Powers who were clearly far from
planning war against her. The attack on members
of the Northern Armed Neutrality of 1800-01 was
explained as due to the threat of the four Nordic
Powers gaining superiority over the British in
seapower, though the threat hardly existed on paper and even less on the waters of the Baltic.[125]
This and the attack on Denmark in 1807 were
essentially due to the British Navy's "paper work."
The Navy calculated that the safe margin of British seapower superiority must not even remotely
be endangered and that such a threat must be
removed in time, must be "Copenhagened," to
use Lord Fisher's later language. The Danish
fleet of 1807 was carried away intact, "which
otherwise would have gone to Napoleon." Of this
even modern liberal British historians remain
convinced,[126] trusting to Canning's assurance
of 1808 that this "pro tanto [diminished] the
means of the enemy, whilst it added to our means
of security."[127] This assumption was sufficient
to justify the expedition in Britain and on the Continent. In Britain, convictions were strong that
"if England had not anticipated Napoleon, he would
have done so, and used it against England"
(Malmesbury),[128] that "if Ministers did not deserve to be impeached for doing what they had
done, they would have deserved impeachment for
not doing it" (Cobbett).[129] On the Continent, the
constant friends of Britain and foes of Napoleon
applauded "the wisdom and forethought" of the
Danish expedition and hoped that, for the sake of
Europe, Canning would never make peace with
Napoleon,[130] as they themselves might be
forced to do. Inhibitions against preventive war
almost inevitably weaken during the spread of
a series of wars, such as the Napoleonic or Hitlerian wars.

THE NINETEENTH CENTURY AND PREVEN-
TIVE WAR

The nineteenth century, at least in its earlier
part, was thought to be "a century of restoration" (Ranke). The Revolution, since its consequences could not be reversed, could at least be
prevented from again raising its gorgonic head.
To this end, preventive-suppressive actions, essentially international police measures in nature,
were undertaken by members of the Holy Alliance
against Naples (1821-27), Spain (1823), and
Hungary (1849).

International law was to be restored after the
numerous slights and injuries it had suffered during the Revolution, while the rules of maritime
warfare remained as vague as suited the British

interest. The more conservative version of international law, as taught for example at Göttingen, long a university for future diplomats and other high state servants, by generations of the Martens family, ruled on "the justifiable reasons for war" that "no violation of a simple duty of morality, policy or decency, considered by itself, can be a justifiable reason for making war. But every act that impairs the independence of another nation and the free enjoyment of its rights acquired either by occupation or treaty, whether such act takes place in the past, the present, or is to be feared in the future, can be a justifiable reason for war among nations if, after having vainly tried the more peaceful ways, one arrives at last at this extremity."[131] Southern German university Liberalism wanted to go farther in the outlawing of preventive war. For Robert von Mohl, "only a war of defence [taken in the juridical, not the strategical sense] is allowed under law."[132]

The war-makers of the century—diplomats, military men, sailors, publicists—had to pay renewed respect to the strong aversion of the Liberal bourgeoisie towards preventive war. If they wanted to make or publicly advocate war, they had to avoid even the appearance of intending it as a preventive measure. What to some military minds still seemed the most advisable kind of war had also become the most forbidden war. It acquired this character even more definitely with the spread of constitutionalism, which, by reserving much of the war-making power for the parliaments, seemed to make preventive war a thing of the past. Unfortunately, more features of the old absolutism extended over into the new century than Liberalism was aware of.[133]

The question of a preventive war bothered politicians even in the United States, remote as it was from the center of military competition. Early in 1848 Lincoln's partner, Herndon, had argued that the President, as sole judge of the necessity of warding off an impending invasion, might lawfully invade the territory of another country. Abraham Lincoln protested strongly against such an assumption:

> Allow the President to invade a neighboring nation whenever he shall deem it necessary to repel an invasion and to do so whenever he may choose to say he deems it necessary for such purpose, and you allow him to make war at pleasure...The provision of the Constitution giving the war-making power to Congress was dictated, as I reason: Kings had always been involving and impoverishing their people in wars, pretending generally, if not always, that the good of the people was the object. This our convention understood to be the most oppressive of all kingly oppressions, and they resolved to so frame the Constitution that no one man should hold the power of bringing this oppression upon us. But your view destroys the whole matter, and places our President where Kings have always stood.[134]

The thought of a preventive war was not altogether foreign to the parties to the Civil War in America, notably during the tense winter of 1860-61. Someone in Massachusetts proposed it to the North: "By trying to gain time we may lose it... One campaign would settle the matter; and it might be finished before haying time."[135]

Prior to the nineteenth century, the military rationale of preventive war had been found in the momentary superiority of the aggressor, a superiority that had possibly escaped the attention of the intended victim. The hope was that one short campaign would decide the issue. The initial military superiority of France under Louis XIV and Napoleon, of Prussia under Frederick II, or the naval preponderance of Britain invited attack on Powers that were almost proverbially unready and slow to organize, such as Austria or Turkey.[136] After 1815, military competition sharpened in the direction of increasing readiness for war and watchfulness. Military power watched military power very closely. This mutual observation, combined with the improving means of communication, made the secret forming of supply depots, the secret mobilization and concentration of troops and other preparations so nearly impossible that, even early in the century, Clausewitz believed the days of the strategic surprise, including the abrupt opening of preventive war, to be over. War at sea still seemed to allow it, as the Japanese attack on the Port Arthur squadron showed. On the whole, however, military thought had concluded by the beginning of the twentieth century that preventive war, if intended as a strategic surprise, was "out of the question as far as the European Continent was concerned...There can be no question, almost, of a particular headstart on the part of an opponent, of playing the praevenire—the time of the strategic surprise attack is over." Thus concluded a Prussian general on the eve of the First World War.[137]

The military competition of the Powers took on different emphases during the nineteenth century. Points of emphasis were the numerical strength of the armies and navies, the size of army budgets, superior organization and leadership, and technical equipment. When, in the cycle of competition, these elements made one Power or group of Powers superior to the expected opponents, who might themselves become superior at a later date, the temptation to plead for or to undertake preventive war remained great. But

burgher-liberal or democratic morality would
no longer permit the undertaking of a frankly
preventive war. As Lord Aberdeen confessed to
John Bright, when he was succeeded by Palmerston in the interval between the battles of Magenta and Solferino: "In former times, English
statesmen would at once have joined the war
against France to prevent her gaining successes
and too much power in Europe, but things are
changed, and it may be for the better."[138]

Whenever war came, the nineteenth century
nations found themselves in a fog--which they
were not always eager to dispel--over the question of the origins of the wars they were fighting
or had fought. In historical approfondissement
they would go from the politically relevant start
back to the origins, from Bismarck and Napoleon
III back to Louis XIV, as Ranke did in 1870. Their
statesmen and diplomats could generally explain
to them that the wars they or their predecessors
had undertaken were unavoidable and had been
brought on by the actions of the enemy. This usually sufficed to make them forget that they had
also chosen the occasion for the war in question
when it offered itself as the outcome of a diplomatic crisis—a term that conveniently deper-
sonalized events. With only a few exceptions, the
wars of the century from 1815 to 1914 were
undertaken with each side believing that it would
win the war. Statesmen and diplomats were
aided in their attempts to make the peacefulness
of their own side believable by the wide-spread
conviction, as the outbreak of war approached,
that war had become unavoidable. In such situations it was forgotten that the avoidance and postponing of war was at least the proclaimed end of
diplomacy.

However, it was not always the peoples—or
their chosen representatives in parliaments—
who most wanted peace. There were occasions
during the nineteenth century when they wanted
war instead, as was the case in Britain on the
eve of the Crimean War. Urged on by popular
desires, various cabinet members came around
to favoring the war with Russia, then finding preventive reasons for their new resolve, thus making themselves "leaders" again with forethoughts
on war. Lord Clarendon wrote to another cabinet member during the final stages of the diplomatic negotiations that "of course, a patch-up
would be the least troublesome thing now: but I
believe would only be playing the [Russian] Emperor's game and allowing him to make monster
preparations for monster objects." Another
cabinet member wanted to hasten the ultimatum
to Russia because he had come to share the popular view that she would seize Constantinople
before Britain was ready to protect it. While
this reasoning was based on military writings

on the strategic importance of the Straits, it
should be remarked that this was not strongly
supported by the services at the time.[139] On
this occasion the military were rather less eager
for war than the civilians. Military war-readiness,
in every sense of the word, was considerably
behind that of the civilians. Hence there was little
or no demand on the part of professional soldiers
for preventive action.

BISMARCK AND HIS CONTEMPORARIES ON PREVENTIVE WAR

The greatest statesman of the century made
the most artful choice of time and circumstance
for starting his three wars. He had originally
gotten off to a bad start when, during his apprentice year as Prussian foreign minister in 1862-
63, he had attempted to talk Russia into a joint
war against Austria. Disturbed by a set-back in
the struggle with Vienna for hegemony inside
Germany, he expressed to Russian diplomats
the reckless view that Russia and Prussia together, by a sudden and unexpected attack like
that of Frederick the Great in 1756, could strike
down perfidious Austria. However, the Russians
refused to give him any encouragement.[140]

After these never-forgotten and never-forgiven
disappointments, Bismarck came to perceive
with near-perfection when both the political-
diplomatic and the military situations most
favored Prussia. In two of Bismarck's wars,
those of 1866 and 1870, the motive of prevention
and anticipation played its role. During the negotiations with Austria early in 1866, when the
outlook for peace seemed to improve under the
influence of the pacific Prussian King, Bismarck, although obedient, remonstrated with
the monarch that if the endeavor to maintain
peace "should be successful now, the danger of
war would threaten us later, perhaps in months,
under more unfavorable circumstances." For
Austria would in the meantime try to get on better terms with France and Italy. The Italian alliance with Prussia was to last for three months
only.[141]

This consideration of the preventive motive
was veiled by language condemning preventive
war in such convincing, even religious terms
that it would equally deceive diplomats and
theologians.[142] Bismarck knew infinitely better than later statesmen the phases through
which military competition was moving. Early
in 1866 he pointed out to a visiting Hanoverian
minister that Austria "had not yet introduced the
needle gun." He hinted that if the Austro-
Prussian conflict should proceed to the extreme,
it would be in Prussia's favor to start a war before Austria reached the point where she had

perfected certain military reforms already under way.[143] At the end of February 1866, he suggested to a Crown Council that it would be wiser for Prussia to start the war than to permit Austria to select the hour most favorable to her. That is, he proposed preventive war.[144] The awkwardness of Austrian diplomacy enabled Bismarck to settle even the burden of guilt on its shoulders.

French politicians, publicists, and generals were vastly disappointed by the short duration of the Seven Weeks' War, for it meant that France was denied "compensations." Convinced of the superiority of French arms, they urged on the hesitant and ailing Napoleon that France undertake a preventive war against Prussia before she developed German military unity. The disillusioning outcome of the Luxemburg crisis of 1867 gave such proposals a new urgency. The War Minister, Marshal Niel, declared to the French Parliament:

> I still believe that I work for peace. The French people has always been very proud, and the Army is made in its image: we have Gallic blood in our veins, we do not know how to bear up for long under a danger that is threatening us; we rather prefer to meet it beforehand. You will not make the French people live in anxiety, suspend its commercial operations, its industry and suffer for long an existence so antipathetic to the nature of its character...it will demand war from you. But if you will give it a good military organization, it will shield itself behind this organization, will not fear the attacks of its neighbors, and since it does not dream of conquests, since it wants to live peacefully at home, it will dedicate itself to its commerce, its industry, its agriculture; it will live in peace.[145]

The argument of the nineteenth-century soldier in parliament, Let us assure peace by providing for a more perfect army! is here strengthened by the argumentation, sincere or not, that such an army would do away with the necessity of undertaking preventive war, the kind of war which the bourgeois world abhorred above all others. But at the same time, Marshal Niel was presenting the proposal of ending war by undertaking one last enterprise, a preventive war. That proposal was one of the paradoxes of Second Empire journalism. Having followed a pacifist line for a number of years, Emile de Girardin, one of the foremost publicists of the age, independent but changeable, veered around in 1867 to demanding war against Prussia. Men, he said, will answer the question, Is there to be war? with NO; events will answer YES. And they will carry the day. As long as France fails to regain her frontiers of 1801, Europe, which robbed her of them in 1815, will be troubled, troubled by more and more excessive armaments.

> Europe is therefore directly interested that France should receive the just compensation which is absolutely due her and which she will demand at the victory if equity does not give it to her. If European disarmament cannot be accomplished except by a supreme effort, then better still immediate war than this continued back-breaking burden; war, however, [should] be preceded by a manifesto addressed to all peoples who are interested in the question which the sabre must solve,...the imperious necessity of putting an end to armaments and of solving, once and for all, in the common interest, all the pending questions which are aggravated by being put off...If war is inevitable, it is better to have it at once when the probabilities of victory are in our favor rather than have it break out two or three years from now when these probabilities will have passed to the opposite side.[146]

The French military experts knew better what the chances for success were at that time. Their war plans for 1867 were purely defensive in character.[147] Moltke was at the same time so confident of the superiority of the North German Confederacy that he would have liked to make the Luxemburg affair the occasion for war with France.

> I think, alas, that this war is absolutely inevitable between now and five years hence; within that period the preponderance of our organization and our equipment, undeniable today, will be levelled off day after day in our disfavor due to France's endeavors. The sooner we come to blows, therefore, the better. The present motive is good. It has a national character; one ought to make use of it, therefore... Better to have the inevitable war with France now, instead of next year; we are not yet ready, but neither are the French; and this year we would have to deal with France alone, whereas next year Austria might possibly take part in the war.[148]

Moltke knew only too well that army reform and the introduction of the Chassepot rifle were bound to improve the relative position of France. Still the Prussian Chief of Staff was willing to submit to Bismarck's political judgment, which concluded against war at the time and on the Luxemburg issue. Moltke thought that Bismarck's reasons were indisputable, but, he added, "they will cost us much blood one day."[149] The Chancellor did not want war over Luxemburg—it was not a cause which would more firmly unite the hardly-yet-joined North and South Germans.

In declining all proposals to make the "inevitable" war now, he put his opposition as to time and cause on the higher plane of morality: "One is not allowed to make war if it can be avoided with honor; the chance of a favorable outcome is not a just reason to start a great war." He wanted to avoid war with France as long as possible, he said in 1867—"for I know that once started, it will never end."[150]

In spite of her various reforms, none of them fundamental, France by herself seemed to Moltke an enemy that Germany need not fear very much. However, a French alliance with Austria, then actually under negotiation, presented a danger that ought to be met in time. Accordingly, his war plans of 1869 envisaged such a constellation. "If Austria arms," he told Schweinitz, now ambassador to Vienna, "we really ought to declare war against France at once so that we shall have settled with her before Austria is ready for war, which will take her three months. For this would be a sure sign that there is an agreement with Napoleon and that the latter intends to attack, something for which he by himself is not strong enough."[151] But Bismarck could meet this danger of Austria's revanche for Sadowa diplomatically, by his understanding with Russia in case of Austrian interference in a war with France.

Bismarck produced his occasion for war through the candidacy of a Hohenzollern for the Spanish throne. This made the French cry out against encirclement. French diplomacy, by its demands for satisfaction, and French national sentiment, by its readiness for war, came to Bismarck's aid. "Il faut en finir: thus it echoes in all France which has had enough of the armed peace," reported the Bavarian minister in Paris on July 12, 1870, noting the sentiment which the journalistic impatience of Girardin and others had expressed or whipped up for years.[152] It made the war seem highly acceptable. It made it appear almost in the nature of a popular preventive war.

Bismarck was careful to avoid any indication of such intentions on Germany's part. He assured Gortchakov, who passed through Berlin during the critical July days, that this war, should it come, would not be a preventive war as far as he was concerned. He had had a council with the generals, including Moltke and Roon, on the 12th. All of them regretted the forbearance with which he had met the arrogant language of France, and they voted for an immediate declaration of war. They argued that all the advantage would be on Prussia's side, were she to start hostilities without further delay. According to Gortchakov's report, Bismarck assured the Russian Chancellor that he was opposed to such a decision. He said that "neither reason nor religion permitted to accelerate the moment of war

merely because a calculation of the chances might prove favorable; that the outcome was always in the hands of a power above that of men; that from one moment to the other an unexpected circumstance might arise which would mark such a measure with the character of a precipitate decision, etc." The gravity of this language, which Bismarck repeatedly used during those days, the gravity of the haruspex rather than that of the distressed Christian, was better designed for the Tsar than for the immediate listener whose "etc." expressed the diplomat's scepticism and impatience with such language. However, Bismarck obtained what he needed from the Russians —the All Clear Signal! He could proceed towards a war with France with the assurance that Austria would not be allowed to interfere.[153]

Once victory has been achieved, nations and their statesmen are not inclined to be squeamish about the character of the war they have just fought. In a Reichstag speech of November 4, 1871, Bismarck came closer to giving public endorsement to the notion of preventive war than he had ever done or was to do. He defended an offensive war undertaken with a defensive intention, a kind of war frequent enough and very effective in most cases. For a country like Germany that could be attacked on three or four sides, he thought, it might be very useful to follow the example set by Frederick the Great in 1756. Under certain circumstances, when faced by an attack in preparation, perhaps by a superior coalition of forces, the German Reich could not wait until the best moment, for the opponent had arrived. In such a case, it was the Government's duty, and it was right for the nation to demand this from it, to choose the moment when the unavoidable war could be fought with the smallest sacrifices and the least danger to the nation.

In fact, he had by that time already threatened France with one preventive war, strictly limited in its purpose, in order to make her keep the peace she had signed in May 1871. Three months later when the signatory, the Thiers Government, seemed in danger of being upset, Bismarck directed the German chargé at Paris (Count Waldersee, the later Chief of Staff) "that if conditions in France should become unsafe, we shall not find it advisable to wait for the French attack but shall on our own part, as soon as the preservation of peace appears doubtful to us, proceed at once to the mobilization of 500,000 men for the purpose of renewing hostilities. But I do not doubt in the least the goodwill of the present Government to keep the peace."[154] Later in the year, however, when the payment of three of the five billions of the war indemnity produced difficulties, the Chancellor decided that non-payment "would not force us to begin war at once, as long as France does not attack us." Germany would rather rely on a prolonged military occupation of French soil as "additional security against military velleities on France's part."[155]

Bismarck's uncertainties about the new peace were revived and sharpened by the economic crisis of 1873. It soon appeared to the German military that France's defeat had not been complete enough and that her recovery, economic and military, had been too rapid. Moltke pondered the idea of a preventive war against her. One year after the signing of the peace treaty, she was already spending heavily on her army while a good deal of the indemnity remained to be paid.[156] The soldiers signalled the indications of military recovery in France to Bismarck, and he showed what they considered "a morbid suspicionness" towards the French. French friends of Ambassador Harry Arnim thought that, were it not for him, such feelings might already have led to a new invasion of France.[157] Should the French think of revanche, Bismarck confided to Odo Russell in December 1873, he would prefer to fight them at once and declare war tomorrow instead of waiting until they felt ready. When the Englishman protested that, considering France's weakness, this would seem inexcusable—before the European Areopagus—Bismarck answered with his characteristic cynical sincerity that a casus belli could easily be found, he had himself had experiences in that respect.[158]

French military reforms went on apace. The Army was now a conscript army, too. One of its generals confided to a Russian friend, late in 1873 (as German diplomats learned in Russia), that one could now look to the future quietly and hopefully. There was only one fear—that Germany might not wait the five or six years necessary to complete France's rearmament. German diplomacy could easily find a pretext for war at the suitable moment.[159] Confidence was growing in France, buoyed up by an economic revival. In February 1875, President-Marshal MacMahon was talking "gaily and sprightly of men, guns and rifles...'This year it is not likely that Bismarck will make war on us, and next year we shall be ready.'"[160]

Meanwhile, Bismarck found his own situation highly irritating. The economic depression, more protracted than in France, was taking the bloom off the fruits of victory. His enemies—ultramontanism at home and in the Catholic countries, French desires for revanche, even Emperor William and his family—seemed to conspire against him. Bismarck was always ready to believe that his enemies, even the most dissimilar, could form a coalition against him. The Kulturkampf seemed to be merging with the opposition of all other foes, diplomatic, military,

and political. In his nervousness, Bismarck considered that these threats would force him "to take warding-off (Abwehr) measures against France into consideration," should an ultramontane government come into power there.[161] He issued a threat to the French Government—although Harry Arnim may not have delivered it. He warned that if they would not call the Bishop of Nancy to order, who was having prayers said for the reunion of the lost territories, there might be the possibility of a military clash. In October 1873, Bismarck had put it this way: "No government, once it had come to consider war to be inevitable, contrary to its desire, would be so foolish as to leave it to the enemy to choose the time and occasion for it and wait for the moment most agreeable to the enemy. The German business world was demanding a clear political horizon; even before 1870 it had on many occasions expressed the view that the outbreak of war was less ruinous to it than the unending threat of a war."[162]

Dark suspicions in politics seek and readily find their confirmation in concrete facts. In February 1875, Bismarck learned, obviously from the General Staff, that, in connection with French army reforms and reinforcements, German dealers had received orders to buy 10,000 German saddle horses at any price. Without verifying the information, he ordered the Paris embassy to report on the situation, with a view to putting an embargo on horses. While there was no reason to expect war within the coming year, the loss of 10,000 horses might inconvenience Germany, were she to mobilize three years hence. Both ambassador and military attaché reported that an immediate war was not likely, that French politicians knew by now that the occasion for the war of revanche had to come in connection with events outside France, that the proposed embargo would not have much effect on the actual reorganization of the French Army. The embargo was nevertheless imposed "in order to throw difficulties in the way of their reorganization and delay its completion and thereby put off as long as possible the war of revanche that the French were so evidently preparing for," as Bismarck told the British.[163]

The French Government decried the measure as a challenge to its peaceful intentions. It tried to convince foreign governments and the public that not France but Germany was seeking a renewal of the fight and that its latest army bill was a necessary measure of defense. The German press responded that the strengthening of the French Army brought the conflict so much closer that it could not be postponed for very long. Actually, according to the reports of the German military attaché in Paris, it did not bring the threat of war appreciably closer.[164] Following press reports clearly provided by the General Staff, the Kölnische Zeitung, on April 5, pointed out the tendencies toward a clerical-monarchical restoration in France, and toward the forming of a Catholic League against Germany— all signs of "an immediate preparation of the war of revanche." The article was written by the chief of the press section of the Wilhelmstrasse, Aegidi, and had been handed to the newspaper with the remark that "every word in it had been put on the scales as in a State paper." On April 6, Bismarck told the Berlin correspondent of the London Daily Telegraph: "I have cut off the spurs of the Gallic cock, but he is still a very dangerous bird. If he thinks me a patient lamb that is going to wait until his spurs have regrown, so that he can tear my hide, he commits the greatest possible error. This time, I shall not have that much patience— not as much as I have shown before. We shall anticipate him. He shall have no chance."[165]

The crescendo in this press concerto was produced by the famous "Is War in Sight?" article in the Berlin Post of April 9. The paper was known to be close to the Reich Government and the article was promptly ascribed to the Wilhelmstrasse. It had actually been written by a member of the Chancellor's press bureau, though, as it was later emphasized, without any express or standing order from any superior. The article considered the danger of a war of revanche as immediately impending, a danger to be met beforehand and promptly by a preventive war on Germany's part. Some observers took a narrow, and indulgent, professional view of the article. They thought that it was designed, like others of its kind, "to justify Germany's great preparations against the peril of the united forces of Papacy and France."[166] The diplomatic world was deeply disturbed and discerned Bismarck's own directing hand behind the press campaign or, in the mildest of judgments, his uncontrolled nervousness. "It was the business of a giant to be good-natured and tractable, above all not to have nervous fits like those of the Post," wrote Sir Robert Morier to the German Crown Prince. He readily identified the Chancellor with the press and deemed "the hysterical giant a terrible neighbor to a company of pigmies."[167]

Still other alarming newspaper and magazine articles followed. Some of these expounded the lessons of preventive war as undertaken by Frederick in 1756. Professors whose Liberalism was being fast consumed by nationalism, like Sybel and Treitschke, were "riding high on the war horse."[168] Without receiving any public or private démenti from the Chancellor, these various papers and persons expressed the conviction that one more struggle would be neces-

sary before the new Reich could "settle down to the undisputed enjoyment of her unity and independence." Moltke threw further fuel under the boiling cauldron, which Bismarck would still not remove from the fire. He told the politicians in Berlin that the French Army would be ready in 1877 and asked them: "How would the country take it if he should start an offensive war before the year was over?" Treitschke, learning about this, thought things were "highly ominous in politics...It would cost now 100,000 men less than in 1877! Thus it stands. For a year the thing can still be put off; hardly any longer. The alliance between Gambetta and the Conservatives is concluded, the French Line stronger than the German by 172 battalions."[169] Contrary to his usual reticent habits, Moltke made the rounds of Berlin society like any vulgar alarm-bearer. He as well as the Wilhelmstrasse warned the Belgian minister that France would carry her attack on Germany through Belgian territory. With or without Bismarck's foreknowledge, he paid a visit to Ambassador Odo Russell (on May 2) to explain to him, who could see no cause or necessity for a war, why it was bound to come. Taffs has summarized their conversation in the following words:

The answer came pat. No one hated war more than Moltke, but France would force it on by her armaments. Reminded that Decazes denied that the army reorganization threatened the peace of Europe, Moltke replied that he knew far too much about military matters to put any faith in mere peaceful assurances... He envied the French their patriotism which was ready to satisfy the War Department's demands, and contrasted it with the lack of loyalty shown by the Democrats in the Reichstag, "who endeavored to resist and refused the most necessary expenses for the German Army...Germany wished for peace and had no need for conquest by aggression, but Germany required more than any other nation an army organized for defence, because she was placed in the centre of Europe and could be invaded from all sides...Germany must be ready to anticipate hostile intentions and alliances on the part of her neighbors."

When Russell said that no one intended to attack Germany, and should France hope to do so later, she would not find allies if she broke the peace again as in 1870, Moltke countered: "He could not admit that peace was broken by the power that marched first, it was the power that provoked the necessity for defence in others which must be held responsible for war." This, Russell thought, "sounded like a war to prevent war" and suggested that diplomacy might at least try to do what it could to keep the peace. To this Moltke replied that "if the great powers would come out openly on the side of Germany and prove to France how futile were her dreams of revenge, war might be avoided for ever. England particularly might assist, owing to her great influence in France, but he personally placed little faith in diplomacy owing to the unaccountable hatred and suspicion shown towards the German Empire."[170]

Treatment of the "war-in-sight" episode in the history of diplomacy has not, on the whole, put it into the large context which it requires. It has been explained merely as the outcome of Bismarck's irritation. Actually, it represents a recurrent phenomenon, the post-war attempt on the part of the victor to avert the recurrence of war, a war of revanche, through a concert of the Powers against the recently defeated country. Moltke's suggestion that the Powers, notably England, should help keep the peace by giving France to understand how hopeless her dreams of revanche were, pointed to such a grand design. In fact, Moltke must have acted as the agent of Bismarck's diplomacy on the occasion. The ultimate intention of this diplomacy in 1875 was to force France, by means other than immediate German armaments and alliances, to forego her rearmament program. An alternate way was to bring "Europe" to warn France of the consequences of rearmament, the first of which in point of time was the threat of preventive war by Germany. Should the threats and warnings prove successful, the military inferiority of France might be perpetuated for a long time to come and thus avert an armament race and the necessity of exclusive alliances.[171] The notion (usually utopian) of making, threatening, or allowing preventive war on the part of some international Areopagus against the likely disturber of the peace makes its appearance once more, conjured up this time by the one who was usually considered the greatest embodiment of Realpolitik.

The first obstacle to the acceptance of Bismarck's design lay in his overly threatening attitude toward France. To all appearances, his approach promised immediate preventive war rather than ultimate peace through war prevention. The neutrals came to share a good deal of the shock designed as therapy for France alone. In the foreign capitals she found far more sympathy than Bismarck had expected, particularly in St. Petersburg and London. The rather obtuse British Foreign Secretary, Lord Derby, was very easily shocked. Summing up the case against Bismarck for the benefit of the Queen, he declared:

The language which he and his agents have been holding all over Europe is, substantially, to the effect that, if France attempts to reassert her position as a great power, she must be attacked and crushed. The Count von Moltke is understood openly and publicly to hold this language.

Lord Derby does not conceal from himself that the prevalence of these ideas, if they do prevail in Germany, constitutes a serious danger to Europe. Moral force does for much in these days, and the sympathy of nations is always with the attacked party. In the last war, France was the aggressor, and the opinion of Europe went with Germany. If the parts are now to be reversed; if France is to be attacked without provocation, merely in order that she may not have an opportunity of making herself troublesome hereafter, there will be in all countries, and in no country more strongly than in England, a protest against the abuse of force, and a common jealousy, inspired by the sense of a common danger.[172]

The Queen approved that Russell be instructed to intervene in the interest of peace and that the other Powers be invited to join. And she did not keep her Government from admitting in Parliament that they had believed in the seriousness of war rumors and had therefore offered their good services in Berlin. This gave Emperor William occasion to complain to her. He was pained to learn that she could consider him the disturber of the peace in Europe, a thing she ought never to have credited for a moment from her knowledge of his character. No one knew better than he that whosoever provoked war in Europe would have all public opinion against him and would find no allies, no well-wishing neutrals, but only opponents. The statements ascribed to Moltke, William explained, were due to the natural desire of any one in conflict with another de se mettre en avantage. The Queen insisted that, from her information, there had been others as well in Berlin, close to the monarch, who had made statements similar to Moltke's, but gave no names—"unfortunately," remarked Bismarck, who wondered from which side such "vigorous untruths" had reached Windsor. The Chancellor assured the King that while it might not be conducive to peace to leave France in the belief that she would never be attacked, regardless of what she might do, he would never advise His Majesty to make war at once just because it was probable that the enemy would soon begin it. One could never know beforehand the ways of divine Providence. "But," he added, "it is also not useful to give the opponent assurance that in any case one would wait for him to start the attack."[173]

Austria and Italy, the future Triplice partners, declined to help in "saving the peace" in Berlin.

Gortchakov, however, proved so eager to rescue the peace—which Bismarck considered was never threatened—that Bismarck never forgave him his "superfluous peace-making." He was a little more forgiving towards Russell. Since it now seemed useless to reveal his grand design, he laid the basis for a fable convenue of the episode. The whole alarm, he stated

> has been engineered by the press, and possibly by speculators exploiting the unfavorable impression created in military circules by the rapid reorganization of the French army. Military men naturally enough discussed the possibilities of the situation and the advantages of forestalling attacks, but he entirely dissociated himself from this policy. He did not subscribe to that "Up and at them" principle and so long as the defence of Germany against her enemies was entrusted to his care, his motto would ever remain "Let them come."[174]

The episode of 1875 represents Bismarck's worst, if least obvious defeat. He who had thought to encircle France with a ring of opinion hostile to her rearmament now found that he was himself almost encircled by hostile opinion, headed by England and Russia, the two countries who were presumably Germany's best friends. Little mindful of the ultimate consequences, they preferred the regrowth of France as a factor in the balance of power. They endorsed her "very natural" rearmament while denying once more the justification for preventive war, even for the sake of firmer peace. Their stand in 1875 provided, in a negative sense, the preparation for Bismarck's later alliance system.[175]

OTHER SEATS OF PREVENTIVE WAR IDEAS

Following the rather upsetting episode of the "war in sight" crisis, Bismarck became increasingly emphatic in his public and private statements on preventive war. Sometimes he even used quasi-religious affirmation, such as that "one can never ascertain beforehand with sufficient certainty the ways of Providence."[176] "We have to wait, rifle at rest," Bismarck told one of his confidants in 1877, "and see what smoke clouds and eruptions that volcano of Europe will bring forth. A policy like that of Frederick at the outset of the Seven Years' War we shall not follow—suddenly attack the enemy who is preparing the attack. It seems, indeed, to break eggs out of which very dangerous chickens might arise." Bismarck now preferred to make use of alliance arrangements for the prevention of war.[177] And so in time his credit as preventer of war was restored, at least among friends and neutrals.[178]

Preventive wars cannot easily be undertaken by an alliance or coalition. Preventive wars are essentially wars of a single autocratic power acting alone or in absolute dominance within a coalition. Whatever Napoleonic ambitions were ascribed to Bismarck during the 1875 episode, he had in later years no intention of using his own position within the alliance system to stage a preventive war. In fact, his alliance system was a substitute for making preventive war. Austrian desires in that direction got no encouragement from him. His alliance system dampened thoughts of "prophylactic" wars, even after the ten years of improved Franco-German relations came to a close with the fall of the Ferry cabinet in 1885, when French military policies were redirected from colonialism towards the Vosges. Sinister sparks flew from the contact of groups of revanchards and Russian soldier-politicians, while those conservative Russians who cared to maintain the Three Emperors' Alliance were inviting Germany to terminate the so-called peace of 1871, which no Frenchman recognized.[179]

Austro-Russian conflicts, involving Germany in spite of Bismarck's diplomatic arts, had led to thoughts of war on both sides. To Russian military circles, the end of 1887 seemed a favorable moment for war against Austria, which was then being equipped with a new rifle.[180] In Austria, Crown Prince Rudolf and the military men of his entourage were eager for their country to fight Russia "as long as this still offered definite military advantages." If Austria did not fight, it might as well abdicate its position as a Great Power.[181] The German General Staff, where Waldersee had become the balance wheel after his appointment as quartermaster-general, concluded that Russia was arming for immediate war and was already preparing the concentration of her forces in the direction of the western frontier.

Preserving his independence even from the greatest experts, Bismarck called these conclusions what they obviously were, "premature." He was just as unwilling as he had been in 1867 or in the 1870's to agree to any aggressive proposals on the part of the general staffs in Berlin and Vienna. "As long as I am minister," he said, "I shall not give my approval for a prophylactic attack on Russia, and I am also far from advising it for Austria, as long as she is not absolutely certain of English cooperation." England's help would make the odds against Russia overwhelming and would bring Italy and Turkey into the front against her. But Austria must not be encouraged to seek quarrels. He refused to share the soldiers' conviction that war was unavoidable, and he refused to look for a motive "to start war today for no other reason than the great probability that it might take place later."[182] General von Schweinitz, one of his most reliable diplomatic helpmates, took an equally determined stand, as soldier and as diplomat, against the military. Not the least of his reasons was his conviction that in a war against Russia even the appearance of aggression had to be avoided. For Germany to appear the aggressor "would double the power of Russia and reduce our own by half, for while the peace-loving Russian people would be stimulated to the highest sacrifices by an invasion, the necessity for leading a winter campaign with all its sacrifices would be apparent neither to the Bundesrat nor to the German nation."[183]

Like many another conflict in politics, the one over preventive war in Germany in the late 1880's was one between the generations. The older generation was represented by William I, Bismarck, and Schweinitz. Even the majority of the Prussian generals in command of army corps, as Waldersee noted early in 1887, were against war with Russia and/or France. Waldersee plaintively claimed that a war that would really permanently cripple France or Russia could not be expected from an octogenarian emperor and a septuagenarian chancellor (whereas the octogenarian chief of staff might have been persuaded in its favor).[184] Those of the younger generation who were in favor of war had taken Prince William, the future emperor, in tow. They included young officers and a few diplomats,[185] and, despite his riper years but in keeping with his ever lively neurosis, Professor Treitschke. In January 1887, Treitschke thought "the situation very serious and a war with France completely certain unless something absolutely unexpected should occur. Should we, indeed, wait until Boulanger has spent his eighty millions for the armor-plating of the Eastern fortresses? As yet, our siege guns are still superior to the brick walls. Hence we must strike, if it cannot be avoided honorably; however, this war is and remains a fearful misfortune, even though I do not doubt victory in the least."[186] The layman's belief that the possibility of victory depends on one single item of technical superiority is one of the worst aspects of lay interest in military problems. Those who most wanted this war were forced to realize, more clearly than political professors, that the threat to peace was not really as great as they wished.

There is everywhere belief that war will break out any day [wrote Waldersee at the same time as Treitschke]. But this is not so. The directing personalities in France are frightened and make friendly assurances; much will depend on whether they can rid themselves of Boulanger...Through my expressing bluntly that we must make use of the present still favorable conditions in order to. bring on the war with France, I incur in many quarters the reputation of being a

wicked man. But that I'm right is a fact and is also recognized by many.[187]

The wisdom, or at least the power of the gerontocracy that ruled Berlin until 1888 or 1890 denied the partisans of preventive war the opportunity for it. The alliance partner in Vienna was left no doubts about this.[188] Bismarck took an emphatic stand against preventive war proposals when a new and larger Army bill came up early in 1887. The Reichstag's approval could be won, if at all, only by the most peaceful assurances on the Chancellor's part. While he would not exclude the possibility that the Reich, like Frederick the Great after the first two Silesian wars, might have to defend its achievements in a still broader conflict, he would not admit that uncertainty about the future gave one the right to make war in the present. "The idea of undertaking a war because it might be inevitable later on and might then have to be fought under more unfavorable conditions has always remained foreign to me, and I have always fought against it...For I cannot look into Providence's cards in such a manner that I would know things beforehand" (Speech of January 11, 1887).

In private talks during the same period, the Chancellor admitted that he considered the situation more threatening. He was fundamentally convinced that war with France was inevitable in the long run. The peace of Frankfurt had brought no healing; the wound, the loss of Alsace-Lorraine, was open. France would attack Germany when the occasion presented itself. In the face of this ultimate certainty of war, the military demanded war immediately, before French military reorganization would have a chance to be completed. During the lifetime of the old Emperor, Russia would not do anything against Germany. Later, her mood might change. Postponing the war would not avert it but would only diminish Germany's chances to win it. By his determination to withstand the demand of the generals for immediate hostilities, he, the Chancellor, incurred grave responsibility. For should the postponed war break out after all, German defeat would be ascribed to him. Having restored German unity, he would now risk the humiliation of compromising the Reich's future existence and security. Despite such arguments, Bismarck was determined to oppose the military demand for immediate war. In view of this opposition, they wanted at least another Septennat, a seven-years' army bill.[189]

All the weight of gerontocracy, that of Moltke's excepted, was thrown into the scales against the proposals for preventive war and against all other ideas of aggressive war. The Austrians were told by the Bismarcks that Old William I "would never participate in an aggressive war of any kind."[190] To one of the most dangerous hotheads in favor of preventive action, namely William, the Crown

Prince of 1888, the Chancellor delivered an emphatic privatissimum as part of his ever-incomplete political education. While the general staff officers maintained that Germany could hope "to smash" Russia through a preventive war, Bismarck argued that such a war would only demonstrate the indestructibility of that vast and inaccessible country and mark the instilling of yet another nation with the spirit of revanche. Russia represented a danger against which Germany must maintain protective dikes. To the Crown Prince's objection that, should the dike break, there would be a vast inundation, the old Deichhauptmann of Schönhausen answered that "if we cut the dike ourselves, it would come still earlier."[191]

The Chancellor had his misgivings about the future William as a governor. Might he not prove to be another Frederick II, so eager for the rendezvous with fame that he might seek preventive war? "There is no need for another Frederick the Great in the future" of Prussia-Germany, Bismarck said on March 22, 1888, the birthday of the first Emperor.[192] The last Hohenzollern continued to accept these political homiletics of the first Chancellor for only a little while longer. By the end of his first year of governing, he threatened that "if Bismarck does not come along against the Russians, our ways must part."[193] Even when out of office, in the Hamburger Nachrichten and then posthumously in his Gedanken und Erinnerungen, Bismarck continued his warnings against a preventive war on Germany's part, whether the Emperor or the generals wanted to hear them or not.[194]

The tension of the European world around 1890 was between the distant poles of the conservator, the role Bismarck had grown into, and the rising annihilators so diversely represented by William II, the Pan-Germans[195] and Friedrich Nietzsche, all possessed with the "will to power." Bismarck's action and speeches against preventive war, with which he regained the confidence of the burghers and his own class-fellows, were for Nietzsche mere "court preacher's tartufferie." For the coming century the philosopher wanted none of the unwarlike views of his "late friend Galiani," including the latter's views on prévoyance as the cause of wars in Europe. He himself was not afraid "to predict a few things and thereby, possibly, conjure up the cause of war...The time of quietude and chinoiserie which Galiani predicted for this century is over." Instead he would put the decision before Europe and see whether "its will for doom is willing."[196] (It would be, as soon as the vulgarians and "terrible simplifiers" had caught up with the philosopher).

As Emperor, however, William II never went beyond marginal notes and militaristic talk in the pursuit and advocacy of preventive war. He never gave Waldersee the chances he sought. After a short three-year term as chief of the General Staff, he was replaced by Schlieffen. During Caprivi's term (1890-94), the Wilhelmstrasse felt that a preventive war started by Germany was quite impossible, considering the European power constellation. "For the case of the next war we must consider what stand public opinion, at home or abroad, will take upon it. There as well as here, no one would understand why one now [1891] should consider peace so rotten that one should prefer war." Entering upon preventive war, it was thought, would estrange England and possibly Italy.[197]

The consequences of the surrender of Bismarck's artful reinsurance system were the Franco-Russian alliance and the prospect of war on two fronts. Caprivi decided to meet them soberly and promptly by a rejuvenated army with a service term of two instead of three years, and not by a preventive pounce.[198] There was no immediate threat to point to in justification. "I cannot appear with a 'War-in-Sight'" Caprivi declared with a slightly ironic reference to his predecessor—who did so much to make his high office disagreeable—when he came to introduce the Army estimates (November 23, 1892). "There can be no talk of that; I shall not rattle the sabre; I shall refrain from all painting black in black." Germany was saturated, wanted no conquests; could not absorb them; could not afford to win more colonies. But she must watch two lovers, Russia and France, "playing with fire; they light up bonfires from time to time and sparks fly across our backyard. We have reason to keep our fire-fighting equipment in order and if it appears deficient to us, to complement it. We shall attack neither France nor Russia, but we want to mobilize all means at our disposal in case these two states should approach one another more closely, in order to repel a possible attack" on two fronts. Germany was resolved to meet such a danger by a stronger army, rather than attempt to put "an end to the difficult situation in which we live, by a preventive war," a war that could offer no reward in the case of a German victory, not even a twenty- to thirty-years' period of quiet. "Once returned home, would we not be forced to arm again in a manner presumably much more costly, more onerous than the present?" Caprivi asked. "If we should return home exhausted after a long prophylactic war, would there not be other people who might perhaps be inclined to take advantage of our weakness? I am firmly convinced that even after the fortunate termination of a prophylactic war our condition would be considerably more unfavorable than at present."

The state that increases its military expenditures is usually accused of starting a new cycle of arms competition. But there is much that offers itself in defense of Caprivi's Army Bill. While it may have contributed to further crystallization of the Franco-Russian alliance, it was designed to meet not only the constant rise of Russian military force against the Eastern dikes of the Central Powers, but also a preparedness on the part of the French Army that was sufficient to encourage desires for a preventive war on France's part. No one was in a better position to know this than Freycinet, who, as war minister, was the organizer of the recent reforms. According to him, France could look forward with relative serenity to the complications that the nation believed were threatening her.

> Certain people even thought that as far as we were concerned, the moment would not have been ill-chosen. In 1890 and '91, while our armaments were finished...I heard whisperings more than once that since the war was inevitable, it would be better to run the risk immediately. I was myself at the time Prime Minister and believed also that our situation was good; but such a temptation, one will believe me, has never even touched my thought. Who would unchain a preventive war?[199]

Which is to say that, even in a democracy, wishes for a preventive war may arise and find voice, but a democratic politician must avoid even the appearance of wanting or starting any aggressive war.

By 1897, Waldersee's anticipatory politics were being aimed at the interior threat posed by the Social Democrats. According to Waldersee, the State must never "leave the choice of the time for the beginning of the great settlement [to the Social Democratic leaders] but must rather accelerate this! As yet, the State is certainly in a position to suppress any insurrection." This is an example of the rarely-heard demand for a preventive civil war. By 1903, Waldersee, now seventy-one years old, had come to the conclusion that the war that even as recently as ten years before he had wished to see must now be viewed as a highly risky enterprise for Germany, considering the military inefficacy of his one-time pupil, William II. But before his days were over, he was to witness one war that he could pronounce a model preventive war. "Japan," he wrote, "has rightly recognized the point of time for striking and has succeeded in making herself master of the sea within a few days and in gaining a free hand for the transportation of the Army to the mainland."[200]

As Emperor, William II showed far less desire for a preventive war than he had in his Crown Prince days, though the thought occasionally broke out in his marginal remarks.[201] Theodore Roosevelt, writing from his office in the Navy Department in 1897, was more eager than the Kaiser himself to have Germany fight Russia in a preventive war—a war that was also to keep

Germany from foolish enterprises in the zones covered by the Monroe doctrine. "This war she could have made easily a few years ago, while now every year she waits to strike is just so much against her." Were he a German, he would strike. "As an Englishman," he wrote, "I should seize the first opportunity to crush the German Navy and the German commercial marine out of existence."[202]

Only once before 1914 was William II confronted with the decision of whether or not to undertake a war of preventive nature. That was in 1905-06. As a consequence of the defeat of Russian power in the Far East, Germany was once more in the superior military position she had held immediately after 1871. France was, militarily speaking, nearly alone. She was exposed and the newly acquired British ally, as then organized for war, could help but little. (This obvious military fact did not keep certain British navalists from advocating a preventive war against the German Navy.)[203] British intervention could not have had an immediate and decisive effect on Continental warfare at the time, although its power to stay in a war was probably not taken into due consideration by Schlieffen and others.

At the time of its signature, the long-run military implications of the new Entente had hardly been considered by the Wilhelmstrasse, nor, in all probability, by British diplomacy. It was Schlieffen who finally pointed them out to his old intimate Holstein. He made Holstein realize the full impact of his earlier mistaken belief that Britain would never let herself be attracted to the Franco-Russian alliance. Given the state of documentation, it may still be impossible to say whether Holstein or Schlieffen first drew warlike conclusions from the new power alignment in the world. However, since the end of 1905, or perhaps earlier, their lines of thought had converged.[204] From the end of 1905 on, Schlieffen's plans took the most unfavorable prospect into account—with Britain, Belgium, Italy, Serbia and Rumania added to Germany's enemies. After the revolutionary troubles had broken out in Russia, Holstein was "convinced we ought to try, with all our energy and with a resolution shrinking not even from the most extreme, to break the ring of the other great Powers before it strangles us. Hence the Emperor's Tangiers voyage!"[205]

A more provocative gesture than the appearance in person of the Emperor in this zone of imperialist competition could hardly have been invented, and very few contemporaries could imagine that the traveling Kaiser had not devised it himself. As must have been expected in Berlin, there were plenty of people in France, from Delcassé down, who had no wish for a peaceful settlement with Germany and who until their dying day would regret that France had not declared war on the occasion of the Tangiers visit.[206] And British policy at that time, even if Delcassé overstated the amount of help he had been promised by London, was not exactly discouraging. And inside Germany, the pressure for preventive war was of considerable strength though it was strangely incoherent. It included great names as well as the nameless. The Russian military attaché in Berlin at the time was persuaded that there existed a whole military party that wished for war, largely in the hope of thereby combatting Socialism, which had begun to undermine discipline and authority inside the Army. The war party was recruited from among the regimental officers and from the highest ranks as well, including Schlieffen himself. All of them thought that "a campaign would be necessary to get everything in hand again." By the end of 1905, this kind of agitation no longer seemed very prevalent to the outsider.[207]

December 1905 saw the diplomatic preparation for Algeciras and Schlieffen's official planning in preparation for war. Uncertain if not hopeless as to the outcome of the diplomats' conference, "very many" in Berlin either expected or wished an armed conflict by the spring of 1906.[208] Schlieffen belonged to this group, but it cannot be said of him, or of anyone else, that he headed it. The invisible Holstein kept on driving towards it longer and harder than anyone else. According to a (much later) letter of Bülow, Schlieffen "never once recommended to me a preventive war or attempted to push me in the direction of war."[209] Still, Bülow was aware of the pressure on him—it came most directly from or through Holstein. The proposals that Schlieffen had in mind at the time seem to have been these: "Let that Germanophobe Delcassé, who would like to dwarf us, pursue his policy of catastrophe! Let the French run up against us while we are in this military situation which is so favorable to us! 'Let them come!'"[210] To make them come was up to the diplomats.

The history of preventive war at this juncture is handicapped by the fact that there is no contemporaneous document of any outright demand for such a war in 1904-06. All the materials on this point are to be found in the literature of memoirs.[211] It appears that during a meeting presided over by the Chancellor in the autumn of 1905, Schlieffen, when asked by Bülow, stated: "From a military point of view, I see the only solution in an immediate war with France. England is still weakened by the Boer War, Russia still tied down by her war with Japan, and France stands isolated, and with her alone we shall easily finish."[212]

This view was in keeping with Schlieffen's war theory. Whatever its appearance, it was predicated on the preservation of the status quo at home and abroad, indicating a conservatism in politics and military ideas that looked for preservation through a short preventive war.[213] War in itself, however, was not a conservative measure, nor was

that piece of house-breaking, the march through Belgium. The plans to move through Belgium were fully worked out only after the Moroccan crisis had been settled, or postponed. Schlieffen's mobilization plans for 1906, which date from December 1905, include for the first time the march through Belgium.[214]

In addition to Schlieffen's advice, Bülow had asked various governmental personages about their opinions for and against war. He found the most enthusiastic wish for war on the part of the War Minister, General von Einem, who told the Chancellor that the Army was ready to strike, the commanding generals good and in part even outstanding. (Among them were Hindenburg and von der Goltz, both of whom favored a preventive war against France.)[215] "You can always rely on the Army, Count, and altogether base your policy on it," von Einem told him. He did everything, he writes in his memoirs, "to stiffen the Chancellor's backbone in his diplomatic struggle against Delcassé, in my dearest hope to settle the whole issue with the sword. Conditions at the time were so favorable to us, militarily speaking, as never before." Bülow appeared to be of the same opinion at the time, and even William II seemed momentarily ready for war, though he told the War Minister with great determination: "I do not love war and should not like to make one, unless it is absolutely necessary." It was the Emperor who disappointed Einem's hopes for war as well as Bülow's diplomacy by bluff and threat of war, and Holstein's urge for preventive war. He even told various Frenchmen—as he somewhat later told his assembled generals, who did not all forgive him their disappointment—that he would not make war or mobilize on account of Morocco.[216]

Going beyond the discreet bureaucracy in gathering opinions as to the best Moroccan policy, Bülow asked the leader of the Prussian conservatives, von Oldenburg-Januschau, a pure-water Junker, what the public thought about Morocco. The practical politician answered that Morocco was not a beautiful casus belli, but that the new Anglo-French alliance was; indeed, everyone down to the last farmhand in Januschau would understand that. Oldenburg did not favor territorial acquisitions in distant Morocco but thought that a preventive war was worth contemplating, for the Anglo-French alliance gave him great concern.

I saw the moment approach when with no one to fall back on we would one day stand alone, ringed in and a victim to numberless enemies... When I hinted to Bülow about the possibility of a preventive war, I did so because, on the basis of the reports that were before him as the responsible Chancellor, he ought to know and decide whether there existed a coalition against us. Only when and if that was above doubt, a preventive war for the Reich's sake seemed to me imperative. This moment, I considered, had arrived, if not in 1905, then in 1908 [during the Bosnian crisis].[217]

Because Holstein, the first to conceive of Morocco as the occasion for a preventive war, was the last to give up his pressuring for war, he was the first to lose office. His retirement was promptly followed by that of Schlieffen, whose advanced age, seventy-three, provided the cloak for the liquidation of all toying with the idea of preventive war. Von Einem survived in office, although he made no bones about his low opinion of Bülow's later Moroccan policy as "far too pacific."[218] Quite a few German military writers have dated Germany's defeat in the First World War from Schlieffen's retirement and the unfought preventive war of 1905. One of them compared the author of the study of Cannae, the pattern for the modern battle of decision, with Hannibal, and quoted Theodor Mommsen on Carthage and the Barkides:

> When a weaker State is threatened by certain war, though it may be indefinite in time, the wiser more resolute men who at once make ready for the inevitable war and want to start war in a favorable hour and thus conceal the political defensive by the strategic offensive will everywhere find themselves hemmed in by the lazy and cowardly mass of the money servants, the senile, the thoughtless who think of nothing but gaining time, merely for the purpose of living and dying in peace, of postponing the final battle at any price.

This very thing had happened to Schlieffen. And thus the First World War was lost for Germany when it might have been won, during the first Moroccan crisis. "The pacifism of the German Government, indeed of the whole people allowed the last opportunity to go by unused. Bismarck's warnings against preventive war had contributed their share. Whether he would have adhered to his opinion under the changed conditions might seem doubtful."[219] Thus German politico-generals expressed their opposition to the authority of the dead Bismarck and to the warnings of his political testament against preventive war.[220]

The idea of preventive war, as one of the arcana of government, has a secret tradition stronger and more unbroken than the public one. Palmerston and Russell, with all the preventive notions they entertained against a victorious North during the American Civil War, could not very well publicly pronounce these notions, because they ran counter to the forces of British Non-conformism. Nor could Napoleon III admit to his preventive motives, for they ran counter to his aim of winning over British Liberalism to the side of the Second Empire.[221] Seward's proposal for starting a foreign war in order to prevent and avert the civil war at home was made in secrecy; its author could not confront the public morality of the day with such a notion.

The contradiction between endorsing preventive war on one occasion before one audience and repudiating it at another time with greater publicity can be illustrated by the case of Arthur Balfour. As Prime Minister, near the end of 1904, he was reported to have said with regard to the author of a London newspaper article proposing a coup a la Copenhagen against the German fleet: "Arnold White ought to be hanged" for having made such a suggestion, either at all or publicly.[222] On the eve of the Second Hague Conference, then out of office, he told the friendly ambassador, Henry White, "somewhat lightly" and as if won over by Fisher's ideas of "Copenhagening":

> "We are probably fools not to find a reason for declaring war on Germany before she builds too many ships and takes away our trade." White: "You are a very high-minded man in private life. How can you possibly contemplate anything so politically immoral as provoking a war against a harmless nation which has as good a right to a navy as you have? If you wish to compete with German trade, work harder." Balfour: "That would mean lowering our standard of living. Perhaps it would be simpler for us to have a war." White: "I am shocked that you of all men should enunciate such principles." Balfour (again lightly): "Is it a question of right or wrong? Maybe it is just a question of keeping our supremacy."[223]

At about the same time, and again a few years later, the same Balfour, still out of office, told the German ambassador, who was honestly concerned with bettering Anglo-German relations and who knew that at least a few Englishmen had publicly favored a preventive war against Germany and thus had given German navalists additional food for their agitation, that he, Balfour, "considered such a war reprehensible. No government in England would be able to undertake a preventive war, considering public opinion. The altogether isolated voices to the contrary were without importance."[224] Still later, on July 29, 1914, Balfour met with Fisher, who was able to remove the Conservative leader's last doubts as to the inevitability of war, even "before the Cabinet knew it."[225] Was the war inevitable, in Balfour's mind, because of the necessity of a preventive stroke against growing Germany?

That the idea of a preventive war was or seems so largely a German one, in spite of Arthur Balfour and certain British naval men, to whom we shall revert in time, has various reasons. In the Second Reich, the Army and later the Navy were so powerful and their officer corps so close, if not superior to the holders of political power, that their professional suggestions in favor of such a war came up for consideration inside governmental circles, as well as outside from time to time. In Germany, the proponents of preventive war were franker and more outspoken than their peers in other countries, where the strong popular aversion to preventive war forced discretion upon those entertaining similar notions, whether they were military or naval men or civilian militarists.

The relatively ample, and for this reason easily misleading documentation on German discussions of preventive war was part and parcel of the governing habits in the Second and Third Reich. There was frankness in the discussion of measures apt to prove most incriminating in later political contests or before history.[226] The governing statesmen and politicians of other Powers knew far better how to keep such dangerous notions to themselves and knew better than to put them on paper.

In Italy under the last Savoyards, diplomacy preserved enough of Renaissance amorality in politics to permit the occasional proposal of preventive war, even to friends and allies. The latter insisted, however, that if Italy wanted to have their sympathy and aid, she must avoid even the appearance of being the aggressor.[227] The Italian ambassador in Paris, Ressmann, thought that the outrageous incident of Aigues-Mortes (1893) offered the Triplice a good occasion to unleash war, which was overdue and "in any case inevitable." The German recipient of these confidences would not admit that war was inevitable and that no peaceful settlement could be found. "In any case," he argued, "even a war favorable in its outcome to us Triple Alliance partners would weaken us more than the armed peace does, but an unfortunate war would practically annihilate us, hence all endeavors must be directed toward the preservation of peace. The more all of us, friends and enemies, arm for war, the more unlikely its outbreak. The peace which by now has undergone a twenty-two years' test, would be preserved as before." But the Italian was more pessimistic: considering French obsession with the idea of regaining Alsace-Lorraine, war could perhaps be postponed, but not forever.[228] German apprehensions about Italian forwardness were shared by British diplomats. They viewed with alarm Italy's desperate inclination "to run amuck at [sic] France at any hazard, in the expectation that neither their allies nor England would allow them to be destroyed"; but they also came to share Berlin's hope that, as in their daily life, the Italians would not necessarily proceed from shouting and gesticulating to actual blows.[229]

When the Japanese entered the circles of Western diplomacy, they felt no native inhibitions with regard to preventive or aggressive war. On the eve of the Chinese-Japanese War of 1894, they shocked Secretary of State Gresham by telling him that "our situation at home is critical and war with China would improve it by arousing the patriotic sentiment of our people and more strongly attach them to the Government."[230] But it did not shock the German ambassador in London when his Japanese colleague Baron Hayashi informed him that the view was quite general in Tokyo that war with Russia was inevitable and that a great number of influential politicians were of the opinion that the moment had come to play the praevenire with regard to Russia and strike as soon as possible. Japanese generals were agreed that their army could not be beaten during the next two years and the admirals that the Japanese fleet, even alone, was superior to the Russian, which would have to be put out of the way before the army could be landed on the continent.[231]

The alliance negotiations with England did not seem to discourage Japanese preventive war intentions. The Japanese were careful to exclude the provision of "previous consultations" with the ally in case of conflicts, as they "would be fatal to prompt action" and might permit the very "events which they desired to anticipate" to come about. When they struck in February 1904, they felt driven to action by the daily strengthening of Russia's military position in the Far East, which the slowness and peaceful assurances of Russian diplomacy seemed designed to aid.[232]

The victorious Japanese incurred the suspicion of Westerners for long afterwards that they were more ready than other Great Powers to disregard inhibitions against undertaking preventive wars. How far the Roosevelt Administration based its aggression-inviting attitude before Pearl Harbor on this Japanese proclivity may long remain a matter of controversy. At any rate, the administration was warned about it by more than one diplomat before 1941, who believed them quite able and ready to proceed to a war opening, as in 1904, on the strength of the belief that they had to be beforehand.[233]

The governors of more democratic countries had to pay greater respect to the horror with which the peoples had come to surround the idea of preventive war. In respecting or circumnavigating such zones of moral judgments, they gained, possibly at the cost of foregoing some military advantage, a factor of morale in case of war. By 1911, the German intention to march through Belgium was a well-known international secret, known even in America.[234] Nevertheless the French, and even more the British Government "had always felt repugnance at contemplating (prévoir) a preventive occupation of Belgian territory," as Poincaré writes in his self-defense, "and no one can forget that in 1914 there was neither in London nor in Paris thought of being beforehand."[235] In reality, failure to occupy Belgian territory by French forces was a necessary consideration in the war plans urged upon the French by British soldiers like Henry Wilson. They were perfectly aware that without the foreseen rape of Belgium the British people could not be brought into the war at the side of France. One of the first questions put to the French in the negotiations on British military assistance was whether it could be assumed that France "will not violate Belgian neutrality, unless compelled to do so by a previous violation on the part of the German armies?" The answer was, of course, in the affirmative. In November 1912, Wilson repeated the warning to the French General Staff "not to yield to the temptation it might [and did] feel at one time, to conduct a preventive offensive through Belgian territory."[236]

"COPENHAGENING"

"But this policy of a 'preventive war' was never even seriously considered by responsible British statesmen."[237]

The memory of Sir Francis Bacon's dictum about justifiable preventive war and of Nelson and the coups of 1801 and 1807 against Copenhagen remained so vivid, even without such literary refreshers as Mahan's Life of Nelson, that British navalists of the nineteenth and twentieth centuries recommended at various stages in the naval competition that similar measures be repeated against navies threatening their country's naval supremacy or relative military standing.[238] The memory of the intended victims of such coups was equally vivid. They feared that such attacks were being planned and would be launched against their budding fleets before the latter had passed through the period of high vulnerability, the "danger zone." The neurotic Treitschke, who believed that he would live to see the fall of English naval supremacy, "obviously a thing belonging to the past century," was afraid as early as 1876 that "those beefs desire nothing better than to destroy our rising sea power."[239] This was a hypermetropic fear that had no basis in Bismarck's or Caprivi's naval policy or that of the British at the time.

The larger part of nineteenth-century English opinion on international morality and the hardly ever disputed supremacy of the British Navy kept the "Copenhagening" idea shelved. But the political amalgam of Darwinism, Imperialism, and the seeming or real threats to naval supremacy led,

towards the end of the century, to the restatement and advocacy of this idea by British Navy and Army officers and their publicistic following. Reverting to the "Battle of Dorking" ideas of an earlier generation of British soldiers, the British military attaché in Berlin in the 1890's, Grierson, was convinced on the basis of his personal experiences among the Germans that "we must go for the Germans, and right soon, or they will go for us later. A pretext for war would not be difficult to find, and I don't believe that even Russia would stand by them."[240]

The Army rather than the Navy can claim priority for British preventive war proposals against Germany. The Navy's immediate enemy for the larger part of the nineteenth century was France, who had a considerable navy close-by, colonial ambitions, and an ally whose naval power was readily added to that of her own in all the British admirals' calculations of anti-British strength. During the last quarter of the century, naval competition had more and more come to be stated in terms of tonnage and thickness of armor plate. In this competition, it was feared and calculated that the British might lose their supremacy at a foreseeable date unless they outbuilt the competitor or took preventive action against him in time. Experts such as the American naval constructor R. P. Hobson recommended such action to the British in 1895, unless they were prepared to lose their supremacy to the French within the next fifteen months. At that time, such proposals found only small acclaim in British admiralty circles, though naval writers took it up and suggested that if "European Powers do not stop the building of warships, an ultimatum should be sent to them by some modern Pitt, and, if not attended to, British fleets should be sent to destroy them in foreign ports and dockyards, à la Copenhagen and the Basque Roads."[241]

The existing preventive action school inside the British Navy, with a considerable backing from the press, never obtained governmental approval. That it did exist the public at home and abroad could surmise, even if the Government insisted in Parliament that "such an idea never entered into the mind of the Government of this country...People abroad are incredulous, but they ought to know that such a war undertaken in such a spirit would have been against the whole tradition of this country, and would have been against the whole moral sense of this country." The "laughter from the Irish members" which greeted this declaration by the First Lord of the Admiralty would have been even heartier had they known that in October 1898 a considerable number of cabinet members, including the First Lord, had been in favor of war—since "the row would have come, it might just as well come now as later."[242]

Among the restraining influences was doubtless the desire to avoid even the appearance of undertaking a preventive war. This would be damaging at home and abroad. There were many abroad who feared, and some who hoped, that England would undertake such a war against France.[243] It was believed that Salisbury alone had averted war, that it would have come had Rosebery and the Liberals been in power at the time of Fashoda—because they wanted war "in order to prevent a possible coalition of the [other] naval powers."[244] When Waldersee, who always thought in terms of preventive wars, was told this by the German ambassador in Paris, he concluded that "naturally, the German Navy, should it grow very considerably, would become just as discomforting to the British and they would start a conflict with us as well. The best means against that would naturally be the early conclusion of an alliance between Germany, Russia and France. But in this I cannot believe."[245]

Before the naval competition veered toward Anglo-German antagonism, the First Hague Conference took place. It did not in the least lessen the arms race, though it occasioned, as not a few international peace conferences have done, the proposal of applying force in a preventive war, including war in favor of general peace, or, more closely inspected, for the maintenance of the status quo.[246] A British M.P. suggested at the time that the United States, Great Britain and possibly Japan should make their combined naval power so absolutely supreme that they could order the other naval Powers to sell out their ships. Should they refuse, their vessels would be captured on leaving port. "That would settle the peace of the world." And at least one of the British service journals was also attracted by the idea of a preventive war to check naval competition.[247]

Such proposals were not at the time aimed particularly at the still small German Navy that Tirpitz had begun to construct. But he had to run the "risk" that a navy of increasing size would arouse British proposals for counter-measures, including a timely preventive war, long before a German Navy would be strong enough to attack the British fleet. Although a sensational journalist like Arnold White, a close friend of Sir John Fisher, had voiced an early demand for such a war on Germany (Daily Mail, July 24, 1902), it was rather surprising to Germany that the more general outcry against the German peril did not develop until the end of 1904. At that time, various London publications advocated preventive action against the German fleet, "a navy without an excuse." Once this fleet had been destroyed, the peace of Europe, held by England either in combination with France or the United States or both, and the freedom of the seas, would be guar-

anteed. The time was near "for the mistress of the seas to decide in her own interests, which are identical with the peace of the world, what shall be done with the German fleet" (Vanity Fair, November 10 and 17, 1904). Other publications took up the hue and cry, including the Army and Navy Gazette, whose character as a service journal gave its words even more weight abroad than at home.[248] There was plenty of unguarded talk in British naval circles, including the lady members, one of whom told the German naval attaché that war would have to be declared on his country soon. At present, she reasoned, Germany possessed only a few ships, which the British Navy could easily dispose of, "but in a few years you might be strong and we would lose too many of our ships" in the attempt—"just the two years," William cried out, "which we would have still needed in order to be ready." He was frightened enough by a suspected British attack to order some of his ships back to home stations and to demand that his diplomats, as his sailors had whispered to him, meet this British "Copenhagening" by a German counter-Copenhagening. Diplomats and Edward VII had to go to work to smooth sea dogs' bristles, or goose pimples.[249]

A speech by Sir Arthur Lee, Civil Lord of the Admiralty, of February 3, 1905, a "most indiscreet and improper speech" as the Liberal leader Campbell-Bannerman later called it,[250] set off another series of Anglo-German scares and recriminations. In his speech, intended probably to assure the audience of the arch-readiness of the Navy, Lee declared that if war across the North Sea "should unhappily be declared, the British Navy would get its blow in first, before the other side had had time to read in the papers that war had been declared." This could only be understood as meaning that the fleet would be on its way before the war declaration was in German hands and would possibly strike even before that. The shaky Balfour cabinet did not dare correct its Civil Lord, the liaison officer with the naval circles around Fisher.[251] Nor could it identify itself with statements such as the Daily Chronicle's to the effect that if the German fleet had been destroyed in October 1904, there would have been peace in Europe for sixty years, that "for this reason we think the statements by Mr. Arthur Lee, provided they were made by order of the Cabinet, a wise and pacific enunciation of the unshakeable determination of the mistress of the seas."[252]

Not long before his East Leigh speech, Lee had assured Roosevelt, as the latter told the Germans, "quite definitely that Germany was planning an attack on England." The President concluded from other communications that there was widespread fear of such German aggression in England, while other Englishmen close to him, like Spring Rice, hinted that Germany's true object was America.[253] There was both fear and boldness in the strong men of 1904-05.

Fisher had been talking preventive war against Germany almost since his appointment as First Sea Lord in 1903. He was guided by the influence of publicists like Arnold White rather than by any plans formulated for such an enterprise. Several of his designs against Germany had a certain fantastic quality, such as that of destroying the German fleet inside the Kiel harbor during the First Moroccan crisis.[254] Whether or not this was part of the promised British support that Delcassé had banked on is not known. The ministers, first the Conservatives, then the Liberals, allowed Fisher, the outstanding naval reorganizer, to keep on talking in this irresponsible manner—it seemed entirely harmless, unreal, "private." But it could not be so private that the Germans would not learn about it. They naturally concluded that he meant what he said and that his Government did not really disavow him in this, in spite of some British assurances that "nobody listens to the wild talk of Fisher."[255] This mischief received public support when a British admiral told the Germans in an article published in a German review in May 1905, that, much as he regarded an Anglo-German war a great calamity, he "would sooner see such a war break out tomorrow than see it (if it really must come) postponed for a series of years when Germany will be stronger by sea and it may be possible for her to obtain an advantage over us."[256]

The continued Anglo-German naval competition, increasingly burdensome and hence irritating, produced on the English side either proposals for a halt in the race or exasperated proposals for preventive action against the danger of tomorrow. From time to time, articles and letters were published even by the responsible press which raised the question as to whether or not the increasing danger of the German fleet should be fought now, in 1905, 1906, etc., under favorable conditions, rather than later. Fisher did not relent in his "Copenhagening" campaign behind the scenes. He put the proposal before Edward VII in the spring of 1908. He outlined how the German battleships were either to be sunk inside Kiel harbor or "treated like rogue elephants and, with some females in the shape of our battleships on each side, hustled out of that harbor as prisoners." The King dismissed his "first and principal aide-de-camp" with a good-humored "Fisher, you are mad," which commentary Fisher gleefully told around town.[257]

Fisher with his preventive war ideas did not stand alone among British defense officials. His and King Edward's close friend, Lord Esher of the Committee of Imperial Defence, shared them for political and military-technical reasons. So he informed the French, who eagerly received such confidences. For him it was axiomatic, by November 1908, that in case of a Continental war, the British Government

> would be led, by the force of things, to intervene...Germany will be our competitor and rival and, sooner or later, the opposition of our interests will lead us into conflict. Much better that it should come about today while we remain faithful to our policy [of the entente with France] rather than postpone the day it is falling due and thus alienate France and possibly prepare for ourselves terrible reprisals. This would as well be for our fleet an exceptional occasion to annihilate the German fleet before it can become a real menace to us.[258]

What the Germans learned about such proposals served not only to bolster Tirpitz' agitation but also to give pause even to such not overly thoughtful statesmen as Bülow. Might not the proposal of a preventive war on the other side of the North Sea, as yet entertained only by a small upper-class group, eventually get hold of the minds of the British people and thus sanction this dreaded war? Would it not be desirable to slow German naval construction? In the ensuing battle between the Chancellor and the diplomats on one side, and Tirpitz and the Emperor on the other, with the Army a thoughtless neutral, Bülow, whose position with William had been previously shaken by the Daily Telegraph affair, gave up and retired.[259]

His successor, soon realizing this same danger, which the Wilhelmstrasse pointed out to him, encountered the same obstacles at home. He was not much more successful in his attempts at an Anglo-German understanding: it proved unobtainable. English publicists like Spenser Wilkinson pointed out and interpreted the "writing on the wall" as meaning that war with Germany was unavoidable,[260] a fatalistic conviction to which even peaceful ministers like Lloyd George occasionally succumbed. He told Henry Wilson during the Moroccan crisis of 1911 that "he was quite in favor of war now."[261]

A quantitative and qualitative analysis of public and private opinion before 1914 as to a preventive war by England against Germany and her navy could hardly fail to conclude that no broad popular sentiment favored it; that definite groups such as the City and business generally, on both sides of the North Sea, were opposed to it and certainly did not call for it in 1914 or before. The Tirpitz group and the German soldiers nevertheless insisted that business was the truly hostile factor in Anglo-German relations and that business competition brought on the First World War.[262]

Walter Rathenau, a businessman whose experiences after 1914 were to turn him into a statesman, and who had even earlier shaken off the muteness and political illiteracy of his peers, struck somewhat deeper in his analysis of Anglo-German relations as of 1912.[263] As Rathenau saw it, England, the cleverest and most truly political nation on earth, understands the situation perfectly. She does not really hate Germany, but senses in her rise a fourfold danger: (1) she feels out distanced in industrial technique; (2) she thinks she is obliged to interfere against any preponderant Power that evolves on the Continent; (3) her colonial structure would be inwardly shaken, should her absolute dominion of the sea lose the authority of an historical dogma; (4) competitive armament is too expensive and, in the light of constantly changing technology, uncertain in its outcome. The war England would have to undertake would, therefore, be a preventive war. But such a war would have no certain sequel, not even in the case of a definite German defeat. The final result would only benefit America.

Such thoughts ranged ahead of those of most statesmen[264] and politicians, ahead of the preventive war schemes of sailors and soldiers who prided themselves on their forethought. Politicians knew better than soldiers and sailors that a popular approval of their nations' entry into war was more important for success than any military advantage to be won by surprise attack.

AUSTRIA'S LAST WAR—THE PREVENTIVE THAT SPELLED FINIS

The basic and soundest idea of Austria's governors after 1866 was conservative, namely the maintenance of her status quo as a Great Power in Europe and as a supra-national monarchy through the maintenance of peace. That idea had led them along peaceful ways for many years after 1866, despite some proposals for preventive action to retain or bring back to submission "the servant peoples who were shaking their shaggy caryatid heads" (Hebbel) and who maintained cultural, religious, or outright subversive ties not only with Austria-Hungary's enemies—Russia and Serbia—but with her allies, Italy and Rumania, as well. Austria's readiness for peace was strengthened by her relatively weak position in the arms race. Her economy forbade, or seemed to forbid, a more complete utilization of her manpower and industrial war potential. Her position in Europe was further weakened by the imperviousness of Western nationalism to the idea that this seemingly outdated monarchy might be carrying out in its own clumsy way a European mission in the Balkan East. Instead the West encouraged, officially and unofficially, the nationalism of the Balkan peoples and eventually came to consider them, as Pan-Slavism had already begun to do, in terms of military usefulness.

Such Austrian predicaments produced repeated proposals for preventive wars, including one against a so-called ally—Italy. This would have been a novelty in the modern history of the idea of preventive war. Austria's distrust of Italy, stirred by the Irredenta, did not end with the forming of the Triple Alliance in 1882. During the winter of 1877-78, her Chief of Staff, Beck, worked out a plan of concentration and operations against Italy. While he emphasized the purely military character of his memorial and was himself generally averse to the notion of preventive war, Beck on this occasion indicated something of a desire for such a war.[265] Plans for the concentration against Italy, alone and in combination with Russia, remained prepared thereafter in Vienna. By 1886, Archduke Albrecht, the victor of Custozza and designated commander-in-chief in case of war, came to regret that in 1879 or 1880 no serious use had been made of these plans for a preventive war against such an unreliable ally. "We would have peace now in that direction; but as it is, we are tied down in every direction because there is always Italy in our rear."[266]

Italy's prolonged conflicts with France, plus a temporary calming down of Irredentist effervescence, allowed Vienna to disregard for a time the danger of a war on two fronts and concentrate on the Russian military threat. The Russian threat seemed constantly on the increase during the 1880's and led to a prolonged diplomatic crisis from 1886 to 1889. While Bismarck admitted the threatening and challenging character of the Russian military measures and of Pan-Slavism to both the Central Powers, he turned down all Austrian proposals to meet the impending Russian attack by a counter-attack on their own part. Only when attacked could Austria expect German armed assistance. Even less than Austrian civilian governors could the Austrian soldiers, as well as Moltke and his adlatus Waldersee, bring themselves to approve of Bismarck's careful diplomacy. It seemed diametrically opposed to the strategic requirements of the situation. Russia's vast potential was as yet undeveloped, her armaments incomplete. Therefore, the military reasoned, let us make use of the headstart while we have it. When the downfall of Boulanger in November 1887 promised a continuance of peace, Waldersee assured the Austrian military attaché that the pause would not last beyond the next spring. Then war would be inevitable; for Germany as well, the greatest danger was now in the East. The best thing would be, regardless of the hardships of a winter campaign, to meet the Russian attack beforehand. And Moltke no less favored prompt unleashing of the attack against Russia.[267]

Giving way a little to Austrian pressuring, Bismarck agreed that general staff conversations should take place in order to discuss what the two partners were to do if and when—and then only—the casus foederis had arrived, an attack by, and not on, Russia. He strongly opposed all Austrian attempts "to shift the casus foederis as if it were to exist at all times." Such a shift would only serve to strengthen Austrian desires for war. He would never agree that the decision as to the casus foederis be taken out of his hands or be defined or fixed by means of a military convention such as the Austrians proposed. The Austrians would have provided for a putative defense. For example, continued Russian armaments might lead to attack on one's own part in order to be protected against the dangers of an overpowering surprise assault. Moltke, recently informed of the existing Reinsurance Treaty with Russia, had to point out to the disappointed Austrians how difficult it was to win over the Chancellor to the idea of an aggressive war. The latter remained unconvinced that "the war must take place."[268]

The last twenty years of Beck's long regime in the General Staff were characterized by what scornful critics called military muddling through—the actual Austrian terms are untranslatable. Then came the era of Conrad, his successor from 1906.[269] "My whole activity as peacetime Chief of Staff," he writes in the first sentences of his memoirs, "was crowded with conflicts resulting from the fact that my fundamental views of politics and their conduct were in opposition to those held by the deciding personalities. I saw the Monarchy threatened in its existence by unmistakable dangers. My opponents either did not value these to their full extent or believed that they could escape them by a waiting attitude. I, however, was convinced that this could only be done by preventive action."[270]

Considering the obvious Russian, Rumanian, Serbian and Italian appetites for the Austrian heritage, it was Conrad's basic idea to "throw these enemies of Hapsburg into the dust" individually, one after the other, as occasion offered. Italy's secret but obvious defection from the Triplice, after 1903-04, and the new encouragement given the Irredenta by Rome provided Conrad with enough provocation for his first proposal for a preventive war. "Military superiority was momentarily still on the side of the Monarchy; therefore it seemed advisable to make use of the situation before it changed around in its disfavor." But his proposals "to settle accounts" with Italy ran up against the firm resistance of the Emperor and his foreign minister, Aehrenthal. The heir to the throne, Francis Ferdinand, would have welcomed

such a settlement then and even somewhat later, but as Conrad told one of the military attachés: "Aehrenthal is working only with freemasons and Jews and keeps the Monarchy from settling accounts with Italy before it is too late."[271] The Emperor's strong No prevailed. "Austria had never started a war," he said—a maxim which Conrad took the liberty of countering with the remark: "Unfortunately, Your Majesty."[272]

Conrad found less rather than more opposition to his preventive war notions in Berlin after Aehrenthal and Bülow, far less cautious supervisors of the direct wires between the two general staffs than the Bismarcks, had given permission for establishing closer staff contacts during the Bosnian crisis.[273] Ever since Conrad's first visit to Berlin in May 1907, Moltke had gained the impression that he was dealing with a friend of Germany, "a quiet, clever and reasonable man whose open and reliable character arouses unconditional trust"; that unfortunately Austro-Italian tension ran rather high and was viewed very seriously in military circles in Vienna where it was thought that a warlike settlement of the existing differences was sooner or later unavoidable; that Francis Ferdinand was in close contact with Conrad and was denying that he would pursue a Slavophile policy after his accession to the throne.[274] Moltke was far from discouraging when, during the Bosnian crisis, Conrad informed him of the Austrian plans for the concentration. Moltke assured him that in the case of an Austro-Italian war, Germany would protect Austria in the rear and that according to German military opinion, Italy was unable to make war, now or for the next two or three years to come, and that the intention of playing the praevenire was, militarily speaking, an ideal one. In the case of a conflict with Serbia, the Austrian assurance that no territorial acquisitions were contemplated would keep Russia from intervening.[275] Even if this was only meant to give encouragement after the event, it must have served to build up and strengthen in Conrad his increasingly maniacal idea of making preventive war and relying in this on German approval.[276]

The same effect must be ascribed to a private letter of Moltke's of April 19, 1909, in which he expressed regret over the "unused opportunity" for war, one that would not soon return:

I am firmly convinced that we would have succeeded in localizing the war between Austria and Serbia; after its victorious close the Monarchy, consolidated within, strengthened without, would have gained a preponderance in the Balkans which could not easily have been shaken thereafter. Even if Russia had become active and a European war had resulted, the conditions would have been more favorable for

Austria and Germany now than they are apt to be a few years hence. Still, let us look confidently to the future. As long as Austria and Germany stand shoulder to shoulder, each prepared to view the welfare of the other as the tua res agitur, we shall be strong enough to break any ring around us.[277]

Only the most lenient judgment will call these well-wisher's statements mere friendly commentary on a recent maneuver that had not quite come out as its directors hoped. The fact that there was no sign of disapproval from Berlin—where they could not afford to estrange the last remaining ally—could only serve to give the Austrian general the encouragement which he did not always find at home to persevere in his preventive war ideas.[278]

The war party at home, in which must be included some of the younger Austrian diplomats, had done what it could to prolong the Bosnian crisis and make it result in war with Italy or Serbia or both. An article published in Danzer's Armeezeitung in January 1909 deeply shocked Italian army circles. The author frankly declared that just then, after the Messina earthquake, which had cost Italy 100,000 lives and a great part of the national wealth, was the time for action against Italy. One had been naïve enough to spare Russia during the war of 1904-05; the same error must be avoided with regard to Italy. Sooner or later there would be war between her and Austria; hence the sooner the better.[279]

Behind the scenes, Conrad continued in his attempts to persuade influential personalities to support his preventive ideas. He said to Francis Ferdinand, through an aide, that although "every war was an uncertain thing, this was no reason to avoid it if circumstances so commanded, even if one should be uncertain about its outcome."[280] This code duello stand on war, which did not take into consideration the problem of survival in defeat, seemed unconvincing to most of the more responsible governors of Austria, and notably to the Emperor. Conrad tried to convince him that a "settlement" with Serbia was inevitable. Russia merely wanted to gain time in order to strike when it suited her. At present, Germany was a loyal ally, France uninclined to go to war. He called it "lightheartedness to start an unjustified war, but it was something else again to pass over an occasion and then have the war brought on under miserable chances." Somewhat perversely, Conrad thought, Aehrenthal, who had himself precipitated the Bosnian crisis, denied him the use of the occasion for a preventive war and was only willing to let him have a bigger army, which would have satisfied many a chief of staff. Aehrenthal told Conrad that "the Monarchy

stands in need of a strong Army, not for the purpose of settling conflicts, which might perhaps become acute at a later time, by a preventive war, but for the eventuality that the honor and integrity of the Empire become endangered or that its vital interests can no longer be preserved in a peaceful manner."[281]

Italy's systematic preparations for war with Turkey in the summer of 1911 gave Conrad the occasion to return to his proposals for preventive war against the false alliance partner. "To be deterred by outdated treaties entered upon without foresight and by diplomatic scruples would be suicidal." But Aehrenthal sharply opposed his views on existing treaties. Since 1902, Austria had promised Italy a free hand in Tripoli; a contrary policy now would expose her to the censure of treaty-breaking. "Military preparations have to suit the exigencies of foreign policy, not vice versa. A waiting policy recommends itself not only as regards the very complicated situation in Europe, it is also imperative as long as our army reform is incomplete, the navy not fully constructed and the state treasury no better funded than at present."[282]

Both foreign minister and chief of staff argued before the throne, where Conrad was sharply rebuked: "My policy is a policy of peace. To this all must conform. It is in this sense that My foreign minister pursues My policy. It might be possible that things lead to war, even probable. But it will not be made until Italy attacks us." Conrad: "If only chances will then favor us!" His Majesty: "As long as Italy does not attack us, this war will not be made. As yet, we merely have a war party."[283] This party's headquarters was the General Staff; the headquarters of the peace party was the Ballplatz. The heir to the throne now sided with the latter. Convinced that the Danube Monarchy could not be exposed to such "trials of strength,"[284] he lent his support to Aehrenthal and together they obtained Conrad's removal from the General Staff (November 1911).

Bülow's dismissal, the ex-Chancellor himself thought, "had created more satisfaction than chagrin" in Vienna, notably "among the military exaltados like Conrad, who took it amiss that I had interfered energetically with their inclination towards a cheerful war, today against Russia or Italy, tomorrow against Serbia or Rumania."[285] Bülow's fall had removed one obstacle to the return to preventive war ideas. With the death of Aehrenthal (February 17, 1912) a second more immediate block on the road to war disappeared. Shortly thereafter (December 1912), Conrad was back in his old position again with his old preventive war ideas. They were "in the air" at the time, and he was by no means the only one to cherish them. Powerful Pan-Slavist circles almost overcame the Russian Government and forced it to undertake "preventive precautions," such as partial mobilization against Austria. The only thing lacking was a good and plausible cause for war, according to neutral (i.e., Belgian) judgment. Without that "it was impossible to provoke a war which must necessarily lead to a general conflagration...It is obviously the Serbian question which must furnish it...The Russian Army wishes for war. It sees in war the occasion for redeeming the Russo-Japanese campaign. The stake in the latter left the Russian people cold; anti-Austrian animosity, however, unites all the classes of the nation...One expresses less the desire of supporting Serbia and rather that of 'settling accounts.'" In Vienna, "the military party profited from this situation and pronounced loudly that the Serbian question must be given a definitive solution, and in fact they arm as if war were absolutely imminent...The change in the Ministry of War and above all Conrad's return to the post of Chief-of-Staff have only made this state of mind more acute."[286]

Conrad at once began to throw his spell over Berchtold, the new man at the Ballplatz. It was a spell somewhat similar to the spell that Holstein held over Bülow, the spell exercised by the hard-working official over his lazy superior, who eventually succumbs to the monomania of his subordinate to whose basic ideas everything seems to revert because he himself always reverts to them. Berchtold was told that a passive and patient attitude on Austria's part during the Balkan crisis would merely result in a deterioration of her position. "Only way for a solution: overthrow of Serbia by war without fear of the possible consequences of such a step...If the Monarchy does not settle this life-and-death question now, it will be forced to solve it within a short time and under much more unfavorable circumstances."[287] Other generals came to support Conrad's stand, such as Potiorek, who added his voice to the appeal for war now. The two army corps under his command were, he said, "sharp tools, ready for use. I can employ them with confidence now, if that should be granted to me. But just as honestly I must say that I would not have the same confidence in the future if the present crisis should be settled peacefully" in a manner neither fully convincing nor satisfactory, even to the masses.[288] Instead of being removed for his admitted incompetence and inability to keep his troops in good shape for very much longer, Potiorek continued in his old position. He was the officer responsible for the failure of police protection for Francis Ferdinand in Sarajevo and for the disastrous opening campaign in Serbia in August 1914.

The chief of staff and the war minister endeav-

ored to bring the other ministers into agreement on a more aggressive policy against Serbia. Berchtold and the majority of the ministers held out against this pressure. They argued that there had been a recent relaxation in the international situation; that Serbia was in no position to undertake warlike action against Austria; that the Ballplatz could not approve of an aggressive policy against Serbia without the risk of complete isolation in Europe. An attack on Serbia "without some tangible reason understood by public opinion in Europe" was out of the question.[289]

But Berchtold, a much weaker man than the robust Aehrenthal, fell gradually under the spell of Conrad's tenacious serviam esse delendam. He would protest feebly (as if the reasons against war to be derived from the arsenal of arguments provided by his own ministry were insufficient) that Austria was much too backward in her artillery equipment. This would make "the game of hazard even more ungemütlich"—but for Conrad that was no reason for not entering the fray.[290] Conrad threw himself into the role of hypnotizer, or masseur or whatever else the late scions of an aristocracy may be in need of; but he could not keep Berchtold away from more peaceful influences, including that of Francis Ferdinand.[291]

German warnings spoiled Conrad's and Berchtold's ideas of a preventive war against Serbia during the crisis of July-August 1913.[292] But all too soon Serbia and her officer-politicians again provided the Berchtold-Conrad team with new provocation by holding on to territory that "Europe" had assigned to Albania. In October 1913, Conrad once more proposed preventive action to the Ministers, action that seemed particularly urgent to him at the time in order to impress Rumania, who was being wooed away from the Triple Alliance by Russia. They considered and argued it in the manner of a prelude to 1914. While the ministers favored postponement, Conrad told them that peaceful settlement with Serbia was henceforth out of the question. Only force would be effective. He reiterated his belief that war should be undertaken as soon as the chance presented itself: "Most wars are lost by those who miss these chances, and all postponing is, from a military standpoint, merely worsening conditions. If we keep on waiting, this would call for the extreme development of our military potential."

We note that this time, and for a change, preventive war was suggested as the way to avoid the later contingency of a far more absolute war, involving burdens which the structure of the Monarchy might well prove unable to bear.[293] On the next occasion, it was urged in order to prevent the growth of Pan-Slavist sentiment inside the Austrian Army. Reservists of two Bohemian regiments had mutinied during the partial mobilization of 1912-13. As the Austrian official history of the First World War notes: "There was forceful reason for Conrad to include among the motives for a preventive war the fact that the Army was as yet still reliable from a national standpoint but that one could not say how long this state would continue."[294] Reasons for preventive war accumulated rather than vanished. The courage of civilian ministers, including Berchtold, did not live up to Conrad's wishes for war and the Anschluss of Serbia. They satisfied themselves with a cheap and reckless diplomatic success over that country.[295] But the recipe of preventive war as the nostrum for the woes of a moribund Austria remained constantly before its governors. Conrad would never let them forget it. His "far-sighted measures" for the case of war in the Southeast found various blank check endorsements at this time—by William II,[296] by Count Czernin, subsequently foreign minister and since 1913 minister at the forlorn post of Bucharest. Czernin had become alarmed by Rumania's rapid movement out of the orbit of the Central Powers. One way to stop her might be Conrad's war against Serbia minus Conrad's idea of annexing that kingdom to Austria. No one wanted "still more Serbs" inside the Monarchy, but they and their territory might be fed to Rumania, Albania, Bulgaria and Greece at the close of a victorious war "which must reduce Serbia to a minimum."

> I think that in politics one must not consider a warlike preventive measure merely from the standpoint of "swallowing." One has called Serbia the "European appendix." Let us stick to this fitting comparison. No one has an appendix removed for gastronomic reasons—one undergoes an operation not on account of its further use but to have quiet at long last. By this I do not mean to propose provoking a war with Serbia today or tomorrow. But I think it would be in our interest to make it a little harder for Serbia to digest her new territories, in particular Macedonia.[297]

The whole suggestion in its descent from the bold general proposal to the piddling proposal for execution might well be considered an epitome of Czernin's diplomacy.

Some of Serbia's politicians admitted in their franker moments that there was provocation if not cause for a war in the South Slav agitation. Before he departed from Vienna in July 1914, the Serbian Minister there gave the French ambassador to understand

> that growing conditions of unrest in the Southern Slav provinces of the Dual Monarchy were

such that the Austro-Hungarian Government were compelled either to acquiesce in the separation of these provinces or make a desperate effort to retain them by reducing Serbia to impotency...Time was working for Serbia, and within three years Southern Slav provinces would be ready to rise against Austria without Serbia having to raise her little finger. Austria realized she could wait no longer...[298]

The Western Powers, then and earlier, found nothing to counteract the undermining of the Double Monarchy by Balkan nationalism and conspiracy. They had no appreciation, until too late, of Austria's ancient eastward mission. But in the perspective of universal history, their culpable negligence contributed nearly as much to the final "success" of Conrad's antique preventive war ideas as did the loose handling of the reins of the alliance in Berlin after Bismarck.

THE FIRST WORLD WAR—A PREVENTIVE WAR?

Well before 1914 Conrad was known in the various European capitals as the zealous partisan of preventive war,[299] which the Russians on their part interpreted as a war that "should be imposed on Russia at a moment when she would be only insufficiently prepared."[300] It could not have surprised Conrad to learn that foreign officers also had their preventive war ideas, that, early in 1914 "in Russia a strong party pressed for war, pointing to the dangerous interior situation," and that the Russian military attaché at the Porte "in all his reports considered an early war against Turkey as absolutely necessary since without it a dangerous strengthening on her part must be feared,"[301] presumably as a result of the labors of the Liman von Sanders military mission.

Aside from old-fashioned Austria, the other Great Powers on the eve of 1914 expected their general staffs not to raise the issue of preventive war and were on the whole correct in their expectation, though the stand the younger Moltke and his aides took on it is not unequivocally clear.[302] While there can be no doubt that they considered Germany's position for waging war more favorable at some times than at others, that professional opinion did not result in attempts to press the civilian governors in the Reich to bring it on, at least not after the half-hearted attempt in 1905-06. The encouragement given to Conrad by Moltke was in the nature of condolence over diplomatic events that might have led to war. He did not press him to act more vigorously during the course of crises that might bring on a war. Moltke shared the belief that many generals held: "the great war" was inevitable, sooner or later.[303] After such crises as 1909 and 1912-13, he expressed regret that they had not brought it on. At other times, he insisted that the attack must come from the other side. Some of this was virile posturing on the part of a sick man who refrained from urging any specific preventive war but readily endorsed the idea of one. As far as Conrad was concerned, the correspondence of the two chiefs of staff only strengthened the preventive war virus in Vienna. It was fully alive and active when the shots of Sarajevo fell.

Conrad was not the only tempter to approach Moltke with the image of a preventive war. The Italian Chief of Staff, General Pollio, was either the Italian most faithful to the Triplice or the most deceptive decoy that Italian diplomacy employed for misguiding Berlin and Vienna. He told the Germans in April 1914:

> The ring which is forming around the Triple Alliance is being strengthened from year to year, and we are mere placid lookers-on! I really believe that the years 1917 or 1918 which are named everywhere [partout, mais partout] by the enemies of the Triplice as the date for a general breaking-loose are not merely a product of fancy. They might very well have a realistic background! Shall we now really wait until the opponents have finished and are ready? Is it not more logical for the Triplice to throw all false humanitarianism overboard and start a war, which will be forced upon us, in our own good time? And therefore I ask, and I think altogether in the spirit of your great King Frederick when in 1756 he broke the iron ring of his enemies: Why do we not start this inevitable war now?[304]

Moltke was careful not to respond to this invitation. Pollio died immediately after Sarajevo, followed a few weeks later by Grierson, another early high-blood-pressure proponent of preventive war. And Moltke, who at least had never condemned the preventive idea, broke down under the burden of supreme command before the Marne battle was over. Among the four high-placed generals favoring preventive war, only Conrad long survived the death urge that must be a strong factor in wishing for war before its time.

The shots of Sarajevo convinced many persons in the governments of the Central Powers that valid cause for a war against Serbia had been provided. Enemies of the Central Powers, at the time or later, were equally convinced that the latter would use the occasion for starting a preventive war. This suspicion, largely formulated after rather than during July 1914, was to form an important part of the indictment against the Central Powers as the losers in the war. In it figured writings like those of Bernhardi, who had maintained since 1911 that Germany could

not remain forever on the strategic defensive but must take the initiative as Frederick had done in his day.[305] But the same charge figured in the counter-accusations directed against the governments or individual statesmen of the Entente by Germans and also by some of their own countrymen.[306] Before the war was over, enemies of Poincaré were accusing him of having "unleashed the war because the people in favor of the Three Years' Service Law believed there was an interest in making the war before its opponents had time to modify the law."[307] Besides, in the opinion of many, including her allies, France at the beginning of 1913 was, of all the Great Powers, able "to go to war with relatively the greatest confidence. France has, as the saying goes, resurrected herself. She has, rightly or wrongly, complete confidence in her army: the old fermenting hate [against Germany] has been reawakened, and France might very well believe that circumstances are more favorable today than they would be later on."[308]

This return to the three-years' term, which had been given up in 1905, was in answer to the German Army Bill of 1913. There was still a measure of moderation in the German bill, considering the constantly deteriorating military position of the Central Powers. But to the French military observer on the spot, Colonel Serret, it betrayed the thought entertained in the Red House, stronger now than ever, "of breaking France's backbone by a preventive war."[309] Whatever the truth behind such allegations, it was never amiss to put the opponents' wicked intentions on record. And preventive war was the most sinister design of all.

The transmutation of diplomatic observation and reporting into opinion and moral judgment on the potential enemy's preventive war-making can be observed in the Berlin memoirs of the Belgian Minister, Baron Beyens (1912-14). During the visit of King Albert to Berlin in November 1913, his host, in order to appear his martial best, declared that "war was inevitable and near," largely due to the restless policy of France. This outburst was imparted to the French ambassador and the latter's report figures in the French Yellow Book on the outbreak of war. Later, when composing his memoirs, Beyens came to wonder what might have been in the Emperor's mind at the time. "Did he simply want to justify in his own eyes a preventive war against France which was guilty, as he hoped he would make others believe, of meditating a war of revanche against Germany? Was he already concerned, as nearly all Germans were since 1914 and continued to be beyond the débacle of the Hohenzollern, with repudiating the responsibility for the bloodshed and placing the responsibility on their enemies? The duplicity in this calculation would be quite in keeping with his character."[310] Beyens the memoir writer discovered portents of preventive plans against Russia that Beyens the contemporary reporter had not seen.[311] Germany's unconditional siding with Austria during the July crisis the later Beyens interprets as betraying the plan for preventive war. As he remembers the July days: "We approach promptly a general conflict, a preventive war which is willed by Imperial Germany dragging along her accomplice, the war announced a few months earlier to King Albert." By July 28, Cambon, his colleague and mentor, came to share this view of a preventive war meditated and prepared by Germany which only England by her immediate intervention could now avert.

On August 3, Beyens asked the Minister of Bavaria to Berlin, Count Lerchenfeld, why people in Munich were so enthusiastic for war. Lerchenfeld replied: "What do you want, they crush us with taxes in order to increase the Army and Navy without end. We are told that the moment has never been, and for a long time to come will not be so favorable. France and Russia are not ready militarily speaking, whereas Germany possesses a smashing superiority. One must make use of it."[312] This was further proof for Beyens of "premeditation on the part of the General Staff and the German Government." The only direct admission of preventive war intentions that Beyens was to receive occurred during his last meeting with Secretary of State Jagow (August 4) who told him: "We learned that the French Army was preparing to march through Belgium and to attack us in the flank. We had to prevent this." When the Belgian remonstrated: "But you are in direct contact with France along a frontier of two hundred miles' length. What need is there, in order to settle your quarrel, to make a detour through our country?" Jagow answered that the French frontier was too strongly fortified for a frontal attack and "we are obliged to act as fast as possible before Russia has the time to mobilize her army."[313] The German march through Belgium constituted preventive action by one of the belligerents against a neutral, following the first declarations of war, accessory preventive war, so to speak. Bethmann Hollweg was speaking in a worthy tradition when he admitted publicly that this was unjust, and called for reparations. And this was the only prophylactic war the Chancellor agreed to, as even his sharp critic Bülow admits.[314]

The more acute the hostility, the greater the polemic readiness to ascribe preventive war intentions to an opponent, be he national or class enemy. International Social Democracy, in 1914 and after, could make such a condemnation, as sweeping as any propagandizing diplomat, with this difference: its condemnation was apt to be directed against more than one capitalist belligerent. As the foremost Marxist theoretician in Germany at the time, Karl Kautsky could not at first find any sense in Germany's policy of July 1914 except the pursuit of a conscious plan to bring on the world war. "This war was explainable only as a preventive war." Afterwards, when the German Revolution opened the Berlin archives to him and he came to study the original documents, he was "very much surprised...My original concept proved untenable. Germany has not worked deliberately in the direction of the world war. She has tried in the end to avoid it."[315]

The judgment of the man who was to become Kautsky's sharpest ideological opponent, Lenin, on the responsibility for the First World War and the preventive feature in it was rather contradictory. He had written to Gorki in 1913, during the Balkan crisis, that while a Russo-Austrian war would be very useful to the cause of revolution in Western Europe, it could hardly be hoped that the two emperors would grant the revolutionists this favor.[316] At another time, in the autumn of 1914, he thought that "the German bourgeoisie, while circulating fables about a defensive war on its own part, in reality chose the moment most opportune for war from its own standpoint. It has profited from the latest developments of war technology, while looking forward to the new armaments which Russia and France have in view or are preparing."[317] More generally speaking, he held that the war "was not an accidental one, that it had been prepared by the entire character and development of bourgeois society" and "must be transformed into a resolute conflict between the proletariat and the ruling classes." Only a few months later, in February 1915, Lenin thought that the Central Powers were really the victims of "the predatory designs of the English, French and Russians. 'We know that for decades the three blackguards (the bourgeoisie and the governments of England, France and Russia) had been preparing to attack Germany. Shall we evince surprise that the two other blackguards started the attack before the first three received the weapons which they had ordered?"[318] This explanation would still make the war as undertaken by the Central Powers a preventive war, but a justifiable one in the world as it existed.[319]

If the war was started by one side or the other as a preventive war, did that make it a particularly unjust war? The official Allied war guilt accusation against Germany, in spite of its vindictiveness, did not specifically raise this point. It would have been hard to "prove." For their part, French and British statesmen and diplomats were far too well-educated in discretion and too well aware of the public feeling against preventive war to admit to any such wish. The one leading politician who, speaking to intimates, came closest to demanding it as a war that was better fought in 1914 than later was Winston Churchill, the youngest member of the Asquith cabinet. On the evening of August 1 a message reached him amidst a group of friends, announcing a postponement of the German ultimatum to Russia. Beaverbrook greeted it as a sign that a European war might be avoided after all. Churchill, in Beaverbrook's words, thought

> that this was only a postponement and that it was bad news, not good news... "The German staff," Churchill said, "have absolutely promised their government a swift military decision, first against France and then against Russia. They may be right, or they may be wrong, but if their Government believes them, it will declare war, whoever is against them." He argued that the German menace had to be faced and fought out some time or other. It would be impossible for British statesmen ever to plan out a peaceful progress for the nation until it had been settled once and for all if Germany was to control the German Ocean. You were not really avoiding war—you were simply postponing it.[320]

This is a flat denial of the dictum that a war postponed is one war less.

There is only one "sufficient" explanation for the outbreak of the war in 1914, the belief of the soldiers and sailors of all the Powers and of the statesmen acting on their advice—not the advice of the moment, but the long-continued advice and implanted conviction—that the war could be won by their own side. The soldiers everywhere during the last July days were "of the best courage." In Berlin, the military reasons given for this feeling of confidence were the superiority of German artillery and infantry rifle, and the insufficient training of certain French units.[321] The Bavarian military attaché in Berlin reported, on somewhat dubious evidence and certainly not on the strength of any direct and recent communication from Moltke to him, that against Bethmann's attempts to "put the brakes on," Moltke was "exerting all his influence in favor of taking advantage of the exceptionally favorable opportunity for striking a decisive blow." France was momentarily handicapped, Russia over-confident, the season of the year favorable, the training of the German recruits of the 1913 class completed.[322] This was the talk of the next-to-the-top echelons of the Berlin military and diplomatic hierarchy, the only ones who had time and leisure to see and inform and encourage the representa-

tives of a federal state in the Reich capital.[323] It was the talk of the ever-ready soldiers, based on what were considered the most recent advantages gained by Germany in the armaments race. It might have emanated from Moltke earlier in the year, although he did not pronounce himself in favor of preventive war during the July crisis. He had been away from Berlin since May, in search of a cure. After his return (July 25) he made various moves, without mentioning the preventive war motive, that were bound to strengthen Austrian willingness to incur the risk of a general war. He was above all concerned to prevent the maneuvers of the diplomats from wasting the precious hours of head-start on which German mobilization time-tables were based.

While Moltke's stand on preventive war during the July crisis remains somewhat doubtful, there was something like a "youth movement" in favor of it in Berlin and Vienna. Leaders of the German economy like Ballin and Gwinner learned about it during the early days of the war, if not earlier, and became alarmed lest word of such intentions hurt Germany's reputation.[324] A German publicist, Dr. Victor Naumann, visiting at the Ballplatz without any official character or mission, told his hosts on July 1 that he had noted in Berlin Army and Navy circles and also in the Wilhelmstrasse that "the idea of a preventive war against Russia was not as completely condemned as it had been a year ago." They believed that they could be sure England would not interfere in a European war. Wilhelm von Stumm (director of the Political Section of the Foreign Office, Holstein's old post) had spoken very seriously to him of the threat posed by Russia's armaments and had termed the war "'which Germany could have if she wanted to,' as not impossible." Count Hoyos, the recipient of this confidential gossip, had long been one of the most active war-hounds at the Ballplatz.[325] He replied that "these dispositions at any rate were for us not unwelcome if we should get into the necessity of undertaking something against Serbia." That, Naumann nodded, was the very thing he had wanted to suggest.[326]

There were other observers of the hankering among the younger Berlin governing set for preventive war in the summer of 1914. The Russian chargé discussed it with the Italian ambassador (July 27). He personally did not believe that Germany wanted war, although her Government was supporting Austria so strongly that one could not help wondering if the war party had got the upper hand and "whether we were not facing the triumph of the idea of the Präventivkrieg [German in the original] for which the German Crown Prince twice during the past month had expressed his sympathy." This prince was "an unbalanced personality who would like to act independently and considered himself a military genius." His reported arrival at Potsdam was by no means to be welcomed. The Italian protested vigorously: he could guarantee that the German Government did not want war and was deeply distressed about the situation.[327]

A similar "youth movement" in favor of preventive war was at work in Vienna. Various "younger diplomats" at the Ballplatz wanted war and for this purpose wanted King Karol of Rumania to be kept from working for peace in St. Petersburg and Belgrade, "lest we be cheated of the warlike settlement once again." [328] The Hungarian Counts, Hoyos and Forgach, in Berchtold's most intimate entourage, were part of this group. So was the representative at Belgrade. He was concerned that the Serbian Government might once more avert war by promising to be good and loyal, when actually "one could hear from every second Serbian officer that within a couple of years at the latest the dance against us would start and the war that one wants to make would not even spare the child in the mother's womb." There was no reluctance about this among the older Serbian officers: according to them, Serbia would attack Austria if the world war should break loose. "But not now, for God's sake, not now"; Serbian armaments must first be made more nearly ready.[329] With this war cry chimed the vieillesse verte of the Austrian Ambassador to the Quirinal, Count Merey, who thought it "truly fortunate if war with Serbia should come. Should the European conflagration grow out of this, it would merely prove to me that it was in the air, had to come sooner of later on some occasion, and there is hardly any doubt that the present moment is more favorable than a later one for the Triple Alliance." He congratulated his friend Berchtold, but only on condition that war not be averted at the twelfth hour—that would be tantamount to a catastrophe.[330]

Conrad applied stronger pressure on the effete Berchtold from a closer vantage-point: now was the hour to strike if the old Monarchy was to be saved, the hour which was left unused in 1908-09 and again in 1912. "New forbearance, even now following Serbia's terroristic deed, would unleash inside the Empire those tendencies which, under the form of South Slav, Czech, Moscophile, Rumanian propaganda and Italian irredenta, [were] already rocking the old structure. Hence there remained nothing for the old Hapsburg monarchy but to cut the knot with force."[331] These high voltage applications from the military power station were burning out the last resistances against war in Berchtold, who was assured that "even for the great war the possibility of a victorious outcome [does] exist."[332]

What more expert advice and encouragement

did a bad diplomat need? Now he could advocate "the sharpest measures against Serbia, though that might result in war with Russia." Was not Russia pursuing a policy in the Balkans that was bound to make Austria's position increasingly worse and was apt to confer greater strength on that "magnetic power" exercised by Rumania and Serbia over the Rumanians and Yugoslavs inside the Double Monarchy? The logical conclusion from this was that Austria should anticipate her enemies and stop the evolutionary process already in full swing by a timely settlement with Serbia, something which would not be possible later on. Of all the ministers assembled on July 7 to consider the ultimatum to be addressed to Serbia, only Tisza, the Hungarian Prime Minister, contradicted the preventive war argument. War need not be made now, he urged. It could be made under better conditions at a later date, when Germany's relative position would be still better. Berchtold insisted on his and Conrad's war: "One had to reckon with the fact that the enemy side was preparing a fight to the finish against the Monarchy."[333] The war to prevent the falling apart of Austria-Hungary was initiated. No serious consideration was given to the thought that perhaps its preservation was impossible except through maintaining the peace!

PREVENTIVE WARS CONSIDERED, 1914-1933

Once a war is under way, many of the existing barriers to preventive action vanish. A variety of measures taken by the belligerents of the First World War were contemplated, planned, and executed as essentially preventive, even against or by parties that were not belligerents. Others were interpreted as preventive in their intent and purpose. A few examples follow.

In 1915, when Bulgaria was taking the final steps into war at the side of the Central Powers, Pasić proposed in Petrograd that she be confronted with an ultimatum from the Entente to halt her mobilization, along with the threat that troops would be landed from the Black Sea if she did not comply within twenty-four hours. He also wanted permission for the Serbs to attack Bulgaria, as the only proper strategic move. But Sasonov withheld his permission; that would be just as serious a crime as the Bulgarian offensive that the Serbs were trying to anticipate. Such an irreparable step would cost Serbia the support of the Allies as well as that of the Greeks (which they did not obtain in the end).[334] Sasonov could well afford to be so highly moral—no Russian troops would have been available for landing in Bulgaria anyway.

The one great step that was to decide the outcome of the war, America's participation, has been explained by some friends as well as foes of Wilson as due to his and America's intention of preventing a German victory and its foreseeable effects. Colonel House had feared these very early and also later in the war: "If Germany wins, it means the unspeakable tyranny of militarism for generations to come...Germany's success will ultimately mean trouble for us."[335] As a long-time diplomat, Lord Bertie could see no other reason for Wilson's entry into the war except to avert such an eventuality,

> to save America. It was not the "Lusitania" which brought him in...What the President thought was that France and England would be defeated and crushed and then would come the turn of America to be attacked by Germany, and there would not be any French Fleet or Army or British Fleet or Army to come to the aid of America, whose ports would be bombarded, her islands captured and sea-coast towns destroyed after the defeat of the American Fleet.[336]

Considering American ideological preparedness—in one sense, and unpreparedness in another—Wilson could not invoke the preventive war or the related balance-of-power motive for America's entry into the war. America's entry had to be pitched on the "right to sail the high seas"[337] and other high motives.

The peace instruments, formulated and signed but not ratified by all participants of that "war to end war," permitted war to be made in the future in order to prevent and stop aggression, through the League of Nations. This idea had been voiced in American war-time discussions of a peace league. As early as 1916, a university philosopher—one of the usual bearers of political ideas in desuetude—had suggested that "we may now take a further step and justify offensive war, when undertaken in the interest of an international system or league of humanity. For a century or more, this greater cause has stirred the imagination of men."[338] But the United States would not ratify such proposals, vaguely embodied as they were in the League Covenant.

To French circles, the Versailles Treaty itself, rather than the League of Nations, was designed to prevent or break any possible German resistance to the execution of its stipulations. Hence the march into the Ruhr and other military measures. But these met with so many frowns from the Anglo-Saxon Powers that it became inadvisable to continue such interpretation long beyond 1923.[339] In fact, France's Rhine and Ruhr policies at that time wrecked forever after all possibility of preventive action in the same direction, even should they be more truly in the interest of peace. The growing disbelief in the Treaty, even inside

France, while allowing no textual revision, at the same time prevented the building of a French Army for the full maintenance of the Treaty. Such an army "might have implied the necessity of energetic intervention à titre préventive or in support of an ally that might be attacked," an army that would have been a means for the permanent execution of that Treaty.[340]

Within Germany, this Rhine-Ruhr policy undermined what little belief there had been in the Versailles Treaty as the basis for peaceful relations and encouraged the first post-1919 war plans in the Reichswehr. Preparations for mobilization were undertaken in all the Wehrkreise in 1923. And Seeckt "did not even reject altogether a preventive war" to be fought, together with Hungary and Austria, against France's ally Czechoslovakia in case of an open Franco-German conflict.[341] Thus the first objective for the regrowing German military power was earmarked at an early date.

One of the other enemies of the peace treaties of 1919-20 was Russia, a non-signatory, and the Third International. On repeated occasions the latter declared war inevitable as long as the bourgeoisie remained in dominance. Two kinds of war might occur—reactionary imperialist war between two or more bourgeois states or war against Soviet Russia. The question of justice depends, then, not on who is the aggressor but on what interest is being served. In the official language of the International,

> it is only imperialists who make reactionary war. As opposed to them, proletarian dictatorship leads a revolutionary war, for the sake of Socialism, in the interest of the world proletariat...The proletariat supports and leads all national, revolutionary wars, all wars of Socialism against imperialism, and organizes the defence of each national revolution, of every State in which the proletarian dictatorship has been established...In the wars of the imperialist powers against the revolutionary States, the question of the appearance of being on the offensive ought to be envisaged in a historical and political sense. The one that attacks first is not necessarily the one that undertakes an unjust war; injustice is on that side which represents reaction.[342]

It was not the resolutions and activities of national sections of the International that made possible the survival of Soviet Russia through the perilous years after 1918, but rather the conflicts of the Western Powers that could not be subordinated by the preventive war arguments of the proponents of an anti-Bolshevist crusade. Such a war was actually tried once, by Pilsudski's Poland in 1920. Pilsudski observed what he considered to be strenuous Bolshevist preparations for a surprise attack on Poland, after the White armies of Kolchak, Denikin and Yudenitch had been disposed of. He feared that Russia wanted to join hands with the revolutionary forces of Germany still in ferment at the time, across the fallen body of Poland. In supreme command of the Polish forces, Pilsudski "decided to anticipate the enemy's onslaught by an offensive of his own, since attack is the most effective form of defence."[343] Judging from the initial easy successes of the Poles, Bolshevist preparations had not gone very far. But soon they gathered enough strength to throw the Poles back to the Vistula, though no further. An uneasy peace was patched together by the two exhausted parties.

PREVENTIVE WAR AGAINST NAZISM?

Fascism postulated that "the offensive war is the decisive war," more specifically that "on the enemy must be inflicted as quickly as possible the greatest damage thinkable." Hence the necessity of opening the air war, the decisive war of the future, with a sudden attack against the opponent.[344] Fascist war doctrine shunned the political odium of outright advocacy of preventive war, except by extolling such wars of the glorious past. But Fascist political morality betrayed at an early date a weakening or absence of the usual inhibitions against preventive war. As long as such military doctrines remained restricted to Italy, they were not taken very seriously. But the advent of the Nazis to power in 1933 changed, or ought to have changed, such complacency. By all auguries, Nazism promised the rebuilding of a military power dangerous to Europe and the world, if and when Germany were taken in hand by the Führer who had for a long time openly argued in favor of aggressive, preventive wars.[345]

In the states surrounding the Third Reich, there were various statesmen and soldiers, perhaps more of the latter, who realized at an early date the dangers to be expected from Hitler. Some of them proposed to their own and to friendly and allied governments, though hardly at all in public, that these dangers be met in time by suppressive measures, including a preventive war. The first known suggestions of this nature came from Pilsudski's Poland. As early as May 1933, Polish officer circles of high and low rank considered war between their country and Germany inevitable. Poland could emerge victorious from such a clash only if it took place at once, with Germany still unprepared and beset by political troubles at home.

According to Czech reports from Warsaw, "the thought of preventive war counts among its partisans not only Marshal Pilsudski but also the general staff which has already undertaken certain measures along the frontier," such as concentrating cavalry in the direction of the German-Lithuanian frontier and in the Corridor.[346] Paris was approached with proposals for such a war. At the same time, United States Ambassador Bullitt was urging French politicians and publicists: "If you don't make preventive war, France is lost."[347] French official and military circles gave the Polish proposal a certain amount of consideration as a plan for the spring of 1934. "The idea is to catch Germany and seize the Rhineland before it is too late." However, on second thought, they (including the Rightists) came to fear that public opinion was too much against war, above all preventive war, although it might at the time have meant little more than a punitive expedition to or beyond the Rhine. But the fear was great that even such a war might broaden into a general conflict.[348] Besides, very few politicians in Britain would favor the idea.[349] Only after Paris finally turned down Pilsudski's proposals for a preventive war did he come to an agreement with Hitler, including a non-aggression pact and an assurance of the territorial status quo for ten years, during which he hoped to see Poland's troublesome German minority "liquidated."[350]

When Hitler came to such terms of postponement with Pilsudski, he was fully aware of the Polish proposals for a preventive war against Germany. In fact, the widely shared secrets of these proposals helped Hitler to consolidate his own position during the first months of his regime. If these secrets were not as true as was widely believed, they were still highly ominous, and useful to some. All the remaining Reichstag parties were informed about them, and they voted resolutions in March and May backing the new Chancellor. "The Social Democratic Party made the very great patriotic sacrifice of voting together with all other parties in favor of a resolution expressing, in cautious terms, the unanimous intention on the part of the Reichstag to oppose an action such as Pilsudski had proposed to the French." This vote may have convinced the French that there was no hope of finding a welcome for any notions of a preventive war against Hitler anywhere inside Germany. It also helped Hitler to consolidate his position at home when he most needed strengthening, in his relations with Hindenburg, with the Reichswehr, and with the German people.[351]

Pilsudski was merely one, if perhaps the bluntest, of several soldiers to arrive at the conclusion during those early years that military necessity called for a timely preventive war against a rearming Germany. One catches glimpses of this professional view on various occasions. A group of British, American, French and Polish soldiers assembled in Lisbon in the summer of 1938, where the British were trying to reform Portugal's army and make her buy British instead of German arms. Members of the British mission were, as they said, "completely aware of the German and Italian bluff" and were convinced that "we should start the war, and at once." Germany seemed, and actually was still basically unequipped for war; her ally Italy was even worse off. A war seemed unavoidable in the future. Much better, therefore, to start it right then when it would mean less danger and when England, thanks to Roosevelt, could look forward to close cooperation with America. The commander of the French Atlantic fleet, visiting in the Tagus, was persuaded that the political circles and the press of the French Right were unduly fearful of Germany, that "the greatest fault was the pacifism of the democracies, for due to it one cannot start war as the first. In this manner the most valuable trump card, that of surprise, is played away to the enemy. But there has already been some progress beyond that point."[352]

The various public warnings against German rearmament were, without exception, careful not to propose preventive war as a means of halting it. Communists at the time might call Fascism "preventive counter-revolution, directed against the onward movement of world revolution," but Litvinov's proposals for armament controls and peace leagues did not mention any such preventive proposals, even from afar.[353] And neither did Winston Churchill. In March 1934, he discussed in Parliament Britain's backwardness in air power as compared with that of France and Germany. He pointed out that Germany was "arming fast and no one is going to stop her." Still he emphatically declared that "no one proposes a preventive war to stop Germany breaking the Treaty of Versailles...not even the French" who "remembered the preventive war which Bismarck had sought to wage in 1875." No party or politician in Britain dared to work up sentiment for a preventive war against Germany in the face of the public's desperate clinging to the League of Nations while their government was jettisoning the rest of the Versailles Treaty.[354]

"When Britain and France in this period [the mid-'30's] were so superior in strength and Germany so inferior, how did they permit Germany to gain superiority and threaten their very existence?" This riddle was formulated by only a few at the time and by the many only after the outbreak of the Second World War. Only after its close did Secretary Hull give his own explanation:

The truth was that neither Britain nor France wanted a preventive war. In Britain the isolationist sentiment was about as strong as it was in the United States. France had tried preventive measures when she invaded the Ruhr in 1923. The result was bitter opposition and the fall of the Poincaré Government. The French Government thereafter was unwilling to embark on a preventive war...Here we are face to face with a basic weakness of democracies, or of governments in which the people have an important voice. With all their riches of God's blessings in so many ways, they most unfortunately have a record of moving slowly—too slowly—in the face of external dangers either imminent or seriously threatening. If [during the 1930's] the nations standing for peace had taken concerted action to arm adequately, they might have demanded a showdown with the bandit nations, Germany, Italy and Japan, and averted the recent world war.[355]

Questions not raised in their own time and answers given to them after the event do not usually provide satisfactory historical explanations. The nations after 1919 or 1933 were not so much confronted with the image of another world war, but rather with the order embodied in the treaties of 1919-20. All sides had come to consider this order, rightly or wrongly, as unjust and unsatisfactory. Even a small-scale preventive war would have been deemed unjustifiable to maintain it. "Fight for Danzig?" expressed the doubt even of Frenchmen about Versailles.

The Germans were fully aware of the strength of their own version of war-guilt and encirclement and based much of their daring policies on it, beginning with the Rhineland remilitarization in 1936. While their high-ranking generals were panicky lest the French re-occupy that province, Hitler banked on British unwillingness to see that done, even under the guise of sanctions. Politicians of the last war, like Lothian and Edward Grey, had protested against such measures. Grey disliked the "idea of resorting to war to prevent war."[356] As spokesman of the Cliveden set, Lord Astor warned the Government against taking measures that "would be equivalent to a preventive fight against Germany." As proof of Hitler's peaceful intentions, he referred to a letter addressed by the latter to himself. The head of the National Socialist Government, he concluded, ought to be supported in his endeavors to save Germany and Europe from the Communist revolution.[357]

Again, as in 1933, Poland offered to go to war, together with France, on the night of the Rhineland occupation. And Yugoslavia promised to order mobilization of her forces, should France mobilize.[358] "All the faults of the past could have been repaired in one day and without striking a blow. A divinity ruling France and applying the principles of the economy of forces would have waited perhaps until the 7th of March in order to act, but on that date it would have struck with its right hand."[359] The French soldiers were ready to mobilize and face the consequences, but they insisted on complete mobilization and not merely a partial one. The ministers hesitated, disagreed, and allowed the last militarily safe occasion for stopping Hitler to go by unused. He and the other Axis Powers, the "ten per cent who are threatening a breakdown of all international order and law" as Roosevelt put it, could not be "quarantined." The governors of Western Europe would not take this broad American hint at prevention.[360]

The hesitations about taking the step into preventive war were considered to be essentially bourgeois, not only by the Communists but also by the Fascists.[361] They thought that the basic weakness in the bourgeois was, as in the non-soldierly civilian, to shrink from aggression, the supreme motivation and form of war. The bourgeois, as a German militarist writer put it, "knows only defensive war: that is to say, he does not know war at all; by his innate nature he is separated from all that is the essence of war."[362] German writers knew no restrictions on the discussion of preventive war. As a new handbook for the Wehrmacht re-defined it:

[Such a war] originates when a State, in view of an ever-sharpened tension, resolves to anticipate the adversary and bring to a settlement a conflict considered unavoidable, at a point of time favorable and under conditions profitable to itself. Besides, it is of the essence of preventive war that the driving element is to be looked for in political or military reasons rather than in any others. An exceptionally favorable political situation or a considerable war-technological headstart in offensive striking power might give a resolute State leadership occasion for striking that was sooner or later inevitable...[This Frederick did in 1756] and world history has justified him...The heavy risk of a preventive war will either be incurred light-heartedly by a gambler without a conscience or responsibility or else by a heroic born leader who, after heavy soul-searching debate within himself, with a full sense of responsibility, comes to such a resolution. In no case should it be undertaken by the mediocrities who are all too often found in positions of national leadership.[363]

While the chiefs of the Reichswehr, Fritsch and Beck, did not discourage such morale-boosting writings, these writings were more in the new Nazi spirit than in keeping with the caution with which these leaders wanted to see the Army rebuilt. Fritsch and Beck were far from entertaining thoughts of preventive war, even if this meant war waged by Germany against one enemy alone. To them, a simple two-sided war no longer seemed feasible. Beck, a son of German industry, held that, in an age of world economy and worldwide competition, every war, including a preventive war against one neighbor, would lead to a war on more than one front. And such a war was beyond Germany's strength, as the unforgettable experience of 1914-18 had demonstrated.[364] To Beck and the conservatives of the Reichswehr, the problem was whether either the foreign Powers or the Nazi party would allow them to proceed with the caution that they proposed in rearming. Both the foreign Powers and the Nazi party failed them, though in different ways.

As early as June 1937, the more pliable Blomberg, Reich Minister for War and Commander-in-Chief of the Armed Forces, issued a "directive for the united preparation for war by the Armed Forces," to be valid for the coming year. The directive was clearly inspired by the Führer himself. It stated that, considering the general political situation and the almost complete absence of desire for war and the deficiencies in war preparations in the countries around Germany, including Russia, the Reich need not fear an attack on itself from any side. While Germany on her part had just as little intention of starting a European war, the politically fluid world situation might not exclude surprising incidents and hence still called for preparedness on the Wehrmacht's part. Among the possible wars was Case Green, war on two fronts with its center of gravity in the Southeast. Such a war "can begin with a surprise German operation against Czechoslovakia in order to parry the imminent attack of a superior enemy coalition. The political conditions for such an action must be created beforehand in accordance with international law."[365] The world was to learn later how this "Fridrician" situation was to be "created," while inside the Wehrmacht the cautious leaders had noticed that wars that they had considered impossible were no longer so regarded by the Führer himself.

The passivity of the Western Powers proved to most of the German officers that Hitler was a genius—fit even to start a preventive war—rather than a gambler. Nazi leaders did not fail to drive the dubious lesson home. Speaking to Wehrmacht officers undergoing political indoctrination in January 1937, Rudolf Hess explained what an exceptional performance it had been for the Führer to free Germany from the bonds of the Versailles Treaty without military complications, and to re-occupy the Rhineland. He believed that the continued hope for an impending breakdown of Germany due to economic difficulties had made the foreign nations hesitate until they had missed the moment when they might successfully have gone to war themselves.[366] This waiting for economic difficulties had a certain reason behind it. But it was not considered whether economic difficulties might drive Hitler into war instead of toward greater peacefulness.

On a still higher level of indoctrination, Hitler himself opened the vistas of his ultimate intentions to his highest military commanders. In the autumn of 1937, he explained to them that the basic aim of German policy was the defense and preservation of the mass of the people and its Lebensraum. The German nationality was decreasing in Czechoslovakia and Austria. Stagnation was setting in. Autarchy on the basis of the territorial status quo was perhaps impossible. Foreign trade was not a cure but rather a source of continued uncertainty. "There was only one way for the solution of the German problem, force, and that was never without risk," as Frederick's Silesian wars and Bismarck's wars of 1866 and 1870 had shown. Once the question of the application of force had been decided, two questions still remained: the When and the How. War should not take place later than 1943-45, for a change in Germany's disfavor was to be feared after that time. The rearming of the Wehrmacht and the forming of the officer corps were nearly-finished tasks. Equipment, materiel, and arms were up-to-date; a longer waiting period would make them obsolete. The "special weapons" could not be kept secret for ever. More reserves could not be drawn from the older yearly classes. If the Reich did not act before 1943-45, the food problem would become critical—admittedly a point of weakness for his regime. Besides, the world was expecting Germany to strike and had increased its counter-measures from year to year. Waiting beyond 1943-45 was impossible for still other reasons: the large Wehrmacht could not be maintained forever. The standard of living threatened to become lower and the number of births to decrease. The National Socialist movement was growing older, and so were its leaders. Should he, Hitler, remain alive, it was his firm resolution to solve the German "space problem" not later than 1943-45, that is to say, before his fifty-sixth year.

An earlier moment for action might come if France should become absorbed by events at home or abroad. In that case, Czechoslovakia and Austria would be overrun at once.[367] More and more, Czechoslovakia came to be singled out as the first foreign objective for the German drive. A casus belli had to be built up:

A strategic surprise attack out of the blue sky without any cause or possibility of justification was to be avoided since this might provoke a world opinion hostile to Germany, which might lead to a disquieting situation. Such a measure could be used only once, when it came to getting the last remaining enemy on the Continent out of Germany's way. Action must be preceded by a period of diplomatic discussions gradually sharpening up and leading to war, unless an incident like the assassination of the German minister to Prague should furnish the occasion for lightning-like action.[368]

The final German plans for the "Green" case, the war against Czechoslovakia, were based on the safe and comfortable assumption that "the danger of a preventive war against Germany on the part of foreign states does not exist."[369] However, Hitler would not march on October 1, the date he had set on May 28, unless he could be certain that France would be as unlikely to march then as during the Rhineland and Austrian occupations.[370] He could be certain that Britain would not stir, for Hitler knew of a Czech report from London giving the following estimate: "Even if the plan of a preventive war against Germany entirely harmonized with the views of the British Opposition, Chamberlain and Halifax can beat the trumps in the hands of the opposition by means of convincing counter-arguments."[371]

According to Gamelin, the Munich settlement was the consequence of France's failure to march. She could have done so with good hope of success, Gamelin assured Prime Minister Daladier and the British ministers.[372] In this case, Germany would have backed down.[373] The French ministers would not believe their foremost military counselors and would do nothing without British approval. Thereby they lost a considerable military potential on Germany's eastern flank. They failed "to strike when the military feasibility still existed, only to declare war at a moment when the situation had become practically hopeless for the French Army."[374]

The polite and often effective fiction of more civilized ages, that diplomatic crises are caused by both sides to a quarrel, became too threadbare to hide the patent fact that the conflict with Czechoslovakia had been manufactured by Hitler alone. Even viewed from far-away America, his provocation was so obvious and his aggression so revolting that a veteran isolationist like Senator Norris, the only surviving member of Congress who had voted against America's entry into the First World War, publicly stated during the September 1938 crisis that, faced by such a situation, he would be among those who "would consider a preventive war against the Fascist nations." This stand caused a sensation in Washington and promised to have considerable effect on the sentiment in the Middle West, the German chargé in Washington reported. He warned that this signalled the impending end of another cycle of American isolation, like that of 1812, or that of 1917 which, by German and some other explanations, "came to pass in order to prevent a threatened shifting of the balance of power in Europe, which would have had a serious effect upon American political and economic importance in the world." It must not be forgotten in Berlin, he added, that Anglo-American relations were much better than they had been in 1914 and after:

> If England is involved in a life-and-death struggle, America will, as in 1917, seek by every possible means to prevent the defeat of England, because this would result in a shifting of the balance of power in Europe and Asia, which would directly affect America. Herein lies America's vital interest, which she already feels to be threatened by the urge towards expansion and the desire for power of the totalitarian States.[375]

This report, as so many reports, combined the Nazi diplomat's duty of warning against America's possible steps with a skin-saving deprecation of any justification for such steps that might have been read into the report.

Hardly had Chamberlain returned from Munich when a hostile Nazi press campaign got under way. The Western Powers, shouted the Nazi press on orders, indicated that they were planning a preventive war against Germany. She would not view such a new wave of armaments with indifference. All this was due to the attitude of the Germanophobe elements in France and Britain who hoped that the great problems raised by authoritarian governments could be suppressed by a preventive war on their part. Such intentions were forcing the Reich Government to examine whether or not the new British armaments were getting out of step with those of Germany, an examination from which Germany would have to draw the necessary consequences.

Fascism south of the Brenner Pass caused a parallel campaign to get under way. In the Informazione Diplomatica (October 12, 1938) Mussolini himself, in the role of an anonymous writer, pointed to the existence of

> strong groups in Britain and France who want war against the totalitarian States. [However], responsible Roman circles emphasize that the proponents of preventive war are too late.

Misguided by their blinding hatred, they may dream of a preventive war; but to attempt it means to envisage an extraordinary risk. Nothing can be done any more now against the Italo-German bloc of 125 million people, a bloc with a yearly population increase of one million that disposes today of imposing forces and favorable geographic and strategic positions on land, in the air, and on the sea, a bloc of material and spiritual solidarity.

The logical consistency of this argument was somewhat doubtful: if the Axis Powers were already as superior in strength as Mussolini maintained, how could they accuse or suspect the other powers of planning preventive war? The essence of preventive war is for the aggressor to attack when he is at least temporarily stronger. In the logic of the thing only the stronger group, the Axis by its own proclamation, could now think of making preventive war.[376]

PREVENTIVE MOVES AND CONSIDERATIONS IN WORLD WAR II.

The European Sector.

The success of Munich went to Hitler's head like gambler's luck. His star seemed in the ascendant, confirming him in his determination to bring on the always unavoidable war while he—and Mussolini and Franco—were still in the prime of life. As he told an assembly of his top military commanders on August 22, 1939, there was no one who possessed the German people's confidence as much as he did. The future was not likely to produce another man with so much authority. "My existence is therefore a great value factor. But I might be removed at any time by a criminal or an idiot." All these fortunate circumstances might not exist two or three years hence; better, therefore, to have the great explanation now, when, besides, there is not one single great man on the opposing side. The old adage of pre-Freudian days about preventive war as the rush to suicide out of fear of death came true in the resolution of this maniacal post-Freudian leader, the like of which had not held power since the late Roman emperors. Never, though, was there a suicide who insisted on taking so many with him into death.

Besides his own indispensability, there were more objective and compelling reasons for war in the summer of 1939. As explained by Hitler at the time:

> Our economic situation due to the restrictions is such that we can see it through for only a few years more...We have nothing to lose, only to gain...Our opponents risk much and can gain but little...The probability is still

great that the West will not interfere [in the war against Poland]. We must take on the gamble with brutal resoluteness...We are faced with the hard alternative of either striking or the certainty of being destroyed sooner or later...It is a great destiny...I am only afraid that some Schweinehund may submit a mediation plan at the last moment.

None of the generals present protested or resigned or shot at Hitler or himself. "The few doubters remained silent. Göring jumped on the table. Bloodthirsty thanks and bloody promises. He danced around like a savage."[377]

While the technology of warfare was in the most advanced stage, the underlying urges, including the urge to preventive war, went back to the primeval, an unevenness of evolution that in itself did not augur well for Germany. Whether filled with forebodings after the close of the Polish campaign or misled by the easy successes, the generals found themselves once more addressed in the same style by Hitler: "I will be accused: fighting and again fighting. I see in fighting the fate of all human beings. No one can escape battle unless he wants to be defeated." The rising German population demanded more living space. Since 1871, England had stood in Germany's way. "Bismarck and Moltke realized that one would have to march once more... Moltke was at times in favor of preventive war" (but never against England!). The time for further moves was still propitious, but might not be six months hence. Hitler's own person, recently threatened by a plot, was

irreplaceable...I am convinced of the power of my thought and of my resolution...Time works in favor of the enemy. At the moment, a relation of strength prevails which cannot be improved in our favor, but can only change in our disfavor. The enemy will not make peace at a moment when the relation of strength is in our disfavor. No compromises. Severity against oneself. I shall attack and not capitulate. The destiny of the Reich depends on myself alone.[378]

This sense of destiny led to further moves of a preventive nature against enemies and neutrals, suspecting or unsuspecting, who wanted above all to stay neutral. As soon as the Polish campaign was over, Hitler was determined to attack France, which had stayed on the defensive throughout September. He told the army commanders and their chiefs of staff in September and October that it was "unbearable to wait for the attack by the Western Powers," considering the exposed situation of the Ruhr region. Belgium was not a sincere neutral, since all her defenses

were directed against Germany alone. There was information that a march into Belgium had been agreed upon by the French and British General Staffs, that it was impending, that Belgium had given her assent. "Under no conditions must the enemy forestall us...The greatest speed is required." Aware of the fatal consequences of the 1914 violation of Belgian neutrality, the generals stalled. They preferred to base their opposition on the incompleteness of German armaments and on weather conditions. A severe winter season and the Führer's belief that his intentions to attack had become known to the enemy put off the preventive war in the West until later.[379]

Another object of preventive war-making had been brought to Hitler's attention, one that had not attracted war-makers for 125 years, Norway. Her cautious governors, while inclined to believe that, as a belligerent, Britain might be willing to provoke the Germans into war-like action in Norway's territorial waters, were still unconvinced that she had any intention of landing on her soil. While the German Minister at Oslo reported that Norway was determined to remain neutral, he also thought her continued neutrality would be in Germany's interest. The Swedes likewise expressed disbelief in any impending action of the Western Powers in Scandinavia and told the Germans so: they would defend their own neutrality against all comers. They actually made preparations against an attack by the Allies on the Gallivare orefields, even though they feared German more than Allied preventive intentions regarding Scandinavia.[380]

Viewing the Scandinavian countries through military eyes, the Allies (including France) and the Germans came to surprisingly identical conclusions, a case, for once, of purely military judgment.[381] At nearly the same time both sides began to consider how to take Norway and Sweden into the war. Perhaps there was a slight head-start on the Allied side. The German Naval War Staff had been worried about the maintenance of communications with Scandinavia as early as the first month of the war, when they learned about special activity on the part of the enemy secret service in Norway. This gave them "a motive for increased vigilance." Early in October 1939, the Naval War Staff began to study the problems of Norway more specifically, how it might be kept from falling into British hands and whether—perhaps with Russian assistance— Norwegian bases might be obtained for Germany. These matters were then brought to the attention of Hitler, who indicated that he would take them into consideration. At this time there is not much indication, judging from the ample German record, that fears of a British move against Norway dominated German ponderings.[382]

Whether the British had then or later any indications of German intentions the far more meager Allied records do not allow us to say.

During the winter season, the vital German ore shipments from Swedish mines passed through Norwegian waters. Plans to interfere with these shipments had been under consideration by the British War Cabinet since September 19, a fortnight before Admiral Raeder put his name to the first German memorandum on a German invasion of Norway. In calling for the preparation of the necessary plans, Churchill referred to the probability of Germany spreading the war to the Scandinavian countries, which would only accrue to the Allies' advantage. He advocated anticipating them, even though that would mean a violation of neutrality.[383] Like most of the German planners, Churchill was aware that Germany had more to gain from Scandinavian neutrality, if it were safely preserved, than the Allies. A German aggression would, he reasoned, be very helpful in "the final tribunal [which] is our conscience," a court of last resort which should overrule all protests by the small countries whose battle Britain was fighting and who must be helped, if necessary, against their own will. The Cabinet was still far too Chamberlainian to be stirred, though they did authorize the military to study the operational implications of intervention in Scandinavia. The Russo-Finnish War, Russia's "preventive attack" as friends of the Soviet Union termed it, provided an additional complicating factor.[384]

By the year's end, the French ally had been informed that the dispatch of a brigade to Narvik was being studied, under the direction of General Ironside. He had duly warned that such an action was likely to set off a German counteraction against Sweden and Denmark and that timely preparations against such an action were required. This was perhaps not a bad thing in itself, Gamelin thought, since it might keep the Germans from opening decisive operations on the Western fronts, which he always considered to be in a firm junctim with events in Scandinavia.[385] At the meeting of the Allied Supreme War Council in Paris on February 5, 1940, attended by Chamberlain, Halifax, and Churchill, plans were approved that envisaged the service of three to four divisions with the Finns. Norway and Sweden were to be persuaded to grant free passage to these forces which were "incidentally to get hold of the Gallivare orefields" (Churchill). The operations were to start during the third week of March at the latest, it was thought.[386] But before that, on March 12, Finland made peace with Russia.

The Allies' rather bold preventive ideas were not directed against Germany alone. In the March 28 session of the Supreme Council, they agreed that "every attempt of the Soviet Government to obtain from Norway a position on the Atlantic coast runs counter to the vital interests and would elicit due counter-measures." In the meantime, the Altmark incident of February 16 had "sharpened everything in Scandinavia" (Churchill). This first real violation of Norway's neutrality, a British measure, presaged worse to come. It spurred German preparations, including the appointment of a military commander for the Norway expedition. He was told by Hitler that the latter had information that the Allies were intending to land in Norway and that Germany's operation "should prevent British encroachment on Scandinavia and the Baltic, should guarantee our ore base in Sweden and give our Navy and Air Force a wider starting line against Britain."[387]

According to documents that fell into German hands in France later in the year, the Allied Supreme Council decided on March 28 that, in addition to measures against German shipping in Norwegian territorial waters, an occupation of Norwegian soil was to be prepared.[388] The embarkation was intended for April 5, 1940. Operational orders, some of which later came into German possession, dated April 2, 6, and 7, were worked out. These included "preparations for the occupation of the Northern Swedish orefields outside Narvik," implying that Swedish neutrality would be violated.[389] In connection with Allied operations, the British began to lay minefields outside Narvik on April 8, twenty-four hours before the arrival of the German landing forces in Norway.[390] The London Admiralty was confident at the time that it would know how to prevent the landing of the German forces then en route.[391]

The Germans promptly maintained that they had by their own measures prevented British landings at the very last moment. They had, however, precise foreknowledge of the Allied plans when they proceded to "Copenhagen" Denmark and Norway. They were never quite certain who would be the first to land. They had, however, argued from the same military premises—hence the coincidence. In historical judgment—we come to the so-called legal one later—it must appear that of the two intended and prepared housebreakings, the German one was the luckier. The Allied failure, on the other hand, enabled them to pose as policemen and judges.

While an absolute neutrality of the Scandinavian countries always seemed the most desirable thing for Germany, Admiral Raeder thought it highly dubious that it would or could be indefinitely maintained, as against either Britain or Russia. British occupation would not only endanger or stop altogether German ore shipments from the North but would also flank all movements of the German Navy, with a "militarily decisive" effect on Germany's war endeavor, and might also mean an extension of the war to the Baltic (February 23, 1940). There were still various ups and downs in the German resolution. Actual preparations were cloaked in the greatest possible secrecy so that "the Scandinavian States as well as the Western opponents would be taken by surprise." Preparations began around March 20, when Hitler expressed his desire for haste to the military commander of the expeditionary force. He must hurry up with his work; the Führer was "very worried that an English operation would preclude ours."[392] A week later, the Navy informed him that "the danger of a British landing in Norway is no longer acute," but that the threat of British interference with ore shipments destined for Germany continued and that the plans for the German landings should be adhered to.[393] On April 1, Hitler gave orders that the invasion of Denmark and Norway be made on April 9, with advance sections of the German fleet sailing from Germany on the 7th.

The uncertainty and paucity of information in their possession did not keep the Nazis from declaring to the Danes (and similarly to the Norwegians) that they

> had positive proofs that Great Britain intended to occupy bases in Denmark and Norway, and Germany had to safeguard Denmark against this. For this reason German soldiers were now crossing the frontier and landing at various points in Zealand, including the port of Copenhagen...The Reich Government had got into its possession undeniable proof that England and France intended to occupy by surprise and within the very next days certain territories of the Nordic States [something which the Danes themselves, even if inclined to do so, were too weak to avert].[394]

The recent appointment of Churchill, the greatest of "warmongers" according to the Nazis, as virtual director of British warfare, his declarations that he would not be detained by "legal decisions or neutral rights," that "it would not be fair, if, in the fight for life or death, the Western Powers adhered to legal agreements" (March 30, 1940), provided additional reasons or pretexts for Germany to forestall English aggression.[395] Whatever the politics behind the German enterprise, to the professionals it was of all Hitler's preventive wars "the only one which a military man had advised Hitler to carry out for reasons of strategic necessity."[396] More exactly, it had been an admiral, reminding one of the fact that, in the form of "Copenhagening," preventive war ideas have been hardly less familiar to sailors than to soldiers.

The British were determined not to be behindhand in their next preventive counter-move. On May 10, 1940, they occupied Iceland, a Danish dependency with a large measure of self-rule. When the government of Iceland protested the measure, the British defended it with the following statement:

> After the German occupation of Denmark, it has become necessary to count on the possibility of a sudden German advance to Iceland. It is clear that the Icelandic government, in view of such an attack, even if it was only carried out with very small forces, would be unable to prevent its country from falling into the hands of the Germans completely.[397]

Still more in the style and tradition of "Copenhagening" were the British Navy's actions against units of the recently-allied French Navy. At Mers-el-Kebir and Dakar (July-September 1940), ships were taken under fire and 1300 French sailors killed in order to keep the ships from falling into Nazi hands, a danger not too immediate at the time.[398]

Holland and Belgium were to be the victims of the next preventive war move on Germany's part. The commanders-in-chief wanted to avert this extension of the war. On November 23, 1939, Hitler told them:

> When the French Army enters Belgium in order to attack us, it will be too late for us...We must anticipate them...I have to choose between victory and annihilation. I choose victory. Greatest historical resolution, comparable to that of Frederick the Great before the First Silesian War. Prussia owes her rise to the heroism of one man...I shall attack France and England at the most favorable and earliest moment. Violation of Belgium and Holland is of no importance. No one thinks of that, once we have won...If we don't violate their neutrality, England and France will do it.[399]

In a way they were doing so already, the Germans contended, by their constant flights across the Netherlands and, as they later pretended to have found out, by offering assistance against Germany in Brussels and the Hague.[400] In those two capitals, however, there was little readiness to give up neutrality and to be "helped preventively," which unfortunately was the only way in which they might have been helped.[401] In opening the war in the West, Hitler was also anticipating American moves. At least Ciano was told that Germany had to obtain victory as soon as possible on account of the "hidden threats of American intervention."[402]

In the diplomatic note handed over by the German minister in Brussels on May 10, it was maintained that Germany felt obliged to march in "in order to anticipate the planned invasion of Belgium, Holland and Luxemburg by England and France, directed clearly against Germany," and thus to assure the neutrality of these three countries. While it is uncertain what "proof" of the Western Powers' preventive intentions the Nazis possessed at invasion time, they subsequently captured some of Gamelin's papers showing that he had not only advocated an energetic attack on Germany, including a march into Belgium at the beginning of the war as the only way in which Poland might be helped, but that he had also discussed plans for moving the defense lines forward to Antwerp-Brussels-Namur with British military authorities. This seemed to point to the importance of Dutch and Belgian territory as a base for the resumption of the offensive against Germany, and especially the Ruhr. Gamelin had in fact told the French ministers that "it was of vital importance to march into Belgium" (November 16, 1939).[403]

Hitler's preventive war moves had to be explained to the German people, to the rank and file of the Wehrmacht, and to the world at large in other ways than they were to the generals. They were told after the event how every move had been undertaken to forestall the enemy and had succeeded just in the nick of time—"only ten hours in advance of an attack on Norway planned by the Western Powers" according to the German High Command's communiqué of April 10. Documents captured afterwards, they were told, indicated that this margin of prevention had been even narrower.[404] The Führer's genius had again and again combined "anticipation and initiative."[405] This was the propaganda stereotype. It was imitated by Mussolini in the propagandistic preparation of his war against Greece in 1940, which was said to have become necessary in order to prevent the use of Greek bases by the British fleet.[406] The invasion of Yugoslavia on April 6, 1941, was undertaken, as Ribbentrop explained, because "England was about to commit another war against Europe."[407]

Hitler's preventive designs against the other end of Europe, the Iberian Peninsula, lent themselves less well to public announcement and self-glorification. He entertained hopes, particularly during the winter 1940-41, of bringing Franco into the war. This would drive Britain out of the Western Mediterranean by taking Gibraltar from her and shutting the Straits.[408] But Franco preferred to evade most of what Hitler considered his obligations for services rendered in the Civil War.

The sudden but long-prepared attack on Russia on June 22, 1941, an enterprise fraught with the most fatal consequences for the Third Reich, called again and again for explanations by the Führer and his Myrmidons. It had been prepared in deep secrecy, although hints of the Führer's intentions had been given to the planners as early as July 1940.[409] The first directives for the annihilation of the new enemy "in a quick campaign, before the end of the war with England," were issued on December 18, 1940 (Fall Barbarossa). The preventive motive for the attack was stressed. The newly-won ally, Finland, smarting under the onerous peace of 1940, was told—as if she needed additional argument—of the prospects of Russian attack and that German defensive measures were necessary to counter these. Hence the "important intention to anticipate the Russian plans of attack" (May 22, 1941).[410]

Hitler justified the attack to his closest entourage as part of "the Chief-of-State's duty to strike the first blow whenever he considered a war inevitable." Russia had been preparing her attack. She had barely been kept out of the Rumanian oil fields, where she would have been in a position to choke off Germany's oil supplies altogether by the spring of 1942. "Proof" of hostile intentions against Germany was later found among the papers of Stalin's captured son, in which Russian officers mentioned a forthcoming "promenade to Berlin." Had he, Hitler, listened to his badly-informed generals—not to mention diplomats[411] —and had he waited until the Russians had started their own preventive offensive, there would have been no stopping their Panzers on the excellent road system of Central Europe.[412]

The new war raised great anxieties among the people no less than among the generals. It had to be explained to the Germans. As Hitler opined before the attack, they would not grasp the need for a new preventive war—a people always had to be forced into what was necessary for its own fortune and life.[413] The explanation was in the manner they had been taught to expect: the war was the outcome of the Führer's foresight, omniscience, and fatherly care for Germany and Europe. Much of the appeal was based on the old mass sentiment or grande peur, fear in the face of danger from the East, a fear at least as old as the Mongol invasion of 1241. The danger of "Red Communism" was now combined with the older "Yellow Peril." This danger had once more reared its head and the Führer had given orders to meet it beforehand and at the very moment it was to strike. That was the tenor of the first dozen Wehrmacht communiqués on the war in Russia: "As a defense against the danger threatening from the East, German forces at 3 a.m. on June 22 charged into a mighty mobilization of enemy forces." They "smashed into the midst of the Russian Army which had completed its mobilization...At the last minute, Middle Europe was spared an invasion, the consequences of which cannot be conceived. The German people are duty-bound to give deepest thanks to their brave soldiers."[414] In the first speech after a long interval of silence, Hitler explained to the German—and European—peoples that he had not wanted the war. He had nevertheless been prepared for it in all respects, save one: "We had no idea how gigantic the preparations of this enemy were against Germany and Europe and how immeasurably great was the danger, how by the skin of our teeth we have escaped the destruction not only of Germany but of Europe...This would have been a second storm of Ghenghis Khan."[415]

By autumn, the war in the East had become "a hard and relentless" one, and Goebbels, as the strategist of German propaganda, felt called upon to explain to the masses why it had come to that:

> When you know you are facing a pitiless adversary who is aiming his rifle toward you to fire from his most favorable position, the best policy is to anticipate his shots. A national leadership acts without responsibility when it simply lets matters come to a head without realizing the danger, then calls for arms when they have already lost their sharpness...Could anyone believe that London would have left us in peace, or that the Soviet Union would for certain decide that it would build up revolutionary armies just for fun? No. We would still have had to take up arms in a few years, but with the difference that our enemies, having learned much through the experiences of the Polish campaign, would have faced us with arms that we could not have matched.[416]

Most of the professional soldiers of the Third Reich considered the attack on Russia to be fully justified from a military point of view. This was true of Jodl, Keitel, Manstein, Hoth, Halder and others, even in their testimony before the Nuremberg tribunals. According to Jodl, the war against Russia was "undeniably a purely preventive war. What we found out later on was the certainty of enormous preparations opposite our frontiers...Although we succeeded in a tactical surprise as to the day and hour, it was no strategic surprise. Russia was fully prepared for war." Considering their own numerical inferiority, the Germans could not have remained forever on the defensive in the East. Had they waited for the Russian attack, they would have been lost. If the political premise was correct and a Russian attack did threaten, the preventive attack was called for and justified from a military point of view. They based their military labors on this assumption.[417] To a prosecution question as to whether, in the exercise of his functions, he had advocated a German war of aggression, Keitel answered that under certain conditions he had favored it "in order to prevent a definite aggression on the part of the adversary."[418] For Manstein, the June attack on Russia was "the only way out. The Soviet was a great potential threat even in 1940, and it would have become an active one as soon as we tied down our forces against Britain."[419]

To a technical expert—and minor war criminal—such as Panzer General Hoth, it had seemed that Russia, judging by her continued expansion since 1939, would not forever miss the opportunity of going to war against Germany. Hence the problem from the military point of view was whether or not Germany was to leave it to Russia to choose the time to act. In 1940-41, Germany had forces available for war in the East, something that might change in a year or two with the advent of a two front war (with the accession of America?). To decide whether Russia seemed intent on attacking Germany was up to the only one who had all the proper information, political and military—Hitler. "The last available date" was 1941, Hoth thought, both in 1941 and in 1949. In 1941, "Germany still had a chance to keep Bolshevism away from the frontier of Europe," though it was another problem still whether Germany and her allies at that time were capable of coping with this European task.[420] This willingness of the expert to admit Hitler's premises in favor of preventive war was tempered by horror at the thought that the Reich would now have on its hands the very kind of war that Hitler had always promised he would never allow to come, the war on two fronts. At the first indications of Hitler's designs against Russia in July 1940, some planners even went so far as to push the landing operation plans against Britain in order to avert war in the East. Beyond that, they had little or no opportunity to take issue with Hitler. As General Leeb put it: "Hitler distrusted us and in the final analysis it was primarily a political question. He distrusted us even in military respects, let alone in political respects."[421]

Even to Halder, a general antagonistic to Hitler well before Nuremberg, the Russians' increasing preparations seemed not only to justify but to demand preventive action, although reports on Russian strength, as submitted by the military attaché in Moscow, and other considerations were not without dissuasive effect on him. By the time of Nuremberg, if not soon after the German attack in June 1941, it was clear to Halder that the Russians had actually been completely mobilized in the assembly area at the time of the attack, "that by mid-1941 they were just about to attack." He said they had been more ready for the attack by one or two months than German intelligence had presumed. It was their own misfortune that they had to wait for orders from the Kremlin instead of meeting the German attack before-hand.[422]

All opposition inside the Reich to the attack on Russia was feeble. Ribbentrop even remembered a bit of Bismarckian advice against preventive war, which was lost on Hitler and Goering.[423] The admirals saw no urgent necessity for making preventive war against Russia in 1941, for it could wait until after the victory over England.[424] They took exception, though they did not form an active opposition, to Hitler's plans when they were admitted to his resolutions. As far as Goering knew, the final crystallization of these plans went back to Molotov's Berlin visit in November 1940. At that time, Hitler concluded that Russia "was getting ready for an attack on Germany." He was also afraid of the continued threat in the rear to any serious enterprise against Britain, which perversely enough declined to come to terms with Germany. And he feared the increasing armaments in the United States, where Churchill expected to obtain still more support for Britain. Goering, according to his testimony at Nuremberg, advised strongly against starting a war against Russia at the moment or for a short time to come. He was not moved, as he said, by "considerations of international law or similar reasons," but only by political and military ones. He advised Hitler to avoid the war on two fronts and to divert Russia against the British Empire, before the United States, led by Roosevelt or Wilkie, could enter the war on Britain's side. But it was in vain.[425]

All the black magic of prevention had not been able to bring victory. But if the formula had failed, Hitler still would not discard it. When he unleashed his last offensive strike in the Battle of the Bulge, he still endeavored to justify himself, this time to the generals who were to command, with the preventive motive that had ruled his moves ever since 1939:

> We are in the midst of a struggle which had to come inevitably, earlier or later. There remained only one question to clear up—whether the point of time for it had been chosen fortunately...The objection that we acted too preventively has to be dismissed at once. All successful wars of mankind, Gentlemen, have been preventive wars. He who realizes that a war is inevitable and does not make use of the moment which he himself thinks is favorable, is sinning against his own people...But to that must be added the military factor...We had for once the great fortune of having established by a gigantic endeavor a full superiority in most fields of armaments...But it

was clear that this superiority could only be of a transient nature...A more fortunate moment than that of the year 1939 could not be thought of. There was still another momentum to be considered, and that one is decisive for me personally...I have gained the conviction that during the coming ten, twenty, perhaps fifty years no man will arrive in Germany who has more authority, more influence over the nation and more readiness for resolutions than myself...And finally, psychological momenta, that is to say mobilization of German popular strength. You cannot distill enthusiasm and readiness to sacrifice like other things and put it in bottles and preserve it. They arise once during the march of a revolution and fade away again by and by...The longer war lasts, the harder the test. At the time when hopes for victory dwindle, tests are not undertaken with the will-power with which, for instance, a fortress fights that can still hope for relief. It is therefore important to rob the enemy of his confidence in victory by making it clear to him by offensive strokes that...success of his plans is impossible...whatever he does, he can never expect a capitulation, never, never...There is one more thing to consider: never in world history were there coalitions formed of such heterogeneous elements, with such divergent aims, as that of our enemies. Those who are our enemies are the greatest extremes imaginable today: ultra-capitalistic states on the one side, ultra-Marxist on the other. From hour to hour these contradictions become more acute. If quite a few strokes are put in at this point, it can come about at any moment that this artificially-maintained common front suddenly collapses with a tremend-ous thunder-clap...[426]

The disintegration of the anti-German coalition, expected as part of that already much overdrawn imitatio Friderici, did not come about while war lasted. And Roosevelt's death in 1945 never brought the miraculous parallel to the Tsarina Elizabeth's death in 1762 that Hitler and Goebbels had hoped for.

Japan and her Preventive War

Under the conditions of military-naval competition, the temptation to undertake preventive war will always be greatest on the part of the Power that has more fully developed its own military potential at a given time and at the same time realizes that this potential is basically less than that of the Power or Powers with which it considers itself to be in compeition. It is the momentary superiority that furnishes the great temptation for such a war. Hence the urges for preventive war on the part of Germany, Japan, and Italy, with their basically slender war potential as compared with that of Russia, America, Great Britain and China.

During their war for the control of China, the Japanese could never quite make up their minds as to whom they would have to envisage as their next or as their ultimate enemy. The conflict was largely due to differences between the army and navy. For the army, Russia was originally the chosen enemy. She was to be fought in due time, with little or no assistance expected from the navy. If the Japanese military clique "foresee an eventual clash as inevitable," Grew reported in July 1933, "it is quite possible that they may intend to strike before Soviet Russia gets stronger —and the time element is all in favor of the latter."[427] For reasons that are more imperalistic than strategic in the final analysis, Japanese hostility eventually settled on the United States as its number one enemy. By the end of 1940 it had become increasingly clear to Ambassador Grew "that we are bound to have a showdown some day, and the principal question at issue is whether it is to our advantage to have that showdown sooner or have it later." As Grew wrote to Roosevelt:

The chief factors in the problem would seem, from this angle, to be:
(1) Whether and when Britain is likely to win the European war;
(2) Whether our getting into war with Japan would so handicap our help to Britain in Europe as to make the difference to Britain between victory and defeat.
(3) To what extent our own policy in the Far East must be timed with our preparedness program and with respect to the relative strength of the American and Japanese navies now and later...
Unless we are prepared...to withdraw bag and baggage from the entire sphere of a "Greater Asia including the South Seas" (which God forbid), we are bound eventually to come to a head-on clash with Japan...The principal point at issue, as I see it, is not whether we must call a halt to the Japanese program, but when...[428]

The anti-American clique in Japan informed their Axis partners that they had chosen America as their number one enemy, with Russia removed to second place.[429] Mussolini and Hitler hardly demurred when Foreign Minister Matsuoka came to explain his reasoning to them in the spring of 1941: he had always maintained at home that if Japan kept on "drifting as she was now, war with the United States was sooner or later inevitable." According to his view, this conflict was bound to come. Why, he had argued, should not

Japan act resolutely at the right moment and run the risk of a war against America? In this very way she would eliminate war, perhaps for generations to come, particularly if she should win control of the South Sea. Many people in Japan, however, hesitated to follow these trains of thought. Such circles considered Matsuoka a dangerous man with dangerous thoughts. "Still, he kept insisting that if Japan pursued her present ways, she would have to fight one day and that would happen under more unfavorable circumstances than at present." The Führer was all encouragement. He pointed to his own felicitous inspirations and his boldness in risking war while he was still young and vigorous. He did not contradict Matsuoka's conviction that America would enter the fight against Japan at the very moment when she became convinced that Japan was in the war for the purpose of aiding in the destruction of Great Britain. (This was something from which many Japanese, with their Anglophile education, shrank.) Instead of reminding his visitor that the United States might possibly be less concerned over the destruction of Russia, Hitler and Ribbentrop were encouraging. The two Anglo-Saxon Powers together might one day turn against Japan. However, America would stand alone against Japan if Britain were destroyed and could then do nothing against Japan. Winning this approval, Matsuoka promised to win over the Emperor, the Premier, and the ministers to his views.[430]

The Army and Navy agreed on going to war against America before she should become too strong—"because Japan was convinced that war between Japan and the United States was unavoidable," as the Chief of the Naval Staff, Admiral Nagano, later explained his orders for the attack on Pearl Harbor—and before Japan herself became too weak, as the advocates of war stressed, pointing to the "gradual impoverishment of military supplies and resources" due to the American embargos.[431] In vain had the peace party argued that it seemed "extremely foolish to make such a great sacrifice as a war against America and Britain for the sake of such goods, that it might be averted by the building up of domestic substitute industries." Suzuki, the President of the Planning Board, agreed, "but added that opening hostilities was a matter of domestic politics."[432] That is to say, the domestic position of the Army and Navy was so strong that their war had to be conceded to them. The surprise attack was planned and the Navy mobilized, unobserved by the Anglo-Saxon diplomats.

In the flush of their initial victories, the Japanese assured their German Axis partner that it was only "natural that one day Japan would have to beat Russia as well, since without that a new order in Eastern Asia was impossible."[433] In the meantime, their non-aggression pact with Russia was to remain in force, allowing them to avoid the war on two fronts, something it was hoped that the Axis partners would understand. And Hitler proved understanding, at least in public declarations. In striking at America, they had only done what he himself had done before. "Providence allowed me to strike two weeks or more before our enemies, the Russians, were ready for us. We can congratulate ourselves that Japan, when her time had come, acted in the very same manner."[434]

Preventive war is an undertaking that can least stand the anticlimax of failure. It can only hope to find its justification in success. In the light of the setbacks suffered in 1942, the dictators' claim of having acted with foresight assumed a hollow ring in their speeches. The claim was finally discontinued, except by Hitler. In December 1942, Mussolini told the Italians for the last time that the menace in the East had to be combatted in time. "If we had waited, events might have shaped differently...Japan did not wait before striking shattering blows at America...If there was anyone who wished for war, that man is Roosevelt. Japan could not stand by and let the U.S. fire the first shot. America expected to annihilate Japan in two or three weeks."[435]

Democratic Preventive War?

The governments grouped as "democratic" for the purposes of a coalition that had not much more in common than their enemies, contrary to many fond American beliefs, were obliged to apply terms such as "preventive" to their measures much more sparingly than their foes. All of them had to pay respect to old democratic suspicions about preventive war, and none more so than the Government of the United States before Pearl Harbor, despite its early determination to prevent the Nazis from achieving ultimate victory.[436] Forced to overcome, by-pass, or disregard such inhibitions, the anti-Axis Powers considered a number of preventive actions, some singly, some concerted, either as belligerents against neutrals or as still-neutrals against belligerents.

Even before the victorious Germans had reached the Channel coast, members of the American General Staff proposed to their chief that the United States "take immediate steps to acquire British and French possessions in the Atlantic," to take them into protective custody before the Germans could occupy them. Plans for American measures "to protect such [possessions] from falling into the hands of Germany by surrender or cession" were worked out promptly and thereafter kept up-to-date. The dreaded German move in South America would make it necessary for the United States "to anticipate action by the preventive occupation of airfields and ports" to the southward.[437]

Once France had quit the war (as far as an onerous armistice allowed her to quit), Britain was determined to prevent the employment of any remaining French strength by the Germans or, later, by the Japanese. She tried to obtain control over or at least neutralize the scattered, nearly intact French Navy by "Copenhagening" measures (Oran, Dakar, Alexandria). German advance personnel began to infiltrate French-held Syria, whence they might threaten British control of the Middle East. Early in June 1941, so-called "Allied forces crossed the frontier into Syria with the object of eliminating German personnel and influence from certain areas in which they are securing a dominating position through continued infiltration."[438] The hoped-for cooperation of the Vichy French in Syria materialized slowly. Their resistance forced the invaders "to use force to prevent obstruction to our advance." For several days, the Vichy forces could not understand the protestations of the invaders that their object was "to counteract German infiltration and forestall the arrival of more important German forces."[439]

The American Government was hardly less eager than the British to keep Petain's announced policy of "collaboration" from developing into military assistance to the Germans. In Washington, "U.S. officials instantly foresaw as probable the throwing open of French bases in North Africa to Germany and perhaps eventual use of the French fleet on the side of the Axis powers." Both possibilities were major considerations in the determination of United States policy toward the Vichy Government. Roosevelt in effect appealed to the French people, over the heads of their own Government, not to support Petain's policy. He intimated that "the United States would feel free to take preventive measures." He gave orders to put Coast Guard men on board French merchant ships in American ports (May 15, 1941).[440] American aid to Britain eventually extended to relieving the latter of some of the preventive steps taken against Germany. Beginning on July 7, 1941, American forces arrived in Iceland to relieve the British, who were needed elsewhere "in order to insure the adequate defense of that country." "The United States," Roosevelt told Congress, "cannot permit the occupation by Germany of strategic outposts in the Atlantic to be used as air or naval bases for an eventual attack against the Western Hemisphere." At the same time, he sent "substantial forces of the United States" to the bases acquired from Britain through Lend-Lease in Trinidad and British Guiana "in

order to forestall any pincers movement undertaken by Germany against the Western Hemisphere. It is essential, he said, "that Germany
should not be able successfully to employ such
tactics through sudden seizure of strategic points
in the South Atlantic and the North Atlantic"
(Message of July 7, 1941).

Not announced at the time was the fact that
originally, in May 1941, the U.S. Navy had received orders from its Commander-in-Chief
to prepare an expedition for the seizure of the
Azores in order to forestall a Nazi landing there.
The participants in the Atlantic Conference had
agreed on this plan, as well as on a British
occupation of the Cape Verdes, which Roosevelt
had recently mentioned in one of his "fire-side
chats" as potential bases for use against the New
World.[441] This was designed to evoke in the
brave New World some of the fears necessary to
make his policies acceptable. It was a psychological rather than a strategic move on Roosevelt's
part, designed to bring America "nearer a shooting war," as the Republican opposition at the time
surmised. His own Party's approval was unconvincing from a military point of view, with the
possible exception of the support of Senator
George, who believed that the occupation of Iceland was "to test the real intentions of the Axis
powers toward the Western Hemisphere."[442]
Hitler, at times, had indeed contemplated occupying some Atlantic islands—not specifying which
ones—"with a view to a future war against America." But the generals had protested: there had
been quite enough extension of the war without
that.[443] The military argument in favor of the
American occupation of these outposts, including
Dakar, was never very convincing. None of them
assumed any great strategic importance during
the rest of the war. Still, the planners of the war
on both sides of the Atlantic were in strange coincidence: American occupation of the Azores was
set at one time for June 22, the very date of Hitler's invasion of Russia. When the plans were
discarded, it was done in view of the fact that Iceland constituted enough of a pretext for the entangling aims of Roosevelt's strategy in the
Atlantic.[444]

The policy of the Roosevelt Administration in
the pre-Pearl Harbor period forms one of the
strangest chapters in the history of the idea and
practice of preventive warfare. Its intent was
clearly preventive. As Secretary Ickes put it to
the President: "It may be difficult to get into this
war the right way, but if we do not do it now, we
will be, when our turn comes, without any ally
anywhere in the world" (June 23, 1941).[445] The
right way meant avoiding all appearance of having
preventive war intentions. Roosevelt sought to
keep the Axis from winning the war, without or

before America's entry into it if possible, and
to spare the United States either "complete preparedness" for all foreseeable time or the "life
of a bug in a bottle" under Hitler's thumb.[446]
But since the long democratic tradition against
the waging of preventive war obviously persisted,
no public statement could ever concede or avow
such intention. This preventive intention was
first concretely expressed by aiding the peoples
who were resisting Hitler, so that they would not
be "knocked out of the war one by one before
our turn came and that we would [not] ultimately
be left to face the onslaught alone."[447] In doing
this, the prerogatives of the Commander-in-Chief
were extended beyond all precedent. The self-
silencing of most critical commentary on Roosevelt's published justifications of his measures,
many of which were hardly "short of war,"
was of inestimable help. Criticism was still
possible, but it allowed an autocratically-inclined
President, in a new kind of absolutism, to act in a
preventive undeclared war with the more or less
tacit consent of the governed.

Modern conditions of warfare, Roosevelt warned,
would not permit the United States to wait until it
was physically attacked "before starting to shoot."
According to him, an attack "begins as soon as
any base is occupied from which our security is
threatened" and "that base may be thousands of
miles away from our shores...The American Government must, of necessity, decide at which point
any threat of attack against this hemisphere has
begun; and to make their stand when that point has
been reached...Our best interests are served by
helping all others to resist, instead of waiting for
them to fall and finding ourselves the next in line
for Nazi attack."[448] To him, peace and bond with
Hitler were as impossible as with gangsters or
outlaws; that is to say, the Rooseveltian world of
law—alas, weak in structure—excluded the Axis,
as much as older realms of law had excluded and
proscribed pirates or the Turk.[449] While often
holding an opinion of Hitler that was little if at
all higher than Roosevelt's own, the isolationists,
whom the President scorned as ostriches with
their heads in the sand, thought it possible to defend America closer to home, thought in fact that
America could not be attacked at all.[450] In their
opinion, the United States still enjoyed the option
of staying out of the lawless strife that went on
outside the Western half of the world.

The strategic aims pursued by Roosevelt were
not determined by any democratic process, except by the most general one: he was the elected
president. Beyond the President's closest entourage, the discussion of strategy was less
than semi-public. The opposition, largely Republican, entertained highly justified suspicions
about the President's intentions, which were only

heightened by the lofty and contemptuous manner with which those in power responded to queries. Early in the war, Congressman Tinkham (Rep., Mass.), a member of the House Foreign Affairs Committee, asked Secretary of War Stimson, who had assured the Committee that "you can safely lodge responsibility with the President," whether the Administration "had any idea of waging a preventive war." Stimson answered that there was "no suggestion of attacking a belligerent for the purpose of preventing [preventive?] war."[451]

It would not be easy to ascertain whether the old taboos against preventive war were dying in the American people or whether the dexterous leadership of Roosevelt in the face of an unprecedented danger had merely silenced or numbed it.[452] Surveys made by the Bureau of Public Relations of the War Department's Intelligence and Analysis Branch during the years before America's entry into the war, a pulse-taking presumably carried out for the political guidance of the Department's high officials and officers, indicate that an attitude accepting the possibility of preventive war was growing. Avoiding the usage of the still opprobrious term, the first of these questions, repeated at irregular intervals, was: "Should we risk war if necessary to stop Japanese aggression?" The Yes answers were 6% in July 1939, 39% in February 1941, 40% in March 1941, 51% in June 1941, 70% in September 1941, and 64% in November 1941. The positive answers to the question: "Do you think it is more important to defeat Hitler than to stay out of war?" were 44% in September 1939, immediately following the beginning of the war; after that, they sank to 29% in October 1939, rose after the fall of France to 39% in July 1940, to 47% in August 1940, to 52% in September 1940, and, after a decrease in October to 50%, rose to 60% in December 1940, and to 68% in January 1941. Sinking slightly to 67% in April 1941 and to 62% in May, it was again 68% by November 1941. The closely related question, "If the Axis wins the war, do you think it will attack us sooner or later?" received positive answers as follows: 63% in October 1939, 55% in July 1940, 60% in December 1940, 61% in March 1941, 62% in April and May 1941.[453]

With an eye on such political weather charts, it was possible for President Roosevelt to challenge the Nazis more and more frequently in the Atlantic, by stepped-up provocations and by measures taken against their submarines. At the beginning of the third year of the war, he called it the Nazis' design "to abolish the freedom of the seas and to acquire absolute control and domination of the seas for themselves." The time had come "for prevention of attack...When you see a rattlesnake poised to strike, you do not wait

until he has struck before you crush him. The Nazi submarines and raiders are the rattlesnakes of the Atlantic" (September 11, 1941). Sometimes the examination of words allows a shortcut political analysis: the imagery betrayed two things—the strike against the poised rattlesnake is the ancient simile in favor of preventive war, into which the President evidently wanted to bring the American people. He must have thought he had brought them far enough along the road to permit his using the faulty, though strong, image of the "rattlesnake of the Atlantic."

The next incident in the undeclared war against the Nazis was the torpedoing of the U.S. Destroyer Kearney in the North Atlantic by a German submarine (October 16-17, 1941). The Administration declared that the Nazis had "fired the first shot." Actually, the vessel in question had been dropping depth-bombs against German submarines. According to isolationist commentary, the incident could cause no surprise: "The United States having taken a position in the center of submarine activities by action of President Roosevelt...There will be war very shortly, as planned by President Roosevelt at least as far back as 1938." Speaker Rayburn, on the other hand, thought that the incident "justifies statements by many of us that the United States is in danger of attack. It looks like it's a direct attack on the United States when there's an attack on one of its vessels."[454]

On October 27, Roosevelt gave his own lurid account of the Kearney incident. I had "wished to avoid shooting," he said. But now America herself had been "attacked. The USS Kearney is not just a Navy ship. She belongs to every man, woman and child in this nation...Hitler's torpedo was directed at every American." It had betrayed Hitler's intentions, as did a secret German map (never published, it would seem) in his possession, which revealed Hitler's plan to put all of South America under his thumb; another German secret document which was even more hair-raising revealed Hitler's aim "to abolish all religions" in case of victory.[455] Roosevelt's appeal to the crusading spirit to prevent such a threat to Christianity was aimed at the same stratum of sentiment as the appeals of Fuller and Defoe before him.

Congress, however, remained in opposition to full and open war in the Atlantic. It retained constitutional control over the declaration of war, in spite of the mastery over public opinion that the President had won. He knew, as he later declared, that by December 1941 the American people were "spiritually prepared for war on a world-wide scale."[456] A vote taken at the Cabinet meeting of November 7, 1941, "as to whether it was thought the American people would back us up if it became necessary to strike at Japan, in case she should attack England in Malaya or the Dutch in the East Indies" found the Cabinet "unanimous in feeling that the country would support such a move."[457] But it still required the attack on Pearl Harbor, the strong provocation that was not forthcoming in the Atlantic, to overcome Congressional opposition to all preventive war argumentation and to extend American participation in the war. Japanese action freed the Roosevelt Administration of all further need to seek the war. The Japanese had brought it to the very soil and waters of America.

It would have been very hard to enter the war in any other way, as Secretary Hull, for one, admitted in his memoirs. Was a preventive attack possible, asked Hull? "Democracies do not engage in preventive attacks except with great difficulty." Had the President gone before Congress to ask for a declaration of war against Japan following their invasion of Indochina, "he could have made a good case concerning the dangers to us inherent in Japan's course of aggression." But, considering the mood of Congress, he might not have obtained a declaration of war. "Nor would the military and naval authorities have been ready for a preventive attack. The fact that they pleaded for more time solely to prepare our defenses in the Pacific was proof in itself that they were not prepared to take the offensive."[458]

While they might not have been ready for the strategic offensive, the American armed forces, in the political atmosphere engendered by the Administration, had obtained nearly all they had demanded. Since the early stage of the war, some officers had urged that "we must become better prepared if in the future we want to prevent any foreign power from committing an act of aggression against us."[459] Near the end of the first year of the war, General Marshall, the Army Chief of Staff, could state that "for the first time in history we are actually trying to prepare for war before actually becoming involved."[460] This preparation had called for time and the avoidance of any premature provocation of war with the Axis, which "would ultimately be inevitable," of which Stimson and Marshall were convinced at least by early November 1941. By this time the Chiefs of Staff, while believing that further waiting could still improve the relative position of the United States, "had urged military action if Japan attacked territory whose security was vital to us and in this connection specified American, British or Dutch territory"[461] in the Far East, for the defense of which cooperative plans had been arranged with the Powers in question. As far as military readiness was concerned, the services were in agreement on all attempts to

maneuver "the Japanese into firing the first shot without allowing too much danger to ourselves."[462] Thus the American governors and soldiers would obtain for themselves the moral advantage of not becoming the aggressor. Clothed in the form of an order, such an admonition went to General Short in Hawaii (November 27): "If hostilities cannot be avoided, the United States desires that Japan commit the first overt act."[463] Considering the record of Japan's war openings by "sneak attack," such an act could almost certainly be expected. And it was invited insofar as fewer precautions against this contingency were made than were possible.

When, on December 6, 1941, intercepted Japanese messages were brought to the President, he said after reading them: "In substance, 'this means war.'" He did nothing to intercept the attack; he waited for it, like the lame hunter waits for the game. When his intimate, Harry Hopkins, somewhat more bluntly expressed the view "that since war was going to come at the convenience of the Japanese, it was too bad we couldn't strike the first blow to prevent any sort of surprise, the President said in effect: 'No, we can't do that. We are a democracy of a peaceful people. We have a good record. We must stand on it.'" But nothing was done after this, no warning was given to either the Japanese or the American outpost commanders,[464] nothing was done to endanger the great advantage of being, or appearing to be the non-aggressor.

None understood this better than the British, America's sub rosa allies awaiting her open entrance into the war as calmly as they could. They carefully refrained from any action that might provoke or give justification to Japanese actions or, on the other hand, to American isolationism. It was a notable display of nerve when their commanders in the Far East, emphatically forewarned, refrained from attacking a Japanese convoy lying off the Malayan coast on December 7, 1941, obviously ready to strike. As the commanders on the spot wrote in their final dispatches about the disastrous Malayan campaign and about their own motivations on the very eve of it:

War had not broken out; Pearl Harbor had not been attacked, and the United States was still neutral: there was grave risk that the Japanese might stage a bait in order to seduce us to strike the first blow and by doing so reinforce that section of the American public which was then strongly opposed to America's entering the war, a danger against which all in Malaya had been warned emphatically by General Headquarters.[465]

So strong is the automatism of preventive action in the military mind that Japanese aggression was promptly followed by a preventive move on the part of the attacked—the landing of an Allied force in Portuguese Timor. It was explained that, in view of Japanese submarine activities just off that neutral island, "it became an unavoidable necessity to take steps to safeguard this territory against Japanese aggression and to forestall use of it as a base from which attacks could be made on Allied territory and communications."[466] For a similar purpose and with a similar explanation and perhaps a similar squandering of forces, Vichy-controlled Madagascar was occupied by a British army and naval force beginning on May 5, 1942, with the declaration that "the United Nations had decided to forestall a Japanese move against the French naval base of Diego Suarez."[467]

The authority behind this preventive action was a new one, the United Nations. The Allies for the first time asserted the prerogative of invoking the beneficent force that utopians have tried for so long to vest in an international authority. In both these cases, the assurance was given by the invaders that the titles of the neutral owners would not be disturbed at the end of the war. The same assurance, not entirely convincing to the French defenders, was given by President Roosevelt on the occasion of the landings in North and West Africa:

> In order to forestall an invasion of Africa by Germany and Italy, which if successful would constitute a direct threat to America across the comparatively narrow sea from Western Africa, a powerful American force...is today landing on the Mediterranean and Atlantic coasts of French colonies in Africa...This combined Allied force, under American command, in conjunction with the British campaign in Egypt, is designed to prevent an occupation by the Axis armies of any part of Northern or Western Africa and to deny to the aggressor nations a starting point from which to launch an attack against the Atlantic coast of the Americas. In addition, it provides an effective second front assistance to our heroic allies in Russia.[468]

Why so little prominence was given to the true motive, the opening of the second front, and so much to the less credible preventive motive, is not apparent. Was it to demonstrate to the American people the foresight shown by the American command, from the President down, in forestalling a new, although unlikely, Axis move? Was this still considered more acceptable than the opening of the second front? Were the French expected to believe the first assertion rather than

approve of the second? In any case, they had to provide the battlefield both in Africa and on the continent of Europe. The Axis Powers, acting like mechanical chessplayers, moved into the as yet unoccupied parts of France.[469]

THE LEGAL STANDING OF PREVENTIVE WAR: NUREMBERG

The court set up for the trial of the major Nazi war criminals, the International Military Tribunal, was a court in which only the Russian members were soldiers, and they were of the judge-advocate variety. Some of the American members of the Prosecution were temporary soldiers. The nomenclature used could thus invite the accusation that drumhead justice was being meted out, or it could provide civilian jurists with a cloak for unprecedented measures. In any case, the trials were to be "a continuation of the war effort of the Allied Nations," according to Justice Jackson.[470] In the absence of neutral justices, this would inevitably mean a continuation of Allied war propaganda and its tenets. And in the absence of truly military members, it meant that no expert military opinions on preventive war would be voiced in or appreciated by the courts.

The proceedings brought to light a vast amount of material on the so-called war crimes of the accused from their own super-abundant records.[471] Hardly anything about possibly comparable actions of the Allies, including their preventive war ideas and measures, was brought forth. With regard to preventive war as a crime, the jurists who were preparing the structure, procedure, and some of the law of these Nuremberg courts were in a certain dilemma from the outset. The opinions of international lawyers—there were practically no relevant formal judgments—on preventive war were only partly in harmony with the general but hazy public condemnation of preventive wars as the most aggressive and the least permissible kind of war.[472] Instead, the Tribunal was forced to build the accusation of criminal peace-breaking on the Briand-Kellogg Pact and its supposed outlawry of war.[473] Early in the formation of the Statute for this court, the British lawyers, more bothered than others by the absence of precedent,[474] raised the question as to whether Hitler's several "unprovoked attacks which, since the original declaration of war, he has made on various countries," were really "war crimes in the ordinary sense," crimes under international law. This uncertainty gave the defense an unwelcome "opportunity of basing arguments on what has happened in the past and what has been done by various countries in declaring war which resulted in acquiring new territory, which certainly were not regarded at the time as crimes against international law."[475] They might have had Russia's two wars against Finland in mind. (Leaving them unmentioned at Nuremberg was among the greatest feats of discretion achieved there.) As American representative, Justice Jackson was rather impatient with such hesitations, which he called "sterile legalisms developed in the age of imperialism to make war respectable." He wanted to see things brought back to the doctrine of Grotius, with its distinctions between just and unjust war, between war of defense and of aggression, a distinction re-established by such documents as the Kellogg Pact.[476]

On the strength of this distinction, American officials such as Stimson and Jackson himself, as Attorney General, had explained the otherwise unneutral American support of the Allies before the entry into the war.[477] Before the Briand-Kellogg Pact, all war-making had been legal; but that pact had once more invoked Grotian standards, a remarkable piece of historical unreality. In the pre-trial discussions with his fellow-lawyers, Jackson admitted that the Pact had probably frozen an unsatisfactory political status quo, as far as the Germans were concerned, but held that war was definitely not redress for that. He avoided the question as to whether there had been any practical means of redress in existence. Jackson's "definition of crime did not involve causes: it involved only actual aggressive war—the attack." Such a pre-trial ruling was intended to keep the Defense from bringing about a "general trial of German grievances." This contingency had to be met by skillful drafting of the Statute of the Court, as otherwise it might be thought that the nations conducting the trial were afraid of something. Instead, this possibility was to be excluded by an article saying that no political, military or other consideration could serve as an excuse or justification for aggression. Any German attempt to say, by way of excuse, that, although they had attacked, they had done so only for imperative reasons, must be suppressed as something awkward to litigate, as causes of war are apt to be.[478] Perhaps this is New Deal justice—the overriding of precedent, the fight against the "nine old men" who successfully stood out for precedent against administrative absolutism—transferred to the international scene, where no carefully administered law stood in its way. It is also New Deal jurisprudence without the tempering of justice with humanitarianism in which it usually prided itself. The Russian representative on the pre-trial committee was able to give his full assent on this point: the trial must not be allowed to be used for propaganda by the Germans but only for their punishment, as ordained at Yalta.[479] He saw no reason to go behind the "new law" as laid down by the declarations of the Allied statesmen at the Moscow and Yalta conferences, which had settled the question of identifying a war criminal. "The fact that the Nazi leaders are criminals has already been established. The task of the Tribunal is only to determine the measure of guilt of each particular person and mete out the necessary punishment—the sentences."[480] The often-underlined divergence of Western and Soviet law could not have been put more bluntly. The Soviet jurist in effect told the Westerners: Why should one consider precedents when the criminal whose guilt is clear because he is an enemy of the Soviet State—and its Allies —is at hand to be sentenced?

The British were far less at ease: they foresaw that when the case of Norway came up, the Defense, in spite of a clearly aggressive German attack on that country, might say that this was done in anticipation of a British measure against Norwegian neutrality. Definitions would have to be found to keep such awkward questions from being raised. Jackson eagerly agreed to the suppression of the historical-political issues, or fact-finding: "If we should have a prolonged controversy over whether Germany invaded Norway a few jumps ahead of a British invasion...whether France in declaring war was the real aggressor, this trial can do infinite harm for those countries with the people of the United States. And the same is true of our Russian relationships."[481] This was a way of saying that war-time convictions instilled in the American people must not be upset by the findings of the international court to be set up at Nuremberg. "Crimes against peace" were defined with such domestic political ends in view. They covered "planning, preparation, initiation or waging a war of aggression or a war in violation of international treaties, agreements or assurances, or participation in a common plan or conspiracy for the accomplishment of any of the foregoing." In finding out whether or not these crimes had been committed, the Court was "to rule out irrelevant issues and statements of any kind whatsoever."

As had been foreseen, the Defense at Nuremberg raised the patent protest that under international law as it had existed in 1939, no law or court could punish anyone who had launched an unjust war. Under general international law as heretofore known, they argued, there was no distinction between forbidden and unforbidden war; heretofore there had been no organ to designate the aggressor[482]—except, as the Defense was almost too polite to point out, the victor to whom go not only the spoils but also the power to name the defeated as the aggressor. While no kind of excuse could be brought forward to defend the Nazi aggression against Denmark in 1940, a fairly convincing case was made out during the trial to suggest that Norway was invaded because it was believed by the Germans that the Allies were about to undertake a similar measure.[483] This, the British prosecution declared, "even if it were true, would be no answer, but the German documents completely dispose of the suggestion that it was for such a reason that the Germans violated Norwegian neutrality...All the alleged intelligence reports contain no information which comes within miles of justifying an anticipatory invasion based—you might think it laughable—on the doctrine of self-preservation."[484] For the lawyer bent on prosecuting a beaten foe, there is no uncovering of all the cards after the game has been played. The Russian prosecutor was equal to the British in withholding from the historian any information regarding the Russian plans in 1941 or later. And Justice Jackson, as prosecutor, was bold enough to state that "even if it could be shown—which it cannot be—that the Russian war was really defensive, such is demonstrably not the case with those wars which preceded it."[485] The contention of some of the defendants, the Russian declared, that the attack on his country was a preventive measure was "to such a degree unconvincing and contradictory to the irrefutable evidence presented in court" from German documentation that he saw no need for occupying the Court's time with that.[486]

The judges saw no reason to insist on documentation from the Allied side as to their own intentions in the case of Norway. Hence they denied all plausibility to the German counterclaims on the point of preventive war. They went so far as to say that it could not be determined "with exactitude how widely the view was held in influential German circles that the Allies intended to occupy Norway" but insisted that when the plans for an attack on Norway were being made, "they were not made for the purpose of forestalling an imminent Allied landing, but, at the most, that they might prevent an Allied occupation at some future date."[487] No credence whatsoever was given to the German preventive war argument in the case of the other attacked countries.

In the Tribunal, the maxim that the rule of nemo potest judex in re sua has no place in the law of nations[488] was illustrated in its extreme. Legislator, prosecutor, and judge were brought together in an identity that had not been reached since the days of tribal warfare.[489] The Tribunal did not declare preventive war per se illegal or criminal. It was left open whether such a war might be justified in cases of imminent danger by saying that "preventive action in foreign territory"—it did not say "preventive

war"—"is justified only in case of 'an instant and overwhelming necessity for self-defense, leaving no choice of means and no moment of deliberation,'" as in the case of the Caroline.[490] Whether this case, which had occurred in peacetime along the badly-policed frontiers of civilization, was truly relevant to the issue at Nuremberg seems highly doubtful. The more relevant case of the British act of "Copenhagening" in 1807 was left unmentioned, perhaps because there has always been fundamental disagreement over its justification between British and Continental publicists.[491] In fact, no actual case of a justifiable preventive war was cited, nor was any war condemned outright except those undertaken by the Germans since 1939. Preventive war remained lawful under certain conditions. The main though undeclared condition which a later proponent of war should never forget, is that it must either be won or at least brought to a stalemate.

Due to the inaction of the various judges at Nuremberg, and in spite of urging on the part of the Defense, the problem of preventive war under international law remains clouded, overshadowed by the blanket indictment of forbidden "aggressive wars."[492] As far as this state of things concerns military planners, it is cruel enough. It becomes highly advisable for them never to put on paper any proposals based on preventive considerations, unless they can be certain of victory for their side and thus escape the jurists and their ex post facto legislation. It reminds one of Hitler's dictum, pronounced on the eve of 1939, that "what matters is not whether you are right but that you are victorious."[493]

UNITED NATIONS FOR THE PREVENTION OF WAR (INCLUDING PREVENTIVE WAR)

"Militarism has flourished far more widely and obstinately in Germany than elsewhere, but it is a plant which knows no national boundaries; it grows everywhere. It lifts its voice to say that war between East and West, or Left and Right, or White and Yellow is inevitable. It whispers that newly devised weapons are so terrible that they should be hurled now lest some other country use them first. It makes the whole world walk under the shadow of death."[494]

Well before the entry of the United States into the Second World War, its Government had outlawed Hitler. On the eve of the war, its Secretary of the Navy, Frank Knox, had told the American Bar Association that "the ultimate defeat of Hitler and the re-establishment of international law go together."[495] The Nuremberg trials, not then foreseen, were to signify this return to lawfulness. But even in 1941 it was thought that the power of the United States, once it had brought about this return to law, must not again be dismantled. The world, said Knox, had "grown so small, so interrelated, so interdependent...that the great law-abiding, peace-loving nations must take power into their hands and keep it there for a long time to come to prevent the inauguration of another world war." For Knox, the interventionist politician and departmental spokesman, the force to be applied for the good of the world would lie in the combination of the American and British navies as the instrument for the control of the seas. The two were to form a nucleus to which other nations of "similar peaceful inclinations and lacking aggressive designs" would be joined. This would mark the beginning of the restoration of international law, the creation of a system "in which an autocratic aggressor would no longer have the time factor in his favor, would no longer be able to determine when to act and keep his preparations hidden until the hour of striking." Democracies inevitably move slowly except for their ever-ready freedom-preserving navies.

Once thrown into the war, even the leaders of the Republican Party, the stronghold of the isolationists, were determined not to lag behind in their declarations in favor of "whatever cooperative organization perpetuating existing unity may be agreed upon." They favored "responsible participation by the United States in a post-war cooperative organization among sovereign nations to prevent military aggression and to attain permanent peace with organized justice in a free world." The stipulation was added, of course, that the vital interests of the nation must not be foregone nor its sacred institutions infringed.[496]

Such hopes and such reservations were embodied in the Charter of the United Nations, first outlined by representatives of the Big Four during the Dumbarton Oaks Conference (August 21-October 7, 1944). The preliminary results achieved there were publicly defended by officials of the State Department: they were not perfect, but, like the American Constitution, they could be improved by the amending process. Certain obligations had to be undertaken in order to help maintain peace

> so that our nation could be protected from the ravages of war. We would agree to settle all our disputes peacefully and we must be willing to commit some of our military forces in order to prevent a new batch of international gangsters from breaking loose. But that can hardly be called a sacrifice. It's more like an insurance policy.

The Dumbarton Oaks proposals represented "the highest point yet reached in international democracy." While the League of Nations had had no means of giving force to its resolutions, the new organization would have extensive forces at its disposal. They were to be applied at the direction of a Security Council, which would certainly "act if we were faced again by the same kind of situations that arose in Germany and Italy under Hitler and Mussolini before the war, and this time we would take action before a war can get started."[497]

The San Francisco Conference (April 25-June 26, 1945) and the drawing up and signing of the UN Charter took place in the flush of common victory. In the Charter, the peoples of the United Nations declared themselves determined "to save succeeding generations from the scourge of war," to unite their strength in order to maintain international peace and security and to insure that armed force would not be used, save in the common interest. One of the nineteen chapters of the Charter was dedicated to "action with respect to threats to the peace, breaches of the peace and acts of aggression." A Security Council was to determine the existence of any threat to peace, breach of the peace and act of aggression, prevent aggravation of a threatening situation, and, if necessary, apply armed force for the maintenance or restoration of international peace and security. Military forces were to be put at the disposal of the Council by member states "for combined international enforcement action." Such preventive or enforcement measures against any state were not to "impair the inherent right of individual or collective self-defence if an armed attack occurs against a member of the organization until the Security Council has taken the measures necessary to maintain international peace and security."

The organization of forces for peace was wrongly envisaged and badly executed. The real conflicts in the world of 1945, between democratic capitalism and pseudo-democratic communism, were overlooked. The Charter had preserved Russian concentration for the world class war better than it had provided for the possibilities of a future counter-concentration of the Western Powers. On this point, the war coalition had induced a temporary, almost hysterical blindness in the governors of the United States. They proved unable to transform the greater power of the United States at the end of the war into either a better peace organization or a militarily superior position.

It is hardly proof of American political acumen that this neglect was first discovered and pointed out by military officers of the United States. According to the Socialist Norman Thomas, in 1944-45 Washington already "buzzed with gossip that war with Russia was a paramount subject of discussion in the armed forces, with some officers, especially in the Navy, believing that since war is so likely we had better have it soon while we, rather than the Russians, are at the top of our strength.

All this, mind you, while our two countries are still allies, engaged at San Francisco in making a charter for permanent security."[498]

That such awareness of conflict first arose among military men was perhaps unfortunate. It enabled those friends of peace and of Russia, who insisted that both friendships must go together, to decry such warnings as militaristic. At an American-Soviet love feast in November 1945, probably the last with full participation on the American side, ex-Ambassador to Moscow Davies denounced "a few militarists—not among the great war leaders—in this and other countries who advocate war with Russia now rather than later." Such talk was to him "insanity" and amounted to "throwing dynamite around."[499] But warnings that the United Nations provided poor insurance against war came not only from military men and militarists. Bridge-expert Ely Culbertson warned the United States Senate, holding hearings on the ratification of the Charter, that this document must be amended by provisions for national disarmament and the creation of a UN armed force. "We are facing within the next five or six years," he warned, "a preventive war by the capitalistic world to eliminate the threat of the rising Russian giant state. And if this war does not take place, then we are facing in fifteen or twenty years a war for the control of the world by Communist Eurasia, led by Russia."[500]

To some Americans, dissatisfied with the outcome of the war and exasperated over the spread of Moscow-centered Communism, the temporary monopoly of the atomic bomb held by the United States seemed to offer the supreme weapon for fighting a preventive war against Russia. If controls of atomic energy were solely based on the assumption of inevitable war, then (Robert M. Hutchins, Chancellor of the University of Chicago, told a Senate Committee), "we ought to start one right now because we are in the best position to win it. The assumption that there is going to be a war would lead to the conclusion that we had better start the war this morning, because only this morning can we be sure of having supremacy in atomic bombs."[501] For those who still thought that the zero point in the rapid development of the law of diminishing returns from war had not yet been reached, this seemed logical. Some of the American proponents of such a war saw no other alternatives than fighting the Soviets soon or making peace with them largely on their own terms. The military chances for a Russian defeat seemed hopeful to some, dubious to others.

Russia was only slowly to lose this character of a "friendly ally" in the minds of the ex-partners of the recent war coalition. It was perfectly safe for the Russian governors to continue to act on this assumption for at least a limited number of years, perhaps until Russia also had the atomic bomb. They hardly even needed the help extended by such American friends of the Soviet Union as Henry Wallace. Relegated to the position of Secretary of Commerce, Wallace protested that "a school of military thinking" was advocating "a preventive war, an attack on Russia now before Russia has atomic bombs," a war that they thought necessary to save civilization because they believe that once several nations hold atomic bombs "a war which will destroy modern civilization will result and no nation or combination of nations can win such a war." To Wallace, such thought seemed "not only immoral but stupid." Since he gave no names of any advocate of preventive war, he made it easy for the Secretaries of War and of the Navy to deny that there was any basis for Wallace's accusations. They knew of no responsible Army or Navy officer "who has ever advocated or even suggested a policy or plan of attacking Russia. There is no such military thinking in the War and Navy Departments."[502] The already evident disunity inside Truman's Cabinet was soon to lead Wallace to more or less involuntary resignation from office.[503]

What Wallace had in mind were probably statements like that of General H. H. Arnold: There is only one defense against the atomic bomb, "hit it before it starts...I don't like the word 'defense.' We should shoot to insure the security of the Americas...This country should capitalize [whatever that may mean] on the atomic bomb, if necessary to assure world peace."[504] Another officer of the Air Force, Lieutenant General Ira C. Eaker, deputy commander of the Army Air Force, predicted later in 1946 that "the next war would be a short war of unparalleled destruction, that the first blows would be struck through the air, and that to prevent destruction of this country in event of such an attack we must strike the enemy first." (Is striking an attacker first logically possible?) "If we are to prevent the launching of atom bombs, guided missiles, or super-rockets against our industrial establishments, we must have a force ready to destroy these weapons at their source before they are launched. The only such weapon we have in the United States today is our long-range bomber force."[505]

It proved to be a great weakness on the part of the democratic governments of the West that, unlike the Soviet Government, they could not at once, even if they had wished, put up a bold front against the ex-partner of the war coalition. They could only stay armed, or rearm, despite considerable opposition at home and hope, as Winston Churchill did—at least publicly—that the Russians would be impressed by it.[506] By all public signs, they were not impressed. Parallels were drawn between the Russian and the German menace, between 1946 or

1948 and Munich.[507] Munich could so easily have been avoided by preventive action in 1933 or 1935 if people had only heeded Churchill's warnings in time. Churchill himself was saying that "there never was a war in history easier to prevent by timely action than the one which has just desolated such great areas of the globe. It could have been prevented without the firing of a single shot."[508] Such speakers were accorded the favorite Soviet epithet of "war-mongers" and accused of advocating a preventive war.

The exasperated feeling about the Russian sit-down strike against peace, performed inside the structure of the UN, and the conspicuousness of having a weapon that could not be used except for ineffective demonstration finally led to the North Atlantic Pact. Although justified as one of the regional pacts envisaged by the UN Charter, this was the first exclusive alliance in the post-war period. With the production of the first atomic bomb by the Russians, the United States lost a monopoly it had been unable to use—one of the most fruitless monopolies in history.[509] The United States had wrung no discernible concession out of the Russians.

The conditions under which military competition was carried on in the post-war world induced various fears and fearful proposals. Ex-Premier Paul Reynaud was concerned as to whether the gigantic American-Russian conflict, dwarfing and overshadowing European issues, would not lead the United States into staging a preventive war. In 1947, he pointed out, the United States was in a position of overwhelming superiority, but in twenty years the population increase would bring the Russians to 250 millions, the Americans to only 165. The next economic crisis might strengthen the American inclination to go to war. There had never been an armaments race that had not ended in war.[510] Even some British officials, who knew better, or should have known better, believed that the United States was leaning "toward the idea of a preventive war in the near future, before Russia gains in relative strength."[511]

Such European fears and suspicions were entertained most strongly among Communists and fellow-travelers, and among those in France who believed that the United States, whatever her intentions, could not even "defend Europe préventivement," that it would be promptly overrun by the Red armies and that it was therefore better to start collaboration, with the Russians this time, through the French Communist Party.[512] These views were brought to the United States for confirmation by a French visitor early in 1947. The guest, a philosophe of the Existentialist school, Simone de Beauvoir, could not help finding a widespread feeling among Americans that war with the U.S.S.R. was inevitable. While such a war appeared horrible enough to those whom she encountered, it still filled them with a hope of success, provided the United States did not wait for the Russians to start such a war at a later and more unfavorable time. She found a prevailing sentiment of resignation to war, a sentiment that she considered to be the prime factor in making a war possible.[513] Such reporting on American inclinations towards a preventive war were only too willingly listened to by the French in their mood of war-weariness, "neutralism," and apathy.[514] In order to combat it, Foreign Minister Schuman, the most enduring figure in French post-1944 politics, gave assurances that France was totally averse to the ideas of a preventive war.[515]

Advocates of a preventive war on America's part were forced to realize, more or less regretfully, that there was no detonator within democratic society to set off such a war, unless a constitutional change could be effected, or at least unless the already very full powers of the President as Commander-in-Chief could be further strengthened or stretched. That change seemed a prerequisite to some military men for the successful undertaking of a preventive war in the atomic age. Emphasizing the need for secrecy and speed in the opening of such a war, Colonel Louis E. Coira of the Air Force Operations Division concluded that the President "must be prepared to accept the responsibility for issuing the order [for a] preventive war." He could do so by executive decree as others had done before him—Polk by sending troops into disputed territory in Mexico, Wilson by the occupation of Vera Cruz in 1914 and again in 1918 by sending troops to Siberia.[516]

Since traditional democracy could not undertake "anticipatory retaliation"—a euphemism occasionally used for preventive war[517]—other arrangements for war-making, including a President-dictator, seemed to be called for. Some publicists agreed with the airman. As a science writer who had done much to popularize the atomic bomb, William L. Laurence proposed that the United States initiate a new approach to the stalemated problem of atomic control. We should propose, he thought, that any nation refusing to renounce its sovereign right to manufacture such bombs makes herself thereby an aggressor nation subject to the UN Charter sanctions. As against such aggression, Congress should authorize the President, after secret consultations with the Cabinet, the Chiefs of Staff and the two Foreign Affairs Committees of Congress, "to take whatever action is necessary to meet the challenge of the aggressor," who was to be prevented from continuing the production of atomic bombs and similarly dangerous war materials. This would be saying in effect to the Kremlin: we are compelled to "destroy your atomic plants before they are ready to operate...if that

means war, it will be a war you will force on us
by your insistence on an atomic armament race
which must inevitably lead to war anyway...under
the circumstances it would be to our advantage to
have it while we are still the sole possessors of
the atomic bomb." Still, the writer denied preventive war intentions. "Does all this mean that we
should fight a 'preventive war' now, before Russia
catches up with us? Emphatically no!"[518]

The elder statesmen shrank in horror from such
bare-faced proposals of preventive war to be undertaken by the United States. Ex-Secretary of
War Stimson, who had witnessed the great extension of the executive power for war purposes during his service in the Roosevelt Cabinet, termed
such a proposal "worse than nonsense; it results
from a cynical incomprehension of what the people
of the world will tolerate from any nation...We
could not possibly take that opportunity without
deserting our inheritance. Americans as conquerors would be tragically miscast."[519] Preparing
to testify in favor of the Marshall Plan, the alternative to war (including preventive war), John
Foster Dulles pointed out that Russian post-1945
policy of "not war, not peace" was indeed dangerous to peace in its assumption that "the other fel-
low has great self-control." In spite of such a
challenge, it was, he said, still unthinkable that
the United States would start a preventive war,
largely because such a war would expose her free
institutions "to the utmost peril." In considering
her world situation, "military factors were not to
be ignored, but in accordance with American tradition, let the military be an instrument of national
policy, and not itself the maker of that policy."[520]

The Truman Administration allowed more liberty of speech and discussion to the military advocates of preventive action than is usually deemed
good for the conduct of foreign affairs. Clearly
it was hoped that the Russians would be intimidated. Instead, they were merely furnished with
ample occasion to attack the United States for its
militarism. With a show of righteousness, the
Soviet Government protested in Washington that
the warlike statements of Americans violated a
UN General Assembly resolution against war propaganda. The answer given was that there still
was freedom of discussion in the United States.
More publicly, Soviet Deputy Foreign Minister
Vishinsky attacked the Western Powers at the
Paris meeting of the United Nations in November
1948 as "war-mongers" and preparers of a "Pearl
Harbor for the USSR." He mentioned by name a
long list of enemies of the peace and of the Soviet
Union, including Winston Churchill, William Laurence and General George C. Kenney, former
chief of the U.S. Strategic Air Command.[521]
Vishinsky served warning on all of these that "the
peace-loving forces of the world" would prove

mightier than the forces of reaction and aggression.[522]

The atomchiks were too valuable a target for
Russian propaganda to be given up soon. The Russians kept on saying that this or that person or
group in the United States, including scientists,
were "advocating the launching of an atomic war
against the USSR."[523] When the announcement
of an atomic explosion on Soviet territory upset
the long uncomfortable belief in American atomic
superiority, the Daily Worker asked: "Will the
monsters who advocate a 'preventive war'-Pearl
Harbor attack on the USSR now clamor for an immediate war?"[524] No monster seems to have
done so.

A definite advantage lay on the Russian side in
this conflict of propaganda. For even if there had
been Russian military proposals addressed to the
Kremlin to make war at a favorable time, they
would never have been aired in public. Hence the
appearance of a greater desire for peace on the
Russian side. Russia proceeded to make use of
appearances in "Peace Petitions" and "Peace
Congresses." Besides, preventive proposals were
outside the tenets of Communist belief and established propaganda. A Russian scientist was asked
by a "Liberal" American journalist: "If Russia had
the atomic bomb, do you think now would be a good
time to attack these reactionaries" in America who
are misleading "the people?" The Russian scientist was deeply shocked. "It is a basic concept of
our thinking," he replied, "that wars are started
by capitalist nations" (which would presumably include Finland). Besides, "there are so many basic
conflicts inherent in the capitalistic system that
the ultimate victory of socialism is assured."[525]
The consistency or fatalism of Marxism as taught
in Russia is strong enough among the indoctrinated
to exclude the consideration of preventive war just
as completely as among the more strictly predes-
tinarian Calvinists.

In point of fact, preventive measures on this side
of the "Iron Curtain" were limited to the sphere of
police action, such as the spy trials or the mass
arrests of suspected Communists in Greece in July
1947. A week before the arrests took place, the
Greek Government asked the American Ambassador
in Athens for advice. The ambassador was told that
his Government "would have no objection to preventive measures if they were considered necessary in
the interests of Greece which was a sovereign State."
Afterwards, the Ambassador was somewhat surprised
at the extent of this preventive measure.[526] There
are apt to be more preventive measures in the cold
war and no doubt the West will continue to leave the
lead to Communism. Liberalism remains under
definite inhibitions with regard to war-making. The
West is forced to arm and keep armed for more
eventualities than the opposite camp, with its

continued initiative. This enforced passivity helps to explain the belief "that we have learned the importance of military strength as a means of preventing war...in the conviction that a sound military system is needed in time of peace if we want to live in peace" (President Truman to Congress, March 18, 1948).

The authoritative military answer to preventive war proposals in the United States was given by the chairman of the Joint Chiefs of Staff, General Bradley, whom Vishinsky had included in his list of war-mongers. Bradley assured a Congressional committee in October 1949 that "we are never going to start a war," and that his and his colleagues' strategy was therefore based on the assumption that the United States would wait to be attacked. This was something that sober-minded military men had told the public before.[527] But, he added, after allowing the enemy the first stroke, "we will have to carry the war back to the enemy by all means at our disposal."[528] This strategy, whether due to the mandates of American policy or to professional resignation, marked the end of a definite phase of the "cold war," the phase during which the United States held the monopoly of the atomic bomb but was unable to use it.

The war in Korea, undertaken on Moscow's orders, made America regret still more poignantly that only Germany and Japan had undergone debellatio, and it aroused once more the feeling for preventive war against the Communist bastion. At least two of Acheson's colleagues in the Cabinet, Secretary of Defense Louis Johnson, in private talks, and Secretary of the Navy Francis P. Matthews, in a speech at the Boston Navy Yard, suggested that the United States should be willing to pay "even the price of instituting a war to compel cooperation for peace." This was generally understood as a proposal to launch a preventive war against Russia. The State Department hastened to repudiate the idea as not representing official American foreign policy, for which it was responsible and which did "not favor instituting a war of any kind." The United States could not hope to find support abroad if it should become in any way identified with such proposals, "playing right into the hands of the Russians," who on their part termed Matthews "one of the most thick-skulled, most reactionary armor-bearers of Wall Street."[529]

The Korean War demonstrated that the deterring effect of the atomic bomb was quickly diminishing. Some American soldiers, more concerned with the direct competition between the United States and the USSR in the production of atomic bombs, advocated the preventive drop of this weapon on Russia before she had produced enough bombs to make it worthwhile for her to drop them on American targets. Major General Orvil A. Anderson, command-

ant of the Air War College, expatiated in classes and publicly on how a preventive war through the use of strategic air force could and should be carried out, since Russia herself would use the weapon once she was ready. He believed that soldiers had a right to advise the State Department on this, since the State Department "can't think clearly." Taking the "cold war" metaphor literally, the General considered that he was not advocating preventive war, which logically refers only to the opening of a war. For the duration of a war the preventive move is not only permissible but imperative.

Since we're at war, damn it, I don't advocate preventive war, I advocate the shedding of illusions. I advocate saying to Stalin: "Joe, you're not kidding anybody. You are saying you are going to destroy us." And if he says "yes"—and he has been saying "yes" all the time—we must conclude civilization demands that we act. Give me the order to do it and I can break up Russia's five A-bomb nests in a week.[530]

The General's superiors suspended him from his office and later dispensed with his services altogether, explaining that the Air Force's primary purpose was "the prevention of war" and not the execution of a preventive war. The difficulties and possible failure of such a war had not been too well considered by its advocates.[531]

The Truman Administration had to contend with an influential school of political soldiers, not overly respectful of the boundaries of the policy-making domain usually reserved for civilian control. It had to contend with militarized politicians such as Louis Johnson and Francis P. Matthews, and even with an occasional representative of the Church militant, of which Matthews was known to be a devout member.[532] These men were ready to discard the older American tradition against "aggressive or preventive war" as outdated. But such wars, President Truman was eager to reiterate, were "the weapons of dictators, not of free democratic countries like the United States, arming only for defense against aggression."[533] Men who prided themselves for holding to the best traditions of democracy echoed the conviction that no preventive war should be undertaken, even as part of the so-called "cold war."[534] Unfortunately, however, arming and rearming are necessary "as a dose of preventive medicine aimed at forestalling a new war" (Attlee).[535] A whole barrage of speakers, civilian and military, had to offset statements by American politicos in and out of uniform in favor of preventive war against Russia.[536] General Bradley assured the American people and armed forces alike that "we will not provoke a war against anybody. And we will not wage a preventive war against an archenemy. But there is one price we will not pay—appeasement."[537] As against the Soviet "program

of world domination," declared Assistant Secretary
of the Army Karl R. Bendetsen, "our concept must
be twofold—military strength to deter aggression,
to buy time, and an affirmative coordinated political, economic and psycho-social program to win
the war for men's minds"; this does not mean all-
out mobilization for war, or preventive war, but
rather "a program preventive of war."[538] As director of American diplomacy, Secretary of State
Acheson declared that proposals in favor of a preventive war were "self-defeating. It is only among
those who have lost their sense of proportion about
the purpose for which we need to build our military
strength that talk of preventive war is possible.
Only among those who have lost sight of our goals
can there be wisdom in self-destructive hyster-
ia."[539]

As Secretary of Defense, General Marshall, a
thoroughly constitution-imbued soldier, pointed
out that the United States was not "a nation that
can move into the conflict in a moment, without
any formal declaration" of war. We thus deny ourselves a position of immense military advantage,
which an aggressor would have. American constitutional processes exclude that: "It is inconceivable that we could have a surprise attack and gain
the advantages of such a sudden procedure. With
the debate in Congress that can't be done." However, he added, the moral plus of the non-aggressor will in the end outweigh the military advantages accruing to the maker of preventive war.
The Korean experience induced still other queries.
For example:

> Senator Cain: "May I ask if you believe in a
> preventive war?" General Bradley: "I do not,
> because I do not believe that is a solution."
> Cain: "May I ask if the Korean War...has not
> become a preventive war?" Bradley: "Well,
> in a way it may have; not a preventive all-out
> war, but I believe that by taking this action in
> Korea we may have postponed or avoided a
> third world war, because one appeasement
> leads to another until eventually war is in-
> evitable."[540]

If the assurances contained in these remarks
did not persuade the Russians of America's unwillingness to wage preventive war, they did prove
convincing to the British, her best ally, and the
Canadians, her next best ally.[541] Churchill went
so far as to declare that, if war should come, it
would be due to the Russians wanting it. As leader
of the Opposition, Churchill told the Commons on
November 30, 1950, that the Soviets had "repeatedly been assured that the United States would not
fight what is called a 'preventive war.' The United
States have expressed the general opinion of the
civilized world upon that aspect. On this basis,
the war, if it ever comes—which God forbid—will

come at the moment of their [the Soviets'] choice."
Unfortunately, he added, the restraining influence,
the possession of the atomic bomb by the United
States, will work less well the more the Soviet
stockpile of that weapon grows.[542]

Such political speakers have less hesitation than
a soldier might have when confronted with a logical inconsistency in the use of political metaphors.
For as far as the commonly so-called "cold war"
is war, there can be no more preventive war. There
can be only preventive moves within the war. War
has already begun, and not by any obviously preventive move on either side. It has begun merely
because the last war was not turned into peace.
Instead the class war was resumed with more
military means.[543] War is under way and therefore all preventive moves seem justifiable meas-
uses of war while it lasts. But this follows only if
cold war is war, bellum apertum, and fighting it is
bellare bellum. Some of the moves in this cold war
are clearly of a preventive nature, whether or not
they are declared as such.[544] Still other moves
are publicized as preventive war measures. The
Chinese Communists perhaps went furthest in admitting the preventive nature of their warfare when
they declared at the seat of the UN organization that
their own armed intervention in Korea was "due to
the view of the Chinese people" that if an aggressor
in Korea, such as the United States, should be allowed to bring his aggression to a successful close,
his next step would certainly be still further aggression against China herself.[545] Coming from a
Communist spokesman, that was a remarkably
traditional military justification of a preventive
war. It may have been deliberately chosen in order
to provoke military minds in America, notably
those who had been flustered by intervention on the
part of Red China.

Arguments in favor of preventive war combine
strategic necessity with the momentary military
superiority of one's own side. Weighing against
such advantages is the difficulty of justifying such
a war of utmost aggression inside a democracy,
where "thought-control" on questions of war responsibilities and war guilt remains incomplete.
The agitation stirred up in America by military
minds in favor of waging preventive war during
the time when she held either the monopoly of the
atomic bomb or the vastly superior number of
them, found her "faithful in temptation." (And was
it "imputed unto her for righteousness?") Whether
the Soviet governors would be inclined to let temptation go by in a similar situation will depend very
largely on their convictions as to the inevitability
of open and full war between the Communist and
the capitalist systems and on their estimates as
to its outcome. If the convictions inherited from
Lenin should remain strong, they might well choose

the moment of their side's actual or seeming superiority to launch the inevitable war preventively. The temptation for such a military measure would have its strong and continued root in ideology, a breeding ground of war easily as dangerous as interest.

NATO is the inscription on the tomb where many of the best Western hopes in the United Nations lie buried. It was torn apart by the utter opposition of the two giant Powers, Russia and the United States. They are considered by many in their respective camps as strong enough to force their followers into war, even preventive war, though obviously such followership is far more automatic in the Communist than in the capitalist camp. And historically speaking, coalitions have proved a deterrent from rather than a stimulant toward the undertaking of preventive war. Military organization, the "infrastructure" of the Eastern camp, was far advanced when a similar organization was brought under way in the West and a counter-force formed. Its aim, as declared by the diplomats, was not "military strength for its own sake," but only to provide enough "military strength to be secure against aggression." A "vacuum of weakness," as Korea has shown, constitutes a "fatal temptation to autocracies determined to expand." As Acheson has put it:

> For this reason, we seek to build forces adequate to deter aggression or to meet it. We do not seek to create greater strength than we need for this purpose, we do not desire military forces great enough to launch a preventive war.[546]

With this declaration on strength and weakness— not so strong as to be tempted into preventive war, not so weak as to invite aggression—the restless idea of the preventive war has reached the latest station on its way through history. It is kept under control for the moment by the reins of adverse democratic convictions and estimates of indeterminate though not vastly differing ratios of military strength.

FOOTNOTES

1. For definitions, see article on "Präventivkrieg" in Herre's Politisches Handwörterbuch, II, 356, and article in Meyer's Konversationslexicon. The editions of 1928 and 1940 define preventive war as "a war which is being undertaken in order to make impossible the foreseeable [or feared] attack of an enemy." (The words in brackets were added in the 1940 edition.) Like most political terms, "preventive" has its uncertainties of meaning and allusion. The original Latin praevenire is "to come before" or "go before" in space or time, as in the older English usage—"God prevents [goes before, guides] us with His grace." When followed by the accusative, it also means "anticipate," as in "More preventus" (Ovid), prevented by death, or as in "I prevented [anticipated] the dawning of the morning" (OED). For the very common modern misunderstanding of the phrase "Prevent us, O Lord, in all our doings," which appears in the Anglican Book of Prayer, see Time, March 31, 1952.

2. Thucydides, Peloponnesian War, Book VI, 18 (Bohn's translation, p. 390).

3. Haldane, An Autobiography, p. 196. See also his Before the War, pp. 170 ff.

4. Cited by Lagorgette in Le rôle de la guerre, p. 633.

5. See, for instance, Thomas Mann's defense of Frederick the Great's entrance into the Seven Years' War, in Friedrich und die grosse Koalition. Cf. Friedrich Meinecke: "Frederick the Great had already been truly German in that he, who bore Machiavelli and anti-Machiavelli in his soul at the same time, alternately professed...the one or the other, with an incaution that as a rule was foreign to the Anglo-Saxon as well as the Latin mind. For it is the incautious verities that tempt the German, whereas the Western European, from a sense of unconscious expediency, often prefers conventionality to the naked but dangerous truth—perhaps even more so in modern times than earlier when Machiavelli and Naudé had not hesitated to bare the nakedness of political man." Meinecke, Die Idee der Staatsräson, p. 491.

6. Trials of War Criminals, X, 1019; cf. also X, 1042.

7. Colonial Records, I, 207.

8. Brinkmann, Soziologische Theorie der Revolution, p. 42.

9. William Goodwin considered the fact "that our neighbor is preparing or menacing hostilities" not a justifiable reason for war. Enquiry Concerning Political Justice (1793), II, 143.

10. "Peoples have no appreciation of aggressive wars, but on the contrary one for a struggle for the maintenance of their life. In a declaration of war they easily discover the will for aggression." Ludendorff, Der totale Krieg, p. 87.

11. See Romier, "La Saint-Barthélemy, les évènements de Rome et la préméditation du massacre," Revue du XVIe Siècle, I (1913), 523 ff.

12. "Even from a war won by the anti-Communists the Holy See expects neither the preservation of religion nor the triumph of Christianity, but on the contrary the uprooting of religious belief, the strengthening of anti-Catholic minds and anti-Catholic forces." Pius XII in Osservatore Romano, June 24, 1951.

13. According to Francois Mauriac, Mrs. Clare

Booth Luce, on November 12, 1949, "tried us out on the preventive application of the atomic bomb," much to the horror of himself and his friends. The Times Literary Supplement, March 20, 1953.

14. Monsignore Ancel, suffragan to Cardinal Gerlier, Primate of France, in a series of articles published in the diocese weekly L'Essor at the end of 1951. We are using a condensation of the articles which appeared in Die Zeit, (Hamburg), on January 3, 1952. For opposite Catholic viewpoints, see below, n. 532.

15. See below, n. 384.

16. For Ambassador Bullitt's view (in 1935) that this position of strength would be reached by 1950, see U.S. Foreign Relations, The Soviet Union, 1933-1939, pp. 225 ff.

17. Kisker (ed.), World Tension. The Psychopathology of International Relations, pp. 59, 67 f.

18. During the early stages of the War of the League of Augsburg, which Louis XIV had aggressively started, the French ambassador in neutral London told his Austrian colleague: "Neither the one party nor the other keeps treaties longer than suits their interest. We had to fear an invasion from Germany and therefore had to be beforehand. But we are ready to change the present standstill into a peace." Klopp, Der Fall des Hauses Stuart, IV, 216.

19. Lieber, Manual of Political Ethics, II, 447.

20. The precedent Lieber very likely had in mind was the case of The Caroline in 1837, to which we shall return later on.

21. "Peace has to submit to the demands of war. War is the secret overlord of our century. Peace has merely the importance of an armistice between two wars." Review of Ludendorff's Der Totale Krieg in Deutsche Wehr, December 1935.

22. Ariosto, Orlando Furioso, Bk. XXXI, 79-81.

23. Ammianus Marcellinus (330-400) lists a category of Roman soldiers under this denomination.

24. To Clarke, November 5, 1807. Cited by Ollivier in L'Empire libéral, XV, 359.

25. Krauss, Theorie and Praxis in der Kriegskunst, pp. 43 f.

26. December 12, 1944. Heusinger, Befehl im Widerstreit, pp. 373 f.

27. Demosthenes, as defender of preventive war, left a long tradition behind him. He was invoked by Chancellor Bacon as one who "exposes to scorn wars that are not preventive." He was called to the attention of American Senators considering American policy in the Far East by the well-read General Wedemeyer and ex-Secretary of Defense Louis Johnson.

Military Situation in the Far East, pp. 2566, 2693.

28. De Bello Gallico, I, 2.3; T. Mommsen, Römische Geschichte, pp. 802 ff.; Delbrück, Geschichte der Kriegskunst, II, 425 f. For similar preventive, and unjustified, attacks by Caesar on the Belgae in 57 B.C. and on German tribes on the lower Rhine in 56-55 B.C., for which he was severely censured by the Senate, see Mommsen, pp. 817 f. Cf. Plutarch, who praises Caesar for having engaged the Germans of Ariovistus rather "than to sit still and wait their time."

29. Suetonius, Julius Caesar, xxiv; Cicero, Offices, I, xi, xxiv. For Cicero's protest against preventive murder, see For M. Tullius, xxiv, 56.

30. For details, see Erdmann, Die Entstehung des Kreuzzugsgedankens, pp. 3 ff.

31. For the absence of inhibitions against preventive war in Moslem conquest, see Ranke, Weltgeschichte, VI, 104 ff.

32. For the defensive war theory in Byzantium, see Military Institutions of Emperor Leo III (680-740). A convenient text is in Liskenne and Sauvan, Bibliothèque historique et militaire, III, 453, 526, 540, 548.

33. Gibbon writes, with reference to a war between East Romans and Saracens in 717: "To prevent is safer, as well as more honorable, than to repel an attack," but that an "intended generous enterprise was defeated by the cowardice or treachery of the [Roman] troops." Gibbon, Decline and Fall of the Roman Empire, II, 793.

34. Richerus, Historiae, I, 8-11.

35. Erdmann, Die Entstehung des Kreuzzugsgedankens, pp. 107 f., 314.

36. For preventive actions of the Saracens against intended crusades (in 1011), see Ibid., p. 105.

37. Fuller, Historie of the Holy Warre, Book I, Chap. ix. According to OED, Fuller offers the first usage of "preventive war" in English. For a most recent discussion of "la guerre sainte et la croisade," see Journet, L'Eglise du verbe incarné.

38. Decembrio, Leben des Filippo Maria Visconti und Taten des Francesco Sforza, p. xxii.

39. Silvius, De rebus et gestis Friderici III (Geschichtsschreiber der deutschen Vorzeit, Vol. 88, 182 f.).

40. For details, see Hobohm, Machiavellis Renaissance der Kriegskunst, II, 6 f., 590 f.

41. Cited by Lagorgette in Le rôle de la guerre, p. 279.

42. Mesnard, L'Essor de la philosophie politique au XVIe siècle, pp. 105, 112, 117. Cf. Vitoria: "Unica est sola causa iusta in forendi bellum iniuria accepta."

43. Gentili, De Jure Belli, libri tres, Book I, chap. xiv. These quotations are from the

English translation of the 1612 edition by John Rolfe.

44. Bacon, "Of Empire," Essays of 1597, XIX.

45. Iblher, Vor der Entscheidung, pp. 125 ff. Lünig, Das teutsche Reichs-archiv, VI[1], 359 ff. In a way, the Swedish policy of prevention received its justification from Samuel Pufendorf in Elementa jurisprudentiae universalis of 1660 (Book II, §12) and De jure naturae et gentium of 1672 (Book II, c. V, §6).

46. 1635. Richelieu, Lettres et papiers d'Etat, VIII, 214. Cited by A. Sorel in L'Europe et la Revolution française, I, 59. For the approval of preventive wars by the publicists of Richelieu's day, as permissible wars which "must be considered just or unjust according to the profit or damage which the State may receive by their execution," see Albertini, Das politische Denken in Frankreich zur Zeit Richelieus, p. 179.

47. Richelieu, Testament politique, I, 33, 276; II, 76 and passim.

48. T. and D. Digges, Foure Paradoxes; or politique discourses (1604), pp. 96 ff.

49. Monk, Observations upon Military and Political Affairs (1671), pp. 8, 11.

50. See article on Thomas Fairfax in DNB.

51. Carlyle, Cromwell's Letters and Speeches, II, 151.

52. March 30, 1664. Pepys, Diary, IV, 93.

53. Cobbett, Parliamentary History, IV, col. 292.

54. Pepys, Diary, IV, 123.

55. Lord Lucas in House of Lords, February 22, 1670. Cobbett, Parliamentary History, IV, col. 475.

56. Lefèvre-Pontalis, Jean de Witt, II, 146.

57. Klopp, Der Fall des Hauses Stuart, I, 296.

58. A French magistrate of Richelieu's time claimed that "the person of the sovereigns enjoys a kind of divination, their prescience participating of the privilege of prophecies and the certitude of oracles." Vicomte d'Avenel, Richeleu et la monarchie absolue, I, 178. In 1654, Charles X Gustav of Sweden had the Great Elector told that "God did no longer speak to men through prophets or dreams; princes must now recognize, in the fortunate opportunities which He was offering them, His call." Droysen, Geschichte der preussischen Politik, III, 193.

59. Descartes, Oeuvres, IX, 387 f.; cited by Sorel in L'Europe et la Révolution française, I, 28.

60. Mignet, Négociations rélatives à la succession d'Espagne, I, 327.

61. Rousset, Histoire de Louvois, II, 18 f.

62. Mignet, Négociations rélatives à la succession d'Espagne, III, 318.

63. Ibid., III, 226.

64. Klopp, Der Fall des Hauses Stuart, IV, 70, 122.

65. Bourgeois, Ezechiel Spanheim, p. 366.

66. Text in Dumont, Corps universel diplomatique du droit des gens (1726), VII, 170.

67. Grimblot, Letters of William III and Louis XIV, I, 471.

68. "Argument shewing that a Standing Army, with consent of Parliament, is not inconsistent with a Free Government" (1698). Sutherland, Defoe, pp. 60 ff.

69. "The Danger of the Protestant Religion Consider'd" (1701). Ibid., pp. 65 f.

70. Cited by Horace Walpole in his Letters, VII, 207.

71. Les intérêts présens et les prétensions des puissances de l'Europe, I, 394. See also Meinecke, Die Idee der Staatsräson, pp. 320 ff.

72. Locke, Essay on Civil Government, §124

73. Barbier, Journal, II, 429.

74. To answer such questions, Frederick II had a pamphlet written and distributed in 1756 which dealt with the problem of the true aggressor and the right to undertake preventive war. Sybel and Schmoller (eds.), Preussische Staatsschriften, III, 437 ff.

75. This is based on Gundling's Ausführlicher über D. Io. Buddei Philosophiae, Part III, Die Politiae, p. 26, and his Ausführlicher Discours über das Natur- und Völker-Recht pp. 109 ff.

76. Vattel, Droit des gens (1758), cited by Lagorgette in Le rôle de la guerre, p. 279.

77. Cf. the following instruction to the French ambassador in Vienna in 1749: "The King having no other aim but the tranquillity of Europe on the basis of the Peace Treaty concluded at Aix-la-Chapelle (1748), desires nothing but to cement and make perfect this work in preventing and removing, in combination with other great powers, all that might start up again the fires of war." Recueil des instructions données aux ambassadeurs de France (Autriche), I, 286.

78. de Broglie, Le Secret du Roi, II, 83.

79. Meinecke, Die Idee der Staatsräson, pp. 358 f.

80. Voltaire to Frederick, May 15, 1749: "Il [Frederick] prévoit d'un oeil pénétrant,/ Il combine avec prud'hommie,/ Avec ardeur il entreprend;/ jamais sôt ne fut conquérant,/ Et pour vaincre il faut du génie." Briefwechsel Friedrichs des Grossen und Voltaire, II, 259.

81. Meinecke, Die Idee der Staatsräson, p. 361.

82. Ibid., p. 371; Berney, Friedrich der Grosse, p. 102.

83. Politische Correspondenz Friedrichs des Grossen, I, 222, 225.

84. To Prussian Minister at St. Petersburg, March 30 and May 3, 1744. Ibid., III, 118.

85. Ranke, Preussische Geschichte, III, 173 f.

86. Harcourt-Smith, Cardinal of Spain, pp. 211 ff.; Williams, Stanhope: A Study in Eighteenth Century War and Diplomacy, passim.

87. Ruville, William Pitt, I, 364 ff.
88. Lord Mansfield, leader of the House of Commons in the war-making Newcastle administration, confessed to the French ambassador in London twenty years later that the Government "made war at the time without wanting to, without being able to, but only because it believed at the time that France was determined to undertake it against England as much as the court of Vienna was resolved against that of Berlin; hence it was necessary to be ahead of her and thus assure to oneself from the outset successes fit to excite the minds and obtain ways to undertake it with advantage." Doniol, Histoire de la participation de la France à l'établissement des Etats-Unis, I, 223.
89. Sybel and Schmoller (eds.), Preussische Staatsschriften, III, 133; Politische Correspondenz Friedrichs des Grossen, XII, 119 f.
90. de Broglie, Secret du Roi, I, 162.
91. Politische Correspondenz Friedrichs des Grossen, XIII, 75, 104 ff.
92. For Winterfeldt, see Varnhagen, Leben des Generals Hans Karl von Winterfeldt, pp. 112 ff.
93. Arneth, Maria Theresias erste Regierungsjahre, IV, 484 f.
94. For a recent non-German conclusion as to Frederick's situation in 1756, see Butterfield, History and Human Relations, pp. 209 f. It is "clear that the conspiracy [of his three enemies] had been more dangerous than Frederick ever knew."
95. Williams, Carteret and Newcastle, pp. 211 f.
96. See Beust (ed.), "Observationes militares oder Kriegs-Anmerkungen," one of the early military periodicals, cited by Jähns, Geschichte der Kriegswissenschaften, p. 1465.
97. Cited by Rothfels in Clausewitz. Politik und Krieg, pp. 37 f.
98. Easum, Prince Henry of Prussia, p. 36; Hegemann, Fridericus, pp. 378 f.
99. Doniol, Histoire de la participation, I, 604, 609; II, 81, 286, 459, 464, 670 f., 804 f.; III, 161.
100. Mémoires sur Carnot. Par son fils. I, 36, 132 f.; II, 500 f.; Dupre, Lazare Carnot, pp. 32 f.
101. Kraus, Das Problem internationaler Ordnung bei Immanuel Kant, p. 36.
102. See Kant, "Mutmasslicher Anfang der Menschengeschichte," in Kleinere Schriften zur Geschichtsphilosophie, Ethik und Politik, p. 62.
103. Masson, Le département des Affaires étrangères pendant la Revolution, p. 130.
104. Michon, Robespierre et la guerre révolutionnaire, pp. 21, 36, 65, 98.
105. A. Sorel, L'Europe et la Révolution française, II, 361. Cf. I, 29 f.
106. "Il faut marcher les milliers d'hommes que nous avons sous les armes, aussi loin que les porterons leurs jambes, ou bien ils viendront nous couper la gorge" (Roland, 1792). Cited by Sorel, Ibid., III, 151.
107. Ibid. II, 362, 413.
108. Michon, Robespierre et la guerre révolutionnaire, pp. 38, 44, 52, 77.
109. Condorcet, Oeuvres, X, 455; Welt als Geschichte, II (1936), 60 f.
110. La vie et les mémoires du Général Dumouriez, II, 217 f., 222.
111. Dumouriez, Nouveau tableau spéculatif de l'Europe, p. 74.
112. Text of the French note in Revue de Génève (1921), pp. 147 f.
113. Derrécagaix, Le Maréchal Berthier, II, 25; Correspondance de Napoléon, XI, 97; A. Sorel, L'Europe et la Révolution française, VI, 440 ff., 452.
114. Mémoires du Chancelier Pasquier, I, 291.
115. Berthezène, Souvenirs militaires de la Republique et de l'Empire, I, 298 f., 308.
116. Las Cases, Memorial de Sainte-Hélène, III, 155.
117. Berenhorst, Betrachtungen über die Kriegskunst, pp. 550 f.
118. Ranke, Denkwürdigkeiten Hardenbergs, I, 392.
119. Memoire for Archduke John, September 4, 1804. Fournier, Gentz und Cobenzl, pp. 282 f.
120. Bryant, The Years of Endurance, p. 263, citing the sentiment expressed in Lloyd's Evening Post (August 1798) on preventive war: "To avert by anticipation a meditated blow where destruction would follow its infliction is surely justifiable."
121. Speech on Expedition to Copenhagen, February 3, 1808. Canning, Select Speeches, pp. 63 f.
122. Desbrière, Projets et tentative de débarquements aux Iles britanniques, IV, 248 ff.
123. A. Sorel, L'Europe et la Révolution française, VI, 266, 290, 295; Bryant, Years of Victory, p. 34.
124. Ponsonby's motion relative to the Copenhagen expedition, February 3, 1808.
125. After the event, Canning wrote to a British diplomat: "I know you will approve of the operations off Copenhagen, by which a Northern Confederacy, an invasion of Ireland, and the shutting of the Russian ports have been prevented." Bagot (ed.), George Canning and his Friends, I, 234. For a recent discussion of "Copenhagening," see article by A. N. Ryan in English Historical Review, January 1953, No. 166.
126. Trevelyan, British History in the Nineteenth Century, p. 120.
127. Canning, Select Speeches, p. 67.

128. Diaries and Correspondence of the First Earl of Malmesbury, IV, 397.
129. Bryant, Years of Victory, pp. 200 f.
130. The Austrian Ambassador to London, Starhemberg, cited by Butterfield in The Peace Tactics of Napoleon, p. 325.
131. Martens, Précis du droit des gens moderne de l'Europe, Book III, chap. iii, §265.
132. Encyclopädie der Staatswissenschaften, p. 454. For the mid-century viewpoint, see the article "Guerre" in Block, Dictionnaire de la politique.
133. For a pre-1914 formulation of the outlawing of preventive war by constitutional means and its possible military disadvantages (though not the moral advantages), cf. the following by a French writer: "The true aggressor, who assumes the responsibility for the rupture of peace, is not the one who declares war or invades enemy territory; it is the one whose policy makes the war inevitable. That one of two peoples which, when it is provoked or threatened in its existence, anticipates by carrying the war beyond its frontiers, makes proof of its wisdom: it puts the lucky chances on its own side by getting hold of the ascendency, and draws the neutral countries into its interest. I know very well that we cannot act that way, tied down as we are by the terms of our constitution." Bapst, Le Maréchal Canrobert, VI, 599.
134. Nicolay and Hay (eds.), Complete Works of Abraham Lincoln, I, 351 ff.; II, 1 ff.
135. Stamp, And the War Came, pp. 259 ff.
136. Mehmet Ali of Egypt went to war against the Sultan in 1838 in order not to allow Turkish army reforms to go too far and endanger his own military superiority. Encyclopedia Britannica (11th ed.), XVIII, 80.
137. Gossler, "Das Praevenire," Deutsche Revue, Vol. 39 (June 1914), 257 ff.
138. Diaries of John Bright, pp. 238 f.
139. Martin, The Triumph of Lord Palmerston, pp. 217 f.
140. R. L. Lord in American Historical Review, XXIX, 47. In 1862, Moltke proposed that Prussia undertake a war in the preventive style of Frederick the Great against Austria, France and Bavaria. Görlitz, Der deutsche Generalstab, p. 107.
141. Meyer, Bismarck, pp. 285 f.; Kohl (ed.), Kaiser Wilhelm I und Bismarck, pp. 136 ff.
142. In 1917, the foremost church historian of German Protestantism, Karl Holl, wrote that "after 1870 Bismarck has tirelessly striven to prevent the warlike collision by a fair consideration of the vital necessities of other States. For this very reason he was a declared opponent of preventive war."

Holl, Gesammelte Aufsätze zur Kirchengeschichte, III, 156.
143. Srbik (ed.), Quellen zur deutschen Politik Oesterreichs, V^1, 179.
144. Ziekursch, Politische Geschichte des neuen deutschen Kaiserreichs, I, 149.
145. December 23, 1867. de La Tour, Le maréchal Niel, p. 262.
146. Ollivier, L'Empire libéral, X, 290 f.
147. Delbrück-Daniels, Geschichte der Kriegskunst, VI, 30.
148. Moltke, Gesammelte Schriften, V, 297; Aus dem Leben Theodor von Bernhardis, VII, 358.
149. Ritter, Lebendige Vergangenheit, p. 124.
150. Meyer, Bismarck, p. 356.
151. Schweinitz, Denkwürdigkeiten, I, 249.
152. Ziekursch, Politische Geschichte des neuen deutschen Kaiserreichs, I, 309. The Goncourts noted that "when France begins to feel something like fighting the city police, the government, whatever its nature may be, if it is intelligent, must make her battle the foreigner." August 6, 1869. Journal des Goncourt, III, 227.
153. Clark, "Bismarck, Russia and the War of 1870," Journal of Modern History, XIV, 202.
154. G. P., I, 37; Waldersee, Denkwürdigkeiten, I, 139.
155. G. P., I, 63.
156. Taffs, Ambassador to Bismarck, pp. 8 f.; Görlitz, Generalstab, p. 129.
157. December 12, 1873. Journal des Goncourt, V, 98.
158. Eyck, Bismarck, III, 156.
159. G. P., I, 146.
160. February 7, 1875. Journal des Goncourt, V, 181.
161. January 23, 1874. G. P., I, 147.
162. Ibid., I, 137.
163. Ibid., I, 155 f.; Slavonic Review, IX, 343.
164. G. P., I, 159.
165. Cited in Neues Tagebuch, October 22, 1938.
166. Except for the continued rearming of the German infantry with the Mauser rifle (since 1873), there was no considerable military measure under way at the time. The assertion of the Russian Chief of Staff, Obrutchev, in August 1892, during the negotiation of the Franco-Russian military convention, that in 1875 the Germans had called reservists to the colors by individual orders and had thus practically mobilized without an order of mobilization, seems to be without foundation. Doc. dipl. fr., 1st series, IX, 660.
167. Wemyss, Memoirs of Sir Robert Morier, II, 337.
168. Bamberger, Bismarcks grosses Spiel, pp. 310 f.
169. Treitschke, Briefe, III, 414.

170. Taffs, Ambassador to Bismarck, pp. 634 f.
171. This is the thesis of the most recent Bismarck biography. Eyck, Bismarck, III, 167 f., 176 f. It was the view for which only Austrian diplomacy showed some understanding in 1875. Wertheimer, Andrassy, II, 240.
172. The Letters of Queen Victoria, 2nd series, II, 389.
173. Kohl (ed.), Wilhelm I und Bismarck, pp. 256 ff.
174. Slavonic Review, IX, 641.
175. The following titles may be mentioned from the ample literature on the "war-in-sight" episode: Gavard, "L'Alerte de 1875," Le Correspondant, November 10, 1893; Herzfeld, Die deutsch-fränzosische Gefahr von 1875; Trützschler, "Bismarcks Stellung zum Präventivkrieg," Europäische Gespräche, I, 185 ff.; Lajusan, "L'Alerte diplomatique du printemps 1875," Revue d'histoire moderne, I, 368 ff.; Noack, Balkanproblem und Präventivkrieg unter dem Fürsten Bismarck; Taffs, "The War Scare of 1875," Slavonic Review, IX, 335 ff., 632 ff., and his Ambassador to Bismarck, chap. v.
176. G. P., I, pp. 189 f.
177. To Lucius von Ballhausen. Bismarck, Gesammelte Werke, VIII, 120.
178. When excitement over the Skobolev affair misled the press into asserting that Bismarck was preparing an attack on Russia, the British ambassador in Berlin remained convinced that "nothing could be more contrary to the truth. Bismarck wants peace and wants to prevent war." Annual Report of the American Historical Association (1942), II, 256.
179. February 1887. G. P., VI, 1249.
180. Ibid., VI, 1152 f., 1168.
181. Ibid., VI, 1175.
182. Ibid., VI, 1163-65.
183. Schweinitz, Denkwürdigkeiten, II, 350 ff.
184. Waldersee, Denkwürdigkeiten, I, 263.
185. For the diplomats, see Ziekursch, Politische Geschichte des neuen deutschen Kaiserreichs, II, 208.
186. Treitschke, Briefe, III, 587.
187. Waldersee, Denkwürdigkeiten, I, 311.
188. December 27, 1887. G. P., VI, 1186.
189. Zur europäischen Politik (Belgian Documents), V, 166 ff.
190. G. P., VI, 1193.
191. May 1888. Ibid., VI, 1339-41. Bismarck, Gedanken und Erinnerungen, III, 135 ff.; Waldersee, Denkwürdigkeiten, I, 395.
192. Cited by Hegemann, Fridericus, p. 100; Bismarck, Gedanken und Erinnerungen, III, 121 ff.
193. Meyer, Bismarck, p. 679.
194. Ziekursch, Politische Geschichte des neuen deutschen Kaiserreichs, II, 430; Bismarck, Gedanken und Erinnerungen, II, 114, 202 f., 205, 258, 296.
195. A Pan-German brochure of 1900 declared that "Bismarck's weak-loined shying from preventive wars is a personal senile phenomenon." Cited by Oncken in Das alte und das neue Mitteleuropa, p. 56.
196. Nietzsche, Wille zur Macht, pp. 92, 95 f., 137, 688; for Galiani, see supra p. 263.
197. G. P., VII, 1566.
198. In February 1892, at the time of a Russian hunger epidemic, Secretary of State Marschall told the Belgian minister to Berlin that nothing would disturb the peaceful policy of the Central Powers as long as Russia had not emerged from her state of distress. A ranking officer had recently told the Tsar that it was impossible to mobilize the Russian Army at that time. In St. Petersburg, they imagined that Germany intended to profit from Russia's misfortune and provoke a war, prepared for the spring. This was only proof of their bad conscience. "Germany would never undertake a prophylactic war. Besides, she had nothing to gain from victories." Zur europäischen Politik (Belgian Documents), V, 112 f.
199. Freycinet, Souvenirs, p. 414.
200. Waldersee, Denkwürdigkeiten, I, 388; II, 219, 236.
201. At the end of 1908, William II thought that, considering the unfinished state of Russian rearmament, "it would, from a military standpoint, be the best moment for us to settle accounts with the Russians" and to strike preventively as Frederick had done in 1756. G. P., XXVI, 9149, 9152.
202. To Spring Rice, August 13, 1897. Gwynn, Spring Rice, I, 228.
203. G. P., XIX, 6149 ff.
204. For the context of Schlieffen's plans and Holstein's urge for war, see Rassow, "Schlieffen und Holstein," Historische Zeitschrift, Vol. 173, 297 ff.
205. Lancken-Wakenitz, Meine dreissig Dienstjahre, p. 65.
206. G. P., XXI, 7340.
207. Doc. dipl. fr., 2nd series, VIII, 377.
208. Hammann, Bilder aus der letzten Kaiserzeit, p. 45.
209. Süddeutsche Monatshefte, March 1921.
210. Freytag-Loringhoven, Graf Schlieffen, p. 141.
211. Rochs, Schlieffen, pp. 67 f.; Bauer, Der grosse Krieg in Feld und Heimat, pp. 4, 76 f.; Der Weltkrieg. Kriegsrüstung und Kriegswirtschaft (Reichsarchiv), I, 79.
212. Lancken-Wakenitz, Meine dreissig Dienstjahre, p. 57; Foerster, Schlieffen und der Weltkrieg, I, 23.

213. For Schlieffen's reactionary political views, see Oldenburg-Januschau, Erinnerungen, pp. 111 and passim.

214. Wissen und Wehr (1939), p. 18. The idea of violating Belgian neutrality had been taken for granted since the 1890's.

215. Görlitz, Generalstab, p. 181.

216. Nevins, Henry White, p. 324; Zedlitz-Trützschler, Zwölf Jahre am deutschen Kaiserhof, p. 173; Faramond, Souvenirs d'un attaché naval, p. 101; Einem, Erinnerungen eines Soldaten, pp. 110 ff.

217. Oldenburg-Januschau, Erinnerungen, pp. 121 ff.

218. Doc. dipl. fr., 2nd series, VIII, 388.

219. Eisenhart Rothe, Im Banne der Persönlichkeit, pp. 40 ff. See also Gröner, Das Testament des Grafen Schlieffen, pp. 5 f. and passim.

220. See Bernhardi, Germany and the Next War, chap. ii, "The Duty to Make War."

221. For the motivation of Napoleon's intervention in Mexico as a preventive measure against later actions of the United States, see Vagts, Mexico, Europa und Amerika, p. 89.

222. G. P., XIX, 6140.

223. Nevins, Henry White, pp. 257 f.

224. G. P., XXIV, 8215; XXVIII, 10371.

225. Dugdale, Balfour, II, 78.

226. As a lawyer in complete ignorance of German governing habits and in search of incriminating evidence, Justice Jackson, in building up first the International Tribunal to sit in Nuremberg and then the case of the prosecution, was surprised at the vast amount of incriminating material in the captured German documents. As he told the jurists who were preparing the statute for the Tribunal together with him: "I did not think men would ever be so foolish as to put in writing some of the things the Germans did put in writing." International Conference on Military Trials, p. 211.

227. 1887. Letters of Queen Victoria, 3rd series, I, 268; Cecil, Life of Salisbury, IV, 21.

228. G. P., VII, 1450.

229. B. D., II, 287; G. P., VII, 1451.

230. Europäische Gespräche, IX, 298.

231. G. P., XVI, 4826.

232. B. D., II, Nos. 116 and 294.

233. Cf. statement by Sumner Welles for FDR, on April 27, 1938, at a time when the Russians tried to have a super-Dreadnought built in American shipyards. Since the vessel was to be based on Vladivostock, Welles thought that "its construction might even encourage Japan to attack and capture Vladivostock before the completion of the ship, so as to prevent it from being based on a port sufficiently near to threaten Japan." U. S. Foreign Relations. The Soviet Union, 1933-1939, p. 684. For Ambassador Grew, see p. 321.

234. Roosevelt-Lodge Correspondence, II, 409.

235. Poincaré, Au service de la France, I, 227.

236. Renouvin in Coville and Temperley (eds.), Studies in Anglo-French History, pp. 161, 163; Joffre, Mémoires, I, 125 f.; Doc. dipl. fr., 3rd series, V, No. 53. For French intentions to march through Belgium during the 1890's, see Europäische Gespräche, X, 80.

237. Encyclopedia Britannica (13th ed.), III, 1035.

238. Bacon, Fisher, II, 76.

239. Treitschke, Briefe, III, 421, 426.

240. Macdiarmid, The Life of Lt. Gen. Sir James Moncrieff Grierson, pp. 101 ff., 132 f.

241. Marder, The Anatomy of British Sea Power, pp. 231, 325.

242. Ibid., pp. 331 f.

243. For William II, see G. P., XIV, 3913, 3916.

244. Ibid., XIV, 3927.

245. Waldersee, Denkwürdigkeiten, II, 425.

246. Vagts, Deutschland und die Vereinigten Staaten, p. 1968.

247. Marder, The Anatomy of British Sea Power, p. 342.

248. G. P., XIX, 6154.

249. Ibid., XIX, 6126, 6149 ff.; Marder, The Anatomy of British Sea Power, pp. 496 ff.; Bülow, Denkwürdigkeiten, II, 66 ff., 79 f.

250. G. P., XXIII, p. 45.

251. The best treatment of the episode is in Europäische Gespräche, X, 185 ff.; see also Hallgarten, Imperialismus vor 1914, I, 497.

252. Cited by Bülow in Deutsche Politik, p. 35.

253. G. P., XIX, 6287 f.

254. Bacon, Fisher, II, 81 f.

255. G. P., XIX, 6249; XX, 6887; XXIV, 8212, 8215.

256. Marder, The Anatomy of British Sea Power, pp. 498 f.

257. Bacon, Fisher, II, 74 f.; Harris, Spender, p. 123.

258. Report of French military attaché in London, November 9, 1908. Doc. dipl. fr., 2nd series, XI, 933.

259. G. P., XXVIII, 10235, 10242, 10244, 10247 f., 10251.

260. Ibid., XXXI, 11549.

261. Callwell, Sir Henry Wilson, I, 103.

262. A big business man in Germany who conceived Anglo-German competition in more violent terms than most others told the Prussian minister of war in November 1911: "If we have another hundred years of peace, we shall have killed England." The general asked whether he believed England would wait patiently those hundred years. The World War was a clear answer. Stein, Erlebnisse, p. 122.

263. In his pamphlet, England und Wir (1912).

Reprinted in Rathenau, Gesammelte Schriften, Vol. I.

264. In April 1914, Chancellor Bethmann Hollweg spoke in favor of "a policy without war" and about the dangers of a preventive war. Germany's national wealth was increasing so rapidly that she would overtake all other nations within ten to fifteen years. "Then our position in world policy, which in the final re-result is economic policy, would be secure. Our task would be to wind our way through this period without great conflicts." Tirpitz, Erinnerungen, p. 233.

265. Glaise-Horstenau, Franz Josephs Weggefährte, p. 186.

266. Ibid., p. 282.

267. Ibid., pp. 297 ff., 310.

268. G. P., VI, 1184-85, 1190-97; Glaise-Horstenau, Franz Josephs Weggefährte, pp. 312 ff.

269. In addition to his voluminous memoirs, Aus meiner Dienstzeit, other literature about Conrad includes: Pribram, The Secret Treaties of Austria-Hungary, II, 144, 156 ff.; Kern, "Conrad und Berchtold" in Europäische Gespräche, II, 97 ff., and the same author's "Die südslawische Frage und die Wiener Kriegspartei" in Schmoller's Jahrbuch, Vol. 48; Urbanski, "Conrad und der Präventivkrieg gegen Italien" in Berliner Monatshefte, March 1930.

270. Conrad, Aus meiner Dienstzeit, I, 13.

271. Ibid., I, 63 f., 509 f.; Giesl, Zwei Jahrzehnte im Nahen Orient, p. 190.

272. G. Conrad, Mein Leben mit Conrad von Hötzendorf, p. 66. A psychological interpretation of history can easily find a definite personal motivation in Conrad's proposals for war. He was deeply in love with a woman whom he could hope to marry only if he should return victoriously from a war, as he wrote her in December 1908. "But what if things go differently and drag on in a vile peace...." Ibid., p. 31.

273. G. P., XXVI, 9156, 9160.

274. Ibid., XXI, 7169 f.

275. January 21, 1909. Conrad, Aus meiner Dienstzeit, I, 142.

276. The more innocent explanation is that Moltke wanted at the time to encourage the weaker alliance partner and to make him maintain a heroic attitude, possibly leading to further Austrian armaments, which were in the German interest, while at the same time he expressed in his office the hope that Austria would not provoke Serbia too much and would give Russia no excuse for active interference. Schäfer, "Wollte Moltke den Präventivkrieg?" in Berliner Monatshefte V (1927), 545 f.

277. Conrad, Aus meiner Dienstzeit, I, 165.

278. See the polemics on this between Schäfer and Lutz in Berliner Monatshefte V (1927), 543 ff., 1107 ff., 1120 ff.

279. Oesterreich-Ungarns Aussenpolitik, I, 947. According to Veit Valentin, Italian mobilization orders had been prepared when the Messina catastrophe occurred, necessitating their cancellation. Valentin, Deutschlands Aussenpolitik, pp. 84 f.

280. Conrad, Aus meiner Dienstzeit, I, 148.

281. Ibid., I, 161 f., 253.

282. Ibid., II, 172 ff.; Oesterreich-Ungarns Aussenpolitik, III, 2644, 2890.

283. November 15, 1911. Conrad, Aus meiner Dienstzeit, II, 282.

284. Glaise-Horstenau in Die grossen Deutschen, V, 509.

285. Bülow, Denkwürdigkeiten, III, 363.

286. Belgian reports from Vienna, November 24 and December 16, 1912, and from St. Petersburg, December 16, 1912. Zur europäischen Politik, IV, 101, 110, 113.

287. December 16, 1912. Conrad, Aus meiner Dienstzeit, II, 395 f.

288. Ibid., II, 397.

289. Oesterreich-Ungarns Aussenpolitik, V, 5059.

290. Conrad, Aus meiner Dienstzeit, III, 19 f.

291. Ibid., III, 127; G. P., XXXIV, 12788.

292. For details, see Fay, The Origins of the World War, I, 448 ff.

293. Protocol of Ministerial Council, October 3, 1912. Oesterreich-Ungarns Aussenpolitik, VII, 8779.

294. Oesterreich-Ungarns letzter Krieg, I, 41.

295. Conrad, Aus meiner Dienstzeit, III, 442 ff.

296. Oesterreich-Ungarns Aussenpolitik, VII, 9096.

297. Ibid., VII, 9463; Fay, The Origins of the World War, I, 491 f.

298. B. D., XI, 172 f.

299. Paléologue, Journal de 1913-1914, p. 111.

300. Danilov, La Russie dans la guerre mondiale, p. 26.

301. Oesterreich-Ungarns Aussenpolitik, VII, 9213.

302. An unsatisfactory monograph on this problem is by Kloster, Der deutsche Generalstab und der Präventivkriegsgedanke, pp. 13 ff.

303. In 1907, one of the commanding French generals, Baillard, declared in a public speech that war between France and Germany was unavoidable; when he was transferred shortly thereafter, it was stated that this was not done with punitive intention. Valentin, Deutschlands Aussenpolitik, p. 95.

304. Berliner Monatshefte V (1927), 395 ff., 407.

305. Bernhardi, Germany and the Next War, pp. 279 f.

306. "What is official Britain waging but a preventive war?" Morel, Truth and the War, p. 57.

307. Judet, George Louis, p. 299, quoting Paul Deschanel. See also Ziekursch, Politische Geschichte des neuen deutschen Kaiserreichs, III, 255.

308. Siebert, Schriftwechsel Benckendorffs, III, 118.

309. Chastenet, La France de M. Fallières, p. 361.

310. Beyens, Deux années à Berlin, II, 33 ff.

311. Ibid., II, 144, 183; Zur europäischen Politik (Belgian Documents) IV, 183 ff.

312. Beyens, Deux années à Berlin, II, 267, citing also Lerchenfeld's letter of July 31. Deutsche Dokumente zum Kriegsausbruch, IV, 151.

313. Beyens, Deux années à Berlin, II, 270. The ultimatum to Belgium had been drafted by Moltke as early as July 26. It presumed a French intention to advance against Germany through Belgium, which would be unable to resist this invasion. This made it "a dictate of self-preservation for Germany to anticipate the hostile attack." Deutsche Dokumente zum Kriegsausbruch, II, 376.

314. Bülow, Denkwürdigkeiten, III, 160 ff.

315. Kautsky, Sozialisten und Krieg, p. 434.

316. Shub, Lenin, p. 129.

317. Potiemkine, Histoire de la diplomatie, II, 264.

318. Shub, Lenin, pp. 134 f.

319. Ibid., p. 192. For the Pan-Slavist accusation that the Central Powers had started the preventive war against Russia, see Slavonic Review, VI, 287.

320. Beaverbrook, Politicians and the War, I, 34 f.

321. Count Lerchenfeld to Bavarian Prime Minister, July 31. Deutsche Dokumente zum Kriegsausbruch, IV, 151.

322. July 29. Dirr, Bayerische Dokumente zum Kriegsausbruch, p. 221; Fay, The Origins of the World War, II, 497 f.

323. The following is a retrospective statement from these circles: "We ourselves had the firm intention to avoid a preventive war under any condition. A light-hearted preventive war is certainly a crime. But whether its rejection as a matter of principle is right must be doubted. In any case, it was illogical to allow Austria-Hungary the possibility of starting such a war." Gleich, Vom Balkan nach Bagdad, p. 16.

324. Tirpitz, Ohnmachtspolitik, p. 64.

325. Conrad, Aus meiner Dienstzeit, IV, 79; Fay, The Origins of the World War, II, 218, 221 f.

326. Oesterreich-Ungarns Aussenpolitik, VIII, 9966. Naumann later testified that neither Stumm nor his superiors, Jagow and Bethmann, would ever advocate a preventive war, even in the light of the ever increasing Russian armaments. Valentin, Deutschlands Aussenpolitik, p. 164.

327. Die internationalen Beziehungen, 1st series, V, 350. Cf. Deutsche Dokumente zum Kriegsausbruch, I, Nos. 84, 105, 132 f., for the reprimand directed at the Crown Prince for his inflammatory statements.

328. Conrad, Aus meiner Dienstzeit, IV, 79.

329. Oesterreich-Ungarns Aussenpolitik, VIII, 10124.

330. July 29, 1914. Ibid., VIII, 10991.

331. Conrad, Aus meiner Dienstzeit, IV, 31 f.

332. Ibid., IV, 124.

333. Protocol of Ministerial Council, July 7, 1914. Oesterreich-Ungarns Aussenpolitik, VIII, 10118.

334. Die internationalen Beziehungen, 2nd series, VIII, 540 f., 709.

335. Beard, Rise of American Civilization, II, 612. Similarly, Lansing, War Memoirs, p. 103; and Houston, Eight Years with Wilson's Cabinet, I, 236 f.

336. Bertie, Diaries, II, 316.

337. Bailey, Wilson and the Peacemakers, p. 14. The U-boat argument showed its weakness when the Paris Peace Conference did practically nothing to remove this presumable cause of war.

338. Ralph Barton Perry, The Free Man and the Soldier (1916).

339. Early in 1922, Curzon had declined a security treaty under which France would have been given the right "to forestall the danger of indirect German aggression." Nicolson, Curzon, pp. 241 f.

340. Gamelin, Servir, II, 26.

341. Rabenau, Seeckt, I, 330.

342. Resolutions of the Sixth Congress of the Third International, Moscow, August 1928. Cited in Revue des deux mondes, May 15, 1929, pp. 268 f.

343. Dr. Vaclav Lipinski, Polish ambassador to Berlin and editor of Pilsudski's Erinnerungen und Dokumente, cited by Wollenberg in The Red Army, pp. 121 f. See also Goul, Toukhatchevsky, Maréchal Rouge, pp. 156 f.

344. Visconti-Prasca, La guerra decisiva (1933); Douhet, Il dominio dell'aria (1921). For the opposition of the elder generation of German military commanders to the Douhet doctrine, see Trials of War Criminals, X, 530.

345. "Reichswehr und deutsche Politik" in Nationalsozialistische Monatshefte, June 1930, reprinted in Militärwissenschaftliche Rundschau, 1944, No. 1, for purposes of morale-building.

346. Czechoslovak report from Warsaw, March 10, 1933. Europäische Politik im Spiegel der Prager Akten, p. 24.

347. Pertinax, Les Fossoyeurs, II, 89.

348. Ambassador Dodd's Diary, p. 74, entries of

January 22 and March 2, 1934. In the Sénat Lemery cried out: "La guerre préventive, mais nul n'y songe et le mot seul nous fait horreur" (January 12, 1934). Wolfers, Britain and France between Two Wars, p. 60.

349. Documents on German Foreign Policy, Series D, II, 568.

350. Europäische Politik, p. 73.

351. Brüning, "Ein Brief" in Deutsche Rundschau, July 1947. A very recent discussion of Pilsudski's preventive war ideas against Nazi Germany—"The Rise, Spread and Refutation of a Legend"—concludes that there were no serious intentions of that kind in Poland. Celovsky in Welt als Geschichte, XIV (1954), 52 ff.

352. Report of Polish military attaché in Lisbon, August 8, 1938. Drittes Weissbuch der deutschen Regierung. Polnische Dokumente zur Vorgeschichte des Krieges, No. 2.

353. Günther, Der Herren eigner Geist, p. 49.

354. Churchill, The Second World War, I, pp. 5, 112, 177 f.

355. Hull, Memoirs, I, 383 f.

356. Cited by Feiling in Chamberlain, p. 261.

357. Potiemkine, Histoire de la diplomatie, III, 574; Churchill, While England Slept, p. 255.

358. Statement of Henry Berenger, chairman of the French Senate Foreign Affairs Committee. N.Y. Times, November 18, 1938.

359. Pertinax, Les Fossoyeurs, II, 99 f.

360. Roosevelt's speech in Chicago on October 5, 1937.

361. From 1936 on, French diplomacy was instructed to ignore all Russian hints of a preventive war against Germany. Coulondre, De Staline à Hitler, pp. 13, 20 f., 30, 32, 47.

362. Jünger, Krieg und Krieger, p. 58.

363. General Taysen in Franke (ed.), Handbuch der neuzeitlichen Wehrwissenschaften, I, 173. Cf. Farago (ed.), The Axis Grand Strategy, pp. 23 f.

364. Görlitz, Generalstab, pp. 410 f.

365. Nazi Conspiracy and Aggression, III, 295 ff.; Trials of War Criminals, X, 490 f.

366. Text in Neuer Vorwärts, October 10, 1937.

367. Trial of the Major War Criminals, XXV, 403 ff.

368. April 22, 1938. Ibid., XXV, 416 f.

369. At a ceremony at the tomb of Dollfuss' assassins, Hess declared that "there is no longer any possibility for other powers to march into Germany; now, the other powers rather fear that Germany might march into their territory." Neuer Vorwärts, April 17, 1938.

370. June 18, 1938. Trial of the Major War Criminals, XXV, 445.

371. July 31, 1938. Documents on German Foreign Policy, 1918-1945, Series D, II, 568.

372. Pertinax, Les Fossoyeurs, I, 9 ff.

373. Keitel at the Nuremberg Trials. Trial of the Major War Criminals, XXXIX, 14.

374. Ritter, Lebendige Vergangenheit, pp. 343 f. (in a lecture of 1941).

375. Report of chargé d'affaires in Washington, September 12, 1938. Documents on German Foreign Policy, Series D, I, 727, 730.

376. Neues Tagebuch, October 22, 1938.

377. Trial of the Major War Criminals, XXVI, 338 f.; Nazi Conspiracy and Aggression, VII, 754.

378. Trial of the Major War Criminals, XXVI, 327 ff.

379. Westphal, Heer in Fesseln, pp. 121 f.

380. Trial of the Major War Criminals, XXXV, 537 ff.

381. Admiral Darlan later told the Germans, as well as Ambassador-Admiral Leahy (see Leahy, I Was There, p. 12) that in December 1939 and again seven weeks before the German invasion of Norway, he had proposed to the British Admiralty "to occupy Narvik and Trondheim which at that time would have been possible with weak forces." But they proved "hopelessly inefficient and unreliable ...unable to get approval of the operation until it was too late." Martienssen, Hitler and His Admirals, pp. 246 f.

382. Trials of War Criminals, X, 356 f., 750 ff., 783 ff.

383. Churchill, The Second World War, I, pp. 421 ff., 474 f.

384. Schuman, Night Over Europe, p. 409. According to H. G. Wells, there was "much to be said for the preventive security measures being taken by the Soviet Government. I see no reason for blaming Russia." The Russians had admitted a certain amount of preventive motivation in their attack on Finland. Molotov stated in a radio address (on November 30) that "inasmuch as further provocations could be expected from the Finnish regime and militarists, the Soviet Union had come to the conclusion that it could no longer maintain normal relations with the Finnish Government,"—that is to say, it was going to war. U.S. Foreign Relations. The Soviet Union, 1933-1939, p. 797.

385. Gamelin, Servir, III, 195, 199, 317. On April 9, when the Germans landed in Norway, he proposed to act against them by way of Belgium.

386. Churchill, The Second World War, I, pp. 442 f.; Gamelin, Servir, III, 201.

387. This was similar to the directives (issued on March 1) for "Fall Weserübung," the code word for the Norway expedition. Martienssen, Hitler and His Admirals, p. 50.

388. Gamelin, Servir, III, 297. Gamelin's version of plans and events would make it seem that all Allied preparations and action depended on the German steps that might follow the British mining of the Norwegian Leads. I have found no documentary evidence for the statement that the Western Allies postponed their own embarkments from the 5th to the 8th of April, when they concluded from the concentrations of German shipping that the Nazis entertained intentions similar to their own, "in the hope that they could leave the lead to the Germans in the violation of Norwegian neutrality." Görlitz, Der zweite Weltkrieg, p. 108.

389. Nazi Conspiracy and Aggression, Suppl. B, 647 ff.; Gamelin, Servir, III, 317; Trials of War Criminals, X, 772 ff.

390. Documentation from the Allied side is still very unsatisfactory as to exact intentions against Norway and Sweden. The most searching examination of the Allies' case is in Hankey, Politics, Trials and Errors, pp. 6 ff., 70 ff., and in Derry, The Campaign in Norway. See also Skodvin, "German and British-French Plans for Operations in Scandinavia," Norseman, December 1951.

391. Gamelin was told this by General Ironside. Gamelin, Servir, III, 304.

392. Nazi Conspiracy and Aggression, Suppl. B., 639 ff., 1536 ff.

393. Martienssen, Hitler and His Admirals, pp. 53 f.; Trials of War Criminals, X, 766.

394. Nazi Conspiracy and Aggression, VIII, 410 ff. Text of German ultimatum to Denmark and Norway.

395. Trial of Major War Criminals, XXXV, 200 ff.; Nazi Conspiracy and Aggression, Suppl. B, 649; Britain's Designs on Norway. Selections from the Fourth German White Book (1940).

396. Statement of the Defense for Jodl, Nazi Conspiracy and Aggression, Suppl. B, 768. · Answering the query of the Defense in one of the minor war criminals trials whether he, in March-April 1940, was "under the impression that this operation was a justified preventive measure," Admiral Schniewind answered: "Yes, I had that impression at the time, and even today it is my opinion that this operation was militarily necessary and justified." Trials of War Criminals, X, 797.

397. It seems that the Germans had no intentions of landing on Iceland. At least none were brought out by the prosecution at Nuremberg.

398. Hankey, Politics, Trials and Errors, pp. 14 f.

399. Trial of Major War Criminals, XXVI, 327 ff.; IX, 318 ff.; Trials of War Criminals, X, 21, 177; Nazi Conspiracy and Aggression, Suppl. B., 756.

400. Dokumente zur Kriegsausweitungspolitik der Westmächte, Fifth German White Book.

401. The Dutch Minister to Washington stated, on April 17, that his Government "will not admit any preventive protection for any part of the country, from whatever side it may be proposed." Schuman, Night Over Europe, p. 483.

402. May 4, 1940. Ciano Diaries, p. 243.

403. Trial of Major War Criminals, X, 456 f.; XI, 218; XVIII, 402.

404. Britain's Designs on Norway, p. 35.

405. Kris and Speier, German Radio Propaganda, pp. 83, 289 ff.

406. The Greek White Book (1942), pp. 109, 113.

407. Schuman, Soviet Politics, p. 405.

408. Directive of November 12, 1940. Trials of War Criminals, X, 23.

409. Ibid., X, 25.

410. Ibid., X, 998.

411. Early in June 1941, the ambassador in Moscow still reported that Russia "will only fight if attacked by Germany... All military preparations have been made quietly—as far as can be recognized, only defensive." Ibid., X, 109.

412. May 18, 1942. Hitlers Tischgespräche, p. 155.

413. Görlitz, Der zweite Weltkrieg, I, 268.

414. AP dispatch from Berlin, June 29 and October 9, 1941.

415. "Winterhilfe" speech of October 3, 1941. N.Y.Times, October 4, 1941.

416. Article in "Das Reich," translated in N.Y. Times, November 7 and 10, 1941.

417. Trial of Major War Criminals, XV, 394 f.

418. Ibid., XXXIX, 14; N.Y. Times, August 15, 1946; Nazi Conspiracy and Aggression, IV, 594.

419. N.Y. Times, August 11, 1946.

420. Trials of War Criminals, X, 1014 ff., 1023 f., 1037.

421. Ibid., X, 1039.

422. Görlitz, Der zweite Weltkrieg, I, 206; Trials of War Criminals, X, 1011 ff.; XII, 1307, 1312.

423. Trial of Major War Criminals, X, 112.

424. Ibid., XV, 393; XXXIV, 710 and passim; Nazi Conspiracy and Aggression, Suppl. B, 653.

425. Trial of Major War Criminals, XV, 342 ff. Nazi Conspiracy and Aggression, Suppl. B, 760 f.

426. December 12, 1944. Heusinger, Befehl im Widerstreit, pp. 373 ff.

427. Grew, Ten Years in Japan, p. 95.

428. Grew to Roosevelt, December 14, 1940. Ibid.,

pp. 359 f. See also pp. 370 f., February 7, 1941.

429. They hinted that war might be opened by "a preventive attack on Singapore as the best way of impeding American operations in the Pacific as well as adding to Britain's difficulties." Langer and Gleason, The Undeclared War, p. 319.

430. Trial of Major War Criminals, XIX, 73 ff.

431. AP dispatch from Tokyo, October 25, 1945.

432. Memoirs of Prince Konoye. Pearl Harbor Hearings, Part 20, 4012 f.

433. Ambassador General Oshima to Hitler and Ribbentrop, January 3, 1942. Trial of Major War Criminals, XXXV, 102.

434. Speech of January 30, 1942. N.Y. Times, January 31, 1942.

435. Ibid., December 3, 1942.

436. For Roosevelt's early determination to save Britain for the reason that "a conquered England, her lands and shores in the possession of Germany, meant the end of America's security," see Creel, Rebel at Large, p. 323. While the traditional inhibitions against preventive war remained, the general attitude of the American people towards the belligerents was in favor of Britain and France, well ahead of the outbreak of the war. A public opinion poll of October 1938 favored them by twenty to one. Forty-eight per cent of the voters believed that they would have to fight Germany once more during their lifetime. Hartley, Our Maginot Line, p. 114.

437. Watson, Chief of Staff, pp. 105f., 110f., 115f.

438. AP dispatch from Cairo, June 8, 1941.

439. Communiqués from British Middle East Headquarters, June 12 and 16, 1941.

440. N.Y. Times, May 16, 1941.

441. Beard, Roosevelt and the Coming of the War, pp. 461 ff.

442. For these statements, see N.Y. Times, July 8, 1941.

443. Trial of Major War Criminals, XV, 397 f.; Trials of War Criminals, X, 23.

444. Watson, Chief of Staff, pp. 333, 363, 487.

445. Langer and Gleason, The Undeclared War, p. 538.

446. Speech of Attorney General Robert H. Jackson. AP dispatch from Albany, N.Y., June 5, 1941.

447. Statement of Secretary Stimson before Senate Pearl Harbor Committee. N.Y. Times, March 22, 1946. For the ideas of the General Staff, see Watson, Chief of Staff, pp. 353 f.

448. N.Y. Times, October 31, 1941; Beard, Roosevelt and the Coming of the War, pp. 636 f.

449. Germany did "not fit into any pattern of arbitration of differences or peaceful settlement of conflicts," Attorney General Jackson told a class of law students. AP dispatch from Albany, June 5, 1941.

450. During the debate of the Draft Bill in the Senate, Senator Wheeler expressed himself in the following manner on August 8, 1940: If I believed that the Axis powers were going to come over here and take over the U.S. and that "Germany was going to attack us, then I would not simply vote for these appropriations, and I would not simply vote to call out men for training or to conscript them. I would vote for a declaration of war, because if the fact is that if England is defeated, we are going to be attacked by Germany, then, of course, we ought to vote for a declaration of war." N.Y. Times, August 10, 1940.

451. N.Y. Times, January 18, 1940.

452. A Gallup poll in the autumn of 1939 showed that twenty-nine per cent of those questioned held that the U.S. should enter the war, should Germany appear to be victorious. Nevins, The New Deal and World Affairs, p. 195.

453. America and Aggression (1931-1941), prepared by the Bureau of Public Relations, Intelligence and Analysis Branch, War Department. There are no indications given as to who was polled by whom and in what manner. The intervals of questioning are irregular.

454. AP dispatch from Washington, October 17, 1941.

455. Peace and War: United States Foreign Policy, 1931-1941, pp. 767 ff.

456. Broadcast of April 1942.

457. Statement of Secretary Stimson, N.Y. Times, March 22, 1946.

458. Hull, Memoirs, II, 1104.

459. Rear Admiral C. H. Woodward, Armistice Day Speech. N.Y. Times, November 12, 1939.

460. Ibid., June 5, 1940.

461. Stimson's statement, Ibid., March 22, 1946.

462. Stimson's diary, November 25, 1941. Beard, Roosevelt and the Coming of the War, pp. 517 ff.

463. Ibid., p. 525.

464. N.Y. Times, February 16, 1946; Beard Roosevelt and the Coming of the War, pp. 550 f.

465. N.Y. Times, February 27, 1948, following the texts in the London Gazette.

466. Communiqué of the Government of the Netherlands Indies, December 18, 1941. N.Y. Times, December 19, 1941.

467. UP dispatch from London, May 5, 1942.

468. N.Y. Times, November 8, 1942. Somewhat similar statements were made in messages of the President to the Resident-General at Tunis and to the Bey of Tunis. AP dispatch from Washington, November 9, 1942.

469. An Italian High Command communiqué stated that "in order to defend the Southern French coast from British and American landing attempts, troops of the Fourth Army started moving yesterday into Unoccupied France," including Corsica. N.Y. Times, November 13, 1942.

470. Nazi Conspiracy and Aggression, Suppl. A, 8.

471. Jackson during the Conference session of July 13, 1945: "I did not think men would ever be so foolish as to put in writing some of the things the Germans did put in writing." International Conference on Military Trials, p. 211. Compare Ribbentrop's final plea: "Out of more than 300 Defense documents, more than 150 have been turned down without cogent reasons. But the archives of the enemy and the Germans were inaccessible to the Defense." Nazi Conspiracy and Aggression, Suppl. B, 190.

472. For a discussion of preventive war as a permissible form of intervention, see F. Smith, International Law (5th ed.), pp. 88 ff.

473. For the view that the Kellogg Pact does not forbid but rather sanctions war, see Borchard, "The Kellogg Treaties Sanction War," Zeitschrift für ausländisches öffentliches Recht (1929), pp. 126 ff.

474. This had led to the resignation of Sir Cecil Hurst as Chairman of the UN War Crimes Commission early in 1945. See War and the Working Class (Moscow), February 1, 1945.

475. International Conference on Military Trials, p. 19.

476. Ibid., pp. 51 f. For a very sound statement of the Defense at Nuremberg concerning the failure of Grotius' doctrine of war and the causes for it, see Nazi Conspiracy and Aggression, Suppl. B, 40.

477. International Conference on Military Trials, pp. 127, 299, 363.

478. Ibid., pp. 274, 302.

479. Ibid., p. 84.

480. Ibid., pp. 303, 317, 387.

481. Ibid., pp. 303, 305 f.

482. Nazi Conspiracy and Aggression, Suppl. B, 1 f., 13, 159.

483. Ibid., Suppl. B, 640 ff. Cf. also closing statement of the Defense for defendant Admiral Schniewind: "I have proved...through an accurate comparison of German and Allied measures that their plans and preparations ran completely parallel and that Germany reached her objective only a hair's-breadth before her enemies. From the very beginning...the objective of the German leaders was to prevent a threatening occupation of Norwegian sovereign territory by the Allies. The intention of the Allies, on the other hand, was solely to cut Germany's supply line, which was protected by international law, by an act contrary to international law." Trials of War Criminals, X, 394.

484. Nazi Conspiracy and Aggression, Suppl. A, 83 ff. For the statement of the Defense on this point, see Trial of Major War Criminals, XVIII, 408 f.

485. Nazi Conspiracy and Aggression, Suppl. A, 32.

486. Ibid., Suppl. A., 223.

487. Nazi Conspiracy and Aggression. Opinion and Judgment, pp. 36 f.

488. Smith, International Law, p. 88.

489. Justice Jackson took care that the agreement on constituting the Tribunal was kept in the form of an executive agreement on behalf of the President as Commander-in-Chief, thus avoiding ratification and discussion by the United States Senate. International Conference on Military Trials, p. 118.

490. Nazi Conspiracy and Aggression. Opinion and Judgment, p. 36. In this case (1837), Canadians in insurrection, together with their American confederates, had used the Caroline, an American vessel, for the transport of men and munitions from American to Canadian soil. Canadian forces had seized her within American territory and had set her adrift over Niagara Falls. In the ensuing exchange of notes, Great Britain claimed that the measure was justified as a measure of self-defense, and both Governments agreed in the end that authorities on the British side "did nothing unreasonable or excessive, since the act justified by the necessity of self-defence must be limited by that necessity and kept clearly within it." J. B. Moore, International Arbitration, III, 2419 ff.

491. Birkenhead, International Law, pp. 89 f.

492. Trials of War Criminals, X, 395. The services of the Defense to the clarification of international law historiography should not be left unmentioned, even if judges and prosecutors left these largely unappreciated, or at least unconsidered.

493. See in particular the statements of the Defense for Leeb: "The arbitrary nature of that idea which attempts to hold military commanders responsible for vital decisions of the political leaders of the state from the point of view of a crime against peace appears nowhere more strikingly in evidence than where the problem of preventive war

exists...In this trial it is of no importance whether Hitler was personally convinced of the necessity for a preventive act. Our interest can only lie in determining what the attitude of the defendants was when they carried out his orders. They had no reason to assume that Hitler was deceiving them in this respect, especially since the political and military situation spoke for the correctness of his theory of a preventive war." Ibid., X, 383 f.

494. Brig. Gen. Telford Taylor, Closing Statement for the U.S. on General Staff and High Command. Nazi Conspiracy and Aggression, Suppl. A., 323.

495. N.Y. Times, October 21, 1941.

496. Report by Republican Post-War Advisory Council, Mackinac Island. Ibid., September 8, 1943.

497. Radio broadcast by members of the State Department, including Joseph C. Grew, Alger Hiss and Archibald MacLeish, March 2, 1945. Ibid., March 3, 1945.

498. Annals of the American Academy of Political and Social Science, September 1945, p. 67.

499. N.Y. Times, November 15, 1945.

500. Time, July 23, 1945.

501. N.Y. Times, January 26, 1946. Hutchins, of course, was not himself arguing for a preventive war.

502. Wallace's letter was dated July 23, 1946. It was published by the White House, together with the undated letters of the Secretaries of War and Navy, on September 18, 1946. N.Y. Times, September 19, 1946. The diaries of Forrestal, which are usually so revealing, contain only one reference to the preventive war proposals: On April 23, 1948, Robert A. Lovett summed up Russia's position toward the United States "as being of a dual nature at the moment: (1) constant probing to find out the solidity of our intent; and (2) a reflection of their own fear of a preventive or aggressive war on our part. Two things he felt were contributing to their motivations—the over-excitable statements, some by military people, on a preventive war, and the activities of Henry Wallace and his proposal that the President sit down with Stalin and make a world agreement." Forrestal Diaries, p. 424.

503. A glowing tribute is paid to Wallace by the late Louis Adamic. But for him, he writes, "the Pacelli-Churchill-Baruch-Dulles-Byrnes-Vandenberg-Spellman American policy" might have produced a preventive war in 1947. Adamic, The Eagle and the Roots, pp. 72 f.

504. N.Y. Times, January 14 and February 14, 1946.

505. Ibid., November 21, 1946.

506. "From what I have seen of our Russian friends and allies during the war, I am convinced that there is nothing they admire so much as strength, and there is nothing for which they have less respect than for weakness, especially military weakness." Churchill's speech at Fulton, Missouri, on March 5, 1946.

507. A letter-writer to the N.Y. Times cited Churchill on Munich: "There is no merit in putting off a war for a year if, when it comes, it is a far worse war or one much harder to win." N.Y. Times, September 19, 1948.

508. Churchill's speech at Fulton, Missouri, on March 5, 1946.

509. See Professor Harold C. Urey, N.Y. Times, October 22, 1946.

510. Ibid., July 26, 1947.

511. Time, October 4, 1948.

512. For this type, see Fabre-Luce, Journal de l'Europe, 1946-1947, p. 121.

513. de Beauvoir, Tag und Nacht in Amerika (transl. of L'Amérique au jour le jour), p. 342. For the advocacy of preventive war by American writers, see Eliot, If Russia Strikes (reviewed by Ely Culbertson in New Leader, June 11, 1949); Maxwell Anderson in N.Y. Times, March 8, 1948; and James Burnham, The Coming Defeat of Communism (1950).

514. The French Institute of Public Opinion, sampling political views among Communists voters in the spring of 1952, found that sixty per cent believed that the United States was preparing a war of aggression. Time, June 30, 1952.

515. Before the National Committee of his (Schuman's) party, the Christian Democrats. Frankfurter Allgemeine Zeitung, January 16, 1951.

516. Cited from Air University Quarterly in Chicago Daily Tribune, February 23, 1948.

517. Time, April 4, 1948.

518. Saturday Evening Post, November 6, 1948.

519. Quoted from Ladies' Home Journal in Time, April 4, 1948. Another protest against preventive war was voiced by Thomas K. Finletter, chairman of the President's Air Policy Commission. N.Y. Times, March 25, 1948.

520. N.Y. Times, January 18, 1948. Cf. Acheson's speech at Dallas, Texas, June 13, 1950: Preventive war might have been "considered in earlier times and by another type of government and people than ours...All

responsible men must agree that such a course is unthinkable for us. It would violate every moral principle of our people. Such a war would necessarily be incredibly destructive. It would not solve problems, it would multiply them."

521. Kenney was quoted as saying: "The question of today is quite simple and direct: When will the Communist crowd start 'Operation America'?....It will be as soon as they feel they can win." Newsweek, May 17, 1948.

522. Speech before the UN Assembly's Political Committee, Paris, November 13, 1948. N.Y. Times, November 14, 1948.

523. For the case of an unjustified attack by the Soviet journalist Fadeev, see New Leader, March 19, 1949.

524. Cited in N.Y. Times, September 25, 1949.

525. Lauterbach, Through Russia's Back Door, pp. 153 f., 195.

526. N.Y. Times, July 13, 1947.

527. Vice Admiral D. E. Barby, commander of the U.S. Fourth Fleet, quoted in Ibid., October 13, 1946.

528. Time, October 31, 1949.

529. N.Y. Times, August 27, 1950; for the Russian reaction, see Ibid., September 4 and 11, 1950; for Johnson, see Ibid., September 1, 1950. The Department of Defense stated that Matthews's address "had been cleared for security only," but not for "policy and propriety."

530. Time, September 18, 1950.

531. N.Y. Times, September 2 and 12, 1950. For a discussion, see Hanson Baldwin in Ibid., September 1, 1950: Preventive war "is a course of political bankruptcy and moral frustration that would be militarily ineffective and which would lose for the United States the very values we are trying to defend."

532. Rep. Carl T. Durham (Dem.), Chairman of the Joint Congressional Atomic Energy Committee, stated that if Russia should try to bankrupt the U.S. through the use of the satellite nations, "if it becomes clear beyond all doubt that that is the Russian policy, then I say that we have no alternative but to go to war with Russia, in which event we must pick the time and place." Ibid., August 14, 1950. The Very Reverend Edmund Walsh, vice-president of Georgetown University, writing in the Washington Star, stated that "neither reason nor theology nor morals require men or nations to commit suicide by requiring that we must await the first blow from a power with no moral inhibitions and when, as in the case now under consideration, the attack would

surely include bombardment by atomic missiles." If the United States had sound reason to believe, had moral certitude that an attack like that on Pearl Harbor was being mounted and was ready to be launched against the United States, the President would be morally justified in striking first with the atomic bomb. N.Y. Herald-Tribune, December 25, 1950.

533. Speech by Truman of September 1, 1950.

534. "America rejects the theory of preventive war as the answer to Soviet aggression. We could not live with ourselves nor stand before the world as a defender of human freedom and of the worth and dignity of the individual if we accepted the moral responsibility for launching a war of aggression." Roy Reuther, Coordinator of Political Action of the UAW, CIO. N.Y. Times, October 14, 1950.

535. Ibid., September 10, 1950.

536. General Eisenhower's speech in Dallas, Texas, on November 11, 1950: "When people speak to you about preventive war, you tell them to go and fight it. After my experience, I have come to hate war. War settles nothing."

537. Combat Forces Journal and Reader's Digest for October 1950.

538. N.Y. Times, November 18, 1950.

539. Ibid., November 10, 1950. Cf. President Truman, who had "no patience with people who talk about 'a preventive war.' There are a few misguided people who want war to straighten out the present world situation. But fortunately these people are a very small even though vocal minority, and they have no power." Hillman, Mr. President, p. 245.

540. May 22, 1951. Military Situation in the Far East, p. 954.

541. For an attack of Prime Minister St. Laurent on advocates of a preventive war against Russia, see N.Y. Times, March 17, 1952.

542. Parliamentary Debate, 5th series, Vol. 401, 1332 f.

543. Malenkov, at the meeting which set up the Cominform, speaking with regard to the post-war situation: "The center of class struggle has shifted to the international scene." Cited by Smith in My Three Years in Moscow, p. 323.

544. Cf. the preamble of the Russo-Chinese Treaty of February 15, 1950: "Filled with determination jointly to prevent by the consolidation of friendship and cooperation between the USSR and the people of the Republic of China...a repetition of aggression on the part of Japan or any other State which

should unite in any form with Japan in acts of aggression...."

545. "An aggressor who invades Korea today will certainly invade China tomorrow."

Statement of General Wu, December 16, 1950, in New York City.

546. Lisbon meeting of the North Atlantic Council. <u>N.Y. Times</u>, February 21, 1952.

The Promise of Victory

"Melior tutiorque est certa pax, quam sperata victoria."
(Certain peace is better and safer than hoped for victory.)
Livy[1]

The most portentous advice military spokesmen can give to their own governments or to an ally concerns the prospects of victory in an impending war. In the councils and deliberations where the choice between peace and war is still a free one, the voice of caution will warn that the outcome of any war is apt to be uncertain, more so than it would appear to be at the start, that even an indifferent peace is preferable to the uncertainties of war.[2] Three and a half centuries ago, Lazarus von Schwendi warned that "war must never be started unless one saw more hope for gain and victory than one had fear for damage and loss."[3] These views of naïve times, commonplaces of governing as they were, were very much in need of restatement after 1914, when the peoples were told by their governors either that the enemy had started the war deliberately or that both sides had skidded into war due to unfortunate alliance systems. Actually, there is enough evidence to justify a pre-1914 German diplomat who stated that "wars, as a rule, are undertaken only if one believes he is certain of victory."[4] Or, as it was stated in Biblical times: "What king, going to war against another king, sitteth not down first, and consulteth whether he be able with ten thousand to meet him that cometh against him with twenty thousand? Or else, while the other is yet a great way off, he sendeth an ambassage and desireth conditions of peace?" (Luke XIV, 31-32).

The majority of wars have been started by the aggressor party in the full persuasion of its own superiority over the intended victim. A number of wars have, however, occurred between more nearly equal parties at times when their readiness for war was practically equal, usually high, on both sides. This was the case in 1859, 1870, 1904, and 1914, when military advice as to the outlook for victory[5] on both sides had produced a superiority complex that possessed not only the military but also the civilian governors and the people of the nations concerned.[6]

Military advice in favor of undertaking a war will be given in one of two ways: (1) War ought to be sought because the situation is particularly favorable; (2) War need not be feared and shunned. In July 1914, the first kind of advice was given and taken in Vienna, while elsewhere the second was given to or was already believed in by the governors well before Serajevo.

The certainty of victory, which must not be less than seventy per cent (according to one of Napoleon's maxims), has been generally established before war in the common councils of civilian and military leaders—or in despotic times in the head of a single governor—usually at the moment when a diplomatic crisis had reached its acutest stage and peaceful settlement appeared either unobtainable, inadvisable, or undesirable. At such moments, councils presided over by the head of state have discussed the pro's and con's of an impending war and have either voted on the issue or given their advice to whoever had final authority. Under such autocrats as Frederick the Great and Napoleon I or the duces and Führers of Fascism, only the minimum of deliberative advice was received, while the deliberative and consultative processes of communist totalitarian government ahead of war remain undisclosed.

After a century of more or less well-recorded deliberations before the entry into war, such deliberations were—strangely, as it would seem to some—dispensed with by most of the participants in the war of 1914. They were unnecessary, largely because the certainty of victory had been ascertained in different ways and previous to the month of July 1914. But this was so contrary to expectations that American Ambassador Morgenthau, or his informants, had to invent a Prussian Crown Council which was said to have decided in favor of war early in July 1914. Again, such councils were completely dispensed with in the war-making Third Reich, where deliberative "defense" councils had been provided for but were not used; yet the case against the major war criminals as elaborated by the Anglo-Saxon jurists assumed their "conspiracy" against the peace. Actually, if there was "conspiracy," it was the strange one in which the co-conspirators had no deliberative or protesting voice. When Hitler said (on August 22, 1939) that "for us it is easy to make decisions," he used the plural majestaticus and Goering used the plural modestatis when he "answered with thanks to the Führer and the assurance that the armed forces will do their duty."[7]

Responsible military authorities are inclined to offer the civilian governors either an outright promise of victory or the assurance of being ready for war, technically speaking. These two assurances mean much the same thing to the civilian, but not to the soldier, if the war is lost by his side. In the discussions about guilt and responsibility following a war that has been lost, the military are inclined to stress that their earlier assurances were only of reasonable or relative war-readiness and did not imply a promise of victory. But far-reaching assurances as to the certainty of victory are apt to be remembered in post-war discussions about their authors, such as the emphatic declaration of French War Minister Marshal Leboeuf in the spring of 1870: "So ready are we that, if the war lasts two years, not a gaiter button would be found wanting."[8]

COUNSEL ON WAR: 1854, 1859, 1864, 1866

The influence of soldiers' and sailors' advice on the resolution for or against a war under consideration has varied greatly. There was exceedingly little military influence in Britain and France on the decision to go to war against Russia in 1854. Aberdeen and others were unable to stem the mass urge for war, while Palmerston made himself the engineer of these pressures, quite mindless of the question as to whether or not the British or French armies were prepared for war, a war to be fought God knows where. The British Army thus went to war in passive obedience, as did the Six Hundred in the subsequent charge into "the valley of death."

The war of 1859 was preceded by much military advice in favor of it, too much as far as Austria was concerned. In their technical preparations for the war, the French generals, who were confident of victory, bowed whenever political considerations demanded from them measures that were inadvisable from a purely military standpoint.[9] Austria's blundering precipitation of the war was due to the advice from Francis Joseph's generals, notably Gruenne, head of the Military Cabinet, to the exclusion of civilian counsel. If left to his own insights, the foreign minister, Count Buol, might have averted the Italian war, but as he said after it had been lost: "What could I do? I was against the war. But all our generals said that we were invincible. Could I keep them from making it?"[10] Which is as much as to say that a war that promises to be successful by common military judgment must not be shunned.

Bismarck was convinced, at least by the end of 1862, that the Schleswig-Holstein problem could "be solved in a manner desirable to us only by war." Within a few days after accepting office as Foreign Minister, he sought the professional opinion of the War Minister on the military advisability of war with Denmark.[11] Militarily, this war was an extremely simple proposition, infinitely more simple than the diplomacy that made Prus-

sia's and Austria's undertaking it without interference from the neutrals possible. Basing her defiance on the hoped-for support of the neutrals, the little Kingdom of Denmark plunged into a popular but hopeless war in which no outside help was forthcoming.

Prussia's and Austria's joint victory was only the first step towards the gaining of the Duchies for the former. Shortly after the war had been won, Bismarck made inquiries about the military strength of Italy as a possible ally against Austria.[12] Uncertain in his aging mind, King William I summoned a Crown Council for May 29, 1865, to discuss the danger of a war with Austria. Without telling Bismarck beforehand, he had his aide-de-camp general, Edwin von Manteuffel, and Moltke, the Chief of Staff, participate in the Council. Manteuffel had just swung around to favoring war against Austria, which he had earlier thought contrary to Prussia's best interests. Much to Manteuffel's surprise, Bismarck spoke with moderation, even though he judged the outcome of such a war quite confidently, given Austria's precarious military and diplomatic situation. The Prime Minister put the decision up to the Monarch, who then turned to Moltke and asked what the Army thought about the annexation of Schleswig-Holstein. While declining the role of spokesman for the Army, the Chief of Staff personally considered annexation the only wholesome solution; as far as he had heard, the Army also favored annexation. Prussia need not fear a war arising from such a policy.[13]

After several attempts (sincere only on Austria's part) to preserve the alliance of 1864, war was discussed again by the councils on both sides. The Ministers of Finance and Commerce, spokesmen of Austria's shaken economy, implored Francis Joseph to find a peaceful solution to the Duchies problem. He promised to abstain from military preparations for the time being, except on paper. A Prussian Crown Council, to which had been added several generals, as well as the ambassador to Paris, was more bellicose. Only the Crown Prince protested against the "fratricidal war." All the other participants were in favor of war as the only way of settling the German problem. Moltke had made the alliance with Italy that would force Austria to fight on two fronts, the military condition sine qua non.[14] Strategy and diplomacy were in perfect unity: Bismarck needed the alliance with Italy, Napoleon's protégé, in order to make the Emperor sympathetic towards Prussia rather than towards Austria. Without intervention victory would come promptly and war would be short—four weeks only, Bismarck had once foretold.[15] Diplomacy would be allowed to resume its work at once.

During April the outlook for war became dimmer, due to Austria's conciliatory attitude and to anti-war sentiment in Prussia and elsewhere. Bismarck and Moltke remained in favor of war, the sooner the better. Austria was ready to reduce her armaments against Prussia in the North, but not in the South, where Venetia was threatened by continued Italian troop concentrations. In order to meet this danger, the Austrian War Minister demanded mobilization of the Southern Army, and, although fully aware of the excuses this would offer to Prussian policy, the Emperor agreed. Venetia must be protected, whatever the political consequences. The limited local military consideration won out over the larger comprehensive diplomatic argument that Austria, as she was constituted, could be preserved only by staying at peace.

Very few of Austria's soldiers realized, then or later, that the survival of Austria depended on peace rather than on war. Ludwig von Gablenz, the military governor of Austrian-administered Holstein, was one of the few soldiers aware of this fact in 1866. He worked long and hard for a peaceful settlement with Prussia. At last he resigned himself to war as the soldier's ultimate duty, even in a war so hopeless for Austria:

> As a soldier, one must always wish for and preach war; at least as a lieutenant one must do that; as a general and good patriot I believe, however, that if we can maintain the peace without drawing up the armies, the latter modality should be preferred. However, once we have spent the money in order to bring the Army on a war footing, then one should fight out this grandiose duel without blinking an eye, even if the advantages for us in the most fortunate case may not be very rosy.[16]

"ARCH-READINESS" IN 1870

The war of 1866 was not lost by Austria alone. France banked on Austrian victory, or at least on a long drawn out war with ample occasion for intervention.[17] When Bismarck denied them "compensations," Napoleon, and even more the generals of his entourage, became aware that they were also losers. When the Prussian military attaché, von Loë, returned to Paris from the Bohemian theater of war, Frossard, a court general, greeted him with: "Now Colonel, what about the compensations? What shall we get out of this?" When the Prussian replied that he saw no justification for such claims on France's part, since she had not fought in the war, Frossard insisted: "You are jesting; for you know very well that we had an observation army of 300,000 men along the frontier, enough to keep you from continuing the war." But von Loë replied: "General, you know as well as I do that France found herself so short of military force that she was not in a condition to make war ...the consequence of Mexico."[18] This disap-

pointment over a war left unfought, over the loss of what the Germans considered "unearned increment," rankled deeply with the French, and most of all with her generals. On a visit to Paris in 1867, Marshal Vaillant frankly told Bismarck: "Do not deceive yourself, bayonets will have to be crossed...We are like the cock that does not want others to crow louder than himself." Bismarck replied, "Well, we shall be at the rendez-vous."[19] Even if the "easy" war of 1866 had escaped them, most of the French generals remained persuaded that victory was theirs any time they wanted it. This conviction persuaded Napoleon III to declare in a speech from the throne early in 1867, that "the constant aim of our efforts has been reached; France's military resources are henceforth equal to her destinies in the world."[20]

With this readiness for war went remarkably little critical examination on the part of the French Army. Almost universal acclaim by the press, parliament, and the Army itself prevented some of the most necessary reforms.[21] Trochu, one of the few serious reformers among the Army officers, addressed himself directly to this point:

> The chauvinism born under the First Empire, nursed under the subsequent governments, master of the public spirit under the Second Empire, is a national, constitutional, endemic, epidemic, hereditary disease. It is dangerous to the highest degree for it substitutes the legend of the certainty of victory for the patient efforts of reflection, comparison, preparation, assiduous labor which are necessary to merit victory.[22]

The ready and uncritical promise of victory came to stand in the way of French victory in 1870. The French Army assured everyone who wanted to hear that it was fully prepared and ready for war. Addressing himself to the legislature and to the Emperor in March and April 1869, the War Minister declared that "at no time has the Army received a more complete training for war...We can never be surprised. We have an excellent, well-instructed Army, full of ardor, perfectly organized...It wants nothing. We are so ready that one must be three times wise in order not to declare war. To have such an Army and still not make war, that is virtuous...Today, whether we are at peace or at war, that makes no difference to the Minister of War: he is always ready...You, Sire, have the most beautiful army in the world."[23] From afar, Niel was somewhat less confident at that time. He told the Empress Eugénie that, obedient to her eager desire to bring the Army into a state where it could contend with the Army of the German Confederation, he had done his part. He was ready but she was not, meaning that the necessary foreign alliances had not been concluded. He was not against

war, not in favor of the indefinite postponement of
war with North Germany. There was merely an
armistice between her and France, with each side
barely holding its fire.

Niel did not live to see the war. In February
1870 his successor, Marshal Leboeuf, reiterated
the Army's "arch-readiness" for war and assured
Napoleon that "we are stronger than the Prussians
on the peace footing as well as on the war footing."[24] He still hoped at times that the diplomats
would be able to avert the war. The hope was
shared by his colleagues in the cabinet, who were
able to persuade him to agree to cuts in that year's
budget and in the effectives. This was done by the
same legislators, as some generals complained
after the defeat, who were to push the Government
into a war that had been prepared, if at all, only
contrary to their proposals. "Logic had nothing
to do with this."[25]

The Prussians were not the only enemies of the
French generals. There was also the "Revolution,"
the enemy of most generals during most of the
nineteenth century. It had scored a great success,
inside the army as well as outside, in the Plebiscite of May 8, 1870. When the first news of the
particularly unfavorable Paris vote, including that
of the garrison, arrived in the Elysée, the emperor was heard to say by his military entourage
that "only war could save the Empire from the
Revolution." This was enough incitement to cause
the court generals to entertain the idea of consolidating the dynasty by a popular and victorious
war.[26] What all subsequent accusations and
counter-accusations of the French parties could
not eliminate was the fact of the military and civilian trust in the victory of the French Army, a victory to be achieved even by this Army alone, without the alliances that were still being negotiated
in 1870. At that time, court generals, the only ones
that counted in Paris, assured the Empress herself
that "never has our Army been in a better state,
better provided, better disciplined...Out of twenty
chances at least nineteen are in our favor!...Our
offensive across the Rhine will be of such a lightning-like character that it will cut Germany in two:
Prussia will be just a mouthful; we shall again find
the road to Jena."[27] The generals pledged victory so emphatically that Prime Minister Ollivier
was more certain of the victory than of what to do
with it. Only after defeat did he realize how much
"all our generals and war administrators had
woven a nearly idolatrous cult, which ruled over
us, around the military institutions."[28] The
burning incense of this cult had all but blacked out
the light in which the responsible statesman must
examine the advice he gets from his generals.

The French cabinet assembled to discuss the
Spanish candidacy on July 6. The question was
raised once more, if only as a matter of formality,
as to whether France was actually ready for war.
They received the war minister's assurance that,
although the war would be difficult, it was inevitable
and could be faced with confidence. The Army was
admirable—well-disciplined and exercised, brave,
better-armed than the Prussian in several respects
(Chassepots and mitrailleuses). "Never will France
have a similar occasion for settling its differences
with Prussia!" It was the sense of the meeting that
all future decisions could be based on two facts:
(1) that "our army was ready and in a state to win"
and (2) that France could count on Austria and Italy
as allies.[29]

The brave declarations based on these beliefs
made by the Government in the Chambre won the
greatest possible acclaim among the generals. Old
Marshal Vaillant told the Emperor: "At last the
winding sheet of Sadowa that had stifled us for four
years has been thrown aside. Never will you find
a more beautiful occasion. It must be made use of,
Sire." There was much chauvinism in the Emper-
or's entourage, where the war party and the political Right were dominant. The latter hoped for war
and victory as a way of removing the Ollivier Liberals from power, should they show even the slightest hesitation to go to war. General Bourbaki, who
was considered to be an expert on the Prussian
Army because he had watched it in maneuvers,
assured his hearers that "out of ten chances we
have eight." When, on July 15, the question of war
was put to a vote in the council of ministers, one
of them turned to War Minister Leboeuf before
giving his vote: "Marshal, you see my distress; I
ask you not whether we are ready but whether we
have chances for victory." The answer was "that
we were ready and that we would never be in a
better situation to settle our conflict with Prussia,
that we could have confidence." War was then
voted unanimously.[30]

Bismarck had been in receipt of Moltke's well-
considered advice in favor of war with France ever
since the Luxemburg crisis of 1867: "Nothing could
please us better than to have a war that is inevitable
in spite of everything," even a war that might have
to be fought along two fronts, against both France
and Austria.[31] Moltke prepared the plans for
these wars during the last years of the 1860's, at
the time when French-Austrian-Italian joint operations were under discussion. This view of the inevitability of war with France was not always shared
by Bismarck. "This war I shall shun as long as I
can," he said in 1867, "for I know that once started
it will never end."[32] He preferred to wait, since
the constitutional and military innovations inside
Germany seemed to require more time in order to
reach their full strength for the case of war.

As time went by, he had less reason to fear the
war. He did not in the least withhold this conviction
from the French.

We are free of presumption as well as any desire for war; but we are convinced, after conscientious examination of our forces and those of the possible antagonist, that we are equal to a war with France and that, even though the decision rests in a higher hand, the chances of victory are, humanly speaking, on our side. War per se is always a misfortune; but that it should be a greater misfortune for us than for France is an idea we do not understand...We are as completely prepared as our new organization allows us to be and, for the sake of this organization, have at the present moment no desire to add to our armaments and preparations.

Early in 1869 he wanted no war. He wanted, however, to maintain "the impression of fearlessness" in Prussia's relations with France, who threatened to strengthen her position by a triple alliance with Austria and Italy.[33]

Germany was still more ready when Bismarck used the Hohenzollern candidacy in order to bring on the war. As originally contemplated, the candidacy did not seem a convincing issue for war to some of those who might have to vote on the issue. The problems involved came under discussion at a Crown Council held on March 15, 1870, in which the candidate's father, the Prussian Crown Prince, Bismarck, Moltke, and Roon, and various civilian ministers and secretaries of state participated. One of the civilians asked Moltke: "If Napoleon takes it amiss, we are ready, aren't we?" The general answered Yes, "with comfortable confidence." While the old King would not hear of pushing the candidacy, Bismarck would not give up. He sent his assistant, Bucher, and an officer as emissaries to Spain, the latter to report on the state of the Spanish Army. Since this officer was to be chosen by Moltke, "Bismarck had the game in his hand. For Moltke, who in this case was pulling in the same direction, would certainly find an officer on whom he could rely." The military emissary in fact proved to be a very zealous partisan of the candidacy, pushing it as far and as long as he could. Both returned from Spain, the potential second front in the south, with roseate reports; but still the King remained uninclined towards war.[34]

The French raised their protests against the Hohenzollern candidacy, based in part on the feeling of "encirclement," to use a later term. They did so in such a way that Bismarck was able to represent their opposition in a manner that would bring on the war and at the same time justify it. "National feeling and national honor" as "powers which cannot be measured logistically" were mobilized by him through his editing of the Ems despatch.[35] The original had made depressing

reading for Moltke and Roon, who were dining with him at the time of its arrival. While Bismarck studied it, he put a few questions to Moltke: How far did his trust in Germany's armaments go? In the face of the suddenly emerging threat of war, was still more time required for armaments? The Chief of Staff answered that if there should be war, nothing could be gained by postponing it. Even if it should be impossible to at once cover all German territory on the left bank of the Rhine against a French invasion, German preparations would soon overtake those of France. An early outbreak of the war would, on the whole, be more favorable than delay. Following these final assurances, Bismarck could safely "redact" the public version of the despatch by which he turned what "at first sounded like a chamade into something like a fanfare in answer to a challenge," as Moltke put it. The best of military advice as to the war with France had been at Bismarck's elbow in this hour.[36]

REVANCHE POSTPONED, CONTRARY TO MILITARY ADVICE

In 1875 and 1887, the chances of victory on Germany's part, or that of the Triplice, appeared overwhelming to military judgment. Moltke's advice as to the desirability of making war was, however, neither called for by Bismarck nor acceptable to him. Germany was "saturated." She could not gain anything worth a war that would necessarily make Russia an ally of France. The Chancellor did not want this alliance to be formed, even if the General Staff was not afraid of it. The General Staff in fact urged, through Waldersee as the spokesman of the younger generation, that such misleading ties as the "reinsurance treaty" with Russia should be dropped for the sake of "clarity."[37] When Bismarck's successor did not renew the ties with Russia, he took the measures necessary to preserve the superiority of the German army over any other army[38] and to inspire confidence in German victory in case the war on two fronts should come. This required a stronger army making better use of the vast German manpower potential through the two years' service term, and a diplomacy of silent unwritten understanding with Britain. In Caprivi's time and for some time thereafter, it was still axiomatic in European diplomacy that "just as England's whole existence depended on unconditional superiority of her naval power, Germany's life depended on her army's superiority, for at the very moment when the German Army should lag behind the French in numbers and efficiency, France would proceed to her war of revanche."[39]

Most Frenchmen, military and non-military, were fully aware that, in order to be successful, revanche had to wait for an alliance with Russia.

A few were ready to gamble on a war of revanche
as the way of effecting this alliance. The promise
of "arch-readiness" for war was resumed by
revanche-seeking generals as early as 1885.[40]
This was the rationale, if it can be called that, of
Boulanger's agitation. He told the other ministers
(September 1886): "You can count on the Army,
not a button is wanting." Only too painfully did
this remind the engineers of the Russian alliance,
such as Freycinet, of Leboeuf's promises of
1870.[41] Bismarck knew these views well enough
to openly pronounce his conviction that as soon as
France, for one reason or another, should come
to believe that she was stronger than Germany,
war was certain. Had not Napoleon III declared
war for reasons of domestic politics and would not
Boulanger, should he become the head of the government, act in the same way? (Reichstag speech
of January 11, 1887). Nearly everything that Boulanger did or proposed as war minister served to
strengthen such fears, at home no less than
abroad. When—not suddenly but as announced the
year before—Germany called 72,000 reservists to
the colors for twelve days in February 1887 to be
instructed in the use of the new M.88 infantry
rifle, Boulanger proposed to the Cabinet that
France take counter-action. "But don't you know
that that means war?" he was asked. "Oh yes, I
am ready," was his answer. "If we mobilize by
starting from a peace footing while they mobilize
from a war footing, they will get to the heart of
the country before we are ready...I would rather
have the war with a chance of victory than the uncertainty of a peace that they can break at their
pleasure and thereby smash us absolutely." President Grévy: "You say that by mobilizing I have
one chance out of two to win the battle. I myself
answer you: we have not one chance to win. I do
not allow this question even to be discussed...You
are just what Leboeuf was in his day." Boulanger:
"Then I resign." Grévy: "All right, do it then."
But Boulanger, "cet animal de général demagogue,"
as Grévy called him, was politician enough not to
resign on the issue of a highly dubious promise of
victory.[42]

MILITARY ADVICE FAVORING WAR, 1882-1904

The various wars near the turn of the century
were all undertaken on military advice. Much
military uncertainty preceded the Chinese-Japanese war of 1894. For one thing, neither party had
yet fought with the help of the modern weapons and
organization furnished them by the Western Powers. Yet both sides felt confident. In May 1894,
when Viceroy Li-Hung-chang inspected fortifications and garrisons around the Liaotung Gulf and
the warships stationed there, he and the foreign
press found everything in good shape and ready

for war. The press disagreed only as to which of
the national armament industries had sold China
the best and which the worst weapons.[43] These
loud declamations made no impression on the
Japanese. They had reconnoitred Chinese weaknesses so well ahead of war that they could safely
base their campaign plans on them.[44] They were
eager to use the instrument they had shaped on
European models during the last fifteen years,
which they were certain would give them superiority over their far more conservative enemy. But
China was not deterred when they demonstrated
their superiority ahead of war by a quick and efficient mobilization of the forces that were to intervene in Korea, a mobilization that reminded Western diplomats of the Prussian mobilization of 1866
in speed and exactness.[45] It encouraged the
Japanese still more to know that Russia was as
yet far away and so backward with the construction
of the Trans-Siberian Railway that her military
intervention need not be feared.

While the war undertaken by Japan was carefully
prepared, the American war against Spain was a
military improvisation. As early as December 1897,
Assistant Secretary of the Navy Theodore Roosevelt
urged that the United States declare war on Spain.[46]
Comparison of strength gave the American governors
no pause; only the most conservative circles in Europe could still think of Spain as a Power of some
military importance. The Americans hoped to sweep
the enemy off the continent and into the sea and thus
reestablish isolation. This was, unfortunately, similar to the Boer's hope on the eve of the war of 1899.
When they let themselves in for the war with the
interloping British, they hoped to regain their
apartheid by a successful war with the uitlanders,
whose military power they had held in low esteem
ever since Majuba Hill (1881). That the British
undertook this war, which had to be fought at such
a distance from home, may in part have been due
to their recent victory in a war not fought but won
—the conflict of Fashoda. That incident had led
dangerously close to war, with armaments rushed
to both sides of the Channel. Confidence in victory
was greatest on the British side. The French Navy
was without hope of achieving success through the
commerce-destroying strategy it had prepared, and
it even suspected the more confident Army, directed by a general staff of anti-Dreyfusards, of being
ready for war in order to ditch the more liberal
Navy and then establish a military dictatorship.[47]
Faced with a thoroughly unsatisfactory domestic
situation and with the denial of Russian support,
the French were in no position to undertake the
war.[48]

Russia had been too deeply embarked on her Far
Eastern enterprise to lend a helping hand to her
ally at the time of Fashoda. While the railroad to
the Far East was a single-track affair, the Far

THE PROMISE OF VICTORY

Eastern policy moved on double tracks: one civilian, pursued by the Tsar's ministers, Lamsdorff, Witte, and even Kuropatkin, the war minister; the other military, pursued by the soldier-imperialists, Bezobrazov, state-counsellor and ex-officer, Admiral Abaza, General Voyak, and Viceroy Admiral Alexiev. This clique had won the Tsar over to its forward war-provoking policy in the Far East. It felt Russia's military power to be so superior to the Japanese that the latter's various proposals to settle the conflict by an outright division of zones of influence—Manchuria to Russia, Korea to Japan—were considered sheer presumption on the part of a midget.[49] The Russian military attaché in Tokyo "sent the most sarcastic reports on the condition of Japan's military apparatus. The Japanese Army would," he reported, "probably need hundreds of years before it had acquired the moral basis required to bring it on an equal footing with even the weakest European army. Against such an army a strong cavalry regiment equipped with artillery would win a certain and decisive victory if it should proceed with sufficient speed and energy." All known Russian military and naval opinion by 1903 was penetrated by the conviction that the Russian forces could not be beaten by Japan, either on land or on sea. "I personally cannot admit the possibility of the destruction of the Russian fleet by the Japanese," declared Viceroy Alexiev's naval chief of staff. The military war-wishers were joined by the Minister of the Interior, Plehve, who favored "a small-sized victorious war" as a cure for the evils with which he had to contend at home.[50] The diplomatic representative in Tokyo, Isvolski, was far more cautious in his judgments.

The Russians' confidence was justified to a limited extent by the continuous strengthening of their military position in the Far East. They believed that they would be allowed to wait until strong enough to start war on their own terms. Meanwhile, the Tsar said to the Japanese ambassador on Russian New Year Day, 1904: "Look at the map and compare the size of our two countries."[51] The Japanese were, however, resolved not to allow Russian military strength in the Far East to gain superiority. Certain of being in a better position, they had forced the Russians to halt temporarily in March-April 1901 in their penetration of Manchuria and of the Peking Government, "a great victory" over Russia, as the Foreign Minister reported to the Throne. Russian imperialism soon resumed its forward moves, unwilling to concede to the Japanese in Korea what they claimed for themselves in Manchuria. Japanese resistance was based on the general staff's opinion that, from a strategic point of view, Japan still had an advantage but that a few years' delay would change this in Russia's favor.[52] By December 1903, the Japanese mind was made up for war. The military men generally agreed that Japan could undertake war with a safe degree of hope for victory. The German General Staff agreed: "Unquestionably Russia was not at the present time equal to the Japanese in Eastern Asia and therefore would not now indulge in war," though ultimate victory would still be hers. Japan, if she does not act now, "might lose the last favorable chance."[53]

While there was not "one hundred per cent confidence in victory" on the Japanese side, their most influential statesmen, Ito and Yamagata, had sufficient belief in victory to undertake the war. Ito told Emperor Meiji near the end of 1903 that "Russian forces will certainly not be able to set foot inside Chosen (Korea), and it will be possible for us to hold the Russians for a year along the Yalu River." Should things go wrong for Japan during that year, the United States would intervene in her favor. "'Hence we can commence preparations at once and with confidence in our success.' On hearing this, the Emperor was much relieved, and at council in the Imperial presence on the very same day he announced his final decision" in favor of war.[54]

Although the more cautious among the Russian soldiers would have preferred to postpone the war, they were undaunted and their confidence in the victory of Russian arms complete. On the eve of his departure for the theater of war, Kuropatkin expressed his belief that he could beat the Japanese if he were given one and a half years' time and an army of 400,000 men, of whom he must be allowed to sacrifice 40,000 in dead and wounded. Witte, an arch-civilian, shared his belief.[55]

The military forecasts, other than the Japanese, as to the outcome of the war in the Far East proved mostly wrong. The Berlin General Staff and the Kaiser had believed in eventual Russian victory. The British feared defeat by the Japanese. Admiral Fisher, a constant opponent of the Japanese alliance, even pointed out the exact spot where they would be annihilated.[56] This failure of the professionals ought to have put the diplomats on their guard when contemplating wars, their own and those of others, but it did not perceptibly do so.

COUNSEL FOR AND AGAINST WAR, 1904 AND AFTER

Long before the final defeat of Russia in Manchuria, the change in the world's military balance of power in favor of the Central Powers was so obvious that some of their soldiers considered war against the Entente advisable and victory certain. When asked by the Wilhelmstrasse for his opinion on the military consequences of the recent pact, Schlieffen concluded that "if the necessity of a war with France should arise for us, the present moment would undoubtedly be favorable." Even if the Russian forces were withdrawn from the Far East for such a war, he added, they would not appear as a factor of consequence for months. [57] As recently as 1902, a world war had seemed uncertain in its outcome and without worthwhile gains to the directors of German diplomacy.[58] Now it appeared of greater promise to many in governing circles. Schlieffen, War Minister von Einem, some of the naval officers, and Holstein favored a war with France in 1905.[59] The Kaiser, even earlier than Chancellor Bülow, shied away from it. As he told a German shipping magnate in February 1906, he could make war only if the whole nation stood behind him as they had stood behind his grandfather in 1870. "The Moroccan question does not have such an importance. In a war with France and Britain we could not win anything, only lose."[60] While he might not doubt victory, the war had no worthwhile objective from his point of view.

The Kaiser's preference for peace in 1905-06, in fact whenever the Moroccan question seemed to lead close to war, earned him little credit with his generals and even less credit abroad. When Edward Grey took over the direction of the Foreign Office, his ignorance of the diplomatic situation was only surpassed by his ignorance of military conditions at the time. This made it safe for permanent officials like Crowe to tell the new chief that "the fact that Germany kept the peace in 1905-06 is not due to the pacific character of the Emperor [as the British ambassador in Berlin had been forced to conclude, somewhat unwillingly] but to the armaments of the countries which Germany would have to fight." As Crowe pointed out to Grey, Germany was so militaristic that she would go to war almost anytime that she had a reasonable certainty of winning.[61] Actually, given the military situation of 1904-06 and for several years after, Germany could have undertaken the war with the odds greatly in her favor.

It was a fairly general British conviction, useful for propagandistic purposes, that Germany, and apparently no other Power, would go to war whenever she felt ready and superior. Lord Roberts took up the theme in a public speech of October 1912. He maintained that Britain was so much endangered by Germany that she had to have conscription.

Now in the year 1912, just as in 1870, war will take place the instant the German forces on land and sea are, by their superiority at every point, as certain of victory as anything in human calculation can be made certain.

"Germany strikes when Germany's hour has struck." That is the time-honored policy of her foreign office. It is her policy at the present hour, and it is an excellent policy. It is, or ought to be the policy of every nation prepared to play a great part in history.[62]

The British forces were permeated with the conviction that the balance of power must be preserved against a German military victory over France and that Germany, with her "clumsy and obsolete" army, could be beaten.[63] This sentiment, plus the promise of British support given Delcassé in 1905, indicated that readiness for war was probably greater in Britain than anywhere else at the time. This readiness proved rather embarrassing to the majority in the French Government, the anti-Delcassé group. Early in June 1905, Prime Minister Rouvier would not even consider "the hypothesis of a war." Our military situation, he said, "would lead us to defeat and the Commune."[64] In the Ministerial Council of June 6, Rouvier asked the war and naval ministers whether France could fight and win a war. They answered: "We are not ready from any point of view." The Moroccan Conference demanded by Germany had to be conceded and Delcassé was forced to resign.[65]

The majority of French governors considered the doubtful British offer of military help in 1905 to be an altogether insufficient substitute for the disabled Russian ally. And Russia would remain ineffective for a number of years to come. The French were told this openly by Russian Army circles at the end of 1906 and later. The mere thought of war with the Central Powers at that time

threw every one in Russia, from the Tsar down to the last mushik, into consternation... Russia is much too disheartened, too exhausted, too impoverished, too much divided at home, much too threatened from all sides to resign herself to the idea of a new war, with its governmental machinery kept in disorder by shaky hands...She might well fear and detest the Germans; she cannot help us against them unless she has several years of respite.[66]

The military position of the Central Powers was predominant in Europe for the time being. But no use was made of it until the Bosnian annexation in 1908. And war notions among the members of the Entente camp, already including Italy, were put off until the Casablanca incident of 1908 again gave rise to them. The Russian ambassador in Rome asked Foreign Minister Tittoni whether Italy would attack Austria, should the latter become engaged in war with Russia. Tittoni replied:

No, we could not attack Austria; for we are not now strong enough to do it. But should this eventuality present itself three years from now, it might be different; for between now and then we hope to have sufficiently provided for the reorganization of our military forces.[67]

The annexation of Bosnia brought on the next discussion of general war. Each side wondered whether it could take on a war with the hope of winning it. Generals and admirals were questioned, if they had not already proffered their advice unasked. On August 18, 1908, well ahead of the annexation, the Austrian Ministerial Council discussed the problems involved. The Chief of Staff had to answer the fundamental question as to how well the Monarchy was militarily prepared in case of an armed conflict. Before Conrad spoke, Aehrenthal informed the meeting that Austria "could be absolutely certain of Germany [not that he had asked her] because this power was now dependent on Austria alone," particularly since she had declined to reduce her naval constructions and thus improve her relations with Britain. Conrad considered Austria's most likely enemies to be unready. Russia was in no position to undertake war; Turkey, about to lose even the nominal title to Bosnia, need not be feared; as for Italy, the nominal ally, war with her was "even almost desirable, as the Monarchy at present still possesses military superiority over Italy."[68]

The heir to the throne agreed with Aehrenthal that there should be no war and that the war desires of the "good Conrad" and his provocative entourage should be dampened. With this support, plus the confidence of the military in Austria's strength, the Foreign Minister drove through his annexation scheme without discussing its diplomatic and military implications with the German ally. He presented Berlin with a fait accompli and the necessity of protesting its Nibelungen faithfulness to an alliance which Aehrenthal was cold-bloodedly misusing. As the crisis continued, war sentiments grew, even in the supposedly cooler political climate of Britain.[69] Nowhere did they grow as much as in Serbia, where disappointment over the lost heritage led to bitterness and recklessness. Pan-Slav sentiment in Russia backed her so strongly that Russian diplomacy expressed the fear that if the Serbs were to take desperate steps, it might prove impossible for Isvolski or any other minister to master Pan-Slav pressure for war. "To be unready for war has on various occasions not proved a sufficient reason for Russia to refrain from war," the Russian ambassador in London warned his Austrian colleague.[70]

However, Russian unpreparedness—the unreadiness of the Army, continued fear of internal disturbances, the condition of the railways, the need for quiet and reorganization, the respect for Austrian and German war power—was too obvious to be disregarded, even by the most exalted Pan-Slavs.[71] The Russian War Minister explained this to the Germany military attaché, whom he left in no doubt that the Russian army was not ready for war, that the administrative and other reforms he had initiated would not show full effect for another eight or ten years. Russian weakness was apparent. The Kaiser concluded that "from a military standpoint it was for us the best moment for settling accounts with the Russians."[72] What Aehrenthal learned about the state of Russian armaments only confirmed him in his determination to see the annexation through. Berchtold reported to him from St. Petersburg that Russian high officers had concluded that the armed forces needed three to five more years to be ready for war and could not seriously consider a war before that time. It was safe to disregard the threats of Isvolski and the Russian press, "considering the inferiority and the unreadiness of the present-day Russian Army, of which the Tsar and his Government were very well aware."[73]

As if in need of collectively persuading themselves of their country's unreadiness for war, war councils were held in St. Petersburg in March 1909, during which the generals were asked point-blank whether or not the Army was ready for active intervention. Their answers had to be firmly negative, even to the query as to whether the Army was ready for a defense of Russian soil. The war minister, whose tenure did not long survive his plain speaking, declared that the Army was completely unready for battle. A war now, he added, might endanger the continued existence of the monarchy. These deliberations soon became known at home and abroad. The result was to strengthen everywhere the determination to prove stronger on the occasion of the next great conflict between the two armed camps of Europe.[74] Winston Churchill participated in the conflict of 1908-09 and survived to write his quasi-historical judgment on it. He concludes that Austria's policy and Russia's disappointment became "a penultimate cause of the Great War."[75]

There never was a more foolish investment of money and men than the pre-1914 Germany Navy. It was foolish from the standpoint of providing additional strength, and foolish from a political point of view. The Navy could not conceivably promise victory to German arms—except at a very remote date under altogether unlikely conditions. It could only be a poor auxiliary to German landpower. Tirpitz, its founder and organizer, instead based its strategic justification on the idea of "risk" (Risiko), of making the fleet so strong and dangerous that no enemy would run the risk of attacking it. The political probability of such an attack, whatever the "Copenhagening" ideas of Fisher and a few others, was never very great. Instead of strength, the German Navy provided provocation. It consolidated British determination to stand by the Entente grouping in 1911 and in 1914. German diplomats were not in a position to attack Tirpitz in his obviously preposterous strategic ideas; under German traditions only a naval man could judge naval strategy. The men responsible for the conduct of Germany's foreign affairs nevertheless became at least partially aware of the damaging effects of her naval armaments. They were, however, unable to remove the source of hostility and irritation because, in the final analysis, the Tirpitz Navy, backed by the Emperor and the navophile Reichstag, was never effectively enough opposed by the senior service to bring competitive construction to a halt. The army did not demand for itself what the Navy absorbed in men and money. The wrangle with Tirpitz and the Emperor over the continued building programs, which were threatening to make Anglo-German estrangement definitive, at last forced Bülow to ask the Admiral point-blank about the state of German defense in case of a British attack. What should be done to strengthen armaments if they were insufficient? What should be done to avert a conflict as long as there was no hope to emerge victoriously from it? "Prince Bismarck," he noted, "in times of threatening danger of war...turned to the military authorities in order to learn how the chances of war would be in case of a clash." Bülow consequently arranged for one of the very few interdepartmental discussions in an age of utter departmentalization of the German government. On June 3, 1909, under the chairmanship of William II, Tirpitz and the Chief of the Naval Cabinet met with the Foreign Secretary, the ambassador to London, the Minister of the Interior (Bethmann Hollweg), and the Chief of Staff, in order to discuss Germany's chances in a war with Britain.

Moltke saw little chance of success for Germany in such a war. That was all the support Bülow was to receive from the man who, by asserting the traditional power of his office, might have stopped the Navy. Being a weak character and a court general, and representing an army that was fundamentally "saturated" and therefore wanted relatively little for itself, Moltke dared not speak out. Thus the meeting with the Protean Tirpitz remained barren of the desired results.[76] This was practically the last collegial discussion of armament problems and of Germany's chances of winning a war. Bülow resigned soon after. The later civilian governors acquiesced even more completely in having the soldiers and admirals prepare for the war. The civilians were informed, always more implicitly than explicitly, that the war would not be lost. Confidence in obtaining victory through the armed forces of one's own country as they were constituted at the time was nowhere more taken for granted than inside the government of Germany, where the departments of government were most sharply divided. Once the other departments had helped them to obtain the necessary funds, the responsibility for preparing the war was left to the military authorities, without any serious collegial re-examination of the organization and plans for war.[77]

The Agadir crisis once more brought the statesmen and soldiers of the Entente face to face with the possibility of war with Germany. Their belief in Germany's warlike intentions surpassed that country's actual design, though it was indeed true that Germany was using to excess the threat of war as a diplomatic expedient. Whatever pretenses had been evolved by 1914, statesmen still had to make up their minds in the 1911 crisis whether to accept war or whether to put it off, as a general in war postpones battle to a more suitable moment. The French governors, more than any others, were obliged to consider these alternatives. Early in August, Premier Caillaux asked Joffre, soon to be Chief of Staff: "General, it is said that Napoleon did not give battle except when he thought he had at least seventy per cent chances of winning it. Do we have that seventy per cent if the situation forces us into war?" Somewhat embarrassed, Joffre finally replied: "No, I don't consider that we have." Caillaux's response was prompt: "Good, then we shall negotiate."[78]

The French withheld this admission of comparative weakness from the British. Just a few weeks later, Nicolson described British reports as showing

> that the French army has never been in a better state of equipment, organization, and armament, or been inspired by so strong a feeling of perfect confidence and unity...In short they would enter into a campaign feeling that they were able to meet their adversary on very nearly equal terms, and that the issue will not necessarily be, as I believe many people in Germany consider, unfavorable to the French arms.[79]

If French convictions about unreadiness were not shared by the British, they were by the Russians. During the Franco-Russian chief of staff conversations in August 1911, the still backward state of Russian rearmament was considered as excluding a war against Germany with any certainty of success. The Army would be in a position to strike a blow but not yet a decisive blow.

At nearly the same time the Tsar warned the French ambassador: "Take care to avoid a conflict. You know that our preparations are not complete."[80] This view was shared by the diplomats of the Entente, with exceptions among the British. Thus, Paul Cambon informed the Serbian chargé in London in September 1911 that for France and her allies "the war must be postponed to a more distant date, i.e. to 1914-15. This need for delay was not so much dictated by France's military preparations in point of materiel—that was excellent—as by the still incomplete reorganization of her supreme command. This space of time was needed by Russia as well."[81]

During the Franco-Russian chief of staff conversations of February 1912, Russia's armaments were described as still incomplete. Pointing to the undoubted recent progress in Austrian preparations, the Russian did not consider his own country to be "in a position to sustain a war against Germany with the certainty of success before at least another two years. It would certainly be able to ward off blows, but probably less able to strike decisive blows itself."[82]

The improvements in Austria's old-fashioned military system were largely due to the incessant labors of Conrad von Hötzendorf, Chief of Staff since 1906. He and the majority of the officer corps valued this renascence so highly that they projected various wars in which Austria-Hungary would be victorious, wars with Serbia and/or Italy and even, should these wars not be localized, with all the enemies of the Central Powers. If war did not come soon, Austria would lose her relatively favorable position, a position they thought would deteriorate from 1908 on. Still, the diplomats would not make use of this war power. They were, as Conrad argued, letting a vast capital outlay go to waste. "The sums spent for the war power is money wasted," he maintained, "if the war power remains unused for obtaining political advantages. In some cases the mere threat will suffice and the war power thus become useful, but others can be obtained only through the warlike use of the war power itself, that is, by war undertaken in time; if this moment is missed, the capital is lost. In this sense, war becomes a great financial enterprise of the State." Only a misunderstanding of Clausewitz's theories would lead to contrary conclusions. In that war-philosopher's homeland, the right understanding of his theories had led to the correctly-timed wars of 1866 and 1870. The adaptable Japanese had followed these examples and owed their victory over Russia to that fact. Since the great opportunity had been missed by Austria, it only remained for her to keep armaments on a level with those of her competitors.[83]

Such pseudo-capitalistic proposals to "realize" investments in war preparations were not backed by Clausewitz. And they were too crude to become influential with cautious diplomats, to whom the "insurance" arguments in favor of armaments were far more persuasive. Neither were they won over by the Austrian soldiers' proposal of doing away with Italy's partnership in the Triple Alliance. This alliance came up for renewal in November 1911. As a member of the Vienna war party, the newly appointed War Minister, General Auffenberg, argued that there was no longer any sound military reason in its favor. It obviously would not hold in a general European war. To have no alliance with Italy would be preferable to the existing Triplice, which only kept the parliaments in the dark and made them refrain from granting the absolutely necessary funds for the strengthening of the armies. While no territorial gains beyond small boundary rectifications could be expected from a war with Italy, a victorious war—no other outcome was expected—"always paid."

It is certainly true [Auffenberg admitted] that a war between ourselves and Italy could hardly be localized. But I am adamant in my conviction that Germany and we together would remain victorious over a coalition of England, France, Italy and Russia. The Italian troops have not in the least shown themselves equal to their task in Tripoli...And Russia? She has still a long way to go before her army is brought on a better footing and overcomes the consequences of the Japanese War. Removing her Western troops behind the Vistula keeps Russia, even if she enters the war at the outset, from appearing earlier than several weeks afterwards along the German and Austrian frontiers. By that time, however, the decisive blows will have been struck in other theaters of war and we can face Russia with united and superior forces. Germany and Austria-Hungary hold the interior line. At the decisive moment they can unite two million soldiers in one theater of war—something the others cannot do. I should not like to change places with the French or English Chiefs of Staff when it comes to planning a war between these states and ourselves...I am certainly no optimist but I am firm in the confidence and conviction that we are equal to the great coalition. If we two stick together and stand loyally side by side through all the situations of the war, we shall certainly remain victorious.[84]

By 1914, the promise of Austro-German victory had taken its effect. But the diplomats and other civilians, headed by Aehrenthal, won out in 1911. He won Francis Joseph over to a policy of peace, continued the Triplice, and dismissed Conrad (November 30, 1911), who had tried to persuade him to give up the "utopian" alliance with Italy.[85]

Italy's Tripolitan war encouraged all parties to participate in the coming Balkan wars, including even the Turks in their determination to seek and engage in war. They all expected to emerge from it victorious, on their own strength or with backing from the Great Powers. The longer the Tripolitan war lasted, the better; the two belligerents, both enemies of Slavdom, would be weakened by it. Slavdom must exploit this weakness, for such a situation would not offer itself again for a long time to come.[86] Once the Balkan alliances had been concluded on the basis of this common conviction, the soldiers looked forward "with joy to a rencontre" with the Turks. Even the commercial circles in the Balkan countries, while worrying about the war, preceded as it was by general economic stagnation, preferred war and a prompt decision to a prolonged state of general depression.[87] The Turks, who were soon to sign the peace treaty with Italy (October 18), felt stronger every day and more the equal, if not the superior, of the small Balkan armies. They were justified, Austrian diplomacy thought, in believing that, while their enemies had mobilized their whole strength at the outset and hence had no resources left for a prolonged war, they themselves would be able to assemble more men and material in the long run and thus sustain the war much longer. This only required that they should remain on the defensive long enough at the outset.[88] The Turks were unable to do this. They did not deny the attackers the opening battle by digging in as they had done at Plevna. They suffered a defeat that surprised nearly everyone, the experts most of all—something many a defeat has done to many an expert.[89]

THE CONSEQUENCES OF RUSSIA'S RETURN TO STRENGTH

As far as the opening of the Balkan war had depended on the placet of any Great Power, Russia, taken most deeply into the confidence of the Balkan allies, had given it. The French government, through Poincaré, had promised Russia's Balkan policy "the most sincere and most energetic diplomatic support," but had also warned her that military support could not be expected in case of an Austro-Russian conflict. If Germany should become involved with her armed forces, "the French Government recognized in advance that this would constitute a casus foederis and he, Poincaré, would not hesitate one minute to fulfill the obligations toward Russia which were incumbent on it." Poincaré had received advice from the highest army sources, "informed and responsible personalities," he told Isvolski, who "envisaged with much optimism the chances for Russia and France in the case of

a general conflagration." His optimism was strengthened by the expectation that the united Balkan forces would attract a portion of Austria's armed forces from the Russian front.[90] This enabled him to give Russia his full assurance of French support—a blank check as good or as bad as that which Germany gave Austria early in July 1914, only older.

This French confidence in victory, freely expressed to the ally, was a new feature in the military-diplomatic situation. Military judgment was accepted by the civilian governors without any detailed re-examination, to which a man with a departmentalized mind, like Poincaré, was far less inclined than, say, Caillaux. This allowed the directors of French affairs and then the directors of Russian affairs to contemplate and at last to undertake the general war in Europe with confidence. One of the several "origins" of the war of 1914 lies at this juncture. France was no longer shunning a general war, and Russia was following France. And the British, even if they had not fully known of this step towards the technical possibility of war, would be led by "the irresistible course of events...to armed intervention against Germany."[91]

In Austria, the Aehrenthal tradition, after his death in February 1912, at first proved stronger than the Conrad tradition with regard to the Balkan situation. A ministerial council presided over by Berchtold considered what position Austria was to take in case the Russian-patronized Balkan alliance should go to war. The War Minister pointed out the difficulties of various military actions against Serbia, concluding that "generally speaking actions that might lead to large conflagrations might better be avoided, considering the hardly favorable situation of the Army as regards important material equipment." Both premiers, Austrian and Hungarian, spoke against a war that would call for gigantic sacrifices but from which nothing would be gained.[92] On second thought, however, War Minister Auffenberg discussed the situation with Conrad's locum tenens, Schemua, and asked him to report on the situation and discuss the possibility of conflict with the Russian Army. The Chief of Staff considered Russia superior only with regard to artillery. But in general, he said, "one can conclude that even in a war in which we would have to fight it out with Russia alone [the war most unwelcome to Poincaré] the chances of an ultimate victory are in no way unfavorable." His estimate was based on the assumption that Serbia and Montenegro would remain engaged in war with Turkey and that Russia would not be allowed to get ahead of Austria in her preparatory measures for war.[93]

The belief that Russia was not yet fully ready

for a major war still prevailed, inside and outside Russia, though there was a strong war party
within the Russian Army looking for an occasion
to wipe off the shame of the Manchurian defeat
by beating the Austrians.[94] Much of what the
Russians still lacked in self-confidence they
gained from the French, notably through Poincaré.[95] He gave them to understand that even
such events as a territorial change in Austria's
favor on the Balkan scene would induce France
to enter the field of military operations. It was
a new note of encouragement when, during the
Austro-Serbian conflict of November 1912, Poincaré stated that "it was up to Russia to take the
initiative in a question in which she was principally interested; the role of France is to lend her
the most effective support." As Isvolski understood him, this amounted "to saying that if Russia
undertakes war, France will also, because we
know that in this question Germany will be behind Austria."[96]

France's declared readiness for war made
Russia persevere for many weeks in her mobilization measures against Austria.[97] As to the
reasons for this French confidence, the most
friendly witness imaginable, Sir Henry Wilson,
informed the Foreign Office that the French

> are of the opinion that it would be far better
> for France if a conflict were not too long
> postponed. Their reasons are that if it would
> come now, it would be in consequence of the
> Balkan difficulties, and therefore they would
> be able to secure the wholehearted support of
> Russia. Were a conflict to be postponed and
> eventually to arise over some difficulty be-
> tween Germany and France alone, they had
> some doubts—treaty notwithstanding—whether
> Russia would go whole-heartedly on their side.

The French generals impressed upon Wilson that
Russia was exceedingly strong, both in her military organization and in her financial condition,
and was therefore far less dependent on French
support—in short, that Russia was now well able
to look after herself, and might be inclined to take
a line of her own.[98]

Grey, who wanted Britain to be "no party to
France precipitating a conflict for the revanche,"
took this report as indicative that the French
Government did not share these military sentiments. The Russians, however, understood the
French Government to be less peacefully inclined and in any case considered the French
military to be nearly as politically powerful as
were the soldiers in Russia. By February 1913,
the Russian ambassador in London thought that
of all the Great Powers, France was the one least
opposed to war.[99]

Confidence in victory and the readiness for war

deriving from it were equally high in Berlin and
Vienna. The latter received more encouragement
than discouragement from Berlin for continued
military preparations along the Russian and Serbian frontiers. Moltke told his Austrian counter-
part that the Double Monarchy "could absolutely
count" on German support if Austria were threatened by Russia. The Austrian report states that
Moltke felt it was also "important for Germany's
interests that we should not be weakened. He
grasps fully the seriousness of the situation.
The mobilization of Germany results automatically
in the mobilization of France, and two mobilized
armies side by side create an untenable situation
which will surely result in a conflict." Moltke also
hoped "to finish with France in four to five weeks,
and then turn to the East."[100]

Although persuaded that Russia would not be
ready for another two years, neither Moltke nor
William II made this expectation the reason for
a war in November 1912. They did not propose a
preventive war. But they did hand over an un-
Bismarckian blank check. The Kaiser assured the
Austrian heir to the throne—"not a man of action,"
as Moltke noted on the occasion of his visit to
Berlin—that his support went so far that "if it became a question of prestige for Austria-Hungary,
he would not even fear a world war and that he
would be ready to enter into a war with the three
Entente Powers."[101] It needed the somewhat
brutal methods of Secretary of State Kiderlen-
Wächter to snatch back this blank check from the
careless hands of Berchtold.[102] There was no
such snatcher in Berlin in 1914. Kiderlen died at
the end of 1912. No one in Germany could keep
the Kaiser from talking big, indulging in the
verbosity of a basically weak and only nominally-
directing entrepreneur, who felt that he had the
most efficient office personnel and the strongest
battalions behind him in the world's most terrible
competition. In mid-December 1912, in the most
splendid humor and full of hope for peace, he
voiced once more his approval of Austria's military preparations, even though he did not expect
Russia's warlike intervention. Germany herself
"had made no special preparations for the eventuality of a war; for this was not at all necessary
since the German Army could be ready for war
within six days."[103]

Great Power confidence in victory was crudely
reflected in the Balkans, where the regrouping of
the belligerents after the end of their first round
of war was coming to a head. In spite of their
isolation, the Bulgarians were certain that if it
should come to war with Serbia, such a war would
be "quick and bloody and would result in victory
for Bulgaria." After that, Serbia would not only be
denied a part of the spoils but would have to
agree to frontier adjustments at her expense.[104]

The civilian politicians in Sofia were completely under the spell of the Army, which reported itself "in full war competence," and of the terrorizing Macedonians. Some of them agreed to the attack on the former allies in the hope of thereby accelerating Russian intervention. The ex-allies were ready for them. The Greek foreign minister had spoken constantly "and in the most hopeful manner of war and had given most positive assurances that within a fortnight after the outbreak of the war the Bulgarians would be annihilated."[105] It took somewhat longer than that, plus the entry of Rumania and Turkey into the war, to make the débacle of Bulgaria complete.

The unreadiness of Russia's armed forces for war after 1905 was perhaps the greatest peace-preserving factor in the years before 1914. On the other hand, war-readiness is not in itself absolutely conducive of war. At any rate, it is not as conducive as is the readiness to consider war as a means when specific aims of an imperialist character present themselves. Whatever may be held against Germany's pre-1914 Army, it was ready for war technically far more than politically.[106] To an extent, these motivations can be kept apart, at least as compared with conditions inside the Russian and French armies. Both of these armies were animated by distinct aims that could only be won by a victorious war—Constantinople and Alsace-Lorraine. The absence of imperialistic aims, combined with a social conservatism that kept the strengthening of the Army below what was possible and allowed the waste of men and money for an irrelevant navy, made the German Army peaceful by comparison with the Russian and French. On the other hand, its exactly planned preparations for the case of war made it press for war as soon as a certain amount of preparation in the opposite camp had persuaded its directors that the closely calculated superiority based on ultra-readiness must not be endangered by further waiting.

It was the lure of Constantinople that first made the Russian governors consider undertaking war after the Peace of Portsmouth, in January 1908. On the initiative of the chief of staff, a meeting of the various departmental heads, including the minister of finance, was called in that month. The Chief of Staff suspected "an active movement" in the spring on the part of the Turks, which would not remain restricted to the Caucasian region but would extend at least as far as the Balkan Peninsula. While Isvolski was willing to have Russia's "historical mission" reactivated, Premier Stolypin and Finance Minister Kokovzev protested energetically: a forward policy was impossible for the time being. "A new mobilization in Russia would only strengthen the revolution from which we are just now beginning to emerge...Russia

was in need of a breathing spell after which she would consolidate herself and again assume a position in keeping with her rank as a Great Power." The Premier based his opposition on the War Minister's statement that the Army "could not yet be considered as reorganized." The training had not gone far enough and the Army had suffered from the necessity of employing the troops on the home front against the revolution. "The restoring of order inside the Army and the fortresses would require colossal funds and much more time."[107]

Early in 1914, the Liman von Sanders mission, which seemed designed to keep Russia out of Constantinople and the Straits forever, once more gave her governors occasion to consider whether her armed forces were ready for the eventuality of war. All—in the absence of such "home bodies" as the Interior Minister, whose approval could be dispensed with as constitutionalism receded in Russia—were agreed. Russia and France alone could never give Germany the mortal blow, but a war in which Britain participated "would be fatal for Germany, which clearly realizes the danger of being brought to a social catastrophe at home within six weeks following British intervention." Revolution was so forgotten at home that it could now be hoped to work in Russia's favor inside Germany. Unfortunately, British intervention for the sake of obtaining Constantinople was quite unlikely. In the face of German unwillingness to recall the obnoxious mission, the following question posed itself (as formulated by Kokovzev, now Prime Minister): "Is war with Germany desirable and can Russia undertake it?" Both he and Foreign Minister Sasonov considered such a war undesirable. In answer to the Prime Minister's question as to whether the Russian forces could undertake it, War Minister and Chief of Staff "declared categorically the full readiness of Russia for a duel with Germany, not to mention a duel with Austria. But such a two-sided war was hardly likely," and one could not be certain of obtaining French and British backing for measures against Turkey that might in turn lead to war with Germany.[108]

At this time, the nine-years' period of Russia's declared inability to fight a major war had come to an end. According to War Minister Suchomlinov, the Russian Army was "in 1914 so far prepared that Russia appeared justified in looking a war quietly in the eye. Never before had Russia been better prepared for a war than in 1914. In addition, Sasonov's information about the French and English attitudes towards the conflict were of such a kind that there was for us no reason for faintheartedness. His communications about Italy and Rumania also worked in the same direction."[109]

ALL-ROUND BELIEF IN VICTORY, 1914

The confidence on the part of the military of both armed camps was established well ahead of July 1914. This confidence was imparted to the diplomats and other governors, who accepted it uncritically but not so very wrongly: the soldiers on either side proved nearly right in their prognostications. It was shared so fully that most governments, except the old-fashioned Austrian one, refrained from again discussing their own war-readiness and their chances for victory in July 1914. Confidence reigned everywhere, from the greatest to the smallest of the original participants, well before that July.

The danger to peace arising from such convictions, more general in Europe by 1914 than ever before, rested in the fact that the belief in one's own victory caused a definite weakening in the diplomats' determination to preserve the peace. In no person is this more clearly observable than in Count Berchtold. Within the space of a year and a half, he succumbed completely to the high-voltage of Conrad's demands for war and promises of victory. The belief in military victory was highly enticing to the weak character of the diplomats of 1914. Grey and Bethmann Hollweg, the representatives of the two Powers that had nothing to gain by war, could feel that, if their not overly intelligent, prompt, or honest endeavors in favor of peace should fail, the recourse to arms was always highly feasible. This conviction weakened the eirenicon of diplomacy. The readying for war was also indicated by the increasing care exercised not to appear on the record as in any way responsible for war. Several governments tried to avoid incurring what came to be called war guilt by omitting last-hour councils or votes on the pros and cons of undertaking war. Austria and Britain were exceptions in this respect.

The Austrian soldiers and diplomats marched their ancient Empire to its death because they believed that it could be saved by war. They had been persuaded by Conrad that "there existed even in the great [or general] war the possibility of a victorious outcome."[110] Conrad had drawn up a balance sheet of strengths, showing how unsafe the situation would be if Rumania did not join the Central Powers. In order not to unduly discourage the German ally, Berchtold removed this pessimistic document from the dossier given to his adlatus Count Hoyos for his mission to Berlin to obtain approval for "energetic" measures against Serbia.[111] In going to the Berlin loan office—for a loan of military strength —the Ballhausplatz suppressed such a sobering document. A practical-minded lender might have called for such a document. But Berlin did not.

Instead of examining the balance sheet as the basis of the Austrian demand for the loan that would call for all that Germany had to give, her governors handed over the blank check of "Germany's unconditional support" without haggling, without any new deliberations of cabinet or Crown Council.

Once in possession of this blank check, the Austrian war party proceeded to win over the only staunch opponent to war, Tisza, the Hungarian Premier. He was not easily persuaded that war, including a war against Russia, should be undertaken at that moment. Scoring a diplomatic success over Serbia might suffice. In the Ministerial Council of July 7, Tisza defended the peace; Berchtold and the soldiers, the war. "A diplomatic success would be interpreted as mere weakness," the War Minister declared. "From a military standpoint a war now was more favorable than later when the ratio of strength was bound to suffer in Austria's disfavor." The military were careful to contribute nothing to a discussion about the comparative strengths in the probable course of a general European war that might have been discouraging. They considered the general tendency of armaments in the years to come as "rather in our disfavor." Hence the advisability of "war now."[112]

On the strength of this advice, not seriously questioned, discussed, or examined by any of the civilians present, the Austrian measures against Serbia were decided upon. The same uncritical civilian confidence had reigned for years in Berlin. According to hostile as well as friendly observation, "supreme confidence reigned in military circles in Berlin" from the beginning to the end of the July crisis.[113] The Saxon military plenipotentiary gained the impression from a talk with the Quartermaster-General that the Great General Staff would consider it "a favorable circumstance if war should break out now. Situation and outlook could not be better."[114] The French military attaché in Berlin believed that this German confidence in superiority, the belief that they would "cut through France as through butter" had lately been carried to the point of paroxysm by revelations of shortcomings in France's armaments.[115]

But if scandals in the French Army had given a lift to German soldiers, it had not depressed confidence in the Paris military offices. There the Russian military attaché observed "the general quietness, the satisfaction with one's own labors and the unconcealed joy of putting to use the strategic situation, favorable to them, according to the French."[116] In the higher echelons, there was 'more discretion about the prospects of victory. On the day when the news of the Austrian ultimatum to Serbia reached Paris, War

Minister Messimy told Joffre "that we might possibly have to make war." Thanks to his habit of thinking continually about the preparations for war, the Chief of Staff took "this fearful eventuality without surprise" and answered: "Well, M. le Ministre, we shall make it if it must be." He felt that his own attitude had a calming effect on the Minister, who shook his hand energetically with a "Bravo!"[117] There was thus no last-hour military protest or scruple about going to war; by the judgment of the Chief of Staff the French Government could safely undertake war. The general tendency of French policy prior to 1914, to take on the war if it should come, was no longer considered unsafe from a military point of view.

Russian confidence in victory, provided that England participated in the war, had been established since the turn of the year 1913-14.[118] The Tsar confirmed this when he told Paléologue on July 20 that "unless Germany has lost her reason altogether, she will never dare to attack Russia, France and England combined."[119] Was this also the German military view? Should Germany therefore have refrained from war in 1914, or at least from the invasion of Belgium? Would Germany have refrained from invading Belgium had it known, through an open pronouncement of Grey's, that Britain would enter the war on that issue?[120] These questions cannot be definitely answered. Military judgment in Germany varied, according to mood almost more than according to the latest computation of strengths. Moltke had admitted at least once that Britain's accession to the Franco-Russian alliance would be fatal to Germany.[121] That had been in 1909, and things had not changed in Germany's favor since then. This did not prevent Moltke from considering Britain's participation in the war negligible in 1914.[122]

As a matter of course, British armament was predicated on the possibility of war against the Central Powers in coalition with France and Russia. British sailors and soldiers, men like Fisher and Wilson, felt generally certain of victory in 1914 and well before. Grierson was even persuaded that Germany "would be an easy prey for Britain and France combined." For the French had "guaranteed that, with the help of our 150,000 army, the Germans would be crushed in no time."[123] What Britain's political governors thought about the ratio of strength in July-August 1914 they kept strictly to themselves, then and later. Confidence in victory was not expressed publicly or even discussed in cabinet meetings. The cabinet's belief in victory also dated from before 1914. This was particularly true of the Asquith-Grey-Haldane group, which came to think, only in the light of after-events, that the military had been too confident.[124] The British Gov-

ernment left it to the soldiers to calculate the military strength of the Powers and to establish the mobilization as automatically as they could. The British governors took no last-hour counsel as to whether or not Britain was materially ready for war and victory, only whether they "ought to" go to war.[125] While on the Continent (according to Lloyd Geroge) "each army believed in its own invincibility and was anxious to demonstrate it," the desire of the soldiers to put the machine they had perfected to the triumphant test was of no influence in England. "In this country," Lloyd George writes, "this desire did not count in the estimation of a hair! Our overwhelming confidence in the power of our Navy may perhaps have influenced opinion in certain quarters, but that influence was not decisive" as it was in Germany.[126]

If military confidence in victory was not immediately felt at the time in Britain, it still formed part of Grey's diplomacy which, in the last analysis, was designed for complete victory in war rather than for the maintenance of peace. On July 31 Sir Eyre Crowe put the question at issue on a higher level than English capability of taking part in a war. He pitched the decision as a matter "firstly of right or wrong and secondly of political expediency."[127] But this still reflected an attention to principle based on a strong belief in military victory for his own side, rather than a Don Quixotic loftiness. Which diplomat, if he has his country's interest in mind, can advocate its entry into war without having at the time the certainty of victory, ultimately if not immediately? For if he does not have it, he must urge postponement of the war. Grey and his helpmates had accepted the victory recipe of the combined British-French general staffs as fully as any Continental set of governors. It has been said that "there is one cause of war which the minister of a civilly governed State must be able to avoid: the fixing of a casus belli by joint general staff plans."[128] Grey had taken no precautions against this that would hold in July-August 1914, nor had he kept in mind the possibility, of traditional concern in British diplomacy, that British accession to a Continental group might make the victory of that side too complete. This possibility was seen even at the time by John Morley. He reminded Lloyd George of it, and George admitted only later that he had never thought out the effects of Russian victory in Europe and Asia.[129]

Military judgment assumed such fateful character in 1914 because of the soldiers' and sailors' unanimous conviction that their side could undertake war with a fair hope of victory. For years the desire for more time for military preparation had postponed war more effectively than diplomatic art. Now there was no longer any military reason to postpone it. In 1914, all competitors in the arms race considered themselves ready for war—with this difference: that the military of the Central Powers were convinced they could still win it, though with a shrinking margin of superiority, while those of the Entente Powers believed that now, for the first time, victory was within their grasp. A weak diplomacy could not keep the doors closed against the bloody race.

The conduct of the war from 1914 to 1918 and beyond was replete with military promises and reassurances of victory, so much so that war could not be ended by the action of diplomacy, as the Papacy and Lord Lansdowne proposed, but only by the overwhelming victory of one side. Much of the obstinacy of the struggle was due to the unwillingness of the soldiers on either side to admit that their promises of more or less immediate victory had remained unfulfilled. In striving for victory, war was continued well beyond the limits of most of the measurable national interests.

The bitter taste of the fruits of victory and the still bitterer taste of defeat produced neither general weariness nor disillusionment with the promises of victory given by the military before, in, and after 1914. The first post-1918 victim of such assurances was the ever-optimistic Venizelos. He was ready to undertake the Greek war against Kemalist Turkey. He assured the Big Five in Paris (November 8, 1919) that, should the Peace Conference charge Greece with the task of defeating the recalcitrant Turk, his country, with an army of 325,000 men, could easily defeat Mustapha Kemal, who had only 70,000 men at his disposal.[130] The Greek officers persisted in this over-confidence when, after the fall of Venizelos from power in March 1921, they opened their disastrous offensive without an Allied mandate.

Much of the support given by the Western Powers to the White Russian forces under Kolchak and Denikin was based on the soldiers' assurance that the White cause was quite promising. When Kolchak seemed successful in his advance through Siberia in the summer of 1919, the Allied governments recognized his Provisional Government. They did this against the original advice of the military mission, headed by General Knox, former military attaché in St. Petersburg, following instead the strong urgings of Churchill and Sir Henry Wilson, British Chief of Staff. Knox wired that Kolchak's military failure made recognition inadvisable, but Henry Wilson "would not believe the situation to be as Knox described it. He required Knox to answer clearly whether or not there was any chance of a military success. Everything, he said, depended on that answer, because it was only by promising a military success

that summer that he and Mr. Churchill had been able to persuade the War Cabinet to agree to Kolchak's practical recognition." Under this pressure from home and from above, Knox recanted and reported that success for Kolchak was possible after all.[131]

THE TOTALITARIANS AND THE PLEDGE OF VICTORY

With the rise of the dictators, the counselling function of the soldiers came practically to an end. Instead, the Führer and Duce promised them and their peoples victories that the soldiers considered doubtful or unobtainable. The Nazified generals and lower ranks succumbed to the spell of Hitler as he scored one pseudo-victory after the other. His coups—the remilitarization of the Rhineland, the Anschluss of Austria and Czechoslovakia—could never have been successful if France had interposed, as the protesting Wehrmacht generals were only too well aware.[132] It was only an old code duello convention for General Beck to tell General Gamelin on a visit in 1937: "You are convinced that you will be victorious. We think that we shall be. That is the lot of all good soldiers. But the final upshot would be, in all sorts of ways, the ruin of Europe and of our common civilization. Only Bolshevism would profit by it."[133] The same argument was offered to Hitler by the French ambassador, François-Poncet, during the Czech crisis of September 1938: "You are naturally confident of winning the war, just as we believe we can defeat you. But why should you take that risk, when you can have your more essential demand granted without war?" But Hitler would not assent.[134]

It was an indispensable part of his bluffing to express Germany's readiness to go to war, to insist in each case that her victory was assured. His minions in the Party had to echo his braggadocio. Goering told the assembled German airplane manufacturers (July 8, 1938) that, should Germany be forced to go to war, the great war for which there was a ninety per cent probability, it would be "the greatest hour of destiny ever since there has been a Germany history. And the possibility of victory indeed exists." In case of victory, "Germany will be the greatest Power in the world. Then it is Germany who will dominate the world market. Then will be the hour when Germany is a rich nation. For this goal, however, we have to take risks."[135]

What Goering told the politically ignorant airplane makers Ribbentrop tried to impress on the more sophisticated diplomatic personnel. They were to express a firm belief in German victory in all their conversations with foreign diplomats. In the summer of 1938, they were to tell them that "if necessary we would run the risk of a full-scale war with the Western Powers even now and win it, too," that Germany was provided with the raw materials for a war of no matter what duration, that her aircraft production was superior to that of all opponents. The Secretary of State, von Weizsäcker, a one-time naval officer with the experience of German defeat and capitulation deep in his bones, agreed that it might become necessary to talk to outsiders in such a manner. But he urged that it was still necessary for the Germans not to dupe themselves with such talk. He himself could not believe that the Reich could win such a war, as Ribbentrop maintained. It could not be won from the air, and he doubted Germany's powers of endurance. "Such a war," he thought, "would sooner or later end with a German capitulation." Early in August 1938, Ribbentrop drew up an instruction for the German representatives abroad to guide them in their talks about the Czech crisis. Weizsäcker again protested against boasting of Germany's war-readiness. It was so contrary to the facts that not even the heads of missions could be convinced that, thanks to the Luftwaffe, the Reich was now actually stronger than in 1914, that "we are today so prepared as to be able, if need be, to bring such a war to a victorious end." Such statements, the professional diplomat warned, were only calculated to make fools out of one's own ambassadors. His warning was to no avail. On August 3, Ribbentrop's boastful instructions were sent out.[136]

The conservative Weizsäcker continued the struggle against the Hitler-Ribbentrop gambling. Hitler was beyond the reach of any German warnings, but he could at least force Ribbentrop to hear him. However, Weizsäcker was told by the Minister that it was time for him to acquire that blind belief in the Führer's genius that he, the Minister, had entertained for some years. He must believe in the genius that had achieved such successes as the difficult Rhineland occupation. Weizsäcker's warnings that a German invasion of Czechoslovakia would be followed by a general European war that would sooner or later end in German capitulation went unheeded. Friendly outsiders were no less filled with warnings and forebodings. The Hungarians, while expecting to profit from a partition of Czechoslovakia, thought that the chances for a German victory in a general European war in the autumn of 1938 were less than the necessary minimum of sixty to seventy per cent. To enter war on a lesser chance could not be expected of them. It would be suicidal to enter the war on Germany's side before the spring of 1939, when their own rearmament would have brought its first results. And the well-wishing King of Sweden expressed, together with "his love

for Germany...his grave fear of the inevitability of a German defeat in a world war in view of the present combination of Powers" (September 27).[137] Whether he knew it or not, the Powers were themselves persuaded, largely by British military opinion, that Czech resistance against German attacks was futile and that even the combined military assistance of Britain, France, and Russia could not save her.[138]

Hitler would take warnings neither from friendly parties nor from foreign opponents nor from domestic ones. The German military, judging by truer standards than the Führer, had to put the chances of German victory lower than they did when speaking with foreign soldiers, as in Beck's talk with Gamelin. Brauchitsch, commander-in-chief of the Army, approached Ribbentrop late in May 1938, after he heard rumors that military steps against Czechoslovakia were being contemplated, in order to tell him that the state of German armaments still left much to be desired. The Foreign Minister was somewhat stunned and told one of his subordinates that he had not known of this, that, considering this fact, he was pursuing a wrong policy.[139] Soon after, Hitler ordered a further step-up in German armaments which were to be ready before the autumn for the aggression against Czechoslovakia. Success in Czechoslovakia, though non-military in its nature, further strengthened the Nazis', though not all the generals', belief in Germany's invincibility.

When Ribbentrop arrived in Moscow to sign the non-aggression pact with the Russians, he came, as he told them and as they said they believed, not like the British and French military negotiators to ask the Soviet Union for assistance "in case war should be forced upon the German Government by England. The German Government," he said, "was not in need of assistance for this contingency, but would, in this event, have sufficient military strength to take up the struggle alone against Poland and its Western foes and to carry it to a victorious conclusion."[140] Stalin confirmed the Germans in their hubris, yet personally believing that the initial German superiority would not prove quite as overwhelming as it did and that the struggle of the capitalist Powers would leave Russia in a stronger position than it actually did. The announcement of the British-Polish Pact of August 25 gave the dictators pause, first Mussolini, who now discovered that Italy was not ready for war, and then Hitler. Localized war with Poland alone no longer appeared likely. The German orders for the attack were remanded, although Hitler had just told the French ambassador: "I have, as you know, made an agreement with Moscow which is, I may say, concrete and not theoretical. I believe I shall win. You believe you will win...It greatly depresses me to be

forced to assume that we have come so far."[141]
In this dueller's mood, which he might have
thought he had borrowed from the soldiers, Hitler
went to war, consternated after opening the war
against Poland to find Britain not a mere ineffectual second but ready for war. He received the British ultimatum of September 3 with dismay: "What
are we going to do now?" Then, collecting himself:
"In that case I must talk with the military people."[142] Then he proceeded "to conquer himself
to death." And he took the German people with
him, the people who had been told and persuaded
so long by Goebbels' propaganda: "We believe in
victory because we have the Führer."[143]

The most professionally-minded German generals
had not wanted the war for which they knew they were
not prepared; but they allowed themselves to be
driven by the dictator whom they had helped to
create but could not stop or remove. The Italian
generals were in much the same position. Mussolini's orders, such as the one for the attack on
prostrate France in June 1940, found them "absolutely unprepared."[144]

In April 1939 the Duce had expected war for
1943, following the close of the Rome International
Exhibition planned for 1942, when "turismo" was
expected to help Italian armaments. Badoglio, the
Chief of Staff, protested: even by 1943 the armed
forces, considering their poor state, could not be
ready for war, except perhaps the Navy. When
Mussolini informed him of his resolution to enter the war on Germany's side (May 26, 1940),
rearmament had hardly gotten under way. Badoglio protested violently: "You are perfectly well
aware that we are absolutely unprepared...We
have twenty divisions with seventy per cent of the
necessary equipment and training; and about another twenty divisions with fifty per cent...no
tanks...no stores...not even sufficient shirts for
the Army...It is suicide." Mussolini would not listen: "I assure you war will be over in September
and that I need a few thousand dead so as to be
able to attend the peace conference as a belligerent." The Chief of Staff went to Ciano, the
Foreign Minister, who, when informed about the
entry into war, kept on saying: "Mussolini is absolutely mad." And then both went on serving,
Badoglio on his part to "prevent the mistakes
which Mussolini would make in his complete
ignorance of military affairs."[145]

Compared with 1914, when confidence in victory had reigned on all sides, hopefulness was at
best moderate in all the military staffs and commands in 1939. As an airman, Lord Trenchard
spoke of Britain's "sheer audacity in going to
war" in 1939.[146] Certain war-preparation offices were, however, persuaded by their production
schedules that Britain would be ready to fight on
more or less equal terms by July 1939.[147] By

February 1939, British rearmament inspired
Chamberlain with enough confidence to say that
the Germans "could not make nearly such a mess
of us now as they could then [at the time of Mun-
ich] while we could make much more of a mess
of them." This justified an increasing firmness
on the Prime Minister's part, which his critics,
he thought, applauded without understanding. The
reasons for it were "the connection between
diplomatic and strategic strength which...has
always been stressed by the wisest diplomats
and statesmen of the past."[148] However, the
improved position of strength from which Chamberlain hoped to convince the Germans "that the
chances of winning a war without getting
thoroughly exhausted in the process are too remote to make it worthwhile,"[149] did not impress Hitler. Nor was this achieved by his public
declaration on August 29 that Britain was "ready
for any eventuality," with her air defense "in a
state of instant readiness...the Navy in an advanced state of preparedness."[150]

In addition to the tragic over-confidence in
their own strength, the Poles entered the war in
hopes that France would at once make war beyond
the Maginot Line. In this manner the Poles expected to achieve a joint victory. The French
army chiefs did not share their confidence, nor
did the majority of French civilian ministers.
France was faced with the choice of entering the
war at once, in keeping with treaty obligations, or
refraining from intervention and thereby gaining
time for the further strengthening of French armaments. On August 23, 1939, the Cabinet asked
the military for an answer to the "essentially
military" question of which course to follow. General Gamelin and Admiral Darlan saw no choice
for France but to adhere to her obligations with
regard to Poland. They "indicated that the ground
forces and the navy were ready." But their confidence, which did not extend to the air force, was
so limited that they kept themselves within the
most correct constitutional limits. Gamelin reminded the ministers "that it is not up to the
military to decide whether or not there is reason
to undertake war. They can only say whether it is
possible to undertake it." No more.

Following the defeat of 1940, at the time of the
Riom trials, Gamelin was accused of having made
a statement reminiscent of Leboeuf's declaration
of 1870 that the army was "arch-ready." His
accusers held that when he said "the Army and
Navy are ready," they had a right to understand
him as meaning that he promised victory. As
against these accusations, Gamelin insisted that
he had meant merely that "the Army was ready
for the setting off [déclenchement] of mobilization and concentration." That is, the Army was
more ready than at the time of Munich, when

mobilization had revealed a number of short-comings which had since been remedied. Gamelin protested that he could not have expressed the opinion that the material equipment of the Army was complete. Several of those present knew too well that it was not, even though this fact was not stressed on the occasion, due to the presence of Bonnet. Through him the Germans might have learned of any discouraging statement made. In retrospect, Gamelin writes that

> to have said "the Army is ready," in the ab-solute sense of these terms, would have been sheer absurdity. A modern Army is never "ready." Neither the French nor the German armies were ready in 1914. The morning after the Marne battle, neither of them had sufficient ammunition left to continue the battle along the whole front...In 1939 Germany was ready to attack Poland, but not to act against France. In 1940, she was not ready to attack Britain. On the eve of battle one never, or very rarely, disposes of all the materiel one should have wished for...On the other hand, I know enough history to have refrained from stating once again Marshal Leboeuf's words of sad memory.[151]

The Japanese Army was most unhesitating in promising victory during the 1930's and 1940's. Embarking on war after the China Incident in 1937, the Army informed the throne that "the in-cident would be disposed of in about one month." After four years of fighting, victory had not yet been obtained. The civilian leaders were inclined to remind the Army chiefs of their failure when, following the outbreak of the German-Russian war, they proposed to follow Germany into war. In the words of Konoye, they merely received authorization to occupy French-Indochina "as a consolation prize." The Army continued to press for war, now against the United States and Bri-tain, a war that would also be the Navy's war. The cautiously-moving Emperor, reminding them of the undelivered victory in China, asked for the Army's estimate of the probable length of hostil-ities in case of a Japanese-American War. The Army's Chief of Staff, who had been war minis-ter at the time of the China Incident, replied that "he believed operations in the South Pacific would be disposed of in about three months." When reminded that his victory promises of four years ago had not been fulfilled, the General ex-plained at great length that China's extensive hinterland had prevented the consummation of operations according to plan. But, asked the Em-peror, was not the Pacific even more extensive by comparison? How could the General be certain of his three-months' estimate? He could not answer the simple question and had to give his

assent to some further diplomatic negotiations with the United States. These were resolved upon during an Imperial conference held the next day (September 5-6, 1941). This was the conference whose resolutions, according to Cordell Hull, amounted to "a cold-blooded determination to go to war—one of the most sinister episodes in his-tory."[152]

The bluntness of Japanese politics always led back to a discussion of Japan's chances for vic-tory. Pressed by various civilians, the Japanese generals had to concede that they were prepared for a plunge rather than for a calculable victory. "Sometimes it is necessary fo a man to risk his life in one leap," War Minister Tojo told Prince Konoye. Konoye reminded the general that a metaphor must not be carried too far, that "cross-ing the Rubicon" and "risking the fate of the na-tion" were exciting words, but that "starting a war without seeing the prospect of success is very different from the case of an individual. At last, when one thinks of the 2600-years-old fault-less national policy, one cannot act so irrespon-sibly. Even when criticized as slow or old-fashioned, people like myself cannot act in such a way." The soldiers recalled that no unqualified promise of victory had been given when Japan en-tered upon the two glorious wars of 1894-95 and 1904-1905 and that such a thing as one hundred per cent confidence in victory was not to be had. Konoye reminded them that, in the case of the latter war, there had been reasonable hope of in-tervention by the United States, as the one Power outside the alliance system of that time, should Japan have failed to achieve her expected victory. "However this time," he continued, "there will be no third nation, and there will be no country ready to intervene. Hence any prediction as to future projects is quite impossible. If, in spite of this, our country is to be plunged into war, the decision will have to be made with extreme care and with consideration of the national polity." The Army and the Navy, the latter unwilling to admit its "weakness" and its original unwilling-ness to go to war, continued to press for war. They maintained that men like Konoye were "too well aware of the weak points" in Japan's armor and not well enough aware of the encouraging weaknesses in American preparations.[153]

THE PROMISE OF VICTORY IN AMERICA

Roosevelt had come to consider United States participation in the war as inevitable. However, it was not in the style of Rooseveltian politics to ask the Chiefs of Staff and put question and answer on the record as to whether and when the United States would be ready to enter the war, or what their opinion was as to the chances of Allied victory. As late as November 27, 1941, the military stated emphatically that the most essential thing "from the United States viewpoint is to gain time," that "a precipitation of military action on our part should be avoided as long as consistent with national policy." Stimson, however, noted as early as November 7 that only the President, Hull, and himself were in possession of advice from the chiefs of staff that indicated "how ready we are to pitch in."[154] It was a secret fit only for the few to share—the fewer who knew it, the stronger the impact on the masses when the attack would come, the stronger the belief that their country had been struck while far from ready for war.

It was on the strength of such assurances that Hull could safely pronounce on November 27 that he had broken off the temporary modus vivendi with the Japanese, which would have given the soldiers and sailors still more time for preparations. He declared to Stimson: "I have washed my hands of it and it is now in the hands of you and Knox—the Army and the Navy." With firm reliance on the strength of the armed forces, there remained for Roosevelt only the question of "how we should maneuver them [the Japanese] into the position of firing the first shot without allowing too much danger to ourselves."[155] The Japanese obliged by maneuvering themselves into the position where the President wanted them, enabling him to keep up the appearances that democratic governments find necessary on their way into wars.

To contemplate post-1945 developments leads one far into conjecture. At first, American military superiority, or at least security, seemed assured through the exclusive possession of the atomic bomb, though only a few Americans proposed that their country recapture the vanishing fruits of victory by using this means of warfare. Drawing on the conviction that war with the atomic bomb would not and perhaps could not be made, the Soviet Government proceeded in its imperialistic strides until it finally provoked the Western Powers into alliances and gigantic rearmaments. In the historical context of this chapter, the question naturally arises: Who in Russia promised victory along the road taken and to whom? Did the soldiers assure the Politbureau that it was safe to proceed in the manner chosen, that it was safe, for example, to make war in Korea? If so, did the soldiers not foresee, as they should have from historical experience, that this attempted expansion would provoke a counter-force that might become a greater danger to Russia? Or did the assurance, based on Communist doctrine (though not on it alone) that their rearmament would ruin the Western nations from within, prove persuasive

enough to calm the military professionals and make them accept the Communist recipe as the promise of victory?

The strategy chosen by the Russians for the cold war is one of exhaustion, to use Delbrück's terminology, with annihilation as the final aim. This represents a new combination of means and end. The strategy of exhaustion, with the aim of bringing on peace, has always been closer to diplomacy and its methods and aims than the strategy of annihilation. This was completely misunderstood by General MacArthur in his outlook on the Korean War of 1950-51 when he desired to fight the war in full where it had broken out. The Truman administration, with a more world-embracing view of things, was willing to let the General win the war in Korea with the forces it could put at his disposal. He was unable to deliver victory as promised to President Truman at their meeting at Wake Island (October 15, 1950), when he had expressed his belief that there was "very little chance" of Red Chinese intervention in Korea, that "we are no longer fearful of their intervention," and that he hoped "to be able to withdraw the Eighth Army to Japan by Christmas."[156] Few generals survive nonfulfillment of the promise of victory in office. MacArthur had to be deposed from his viceroyship in Tokyo.[157]

FOOTNOTES

1. Augustus used to say that "a battle or a war ought never to be undertaken unless the prospect of gain overbalanced the fear of loss. For men who pursue small advantages at no small hazard resemble those who fish with a golden hook, the loss of which could never be compensated by all the fish they might take." Suetonius, Julius Caesar, xxv.
2. A German didactic poem of the late fifteenth century puts it this way: "War-making is great painstaking. And nobody knows how it comes out in the end." Cited by Jähns in Kriegswissenschaften, p. 334.
3. Lazarus von Schwendi, Kriegs Discurs (1593). Cited by Jähns in Kriegswissenschaften, p. 540.
4. Monts, Erinnerungen und Gedanken, pp. 232 f. Senator Robert A. Taft, speaking in the Senate on January 5, 1951, did not want to have any U.S. ground forces committed to any avoidable action "unless we are sure it is well within our capacity and almost certain of success." N.Y. Times, January 6, 1951.
5. A problem closely connected with the prediction of victory is that of the probable duration of the impending war. In 1914, the majority of the experts on both sides were agreed that the expected war would, "could be" only short and

that one would be "home by Christmas,"
though Joffre thought early in 1913 that it
would last several years, making at least
one of the men at the Quai d'Orsay cry out:
"Great God! Several years! But civilization
will not survive that!" Paléologue, Journal
de 1913-1914, p. 22.

6. The French cabinet discussed the Spanish
    candidacy of a Hohenzollern prince for the
    first time on July 6, 1870. In these delibera-
    tions, according to Premier Ollivier, "we
    asked ourselves first of all about our mili-
    tary and diplomatic situation. That was the
    necessary first consideration. There is in
    fact a pride forbidden to those who have not
    the strength to sustain it and shameful re-
    signation is imposed upon those who are
    forced by their weakness to swallow their
    pride." Ollivier, L'Empire libéral, XIV, 96 f.
7. Nazi Conspiracy and Aggression, I, 398, 400.
8. Encyclopedia Britannica (11th ed.), XVI, 351.
9. See, for example, Bapst, Le Maréchal Can-
    robert, III, 192 f.
10. Beust, Mémoires, III, 343.
11. Ziekursch, Politische Geschichte des neuen
    deutschen Kaiserreichs, I, 129.
12. Meyer, Bismarck, p. 261.
13. Eyck, Bismarck, II, 51 ff.
14. Ibid., II, 124 ff.; Meyer, Bismarck, pp. 277 f.
15. Meyer, Bismarck, p. 298.
16. Srbik, Quellen zur deutschen Politik Oester-
    reichs, V¹, 305.
17. Ziekursch, Politische Geschichte, I, 153.
18. von Loë, Erinnerungen, p. 268.
19. Hohenlohe, Denkwürdigkeiten, II, 319.
20. Ollivier, L'Empire libéral, XIV, 97.
21. According to Ollivier, it was Thiers, "the
    oracle of oracles," who contributed more
    than anyone else to over-confidence in the
    French Army. Ibid., XIV, 489.
22. Trochu, Oeuvres posthumes, II, 43.
23. Ollivier, L'Empire liberal, XV, 1; X, 376;
    XIV, 98. France, Niel thought, would never
    need as many soldiers as Germany, since
    the individual French soldier was so super-
    ior to the German. Jarras, Souvenirs, p. 30.
24. Ollivier, L'Empire libéral, XIV, 99, 579.
25. Jarras, Souvenirs, pp. 38 f. Jarras was
    Chief of the Intelligence section of the Min-
    istry of War before 1870.
26. Bapst, Le Maréchal Canrobert, IV, 194.
27. Paléologue, Entretiens de l'Impératrice
    Eugénie, p. 139.
28. Ollivier, L'Empire libéral, XIV, 343; XV, 102
    f.
29. Ibid., XIV, 96 ff.
30. Ibid., XIV, 117 f., 252 f., 253, 261, 393.
31. de La Gorce, Histoire du Second Empire, V,
    192.

32. Meyer, Bismarck, pp. 356, 371.
33. Instructions to chargé in Paris, February
    19, 1869. Oncken, Rheinpolitik, III, 114 f.,
    328 ff.
34. Eyck, Bismarck, II, 447 ff.
35. Bismarck, Gesammelte Werke, VI, 33, 349 f.
36. The scene is highly pointed up by Bismarck
    in Gedanken und Erinnerungen, chap. xxii.
37. Preussische Jahrbücher, Vol. 201 (1925),
    268 f.
38. Doc. dipl. fr., 1st series, X, 89.
39. Tittoni to Monts. G. P., XXI, 7216.
40. Ibid., VI, 1223.
41. Ibid., VI, 1200. A French military writer,
    the Commandant de Civrieux, was convinced,
    as late as 1913, that France had never been
    more ready than in 1887 "pour la réparation."
    Civrieux, Le germanisme encerclé, pp. 101
    ff.
42. Dansette, Le Boulangisme, pp. 63 ff.; G. P.,
    VI, 1275.
43. Brandt, Drei Jahre ostasiatischer Politik
    1894-97, pp. 3 f., and his Dreiunddreissig
    Jahre in Ostasien, III, 196.
44. Fieldmarshal Yamagata in Stead, Unser
    Vaterland Japan, pp. 45 f. Cf. dispatch of U.S.
    naval attaché in Berlin, Barber, dated July
    18, 1898: "Probably there never was a war
    for which more careful preparation had been
    made by one of the contestants than that
    between Japan and China, and even after it
    was over the Japanese had an abundance
    of ammunitions and other stores." Barber
    had been stationed in Tokyo in 1894-95.
    National Archives.
45. Doc. dipl. fr., 1st series, XI, 269, 313 ff.
46. Davis, Navy Second to None, p. 70.
47. Langer, Imperialism, pp. 561 ff.
48. Les armées françaises dans la Grande
    Guerre, I¹, 8 f., 10.
49. "Russian giant and Japanese midget, or cur"
    was the simple theme of Russian war propa-
    ganda, in writing and picture. For samples of
    the latter, see Eisner, Der Geheimbund des
    Zaren, pp. 24 f., 97.
50. Wm. Langer in Europäische Gespräche, IV,
    316; Bompard, Mon ambassade en Russie, p.
    66.
51. There are two versions of what the Tsar
    said on the occasion, this one being that which
    he gave to his intimates. The diplomatic ver-
    sion was: "I desire nothing so much as peace
    and I should like Japan to be the ally, and
    not the adversary, of Russia." Bompard,
    Mon ambassade en Russie, p. 45; G. P., XIX,
    5940, 5948.
52. Takeuchi, War and Diplomacy in the Japanese
    Empire, pp. 134 f., 137 f.
53. G. P., XIX, 5931, 5939, 6031.

54. Memoirs of Prince Konoye. Pearl Harbor Hearings, Part 20, 4013. According to Takeuchi, advice in favor of war was far more nearly unanimous, as unanimous as it had been in 1894 and was to be in August 1914 when uncertainty centered on the question of which side to join. Takeuchi, War and Diplomacy in the Japanese Empire pp. 142 ff., 452 ff.

55. G. P., XIX, 6043.

56. Ibid., XIX, 5939, 5971, 6031; Newton, Lansdowne, p. 307; Dugdale, Balfour, II, 280 ff.

57. April 19, 1904. G. P., XIX, 6031 f.

58. July 1902. Ibid., XIX, 5921.

59. "The situation was at that time, militarily speaking, favorable to us as never before; the outcome of a war with France would not be doubtful." Einem, Erinnerungen eines Soldaten, p. 111. For some naval views, see Doc. dipl. fr., 2nd series, IX, 129.

60. Petzet, Heinrich Wiegand, p. 248.

61. B. D., III, 438, 334, 434. For a British military judgment on Germany's "remarkable forbearance" in not attacking France in 1905, see Ibid., III, 196; for a French one, see Civrieux, Le germanisme encerclé, p. 104.

62. G. P., XXXIII, 12245. Roberts denied having made the statement.

63. Ibid., XXI, p. 86.

64. Doc. dipl. fr., 2nd series, VIII, 560 f.

65. Pinon, Histoire diplomatique 1515-1928, p. 593; Anderson, The First Moroccan Crisis, pp. 230 ff.

66. Doc. dipl. fr., 2nd series, X, 493.

67. Ibid., XI, 939. Ex-minister Luzzatti told French Ambassador Barrère that, thanks to her armaments, Italy "within two years would be in a position to get out of the [triple] alliance." Ibid., XI, 943.

68. Oesterreich-Ungarns Aussenpolitik, I, 40, 347.

69. As the German Embassy learned, General French and Admiral Fisher had talked of a general war in connection with the Bosnian crisis as not altogether unwelcome to the Government, while for Fisher it would provide the opportunity to destroy the German Navy. Ambassador Metternich would not believe that this expressed the true wishes of the British Government. "Admirals and generals whose profession is war are at times a little more light-hearted with war and war risk than the directors of a state responsible for its policy." G. P., XXVI, 9124.

70. Oesterreich-Ungarns Aussenpolitik, I, 500.

71. In November 1908, Martchenko, the Russian military attaché in Vienna, received a letter from his superior, the Chief of Staff, saying: "The disarray within the Russian Army which I found on my arrival is such that, if we should march at present, due to taking Serbia's side in her differences with Austria-Hungary, a catastrophe would strike us compared with which that of Tsushima would be child's play." Martchenko, La catastrophe austro-hongroise, p. 110.

72. G. P., XXVI, 9150. Tirpitz would not admit such readiness as far as the German Navy was concerned: Germany could not look forward with confidence to an attack by Britain. Ibid., XXVIII, 10238.

73. Oesterreich-Ungarns Aussenpolitik, I, 998, 1066. Isvolski's threat left Aehrenthal unimpressed. He told the British ambassador that "he knew Russia like his pocket and felt sure that she was in no position to go to war." B. D., V, No. 483, 490.

74. Suchomlinow, Erinnerungen, p. 221; Oesterreich-Ungarns Aussenpolitik, I, 1243, 1261; G. P., XXVI, 9451 f.

75. Churchill, The World Crisis, 1911-1914, p. 30.

76. G. P., XXVIII, 10251, 10306.

77. It was at this time that the Reich Treasury protested against the Navy's continued demands for funds and the Army's continued modesty. G. P., XXXI, 11324.

78. Joffre, Mémoires, I, 15 f.

79. Nicolson to Hardinge, September 14, 1911. Nicolson, Portrait of a Diplomatist, p. 253.

80. Stieve, Schriftwechsel Iswolskis, I, 141; Judet, George Louis, p. 157. The Tsar wrote to Nekliudov: "Do not for one instant lose sight of the fact that we cannot go to war. It would be out of the question for us to face a war for five or six years. We might if it were absolutely necessary accept a challenge in 1915, but not a moment sooner." Nekliudov, Diplomatic Reminiscences, p. 5.

81. Weissbuch betreffend die Verantwortlichkeit der Urheber des Krieges, p. 101.

82. Doc. dipl. fr., 3rd series, II, 88.

83. October 31, 1910. Conrad, Aus meiner Dienstzeit, II, 90.

84. To German ambassador, November 18, 1911. G. P., XXX, 11235.

85. Ibid., XXX, 11238, 11243 f.; Conrad, Aus meiner Dienstzeit, II, 281 ff.

86. G. P., XXXIII, 12254; Stieve, Schriftwechsel Iswolskis, II, 139 f.; Livre noir, I, 267 ff.

87. Oesterreich-Ungarns Aussenpolitik, IV, 3873.

88. Ibid., IV, 4101.

89. Albertini, Origins of the War of 1914, I, 377.

90. September 12, 1912. Livre noir, I, 326.

91. Isvolski, December 5, 1912. Ibid., I, 368.

92. Oesterreich-Ungarns Aussenpolitik, IV, 3787.
93. Helmreich, Diplomacy of the Balkan Wars, pp. 185 ff.
94. G. P., XXXIII, 12215, 12258, 12270.
95. On September 12, 1912, he told Isvolski "with his accustomed gravity of manner" that the experts viewed the chances of the Russo-French alliance in a general outbreak with great optimism. Albertini, Origins of the War of 1914, I, 373 f., 406 ff.
96. November 7 and 17, 1912. Livre noir, I, 342, 346.
97. Ibid., I, 370.
98. B. D., IX, No. 656, with Grey's commentary.
99. Siebert, Benckendorff's diplomatischer Schriftwechsel, III, No. 89. At the Quai d'Orsay, Paléologue, one of the "permanents," noted with relief and satisfaction: "How much stronger is France's diplomatic and military situation now than it was in 1905!" (May 8, 1913). Paléologue, Journal de 1913-1914, p. 127.
100. Schemua's report. Helmreich, Diplomacy of the Balkan Wars, pp. 239 f.
101. Oesterreich-Ungarns Aussenpolitik, IV, 4559.
102. Helmreich, Diplomacy of the Balkan Wars, pp. 243 ff.; Jäckh, Kiderlen-Wächter, II, 191 f.
103. Oesterreich-Ungarns Aussenpolitik, V, 4942.
104. Bulgarian Minister in Belgrade to his German colleague. G. P., XXXV, 13402. Convinced that he knew the value of the Serbian Army better than anyone else, one of the Bulgarian generals told the French military attaché that it could not resist the Bulgarian attack for more than eight days. Doc. dipl. fr., 3rd series, VII, No. 251.
105. G. P., XXXV, 13392.
106. Nothing can be more incorrect than to accuse the German officer corps as a whole of Pan-Germanism.
107. Pokrowski, Drei Konferenzen, pp. 17 ff.
108. January 12, 1914. Ibid., pp. 32 ff.
109. Suchomlinow, Erinnerungen, p. 360.
110. Conrad, Aus meiner Dienstzeit, IV, 121. Conrad had not always believed that this victory was possible. At the end of 1912—and since then the competitive position of the Central Powers had hardly improved—he considered a war against Russia-Italy-France as "the most unfavorable case of war, which must therefore be avoided," a case "one might presume which the direction of politics will never allow to come about." Ibid., II, 445.
111. July 5, 1914. Oesterreich-Ungarns Aussen-
politik, VIII, 248, 249. Gooss, Das Wiener Kabinett und die Entstehung des Weltkriegs, pp. 25 f.
112. Text of protocol in Conrad, Aus meiner Dienstzeit, IV, 43 ff.
113. Report of British military attaché in Berlin, August 1, 1914. B. D., XI, No. 404. The British General Staff informed its Russian counter-part as early as July 25 of its conviction "that Germany pushes Austria towards war because Berlin considers the situation as favorable." Die internationalen Beziehungen, 1st series, V, 53.
114. Report of July 3, 1914. Revue d'histoire de la guerre mondiale, XIII (1935), 257.
115. Doc. dipl. fr., 3rd series, XI, 243.
116. July 30, 1914. Die internationalen Beziehungen, 1st series, IV, 204.
117. Joffre, Mémoires, I, 207. Messimy does not mention this episode in his Souvenirs.
118. Pokrowski, Drei Konferenzen, p. 41.
119. Paléologue, An Ambassador's Memoirs, I, 32.
120. Lloyd George, War Memoirs, I, 86.
121. G. P., XXVIII, 10306.
122. For Moltke's low opinion of Britain's role in case of a continental war in the spring of 1914, see Eckardstein, Lebenserinnerungen, III, 185. This was in keeping with the Kaiser's view—and probably that of the German military generally—that the Reich's power was so overwhelming that it could not be stopped, even if Britain should intervene (December 1912). G. P., XXXIV, 12561.
123. Waters, "Secret and Confidential," pp. 234, 334.
124. "It must be remembered that both British and French military opinion of the highest order...held that the French Army and the BEF would together be able to resist successfully a German attack, even if France and Britain were alone and unsupported by Russia." Grey, Twenty-five Years, II, 68.
125. During one of the earlier phases of Anglo-German naval competition, the German Ambassador to St. James, Count Metternich, imbued with British views, wrote to Berlin: "Wars are no longer undertaken in civilized countries from purely arithmetical-military points of view, because one side feels superior to the other at a given time. This is the case in England as well. There can come moments, however, when the burdens and dangers of peace are felt as being so oppressive that war will be preferred to peace. This may occur in England as well" (November 1911.) G. P., XXXI, 11316.
126. Lloyd George, War Memoirs, I, 59, 50 f.

127. B. D., XI, No. 369.
128. Mendelssohn Bartholdy in Europäische Gespräche, VI (1928), 569.
129. Morley, Memorandum on Resignation, August 1914, pp. 6 f.
130. Documents on British Foreign Policy, 1919-1939, 1st series, I, 236.
131. Zilliacus, Mirror of the Past, pp. 266 f. It seems that Wilson never showed the earlier telegram from Knox to Lloyd George.
132. Cf. Churchill's post-war commentary on the Rhineland occupation: There was "great division in France. On the whole it was the politicians who wished to mobilize the Army and send an ultimatum to Hitler, and the generals who, like their German counterparts, pleaded for calm, patience and delay …If the French Government had mobilized the French Army, there is no doubt that Hitler would have been compelled by his own General Staff to withdraw, and a check would have been given to his own pretensions which might have proved fatal to his rule." Churchill, The Second World War, I, pp. 194 f.
133. Gamelin, Servir, II, 283.
134. P. Schmidt (German Foreign Office interpreter), Statist auf diplomatischer Bühne, pp. 410 f.
135. Trials of War Criminals, XII, 496 ff.
136. Ibid., XII, 797 f., 928; Documents on German Foreign Policy, Series D, II, 504, 527 ff.
137. Documents on German Foreign Policy, Series D, II, 393, 663, 710, 974.
138. Wheeler-Bennett, Munich, pp. 57, 152.
139. Kordt, Wahn und Wirklichkeit, p. 109.
140. Nazi-Soviet Relations, p. 125.
141. Gisevius, To the Bitter End, p. 368.
142. Poole in Foreign Affairs, October 1946, p. 142, on the basis of Paul Schmidt's testimony.
143. Kris and Speier, German Radio Propaganda, p. 9. By the end of 1944, Hitler had learned to state military common sense on readi-ness, telling the generals on the eve of the last German offensive: "You are never entirely ready, the things that were ready are no longer at your disposal but have been used somewhere else." Gilbert (ed.), Hitler Directs his War, p. 170.
144. Ciano, cited by Namier in Diplomatic Prelude, pp. 483 f.
145. Badoglio, Italy in the Second World War, pp. 14 ff.
146. Wheeler-Bennett, Munich, p. 435.
147. Statement of Sir Arthur Robinson, chairman of the Supply Board under the Committee of Imperial Defence. Feiling, Chamberlain, p. 350.
148. Ibid., pp. 394 f.
149. July 30, 1939. Ibid., p. 409.
150. Namier, Diplomatic Prelude, pp. 352 f.
151. Gamelin, Servir, I, 23 ff.
152. Hull, Memoirs, II, 1102.
153. This is based on Konoye's memoirs, translated in Pearl Harbor Hearings, Part 20, 3985 ff. See also Langer and Gleason, The Undeclared War, p. 906.
154. Beard, Roosevelt and the Coming of the War, pp. 448, 508 f.
155. November 25, 1941. Ibid., p. 516 f.
156. Documents of Wake Island meeting, published by the Administration. N.Y. Times, April 21 and May 3, 1951. The version of these promises, "perhaps the most hubristic Famous Last Words of history," that reached Britain was as follows: "Tell the boys when they reach the Yalu River they can all come back; they will eat their Christmas dinner at home." Tom Driberg (Labor) in House of Commons on November 30, 1950. Parliamentary Debate, 5th series, Vol. 481, 1387.
157. "Harmony might have continued to this day if the victory predicted by General MacArthur had materialized." N.Y. Times, April 21, 1951.

Mobilization and Diplomacy [1]

Very few troops, even during the era of the standing army, were so fully prepared and equipped in peace-time as to be able to march at once into the field in case of war. Mercenary troops and navies came closest to this state at certain periods in military history. Most forces required strengthening before marching out, usually by the addition of men trained at an earlier time and by the addition of animals and vehicles acquired in the market or requisitioned from private owners. While this strengthening was a process of addition in the case of the eighteenth-century armies, it has become one of multiplication in modern times. The process by which an armed force is brought from a peace-time footing to a war footing is called mobilization.

The term "mobilization" was first applied only to armies.[2] Navies, generally speaking, were more prepared for war than were land forces. Use of the term dates from the second half of the eighteenth century, when a large part of modern military terminology was established. It comes from the French language, as the most precise and exact language of the day. It was not used in Germany until early in the nineteenth century, much later than the process it described, and it did not appear in England, as far as military life is concerned, before 1850. It seems to have been taken over from the vocabulary of the capitalist market where, as far as English usage is concerned, it dates from the end of the eighteenth century. Just as a capitalist would ready himself for a large-size venture by mobilizing his resources, so a military power would prepare for war, or for the possibility of war, by preparing in advance a plan for the disposal of forces in case of war. The planner's thought was applied in order to ensure economy of means and effort and the ability to achieve superiority over or at least equality with the prospective enemy. And, particularly at times when it was thought that wars would be short and decisions quick, as before 1914, the planners strove above all for speed in mobilization.[3]

That a concept such as mobilization arose in the eighteenth century was in keeping with the fact that society as a whole was no longer constantly at war, as in primitive ages, and only a relatively small part of it was continually under arms. "In rude societies the army was the mobilized community, and the community was the army at rest," as Herbert Spencer put it.[4] In Spencer's own time, only a part of the community remained dedicated to preparing and fighting wars. Mobilization was the most economic and rational process of bringing the forces maintained in peacetime to a war footing.

In the course of time, the term "mobilization" fell into disuse for some kinds of preparations for war. Various military great Powers shunned the use of the term because they wanted to avoid the alarm, if not panic, it was apt to arouse at home and abroad. During periods of international tension, they introduced instead a system of preparatory measures, such as the recall of furloughed military personnel, the early return of troops from maneuvers and training camps to their garrison ready for eventual mobilization, security measures for the stricter guarding or closing of frontiers, the protection of railways and other structures and installations important in war, and strengthening of the peace-time effectives by calling up individual rather than whole classes of reservists. Before 1914, Germany included among the measures for periods of tension the stopping of food shipments to countries like Switzerland, with a view towards seizure should war come. This measure was ordered during the Second Moroccan crisis of 1911 and again on June 26, 1914.[5] The complex of such measures was covered by the centrally-given cue word, "threatening danger of war" (drohende Kriegsgefahr) as a state of affairs probably but not necessarily leading to mobilization.[6]

Prior to 1914, the French had thoroughly systematized the complex of these measures. Over a period of twenty years their General Staff had worked out, in what seemed impenetrable secrecy, the couverture, growing in complexity and in independence from open mobilization.[7] As perfected by Joffre, couverture provided for "measures of precaution," followed by "measures of surveillance," next by "measures of protection," then by "measures of preparatory organization," and lastly by "measures of preparation for operations."[8] Other such measures of preparation and precaution might include keeping formations in frontier districts above full peace-time strength, as was done by France and Germany along their common frontier, or retaining conscripts after their service terms had come to an end, a measure much preferred in autocratic Russia, but also used in democratic America since 1941.

Among the component parts of an armed force, some are always more immediately prepared for war than others. Generally speaking, naval and, in modern times, air forces, are more nearly ready or can be readied for war more quickly than the land forces. Laying up or "moth-balling" of vessels has, however, introduced a somewhat larger difference between the peace and war strengths of navies. But their mobilization quotient—mobilized strength divided by peacetime strength—is always nearer one than in the case of the military forces. The short wars before 1914 were fought with the naval forces almost as they existed at the outbreak, with some auxiliaries drawn from merchant fleets. Eventually, vessels already under construction prior to the war may be added. Ships in commission are "practically mobile, that is to say, they can be brought into fighting condition within a few hours and without outside help."[9] Others, recommissioned, can be manned by recalled reservists.

Mobilization is either general, comprising the totality of the organized forces of a country, or partial, extending only to a limited part of the land and/or naval forces. Not all European wars of the nineteenth century required complete mobilization, nor did most overseas expeditions and colonial wars. For the Danish War of 1864, Prussia and Austria put only a limited number of their army corps on a war footing. Other uses of the armed forces required only partial mobilization. Some of the so-called "observation corps," which the powers mobilized and posted along their frontiers from time to time, were designed to keep watch over warlike events and revolutionary movements in neighboring countries and keep them from affecting their own countries. France, for example, stationed an observation corps of two divisions along the Pyrenées at the time of the fratricidal war between the Christinos and the Carlists in Spain which began in 1834, and another such corps of 70,000 men in the Rhone Valley during the Austrian-Piedmontese War of 1848. During the war of 1866, however, she refrained from sending such corps to either the Rhine or the Rhone, not expecting that the decisive end of the Seven Weeks' War would come so quickly. Prussia put her Eastern Army corps on a war footing during the Polish insurrections of 1830 and 1863. None of the Great Powers considered these measures as opening moves for war, nor did they consider as hostile the mobilizations that the majority of the small neutrals of Europe undertook in July-August 1914, usually with the assurance that the measure was not directed against one or the other side.[10] This armed neutrality through mobilization, costly as it was, was maintained by a number of the European nations throughout the First World War and by Switzerland throughout the Second.

MOBILIZATION PLANS

Mobilization plans are worked out ahead of war by general staffs or, as in earlier times, by such organizations as the Hofkriegsrat in Austria. Civilian officials took an active hand in the elaboration of war plans in the Hofkriegsrat.[11] On the whole, however, civilian participation in such planning unfortunately became more and more restricted, due to the monopolizing tendencies of general staffs. They presumed to know everything about the preparation of war, except possibly its financing.[12] Only with the approach of total mobilization did the civilian administrator and expert return to fuller participation. In the meantime, the civilian governors had become resigned to accepting the mot d'ordre from the military and confining their attention to the administrative measures accompanying mobilization. These included closer supervision or the closing of frontiers, financial measures, embargos and rationing of foodstuffs, feed, fuels and livestock, especially horses.[13] A state of siege was usually declared in the mobilizing country, with a shifting of certain powers, such as censorship, to the military authorities. Along the coasts, the navigation lights would be extinguished or changed in accordance with prepared plans.

Mobilization plans envisage war with one or more likely enemies, reserving certain forces for the observation of neutrals that might enter the war in a later stage. Not all wars of the nineteenth century had been prepared by mobilization plans long ahead of their outbreak. Leaving colonial wars aside, the Crimean and the Spanish-American wars were in this respect the most unprepared wars. Due to the constellation of alliances, most of the Great Powers had only one general mobilization plan as 1914 approached. Only Austria-Hungary had elaborated three such plans—Plan R for the war with Russia and Serbia-Montenegro, Plan B for a war in the Balkans alone, and a third one against Italy and Serbia. Italy's plans were, in 1914-15, and again in 1939-40, as indeterminate as her diplomacy intended to be at the start of a European war.

The first steps towards war, the assembling and equipping of men, animals, and engines, is followed by the "concentration"—again an eighteenth-century term—or initial assembly.[14] The more primitive an army, the earlier its concentration, whereas, according to Scharnhorst, a modern army must "never stand still in concentration but must always battle in concentration."[15]

Generally speaking, concentration has followed mobilization, that is to say, only fully mobilized forces have proceeded to the concentration. However, combinations of the two taking place simultaneously have been undertaken at various times. The purpose is to save some of the time consumed by the sequence of mobilization-concentration. In 1870, the French attempted to combine both, to transport the war-equipped peace-time forces to the frontier at once and have them joined there, fifteen and seventeen days later, by the reservists. Thus they hoped to get a head-start on the Germans, whose arrangements for mobilization and concentration were more orthodox. The French effort miscarried. The forces that first arrived on the Eastern frontier wasted their time and the opportunity of interfering with the German preparations. Their inactivity was ascribed by some to Napoleon's hesitation, by others to the unplanned slowness with which the reservists arrived at the front. The Rhine Army, which ought to have counted at least 400,000 men on July 30, had an effective strength of only 235,800 on August 1.[16] Better organization and discipline made the subsequent French arrangement of the couverture, which combined features of mobilization and concentration, more successful. Still later, total war would combine these two features of war preparation even more inextricably.

Transport for purposes of concentration was largely by railway, the accelerator of nineteenth-century warfare. Ship transport of mobilized forces was impressive only in the beginning.[17] However, it soon became too slow for the tempo of modern war, except in Russia where the Volga served as a military highway in 1914 and before.[18] The motor vehicle brought still greater acceleration of troop movements for concentration and for other purposes—the first German troops to violate Luxemburg's neutrality in 1914 arrived by automobile. But the largest number of troops covering the longest distances were still carried by rail to the regions of concentration, even in and after 1939.

At least on the part of the Great Powers, mobilization and concentration and, finally, the opening of operations, became increasingly one, due to preparations for war on the part of the soldiers, rather than to the demands and wishes of the diplomats. As far as the diplomats still considered the preservation of peace their business, they would have welcomed the possibility of a halt between the three stages.

The relative length of the periods of mobilization proper and of concentration has varied so much in different countries that it cannot even be said that as a rule the one takes longer than the other. Prussia gave mobilization orders on August 9, 1806, and the battle of Jena, preceded only by a few skirmishes, took place on October 14. In Serbia in 1914, mobilization required five days and concentration ten to eleven, instead of eight to nine days as expected.[19] None of the great military Powers could have afforded her tardiness, so bound were they to their schedules, even

if at the expense of elasticity.[20]

In the nature of things, the plans of bulky and unwieldy armies are vastly more inflexible than those of other forces. While navies and air forces have mobilization plans to make them fully prepared for war, their concentration plans can remain far more indeterminate, and their operation plans, unless aiming at such an initial move as "Copenhagening" the enemy fleet, can be left vague or even unprepared beyond the general stationing and distribution of the available forces. Many naval war plans may actually prove to be foolish (such as John Fisher's plan for landing operations in the Baltic) and never see the light of publication because they cannot stand up under it. On the whole, the majority of admiralties, like the British prior to 1914, have preferred not to prepare war operation plans. They leave these to be formulated by the admiral who happens to be commander-in-chief at the outbreak of war, in the certainty "that any plan you draw out in peace will not be carried out in war." Not even the belief shared by many in Britain that Germany had such plans could shake them in this view. In any case, no German enterprise could be staged without some previous warning reaching England.[21]

The relation of war plans to foreign policy is, or ought to be, a close one. It was the hope, or belief, or fear of many that coordination could best be effected by a dictator, such as Hitler. It was thought that he would perform the function of coordinator much better than William II had done before him. Actually, the totality of his ideas about policy and warfare were no better knit together than were those of pre-1914 Germany. The German Navy had its plans for mobilization and concentration, but it was not built according to the specifications laid down by its most likely task in war. It was built as "a well-balanced homogeneous fleet," with not too many of any one type of ship. It had no war plans before it was given a minor role in "Case White," the war against Poland. But, according to a long-time member of the operational department of the Naval High Command,

a plan for the war against England did not exist at all before the beginning of the war. Such a war seemed to us outside the realm of possibility. Considering the overwhelming superiority of the British fleet, which can hardly be expressed in proportionate figures, and considering England's strategical domination of the seas, such a war appeared to us to be absolutely hopeless. The only means by which Britain could have been damaged effectively was by submarine warfare; but even the submarine weapon was by no means being given preferential treatment nor was its production accelerated. It was merely given its corresponding place in the creation of a well-balanced homogeneous fleet.[22]

A strong popular misconception about general staffs assumed, and may still assume, that they are blue-printing shops in which all wars, "possible and impossible," are being planned and prepared for. Corporal Hitler still held this view when he told the German General Staff in March 1938 that he was determined to march into Austria and expected that they were prepared for this possibility. He was considerably taken aback when they told him that, in the absence of any hint from the political offices, the case had not been studied and would have to be improvised.

Actually, the work of general staffs was and is far more selective than Hitler thought. While they collect relevant information about friends, foes, and neutrals, there are too many complexities involved to permit adequate coverage of every imaginable case of war. The work of gathering and digesting all the relevant data for all hypothetical cases of war is too great for any existing organization. In 1940, when the Führer ordered the study of "Weserübung," the code-word for the invasion of Norway, maps had to be bought in Berlin bookstores. The General Staff, whatever data it may have possessed on Norway as a possible theater of war, did not even have adequate maps.

General staffs can only study and prepare the wars most likely to occur. The perfection of mobilization plans against the chosen enemies during the nineteenth century brought a definite rigidity with it. Because the French Army thought Germany to be the only possible enemy after 1871, it was rather surprised by the Fashoda crisis. That crisis found it—more than the French Navy—unprepared for war against Britain. German plans before 1914 were so completely fixed on the two-front war that the war on one front was not contemplated by the Great General Staff. Hence it desired to know from the outset whether France might remain neutral in the case of a war with Russia arising from an Austrian-Russian conflict. In an exchange of ideas with Conrad in 1910, the younger Moltke was particularly emphatic that "at the very moment when mobilization is pronounced, there must be complete clarity as to who is friend and who is enemy."[23] Consequently, he was very upset when the Kaiser, even though only for a moment, demanded that the whole mobilization be re-directed against Russia. Moltke told the Supreme Warlord that this was technically impossible.[24] In order to obtain final clarification about neutral and foe, Moltke had the Wilhelmstrasse ask the French Government on July 31, before German mobilization had been ordered, whether they would remain neutral in case of war with Russia. The answer was, as must have been expected, non-committal yet clear.[25]

The Russian mobilization plans for 1914 were worked out only for the case of a full mobilization against both of the Central Powers.[26] They were based entirely on the soldiers' assumption that war between Austria and Russia would inevitably and immediately involve Germany. The military authorities who had worked out the mobilization plans and kept them up to date were therefore very much upset when, during the July 1914 crisis, they were presented by the foreign minister with the demand for partial mobilization, against Austria only. Diplomatic considerations seemed to require this. The Chief-of-Staff was new to his office. At first he did not seem to think partial mobilization unfeasible. Then the head of the mobilization section of his own staff, General Dobrorolski, explained to him "the absolute impossibility of a partial mobilization of the Army...By what motives was one's strategy to be guided?" he asked. "By political considerations?" No mobilization plan existed for war against Austria alone. It would have been sheer folly from a strategic point of view. Should only the four military districts of Kiev, Odessa, Moscow, and Kazan, comprising thirteen army corps, be mobilized, as the diplomats wished, and should they be marched to the Austrian frontier, some of them would have to move through the unmobilized district of Warsaw in order to attack Austria as she ought to be attacked, from the North as well as from the East. This difficulty would be increased if partial mobilization were to be followed by a general one.[27] Whether war against Austria alone was unfeasible for Russia if undertaken only from the East may well be doubted. That the soldiers could not consider it was due to the fact that it had not been prepared.[28]

The negative experiences of the Crimean War and the wars of 1859 and 1870 on the French side, and the positive lessons of the wars of 1866 and 1870 on the Prussian side, put all continental armies as well as much of diplomacy under "the domination of the plan."[29] The four wars of Napoleon III had produced a crescendo of improvisation, precipitation, disconnection—partly because the first three had seemed so very "successful."[30] The realization of defeat and its causes, however, resulted in France's mobilization for the revanche. With it improvisation, dash, and intuition gave way to methodical laboring among the military, who were also the standard-bearers of revanche. After that, all the military Powers on the Continent—and Britain after 1905—endeavored in their calculations to gain time—weeks, days, minutes—over the expected enemy during the periods of mobilization and concentration. This tendency made all plans more rigid and more monomaniac, if only for reasons of economy. No case could be worked out in

such detail as the one against "the chosen enemy."
From the viewpoint of the soldiers, an added rigidity had entered into the alliance system. On the
side of the military planners, a dictatorship arose
that indicated to the political leaders the point beyond which their conduct had to be regulated by a
regard for existing military plans, in the shaping
of which these civilians had taken no part. Clausewitz' dictum that war is the prolongation of policy
by different means approached its reversal.[31]

Whether the gaining of time would actually add
greatly to the chances for victory, whether the
gaining of time might in actuality favor only one
side and not also the other, whether in the speed-
up of mobilization one might actually hurt one's
own chances of success, given the realities of
terrain and weapons: these questions were never
seriously considered before 1914. Actually, Russia ran into her first defeats by accelerating the
movement of her armies into Prussia; and similarly France by her Lorraine offensive, Austria
by her push forward from the base of Galicia. At
least one statesman came to question the rage for
racing in which the soldiers had indulged, though
only after the close of the great experience. In
the final volume of his work on the First World
War, Winston Churchill wrote:

> The general staffs and those who speak for
> them are prone to emphasize the importance
> of forestalling the enemy in the beginning of
> great wars, and statesmen are at their mercy
> on such questions. Even time, that precious
> talisman of war, may be bought too dearly if
> it leads to the wrong planning of the masses,
> to the erroneous training or organization of
> the troops, or to an untrue conception of the
> character of war, or of the values and propor-
> tions of its physical and moral factors. It is
> with the greatest reserve that we thus throw
> doubts upon the sovereign virtues of celerity
> in striking the first blow. Nevertheless as the
> scale of war rises in magnitude, celerity and
> forestallings at particular points and for par-
> ticular brief periods seem to become less ef-
> fective. After all, the supreme study is the
> general battle and everything should be subor-
> dinated to that. Both the French and Austrians
> would have fared better if they had allowed the
> invaders of 1914 to test for themselves the
> then unmeasured power of modern fire arms.
> Both were nearly destroyed at the very begin-
> ning of the war by precipitate offensives which
> they launched in complete misconception of the
> numbers and movements of their enemies, and
> of the power of their own rifles, machine guns
> and artillery....[32]

Among the reasons for the quickly shifting alliances of the eighteenth century was the absence of

vastly complicated mobilization and concentration
plans tied to such rigid factors as rail lines and
time-tables for the movements of troops. The diplomacy of the railway age to a large extent succumbed to the inflexibility of plans for the case of
wars considered "possible." Preparation of these
plans by the general staffs came to determine to
a very large extent which wars were possible and
which were not. Conrad, the Austrian Chief of Staff
before 1914, expressed it in this way: it was the
vast detailed preparation of mobilization and concentration plans and in particular the planning for
the railway movements "that made it chiefly necessary to prepare oneself for definite war eventualities. It forbade a constantly changing accommodation to an undirected policy by fits and starts, unless one ran the risk of being unprepared in case
of war, being unable to work out an orderly concentration, and being overrun by an opponent working
towards a conscious aim. This would have decided
the war against oneself from the outset."[33]

The motor, built into ground-bound and air-navi-
gating vehicles, brought an emancipation from long-
term planning, while at the same time calling for
even more detailed short-term planning. Diplomacy
could assume a new fluidity if it cared to do so, being less under the dictatorship of fixed plans, but
also falling an easy victim to the short-term and
abrupt planning of reckless dictators. In 1914, the
opening of the war was under the dictatorship of
plans that, from a certain moment of diplomatic
complication, demanded not only that war be fought
but also that it be started as prepared. In 1939, the
opening of the war fell under the Diktat of a totalitarian ruler who wanted war at the time far more
definitely than the planners serving under him.

TRIAL AND CONTROL MOBILIZATIONS.

In order to test their mobilization plans, various
military Powers undertook trial mobilizations before 1914. The process was reminiscent of the pre-
capitalist mind, which cannot fully trust blue-prints
or entries in ledgers but insists on seeing machine
models or specie. Such trials, usually restricted
to an army corps, would range from an inspection
and examination of the supply depots where war
equipment for reservists was stored, to making
the reservists actually join the formations specified in their mobilization orders. Some of these
measures may have been supervisory in intent, as
in Russia where the corruption and negligence of
the bureaucracy was traditional. It was more in
the true spirit of experimentation when, early in
the railway age, Prussia held transportation exercises. In 1862, for example, these took place in the
direction of Hamburg-Lübeck, behind which lay the
theater of the war of 1864.[34]

The pre-1914 Russian Army examined the

practical applicability of its written mobilization plans by control or trial mobilization far more often than any other military Power. In the control mobilization, the written orders for the case of mobilization were locally re-examined, the clothing and other equipment stored, counted and otherwise examined, etc. Whatever the final contribution of these measures to Russia's increased readiness for war may have been—and they were undertaken on a very large scale in 1913-14—they subtracted from her war readiness while they lasted, absorbing a great deal of labor and attention. Trial mobilization, the older of the two measures in Russia, extended to the calling up of personnel, horses, and vehicles, thus making certain units fully mobile. As a rule, the high cost involved forbade this form of test to go beyond a brigade in size and ten days in time. While this measure somewhat increased war-readiness on a local scale, its actual effectiveness was hardly as great as the alarm raised by such measures would make it seem. By comparison, it added infinitely less to Russia's preparedness than certain other measures, such as retaining reservists at the end of their service period. None of the other less autocratic military Powers could strengthen their forces in this way.[35] Certain of the mobilization tests were resumed by Red Russia.

Under normal circumstances, test mobilizations were considered routine matters except by those most directly concerned and most severely hurt in their civilian pursuits. Many of the reservists and Landwehr were uncertain of the meaning and length of their newly-demanded services. They were inclined to drown the shock of being separated from work and family in alcohol.[36] But when such trials coincided, intentionally or accidentally, with international crises, they were apt to add greatly to the already existing tension. The usual errors on the part of the newspapers, mistaking alerts and similar exercises for partial mobilization, and partial mobilization for the beginning of general mobilization, did not improve matters. And they were usually loath to leave any newsworthy "discovery" unreported. The service journals were often equally alarming in their discussion of these events. In May 1914, the Austrian Military Observer (Militärrundschau) warned of the danger of a sudden attack by Russia, whose various trial mobilizations were said to be designed to give her a head-start over her opponents.[37]

Practically every great diplomatic crisis in Europe was accompanied by military measures. The diplomats and even the soldiers preferred to call them "precautions" rather than "preparations."[38] Mobilization and even the appearance of it was avoided. Nothing could have been more ill-timed and provocative than a test mobilization at such moments of crisis.[39] Shortly before the opening of the Algeciras Conference, the Berlin authorities received information that led them to believe that France intended to have a test mobilization of two army corps on her Eastern frontier. Anxious for a peaceful start of the conference, they prepared to ask the Paris Government to postpone it, since such a measure would only serve to acerbate the situation once again. Happily, more correct information received by the Great General Staff revealed the true nature of the French measures and made it unnecessary to raise objections in Paris.[40]

Test mobilizations were usually quickly detected in Western Europe. But that was not equally true within the vast reaches of Tsardom, with its secretiveness in all military matters. Poor reporting, both official and unofficial, led the Indian Government and the India Office to believe that the Russians were on the move towards Central Asia more often than they actually were. When troop movements towards that poorly observed zone were detected, the Russians denied them or explained that they were of a routine nature, or that mobilization plans were being tested. British statesmen like Salisbury accepted such assurances only with the greatest scepticism, "for without a real purpose no government undertakes mobilization exercises on so large a scale."[41]

EARLY MOBILIZATIONS.

Similar to such concepts as reserve, plan, supply, or uniformity, "mobilization" is a modern military concept. While medieval knighthood seemed to be continuously under arms, its forces were almost completely unprepared in terms of organization. Orders to assemble for war traveled slowly and slowly the warriors arrived at the points of rendezvous. Compliance with orders was never too good. When Charles the Bald called up the host against the invading Normans in 845, "many came but not all," according to a contemporary.[42] Annual musters, such as the March or May Field of the Franks, were but feeble forerunners of modern test mobilizations.

The hiring of mercenaries brought a speed-up in mobilization and gave a distinct advantage (never too well exploited) to the first hirer. On the whole, the soldiers of the Middle Ages moved more slowly, generals thought more slowly, and they prepared for war and battle more haphazardly and unsystematically than capital did in its transactions. In the period of the Renaissance, preparation for war became more systematic, possibly as a means to overcome a power inferiority in relation to the contemplated enemy.[43]

The standing army was intended to overcome the wilfulness of the mercenary as well as the financial embarrassments of the State-employer, to which most mutinies and other refractoriness were due. It was also intended to make the soldier a more reliable and obedient war-worker. The superior readiness achieved by such means conferred success after success on the banners of Gustavus Adolphus and Louis XIV, but also gained for them, particularly for Louis, the odium that the aggressor incurs, particularly the continual aggressor, at home no less than abroad. According to Saint-Simon, it was the awareness of the growing criticism among the French bourgeoisie that caused Ludovican France to lose the last and most important of her wars, that of the Spanish Succession. A new délicatesse, says Saint-Simon, no longer permitted France to appear as the aggressor. She insisted on being attacked first, whereas the resoluteness, the courage and the celerity that had marked the opening of the earlier wars, if applied again, would have disconcerted and reduced to impotence the enemies of France before they had made preparations of their own.[44] The war-makers were henceforth obliged to take into account this respect for the opinion of the bourgeoisie, who did not fight the wars of the age but financed them, whenever they mobilized.[45]

The armies of Absolutism were never quite complete in time of peace, least so in the winter season. In the summer season, conscripted soldiers on leave were called in for purposes of re-training and maneuvers, thus bringing the army closer to its war-footing. As a rule, the war strength of the armies of Absolutism was not much greater than its peace-time strength as far as personnel was concerned. Mobilization by the Continental Powers consisted largely of the recall of the many men who were on furlough during the greater part of the year. According to the Prussian mobilization plans of 1789, the war-time strength of 219,751 men was only 24,704 men above the peace-time strength. In 1805, the war strength, as measured by mobilized field forces, was only 193,017 men against a peace-time strength of 234,751, while 69,687 men remained unmobilized as fortress troops, in depots, and as replacement units.[46]

While the wars of Ludovican France, with the exception of the last, were the result of a socio-economic pleonexy, war-making by Prussia was based on a strict economy of means and constant planning and preparations for the case of war. The first detailed plans for mobilization in Prussia were worked out by order of her "Soldier-King" in 1722, not in contemplation of any immediate or specific war. They covered the mobilization of fifty battalions, eighty-one squadrons, the field artillery, a general staff and field chancellery. All were to be ready to march out on the twelfth day following the receipt of mobilization orders. During the mobilization period, the units had to recall their furloughed men, draft drivers, make the officers buy their extra remounts, and receive their field equipment from depots and arsenals. "Magazination" of supplies, from grain and gold to munitions, was one of the main features of Prussian war-planning. Also included were the arming of civilians in case of enemy invasion and measures for the employment of soldiers' wives after their breadwinners had gone to war.

With the rise and growth of general staffs and other peace-time planning institutions during the second half of the eighteenth century, mobilization plans became more and more a foremost concern in time of peace. The Prussian Supreme War Collegium dedicated one of its three sections to mobilization business.[47] Speed-up processes were introduced into army and navy organization, and troop movements became increasingly more reliable, uniform and predictable. They still remained slow in certain countries, most so in Russia and only slightly less in Austria. In Prussia, geographic proximity and an enforced economy of means promoted acceleration. An Austrian mobilization of 1782, with Prussia as the expected enemy, was based on the following time elements: it took sixteen days for the mobilization order issued at Vienna to reach all the troops; for the regiments of the Line to march out in their assembled strength would require three days, while it would take fifteen days in the case of the frontier troops. The frontier troops were among Austria's best. In case the regiments were first to recall their furloughed men and equip them for war, it would take forty-eight to ninety days to get them ready from the date mobilization had been ordered. A somewhat shortened procedure made possible a general marching out on the fifty-second day of mobilization.[48]

Given this availability of soldiers, mobilization, either that of a whole army or of parts only, came to be used more and more frequently for warlike demonstrations by the greater military Powers. It was practically an attribute of Great Power standing to mobilize from time to time.

To mention but a few of the diplomatically-intended mobilizations: In 1788, Gustavus III of Sweden opened the war against Russia, who was already at war with the Turks, in hopes of regaining the lost provinces across the Baltic. Russia called for help from Denmark, as promised by an assistance pact of 1773. Unmoved by the mediation attempts of Prussia and Britain, who feared an increase of Russian power in the Baltic, the Danes invaded Sweden from Norway. Gustavus hurried back from Finland to meet the threat to his capital, while Prussia and Britain threatened Denmark with armed intervention. Prussia ordered mobilization of an army corps, while Britain readied Hanoverian forces. Faced by this threat to Jutland, the Danes agreed to an armistice and later issued a declaration of neutrality in the Russian-Swedish War. The Prussian corps, though mobilized, never had to leave its garrisons.

On a much larger scale, the prolonged Prussian mobilization beginning in 1788, to support the policy of Minister von Hertzberg, led much closer to war. He hoped to exploit the Turkish War, in which Austria was fighting side by side with Russia, to partition Poland exclusively to the benefit of Prussia. Continued successes against the Turks—despite a Prussian officers' advisory mission to Turkey—allowed the Empires to safely disregard this Prussian blackmailing, even after almost the entire Prussian Army had been mobilized against Austria (1790-91). While the French Revolution temporarily reunited the monarchies, the last Partition of Poland brought on a new Austro-Prussian disagreement. Austria, left nearly empty-handed at first, supported Polish resistance against Prussia rather than against Russia. In order to force the Polish parliament to give its sanction to Prussia's share in the spoils, the latter applied the by now traditional means of extortion, a mobilization in the direction of Warsaw.[49]

In all these cases, mobilization of Prussia's forces remained partial for reasons of economy. Even in 1806, when a life and death struggle with Napoleon was impending, a full fifth of the Prussian Army, the forces in East Prussia, remained on a peace-footing—partly for reasons of economy, partly due to the distrust of Russian policy—until a very late date before Jena, where they were absent.[50]

Mobilization as demonstration, used and recognized in ancien régime diplomacy as one of the great "as if's," did not impress the military imperialist, Napoleon. The Corsican upstart saw that the maneuver was not really intended for war. But so did many of the old-style diplomats. Napoleon, however, differed from them in that he did not consider mobilization as the final admonishment to reconsider the terrors of war. In 1805, when Prussia partially mobilized in order to maintain her neutrality against him as well as his enemies, the latter respected it, whereas French troops violated Prussia's possessions on the Main. Patriotic demonstrations thereupon drove Prussia closer to the camp of Napoleon's enemies, but not fast enough to join them before Austerlitz. The irresolution of Prussia's policy lost her friends and only made Napoleon more determined to settle with her. Prussia began to realize this after she had given the demobilization order early in 1806. The order was then rescinded for part of the forces. As one of the King's secretaries wrote the foreign minister, this was done "ostensibly as the only way to bring the King of Sweden [an enemy of Napoleon after Austerlitz] to reason, actually because the King does not want to await developments with his hands and feet tied and because he seems to reproach himself since some time for having recalled his Army too early."[51]

Whether successful or not, eighteenth-century mobilization always proved devastating to the finances of the mobilizer. Frederick the Great had left behind a war treasury of fifty-four million thalers in specie as against a Prussian indebtedness of only twelve million. By 1794, this fund had been completely used up by wars and mobilizations, and Prussia had to resort to loans, subsidies from abroad and other financial make-shifts. Her mobilization of 1805, followed by war, cost another 6.3 million.[52] If mobilization as a diplomatic maneuver failed, the anti-climactic effect on those immediately responsible could be utterly upsetting. In 1790, the Prussian civilian minister charged with directing the mobilization shot himself after the mobilized Army had marched out to war against Austria, a final step for which he would not take the responsibility. He left a note, saying that he did not feel strong enough to be witness to the evil he had set in motion through his own recklessness and want of understanding. His suicide was considered tantamount to a lost battle in Berlin. Prussia was forced to compromise at that late stage in the preparation for war, thereby losing much of the prestige that had survived Frederick the Great.[53]

At that time, the accession of Joseph's conciliatory brother Leopold to the Austrian throne enabled the Prussian diplomats to beat a face-saving retreat. On other occasions, the impasse into which mobilization and counter-mobilization had driven two opposing nations provided diplomacy with one of its most difficult tasks. Usually the most satisfactory solution was for both sides to agree on mutual and simultaneous demobilization. Demobilization pari passu was agreed upon between Russia and Britain in 1878 when mobilized seapower and landpower had faced each other at the Straits. Since questions of mobilization as a rule become questions of public opinion, such settlements are not easily reached. Pan-Slavist opinion in Russia made it extremely difficult to reach an agreement on simultaneous demobilization during the partial mobilizations of Russia and Austria in 1912-13. A peaceful result will not always satisfy an excited public that may feel cheated of a war consciously or subconsciously longed for. Still far more grievous to the mass mind is for one side to be forced to demobilize before the other. Such a severe diplomatic defeat or loss of national prestige rankles long in the popular memory, as in Prussia after Olmütz, or in Serbia after the Bosnian crisis.[54]

MOBILIZATION AND CONSTITUTIONALISM

Issuing the order of mobilization is a most serious and portentous act of state. Even in the case of partial mobilization, it is likely to have vast repercussions at home and abroad. Outside remonstrations against the fact or the intention, whether of the most circumspect or the most peremptory kind, are apt to be rejected as interference with the exercise of national sovereignty.[55] Modern nationalism is inclined to insist upon absolutism in relation to other states, even when tempering it internally.

In the struggle of internal politics during the nineteenth century, the question arose as to whether the power of ordering mobilization ought not to be taken away from Absolutism and what survived of it in foreign offices and armed forces, and be put under the direct or indirect control of the parliaments.[56] Almost as soon as this demand was voiced, it was argued that such control might interfere with the military considerations of promptness and effectiveness. Military measures were bound to suffer from the slowness of parliamentary procedures. Still, it seemed to Liberals and to more leftist parties that governments and diplomats working in secrecy had misused mobilization far too often and too light-heartedly, that to leave them this prerogative was to leave Absolutism one of its essential attributes. (Hence the various cases of mutiny on the part of Prussian Landwehr when called to colors in 1848.) However, the constitutional movement in most countries did not obtain or in the end did not insist upon the right to full control over mobilization. Most parliaments reserved the right to declare war. They refrained, however, from claiming that the right to order mobilization should depend on their previous authorization. They refrained from interfering with the command power of the executive, an interference that might lessen their own country's readiness for war. Defensive war was the only kind of war that Liberalism ever contemplated and such a war, it was recognized, might necessitate mobilization even before a parliament-authorized declaration of war or a state of war could be issued. Most parliaments expected to be called into session as promptly as possible after mobilization measures had been taken, if only in order to approve and finance them.

The Third Republic, reacting strongly against the policies of Napoleon III, arranged matters in such a way that, while the head of the state would decree authorization, not one company could be mobilized without a special law requiring the approval of both chambers. The restriction did not exclude a post factum approval, however. And the restriction itself contributed to the establishing of the couverture as an unauthorized pre-mobilization measure.[57] Even in semi-constitutional Russia before 1914, the Tsar's signature on the mobilization ukase required the counter-signature of the Ministers of War, Marine and Interior, as a check

on absolutism.[58] Even in Britain, where parliamentary control over the executive was the most extensive, it did not cover mobilizations, even though the latter were to be restricted to cases "of imminent danger or of great emergency." The majority of the Beaconsfield cabinet decided that such a situation had arisen with the far-reaching Russian victory over Turkey in 1878, the Treaty of San Stefano, and the Russian refusal to listen to British protests previous to the Congress of Berlin. They decided to call out the reserves and have the Government of India send a force into the Mediterranean via Suez. They found the military plans prepared for the case of mobilization to be disappointingly "meager." At the same time, they decided upon the acquisition by Britain of a station in the Eastern Mediterranean, at the expense of and with or without the agreement of Turkey. Contrary to what was commonly believed at the time, it was on the issue of the acquisition of "new Gibraltars," rather than on the issue of mobilization, that Lord Derby, the Foreign Secretary, resigned from the cabinet. Disraeli remained confident that Derby's resignation and the mobilization of the Army did not mean war; on the contrary, he hoped to avoid war by an energetic attitude. War did not follow the mobilization measures; negotiations with Russia continued. Still, the situation was anomalous. "Rarely had two states found themselves in a more strange condition," Lord Salisbury, Derby's successor, told the German ambassador. For these negotiations were in reality concerned with an armistice that had not been preceded by war. The negotiations had to settle the problem of whether the Russian Army or the British Fleet should be the first to leave the scene of near-war, the vicinity of Constantinople.[59]

There can be little doubt that the vast military powers vested in the President of the United States would enable him to give the order for mobilization if such an order seemed to him to be called for.[60] Actually, until after the outbreak of the "cold war," it has not often been given, due to the absence of mobilization plans. The United States' organization for war has not been along the lines of long-prepared mobilization plans, although contingents of their forces have on occasion been mobilized on presidential orders, as during the participation in the Boxer troubles of 1900. While this perhaps did not constitute war-making, it was nevertheless mobilization. The juridical justification for mobilization by the Federal Government seems to lie in Chief Justice Hughes' dictum (in the Minnesota Moratorium case of 1934): "The war power of the Federal Government is a power to wage war successfully, and thus permits the harnessing of the entire energies of the people in a supreme cooperative effort to preserve the nation." If the "Fathers of the Constitution" did not envisage total war and total mobilization, concepts foreign to the eighteenth century, the American judiciary had done so by 1934 at the latest.

The question of whether measures short of mobilization should come under parliamentary control has been raised, if only occasionally. It was discussed by the North German Reichstag in November 1867. The government of the Bund had demanded a law authorizing it to call up reservists for the purpose of a "necessary strengthening of the Army," even without an order of mobilization. Several members found the quoted term too vague and wanted to have it replaced by the term "Kriegsbereitschaft," readiness for war. But Moltke protested against this proposal; while it might be useful to protect individuals against executive arbitrariness, it still seemed advisable to allow the executive a certain latitude, for the latter might find it advisable to strengthen the effectives without going as far as bringing them up to Kriegsbereitschaft, not to speak of mobilization. If, for example, the Berlin Government had called up reserves on such a basis during the recent Luxemburg crisis, there would have been war, "considering the excitable character of the French nation." Moltke assured the parliamentarians that the Government would never call up individuals but would always call up definite categories of men. And the expensiveness of such measures would also work as a restraint. The bill was then passed as the Government had proposed it and as Moltke had defended it.[61] Whether any mass recall of reservists could actually escape foreign observation, whether its clandestine character would not cause as much alarm as a more openly-announced measure, may well be doubted, considering the existence of military intelligence and general news services.[62]

Parliamentary control over mobilization through the use of the purse strings was largely illusory. There seems to be no case on record of a parliament denying credits for such a purpose, either before or after the event. Austria-Hungary ruined her already shaky finances by the various mobilizations she ordered after as well as before the institution of the Delegations (1867), which acquired control over finances. While her prolonged mobilization during the Crimean War cost her 500 million fl., the much shorter and less complete mobilizations of 1908-09 and 1912-13 involved an expenditure of 180 and 309 million fl., respectively.[63] Still poorer countries came to believe that they could afford mobilization only if it were followed by a "paying" war. The Rumanian military attaché in Vienna told his German colleague in 1913, when his country was on the verge of intervening in the Balkan War, that if his Government should give the order to mobilize, it would at once start military operations since the country could not support the burden of a prolonged state of mobilization without war.[64]

Constitutionalism, if extended to include parliamentary control over war declaration and possibly even over mobilization, might have furnished insurance against the one serious interference with the orderly processes of mobilization that appeared possible before 1914, namely, Socialist counter-mobilization. The Socialist International movement had continually proposed or discussed the general strike against war since at least 1868.[65] The democratic features of constitutionalism, as far as they went, made the Social-Democrats of the various countries—though not the Lenins and Liebknechts—prisoners of the wars supposedly undertaken by "the bourgeoisie." Democratic control did not extend to diplomacy and war-making because the diplomats and war-makers were able to persuade parliamentary majorities that their procedures must not be interfered with if they were to be successful.

The relatively few attempts to protest against the order of mobilization had been fairly alarming to the governments directly and indirectly concerned. In Kharkov, Ekaterinoslav and other Russian cities, several hundred reservists mutinied in September and November 1904 in "protest against the accursed war," and Cossacks had to be employed to return them to obedience. In fact, Russian authorities in some districts resorted to mobilization in order to break the anti-war sentiment among workmen and peasants.[66] The French governors at that time were not free from the fear that, in case of mobilization, many French reservists, "infected with anti-militarism, internationalism and anarchy," might disobey the call to the colors. "We must anticipate serious mutinies among them," the military governor of Lyon told Paléologue in November 1904. French anti-militarism seemed to be at its height during the Moroccan crisis of 1905. France at that time could not meet a German attack, the Chief of Staff informed Quai d'Orsay officials (May 5). Of the 900,000 men she could put in the field, "100,000, possibly 200,000, would refuse to take the field. You've read what Hervé said at the last Socialist gathering: 'Our reply to the mobilization order will be the reservists' strike.'"[67] Such a warning was ominous enough to stifle all thoughts of mobilization in reaction against German procedures, and to make Rouvier and his colleagues rid themselves of Delcassé because of his war-like intentions.

Even if anti-militaristic radicalism had clearly abated in most countries by 1914, the governors still had to take into consideration whether or not the Social Democratic leaders and masses would follow them unquestioningly into war and grant the war credits, through their elected parliamentary representatives, after mobilization orders had been given and war had been declared. Only one lone vote denied the war credits in the Reichstag, Karl Liebknecht's.

France's military experience in the First World War and political totalitarianism in Germany went a long way towards eliminating parliamentary influence over mobilization. After 1919, the French re-worked their mobilization plans in a manner that was to give this always alarming measure not only greater speed but also greater discretion. The Government was authorized to call up the youngest classes of reservists, the so-called "disponibles," without pronouncing mobilization and without previous parliamentary authorization. The Wehrmacht, studying and in part imitating these arrangements, expected that with such measures, plus the mechanization and motorization of forces, the old principle of opening hostilities only after concentration had been perfected would be discarded.[68] The French themselves did not share this expectation.

In totalitarian countries, all "outside" influence over mobilization came to an end. The decision of when and how to order mobilization was taken into the hands of Führer or Duce. The German Reich Defence Law of May 21, 1935, laid down that the Führer and Reich Chancellor could declare a state of defense whenever war threatened. At that time, complete executive power was to be assumed by him and he was in turn to delegate it to the Reich Minister of War. The delegation of this function to a soldier was "to emphasize the prior claims of the immediate leadership in war and to guarantee their fulfillment." Should battle with a foreign enemy become unavoidable, the Führer could order mobilization. Prior to war, he was to appoint a General Plenipotentiary for War Economy, who was to direct total war economy and "to put all economic forces into the service of war leadership and to ensure the economic security of the German people." His work was to begin well ahead of war. Actually, it began at once, with Schacht as the first Plenipotentiary. He and the Reich Minister of War were to determine the preparations for mobilization in closest cooperation. In the terms of official commentary, this law was

to create clear foundations in constitutional law for the transfer of the whole State (Staatswesen) from the state of peace to that of war. In doing this, it has to be taken into account that the state of war can come about abruptly, can arise from a state of diplomatic tensions. Since the period of such tensions must be made use of to the limit of what is diplomatically possible in order to achieve readiness for war in due time, the Reich Defense Law envisages two stages for the passage from a state of peace to one of war: (1) the state of defense, (2) mobilization.

Since official declarations of war were no longer to be expected in a future war, the beginning of the state of war was to coincide with the beginning of mobilization.[69]

DIPLOMACY AND MOBILIZATION

At the end of the Revolutionary and Napoleonic wars, a certain approximation to total, or rather to constant, mobilization was disclosed. From then on, planned mobilization became the first condition for war in Europe. The majority of wars in Europe were militarily planned well ahead of their outbreak, with some notable exceptions, such as the Crimean War. The stabilization of friend-foe relations among the Powers made this possible.

a. Mobilizations under the Impact of Diplomacy, Capitalism, Steam Power, Liberalism, and Reaction

Most of the European war plans of the century from 1815-1914 were based on the expectation of setting into motion the maximum of forces immediately available, in order to obtain a decision within the shortest possible time. The upsetting of the economic life of the belligerent was thereby avoided, as was the danger of intervention on the part of neutrals. This was the essence of the Bismarck-Moltke kind of war.[70] Peace-time organization for war, culminating in mobilization, did not look much beyond the period of concentration and the first battles. Many of the later measures took on the character of improvisation. This was true of the First World War, as it was of the war of 1870-71. Until 1914, thought on the subject of mobilization was bound by the spirit of capitalist economy. Hence the prevailing hopes that long and careful preparation for war would make for victory in the shortest possible time. The short war was the only war compatible with the capitalist system of economy.

The short war appeared to governors and war-makers as the one called for from still another point of view: it was suspected that conscripted peoples, however great or small their share in government, would not support a long war. It even appeared doubtful whether they would approve of mobilization as a useful and "just" measure, or whether they would view the governments that mobilized first as aggressors. In consequence, mobilizations became less frequent during the nineteenth century. They still occurred most often in the absolutist countries, Russia, Prussia, and Austria.

Before 1914, much more so than afterwards, mobilization plans were intended to save a capitalist economy from the unlimited demands of warfare ahead of war. Its production and transportation systems were to be applied to war, though not

earlier than seemed absolutely necessary. Postponement was made possible by plans and preparation for the rapid obtaining of services and goods
following the pronouncement of the order of mobilization. At that moment a process of acceleration would be set off. It was steam power that
wrought the new connection of war and economy,
with railroad lines, often strategically conceived,
indicating where war and peace reached utmost
interpenetration.

The great acceleration of military movements
and timetables through steam power on land was
first demonstrated on a large scale by the mobilization undertaken by the German powers in 1850,
during the crisis preceding Olmütz. This crisis
was due to the continued struggle between Austria
and Prussia for hegemony in Germany. Berlin
took the more liberal stand in the constitutional
problem involved. This was enough to cause Russia to side with Austria and to set some army
corps marching westward from Mohilev and
Dubno. This unmistakable gesture on the part of
the Tsar, protector of all reaction, drove the
Prussian ministers and most of the reactionary
generals, at first very bellicose, to seek negotiations with Schwarzenberg. He forced on them the
humiliating settlement of Olmütz (November 28,
1850), especially humiliating since Prussia was
forced to agree to demobilize first. The mobilization order had found the Prussian Army in an unfortunate position—many units were away from the
garrisons and districts where mobilization was
scheduled to take place, some as far away as
Baden, where they had suppressed the Revolution
of 1849. Its execution, however, demonstrated
considerable superiority of the Prussian preparations over those of Austria. While the effect of this
demonstration might have been lost on the haughty
Schwarzenberg, others were full of admiration.
The French representatives in Berlin commented
that "the rapidity with which she has carried her
army from a peace to a war footing should not be
witnessed with indifference" and neither should
the use of railroads for the transportation of
troops. "You will learn, perhaps not without interest, that what has so much accelerated the
movement of the army mobilization is the fact
that all the orders had been prepared in 1840, at
the time of the Orient crisis, and had been kept
up-to-date until now, in such a way that when the
moment for arming had arrived, only the date and
the signature had to be filled in."[71] Among
themselves, the Prussian military did not think
quite so highly of their mobilization plans, and
the Chief of Staff entrusted Moltke, soon to be
his successor, with the task of re-examining them
and making the necessary improvements.[72]

Not many soldiers outside Prussia had observed the organizational progress under way

there, nor had they considered the problems
involved in the mobilization of conscript armies.
In France, Colonel Trochu pointed out that future
conflicts with conscript armies would assume
proportions and demand measures that would upset all the principles and traditions of strategy
and tactics.

> The fact that will bring a revolution into war
> is that of mobilization...The armies that
> mobilize with the greatest speed and the high-
> est orderliness will attack with the virtual
> guarantee of success, for which the armies
> opposed to them will only rarely be able to
> compensate by the abilities of generals and the
> vigor of troops...Of all military institutions
> today, the methods and procedures of mobiliza-
> tion constitute, therefore, the great factor in
> the wars to come, that upon which the safety
> of the armies will most often depend.[73]

Warnings of this kind were not heeded by the
French Army either before or after the Crimean
War. Its leaders trusted to "the abilities of generals and the vigor of troops," and Napoleon's
theoretical approval of such warnings had no
practical effect. Preparations for mobilization
remained incomplete; there was, for instance, no
army corps organization ahead of war until after
1871. Such forces as were sent overseas to the
Crimea and to Mexico were put together with
peace-time formations, filling them up to war-
time strength by stripping others that remained
behind. The weakening of the cadres that resulted
from the Mexican expedition was still felt in
1870. At the outbreak of the Crimean War, only
twenty-five infantry regiments, brought up to
war strength by drawing upon one hundred others,
could be sent overseas.[74]

Austria's halting policy during the Crimean War,
which only made her enemies and won her no
friends, found its only too adequate expression in
the prolonged mobilization of large parts of her
Army. Some 250,000 men were kept under arms
for several years, first for the purpose of forcing
Russia to evacuate the Danube Principalities and
then to occupy them herself for the duration of
the war, in order "to defend the frontier of said
Principalities against any return of the Russian
forces" (Treaty of Alliance with Great Britain
and France of December 2, 1854). While her armed
neutrality enabled Austria to force Russia to
come to terms with the Western belligerents and
conclude the Peace of Paris in March 1856, it
earned her no gratitude on the part of the latter.
There had been fearful losses within the mobilized
Austrian forces because of cholera, and the
mobilization had practically bankrupted her.[75]

Progress with regard to mobilization, as
demonstrated in Prussia in 1850, did not at first

impress the other European governments enough to bring them to imitate it. Either the soldiers refused to learn or the political governors were afraid of having their hands tied by hard and fast schemata. The preparations for the Italian War of 1859 on the part of France illustrate the effect of constantly changing political resolutions on military preparations for war. The French Army had no mobilization plans, properly speaking, for a war in Italy. At certain times the Army would receive orders from the Emperor that pointed towards war, such as orders to contract for uniforms and other supplies. At other times, and as late as April 1859, counter-orders were issued. Napoleon remained uncertain as to his own resolution for war, like a man planning suicide but shrinking from it after a look down the precipice into which he had intended to jump. Measures of military preparation had not yet attained the state of independence from political resolution or irresolution that general staffs were later to demand and obtain for themselves.

Promptly after Napoleon had given the Austrian ambassador his brusque New Year's greeting, French military preparations began. The marshal who commanded the forces around Lyon received orders to get two of his divisions so ready that, on telegraphic orders, they could be immediately transported to Marseilles and embarked there. "Get everything ready and without noise," he was told. "The movement might not take place, but it might also come about almost at once." Should the order for transportation be issued, it was to be rumored about that the troops were destined for Africa. The Marshal asked if the men on furlough should be recalled. No, that would reveal too much, he was told. "Do not talk; remain, I implore you, more silent than ever" (January 2-13). By the end of February there was less expectation of war. When the diplomatic situation again became hopeless, a new division was assembled between Grenoble and Besançon. Since spring was the usual season for the change of garrisons in the French Army, the war minister was hopeful that this concentration might escape public attention. Still, attempts to hide the preparations interfered with the preparations themselves, such as the buying of horses. A European congress, tentatively planned for the end of March, promised to give the soldiers more time for their preparations. But there was no congress.

Austrian preparations had been far more obvious. Partial mobilization of the forces in Italy and of the Vienna army corps was ordered on February 28. Full mobilization followed on April 5. On April 23, the ultimatum was issued to Piedmont to demobilize within three days. This was made necessary by the constant increase in Piedmontese and French armaments, as well as by the approach of spring, which would open the Alpine passes to the French. While this took the decision out of Napoleon's hands, there was, even after the declarations of war, no war plan. The Emperor called on old Jomini for advice on the conduct of the war in Upper Italy.[76] At the same time, the Austrians, foolishly forcing the issue, remained strangely passive in Italy.[77] They wasted their undoubted initial superiority over the Piedmontese and allowed the French to enter Italy and begin the war with the battle of Magenta (June 4).

Towards the end of the war, Prussia found it advisable to mobilize, largely due to the pressure of public opinion. The public favored Austria as a German power that might have to be defended on the Rhine as well as on the Po. The diplomatic history of this particular mobilization, with the problems it involved for a neutral who might not want to remain a neutral, deserve a summary. The mobilization was under cabinet consideration as early as February. Foreign Minister von Schleinitz, who was more of a Liberal than his successor Bismarck, was asked by the British minister to Berlin whether the Landwehr would also have to be called up in case of Prussia's mobilization. He answered: unfortunately, yes, and that is the crux of the matter, since the mobilized army cannot long remain on such a footing without bringing severe harm to the country. Prussia's military organization is fine for the case of a sudden invasion, but not for a prolonged campaign. In a Crown Council discussing the military measures to be taken by Prussia (February 27), Schleinitz stated that "to find the right measure in military preparations had unmistakably its very great difficulties." On the one hand, it was doubtful, considering French readiness for war, whether mobilization could be postponed any longer, particularly if French intentions were aimed at the Rhine. On the other hand, such an early mobilization would be a provocation to France. There was thus the dilemma of either accelerating the war by an early mobilization, possibly attracting the war to the Rhine and away from Italy, or exposing oneself to a superior enemy's attack by a belated mobilization. The War Minister, who knew more about the state of French preparations, was more reassuring. Prussia's mobilization could well afford to wait for that of France, he said, and still not be late. Should Franco-Austrian relations become much worse, preventive mobilization in Prussia might be advisable, but not unless Paris should become more war-like. The Prince Regent reminded the Council that French concentration around Lyon would make it equally possible for the French to throw their forces either against the Rhine or across the Alps. An embargo on horses was discussed and finally resolved upon, as a measure that one usually takes in crisis periods—or so it was explained to the French.

Austria's first mobilization measures were not encouraging to Prussia: depression was spreading and many people thought war would be a misfortune for Austria. If it had to come, however, better now than later, for "the population finds the present situation, which is totally paralyzing to trade and commerce, so unbearable that by comparison war appears as the lesser evil."

Moltke, the chief of staff, found the military and political situation singularly favorable to Prussia, once the war in Italy had started. From an exclusively military viewpoint, he thought that mobilization, if resolved upon, should be based from the outset on the firm intention of attacking the French in France (May 8). The first Austrian reverses excited much pro-Austrian sympathy in Prussia and the rest of Germany. This led the British representative in Berlin to believe that, unless a peace were to be suddenly patched together (which he considered an impossibility), Prussia would soon mobilize. "And," he added, "you know that mobilizing means war. Germany feels that Napoleon is her natural enemy, that when he has done his work in Italy, he will be on the Rhine, and that waiting a year or two is useless and therefore the sooner the struggle begins the better" (June 11).

On June 12, a partial mobilization was at last ordered in Berlin. The measure was explained to the other European capitals as follows: "Since the events in Italy have suddenly assumed large dimensions, the Royal Government feels the need of taking measures which allow it to give its attitude the weight which the grave character of the situation demands. It is under this condition that it has considered itself as in duty bound to augment its armaments by ordering the mobilization of several army corps." Many thought that this would be encouraging to Austria. The senior of the Prussian generals, Wrangel, told the Austrian minister in Berlin: "Now, my good son, you will be satisfied; within a fortnight we will move to the Rhine and Main. But do not stand still along the Mincio, go forward, under the command of the Emperor himself, with the brave Hess by his side; this is what we expect...One must come to grips with Louis Napoleon, and if he does not give way, march on Paris." On June 22, the Prussian representative at Turin wrote:

We have mobilized six corps, in a kind of sentimental fervor, following the battle of Magenta, without knowing exactly for what, but still in the direction of helping Austria. We shall now undertake large concentrations along the Rhine—

and still nobody wishes that it should come to war...To have the Landwehr battle for Austria's territorial possessions in Italy, no one will risk. There can be no mistake that mobilization alone, not to speak of war, is quite unpopular in the country and can only become more hateful with every day that calls for more sacrifices. As a demonstration, an observation along the Rhine can be useful, but it is an expensive demonstration.[78]

Since neither belligerent was certain of Prussia's intentions, the two Emperors hastened to conclude the armistice of Villafranca (July 11), which came too early for many of the great expectations entertained by the Prussians. "They had mobilized, they had drawn the sabre, even if they had wrapped themselves in a statesmanlike silence as to the enemy against whom it was aimed. Suddenly, there was no enemy any more—but also no friend."[79] Prussia had to demobilize, with empty hands and empty treasury, even if enriched by some military experience gained on the occasion. Many serious defects in the organization of the Army were discovered, Schleinitz confided to the British, "which he trusted to see remedied before its services would be actually required."[80]

b. Prussia-Germany—Model for Mobilization

There were altogether six Prussian mobilizations between 1815 and 1866 that did not result in war.[81] The experience gained by Prussia's governors on these occasions was not only technical but also political. The mobilized Landwehr, for example, had greatly resented being called away from family and business, and being called to uphold anti-Liberal policies with which many of them strongly disagreed.[82] The mobilization of 1859 had come during the slow recovery from the severe economic crisis of 1857. On these occasions, the men of the Landwehr had expressed their resentment by unmistakable demonstrations and agitations, in spite of martial law. This made the governors, political and military, think that the Landwehr as then organized was not a reliable instrument. This doubt led to the Army reforms of 1861-62, forced through against the opposition of the Landtag, which did away with the Landwehr as a separate part of the mobilized army, made the latter more homogeneous, and rejuvenated the Army, while keeping the peacetime service term at three years. Two years would easily have sufficed for technical training; however, the three-year term was regarded as the best and only way of teaching the soldier to obey unquestioningly.

The wars since 1815, notably the Russo-Turkish war of 1828-29 and the Crimean War, had led most military men to believe that an era of strategy of exhaustion, rather than of annihilation, had opened. With approximately equal opponents in the field, no early decisions could be expected, and only the ability of staying in the war while complementing one's own as yet not fully mobilized strength would bring success. "Whosoever is the last to be exhausted remains the winner"; this sums up the dominant thought of the period.[83] None realized better than Moltke and Bismarck that a state and economy like Prussia's could not have fought this type of war with great hopes for success. However, political considerations of all sorts—the hesitation of the Prussian King when faced with the decision to agree to a war that Bismarck and Moltke had carefully prepared, the respect for public opinion, for the neutrals, for Europe—intervened in such a manner that Bismarck the statesman could not permit Moltke the strategist to wage the technically most advisable war, the war of open aggression.

Such a war would have been based on Prussia's superior organization, which made up for her demographic and other inferiorities. Early in 1866, it seemed to Austrian diplomats that Bismarck's adventurous policies left him only the choice between an act of aggression or a defeat at home.[84] Bismarck, however, prepared for success abroad as well as at home, for a victory over Austria not only in the field but in the minds of the people as well. "We must take into consideration the impression which the outbreak of war will make on Europe," Bismarck realized, respecting rather than admiring public opinion. "For under present European conditions war cannot be started by one Power's arbitrary aggression against another. European public opinion is delicate in this respect; it would place itself on the side of the attacked and force even friendly governments to deny the aggressor moral support." Public opinion in Europe and inside Germany had to be convinced that war had become necessary because Austria was opposing the imperative demands for a new order of things inside Germany and was arming with that negative purpose in mind.[85] Mobilization for war on Prussia's part must either be camouflaged or made to appear quite justifiable.

The Austrians were not unaware of Bismarck's intentions and methods. At the outset of the tension, early in 1866, they were determined not to let him succeed with his plan of prolonging the tension indefinitely while perfecting the diplomatic and military preparations of Prussia, at the same time keeping Austria in a position where she could do essentially nothing for her armaments, partly because she had to husband her weak finances, partly because she had to avoid incurring accusations of aggressive intentions.[86] Whatever Austria did to strengthen her forces had

to be explained as altogether unwarlike. When dealing with the peace-minded King and the people, Bismarck systematically exaggerated the Austrian preparations: Austrian armaments were far ahead of Prussia's and were forcing Prussia, for her own security and in order to restore the balance, to proceed to analogous measures and make three army corps ready for war (March 28 - April 3). Yet the Prussian agent, a member of the Great General Staff whom the Austrians caught, had in his possession rather accurate data on Austrian strength in Bohemia, with figures much lower than those that Bismarck used in his argument.[87]

Bismarck's publicistic campaign was aimed at undermining all belief in the statements of the reactionary Austrian Government. He sought to cast them in the role of trying to maintain the highly unpopular status quo embodied in the German Bund, which was so sorely in need of the reforms proposed by Prussia. Unable to compete in this field, an Austrian diplomat cried out in horror: "Instead of the war, revolution is coming. The Man of Blood and Iron wants to solve the German question by reforming the Bund. Risum teneatis! But the thing is very serious and dangerous." What should Austria do in her dilemma? Halt her armaments for the time being? On the one hand, Prussia had partly mobilized and was provisioning her fortresses. She already had a headstart if war should actually break out. On the other hand, if Austria were to go ahead with open war measures, she would only furnish Prussia with the eagerly-awaited pretext for war.[88]

The diplomatic preparation of the war of 1866 presents the first fully developed case of the diplomacy of mobilization. One state prepares for the war it has decided upon, or is willing to accept, while avoiding all indications of such readiness. One state puts the blame for its armament on the prospective enemy, who has started to arm in order to make up for a more or less obvious backwardness. One sees also the last-minute appeal for peace from sovereign to sovereign in the interest of monarchical institutions, endangered by a war that might unleash dangerous sentiments. The unique feature of the Seven Weeks' War was the way in which Bismarck used the German question to stir national sentiments "wherever the German tongue was spoken." His reform proposals for the Bund, including a parliament elected by universal suffrage, were, he said, "the only way to avoid war, since the people wanted a settlement in a peaceful manner and not the pursuance of special interest by a war-like cabinet policy." Austria could promise nothing similar but was bound to stand for Kleinstaaterei, the German counterpart of "states' rights." Bismarck frightened all the status quo interests. Some, like the Bavarians, thought that the situation was becoming so critical that "a simple war might be preferable to the pre-vailing confusion." Others suggested that a mutual demobilization be arranged between Berlin and Vienna. Pressured by the peaceful King, Bismarck agreed to such a mutual disarmament, but neither he nor the Austrians were convinced that war would thus be averted. Should it prove unavoidable, the Austrians argued among themselves, they would need still more armaments. They decided that their acceptance of Bismarck's proposal to restore the status quo in armaments must not fur-nish him with any pretext for war. The Austrian war minister doubted that this was possible, for Bismarck could always find pretexts for not re-turning to the status quo. The appeal from mon-arch to monarch in favor of peace, which Francis Joseph was considering at this stage, seemed as yet premature. "This was always the last step, to be taken only when no other remained, and not before."[89]

Even when halted in the North, Austria's arma-ments remained burdensome enough to make it advisable for Bismarck to prolong the situation, thus making them even more burdensome. But when mobilization was continued in the South, against Italy, he declared that this was putting Prussia in an unfavorable position; since these armaments in Venetia had no real object, they were virtually directed against Prussia.[90] When Austria refused to halt, Bismarck obtained the King's authorization for the order of mobilization (May 4). "In the face of such procedures, he [Bis-marck] could not have passed one quiet night until he had brought the King to restore the balance by mobilizing the larger part of the Army." Bismarck was able to persuade the monarch that the danger of "Austrian aggression" was real. The die was cast, the movement towards war seemed irresist-ible, the machine stronger than the men who had started it. "Conditions once grown into such pro-portions are more powerful than the will of single men and lead to irresistible consequences," wrote the Austrian representative in Berlin upon learn-ing of the mobilization order. "Count Bismarck has several times declared that, once the Prussian Army had mobilized, he could not possibly offer his hand to any other procedure except war."[91]

When Prussia carried out her mobilization, from May 5-12, Austria was ahead of her by five weeks, at least in certain armaments, according to the calculations of the Great General Staff. On June 5, now a fortnight in advance of the Austrians, the three Prussian armies directed against Aus-tria stood ready to strike along the Saxon and Bohemian frontiers.[92] Now "if we are not at-tacked, we must ourselves attack, even if we should thereby become the aggressor," concluded the Chief of Staff of one of the three Prussian ar-mies, reasoning from military premises.[93] But

the dictatorship of strategic considerations and long-prepared plans had not yet begun, even in Prussia. The King still hesitated, hoping that the Austrians would attack. However, they were ad-vised by their friends not to march before they were ready but rather to pocket three slaps in the face if necessary.[94] As Bismarck saw it, in re-trospect: "To beat the Austrians was no art. I knew they were not prepared and that I could rely on the Prussian Army. The difficulty was to get the King across the ditch. That I succeeded in this is my achievement and for this I may claim the thanks of the country."[95] This had taken much time, time which poor observers (notably the French) thought had actually been required to per-fect Prussian mobilization and concentration, which was to be completed by June 5 at the latest. From then on, much "valuable" time was wasted by the King's hesitations. Only after some more outside provocations, including the resolution of the major-ity of the Bundestag to mobilize against Prussia as the peace-breaker (June 14), was he induced to give the order to attack.

When Bismarck resolved upon war in 1866, he had ascertained well in advance that Prussia's Army was ready. "The greatest of all Junkers" was, however, sufficiently familiar with things military to presume a military judgment of his own—too much so, the soldiers often thought, when he seemed to reach over into the sphere they be-lieved to be their own. Things were quite different in France (before 1870), where the army was trusted implicitly. Without ever having examined the pre-pared mobilization measures and war plans of the army, the civilian governors and politicians in and before July 1870 were firmly convinced that its prestige and impetuosity and declared readiness for war assured victory to France, so much so that not even the délicatesse of endeavoring not to ap-pear as the aggressor (of which Saint-Simon had spoken) was observed by them. The Premier at the time, Emile Ollivier, later wrote, when he had become the historian of the Second Empire in its short Liberal phase:

> [we had decided] to take the part of courage... and our declaration of war was prefatory to an immediate offensive operation; between it and the first battle there was to be no more interval than between lightning and thunder. They [the military] gave us the assurance that it would be so, and it is not our fault if it was not follow-ed up, as had been promised, by a quick opening of the campaign.[96]

Actually, the French government had generally paid little or no attention to the ties between politi-cal action and military strength and preparations. The bourgeoisie of the "Liberal Empire" trusted the soldiers implicitly, too much, as they often realized after 1871. During the first July days, the Duc de Gramont, the Foreign Minister, told the British ambassador, whose government was eager to help preserve the peace, that France had already begun war preparations, when actually none had been undertaken. While he had hoped to thus accelerate the peace efforts of the British, the latter actually became discouraged, believing that peace had already been lost.[97] Napoleon did not issue the first orders in the direction of war until the 9th and 10th of July—an order to MacMahon, commanding in North Africa, to embark as soon as possible the troops that were to take part in the Continental war; to artillery and engineering officers to inspect the state of the fortresses in the Northeast; to the administrative services to start buying supplies, etc. He gave the Austrians and Italians to understand that he was expecting their support.[98] Ollivier told the Austrian ambassador: "Within a fortnight we shall have 400,000 men on the Saar, and this time we shall make the war as in '93, we shall arm the people and they will rush to the frontiers."[99] There was little or no organizational reality behind this bluster, not even certainty as to how much actual force French policy would immediately have at its disposal.[100]

There was such a rush of blood to the governing heads in July 1870 that it was practically forgotten how much the problem of mobilizations and their comparative speeds had been discussed in the alliance negotiations with Austria and Italy. It had been calculated that Prussia would need three weeks to mobilize an army corps and one week for transport to the frontier, and that her offensive across the Saar could take place only seven weeks after the beginning of mobilization. These expectations were based on an erroneous interpretation of the opening of the war in 1866. It was calculated that Austria would need six weeks to mobilize and concentrate her far-flung troops, provided she undertook certain preparations even earlier, such as the buying and transport of horses and supplies. Conditions in Italy were even worse. Considering her financial exhaustion and the ill-will of her population, she would need a whole month of secret preparations and then four weeks more before even the first division could stand ready at Verona. It would take another four weeks for ten more infantry divisions to be readied.[101]

These factors, discussed at length in the earlier alliance negotiations, were dismissed in July in the expectation that France could win or at least safely start the war by herself. The alliances were far from being concluded and far from military implementation, whereas the Prussians and their allies inside Germany were ready and firmly tied together. There was a strong party in Bavaria in favor of armed neutrality. The King, though

recognizing that the casus foederis had arrived, still wanted to discuss the matter with his foreign minister, who was absent. The war minister informed him on the 15th that unless he was authorized to send out the mobilization order the next day, he must decline the responsibility. The King bowed to this time-table exigency and gave the authorization that the soldier demanded without consulting the foreign minister.[102]

In spite of the variety of federalisms in Germany, the right persons held the right views as to what preparations were necessary to wage a successful war. Germany's unity in planned action contrasted sharply with the improvisations and indecisions of supposedly-centralized France. On July 11, when a ministerial council was about to resolve upon military preparations, a telegram arrived from Benedetti, the ambassador to Berlin, warning that war was inevitable, should France undertake military preparations. The council thereupon decided to postpone such measures, unaware that the Emperor had already ordered some of them. This became known when the Marine Minister insisted on calling up 6,000 naval reservists, for which he had the Emperor's permission, and threatened to resign unless the order stood. The civilian ministers conceded.[103]

The division of councils continued in Paris. On the evening of the 11th, Napoleon asked the Austrian ambassador, Metternich, whether or not he thought the situation should be exploited. The Austrian encouraged him and learned that the Emperor would decree first degree mobilization on the following day. "He believes that will make the war inevitable," Metternich reported to Beust. "You see that one wishes to march, thinking rightly, I believe, that one will never find a better occasion and that the German problem is not involved and that one is ahead of Prussia by ten days." On the morning of the 12th, the Emperor gave orders to begin the mobilization; troop movements, prepared in advance, were to start at once. As the Austrian military attaché reported the situation, the French Army expected to have 200,000 men assembled in and around Strasburg and Metz in a fortnight and to be ahead of the Prussians by marching into Luxemburg. "They want the war absolutely, excitement very great, the cause popular, however dangerous the operation; Empire would never again combine so many advantages and never again win such a headstart in point of time. Count Bismarck has only the choice between war and a second Olmütz."[104]

The calling up of reservists was countermanded on the 13th, while all other preparations continued. When Benedetti was instructed to ask the King of Prussia to give the assurance that the issue of the Hohenzollern candidacy in Spain would never be renewed, War Minister Leboeuf broke into the council room "like a madman: 'What now?' he asked. 'What about those guarantees? The quarrel is beginning again, then, and I do not know? But I have stopped my preparations! You do not know what terrible responsibility is resting on me! This cannot go on, I must know absolutely this very morning [the 13th] whether it is peace or war!'" He demanded the immediate calling up of the reserves; after that, diplomacy might do as it wished. "Each day that you make me lose puts the fate of the country in jeopardy." To the civilian ministers, the calling up of the reservists, the main step in French mobilization, meant war with Prussia at once, as Benedetti had warned them. The problem as they saw it was this: Should France back up her demand for a guarantee that Prussia renounce the Spanish candidacy for all time by calling up the reserves, or would this measure merely make war inevitable? The council was divided, with eight votes out of twelve, including that of the two defense ministers, in favor of the more peaceful alternative, possibly also in favor of still "gaining time" over the Prussians.[105]

The question of which side was gaining by "gaining time" was largely an idle one. When asked by Bismarck on the 13th whether he needed more time, Moltke saw nothing to be gained for Germany if war were postponed. Even if not all German territory across the Rhine could be immediately protected against a French invasion, Germany's war preparations would soon leave the French far behind. On the whole, an early outbreak would favor Germany more than postponement.[106] It was under the immediate impact of this highest military opinion, which agreed with his own, that Bismarck wrote his "redaction" of the Ems dispatch. It went unaccompanied by any specific military measures.

The French ministerial council, meeting after the receipt of the dispatch, could not base its decision on any mobilization measures taking place in Prussia. Although the newspapers reported some moves in Prussia, there actually were none. Still the French War Minister insisted: "If we [do] not want to be preceded, we [have] not a moment to lose." The council was not at once persuaded, but finally agreed that "what had taken place in Berlin constituted a declaration of war, that the only question at issue was to know whether we would bow our heads to an outrage or whether we would hold them erect like men of honor." The reserves were to be called up. The War Minister left the room to give the necessary orders but returned on the way: "Gentlemen, what we have decided is very serious; but no vote has been taken." He wanted a roll-call before signing the order; the vote was unanimous. "Now," said the Marshal, "what will happen no longer interests me."[107] Towards the end of the day, when a

more explicit dispatch from Benedetti arrived, and when a plan for a European congress to avert war had been evolved, the Emperor wrote Leboeuf a note "which, while not containing the order to stop the calling up of the reserves, allowed some doubt as to the urgency of the measure." But it did nothing to halt the mobilization then under way.[108]

The next day the Cabinet went before the Chamber. Premier Ollivier explained the situation and what had led up to it. He asserted that armament had already been undertaken in Prussia—an assertion he later admitted had been incorrect, but had been made on the strength of army reports. "Under these circumstances," he continued, "to try conciliation any longer would...amount to forgetting dignity and prudence. We have neglected nothing in order to avoid war; we shall prepare ourselves to sustain the one which is forced upon us, leaving to each the part of responsibility that falls upon him" (great applause).[109] At the same time, War Minister Leboeuf told everyone "that if no time was lost he would answer for everything; that we would be ready before the Prussians, whose concentration would not be as rapid as was presumed; and that since war would have been imposed upon us sooner or later, it was much better to have it come before the Prussians had changed their rifle and acquired good mitrailleuses, and before the oppositon in France had succeeded in ruining the Army." He buttonholed a parliamentarian to tell him: "We are a few days ahead, don't make us lose that." And when the usually more judicious military attaché, Colonel Stoffel, arrived from Berlin, he also stressed that view: "The Germans are not ready. If we don't lose time, we shall win over them."[110] Even a large part of the Left was won over. One member declared on the 15th, four days before the declaration of war: "If you delay in order to give time for thought, as the Hon. M. Thiers wants, you give the Prussian cannon time to be loaded."[111]

While the parliament of the "Liberal Empire" discussed and ratified the Ministers' resolution for war, the Prussian King returned to Berlin from the historic spa at Ems. His son and the triumvirate of Bismarck-Roon-Moltke met and entered his train at Brandenburg. Bismarck demanded from him the order for the mobilization of the whole Army. William was at first reluctant, loath to incur the responsibility for a war in his old days. And could one be sure of the South Germans? The Chancellor answered him that mobilization was not a declaration of war, that it was nothing but a measure of defense against a French attack, and that France alone was responsible. Moltke told him that this war had been the thought of all his life, that it would be acclaimed in South Germany and that he would march even without the South Germans. The old King was somewhat taken by surprise but, listening to Bismarck as the train sped on, he could say very little against the urgency of the order for mobilization. When the detailed reports of the parliamentary discussions in Paris were shown to him upon his arrival in Berlin, he muttered: "But that's a declaration of war, still another war!" He thought that at least the two Rhenish corps ought to be mobilized, since the French might be before Mayence within twenty-four hours. But his son urged him to order mobilization of all the forces, "because under these circumstances no time must be lost." The King agreed, while still in the waiting-room of the Berlin station, and the Crown Prince announced it at once to the crowds waiting outside. On the 15th, Roon submitted the necessary orders for the King's signature. They were signed on the 16th and published that day.

French mobilization, ordered on July 14 at 8:40 p.m., was soon slowed down by disorder and the absence of comprehensive direction.[112] The original intention was to direct the offensive at the Main as the supposed separation line between North and South, and to compensate for France's numerical inferiority with speed. This plan had soon to be abandoned. The plans for war, supposedly elastic, proved merely to be indecisive. "In the mind of the Emperor and in the councils of his entourage, there were velleities rather than will, notions rather than designs, intentions rather than plans."[113] German mobilization, by contrast, proceeded without a hitch.[114] Once the concentration of 400,000 troops had been achieved without interference from the French, the frontier was crossed and the first notable successes obtained on August 4 and 6.

Some of the neutrals proceeded to mobilize in order to safeguard their neutrality. None did so more completely than Belgium, the object, as Bismarck had revealed, of vague Napoleonic aspirations. Austria, under the frown of Russia and the impact of the French defeats, soon limited her military preparations.

c. Mobilization as an Index of Military Preparedness

Germany's victories in 1870 sooner or later moved all Continental Powers to imitate her staff work and, in particular, her planning work on mobilization and troop concentration. For once the relentless competition among the armies hinged less on a superior model of rifle or cannon than on organization. As the experience of 1878 and the Boer War showed, British Army mobilization was not as well prepared as the increasing closeness of the European continent seemed to warrant. Cardwell's reforms (1869-74) had made a beginning with the forming of a reserve, though

"the powers of expansion" for which they had provided proved insufficient to cope with the demands of the Boer War. Operation plans were quite immature. In 1902, when operations in the case of a war with Germany were considered in the War Office, apparently for the first time, the military attaché in Berlin was asked whether taking Germany's colonies would bring her to her knees.[115] Not until Haldane's Army reforms had been instituted was mobilization prepared with exactitude, an organizational achievement which the Army had been unable to effect endogenously. Haldane was able to do it only after he had been permitted to observe German arrangements in September 1906.[116]

Many of the British arrangements imitated the better part of German organization. Haldane's predecessor, Arnold-Forster, had suggested imitating even the gerontocratic side of it, by giving the British Chief of Staff a tenure longer than the proposed four years. He maintained that Prussia's General Staff had been so outstanding because it had had only three (sic!) chiefs in a century.[117] Germany was the great model for Britain, rather than her ally France, who had herself honored the Germans by imitation. France had taken over many of the victory-tested German mobilization and other arrangements after 1871. Germany and France became the pace-setting pair in the military mobilization race, and both prodded their allies to follow more closely. France tried frantically, and at great sacrifices to her national wealth, to bring Russia to step up the mobilization and concentration of her Army, with such success that mobilization finally came to mean war even for Russia.

Away from this center of competition, mobilization remained much slower and the time distance between it and war greater, except of course in Japan. The Serbs, for example, in their war against Bulgaria in 1885, mobilized the active army and one class of reservists as early as September 21, 1885. On October 1, the Skuptchina convened and received a report on the seriousness of the situation; on October 10, the Belgrade Government explained publicly that mobilization had been undertaken because of the threat to which Bulgaria's coup in Eastern Rumelia had exposed the balance of power in the Balkans; only on November 14 did she declare war.[118]

Geographic and diplomatic isolation allowed the United States to do without such institutions as a general staff and organized reserves, except for the National Guards, until well into the twentieth century.[119] While their absence was only too painfully evident at the outbreak of the Spanish-American War, it did not as yet represent a serious danger. The United States remained reasonably safe, despite the absence of systematic and comprehensive mobilization plans. This state of affairs gave hope to some of the younger members of the Berlin General Staff that a German surprise attack on the United States, at the turn of the century, was not without the promise of at least initial success. So strong was the superiority complex based on German method.[120]

d. Russia as Mobilizer and Russian Diplomacy

On the occasion of the war of 1877-78, as on others, Russia protested that the slowness of her mobilization meant continued peacefulness and readiness to carry on peace talks. Thus she gained time for more preparations in a way undesirable to any opponent other than Turkey. The military time-table of the Russo-Turkish War began with Russian preparations as early as November 1876. Three army corps were mobilized in December but were not ready to move for half a year. Yielding to Pan-Slav pressure, the Government declared war on April 24, 1877, and opened hostilities that same day. Three columns of six army corps, drawn mostly from the Southwest, marched on Bucharest, where the gros was assembled by the end of May. The Danube passage was not forced until June 22. These dates help to explain why it did not seem altogether hopeless from a military point of view for the British Government to consider saving Constantinople. The British Army could be mobilized within twenty-one days, possibly less with certain preparations, and could be landed at the Straits in another twenty-one days. Should the order for mobilization be given at the time when the Russians passed the Pruth, it was calculated that the British forces could arrive at the Straits twenty-two days ahead of the Russians, and still one day ahead of them should the order be given as late as the Russian passage of the Danube. If, however, the order were given at the time of the crossing of the Balkans, they would be sixteen days too late.[121]

The Pan-Slavists, disappointed with the results of the Balkan war, laid the responsibility squarely at the doors of the Central Powers. This resentment resulted in the rearrangement of the garrisoning of the Russian Army after the war. Before, Russia had at times enjoyed her isolation as much as Britain and the United States had theirs. It had been a land-locked isolation, deadly to the invader, such as Charles XII and Napoleon I. But the same conditions that were an advantage in defense made Russian intervention to the West and Southwest slow and cumbersome. The military concomitant of isolation had been to keep the gros of the Russian Army in the interior. Driven by the endogenous pressure of Pan-Slavism rather than by any genuine foreign military threat, Russia broke out of her isolation and filled her border provinces towards the West and Southwest with increasing masses of soldiery.

This peace-time distribution was to compensate for Russian slowness in the war that seemed increasingly probable. In turn, it intensified the diplomatic tension among the three Empires so much that, by 1887, the danger of war was openly spoken of in the highest governmental circles. By that time, Russian peace-time forces were considerably superior to the German forces directly across the border. The latter could, however, be doubled within a few days, while Russian strength would remain on nearly the old footing for weeks to come. During that time the Russians would do their best, as the Tsar openly told the Germans, to interfere with German mobilization and concentration by sending Cossack swarms across the border.[122] The following years brought still more indication of the Russian Drang nach Westen, when places close to the German border like Lowicz, Skiernewice, and Plock were strongly garrisoned. The French embassy in St. Petersburg observed: "The idea that inspires these various changes is evidently to concentrate the troops as much as possible at the points they are to occupy in case of war." That is to say, a considerable part of mobilization and concentration was undertaken in time of peace.[123]

The Russians justified these measures by saying that their "wide spaces made mobilization very difficult and the loss of time they would suffer in case war broke out must be equalized as far as feasible ahead of it."[124] Diplomatic and military circles in Berlin and Vienna, estimating the strength of the Russian forces along the frontiers of the Central Powers to be about 600,000 men, considered it "a veritable mobilization of peace." Germany would be able to meet these forces with a million of her own within a very short time. It was still very upsetting, as a highly-placed Berlin official put it to the French ambassador in 1889, to have to do with a powerful enemy among whom "caprice laid down the law"—that is to say, the will of the Tsar, who had just recently toasted Montenegro as the only remaining ally of Russia and whose arbitrary power remained unfettered by any parliamentary influence.[125]

The logical way of dealing with this far advanced but still basically inert Russian mass was for the Germans to shift the opening offensive in the war on two fronts from the West to the East, trying at the same time to bring their Austrian allies to improve their forces and accelerate their mobilization. The six weeks which they required for their mobilization seemed much too long to Bismarck. Rather than plan towards a preventive war to begin at a set date, he told them to make use of the time still left to them to improve their preparations for mobilization.[126] When the Russians at last became aware of the danger of the German-Austrian pincer movement, which would close on them behind

Warsaw, their soldiers, rather than their diplomats, felt forced to accept if not to seek the French alliance. At times, notably in 1891, they felt at least as much in need of the alliance as did the French.[127] The Russian generals had pushed very considerable parts of their Army so far out on a westward limb that they found themselves in an exposed position from which only the French alliance could extricate them, unless they were willing to pull their troops back. The generals would not consider this at the time.

The very obvious Russian preparations and the German counter-measures as well forced the slow Austrians to share in the speed-up of the war in the East. Their general staff, formed after the cruel defeat of 1866, had remained at first rather backward in the preparation of mobilization-concentration. Rail transports, it had been assumed, could still be arranged during the long mobilization period. General Beck, Chief of Staff since 1881, wrought considerable changes in the old jogtrot by better planning and additional railway construction. (The head of his railway section finally became minister of railways.) Beck's first plan for concentration against Russia reduced the concentration period from forty to thirty-three days. But that was still not good enough. The German Army, according to the plans for 1881-82, intended to cross the Russian frontier with 400,000 men on the twentieth day of mobilization; the Austrians would not be able to do so until the forty-fifth. This time difference meant, according to Beck, that the German ally would at the outset fight alone against the Russian main force. Austria-Hungary would come in much later and only as a reserve army so to speak, intact, but without a claim to a share in what would already have been won and conquered. "This would not be in our political and military interest," Beck thought. "Our Army, if led into the war, needs victories, decisive victories, even if bought at heavy sacrifices; it must stand awe-inspiring, particularly with regard to the Russian neighbor. He must learn to fear it for a long time to come." Hence the demand for a speedier concentration through the construction of railway lines and a regrouping for the concentration. While Foreign Minister Kalnoky embraced these ideas, much opposition on the part of the Finance and Commerce Ministers had to be overcome. By the spring of 1885, the concentration period had been reduced to twenty-one days, by 1889 to twenty, by the end of 1891 to nineteen, thanks to new rail lines, principally in the direction of Galicia, to the doubling of existing tracks, and to better loading and unloading facilities. To achieve the speed-up, a change in the mobilization was also required, which was not without danger in a nationalities state. Mobilization was changed to a territorial basis, as in most other countries,

and reservists were called to formations in or near their home provinces. Thus "national armies within the Army were formed and the spread of Socialist ideas considerably abetted." Subversive elements were gathered together, rather than dispersed as under the old system, in such units as the Prague infantry regiments that deserted in a body to the Russians in the First World War.[128]

Russia had entered the speed-up race in her own way, even before the French alliance, much as if this were an inescapable part of general military progress in which she had to share, whether it added to her security or not. Her Chief of Staff at the time of the founding of the French alliance, General Vannovski, held that even for Russia, "beginning of mobilization cannot now be regarded as a peaceful act; on the contrary, it is the most decisive act of war." Two allied Powers must mobilize simultaneously, and with that diplomatic action must cease.[129] That is to say, mobilization was no longer a diplomatic tool of threat and pressure, as it had been for the greater part of the nineteenth century. Diplomacy must no longer interfere with the orderly processes of mobilization, once the decision to mobilize had been taken. It should be remarked that this claim to the primacy of mobilization over diplomatic peace endeavor was not originally put forth in Germany, the Power with the most advanced and complicated organization for mobilization, but on the part of the clumsiest and slowest runner in the race. There is no indication that Bismarck and his immediate successors would have allowed it. But in the end, how could a sprinter like Germany, knowing that Russia was fully committed to the race, be expected to allow the slowest participant a head-start?

Russia wanted the alliance with France to be directed primarily against Austria. She recognized, however, that if Germany was not the principal political enemy, she was still the foremost military foe. France wanted the alliance to be directed primarily, or exclusively, if that had been possible, against Germany. This complex of enmities eliminated all consideration of mobilizing against any single partner of the Triplice. Once bound by a military alliance, both France and Russia would have to mobilize at once and simultaneously against the Triplice "in case of an aggression, regardless of where it might come from, and [they would have to] begin the war on the first day of mobilization," as War Minister Obrutchev told Boisdeffre, the French negotiator, at their first meeting in Paris in May 1891. "We shall do that," he continued, "and shall push forward our whole cavalry, which is ready and will destroy railroads, etc. Without that we would lose our head-start and our advantages."[130] The Russians would never admit the possibility of mobilizing against "Germany alone" or against Austria alone. In the latter case, Germany would eventually enter the war, even if Russia were attacked by Austria first. Russia also believed, for technical reasons, that partial mobilization was "absolutely impossible."[131]

The other mobilization problem that came up in Franco-Russian staff conversations was the demand directed by either party to the other that the latter speed up its mobilization and concentration. At first the Russians raised this demand. They maintained that the Germans were able to complete their effectives by individual orders to reservists to join the colors. (They were said to have done this during the "war in sight" crisis of 1875.) They would thereby gain a head-start over the French of at least three days. The Russian Chief of Staff wanted the French to start earlier on their concentration, and also to have it take place farther from the frontier. "Increase your rolling stock and try to approximate the Germans on that point," the Russians urged. "How can you, who are so rich, hesitate on that point?" The French negotiator thought that the Russian General Staff, "under the sway of its fears, had allowed itself to be carried away by considerations that are truly too panicky."[132]

The unanimous decisions of the soldiers were presented to the Tsar by Boisdeffre: "that mobilization was the declaration of war; that to mobilize was to force one's neighbor to do the same; that mobilization involved the carrying out of strategic transports and concentration; that to allow a million men to be mobilized along one's frontiers without doing as much oneself at the same time meant denying oneself all possibility of moving later and placing oneself in a situation of an individual who, with a pistol in his pocket, would allow his neighbor to put a loaded gun against his forehead without drawing his own." The autocrat for whose soul the Russian diplomats battled in vain with the soldiers approved of this primacy of military considerations over diplomatic moves and told the Frenchman: "That is exactly the way I understand it."[133]

With the Russian general staff so obviously "under the sway of its fears," the French partner insisted that France and Russia should mobilize simultaneously only in case the Triple Alliance or one of its partners should start a general mobilization. The French, for example, were unwilling to mobilize if Austria mobilized two or three army corps in the wake of some Balkan trouble. They argued that "it would obviously be excessive and contrary to our common interest to oblige us in such a case to at once carry the totality of our forces to points closest to the frontier."[134]

Once France had obtained the instrument so long desired, her soldiers and diplomats began to press the Russians for an acceleration of their mobilization and concentration process. They offered the resources of the French capital market for the purpose of "building strategic railways indispensable for the acceleration of the concentration of their [the Russian] armies and their rapid transport to the most important points in the theaters of operation." The "most important points" at that time included India, in which direction the Russians were also urged to step up their railway construction.[135] But, for many years to come, Russia instead preferred to turn her military energies to the Far East, where they were wasted as far as France was concerned.

Russia, slowly recovering from her Manchurian defeat, could only gradually return to full usefulness in a war with Germany. In their conversations of 1908, 1910, and 1911, the chiefs of staff once more agreed that total mobilization and most cases of partial mobilization of the German Army would bind both Russia and France to mobilize their forces at once without any preliminary conversations.[136] Such conversations would be indispensable only if Austria or Italy should mobilize, partly or generally. This agreement was made still more stringent in August 1913. Henceforth, simultaneous mobilization of both armies was also to take place in the case of any hostile action on the part of the unmobilized Germay Army against one or the other party, a further step in the curtailment of diplomacy's peace-preserving functions.[137] However, instantaneous and simultaneous mobilization was still a long way from that French desideratum, the simultaneous offensive against Germany. The French were convinced that by 1912 their own concentration would be as fast as that of the Germans, and that they would be in a position to take the offensive on the twelfth day of mobilization. However, they still needed quicker Russian support in order to be certain of victory. As late as 1910, the Russian Army was expected to cross the frontier only on the twentieth day of mobilization, as against the eighteenth in 1900. The French urged that the first Russian echelon cross the frontier on at least the eighteenth day. But the ally protested, in February 1912, that they could not undertake war against Germany with any certainty of success for at least another two years. This gave the French some hope that they would soon be able to undertake an offensive shortly after the fifteenth day.[138]

Mobilization prior to war was more closely approximated in 1913. The French increased the service term from two to three years; Russia almost habitually kept her reservists with the colors several months beyond their term; and the German Army Law of July 3, 1913, as the French and Russian Chiefs of Staff interpreted it, would enable the Germans to shorten the length of time necessary for their preparations and give them a few more days to operate in the West against France, before being compelled to throw more forces to the East to meet the expected Russian offensive. Urging his Russian colleague to make the Eastern offensive still more nearly simultaneous with that of the French, Joffre informed him that, due to further acceleration of plans, the French would be able to proceed to the offensive on the morning of the eleventh day of mobilization. As yet, the Russians could start offensive operations only after the fifteenth day. They hoped to shorten mobilization and concentration by another two days by the end of 1914.[139]

From the outset of the alliance, the soldiers of France and Russia left it to the diplomats to make certain that the other side would at least appear as the aggressor. They themselves understood that simultaneous mobilization "would immediately be followed by effective deeds, acts of war; in a word, mobilization would be inseparable from an aggression."[140]

e. The Twentieth Century: Mobilization = War

At the Hague in 1899, Russia had proposed that negotiations be continued even after the start of mobilization and that disputes be settled by arbitration procedures rather than by proceeding to war. For the most part these proposals were inspired by the slowness of Russian mobilization. Most of the other Powers, with higher mobilization velocities, could see nothing but deception in such suggestions. The German representatives were most outspoken in their opposition. Agreeing to arbitration under such circumstances, they argued, would mean that Germany would lose, in questions that might still result in war, "the advantage that quick mobilization grants us and which no other Power can even approximately imitate." That view, according to William II, was "quite correct. That's what the whole swindle is aiming at." As the first German delegate at the Hague explained to the head of the American delegation: "Arbitration must be injurious to Germany; Germany is prepared for war as no other country is or can be; she can mobilize her army in ten days; neither France, Russia, nor any other Power can do this. Arbitration would simply give rival Powers time to put themselves in readiness, and would therefore be a great disadvantage for Germany." British sailors, such as Fisher, also a delegate at the Hague, held similar views as to the initial superiority of the British Navy, which must not be put in jeopardy by arbitration. He declared that "the Navy of Great Britain was and would remain in a state of complete preparation for war; that a vast deal depended on prompt action by the Navy; and that the time taken by arbitration proceedings would give other powers time, which they would not otherwise have, to put themselves into readi-

ness."[141] Fisher's civilian chief in the Admiralty fully shared these views: compulsory arbitration in great political questions would not be in the British interest. The French had been clearly backward during the recent Fashoda crisis. "If at that time a court of arbitration had existed, for whose endeavors in settling the dispute both parties would have been forced to wait for some time, France unavoidably would have perfected her armaments in the meantime and England would have lost the advantage of her superior readiness for war. It was not in the interest of any Great Power disposing of a war-ready navy or army to expose herself in times to come to such a disadvantage."[142]

The Second Hague Conference accepted a convention on the declaration of war which, at least in the form of "an ultimatum with a conditional declaration of war," must precede hostilities. Emperor William's furious remark that this convention was "a stroke against our fast mobilization" and that he would never observe it was sheer superarrogation: there was enough time left for Germany to make use of her superior mobilization as far as it still was superior; and besides, coups preceding a declaration of war were not then on the books of the Great General Staff.[143]

Considerations of superior preparedness always defeated the proposals for arbitration, "cooling off," or conciliation advanced by Secretary of State Bryan. He sought to provide for periods during which military preparedness would remain in status quo—something extremely difficult to ascertain and control, far more so than Bryan seems to have realized. The European governments, tearing along in their armaments race, thought his proposals either gratuitous or naïve and in any case to be explained by America's aloofness from military competition. While Germany showed some readiness to sign such an agreement with distant America, she would never consent to do so with the dangerously close-by European Powers, for that would mean signing away her greatest advantage in case of war. Only Britain and Italy among the European Powers signed a "Bryan Treaty."[144]

To most practicing European statesmen and soldiers the Bryan proposals appeared sheerly utopian and unrealistic, if not pernicious. As Lloyd George put it: "In 1914, mobilization made for war —it meant war."[145] It had acquired this meaning, generally speaking, since the fall of Bismarck. The gradual abdication of the civilian to the military governors meant abandoning endeavors to preserve peace at an increasingly earlier stage of the diplomatic process. It signified an increasing readiness to abstain from interfering with military preparations that often seemed more orderly, better regulated, and more full of promise for a "final" settlement of disputes than endless diplomatic negotiations. Civilian governors, politicians and diplomats, without examining the premises and conclusions of the soldiers, came to accept their view that, as a concomitant of military progress, general mobilization had come to mean war.

This conviction formed the basis of the Franco-Russian alliance. It came to be accepted in Germany, apparently without any discussion whatsoever between soldiers and civilians. The latter unquestioningly shared the view that mobilization on the part of Germany would inevitably lead to war, unless one were to sacrifice German superiority based on greater speed and exactness in mobilization, concentration, and the opening of hostilities. To halt during or at the close of mobilization, even if this might allow the diplomats to act once more in the interest of peace, would cause Germany to lose her cardinal advantage and would throw a monkey wrench into the complicated machinery of mobilization.

It is highly significant that this view was held, and perhaps first introduced, by one of Bismarck's most dangerous enemies, the politico-general Count Waldersee. This ex-chief of staff, Moltke's first successor, stated at the time of the Fashoda crisis that "mobilization of the Army, as we have prepared it, is identical with war." On second thought, this seemed to him to go too far. Preparations, he said, were so exclusively devoted to general mobilization that partial mobilization, for which certain political situations like Fashoda might conceivably call, had never even been considered.[146] Nor was it considered later, as far as is known.

Due to a curious osmosis between professional conviction and public opinion in general, the view that mobilization meant war was widely shared by the people. And it was shared by those whose economic interest caused them to dread mobilization, just as it was by those whose chauvinism caused them to clamor for mobilization. The devising of "security" measures short of mobilization was a slight concession to panicky economic interests.

f. Mobilization in 1914

"There was political danger in the practically hysterical fear of being late, which had evolved in the European General Staffs since 1870."[147]

The various mobilizations connected with the Balkan Wars of 1912-13 had proved deeply upsetting to the peoples of Europe. There was, however, no great search for the party that had started it all, no general attempt to label the initiator as the aggressor—whose identity was only too evident as far as the Balkan Slavs were concerned. The automatism of one measure of mobilization following the other was taken for granted. At the same time, the governments did not lose sight of the problem of how and on whom to throw the responsibility. They realized that the chain reaction of mobilizations in Europe had been incomplete because Germany had not become involved. They realized that she still possessed the highest degree of readiness for war and that once she mobilized, war was bound to ensue. For Germany would not want to lose the increasingly narrow margin of strength needed for the initial victory that seemed to hold the promise of ultimate success in a war expected to be of short duration. It was generally believed that the one first to march, and particularly the first to march into Belgium, would expose himself to the accusation of being the aggressor. This would be an invaluable "moral" asset to the other side, as was realized by the British and to a slightly lesser extent by the French soldiers well before 1914.

Aside from Austria, whose intended punitive expedition into Serbia called for a partial mobilization, Russia was the first state to contemplate mobilization in the crisis of July 1914. Considering governmental dependence on public opinion, it was only in the logic of things, in a world of nation-states, that the government that had to pay the smallest respect to a broad public opinion and that had at the same time the slowest mobilization should be first to make her preparations. On July 24, after the Austrian ultimatum to Serbia had been dispatched, Sasonov proposed to the Chief of Staff, General Ianushkevitsch, that a partial mobilization directed solely against Austria be prepared and announced as a warning to Germany, and even more to Austria. So little did the diplomat know of the instruments supposedly at his command that the soldiers had to inform him that this was impossible. There were no plans for partial mobilization and none had been contemplated since the beginning of the Franco-Russian military alliance. Russian soldier-negotiators had long emphasized the impossibility of Russia's undertaking a partial mobilization in case of war with Austria. Russia must and would undertake general mobilization.[148]

On July 25, Russian maneuvers were called off, and the troops who happened to be away from their garrison were ordered back to where their mobilization was to take place. These movements began on the following day. Comparable orders were given in France on July 27 and in Germany on July 28 and 29. Russian preparations also included the immediate promotion of the graduating class of cadets, instead of in the autumn, and the proclamation of "the state of war" in fortified places and in the Western frontier districts. These measures aroused various alarming reports in Berlin and Vienna about Russia's preparation for mobilization and evoked a German warning on July 26:

"Preparatory military measures by Russia which are in any way directed against us would force us to counter-measures, which would have to consist of the mobilization of the Army. Mobilization, however, would mean war and would have to be directed against Russia and France at the same time, since France's obligations towards Russia are well known to us. We cannot suppose that Russia will unchain such a European war." It was hoped that instead she would passively await Austro-Serbian developments, since Serbia's territorial integrity did not seem to be in jeopardy.[149]

The ministerial council held on July 25 in the presence of the Tsar adopted Sasonov's demand for a partial mobilization. This drove the soldiers to distraction, for, they said, it would interfere with the successful waging of a war that would inevitably include both Austria and Germany. Sasonov answered that the time he hoped to gain for diplomatic negotiations need not be lost for the military. They could use it to execute the measures envisaged by the "Regulations Concerning the Period Preparatory to War." Sasonov was back in the Russian tradition of negotiating diplomatically while arming for war. The previous order specifying that "the proclamation of mobilization is equivalent to the declaration of war," given out in the optimistic belief that Russia had reached a stage of military organization comparable to that of Germany and France, had been rescinded during the Balkan crisis in November 1912. At that time, a military commission in secret session had come to the conclusion that "it will be advantageous to complete concentration without beginning hostilities, in order not to irrevocably deprive the enemy of the hope that war can still be avoided. Our measures for this case must be camouflaged by clever diplomatic negotiations in order to lull the enemy's anxieties to sleep as much as possible."[150]

Detailed regulations for the "Period Preparatory to War" had been in force since March 1913. They comprised two lists of preparatory measures to be taken during "the period of diplomatic complications preceding the opening of hostilities." List One included measures to be taken at once upon the order of the Minister of War, issued with the Tsar's approval. Reservists were to be called for exercises in such a way that they might be assigned to the frontier divisions; territorial reservists were to be used to form units for securing the frontiers, lines of communication, and other lines of military importance. The considerable funds granted by the Duma in March 1914, ostensibly for reservists' training and test mobilizations, were to cover the cost of such measures. Other details covered were the readying of the frontier posts, re-examination of the mobilization orders, instruction of the troops as to enemy uniforms, reshoeing

of horses, restriction and termination of furloughs, restriction of exports of live-stock and foodstuffs, arrest of suspected spies, removal of moneys and securities from the banks of frontier towns, and various naval precautions. List Two allowed the War Minister to go beyond the limit of the funds granted by the Duma. Horses and vehicles were to be bought in the frontier districts; officers' families were to be transported from the frontier to the interior at government expense; freight cars were to be embargoed, harbors closed by mine barriers, and Russian merchant ships destined for military use detained. If this was not already mobilization of the frontier and ports, there was little left to complete it. Compliance with the orders for the preparatory measures was good, and the helpfulness of these measures to Russia's war preparations was far from negligible.

According to Pan-Slavist sentiment, Austria's ultimatum to Serbia of July 23 was above all the expression of her "hostile attitude towards Russia." A few hours before the time limit of fortyeight hours had expired, the Serbs ordered general mobilization. The answer to Austria was cleverly worded, conciliatory as behooves a small Power. However, the mobilization order, becoming known before the answer to Vienna, satisfied the powerful and chauvinistic military element at home. William II later said of the Serbian answer: "A brilliant performance for a time-limit of a mere forty-eight hours...A great moral success for Vienna; but with that all reason for war fell away! After this, I should never have ordered mobilization."[151] But Austria's procrastination had prevented his seeing the reply until the 28th. In the meantime, Austria had ordered mobilization.

On the evening of the 25th, Austria set the 27th as the "alarm day" and the 28th as the first day of mobilization. War was declared on Serbia on July 28. This upset the originally planned sequence of events: on July 22, the Germans in Vienna were told that a declaration of war on Serbia would come after mobilization had been completed. On the 26th, they were told that war against Serbia could not be undertaken with insufficient forces and that only by August 12 could general operations be started. But on the 27th it was resolved to send a declaration of war that day or the next, "largely in order to cut the ground from under any attempt at intervention."[152] Apparently the Austrians believed that a fait accompli would stop Russia, as it had done before, that she was still as unprepared for war as she had been in 1908-09 and 1912-13, that she would be held back by monarchical solidarity rather then driven ahead by Pan-Slavist sympathies.

There was also a foolish hope that this decision might "localize" the conflict so that Austria would only have to fight Serbia-Montenegro. But what if Russia should enter in, at once or later? Would the mobilization at the outset have to be "Mobilization B," "Mobilization R," or some modification of them? Conrad's plans for mobilization and concentration were somewhat elastic, in order to meet such contingencies. The fifteen army corps were divided into four groups: (1) a minimum Balkan group of three corps, sufficient to contain the Serbs in and around Serajevo; (2) a group of eight corps for use against Russia and possibly Rumania; (3) an alternative group of four corps for use against either Russia or Serbia—against Russia if she was to be in the war at an early time, against Serbia if she should remain the only enemy; (4) the Graz corps, to be kept in reserve for use against either Russia or Serbia. These plans made partial mobilization in Austria-Hungary quite feasible. Group (2), closest to the Russian frontier, was to remain unmobilized in the case of war with Serbia alone. Thus Russia would not be provoked. And war-like measures in the direction of Russia were in fact omitted in July 1914.[153] Since this was the case, it seemed only fair to minds like William's that Austria's army, after her two abortive mobilizations because of Balkan problems, for once be given "satisfaction d'honneur and the appearance of a success and the consciousness of having stood on foreign soil. Without that, without a campaign, a very evil anti-dynastic sentiment, highly dangerous, would arise."[154] But this was antiquated sentiment in the world of July 1914, its obsolescence contrasting with the modernity of organization in William's own Empire.

Somewhat optimistically, Sasonov hoped for a few days (July 26-28) to announce partial mobilization as a threat in his negotiations with Austria. Partial mobilization was never actually started, but the announcement of it served as a screen for the measures applied in the "period preparatory to war." When questioned by the German ambassador as early as July 26 about the rumors of mobilization orders for the army corps in the Western provinces, Sasonov denied them. Orders would not be given unless Austria assumed a hostile attitude towards Russia. But he admitted that "certain military preparations" were already being taken "in order not to be surprised."

The German embassy was soon aware that these preparations were extensive; the Russians were "obviously endeavoring to gain time for new negotiations and for carrying out armaments."[155] They were not deterred by Pourtalès' warning that "nowadays to use mobilization measures as a means of diplomatic pressure was highly dangerous; for in such cases, with their purely military considerations, the general staffs got their word in and, once Germany had pushed the button, things became irresistible."[156] These Russian measures made certain endeavors to preserve peace

less promising, such as Grey's proposal of July 26 for an ambassadors' conference of the four neutrals —Britain, France, Italy and Germany. The considerable time required to arrange it would accrue to the military advantage of Russia and to the disadvantage of Germany.[157] Even Grey, with his ignorance of military considerations, took this point into account.[158] Paléologue, French ambassador in St. Petersburg and formerly liaison officer from the Quai d'Orsay to the military offices, was a more experienced diplomat. On the 26th, he feared that "military preparations leave but little time to the action of diplomacy."[159]

The German Chancellor and the Wilhelmstrasse continued in the passive attitude they had adopted towards Austria's moves ever since they had given their blank check of July 5. Until the afternoon of July 27, they were under no influence from the military and naval offices and did not discuss the situation with them. The Kaiser, Moltke, and Tirpitz were away on their summer vacations, and the Admiral had been requested by Bethmann on July 24 not to cause alarm by an early return to Berlin. But all three were back by the afternoon of the 27th, the Kaiser and Tirpitz in haste, Moltke calmly and leisurely, relying on his mobilization schemata. But he also provided the Wilhelmstrasse with a draft of the ultimatum to be addressed to Belgium in case of war.[160] On July 27, Conrad and Berchtold, alarmed by Russian military preparations against Austria, suggested that Berlin warn St. Petersburg that these Russian measures constituted such a threat that counter-measures would have to be taken. They were told that the military reports from Russia were only rumors, as yet unconfirmed.[161]

The military reports about Russian and French preparations, gathered by the Great General Staff and communicated to the Wilhelmstrasse on the 29th, were more substantial than rumors and led to serious warnings in Paris. Germany mentioned that she might have to proclaim a state of "danger of war" which, while not equivalent to mobilization, would still heighten tension. And Germany announced to St. Petersburg that the continuation of Russian mobilization measures would force Germany to mobilize, and "then European war could hardly be stopped."[162] Before this telegram had arrived in St. Petersburg, it was known there that Austria had ordered the mobilization of eight army corps —more than seemed necessary to fight Serbia. Russia considered this step to be partly directed against herself and felt that the mobilization of her military districts along the Austrian frontier was called for. When the German ambassador pointed out how very dangerous this measure would be, Sasonov resorted to the hoary Russian argument that in his country "mobilization was far from meaning war as it did in the Western European

States; the Russian Army would stand possibly for weeks at rest (Gewehr bei Fuss) without crossing the frontier." Pourtalès warned him that "the danger in any military measure was in the counter-measures of the other side. The thought was obvious: the general staffs of Russia's possible adversaries would not want to surrender the advantage of a great superiority over Russia in mobilization; they would press for counter-measures."[163]

These general-staff arguments were submitted to the Chancellor by Moltke. Austria, he pointed out, had mobilized eight corps against Serbia, just enough to undertake the punitive expedition. As against this, Russia was preparing to mobilize twelve corps as soon as Austria should cross the Serbian frontier. Austria would then be faced not only by the Serbian Army but also by a strong Russian superiority and would therefore be forced to mobilize the other half of her Army as well. He elaborated as follows:

The moment, however, when Austria mobilizes her whole Army, the clash between her and Russia will become inevitable. But that is for Germany the casus foederis...Unless Germany wants to break her word and leave her ally to be annihilated by Russian superior power, she has to mobilize. This will have as a consequence mobilization of the remaining Russian military districts. Then, however, Russia will be in a position to say: I am attacked by Germany, and thus assure herself of the support of France, which is bound by treaty to participate in the war when her ally Russia is attacked. The Franco-Russian agreement, so often lauded as a purely defensive alliance only created to meet the aggressive plans of Germany, thus becomes effective and the mutual tearing to pieces of the European States will begin.[164]

It would seem that the soldiers now realized, much more than they had before, the entanglements inherent in the supremely organized mobilization plan. Mobilization had become a competitive process in which Germany seemed bound to lose advantages accrued through peace-time organizational work, with every day of Russian preparation. The increasingly important political consideration of incurring the responsibility for aggression was more and more likely to be assigned to Germany as the mobilizer in Europe's military "heartland." "War guilt" was the price to be paid for organizational superiority, real or imagined. The politics and psychology of mobilization measures were now under contemplation in both camps.

On July 28, when the news of Austria's declaration of war on Serbia arrived in St. Petersburg,

the soldiers saw Sasonov's "optimism vanish at a stroke." He was immediately convinced that a general war was inevitable and informed Ianushkevitch that he must no longer delay with the mobilization of the Army, which he was surprised to find had not been begun sooner.[165] He informed foreign governments that, due to Austria's step, Russia, entertaining no aggressive intentions against Germany, would order mobilization in her four southern military districts on the 29th. Whether he still disregarded military arguments against the unfeasibility of partial mobilization or had resigned himself to general mobilization and general war is uncertain. For the latter case, he had the assurance of France's support and word from Grey that the British Fleet would remain assembled at the close of its maneuvers. "Without volunteering any further explanation, [the Austrian ambassador] repeated his apocalyptical metaphor [to the Tsar]: 'The machine is in motion.'"[166]

On the 28th, the Russian soldiers most directly concerned with mobilization once more considered Sasonov's wish for partial mobilization, concluding that general mobilization was the only feasible thing and that they must win the Tsar's approval for it. The Chief of Staff, now the main force driving for mobilization, saw the Tsar, who gave none of the ministers an occasion to be heard. He obtained the Tsar's signature on the ukase for general mobilization, and possibly also for partial mobilization in case the diplomatic situation should improve, although it remains doubtful whether the soldiers could have executed partial mobilization. They were so certain of the Monarch's assent that, even before his signature had been obtained, they informed the commander of the Warsaw district, and presumably other district commanders as well, that general mobilization was imminent and would be announced presently, with the 30th as the first day of mobilization. A bit more mindful of the political impact of his warning, the First Quartermaster General advised the troops in the Warsaw district to refrain for the time being from committing any sort of hostility that might give Germany ground for ordering mobilization and compromise Russia in the eyes of her allies.[167]

Though in possession of the Tsar's signature, the Chief of Staff called in the German military attaché and assured him on his word of honor that things still stood as they had two days before. Nowhere had there been mobilization, not one man or horse had been called up. While he said that he could give no guarantee as to the future, he did state emphatically that the Tsar, now as before, wanted no mobilization against Germany. Considering the positive information about the calling up of the reservists that was available, the German could see in these solemn affirmations nothing but an attempt to mislead him as to the true extent of

Russian preparations.[168] A word of honor was at best only good in time of complete peace.

Russian diplomacy accomplished little more on the 29th than to camouflage Russia's intention to mobilize in the very near future. Sasonov told the German ambassador that mobilization would be only partial, in the direction of Austria. Perhaps he was still unaware of Ianushkevitch's acts. Later in the day, when he must have had this knowledge, he assured the British ambassador that "the order for partial mobilization was signed today [and] would only be directed against Austria. It was for this reason that it had been decided not to order the general mobilization, which the military authorities had strongly recommended." He captivated rather than alarmed the Britisher.[169] The latter expostulated with his German colleague that "if Russia had not shown that she was in earnest by ordering mobilization, Austria would have believed that she could go to any lengths and thus trade on Russia's desire for peace. A week or more would elapse before mobilization was completed," and even then, Sasonov had said, "Russia would not precipitate war by immediately crossing the frontier."[170] It would be impossible to say with any certainty whether the British diplomat was naïve and backward, the product of an era when mobilization could still be employed demonstratively in the service of diplomacy, or merely an innocentiste anxious to excuse an ally with whom he did not for a moment remonstrate about mobilization.

The task of doing this repeatedly was incumbent on the German ambassador. He told Sasonov that the Russian order of mobilization, if really impending—it must have been rumored all over St. Petersburg by the afternoon of the 29th—would be a serious mistake. While not denying the imminence of the order, the Minister insisted that Russia had been forced by Austria's actions to take this step; "however," he added, "mobilization was far from meaning war."[171] In a conversation with the Austrian ambassador, to whom he often spoke more confidentially than to others, Sasonov later in the day charged the Russian soldiers with the responsibility for the mobilization, which was "of fairly wide extent." It was they who had alarmed the Tsar by their interpretation of the Austrian mobilization to the southward. But it was childish, the Austrian explained, to see a threat to Russia in this mobilization. Then, in a last attempt to establish diplomatic solidarity against the soldiers, he urged putting an end to their nefarious, peace-endangering activities. This, Sasonov confided to him, was not easy, for he himself saw the Tsar only once a week and only thus had he "learned for the first time from His Majesty what the militarists had been urging upon him." This inter-diplomatic exchange of confidences was rudely interrupted by the telephoned news of the Austrian bombardment of Belgrade.[172] After that, Pourtalès called for a third time that day to bring Bethmann's serious warning of the inevitable effect that Russia's continued mobilization measures would have. They would force Germany to mobilize, and then a European war could hardly be postponed any longer. He submitted this message not as a threat but as a friendly warning. Sasonov, much excited, declined to accept it as such. He did not inform the German that Russian mobilization was impending, as he had told the Austrian. And he remarked that Russian mobilization must not be construed as indicating an intention to make war on the part of the Russian Government, but as intended merely to bring Russia to a state of armed neutrality.[173]

Sasonov had come to believe in the inevitability of general war. He agreed with the Chief of Staff and the War Minister that, "considering the slight probability of avoiding the war with Germany, it was necessary to get ready in time and in every way for it, and that therefore one could not risk interfering with general mobilization later by executing only a partial mobilization now." Their general agreement, when telephoned to the Tsar, was confirmed by the monarch, who authorized the necessary steps. The decision was "received with enthusiasm in the narrow circle of those familiar with the business."[174] Then followed the construction of more alibis. London and Paris were given a version of the German warning received in St. Petersburg that was far from truthful. "As we cannot comply with the wishes of Germany," the Russians added, "we have no alternative but to hasten our own armaments and to assume that war is probably inevitable."[175] Germany rather than Austria now had to be made responsible in the opinion of the allies for what was to come.

While the director of Russia's foreign policy had abdicated in favor of military considerations, the Tsar was not yet ready to do so. A telegram from the Kaiser, received on the evening of the 29th, warned against the calamity of a European war, which might be precipitated by military measures on Russia's part.[176] This made him reconsider his approval of general mobilization. Now, on his own initiative, he decided that it was to be cancelled and to be replaced by the seemingly less dangerous partial mobilization. The soldiers warned him about the "technical impossibility" of interfering with mobilization but were unable to dissuade him. The order for general mobilization was stopped at the Telegraph Office and the order for partial mobilization was sent out instead towards midnight of the 29th.[177] The persons who had most to lose by a lost war shrank from the next step in the direction of war. Tsar and Kaiser believed momentarily that they still held the absolute power, which the masses ascribed to them, over the diplomatic and military machinery. For a short moment, fears of the outcome of the war loomed greater than the soldiers' fear of losing the war through belated mobilization. At this fatal hour, the German Military Plenipotentiary, moving in the Tsar's entourage, gained the impression that "they have mobilized here out of fear of coming events, without aggressive intentions, and now are frightened by what they have done."[178]

It was past midnight when Sasonov once more called Pourtalès for a long interview. He attempted to bring the German Government to exert pressure on Austria in order to make her give up some of her demands on Serbia, notably those infringing upon the latter's sovereignty. The ambassador insisted that Austria's declaration that she would respect Serbia's territorial integrity was sufficient. Sasonov protested that allowing Serbia to be turned into a dependency like Bokhara would create serious dangers for Tsardom at home. Now that Russia had resolved upon the fatal first steps towards mobilization, Pourtalès found an exchange of ideas very difficult and once more reminded the Russian of the automatic effect that his country's mobilization would have in Germany, due to the Austro-German alliance. "Sasonov declared that cancellation of the [partial] mobilization order was no longer possible and that Austrian mobilization was responsible for it." The German concluded from Sasonov's words that the Kaiser's telegram to the Tsar had had its effect but that the Minister would work hard to keep the Tsar in hand.[179] In this he was to be successful enough.

The 30th of July was the day for the soldiers to take over in the interest of the smooth working of their mobilization plans and for the diplomats to endeavor to throw the responsibility and the guilt for these measures on the enemy-to-be. During the night, Isvolski gave Sasonov's version of his talks with Pourtalès to the French Government. He explained that it was necessary for Russia to accelerate her armaments and to consider war imminent, in which case he expected the allied support of France and Britain. At the Quai d'Orsay they recommended once more that Russia's military preparations should assume "a character as little obvious as possible." War Minister Messimy told the Russian military attaché that, in order not to give Germany the much-feared pretext, his countrymen might stop mobilization but would still go on with their preparations and even speed them up. They should, however, refrain as much as possible from such spectacular measures as the mass transport of troops, the most observable of all measures.[180] At about the same time, the French informed Grey that a comparison

of French and German military preparations so far showed that "France was resolved that it would not be she who takes measures of aggression." In witness thereof her troops would evacuate a strip of national territory open to sudden aggression, for no other reason than to show public opinion and the British Government that France, like Russia, would not fire the first shot.[181]

The Russian soldiers accepted the order for the "impossible" partial mobilization. Still they wanted the general measure. They found Sasonov ready to support their demand with the Tsar, who had turned it down again on the morning of the 30th. Sasonov saw the Tsar once more in the afternoon and made himself the unreserved advocate of the military demand. He even accepted the political arguments produced by them in favor of general mobilization.[182] This shows how complete diplomatic abdication had become, how fully military-technical considerations had won out over the others. In the afternoon, Quartermaster General Danilov expounded to Sasonov's closest assistant, Basily, a "rather detailed picture of the fatal consequences the partial mobilization that we were about to effect would have." He pointed out that there was still time to pass to a general mobilization without great trouble but that the decision must be taken quickly, possibly not later than the 31st, because otherwise there would be great disorder. "On the other hand," he asked, "if the German Government were fair to us, could it consider general mobilization of our Army, provoked by the policy of Austria, as a threat to Germany's security? Obviously not." It seemed to the soldier that he had won over the diplomat with his argument.[183] Honestly or dishonestly, Danilov forgot that heretofore the Russian soldiers, like most other soldiers, had always considered general mobilization as equivalent to war.

Meanwhile, Sasonov wrestled with the Tsar to obtain his consent for general mobilization. A partial one, he argued, would upset the whole military organization of the country and estrange the allies. "It only remains to do everything necessary to meet war fully armed and under the conditions most favorable to us. Therefore, it is better to call forth a war without fear by our preparations for it, and to continue these preparations carefully, rather than to give an adducement for war out of fear and be taken unawares."[184] The weaker character had the better memory: for an hour the Tsar resisted, aware of the hitherto axiomatic view that general mobilization would bring general war. But finally he gave in and once more authorized general mobilization. Sasonov rushed to the telephone, informed the impatiently waiting Chief of Staff of the decision and told him to smash his telephone and disappear for the day, so that no counter-orders could reach him.[185] Thus peace was sacrificed in the interest of military orderliness—to avert the much-feared sequence of order, counter-order, disorder.

The Russian mobilization order went over the wires at 6:00 p.m. The dreaded confusion expected as a result of partial mobilization was happily averted. And so was peace. The foremost Russian mobilization specialist in 1914, Dobrorolski, put it this way: "The whole plan of mobilization is worked out ahead of time and to the end in all its details. At the chosen moment, one only has to press the button, and the whole machine begins to function automatically with a clocklike precision ...The choice of the moment is determined by a variety of political reasons. But once the moment is chosen, everything is settled; there is no going back; it determines mechanically the beginning of war."[186] And it was taken for granted by the soldiers on all sides that this was so for every one of the allied and counter-allied Powers.[187] The diplomatic profession proceeded to put the blame for the war on the party that had mobilized first or committed the first warlike act.

Apart from Serbia's mobilization, Russia's was the first general mobilization by one of the Great Powers. This was a fact that had to be immediately concealed. On the text of the telegram announcing Austria's general mobilization, Berthelot, one of the permanent officials at the Quai d'Orsay, made a note of the time-table: "Austrian mobilization the 31st in the morning (5 o'clock), Russian mobilization follows (10 o'clock), German Kriegszustand (3 o'clock), summoning of the troops for the French couverture (6 o'clock)."[188] This sequence, not a true one, provided the guiding thread for much of the propaganda to come. A telegram from Paléologue of July 31 was manufactured, announcing Russian general mobilization. In it, the necessary sequence was contained, as rewritten for the French Yellow Book: first, Austria's general mobilization; second, Germany's continued secret preparations over a period of six days; third, Russia's general mobilization in order not to be out-distanced by the Central Powers.[189]

Russian diplomacy had treated the French ally rather cavalierly during these critical days. Considering the repeated assurances that France would stand by her ally, this was safe enough. Partial mobilization was announced to the Paris ministries most concerned by Isvolski and the military attaché, Ignatiev, during the night of the 30th. The attaché asked War Minister Messimy what the French Government's attitude would be. Messimy told him he ought to know that it was beyond his province to give an answer, that it was up to the Cabinet. Following a telephone consultation with the Premier, he told Ignatiev that the Russians ought to refrain

from all asininities and particularly from all noise with the mouth. Mobilizing your Southern

army corps without warning us, even as an answer to Austria's declaration of war on Serbia, is that in keeping with the letter of our accords?...But be careful! Germany is not only your principal adversary, she is in fact the only one, absolutely the only one, as she is ours. Austria does not count, sink that well into your head. Do not fall into the trap which the Germans have put up for you by pretending to defend the Slavs.

Both Messimy and Viviani recommended going slowly with mobilization. But that would not do, answered Ignatiev. "We soldiers know too well that the speed of a mobilization is not something leisurely like drinking a cocktail (ne se gradue pas)! Once ordered and set off, it goes like the mechanism of a well-set clock, following a timetable that no one in the world can change in the least without a commotion of incalculable consequences." Messimy was willing to admit that this was true, as far as mobilization in the narrow sense of the word was concerned. Still, he thought it did not apply to troop transports and concentration. The latter ought to be stopped and the stoppage publicly announced.[190]

All this cautioning must not be interpreted as a readiness on the part of the French to beat a last-minute retreat, as Ignatiev concluded for the benefit of his superiors at home. Messimy was still ready to declare that France was prepared to fulfil exactly her obligations under the alliance. "It would be desirable, however," thought Messimy, "to apply all means to the maintenance of peace, the more so since a postponement of the conflict could only prove useful to us" (referring to Russia); whereas Joffre thought that allowing too much time to elapse might favor the Germans instead. One must conclude from this disagreement among the experts that they either did not know which Power might be favored by additional time or that one of them, the Chief of Staff, was more eager than his nominal superior to have the war come soon. In any case, France continued to ready herself. The third period of couverture—the calling up of the reservists in the frontier corps districts —went into effect on the evening of the 30th, at a time when the corps in question were already practically at war strength. Ignatiev watched with admiration the general calm in the Paris military offices and their "unconcealed joy to be able to make use of the favorable strategic situation."[191]

The French governors did not show the slightest desire to interfere with the effectiveness of the Russian mobilization. They only hoped that it would be carried out as unostentatiously as possible, not only in order to rob Germany of a pretext for mobilization but also in order to avoid making a bad impression on Britain and Italy. On July 30, Jules Cambon warned from Berlin: "It is important not to publish the mobilization measures in France until after they have been decided upon definitely in Berlin, in order that British public opinion, which can play such a great role in events, does not ascribe to us any initiative tending towards war." While the Germans took all possible measures of mobilization preceding the order for general mobilization, they also tried to induce the French to publish their mobilization first. "We must spoil these calculations," Cambon thought, "and not yield to the impatience that will manifest itself in the press and in public opinion in Paris."[192]

The French governors refrained from any warning in St. Petersburg that might have averted the step from partial to general mobilization, a step about which they were not consulted. At the same time, they did everything to make certain of British good will. They presented Grey with an exaggerated list of the many military preparations that Germany was said to have made, claiming that they were more extensive than the analogous French preparations.[193] Although circumspect about the diplomatic couverture, the French governors by no means neglected the military one. This too was diplomatically conceived to captivate British opinion by the famous ten-kilometers' withdrawal from the frontier. The numerous French measures were, indeed, so far-reaching and so close to mobilization that a great soldier like Foch, commanding the Nancy army corps at the time, called them the real thing—"la mobilisation"—before the order of general mobilization had even gone out.[194]

Britain's entanglement in Continental conflicts was less remote than her people believed at the time. Her diplomacy was deeply committed and so were various soldiers. Her Navy happened to be in a high state of readiness for war, technically speaking. On July 25, after Austria's ultimatum to Serbia, the Foreign Office was informed that Sasonov "thought that Russia would at any rate have to mobilize" and that "the step taken by Austria meant war." Grey's adlatus Crowe was ready at once: "We should decide now," he urged, "to mobilize the fleet as soon as any other Great Power mobilizes, and we should announce this decision without delay to the French and Russian Governments." He thought the moment to enlist French support in an effort to hold back Russia had already passed. Mobilization of the fleet would also indicate to Germany the danger to which she would be exposed if England should take part in the war. The British Navy was an instrument of peace. "If we can help to avoid the conflict by showing our naval strength, ready to be instantly used, it would be wrong not to make the effort." Grey was not swept along quite that far. Besides, Churchill had told him that the fleet could be mobilized within twenty-four hours.[195] Churchill decided, on his own authority, that the fleet was to be kept in concentration at the close of the maneuvers, and this was announced on the 27th. The Entente representatives were greatly satisfied with this precaution, while the Germans and Austrians were not influenced in one way or the other.[196]

The permanent bureaucracy around Grey was, of all discernible British groups, the most pessimistic about the outlook for peace. As Nicolson expressed it to Buchanan, "we [the British] would not hesitate to do our duty if we were called upon to take a share" in a general European conflagration.[197] Technical readiness for war was increased on the 28th when Churchill, with Asquith's approval but without asking the Cabinet, resolved to put the fleet in its war station, Scapa Flow. The fleet made its move during the night of the 30th, passing the Dover Straits "at high speed and in absolute blackness," and perfected its "strategic concentration" on the 30th. The British Fleet was as ready as any other European fighting force for the entry into war. Some measures even lacked "legal authority," such as calling the naval reserves when "no proclamation had been submitted to His Majesty." But Churchill and his friends "were quite sure that the Fleet men would unquestionably obey the summons," which the Cabinet subsequently legalized.[198] Although naval preparations are somewhat less visible in their nature than army measures, the British measures did not escape German observation.[199]

During the whole July crisis, Germany was generally considered to be the country where everything was ruled and ordered by organization and preparation for war. The German nation, including the Austrians, trusted the military organization handed down from an elder Moltke to a younger one, though personality should have counted for little as against apparatus. The other nations distrusted and feared it and confounded its technical readiness for war with political aggressiveness. This aggressiveness, which was often enough mere diplomatic ineptitude, was seen as the driving force behind Austrian policies. Meanwhile, Austria went on using the blank check that Berlin had signed early in July. On the strength of it, she thought she might safely proceed to punish "the regicides." It was believed in Berlin that no monarchical state would interfere with such punishment.[200] The conflict would be "localized."

If that hope should fail, there was always the marvelous mobilization, or the unspoken threat of it, to fall back upon. As the crisis proceeded, the mobilizers became upset. While they were not greatly affected by the panic of the stock exchanges, the protests of international Social Democracy against the planned "devastation of Europe" seemed to hold a dangerous threat to undisturbed mobilization. On July 28 the Berlin Vorwärts cried out:

"There is only one answer to the mobilization of
the Powers: the permanent mobilization of the
people!" Such protests, including street demonstrations against war, "must not be permitted,"
the Kaiser decreed on the margin of a report.
"Should that occur again, I shall proclaim the state
of siege and put all the leaders tutti quanti in jail."
At nearly the same time, a mass meeting of the
Paris labor unions was forbidden "because the
speakers want to discuss the ways and means of
how to prevent mobilization." In Italy, who was
determined to remain neutral for the time being,
anti-war meetings passed resolutions "to decree
the revolution should an order of mobilization be
sent out."[201] A Labor anti-war meeting in Tra-
falgar Square on August 2 was unsuccessful, as
Paul Cambon was happy to report from London.[202]
After the murder of Jaurès, international solidarity
against war went to pieces in nearly all national
sections of the Internationale. The mobilization of
Russia made the German Social Democrats, who
"did not want their women and children to become
the victims of Cossack bestialities," vote the war
credits. They were convinced by the German governors that Russia, whom they considered the
greatest threat to Socialism and democracy, was
also responsible for the war.[203]

While the civilian governors were worrying
about disturbances on the home front, Moltke became disturbed by reports of military preparations
in Russia and France. They would make Germany's
military situation "more unfavorable every day and
might have fatal consequences if our prospective
enemies prepare further in all quietude." If the
clash between Austria and Russia should prove
unavoidable, Germany would have to mobilize and
take on the war on two fronts. On the 29th, Moltke
asked Bethmann to clarify the diplomatic situation
and ascertain as soon as possible whether Russia
and France intended to let it develop into a war
with Germany.[204] That same day, it was understood in Berlin military circles that Moltke was
"exerting all his influence in favor of taking advantage of the exceptionally favorable opportunity
for striking a decisive blow," offered by such circumstances as France's military embarrassments
and scandals, Russia's over-confidence, the summer season with the harvests nearly in, and the
completion of the training of the recruits of 1913.
But it was also understood that the Chancellor was
"applying the brakes with all his might, anxious to
avoid everything that might lead to corresponding
measures in France and Britain and start the ball
rolling."[205] On the following day, the brakes
still held. As Bethmann informed the Prussian
Ministerial Council, "the military authorities had
expressed the desire that a 'state of threatening
danger of war' be proclaimed, but he had successfully defended the objections before His Majesty."

The proclamation would have meant mobilization,
and mobilization would have meant war. This conviction reflected a fatalistic and dangerous maxim,
one not taken out of Bismarck's book: "One could
not very well carry on military and political activities at the same time."[206] No military precautions had as yet been taken, except the guarding
of railways and buildings, recall of officers and
men on leave, and the reinforcement of frontier
fortresses. These were ordered by the evening of
the 29th and on the whole were much less extensive
than those that had been ordered in Russia and
France.[207]

It was at this moment that Russia was warned
that continuation of mobilization measures would
"force" Germany to mobilize, and the Kaiser's
warning telegram to the Tsar was dispatched.
Bethmann then made the second of his foolish
blunders, his bid for British neutrality in a Continental war. This was turned down in London as
unhesitatingly as the Tsar's suggestion that the
case of Austria versus Serbia be handed over to
the Hague Court was turned down in Berlin.[208]
The forces that had declined arbitration proposals
before 1914, as something that would interfere with
mobilization, were active in July, and they included
the Tsar's own foreign minister.[209]

Berchtold remained determined to have his war
with Serbia, even when confronted with the image
of a war in which the Central Powers would have
to face four Great Powers.[210] While increasingly
angry with Berchtold, Bethmann never applied the
bluntness necessary to make himself understood
in Vienna. Germany was too much the prisoner of
the weaker alliance partner, who was determined
to use the stronger to the utmost. The true heirs
to Bismarck's alliance conservatism in Germany
were now the Social Democrats. One of their leaders, in an article on "The Limitations of our Alliance Obligations," recalled, as no one else did in
these days, that Bismarck "never thought of following the Viennese diplomats as an irresolute vassal
in an aggressive anti-Russian policy."[211]

"We need your strong pressure on Austria to
come to an understanding with us," the Tsar wired
the Kaiser on the night of the 30th. Almost everywhere the Kaiser was believed to be a stronger
governor of men and things than was actually the
case. But the Kaiser thought that his role as mediator had ended: Russia was now almost a week
ahead with measures said to be directed against
Austria but actually becoming more and more of
a threat to Germany. "It is," he thought, "only a
maneuver to draw us out and to enlarge the head-
start they already have." Another cause for this
pessimism was the increasing tendency of the
diplomats on all sides to place responsibility for
the more and more expected war on the prospective enemy.[212] Diplomacy devoted itself to this

function, at the same time conceding the military more urgency in their demands for mobilization and pre-mobilization measures.[213]

As late as the morning of the 30th, Moltke was still willing to pay respect to political considerations. He sent Conrad word that "Russia's [partial] mobilization is not yet cause for [Germany's] mobilization. Not until state of war exists between Austria and Russia. In contrast to mobilizations and demobilizations which have been customary in Russia, Germany's mobilization would unconditionally lead to war. Do not declare war on Russia; rather await Russia's attack."[214] Up to this point Moltke was in accord with the diplomats, notably the French, in the competitive endeavor not to incur the odium of aggression for their countries. It was a long-settled axiom among Germany's enemies that she would have to pay for her presumed organizational superiority by the odium of the "aggressor" label, which even the German Chief of Staff was loath to incur—until the afternoon of the 30th of July.

Learning that the Russians had insisted that their presumably partial mobilization could not be halted and fearing that they were getting ahead of Germany by about five days on the strength of their preparatory measures, Moltke arrived at the conclusion that the Central Powers were surrendering too much military advantage by waiting for Russia to incur the odium of being the aggressor. At about the same time that Bethmann made his reassuring statements before the Prussian ministers, Moltke told the Austrian military attaché that he would consider the situation critical if Austria did not at once mobilize against Russia. In doing so, Austria must publicly explain the measure as due to the earlier Russian mobilization. "Thereby casus foederis for Germany would arise...Sticking firmly to [the idea of] European war is last chance of preserving Austria. Germany will go along unconditionally."[215] Moltke did not consult or inform the civilian Chancellor about the pressure he was putting on Austria. Military trespassing on the political field could go no further.

Unable to obtain the civilian Chancellor's approval for the German order of mobilization, Moltke turned in a direction where he had greater influence than in Berlin itself, to the alliance partner. The latter, he concluded, must be made more ready for war and be kept closer to the German war plans, which he had never fully communicated to Vienna. There were no military conventions specifying what part of the Austrian forces were to be made available against the common enemy, Russia. Moltke was forced to attempt last-hour improvisations. He offered the casus foederis as the price for Austrian support of his war plans. The free hand, the reservation of the casus foederis until the last moment, the denial of the military

convention which the Austrians had sought more than once: these had been the strong points of Bismarck's diplomacy. They proved to be the weakness, almost the undoing, of Moltke's plans. A maximum of Austrian forces was needed against Russia to insure their success. He did not obtain this maximum in the end, for too many of the Austrian forces were squandered by a court-general operating in Serbia in August-September 1914.[216]

In Vienna, Moltke's advice in favor of general mobilization and Bethmann's warnings against Austrian recklessness clashed. "That is strange! Who is governing? Moltke or Bethmann?" Berchtold cried out. "I was under the impression that Germany was drawing back; but now I have from the most competent military side the most reassuring declaration."[217] With that, "good spirits were restored" in Vienna. It was obvious to Berchtold that Moltke, not Bethmann, was governing in Berlin. Austria's general mobilization had already been resolved, but Moltke's "hint" encouraged Berchtold and Conrad to cling to their war. They obtained Francis Joseph's signature on the final order for mobilization, with August 4 as M-day. Published in the early afternoon of the 31st, the Austrian announcement followed the Russian one by eighteen hours.

Shortly before midnight, Moltke, after receiving intelligence reports that Russian general mobilization had been ordered, had a conversation with Bethmann. The latter had been shaken by military considerations in his determination to work for the preservation of peace, but only for a moment. He decided to try once again to bring the Austrians to reason, to await more definite word of Russian general mobilization, and to put off the decision whether or not to declare "Threatening Danger of War," (demanded by the Chief of Staff and the War Minister) until midday of July 31. Definite word of Russian general mobilization arrived in Berlin at 11:40 a.m. The German Embassy had learned of it earlier in the morning through public announcements in the newspapers and on posters, and not through any official channel.[218] A hurried conference of Kaiser, Chancellor, Chief of Staff and other officials resolved to proclaim "Threatening Danger of War" as a state of pre-mobilization. In order to dissuade Austria from committing too many of her forces against Serbia, this resolution was telegraphed to Vienna with the comment that it "will probably (voraussichtlich) be followed within forty-eight hours by mobilization. The latter inevitably means war. We expect from Austria immediate active participation in the war against Russia."[219]

Military preparations and the conclusions derived from them were so closely drawn that only a few hours later, before the Berlin decision was known in Paris, Joffre, the French Chief of Staff, informed the Cabinet that the French measures taken up to that time, following from afar analogous measures taken by the Germans, particularly during the last forty-eight hours, do not allow us to take any more additional detailed steps beyond those already ordered, without throwing profound disorder into the dispositions provided for the troops of the couverture and for mobilization, particularly as far as railway service is concerned. If the tension goes on and if the Germans, under cover of diplomatic conversations, continued to apply their plan of mobilization,... it is absolutely necessary that the Government should know that, from this evening on, every twenty-four hours' delay in the calling up of the reservists and the sending out of the telegram for the couverture will mean a setback in our plan for the concentration, that is to say, the initial surrender of part of our territory, about 15-20 kilometers for every day of delay. The commander-in-chief cannot accept this responsibility.

Following the receipt of this warning and possibly of the German declaration of the "Threatening Danger of War," the French Cabinet decided at 5:00 p.m. to give the order for marching out the troops of the couverture.[220]

"Threatening Danger of War" in Germany signified a state of siege, authorizing the Government to call up some classes of reservists, suspend certain public services, close the frontiers, and forbid public meetings. It was the last step short of mobilization, since the diplomats accepted the time-table from the soldiers. Unless Russia stopped all war-like measures against the Reich and Austria within twelve hours and gave Germany positive assurance on this point, German mobilization was to follow. If Russia finished her mobilization and Germany failed to move, "East Prussia, West Prussia and perhaps also Posen and Silesia are without protection sacrificed to the Russians."[221] So it seemed to the Germans. In the interest of Germany's military readiness, Bethmann was now willing to forego the "moral" advantage of not declaring war on Russia.

Both the Tsar and Sasonov declared to the German ambassador who presented the German ultimatum that technical reasons did not permit recalling or suspending the order of mobilization. "You have been an officer yourself," the Tsar said to Pourtalès, "and must therefore know that for technical reasons such orders cannot be held up any more." Pourtalès reminded him that the Tsar's omnipotence might yet save monarchies everywhere if he would call such a halt. Under these circumstances "you cannot blame us if we are not inclined to allow Russia a further advantage in mobilization," he told Sasonov when presenting the ultimatum.[222] The Serbian minister

in St. Petersburg got the impression that "Russia now draws out negotiations in order to gain time for the concentration of her Army and, once her mobilization is finished, will declare war on Austria."[223] The Germans were at least entitled to suspect as much.

For the French, who had not advised against one of Russia's steps towards the war, there was only one enemy, Germany. Late in the evening of the 31st, War Minister Messimy, like Pourtalès a former officer, declared to the Russian military attaché "in a tone of hearty enthusiasm the firm decision of the French Government for war." He begged him to confirm once more the hope of the French General Staff that all of Russia's efforts would be directed against Germany, while treating Austria as a quantité négligeable. Germany was not merely "the principal enemy," she was the only one that counted; against her, against East Prussia specifically, Russia's main operations must be conducted, in her own interest as well as in observation of the military convention.[224] The last-hour appeal addressed to the military ally was essentially the same as Moltke's: Adhere to the old understanding now that war is here! If possible, give even more than was agreed to!

There would have been still more reason for such "hearty enthusiasm" in Paris if Grey had only declared himself. While there was anxious waiting for favorable word from England, Joffre pressed for measures to ensure greater readiness. France, he told the civilians, was already falling behind. Considering the inconvenience due to the belated departure of the couverture troops, the order for general mobilization should no longer be postponed. For, he maintained, German preparations, proceeding on the basis of a plan which the French General Staff had gotten hold of, went on apace without any formal order of mobilization. They were nothing less than a discreet form of mobilization, which would thus be completed by August 4, giving Germany an advantage over the French Army of two if not three days. Since French legislation did not permit any further measures analogous to those being taken by Germany, the only means of preparing for all eventualities was the order for general mobilization. The Cabinet was sufficiently impressed or scared by the military argument to contemplate early mobilization. They proceeded to prepare the British friends for its coming. They justified it by the German measures which indicated, it was said, that the Reich "had commenced mobilization properly speaking," that her measures were already "mobilization under another name," that French mobilization was "essentially a measure of preservation" and that "this act of mobilization was purely defensive."[225] Orders for mobilization went to the General Staff at 3:55 p.m. on August 1, with August 2 as M-day. When the order went out to the army corps commanders in the East, they were reminded that, "in view of assuring ourselves of the collaboration of our English neighbors," the order of refraining from action in the ten-kilometer zone must be strictly observed. The Government's proclamation explained that "mobilization is not war, that under the present conditions it is for France the best way of safeguarding peace and that the Government of the Republic will multiply its endeavors to work for a peaceful outcome of the negotiations."[226] Without knowing of the French orders for mobilization, the Germans issued their order of mobilization one hour and five minutes later,[227] at 5:00 p.m.

The time-limit given the Russians by German diplomacy had expired at noon. There could be little expectation that they would suspend their mobilization. A declaration of war was dispatched to Pourtalès at 12:52 p.m., to be presented after a last query as to whether Russian mobilization would be suspended. After receiving a negative answer, the declaration was delivered at 6:00 p.m. From the afternoon of August 1 on, none of the actors on the international stage were more prisoners of the formula that mobilization means war than the men of the Wilhelmstrasse. They never considered, then or before, whether announced mobilization or perfected mobilization had that meaning, whether the few days between the one and the other did not offer a last-minute opportunity for trying to salvage the peace. Not even the soldiers had demanded such promptness.[228] They realized, as did the war-seeking counts of Austrian diplomacy, that it was important "to avoid taking upon oneself the odium of aggression by a spontaneous declaration of war," which made the Austrians, once they had their war, quite loath to declare it. The driving forces behind Bethmann's haste were his "anxieties as to home politics," his concern and ignorance about the possible counter-mobilizers, the German Social Democrats.[229] He thought that they could be expected to march into the field, instead of through the streets in protest against war, if they were shown that the foreign war was directed first of all against Tsarism. "Otherwise I don't get the Social Democrats to come along," he told a great industrial employer, Albert Ballin, who asked him on August 1 why there was such an "enormous hurry" about the declaration of war on Russia.[230]

It was in keeping with Britain's strategic position that she could safely be the last of the Powers to mobilize her Army and in keeping with the political situation of the Asquith Cabinet that she must be the last to do this. On the 31st, Grey told Cambon, who had come for a pledge of British help but did not then obtain it, that the latest news he had was that Russia had ordered general mobilization.

This, he thought, "would precipitate a crisis and would make it appear that German mobilization was being forced by Russia."[231] Grey was waiting for "some new development," which could hardly be anything but German violation of Belgian neutrality. Under the conditions of British politics, this would be comparable to the incitement provided by Russian general mobilization to the hitherto peaceful German Social Democrats. Grey's closest diplomatic assistants, Nicolson and Crowe, urged that in any case, whether or not England planned to intervene, her Army should be mobilized at once. Nicolson urged that "mobilization is a precautionary and not a provocative measure—and to my mind essential."[232] Grey found "much force in this. We ought to prepare." But the decision remained for the Cabinet, which was only moved into war by the only popular cause for British intervention, the German march into Belgium. While this step shocked the civilians, from the majority of the Cabinet members to the man in the street, it was expected by the soldiers of the Western Powers, as much expected as war was assumed to be the unavoidable consequence of mobilization.

It seems uncertain how far the various civilian governors of July 1914 were aware of and shared the soldiers' view of the irresistible equation, mobilization = war, or German mobilization = war.[233] Their last feeble attempts to interfere with it were as futile as a peasant's wish to have a through-train brought to a non-scheduled stop. While the ignorant peasant might shrug his shoulders and agree that the engineer "must be on time," the more powerful governors of 1914 ought to have known that there was danger beyond a certain point. However, they found it just as easy to resign to the demands of the time-table. On August 1, following the receipt of some misleading news in favor of peace in the West, the Kaiser told Moltke: "Now we simply concentrate in the East." The latter answered that that was impossible. "The concentration of an army of millions cannot be improvised. If Your Majesty insists on leading the whole Army eastward you will have nothing but a confused mob of disorderly armed men without supplies." When the Kaiser told him that his great uncle would have given a different answer, Moltke declared that it was "completely impossible to march in any other way than according to plan—strong against the West, weak against the East." And when the Kaiser insisted that at least the one division that was to violate Luxemburg's neutrality should be stopped, Moltke wrote: I felt "as if my heart would break. Again, there was danger that our concentration would be upset. Arriving home, I was all broken up and shed tears of despair." He was relieved to learn later in the day that concentration would take place as planned. But, he wrote, "I have never been able to overcome the impression that this experience made.

Something inside me was destroyed that could not be restored, conviction and confidence were shaken."[234]

The deeper reason for non-interference with mobilization was the conviction prevailing on all sides in July 1914 that, given the proportion of strengths at the time, their own side could be expected to win. (It was different in 1908-09 and 1912-13, when Russia's war-making powers were not yet restored.) To have interfered with the military schedules would have meant endangering the hope and promise of military victory. Mobilization plans were the secretly worked-out recipe for military victory that was promised to the civilians. For the soldiers themselves, mobilization plans were the expression of their hope of carrying order deep into the chaos of war. The conviction that granting freedom to the soldiers was necessary for victory was definitely and firmly instilled in practically all the governors of 1914. For the German soldiers, the promise of victory was more nearly victory for victory's sake than for the Russian, French and Austrian soldiers, who had very concrete political war aims in and before 1914. The apparently rational planning that lay behind the promise of victory was its most persuasive and least-examined argument. Nations have sought and found guilt and responsibility for war mostly in the doings of their enemies, and not in the activities and concepts of specific groups at home and abroad. Thus the "war-guilt" of all the military planners has not been sufficiently examined.[235]

The diplomats, with much less excuse, shared the blind belief of the people in the efficacy of military planning, neither realizing the implications of mobilization in 1914 nor asking whether it could be halted or at what stage it could be halted. Such knowledge did not seem to be a necessary part of their professional equipment. They gave it no forethought. Grey had never suggested to either Russia or France that they refrain from mobilizing. On August 1, he and Lichnowsky discussed whether it would not be possible, at the close of mobilizations and even after the Russians had gone to war, for the French and German armies to remain passive. ("The man is mad or an idiot," the Kaiser marginalized.) Grey, however, realized the difficulty of retaining the military on both sides in a state of inactivity.[236] At this stage, diplomacy could no longer speak of armed force as one of its tools. It had itself become the tool of war, largely run by the military, who were not to release it from servitude for over four years to come. As Paléologue realistically stated: "The time for calculations, for diplomatic tricks is over...There is no longer any personal initiative, any human will which can resist the automatic mechanism of the powers set loose."[237] This

declaration of impotency, if not of bankruptcy, on the part of diplomacy was formulated by one of its most literate practitioners, who was at the same time the most experienced peace-time liaison official between foreign and military offices.

Despite the expectations and hopes that had been placed in the automatism of mobilization, concentration, and initial operation plans, they did not prove to be comparable in effectiveness and exactitude to machines prepared by industrial blueprinting. Hardly had the time-tables of mobilization and concentration gone into effect before one or the other of the belligerents found them insufficient to assure victory to their side, or even to assure their own security. All through the first days of August 1914, the French War Ministry, as well as the French diplomats acting on its behalf, pleaded with the British and Russian allies to accelerate their measures beyond what was called for by the original plans. It was as if some of the mobilization plans had been designed only to get the countries into the war. That the war could also be won according to plan seemed already doubtful. As late as August 9, the French governors begged London to push at least one British division ahead and bring it into the front that was forming. Naturally the War Office had to deny the request: the slightest modification of its transport schedules would cause disorder and the BEF would thus arrive later rather than sooner.[238] Similar French appeals to Russia proved to be somewhat more successful. The commander-in-chief was willing to attack before the concentration of all his army corps had been completed, two days earlier than had been foreseen in the pre-war conversations of the chiefs-of-staff.[239] While this "gain of time" somewhat relieved the French, it pushed the Russians towards their first defeats in East Prussia. It also forced the Germans, as they thought, to detach two army corps from the battle lines in the West and throw them to the East, where they arrived too late for Tannenberg. In the chaos of war, meticulous peace-time planning proved less effective than had been expected.

g. Post-1918: Germany's Return as Mobilizer

Would planning for the maintenance of peace in the anarchy of the world of states prove more effective? The intention of the planners, as laid down in the military terms of the Versailles Treaty, gave a clear indication of the feeling among the Allied and Associated Powers that they had narrowly escaped defeat at the hands of the Germans and their highly organized and mobilized forces and that such possibilities must be excluded for the future. They decreed by Treaty and the Germans accepted on paper that the German forces were to be reduced to a 100,000-man Reichswehr. All measures of mobilization were henceforth to be forbidden and the office mainly concerned, the Great General Staff, dissolved, never to be reconstituted in any form (Articles 159, 160, 177, 178).

That institution soon proved its irrepressible character. With greatly diminished powers and with small forces at its disposal, it returned to its traditional tasks and pursuits. The Reichswehr worked out its first comprehensive mobilization plans for the transformation of the 100,000-man army to a war footing, to become effective on April 1, 1930. After that, these plans were brought up-to-date annually. One of the main concerns was to have civilians and semi-civilians, such as customs and postal officials, share the burdens of this purely defensive scheme. Planning soon had to take an inward turn, towards civil war. In 1932, the Planning Office of the Reichswehr concerned itself exclusively with preparations for the employment of the Reichswehr in internal conflicts. No further plans for strategic concentration were formulated until 1935.[240] (The still-more-reduced Reich Navy had likewise started early on mobilization plans.)[241]

In spite of some notable progress achieved before 1933, the manpower resources within the Weimar Republic that could not yet be mobilized were still too large to allow the soldiers to consider the total mobilization that the most up-to-date concept of war seemed to demand. The mobilizing powers of neither the old nor the reformed General Staff were equal to the task of mobilizing non-military masses. Only National Socialism could be trusted to do so, as well as to suppress the remaining counter-mobilizers, the Social Democrats and the Communists, thereby opening the road to total mobilization in Germany.

MOBILIZATION PLANS FOR TOTAL WAR

(a) France

Germany's ex-enemies were more advanced in preparations for their future mobilizations. They applied the lesson that the World War had taught all the belligerents: their preparations before 1914 had not gone far enough. Even the United States now had mobilization plans, at least for the war industries.[242] France's preparations for mobilization went much further. Anxiety about shrinking population and economic potential, combined with the desire to appear as peaceful as the League of Nations ideology seemed to require, led to the working out of mobilization preparations that avoided the term "mobilization" even more completely than before 1914. They were still further removed from parliamentary control and required no more public decrees or "white posters." Enabling acts authorized the Government to call up the so-called "disponibles," the three

youngest classes of reservists, on condition that it justified the measure before the assembled parliament within eight days.[243] In contrast to 1914, plans for concentration were made highly elastic. As they stood in 1939, they envisaged, in addition to the war beyond the Maginot Line, the following possibilities: Italy's initial neutrality or her immediate entry into war; Belgium's cry for help, or continued neutrality; violation by Germany of Luxemburg's, Belgium's, Holland's or Switzerland's neutrality. These contingencies would become apparent by the time mobilization had been completed.[244] Obviously, the non-aggressor in the war to come had to prepare for more eventualities than the aggressor.

Diplomacy and military preparation were brought into the closest accord. The Foreign and Defense Ministries worked out a volt-metering system under which each of five increases in international tension and conflict, presumably signalled or confirmed by the Quai d'Orsay, was to be followed by definite military measures ahead of full and final mobilization. These were covered by the terms "Alerte," "Sûreté," "Couverture" (simple or reinforced), and "Mobilisation générale." The Nazis found much of this scheme worthy of imitation.[245] And for total supra-military mobilization in France there was the rather totalitarian—as totalitarian or "Jacobine" as the French Revolution had been—Loi Paul-Boncour of 1927. It provided for "the organization of the nation in time of war." It made all French people (regardless of age or sex), French civilian organizations such as labor unions and employers' associations, and capital (though to a lesser extent), liable to war-time service for the preservation of the material and moral life of the country. All necessary preparations were to be made in order to transform the peace-time organization of France into organization for war.[246]

Much of the actual work of preparing for the war in the shape it would assume remained undone, notably in the industrial sector. According to its author, the Loi suffered from an absence of urgency as long as France's military supremacy seemed assured and even later, as well as from "indifference on the part of the General Staff." In March 1938, when its application to the industrial sector was once more discussed and a special ministry of armaments proposed, Daladier, the appeaser, said he wanted no war economy ahead of war. The ministry was actually set up ten days after the declaration of war.[247] In its provisions, as well as in the mind of its not very radical Socialist author, this law breathed the spirit of 1792. It fell far behind in its practical application, however, due to the deep dissensions within French society. And when the front populaire nationalized part of the armaments industry, the arms potential of France was reduced rather than heightened.

Post-1918 mobilization plans generally reached deeper into civilian life and economy, re-approximating the total claims of primitive warfare.[248] The willing or unwilling cooperation of civilian administrators increased greatly, though as a rule the general direction was in military hands.[249] Considering the revolutionary effect of mobilization on the life of nations, its use as a tool of diplomacy had become practically impossible in the most modern states. Only under the relatively simple conditions prevailing in the countries of the Little Entente in the early 1920's could it still be applied in the style of an earlier diplomacy. Mussolini partially mobilized against Germany in 1934, at the time of the Dollfuss putsch, under the influence, as Hitler thought, of the French and the Francophiles inside Italy. But he came to regret this step as "the one and only politically false decision of his life," according to his later and last friend, Hitler.[250]

When Hitler moved into the Rhineland, the French Army proved to be a prisoner of its own mobilization plans. The Government offered Gamelin the calling up of the "disponibles" for the purpose of reoccupying the Saar. But the General told the ministers that this was not enough to meet all possible emergencies, that he must have general mobilization. Actually, he seems to have been loath to set part of the big machine in action when only the operation of the whole had been contemplated and prepared.[251]

(b) Germany

The Germans under Hitler more than followed the French recipe. Their preparation for total mobilization got under way at the end of 1933, presided over by the first post-1918 Chief of Staff, General Beck. He set October 1, 1934, as the date when a first general mobilization plan should be ready; Reichswehr officers and representatives of all civilian ministries and Nazi organizations deliberated on such a plan. They were admonished by Beck to preserve the greatest secrecy about the many remaining weak spots in the German armor. The measures resolved upon covered the financing of mobilization and the opening and later stages of a war; frontier surveillance in case of a conflict; evacuation of civilian population from certain regions; construction of merchant ships, in which the wishes of the Navy were to be heeded; mobilization orders for 60,000 to 240,000 factories, which would still take years to perfect; raw materials supply; power supply; foreign trade ahead of war and in time of war; food supply; rationing; railway and waterways problems; propaganda; requisition of private motor vehicles and other motorization problems; postal questions, including the supervision of mails and communica-

tions; regulation of wages and salaries, and of industrial profits; conscription and musters.

A War Service Act (Kriegsleistungsgesetz) authorized the Government to demand from the German people all personal and material services necessary for making war and assuring victory. A General Plenipotentiary for War Economy was originally to be appointed on M-day. However, in May 1935, Schacht was given orders to begin his labors forthwith and to direct the economic preparation for the case of war, in closest cooperation with the Reich Minister of War. A Law of Popular Service (Volksdienst) called for the conscription of all Germans from ages fifteen to sixty-five who were not in the armed services, for all kinds of personal services. A Law for Public Safety was considered necessary, even though disturbances in case of mobilization were not expected to occur under the new conditions in the Reich. A Reich Defense Committee, the top directive organization, supervised unified mobilization, not only of the armed forces but of the state and the nation as well. Plans were laid down in mobilization books for practically all offices, bringing them into line with the military. The first mobilization year was to start on April 1, 1936.[252]

The general principles for total mobilization, largely evolved by the soldiers and enforced by the Nazis, were as follows: "The armed readiness of the whole nation is the first condition of an effective defense of the Reich. Wehrmacht, economy, State and people are brought from the state of peace to that of war through mobilization...The case of war may arise either abruptly or from a state of diplomatic tensions. Preparation and launching of mobilization must pay due regard to these two possibilities." A State of Defense and a State of War are envisaged, to be declared by the Führer. The State of War may not be proclaimed for reasons of diplomacy, in order to avoid incurring the odium of war guilt, even though war may actually be intended. "A period of tension possibly preceding the case of war must be made use of, within the limits of what is diplomatically possible, in order to achieve war readiness on the part of the Reich." In keeping with this, three stages of mobilization are to be distinguished: (a) The period of tension, which will not be officially declared as such. It will be left to the various authorities to do what they can (while avoiding everything that ought to be avoided for diplomatic reasons) to guarantee the smooth functioning of mobilization and to do as much as possible ahead of it and in preparation for it. (While the Wehrmacht had arranged measures to go with distinct "stages of tension," the civilian mobilization books are not specific on this); (b) Mobilization without public announcement (Case X). This is actual mobilization, concealed by a maximum of camouflage for the purpose of mobilizing the Wehrmacht either partially or totally, or of secretly mobilizing the whole State. The fact of mobilization must not be publicly mentioned in diplomatic negotiations, over the radio, or in the press, so as to withhold from the prospective enemies all legal reasons for the opening of war on their part or cause for their own mobilization; (c) General mobilization publicly announced.

Jodl, one of the principal organizers of the mobilization, explained the new arrangements and the reasons for them to the civilian bureaucrats in December 1935. With heavy sarcasm, he said:

It is well-known that there are no more wars. In spite of that, all States are arming more than ever before. Economic and military sanctions are imposed. In preparation of war, protective measures are being taken that merely serve one's own security. Whosoever pronounces the word mobilization has lost the war in the political field. For this reason, all States shun the word mobilization. We observe as a fact that France, without even mentioning the word mobilization, can mobilize forty divisions. The announcement of mobilization stands at the end of mobilization, no longer at the beginning. These facts are cause and reason for us to deviate from the old sequence of mobilization and, like France, to choose a new terminology.[253]

The proposals, or rather rulings, of the Wehrmacht soldiers on mobilization were clearly derived from their reading of the war guilt literature and were not due to any urging on the part of the Wilhelmstrasse to pay respect to diplomatic considerations. In all the known deliberations of the Reich bureaucracy on mobilization planning, the representatives of the Foreign Ministry remained passive. The diplomatic service was fitted into these plans later than any other branch of German administration. Not until April 1938 did a very secret order go out to all diplomatic and many consular representatives abroad, instructing them to undertake certain preparations with regard to mobilization plans. It read as follows:

Since the work in the field of preparation for mobilization has made further progress at home, in the armed forces, and in all civilian administration, including the Foreign Office, it is necessary now that governmental offices abroad take corresponding measures in their area of jurisdiction and harmonize them with the tasks incumbent on the homeland. The beginning of a period of tension or of a case of mobilization presents authorities abroad with great and difficult tasks in the most diverse fields, such as additions to personnel, the employment of Reich nationals for particu-

lar purposes (ciphering, propaganda, etc.), protection of archives and the destruction of secret documents, cooperation in the planning for war economy.[254]

At first these preparations were wrapped in utmost secrecy, particularly in the remilitarized Rhineland where they were apt to attract too much French attention. In this zone, the Wehrmacht insisted, "camouflage must rank before effectiveness," for "France is only waiting for the moment when Germany should take a new and independent step against the treaties in order to be able to mobilize on her part. The Reich Government is anxious not to furnish such facts..."(1935). By the end of 1935, Keitel, presiding over the Committee for Reich Defense, could express to co-workers his satisfaction that great progress in the defense of the Reich and its legalization—under domestic law, that is—had been achieved. But, he added, much still needs to be done before Germany can make up for the headstart the other nations have gained.

While the OKW did not consider military progress sufficient to undertake the remilitarization of the Rhineland, Hitler, gambling on the indecision of the Western Powers, did. The traditional reflex action in Paris was to discuss mobilization. French forces actually under arms were thought to be insufficient in case active intervention should be intended. Gamelin put them at considerably less than half of what the Germans had immediately available, Reichswehr plus militarized police plus para-military Nazi formations. On the morning of March 7, the day of the German advance into the forbidden zone, Gamelin demanded that at least the first measures of precaution be taken, including the recall of furloughed personnel and the moving of couverture forces into the fortified region by foot marches, while preparing the rail transports for the rest. But could France alone, without allies, safely undertake steps that might lead to war with Germany, the Ministers asked?

There was no confidence on either side among the regulars. It is hard to say who was more doubtful of their own side's ability to wage war, the German or the French generals. Gamelin thought that France would be superior at the outset, but that numbers and industrial potential would favor Germany in a war of longer duration. Besides, France would be alone. On the afternoon of the 7th, the British were already inclined to recognized accomplished fact, although the bolder minds at the Quai d'Orsay were convinced that Britain would follow if France were to act decisively, as Poland encouraged her to do. All that the soldiers obtained from the Cabinet was permission for security measures to be undertaken by the active forces. They wanted to be provided with enough forces to avert an initial setback, and to take pledges, such as the Saar. But Anglo-Belgian unwillingness to participate in such steps and impending elections at home, where sentiments were far from war-like, caused the French Government to decide, after several days of deliberation and consultation, to refrain from all military measures against Germany.[255] This negative decision obliged the French soldiers to begin work on new, still more elaborate and elastic plans for the mobilization and concentration of their forces, which seemed to be decreasing in strength rather than increasing in comparison to those beyond and now west of the Rhine.

By 1935, the Germans had mobilization plans and forces that could be mobilized in a state of sufficient preparation to make the elaboration of plans for their strategic concentration worthwhile. During that year, Case "Red," calling for a defensive Aufmarsch along the Rhine and along the Czech and Polish frontiers, was worked out. Case "Otto," for the eventuality of an attempted Hapsburg restoration in Austria with the help of either Italy, Hungary or Czechoslovakia, seems also to have been prepared at this time. During 1937, when Hitler first indicated his war-like intentions to the Wehrmacht, Case "Green," calling for offensive measures against Czechoslovakia, was mapped out. It underwent necessary changes after the annexation of Austria. In 1939, Case "White" was planned for the war against Poland. In all these cases, interference by the Western Powers, and to a certain extent by Russia, was considered, if not always expected.[256]

The most important new technical factor in these "cases," as in post-1918 mobilization and concentration generally, was the internal combustion motor. Motorized warfare made the beginning of war increasingly imperceptible. Motors idling during the preparation for total war can be turned off at once, if political circumstances make this advisable. But the preparatory state cannot be prolonged indefinitely, since the very substance of the nation is consumed while the "State, armed forces, and the people are being brought to the highest possible readiness for war." Airplane squadrons in many cases call for no concentration in regions near the enemy's frontiers, since they can use their peace-time flying fields instead. This offered the greatest temptation to plan tactical and strategic surprises. The Wehrmacht, pressured by Hitler, was seduced by the new conditions. They cast aside as obsolete old concepts about the opening of war and changed their mobilization-concentration plans accordingly. As expressed by the Chief of the OKW: "Surprise as the first condition of quick and great initial successes will often make it necessary to open hostilities before mobilization or concentration of the army is completed. Declaration of war no longer comes in every case at the beginning of war."[257]

From a military point of view, the danger of opening a war by airplane-and-tank-supported aggression was that the enemy would interfere with mobilization and concentration before their orderly completion. This danger had to be met by couverture in its various new forms—the Maginot Line, manned by increased garrisons; the Siegfried Line, which Hitler ordered to be made strong enough to resist triple or quadruple superiority, though it probably never was; the Russian and German concentrations along the demarcation line in Poland well before 1941. Such forces as the German Grenzschutz and Grenzsicherung were not conceived of as purely passive: the German actions against Memel and rump-Czechoslovakia were carried out by such formations, proceeding to their objectives without previous concentration. Various other uses of such unmobilized but still highly mobile German forces were contemplated. For example, they would have been used had France resisted the move into the Rhineland or had Italy marched in the direction of the Brenner Pass at the time of the Dollfuss murder.[258]

Two army corps were hurriedly mobilized without calling up reservists for the invasion of Austria. In addition, 40,000 SS men, police and other forces were used as a "second wave." On March 10, 1938, Hitler called in the Wehrmacht chiefs, Beck and his deputy Manstein, and told them that he wanted to settle the Austrian question before Schuschnigg could carry out his intended plebiscite on the 13th. He asked what suggestions they had to make, should he decide to march into Austria. Beck considered mobilization of two Bavarian army corps and one Panzer division necessary. Hitler seems to have thought that a General Staff must have plans ready for any and all eventualities.[259] Beck reminded him that "such a case was in no way prepared since the political leaders had never given us even so much as a hint of such instructions. It would be necessary, therefore, to improvise everything." At first Hitler wanted no mobilization at all. Finally he realized that if any such march were intended, troops had to be made mobile at once in order to be inside Austria ahead of the plebiscite. The necessary orders went out after four or five hours of preparation. As an experiment and trial mobilization, the march into Austria demonstrated to the generals, rather than to Hitler, "that matters had not yet reached the stage where a reasonably satisfactory mobilization could be effected."[260]

France and Britain again refrained from all interference. Belgium and Italy could no longer be relied upon by French policy, the one retired into neutrality, the other affiliated with the Germans in Spain. Russia seemed an uncertain military ally, and France herself was paralyzed by a ministerial crisis at the time Hitler marched. The British Navy and the French Army together ought to be the arbiters of the world, Churchill told Gamelin at the time. But if they still were, they were not allowed to show it. At the first news of the German inten- tions, on the 11th, Gamelin asked for authorization to undertake the first measures of an alert. The government en démission would not permit him to undertake anything without a preliminary under- standing with Britain. On the 12th, he obtained from Daladier only the stopping of leaves in the Eastern zone. No other military measures were taken by France at the time, although her gover- nors were told by Gamelin that if she again bowed to Hitler, she would have to intensify her military effort and in particular would have to further ex- tend the Maginot Line on both wings. Germany might well disrespect the neutrality of Belgium and Switzerland.

The fate of Austria made the French governors consider the fate of allied Czechoslovakia, whose strategic position the Anschluss had put in jeop- ardy.[261] What kind of military action in favor of the Czechs could France undertake against Germany? Daladier asked Gamelin at the end of March 1938. A month later, Gamelin pointed out to him the main aspects of a thoroughly bad situ- ation. There was no military implementation of the Franco-Czech assistance pact, concluded years ago without consulting the military. France could undertake all the prepared military measures on her own soil, which provided security to France and menaced Germany. The effectiveness of French help to Czechoslovakia would largely depend on the help given the latter by the Little Entente, Russia, Poland and Great Britain. Such help involved prob- lems which would first have to be ironed out on the diplomatic level.[262]

This outline of the military situation could not really help the French Government in answering the blunt British question: What did the French mean in practical terms by all their declared readiness to come to the aid of the Czechs? The French answered that little or no direct help from France could reach Czechoslovakia. All help would have to be indirect, such as mobilization along the German border in order to retain a maximum of German forces there, and even this was becoming less effective every week as the German West Wall grew stronger. The days were over when it had been thought possible to push across Germany along the Main line, the wasp waistline of the Reich. The outlook for Russian help was doubtful. Support would have to come across Polish and Rumanian territory, on the ground and through the air, and both might be closed to them. Besides, Czech airfields were not numerous enough and not well enough equipped to receive Russian planes before the Germans destroyed them. As early as March 15, a French Cabinet had come to the con- clusion that France could do no more than pin down certain German forces by the offensive action of her mobilized forces, possibly by a maneuver

through Belgium on the strength of Article 16 of the League Covenant. But she could not prevent (empêcher) an action against Czechoslovakia. It was hoped that all these considerations would move the British to take diplomatic action in capitals like Brussels and Bucharest, which they hardly did.[263]

By contrast with the military preparation of the Anschluss, German plans for action against Czecho- slovakia had been fully worked out. But should they be put into effect? And if so, when, and under what circumstances? Hitler discussed these questions at various times with the soldiers and the foreign minister. In November 1937, the soldiers of the older generation, Blomberg and Fritsch, warned that Germany, even with Italy as an ally, could not take on England and France as enemies. France would still be superior on the Western front because her mobilization was superior and Germany's forti- fications vastly inferior. And the Czech fortifica- tions assumed more and more the character of a Maginot Line. As against these down-to-earth military considerations, Hitler even then main- tained that Britain would not interfere in a Conti- nental war and that France would consequently refrain from military action.[264] His convictions led to intensified studies of Case "Green" under the more compliant Keitel's direction, beginning in the spring of 1938.

Three political-military possibilities offered themselves for an attack on Czechoslovakia: (1) "Strategic assault out of a clear sky, without cause or possibility of justifying it." This was unfortu- nately unacceptable, since it would arouse world opinion against Germany. "Such a measure," it was concluded, "is justified only for the removal of the last remaining Continental enemy"; (2) Action following a period of diplomatic disputes, slowly intensifying and leading to war; (3) Light- ning-like action on the basis of an incident—for example, the assassination of the German minister to Prague in connection with an anti-German dem- onstration. In such a case world opinion could be presumed to side with Germany.

The military deductions drawn from these hypoth- eses, more desirable than likely, were: (a) Prep- arations were to be made for political possibilities (2) and (3), of which (2) was considered the less desirable, since the Czechs in this case would take precautionary measures; (b) No loss of time, such as would be incurred by the railway transport of the required troops, must be allowed to interfere with a lightning-like thrust at the best moment for action; (c) In the event of action, partial thrusts to breach the line of fortifications were to be imme- diately undertaken by simultaneous attacks of Army and Luftwaffe; (d) Politically speaking, the first four days of military action were to be considered the most decisive ones. Should no striking military success be achieved in those days, a European crisis must certainly be expected to arise. But faits accomplis would convince outsiders of the futility of military intervention, and interested parties, such as Hungary and Poland, might be tempted by these accomplished facts to ally themselves with Germany in order to share in the loot. For such reasons it was necessary to shorten the period of time between the first penetration and the start of the attack by the forces to be rail-transported to the frontier. Resolute thrusts on the part of a motorized army, interference with Czech mobilization, etc., would be required. Transportation for Case "Red" (France), while being prepared, must be kept separate from that for Case "Green." Concentration against "Red" might cause "Red" to undertake undesirable counter-measures.

MOBILIZATION FOR MUNICH

In the new directives for Case "Green" (issued on May 30, 1938) and for the mobilization year 1938-39, Hitler told the Wehrmacht chiefs that he was "unalterably determined to smash Czechoslovakia by military action within foreseeable time"—beginning on October 1, 1938, as he later specified. To await or to bring about the politically and militarily desirable moment would be the task of his political leadership. Military preparations for readiness at the given moment were to be made at once. They were to aim at the highest possible peace-time degree of preparedness and to provide for the unexpectedly fast execution of the action necessary to create, within the first two or three days, a situation that would discourage all intervention. A mere minimum of forces was to be left along the Western frontier and even less at the other frontiers. The great mass of the army and air force was to be employed against Czechoslovakia.

In giving these directives, Hitler was convinced that Germany need not fear a preventive war against herself by any foreign Power. He assured the generals that he would undertake his action against Czechoslovakia only when firmly persuaded, as he had been during the Rhineland remilitarization and the Anschluss, that France would not march and that England would consequently refrain from intervention.[265]

Following the false alarm of May 21-22, things happened more quickly in Czechoslovakia than contemplated by Hitler's military time-tables. For a time he seemed a prisoner of the mobilization schemata. On September 15, the problem was brought up and discussed in the Supreme Command of the Wehrmacht (OKW). What could be done if, in view of the rapidly changing situation, the Führer should demand an acceleration of the plans worked

out in May? The answer was to the effect that it was not feasible. "The old Plan 'Green' can only be run if everything returns first into its garrisons. Even then, the railway preparations would still take ten days...The new time-table comes into force only on September 28. We are therefore tied to this date, which the Führer himself selected in order to gain the maximum of time for continuing the [fortification] work in the West."

As late as the 22nd, the negotiations with Chamberlain made it still impossible to foresee when Case "Green" would come into effect. It seemed improbable before the 30th. If it came earlier, it would have to be carried out with improvised forces. The 28th, the day before Munich, proved "the most difficult day" for Wehrmacht soldiers like Jodl. Increasingly numerous reports of British and French preparatory measures—France had actually called up nearly 1,000,000 men—seemed to point to at least partial mobilization. In discussions with Luftwaffe leaders, Goering declared that "the great war is hardly avoidable; it could last seven years." But, as described in Jodl's diary, "at 17 o'clock tension eases. The Führer has resolved upon a meeting at Munich with Chamberlain, Duce and Daladier." After that, "Czechoslovakia no longer plays a role as a power factor...The genius of the Führer and his determination not even to shrink from a world war have brought victory once more; and without the application of force. One can only hope that the unbelievers, the weak and the doubters [within the Wehrmacht] are converted and stay converted."[266] Munich was not only a bloodless victory, but also one achieved without mobilization on the part of the Germans.

Czech fears, only too well justified in general if not always at the right hour, had led to a first Czech mobilization in May 1938. At that time the Czechs—having scrupulously refrained from mobilizing during the Anschluss—mobilized and marched up to the German frontiers in the belief, as the Czech Chief of Staff told the German military attaché, that Germany had assembled twelve divisions in adjoining Saxony. Actually no such concentration, no mobilization, no considerable troop movements had taken place inside Germany. Since no intelligence service worthy of its name could have gone so completely wrong, the Wehrmacht surmised that the Czechs wanted to stir up their political allies and make them take a stand against Germany in a sort of test mobilization.[267] If the surmise was correct, the Czechs had grievously miscalculated. France and Britain were not greatly persuaded when the Czech Government explained the measure by pointing out the alarmingly low effective strength of the Army at the time, the necessity of instructing reservists in the handling of new weapons, the internal unrest that had led to an increasing number of armed clashes, and the reports of German troop movements in the direction of the Czech borders. The original intention of calling up five classes had been given up after certain explanations had been received from Berlin. Only one class was actually called back to service.

It was believed in Paris that war had only been averted by Britain's action. Nearly everyone was ready to accuse the Czechs of a serious want of suppleness. Had they informed him beforehand, the British ambassador asked Bonnet? What they had done might justify mobilization on Germany's part. Under this frown, the Czech minister at Paris hastily explained that his government's measures were nothing like a mobilization and that merely one class had been called up for retraining. The somewhat more confident minister to London, the younger Masaryk, thought that "our resolution makes a great impression here." Halifax refused to believe the German ambassador's assurances that his country had undertaken no steps of any kind against Czechoslovakia. It seemed "enormously important" to Masaryk "that no tactical mistake be made that would give the Germans, and the English as well, an occasion to put the responsibility on us" (May 22). More encouraged than cautioned by these foreign reactions, Beneš and his Government decided on the 24th to continue with their measures until full tranquillity had been restored at home. This gave the Poles an excuse for the wrathfulness that was later to be turned towards spoliation: officials of the Warsaw Foreign Ministry sharply censured the Czechs for their military measures, which, they maintained, included the concentration of 70,000 men along the Polish frontier.[268]

The men of Munich did not know how to stop Hitler, but they were at least certain that the Czechs had done wrong to mobilize against a not yet mobilized Germany. "[I] could never quite forgive the Czechs their stunt of May 21," Bonnet said afterwards.[269] The false alert of May 1938 was held against them. According to the diplomats it was an error easily converted into "guilt" and presaged ill, should a similar tension again develop. Ribbentrop had already told the British that if France were opposed to German demands for an independent status of the Sudeten Germans, she might try to attack Germany. And only bad things could be expected from the Poles, who were determined to "recover" Teschen and to block Russian passage through their territory. From a French point of view the Belgian attitude was almost worse. The French ambassador to Brussels was told that the Belgian Army would stage maneuvers along the French frontier in order to demonstrate that, if the French should try to carry help to the Czechs by an offensive against Germany over Belgian territory, they would run up against armed resistance. The French ministers were

even then half ready for Munich. They told their Chief of Staff that the Czechs must not be too intransigent in either the Sudeten or the Teschen questions—and this in spite of Gamelin's reminder that, under the guise of a federative state, Czechoslovakia might be wiped off the map of Central Europe as a military Power. The Germans would then be able to proceed at will against either Poland or France.[270] The Czech mobilization of May 1938 made Hitler even more wrathfully determined to settle the Czech problem, and to avoid being "humiliated" by such a small-Power mobilization and the pseudo-victory that was being cried out for a second time in many quarters of the world.[271]

When the Czechs mobilized for a second time, in the September crisis, they took care not to be premature. Even more than in May, they seemed to look forward to an actual war to be fought at the side of their allies, a war that this group had less reason to fear than Hitler from a military point of view.[272] However, Daladier frowned at the news of their first few measures in the direction of war. He found it unbearable, he told the Czech minister in Paris, that the Czech Government should have made such extensive military preparations without consulting him (September 14). The Czechs learned only too soon (though they found it hard to believe) that the French were informing the British that it was necessary to preserve the peace, even at the price of the Czech Republic. France was unprepared and could not wage war for the sake of Czechoslovakia; the French General Staff had declared France to be so completely unprepared, particularly in the air, that a European war would result in a débâcle.[273] The French ambassador to Hitler, François-Poncet, told his Czech colleague that "the influential factors at Prague" must at last understand that Geneva ideas were no longer suitable for the new age. When the Czech reminded him that the loss of the frontier district, inhabited by the Sudeten Germans, would mean the military destruction of his country, the Frenchman tried to console him. The remainder would be neutralized and guaranteed by the Great Powers, as in the case of Belgium and Switzerland.

Sworn to caution, the Prague Foreign Ministry asked the French on the evening of the 17th how they would view mobilization measures which their General Staff had recommended in view of the reported German troop movements. On the 19th, Paris advised that these be postponed so that there would be a good atmosphere for attempts to preserve the peace. As these attempts seemed to approach failure on the 23rd, the French and British informed the Czechs that they no longer adhered to their earlier counsel. They could "no longer assume responsibility for the advice not to mobilize"; Czechoslovakia must herself decide what she considered necessary in view of the situation. But late in the day, Bonnet, the worst of the men of Munich, told the Czechs that their mobilization would only keep Hitler from making any of the concessions he had vaguely promised Chamberlain when the latter took leave of him earlier that day.

The Czechs promptly announced, through the press and over the radio, that all their military measures had been undertaken with the full agreement of France and Britain. Thus they stopped rumors, systematically spread, that they had mobilized in order to spike any possible understanding between Chamberlain and Hitler. They screwed their courage up high, hoping that the French and British would follow. They argued that "further concessions are no longer possible following completion of mobilization. The military situation is good. We have expected an air attack this very same night. That Berlin has shown restraint up to now is rather a sign of weakness. The eighty German divisions will soon be opposed by forty of our own, provided our mobilization is not disturbed tomorrow and the day after." In accordance with their plans and the advice that could be obtained from London and Paris, the Czechs manned their fortifications with the mobilized forces, "surprising" Chamberlain when they would not move out again at once when he expected them to do so. "It is a misfortune," said Masaryk, "that this stupid, badly informed little man is Britain's Premier."[274] It was with such bitterness that the Czechs faced their "Olmütz," or worse, the end of their national independence. Their resentment over the failure of the West to save even the vestiges of their independence,[275] still nourished in 1945 and after, moved them farther to the East than was compatible with the continued existence of their democracy. As Nietzsche has put it, nothing on earth consumes a man—or a nation—more quickly than the passion of resentment (Ecce Homo).

The Western Powers had painted for the Czechs a much blacker picture of the military situation than was actually the case. Gamelin, never over-optimistic, told the ministers that the democracies could still dictate the peace, if they wanted to.[276] Preparatory measures had been proposed by him since August 29. On that date, the chief of the French military mission to Prague had arrived in Paris with the information that the Czechs were reluctant to call on Russia for help, since this might serve as a pretext for German interference (if not also as a pretext for the Western Powers to refrain from interfering on Czechoslovakia's behalf). On September 2, the Cabinet approved of measures for the preparation of the couverture, of which the Germans were at once informed through their military attaché. By the 9th, the reinforced couverture was under preparation, as the Germans were again informed. Gamelin told

their attaché: "We are obliged by virtue of the measures you are taking to do likewise. Considering the correct attitude your command has always shown to us, I beg you to transmit our conversation at once." The German protested, more dutifully than truthfully, that his country had undertaken no mobilization, whereupon Gamelin reminded him that reservists had been called up and large units had been assembled. On the 12th, the generals discussed with Daladier the question of what military help might be extended to the Czechs. They assured him of their confidence in the Army and in the final outcome of a war, even if Czechoslovakia might in the end only be saved as Belgium, Serbia and Rumania had been saved in 1918-19. It was unfortunate that Belgium would not allow France to attack through her territory. Because of this refusal, it would be necessary to open the French offensive on a narrow front against the Siegfried Line. Although this would make action difficult, it would not make action altogether impossible.

The British-French military and diplomatic discussions in London on the 26th revealed to the British that the French would not fight for Czechoslovakia, and to the French that the British could not yet fight, given the state of their armaments. While Bonnet discouraged everyone, Gamelin found some encouraging features in the military situation, pointing to certain German weaknesses. But he left only "an unhappy impression" on the British, even when he pointed out that to shrink from war now was reculer pour plus mal sauter.[277]

Orders for the mobilization of the British Fleet were given on September 27;[278] the French called up altogether 700,000 men and the British certain Territorial Formations such as anti-aircraft units; in London parks they were digging trenches and distributing gas masks, and the report that the British Fleet had steamed out gave the OKW some anxious moments on the 25th and 26th. However, the early indications of a readiness to give in to Hitler's threats made the actual Franco-British military preparations mere unconvincing gestures. By late September, many Britishers, including experienced diplomats, had come to feel "that war was inevitable, because the wheels of mobilization had moved so fast and so far that they could not be reversed."[279] Munich came as the anticlimax to these fearful expectations and exhilarated the British people by seemingly freeing them from the very jaws of war.

Filled with the same fearful expectations, some of the smaller Powers (such as Holland, Belgium, and Switzerland) who expected to remain neutral and hoped to see their neutrality respected had taken at least preliminary measures of mobilization. The Soviet Union, in spite of her obligations to aid the Czechs, had not moved. Her governors maintained, at least after Munich, that the appeasement policies of Britain and France had made active support of the Czechs so unlikely from the outset that anything like mobilization would have amounted to sheer waste. The Germans took due notice of this abstention as promising "a more positive attitude on the part of the Soviet Union towards Germany."[280]

The Czech catastrophe gave the French a chance to try out their mobilization and to ascertain and repair minor imperfections. Their actual military position, however, was greatly weakened, partly due to the pessimistic conviction that further armaments would completely upset the socio-economic status quo. British preparations for participation in the ever-more-likely Continental war were far more energetic. The army was reorganized and preparations made that would guarantee quick mobilization. Changes were introduced within twelve months, which in more normal times would have required years to perfect. The expeditionary force was to consist of nineteen divisions, as against the original seven proposed by Haldane.[281]

There was not much secrecy surrounding these and connected measures. In fact, in conscious opposition to pre-1914 methods, a fair amount of "open diplomacy" as to military preparations and precautions was displayed by France and Britain in their relations with the Axis Powers. Early in February 1939, when the Italians reinforced their troops in Libya, the French followed suit in their North African possessions and informed the Italians of this through their military attaché in Paris. He, of course, protested that his country's movements were merely indicative of some reorganization.[282] In Britain, the existing arrangements for the calling up of reserves and Territorials were changed in such a manner as to eliminate the alarming reference to an "emergency," used heretofore to justify it. The Nazis were informed of this change and the change explained to them: since it seemed desirable to avoid disturbing public confidence at home and abroad by such a reference to emergencies, it would henceforth be omitted and the British Government would proceed along lines in general usage in the various Continental countries.[283] Other preparatory measures in Britain accompanied or followed these reforms. Conscription was inaugurated and a Ministry of Supply established to handle the production of war materials, stock-piling, and questions of priority (April 1939).

MOBILIZATIONS, 1939-41

A series of tensions began in 1939 with Italian movements in North Africa, which made the French quite seriously consider whether the Fascists were intending to wage war. In Paris, little thought was given to Poland at the time. She had disgusted everyone by her participation in the partition of Czechoslovakia. It was still hoped, however, that she might be defended against German aggression by Russia, possibly against her will.[284] The "liquidation of the remainder of the Czech State," contemplated by Hitler since October 21, 1938, was effected by Wehrmacht forces that remained unreinforced by mobilization, partly in order not to again provoke French counter-mobilization.[285] This event redirected Western attention to the East, where a totally new military situation had been created. France was forced to face new eventualities and to reconfirm the existing loose ties with some of the countries in the Southeast.[286] She and Britain gave Rumania and Greece their joint guarantee, and both concluded a mutual assistance pact with Poland. But they proved too late and too slow to draw Russia firmly to their side.

Like the Czechs, the Poles began their mobilization against German threats early and instinctively. Torn between hopes for the preservation of peace, fear of war, and illusions about their own strength, they began troop movements and partial mobilization as early as March 21, 1939. Four infantry divisions and one cavalry brigade were put on a war footing. This step was due to pressure from the military, who entertained curious notions about the relative strength of the Polish Army. Though irked, the population bore the prolonged state of mobilization and political uncertainty "without any collapse or appreciable deterioration of morale."[287] Two more divisions and one brigade were mobilized on August 14, and on the 21st secret mobilization of the main forces—twenty-eight divisions, eleven brigades, air forces, artillery, etc.—was ordered. On the 25th, the two army corps most directly facing Germany were mobilized. The mobilization was accomplished by individual summons issued to the reservists. Who was deceived by this camouflage, the Polish population, the Germans, or Poland's allies, is hard to say. Considering the extent of the summons, scarcely anyone could be misled.

Ribbentrop gave the Poles early warning that their mobilization measures were not apt to improve relations. He reminded them of "similar risky steps taken by another State," meaning Czechoslovakia.[288] The German ambassador in Warsaw pointed out the damaging effect of these measures on German-Polish negotiations, particularly since they were "without any justification and besides formed a step highly dubious in its effect"; they provoked war sentiment and new clashes with the German minority in Poland. Colonel Beck justified mobilization by pointing to the German demands regarding Danzig. After the precedents set in Czechoslovakia and Memel, these could only be read as alarm signals by his country.[289] In his Reichstag speech of April 28, Hitler denounced the German-Polish Non-Aggression Pact of 1934 and accused "a mendacious world propaganda" of having induced Poland to call up troops, as Czechoslovakia had done a year ago. Germany had not called up a single man and had no thought of proceeding against Poland.

Subsequent German military preparations in the direction of Poland, for which "the ominous word mobilization" was carefully avoided, led the Poles to resolve upon further measures of their own, as Beck told the French ambassador on the evening of August 24th. Word of this could hardly have reached Paris when Bonnet sent Beck a warning that "under the new conditions resulting from the Russo-German Pact," he was particularly anxious that Poland should avoid laying herself open to the charge of being the aggressor. This would play into the hands of Germany, who was seeking to maneuver her into just such a position. Above all, she must refrain from military action in the event that the Germans should take over Danzig or in connection with the border incidents that were constantly increasing. On August 28 the Poles resolved to order general mobilization, which would have covered an additional eleven divisions, consisting largely of Ukrainians and White Russians. The Polish decision was taken in reaction to German concentrations along the Polish borders and the German entry into Slovakia. On the 29th, when the British and French ambassadors were informed of this decision, the British representative protested: the very word "mobilization" would produce the impression that it was Poland who was embarking on war. It would be "extremely desirable" to postpone the public announcement for at least a few hours or at least until the German answer to Chamberlain's mediation proposal in the Danzig and connected problems had been given. The French ambassador had "no objections whatever to the actual fact of mobilization" but supported the Britisher's view. Both had obviously read the 1914 documents and the war guilt literature, rather than the signs of their own time. The Poles bowed to their wishes and put off general mobilization until noon of August 30. When it was proclaimed, the announcement avoided the "ominous word mobilization."

It was largely in deference to the arguments of the French ambassador, as the supposed voice of the French Army, that the postponement had been agreed to. However, his arguments were not supported by Daladier. The latter was not prepared to shoulder the responsibility for a step too reminiscent of the desertion of Czechoslovakia. On the morning of the 30th, he gave the ambassador to understand that he was to blame and that Poland must be sole judge of the necessity for mobilization. When the latter subsequently explained to the Poles that he had merely wanted a few hours' delay, he was informed that the General Staff had found it possible to go beyond his suggestion and postpone mobilization by a whole day. There were technical reasons for this—a mobilization order published late in the day would have caused confusion as to the first M-day.[290] That this postponement, under the existing ratio of strength, was as fatal as it has been described and that it brought Poland's defeat "several weeks nearer" cannot well be accepted.[291] Her mobilization was never even completed, so promptly came the German attack for which Polish general mobilization provided a final pretext.[292]

Poland had been backward in nearly all respects, including the camouflaging of her measures preparatory to war. To quote a moderate and quite friendly judgment:

The Polish Army found itself attacked when it was only at the start of its mobilization and in the midst of concentration. In order not to risk appearing as the aggressor, Poland had put off to the last moment the order for general mobilization. And her system, in this respect, lacked suppleness. It is obvious how great the importance is, from the standpoint of foreign as well as domestic policy, to be able to mobilize and even concentrate without saying so. Germany was past-master in this art and, besides, there is no doubt that only a form of dictatorial government allows this in the most complete form.[293]

Popular judgment everywhere, and, on the anti-Axis side, most military and diplomatic judgment as well, had arrived in 1939 at the point where it assumed that mobilization meant war; that the side that ordered it first had practically ordered war; that governors everywhere must pay respect to such judgments and must not call mobilization—even if necessary for national security and unaggressively conceived—by this name. To follow this rule would, it was thought, deny the opponent most obviously ready for war the opportunity for the propagandistic accusation that the other party had started it, and would at the same time deny an unwilling ally the pretext for withholding his support. Militarily speaking, early mobilization on the part of any of the non-Axis Powers did not have much significance, since the initial military superiority of the Reich was so great by August 1939 that it could not be countered by advancing mobilization dates. The situation in this respect was fundamentally different from that of July-August 1914. But the lessons of 1914 were believed applicable even to such a war-bent opponent as the Third Reich. For once men had tried to learn something from history, but they had learned the lesson wrong (which need not mean that the historians concerned with the problem of 1914 had established wrong findings or passed wrong judgments).

The Russian general mobilization of 1914 could be considered a positive military threat to Germany. It was understandable that Russian mobilization could move Germany to declare war. The mobilization of Poland in 1939, however, was a mere pretext for a war that Hitler had decided upon when Poland would not give in to the German demands for Danzig and changes in the Corridor. Case "White" (war with Poland), as part of the "Directive for unified war preparation of the Wehrmacht for 1939/40," was ordered by Hitler early in April 1939, to be prepared in such a way that operations could begin at any time after September 1. The directive stated that Poland's present attitude made it necessary to go beyond the hitherto elaborated "Frontier Security East" case, largely defensive in character, in order to eliminate once and for all any possible threat from that direction. Should the clash become unavoidable, the aim would be to smash Polish armed strength and to create a situation in the East in keeping with the requirements of Germany's national defense. "The political leadership considers it its task to isolate Poland if possible in such a case, that is to say, to limit the war to Poland." The tendency of France and Britain to dissociate themselves from such Continental complications would help to isolate Poland, while Russia's intervention, if she were in a position to undertake it, would not help Poland at all, since it would mean her destruction by Bolshevism. "Poland's isolation might be the easier to maintain beyond the outbreak of war, the more we succeed in opening the war by surprising and strong strokes and by achieving quick successes... It is the task of the Wehrmacht to annihilate the Polish Wehrmacht. To this end a surprise opening of the attack is to be hoped for and to be prepared. Camouflaged or open general mobilization will be ordered only on the day before the attack, at the latest possible time," if at all. The Luftwaffe, leaving a minimum of forces facing the West, was to be used for a surprise attack on Poland. Its special task would be to disrupt Polish mobilization and to interfere with the enemy's planned concentration. Publicly announced general mobilization should not be expected, particularly if military events should remain restricted to Case "White." Everything would be covered by X-case, partial mobilization without public announcement.[294]

The OKW's preliminary time-table for the attack on Poland was approved by Hitler on June 22. He ordered that the calling of reservists, which was already taking place, should be explained as intended for the autumn maneuvers. Still, the numbers called up were too great to remain unob-

served and to be explained away. This caused "rather marked anxiety among the middle classes" in the Reich. It could be foreseen by July 11 that the number called would reach a full million by the end of August. The various stages of transition from a state of semi-mobilization to a state of war were clearly observed by French representatives in Germany. By July 13, they concluded that "all the measures preparatory to war are being taken. The German General Staff is acting as if they were to be ready by a fixed date which, it would seem, falls due in the course of August, after the harvest has been gathered, the fortifications completed and large numbers of reservists assembled in the camps." Still later, they reported that the stepped-up callings would allow an advanced state of mobilization to be reached by August 15, with two million men under arms.[295] In keeping with her "stages of tension" calendar, France had also called up reservists. When Ambassador Henderson pointed to the numerous German callings as a symptom of the political situation, Ribbentrop's lieutenant replied that "it was a fact that in France and Poland [each or together?] men to the extent of nearly half a million above the normal status were with the colors." He claimed that the calling-up notices published in German newspapers merely represented what all standing armies do in the summer season. And were not the British at the same time in the midst of war preparations and looking, though without signal success, for allies? (July 14).[296]

By mid-August, the Reich's military preparations had gained so much momentum (or so the French thought), that they could be said "to have reached an advanced stage of mobilization," with war psychosis, more fearful than hopeful, spreading among the German people.[297] Unit after unit was pushed into the Eastern regions. The German preparations seemed part of a far from secret mobilization to French and British observers.[298] The Wehrmacht command did not as yet consider them as such. The moment for the equation Mobilization=War had not yet arrived. The Ribbentrop-Molotov Pact, doing away with the threat of the highly undesirable war on two fronts, brought it appreciably nearer. (Poland at best represented only half a front.) On the 22nd, Hitler had told the generals that he would shortly conclude the Russian Pact. Then the way would be "open for the soldier." The only thing to be feared was that "at the last minute some Schweinehund will make a proposal for mediation."

The top-ranking commanders were not carried away by the assurance which had swayed their predecessors of 1914, that, considering the preparations made and the given ratio of strengths, victory was assured. To several among them it was a gambler's guess when they heard Hitler say:

For us it is easy to make decisions. We have nothing to lose, we can only gain. Our economic situation is such that because of our restrictions we cannot hold out for more than a few years... We have no other choice, we must act [now, when the political situation was more favorable than it might be two or three years hence. The creation of a Greater Germany, achieved largely through political bluff, would now have to be tested by war. It was impossible to stand facing Poland indefinitely while both had cocked rifles in their hands. There were chances that the West would intervene, but that risk must be accepted]. The alternative is either for us to strike now or ourselves be destroyed sooner or later.[299]

On the 23rd, Jodl, a creature of Hitler and the strongest military believer in his "genius," was ordered to Berlin to take over the post of Chief of the Operations Branch of the Wehrmacht, a post he had been selected to fill in the case of war.

When the news of the impending German-Soviet Pact reached Paris, Daladier, at his wits' end, spoke of general mobilization. Two other ministers, Mandel and Reynaud, were also in favor of it for political reasons, while President Lebrun did not as yet consider it necessary. "I am not asking for it," said Bonnet on August 22, presumably voicing the diplomatic viewpoint. The question was put off for two days. At the request of Bonnet, who wanted to know whether the military chiefs considered "that we could, or could not, face a war," the Ministers discussed the question of France's preparedness with the three chiefs of staff. Gamelin did not consider it proper to indicate in Bonnet's presence the deficiencies "which still existed in our armament and in our industrial mobilization." He feared that, through Bonnet, the Germans would soon learn whatever he said. Instead, he and Admiral Darlan declared that "the Army and the Navy were ready. In the early stages of the conflict they can do little against Germany. But French mobilization by itself would bring some relief to Poland by tying down a considerable number of German units at our frontier." Gamelin considered an early mobilization equally desirable for France's own sake. If Germany should destroy Poland as she had Czechoslovakia, and then should turn all her might against France, especially if she attacked through Belgium, France might find it very difficult to mobilize and concentrate her armies, might in fact hardly be able to enter the struggle. France's hope lay in a prolonged war in which British troops and American equipment would come to her rescue. France had an interest in making her entry as late as possible so that her concentration would be as far advanced as possible for the case of a "strategically defensive war."

Such a war would not, of course, preclude counter-strokes and counter-offensives for the relief of the ally in the East, from whom "honorable resistance" was expected, though little more. Poland expected far more from France than the French expected to give.[300]

On the 23rd, Ambassador Henderson showed Hitler Chamberlain's letter announcing British precautionary measures. They were rendered necessary, the letter explained, by the military movements reported from Germany and by the seeming conviction in some Berlin quarters that the German-Soviet Pact would make British intervention on Poland's behalf a contingency that need no longer be feared. At the same time, Chamberlain offered British mediation in the Danzig and related issues. The "excitable and uncompromising" Führer blustered that he would respond to mobilization in the West with the mobilization of Germany. Henderson: "Is that a threat?" Hitler: "No, a measure of protection." Britain, he said, had poisoned the atmosphere by spreading false rumors about German mobilization and by keeping the Poles from agreeing to reasonable German proposals. In his written answer to Chamberlain of the 23rd, he threatened that if Britain and France should carry out mobilization measures against Germany, despite the fact that the latter had no intention of attacking either of them, he would order the immediate mobilization of the German armed forces.[301]

On the 24th, Hitler was still pondering Chamberlain's combined offer and warning. He was uncertain, he told the soldiers, whether England, with whom he wanted no conflict, might not be serious this time. Nor was the situation as yet propitious for the announcement of general mobilization. Six hundred and fifty German merchant vessels of three million tons were on the high seas, a large part of them liable to fall into British hands. They received warning on the 25th to seek the nearest safe port. As far as was known or suspected in Berlin, Britain had ordered "quiet mobilization" on the 23rd, while France had reached "States of Tension Numbers One and Two," but would not enter State Number Three until the 25th. Convinced that Britain would not intervene in Case "White," Hitler gave orders on the 25th for the pre-arranged camouflage and partial mobilization required for that case. The 26th was the first day of mobilization, and 4:40 a.m., sunrise, was Y-time, the hour to strike. Various precautions accompanied the mobilization measures: Germans in Poland were warned to leave; five more Luftwaffe groups were transferred to the East, and civilian air protection (Luftschutz) in the East was called out; telephone connections with the Western capitals were cut for several hours in the afternoon; foreign military attachés were forbidden to leave Berlin without prior authorization, in order to keep them from spying on German preparations, as they had done in 1938; most private air services were suspended; rationing was set to begin on the 27th. Comparing the state of preparations in other countries with their own, the Germans ascertained that the fourth state of tension prevailed in a number of localities in France, that the Italian Army in the Po valley had been brought to war strength, that pre-mobilization was taking place in Holland and partial mobilization in Bulgaria and Rumania.[302]

The form of mobilization chosen in Berlin did not include economic mobilization. When the officers concerned with this particular task pointed this out, their protests were overruled by the OKW, which did not think that war against Poland called for general mobilization. And political reasons made anything more than partial mobilization inadvisable. Thus economic mobilization got off to a bad start, with many features of the prepared plans not coming into effect until 1943. Still, as the military chief of Germany's war industrial planning, General George Thomas, expressed it from the perspective of 1944: "History will know few cases of a state which, in time of peace, had already aimed so consciously and in such a deliberate manner at the requirements of war as was necessarily the case in Germany between the two world wars."[303]

The long-postponed British-Polish Mutual Assistance Pact was signed in the late afternoon of the 25th. News of the signing reached Berlin around 6:00 p.m. This followed on the heels of Mussolini's communication that, while he would stand by Germany, he could not mobilize at the time and, in order to mobilize later, would have to beg large supplies from her. These two communications made Hitler cancel the orders for the attack on Poland. "Stop everything at once... I need time for negotiations," he told the OKW, which issued the counter-orders at about 8:30 p.m. without causing too much of the generally expected disorder. Only a few small units on the Polish border were not reached in time. Their action added a few more frontier incidents to the record. Temporarily, none were more relieved than those German generals who were in opposition to Hitler and a second world war.[304] On the 26th, "all decisions on possible military action were suspended, at first without any time limit." On August 30, according to Keitel, "the day for the attack was again postponed for twenty-four hours." The reason given to the soldiers was that a Polish plenipotentiary was expected. From then on, "no further change in the military instructions occurred."[305] The final decision to open hostilities against Poland on September 1 was made by Hitler at 12:40 p.m. on the 31st. Y-time was set for 4:45 a.m., fifteen minutes later than on August 26, to correspond with the later sunrise. There was

no previous declaration of war, no general mobilization. As the Führer's final directives explained: "After all political possibilities for the removal of an unbearable situation along Germany's Eastern frontiers in a peaceful manner have been exhausted, I have resolved upon the forceful solution... In the West, it is important to leave the responsibility for the opening of hostilities in an unmistakable manner to England and France."[306]

From then on, the endeavors of the diplomats were little more than exercises in the art of war guilt imputation. The British were frank in stating that they would not repeat Grey's possible mistake of 1914, when he left Britain's position towards a Continental war unclarified. They wanted to avoid the repetition of such a tragic misunderstanding by openly declaring their support of Poland. This, Hitler chided them, was giving Poland the blank check that Bethmann had handed the Austrians early in July 1914. British intervention had produced nothing except Poland's mobilization, Ribbentrop told Henderson late on the 30th. Henderson retorted that the Poles had mobilized only because of Germany's mobilization, the existence of which the Führer had admitted to him the day before.[307] At midnight of the 30th, Ribbentrop "gabbled through" to Henderson "Sixteen Points" for a solution of the Danzig and Corridor problems, including a plan that would allow Germany and Poland to demobilize. These, however, were intended for a German White Book, rather than for serious negotiations.[308] They formed part of Germany's psychological mobilization, which started much earlier than it had in 1914. Frontier and other incidents, which in 1914 proved much less numerous than expected, were now provoked by Nazi organizations; and reports on "intolerable provocations" were spread in order to raise the fever heat of the German people.[309] In his Reichstag speech a few hours after the outbreak of hostilities, Hitler accused the Poles of having met his conciliatory proposals by acts of terror against the Germans living in their country, by early mobilization measures, and finally by general mobilization. An uninformed people like the Germans of the Third Reich could be made to believe that the party which was said to have mobilized first was most guilty of war.[310]

British mobilization was ordered on the morning of September 1. French mobilization, preceded by the couverture générale, was ordered the same day. "The Government has thus placed France in a position to act in accordance with her vital interests and with our honor," Daladier told the legislature on September 1, the day of the capitulation at Sedan. Peace still prevailed between Germany and the Western Powers. An ultimatum presented to Germany to halt all aggressive action against Poland and to prepare to withdraw from that country was ticking off its time-limit. Bonnet still hoped for

Italian mediation, while Gamelin valued general mobilization as a threat to Germany, as a starter of France's war production, and as the first condition for getting the forces ready, even if the situation should result in another Munich. The British sense of obligation towards Poland, considerably higher than that of most French soldiers and politicians, did away with all remaining hopes for another Munich. Since Hitler did not interfere, French mobilization was perfected without a hitch, (aside from local shortcomings in clothing and encampment).[311]

Various other European nations initiated or completed their mobilizations, most of them in the hope of being able to better preserve their neutrality if more fully armed. When Russia first mobilized large numbers of the Red Army, it was for the purpose of participating in the Fourth Partition of Poland. This took place much sooner than the Russians had expected, due to a German victory achieved in days, when the Russians had thought of it in terms of weeks. In order to gather the Russian share of the spoils, heavy demands were made upon the Red Army by the Politbureau. By September 10, three million reservists, age groups up to forty-five, had been called up. Mobilization was accompanied by the usual scares and scarcities.[312] Once the harvest had been gathered, which involved some difficulties, the still incompletely mobilized Red Army proceeded to take over the small Baltic States, to attack Finland, and to prepare itself for the coming conflict with Hitler. The Germans complained that the Russians were concentrating "needlessly large numbers of divisions in the Baltic," and, by mid-May 1941, were maintaining stronger forces along the Western frontiers than ever before in Russian history.[313]

In the wake of Germany's victory in the West, Italy proceeded to full mobilization in the latter half of May 1940. According to the observations of foreign military attachés, preparations were "sufficient [by May 26] to enable Italy to enter the war; the rest can be completed after the beginning of military operations."[314]

Following a far from glorious participation in the last stages of the war against France, Italy concentrated considerable land forces along the Albanian-Greek frontier during the second half of August. A series of incidents and provocations were staged by the Fascists, leading to a most humiliating ultimatum addressed to Athens. When this was turned down, the incendiaries opened the attack along the burning frontier at sunrise on October 18, 1940.[315] Germany unwillingly followed the Axis partner into the Balkans, overrunning Yugoslavia and Greece before she had even concentrated her forces.

In the "fluid" situation that had been created

by Germany's actions, the totalitarian Powers, Russia, Italy and Japan, mobilized increasing numbers of their armed forces.[316] Not all of this power, they thought at first, would have to be spent in military action which, as Molotov agreed with Hitler (November 12, 1940), was vastly more expensive than peaceful means.[317] Until the last the Russians hoped to get by without a war with Germany. Yet, cautiously, they called up more and more troops. When another such levy took place in the first half of June 1941, Molotov explained to the Germans that this was nothing beyond the usual summer-time calling-up of reservists and that "the impending maneuvers meant nothing but a training of the reservists and a check on the operations of the railway system which, as is known, takes place very year." Consequently, it was "at least nonsensical to interpret these measures of the Red Army as an action hostile to Germany" (June 14).[318]

MOBILIZATION OF THE UNITED STATES

Realizing that America's security, in the long run, was not likely to be preserved by peaceful means, her Government undertook various preparatory steps for the entry into war. In doing this, care had to be taken to avoid calling them by any name resembling mobilization. Mobilization was still something un-American. Mobilization in the United States had to take place under another nomenclature, except in the industrial field, where it had been prepared for a long time. Serving as an "arsenal to the democracies" proved to be, as it was intended to be, a measure of pre-mobilization, and so did the Selective Service Act of 1940 in the field of military manpower procurement. To this extent, the United States had prepared and started mobilization of her forces prior to Pearl Harbor. To this extent it was ahead of 1917, when not much more had been brought to a war footing than the military forces stationed along the Mexican border.

The war-to-end-war mentality had been so far abandoned that the Selective Service Acts provided for future military mobilization. They included obligations for ex-servicemen to serve for five or six years in the reserves following their discharge, and to remain subject to recalls for training purposes. The ever-closer approximation to long-existing European arrangements was due to the radical change in America's strategic position. Her fate no longer seemed to depend on the last sixty days of a war but rather on the first sixty days of participation.[319] The existing arrangements, however, did not as yet provide the United States with reserves so organized that millions of trained men could be mobilized at a moment's notice. Even during the Korean campaign, the calling up of some 200,000 reservists took place by individual notices. The procedure was slow and cumbersome and produced great individual hardships while not at once producing a commensurate addition to fighting strength. The arrangements made for using these men proved far from adequate, and there were too many reservists merely "sitting around" in offices, barracks and camps. Others were made nearly unemployable by the uncertainties of the recall system.[320] These were some of the shortcomings of American mobilization in the early 1950's. Mobilization was in itself "an entirely new endeavor in American democracy."[321] The time for the elaboration of more exact mobilization plans, in order to facilitate the more instantaneous calling up of reservists to complement a proposed two-and-a-half to three-million-man standing army, had clearly arrived.[322] The hour had also arrived for preparing the mobilization schedules of the multinational forces, whose simultaneous employment, beginning with mobilization, had to be contemplated by the coalition of the North Atlantic Powers, doubt persisting as to whether these coordinations had yet gone as far as arranged for between the United States and Canada.[323]

As part of American rearmament, mobilization long before war—intended to prevent war, diplomatically speaking, as much as for the eventuality of war, militarily speaking—had to be undertaken in earnest. However, the announced intention to mobilize was bound to be ineffective as far as Moscow was concerned. Such a move could be understood as a diplomatic gesture only in a system of states filled with an identical world outlook, such as had been the case in the eighteenth century. It did not stop Russian-Communist expansion in the Far East, even if it proved encouraging, and frightening at the same time, to the Western European nations. In the last analysis, Russia's iron-faced indifference in the face of American rearmament and mobilization evinced considerable awareness on her part of the ruinous economic effects that mobilizations had had on the mobilizers in the past. Forcing the foremost capitalist nation into a state of permanent mobilization of large parts of its population and industries promised to effect that undermining of capitalist economy from within that had failed to come about as a consequence of the cyclical upheaval for which Moscow had so ardently hoped. The wastefulness of most American military measures gave great promise that such Russian hopes might yet be fulfilled. These hopes were far greater than any Russian fears of being overtaken by America in the armaments race. The Politburo did not have to take that risk too seriously. The essentially anti-war sentiment of American policy would scarcely permit her to exploit a temporary or permanent superiority in arms. Since the Ameri-

cans had not made use of the A-bomb at the time when it was their monopoly, it was not likely that they would make use of a position of superiority that was even less obvious. Forcing the class enemy into mobilization measures, more costly now than ever before, is the latest stroke in the grand strategy of international class warfare.

Mobilizations have always wrought great hardships on the nations undertaking them. The Russian hope in forcing the United States and others to start on a competitive mobilization race is that the peoples under their own control can be forced to bear these hardships far more easily than the "spoiled" Americans, with their high standards of living and political criticism. It can also rely fairly safely on the West's inability to make friends behind the "Iron Curtain" in a manner that would really sap the Russian war potential, that is, by inciting the opponents of Sovietism to desertion en masse. Western immigration policies offer them no escape routes! The nationalism of the democracies does not allow for the reception and employment of hundreds of thousands of fugitives from Communism.[324]

With the partial mobilization of America as a feature of the stalemate in the "cold war," a state of prolonged though still only partial mobilization has been reached throughout the world. A return to the practices of earlier ages seems to be impending. In various periods of history, constantly mobilized forces have stood arrayed against each other and have fought small wars along the frontiers of civilization: the Roman limes, the outposts of Byzantium, the Austrian "Military Frontier" against the Turk as the enemy of Christianity and later against Balkan brigandage. The Austrian Militärgrenze, an institution lasting from 1527 to 1848, makes highly dubious such statements as Toynbee's (A Study of History) that "when a frontier between civilization and barbarism stands still, time always works in the barbarians' favor." An absolutely static character of defense, sheer "containment," might indeed be self-defeating, even in its function as couverture to permit the completion of mobilization in America and elsewhere. But, as past examples show, this is not necessarily true with regard to a politically activiated military frontier of civilization.

FOOTNOTES

1. There has been little recent literature on mobilization. Among the older writings one might mention E. Pascal, La mobilisation (1887), and A. Froment, La mobilisation et la préparation à la guerre (1887).
2. Aston, Sea, Land and Air Strategy, pp. 42 ff.
3. Cf. article on "Mobilisation" in Dictionnaire militaire, II, 1916: "Mobilization is the passage from a peace footing to a war footing, a period

during which an army must be provided with everything it needs in order to march into the field and begin active operations at once. It is naturally important that this period should be as short as possible because on its good and complete performance will often depend the fate of the first encounters."

4. Spencer, Sociology, I, para. 515.
5. Joffre, Mémoires, I, 212.
6. The French military believed that there was still another German measure of preparing mobilization, something France did not have —a "hint" to members of the reserve to get ready. This they thought was possible only in a disciplined country like Germany, where the secret could be kept. In France, a similar measure would become known at once through the press. No such measure actually existed. Doc. dipl. fr., 3rd series, VI, passim; Berliner Monatshefte, XIII, 60.
7. Some of these arrangements formed the subject of the famous bordereau in the Dreyfus case. Gamelin, Servir, II, 199.
8. Messimy, Mes souvenirs, pp. 131 f.
9. Franke (ed.), Handbuch der neuzeitlichen Wehrwissenschaften, I, 736.
10. For Swiss declarations in 1914, see Doc. dipl. fr., 3rd series, XI, 100.
11. Jähns, Geschichte der Kriegswissenschaften, pp. 2289 ff., 2684.
12. For French financial preparations as part of mobilization before 1914, see G. P., XXI, 6942. For the German ones, see Der Weltkrieg 1914-1918: Kriegsrüstung und Kriegswirtschaft (Reichsarchiv) Vol. 1, with appendix.
13. The heavy buying of horses by or for the military authorities was among the first visible preparations for war during the eighteenth and nineteenth centuries.
14. The German term Aufmarsch, or "marching up," in certain predetermined regions in the direction of the frontiers is the more precise one, for concentration in the more exact sense takes place only on the battlefield. Manstein gave the following definition of "forming-up" or concentration for the benefit of the Nuremberg Tribunal: "A plan according to which troops, in the event of a threat of war, are ready along the frontiers, that is to say, a plan for the event of threatening political conflagration. Whether it may lead to war or whether from this formation one would enter into a war has actually nothing to do with the concentration plan. It merely states how the troops are to be assembled and, in the event of war, what would be the first tasks for the army groups and armies." Trial of the Major War Criminals, XX, 602.

15. Cited by Görlitz in Der deutsche Generalstab, p. 39.
16. Ollivier, L'Empire libéral, XV, 111, 178, 314; Lebrun, Souvenirs militaires 1866-1870, pp. 116 ff., 193, 211.
17. Troop transports over the British canal system in the early nineteenth century not only reduced fatigue considerably but also cut marching time from over fourteen to seven days in the movement of a body of troops from London to Liverpool (1806). Pratt, Railpower, p. 1.
18. Deutsche Dokumente zum Kriegsausbruch (hereafter cited as D. D.), II, No. 333.
19. Doc. dipl. fr., 3rd series, XI, 479 f., 557.
20. It seems doubtful whether the Russian War Minister was justified in saying, on August 3, 1914, that Russian mobilization on the one hand was executed with a perfect regularity and, on the other, that some hours had already been gained over the original schedules. Ibid., XI, 509.
21. Bacon, Lord Fisher, II, 33 ff.
22. Admiral Wagner before the Nuremberg Tribunal. Trial of the Major War Criminals, XIII, 445.
23. Oesterreich-Ungarns Aussenpolitik, II, 1987.
24. This was on August 1, 1914. Moltke, Erinnerungen, Briefe, Dokumente, pp. 19 ff.; D. D., III, 575.
25. D. D., III, 491, 528, 571.
26. For a more detailed discussion, see below pp. 397-399.
27. Dobrorolski, Die Mobilmachung der russischen Armee, 1914.
28. Suchomlinow writes in retrospect that "it was a great fundamental error on Kuropatkin's part to have tied himself already in peace-time to one definite case of war, to direct the whole peace training and administration to this one case only. Once this case did not arise exactly as expected, as it had been contrived to the last detail in the chancelleries, the whole apparatus was endangered," as by the war in the Far East in 1904-05. Suchomlinow, Erinnerungen, p. 215.
29. Schulte, "Die Herrschaft der militärischen Pläne in der Politik," Süddeutsche Monatshefte, September 1924.
30. Trochu, Oeuvres posthumes, I, 69 f.; II, 350 ff.
31. For this complex of questions, see the Schulte article referred to above (n. 29).
32. Churchill, The Unknown War: The Eastern Front, pp. 89 f.
33. Conrad, Aus meiner Dienstzeit, I, 364 ff.
34. Görlitz, Der deutsche Generalstab, p. 100.
35. For details, see Frantz, Russlands Eintritt in den Weltkrieg, pp. 17 ff.
36. The experiences with excessive drunkenness

during trial mobilizations in Russia before 1914 led to the prohibition of the sale of alcoholic drinks in all districts where mobilization took place in 1914, and eventually to wartime prohibition in Russia. Die internationalen Beziehungen, 1st series, V, 100 f.

37. Ibid., III, 116.

38. G. P., XXI, 6942, 6945.

39. Cf. Boulanger's proposal for a test mobilization in the East of France in 1887. The mobilization as he planned it, but not as it was actually held, was perhaps the most provocative one ever proposed. See chap. X, p. 291.

40. G. P., XXI, 6937.

41. January 1900. Ibid., XVII, 5212.

42. Lot, L'art militaire et les armées au moyen age, I, 98.

43. Cf., for example, Oman, History of the Art of War in the Sixteenth Century, pp. 297 ff.

44. Cited by Ollivier in L'Empire libéral, XIV, 550.

45. Prussia, as the smallest and poorest of the Great Powers, with a penurious citizenry, could least rely on financing a war by loans at home or abroad. She therefore kept a war chest ready in time of peace. A grand treasury for war amounted to thirteen million thalers in the summer of 1756, and a small one, as part of the annual budget since 1750, to 700,000 thalers for mobilization purposes. Jany, Geschichte der preussischen Armee, I, 748; II, 214.

46. Ibid., III, 181, 391.

47. Görlitz, Der deutsche Generalstab, p. 23.

48. Jähns, Kriegswissenschaften, p. 2292.

49. For details, see Jany, Geschichte der preussischen Armee, III, 181 f., 217 ff., 315.

50. Ibid., III, 523.

51. Ibid., III, 523.

52. Pantlen, Krieg und Finanzen, pp. 10, 17.

53. Droysen, Abhandlungen zur neueren Geschichte, pp. 194 f.; Jany, Geschichte der preussischen Armee, III, 225 f.

54. See the numerous references to Olmütz in Bismarck, Gedanken und Erinnerungen.

55. Oesterreich-Ungarns Aussenpolitik, IV, 4017.

56. In the Second German Reich, the order for a mobilization called for the Chancellor's counter-signature. William II, surrounded by his mariners, wired the German ambassador in London that if Britain should move still more ships from the Mediterranean to the North Sea, this would be considered as a threat of war and would be answered by a larger naval bill and possibly mobilization. Chancellor Bethmann at once submitted his resignation, since he would not take the responsibility for such a policy (March 1912). Jäckh, Kiderlen-Wächter, II, 158 ff.

57. G. P., VII, 1563; article on "Mobilisation" in Grande Encyclopédie.

58. Fay, The Origins of the World War, II, 454.

59. Monypenny and Buckle, Disraeli, II, 1134 ff.; G. P., II, 373, 375, 392.

60. For these, see Corwin, Total War and the Constitution.

61. Ollivier, L'Empire libéral, X, 30 f.

62. According to later French and Russian statements, Germany called up considerable numbers of reservists during the "war in sight" crisis of 1875, thus "practically" mobilizing. I have found no confirmation of this in German sources.

63. Helmreich, Diplomacy of the Balkan Wars, p. 462; G. P., XXXIV, 12621.

64. G. P., XXXIV, 12667.

65. For the problem in general, see Kautsky, Sozialisten und Krieg.

66. Paléologue, The Turning Point, pp. 114, 128, 146.

67. Ibid., p. 240.

68. Franke, Handbuch der neuzeitlichen Wehrwissenschaften, I, 734 ff.

69. The texts are to be found in Trial of the Major War Criminals, XXX, 59 ff.; cf. Görlitz, Der deutsche Generalstab, p. 423.

70. Theodor von Bernhardi in a lecture of 1867. Aus dem Leben Theodor von Bernhardi's, III, 439. Bernhardi was the military author closest to Moltke at the time.

71. December 12, 1850. Guichen, Les grandes questions européennes, II, 50.

72. Görlitz, Der deutsche Generalstab, pp. 96 f.

73. Trochu, Oeuvres posthumes, II, 191 f.

74. Bapst, Le Maréchal Canrobert, II, 86 ff.

75. Count Buol, the foreign minister, admitted to the Russian ambassador at the outset of the conflict that, considering the onerous conditions under which Austria obtained her loans, she was on the way to bankruptcy. And still, Austrian policy stuck to its fatal course of ruining the Empire in the pursuit of her Balkan "mission." The Russian found "the situation here most singular and inexplicable, even for those who see the inside of the cards. The Emperor says all the time there will be no war; the whole Army trembles at the thought of a struggle with us, and all propertied people think the same way, and still, in spite of everything, Buol directs things straight into war while always saying there will be no war" (May 28, 1854). Hoetzsch, Meyendorff, III, 169 f.

76. Bapst, Le Maréchal Canrobert, III, 216 ff.; de La Gorce, Histoire du Second Empire, III, 4 ff.

77. The principal author of this was Francis Joseph's aide-de-camp general, Count Gruenne,

who, behind the back of the ministry, caused the Emperor to present Piedmont with the ultimatum by which Austria incurred the odium of the aggressor, which Cavour was so eager to pin on her.

78. Aus dem Leben Theodor von Bernhardi's, III, 244.

79. Eyck, Bismarck, I, 329.

80. This is based on Die auswärtige Politik Preussens, 1858-1871, Vol. 1, notably pp. 256, 276 ff., 284, 318, 345, 371, 390, 401, 405 f., 412 f., 506 f., 551, 653, 655 f., 658, 668, 788.

81. Ziekursch, Politische Geschichte des neuen deutschen Kaiserreichs, I, 34.

82. Valentin, Geschichte der deutschen Revolution, II, 275 f., 472.

83. Prussian War Minister von Bonin, before 1858. Ziekursch, Politische Geschichte des neuen deutschen Kaiserreichs, I, 176 f.

84. "250,000 men can be in the field against Austria within six weeks, whereas our State, quite apart from its bad financial situation, would need three months for the same demonstration of strength." Srbik (ed.), Quellen zur deutschen Politik Oesterreichs, V¹, 219 f.

85. Bismarck, Gesammelte Werke, V, 399.

86. Srbik (ed.), Quellen zur deutschen Politik Oesterreichs, V¹, 347.

87. Ibid., V¹, 374, 383, 395, 402, 411, 446, 452, 466 f.

88. Ibid., V¹, 448, 441.

89. Ibid., V¹, 495, 498 f.

90. Ibid., V¹, 534, 543, 547, 552 f.

91. Ibid., V¹, 585, 609.

92. von der Goltz, Volk in Waffen, pp. 166 f.

93. Blumenthal, Tagebücher, p. 10.

94. Beust, Mémoires, I, 290.

95. Ziekursch, Politische Geschichte des neuen deutschen Kaiserreichs, I, 168 f.

96. Ollivier, L'Empire libéral, XIV, 500 f.

97. Ibid., XIV, 160.

98. Ibid., XIV, 190.

99. Oncken, Rheinpolitik, III, 403.

100. At one time, General Leboeuf, the war minister, promised that "in a fortnight we shall have an army of 415,000 men," at another that 250,000 men would be ready to strike in a fortnight with another 50,000 eight to ten days later, and, at still another moment, speaking to the Emperor, that 350,000 men would be marching within a fortnight. Ollivier, L'Empire libéral, XIV, 98; de La Gorce, Histoire du Second Empire, VI, 226 f. Oncken, Rheinpolitik, III, 403.

101. Lebrun, Souvenirs militaires, pp. 116 ff.

102. Ollivier, L'Empire libéral, XIV, 219 f.

103. Ibid., XIV, 194 f.

104. Oncken, Rheinpolitik, III, 427 f.

105. Ollivier, L'Empire libéral, XIV, 285 ff. On July 18, after the die had been cast, the Duc de Gramont told the Danish minister: "We are ten or eleven days ahead of the Prussians in the matter of military preparations; we would have had even more of a headstart if it had been possible for us to draw out the negotiations as we wished. Unfortunately, there came that insult from the King of Prussia which has necessarily resulted in a prompt cessation of all discussions." Oncken, Rheinpolitik, III, 456 f.

106. Bismarck, Gedanken und Erinnerungen, end of chap. xxii.

107. Ollivier, L'Empire libéral, XIV, 358 ff.

108. Ibid., XIV, 366.

109. Ibid., XIV, 400, 420.

110. Ibid., XIV, 451, 624.

111. Ibid., XIV, 447.

112. The general commanding the Marseilles military district wired the War Ministry: "9,000 reservists here; don't know where to put them. To gain breathing space shall send them all to Algiers on the transports available in port." von der Goltz, Volk in Waffen, p. 164.

113. de La Gorce, Histoire du Second Empire, VI, 325 ff.

114. Lehmann, Die Mobilmachung von 1870-71, (Bearbeitet im Kriegsministerium).

115. Waters, "Private and Personal", pp. 240 f.

116. Haldane, Before the War, pp. 21 ff. For a German military report of British mobilization in 1905-06, see G. P., XXI, 6946; also, Kluke, Heeresaufbau and Heerespolitik Englands, pp. 112 ff.

117. Arnold-Forster, The Army in 1906, p. 394.

118. Doc. dipl. fr., 1st series, VI, 84.

119. Emory Upton, one of the young generals of the Civil War, wrote from Berlin in 1876: "When Germany fought France, she put her army on a war-footing in eight days, and in eight days more she had 400,000 men on French territory. It took us from April 1861 to March 1862 to form an army of the same size at an expense of nearly $880 millions. We cannot maintain a great army in peace but we can provide a scheme for offering a large force in time of war, and such a scheme is deserving of study." Michie, Life and Letters of Emory Upton, pp. 386 f.

120. Vagts, Landing Operations, pp. 496 f.

121. Monypenny and Buckle, Disraeli, II, 973 f.

122. January 27, 1888. G. P., VI, 1176.

123. Doc. dipl. fr., 1st series, VIII, 286.

124. Grand Duke Vladimir to Herbert Bismarck, December 1, 1888. G. P., VI, 1355.

125. Doc. dipl. fr., 1st series, VII, 432.

126. G. P., VI, 1186.

127. Doc. dipl. fr., 1st series, VIII, 580.
128. This is based on Glaise-Horstenau, Franz Joseph's Weggefährte, a biography of Beck. See also Cramon, Unser oesterreichisch-ungarischer Bundesgenosse, pp. 9 f.
129. May 1891. Langer, Imperialism, I, p. 34.
130. Doc. dipl. fr., 1st series, VIII, 378.
131. Ibid., IX, 655. Cf. above, p. 380.
132. Ibid., IX, 661 f.
133. Ibid., IX, 680 f.
134. Ibid., X, 10 ff., 16.
135. 1901. Ibid., 2nd series, I, 145 f.
136. Ibid., XI, 787 f.
137. Stieve, Schriftwechsel Iswolskis, I, 138; III, 273.
138. Doc. dipl. fr., 3rd series, II, 86 ff.
139. Suchomlinow, Erinnerungen, p. 265.
140. Report of French military attaché in St. Petersburg, July 16, 1892. Doc. dipl. fr., 1st series, IX, 599.
141. G. P., XV, 4276 ff.; A. D. White, Autobiography, II, 265.
142. G. P., XV, 4330.
143. Ibid., XXIII, 7963.
144. Ibid., XXXIX, 15707; Bailey, Diplomatic History, pp. 593 f.
145. Lloyd George, War Memoirs, I, 40.
146. Waldersee, Denkwürdigkeiten, II, 420. For a German military view of 1907 that mobilization was tantamount to a declaration of war, see Unger, Blücher, I, 263.
147. Geyr, Erinnerungen eines Militärattachés, p. 138.
148. Doc. dipl. fr., 1st series, IV, 32. For the problem in general, see Florinsky, "The Russian Mobilization of 1914," Political Science Quarterly, XLII, 203 ff., with a reply by Wegerer, Ibid., XLIII, 201 ff. And cf. above, p. 380.
149. D. D., I, 219.
150. Frantz, Russlands Eintritt in den Weltkrieg, p. 236.
151. D. D., I, 271.
152. Ibid., I, 138, 213, 257.
153. Fay, The Origins of the World War, II, 351 ff., with map.
154. D. D., II, 293.
155. Ibid., I, 230, 242.
156. Oesterreich-Ungarns Aussenpolitik, VIII, 10758.
157. D. D., II, 290, 339; Fay, The Origins of the World War, II, 386.
158. Benckendorff to Sazonov, July 25. Grey's proposal to halt the various mobilizations, except the Russian and the Austrian, "would in his opinion be a way of feeling Germany's pulse...I believe he expects little effectiveness to come from the method he has devised. He doubts—as he has admitted to me in all
confidence—that Germany will give up the advantages of the speed of her mobilization." Die internationalen Beziehungen, 1st series, IV, 52.
159. Doc. dipl. fr., 3rd series, XI, 89.
160. Dated July 26, received July 29. D. D., II, 376.
161. July 28. Ibid., II, 281, 299.
162. Ibid., II, 341 f.
163. Ibid., II, 343.
164. Ibid., II, 349.
165. Dobrorolski, Die Mobilmachung der russischen Armee, p. 23.
166. Paléologue, An Ambassador's Memoirs, I, 40.
167. Fay, The Origins of the World War, II, 452 f.
168. D. D., II, 370.
169. Cf. Paléologue, An Ambassador's Memoirs, I, 41 f. Paléologue said to Sazonov on the 29th: "The die is cast as far as Berlin and Vienna are concerned. It's London we must think of now. I ask you not to resort to any military measures on the German front and even to be very cautious on the Austrian front, until Germany has definitely shown her hand. The least imprudence on your part will cost us England's help." Sazonov: "That is my opinion, too, but our General Staff is getting restless and even now I am having great difficulty with them."
170. B. D., XI, No. 276.
171. D. D., II, 365.
172. Diplomatische Aktenstücke zur Vorgeschichte des Krieges 1914, III, 19.
173. D. D., II, 342, 378.
174. Die internationalen Beziehungen, 1st series, IV, 161 f.
175. Livre noir, II, 289; B. D., XI, No. 300. Sazonov gave Paléologue and Buchanan his own version of his last conversation with Pourtalès, to whom he had said, he maintained, that Germany was "being animated by desire of gaining time to complete her military preparations." Such preparations, he told the uncritical allies, were already being made against Russia, notably in the direction of the Gulf of Finland. B. D., XI, No. 302. This seems sheer invention.
176. D. D., II, 359.
177. Fay, The Origins of the World War, II, 465 f.
178. July 30, p.m. D. D., II, 445.
179. Ibid., II, 401, 412.
180. Doc. dipl. fr., 3rd series, XI, 261 f.
181. Ibid, XI, 271 f.
182. Dobrorolski, Die Mobilmachung der russischen Armee, p. 28.
183. Danilov, La Russie dans la guerre mondiale, pp. 42 f.
184. Schilling's Diary, p. 65. Cf. Paléologue's version: "Your Majesty and the Government

will have done everything to spare the world this terrible visitation. But now I feel certain that diplomacy has finished its work. We must henceforth think of the safety of the Empire. If your Majesty stops our preliminary mobilization, all you will do is to dislocate our military organization and disconcert our allies. The war will break out just the same—at Germany's appointed time—and will catch us in hopeless confusion." Paléologue, An Ambassador's Memoirs, I, 45.

185. Schilling's Diary, pp. 64 ff.
186. Dobrorolski, Die Mobilmachung der russischen Armee, pp. 9 f.
187. See the discussion in Fay, The Origins of the World War, II, 480.
188. Doc. dipl. fr., 3rd series, XI, 431 f.
189. Ibid., XI, 432; Fay, The Origins of the World War, II, 476.
190. Messimy, Mes souvenirs, pp. 181 ff.; Fay, The Origins of the World War, II, 484 f.
191. Die internationalen Beziehungen, 1st series, IV, 202, 204.
192. Doc. dipl. fr., 3rd series, XI, 287.
193. Ibid., XI, 271 f.; B. D., XI, 201 f. Bertie to Grey on July 30: "The French, instead of putting pressure on the Russian Government to moderate their zeal, expect us to give the Germans to understand that we mean fighting if war breaks out. If we give an assurance of armed assistance to France and Russia now, Russia would become more exacting and France would follow in her wake." B. D., XI, 203.
194. Doc. dipl. fr., 3rd series, XI, 379.
195. B. D., XI, No. 101.
196. Fay, The Origins of the World War, II, 493.
197. Nicolson to Buchanan, July 28, 1914. B. D., XI, No. 239.
198. Churchill, "The Mobilization of the Navy," chap. x of The World Crisis.
199. D. D., III, 372, 524, etc.
200. Ibid., II, 288.
201. Ludwig, Juli 14, pp. 117, 123; Bloch, "Les Socialistes allemands pendant la crise de juillet 1914," Revue d'histoire de la guerre mondiale, October 1933.
202. Doc. dipl. fr., 3rd series, XI, 482.
203. Bloch, Les causes de la guerre mondiale, chap. xiv.
204. D. D., II, 349.
205. Report of Bavarian Military Plenipotentiary, July 29, 1914. Dirr, Bayerische Dokumente zum Kriegsausbruch, p. 221. How far the Moltke-Bethmann conflict was real is uncertain. See Berliner Monatshefte, V, 1107 ff. The French ambassador in Berlin was told by another ambassador, probably the Italian, who had it from the Undersecretary of State in the Wilhelmstrasse, that "the military authorities pressed hard that mobilization be decreed because backwardness would deprive Germany of some of her advantages. However, up to now, it had been possible to combat the haste on the part of the General Staff which in mobilization sees war" (July 30). Doc. dipl. fr., 3rd series, XI, 287.
206. D. D., II, 456.
207. According to a telegram of the German ambassador, dated July 29, Viviani "did not deny military measures of precaution, but emphasized small extent and discreet execution. They were a long way from mobilization. He would not find it disquieting if we should do the same. However, measures on our part would be regrettable on account of alarming effect on public opinion." Ibid., II, 367.
208. Ibid., II, 361, 391.
209. Fay, The Origins of the World War, II, 503.
210. Conrad believed that there was "even for the great war the possibility of a victorious outcome." Conrad, Aus meiner Dienstzeit, IV, 121.
211. Kautsky, Sozialisten und Krieg, p. 438.
212. D. D., II, 390, 399, 407, 441.
213. Particularly outstanding in this respect are the endeavors of the French: the two Cambons—Doc. dipl. fr., 3rd series, XI, 287, 301, 523; and Poincaré—B. D., XI, No. 403.
214. Conrad, Aus meiner Dienstzeit, IV, 151 f. See also Schaefer, "Generaloberst von Moltke in den Tagen vor der Mobilmachung und seine Einwirkung auf Oesterreich-Ungarn," Berliner Monatshefte, IV, 514 ff.
215. Conrad, Aus meiner Dienstzeit, IV, 152; for complete text, see above, p. 406
216. When Conrad, before learning of the Russian mobilization, had believed he would see the war against Serbia through safely, Moltke begged him not to divert strong forces from the main struggle against Russia by a Serbian side-show. Austria's main force was needed against Russia "because the German rear covering forces are inadequate against a decisive Russian advance...Is Austria going to leave us in the lurch?" See Schaefer in Berliner Monatshefte, IV, 540 f.
217. Conrad, Aus meiner Dienstzeit, IV, 153.
218. D. D., II, 473.
219. Ibid., II, 479.
220. Doc. dipl. fr., 3rd series, XI, 335 f.; Fay, The Origins of the World War, II, 531.
221. D. D., III, 488, 490, 529.
222. Ibid., III, 535 f.
223. Berliner Monatshefte, IV, 836.
224. Livre noir, II, 294; Messimy, Mes souvenirs, pp. 186 f. Already on the 28th Joffre had expressed to Ignatiev "full and spirited readi-

ness loyally to fulfill the duties under the alliance." Die internationalen Beziehungen, 1st series, IV, 229; V, 140.

225. Doc. dipl. fr., 3rd series, XI, 386 f., 419, 427 f.; B. D., XI, 252.

226. Doc. dipl. fr., 3rd series, XI, 410, 412, 419.

227. Doc. dipl. fr. gives 3:55 (XI, 410), B. D. gives 3:40 (XI, 425) and Fay 3:45 (II, 533) or an hour later by Central European time.

228. Tirpitz, Erinnerungen, pp. 241 f.

229. Bülow, Denkwürdigkeiten, III, 168.

230. Kautsky, Sozialisten und Krieg, p. 427.

231. B. D., XI, No. 367. This passage was suppressed in the British Blue Book of 1914.

232. Ibid., XI, No. 368 f. For Nicolson, an unconfirmed report of Germany's violation of French soil on August 1 "clearly constituted her the aggressor...We should mobilize today [the 2nd] so that our expeditionary force may be on its way during next week. Should we waver now we shall rue the day later." Ibid., Nos. 446, 473.

233. Cf. the commentary by one of Moltke's assistants, General von Kuhl: "The terrible days of the end of July 1914 were grave for the Great General Staff. Announcement of mobilization signified world war, which one did not want to unleash under any conditions as long as it could be somehow avoided. But each postponement in the proclamation of our mobilization would bring us into a disadvantageous situation as compared with our enemies, which could not be repaired. The heavy responsibility of fixing the exact moment when the military necessity would arise to give the order for mobilization was incumbent on the Great General Staff." Kuhl, Der deutsche Generalstab, p. 119.

234. Moltke, Erinnerungen und Briefe, pp. 19 ff.

235. In October 1916, after the close of the bloody Somme battles, Grey proposed that the questions as to whether the original Russian mobilization should be considered aggressive and as to whether any Power other than Germany had planned to attack through Belgium be put before an impartial tribunal. This was never done. For details, see Mowat, Diplomacy and Peace, pp. 34 f.

236. D. D., III, 596; B. D., XI, No. 419.

237. Cited by Ludwig in Juli 14, p. 187.

238. August 5, 1914. Paléologue, An Ambassador's Memoirs, I, 61 f.

239. Messimy, Mes souvenirs, pp. 179 ff.

240. Trial of the Major War Criminals, X, 488; XVII, 628; XX, 602; Görlitz, Der deutsche Generalstab, pp. 375 ff., 390; Westphal, Heer in Fesseln, p. 59.

241. See, e.g., Trial of the Major War Criminals, XXXIV, 471 ff.

242. See, e.g., Army and Navy Journal, December 5, 1925, for the 1920's. The later General Warlimont, one of the Wehrmacht specialists on industrial mobilization, studied American preparation on the spot in the late 1920's. Görlitz, Der deutsche Generalstab, p. 375.

243. Gamelin, Servir, II, 199, 205.

244. Ibid., III, 2 f.

245. Ibid., II, 199; Jodl before the Nuremberg Tribunal, Trial of the Major War Criminals, XV, 347.

246. Paul-Boncour, Entre deux guerres, II, chap. vi. A convenient law text may be found in Europäische Gespräche, V (1927), 299 ff.

247. Pertinax, Les Fossoyeurs, I, 147 ff.

248. When Italy invaded Ethiopia in 1935, the following order of mobilization went out from Addis Ababa: "All men from fourteen to eighty report, bringing weapons. Married men bring wives to cook and work. Single men bring any convenient woman. Men found at home will be shot." Corwin, Total War and the Constitution, p. 5.

249. For discussions about mobilization for total war, see Bley, Moderne Heere—Moderne Waffen, pp. 52 ff.; Farago, The Axis Grand Strategy, pp. 47 ff.

250. April 9, 1942. Hitler's Tischgespräche, p. 272. In his aggression against Ethiopia, Mussolini avoided as long as possible pronouncing the term "mobilization." When the Ethiopians pronounced it first, de Bono, the leader of the enterprise, was much relieved: "From now on, no one can say any more that we have not been provoked." De Bono, Das Jahr XIV, p. 67.

251. Pertinax, Les Fossoyeurs, I, 9 f.; Gamelin, Servir, II, 129 ff.

252. Trial of the Major War Criminals, XV, 347 f. The protocols of the interministerial discussions on mobilization plans are in Ibid., XXXVI, 381 ff.; XXVII, 389 ff.

253. Ibid., XXXVI, 463.

254. Ibid., XXXII, 409 ff.; XIV, 296.

255. Gamelin, Servir, II, 199 ff., 218.

256. Testimony of Manstein and Jodl at Nuremberg. Trial of the Major War Criminals, XX, 602 f.; XV, 357; Görlitz, Der deutsche Generalstab, pp. 434 f.; Westphal, Heer in Fesseln, pp. 67 ff.

257. Study by the Chief of the OKW, April 19, 1938, on organization problems in war. Trial of the Major War Criminals, XXXVIII, 50.

258. Ibid., XXXIV, 477 ff.

259. Shortly after the Anschluss, Premier Léon Blum suggested that France imitate Hitler's action in Austria and force Franco to dismiss all foreign military help at once by an ultimatum and the threat of French intervention. The Army informed him that although separate

mobilization for the Northeast (Germany) and Southeast (Italy), as well as for North Africa, had been prepared, this was not the case for the Southwest (Spain). Gamelin, Servir, II, 325.

260. Trial of the Major War Criminals, X, 504; XV, 604 ff.; XXVIII, 371. For the military interna of the Anschluss, see Heusinger, Befehl im Widerstreit, pp. 26 ff.

261. At the time of the Anschluss, the Czechs had carefully abstained from mobilizing, though rumors had circulated that they were, which alarmed the Germans. Prague accepted Goering's assurances that it was altogether a family affair and that, on his word of honor, Czechoslovakia had nothing to fear from the Reich, provided she did not mobilize. Wheeler-Bennett, Munich, pp. 25 f.

262. Gamelin, Servir, II, 315 ff.

263. Ibid., II, 322 ff.

264. Trial of the Major War Criminals, XXV, 402 ff.; Görlitz, Der deutsche Generalstab, pp. 467 ff.

265. Trial of the Major War Criminals, XXV, 445 ff.

266. Ibid., XXVIII, 379 ff.

267. Ibid., XV, 357. For a pro-Czech version, see Wheeler-Bennett, Munich, pp. 55 ff. No German mobilization or large-scale military movements had actually taken place. See report of British military attaché in Berlin. Documents on British Foreign Policy, 3rd series, I, 358.

268. Europäische Politik im Spiegel der Prager Akten, pp. 106 ff.

269. Werth, The Twilight of France, p. 176.

270. Gamelin, Servir, II, 334 f.

271. According to Jodl's diary, Hitler had decided, on April 21, 1938, "not yet to touch the Czech problem. This intention is being changed by the Czech concentration of May 21 which takes place without any threat on Germany's part and even without any apparent motivation. Due to Germany's keeping quiet, this results in a loss of the Führer's prestige which he is not willing to suffer for a second time. Hence on May 30 the new directive for 'Green.'" Trial of the Major War Criminals, XXVIII, 372.

272. Ibid., XV, 360 f.

273. Reports of Czech ministers in Paris and London, September 14 and 20, 1938. Europäische Politik im Spiegel der Prager Akten, pp. 122, 124; Lockhart, Comes the Reckoning, p. 17; Feiling, Chamberlain, p. 356.

274. Europäische Politik im Spiegel der Prager Akten, pp. 122 ff.

275. When Hitler took the Czechs under his "protectorate," he sent the Italians "word that he acted because the Czechs would not demobilize their military forces, because they were continuing to keep their contacts with Russia, and because they mistreated Germans. Such pretexts may be good for Goebbels' propaganda, but they should not use them when talking with us." Ciano, Diaries, p. 43.

276. Pertinax, Les Fossoyeurs, I, 10.

277. Gamelin, Servir, I, 23; II, 341 ff.; Feiling, Chamberlain, chap. xxviii.

278. According to Wheeler-Bennett, the First Lord of the Admiralty, Duff Cooper, tired of waiting and delay, gave the order for the Fleet mobilization on his own authority, which was two hours later endorsed by Chamberlain. Wheeler-Bennett, Munich, p. 168.

279. Lockhart, Comes the Reckoning, pp. 10 f.

280. Documents on German Foreign Policy, Series D, IV, 602 ff.

281. Secretary for War Hore-Belisha in House of Commons, March 8, 1939.

282. Gamelin, Servir, I, 389 ff.

283. Memorandum of British Embassy, Berlin, April 20, 1939. Zweites Weissbuch der Deutschen Regierung, No. 251.

284. Gamelin, Servir, I, 391 ff.

285. Documents on German Foreign Policy, Series D, IV, 99 ff., 186.

286. Daladier in the Chambre, March 19, 1939.

287. German report from Warsaw, August 1, 1939, Zweites Weissbuch, No. 444.

288. March 26, 1939. Ibid., No. 208; Namier, Diplomatic Prelude, pp. 97 ff.

289. Zweites Weissbuch, No. 211.

290. Namier, Diplomatic Prelude, pp. 349 ff.

291. General Anders speaks also of an American démarche in favor of postponing general mobilization in An Army in Exile, p. 2.

292. Hitler's Reichstag speech on September 1, 1939.

293. Gamelin, Servir, III, 46. This overlooks the fact that Poland was dictatorially governed for all military purposes.

294. Trial of the Major War Criminals, XXXIV, 380 ff., 428 ff. (for the Navy).

295. French reports from Berlin, June 27 to July 25, 1939. Namier, Diplomatic Prelude, p. 235.

296. Zweites Weissbuch, No. 440.

297. Namier, Diplomatic Prelude, p. 270.

298. The French had called up one class of reservists before mid-July, equivalent to seventy-five battalions of infantry; Spanish refugees were formed into units to perform military labors, etc. Gamelin, Servir, II, 442. On August 22, the British Cabinet, taking note of the German-Russian pact

and certain military movements inside Germany, resolved to assemble Parliament and submit to it an Emergency Powers (Defense) Bill, giving the Government new powers to meet the situation. Certain Army, Navy and RAF personnel, as well as personnel of the Air Protection and Civilian Defense services, were called up, embargoes put on certain raw materials, etc. Zweites Weissbuch, No. 453.

299. August 22, 1939. Görlitz, Der deutsche Generalstab, p. 499.

300. Namier, Diplomatic Prelude, pp. 290 ff.; Gamelin, Servir, I, 23 f., 35.

301. Zweites Weissbuch, Nos. 454 ff.; Schuman, Night Over Europe, pp. 302 ff.

302. Trial of the Major War Criminals, XXVIII, 390.

303. Ibid., XXX, 263, 280.

304. Ibid., X, 271, 514; XXXIV, 678; Görlitz, Der deutsche Generalstab, pp. 500 f.

305. Trial of the Major War Criminals, X, 515; Namier, Diplomatic Prelude, pp. 318 ff.

306. Trial of the Major War Criminals, XXXIV, 456 ff., 678; Namier, Diplomatic Prelude, p. 379.

307. Schuman, Night over Europe, p. 343; Zweites Weissbuch, No. 466, omits Henderson's retort.

308. Schuman, Night over Europe, pp. 343 ff.; Zweites Weissbuch, No. 466.

309. For details, see Namier, Diplomatic Prelude, pp. 314 ff.

310. Zweites Weissbuch, No. 472.

311. Gamelin, Servir, I, 24, 36 f.

312. Nazi-Soviet Relations, 1939-1941, pp. 90 ff.

313. Ibid., pp. 331, 342.

314. The Greek White Book (1942), p. 51.

315. Ibid., pp. 90 f.

316. Japan had mobilized parts of her land and sea forces successively over the past years. The final mobilization of the forces to be unleashed in December 1941 was completed by mid-August.

317. Nazi-Soviet Relations, p. 230.

318. Ibid., p. 346.

319. "What we are able or not able to do within the first sixty days of another war will be decisive in its determination of our ability to carry the war to a successful conclusion." Eisenhower's final report as Chief of Staff to the Secretary of the Army, February 17, 1948.

320. For criticism, see Hanson Baldwin in N. Y. Times, August 25, 1950.

321. Mobilization Planning and National Security (1950-1960), Senate Document No. 204, I, 18.

322. In October 1950, Secretary of Defense Marshall set up a committee of civilians and soldiers to study and make recommendations as to the problems "involved in using reserves to carry out the long-range build-up of the armed forces that will continue even after victory in Korea." It was said that he was disturbed by "evidence that the outdated reserve rolls were not a true index of reserve maneuver." N. Y. Times, October 27 and 28, 1950.

323. Mobilization Planning and National Security, pp. 50 ff.

324. E.g., Senator Lodge's vain attempts—until the end of 1950—to move Congress to authorize the military employment of anti-Communist aliens by the U. S.

General Staffs and Foreign Offices in Time of War[1]

With the change from peace to war, general staffs and their chiefs (though not quite as regularly) become the executors of their own peace-time plans. Before 1939, the director of plans was not often denied the actual supreme command in the field. In Russia in 1914, the Grand Duke Nikolai, commander of the St. Petersburg military district, was made supreme commander of the field armies, but this was due to dynastic considerations. Elsewhere—in France (Joffre in 1914), in Austria (Conrad in 1914), in Germany (the two Moltkes, in 1870 and 1914)—the chiefs of staff assumed direct command, assisted by their general staffs. The general staff might split into a staff for the field army and one for the home army, or else the staff as a whole would remain in remote control. The second arrangement was preferred in Washington in 1917 and again in 1941. The majority of foreign ministers have likewise remained in office during war, sometimes lasting as long as the army commanders, sometimes outlasting them. Their duration in office has often reflected their war-time success.

It has often been claimed by military commanders, their staffs, and their partisans that, once war has been declared, the toga has to cede to the military uniform, that political considerations must not be allowed to interfere with strategy, that commanders must not be disturbed in the execution of their plans by the demands or desires of the civilian governors, including diplomats, lest victory be endangered. "Politics must not be allowed to interfere with operations," as Moltke put it. His seemingly selfless authority exercised a dangerous influence not only inside the Second Reich but also beyond, down to MacArthur in Korea from 1950 to 1951.[2] Moltke conceded that policy must have a decisive influence on the beginning and ending of war. However, strategy "must be completely independent in its action" from policy for the duration of the war. Strategy must always strive for the highest aim obtainable by the means at its disposal, leaving it to policy to raise its demands in accordance with military successes, or to deflate them in accordance with military reversals.[3] Stalemate or defeat was not even theoretically envisaged.

It was in deference to this view that the Great Power governments of 1914 sent their armed forces into the war, that French War Minister Messimy gave Joffre, generalissimo of the armies of the Republic, "absolute liberty of action for the execution of his plans."[4] This liberty had to be curtailed when it was seen that victory would not be immediately forthcoming. When the civilian governors had to intervene, the always painful problem arose: how to replace the field commander who, though not defeated outright, still proved unable to deliver victory? The problem is a recurrent one. Governments shrink from recalling generals because that may seem like admitting defeat, to their own peoples or to the enemy. They shrink from seeming to interfere with the conductor of operations who will maintain, before and after his relief, that victory was near and would have been achieved if only he had not been interfered with, if only his government had followed his suggestions.

Schism and conflict between the political and the military appeared as soon as the complexity of governing had forced a division of labor upon the governors. The schism was difficult to bridge by unity of policy and strategy in time of peace, and still more difficult in time of war. This disunity could sometimes be avoided by combining the direction of war and policy, as was done by Gustavus Adolphus, Cromwell, Richelieu, Frederick II, Napoleon I, and Hitler. Whether the results were happy or unhappy, their example produced an historical mirage that has more often misled than guided later generations.

While absolute governors make short shrift of unsuccessful generals, the problem of their removal has long plagued democratic governments.[5] But only the British seem to have drawn practical and general conclusions from their experience.[6] They curtail the imperium of the field commander from the outset. American officers in World War II expected maximum freedom and discretionary power for the field commander in the exercise of his command. During the arrangements for setting up a joint supreme command for Operation "Overlord," Churchill bluntly told them:

> In practice it is found not sufficient for a Government to give a General a directive to beat the enemy and wait to see what happens...The General may well be below the level of his task ...A definite measure of guidance and control is required from the Staffs and from high Government authorities. It would not be in accordance with the British view that any such element should be ruled out.[7]

Given the increased independence granted to commanders in time of war, they have usually been willing to concede with Clausewitz that the subordination of political viewpoints to the military is preposterous, for it is policy that has produced the war. It furnishes the sense; war merely the instrument, and not vice versa. The only thing possible, therefore, remains the ranking of the military point of view below the political one.

Some practical regard has been paid to the political situation in most modern wars.[8] Wellington, for example, was a general who was fully aware, even without a reminder from his government, that the commander in a local theater must keep in mind the exigencies and political considerations involved in such a complicated war as was being fought by the widespread coalition against Napoleon in 1813-14.[9]

Insubordination in relation to policy has, however, grown inordinately during the century since Clausewitz. In practice far more than in theory, the elder Moltke showed himself increasingly deaf to the war-time considerations put forth by the director of policy. He stood halfway between Clausewitz and Ludendorff. The latter came to claim that "all policy has to serve the war," both practically and theoretically.[10]

In the United States, Lincoln replaced field commanders wholesale, even if reluctantly. Since his day, American generals have been left with wide powers, if only because of their luck, and MacArthur exercised them in Korea as Far Eastern theater commander. He could not produce victory in a war that seemed unlikely to result in victory, and his procedures and suggestions interfered with the cautious steps forced upon his Government. His stubborn and publicly-expressed ignoring of Washington's wish to give this war a merely local character led to the General's recall, under conditions that seemed unprecedented to him and to many of his countrymen.[11]

In his Tactical-Strategical Essays, the elder Moltke conceded that strategy must serve the purposes of policy, but must remain completely independent from it in its own action. On another occasion, he expressed regret that military action could not always be independent of policy. Bismarck's insistence upon the absolute supremacy of political considerations and of the political direction, even in time of war, had taught him at least that much. The lesson, however, did not stick with such successors as Waldersee and Ludendorff, who demanded that, in war, the whole of politics must serve the purposes of war as directed by the military. Such a demand comes close to "war for war's sake" which Foch, considering his democratic employers, was always careful to forswear.

Such militaristic velleities easily arose where the policy-makers were weak in character or weak because of the structure of government and politics. During the night of August 2, 1914, the German Chancellor informed the military men—Moltke, Falkenhayn, Tirpitz—that war seemed inevitable. Their first reaction was to complain among themselves about the inadequacy of the Reich's political direction. "Moltke opined that he must now take the political direction in hand." He wrote what Tirpitz called "a political recipe for the Foreign Office," a prescription which should be filled by the political pharmacists. It included the suggestion that Turkey be brought into the war on Germany's side as soon as possible, and eventually Sweden, Norway, Bulgaria, and Persia as well. It suggested stirring up insurrections in various British-controlled regions—in case Britain were to join Germany's enemies. Japan was to be invited to use the favorable occasion, while Russia had her hands full in Europe, to help herself to all she aspired for in the Far East. Italy, which the General had by no means written off, must be made to clarify her stand on her obligations under the Triple Alliance.[12] Neither the naïveté nor the obviousness of most of these suggestions nor the fact that Moltke failed to win the Marne battle shook the high authority given him and his successors.

Due to the civilian governors' increasing ignorance of military things, or their lack of self-confidence, they have been inclined to grant vast wartime powers to military men and at times to concede to the latter more knowledge of the war to come than has in the end proved justified. The surrender of such powers to military commanders in time of war has often presented great dangers to the governments granting them. Generals might turn against their political superiors, might in extreme cases not only disobey but also betray and overthrow them. Hence the need for war-time controls over the military, such as the supervision of the condottieri in Renaissance Italy, some of whom were put to death by their employers on the mere shadow of suspicion.[13] Other controllers of the generals were the Dutch Field Deputies during the Ludovican wars, the revolutionary emissaries with the French armies of the 1790's, the political commissar in the Red Army and in the Reichsheer from 1944 on. The dangers from the fronde inside the French army under Louis XIII were so great that Richelieu felt that he must himself conduct the siege of La Rochelle (1628) and the campaign in Savoy (1629). As Ranke judged him later: "It was not a case of vanity for Richelieu to keep the supreme command of the army in his hands; the situation was so dubious and difficult that political and strategic leadership had to be combined in each case. The direction of military movements had to be at the same time the secret of the highest statesman," whatever the soldiers might say about the command being exercised by a prelate. The King's first minister could not entrust the King's army to commanders such as Montmorency, who pursued his own political ideas until he ended on the block.[14]

ROLE OF CONSTITUTIONAL COMMANDERS-IN-CHIEF

The preferred constitutional solution of conflicts between policy-makers and strategists has been to make the monarch or elected head of state the arbitrator between them. In Britain, the military commanders have usually been the trusted men of the cabinet, such as Marlborough until the fall of the Whigs (1711), and Wellington; no king has gone to the field since George II and Dettingen (1743). In some great wars of modern times—notably the Wars of Liberation and the wars of 1859, 1866, and 1870-71—various monarchical commanders-in-chief have accompanied the army supreme command, as have some of the most important ministers. Clausewitz, still under the impact of the experience of the Wars of Liberation, when the monarchs and ministers had followed the armies closely, advised that

if war is to correspond completely with the intentions of policy, there remains, unless statesman and soldier are united in one person, only one good remedy: to make the foremost general a member of the cabinet in order to have the latter participate in the main moments of his action. This again is only possible if the cabinet, that is to say, the government, finds itself in the neighborhood of the scene of action so that things can be settled without perceptible loss of time.

William I, Bismarck, and War Minister Roon followed the wars of 1866 and 1870-71, as well as the not less important one of 1864, in GHQ, formed part of GHQ, and resided where it resided. So did Napoleon III in 1859, and in 1870, until Sedan. And he frightened the generals stuck before Sebastopol with the threat that he might come out there. Francis Joseph stayed away from the wars, which his armies lost, except the one in 1859, when he was on hand to directly conclude a preliminary peace with Napoleon. Tsar Alexander II returned from the war of 1877-78 after a short stay in the Balkans, whereas his grandson stayed continually in GHQ from September 1915 on. The American Civil War took place so close to Washington that Lincoln was almost within the camp of the main army fighting in Virginia.

There was much that was deceptive in the arrangements for a GHQ with the commander-in-chief and the heads of government forming part of it. William I, for example, exercised his authority over generals and ministers only reluctantly, under the strong thumb of Bismarck. Still, as written up by monarchist historiography, the arrangement was considered a part of the recipe of victory inherited from 1870-71.[15] It was resumed in 1914 when William II, the Chancellor, and the War Minister again formed part of GHQ.[16] But the monarch's authority proved far below even the minimum advised by his ancestor, Frederick the Great, who had written (in his Anti-Machiavell):

The task of defending the State is so highly responsible that the Prince ought to entrust it only to himself; and duty no less than interest requires him to venture his own person...However, not everyone is born to be a general...Still, the presence of the prince in the camp will serve to lend the orders of an efficient general the emphasis of the highest authority. In doing so, the prince only serves one of his duties: maintaining discipline, order and subordination within the army.

In William II's time, the monarch's active role in the German GHQ was at an end and his political function as mediator and umpire in the conflicts between military and civilian offices nearly at an end before the war had begun.

The seeming successfulness of the institution in the earlier German wars had given it at least one sincere imitator—Japan since the Meiji era. There, in time of war, the supreme military command was concentrated in the Senji Daihonei, Imperial Headquarters, although the Emperors did not actually proceed to the theaters of war. This arrangement served to ward off civilian interference.[17] The Emperor was to "exercise personal command," which boiled down to such arrangements as the "immediacy" position of the Army and the Navy Chiefs of Staff under him. He served as a most precious paravent for the ascendency of the military, sanctioning their self-will and independence of action, particularly in the later stages of Japanese imperialism. Surprisingly, enough life remained in the institution of the Emperor to help bring on the armistice negotiations against the wilder wishes of the military to resist to an even more bitter end.[18]

For the most part, Mussolini stayed away from Fascism's wars. Hitler was away from home most of the time, but was also very careful to avoid the vicinity of the war fronts. He escaped from the realities of both fronts to his GHQ. There he surrounded himself with two groups of aides, one composed of Party members, among whom the Imperial Pictorial Reporter (Reichsbildberichterstatter) ranked easily as high as Ribbentrop or any other Foreign Office representative, and the other composed of soldiers, forming the Führer's military staff.[19]

FOREIGN OFFICE REPRESENTATIVES IN THE FIELD

In a number of modern wars, foreign offices have had their representatives with the armies in the field. In 1866 and 1870, the Wilhelmstrasse placed young and adroit diplomats, such as Radowitz and Count Harry Arnim, as observers with Prince Frederick Charles of Prussia, one of the most headstrong army commanders. This was ostensibly done in order to give advice to the Prince and his staff on matters concerning the international law of war. During the First World War, the Wilhelmstrasse maintained a special representative in GHQ and another in the entourage of the Kaiser, who resided in GHQ most of the time. A military section in the Foreign Office for purposes of liaison was set up in the summer of 1916, headed by one of the most politically astute members of the Great General Staff, Colonel von Haeften.[20]

The Russian foreign ministry had a diplomatic bureau in GHQ from 1914 on. Its directors became highly critical of the military and their conduct of the war. The Japanese Foreign Ministry sent one of its highest officials along on the Siberian expedition of 1918-19, which the Army had wanted more than the diplomats, in order to take charge of the diplomatic end of the expedition.[21] The first Ballhausplatz representative with the Kaiserlich und Königlich Armeeoberkommando was Baron Giesl, minister to Belgrade until the end of July 1914 and military attaché prior to that. His antecedents were still not sufficient to keep him on good terms with Conrad, who considered him "the secret agent of the Foreign Ministry for purposes of direct reporting, a kind of detective bureau for supervising the AOK." His instructions charged him with "reporting regularly on the general political situation and explaining the most essential military events and occurrences." They also specified that he should be kept informed of the political situation and should in turn inform the AOK. He was to be heard by the AOK on "all questions of international law, notably those which concern the exercise of powers in possibly occupied enemy territory." Giesl's reports, written and oral, reached Vienna much more promptly than Conrad's own. This was especially true in August and September 1914, when Austrian successes were rare. And his reports were far more elaborate than those of the AOK. In fact, the Emperor used to say: "Tomorrow comes Giesl; and then we shall hear the truth." This infuriated Conrad, who obtained the imperial order that Giesl was no longer to report on such things as "operative intentions," about which he could learn only through "illegal channels," but was to restrict his reporting to what had already happened. "Should Giesl with his diplomatic aides still continue in such reporting, I shall

remove him," Conrad threatened from GHQ. He admitted, however, that his own reports had perhaps been overly scant and overly discreet, quite in contrast to his peace-time verbosity. He promised the Emperor to reform, but he remained utterly reticent in his relations with the Ballhausplatz and other governmental departments in Vienna and Budapest.

Giesl lasted only until January 1915, when Conrad obtained his removal on the usual military pretence that, due to his activity, operative secrets were being endangered. Actually he did so in order to rid himself "of undesirable advice and other influences" which had become particularly pressing during the opening of the Serbian campaign in 1914 and during the Russian attack on the Carpathian front in 1914-15. On the former occasion, ancient animosity against the Serbs had misled the Foreign Ministry into an over-emphasis on this particular theater of war.[22] The Ballhausplatz was "consumed with impatience for a military success, which, however, due to the low efficiency of the railways in Southern Hungary and Bosnia, naturally kept them waiting." For the diplomats, "a considerable setback at the hands of little Serbia was undoubtedly far more fatal than a defeat at the hands of overpowering Tsardom. It would undermine the prestige of Austria-Hungary in the eyes of all the world, and particularly in the Balkans where a success was so much needed in order to gain allies." Under such political considerations, more Austrian forces were entrusted to a political general in the opening campaign against Serbia than was justified by the supreme concern for the main theater of war.[23] This was the most erroneous and perhaps the most direct example of the continuation of "policy with other means."[24]

BISMARCK AND THE FIELD COMMANDERS

Both the American Civil War and the German wars from 1864 to 1871 were not only wars of union and reunion; they were also (as is not usually realized) wars in which the supremacy of civilian considerations over military arguments became assured.

Bismarck had his first experiences and first conflicts with military field commanders during the Danish war. He, as well as the King, had remained in the capital until nearly the end of the campaign. (The Prussian Government as well as the Austrian had diplomats as civilian commissars with the allied Army in Schleswig-Holstein.) For reasons of rank, the supreme command had been entrusted to Field Marshal von Wrangel, suppressor of the 1848 Revolution in Berlin, but a mere child in politics and now an octogenarian. Unaffected by Bismarck's subtle diplomacy, he submitted his own views on the complicated question of the Duchies to the King early in the war: "The soldier with the sword in his hand ought not to pursue politics; still, trusting to Your Majesty's graciousness, I dare to submit my views on the European political situation." His advice, completely contrary to Bismarck's intentions, was for the two allied governments to recognize and proclaim the hereditary prince of Augustenburg as sovereign in the Duchies. Such an action, Wrangel thought, would paralyze the German Bund and the small German states "in their revolutionary policy. The democratic party, which is undermining the whole of Germany ...would then shrivel up." The two great German Powers would then dominate the situation, and a strengthened Germany would be able to sustain any war with either France or Britain. "Only in the strict observation of this policy," he concluded, "can be found the salvation of Germany and, more especially, of our own dear Fatherland." He received his answer from Bismarck, who reminded the Field Marshal that it had been arranged with Austria that the succession in the Duchies must not be prejudiced by any action or demonstration, and that the military authorities must not tolerate any such action, by whomsoever attempted.[25]

As the victorious armies approached the frontiers of Jutland, or Denmark proper, the Austrians, through their civilian representative in Wrangel's headquarters, proposed that the line not be crossed for the time being, in order not to provoke intervention on the part of the European Powers. Rather brusquely, Wrangel's chief of staff asked the diplomats to omit all such communications, which he considered to be non-avenu. "For us and for our operations," he added (with Wrangel's full approval), "only military considerations and necessities can be determinative." The next day (February 15), Wrangel received telegraphic orders from the King, signed by the War Minister, that the frontier must not be crossed until further orders. Although he did not share the Austrian fear of European complications, Bismarck supported the suggestion of stopping at the frontier for the sake of the war coalition. In spite of the royal orders, Wrangel's advance guards nevertheless crossed the forbidden line three days later. "Military necessity" on this occasion was even more spurious than on others. As the Wilhelmstrasse ascertained, Wrangel and his staff had never even informed the vanguard of the royal order. He later explained that earlier orders for these troops had never authorized them to undertake such an advance. As for ordering these forward troops back to German soil, "military necessity" would not allow that. In order to captivate the King and make him side against the diplomats who wanted his removal, Wrangel telegraphed that "to recall the Prussians from their career of victory is quite impossible for me, for the curse of the Fatherland would strike even my grandchildren. The diplomats may counsel such a thing, but they may be sure that their names

will be affixed to the gallows." And couldn't he expect to soon receive the King's orders to advance still farther North?

In Berlin, Bismarck stressed to the King how imperative it was to remain in close understanding with Austria, who was hesitant about a further offensive. He suspected that Wrangel had somehow learned that it was intended to replace him and that the old general, thus repaying the King's indulgence, was preparing a resounding exit, making himself popular with the Army and the people by publicly pretending that his retirement was due to wicked diplomacy. In order to avert such theatrics, the Prime Minister proposed that he be called to Berlin for consultation about further operations, while at the same time temporarily suspending all operations. "The old gentleman's strong language and the open refusal to obey makes me fear that he may commit some dangerous arbitrary action" unless removed from the scene in Schleswig. Afraid of hurting Army sentiment, the King, while admitting to Bismarck that Wrangel's language was unbecoming, would not call him away from Schleswig and merely repeated his earlier orders not to advance until further notice. Meanwhile, the diplomats in Wrangel's headquarters were having a fairly unpleasant time, being told to reside anywhere except at headquarters, "where there is nothing for the gentlemen of diplomacy to do."

Actually there would have been work to do, if Wrangel had only accepted diplomatic advice when he took it upon himself to send a direct communication to the Swedish Government and King, in connection with Swedish volunteers serving in the Danish Army. This direct action, Bismarck informed the Field Marshal, was "not in conformity with the policy pursued by the Royal Government under the King's own orders. I know from Your Excellency's own communications that your views on foreign affairs do not conform throughout with my own. I may add that my own opinion as to how the war on the Cimmerian Peninsula ought to be made does not always agree with what is being done under Your Excellency's orders. Still, I shall never permit myself to send military orders to one of the officers under Your Excellency's command." Should not Wrangel likewise refrain from interfering with business not his own?

In order to keep the Austrian ally in good humor and to re-cement some of the porcelain that the old cuirassier was breaking, Bismarck sent one of Prussia's diplomat-generals to Vienna on a special mission. He was to tell the timid Austrians that the ill-will of Europe need not greatly be feared and that the pride of the two armies, which naturally could show itself only in time of war, must also be respected. Their disregard of the frontier line here and there, which Bismarck regretted the more since it had taken place contrary to orders, "only showed how difficult it is to appreciate from a military standpoint the weight of such delicate measures."

As a proven friend of the Army, Bismarck understood only too well that, after nearly fifty years of peace, its officers were eager for action, anxious to win laurels, to shed blood in order to refurbish the lustre of Prussian arms and to outdo the temporary ally. Still, he found it necessary to have Wrangel, who was sending cavalry patrols farther into Jutland, reprimanded by the War Minister for having again acted "contrary to the very concise royal orders, on the exact observation of which the Ministry of Foreign Affairs bases its statements to foreign cabinets...Under these circumstances," the Minister continued, "and in order to direct our foreign affairs safely and without the appearance of ambiguity, I must consider it absolutely imperative that the renewal of such steps be prevented by resolute measures." These express orders still did not put an end to Wrangel's self-willed interference with Bismarck's fine-spun diplomacy. Bismarck at last obtained his recall during the armistice in May. His military ineptitude, playing havoc with Moltke's ideas for this "experimental war," had become as obvious as his political elephant steps in the china shop of diplomacy.[26] Only years later was there a reconciliation, in the interest of harmony within the Prussian ruling stratum, when Wrangel somewhat shame-facedly approached Bismarck with these words: "My son, canst thou forget ever?"—"How should I start forgetting what I have gone through?"—"Canst thou forgive?"—"With all my heart." They shook hands and were friends again, as in old times when they had fought together in the 1848 Revolution.[27]

The Prussian Army, anxious to wipe off "the shame of Olmütz," found a new self-confidence in 1864. The propensity toward annexations, starting with the Duchies, was constantly on the increase and gave Bismarck much trouble, even when he shared in this propensity. Membership in the same ruling class, by birth and from conviction, at times made it harder rather than easier to keep the militarism of Prussian Junkerdom under control. While the victorious Army would have preferred to carry the war of 1866 to a triumphant conclusion, it still accepted the quick peace and safety that Bismarck snatched from the triple nettle of war, possible French intervention, and Army ultraism. Army acquiescence went even somewhat beyond Bismarck's expectations. This may help to explain his later tales, which in part at least are Phantasiestücke, about the violent resistance on the part of the Army to his diplomacy of July-August 1866, the "tensions" between him and the General Staff, and the battling with generals who could not get enough of war and annexations.[28]

Bismarck's conflicts with the military were those of the prime minister who was also foreign minister. Conflict became more genuine and truly serious during the war of 1870-71. The military treated him badly as to quarters and military information. They allowed him no part in the composition of the daily communiqués, which was, after all, a politicum. The "demi-gods" of the Great General Staff, Moltke's aides, denied him information about intended operations. They pretended that such super-secrets were not well enough preserved by one who wrote everything home to his wife. In her salon, they said, their secrets would be divulged to Russian and British diplomats and thereafter handed on to the French. The motivation was childish, the intention clear: even the highest official of Prussia and Germany was to be excluded from knowing about and possibly influencing future operations. The secret of operations was not to be shared by the statesman. Highly irritated by this military hubris, Bismarck threatened that he, heretofore disposed to do everything for the military, would join the advocates of parliamentary government in the future and would take his seat on the extreme left if the soldiers continued to make trouble for him.[29] He voiced his complaints everywhere. But this was simply proof for the proud generals that having risen "to such heights, he finds it quite unbearable to be forced to play a secondary role here"(in headquarters). "That others...are able to achieve something and that there are things which another man understands better than he, for a change, seems to him an unjustified presumption...The policy of the Chancellor is no concern of ours."[30]

The conflicts, open and latent, between Bismarck and the General Staff, extending now to Moltke, came to focus finally on the question of bombarding Paris. For diplomatic and political reasons—in order to cut short the time during which highly unwelcome neutral intervention might be offered and to discourage the French from undertaking further armaments—Bismarck wanted to have the bombardment started as early as possible. "As it is," he thought, "the Parisians imagine that we are forbidden to open fire by London, St. Petersburg, and Vienna; while on the other hand, the neutral Powers believe that we are not able to do so. The true reason, however, will be known at a future time. One of its consequences will be to lead to a restriction of personal rule."[31] The last allusion was to the Chancellor's dissatisfaction with the Supreme Warlord's lack of concern for political considerations at this juncture. Unfortunately for Germany, this dissatisfaction with the Supreme Warlord did not find expression in the constitution for the new Reich.

Bismarck's demands for an early bombardment of Paris appeared "ensign-like" to the General Staff, and his offering of military advice to soldiers sheer presumption. It was "a shame that such a politician should have more influence than an army leader," Manteuffel grumbled.[32] And Moltke himself thought that a strong fortress city like Paris should first be invested and if possible forced into surrender by hunger, that hunger might even take effect before the artillery attack. Consequently, the Army command was in no hurry; after Bismarck had obtained the Royal order that the bombardment was to start, it did less than it could have done to accelerate the transport of necessary siege artillery and ammunition. Hunger actually had greater effect than the artillery bombardment, (though it took longer than the soldiers had expected), forcing the surrender, after some sorties had failed, on January 26, 1871. However, as we now know, the actual danger of neutral intervention was never very great. Beust was quite right when he lamented: "Je ne vois pas l'Europe."

Before the surrender had been secured, the conflict between Bismarck and the generals assumed dangerous dimensions.[33] The Crown Prince, seeing that his father was unable to cope with this problem, tried to mediate in the interest of country and dynasty. He was not immediately successful. As one of the almost-Liberal officers at GHQ described the situation that had developed between Bismarck and Moltke:

> Their basic dissimilarity has set them apart; they stand in sharp opposition, and only with great endeavor is it possible to keep business going at all. Moltke is the man of stately quietude, Bismarck the passionate politician, the former coolly contemplating the matter, the latter always firmly attacking the persons concerned. The fight has even broken out inside the General Staff, because Bismarck knows how to bribe and govern people. King and Crown Prince are very unhappy about this conflict, but have no means of settling it.[34]

King William was less than fully qualified to coordinate his powerful servants and dissolve the impermissible conflict of policy and strategy, to make them understand that the military chief must consider political requirements and that the political chief must consider what is militarily possible. The capitulation of Paris, traditionally the concern of the military, was largely arranged by Bismarck. The preliminary peace brought about some reconciliation, perhaps more than was good for the peace that was to follow, for Bismarck now began to listen to the generals' advice and strategic reasoning about peace conditions.[35]

It was high time for Bismarck to move: the military simply did not know how or whether to end the war they were making.[36] Early in January 1871, the Crown Prince asked Moltke what he was planning to do once Paris had fallen. Moltke answered to the effect that the war would be carried on with the newly available troops and would be pushed into the South of France in order to lay hands on the remaining resources of the French Republicans. "We must fight this nation of liars to the last and finally bring it down."

Crown Prince: "And then?"
Moltke: "Then we must dictate the peace as we want it."
Crown Prince: "And if we ourselves are bled white?"
Moltke: "That will not happen, and even if it should, we shall have won the peace fighting."
Crown Prince: "If, however, all these combinations do not harmonize with the foreign policy situation and the latter forces us to act differently?"
Moltke: "Well, then a new situation arises and we must make our operations suit these."
Crown Prince: "But do you know what the present political situation is and whether it is politically advisable to proceed in accordance with your suggestions?"
Moltke: "No, for I have to concern myself only with military things, and if His Majesty orders differently, I shall arrange my proposals in accordance with that."
Crown Prince: "If it were a matter of a few army corps only, I should be able to share your view, but since it is a matter concerning the whole German Army, it is imperative for you to try to keep in contact with the political intentions of the Government of the King in order to adapt your own propositions to these. It appears to me therefore urgently necessary—first, that you inform the Chancellor of all decisive operations, second, that already at this time all eventualities that may arise, once Paris has fallen, be discussed...."
Moltke: "Count Bismarck wants to be informed about the military measures, and that does not go—for I cannot inform him about what is to happen before it is decided, and even then the secret must be preserved. Besides, this is none of Count Bismarck's business, and he only wants to interfere everywhere and give orders. He thinks that by my own orders I want to interfere with his prerogatives."
Crown Prince: "But all that is not sufficient reason to leave such a serious task as the settlement of a war undiscussed; your responsibility for not shirking such a duty is as great as Count Bismarck's."

The Crown Prince then offered to serve as a mediator between the two. "For, don't be angry with me, things cannot and must not remain in this state. We must try to come to an agreement on what to do with

Paris, once it opens its gates, and on what we want or can undertake afterwards, and then submit joint proposals to the King." Moltke, who had tried to cut the inquisition short almost from the outset, finally broke it off with a dry "At your orders."[37]

William I was unhappily caught midway between the achievers of military success, who wanted a "war of extermination," and the political empire-maker, who now wanted peace. He at last broke the impasse by establishing Bismarck's—and every reasonable political leader's—claim to political supremacy. Without hearing Moltke again, he gave out two cabinet orders (January 25, 1871). In the first, he "repeated his expectation" that the General Staff would "communicate as soon as possible any information of importance to the Chancellor in order to keep him constantly informed about the larger war operations." In the second, he ordered that, before entering upon any correspondence with members of the French Government, the decision of the monarch was to be obtained as to whether or not this ought to be made the subject of discussions with the Minister of Foreign Affairs. After composing an irate remonstration involving his resignation and the suggestion that Bismarck might as well take over the military direction of the war, Moltke thought better. He swallowed the order and let Bismarck enter upon negotiations with Jules Favre, the French emissary. The negotiations soon proceeded from the military business of capitulation and armistice, cut short by Bismarck, to the preliminaries of a peace, "without paying any more respect to General Moltke and the General Staff."[38] Nothing can so much emphasize his superior talents for peace-making than a comparison with the slowness of peace-making after 1918 and 1945.

CONFLICTS IN RUSSIAN HEADQUARTERS, 1877-78

Bismarck owed his triumph over the military to his greater influence over the Emperor-King and to his constant presence in the GHQ. How such conflicts between opposing groups within the ruling class develop and are settled less fortunately was demonstrated in the Russian camp during the war of 1877-78. There, a military party—which included the War Minister Miljutin (whose ascendency over Gortchakov had already begun), the Chief of Staff Obrutchev, generals such as Gurko and Skobelev and General Count N. Ignatiev (ambassador to Constantinople before the war)—was in conflict with the diplomatic party, formed by Gortchakov, Shuvalov (the ambassador to London), and Grand Duke Nikolai, commander of the Balkan Army and brother of the Tsar, for whose soul both parties were contending. The scene of the clash was divided between St. Petersburg, where the Tsar had

returned after a sojourn with the troops, and the GHQ located at Adrianople. Ignatiev arrived at Adrianople in February 1878 with instructions from the Tsar. They contained no clear order to advance on Constantinople, as the Grand Duke read them and explained to Ignatiev. Nevertheless Ignatiev tried to push him on, despite the poor condition of the Russian Army and the danger of open conflict with Britain. "God forbid! Look here," exclaimed the Grand Duke. "Are you going to saddle us with another war with England? It's time to stop all military operations and go home." Ignatiev replied that the best way of avoiding complications was "to take account of the strategic considerations and pay no attention whatever to warnings and wishes coming from London, or even from our Foreign Minister." Unmoved, the Grand Duke proceeded to conclude an armistice with the Turk, even though (as Ignatiev discovered) he had been in possession of a telegram from the Tsar at the time, "inviting" him to resume his advance in the direction of Constantinople. Ignatiev urged him to denounce the armistice and resume action, but the fact that there were still no "orders" from St. Petersburg and that rather disturbing information had been received from Gortchakov and Shuvalov made any further advance seem inadvisable to the Grand Duke.

While British and Austrian diplomatic resistance was stiffening and a British squadron appeared at the Dardanelles, an order to resume the offensive against Constantinople arrived from St. Petersburg. It resulted only in half-measures, including the occupation, with Turkish agreement, of San Stefano, described as a suburb of Constantinople in the dispatches to Alexander II. The Grand Duke ignored suggestions from the capital that, in view of the "almost inevitable rupture with Britain," the shore of the Bosporus be occupied and other measures taken to anticipate the arrival of a British landing force. He pointed out all the difficulties and asked for "definite orders" as to whether or not the Turkish capital was to be occupied. As the representative of the war party, Ignatiev tried to drive him on and make him accept the wishes of the War Minister. Nikolai's staff in turn pointed out the threat posed to the Russian rear lines by the British squadron, which by now had steamed through the Dardanelles, and by Austria, which could easily disrupt the far-extended land communications. "You are out of your head," the Grand Duke told Ignatiev. "You absolutely want to drag us into a new war with England. That's what your designs are leading to." The image of the Hagia Sofia, conjured up by Ignatiev, made no impression, nor did his information from inside Constantinople that the Turks were completely exhausted and ready to let the Russians march in.

In the end, Ignatiev engineered the breaking of

the armistice and the dictated peace of San Stefano. He found that "the desire of headquarters to end the alarms and privations of war as soon as possible and to rest on their Turkish laurels in their own country" was an extraordinary hindrance in his final negotiations, "the more so as those surrounding the Grand Duke, and even His Highness himself, found our demands to the Turks excessive and advised their reduction." This was something that the Berlin Congress was to do, thus arousing the deep resentment of the Russian Army and the Pan-Slavs. While Miljutin and his party obtained the recall of Nikolai, their opponents in turn had Ignatiev removed and shelved in the hour of his triumph.[39] Such are the ways of harmonizing the conflict between strategy and imperialism under an autocracy, under a supposedly strong monarchy. Actually, the monarchy was no stronger than the difference of strength between the two strongest groups "serving it."

FIELD COMMANDERS AND FOREIGN OFFICES IN WORLD WAR I

A fairly common war-time disagreement between policy-makers and strategists, increasing in incidence and violence as war became global, was that relating to the choice of the main theater of war. The choice is still more perplexing to war coalitions. Whether the military preferences as to Enemy Number One are always purely strategic, in the sense of being supra-political, may well be doubted, but once they are fixed, the investment of forces becomes far more inflexible than many capital investments. Little or absolutely nothing is left to spare for the maintenance or opening of promising side-shows. For this reason, war-time proposals originating in diplomatic calculation for the use of even relatively small forces have usually run up against unbending military resistance, more often than not based on sound military grounds.

One of the most embarrassing problems confronting Russian war imperialism in 1915 was the conquest of the Straits. Should the Western allies be allowed to win it without the cooperation of even a Russian token force? Might not Constantinople in such a case be denied to Russia forever? After operations at the Western exit of the Straits had started, Isvolski suggested from Paris that Russia prepare to play the preponderant role in the occupation of Constantinople. The Stavka regretted the absence of Russian forces. However, their absence was inevitable, partly because such forces were not available, partly because operations undertaken at the Dardanelles were so much more promising than those that might be attempted at the Bosporus. "Besides, the relative number of Allied forces employed can in no case serve as the basis for later territorial acquisition, since the operations against

the Dardanelles form only a partial operation within the framework of the World War. The distribution must be in conformance with the vital interest for which the Allies are battling." And Russia had done and was doing so much in the common cause—elsewhere.

But the thought that Russian forces were not participating in the struggle for Constantinople rankled in Russian hearts, even during the summer of 1915 that was so disastrous to Russian arms. It was arranged that a token force of 4,500 men be brought by the British from the Far East in order to participate in the fight in the Dardanelles. Late in June, Quartermaster Danilov told the representative of the Foreign Ministry in GHQ that

as a Russian, he could not suffer the thought that no Russian troops would be present at the entry into Constantinople. And if our detachment should make trouble for the British, who simply did not wish to have them by their side when marching into Constantinople, that need not bother anyone. That is a political question and not a military one. As to that, the supreme commander, the Chief of Staff and myself feel the same way. Should Sazonov want to take it upon himself to make it clear to all Russia that one must suffer to have Constantinople taken without any participation of our troops, that is his business. But we soldiers do not want to be accused of having been unable to spare even 4,000 men for this operation.

Both the diplomat and the soldier were filled with the sense of "Russia's historic mission"; both would have liked to conquer Constantinople with Russian forces alone, something the British would not have opposed at that time. "But," wrote the diplomat, "since it is impossible to give satisfaction to this feeling, we find ourselves at variance. While Danilov is reconciled to the idea of our 'symbolic' participation, I personally find it rather unpleasant to let Russia play the role of the fly in the fable, sitting on the horns of the oxen and saying: I have also ploughed. I should have preferred not to have our troops participate after all."[40] The token force did not appear on the scene until after the liquidation of the Dardanelles enterprise had taken place.

The Foreign Ministry wanted military implementation in still another sector of Pan-Slavism. At its demand, another token force departed in the direction of the Straits: Russian troops were to fight side by side with the Serbs. While the Stavka considered such Slav brotherhood-in-arms desirable in itself, it could not make troops available in any considerable numbers. It was regrettable, they said, that Isvolski and the Finance Minister had started negotiations with the Serbs in this matter, which was decidedly not within their competency. Only continued begging on the part of the Serbs induced the Supreme Commander to send a brigade of second-line troops and a cossack regiment to their theater of war "exclusively for the purpose of moral encouragement." More was not available, due to the shortage of rifles rather than of manpower.[41]

Several of the commanders of the First World War were more imperialistic than the diplomats, more so than proved good for their strategy. The worst sinner was Ludendorff, who kept nearly one million men to guard the proposed annexations in the East at the time of his offensives in the West. He was the military repudiator of the "outdated" ideas of Clausewitz, especially the idea that policy, notably foreign policy, must be ranked before war itself. As the Moltke of the Second World War, the executor of Bernhardi's rather than of Clausewitz's ideas, he made war as total as he could in his time.[42] With the arrival of total war, wrote Ludendorff, "the essence of war has changed, the essence of policy has changed; hence the reaction of policy to the conduct of war must also change. All of Clausewitz's ideas are to be turned upside down. War and policy serve the preservation of the people's life, but war is the highest expression of the folkish (völkisch) will to life. Hence policy has to serve the conduct of war."[43]

Political control inside the Second Reich was weak, from the Kaiser and the Chancellors down.[44] Ludendorff became "the unchained general," backed by the gerontocratic make-believe authority of Hindenburg, driven by a ruthless energy as well as by the colonels of the General Staff.[45] He interfered with nearly all branches of government and administration, making and unmaking chancellors and foreign secretaries, a veritable war dictator. Those in the Reich who had most to lose by this undermining of its old structure—men like Rupprecht, the Bavarian Crown Prince, or Prince Max von Baden, or Secretary of State Kühlmann, son of a Baghdad Railway director—naturally became most concerned about this fatal role. "Ludendorff must be absolutely restricted to his military field," Rupprecht wrote his father in July 1917, when he was an army leader in the field. "He must not be allowed to interfere in questions of domestic and foreign policy; quite apart from other disadvantages, the direction of military operations is suffering from that." Ludendorff was "a man of will, but no coolly contemplating statesman." He tackled political problems for which he was not prepared. He did not perceive, as an harassed diplomat like Czernin would, that while the military situation of the Central Powers still did not seem unfavorable in August 1917, "war was in a race with the revolution," that a status quo was probably the best the Central Powers could obtain. But

to Ludendorff "Germany had lost the war if she made peace without gains."[46]

Diplomats had little influence over Ludendorff as long as there was still some hope for military victory. Although the original civilian members of GHQ, the Chancellor, and others returned from the field to Berlin and the pursuit of war-time home politics, representatives of the Wilhelmstrasse stayed behind as liaison officers. It was they who had to receive and transmit Ludendorff's insolences and annexationist demands to Berlin. Like all the diplomats in the Reich, they found themselves under the supervision of the OHL in their ciphered telegraphic communications.[47] The diplomats attempted to win over the Kaiser and make him tell the generals of the OHL "that, considering the continued great difficulties raised by the General Staff, one would in the future...call upon it only as far as purely military interests were concerned." The attempt failed. The Kaiser showed even less courage than his grandfather had shown in 1871. He listened instead to military denunciations of the pleasure-loving diplomats who, instead of ramming a victor's peace down the throats of the reluctant Rumanians, went duck-hunting.[48] Only after Ludendorff had realized that the game was up and the war lost did the diplomats in GHQ regain a modicum of usefulness —to transmit to Berlin, beginning on October 1, 1918, his urgent demands for an armistice.

The complete and prolonged subordination of political considerations to what was so readily admitted as "military necessity" made the loss of the war more ruinous to Germany, if it did not in fact make her lose the war.

At the same time, civilian-political superiority was never seriously questioned on the Entente side. It greatly helped to win the war. Many if not most of the soldiers on the Entente side, however, were not willing to admit that the war services of the civilians had been of positive value, least so in their influence on strategy. They pointed out such failures of civilian strategic initiative as the enterprises undertaken at the Dardanelles and at Salonika. The least initiative came from the several foreign offices. Considering the diversity of the final war aims, which engendered some distrust among the allies on both sides, the demands for the exercise of the specific talents required for successful coalition warfare were filled fairly satisfactorily in both camps. Both groups of the original belligerents were able to add some allies to their side as the war went on. The attempt of the German diplomats to keep such a powerful neutral as the United States out of the war was doomed to failure by (1) the low opinion of America's war potential entertained by German generals and admirals and (2) the military determination to use the very form of warfare that was bound to bring the United States into the war against them, submarine warfare.

The usual attempts made during wars of coalition to embroil the members of the opposing group, to detach one of them from the coalition, were made by both sides.[49] German agents negotiated with Russian agents in neutral Stockholm until the Central Powers' promise of future independence to the Poles (given in the vain hope of obtaining Polish army corps for the war against Russia) made the Russian reactionaries, who had favored the negotiations, give up all notions of a separate peace. Agents of the Entente met with those of war-weary Austria without German foreknowledge in order to seek a separate peace, until the OHL took the situation in hand and strengthened the German grip on Austria.

Ludendorff, rather than the several Chancellors and the Wilhelmstrasse, usurped the formulation of Germany's official war aims. They were annexationist in both East and West. They were to be achieved by unrestricted U-boat warfare and the 1918 offensives. By May 1918, even before the last of these had failed, Ludendorff found that "it was due to the maladroitness of our diplomats that they have not entered upon negotiations with our enemies as they ought to have done long ago." He completely forgot that the OHL had earlier vetoed all "peace offensives." Now the OHL could no longer believe in final victory. They did not, however, draw the necessary conclusions, nor did they allow anyone else to draw them and seek an armistice. As Prince Rupprecht wrote at the time: "It is ostrich policy which is being pursued amongst us."[50]

The OHL was unable to make peace. It could not attain the Pan-German victory peace (Siegfrieden) which it had promised and which was the only one it could imagine. Nor could it attain the peace of negotiation (Verständigungsfrieden). As long as the OHL still thought victory possible, it would not permit anyone to seek, and hardly even to discuss, a negotiated peace. When the OHL finally had to admit that the possibility of victory had disappeared, a negotiated peace was no longer possible. Peace after defeat was never even considered by Ludendorff. On the eve of the March 1918 offensive, when Prince Max von Baden, the later Chancellor, asked him what would happen if it did not succeed, the General answered: "In that case Germany must just go under."[51] She came close to that point in 1918, without yet reaching the zero point to which that other hasardeur, Hitler, was to reduce her. Ludendorff finally asked the civilians to obtain an armistice as quickly as possible.

WAR-TIME ECLIPSE OF DIPLOMACY, 1939 AND AFTER

As far as the Second World War was a reprise of the First, this was nowhere more the case than on Germany's part. Nothing had been learned, either from Bismarck's successes or from Ludendorff's disasters. Diplomacy was assigned only the most subordinate role in Hitler's scheme of war. In the summer of 1942, when Rommel stood at the gates of Egypt, Hitler told the representative of the Wilhelmstrasse that his office "must not presume to send a minister-resident to Alexandria or Cairo in case they should be occupied. They had a generalissimo there in the person of Rommel, who had covered himself with such undying glory that it would be absurd on the part of the Foreign Office to want to interfere with things."[52]

The example of the dictators as war leaders spread, necessarily or not, to practically all belligerents. The unity of policy and strategy was firmly established in the heads of state. By no means did this necessarily signify the triumph of political over military policy. In many countries, it resulted in extensive neglect of diplomacy in its best traditional functions and its degradation to handmaiden services such as spying.[53] In general, the role of the diplomat in total war has been limited to the role of servant of war. Ought he to be satisfied with this role? There runs throughout Secretary Hull's memoirs a muted complaint about the near-elimination of himself and his Department from most of the major political negotiations after the entry of the United States into the war—an exclusion only more disappointing to the Secretary after the role he had been made to play in bringing the Japanese to Pearl Harbor. This exclusion went far beyond the self-abdication that Hull himself had vowed immediately after Pearl Harbor. He told his associates "that the role of the State Department from now on [is] to contribute to the war effort," that he wanted everyone "to cooperate to the full with the War and Navy Departments and all war agencies, and to place at their disposal all our facilities." "For the duration," he would not hear any complaint from members of the Department that military or naval personnel were "doing something wrong." To his way of thinking, they were "the fellows who are taking responsibility for the strategy and conduct of the war. They have a right to our fullest cooperation." That they were accorded superiority rather than mere cooperation was made abundantly clear by Hull's exclusion, after Pearl Harbor, from Roosevelt's War Council, in the meetings of which he had participated rather fully prior to Pearl Harbor. Hull writes:

After Pearl Harbor I did not sit in on meetings concerned with military matters. This was because the President did not invite me to such meetings. I raised the question with him several times. It seemed manifest to me that, in numerous important instances, the Secretary of State should sit in on the President's war councils, particularly on those of a combined military and diplomatic nature, for it was obvious that scarcely any large-scale military operations could be undertaken that would not have diplomatic aspects. I feel it is a serious mistake for a Secretary of State not to be present at important military meetings.

But Roosevelt would not hear of it. He would not admit that Hull was, by comparison, far more completely shut out from international war-time negotiations than his British counter-part, Anthony Eden, or his Russian counter-part Molotov.[54]

Hull and his Department did not participate in many of the Roosevelt-directed war policies. They remained uninformed of some policies "which had widespread diplomatic repercussions," such as the dealings of the American generals with Darlan or the agreements entered upon by Roosevelt at Casablanca. When Hull asked Admiral Leahy for the latter, he was told "that no copy was available for us." Such by-passing was to hamper the State Department in subsequent negotiations. It again illustrated Hull's contention, "advanced to the President on many occasions, though unsuccessfully, that fundamental military decisions often [have] diplomatic angles and reflections" and that he should therefore know about them. In American war-time policy-making the civilian militarism of the President, with the "unconditional surrender" formula as its final expression, overruled the timid claims of diplomacy.[55]

The Department of State had no say in the development of the fatal new weapon, the atomic bomb, and little more say in its use. It does not appear that the State Department representative on the committee that was to advise War Secretary Stimson as to whether the bomb should be dropped on a Japanese city with or without "specific warning" raised any objections to its proposed use. Whatever the consequences, political and otherwise, the ultimate responsibility for the recommendation to the President that the bomb should be dropped without warning was shouldered by Stimson, who had in this the support of all his senior military advisers, with their "insistence on the shock value of the new weapon."[56]

To themselves and to the President the latter's intimate advisers justified the exclusion of the State Department in the same manner as had the "demi-gods" of the German GHQ in 1870-71, who had tried to have Bismarck excluded from all foreknowledge of operational plans. Both were declared to be "bad security risks," to use current American lingo. Sherwood has expressed this point of view clearly:

The archaic and disjointed machinery of the State Department and the Foreign Service [as compared with British and Russian arrangements] was woefully unable to cope with the requirements of a global war in which the United States had suddenly assumed the position of a pre-eminent world power. There was, for one thing, the essential question of security, since most important policy decisions were linked directly or indirectly with military plans, and the State Department machinery was full of leaks as well as creaks. That is why both Roosevelt and Hopkins sent all of their vital messages through military communications instead of through the regular diplomatic channels which would have kept the State Department and the various embassies and legations informed as to the progress of the correspondence.[57]

Total victory seems the logical outcome of total war to pseudo-logicians, and unconditional surrender its seal. It was in the logic of Hitler's warfare, and war-dictator Roosevelt could not be dissuaded from it.[58] Unconditional surrender is traditionally the demand of soldiers—and almost as traditionally it increases the bitterness with which the enemy reists.[59] By 1945, unconditional surrender was not demanded by either the Western diplomats or by the military, who had come to doubt its wisdom.[60] But it was upheld like a ghastly banner by Roosevelt and, when it sank from his hands, by Truman.[61] It was "accepted with alacrity" by the Soviet Union, "probably because a completely destroyed Germany would facilitate Russia's postwar expansion program."[62] It was part and parcel of the self-destruction of the Western world, calling in the Eastern in order to make it more complete. The disregard for diplomacy during the war, observable everywhere in the West, greatly contributed towards making the war a total one. The more or less complete annihilation of the enemy was a war aim that had not usually been among the war aims of an older diplomacy.

DIPLOMACY IN THE COLD WAR

The hope of the masses who clung to the formula of unconditional surrender—that it would end war far more finally than a negotiated surrender—was soon disappointed by the outbreak of the "cold war." Anglo-American policy had invited this warfare as much as Russo-Communist ideology had incited it, for Roosevelt and his captive, Churchill, had neglected—for the sake of smooth coalition, complete victory and utopian peace—precautions usually entrusted to the care of diplomacy. They were put aside, almost contemptuously by Roosevelt, who had always vaguely hoped that it would be possible to come to an understanding with Stalin.

The new enmity raised altogether new problems

regarding the cooperation of diplomacy with military staffs and commanders. Since the situation was largely conceived in strategic terms, diplomacy never regained its old supremacy and became instead the servant of the strategists in many respects, though never to the extent that an old-style commander like MacArthur in Korea expected. The situation characterized by the metaphor "cold war" added still further to the bewilderment of a military commander such as MacArthur: the various near-war conflicts occurring all over the globe only proved to him that open aggression had to be met with full force. He was entirely correct in his view that the conflict could scarcely be conceived on a larger and more absolute scale. How could the Western Governments, in the face of this, still adhere to their determination to fight only on the most restricted scale?[63] A dictum of Clausewitz brings out this dilemma: "The more magnificent and stronger the motives of war, the more they comprise the whole existence of the peoples involved, the more violent the tension which precedes war, the more closely will war approximate its abstract shape, the more its objects will be the destruction of the enemy, the more closely military aim and political purpose will coincide, and the more purely warlike, and the less political, war appears to be."[64] With a conflict of ideals approaching the intensity of a war of religion, the primacy of politics becomes increasingly difficult to maintain, in cold war as in hot war.

FOOTNOTES

1. For the broader aspects of civilian-military war-time relations, see Herring (ed.), Civil-Military Relations; Bourget, Gouvernement et Commandement; Moser, Die obersten Gewalten im Weltkrieg; most recently, (too late for extensive use), see Ritter, Staatskunst und Kriegshandwerk (1954).
2. "Die Politik darf sich in die Operationen nicht einmischen." Cited by Foertsch, Kriegskunst heute und morgen, pp. 27 f.
3. Kuhl, Der deutsche Generalstab, pp. 180 f. While Kuhl admits that these dicta are no longer valid in modern times, when political conditions, including home politics, can exercise their influence on operations, they must still stop short of influencing the choice of the military means for attaining the objectives set. This was written after the struggle over unrestricted U-boat warfare and before the discussions of the atomic bomb!
4. King, Generals and Politicians, p. 15.
5. For the interna of the removal of Soviet commanders in World War II, see Kalinow, Sowjetmarschälle haben das Wort, passim.

6. For Queen Victoria's protests against the civilian ministers' interference with quarreling and against ineffective generals in the field during the Boer War, when intervention from home was imperative and she herself was not above making suggestions as to the conduct of the campaign, see Newton, Lansdowne, pp. 178 ff.
7. Harrison, Cross-Channel Attack, pp. 108 f.
8. Contrast Japan. Following the Mukden incident of September 1931, the Japanese cabinet announced publicly that it would follow a policy of "non-aggravation," that orders in keeping with it had been dispatched to the Kwantung Army. Immediately thereafter, the military "Big Three"—the war minister, chief of staff and inspector-general of military education—met in order to discuss the scope of future military operations, stating (also publicly), as a result of their deliberations, that "the army need not consult the cabinet as to the measures to be taken to meet the exigencies of the future, but would leave it to the commander-in-chief of the Kwantung army to exercise his discretion." Following another military conference, it was announced that "the army agrees with the government in its policy of non-aggravation, but desires to point out that the non-aggravation of the situation does not necessarily mean the non-enlargement of military operations." While the civilians in the cabinet still struggled for their concept of non-aggravation, the Kwantung Army proceeded to strengthen the forces in Manchuria by troops from Korea, whose dispatch, by all other concepts, would aggravate the situation. Takeuchi, War and Diplomacy in the Japanese Empire, pp. 351 ff., 458, 467.
9. Cf. his letter of November 22, 1813, to Dumouriez, with whom he occasionally discussed military questions of a general nature: "Perhaps, if I regarded Spain only, or even if I looked at Spanish affairs merely under a military aspect, I should have gone there, for there is no doubt that Bonaparte sticks to Catalonia and keeps open the facilities for re-entering Spain. However, the purely military view must cede to the political, considering the hopeful successes in Germany." These made it far more important to the Allies, and even to Spain, that he should carry the war deeper into France rather than bother to start a campaign of besieging fortresses in Spain. Wellington, Dispatches, XI, 309.
10. Foertsch, Kriegskunst heute und morgen, pp. 24 ff.; Oncken, Politik und Kriegführung, p. 72.
11. Cf. Secretary Marshall's testimony before Senate Committee (May 7, 1951): The conflict with MacArthur arose "from the inherent difference between the position of a field commander, whose mission is limited to a particular area

and a particular antagonist, and the position of the Joint Chiefs of Staff, the Secretary of Defense, and the President, who are responsible for the total security of the U.S., and who, to achieve and maintain this security, must weigh our interests and objectives in one part of the globe with those in other areas of the world so as to attain the best over-all balance." Military Situation in the Far East, p. 325; see also p. 354.

12. Tirpitz, Ohnmachtspolitik, p. 221; D. D., III, 662.

13. Semerau, Die Condottieri, p. 12 and passim.

14. Ranke, Französische Geschichte, II, 416 f. and passim.

15. In 1891, one of Moltke's pupils, Max Jähns, thought "it not impossible that at one time the existence of the Central European world of peoples will be tied up with the existence of such a GHQ in which may converge the threads of the policy of diverse Great Powers and those of the strategy of several national armies." Jähns, Kriegswissenschaften, p. 2863. No arrangements for the unity of command were ever made between Berlin and Vienna. Early in the First World War, both high commands were in close geographical proximity, at Plessen and Teschen, but Emperor Charles removed the Austrian command to the vicinity of Vienna, marking the attempt at greater independence which resulted in the Sixtus episode. G. Conrad, Mein Leben mit Conrad von Hötzendorf, pp. 156 ff.

16. For the composition of the German GHQ in 1914 and later, see Cron, Die deutschen Heere im Weltkriege, pp. 4 f. The civilian officials, in addition to the Chancellor, were representatives of the Wilhelmstrasse, and the Chief of the Secret Civil Cabinet, i.e., the chief of civilian personnel. Not all remained for the duration of the war.

17. Takeuchi, War and Diplomacy in the Japanese Empire, pp. 16, 142, 456.

18. Kase, Journey to the "Missouri", pp. 234 f., 248, 252 f.

19. For a description of Hitler's GHQ as of the end of 1939, see Dietrich, Auf den Strassen des Sieges. For later times, see Hitlers Tischgespräche.

20. In addition, there was a representative of the Chancellor with the OHL and an OHL representative with the Chancellor. The latter was Colonel von Winterfeld, former military attaché in Paris. For details, see Max von Baden, Memoirs, I, 83 and passim; and Schwertfeger, Das Weltkriegsende, pp. 40 f.

21. Takeuchi, War and Diplomacy in the Japanese Empire, p. 78.

22. Giesl, Zwei Jahrzehnte im Nahen Orient, pp. 275 ff.; Conrad, Aus meiner Dienstzeit, IV, 248 ff., 485, 671, 693, and passim.

23. For details, see Oesterreichisches Ministerium für Heereswesen, Oesterreich-Ungarns letzter Krieg, I, 18 ff., 60, 95, 147, 155 f., 321 ff.

24. This also includes entrusting the war against Serbia to Potiorek. Since he had been Conrad's rival for the post of Chief of Staff, it seemed only fair to give him the second most important post and his own little war.

25. Die auswärtige Politik Preussens, 1858-1871, IV, 514.

26. This is based on Ibid., IV, 550, 546 f., 569 f., 573 f., 592 f., 547 f.; and Bismarck, Gesammelte Werke, IV, 328 f., 352 f., 432; XIV, 665 f.

27. Bismarck, Gedanken und Erinnerungen, I, 372.

28. This is based on Bethcke, Politische Generäle, pp. 4 ff., 66 ff.; Roloff, "Brünn und Nikolsburg," Historische Zeitschrift, Vol. 136 (1927); Bismarck, Gesammelte Werke, VII, 140, 234, 286.

29. Busch, Bismarck. Some Secret Pages, I, 324. Bismarck to Waldersee, November 16, 1870: "Why don't the military inform me of all that is important? In 1866 it was different. At that time I was called in on all discussions. And that is as it ought to be. My business demands that: for one thing, I must be informed about military events in order to conclude peace at the right time." Rehlen, Bismarck, p. 149.

30. Blumenthal, Tagebücher, p. 199; Foertsch, Kriegskunst, p. 28. Blumenthal was chief of staff of one of the armies.

31. November 28, 1870. Busch, Bismarck, I, 334.

32. Meyer, Bismarck, p. 431.

33. War Minister Roon was the notable exception; his office had taught him to think most politically of all.

34. January 24, 1871. Stosch, Denkwürdigkeiten, p. 227.

35. This is based on Busch, Das deutsche Grosse Hauptquartier; Blume, Die Beschiessung von Paris; Bethcke, Politische Generäle, pp. 12 ff.; Eyck, Bismarck, II, 516 f., 530 ff.; Schmitthenner, Politik und Kriegführung, pp. 266 ff.; Meyer, Bismarck, pp. 429 ff.

36. Waldersee wrote home in early February 1871: "As far as my desires are concerned, things could go on for a long time to come; but I do admit that enough blood has been shed, everything considered. The feeling, however, of seeing the moment approach when peace comes is in any case depressing. Soldier's life is after all most beautiful in the field." He had to admit that his own life had been particularly beautiful; he had hardly seen any fighting, no camping, had had full meals every day, no wounds and no sickness. Waldersee, Denkwürdigkeiten, I, 124, 164.

37. Oncken (ed.), Grossherzog Friedrich I von Baden, II, 300 ff. Kaiser Friedrich III, Das Kriegstagebuch von 1870-71, pp. 319, 325.

38. Haeften, "Bismarck und Moltke," Preussische Jahrbücher, Vol. 177 (July 1919).

39. This is based on Onou, "The Memoirs of Count N. Ignatiev," Slavonic Review, XI, 110 ff.

40. Die internationalen Beziehungen, 2nd series, VII, 477 ff.; VIII, 148.

41. February 1915. Ibid., 2nd series, VII, 134 f. The same dilemma, within the frame of reference of the Third International instead of Pan-Slavism, faced Lenin in the summer of 1920. While the Red Army was advancing on Warsaw, Bela Kun proposed to him that the revolution in Hungary be reopened by sending a number of Russian battalions there. The peasants and workers would join the intervening force and overthrow the Horthy Government. Lenin rejected the proposal, telling Kun that "his demand is too much. We have a first class war on with Poland, which is aided by the Entente; and besides, my people are tired." Lewis Corey in the New Leader, June 25, 1951.

42. According to Bernhardi, "the military demands superimpose upon the political ones... Diplomacy has no other task but to support the conduct of war as far as possible...It must comply with the latter's wishes and completely give up the idea of undertaking anything without regard to it. Statecraft must, therefore, restrict itself to preparing military success and making use of it, and this in accordance with directives emanating from the military side." Bernhardi, Germany and the Next War.

43. Ludendorff, Der totale Krieg, pp. 3 f., 10.

44. "The position which the war gave to the political direction with regard to military operations on land and sea was determined by things themselves. It was impossible for the military layman to presume to judge on military possibilities, not to mention military necessities." Bethmann Hollweg, Betrachtungen zum Weltkrieg. Bethmann "did not regard it as his duty to make his influence felt in the imposition of a political aim on great strategical decisions." Max von Baden, Memoirs, I, 72. Hertling to Prince Max: "The idea was intolerable that he should be the man who stayed the hand of the Supreme Command [by a peace offensive early in 1918]. He had unbounded confidence in the two army commanders. They would, he believed, create a military situation from which peace must automatically result, and that a better peace than was attainable today." Ibid., I, 252.

45. By the summer of 1916, the military members

of GHQ were highly dissatisfied with Falkenhayn who, in order to warn the Kaiser against Hindenburg, had called the latter "a new Wallenstein." Rupprecht, Kriegstagebuch, I, 494.

46. February 5, 1918. Czernin, Im Weltkriege, p. 334.

47. The OHL "read not only the ciphered dispatches of all foreign missions but also those which the Auswärtiges Amt sent to its representatives abroad—a state of things which resulted sometimes in the most incredible situations and difficulties." Kühlmann, Diplomaten, p. 80.

48. Bredt, Der deutsche Reichstag im Weltkrieg, pp. 202, 254, 290 ff.

49. Cf. Frederick the Great, "General Principles of War" (1748): "The most difficult projects for a campaign are those where one has to oppose many strong and powerful enemies at the same time. In such a case one must take recourse to policy and try to set the enemies at variance or to detach one or the other by advantages, if they can be brought about. On the military side, one must in such a case know how to lose à propos, for he who wants to defend everything at the same time will defend nothing." Cited by Jähns in Kriegswissenschaften, pp. 1942 f.

50. Crown Prince Rupprecht, Mein Kriegstagebuch, II, 240, 243 f., 320, 324, 400 f.; III, 14, 18 f.

51. Max von Baden, Memoirs, I, 258.

52. Hitlers Tischgespräche, p. 109.

53. Hull, Memoirs, I, 951 f.; II, 1185, 1201 f. and passim; Leahy, I was There, pp. 115, 226, 257; Military Situation in the Far East, 2553 ff.

54. Roosevelt insisted on Eden's absence from Casablanca because he did not want Hull there. Sherwood, Roosevelt and Hopkins, II, 261 f.; cf. Hull, Memoirs, II, 1109 ff., 1174, 1196, 1367 and passim.

55. Hull, Memoirs, II, 1110, 1196, 1367, 1570, 1578 f. and passim; Leahy, I Was There, p. 145. From the viewpoint of administration, the authors of a Brookings Institution report have this to say: "During this whole period [since Pearl Harbor] the position of the Department of State and the Foreign Service in the field of foreign affairs as a whole was far from central...The Department found it increasingly necessary in 1942 and 1943 to insist on its prerogatives respecting foreign policy, and to seek an active coordinating role in order to maintain them [with but little success]. Under the emergency pressures of the war and postwar period, the monopoly of the diplomatic mission was seriously breached." The Aministration of Foreign Affairs, pp. 19 f., 243.

56. Hull, Memoirs, II, 1110; Stimson and Bundy, On Active Service in Peace and War, chap. xxiii.

57. Sherwood, Roosevelt and Hopkins, II, 372 f.

58. Trial of the Major War Criminals, XXXIV, 426.

59. "But nothing less being asked of them than unconditional surrender, they absolutely refused it and declared they would defend themselves to the end." Grose, Military Antiquities (1786), I, 184.

60. See, e.g., Ambassador Weizsäcker's testimony, N. Y. Times, June 15, 1947.

61. Proclamation ending hostilities, December 31, 1946.

62. Deane, The Strange Alliance, pp. 162, 166.

63. When shown a speech by Assistant Secretary of State Dean Rusk, saying that the United States was trying to resist aggression and yet avoid a general war, MacArthur declared: "That policy seems to me to introduce a new concept into military operations—the concept of appeasement, the concept that when you use force you can limit that force...If you practice appeasement in the use of force, you are doomed to disaster." Time, May 14, 1951.

64. Clausewitz, On War, p. 17 (Modern Library Edition).

Strategy and Diplomacy

If strategy were, or could be, truly and simply "the practical application (or adaptation) of the means placed at a general's disposal to the attainment of the object in view" (Moltke), the distinction between strategic and diplomatic outlook would not be as doubtful as it has so often proved to be. Diplomacy would simply put to practical use the means put at its disposal. The diplomat would serve the country's outward interests, including its security, by means short of war, while the strategist would serve the same ends with military means in time of war and by war preparations in time of peace. The farther removed from battle —in time rather than in space—the more the objectives of strategy and diplomacy will coincide. Or perhaps they will only seem to coincide, for such matters are not discussed ahead of war. Diplomatic and strategic aims will most often come into conflict in time of war, particularly if victory should be doubtful. Even if there is an arbiter or unifier above their conflict, the solution arrived at will often be in the nature of a compromise, and each side is likely to hold that there has been interference with its own assigned field of activity.

Can strategic judgment claim greater objectivity, as is often believed? Is what strategy wills more clearly determined by the object to be attained than the aims of diplomacy? Has an object of world policy great strategic importance if the strategists, all or many or a few, claim that it has? Even a cursory examination of such a matter of dispute as the Baghdad Railway makes this seem doubtful.[1] Was it considered above everything else as a strategic road? Whose interests and strategic ends was it to serve? And whose security did it threaten? Did it constitute a threat to India's security? The India Office soldiers thought so for a long time, and the Foreign Office shared this view until 1913-14, when it arrived at an understanding with Germany regarding the line.[2] Did it constitute a threat to Russian security? The Russian General Staff believed that it did, until a Russo-German agreement of November 1910 implied that it did not. The French never ascribed much military significance to it but, as Turkey's oldest creditors, were eager to share in the enterprise. Would the Russians allow them to do so? Could France persuade her ally that the line had little or no strategic importance?

In 1906, the French Government resolved to let French capital participate in the financing and administration of the enterprise. The French ambassador in St. Petersburg presented himself first of all to the newly appointed Russian chief of staff, General Palitsin. The ambassador was aware that "objections based on strategic considerations are in effect the ones most difficult to overcome, first because one is most of the time not even permitted to discuss them, and then because the officers who have raised them often make it a point of honor to uphold them. It is therefore necessary to be beforehand. It is the more necessary to do this, and thus captivate the new chief of staff in favor of our view, since at an earlier time the Ministry of War showed itself unfavorable." Palitsin gave most satisfactory assurances: there was no objection to French participation on the part of the Russian military administration.[3] That hurdle taken, Witte was won over; even if he was no longer in power, he could still interfere with the French plans, should he renew his earlier opposition to the Baghdad line. And at last Isvolski came around.[4] By 1914, the governing circles of Europe had persuaded themselves that the line was not primarily a strategic one. One ineluctable strategic fact less in the world![5]

The theoretical differentiation between diplomacy and strategy has always been made more difficult by the theoretical emphasis on their necessary union, as well as by the practical claims of the professional or non-professional strategists and the diplomats. Both strategy and diplomacy are embedded in policy and politics, both in wartime and in peacetime.[6] They are so interpenetrative that Jomini, a military theoretician, distinguished between (a) military policy (politique militaire) and (b) policy of the war (politique de la guerre). The first has as its object the military combinations of a government that determine the relative importance of the various theaters of war, the kind of war to be undertaken (defensive or offensive), and the choice of generals for the theaters of war. The second covers everything that concerns diplomacy in an actual war, judging whether a war is opportune or indispensable, obtaining alliances, etc. In a modern reformulation: policy of war has as its object the relation between war and diplomacy; military policy, the relation between war and strategy. Both form part of "the science of supreme command."[7]

While modern tactics began with the introduction of fire-arms, modern strategy might be said to date from the time when the national state was taken as the base from which to calculate and to act. In spite of the many military definitions of strategy and tactics, which often seem designed to exclude the political factor, both tactics and strategy have nearly always acted within the fluidum of politics. Neither tactics nor strategy evolved along sheer rational-technological lines. Social stratification inside the armies, for example, interfered with tactics that ought to have been based on the technology of the arms and other equipment of the combatants.[8] And only too often strategy as the general's art turned out to be something that was heavily conditioned by the general's political tendencies, of which he himself might be unaware.

Almost as soon as theoretical separation and practical differentiation were attempted, they proved untenable. As Foch once observed, referring to the age of Louis XIV: "The relations between policy and war were already too close for the two activities to possibly ignore one another."[9] Tactics were dominant until the French Revolution, reflecting a sharply stratified society. Then, as the foremost Austrian commander against the French, Archduke Karl, put it:

> Because of the excessive increase of armies, tactics lost in value, and the strategical design of the operations (rather than details of maneuver) became the decisive factor in the issue of a campaign. The strategical design, as a rule, depends upon the decisions of cabinets, and upon the resources placed at the disposal of the commander. Therefore the leading statesmen should either have correct views of the science of war or should make up for their ignorance by giving their entire confidence to the man to whom the supreme command of the army is entrusted. Otherwise the germ of defeat and of national ruin may be contained in the first preparations for a war.[10]

Strategy started with the standing armies and the competition between them, an outstanding characteristic of the European state system. Before the rise of permanent forces, war waited for the armies to come and fight it; now, the armies were ready and waiting for—if they did not accelerate or precipitate—the war.[11] There was increasingly more planning, thought and material preparation in contemplation of war. Making use of new statistical data and methods, there was constant comparison of existing and, later, potential forces, until the conviction was established that in the "system of states" no nation could remain hors de choc if another undertook or contemplated some weighty measure of armament, whatever protest the isolationists might make.[12]

Strategy is the plan for the war-time application of the power available to a government. It has increasingly come to include the pre- and post-war application of such power as well. Those who think most strategically, if not most militaristically,

hold that, in order to be at all successful, diplomacy needs power, that all important policy is Machtpolitik. The extreme Old World view of Machiavelli is represented in the New World by Theodore Roosevelt. Roosevelt told young naval officers that diplomacy is "utterly useless where there is no force behind it; the diplomat is the servant, not the master of the soldier."[13] Such a claim, although more often raised by military men in conscious or subconscious self-justification, is still supported by numerous civilians, politicians, or ideologists.[14]

While much political advantage has been gained under "the silent pressure" of sea and other power, the diplomatic successes achieved without the use of military power have, on the whole, proved more durable.[15] But to this statement must be attached the proviso that the peaceful must always look to their military resources in order to curb the sporadic outbreaks of power virulence such as occurred in the times of Louis XIV, Napoleon, and Hitler. Each of these was at one time wielder of the superior power; his striving for still more power eventually united a coalition of the nations less obsessed with power, which had become aware of the need to forge the power of resistance. Since 1944, the expansion of Communist power has brought painful evidence to Anglo-Saxon political leaders of "the relation of military power to diplomacy." The expansion of Communism has produced an awareness that power is "needed until we are sure of a reign of law," that some states will "not respond to anything except power," that this fact had been overlooked during and immediately after the war due to "American failure to realize that military and political action had to go hand in hand."[16] Differently put, military power becomes the more necessary and the more effective, the less the members of a state system prove homogeneous. The highly deceptive war-time use of the term "democracy" to designate the members of the anti-Hitler coalition only put off the day when this was recognized in the United States.

Where politics seem to have been eliminated in favor of strategy, leaving the commander on land or sea a free hand, it usually turns out that his politics, unless they coincide with those of his government, have merely replaced those of the civilian governors. In such cases a military dynamism evolves that causes the supreme political-military director to neglect the most obvious political considerations. Thus Napoleon neglected the diplomatic possibilities in 1813, even though his war could have been won only with the help of diplomacy. There are temptations towards l'art pour l'art in war-making, temptations or suspicions which Foch turned aside with his comment: "Je ne fais pas la guerre pour faire la guerre."

Generally speaking, parliamentary and democratic

governments have warded off the dangers implicit in the attempted separation of war and politics somewhat better than have the military monarchies.

If war is to be the "continuance of policy by other means," there has to be preparation for the continuance of policy through the war and after it, as well as for the change to war, if war is to be at all successful. There has to be "peace strategy."[17] There must be at least a minimum of cooperation so that the statesman will not begin a war that the soldier, given the means at his disposal, cannot fight and even less win. Conrad, arch-militarist and erstwhile advocate of preventive war, has stated the rational bases of state policy with considerable perception: "The minister of foreign affairs has to keep in mind never to allow policy to drift into a direction which could lead to conflict with a superior power or group of powers, militarily speaking. Besides, he has to consider that the work of preparing for war is tied down for a long period, hence cannot be changed abruptly. This requires a policy with far-reaching, clear-cut and consistently pursued objectives and a perfect statesman to direct it."[18] The soldier on his part must not fail to prepare for the wars in which the statesman's policies may result, and he must not prepare for wars that the latter does not contemplate or intend.[19] "None of the principal plans which are required for a war can be made without an insight into political relations" (Clausewitz).

Political circumstances are a highly variable factor, not conducive to the steady organizational progress that officers as large-scale organizers would like to apply to the forces under their command. One might distinguish between armed forces that are built up predominantly in response to endogenous urges and others that result from exogenous pressure.[20] So-called "cabinet wars" were undertaken on the assumption that armies and navies were prepared for war with every conceivable enemy, although it was often proved that they were not. But they were mobile, at least psychologically speaking, even if religious sentiment might still interfere to a certain extent. Modern forces are closely akin to large-scale industrial organization: to enable them to undertake war they must have production schedules and be allowed the time to fulfill these.

SELECTION OF FRIEND AND FOE

The use of mass armies in the nineteenth and twentieth centuries was and is to a large extent predetermined by their size, by installations like fortresses, Maginot lines and strategic railways, and by inflexible plans for the opening of war. They are also limited by the psychological impedimenta of national and class animosities that have come to dictate policy to a greater extent than ever before.

In keeping with long-term alliances, the strategic plans for likely coalition wars are settled and perfected over a long period of years.[21] A volte-face in a country's alliance and treaty system, such as the Nazi-Soviet pact of 1939, demands improvisation of plans and bewildering shifts in sentiment.

In this respect, Italy-Savoy holds the record among the Powers.[22] Nothing in alliance diplomacy was ever more equivocal than her shifts among the pre-1914 alliance groupings. From 1902 on, following her secret understandings with France, she stopped all major military preparations against the latter.[23] Still, her new friends, or the majority of them, preferred that she stay within the Triple Alliance. In that way she might mislead, if not the German and Austrian diplomats, at least the German and Austrian peoples, who continued to believe in the Triplice as a guarantee of security, and at times the Berlin General Staff as well. And the peoples of the Entente Cordiale still believed that the continuance of the Triplice was a threat to their security. Inside the Triplice, Italy tried to work as a dissolvent. Her wait-and-see diplomacy was also part of her usual military unpreparedness, which was particularly extensive in July 1914, when the effects of the Libyan War had not yet been overcome and large forces were away in Africa and the Dodecanese. According to her chief of staff at the time, Italy "was not even ready for a defensive war with one single great Power."[24] To state things differently, Italy's governors had waited until the last possible moment to choose enemies or friends in war—Italia fara da se. If and when the choice is made, rightly more often than wrongly, the civilian governors, rather than the military, have usually made the supreme decision. Pollio might have disagreed with the civilians in 1914, had he lived; Badoglio before and in 1940 and again in 1943 opted for the West instead of the North as Mussolini had done.

The choice between friend and foe is not always obvious. The diplomats are not always the first to decide who is the enemy and who must therefore be the friend. In the formation of the pre-1914 alliance system, it was the British soldiers who first "became convinced, and stated so officially, that instead of regarding Germany as a suitable ally, we ought to look upon her as our most formidable rival, and that the contingency of war with her ought to set the standard of our military requirements." This was the conviction of several officers in the British War Office by 1901. They found, however, that it "was not yet shared by those responsible for laying down policy."[25] In 1919 and later, when no more enemies seemed left, Sir Henry Wilson was almost plaintive: the Navy had a two-power standard whereas "we soldiers had no standard...War could not be considered in the abstract, an enemy must be named and plans considered."[26]

Armies and navies have enemies in most periods of their existence, as often as not enemies of their own choice and partly at least of their own making. The problem of finding and making enemies was of the greatest urgency for the German and American navies, both infected by Mahanism, during and after the 1890's. Their urges to expand had to be justified by external enemies.[27] In the nature of things, these could not be "hereditary enemies," such as the German armies had in France. The choice of new ones had to be made plausible to various persons and groups at home. In Germany, these included the Emperor, the diplomats (who in Germany remained skeptical),[28] the General Staff, careless about the diplomatic and military consequences of naval construction, the uncritical Reichstag, and the still more ignorant masses. In pre-Pearl Harbor America, Japan was Enemy Number One for the Navy. Somewhat over the Navy's opposition, it was settled as early as February 1941 in the Anglo-American staff conversations that, for strategic reasons, Germany must be the enemy on whom the main weight would be thrown. There was no shift of focus after the Pearl Harbor shock, despite the temptation to follow public indignation and the Navy's itch to make Japan Enemy Number One.

DIPLOMACY AND THE WAR ON TWO FRONTS

One of the fundamental military demands put to the alliance-making and alliance-preventing diplomats is the demand for a constellation that eliminates the war on two or more fronts, or, better still, one that makes it possible to encircle the enemy or enemy-grouping. The war on two fronts is the soldier's nightmare as much as its peacetime preparation (the encirclement by way of alliances) is the cauchemar of any watchful diplomat. Ludovican and Napoleonic France, Frederician Prussia, Austria in 1866, the Central Powers in 1914, the Third Reich in 1941, and Japan after Yalta, became the objects and victims of such encirclement.

It was the miracle of Bismarck's diplomacy to have eliminated the dangerous threat of a Franco-Russian alliance; geopolitically speaking, Germany's location in the heart of Europe invited encirclement. Most of the Austrian diplomats and soldiers welcomed the alliance with Germany, and later, with Italy, despite the bitter memories of 1859 and 1866, because it promised to free them from another war on two fronts. Another such war, a war on one-and-a-half fronts so to speak, subsequently opened up, with half a front on the Balkan side. While they had prepared concentration plans for such a case, the Austrian soldiers

hoped during the 1870's that the diplomats would never allow things to go to such extremes. "That one may become reconciled to the idea of fighting simultaneously on two fronts, in spite of the bitter sufferings of 1859 and 1866, I consider absolutely impossible," Archduke Albrecht, the victor of Custozza and commander-in-chief designate, wrote in November 1879, a few weeks after the signing of the alliance with Germany. "It is up to diplomacy to avert such a thing from the outset, and it can always do so, if it is tolerably attentive and foresighted."[29]

Bismarck's reinsurance against a war on two fronts was dropped in Berlin without any protest from Austria. The military strength of the Central Powers would still have sufficed to fight this dangerous war, provided Britain remained neutral. She forsook this position in 1904 and was thereafter kept from resuming it by German naval construction. For a time, the Russo-Japanese War relieved the Central Powers of the threat of a war on two fronts. As Schlieffen reminded the German governors in 1904, a state fights such a war only unwillingly, even if in a position to do so from a military point of view.[30] After some hesitation, which found its diplomatic expression in the Bjoerkoe episode, the Russians resolved to forego revanche in the Far East, make that front one of minor importance, and turn their main force against the Central Powers. By 1909, William II reported to the Austrian heir that he had heard the Russians say:

> We are not strong enough for a war on two fronts, therefore we want to liquidate affairs in the East to be in a better position to deal with the Balkans and the "rotten West."[31]

Only now did the Russian alliance begin to promise a firm second front against Germany, as France had always hoped it would. The first front, in the West, had already been strengthened by the Entente with Britain. Diplomatic fronts hardened into military ones. The German attempt to break out of this ring to the southeastward by a military reconstruction of Turkey failed; the Turks and Bulgarians did not give the Central Powers the additional power which the United States lent to Britain and France in 1918.[32] The other attempt to break out of this ring, the violation of Belgian neutrality, likewise failed.

The march through Belgium, as well as the military reconstruction of Turkey through the Liman mission, were the brain-children of the General Staff. The plan for the unconditional march through Belgium was submitted to the Chancellor in December 1912.[33] The military reasoning went as follows:

> Unless the political situation of Europe changes, we shall always be forced, due to Germany's central location, to make front in several directions

and consequently to remain on the defensive with weaker forces on the one side in order to be able to assume the offensive on the other. This side can only be France. There is hope for a quick decision here, whereas an offensive war deep into Russia would be without a foreseeable end. In order to be on the offensive against France, it will be necessary, however, to violate Belgian neutrality. Only through a movement cutting across Belgian neutrality is there hope of our being able to attack and beat the French Army in the field.

In spite of the opposition of the British expeditionary forces and the Belgian Army, Schlieffen thought that such an operation would still be more promising than a frontal attack on France's fortified eastern frontier.[34]

German diplomacy, Bismarck not excepted, had never approached the problem by presenting its own reasons for the choice of Enemy Number One in a war on two fronts. Instead, the diplomats bowed to the choice of the military experts. In France this choice, although it was at most times automatic, was at least theoretically reserved for the government. A Ministerial decree of October 28, 1913, declared that the government alone assumes

the care of the country's vital interest and is qualified to fix the political aim of the war... In case the struggle extends to several frontiers, it designates the principal adversary against whom the larger part of the national forces must be directed, it distributes accordingly the means of action and resources of all kinds and puts them at the disposal of the generals who are charged with the supreme command in the several theaters of operation.[35]

Since the march through Belgium presented the only recipe for victory offered by the German General Staff, the directors of policy felt that their "resolutions stood under the constraint of military necessity" (Jagow). These "resolutions" never went so far as to give the plan formal approval, nor did they ever consider its hazardous character. Moltke never clarified the situation by insisting on such an approval from the political offices. He left them uninformed as to the details of his plans, including the coup de main against Liège, until the first days of August 1914, by which time Bethmann had been too far swept along to protest.

Jagow, the director of the Foreign Office, had warned Moltke in February 1913 that the march through Belgium would bring the British into the war. He explained after the war that the civilian part of the Reich Government had resigned itself to fate when told by the General Staff that a change in their plan, such as omitting the march through

Belgium, was impossible and that in fact this plan was the only possible one. "Could the Chancellor at all shoulder the responsibility of forcing the abandonment of a war plan which alone, according to military judgment, could bring victory?"[36] While a Bismarck would have shouldered this responsibility, his last successor, given the 1913-14 structure of German government, was unable to do so. No state reasoning proceeding from the premises of foreign policy and security could shake off the incubus of the German Navy which the Kaiser, the Navy itself, and the Reichstag wanted, and against which the powerful Army did not protest.

The French military build-up of the Slavic Near East was begun in 1918 in order to keep Germany encircled after Russia had dropped out of the war. This proved to be only a poor substitute in the end, partly for the reason that it was never used when it could have been of use, before it had shrunk into military insignificance by comparison with re-strengthened Russia and Germany. For the Reichswehr, this ring was a haunting reminder of the First World War as a two-front war—hence Seeckt's policy of a close understanding with the Soviets, hence the firm view held by the first post-war Chief of Staff, General Beck, that Germany was in no position to fight such a war. Hitler dismissed this Heulboje, this howling buoy, as he called the warning voice. He told the generals that he would never repeat the Kaiser's fatal mistake of allowing a two-front war to come about. And he persuaded many of them of his "genius" by avoiding this war in 1939 through the pact with the Soviets. The older generation feared that his initial gambler's luck would only serve to postpone defeat. It seemed sheer madness to them to open a new front by the attack on Russia in 1941. The Wehrmacht had been forced to come to Italy's help in the Balkans and in Africa. Russia represented the third or fourth front! Hitler rushed into the side-show wars because Britain had refused to come to terms with him following the fall of France in 1940, thus denying him the opportunity to close the Western front and open the Eastern as he had considered doing as early as June 1940.

It was the security existing at the center of the inner line that enabled the United States to make a free choice between its two main enemies in World War II and then to turn with the gros of its strength against Germany first. The inevitable slowness of American arming gave Hitler his last respite; it had to run its time, in spite of the Russians' clamor for an early opening of the "second front." They practically specified in their demand, at Teheran and on other occasions, that this front be formed in the West, and not in the Mediterranean. Happily for the Russians, the American planners, for logistic and connected reasons, agreed with these far-seeing Russian wishes rather than with the British proposals to carry the war beyond the

Adriatic.[37] It was America's turn to call on Russia at Yalta for the opening of a new second front, in order to get Japan into a vise.[38]

Nothing is more costly in politics than the superfluous. Japan was about to fall along the first front without the opening of a second. By their invitation, the Americans simply enabled Russia to move into new favorable positions for the war that her governors had never dismissed from their thoughts—class war on the international scene. In this new-old war, the second front, a line of foci, is opened behind the enemy's frontiers where Communist parties and partisans operate. In addition, conflagrations are started here and there along the capitalist perimeter (Greece, Indochina, Korea). They force the capitalist Powers to form costly lines of containment. The supreme aim of the Western Powers in this conflict was to keep open war restricted to a minimum of fronts and to small fronts, an idea not traditionally a military one, as the actions, perplexities, and proposals of a traditional local commander such as MacArthur betrayed only too clearly. While Washington left him considerable latitude, the policymakers were duly apprehensive that "in exercising his discretion, he would do so in the direction of enlarging rather than confining the conflict."[39] They therefore ordered him to refrain from such measures as hot pursuit into Manchurian territory and bombardment of places close to Russian soil that might provoke war on broadened or additional fronts.[40] Such a war had to be avoided, at least until the positions around the Soviet Union, formed out of military alliances and a strategic system of bases, had become firmer and more nearly complete.

In so-called "cold war"—partly called so because the idea gives many people the frissons— fronts are different from those drawn in national war. Russian propaganda, directed at the many innocents at home and the fewer innocents abroad, protests against the "encirclement" of the "homeland of socialism." Their propaganda appeals to the old anxiety complex underlying the preparation for war on two or more fronts. The capitalist side substantiates its appeals by pointing to the "enemy in our midst." These are the anxiety situations that in a sense have determined the forming of fronts in the post-1945 world.

SEASONABLE AND UNSEASONABLE WARS

The demands of diplomacy and the demands of the military are reciprocal. The foreign minister will ask whether or not naval or military units are available for demonstration purposes and thus give emphasis to demands presented or to be presented to a foreign government. Or he may request that the military commands omit or postpone certain contemplated movements of their forces that are likely to be misconstrued abroad. The most portentous question he can ask concerns the readiness for war and the expectation of victory in a contemplated war. In return, the military will demand that no war be undertaken while they are unready for it.[41]

Before war became an all-season possibility, military and hence diplomatic moves were very much under the dictatorship of the weather, from which only an occasional early military reformer such as de Saxe tried to emancipate them.[42] In August 1789, Hertzberg, the director of the ambiguous and irresolute Prussian policy between the first two partitions of Poland, recommended that King Frederick William II make use of the engagement of the two Empires in a war with Turkey and force them to agree to Prussian partition and territorial exchange proposals. For this purpose, Hertzberg proposed the assembling of strong Prussian forces in the direction of their frontiers. The King declined—because the season was too far advanced. When the good weather season returned, the good political season was over. The demonstration as undertaken in the spring of 1790 left the two Emperors, who had in the meantime achieved great successes in the Balkans, quite unimpressed. It proved so anticlimactic that the director of Prussian mobilization shot himself.[43] Napoleon I's attempts to overcome the dictatorship of the weather were not uniformly successful. Napoleon III was least eager to imitate him in that respect. The latter had taken a pro-Polish stand during the insurrection of 1863, but found Russian resistance stiffening as the winter season approached, making Russia nearly unassailable.[44] At nearly the same time, Bismarck asked for the General Staff's opinion about the prospects, should the two German Powers, Prussia and Austria, be forced to consider war. "The question whether and how far special regard has to be paid to the seasons and whether the winter season must be considered as specially favorable to our own interest in case measures are undertaken against Denmark I should like to see particularly treated in Lieutenant-General von Moltke's answer."[45] The war against Denmark was started in February 1864.

During discussions between the Austrian and German General Staffs in the 1870's and 1880's, the question of the most favorable season for a war against Russia was constantly considered. The usual conclusion imparted to the diplomats was that, on the whole, a winter war was impossible, at any rate more impossible for the Central Powers than for Russia.[46] The Austrians considered themselves even less well prepared for a winter war than the Germans did. As Andrassy was about to depart for the Berlin Congress of 1878, Archduke Albrecht, the army commander, reminded him that a campaign against Russia starting in the late autumn would promise little success. Should war become inevitable, Austrian diplomacy must put off the outbreak of hostilities until the following spring; only at that time of year could a campaign be undertaken with any hope of success. But Andrassy did not look for war at any season.[47]

The Napoleonic disaster in Russia, partly due to the late opening of the campaign, furnished the most impressive lesson of the nineteenth century about winter campaigns, though a number of wars at the same time demonstrated that war was feasible the year round.[48] In the eighteenth century, wars usually opened when enough grass had grown to feed the horses. In the nineteenth century, the most appropriate time for opening a war was thought to be when the crops were in. The men called up for duty the preceding autumn would be in perfect training, the grain supply would be assured, and enough of the good weather season would still remain for a promising campaign. Some diplomats, including Grey, and some propagandists and historians have "explained" the fact that the First World War began in late July as due to such calculations on the part of the Germans. After all, they had started the war of 1870 in a similar way, at a similar season.[49] Actually, by 1914 war had become largely emancipated from the weather, if not also from diplomacy, which is not meant to say that weather and seasons are now without influence either on operations or on the decision to begin war. The Fascists timed their coups with an eye to the most favorable season. Action against Ethiopia was resolved upon in Rome in 1934 and slated to start in October 1935, at the close of the rainy season. In March 1935, de Bono, the chosen leader of the enterprise, wired from Eritrea that the chosen time was still appropriate.[50] The British Government, among the opponents of the Italian venture once it had started, gambled on a time factor. "If before the rains in Abyssinia set in towards the end of May, Abyssinia's resistance is fully crushed, it will mean a disastrous defeat to British policy"; so ran Hugh Wilson's report to Hull.[51] Italian success was achieved before the rains came, and the collective security endeavors, directed by Britain, crumbled.

At the beginning, Hitler paid more attention to the meteorology of politics and war than he did towards the end of his career. When he determined in April 1938 to solve the Czech problem by force if necessary, mid-October was "set as the latest possible date on account of flying conditions."[52] The Polish problem was to be "clarified," one way or the other, by the end of August 1939. If there was to be fighting, it would have to take place in September. Later in the fall, Germany's

heavy motorized forces, necessary for the deep thrust into Poland, could not be used. And while a severe winter would still allow certain military operations, Luftwaffe activities would come nearly to an end. "Consequently, the deadline had to be the end of August."[53] The winter weather of 1939-40 proved to be a main deterrent to the Führer's intentions to attack in the West immediately after the close of the Polish campaign. It provided the only reason why the advice against war in the West found a hearing at all. "When the winter was over, nothing could be done to stop the attack."[54]

IMPOSSIBLE WARS[55]

Unseasonable wars are not the only ones that military men have hesitated to undertake for military reasons. There are numerous impossible wars, fought and unfought, on record.

The director of Prussian foreign policy, General von Radowitz, relying on his own military judgment, had brought things to the brink of war with Austria in 1850. The war minister informed him bluntly: we cannot go to war; we could not mobilize in time, if at all; we could not prevent the Austrians from occupying Berlin.[56] Prussia had to back down at Olmütz in a manner that many, including her own army, thought discreditable and dishonorable.

Even such a cautious statesman as Salisbury called on at least one occasion for a military measure that was deemed unfeasible by the spokesman for the Navy because it might lead to war. When his patience with the Turks in the Armenian question of 1896-97 had been exhausted and he proposed to send a demonstration squadron inside the Dardanelles, Goschen, First Lord of the Admiralty, protested in the Cabinet. Did Salisbury know for certain, he asked, what the French and their fleet would do in such a case? When he answered No, Goschen declared that if the French should blockade the Straits while the British were inside, the latter would find themselves in a mouse-trap, cut off from their munitions and other supplies. He would, therefore, give no orders for such a move. Somewhat chagrined, the Prime Minister desisted: "If your ships are made of porcelain, I must needs pursue another policy."[57] The British Navy was better prepared for the next conflict. At the time of Fashoda and after, it was at such full readiness that Delcassé felt forced to give in: "We must avoid a naval war which we are absolutely unable to sustain."[58]

Another war proposition turned down by the military chieftain as impossible or at least unprofitable was submitted to Foch in 1922, not long before the march into the Ruhr. One of the politicos in Paris sounded him out on the possibilities of a march to Berlin as the measure to bring

Germany, acting in obvious bad faith and not living up to any of her obligations, to her knees. The French Government was thinking of such a measure. Hence the consultation, indirect at first, with Foch. "We are thinking of reopening military operations, having our troops advance, if necessary, as far as Berlin, the capital. Once there, we shall find the means of forcing Germany to render us what she has promised. What do you think about that?" he was asked. The Chief of Staff led the visitor before the map of Europe, pointing out the equal distance of Paris and Berlin from the Rhine, some five hundred kilometers, a line of communication that would have to be held. The active force could easily dispose of the Reichswehr, he said, but the étape would have to be held by two or three yearly classes of reservists who had yet to be mobilized. Had he considered the effect this measure, coming after fifty-two months of war, might have on the French people, on the former allies, and on the neutrals? Furthermore, if the Germans should retire to the East and put up resistance there, on the Russian model, what did the visitor and his friends propose to do then? Would they have them pursued? and how many men would be needed for that?

Thus for an operation the benefits of which are highly dubious and problematic, you run risks of all sorts, risks that are unfortunately real, inevitable. Are we going to repeat the errors and follies of Napoleon? On my part, I consider the projected operation as one of the most imprudent, most dangerous ones. I disapprove of it from the outset. I shall refuse to give it my endorsement.

These protests, according to Foch, sufficed to stifle the plan for a march to Berlin. There was only a march into the Ruhr, which Foch himself proposed, but with results with which he was soon to be disappointed.[59] Several of the military measures taken against Germany that France thought legitimate by the terms of the Versailles Treaty proved impossible for one reason or another.[60]

More serious than the military declaration—timely or belated—that an intended diplomatic enterprise is impossible, is the military statement to the political chief that a long-pursued, traditional, fundamental line of policy must be given up as no longer tenable. Czechoslovakia had begun its existence in 1918 as a thorn implanted in the flank of Germany. Beneš had told the Allies in the autumn of 1918, in order to win their favor, that "Bohemia pushes itself into the body of Germany in such a manner that it has a position, strategically speaking, of capital importance." The French General Staff had assigned this very role to Czechoslovakia, even pre-natally. This state-to-come was, in their view, "unequivocally and necessarily anti-German. Destined to absorb the German elements of Bohemia, it threatens the heart of Germany." But even at that time, the patrons of Czechoslovakia realized that this "anti-German barrier" could not survive without the continued protection of the Western Powers unless Germany continued to remain weak.[61] Both assumptions had been invalidated by 1938 at the latest. The Czech Chief of Staff stated this fact to President Beneš, who still relied on the hope and promise of French and Russian help, "in a very stormy conversation" which took place in April 1938. The general reportedly told Beneš quite clearly "that Czechoslovakia's military position was absolutely untenable, since neither Russia nor France could send her direct aid. It was therefore time to abandon the policy hitherto pursued by Prague and to seek an understanding with Germany."[62] Beneš dismissed the Chief of Staff as "Fascistic" and continued to rely on outside support until the time of Munich.

Not unlike other diplomacies, that of the United States has occasionally assumed positions that were untenable from a military point of view. This must be said of most of its Far Eastern policy. Nearly from the outset of American control, the Philippines were considered indefensible against Japanese aggression, though military opinion has been somewhat varied on this point. MacArthur's plans for their defense displayed some confidence that he could develop the forces there in order to stop the Japanese on the beaches.[63] Even more of a "lost hope," diplomatically and militarily speaking, was another American ward in the Far East, Korea. Independence had been promised her at Cairo (1943) and at Potsdam (1945). It proved "a commitment almost impossible to back up militarily."[64] At the same time that these pledges were given (to which Soviet Russia had also subscribed), United States policy in the Far East made Russia strategically paramount on the Asiatic continent by giving her free entry into Manchuria. Korea was thus under continual threat. When both Russia and the United States evacuated the two halves of Korea in 1949, the State Department found the Army agreeable to the proposed measure. The decision was approved for good military reasons—and not simply because the decision had been reached on the highest policy-making level, as Secretary of Defense Louis Johnson wanted to make it appear. South Korea was indefensible. As expressed in 1949 by a former Deputy Military Governor of that zone: "If the Russians decided to do so, they could take over South Korea without any great military difficulty. They are right there with large armies. Any troops that we have there would suffer another Bataan."[65] They nearly did at Pusan in 1950.

On such occasions, when political decisions have to be made in the face of clearly unfavorable military conditions, military advisers can often bring the belligerent politico to reason and make him shrink from war or the possibility of war. If in spite of all military advice the director of policy insists on seeing the impossible done, it must either turn out that what by orthodox judgment was thought impossible was feasible after all, or military disaster will result. In 1895, General Baratieri with his 20,000 troops remained inactive while swarms of Ethiopians gathered around. Premier Crispi, in the throes of a prolonged economic-political depression, tried hard to push the general into "un azione resolutiva." For this the latter felt thoroughly unprepared, considering the forces at his disposal. But Crispi was in great need of a military success to maintain himself in power and to justify the vast expense already incurred in the Abyssinian venture. He telegraphed sarcasms to the hesitant general (such as "your campaign is military phtisis") and dispatched another general to take over Baratieri's command. When the latter learned about this, he resumed the offensive that ended so disastrously at Adua, this causing Crispi's fall and practical retirement from politics.[66]

Still another kind of impossible war is the one that is not prepared. For example, when the North Koreans struck, and the directors of policy asked for military support of South Korea, there was no plan in Washington for such a contingency. "So," as Louis Johnson said later, "it was a case of rather shooting from the hip...of doing with what we had in that area at that time, what could be done, and everyone recognized that."[67]

Diplomats and politicians are not the only ones who have demanded and obtained the undertaking of impossible wars. A number of such wars must be attributed to more or less exclusively military urging. Japanese war-making in Manchuria and China in the 1930's was undertaken against the original intentions of the country's diplomats and to the subsequent regret of many of them. The Japanese ambassador to London, for example, poured out his woes, even to such a dangerous recipient of confidences as a Nazi negotiator, saying that

in China Japan had engaged on a task which overemployed her forces to the full. The military leaders had not followed the advice of the Foreign Minister in Tokyo. The struggle had assumed proportions which no one had intended...There was such tension in Japan's State finances, currency and taxation that social repercussions were inevitable...[68]

From "a strictly military point," MacArthur considered it necessary to broaden the war in Korea in 1951. General Marshall and the Washington Chiefs of Staff agreed with the State Department's view that MacArthur's proposal was inadmissible, since it might extend Soviet participation in the war. They also reasoned, in the words of General Bradley, that for such an extended war Korea was definitely

a poor place to fight...The fundamental military issue that has arisen is whether to increase the risk of a global war by taking additional measures that are open to the United States and its allies. We now have a localized conflict in Korea. Some of the military measures under discussion might well place the United States in the position of responsibility for broadening the war and at the same time losing most if not all of our allies...We feel that we are not in the best position to meet a global war...that we are improving all the time our own position, and that of our allies, and we would like very much to avoid a war at this time, not only as to our own readiness, but the longer you can avoid a war the better the chances you have in avoiding it altogether, in the end...If we can fight this limited action in Korea without its being spread, we may be going a long way toward avoiding World War III....[69]

Washington did not want such a war—and it is hard to say whose reluctance in this respect was greater, that of the diplomats or that of the military. MacArthur, on the other hand, considered that the war he had been ordered to fight was an impossible one, judging by "true" military standards. He felt that certain orders given him were "not a mission" that could be performed. He felt that the politically inspired and conditioned demands sent out to him by the Chiefs of Staff introduced "a new concept into military operations—the concept of appeasement, the concept that when you use force, you can limit that force," instead of always applying it to the full in order to achieve military victory. He complained, publicly almost more than to his superiors, about "abnormal military inhibitions" which made "a military stalemate seem inevitable" and which stood in the way of victory. Instead of aiming for victory, there prevailed "the concept of a continued and indefinite campaign in Korea, with no definite purpose of stopping it until the enemy gets tired or you yield to his terms...That introduces into the military sphere a political control such as I have never known in my life or have ever studied." It was to him a perverse kind of war in which the commander was denied the use of possibly decisive weapons, "war applied in a piecemeal way, [so] that you make half war, and not whole war."[70] He did not understand that

war, as Clausewitz put it, "is a thing that sometimes is more war, sometimes less." There have
actually been wars that were "less war," even if
not particularly glorious ones. There have been
attenuated wars, often the result of the disappointing outcome of recent total wars. One such
war was the War of the Bavarian Succession,
which Frederick the Great waged without one
battle, following the many battles of the Seven
Years' War. Such wars are not usually covered
in the courses on military history that are given
to future military officers.[71]

STRATEGIC AND POLITICAL OBJECTIVES

Neither the complete independence of the diplomatic and the military departments nor the
practice of one acting as the handmaiden of the
other serves the best interests of the state. But
often, if not usually, unity in practice has been
difficult to achieve, even for the greatest and
most powerful statesman. "If I had only for five
minutes the power to say: Thus it shall be, and
not otherwise!" Bismarck sighed as he struggled
with Moltke, the General Staff, and the King during the siege of Paris. "That one need not have to
bother with the Why and the Wherefore, need not
have to demonstrate and beg for the simplest
things!"[72]

The soldiers' ideas of this interdependence
have generally tended toward simplification and
have tended above all to establish the independence, if not the superiority, of the military
branch in time of war. General von Verdy du
Vernois, a former Prussian minister of war and
member of the Great General Staff, was imbued
with a sense of superiority with regard to the
German arrangements. He developed his ideas of
the desirable practical relation between strategy
and diplomacy in a letter to the Austrian Chief of
Staff, General von Beck, in 1896. He wrote:

That the campaign plan—or better still, the initial assembly plan—must be the General Staff's
own work, is obvious. But in order to prepare
everything in time, it is absolutely necessary
that the Staff always be kept informed of the
political situation by the director of foreign
affairs. Also, the latter in his political action
must reasonably go only as far as there is
power available to see it through. He must not
enter upon an action, still less drive matters
to an extreme, without the most intimate understanding with the chief of staff. The general plan
of campaign—if it comes to execution—can be
withheld from him as little as from the war minister, who has to put all things into readiness.
But with that a point has been reached which
easily brings about interference from other
sides regarding the directives to come from

the Monarch (as commander-in-chief). One
has to suffer this as far as political considerations and military operations are in unconditional interdependence, for some military measure may be very useful in the momentary
[military] situation but might prove very harmful, politically speaking, as regards neutrals
for instance. Coöperation on the part of the
foreign minister is therefore inevitable at the
beginning and almost more so at the close of
operations, and also under certain conditions,
during the war. But with iron energy the Chief
of Staff must insist before the Commander-in-
Chief that in his presence no statements on
operations are to be made by anyone except
himself.[73]

Strategy is deeply rooted in a country's peace-
time conditions and influences. It is a moot point
as to which is more conditioned by peace-time,
strategy or tactics. On the whole, foreign policy
has closer connections with strategy, while domestic policy, societal stratification, weapon
technology, etc., are co-determinants of the various tactical systems. Considerations of domestic policy throw their spell over such a question
as the setting-up and use of SS divisions in Nazi
Germany or the balance within the army services of the United States.[74] In fact, considerations of domestic policy may almost suffice to
beat an army from within—they may be said to
have done this to the Austrians in the war of 1859.
The Austro-Hungarian Army, considered to be
the only safe instrument left for use against "the
Revolution," was much better prepared at the outbreak of the war than the Franco-Sardinian forces.
But its leaders did not possess the courage to march
it deep into Piedmont, because that region was
considered a hotbed of revolution. No requisition-
ing of food and fodder was allowed the troops because it was feared that their discipline might
suffer and because it might arouse the civilian
population. When a few cavalry patrols were killed
by Italian peasants, patrol activity was practically
stopped. Fear of partisan activity was far greater
than was justified. Fear of desertion by the non-
German elements was so great that no skirmishing
was allowed. Pessimism was so strong that none
of the strong positions in Lombardy were considered tenable. Actually, as historians have concluded, "only the strategic and tactical indecision
on the part of the leaders, going back to domestic
political inhibitions and not to any mutinous sentiment, has covered these brave troops with
shame."[75]

In another quarter, the fear of revolution soon
resulted in bad strategy, that of MacMahon's movements into the sack at Sedan. The purpose of the
maneuver was to relieve Bazaine, invested in

Metz by the Germans, and join him for a decisive battle. In starting on this march from Reims, MacMahon acted against his own better judgment but under the impact of a telegram from the War Minister in Paris, saying: "If you abandon Bazaine, there will be revolution in Paris, and you yourself will be attacked by all of the enemy's forces." The movement, very difficult to execute, was so contrary to all strategic thought that only one of Moltke's assistants guessed it: though inadmissible from a military point of view, it might still be explained by political considerations. "It is impossible, it would be foolish," Moltke opined. As a result of this opinion, his own decisions were made somewhat belatedly.[76]

The demand for the immediate security of the homeland at the opening of operations has led not only to the building of large permanent fortifications but also to the holding in reserve of large numbers of troops for the couverture, or of large numbers of ships for coastal protection. Usually these large numbers have been too large. Moltke's original plans for the war against Austria in 1866 provided for the concentric march of several armies into Bohemia, leaving the extreme left wing and the province of Silesia uncovered. The King's own son and other high Prussian dignitaries argued that this would leave the province exposed to an Austrian invasion. This reasoning, rather than Moltke's argument that Silesia could not be better protected than by a Prussian victory inside Bohemia, swayed William I. He ordered that one of the armies be placed much further to the left than Moltke had intended. As it turned out, and as Moltke had expected, the Austrians were far too slow in their movements to attempt an invasion of Silesia. The last-hour change merely endangered and delayed Prussian victory. As Schlieffen put it: "If anything could endanger Silesia, it was the measures taken for its protection."[77] Similar considerations prevailed, with worse consequences, when Schlieffen's original Plan was altered by his successor. The right was weakened in order to give better protection to Alsace-Lorraine. And on the eve of the battle of the Marne in 1914, several German army corps were withdrawn for the protection of East Prussia. The same kind of thinking led the British, in and after 1914, to retain divisions at home for use against the unlikely danger of a German landing when these divisions could have been better used on the Continent. Strategy suffers whenever a specific interest, such as that of the East Prussian Junkers in 1914, prevails over the national one.

The greatest declination from true military North is easily brought about by over-emphasis of the immediate political objective. Constantinople has perhaps most often provoked this demand for the direct grasp, or the fear of it. In May 1890, the British and German diplomats were so absorbed by the problem of the Straits that they assumed Russia would surely open the expected war with an attack on the Bosporus. Chancellor-General Caprivi had to remind them that by true military reasoning the assumption was a false one. Instead, Russia would first have to fight Austria, who was unwilling to suffer that Bulgaria or Constantinople should become Russian, and Germany as well on her Western front. "The final decision in the main theater of war also decides over the more unimportant military fields of action."[78]

Some of the objectives of the opening moves of wars have been far too politically conceived to be either advisable or realizable from a military point of view. The result has usually been an unsound distribution of forces. The political urge resulted in "the rage for the capitals" in 1914, and later, in the desire to liberate certain populations.[79] Such hopes attracted more French forces to Alsace-Lorraine in August 1914 than would have been necessary to pin down German forces. Their appearance, it was hoped, would "facilitate the insurrection of the Alsatian population who had remained loyal to the French cause." Actually, the welcome remained somewhat below expectations.[80]

Russia's opening strategy in 1914 was ideologically based on a combination of the "rage for capitals" and Pan-Slavism. As recommended by Joffre, its objective was Berlin, by way of Posen, "whose population was akin to our own," and Upper Silesia, with Bohemia and Moravia, in the midst of Slavic populations, as pivot points.[81] Meanwhile, the soldiers had to fight off the demands of the civilians for at least a token force to participate in the capture of the Straits.[82] The experiences of the earlier belligerents had taught the Rumanians nothing. When they entered the war in 1916, they went at once after their political objective, Transsylvania. "I am afraid," the British ambassador in Paris soon noted, "that the Rumanians are in a parlous condition, but they did what others of the Entente did, they made for what they coveted instead of doing what was militarily advisable. We went for Mesopotamia unprepared. The French led off by going into Alsace."[83]

Political obsessions were the besetting sin of Hitler's strategy, which ran contrary to the advice of his generals in the war with Russia. The best, or boldest German plan proposed a moderate advance on the left wing between the Gulf of Riga and the upper Dnieper. Meanwhile a strong Southern group was to push through the Ukraine into the Donets basin and from there northward in order to force the Russians into the battle on an unexpected front. Hitler would not hear of such a plan or of Moscow, the political and communications center, as the main objective. He considered Leningrad, where the Red Revolution had started, and Stalingrad, where the tide of civil war had turned against the Whites, as the pivotal points of Red Russia. It would take considerable time and space to settle whether or not these aims were more than results of the Führer's political notions.

Like other conquerors before him, Hitler considered the gaining of capitals as the crown of victory, though the loss and destruction of a capital has by no means always meant that.[84] In a number of cases it has galvanized rather than terminated resistance. The possession of Moscow in 1812 did not confirm Napoleon's victory; it started him on his fatal road to defeat. The burning of Washington in 1814 did not hasten the peace. The occupation of capitals like Pretoria and Bloomfontein during the Boer War, of Brussels, Belgrade, and Bucharest during the First World War, of Warsaw, Oslo, Paris and many others during the Second, made them symbols of continued resistance, rather than of final surrender. And what the final "sense" of the joint occupation of Berlin and Vienna since 1945 will be, no political prophet has yet pronounced. On the other hand, Bismarck's veto against the entry into the enemy capital of Vienna in 1866, open as it lay to the Prussians, was one of the rarest war-time victories of diplomacy over the military desire for a complete triumph. Though not otherwise a politician much guided by precedence, Lloyd George entertained vague notions of imitating Bismarck and therefore opposed carrying the final offensive of the Western Powers to Berlin. Pershing alone among the military leaders opposed him.[85]

American strategy, if we may for once generalize over one hundred and seventy-five years of history, has usually been obsessed by the rage for capitals. The British had good reason, after Benedict Arnold's assault on Quebec in 1775-76, to worry about the security of this provincial capital and to fortify and refortify it from time to time against an American advance. While Zachary Taylor halted at Monterey in September 1846 and concluded an armistice, the Polk administration, without more definite plans of its own, ordered him to cancel the truce. The resumption of hostilities resulted in nothing but an indecisive spreading of the American forces over the vast deserts and mountains of Mexico, until Scott made the Administration adopt his plans for advancing on the capital from the sea side, from Vera Cruz. "Scott knew," as Ganoe puts it, "that there was only one way to gain a speedy peace. It was to strike at the heart and center of the hostile country with the largest force obtainable." However, after he

had fought his way upward from the coast and was almost within sight of Mexico City, Scott

did one of the most loyal and self-sacrificing things ever done by any man in high position. Although the way to the city now lay open, he forsook the personal glory of capturing the capital of the enemy's country because he felt wisely that such action would not so quickly "conquer a peace." The political conditions were such that a successful assault would mean only a postponement of a permanent settlement and the unnecessary sacrifice of many soldiers.[86]

At this point Scott agreed to Mexican proposals to halt hostilities with a view to opening peace negotiations. When a fortnight had been wasted by Mexican procrastinations, hostilities were resumed and the capital taken by storm.

A more popular than truly strategic objective in the Second World War was Tokyo. Admiral Halsey, more than any other, made it popular with his proclaimed hope of one day riding into that capital on the Emperor's white horse. And for him, life and forty-five years of naval career "reached its climax on August 29, 1945" when he steamed into Tokyo Bay on board the Missouri.[87] America's aiming at other capitals, such as Berlin, Vienna, and Prague, was muddled. It was thought in Washington that military considerations spoke against taking possession or co-possession while the fighting continued. When Churchill and the British Chiefs of Staff urged Roosevelt to reverse Eisenhower's decision not to aim for Berlin, he declined, declaring that military considerations were primary and the grasp for Berlin a prestige measure not worth the additional military sacrifices.[88] Political considerations as to the postwar roles of such capitals were so uncertain that no timely steps were taken to assure full and free access to them.[89]

In the cyclical changes from the strategy of exhaustion (Ermattung) to the strategy of annihilation (Niederwerfung), which may be accompanied by a change in the respect paid diplomacy, the aiming at capitals is one of the outstanding characteristics. The French Revolution and the influence of Napoleon started the modern rage for capitals.[90] Generally speaking, this practice had been foreign to eighteenth-century warfare. Berlin was occupied temporarily during the Seven Years' War but soon evacuated for fear of over-extending the occupants' lines. During the Second Silesian War, Frederick the Great had intended to fight the decisive battle under the walls of the Austrians' capital, "pour leur mettre le pied sur la gorge," as he boasted at the time.[91] He got as far as Prague, but was then forced by mere maneuvering on the part of the Austrians, who always denied battle, to evacuate Bohemia and retire to Silesia with a decimated and worn-out army. He had been unable to feed his army and stop desertion, which was quite unprecedented, even for his armies (1744). Such experiences with over-extended lines of supply and lack of cohesion demonstrated the inadvisability of aiming at distant capitals. These experiences were altogether in harmony with, if they did not set, the style of diplomacy of the age. The partners of the coalition against Frederick had originally intended to annihilate him, or at least reduce him to the status of the margrave of Brandenburg. The strategy of exhaustion, which prevailed until the French Revolution, taught them better and persuaded them that, at least in Western Europe, no violent or vast territorial and political changes could or should take place.[92]

The belief of the soldier that the international problem that has "caused" the war will be the more permanently solved, the more complete the victory, tempts him to carry war to the utmost point of annihilation. Hence the urge to force the enemy into "unconditional surrender." This conviction has been shared by politicians and the masses, but is probably still more common with the soldiers. "Germany is ended! There is no Germany now! There are Germans but no Germany. It is finished!" Foch cried out in exultation at a victory dinner in 1919. Lloyd George, however, "was not quite sure that he was right."[93] They are rare soldiers who, as General Wedemeyer, would declare soon after victory that they did not "believe the military have ever solved an international problem, nor will. It just expands, perpetuates and breeds hate and suspicion."[94] Equally rare are those who, as General Kleist, would declare soon after defeat that "our mistake was to think that a military success would solve political problems. Indeed, under the Nazis we tended to reverse Clausewitz's dictum, and to regard peace as a continuation of war."[95]

The clash of opinions over the importance of enemy capitals as strategic objectives represents merely one of the conflicts bound to arise among partners in a coalition war. Of all types of war, this is the one in which it is most likely that political aims will crowd out and repress strategic aims. And even if this is not intended, the other partner or partners will still suspect it, will try to spare their own forces and sacrifice those of the ally. Largely in order to dispel such distrust, which could easily harm the coalition, the supreme command, if there is one, will be given to a general of the country that contributes the larger part of the forces to the common venture.[96] Or forces of equal strength will be invested in joint enterprises of a somewhat hazardous nature.[97]

The Second World War brought the problems of coalition warfare to a culmination.[98] Coalition stood against coalition, but only at the begin-ning could Hitler echo Napoleon's wish: "Give me a coalition to fight." The common totalitarianism of the Axis Powers did not result in a joint global strategy, nor did the "democracy" of their opponents.[99] On both sides, friction detracted from the effectiveness of combining forces, even in the case of the relatively most harmonious partnership, that of the British and the Americans. The Americans, from Roosevelt down, brought to this partnership a strong distrust of British imperialism, which they had long suspected more than Russian imperialism. The continued British opposition to the cross-Channel attack on Germany was resented by the American planners as contrary to "sound strategy" and as due to political considerations. It added to the irritation that the British never brought forth the political arguments but rather argued their preference for the war around the Mediterranean along strategic lines.[100] These and older experiences resulted in the attempt, embodied in NATO, to overcome the difficulties of a war of coalition well ahead of its outbreak.

POST-WAR USE OF ARMED FORCES— "DEBELLATIO" AND "REBELLATIO"

Conclusions as pessimistic as General Wedemeyer's can well be drawn from historical experiences with occupation of enemy soil after the close of hostilities. The usual reason given for such occupation has been debellatio: victory is intended to make the enemy unfit for further war.[101] The actual result has far too often been rebellatio, "a renewal of war, especially by a subdued people." Debellatio has never yet proved a satisfactory method for establishing a lasting peace. Generally speaking, eighteenth-century diplomacy did not believe in continued military occupation. The soldiers of the French Revolution and Napoleon, however, made extensive use of it, with the most embittering effect on the populations affected. No one realized this better than the conservative soldier-statesman, Wellington. He was commander-in-chief of the Allied troops left in France in 1815, for a maximum period of five years. Almost from the outset, he urged the governments to shorten this period in order not to create new enmities, as the Prussian methods and proposals for continued control of France threatened to do. Although, according to Castlereagh, the Prussian soldiers still proved uninclined "to go home and commence a civil life," the Aachen Congress (1818) reduced the occupation period and settled the reparations question so that it could not be made a pretext for prolonged occupation.

Bismarck cut short the stay of Prussian troops on Austrian and other soil following the Seven Weeks' War of 1866, and proved quite ready to

accelerate the evacuation of France after the
Treaty of Frankfurt by agreeing to faster payments
of reparations. But if these measures were
lessons, they were lost upon the Liberal statesmen who were making peace in Paris in 1919.
These statesmen fell under the spell of soldiers
who, cheated of their entry into Berlin, were able
to convince them of the great usefulness of prolonged occupation for the purposes of German
debellatio. This proved on the whole to be a very
pleasant procedure to the occupying forces and
notably to the imperialist ego of some of their
commanders.[102] The Americans at home, however, became thoroughly disgusted with the details
of the inter-allied Wacht am Rhein and the entanglements with French procedures.[103] The Republican Administration recalled the Rhineland force
in 1923 as the French marched into the Ruhr. The
French occupation of the Ruhr was their greatest contribution to German psychological rebellatio.[104]

Continued military occupation of Germany and
Japan after World War II, up to fifty years if
necessary, figured among the suggestions for
peace made by American statesmen like Hull.[105]
Although he was a Southern Democrat, he did not
seem to consider the experience of the prolonged
occupation of the South after the Civil War as in
any way relevant. In the anticipation of victory,
such a measure seemed called for in order to
avert rearmament of these "warlike peoples."
This was to be partly achieved by an army-di-
rected re-education.[106] It took some time before it was realized that this did not require
large military forces, that these forces might
have been used to greater advantage elsewhere.
It would have been better to have forces in China
from 1945 on than to have them in Japan.[107]
The purpose of occupation soon had to be changed
—as soon as the motives for Russian occupation
were fully realized. Henceforth occupation was to
be for purposes of strategic security, which
neither Russia nor America could any longer find
in the isolationism which they had attempted in the
past. "There should be no thought among us of
quick withdrawal from Europe or Asia," Secretary Hull warned his countrymen after his retirement from office. "We cannot withdraw, for where
can we go? The world is with us, here and now,
and all about us. It is in our front yard, in our back
yard, at our side porch. To withdraw from Europe and Asia is to pull Europe and Asia in upon
us."[108] Such a statement is not far from the
complete abdication of diplomacy in favor of
strategy.

Neither in 1919 nor in 1945-46 did public sentiment greatly favor prolonged military occupation,
particularly in the Anglo-Saxon countries. Par-
ents and wives wanted "the boys home" and there-

fore insisted upon prompt and perhaps too prompt
demobilization following the close of hostilities.
At the beginning of 1919, the demobilization of
the BEF was going too fast, in the judgment of
the Army officers headed by Henry Wilson. They
forced Lloyd George to come out in the open and
make it clear to the country that the war was not
yet over. "He must," they urged, "crush the poi-
sonous part of the Press," which was pressing
for faster demobilization; "he must say the war
is not over. He must prepare the public mind for
armies of occupation in India, Gibraltar, Malta,
France, etc."[109] Some of these occupation troops
were to guarantee the beginnings of the new order
laid down in the Versailles Treaty, including the
supervision of plebiscites in certain contested
regions. Lord Bertie, a diplomatic pessimist,
was convinced well before the Peace Conference
that "a plebiscite can always be worked by the
occupying military force in the direction
desired."[110] French troops in Upper Silesia
did their utmost to throw the plebiscite there to
the Poles. They were, however, much less successful along the Rhine, where their attempts at
plebiscites by putsches were stymied by the other
occupation Powers or by the resistance of the German population.

The world before the Second World War was at
times aware of and respected certain supra-national considerations and interests which put a
limit on destructiveness. The knights of Europe
spared the lives of the knights they captured,
though not of peasants caught arms in hand.
Modern armies bound themselves by the Hague
Conventions—from which Soviet Russia held aloof
—to give decent treatment to their prisoners of
war. Staffs often left enemy staffs unmolested by
artillery fire, though they knew of one another's
location. Armies would even spare one another's
industries, to a certain extent. Monarchs of the
ancien régime "wanted to make war but they did
not want to destroy one another," as a Prussian
diplomat explained to the Directoire, after revolutionary France had first begun to feel tired of
war and before Bonaparte had pulled her out of
the mood.[111] As an Internationale, monarchism
lasted much longer and proved much stronger
than any other, except that of the Catholic Church.
Metternich would have been willing to salvage the
upstart Bonaparte dynasty if only the first Napoleon had been more reasonable. Bismarck was
perfectly willing to facilitate a restoration attempt
by the third Napoleon. Hirohito was spared in
1945 so that he might play his role in a governable
post-war Japan, Western monarchical style.[112]
The Russians and their friends in the United States
would have liked to treat him as a war criminal.
Even the discredited Savoy dynasty was of some
service in ousting Mussolini and bringing an

armistice closer. Such survivals could provide the diplomats with starting points for peace talks.

From the outset, war-making capitalism has proved to be full of contradictions as to destruction and preservation in and by war. The alliance of the capitalist Powers with Bolshevism came close to producing the self-destruction of the former. In the United States, the most destructive post-war plans, plans that could only serve the purposes of Communism, were hatched and propagated by the Treasury Department, the one department that ought to have looked most closely to the preservation of capitalistic concepts. Not before the Morgenthau Plan had found a certain amount of acceptance did such weak defenders of the primacy of diplomacy as Hull and Stimson reassert the prerogatives of their offices. Even then they argued only in the interest of winning the war—knowledge of the Morgenthau Plan might prolong German resistance—and not with a view to any reasonable post-war settlement. For that problem they unhesitatingly ascribed a large role to the military as occupants, with no doubts raised as to their qualifications.[113]

As post-war developments almost immediately showed, the destruction of the Axis enemies had been carried too far by the West.[114] This was partly caused by the fact that war-time diplomacy in America and Britain had been made powerless by Roosevelt and had become oblivious of its irenic mission. The diplomats had not protested, had, for example, not even cared to inform themselves about such revolutionary developments as the atomic bomb.[115] As far as the available historical record shows, the diplomats of the anti-Axis coalition in its Western-capitalistic sector never realized, as earlier ages had, that destruction by war may indeed go too far. Even the presence of Communism, which is annihilation itself, did not serve as such a reminder until several years after the close of hostilities. Only then did the governors of the Western world—and some soldiers earlier than many diplomats—become sufficiently aware of the presence and workings of a force aspiring for the destruction of the capitalist order. The Western states, "for the duration," had forgotten to consider whether some forces similar to their own might not survive inside the Axis countries and whether, in the interest of the future, these should not be spared. For this, a firm amalgamation of political and tactical-strategical concepts and practices would have been required. The separation of political and strategic activities had been overcome much earlier and much more thoroughly by the Communists in Russia. Its directors knew none of the hesitations that Washington civilian and—to a far lesser extent—military offices betrayed about turning the

recent enemy, notably his scientists and his manpower, to military use.[116]

THE UNITY OF POLICY AND STRATEGY

Victory increases by concord.

And, therefore, it is really nonsense to discuss considering military matters apart from the diplomatic because the diplomatic fixes the objective.[117]

None of the principal plans which are required for war can be made without an insight into the political relations. (Clausewitz)

The unity of policy and strategy is axiomatic in statecraft. The need for unity has been proclaimed again and again by civilians as well as by soldiers, by Liberals, Democrats and Conservatives, as well as by Totalitarians.[118] The mere fact of reiteration indicates that this imperative has at times been forgotten or disobeyed. The practical governmental-administrative problem through the ages has been how to establish and maintain unity between the largely civilian components of government, entrusted with policy-making in general, and the military offices, which are to provide for the case of war. As seen from the civilian side, the unifying concept is policy; viewed from the military side, it is "grand strategy," a post-Clausewitzian concept and not a fortunate one in all respects, despite the wide acceptance it has found in America.[119]

The institutional solution has been looked for in the combination of political and military leadership in the hands of a monarch, dictator, or constitutional commander-in-chief, as well as in various collegial arrangements between military and civilian officials who are to prepare or wage war together. In order to make this unity more harmonious and durable, it has been held desirable for the politician to know something of strategy and for the military men to be thoroughly penetrated by the policy of their government.[120] But even such a minimum demand has appeared impossible to attain in periods of specialization, when soldiers and sailors have readily called their political superiors amateur strategists, and politicians have almost as readily called military men amateur politicos.

Unity must overcome the departmentalism that the division of labor nearly always produces. The traditional unifying practice has been the handling of all foreign business of state through the foreign ministry and its organs abroad. It was understood that nothing would be done by any governmental agency abroad without at least a minimum of its cooperation, knowledge, and supervision. It was assumed that personnel acting in a foreign country would have to come under the authority, direction or supervision of the chief of mission in that country. The very minimum an embassy would do was to introduce the non-diplomatic agents of its government to the offices of a foreign government with which they were to deal.

In recent years, the increase in the number of agencies having to do with the administration of foreign business has been unprecedented. With military and other personnel vastly outnumbering diplomatic personnel, old-style diplomatic control no longer seems feasible.[121] At the same time, the coordination of diplomatic and military work has become more imperative than ever. By 1951, a situation developed in the United States that caused administration experts to conclude that the Department of State "should not take over all foreign affairs work," that "even in the field of negotiations there can be no monopoly for the Department of State"; the latter, however, should maintain a review of all such work, wherever it is being carried on. The experts would not go so far as to embrace "the thesis that as a general rule the Department of State should not be given responsibility for the operation of specific foreign programs," as some had proposed. But they preferred that "the administration [they were not concerned with the problem of initiation] of military and economic aid should be carried out jointly by the Department of Defense, the Economic Cooperation Administration and the Department of State. Some form of central coordination or direction must be provided, but the method by which this is to be done with sufficient effectiveness is a matter of great difficulty and complexity," perhaps necessitating a coordinator directly under the President.[122]

The threats to unity lie not only in the often so-called fundamental opposition between military and civilian outlooks. One of the greatest dangers lurks in the tendency—not a failing which can be termed typically civilian or military—to over-value the diplomatic scene or the theater of war of one's immediate concern. This may be only a side-show and not the main theater where, under most conditions, the enemy's main force must first be met. Other dangers are hidden in the hope that, at a time of pan-hostility, a desirable small war can be localized, or in the habit of seeing only one danger when there are others as well.[123] The latter temptation is particularly great in the case of the proconsuls of far-flung empires. Over many decades, the Government of India, usually under the influence of its military advisers, was more afraid of the Russian forward thrust through Central Asia than they need have been from more general military reasoning. And they were inclined to overlook other regions of conflict between Russia and Britain, notably in the direction of the Straits.

When Lord Salisbury was Secretary for India in 1877, he found it necessary to remind the Viceroy that he should not listen too much to the soldiers in Simla. "No lesson seems to be so deeply inculcated by the experience of life as that you never should trust experts. If you believe doctors, nothing is wholesome; if you believe the theologians, nothing is innocent; if you believe the soldiers, nothing is safe. They all require to have their strong wine diluted by a very large admixture of insipid common sense...Soldiers are dangerous advisers as to a military policy."[124] Many of the soldiers' fears of the Russians were proved groundless by the many shortcomings that this foe had shown in its war with the Turks of 1877-78, or so it seemed to Salisbury. As the danger of Anglo-Russian war in Europe over the Straits increased, the Viceroy was again told by Salisbury that there must be one policy only, centered in London. The Secretary "suspected the soldiers of trying to force his hand, noted the preparations that were being made and begged the Viceroy to see to it that 'the muskets do not go off of themselves...In the present excited state of the military mind it is of the first importance not to leave the military men the chance of becoming practically the arbiters whether there should be peace or war.'"[125]

These examples from the past serve to put the 1950-51 conflicts between General MacArthur and the Truman Administration in an historical perspective that the American public did not have at the time. Once put in that context, they seem typical enough, except in the cumulation and protraction of the disagreements. When questioned by one of the Senators (May 4, 1951) as to the relation of political and military responsibilities in peace-time and in wartime, General MacArthur said:

The general definition which for many decades has been accepted was that war was the ultimate process of politics; that when all other political means failed, you then go to force; and when you do that, the balance of control, the balance of concept, the main interest involved, the minute you reach the killing stage, is the control of the military. A theater commander, in any campaign, is not merely limited to the handling of his troops; he commands that whole area politically, economically, and militarily. You have got to trust at that stage of the game when politics fail and the military takes over; you must trust the military, or otherwise you will have the system that the Soviet once employed of the political commissar, who would run the military as well as the politics of the country.

Congressional hearings and investigations are not the appropriate place for theoretical definitions, and when questioned the day after, MacArthur narrowed his statement. It was, he said, "meant to convey the idea that there should be no non-professional interference in the handling of troops in a campaign."[126]

These semi-theoretical statements stand at the temporary end of an interminable discussion about the relations and the distinctions between diplomacy and strategy. The most succinct contribution to the discussion is still that of Clausewitz. As a philosopher of war, he felt impelled to state as a fact and then to overcome by theoretical discussion the sharp military-political dichotomy that was beginning to develop in Prussian affairs, the dichotomy that was in the end to destroy Germany. Within nations where this conflict was less acute, at least at most times, a similar discussion of the same problem can remain much less clear-cut. Jomini, for example, would "scorn the sharp distinction so often asserted between diplomatic and military considerations" and prefer a unity of outlook. Mahan was later to embrace this "precious truth" as "one of Jomini's great gifts."[127] Mahan made the best and also the worst of it in his own teaching and counselling of governments. He exercised the most fatal influence in Wilhelminic Germany, where the dividing line between strategy and diplomacy had become the last dyke for a minimum of civilian co-determination in Reich affairs.

In the theoretical discussion with which Clausewitz overcomes the dichotomy in policy that he had posited between the military and civilian elements, he himself gives as fine a statement of the unity of policy as can be written. Unity, he says, is

> the conception that war is only a part of social intercourse, therefore by no means an independent thing in itself...is nothing but a continuation of political intercourse with an admixture of other means...Does the cessation of diplomatic notes stop the political relations between different nations and governments? Is not war merely another kind of writing and language for their thought? It has, to be sure, its own grammar, but not its own logic. Accordingly, war can never be separated from political intercourse, and if...this occurs anywhere, all threads of the various relations are, in a certain manner, broken, and we have before us a senseless thing without an objective, [a war that would be] entirely war, entirely the unbridled element of hostility.[128]

Unity must also prevail in the planning of war. In preparing for war, as Frederick the Great

emphasized, statecraft and the art of war must go hand in hand![129] For Clausewitz, it was "not permissible to have two or three points of view, from which things might be regarded, now with a soldier's eye, now with an administrator's, now with a politician's." All standpoints and interests must be united and reconciled by policy as the representation of all the interests of the community. Policy must not give way to purely military considerations, as it tends to if and when wars assume the character of struggles for life or death. He argues:

> It is an impermissible and even harmful distinction according to which a great military event or the plan for such an event should admit a <u>purely military</u> judgment, as is frequently done by cabinets; but still more absurd is the demand of theorists that a statement of the available means of warfare should be laid before the general, so that in accordance with them he may draw up a purely military plan for the war or the campaign. General experience also teaches us that in spite of the great diversity and development of the present system of war, still the main outlines of a war have always been determined by the cabinet, that is, if we would use technical language, by a purely political, and not by a military organ. This is perfectly natural. None of the principal plans which are necessary for a war can be made without an insight into the political conditions, and when people speak, as they often do, of the harmful influence of policy on the conduct of war, they really say something very different from what they intend. It is not this influence, but the policy itself, which should be found fault with. [The policy might not have been as faulty had it been realized] that a certain knowledge of military affairs is essential to the management of political intercourse...If war is to correspond entirely with the intentions of policy, and policy is to accommodate itself to the means available for war, in case statesman and soldier are not combined in one person, there is only one satisfactory alternative left, which is, to make the commander-in-chief a member of the cabinet, that he may take part in its councils and decisions on important occasions.[130]

The immediate post-Napoleonic era, when Clausewitz drew his conclusions, was one of a new consolidation of the traditional ruling groups within the military and civilian bureaucracy. The nobility dominated, admitting only as many sons of the bourgeoisie as were necessary to furnish supplementary brains for the organization and running of such large-scale enterprises. That is to say, originally the organizing intelligence in such offices as the general staff did not also rule.[131] In Britain, this consolidation of the ancient powers, surviving Reform Bills, etc., gave the ununiformed members of the ruling stratum a long-lasting amateur status in military affairs. (Sometimes the results were fortunate, as in the cases of Cardwell and Haldane.) In most Continental countries, the community of power between civilians and soldiers rested on the understanding that the former would concede their incompetency in the military field. This admission preceded the increasing technicality of the military profession, although it still did not move a Bismarck to refrain from passing military judgment. He realized only too clearly that the soldiers' claim to exclusive competency was a bid for power that the supreme statesman must not concede them.

The "separation of the toga and the sword," which had been united in Rome, in the Middle Ages, and in rulers like Frederick and Napoleon, did not go unobserved and uncriticized, even as it began. While the majority took it for granted that "separation" was part and parcel of the inevitable process of division and specialization of labor, a soldier like Clausewitz or an occasional political scientist warned against it as

a bad invention of modern times, devised by rivalry and envy, originally agreed to by distrust and mediocrity and retained by habit. The result could only be to make new enterprises puny and fruitless. This is particularly true in the most recent times, when it was believed that the shortcomings of ministerialism could be cured by collegial arrangements. Actually nothing was achieved except that, with legislative chambers on the one side and ministerial boards on the other, sovereignty became completely isolated, all unity destroyed and an all-consuming bureaucracy produced, within which only writing machines could be created, but no statesmen...The successes of Rome and also the Middle Ages testify how fruitful unity in the direction of policy and war (Kriegswesen) can be. How puny, however, are the successes since the separation of policy and the art of war has come about![132]

Theoretically speaking, the practitioners themselves as a matter of course admitted the necessity of unity rooted in policy. Early in his career, Moltke stated that political questions are the premises of military conclusions.[133] But in the actual conduct of war he came to insist that, once military measures had been set in motion, they should not be interfered with by political considerations and demands. Theoretically far more than practically, the military have been aware of the dangers of departmentalism and

the need for overcoming it by fundamental and continuous agreement between the directors of policy and the military leaders. As one general put it, "the General Staff is entitled to expect that the Government shall keep it fully au courant with the political conditions of the day...There should be at all times an intimate understanding between what has been called the 'brain of the army' and the civilian executive at the head of the State."[134] In return, the civilian governors should be entitled to expect that the military share their basic policies and inform them of military limitations. Despite fundamental agreement, some friction nearly always remains, making it doubtful whether the description of the U.S. Navy, for example, as "a precision instrument of diplomacy to help maintain peace" is a very realistic one.[135]

Even MacArthur was willing to admit that "it is quite impossible to draw a line of differentiation and say this is a political and this is a military situation. The American Government," he concluded, "should have such coordination so that the political and military are in coordination."[136] His superiors in Washington became still more aware of the "intermingling of political necessities along with military directions," an intermingling that took place inside such bodies as the National Security Council.[137] MacArthur's chief, Bradley, was presented with the question as to whether it was still

possible, in view of the global problems of the United States, to draw the line of demarcation that is attempted to be drawn between the strictly military on the one hand and the strictly diplomatic on the other, or are they so intermingled and commingled that as Joint Chiefs of Staff you have to look at the security of our country and make plans to protect the security of our country from the standpoint of the overall problem—diplomatic, military, including every other conceivable factor?

His answer had to be:

We have to take all those into consideration. However, in some cases before a decision is arrived at, we are called upon merely to submit the military side of the question and somebody else presents the other side, the additional points—that is, the political and diplomatic—and then the man making the decision weighs all those things—sometimes there is conflict, sometimes there isn't—and arrives at the decision...Naturally, the Joint Chiefs of Staff have to know considerable about the diplomatic and political implications of these questions also.[138]

The older kind of world policy had received practically no true strategic implementation at any of its foci. It had largely been concerned with imperialism, that of the services included, rather than with genuine security. Now, with an imperialism in the world that is proceeding along the lines of a centrally-directed strategy and tactics, security has to be bought and war-planning and war-making have to be contemplated from the counter-center of Washington over a world-wide scene and in various strata and media.[139] Under such conditions, the unity of policy and strategy acquires an unprecedented importance.

FOOTNOTES

1. For the fantastic ideas of contemporary publicists about the Baghdad line, see Pratt, Rise of Railpower, chap. xx.

2. See, e.g., G. P., XXIV, 8212.

3. Perhaps this agreement was an expression of the pro-German views that caught part of the Russian General Staff immediately after the close of the Russo-Japanese War. Doc. dipl. fr., 2nd series, X, 418 f.

4. Ibid., X, 131 f.

5. The discussions about the strategic importance of Formosa in the 1950's offer numerous parallels, and may offer still more in times to come.

6. "There is no question that foreign policy is a function of defense and vice versa" (September 2, 1948). Forrestal Diaries, p. 497.

7. Grouard, "Stratégie et politique militaire," Revue de Paris, December 1, 1922, pp. 581 ff.

8. Here is an illustration: During the discussion of the reforms for the French Army, beginning in 1871, even such an exclusively technical question as the choice between the battalion with six and the one with four companies became identified with political viewpoints. The Left, generally speaking, opted for the formation which seemed to favor the dispersed order. The Right preferred the formation with the closed order. The former put their confidence in the individual and liberated him from the ranks; the latter could only see him as constantly submitted to the constraint of authority. "Just as democracy presupposes the fullest unfolding of the human personality, modern combat demands the intensive development of the soldier's individuality." Monteilhet, "L'avènement de la nation armée," Revue des études napoléoniennes, XIV (1918), 131 f.

9. Cited by Bourget in Gouvernement et commandement, p. 6.

10. Cited from his Ausgewählte Schriften by Wilkinson in War and Policy, p. 105.

11. About 1660, "there were here and there, and not only in France, standing regiments which

waited in peacetime for war." Berenhorst, Betrachtungen über die Kriegskunst, p. 141.

12. Campbell-Bannerman, as a member of the Hartington Commission on British Army reforms, dissented from some of his colleagues' recommendations, notably those in favor of a general staff, saying that "it was not necessary for us continually to be studying our neighbors' strength and weakness; and that 'in any of the smaller troubles into which we might be drawn...the plan of campaign must be governed by the particular circumstances, and would be left (I presume and hope) to be determined by the officer appointed to direct operations.'" He held "that for giving advice to the Secretary of State for War the officers who were in touch with the actual executive work of the Army were in a better position to do so than those who 'sit apart' and cogitate on the subject" (1890). Verner, The Military Life of George, Duke of Cambridge, II, 360 f.

13. Bishop, Theodore Roosevelt and his Time, I, 74 f.

14. Voltaire for one did not think highly of diplomacy. "The true charter of liberty is independence maintained by the strength of arms. The treaties which secure this natural privilege are signed by the point of the sword. If it is a matter of peace treaties, the sabres of the grenadiers cut the necessary quills. Roman virtue does not achieve much these days. The richest wins—that is not noble, but is true. The ministry of foreign affairs is dependent on those of war and of finance. Have money, then you have victory! Then the ministry can do all it wants to. Wealth, derived from industry and commerce, a large army and (as in the case of France) a strong fleet—that is the only basis of flourishing states. There are no political secrets beyond that." Cited by Sakmann in Voltaire's Geistesart und Gedankenwelt, pp. 362 f.

15. By 1752, after the first two Silesian Wars, Frederick the Great concluded that "acquisitions made by the pen are always preferable to those achieved by the sword." Cited by Berney in Friedrich der Grosse, p. 231.

16. Forrestal Diaries, pp. 25, 154, 496. Cf. Senator Lyndon B. Johnson: "I assume that the policy of the State Department is determined largely by the strength of our services and what it can do if it should be called upon to do it" (June 1, 1951). Military Situation in the Far East, p. 1777.

17. A term used by Sir George Aston in his Sea, Land, and Air Strategy, pp. 5 ff., and again by Admiral Karlgeorg Schuster in "Einfluss der Politik auf die Kriegsführung," Zeitschrift für die gesamte Staatswissenschaft, Vol. 97, 1 ff.

18. Conrad, Aus meiner Dienstzeit, I, 303.
19. The secret French-Italian agreement of 1902, which promised France Italian neutrality, was not made known to the French General Staff until 1909. For nearly seven years, then, France had continued a very considerable military force along the Alpine front for no good purpose, except to keep the Germans—and the Italian Chief of Staff?—in the dark about the Triplice partner. Joffre, Mémoires, I, 103 ff.
20. The rebuilding of the post-1918 German Army would have been unthinkable without Reichswehr pressuring of various sorts. Since the majority of civilian politicians did not particularly want a big army and saw no immediate reasons for it, Seeckt provided its raison d'être. "The State that wants to have prestige in the world, wants to conduct foreign policy, stands in need of a reliable, i.e., a trained and equipped army. Since it cannot foresee far in advance just when the army will be used, it needs a standing army. This maxim is almost banal, self-evident, but today its correctness, proven by the history of all times, must be strongly emphasized, considering the attempts made to obscure it." Memorandum of February 17, 1919. Seeckt Papers, National Archives. Cf. also Rabenau, Seeckt, II, 184, on the sword as ultima ratio regnorum.
21. The alliances concluded before the wars of the eighteenth century were often concluded only a few weeks before their outbreak. The Austro-German alliance was concluded thirty-five years prior to 1914, the Franco-Russian twenty-three and the Anglo-French entente ten.
22. Very soon after the conclusion of the war alliance of 1866 with Prussia, which was limited to three months, and after the inglorious defeat at the hands of the Austrians at Custozza, Italy began to negotiate an alliance with France and Austria against Prussia-Germany, which only the prompt German victories of 1870 kept from final conclusion. During the summer of 1870, ossuaries and cemeteries on the battlefields of 1859 and 1866 were consecrated and, in an exchange of toasts, General Govone, the negotiator of the treaty with Prussia of 1866, greeted Francis Joseph as "il nobile e valoroso alleato dell'Italia" and the Austrian military attaché in return drank to "la bella, la prode, la valoroso Armata italiana." Oncken, Rheinpolitik, III, 383.
23. Stieve, Schriftwechsel Iswolskis, II, 373.
24. For details, see Cadorna, La Guerra alla Fronte Italiana.
25. Robertson, From Private to Field-Marshal, p. 134. The view of General Grierson was similar.
26. Callwell, Sir Henry Wilson, II, 298.
27. See Kehr, Schlachtflottenbau und Parteipolitik, for the double uncertainty of the German Navy: what types of ships should they build and against whom?
28. "The Navy is and remains unfortunately a disease of our all-highest master, and only a war and the small importance of the Navy that it will doubtless demonstrate will be able to prove curative in this respect." This was the opinion of a general and ambassador as early as 1891. Wedel, Zwischen Kaiser und Kanzler, p. 166.
29. Glaise-Horstenau, Franz Josephs Weggefährte, p. 246. Four years later, Albrecht, contemplating an anti-Austrian alignment from Russia to Italy, including the small countries from the Pruth to the Adriatic, concluded that "diplomacy must mobilize everything in order to avert a misfortune of that kind." Ibid., p. 293.
30. G. P., XIX, 6031.
31. American Historical Review, LVII, 340.
32. For American approval of Czechoslovakia's role in the continued encirclement of Germany, see State Department memorandum on "The Slavs of Austria-Hungary" (May 9, 1918, signed by Putney), cited in Pergler, America in the Struggle for Czechoslovak Independence, pp. 78 ff.
33. Schlieffen's original calculations envisaged the possibility of a French invasion of Belgium prior to a German one that was to take place on the tenth or twelfth day of mobilization; the Great General Staff was in the possession of such plans in 1895. Europäische Gespräche, X, 80. The new feature of a coup de main against Liège, to be undertaken as soon as possible following the outbreak of war, was introduced in 1912.
34. Memorandum of December 21, 1912. Reichsarchiv, Kriegsführung und Kriegswirtschaft, (Anlageband), p. 163 f.
35. Bourget, Gouvernement et commandement, p. 110.
36. For details, see Hemmer, Die deutschen Kriegserklärungen von 1914, pp. 8 ff., 107 f., 113 and passim.
37. For details, see Harrison, Cross-Channel Attack, pp. 24, 121, 123, 125.
38. For the American motivations, see Dean Acheson's testimony of 1951. Military Situation in the Far East, p. 1845.
39. Dean Acheson. Ibid., p. 1783.
40. For details, see Ibid., pp. 1723, 1760, 1763 f., 1958 f., 2260, 2275 f.
41. Late in November 1941, when "diplomatically the situation was virtually hopeless," the Secretaries of the Army and Navy and the Chiefs of Staff were still pleading with Hull "for more time in which to prepare our resistance." Hull, Memoirs, II, 1071.

42. Jähns, Kriegswissenschaften, p. 1508.
43. Jany, Geschichte der preussischen Armee, III, 221 ff.
44. Report of Prussian Minister in Paris, June 13, 1863. Die auswärtige Politik Preussens, III, 623 f.
45. Ibid., III, 110 ff.
46. G. P., VI, 1151, 1159 f., 1165; VII, 1496.
47. Wertheimer, Andrassy, III, 107.
48. Tarlé, Bonaparte, p. 259. When, during the hard winter of 1941-42, some German "imbecile" set off the ominous rumor that Hitler had started the fatal attack against Russia on the same day as Napoleon, June 22, the Führer had it announced that Napoleon had not started until the 23rd (actually, on the 24th). Hitlers Tischgespräche, p. 186.
49. Schmitt, The Coming of the War 1914, II, 136.
50. For details, see de Bono, Das Jahr XIV.
51. From Geneva, April 20, 1936. Tansill, Back Door to War, p. 254.
52. Trials of War Criminals, XII, 798.
53. Hitler to Ciano, August 13, 1939. Ibid., XII, 1169.
54. Secretary of State Weizsäcker, Ibid, XII, 1169.
55. For this problem, see Binder-Krieglstein, Krieg ohne Chancen, Vol. II of his Psychologie des grossen Krieges.
56. Bismarck in the Reichstag, January 24, 1882. Gedanken und Erinnerungen, I, 81 f.
57. G. P., XII, 2934.
58. Renouvin, Préclin, and Hardy, L'époque contemporaine, II, 474; Langer, Imperialism, pp. 561 f.
59. Recouly, Le Mémorial de Foch, pp. 142 ff., 266 ff.
60. Compare France's reaction to Germany's remilitarization of the Rhineland, chap. XII, pp. 415-416.
61. Hölzle, Der Osten im ersten Weltkrieg, pp. 194 ff., on basis of French documents.
62. Documents on German Foreign Policy, Series D, I, 1082.
63. Waldrop, MacArthur on War, pp. 308 ff.; Vagts, Landing Operations, pp. 646 ff.
64. Hanson Baldwin in N. Y. Times, July 10, 1950.
65. Ibid., September 1, 1950.
66. Langer, Imperialism, pp. 272 ff.; Gleichen, A Guardsman's Memories, p. 18.
67. Testimony of ex-Secretary of Defense Louis Johnson. Military Situation in the Far East, pp. 2671 f.
68. Documents on German Foreign Policy, Series D, II, 466 f.
69. Military Situation in the Far East, pp. 730, 878, 896, 998 f.
70. Ibid., pp. 31, 39 f., 60, 68, 571.
71. During the commotion over MacArthur's dismissal, it was recalled that American history also included one partial war, the one made at sea against France in 1798.
72. Meyer, Bismarck, p. 436.
73. Glaise-Horstenau, Franz Josephs Weggefährte, pp. 469 ff.
74. "The influence of politics upon strategy had nowhere been more sharply emphasized than in the Navy B-36 hearings before the House Armed Services Committee...The members of the committee are themselves, of course, representatives of two political parties. Each member considers, as he must under our form of government, his constituents back home. Some committee members from states like Texas, where there are great Air Force installations, and where the B-36 Consolidated bomber is built, are pointedly sympathetic to the Air Force in their questioning of witnesses. Others, from 'Navy States,' are sympathetic to the Navy." Hanson Baldwin in N. Y. Times, October 11, 1949. He adduces other "proof of the fact that the overtones of politics shade and influence even technicalities and tactics."
75. Delbrück-Daniels, Geschichte der Kriegskunst, V, 285.
76. Ollivier, L'Empire libéral, XVII, 345 f.
77. Tschuppik, Ludendorff, pp. 26 f.; Holborn in Earle (ed.), Makers of Modern Strategy, pp. 181 ff.
78. G. P., IX, 2087.
79. For a discussion of capitals as objectives in war, see Aston, Sea, Land and Air Strategy, pp. 72 ff.
80. Les Armées françaises dans la Grande Guerre, I, 55, 96 f., 144.
81. Danilov, La Russie dans la guerre mondiale, p. 129. Traditional French pro-Polonism had long been written off in favor of the alliance with Russia. Repelled by France and the repressive measures of Russian administration, the most war-like Poles, such as Pilsudski, were inclined towards siding with Austria, their most friendly enemy, relatively speaking. Though French politicians might still turn their liberal sympathies towards Poland and wish to have it share in the reforms which the Russian Revolution of 1905 seemed to promise, the French military attaché in St. Petersburg warned against such hopes as contrary to the best French interests. An autonomous Poland would upset all Russian plans of concentration against Germany and Austria. Could France wish for that? Fortunately, the Russian chief of staff understood this dilemma and assured him that such Polish aspirations would be disapproved by the vast majority of the Russian nation. As was required by her military situation, Russia would remain one and indivisible. Doc. dipl. fr., 2nd series, VIII, 231 f.

82. See above, chap. XI, p. 445.
83. October 13, 1916. Diary of Lord Bertie, II, 44.
84. The aiming of Hitler's V-Vergeltung (retaliation) missiles at London was wrong from a strategic point of view. They ought to have been directed at the embarkation ports of 1944, at Plymouth, for instance.
85. Mott praises Pershing "who alone foresaw that any termination of the war short of complete surrender would be unfortunate" (1937). Mott, Twenty Years as Military Attaché, pp. 261 ff. In the autumn of 1918, Woodrow Wilson was urged by Masaryk to carry the war on to Berlin and there force the German Army into complete surrender. Die Weltrevolution, p. 313.
86. Ganoe, History of the United States Army, pp. 216, 223; Nevins, Ordeal of the Union, I, 3 f.
87. Admiral Halsey's Story, I, 289 f.
88. Statement by Army Historian Forrest C. Pogue. American Historical Review, LVII, 807 f.
89. For a discussion of this error, see Baldwin, Great Mistakes of the War, pp. 45 ff.
90. In the summer of 1795, when the Directoire asked the topographical section of the War Ministry to elaborate a plan of war against Austria, the resulting plans, Bonaparte's brainchild, proposed that the French mass armies strike at the heart of the Monarchy by advancing along the Danube and Po rivers in order to "dictate" the peace at the gates of Vienna. While the campaign of 1796 was not fought in accordance with such plans, those of 1805 and 1809 followed the direction of the Danube and ended with the two peace dictates of Pressburg and Schönbrunn, after Vienna had been taken.
91. Politische Correspondenz Friedrichs des Grossen, III, 136.
92. Eighteenth-century subjects would not always understand such moderation, and the supreme grumbler among the British, Dr. Johnson, once remarked that "the king who makes war on his enemies tenderly distresses his subjects most cruelly."
93. Riddell, Intimate Diary, p. 106.
94. Military Situation in the Far East, p. 2440. The Annales Mettenses (747 A.D.) tell of Charlemagne's brother Karlman, who, after having slain thousands, became melancholy and entered a monastery, where he was employed as a goose-herd; when he could not save one of his herd from a wolf, he realized how little he was qualified to be a leader of men. Thus the Monkish tale.
95. General von Kleist to B. H. Liddell Hart in the latter's The German Generals Talk, p. 194.
96. Soon after the close of World War I, Maurice Barrès noted: "If Foch had not wound up in 1918 but had waited until the spring of 1919...

had waited for the arrival of fifty American divisions, Pershing would certainly have claimed the command over everything." Barrès, Mes Cahiers, XII, 305.
97. 314,514 troops had been landed in the U. S. Zone in Normandy and 314,547 in the British Zone by the end of June 18, 1944. Harrison, Cross-Channel Attack, p. 423.
98. See Langer, "Political Problems of a Coalition," Foreign Affairs, October 1947.
99. Mussolini to Badoglio: "The Germans are terrible as enemies and unbearable as friends." Badoglio, Italy in the Second World War, p. 112.
100. Harrison, Cross-Channel Attack, pp. 26, 96.
101. The Germans announced that the 1940 armistice with France was intended to make it impossible for France to resume hostilities, to enable them to carry on the war against Britain with France as the base, and to create the first conditions for a constructive peace. Görlitz, Der Zweite Weltkrieg, p. 140.
102. The worst of these proconsuls was General Mangin, who set himself up as viceroy in Mainz, and who was much admired by his compatriots. "Il n'y a qu'avec lui qu'on a vraiment l'impression d'être vainqueur. Et pourtant il n'ordonnait aucune violence contre les habitants." Andriot in Revue d'histoire de la guerre mondiale, XIII (1935), 66.
103. For the combined military and political reasoning against prolonged American occupation, see March, The Nation at War, pp. 109 ff.
104. For the idea of 1920 of setting up "a respectable and docile Turkish Government at Constantinople, preserved from its hereditary vices by a military cordon of the Powers— including a permanent British garrison of 10,000 to 15,000 men" and Curzon's judgment of it as "a chimera," see Nicolson, Curzon, p. 113.
105. Hull, Memoirs, II, 1617.
106. For MacArthur's claim of what American occupation in Japan has achieved, see Military Situation in the Far East, pp. 310 ff. The Japanese "are in our camp strategically, economically, financially, and to some extent spiritually."
107. Cf. General Wedemeyer's testimony: When MacArthur occupied the Japanese homeland, "it turned out that they were docile and cooperative, but he had no way of knowing at this time, and he required those divisions in his occupation of Japan; and he refused to make them available to me [in China]." Ibid., p. 2415.
108. Hull, Memoirs, II, 1739. During a visit to Vienna in June 1952, Acheson told a news conference: "The business of troops and

occupation is something Americans don't
enjoy. We want to terminate it as quickly as
possible...Make no mistake about it, of the
four powers in Austria three want to go
home." N. Y. Times, July 1, 1952.
109. Callwell, Sir Henry Wilson, II, 161.
110. Diary of Lord Bertie, II, 145, 147.
111. "Entre monarques on veut guerroyer, mais
on ne veut pas se détruire." Cited by Ollivier in L'Empire libéral, XVII, 553. Eighteenth-century tactics did "not at all aim at
smashing the enemy forces but at pushing
them out of certain positions. In keeping
with that, strategy did not aim at the destruction of the enemy's forces but rather at the
gaining of certain terrains...and did not
really intend the debellatio of the hostile
state, i.e., to make him actually unable to
continue the war, but rather to move him, by
holding some of his territory in pawn, to conclude a favorable peace. Even such an aim
seemed at times too highly put to the governors of states and armies: sometimes they
would be satisfied with mere demonstrating."
Jähns, Kriegswissenschaften, III, 1919, 2029.
112. At a secret White House meeting during the
war, Roosevelt discussed with a number of
advisers, including Senator Elbert Thomas
as an expert on Oriental affairs, the proposal
to destroy Hirohito by an air attack on his
Tokyo palace. The political arguments against
the obviously military or naval proposal were
so strong that the plan was dropped. N. Y.
Times, August 12, 1947.
113. Hull, Memoirs, II, 1604 ff.
114. Zhdanov at the founding of the Cominform in
Warsaw, September 1947: "The military destruction of the bloc of the Fascist powers has
sharply changed the relation of strength between the capitalist and the socialist states
in favor of the latter." Cited in Die Zeit,
(Hamburg), July 19, 1951.
115. Cf. Hull's remarks: "I was not told about the
atomic bomb. Occasionally someone gave me
a veiled hint, but I did not press any questions." Hull, Memoirs, II, 1110.
116. One of Washington's earliest proponents of
Germany's and Japan's rebellatio was General Wedemeyer. He was soon recognized
as such by the Communists. When his ideas
found no hearing in the capital, he had himself transferred to a troop command. Military Situation in the Far East, pp. 2310 f.,
2385, 2449, 2452; for opposition from the
State Department, see Ibid., pp. 1468 f.
117. Senator Green, June 27, 1951. Ibid., p. 3036.
118. Cf. Visconti-Prasca, La guerre décisive,
pp. 1 f., 8.
119. A Brookings Institution report defines it as

a complex that "looks beyond war to the subsequent peace, includes all factors that will
affect the peace, and extends to the relations
of a nation to its allies and neutrals as well
as to its opponents. Grand strategy and the
national security policies to which it is related are matters for decision by government
in the largest sense and not by any single
department or interest." The Administration
of Foreign Affairs, p. 155.
120. The Department of State sends a number of
its members to the War College for this purpose. Here officers of the three armed forces
are schooled for "joint staff and command duties of the highest level in behalf of national
security" (according to the U. S. Government
Manual). McCamy, The Administration of
Foreign Affairs, p. 110.
121. As of September 30, 1950, some forty-three
governmental departments and other agencies
engaged in overseas activities employed a
total of 74, 879 civilian personnel, American
and non-American, of whom 51,204 were in
the service of the Defense Department.
Brookings Institution, The Administration
of Foreign Affairs, pp. 248 f., 344.
122. Ibid., chaps. xix, xxi, p. 229.
123. For the proposal of the Russian Minister of
War in 1906-07 for a little war against Turkey, see Stieve, Schriftwechsel Iswolskis, II,
312.
124. Cecil, Life of Salisbury, II, 152 ff.
125. Ibid., II, 157 f.
126. N. Y. Times, May 5-7, 1951. When still in
Tokyo, MacArthur told a British correspondent that "it was not the soldier who had encroached on the realm of the politician, it
was the politician who had encroached on
that of the soldier." Time, April 23, 1951.
127. Puleston, Life and Work of Mahan, p. 78.
128. Clausewitz, "War as an Instrument of Policy,"
chap. vi (B) of Book VIII, On War, pp. 594 f.
129. Frederick the Great, "General Principles of
War" (1748), cited by Jähns in Kriegswissenschaften, p. 1941.
130. Clausewitz, On War, p. 599. His original version, before the "editing" by a brother-in-law,
was: "...that he may take part in all the important moments of its activities." Ritter,
Staatskunst und Kriegshandwerk, p. 92.
131. Until 1859, if not later, the chiefs of staff in
Austria were outsiders, whereas "the commanding generals were born as such," not
made. "If in the cradles of the princes and
counts there was also placed a little talent,
a little of the blithe courage of the horseman,
then the attainment of the highest military
posts could be predicted with confidence,
provided they chose a military career. That

a general must...also have profound expert knowledge, of this one did not seem to be aware at the time when this system was in usage." Article on "Karl Ludwig Graf Grünne" in A. D. B., Vol. XLIX, 602 f.

132. Werklein, Kriegskunst und Staatskunst, pp. vi f.

133. Memoire of February 8, 1859, cited by Eyck in Bismarck, I, 324.

134. Callwell, in Encyclopedia Britannica (13th ed.), III, 632.

135. Admiral Radford, Vice Chief of Naval Operations, speaking at Chautauqua, N. Y., N. Y. Times, July 11, 1948. Similarly, Rear Admiral Walter Boone, when on the way with the U. S. Aircraft Carrier Boxer to strengthen American units in the Philippines: "I have no 'shoot' orders but we are fully prepared for any eventuality and have a full allowance of ammunition...The Navy's mobile airpower in the Western Pacific is one of the principal instruments of U. S. diplomacy." Time, January 30, 1950. Major General Laurence Kuter described the Berlin airlift and strategic air transport generally as "a conspicuous expression of American airpower, peace power and an effective weapon of diplomacy." N. Y. Times, January 25, 1949.

136. Military Situation in the Far East, pp. 289, 45.

137. Secretary of Defense Marshall. Ibid., p. 360.

138. General Bradley in answer to query of Senator Smith (N.J.), Ibid., p. 898. Cf. General Collins (Ibid., pp. 1364 f.), and Barr: "If the military man only considered the military factors and went ahead and acted upon them, he probably wouldn't remain a military man very long." Ibid., p. 3018.

139. Senator Morse: "Is it not true, that we no longer in the world can fight a war on a strictly military basis, but that we have to fight it also after giving consideration to diplomatic problems?" Bradley: "That is correct, and certainly your objectives in a war are not entirely military. In other words, the end results of a war are a combination of military and political considerations, and you use the military to obtain your political objectives." Ibid., p. 899.

Generals and Peace-Making

" 'Tis safest making peace with sword in hand."
George Farquhar,
Love and a Bottle (1699).

War, at least modern war, implies the breaking off of all open relations and negotiations between belligerents. A first step towards the resumption of these relations is most often taken through action on the part of the commanders of field armies. The official action may be preceded by limited suspensions of hostilities, including thoroughly unauthorized "fraternizations" at the strictly local level.

ARMISTICE AS THE BEGINNING OF PEACE

Field commanders, acting on their own initiative or on general or detailed directives from their home governments, have usually engineered the beginning of the end of wars by terminating actual hostilities. This opens the way to peace negotiations, unless hostilities are resumed or the defeated belligerent is deprived of his treaty-making sovereignty. Only rarely in modern times has a war been terminated over the generals' heads, by a peace unpreceded by an armistice.

In earlier times, field or theater commanders customarily acted with considerable independence in terminating hostilities, though at the risk of being disavowed by their home government. Cumberland at Kloster Zeven in 1757 and Zachary Taylor at Monterey in 1846 were disavowed, whereas York at Tauroggen in 1812 was upheld. Since the invention of the telegraph, home governments have increasingly participated in or even initiated negotiations leading to armistices and truces of a more than local nature.[1] Their supreme concern has been to keep so-called political matter out of negotiations between the military.[2] Where it suits them, however, governments gladly leave the disagreeable aspects of ending hostilities to the triumphant military. Where possible, a general of the defeated army has been given the task of concluding or attempting a peace. On September 2, 1870, Napoleon III, according to Bismarck, demanded "a more favorable convention." Bismarck said he "could not enter upon negotiations about that, since this was a purely military question in which Moltke must be heard. They could, however, talk about a possible peace." Napoleon answered that "he was a prisoner of war and thus not in a position to make any decisions on that."[3]

Because of the all-pervasiveness of political considerations, the participation of the home gov-

ernments in the preparation, negotiation, and formulation of armistices eventually came to have but few limits.[4] The negotiators of armistices became plenipotentiaries with the most restricted full powers and the most detailed instructions. This was obviously the case during the many months of negotiations for an armistice in Korea. At least one kind of peace-making by generals came to an end with such procedures. So also ended the politicians' excuse, used by Thiers, that "if peace treaties were generally impolitic, that was due to the fact that they had most often been dictated by victorious generals."[5]

MILITARY WISHES REGARDING PEACE TREATIES

In modern times peace dictates or the suggestions of generals have been made in the various capitals rather than in the field. There the military formulate and present their proposals for at least the military sections of the peace treaties which are to be negotiated by the civilians. The military have usually exerted their most lasting and often their most fatal influence on peace-making by their advice on the drawing of frontiers. They have frequently maintained that the great peace conferences and congresses have too often come to decisions on frontiers "without asking the generals," that they have ignored "military and political geography," that this has resulted "in so many worthless treaties, produced in the bare chancelleries of these clever people."[6] Military pressure for "better frontiers" has nearly always proved synonymous with the desire for territorial expansion. Many of the frontiers drawn by the military, since the time when they first obtained what often amounts to overruling determination in this matter, have given diplomats occasion for putting the blame for later frontier difficulties squarely on the military and their insistence on having defensible strategic frontiers. Bismarck held Moltke responsible for having forced him to include Metz in the German conquests of 1871.[7] And Dean Acheson indicated that the unfortunate 38th Parallel in Korea went back to a military proposal.[8]

When the diplomatic negotiators would or could not obtain such "frontier corrections," the soldiers groused about the "bad peace." Practically every modern peace treaty has found disfavor with large or small groups of military men who have felt that their wishes and advice were neglected.

Officers of armed forces actually or seemingly near victory have insisted that only full victory, and not negotiations, can give peace—victoria pax non pactione parienda est (Cicero). They have pressed for more participation in the making of peace, while those on the defeated side have endeavored to avoid participation in the necessarily painful if not shameful negotiations that precede a peace. Bismarck realized at an early date that the participation of military personnel in such negotiations was likely to have a long-lasting antagonizing effect on the beaten army. He tried to reduce this effect to a minimum in his dealings with the French in 1871. Needless to say, this did not prevent the French officer corps from becoming the culture-medium of revanche. The Russian delegation to the negotiations at Brest-Litovsk included nine army and navy officers, who were taken along as strictly technical advisers by the Bolshevist negotiators. One of them found the terms agreed upon by the Bolsheviki so humiliating to Russia that he committed suicide in Brest. The triumph of the military of the four Central Powers found its partial expression in the signature of five military men on the Treaty concluded there. This was done in order to satisfy the wish of the German generals and admirals to be heard in the peace-making negotiations. At the outbreak of the war in 1914, Tirpitz had been assured that the military would be heard in the making of the future peace. This assurance was reaffirmed in April 1915 by the Emperor's naval cabinet chief.[9] Hindenburg reminded William II even more directly, during the Brest negotiations, which did not seem to promise satisfactory new frontiers to Germany, that William himself "had graciously ordered" that he and Ludendorff were "to participate in a responsible manner in the peace negotiations," that William had thereby conferred upon himself (Hindenburg) and his Quartermaster-General "the right and the duty to help watch that the result of the peace is in keeping with the sacrifices and performances of the German people and army and gives us such strong frontiers that our enemies will not soon again dare to unleash a new war."[10]

Later in 1918, when the tide of war had turned against Germany, the OHL was far less eager than at Brest and Bucharest to have any of its representatives participate in the armistice and peace negotiations. The civilians in the revolutionary government obligingly took the onus of defeat on their shoulders. A civilian, Erzberger, headed the armistice delegation and was later murdered for his pains by a military assassin.[11] The German Army was soon relieved to learn that

the general on the armistice commission had "the good taste of not wanting to work any longer with Erzberger" and that a French general "was taking care of the German military interests" instead of a civilian member of the delegation. When Seeckt became military representative on the peace delegation in 1919, the beginning of the end of German disarmament was in sight, even though nothing more could be salvaged than the 100,000-men Reichswehr.[12]

In 1945, the "democratic" allies, persuaded that they had learned a lesson from the experience with the Germans in 1918-19, insisted upon and received an armistice delegation composed exclusively of military personnel. The conditions imposed were so crushing that one of the delegates put himself to death immediately after the signing of the armistice. Under the customs of war introduced in 1945, he might have become a "war criminal," as happened to the principal military delegate of the Japanese surrender mission, General Umezu. When this soldier, who had opposed surrender to the last, learned of his new assignment, he at first threatened to commit hara-kiri should the job he forced upon him. Only the orders and persuasion of the Emperor made him accept the odious duty. After he had performed it, an American court sentenced him to a life-term in prison.[13]

The motivations leading to armistices have usually been both military and political in nature. Military defeat may appear obvious and final to the defeated side—the South in the American Civil War, France in 1871 and 1940, Germany in 1918 and 1945. Or defeat may seem reparable only at an inordinate price—as was true of Russia's situation in 1905, which was further complicated by a revolutionary situation at home. There may be reasons for not attempting to achieve a complete victory that in itself seems possible of attainment— the British view as to the war of 1812 with the United States.[14] War-weary populations may make a war's continuation inadvisable and may provide defeated military leaders with convenient scape-goats as well. On the victorious side, civilians in war governments may be burdened with the post-war reproach that they did not allow the military victory to be carried to its "logical" end. For generals like Pershing and Tasker Bliss in 1918 or 1919, this would have meant "unconditional surrender" and an armistice signed in Berlin, at whatever cost of Allied and German soldiers' lives.[15] Some American officers in 1918 were as little tired of the war as Swedish officers had been at the close of the Thirty Years' War, when they cursed the peace negotiators of Münster-Osnabruck. Both groups thought that more could be gained by more war.

This was not the view of Haig or Generalissimo

Foch in 1918-19 or in the years that followed. But this does not mean that the latter approved of the peace terms. Defending himself and his actions of 1918 in the face of the disappointment over the outcome of Allied victory and peace in the 1920's, Foch asked an interviewer:

> What is an armistice? It is a suspension of hostilities which the victor grants the conquered in order to avoid useless effusion of blood and to discuss in the meantime the conditions of peace which he is in a position to impose. For war is a means, not an end. One does not make it in order to carry off victories—but only in order to impose one's will, one's whole will, on the conquered...What good would it have done to continue conquering if the enemy accepted, militarily speaking, all our conditions? He was absolutely forced to bow to all our demands. Now that is precisely the sign of a good armistice. The victor who signs it has the right and the duty to demand of the conquered all that makes it impossible for the latter to continue the struggle. But what would have been gained by demanding more?....
>
> The Allies have discussed the peace treaty among themselves. This treaty in my opinion was bad, very bad for us. It did not assure us of either of the two things to which we were entitled: reparations and security.[16]

Anything but a Siegfrieden was unthinkable for either side in 1918. No negotiated peace, such as generals have occasionally initiated in order to crown their military successes on the battle fields with peace, was possible.

MILITARY INHIBITIONS AGAINST PEACE-MAKING

Breaking off a battle is not an easy step for a general to take. Breaking off a war is even less easy, despite indications that victory may have become uncertain. It requires a form of courage that the peace-intending diplomat is inclined to call "civilian." It would have been in the logic of the Schlieffen Plan—based on the view that a long-drawn-out war was unbearable—if, after the failure on the Marne, German Army leaders had suggested that their Government enter upon peace negotiations.[17] What happened instead? On September 8, 1914, the Crown Prince urged Falkenhayn, the War Minister, and others to do their best to prevent "a rotten peace" such as high financial and industrial circles in the Reich were said to be seeking. Falkenhayn's answer was: "It would be vain to talk about peace. Germany could not very well offer it as long as no enemy stood on German soil...and the others would certainly not offer it. The whole talk of peace was based on an erroneous view of the opponents' psychology."[18] It was also

based on an erroneous view of the German officers' psychology. They now shifted their hope of winning the war from a strategy of annihilation to a strategy of attrition. Falkenhayn stated, before Verdun, that the war would still last a long time and that victory would go to the one who stuck it out the longest. Rupprecht of Bavaria, a commander who had more to lose than the war, was more ready than the soldiers to admit that this pronouncement was a military testimonium paupertatis. As late as June 1918, Ludendorff would not admit the possibility of German defeat. His last political success was to obtain the removal of Foreign Secretary Kühlmann because the latter had told the Reichstag that "through a clear military decision alone, without diplomatic negotiations, an absolute end could hardly be expected" (June 24). This statement struck the OHL "like a bombshell and set off the greatest indignation."[19] As a recent historian has said of Ludendorff, "he had enough despair to go on fighting, but not enough courage to end it."[20]

Concluding peace over the heads of generals usually infuriates them. When Napoleon III very suddenly made the Peace of Villafranca, nearly all of the French generals "were surprised and many expressed their wrath." Leboeuf cried out before his staff: "This making of peace means turning us into fools. Why? Everything went according to wish. And what will our Allies say to whom we promised the Adriatic?" Another general described the peace as nauseating and said that the Army had been robbed. But on second thought their emotions calmed down. Everybody was happy to be home once more, and dubious about the wisdom of going on with the war only to get killed for the sake of the ungrateful Italians, who had done so little to help in the war fought for their own independence. Only a general like Fleury, with his insight into political conditions, realized even before Solferino that Europe might intervene in order to keep Austria from being too deeply humiliated. The other Powers, after all, would not want to see Napoleon as arbiter of the Continent.[21]

Generals have often expressed their own opinions as to when or when not to make peace. In many cases, these opinions have been in conflict with those of the political directors of policy and have on occasion interfered with the latter's own plans and ideas. It could only strengthen French intransigence when, in July 1918, Pershing told the French liaison officer with the American Army in France:

> The Allies must not allow themselves to be caught by possible proposals of the Germans who after the failure of their attacks might seek a compromise peace. If the Germans want peace, this is not the moment to grant it to them. The

man who has committed a crime must undergo his punishment. The same with nations who have committed crimes. No negotiations ought to be entered upon before the Germans have suffered their punishment, which ought to be inflicted upon them in the military way. It is in this sense, therefore, that I shall act towards my Government. I am assured, incidentally, that President Wilson is of the same opinion. I hope that by the autumn of this year the Americans will be sufficiently numerous and sufficiently organized for a powerful offensive, designed to make the Germans feel their force, in order to start with the punishing.

Two weeks later, Poincaré, much emboldened, could speak to Pershing about "the necessity of assuring a definite peace through a complete victory." Pershing was very happy to see the Lorrainer take this stand and quite ready to incur possible losses, even high ones, in order to achieve complete victory.[22]

Captured generals, sometimes interpreting their personal defeat as a portent, have on several occasions served as a one-man peace mission from the captor to their own government. Taken prisoner at Lawfeldt in 1747, British General Ligonier, of French descent, began the first talks of a peace with his captor, German-born Marshal de Saxe. These talks continued after his exchange, leading to the general peace of Aachen in 1748. Even if it seemed to be an unfruitful peace, it nevertheless ended a senseless war.[23] Saxe had wanted France to gain some of the territories he had occupied. "I have maneuvered in order to make conquests," he said; "I shall now combat in order to make peace." But Louis XV would not hear of it: "I recognize very well the style of generalissimos: their policy is one of red-hot shot." He wanted instead to make a king-like peace.[24] In 1918, the Turks sent their British captive of Kut-el-Amara, General Townshend, across the lines to carry the request for an armistice. And Badoglio put out his armistice feelers by releasing British General Caron de Wiart, of Belgian descent, and sending him to Lisbon, where negotiations eventually started.

The sensibleness of a war might well be measured in adverse ratio to its length. This would make the wars of 1859 and 1866 history's most reasonable wars. The shorter a war is intended to be, the more ready statesmen must be to start negotiations promptly. In doing this, however, they may run up against a dangerous dynamism inside the armies. The Generals will want to bring war to a close in keeping with the "laws" of strategy. Throughout the Wars of Liberation, the diplomats on either side were far more ready to enter upon negotiations than either Napoleon or most of the

Allied generals, notably some of the Prussians.[25] The soldier in Napoleon was loath to end war as long as there was even a slight chance left of battling, to say nothing of victory. The soldier won out over the statesman; he succumbed, unable to retain his Empire even on the reduced scale that was more than once offered to him by Allied diplomacy.

Their splendid successes in the wars of 1864 and 1866 provoked a similar hubris in the Prussian officers. They developed an argument by which they hoped to master Bismarck, according to which "the Minister of Foreign Affairs only regains the word when the army direction thinks the time has arrived to close the temple of Janus." They forgot altogether, as Bismarck thought, the warning expressed by the double-faced nature of that god; the government of a belligerent state must also look in directions other than the theater of war. According to Bismarck, "the task of the army directorship lies in annihilating the hostile forces. But the purpose of the war is the achievement of peace under conditions which are in keeping with the policy pursued by the State. Ascertaining and limiting the objectives to be reached by the war and counselling the monarch with regard to these is and remains, during the war as well as ahead of it, a political task."[26]

"DEBELLATIO"[27]

The measures proposed by one side or the other for the debellatio of the enemy have been another common source of military-diplomatic disagreements over peace-making. Such measures include disarmament of the enemy, restriction by treaty of his future forces, demilitarization of certain regions or places, and occupation of his territory after the signing of the peace. While the soldiers have often nourished firm (if unanalyzed) notions as to the effectiveness of continued occupation, the great diplomats have entertained far fewer illusions. The French Revolution and Bonaparte may be considered as the inventors of the combination of supervising disarmament and exacting reparation payments through prolonged military occupation. The revolutionaries also thought that this would serve to implant the seed of liberty abroad. The Emperor continued his occupation of Prussian territories after the Treaty of Tilsit (1807) under various pretexts, but actually in order to exact reparations and at the same time supervise Prussia's disarmament down to 42,000 men. The net result was less in achieving efficient supervision than in earning the undying hatred of the Prussians. Of all the Allies against Napoleon in 1813-14 and 1815, they were the most eager to apply this same treatment to France. The Prussians were, as Castlereagh put it, reluctant "to go home and commence a civil life." They reasoned, he wrote in 1818, "as if Bonaparte was still on the throne of France and as if the French Army was capable of effectuating a coup de main as formerly...Their irritability and taste for demonstration is more likely to excite the military spirit in France and augment our danger than to add security to the general interests." The supremacy of diplomacy in the councils of Europe was great enough to overrule all the proposals of the Prussian soldiers for continued occupation and other controls over France.[28]

Most other settlements of nineteenth-century wars, as far as they envisaged any peace-time occupation of ex-enemy territory, kept these periods short, or reduced them below what was originally stipulated. These decisions were largely due to the diplomats, who more often than not disagreed with the soldiers as to the execution of the old Roman imperative, addressed to both, to spare the conquered and render the proud unwarlike.[29]

MILITARY CONSULTATION ON PEACE-MAKING

Once hostilities had been brought to a close by the military, with or without prompting or assistance from the diplomats, the latter, until fairly recent times, would then dispense with the services of the military, even as "experts," during the peace negotiations proper. The great historical peace conferences and congresses—Münster, Utrecht, Vienna (1814-1815), Paris (1856), and even the London conference dealing with the Balkan peace (1912-1913)—did without soldiers as delegates or experts. When Wellington went to Vienna in order to replace Castlereagh, who was needed at home, he acted as the conservative statesman. Resentment over the exclusion or disregard of military advice habitually found its expression in the subsequent complaint that the pen had once more signed away what the sword had won. In spite of Prussia's very substantial gains in the settlement of 1815, Blücher, the most drastic spokesman, or grumbler, of her army, cursed the politicians as "poor judges of men." The Vienna Congress, he wrote, "resembles a small town fair whither each drives his cattle either to sell or to barter. We have brought there a first-call bull and got in exchange only a shabby bullock."[30]

Thoroughly familiar with this kind of dangerous grousing,[31] Bismarck took care to check over Moltke's proposals for the capitulation of Paris and for the peace conditions best ensuring the strategic security of the new Reich before the latter embarked on negotiations with the French representatives in 1871. All of Moltke's proposals were far from moderate; those for the capitulation of the capital were tantamount to unconditional surrender.[32] As a condition for the peace, the Chief of Staff demanded Alsace and Lorraine and a whole strategic glacis farther West, which was to include places such as Nancy, Luneville, Briey, Belfort, and Montbeliard, some of them focal points of the later French fortification system. If these places had been put in German hands, later French revanche desires would have been under a great handicap. Bismarck himself never wanted as much. He would even have given in on the demand for Metz and French-speaking Lorraine, had the French remained adamant on this point.[33] And as early as the summer of 1871, he was willing to admit that perhaps too much had been taken for reasons of strategic security. "I am under no illusions," he told the first French diplomatic representative in Berlin.

It is absurd for us to have taken Metz, which is French. I did not want to keep it for Germany. The General Staff asked me if I would guarantee that France would not take revenge. I replied that, on the contrary, I was quite convinced that she would do so and that this war would not be the last to break out between Germany and France, but that it would be followed by many wars. "If that is so," they said to me, "Metz is a glacis behind which France can place 100,000 men. We must keep it." I could say the same about Alsace and Lorraine. If peace is to be durable, it was erroneous on our part to have taken it [them?] from you, because for us these provinces are an embarrassment... In taking from you Metz and a piece of Lorraine, the Emperor, my master, and the military who have inspired in him this resolution, have committed the most grievous political fault.[34]

But all such admissions that demands based on military security had sown political insecurity remained Platonic and were never intended as an offer to return part or all of these provinces to the Third Republic. And even had they been so intended, there would still have been no guarantee that this would have smothered French desires for revanche.

The "Prussians of the Far East," eager warmakers in 1894 in the civilian as well as in the military sections of their government, were confronted before long with the problem of when to terminate the war. In spite of the threat of a foreign intervention hanging over their heads, of which the foreign minister was aware as early as October 1894, the attempts to open armistice and peace negotiations were postponed until the end of March 1895. This was partly due to the intransigent demands raised by the high command. While Prime and Foreign Ministers, always fully

conscious of the threat of intervention, wanted to
forego all continental acquisitions, "high military and naval officers pressed upon the cabinet
to demand what they regarded as legitimate
fruits of their operations," including the cession
to Japan of the Liaotung peninsula. The argument
that greater strategic security would thus be acquired apparently played a small role in comparison with the drive for imperialistic gain. When
the long-dreaded "advice" (to cede Liaotung back
to the Chinese) of the three interveners arrived
on April 23, their superior military strength was
so obvious that war and naval ministers counselled in favor of accepting it.[35]

After the victory at Mukden in March 1905, the
Japanese General Staff was first to realize that
the country was in danger of conquering herself
to death. To continue war for another year would
call for an additional 250,000 men and one-and-
a-half billion yen, which would have to be raised
by foreign loans that were not likely to be forthcoming. The chief of staff of the field army, returning to Tokyo after the Mukden incident, told
the military and civilian authorities that "those
who had started the war should know when to stop
it." He urged that they seek an early opportunity
to open negotiations leading to peace. After American friendly services had brought the belligerents
together, the threat to the peace came from Japan's
diplomats, who ran up against Witte's obstinacy
at Portsmouth. They considered breaking off
negotiations and resuming war. It was the military argument and judgment that forced the signing of the treaty. And the Japanese government
needed military force to control the over-expec-
tant masses who were unwilling to acquiesce in
the disappointing peace.[36]

MILITARY ANNEXATIONISM

The annexation of Alsace-Lorraine made the
Berlin General Staff feel just as territorially
"saturated" as most Germans of the period. Annexationism, however, had other loci within the
body politic, notably, as in many other countries,
in the naval offices. Inspired by Mahan's writings,
they clamored for naval stations in all parts of
the globe. Strategic "justification" for the various
territorial changes that took place between 1871
and 1914, as well as for farther-reaching aspirations, was never lacking. At the outbreak of the
First World War, many officers were far better
prepared for the opportunities to acquire more
real estate than for the technical problems that the
war presented. This land hunger was stirring long
before victory was assured. Everywhere on the
European continent, the military presented their
demand that strategic improvement of their countries' frontiers be taken into consideration in the

treaties and understandings with old and new
allies, as well in the future "victory peace"
(Siegfrieden).

Italy was promised territorial acquisitions at
the expense of Austria-Hungary, based on ethnographic as well as strategic considerations,
when she signed the Treaty of London of April
26, 1915. At that time, the Russian Foreign Ministry and the GHQ were discussing the partition
of Austro-Hungarian Bukovina, some of which
was to go to Rumania as part payment for her expected entry into the war on the Entente side. The
Russian military wanted a frontier running along
a mountain crest line in the Carpathians, which
would dominate Hungary and its plains. The diplomats reminded them that strategic considerations
were not the only basis for a satisfactory boundary zone, that security had also to be based on
those friendly neighborly relations which are best
guaranteed by the absence of "irredentism."
And besides, the Rumanians would enter the war
only if assured of the exact territorial gains they
would receive. Bringing this conflict between
ethnographic-political and strategic frontier-
drawing before the Tsar, the Chief of Staff enumer-
ated the numerous arguments against the purely
ethnographic settlement preferred by the diplomats.
According to him, the strategic, political, economic, and religious conditions of the zone in question spoke against the ethnographic argument. The
population was of such a mixed character in places
that a distinct line of separation could not possibly
be drawn, while the zone was united by the Orthodox religion and the common hatred for the "Jew-
ish-German yoke."[37] The Bukovina and adjoining Carpatho-Russia were freed from all such
uncertainities, not by the White Tsar but by the
Red one. Thirty years later, both were added to the
homeland of Socialism for its greater strategic
security, and the ethnographic problem was solved
by the extermination or expulsion of minorities.[38]
In 1915, the strategic considerations voiced by the
Stavka helped to keep the Rumanians out of the
war for still another year.

The demands of the German General Staff for
strategic annexations came relatively late in the
war—another sign that it had not been imperialist-
annexationist-minded before 1914. Only with
Hindenburg-Ludendorff in the Supreme Command
(OHL) did Pan-Germanism in its strategic guise
receive the official military stamp of approval.[39]
The demands that finally developed were for the
correction of frontiers at the expense of France,
who was to surrender the industrial basin of
Briey-Longwy, for control over Belgium, and
for a "protective belt" for Upper Silesia and West
and East Prussia.

Ludendorff was fully determined to extend his
virtual dictatorship in German politics to dictating

the peace-making. He and his staff proceeded on the conviction that the waging of the war had gone so far beyond the purely military frame of reference that the organizer of the war—meaning Ludendorff—could no longer remain a subordinate of the political director but had to assume that role himself.[40] The German delegation to Brest-Litovsk included both military men and civilians. The Chief of Staff of the army in the East (Oberost), Major General Max Hoffmann, as "special representative (Sondervertreter) of the OHL," was yoked together with the Secretary of State for Foreign Affairs. The latter was to be kept from signing away what the soldiers believed they had won. Although militaristic enough in his conference manners, even Hoffmann could not bring himself to justify all of the OHL demands for annexations. Part of these Hindenburg said he needed "for the maneuvering of his left wing in the next war," while Ludendorff wanted other parts in order to make sure of a more ample food supply for Germany in case of such a war. Hoffmann tried to urge the Kaiser, who was poorly filling the role of arbiter which had been given him in the Second Reich, to oppose so much annexation. The Kaiser was willing to agree. The dioscuri of the OHL fumed at what they considered to be Hoffmann's insubordination, regretting perhaps that they had not made General von Bernhardi their peace delegate, as Hindenburg had contemplated.[41] Hindenburg and Ludendorff threatened to resign if the Kaiser disregarded their opinion in this matter, "a matter of vital importance for the existence of the German Fatherland." All moderation crumpled before this threat of the then two most popular persons in the Reich.[42]

The manner in which the peace negotiations in Bucharest (March-May 1918) were conducted displeased Ludendorff no less. He thought that the German negotiators did not sufficiently exploit the recent victories in the West, which should have been at once recoined into diplomatic specie. Instead, he thought, they left the Rumanians under the impression that they might one day be able to reopen operations and that the four Allies were hopelessly divided. Hindenburg was made to sign a letter to the Chancellor, saying that

continuing negotiations in the present manner endangers the interest of the directorship of war and of our peace-time economy. The Rumanians must be presented with an ultimatum. Basing ourselves on our military successes in the East, we need not fear a breakdown in the negotiations. In any case, I have already given orders that for the time being part of the divisions designated for the West will remain in Rumania in order to give our demands more force...The war and power situation with regard to Rumania is such that everything would have been obtained if Your Excellency's representatives had acted in keeping with it.

Buoyed up by his initial successes in the West, Ludendorff explained to the Chancellor, over the name of Hindenburg, his

views on the mutual relations of military situation and diplomatic action. It is up to diplomacy to make immediate use of the favorable military situation. We have too many enemies in this war and the favorable picture can be changed too quickly by events in one or the other of the many theaters of war for diplomacy to wait, at a time of military success, for a politically favorable moment. General Ludendorff was, therefore, fully justified when, early in February, he pressed for opening negotiations with Rumania in order to make full use of the momentum of strength inherent in the favorable military situation and the locally available forces which were already partly earmarked for the Western front.[43] In Rumania, the military means of power have constantly stood behind the German negotiators. The negotiators, however, have only made use of this momentum of strength under pressure from the OHL. In Bucharest as well as in Brest, we have seen that as soon as German diplomacy became conscious of this momentum of strength, it succeeded within the shortest time in putting down the delaying attempts of our enemies and obtaining the peace.

The voice of diplomatic reasoning was that of Kühlmann. He was far from certain that the peace order in the East would be of a permanent nature, but he was a weak force in the Second Reich. The voice of traditional, aristocratic, diplomatic reasoning became audible in the war only at certain moments, as, for example, when the Vatican offered its peace mediation and when Lord Lansdowne's letter in favor of a peace of understanding was published on November 29, 1917. But such voices were promptly drowned out by the demands for a victory peace, for security through annexations, for one-sided disarmament, and for reparations.[44] From the time of the Germans' first request for an armistice, addressed to Woodrow Wilson on October 6, 1918, military counsel on the conditions for the armistice and for the peace to follow abounded in the West. According to Foch, "it was advisable that without delay the military counsellors be given the floor."[45] They tried to hold the floor with their advice, recommendations and occasional threats, although their ascendancy never became as dictatorial as military counsel on peace questions had been in Germany a year earlier. Not all of them were eager to shut the temple of Janus or to keep it shut. Having been the last to come into the war, Pershing was most radical in his suggestions to carry on with the war and sign the armistice only after "unconditional surrender" at Berlin. Generals and admirals were notoriously slow to allow humanitarian sentiment and practice to flourish again after the moratorium they had suffered during the war.[46] The five weeks that elapsed before the armistice could be signed, while military advice on the armistice was being obtained, resulted in conditions that civilians could not have made worse had they tried. It became more difficult for the civilian governors to attain or maintain a position where for once in history there would be "a victor superior to his success."[47]

Several of the makers of the Paris treaties arrived with what they considered to be highly enlightened notions about peace. Some of their ideas had been derived from a contemplation of the more unfortunate examples of peace-making under the influence of military or strategic reasoning. Wilson was more firmly grounded in his Liberal beliefs than in a correct knowledge of the history of peace-making. He declared, when the question of Danzig was being considered, that soldiers should have nothing to do with boundary-drawing. And during the discussions on Fiume, he declared that "the strategic argument is very dangerous; the treaties of 1815 [!] and 1871 were drawn up by military men; they were responsible for the annexation of Alsace-Lorraine; it is the military who have led us from one disaster to the other."[48] Strategic arguments could not even be considered against such firm convictions.

Short of the detailed analysis that has not been undertaken, it would be unsafe to say which were more fatal: the disagreements between the civilian and military peacemakers over the French soldiers' demand for the Rhine, or their agreements on the creation of the French satellites, with their impossible military tasks, and on the 100,000-men Reichswehr, which implanted the anti-democratic virus in the weak system of the Weimar Republic. Various actions of the soldiers in the implementation of peace-making undermined the peace, disrupted the cohesion of the war coalition, and aroused those sentiments in which wars of revanche have their beginnings.[49]

Foch and his comrades in and outside France were convinced that any peace preferred by the Allied and Associated Powers could be forced upon the Germans, that sufficient military means were available "to overcome all difficulties likely to arise from the signature of the Peace." The rarer general, such as Tasker Bliss, warned its authors that the Treaty might prove indefensible for moral and even military reasons. For "the peace which may not be defended in the name of right before the world always calls forth new resistances against it. Nobody will be capable of subscribing to it with good conscience for it will not be able of fulfillment. Nobody would be able to take upon himself the guarantee of its execution which ought to lie in its signature."[50]

The peace that had been denied Ludendorff because of the defeat of Germany in 1918, peace through Lebensraum annexationism, Hitler, who was more the heir of Ludendorff than either of the two was willing to admit, hoped yet to achieve. As in Ludendorff, the "general" in Hitler had been repressed by the imperialist from the outset of his mad career. Almost until the end he continued to give orders to cling to "real estate" instead of ceding terrain in an elastic defense. His wild annexationism went so far beyond military considerations and reality, was so much the Party's own affair that, as far as one can see, the generals were never asked to state their views on a desirable post-war order for the Third Reich.[51] The officers' putsch of 1944 was their own way of seeking peace, as was Badoglio's more successful defection from Mussolini. They had long known that their side could not win the war.

The Russian military must have had full opportunity to state their own concepts of Russian security, though it is impossible to say or even guess which side, the military or civilian marshals, suggested most eagerly and determined most strongly the new Russian territorial expansion as the basis for Russian security. It began with Moscow's participation in the Fourth Partition of Poland, as complete as the Third had been. And necessarily so, as Stalin said at the time, since an independent rump-Poland would only create frictions between Russian and Germany.[52] This marked the full resumption of the traditional expansionist tendencies, "hunting for the frontier" as it had been called in the Berlin General Staff in the 1890's. War was waged against Finland when she refused to accept the territorial and strategic demands made of her, demands justified by the need for the greater security of Leningrad, Russia's second capital.[53] There is no other war on record that was undertaken for "purely strategic" reasons, undertaken by civilian governors who had themselves become fully strategic-minded. And a Pan-Slavism was resumed in the direction of the Balkans that was, as in the past, strongly military and utterly non-Marxian.

The Russian penchant for conquest and control was little understood in London, and still less in Washington, partly because the governors and soldiers believed they could not afford to understand them. They felt in need of Russian support for the final victory over Japan, little aware of the possibility of war after the war, of the resumption, from new bases, of the international class warfare that had been only temporarily halted. Thus, for a time, only the Axis and, strangely enough, Britain were considered by America to be imperialistic.[54]

As far as the peace had been prepared before 1945 by the Western Powers, the military and naval men, according to present evidence, were only rarely consulted. Only a few of them had any misgivings as to the ultimate intentions of Russia or as to the wisdom of the "unconditional surrender" demand.

The Joint Chiefs of Staff did not voice any strong misgivings about this demand, which had considerable military implications, nor about Roosevelt's vast concessions to Russia in the Far East.[55] A true artificer of peace might in fact have urged Roosevelt to keep the Russians away from the Pacific. But such remonstrations would have collided with one of Roosevelt's "pet ideas...a plan for a series of strategic bases all over the world to be controlled by the UN."[56]

This solution was apparently Roosevelt's unrealistic compromise between the war-time demands of the Joint Chiefs of Staff that the Pacific islands be taken from Japan to become American property and Hull's contention that all colonial territories wrested from the Axis Powers should be put in trusteeship with the United Nations.[57] American annexations, according to Hull, would only encourage if not justify Russian claims for similar acquistions.[58] The peace strategy underlying Hull's proposals would have been sounder if Russia's access to the Pacific had not been increased by the concessions made at Yalta. These concessions were made after Hull had gone out of office, and were obviously agreed to by the Joint Chiefs of Staff as the price for Russia's entry into the war against Japan. They dreaded (wrongly, as it turned out) the final phase of the war, the fight for the Japanese homeland. They were so convinced that it might call for extremely high American casualties that they preferred to have Russia enter this war at a high price rather than have her stay out of it. Her staying out might have given her a superior post-war position over an America weakened in the final struggle against Japan.[59]

There could not have been more civilian supremacy in the peace-making of the Western Powers. An insouciance prevailed which was as much military as it was civilian and which left even the bare minimum of military caution unobserved. This is reflected in the arrangements for the supply lines of the Western Allies to Berlin, which enabled or encouraged the Russians to declare the land blockade of that city.[60] The soldiers and sailors were presumably permitted a hand in the writing of the disarmament paragraphs,

already largely disregarded today, in the peace treaties with the ex-Axis partners, Italy, Hungary and Bulgaria. But that was the measure of their participation in peace-making. Whether greater participation on their part would have improved things may seem doubtful, but non-participation provided them only too soon with occasion to grumble. As Forrestal summed it up in April 1947, "it was manifest that American diplomatic planning of the peace was far below the quality of the planning that went into the conduct of the war. We regarded the war, broadly speaking, as a ball game which we had to finish as quickly as possible, but in doing so there was comparatively little thought as to the relationships between nations which would exist after Germany and Japan were destroyed...." The writing of the peace treaties should have been done "while our troops and military power were still evident in Europe."[61]

The initiative in post-war preparations for war came altogether from Russia's side. Even such atrocious, friction-charged arrangements as those for Russian bases within Finnish territory went unprotested—they were to serve the peace.[62] Only after Russia had nearly completed her compact glacis system, which was to reach "from Japan to the Adriatic,"[63] did America proceed to weld the lands and bases stretching around this land fortress into a counter-system. Thus began a process of competition in which the West is still far behind because it started late and with an uncertain mind. This lateness gave the Soviets, as first-comers, the advantage in propaganda: they could accuse the West of encircling them.[64] They displayed a bazaar effrontery in their propaganda, which makes one even more curious about the people to which these arguments may possibly appeal outside Russia than about the beliefs prevailing inside the Kremlin.[65] Roosevelt's illusions about the peace died slowly in Washington and elsewhere in the United States. For a time, military advice on such questions as the acquisition of bases was denounced as a sign of "the growing control of our foreign policy by those who speak primarily for the armed services," of the "preponderant influence that the professional military mentality is exercising in those decisions that are determining the objectives and the methods of our foreign policy."[66] Such possible footholds as Formosa were written off by the State Department, with the Joint Chiefs of Staff concurring.[67] Instead of accepting this obvious invitation to take Formosa, the Red Chinese and the equally Russian-controlled North Koreans preferred to invade South Korea and thus extend the Russian glacis still nearer to Japan. With the Korean War, strategic considerations assumed enough weight in the considerations of the State Department to cause it at last to openly endorse the long-standing military suggestion that the peace with Japan provide for American military bases in that country and for the administration of the Ryukyu and Bonin Islands by the United States on behalf of the United Nations.

While such decisions did not go to the length of MacArthur's proposals, which would have given the Far East the character of the main theater of war, they marked once more the reluctantly accepted ascendancy of strategic considerations in American foreign policy. The rejection of MacArthur's idea also included the rejection of his definition of a "victorious" outcome of the Korean War. He thought of victory as old-style Siegfrieden, victory in the recently-established style of unconditional surrender. The Chiefs of Staff in Washington, in common with the President and the State Department and a number of political leaders, came to reject the idea of a necessarily victorious outcome of the conflict, either because it was unobtainable at the time or because it was not even considered as desirable per se. By spring 1951, there was "room [in Washington] for qualifying the thought that there is no substitute for victory"; that "while we had unconditional victory in the last war, the result had not been entirely satisfactory"; that the idea of unconditional surrender called for re-examination; that the idea of "all-out victory" might well be shelved in the settlement of the Korean conflict, provided such an outcome would still teach aggressors that aggression would not be permitted to succeed. As expressed by Senator Fulbright, this was "a new kind of objective and one that is not surrounded by all the glamour and emotional connections that the old-fashioned victory is surrounded with. It is much easier to appeal to most people's emotions by talking with the language and concepts we used a century ago, but...this objective is just as real, albeit it is a new one, a new kind of objective."[68]

EUROPEAN "REVANCHE"—AND ITS END?

At a later date, it may be possible to describe and evaluate in detail what role the diplomats and what role the soldiers have played in post-World War II re-understandings, in the making of new enemies out of old—not very old—allies and of new friends out of old—perhaps older—enemies.[69] It may be possible to determine how soldiers and diplomats

"Have learnt, though late,
This rule, to hate an enemy as one
Who may become a friend, and serve a friend
As knowing that his friendship may not last."[70]

If the wisdom of the generals as co-makers of peace seems somewhat open to doubt, their role in the keeping of it is far clearer, if more negative. The military officers of the peace-dictating

Powers have usually given advice as to the extent of injury that should be inflicted on the defeated in order to make it impossible for him to seek vengeance.[71] Those of the beaten party have usually kept their "own wounds green" and have kept alive the sentiment for revanche sooner or later, urging rearmament and the search for allies against the victorious nation.[72] Austrian officers, including Emperor Francis Joseph, sought revanche pour Sadowa until 1879, when the civilian governors concluded the alliance with Bismarck.[73] French officers pursued revanche from 1871 to 1914, if not from 1815 to 1919;[74] German officers from 1919 to 1939. Ideas, healthy or deadly, have their birth-place and lodging in specific groups within a society. Military officers have most often given shelter to the idea of vengeance for defeat in war. Is it with them that it is being sheltered today?

As far as the current proposals for a European Defense Community are honestly intended, they can provide a dissolvent of the impulse to revanche, as well as of the fear of revanche itself. For the time being, however, the opposition to rearming and winning over the ex-enemy is lodged with the civilian electorate, mostly in France. Unconvinced of what their own soldiers and those of their allies have termed military necessity, they cling to their fear of a revanchist Germany. By so doing, by denying satisfaction to those elements in German society that are most apt to resent continued dishonor, they weaken at the same time the position of the western-minded German politicians. The French do not realize that they have done this once before, in the years after 1918, to the immeasurable injury of all the West.

FOOTNOTES

1. During the Korean War, General MacArthur "invited the enemy commander to negotiate with him in the field, though he knew that the U.N. itself was trying to lay the groundwork for negotiations looking towards the end of fighting." N.Y. Times, April 29, 1951. Much of the older custom spoke in favor of MacArthur.
2. Early in March 1865, when Grant reported Lee's first desire to come to terms, Lincoln directed him "to have no conference with General Lee, unless it be for the capitulation of Lee's army or on solely minor or purely military matters...You are not to decide, discuss, or confer upon any political questions; such questions the President holds in his own hands, and will submit them to no military conferences or conventions. Meanwhile you are to press to the utmost your military advantages." Ignorant of these instructions, Sherman entered upon armistice negotiations with another Confederate general. He was rebuked and threatened with

dismissal. He duly apologized for what he had done: "I admit my folly in embracing in a military convention any civil matter." Pfanz, "The Surrender Negotiations between Johnston and Sherman," Military Affairs, XVI, 61 ff., cited in N.Y. Times, June 3, 1951.

3. Bismarck, Gesammelte Werke, VII, 336.

4. For the intervention of the various governments in the negotiation of the Italian armistice of 1943, see Hankey, Politics, Trials and Errors, pp. 42 ff.

5. Cited in Doc. dipl. fr., 2nd series, X, 562.

6. The Prince de Ligne to Empress Catherine II, autumn of 1790. Klarwill (ed.), Der Fürst von Ligne, p. 303.

7. Meyer, Bismarck, pp. 438 f.

8. "The division at the 38th parallel was recommended by the Secretary of War, was approved by the Joint Chiefs of Staff, by State, Army, Air Force Coordinating Committee, and was approved by the President." Military Situation in the Far East, pp. 2104 f.

9. Tirpitz, Erinnerungen, p. 467.

10. Ludendorff, Urkunden der Obersten Heeresleitung, p. 452.

11. When the Armistice Commission visited Hindenburg at Spa, on its way to Compiègne, he told Erzberger: "It [is] probably the first time in world history that not soldiers but politicians have concluded an armistice, but [I am] quite agreeable to that, particularly since the OHL [does] not give political directives any more; and in any case the Army [does] need rest." Schwertfeger, Das Weltkriegsende, p. 186.

12. Rabenau, Seeckt, II, 148 f., 159 ff.

13. Kase, Journey to the "Missouri," pp. 5 f., 212, 246 ff.

14. For a discussion of these issues, see Calahan, What Makes a War End?

15. T. Bentley Mott refers to Pershing's proposal admiringly as giving "the measure of his robust sagacity." Mott, Twenty Years as Military Attaché, chap. xxvi. For Bliss, see Bailey, Wilson and the Peacemakers, p. 50. Cf. pp. 479-480 above.

16. Recouly, Le Mémorial de Foch, pp. 30 ff.

17. The 78-year-old General von Haeseler, who had followed the army into the field without holding command, was almost the only one to whom it appeared "that the moment had arrived when the attempt must be made to end the war" (September 29, 1914). Oberkircher, General Erich von Grundell, p. 154. And after the trench war opened on the Western front, Kitchener was perplexed, saying to Grey repeatedly: "I don't know what is to be done; this isn't war." Grey, Twenty-Five Years, II, 72.

18. Zwehl, Falkenhayn, p. 65. Delcassé told Lord Bertie in May 1915 that the German Governor-General in Brussels, von Bissing, was in the habit of saying: "Nous ne serons pas vainqueurs, nous ne sommes pas vaincus, et nous sommes trop fiers pour faire la paix." Diary of Lord Bertie, I, 169; And Bertie noted another mot, ascribed to Churchill, describing the military leaders on the Allied side: "The Generals won't make peace and the Admirals won't fight" (September 17, 1917). Ibid., II, 185.

19. Huber, Heer und Staat in der deutschen Geschichte, p. 414.

20. Foerster, Der Feldherr Ludendorff im Unglück.

21. Fleury, Souvenirs, I, 287.

22. Poincaré, Au service de la France, X, 273 f., 299, 316.

23. Parisians greeted one another afterwards by saying: "You are as stupid as the Peace."

24. Reboul, L'armée in La vie au dix-huitième siècle, p. 107.

25. These, incidentally, provided Clausewitz with much of the experience from which he derived his emphasis on the primacy of policy over strategy.

26. Bismarck, Gedanken und Erinnerungen, II, 118.

27. Cf. the section entitled "Post-War Use of Armed Forces: Debellatio and Rebellatio" in chap. xii above.

28. Webster, The Foreign Policy of Castlereagh, 1815-1822, pp. 161 ff.

29. "Hae tibi erunt artes, pacisque imponere morem, Parcere subjectis et debellare superbes." Virgil.

30. von der Goltz, Volk in Waffen, p. 125.

31. In April 1871, when Miquel, a National Liberal and later Prussian minister of finance, dined with officers of the Berlin Guard Artillery just returned from the field, he found among them great resentment against the Chancellor. They were unanimous that, by the leniency he had shown the French, the most important interests of the new Reich had been hurt and that the peace treaty was a "a real shame." Oncken, Politik und Kriegführung, p. 87.

32. Moltke's proposals for the capitulation included not only the occupation of the outlying forts but of all Paris. All eagles, colors and weapons were to be handed over. The whole garrison, except the officers who were to be freed on parole, 250,000 men, were to be made POW's and transported to Germany. Bismarck passed over all these harsh conditions, except the first, in order not to put off peace, provoke chaos in Paris and undermine the credit of the existing provisional Government in France. Meyer, Bismarck, pp. 433 f.

33. Ziekursch, _Politische Geschichte des neuen deutschen Kaiserreichs_, I, 356.
34. _Doc. dipl. fr._, 1st series, I, 62; II, 582. For similar statements by Field Marshal von Manteuffel, Governor-General of Alsace-Lorraine, see _Ibid._, II, 164, 562.
35. Takeuchi, _War and Diplomacy in the Japanese Empire_, pp. 111, 115 ff.
36. _Ibid._, pp. 149, 153 ff.
37. _Die internationalen Beziehungen_, 2nd series, VII, 622 f., 638.
38. For the Russian aspirations with regard to the Bukovina since 1940, see _Nazi-Soviet Relations_, p. 237 and _passim_.
39. For the latter, see Gatzke, _Germany's Drive to the West_. Cf. Hindenburg to Chancellor, September 15, 1917: "An economic annexation (Angliederung) of Belgium by Germany will not come about without pressure on Belgium following the conclusion of the peace. A military occupation of several years' duration will serve this purpose, which will also be necessary for military reasons if and when England and America will have evacuated France. Germany's position in Liège must extend beyond that. Its main purpose is the direct military protection it is to give the Rhenish-Westphalian industrial region." Bredt, _Der deutsche Reichstag im Weltkrieg_, pp. 140 f.
40. Nikolai, _Nachrichtendienst_, p. 187.
41. F. von Bernhardi, _Denkwürdigkeiten_.
42. For details, see Bredt, _Der deutsche Reichstag im Weltkrieg_, pp. 218 ff.; Wheeler-Bennett, _The Forgotten Peace_, pp. 108 ff. and _passim_; Rosenberg, _Entstehung der deutschen Republik_, chap. vi.
43. Under pressure from Ludendorff, Rumania had been forced to open peace negotiations at once by a German ultimatum of February 6, 1918.
44. Cf. Sir Henry Wilson to Smuts, April 8, 1917, on "the necessity of our beating the Boches to such a point that we can dictate terms—not discuss them." Callwell, _Sir Henry Wilson_, I, 336.
45. Foch, _Memoirs_, pp. 451 ff.
46. The continuation of the blockade against Germany was largely due to the initiative of Allied sailors. When Herbert Hoover approached the commander of the blockade, Admiral Wemyss, with his proposals, backed by the Big Four, to distribute food to the needy of Europe, including the Germans, the Admiral told him: "Young man, I don't see why you Americans want to feed these Germans." Hoover replied: "Old man, I don't understand why you British want to starve women and children after they are licked." _Collier's_, September 8, 1951.
47. In 1919, Clemenceau recalled French peace-making in Napoleon's time as an example not to be imitated. "I would not say that we were very accommodating conquerors throughout that glorious era...A victor superior to his victory was needed, a victor who would be a hero of moderation. Napoleon was not this hero of moderation, nor was Germany." Cited in _La France de demain_ (25e année), No. 215, 142.
48. Callwell, _Sir Henry Wilson_, II, 175; Albrecht-Carrié, _Italy at the Peace Conference_, p. 463.
49. For the revolting methods used in the Saar by "our military administrators educated in the school of Faidherbe, Gallieni, Lyautey," see Barrès, _Mes Cahiers_, XII, 641. For an early American military opinion on the "arrogant and merciless" role of General d'Esperey in Hungary, see Kruger (ed.), _An Undiplomatic History_, pp. xviii ff., 330 f. Cf. Ambassador Houghton to Secretary Hughes, July 27, 1923: "Apparently everything that would arouse hostility, and nothing that would conciliate, has been done. As a result, the Rhineland population today is savagely anti-French." Tansill, _Back Door to War_, p. 29.
50. Baker, _Woodrow Wilson and World Settlement_, II, 496 f., 504, 517.
51. For his ideas about Russia's future, see _Hitlers Tischgespräche_, pp. 64 ff. The ideas of the OKW after Munich about the "new order" in Southeastern Europe were hostile to "the creation of a compact bloc of succession states on Germany's eastern frontier...For military reasons a common Hungarian-Polish frontier was undesirable." _Documents on German Foreign Policy_, Series D, IV, 40.
52. _Nazi-Soviet Relations_, pp. 102 ff., 117, and _passim_.
53. For details, see Schuman, _Night over Europe_, pp. 397 ff.
54. Only belatedly, from 1948 on, did American official statements describe Russian expansion as "imperialist."
55. For doubts about the military wisdom of the surrender formula, see Leahy, _I Was There_, p. 145. The Joint Chiefs of Staff discussed it with the President before Casablanca, and did not protest. Sherwood, _Roosevelt and Hopkins_, II, 602 f.
56. Leahy, _I Was There_, p. 314. The Admiral "could never agree with him on this proposal, and always felt that any bases considered essential for the security of our own country should be under the sovereignty of the U.S."
57. Forrestal often mentions the views of the Joint Chiefs on this. See _Forrestal Diaries_, pp. 8, 28 f., 33 f., 37 f., and _passim_.
58. Hull, _Memoirs_, II, 1488.
59. Testimony of Secretary of State Acheson before Senate Committee, June 4, 1951, _N. Y. Times_, June 5, 1951.

60. <u>Forrestal Diaries</u>, pp. 451 f.
61. <u>Ibid.</u>, pp. 265, 297.
62. For Hull's and Eden's inconclusive discussions with Molotov in October 1943 as to the establishment or abolition of naval and air bases of the Great Powers on the territory of small nations, see Hull, <u>Memoirs</u>, II, 1299 ff.
63. This was the slogan of Titoism before the break with the Cominform.
64. Soviet memorandum on Atlantic Pact. <u>N. Y. Times</u>, April 2, 1949; Vishinsky before UN General Assembly, November 29, 1949; Gromyko before UN General Assembly, April 13, 1949; Cominform communiqué, published November 29, 1949, <u>N. Y. Times</u>, November 30, 1949.
65. See Stalin's answer of 1949 to Ambassador-General Walter Bedell Smith's query as to how far Russia was going to go in her expansion. "Not much further...The Soviet Union has no intention of attacking Turkey...But Turkey is weak, and the Soviet Union is very conscious of the danger of foreign control of the Straits, which Turkey is not strong enough to protect. The Turkish Government is unfriendly to us. That is why the Soviet Union has demanded a base in the Dardanelles. It is a matter of our own security." Smith, <u>My Three Years in Moscow</u>; <u>N. Y. Times</u>, November 7, 1949.
66. Former Under-Secretary of State Sumner Welles before Cleveland meeting of the Council on World Affairs. <u>N. Y. Times</u>, December 4, 1948. A meeting of Democratic party leaders of the Middle West in September 1950 found it necessary to "urge strict adherence to our national tradition of control of the military by civilians and to condemn encroachments of military personnel upon the functions of other departments of government." <u>Ibid.</u>, September 10, 1950.
67. See its directive of December 23, 1949, published in Tokyo by MacArthur's HQ. <u>N. Y. Times</u>, January 4, 1950.
68. With the almost complete agreement of Secretary of Defense Marshall, May 12, 1951. <u>Military Situation in the Far East</u>, pp. 644 ff.
69. The problem of re-understanding among ex-enemy soldiers deserves special treatment. Such a treatment would begin, perhaps, with the tenth-century Waltharius Lied which describes the reconciliation of the heroes immediately following the battle, before their wounds had begun to heal. It would continue down to the post-1918 attempts of General Ian Hamilton and Max Hoffmann. Since the rise of modern nationalism, officers of the victorious state have come to share the popular immediate post-war feeling that the ex-enemy presents a rather hopeless case and must therefore be put on probation and be re-educated.
70. Sophocles, <u>Ajax</u>, I, 678 ff. (transl. by F. Storr).
71. Machiavelli, <u>The Prince</u>, iii.
72. "Even the final decision of a war is not to be regarded as absolute. The conquered nation often sees it as only a passing evil, to be repaired in after-times by political combinations." Clausewitz, <u>On War</u>.
73. For details, see Wertheimer, <u>Andrassy</u>, I, 445, 477, 504 ff.
74. Joffre had his conditions for an armistice, as well as for a peace, worked out as early as the summer of 1916: France was to regain the frontiers of 1798 and was to annex Luxemburg and the Saar. "It seemed just to me to take back from the Germans this piece of territory which Prussia had taken from us in order to punish us for the disaster of Waterloo. The frontier of 1815 was a frontier of the conquered which no longer suited the winners of the Great War." Joffre, <u>Mémoires</u>, II, 369 ff.

Organization for Unity

"Seeming parted, but yet a union in partition."
Shakespeare,
A Midsummer Night's Dream.

The departments of a government are designed to provide in an efficient manner for the greatest possible security of their country, at home and abroad, and for its best welfare. It is expected that departmental organization will serve these ends most effectively and most economically, whether in peace or in war, either under an absolutist system or under parliamentary control. Subject to controls, which they often try to evade, department heads must cooperate with one another by direct correspondence or through such "collegial" arrangements as a deliberating cabinet, a privy council or a crown council.

Such councils consider and decide, alone or together with the parliaments, how much of their country's resources are to be assigned to military security and how much to welfare. The share accorded the latter commonly increases in time of "deep peace" and at moments of inner stress;[1] that given to the former, in time of outer threat. While certain national economies may be able to carry both loads for a period of time, the choice between reduced welfare and increased expenditure for defense requirements is a forced one in certain other economies. A capitalist economy will try to postpone the choice as long as possible by inflationary tactics, rather than adopt some combination of severe taxation and economic controls in order to meet it.

The problem of which department should handle which business of State is less automatically decided by the innate nature of the subject matter than is commonly assumed. Revolutions remind us of that fact when they attempt to redistribute governmental tasks. One German diplomat, caught between the traditional assignment of work and the new one decreed by the Nazis, expressed it in this way: "Of course, you might say that any question might be given an aspect of foreign policy."[2] In war, in contemplation of war, and, above all, in total war, "any question" might also be given a military aspect. A multiplicity of aspects must either result in interdepartmental cooperation or, where bureaucratic "empire-building" is rampant, in conflicts of competency and jurisdiction.

CABINETS, COUNCILS, AND DEPARTMENTS IN DEFENSE AFFAIRS

Policy decisions will be arrived at in common council, subject or not to the usually vague mandate and approval of parliaments, pressure groups, or the still vaguer urges of the people and public opinion. Departments, ministries, and other governmental agencies are the permanent organs for the realization of agreed-upon policies in their specific fields. Since there is no complete separation according to subject matter in government and politics, the work of a single department ought to come, to varying degrees, under the influence of all other departments.

As the most constantly outward-oriented departments, the foreign and defense ministries interact most frequently. The intensity of interaction changes constantly, reaching its acme in time of war, when all other departments become increasingly involved with those concerned with the preparation and fighting of the war. In modern times, the complexities and technical intricacies of affairs of state have been allowed to disrupt the unity of policy in many places. Thus, different interests and differences in world outlook set diplomatic offices and armed services apart, even in societies where a high degree of homogeneity presumably prevails in the ruling strata. Only the highest statesmanship can preserve the unity of policy in the face of the most technical and the most persuasive arguments offered by the various department heads.

In the invidious competition among departments, the fact that the unity of organization for war is itself a factor of strength is liable to be forgotten. In certain periods of history, it has been a most decisive factor. For example, Isocrates (436-338 B.C.) put the following words into the mouth of the Spartan King, Archidamus:

> It is obvious to everyone that we excel the other Greeks neither by the size of our city nor by the number of our population but by the fact that we have arranged our public discipline like that of an armed camp where everything duly hangs together and where the orders of the superiors are punctually obeyed.[3]

The departmental system of the nineteenth century avoided numerous, though by no means all, jurisdictional and power conflicts between the civilian-diplomatic and the military-naval outlooks on world-wide policies. In practice, however, this system was still not the best preparation for or against war. It too often left matters of the most consequential nature to departmental decisions; for example, to mechanisms devised by the defense departments for the case of war. Schlieffen's plan for the march through Belgium was never considered by a Reich cabinet and was only vaguely known to the Chancellors. They never pressed for either more information on it or for a discussion of its merits and likely political consequences. No Chancellor knew, and even William II was not certain, that the Plan, based on a violation of Belgian neutrality, was the only war plan prepared. The British Liberal cabinet from 1906 to 1914 was almost equally uninterested in the details and implications of the Anglo-French staff discussions during that period.

The discussion of the relation between foreign policy and national defense centers on the relations between departments of foreign affairs and defense agencies. The connections of other government offices with matters of defense, however, ought never to be omitted. The question of army remounts, for example, established ties between the war and the agriculture ministries; the question of railroads, between general staffs and railway ministries.[4] Obliged to furnish the "sinews of war," finance ministries and treasuries have frequently protested demands for military funds. More often than not, they have tended to keep armed forces and the expenditure for them at a minimum that military leaders and sometimes their colleagues in the cabinets did not consider safe. Among the most determined advocates of a radical reduction of the French Army in 1814 was the first Finance Minister of the Restoration, Louis.[5] The British Treasury was at many times no less economy-minded when confronted with the military budgets. During the war scare that swept Britain at the end of 1886, Randolph Churchill, Secretary of the Exchequer, held out most strongly for retrenchment. He demanded that the naval and military estimates, already lower than the year before, be reduced still further, in order not to endanger the economic revival that was just then beginning. Salisbury, however, thought that the estimates presented by their colleagues in the defense departments, without "a taint of militarism in their composition," were not unreasonable. He thought it would be "a serious responsibility to refuse the demands of a war minister so little imaginative [we would say: over-imaginative] as Smith." Remaining unpersuaded, Churchill resigned.[6]

Generally speaking, the departments of government in the Second Reich were "militärfromm," like gentle horses when confronted with the soldiers' and sailors' budgets. But it was the Reich Treasury that sounded the voice of reason when the aggravating Naval Bill of 1912 was being prepared by Tirpitz. The latter—to some the "father

of the German Navy," to others "the father of the lie"—had assured the Reichstag and the several Reich offices in 1909 and later that the naval budget would remain steady for a number of years to come. Suddenly, in the summer of the Agadir crisis, without any considerable change in the strength of any of the competing navies, a Flottenverein agitation for an additional squadron got under way, instigated by the Reichsmarineamt itself. New demands on the Reich Treasury were presented by Tirpitz. The Treasurer, Wermuth, protested: funds were not available without new taxes and there were priority claims, notably those of the Army. In arguing against Tirpitz, Wermuth, rather than the Army, made himself the defender of military considerations:

> I cannot by any means renounce the conviction that Germany's position as a Central European land power forces us to concentrate all endeavors on the high efficiency of the Army. By a reduction of the Army budget, a strengthening of the Navy would be bought at too high a price, particularly if the political difficulties resulting from it [meaning the bad effect of a big naval bill on Anglo-German relations] are taken into consideration.

These conclusions, sound not only with regard to Reich finances but also with regard to its security problems, were overruled by the most powerful men in the Reich, the Emperor and Tirpitz. The spineless Chancellor yielded, despite Wermuth's influence, and the Army demanded rather less than the Treasury had invited it to submit. When what Tirpitz contemptuously called his "financial artifices" found no approval, Wermuth could do nothing but resign.[7]

A similar fate struck Wermuth's contemporaries, Caillaux and the Russian Finance Minister, who was also Prime Minister during his last years in the cabinet. V. N. Kokovtsev was the man of peace among his colleagues, and, like Count Witte before him (Finance Minister, 1893-1903, Prime Minister November 1905-May 1906), more in favor of peaceful relations with the Central Powers than the rest of the ministers. Early in 1913, he confided to the Austrian ambassador that he could no longer oppose the military as strongly as he had previously done because of the Balkan complications; but what they wanted vastly surpassed what Russian industry could actually provide. "Les militaires ont toujours les yeux plus grands que l'estomac."[8] Because of his businessman's outlook on politics and war, which made him deny that war with Germany was at all "desirable," he could not last against those Government members who believed that Russia had had enough of a "breathing spell." He was dismissed early in 1914, a few days after the last of the three historic conferences concerned with plans for taking the Straits. He was the only one among the conferees who at least suspected Russia's basic weakness in war, namely her low industrial potential and output. He was dropped, as Sazonov confessed, because he had attempted to cut down the various budgets presented by his colleagues. His successor, who was more accommodating, informed the Duma in closed session that the Tsar was determined to see the military demands satisfied. From now on there was to be no more economizing in the military offices. According to Sazonov, the new man, Goremykin, was "certainly no man of war, but his predecessor had been a man of peace and a financier."[9]

Also aware of the weaknesses in the economy of their countries, the finance ministers of the Axis partners were among the most determined opponents of the wars that the dictators or the military planned and undertook. They did not believe that these wars could be won by their countries. The peace-minded Finance Minister in Japan, Takahashi, was among those killed by military assassins in February 1936. They wanted to keep the way clear for war, and they singled him out for the most brutal form of murder, as if his opposition had been the most annoying to the Army.[10]

During the Weimar Republic, the soldiers complained that the Ministry of Finance "did not show the necessary understanding for the interests of the Reichswehr," despite all it had done to make secret armaments possible. There was no occasion for such complaints under Hitler: Blomberg obtained a completely "free hand in the expansion of the Wehrmacht with regard to financial funds," escaping all budgetary control.[11] The financing of this rearmament absorbed forty-eight per cent of the total Reich budget in the years from 1936 to 1939, while from time to time the Finance Minister, von Krosigk, timidly submitted his views on Germany's inability to wage war.[12]

In Italy, the Minister of Finance and Foreign Currency opposed Italy's entry into the war in 1940 as strongly as did Badoglio. And, to the great annoyance of the Chief of Staff, he had earlier opposed the whole Italian rearmament program. This he had no right to do, as Badoglio himself thought. While the latter "appreciated the lucid and exhaustive explanation of our holdings in foreign currencies," he did not think that the financier had either the capacity or the authority to express opinions on military matters. Mussolini promised Badoglio the necessary funds for rearmament and closed the painful session of the Supreme Defense Council, where Army and Finance had clashed with some embarrassed grandiloquence. Everything must be done, he said, and even more speedily than planned, "because we must not desert history" or miss our rendezvous with Fate. This

did not prevent him from selling four destroyers to Sweden and the first anti-tank weapons produced by Italian factories to other neutrals in order to buy wheat abroad, thereby disposing of equipment which Italy herself greatly needed.[13]

The finance ministers of the Axis Powers were, to say the least, reluctant to indulge in wars that appeared so hopeless from the point of view of their departments. In the race of capitalism towards self-destruction a still stranger phenomenon arose—the Morgenthau Plan, conceived and promulgated by the United States Treasury. This plan would have exposed the heartland of Europe to Bolshevization, thus making it a likely ally for the permanent enemy of the West. Aside from Fascism, political Todessehnsucht (to use the necessary Freudian term) found no stronger expression.

Another problem on which more than one governmental department has at times tried to exert an influence is the peace-time garrisoning of troops and stationing of naval units. Considerations underlying the distribution of forces vary from ignoble pork-barrel politics—the idiom should not mislead anyone into believing that these practices are restricted to America—to concern for the greatest security of border provinces. The pattern of garrisons may reflect external political considerations, as the unfortified frontier between Canada and the United States, or it may reflect considerations originating more exclusively in internal politics. The constant strengthening of the Russian garrisons in the West, following the Russo-Turkish War of 1877-78, demonstratively marked the breaking away of the Russian soldiers from the ancient friendship with Austria and Germany. It seems that the diplomats were not consulted at all about this "purely administrative measure."

The garrisoning of troops and the concentration of naval units in the North Sea were constant preoccupations of the governors of the British Empire when it was in its heyday.[14] American governors became similarly preoccupied as soon as expansion had extended beyond the confines of the continental United States. After 1945, the distribution of American forces, land, sea, and air, became practically the foremost concern of American strategy in the cold war.

Cabinets, pre-constitutional and constitutional, are the usual clearing-houses for the variety of interests and views that come into play in the settling of a government's policy. Where a true "primacy of foreign policy" is established, the foreign minister exercises the strongest influence. At other times, such as at times of economic crises, civilian governors who are entrusted with home affairs may predominate. However, as Napoleon put it, "là où le gouvernement est faible, l'armée gouverne."[15] On critical occasions, cabinets may be enlarged by having non-ministers sit in on their meetings. Or they may be concentrated, as British and American cabinets were during the two World Wars, in order to cut down deliberation and expedite decisions. In certain monarchical countries, notably Prussia, the King presided over deliberative bodies that were somewhat elastic in composition, the Staatsrat (from 1817 on) and later the Kronrat, in which generals, including the chief of staff, joined the regular ministers. Generals and admirals were not always at their best in these discussions, when their cherished plans had to stand up under the relative publicity of a council's discussions.[16] Nevertheless, their presence provided the civilian heads of government with the possibly required alibi. They could say to the warriors on subsequent occasions: Well, you had the opportunity to warn us earlier.

All governments and constitutions have wrestled with the problem of effecting that unity of policy and purpose that best ensures the national interest and security, the most fruitful consideration and harmonization of interests, and the best application of available strength for national security, either by preserving the peace, through armaments or disarmament, or by proceeding to war at the right time and on the right occasion. Under an absolute government, this unity was established by the monarch with his unlimited powers. Unless he was a Frederick the Great or a Napoleon, he either presided over the meetings of ministerial and other councils or took counsel separately with heads of departments "in his cabinet." The quality of the unity achieved depended largely on the monarch's entourage, whether predominantly military or civilian. The conventional description of an autocrat of the eighteenth, nineteenth or twentieth century "surrounding himself with soldiers" actually meant that the soldiers had managed to surround the throne. The moves to gain parliamentary control were designed to wrest this decision from the monarch and his irresponsible entourage. The American Declaration of Independence, as a tally of complaints elaborated by the Colonists against George III, accused him of having "affected to render the Military independent of and superior to the Civil Power." After achieving independence, the Americans provided for a governmental center of unity in the office of the President. They vested in him the executive power, which included the commander-in-chief-ship and the treaty-making power; and, somewhat less definitely, they provided for his presiding over the executive departments. Presidents have filled the office of civilian commander-in-chief with varying zest, gladly, like the Roosevelts, or reluctantly, like McKinley.

The strong anti-military reaction that followed the revolutionary period in both Anglo-Saxon countries resulted in the conviction of large groups of civilians that not only was military influence per-

nicious but that they themselves were possessed of sufficient military understanding and talents to justify the claim for civilian supremacy, which was the best unifying concept.[17] In Britain, generals and admirals were kept out of the Government: for about one hundred and fifty years, Conway, Wellington and Kitchener were the only generals to be made Cabinet members.[18] "Although General Conway sat in the House of Commons in 1783 and the Duke of Wellington in the House of Lords in 1843, and each was a member of the Cabinet while he held the command of the Army, yet the constitutional usage is one of absolute exclusion on the part of the Commander-in-Chief from all political action, and from all political parties in the State."[19] In the United States, such exclusion was never as radical, partly due to the fact that the distinction between civilians and soldiers was never as sharp. Even before General George C. Marshall was made Secretary of State and of Defense, an occasional ex-officer had been made Secretary of War. While the National Security Act of 1947 provided that a civilian must be head of the National Military Establishment, this was readily waived only three years later in favor of Marshall.

In order to have representatives of the armed forces or experts on military-strategic considerations in the government, the majority of the Great Powers made it a rule that generals and admirals should serve as heads of the defense ministries. France did so until 1870, Prussia-Germany and the other German States until the end of the Second Reich; and the practice was common in Tsarist Russia, Austria-Hungary, Japan, Italy, and in many of the smaller nations. The Third French Republic remained perpetually uncertain as to whether civilians or military men should be at the head of the defense ministries. Following the displays of excessive militarism in the period of Boulangism and in the Dreyfus affair, a series of civilians took over, in the war ministry more often than in the marine ministry. After 1918 and 1945, the majority of the defense ministers were civilian parliamentarians.

Many of these arrangements may be traced back to the horrified reaction against the excesses of Napoleonic imperialism and militarism. Such experiences moved the civilians, who had once more obtained the governance of Europe, to bring the military into the general framework of government and administration and thus withdraw military affairs as far as possible from a position of "immediacy" with the monarch. As member of the cabinet, the war minister was to rank highest among the soldiers, at least politically speaking. All military affairs were to be concentrated in his office and he was to bring them to debate within the cabinet, rather than settle them with the monarch.

Needless to say, this control was never complete. Uncontrolled influences and offices survived and grew, such as the "military cabinets" or the Chiefs of Staff in Prussia-Germany and Austria.

For the greater part of the nineteenth century the war minister was supreme over the chief of staff in most countries. The Prusso-German victories from 1864 to 1871, however, were largely credited to the chief of staff. On the strength of these victories, the chief of staff escaped ministerial control and was given a position of "immediacy" with the Emperor-King. A somewhat similar release from ministerial control took place in Austria. The bustling Conrad obtained an imperial order that, in political questions having to do with operative war preparations, the chief of staff be authorized to treat directly with the foreign minister without the participation of the war minister.[20] In 1903, when the United States Congress established a general staff, it made its chief "the principal Army adviser to the President," as well as to the Secretary of War. This position of "immediacy" was not fully exploited until President Roosevelt, in his conduct of the Second World War, largely cast aside the civilian Secretary of War and dealt directly with the chiefs of staff in a way that was not very much different from the custom that prevailed in various military monarchies.[21]

THE SUPREME WARLORD

Cabinets as unifying centers have evolved in opposition to influences tending towards absolutism of various kinds. That is to say, they have evolved in a process of political struggle for power rather than in a competition for superior organization of available power. On the whole, they have functioned best in periods of political good weather. When encountering rougher seas, cabinets have often been reduced to an inner cabinet of a few men, or have been replaced by one man as unifier, somewhat along the lines of the Roman temporary dictatorship. Unification of power under one man may result from war, revolution, or the persistent endeavor of militaristic groups at home. The army, in peace as well as in war, may consider that its own interests are best served by a monarch or other supreme warlord, well aware that "they who possess the prince possess the law" (Dryden, 1682). At the same time, the army in the militarized state will defend its power position by claiming organizational superiority even beyond the purely military sphere.[22]

In pre-, extra- or post-constitutional times and places, the necessary unity of policy and strategy has often been established, actually or seemingly, through the institution of the absolute monarch or the dictator as commander-in-chief of the armed forces and director of all policies. Absolutism, in the narrow meaning of the word, was originally an instrument designed to break the self-will of armed feudals and mercenaries by establishing a central authority.[23] It has been said of such an autocratic system that it is "superior at least in time of war because it admits of a closer alliance between policy and strategy than any other."[24] Many soldiers, even great soldiers like Moltke, have preferred it for this reason. In actuality, it has not proved to be an infallible prescription for victory. Absolutistic governing was often reduced to a vicious competition of ministers and other officials for the favor of the ruler. He in turn most often preferred to meet ministers and other counsellors singly in his cabinet, rather than have them meet together under his presidency or in his absence. The results were sometimes disastrous, as became most manifest in wars. With much justice, Torcy, who was Louis XIV's foreign minister for many years, ascribed the faults and final defeat of the Sun King's policies "principally to the small credit in which the Ministry of Foreign Affairs was always held during Louis' reign. The other ministers were always more listened to than he, particularly the War Minister and the Superintendent of Buildings."[25] Centralism under Absolutism was of a highly deceptive nature. Unless the monarch exercised his powers in a comprehensive manner, departmentalism ran rampant, notably among the military, whose love for independence is far stronger than their vaunted hierarchism.

Various arrangements ensured not only that the officers would obey the supreme warlord, ostensibly and ostentatiously, but also that the latter would listen to and often obey the military views and wishes carried to his ear by the many military aides in his entourage. At any given time, it would depend on the power situation and the monarch's character whether or not this influence was exercised without incidents and violent clashes. In extreme cases, officers' rebellions, depositions, and assassinations would occur. The coups were usually performed by officers from the "life" or "body" guards. The most recent attempts to temper tyranny by assassination or deposition were made by the general staff circles from which the Fascist dictators had wrested the conduct of the war. Badoglio helped to remove Mussolini in 1943, and German officers, with less success, attempted to execute their conspiracy against Hitler in 1944.

The complexity of political issues and of the practical preparation for and conduct of war made some consultative inter-administrative arrangements necessary, which even the most extreme assertions of Absolutist power could not abolish or greatly change. The Austrian Hofkriegsrat (Aulic Council) lasted from 1556 to 1848, when it was at last replaced by a war ministry. Other Powers had established their war ministries, variously named, much earlier, as the office in which the administrative and strategic functions, as well as the relations with the other branches of government, were to be taken care of. Through the war minister much—in some countries, all—military business "came into cabinet" for collegiate discussion and decision. In some places, notably in Prussia-Germany, Japan, and Spain, zones of "immediate" relations between the heads of state and various armed forces officials, from the chiefs of staff down, remained or were re-established. In this way, a number of subjects were exempted from ministerial, not to mention parliamentary, control.[26] The preference of the military for central authority and hierarchy as a guarantee against non-military influence was not uniformly strong enough to stifle the desire for independence on the part of individual officers: some forty military and naval office-holders reported directly to William II as Supreme Warlord, and the Japanese Army directorate under the Mikado was tricephalous, with a Chief of the General Staff, a War Minister and an Inspector-General of Military Education in coordination.[27] While each pursued his own special interest—as well as defended the common interest against the civilians—they generally agreed that the holder of the constitutional Kommandogewalt was the last to whom actual command in war should be left.[28]

What matters of military policy were to be discussed in interdepartmental meetings? Was the list of included topics longer than that of forbidden ones? While the military participants were ready to learn of the possibility or difficulties of financing peace-time establishments or war-time expenditures, they balked at disclosing, leave alone discussing, their war plans. They maintained that civilians either would not understand them or would not keep them as secret as they must remain. Civilians had participated in the war planning in the old Austrian Aulic; there prevailed throughout the nineteenth century, however, a growing tendency to exclude them from such knowledge, despite Clausewitz's advice against a "purely military judgment" on a great military event or plan.[29] Even during the last, the so-called "Liberal" phase of the Second Empire, the altogether insufficient plans for the war against Prussia-Germany were fixed without the participation of the Ministerial Council. Napoleon III, according to his last Premier, "insisted stubbornly on having everything concentrated in his hands and on keeping us [the Ministers] on the outside."[30] How far ministers and ministries were informed of secret plans of the general staffs elsewhere we shall observe from time to time and from place to place.

The constitutional cabinet system as a way of achieving unity of policy and strategy often remained ineffective or was by-passed by so-called Military or Naval Cabinets in Germany and Austria, or by the sovereign's maison militaire. The fondness of the military for constitutional systems has always been moderate, often due to their inability to make their points strongly in mixed discussions. They have preferred different ways to obtain their wishes, and have found autocratic or semi-autocratic regimes most conducive to their interests or inclinations and hence worthy of being sustained by the force or prestige of arms.[31] Many officers, even outside the autocratic countries, have considered a hierarchical structure, with a supreme war lord at the point of the pyramid, the guarantee of the predominance of the military sector.[32]

It is probably due to the informality and unsystematic nature of these arrangements that political scientists have neglected to treat, at length or in depth, the influences, pernicious or otherwise, exercised by the military on governments and politics. The secret history (secret largely because unwritten) of the relations between heads of states and army chiefs can only be indicated here by a few "guiding fossils" from the record. In most cases, the supposedly autocratic emperors were aware, made aware when necessary, of their dependency on their armies. From various vantage points, army politicos constantly worked with, through, and on the monarch, most so when a decision on peace or war was required.[33] When Russian-Japanese relations neared their breaking point early in 1904, French diplomacy, not the least bit interested in having a Far Eastern war, still believed that war could be averted. William II, who was professionally familiar with military pressuring, doubted this, for if Japan became provocative and the Tsar backed down, "he would become impossible to his Army."[34] He realized, at least subconsciously, that monarchs of his own kind were not fundamentally employers but employees of the armed forces of their countries. In a way, William's shift of interest to the new Navy in the late 1890's was an attempt to emancipate himself from the earlier tutelage of the Guards and the General Staff. The attempt ended in his falling into an even stricter dependency on Tirpitz. When, in the later years of his reign, he inclined towards greater peacefulness, he thereby exposed himself to the Crown Prince's open competition for the Army's favors. Generals were heard to say that he had twice made Germany appear ridiculous, on the occasions of Algeciras and Agadir; the next time they, the generals, would not allow him to back down but would force him to fight it out, whether he liked it or not.[35]

During the First World War, William II tried to play his constitutional role by observing a maximum of discretion in his dealings with the all-powerful military. (He marginalized on an article of the Frankfurter Zeitung at this time: "Policy has to keep its mouth shut in war-time until strategy permits it to talk again."[36]) Nevertheless, he still infuriated

Ludendorff and his politico-colonels, among whom Max Bauer was heard to say that the fatal and inept monarch ought to be dethroned.[37] Political terror lurks in unsuspected places, and the supposed "kings of terror" are not always immune to it.[38] And if the supreme warlord is not terrorized by "his" officers, he may finally get tired of their constant pressuring and respectful importunities. Just after a parade in the year preceding his death, Alexander I intimated to his entourage, for the first time, that he was somewhat disgusted with military affairs. "You find me tired?" he asked. "That is because after having done so much for the Army, I often think how little has been done for the rest. That thought weighs on my heart like ten pounds and that's what puts me into the state you find me in."[39]

The most effective grave-diggers of old Austria were her military politicos, first the members of the aristocracy, then the ambitious professionals of the Conrad type. They did not understand until it was too late that their old-fashioned empire could only be preserved by peace and not by the wars that they were influential in bringing about. For a considerable period of time prior to the war of 1859, the Emperor's Military Cabinet, headed by his aide-de-camp general Count Grünne, worked together with other generals for the removal of the peace-minded foreign minister, Count Buol. His unfortunate direction of foreign affairs, they warned the Emperor, "foretold great calamities for the Empire." While Buol kept on trying to obtain a diplomatic settlement, the soldiers pressed for an early declaration of war against France and Piedmont. No diplomatic arts could preserve the peace, they argued. Further attempts would only let the most favorable time for Austria to strike slip by. Finally impressed, Francis Joseph asked old Metternich for his advice. The latter also pronounced against Buol, whose repeatedly profferred resignation was then accepted. "God be thanked, at last! We have worked long at that!" exclaimed Count Crenneville, one of the court generals.[40] Even earlier, Francis Joseph, acting on Grünne's advice and without Buol's knowledge, had given orders to present Piedmont with an ultimatum to disarm within a few days. This provided Cavour, who was eager for war, with the hoped-for provocation. Grünne's influence did not end there: on his advice, the command in Italy was given to Count Gyulai and not to the better-suited but far more lowly-born Hess. Hess remained as chief of staff, a post so technical in nature that the high nobility itself could not fill it.[41] The bearers of the greatest names in Austrian history—Wimpffen, Clam-Gallas, Liechtenstein—were the worst defeated and the worst defeatists. Only a commoner like Benedek emerged with some credit

from the campaign of 1859. A thorough revirement took place soon after, which included the dismissal of one hundred and thirty-five generals. They had been led into outer darkness by Grünne, who was held responsible for much that had resulted in the battle of Solferino. The military camarilla around the Emperor was supposedly re-formed, with Count Crenneville as successor to Grünne. In Prussian and many other eyes, he above all others was the driving force on the Austrian side behind the equally unfortunate war of 1866.[42] It was he who made Benedek accept the command in Bohemia that the modest commoner had not wanted. The defeat of the commoner at Sadowa was the only triumph scored by Austrian aristocracy in the war against Prussia.[43]

In agreement with wide circles of the French people, the army of the Second Empire enthroned Napoleon III as the head of state. Military and civilian powers were combined in him in a manner similar to the glorious arrangements of the First Empire. The Empire fared well enough under his fake aegis, and no one protested the various improvisations and vagaries of his policies and their impact on military measures until it was too late. Napoleon never corrected the soldiers' vague though persistent pseudo-Napoleonic outlook on German affairs. The soldiers in particular were filled with expectations of pro-French sympathy from the people who had so recently been annexed by the Prussians and who were now somewhat unwillingly allied with them.[44] Napoleon's own vague ideas on nationality were discarded by the generals in favor of security when it came to German affairs. In case of war, the French offensive was to be directed towards the confluence of Rhine and Main, whence it would push upward from the Main in order to separate North and South. They would then join hands with an allied Austria somewhere around Nuremberg and afterwards repeat the battle of Leipzig, thus restoring Napoleonic gloire. The few friends of France inside Germany, and Beust in Vienna, had warned in vain that France should not count on sympathy south of the Main, that German nationalism was too strong, that France's best military chances lay in keeping the Southern contingents from uniting with the Prussian forces, in which case they would actually come under Prussian command. Once the first battle of the united forces had taken place, it would be too late. Neither the vague French plans nor the poor execution of them nor the diplomatic preparations of 1870 were in keeping with this strategy. When Napoleon arrived at the headquarters of the field army, the generals received him with the question: "Well, Sire, how do we stand with Austria?" "One negotiates," he said. "One negotiates!" they replied, "but in two or three days we must start operations; if we don't advance, we shall be attacked" (July 31). They were attacked at Wörth and Weissenburg on August 4 and 6.[45]

Bismarck's position in Prussia-Germany was fundamentally that of a constitutional civilian mayor of the palace who had constantly to reassert his control over King and Army. The army might have served his politics better during the war of 1864 than it actually did. Still, the next war was prepared and started in perfect harmony between him and the generals. He had even intended to send Moltke to Florence to act as negotiator of the Prussian-Italian alliance of 1866 against Austria. His instructions had already been worked out when word came that General Govone was en route to Berlin to treat there.[46] During the last days of peace, the generals, Moltke, Roon and others, gathered regularly around Bismarck in the evenings at the Wilhelmstrasse and, according to one of his closest collaborators, "never was there such complete harmony between Bismarck and his colleagues and the generals as during those days of hopes for victory."[47] But what the generals considered to be interference in the war on his part, namely his determination to bring it to a close before it was "fully won," brought them into violent conflicts with him. He complained that, after the peace of Nikolsburg, the generals treated him like a traitor who had spoiled everything the Army had won. Many hated him and avoided him for this reason.[48] There is reason to assume that some of Bismarck's stories of his conflicts with the generals and the General Staff are, for various reasons, exaggerated. For one thing, Bismarck was quite obviously jealous of the military giants who claimed for themselves the larger share of the credit for the successes in Prussia's three wars. Nevertheless, these stories indicate how seriously and how constantly the problem of the unity of policy and strategy and the supremacy of policy over strategy bothered him. The Prussian generals did not seem to read Clausewitz any more, and the warlord did not always function well, that is to say he functioned not promptly but only after much prompting.

In the new German Reich, the unity of foreign relations and defense policy was maintained as long as Bismarck stood on the bridge to steer his perilous course. He continued his control over the aging supreme warlord and, through the latter, over the soldiers, increasingly difficult as this proved to be.[49] And although he did not agree with the heir to the throne in all respects, the two of them still shared the conviction that soldiers must not interfere with diplomacy.[50] The primacy of diplomacy was carried to the extent of deciding, perhaps too hastily even, when and with whom Germany was to conclude new

alliances for her greater security. Neither the Emperor nor the military were consulted in advance, nor was so-called military necessity deeply considered. Only after he had concluded the alliance with Austria in 1879 did Bismarck obtain Moltke's endorsement. Moltke duly testified that the Reich's security urgently necessitated this measure, that the threat from Russia, who was concentrating more and more troops against Germany, was serious. He did this in order to break the old Emperor's opposition, while at the same time other military men, like the Prussian war minister, considered Russia's peace-time concentration much more lightly. Still others, like Manteuffel of the reactionary school, would have preferred an alliance with the old friend Russia, rather than with Austria.[51]

Publicly no less than behind the scene, Bismarck left no doubt as to the primacy of his office. He declared in 1885 that all those who believed that political direction in Germany was in any way subordinate to the views of the General Staff were wrong.[52] His interference stopped short only of determining the Generals Staff's strategic plans after 1871. Moltke's plan for the war on two fronts envisaged that Prussia would remain on the defensive against France, relying on the strength of Germany's fortress system. The Russians, who had concentrated their masses in the West, close to Austria and Germany, were to be tackled first. Bismarck, however, would have preferred to open the war with an offensive in the West, "because in Russia there were no worthwhile objectives by the possession of which the war would be terminated."[53] Meanwhile, he left no doubt in the minds of the partners to the as yet unformed coalition, which already gave him nightmares, that military plans to oppose it did exist.[54]

It was with high confidence in his ultimate control of things that Bismarck allowed the chief of staff to be increasingly emancipated from the war minister's control. This was formally recognized in 1883 when Moltke came into a position of "immediacy" with the commander-in-chief, a relationship which all important military officers in the Reich sought to obtain and too many of them managed to effect.[55] As long as such a position was filled by a "non-pusher" like Moltke, who "modestly" said that the Emperor would know to call him when he needed him, such a position and arrangement appeared innocuous enough. But it became dangerous to Bismarck and his successors when ambitious young men, such as Waldersee, Moltke's successor-designate, took over. Waldersee did not wait to be called on by the successors of William I. Bismarck himself had provided for an archimedean point in Reich government from which he could be levered out of his own powerful position with the help of a chief of staff.

Bismarck soon became aware that the incumbents of this newly independent office threatened to take into their hands one of the vital decisions in Reich affairs, that of the casus foederis. In 1887, the two General Staffs in Berlin and Vienna wanted to open direct discussions that might conceivably touch on this question. Bismarck sent emphatic warning to his colleague in Vienna that the two of them "in their office as ministers of foreign affairs could not transfer their powers, even in subordinate affairs, to military persons on either side without endangering the business for which they themselves were responsible." He begged for help in making it impossible for any international agreements to be arranged "from the purely military side without their own mutual knowledge and permission."

Neither minister [he cautioned] can abdicate, totally or partially, in favor of negotiating officers; rather they must keep the direction of business in their own hands and allow no doubt that international agreements which take place without their written agreement, cannot be considered as binding in their parliaments. It is in the interest of peace to adhere to this manner of conducting affairs since both ministers, naturally, will be more peacefully minded than their military compatriots...Military correspondence could only have an informatory, but no contractual, character.

Kalnoky dutifully agreed that the power of giving political advice to the monarchs must never escape from the directing ministers and pass over to the general staffs.[56] Bismarck was fully aware that this line of separation was never a very sharp one, for which reason he preferred to push his own jurisdiction as far over into the military field as he could, with a courage and confidence that his successors could not muster.

Compared with Bismarck's personal over-all direction, collegial arrangements for the discussion of and decisions on German defense questions played only a minor role. Military and civilian officials were assembled in the National Defense Commission (Landesverteidigungs-Kommission) to consider, under the chairmanship of the Chief of Staff, such problems as the construction of the Kiel Canal and its alternative, the doubling of the Reich Navy. Again, Bismarck's and Moltke's stands were diametrically opposed. After the canal project had been vigorously opposed by the majority of the soldiers and sailors throughout the 1870's and most of the 1880's, Bismarck went before the Reichstag with it. And when a Liberal member correctly pointed out that the initiative for it had come neither from

the military nor the naval offices but had originated in the Reich Chancellery, the War Minister admitted it. "We entertain no professional jealousy," he said, "as to who is mainly responsible for such a bill."[57] The Reichstag by a large majority voted funds for the construction, which in a short time came to justify all the civilian arguments in its favor, including its value for the Reich's military and naval defense.

Bismarck's successor, Caprivi, was a general. Bismarck himself had wanted to make him Moltke's successor instead of Waldersee, who in turn thought he would wait for the chancellorship until Caprivi had been used up in that office, which would not take long.[58] On being introduced to Bismarck's system of treaties, Caprivi found it "too complicated" and thought he would have to simplify it.[59] He by no means simplified things, as might have been expected of a general in politics. "Unimaginative" by comparison with the over-imaginative young Emperor, he, the life-long soldier, preserved the unity of direction in the diplomatic and defense problems of the Reich, endangered as it was from the military side. While dropping the artful Reinsurance Treaty with Russia as the supposed barrier against the war on two fronts, he prepared against this same contingency not only through military reorganization but also through diplomacy, by maintaining a good understanding with Britain.[60]

Various half-hearted attempts were made to establish unity in the Reich, if need be through "constitutional cooperation," by allowing the Reichstag a greater share in governing. Even such an unlikely man as Holstein would have preferred this to the Wilhelminic regime of utter governmental dispersion.[61] The three last Chancellors, however, resigned themselves to a modus vivendi with the numerous military and naval offices that were in positions of "immediacy." This simply put the seal of approval on a concept of unity that was tantamount to inter-bureaucratic conflict and occasional log-rolling. The split with Britain developed because the Navy had to have its ships and the Army its Schlieffen Plan, regardless of consequences that at least some of the German diplomats foresaw and foretold.[62] As the nominal head of the Reich, the Emperor was completely unsuited to control the multiplicity of offices and officials who reported to him directly. Under his pseudo-dictatorship, the Reich was turned into a concern in which units and branch offices became stronger than the whole that would one day have to enter into war-time competition. And the war threatened to be total, even if the Schlieffen Plan was, in the last analysis, intended to avert that Gorgonic fatality. In spite of William's amateurishness, the Army suffered him, flattered him, treated him almost as a valuable publicity and sales agent.[63]

The Wilhelmstrasse found that when William was called upon to act as an arbiter between their proposals and the demands of the Army and Navy, he generally decided in favor of the services.[64] For this reason they avoided, as far as they could, bringing anything to him for decision. After Bülow had lost out in his fight with Tirpitz, he resigned from his office. His successor, Bethmann, losing out against the same opponent, also resigned in office. The attempts of the Wilhelmstrasse to re-establish civilian supremacy came to an end with the death of Secretary of Foreign Affairs Kiderlen in 1912.

The crux of the matter lies in the relation of the Foreign Office to the war plans prepared by the armed forces. The Schlieffen Plan had been conceived in 1894 and thereafter elaborated upon.[65] There had been no discussion of the plan with the Wilhelmstrasse. Information—if any was given—was oral, as was meet in the matter. Schlieffen and his successor broached the plan "casually and in conversation" to Chancellor Bülow. Talking to the latter sometime in 1904 or 1905 "about the chances of a possible war, Schlieffen explained that in case of war with France and Russia, we would have to strive to beat down France first of all. The surest way of doing this was by way of Belgium." Bülow answered that he was well aware of this. He insisted, however, that for weighty political reasons this road could only be taken after Belgian neutrality had been violated first by Germany's enemies, a condition Bismarck had always insisted upon in order to preserve British sympathies. Germany must not sacrifice her reputation as a strict observer of treaties. Schlieffen emphasized his belief that, in case of war, the French, and possibly the British, would at once march into Belgium. Bülow apparently never raised the embarrassing question as to how Schlieffen would act if they did not march and whether there was an alternative plan in this case. Schlieffen published an article after his retirement which many read as meaning that the German High Command was counting on the march of German troops through Belgium as something highly probable, if not axiomatic. His successor denied this when speaking to the Chancellor in January 1909, far from truthfully.[66] Neither then nor in 1912, when both Chancellor and Wilhelmstrasse were somewhat more fully informed of the plan, did they raise the question as to whether or not this was the only plan for war in the West and whether it would only be executed if Belgium had been first invaded by France and Britain.[67]

The French and British General Staffs and the Quai d'Orsay knew at least as much as the Wilhelmstrasse about the inflexible character of the Schlieffen Plan.[68] They predicated their plans on German violation of Belgium: the French armies would have to await the German move rather than march into Belgium, as they felt tempted to do for various military reasons. The unity of defense and diplomacy had been firmly established in France since the time when the violent dissensions that smoldered between soldiers and civilian governors in the Boulanger and Dreyfus crises had been overcome.[69] This unity functioned through the cabinet system, as well as through the especially close and highly organized collegial relations between the Quai d'Orsay and the defense departments.

The relations between the diplomatic-political and the military-naval offices in Berlin were on the whole schiedlich-friedlich, peacefully separate. There was no indication on the eve of 1914, as has been maintained, of "a tendency for the General Staff to attempt to direct, and even partially to succeed in directing the policy of the Government,"[70] though this might be said of the Reich Navy and of the General Staff at the end of July 1914. To say that before 1914 "among the Great Powers [generally, there] was close liaison between the Foreign Office, the Admiralty and the War Office," that "consequently, there was a rapid reaction of armies and fleets to any changes in the diplomatic situation," is a highly dubious statement.[71] Applied to pre-1914 Germany it is downright wrong. Her politicians and diplomats relied on the credit of the Army, established in three successful wars, and not on a Bismarckian-controlled use of it.

The General Staff strongly believed that it could win any war that might confront Germany as she was then organized for war.[72] This confidence and over-confidence resulted in an attitude of reactionary conservatism and in an absence of criticism, which a little understanding of the Reich's defense problems ought to have stirred.[73] There was more than a little reason for doubt. By 1914, the fortress system was illogical to the point that it was strongest where the first German attack was to be undertaken, in the West, and weakest where the enemy offensive had to be expected, in East Prussia.[74] As war approached in 1914, the responsible director of German policy, who knew little of the Army's plans and who had never fully considered their political implications, found it a civilian interference with a military plan declared to be imperative, "a responsibility not to be borne."[75]

COLLEGIAL ARRANGEMENTS FOR DEFENSE IN THE FRENCH REPUBLIC

The constitutions of the Second and Third French Republics made the President commander-in-chief, saying that he "disposes of the armed forces." The constitution of 1850 added "without his ever being able to command in person," a restriction dropped in 1875 to please the then President, Marshal MacMahon. There were no specific regulations as to the actual exercise of the supreme command, and the unifying role of the presidency remained secondary. This role was instead assumed by the cabinet and various inter-ministerial committees.

From 1874 on, the Third Republic had a General Staff, an acquisition largely due to the bitter experience of defeat in 1870-71.[76] But the politicians never trusted the General Staff with the exclusive and unilateral preparation of war. They passed judgment no less than seventeen times between 1871 and 1914 on the war plans worked out by the military.[77] Foreign military affairs, together or singly, were more constantly discussed and decided around the cabinet table in Paris than in any other Great Power government. This harmony was reflected in the activities of the Republic's diplomatic and military officials at home and abroad, for instance in the final stages of the pénétration of Tunis. The imperialist processes had produced some military-diplomatic friction in the earlier phases of the Tunis project. In order to carry this project to its culmination in 1882, the foreign minister admonished the diplomat on the spot to display the cooperation and good-will in dealing with the army authorities that were indispensable for the purpose:

My colleague, the War Minister, represents the Army in the Council of Ministers, in the same way that I represent its policy, and the unity of the resolutions arrived at by the Government must be reflected in the harmony between the agents entrusted with its execution. I know that you yourself are fully disposed to allow our brave and expert generals to play the role for which they are competent; and they, on their part, will never think of infringing upon yours. Since the two fields are thus perfectly distinct, there is no occasion for conflict between functionaries animated by an equal patriotism; but should it by accident occur, I beg you to inform me about this at once so that I am acquainted with it immediately.[78]

The more often the governments changed, the more firmly the bureaucracy entrenched and intertwined itself. The close and constant cooperation of the permanent officials in questions of national defense was organized, from October 1901 on, in the Commission secrète des instructions de guerre. The purpose of the Commission was to plan the measures—police, intelligence, espionage, liaison—which were to be taken jointly by the Ministries of Foreign Affairs, War, Marine, and Interior (Police) in case of war. Representatives of these offices, excepting the Police, which was only called in on special occasions, met regularly once a month at the Quai d'Orsay for a number of years, under the chairmanship of Paléologue, the deputy political director. At critical moments, they would re-examine all the arrangements made for the eventuality of a general European war. In their November 1905 meeting, for example, they reviewed such measures as watching the German frontier, where preparations for a general mobilization would be difficult to conceal; watching German army concentrations, notably in the vicinity of Cologne, Aachen, Malmedy, Trier; organizing an intelligence service on German soil and communications with it via neutral countries, etc. These collegial arrangements represented a definite reaction to the thoroughgoing division of labor that was elsewhere keeping diplomatic and military officers apart.[79]

The Conseil supérieur de la défense nationale, functioned on a higher or policy level. It was set up under the impact of the First Moroccan crisis by a Decree of April 3, 1906, and was charged with the study of all questions relating to the national defense as far as they called for the cooperation of the various ministries. It underwent reorganization during the Second Moroccan crisis by a decree issued on July 28, 1911, the same day that Joffre was appointed chief of staff. By the new decree, the Conseil was to meet at least twice annually and was to be composed of the President of the Republic, the Premier (presiding), the Foreign, Finance, War, Marine, and Colonial Ministers and, in consultative function, the Chief of the General Staff, the general presiding over the consultative committee for the defense of the colonies, plus various admirals and high civilian functionaries.[80]

From this Council Joffre demanded (though he did not fully obtain) clarification of France's position in relation to the other Powers of Europe in the event of war. The engineer among the pre-1914 chiefs of staff wanted this information so that he could base his war plans on it. Joffre submitted his plea in the following way:

Our war plan is a function of France's position regarding the other nations. It is up to the Government to define the aim to be achieved, to lay the foundations for the war plan, while leaving all initiative to the competent ministries to prepare the means of execution, and to the generals, commanding the armies, to lay down their projects of operations. The preliminary tasks ought to be undertaken in collaboration with all ministerial departments...Above all, and ahead of any elaboration of the war plan, the foreign political situation must be clearly outlined by the Minister of Foreign Affairs.

Conversely, the latter ought to be exactly informed of the military and naval resources of the European Powers, because of their repercussions on foreign policy.

This exchange of information had heretofore been imperfect. The General Staff was uninformed as to the actual agreements with Britain, as to the Government's stand on Belgian neutrality, and, until only a few years previous, as to the degree of intimacy with Italy.

A meeting of the Conseil supérieur of October 11, 1911, discussed some of the questions posed by Joffre. The Foreign Minister, de Selves, declared that, according to his view, "it was up to the War Minister to indicate what his intentions for the case of war and his plans were; the Foreign Ministry would then respond by making known the diplomatic possibilities. In diplomacy," he added, "one bases oneself on probabilities, never on certainties." That diplomatic evasiveness must have appeared to Joffre like putting the cart before the horse. Supported by the President, Fallières, he asked for more certainty, more neatness, a firmer ground on which to base his planning. There was the question of Belgium: from a sheerly military point of view, France's interest lay in carrying the war into Belgium. That problem, however, lay above all in the diplomatic field. The Foreign Minister said that he had discussed this problem with Joffre's predecessor during the recent war scare and that they had agreed that France should herself be ready to push into Belgium if the Germans should violate her neutrality first. But he would not make such a statement in writing, preferring a system of conferences between representatives of the Quai d'Orsay and the War Ministry. Prime Minister Caillaux backed him up firmly in this—nothing in writing.

The Conseil, as Joffre saw it, refused to assume the responsibility incumbent upon it. In the end it was agreed that a conference between representatives of the War and Foreign Ministries should soon take place "with a view to establishing an understanding on questions of a diplomatic nature that are liable to influence operations. There would also be conferences between War and Finance Ministries regarding war financing during the first months after mobilization. In these discussions the diplomats, instead of outlining the foreign political situation for the benefit of the soldiers, largely accepted the soldiers' views of the situation, correcting them only in certain respects. With regard to Switzerland, for instance, the Foreign Office thought that she would defend her neutrality less energetically against Germany than the General Staff believed to be the case. A number of delicate questions, such as the binding

character of the entente with Britain, remained unanswered.[81] Joffre was left with some uncertainties for his war planning, of which British soldiers like Henry Wilson were to relieve him better than France's own diplomats.[82]

With the arrival of the war, the Conseil supérieur lost much of its importance in comparison with the position of the commander-in-chief, Joffre. Flexible in composition, it took in various other ministers, convinced of the war-time importance of their offices, including such old ministrables as Freycinet and Leon Bourgeois. Although both proved of "good counsel" according to the soldiers, they made the body even more of a discussion group, and the more that was said the less action ensued. By the end of 1915, Joffre, who had to spend a great deal of time in these deliberations, was ready to cut down the discussions in order to help prepare for the unitary command over all Allied forces that he hoped to assume in the near future.[83] As Joffre saw things, the Government had all of the country's resources at its disposal, determined all activities, military, diplomatic, economic, and gave the war its general direction. In the pursuit of the various objects set for him in the various theaters of war, the commander-in-chief had to distribute and assign the resources put at his disposal. The problem proved infinitely complicated in practice, for it was difficult to draw the line of separation between the domain of pure policy and that of strategy, particularly in a war of coalition.[84]

The practical difficulties of war government could not be solved by making Joffre, who unfortunately did not deliver victory, the "papa" of the war, nor could theoretical clarification be obtained by any pseudo-patriarchalism. The more thoughtful officers on his staff, including those employed in liaison duties between him and the Government, realized

that policy and strategy [must] march hand in hand. Policy determines the aim, strategy executes. During action, however, policy must follow strategy step by step. It is policy that starts strategy off, slows it down, even halts it. Policy, well-conducted, and in constant liaison with strategy, doubles the results obtained by the latter. To enable it, however, to act effectively, it must always know of what strategy is capable, the effect it can produce, when, in how much time, etc. Equally, strategy ought to know the purposes and means of policy. In one word, the most beautiful combinations will always fall flat unless propped up by strategy. Conversely, all the combinations of strategy will crumble if policy runs counter to them.

This reasonable re-statement by Colonel Herbillon of the relations between policy and strategy found, however, that the organ was missing which would assure the close liaison between the two, a director of the whole. "How can there be, without that, the indispensable coordination of efforts? In a war like the present one, given the extension it takes every day, one must look from on high in order to see far. Is there, for this coalition, an organ charged with study, condensation, unification? If there is not, that means anarchy. All our efforts are in vain."[85] Arrangements inherited from peace-time, such as the Conseil supérieur, could not cope with the demands of the war. Instead, the war resulted in unification under one military chieftain, Foch, combined with a strengthening of the position of the premier, Clemenceau.[86]

THE TSAR OF ALL RUSSIANS

The façade of Russian autocracy was "monolithic." Most of the time this façade concealed an inability to govern on the part of the Tsars, an inability to decide on the many if not innumerable questions brought before them and, in consequence thereof, at most times a rampant, expansionistic, bureaucratic departmentalism.[87] The belated introduction of constitutionalism in 1905 did not fundamentally change the situation. By way of explanation and excuse, foreign governments got from Russian diplomats themselves "a terrible picture of the disorganization of the Russian services—or rather their mutual independence," which sometimes made it difficult to decide whether this décousu made Russian policy more dangerous or less so.[88] The split within the Russian government was a deep one. To a large extent, Russian diplomacy remained internationalist-conservative, in the Vienna Congress-Holy Alliance tradition. The Army, especially since Miljutin's reforms, "cultivated the national spirit more than the chivalrous and monarchical sentiments," and evolved "a general-staff chauvinism" which thought that "the road to Constantinople went by way of Vienna," or, still later, by way of Berlin.[89]

Russian imperialism was officer imperialism. It was a restless, energetic movement, often following no directive from the central Government but rather the ambitions of local governors who resumed the Alexanderzug in Asia for Alexander II. Defeated in the Crimean War, the officers shifted their objectives towards the Southeast, to the Sir Daja and Tashkent. As the Prussian Military Plenipotentiary in the 1860's, who lived in the intimacy of Russian officers, described their motives: "Personal interest, craving for orders and medals, promotion, money, local necessity, hunger and thirst of man and beast for bread, meat, grass and sweet water drove guard officers, heavily in debt, and ambitious and inquisitive General Staff officers, in large part of

German descent, on and on into the 'warm lands.'"[90] When imperialism had once again swung back to the vision of the Hagia Sophia (1877-78) and had been halted there by the Congress of Berlin, it turned westward against the two other Continental empires, Central Asia becoming a secondary theater for the more turbulent ambitions of a Skobelev or a Stoletov. When Stoletov returned from a mission to Kabul to enjoy the admiration of St. Petersburg society, Gortchakov, the supposed director of Russian policy, refused to meet this man who had been sent out not by him but by the military authority for the purpose of driving Afghanistan into war with Britain.[91]

The Russian army had had the ascendency in political influence over the Tsar ever since the Russo-Turkish War of 1877-78. In league with Pan-Slavists, whose own devotion to the Tsars was conditional,[92] the army took on an anti-German bias after the disappointing outcome of the Congress of Berlin. From 1878 on, the Russian military thought it best to express their disapproval by raising the peace-time strength, massing more and more Russian troops against and building fortifications along the German and Austrian frontiers—"getting ready for the war with Europe," as Miljutin put it. There was no sound strategic reason for such measures. Contrary to Russia's interests, they resulted in Moltke's plan for the war on two fronts and the German-Austrian alliance of 1879.[93]

In spite of the boost provided by the Three Emperors' League of 1881, Tsardom was too weak and uncourageous to take a stand against the home-front of soldiers and Pan-Slavists. Rather the Tsars accepted them as their own bulwark. The true conservatives in Germany, Austria, and in Russia itself, however, feared this alliance as the pace-maker of Nihilism and Revolution.[94] They were horrified at the spectacle of such military agitators as Skobelev, who did not hesitate to say that, while he was a faithful servant of the dynasty, the latter was doomed unless strengthened by great successes abroad, and that in the end it might have to be replaced by a Slav-Napoleon like himself. At first, there were only a few diplomats in the Pan-Slav group. Most diplomats, like Prince Orlov, Ambassador to Berlin, warned against using such a "new Garibaldi"—no diplomacy could continue if high military officers like Skobelev were permitted to indulge in oratorical indiscipline. The ambassador to London called him "insane, due to vainglory." However, the autocrat continued in the divide et impera system of governing without using a prime minister to give unity and coherence to the business of state. As one of the Tsar's more sober military aides confided to Bülow, the later Chancellor, the Tsar had forgotten that "we live in difficult times which make a unified and firm conduct of state business absolutely necessary."[95] Alexander could hardly screw up his courage to discipline Skobelev, whose strongest protector was Count Ignatiev, the negotiator of San Stefano and now Minister of the Interior. Death, coming to the aid of the Romanovs, silenced Skobelev when the two Alexanders could not.[96]

Ignatiev was removed from office at the time of Giers' appointment to the Foreign Office, which once more gave the civilian party the upper hand over the new Tsar (1882). The hold proved fairly precarious, for Alexander III had given up resisting the military party by 1885. He seemed ready to go to war with Britain over the Pendjeh incident, a war which the Russian diplomats feared might be set off by a second "coup de tête along the frontier" staged by the unruly officers of the Caucasus Army. To the Central Powers, such hunting for new frontiers in Asia by officers suffering from attacks of boredom and Nihilism was far more welcome than the violent interest they were soon to take in such Balkan problems as the Bulgarian crisis of 1886-87.[97] The officers' activities brought on another "danger of war" and set off new quarrels within Russia, with much of the tension discharged against foreign countries.

The failure of the Kaulbars mission in Bulgaria was a severe échec to the military, and particularly to the General Staff. They would gladly have "substituted" Austria for Bulgaria, and would have preferred a war against Austria to the seemingly necessary military occupation of Bulgaria. The by now usual solution, the Russian soldiers' substitute for war, was the cramming of still more garrisons along the German and Austrian frontiers.[98] This resulted in a new "danger of war" in 1887, which was considered more serious by the General Staffs in Berlin and Vienna than by the diplomats. Whether German, Austrian or Russian, the diplomats admitted, however, that the chaos reigning in Russia constituted a continuous source of war. The Russian ambassador to Berlin called it "a highly dangerous symptom that the Russian military administration was at the helm now, instead of the Ministry of Foreign Affairs; M. de Giers ought not to have allowed things to progress that far. 'De cette manière nous aurons la guerre au printemps.'"[99]

Under such conditions, generals like Obrutchev and Bogdanovitch worked for the French alliances as "volunteer diplomats," as Skobelev had done before them.[100] Only occasionally were they called to order by the Tsar. They undermined Giers' position at home. The following words describe fairly well the role of the foreign minister in Russia at that time:

Neither in society nor personally nor officially has he any ascendancy over his colleagues. He cannot avert vexatious measures of the Finance Minister against the Germans nor suppress, by way of the Ministry of Interior, press attacks against them. Nor does he find in the Ministry of War any protection against the generals who, either as troop commanders, or as high administrative officials, directly oppose his policy, approved as it is by the Monarch.[101]

When Bismarck's successors felt that they could not renew the complicated Reinsurance Treaty with Russia, the first among the Russian governors to lose insurance was Giers and diplomacy in general. There were few if any obstacles left in the way of the alliance with France, which the Russian military had sought more than any other group, and to which the Tsar agreed, partly as a way to put an end to the governmental disorder inside Russia. In former times, military influence on autocracy had taken the form of assassination; now it took the form of a Diktat in the diplomatic field.

The position of the foreign ministry and diplomacy remained precarious until the last days of Tsardom. The chaotic character of tsarist government found a new expression in the conflict over the forward policy pursued by Nicholas II and his military counsellors. They wanted to gain control of Korea as much as Stalin and his advisers did in the 1950's. The more moderate aims and methods of Lamsdorff and Witte, the Foreign and Finance Ministers, could not prevent the setting-up of a widely independent Far Eastern viceroyship under Admiral Alexeiev.[102] The conflict of the governmental "ressorts" brought Russia into the war with Japan, for which she was not yet fully prepared. This conflict continued during the war and contributed to the defeat and to diplomatic difficulties in the course of the war.[103] "The absence of unity in direction" and "the independent and side-by-side working of the individual factors of the governing machinery," although nothing new, still seemed to be among "the most remarkable phenomena in the Russian governing system" to foreign diplomats, whether friends or foes.[104] The German diplomat who made this comment did not see the basic similarity of this situation to conditions in his own country, probably because it was all so much rawer and cruder in Russia.[105]

Military defeat temporarily weakened the influence of the military in Russia. A newly appointed Chief of Staff, General Palitsin, soon complained (November 1905) that the Foreign Minister was not keeping him informed about developments of interest to him and his office, such as a £50,000,000 loan to Japan in which the French ally might participate. Such a loan would help the Japanese, still Russia's enemy, peace or no peace, to strengthen the weakest part of her armor. When informed that merely a £25,000,000 reconversion of an older loan was under consideration, he grumbled that Lamsdorff had dealt with the problem from an exclusively diplomatic standpoint, "only consulting the financial circles and without breathing a word to him, forgetting altogether on the one hand that 'money is the nerve of war' and, on the other, to take into account the relations he ought to maintain regularly with the Chief of the General Staff, following its recent reorganization, on the model of those which Bismarck had entertained with Moltke." Much to the satisfaction of the French ally, this incident had the good effect of establishing regular relations conducive to the good functioning of business.[106] The General's own ideas of cooperation with the diplomats were illustrated when, at the turn of the year from 1906 to 1907, he "almost on his own initiative provoked a war with Turkey along the Caucasian frontier." He naïvely imagined that "a little war" of this kind might remain localized. Isvolski and Prime Minister Stolypin stopped that adventure before it had begun and engineered Palitsin's removal from office soon thereafter.[107]

Such removals are not always easily obtained from absolutist governors or pseudo-autocrats such as Nicolas II and William II. Absolutism can survive longest in personnel policy, something of which the Fathers of the American Constitution were well aware when they made higher appointments and promotions subject to the approval of Congress. As a rule, autocrats are more willing to drop a civilian than a general, whose arms-bearing obedience gives the supreme warlord the same kind of self-satisfaction that a fearsome lion-tamer feels in the presence of an animal who is no longer as dangerous or strong as an ignorant public on the outside believes him to be.

Predilection for the soldier and his advice and argument makes the autocrat a poor chairman to preside over interdepartmental discussions. He usually proves unable to come effectively to the assistance of military spokesmen when they prove to be poor speakers and debaters, unable to stand up to the eloquence of foreign and finance ministers. Consequently the last Tsar and the last Kaiser rarely presided over crown councils.[108] In constitutionalist Russia, the Tsar was still further removed from such councils. He did not participate directly in the three famous conferences of 1908, 1913, and 1914, in which the Straits problem was discussed in the presence of ministers and agents of the defense offices.[109]

BRITAIN: UNITY THROUGH THE CABINET

In British government, civilian-political supremacy and—as was perhaps taken too much for granted—the unity of policy and strategy was guaranteed by the supreme position of the cabinet system. Throughout the nineteenth century, the Cabinet curtailed the remaining prerogatives of the Crown as an actively unifying factor and practically eliminated it as far as the armed forces were concerned.[110] The checks-and-balance arrangements of the various war-preparing and war-making offices, originating in the by now remote experiences with the standing army, were for long periods of time deemed more important than any centralizing arrangements for defense. The latter were attempted from time to time in the interest of higher efficiency. Under the impact of the invasion scare of the late 1850's, for example, a permanent Defence Committee within the Privy Council made the combined operations of Army and Navy the object of its discussions.[111] Soon after the scare subsided, the Committee ended its labors.

There were further complications resulting from the self-will of the service experts, particularly of the extremely powerful Board of Admiralty.[112] The four "naval lords," out of a total membership of six, occasionally exercised the threat of resignation in corpore when they thought it meet to hoist this warning signal against the politicians and their neglect or wrong handling of the Navy according to professional judgment. This extremely strong position, deeply anchored in the British political psyche, stood for a long time not only in the way of a unity of policy and strategy but also of an amphibious strategy, which in the end had to be forced on the Navy.[113]

While it would seem logical that final authority should be centered in the Prime Minister, Salisbury during his second premiership (1886-92) abandoned as hopeless the task of trying to effect this focus, even though Britain's seemingly final and irrevocable entrance into the European armaments race at that time made it more imperative than ever. Caught unawares by the Continental scare of 1886-87, the anxiety of the British public was heightened by public statements of military men such as Wolseley to the effect that a French landing in Southern England was feasible and that, as long as the Navy remained as weak as it was at that time, the Army could not guarantee the safety of the metropolis. Salisbury was ready, more ready than the Board of Admiralty, to admit that serious deficiencies existed. As War Office, Admiralty, and Moltke (whose advice had been solicited) agreed, such an invasion would be possible under certain circumstances. Britain was forced to enter the arms race despite her reluctance. The consequence of the scare, rather than of a strong demand from the Board of Admiralty, was the Naval Defense Act of 1889, which resulted in a considerable raise in naval expenditures. The attitude of the

Board on this occasion, "its failure to appreciate
deficiencies until their existence was driven home
to it by Cabinet cross-examination...presented a
curious inversion of the parts ordinarily played
by service officials and their political masters."
Salisbury thought "the fault [lay] in the constitution
of the Admiralty. The experts—the pedants—have
too much power. They ought to be advisers and
subordinates. They are checks and colleagues.
They claim an undefined power and responsibility,
and their consciences bear them out in resisting,
each man for himself, whatever he does not entirely approve." (They did approve of the exchange
of Heligoland for Zanzibar in 1890.)[114]

For a long time, this checks-and-balances distribution of powers did not seem to provide a
proper place and role for an institution like a general staff. Good Liberals like Campbell-Bannerman feared the politics of that institution so much
that they preferred to forego its military usefulness. For were not general staffs "constantly and
necessarily concerned in watching the military
conditions of their neighbors, in detecting points
of weakness and strength, and planning possible
operations in possible war against them?" To
have such an institution in England might create
a "general military policy," in the ambitious sense
of the word, for which she had no use.[115]

The disasters in the early stages of the Boer
War, which found "our War Office as inefficient as
usual,"[116] demonstrated the need for a thorough
reorganization of Britain's war-preparing and war-
making agencies. The Defence Committee of the
Cabinet was established in 1902. It consisted of
the Prime Minister "with such other members as,
having regard to the nature of the subject to be
discussed, he may from time to time summon to
assist him." The War Office was reorganized in
1904, a Committee of Imperial Defence set up in
1904, and a General Staff established in 1906.[117]
These reforms gave Britain the organization she
would need if she were to participate in the arms
competition into which her Entente policy had
finally brought her.

The unity of policy and strategy became vested
in the Prime Minister, who was enabled to establish a supreme position in all questions of defense.
His position became more and more like that of
commander-in-chief and supreme warlord, leaving
to the Cabinet only a more or less formal last
decision. It cannot be said that there was a unified
outlook during the Asquith Ministry, with Grey
directing, or being directed by the Foreign Office.
Whether the British considered Grey's regime as
a failure of man or of office, they never again allowed a Foreign Secretary to have as much power
and independence as Grey had had. They gave war-
making powers to Lloyd George in the First World
War and to Winston Churchill in the Second that

were almost commensurate with those of the
American President.

AUSTRIA-HUNGARY - "VIRIBUS DISUNITIS"

The armed forces have been co-determinants
as well as servants of their countries' policies.
Their influence, whether or not it is brought to
bear through authorized organs, has varied widely,
but hardly anywhere has it been completely absent.
There have been high tides and low ebbs in this
influence. The high points have not always been
due to the fact that armies and navies consciously
sought more influence but simply to the fact that
at times defense questions objectively assumed
greater weight in a country's affairs, as in the
United States since 1939. In certain countries,
officers of the armed forces have traditionally
dominated their countries' politics. In Austria-
Hungary, the Empire's officers came from the
dominant strata, the Germans, Hungarians and, to
a lesser extent, the Poles and Croats, to the almost
complete exclusion of the Czechs, Serbs and Italians, the Irredentists and unreliables. In no other
country, consequently, did strategy arise so directly from conditions of domestic policy, nor in
any other country did the military so constantly
seek to influence foreign policy. Towards the end,
they wanted to see it directed in a way that would
permit the staging of the preventive war so often
proposed by Conrad. As Winston Churchill has
said: "What Ludendorff became in 1917, Conrad
was already some ten years earlier...that most
dangerous of combinations, a Chief of General
Staff absorbed in Foreign Policy."[118]

Conrad based his interminable proposals on
"the standing order of His Majesty to keep in contact with Your Excellency [the Foreign Minister]
as regards all important political questions."
These, according to Conrad, always called for
more Austrian armaments in preparation for necessary wars. Since the Bosnian annexation Aehrenthal considered the Empire to be "saturated." Her
policy, necessarily conservative, must not provide
for the armaments that Conrad demanded—they
would only give the appearance of an aggressiveness on the part of Austria that was contrary to
the Emperor's peaceful policy, and they would
result in an armaments race for which Austrian
finances were not suited.[119]

Conrad pointed out to the Foreign Minister the increasing strength and hostility of Serbia-Montenegro,
which would have to be taken into account in the
case of a conflict with Russia. If it should come
to such a war, Austrian diplomacy must follow a
course that would require her to leave only minor
forces along the Balkan front. With this Aehrenthal
"very much agreed." He did not, however, agree
with the suggestion that Austria's long-term

policy objective ought to be the Anschluss of Serbia-Montenegro, as a means of preserving her own Serbian-Croatian provinces. While the hostility of the Serbs and the threat of military action on their part in the direction of the Austrian frontiers had to be reckoned with, Aehrenthal considered it still more likely that they would turn first against Turkey's remaining Balkan possessions. In doing so, they would be trying to avoid a war on two fronts. In any case, the aggressive Balkan states would not turn against Austria first. Postponing conflict was no solution in Conrad's eyes, and so-called better diplomatic relations with the Balkan states should have no influence on the concrete preparations for war. He wanted Aehrenthal to seek better relations with Turkey and to make her treat the Albanians better, thus making it possible for Austria to restore her ancient hold on them.[120]

Italy betrayed an intention of entering upon the Turkish heritage ahead of the Balkan States. Months before the actual outbreak of the war in Tripoli, Conrad hastened to point out to the Foreign Minister the possible repercussions that this war might have in the Balkans and the necessity of considering Austrian intervention there. Military preparations would require some time, even though plans had been made for the various possible wars—war with Serbia-Montenegro alone, war with Russia, with Italy, with Russia and Italy. Should the Serbs enter the war against Turkey and make conquests, Austria must unfailingly intervene, possibly by making use of her right of occupation in the Sandjak of Novibazar. Aehrenthal considered it "lucky that we have no such right any more"; it had been given up as part of the settlement with Turkey following the Bosnian crisis. Aehrenthal reminded Conrad, who was always harping back to all that had been left undone on that favorable occasion, that the policy followed in 1908-09 had been that of the two partners of the Double Monarchy and as such had been approved by Francis Joseph himself. His own policy in the Balkans was aimed at maintaining the territorial status quo there. For that reason, military preparations could be omitted for the time being.[121]

The Foreign Minister lost a round in August 1911 when a war minister was appointed who was not his candidate. Aehrenthal offered his resignation, since harmonious relations among the various ministries seemed no longer guaranteed, but was persuaded by the Emperor to stay. He returned to the attack in September when Conrad, with the outbreak of the Tripoli war imminent, proposed preventive war against Italy. The Chief of Staff argued that, once Italy had defeated Turkey, she would inevitably return to her ancient objectives, the Italian-speaking parts of Austria, the Adriatic, and the Balkans. Determined to see the principle

recognized that "military preparations must be suited to the exigencies of foreign policy, and not vice versa," Aehrenthal proceeded to force a showdown, explaining his own position and duties, as he saw them, and those of Conrad to the Emperor:

It is part of the foremost duties of the Minister of Foreign Affairs to entertain friendly and peaceful relations with all foreign governments as long as this can be done without harming the prestige of the State and without sacrificing vital interests. The Chief of Staff has the task of making the necessary military preparations and of insuring the readiness of the Army in view of the political situation of the time and the various possibilities of war. These so very different circles of activity have, however, many points of contact which demand the close cooperation of the directors of foreign affairs with the General Staff. The first condition for this is that there should be a relation of confidence between these two factors and that they should keep strictly within the limits of their competency. Otherwise friction might result that would be damaging to the All Highest's service.

[It is not in keeping with this requirement that Conrad, for many years] has felt called upon to exercise an influence on the conduct of foreign affairs and, going beyond that, does not hesitate to criticize the latter, which means entering upon a field that is beyond his competency. The interference has gone so far that he has posed a sudden war against Italy in April 1907, forgetting that consideration and decision of the question whether and when a war is to be undertaken is first of all up to the Ministry of Foreign Affairs.

After having continually criticized and termed faulty my own policy during the Bosnian annexation crisis, though it had the Emperor's approval throughout, Conrad, determined to put over his own political ideas, had now returned to his plan for a preventive war against Italy, for which no present cause existed. Italy would not even win anything by the acquisition of Tripoli, as Conrad maintained, certainly not in offensive strength. These political ideas he had not merely submitted to the Emperor, the Heir to the Throne, the Foreign and War Ministers; he had also inspired part of the press with them, with the result that the newspapers close to him were using a language that made the conduct of foreign affairs considerably more difficult. He had organized a whole "war party" within the General Staff corps, which was systematically pushing for a war against Italy at the very same moment when the renewal of the Triple Alliance was under discussion.

Since the proposed action on the part of the

Chief of Staff had become semi-public, to say the least, the public abroad and at home had been made aware of the unfortunate fact that there was a fundamental conflict concerning a purely political question between the director of foreign affairs and the chief of the General Staff. This could only prove harmful to the credit of the Monarchy and make relations with Italy very difficult, for whose expansion in the direction of Tripoli Austrian diplomacy had rather prayed these tens of years.

It is high time to establish that the Minister appointed by the All Highest Crown for the conduct of foreign policy remains its competent and responsible director. It is the duty of the Chief of Staff to make the military preparations required for the various possibilities of war without however being entitled to exercise an influence on the coming of this or the other possible war. If these two functionaries remain within the spheres of competency assigned to them by the All Highest service, a mutual understanding about the political and military situation as it arises from time to time will result automatically.[122]

Faced with this bid for the maintenace of the civilian direction of policy, Francis Joseph informed Conrad that "as regards the duties of your office, the principle is valid now as before that at all times all possible war readiness on the Wehrmacht's part has to be striven for. In awareness of that, My Minister of Foreign Affairs directs the efforts of his office within the Monarchy in accordance with the expression of My will and in harmony with My two Prime Ministers."[123] A few weeks later, Conrad was relieved of his office, to the satisfaction of Austria's ally and foes alike. It was an open secret that he had been sacrificed in the interest of better relations with Italy, as well as with the Ballhausplatz.[124] Conrad thought that the directors of policy at the Ballhausplatz found it

really very convenient in time of peace to keep those organs responsible for war-making at arm's length, but put the blame on them should war come about. Diplomats of this school look at the army as an umbrella, which they allow to become full of holes in time of peace and only pull out when the downpour starts. The diplomats of our enemies, however, see in the army the most effective instrument of politics which one prepares for a definite objective, if only for one's own preservation.[125]

Unawareness that the military policy of Conrad and his General Staff was utterly anti-conservative, as Aehrenthal and Francis Joseph realized most of the time, cannot be more completely dem-

onstrated than by Austrian policy leading to the First World War. The General Staff had at last taken the Ballhausplatz in tow. Attempts in this direction had been made during Conrad's temporary absence, demonstrating how institutional his policies were, rather than personal. When the Balkan States were mobilizing for their war against Turkey in September 1912, Conrad's locum tenens submitted to the Emperor his views of "the general political situation as it touches my province." The salient features mentioned by him were: an increase in Anglo-German antagonism; the ineffectiveness of the Great Powers' intervention in the Balkans, where the governments were then uniting under Russian patronage in order to effect the liquidation of Turkey by war; and the untrustworthiness of Italy. What was Austria to do under these circumstances? She must take measures in order not to be surprised by events. These should include preventing Serbia, already under Russian influence, from making territorial gains and effecting union with Montenegro. She should instead be drawn into Austria's power orbit by tariff and commercial unions and military conventions. At the same time, the way should be kept open for Albania. Falling also into Austria's power orbit, she must not be allowed to become a victim of Italy's aspirations with regard to the Adriatic. The situation, he concluded, offered three courses of action from which Austria would have to choose: (1) Austria could call for a Great Power conference. This was likely to result in reform demands addressed to the Turks and was likely to end in failure, considering the basic divergence of Great Power interests; (2) Austria could wait for things to happen and then intervene. In this case Austria might miss the right moment for action and come in last, thereby losing her standing as a Great Power, decreasing her value as an ally, and risking constant danger to her South Slav possessions from the newly-strengthened Balkan states; (3) Austria could act in accordance with independent resolutions, stated openly and in advance. Action would most likely be called for along the Southern frontier, where troops should be reinforced, a state of war declared, and everything prepared for Mobilization B and armed intervention against Serbia if the latter went to war. However, Case B could only be carried out if diplomacy were to assure peace with the other two potentially hostile Powers, Russia and Italy.

The Ballhausplatz and its new director, Berchtold, would not hear of the active and aggressive policy proposed by the Chief of Staff: no Russian or Italian approval of such an Austrian policy could be expected. The shock of the Bosnian annexation was still felt, and it had united most other Powers, as well as the Balkan states, in a common anti-Austrian front. It therefore seemed best to join in on the attempt of the Great Powers to localize the Balkan conflict, without surrendering any of the Monarchy's specific Balkan interests. Premature mobilization would be interpreted as indicating aggressive tendencies on Austria's part and would the more promptly unite other Powers against her. Her forces would thus be prematurely tied down in the South.[126]

In December 1912, Conrad was back in his old office. Austria could no longer do without her best general, as Francis Ferdinand and other influential persons thought. They hoped that Conrad the politician would prove more discreet during his second term of office, a hope that was never justified. Once again he expressed his basic view that

> a state must always pursue positive, that is to say, aggressive objectives. Restriction to the purely conservative side would result in an inevitable setback, since the surrounding neighbors would tend to enlarge their sphere of power...It is a fiction to believe in a status quo [and no military preparations can be built upon it].[127]

Abroad, Conrad's reappointment was considered to be highly ominous, signifying that the war party had returned to power in Vienna and that the higher ranks of Austrian army circles had been further invaded by politics.[128] It was almost futile for Berchtold to assure everyone that Conrad's return would have no influence on the course of Austrian policy.[129] The signs were already ominous enough. When the Austrian press wrote that, before his return, Conrad had promised Berchtold that he would not interfere with politics, Conrad at once gave a resounding démenti. This was promptly followed by Italy's notification that she no longer intended to send an army over the Brenner to the Upper Rhine in the case of a war of the Central Powers (December 18, 1912).[130] Conrad was back in politics all the way. He informed the Austrian military attachés, even less under foreign office control than in other countries, that in his "purely personal view, a warlike settlement with Serbia would be the only promising solution of the problem."[131] For him it remained axiomatic that "the military ratio of strengths reaches far over into the direction of policy; military power factors, concrete war preparations and direction of policy are so intimately intertwined that the labors of my office, as they are incumbent on me, not only justify my dealing with the political situation but are the very first conditions of it."[132]

Even a weakling like Berchtold was not at once ready to surrender the political primacy of his office. He tried to soothe Conrad, who was wrought up over a newspaper article by a nameless diplomat who had written a warning against the war aspirations of the General Staff. Berchtold

assured him that there was "no dualism in the political guiding lines of the influential factors" in the Double Monarchy. In their conservatism, diplomats tried to persuade Conrad that a defeat of Russia would have revolutionary consequences. And a non-Tsarist Russia would be far more dangerous to Austria than the one at that moment.[133] Berchtold emerged victorious from his first clashes with Conrad, which he had not provoked. When the Army proposed that more artillery be put into Semlin, the Hungarian town opposite Belgrade, Francis Joseph at first agreed, provided the Foreign Minister did not think the measure inopportune. Berchtold, however, submitted that, because of the negotiations then going on, he could not approve "a further increase in our military preparedness against Serbia." Events, he said, did not justify the concern shown by the soldiers over a sudden concentration of Serb forces against the Monarchy, whose own preparations had already gone so far as to arouse fear of Austrian aggressive intentions, even in Berlin. New military moves at the present moment could not be justified from the standpoint of the foreign department. The Emperor accepted Berchtold's view and forbade the further arming of Semlin.[134]

Emboldened by this success, Berchtold protested to Conrad against the Army's plan to provide the Albanian tribes with arms and ammunition to be used against the Serbs, who were reluctant to end their occupation of Albania. The Ballhausplatz learned of this plan "in a confidential manner," that is to say, not from the soldiers themselves. If this was really intended, it was particularly improper at a moment when the Serbs, under pressure from the Powers, were at last ready to retire from Albania. "For this reason," Berchtold protested, "I must insist most emphatically, as you will understand, that I be informed in detail about the General Staff's intentions in Albania, in order to reserve for myself the possibility of protesting in time against those measures which seem to me inopportune, or even dangerous from the standpoint of foreign affairs." Conrad was not at once dissuaded. He told Berchtold that he was still considering war-like steps against Serbia, "because I see in the growth of this State a decisive danger for the Monarchy, a danger the harder to remove the later it is attempted. I believe that even the question of the demarcation of Albania's frontiers— unless the Monarchy wants to back down—will lead to a conflict. Should it come to that, it is of the highest importance to tie down Serbian forces by an Albanian insurrection." Hence the plan for arms shipments. Some 12,000 rifles were made ready and one parcel was soon to be dispatched. There could be no question of this being an unneutral act, since Russia, France, and Italy had provided the various other belligerents with arms.

Only after further remonstrations was Conrad persuaded to give up this dangerous and discreditable enterprise.[135]

With the boldness of a rabbit hiding behind the "cavalier's" wardrobe, Berchtold even dared to strike back at Conrad. He reminded him, after reading an expert's article on the serious shortcomings in Austria's artillery, that this relative backwardness was a fact that made the hazardous game of risking war, to which the General's policy was leading, "even more uncomfortable." But Conrad put his trust in the German strength that would pull Austria out of all embarrassments— once she had conquered France in four to six weeks. Such shortcomings (and there were many others) were to him "no reason to speak of a relative battle inferiority in the sense that we would have to shun entrance into war."

Conrad pushed Berchtold closer and closer to the thought of war with Russia, which the Balkan complications would bring on. He pointed out to Berchtold that "if we allow ourselves to be at all times influenced by the fear of a war with Russia, our action, generally speaking, will be so much paralyzed that it is tantamount to digging our own grave." Berchtold's resistance to war was not strengthened by any peaceful success, such as the Bosnian annexation which had helped Aehrenthal in his day. His protests against Conrad's bellicose policies grew weaker and weaker. In fact, he began to take on the role of the strong man who was only held back by Francis Ferdinand, his minister-colleagues, and part of the press. In March 1913, a Great Power blockade of Montenegro was planned in detail, and Conrad proposed to direct Austrian participation in a manner "as if we were to seek war." One of Berchtold's assistants corrected this to read "that we would not shrink from war," but Count Berchtold himself remained silent. To Conrad he appeared more in favor of war than ever before, while Berchtold was content to appear ready to risk war only because he was certain that the Emperor and Francis Ferdinand would ultimately decide in favor of more peaceful measures. When Conrad proposed that Mobilization B be applied against Montenegro, the forces of peace formed front against him. In order to strengthen the peace party, the Emperor sent his Court Marshal to the Cabinet council that was discussing the proposal. This left Conrad in a minority of one. In his rage, he asked Berchtold what right a court official had to participate in such deliberations. Abroad, the peace party was formed mainly by Britain and Germany. Why pay too much attention to them? Conrad asked. Berchtold told him "that the mot de l'énigme is in the fact that the situation is too serious and we are faced by events that threaten the Monarchy in its very existence. We must take all precautions in order not to make the international situation too unfavorable to ourselves." Any independent action on Austria's part at that moment would inevitably lead to war on three fronts, with Russia, the South Slavs and Italy (April 2, 1913).

The fall of Scutari to the Montenegrine besiegers was considered highly detrimental to Austrian prestige, particularly by Viennese society. It was ascribed to "poor Berchtold," and he was criticized in the sharpest terms. So was the Emperor himself to a certain extent, as well as all the men who had shown patience in "spinning along on the European thread." Suffering this Balkan insult seemed to put in doubt Austria's very position as a Great Power and as a worthwhile ally of Germany—these were the inferiority complexes of the ruling society in Vienna. Conrad appealed once more to Berchtold: "Unless the Monarchy wants to altogether give up raising its lowered prestige and preserving its most vital interests, there remains only one thing —to proceed at once towards the solution of this [Scutari] problem and, in doing so, to shake off all restrictions imposed by the Great Powers." All of Conrad's hopes for war, raised once more by Montenegro's unwillingness to evacuate Scutari, were spoiled when, on second thought, King Nikita decided to surrender the place as bidden by the Powers. Conrad was a broken man, "absolutely in despair," according to the highly sympathetic German military attaché.[136]

Between Scutari and Serajevo, Conrad saw various occasions that ought to have brought on war. But he had little hope that they would. Instead they would "only result in a diplomatic Ballhaus comedy and an orgy of perplexity among the dabblers there." He was ready to resign from his office just before the shots of Serajevo exploded.[137] They provided the high voltage currents for war, applied by Conrad to burn out all the remaining fuses in the wiring system of the ramshackle Austrian governmental system.

1914 - 1918

The civilian powers in the three Empires, personally as well as constitutionally weak, resigned to rather than resolved for war in 1914. The arch-civilian consideration as to whether or not anything could be gained by winning a war gave way to the standing military conviction that victory could be won. This conviction prevailed just as definitely where the civilian power was strongest, in Britain and France. In the arrangements between the civilian and military parts of the government in the three Empires, there was, as a critic of German conditions has put it, "not organization, but simply juxtaposition" of the parts. And this was as true during the war as before it. "All reverts to the personal influence which each

of the counsellors succeeds in assuring for himself...Each works in his own sphere, his own ressort, and leaves to the Emperor the task of recon-
ciling his own desires with those of the rest."[138]
All the genuine harmonizing, uniting, and appointing powers of the Crown were gone. The imperial
power was deeply shaken from domestic military
quarters, long before revolutions swept it away.

The relative weakness of the civilian power,
swept along in the blinding chase for victory, made
all intra-European peace endeavors quite nerve-
less. The irenic ethos of diplomacy, of which
Lansdowne's appeal was a reminder, was gone.
All the grim determination to win the war—Durch-
halten! Carry through! as the German imperative
went—nowhere produced a basic reorganization
for the unity of strategy and policy. As a military
writer stated soon after the war: "No nation possessed the grand strategical machinery necessary
to coordinate political thought and military action;
warfare has consequently assumed an almost entirely military aspect."[139]

Judging from post-war developments, neither
defeat nor victory taught the participants very
impressive or penetrating lessons as to the necessity of unity of civil and military policy. A few
lessons learned were embodied in the Weimar
Constitution and in the general tendency, the world
over, to discard the remnants of military federal-
ism in favor of centralism. The winners of the
war, so much satisfied with the fact of victory that
they were inclined to forget about the ways in which
it ought not to have been won, allowed most of their
pre-war practices and arrangements to stand. The
various Totalitarianisms promised that their duces,
assuming a cumulation of offices, would at last re-
unite policy and powers. The most extensive arrangements for unity were made in Russia, on the
basis of conclusions that were derived at least as
much from the premises of class conflict as from
the military defeat of 1917-18. While the details
of coordination may have escaped outside observation, the general tendency was clearly towards
a strict centralism and monolithism—all power
away from the Soviets and to the Politbureau! The
Soviets ratified by constitutional amendment the
Politbureau's proposal for a reorganization of the
Ministries of Foreign Affairs and Defense in February 1944.[140] This reorganization was a result
of the struggle with Hitler but was also a measure
in preparation for the conflict with the remaining
capitalists. Molotov declared that it was intended
to heighten the significance of the Soviet Union
for "the peoples of East and West."[141]

JAPAN, 1939 - 1945

"The fact that the Supreme Command and State
affairs are independent of each other has been a
matter of anguish from generation to generation"
in Japan, according to a relatively Liberal Japanese leader.[142] The separation proved even more
troublesome, once the elements that elsewhere
sparked Fascist movements formed inside the
Japanese Army and made it violently aggressive
at home and abroad. The traditional governors of
Japan were unable to bridge the gap between military and civilian and to overcome "the complete
lack of coordination between Japan's military and
diplomatic action and policies."[143] The Tokyo
Foreign Office confessed again and again to Americans, even if with decreasing sincerity, that there
were two Japans—one Liberal, civilian and peaceful,
the other military and expansionistic. The Foreign
Office hoped and begged for concessions from the
foreign Powers in order to enable them to preserve
a dubious foothold at home.[144] Finally they were
ground to pieces between military demands and
American antagonism.

The traditional role of the Japanese Emperor as
unifier, quite effective during the Meiji era, had
become too weak to serve the purposes of the older
order. The Emperor was "theoretically the sole
source of military authority."[145] When he affixed
his seal of approval to the changes taking place,
however, the old-fashioned character on the seal
could not hide his helplessness. At first, the traditional governing groups had sought to preserve the
old order by such arrangements as having admirals
and generals function as Prime and Foreign Ministers.[146] Of ten Premiers in ten years, three were
admirals—Viscount Saito, 1932-34, Okada 1934-36,
Yonai 1940—and three generals—Hayashi 1937, Abe
1941 and Tojo 1942. Of the twelve foreign ministers
during that period, six were officers. Originally it
was hoped that the civil government could obtain
control of the armed forces by giving these civilian
offices to military or naval men; it was hoped that
the offices would take over the men. In the end it
was the armed forces that got control of the offices.
The ominous turn came when Tojo, who had risen
from the most imperialist section of the Army, the
Kwantung Army, became Prime Minister and War
Minister concurrently, thus combining these two
offices for the first time. And at the same time he
remained an army general. He did not even retire
nominally from the service.[147]

The intervention of the Army and Navy in foreign
affairs became increasingly more direct. At first,
it was simply that the Foreign Office had to refer
various propositions of foreign governments to the
armed forces for approval or other action.[148]
They admitted this to the foreign diplomats, originally with some embarrassment, later as a routine
matter. In the end, there was even more direct
action on the part of the armed forces: the diplomacy of the service attachés, the use of admirals
and generals as ambassadors, and direct negotia-

tions on the part of the services with foreign military and naval offices, with or without the knowledge of the Tokyo Foreign Office. They considered their methods to be very successful in the preparation of war, as they gleefully assured the German war makers. Hitler and Goebbels were filled with admiration for those Japanese who

> prepared everything secretly. We have now heard that Kurusu and Admiral Nomura negotiated in Washington without having the faintest idea as to what the Japanese war leaders were planning. That's a good thing. When you are gambling for the existence of your own people, you should employ all methods of a tricky and superior war strategy. It means, of course, that Kurusu and Nomura played an exceedingly ludicrous role...They deserved making fools of themselves, for these two diplomats have always been the representatives of Japanese appeasement...We, too, have employed such methods again and again. Our ambassador in Moscow also hadn't the faintest idea that the Reich was determined to attack...There is no doubt that one does best if one keeps the diplomats uninformed about the background of politics.[149]

The gangster methods of ruling by division could not even claim superior efficiency and success. With a good deal of justification, one of the duped Japanese negotiators later put the blame for the Pearl Harbor attack and Japanese war policy generally on the "independence" of Japanese military leaders from civilian control, an independence that was "the principal cancer of Japan."[150]

GERMANY AND ITALY, 1919-1945

There was a certain post-war awareness within Germany (even if the war-guilt imputation put upon her pre-war leaders from the outside stood in the way of a fuller realization of the lesson) that many of the constitutional and extra-constitutional arrangements in the governance of the Second Reich had been faulty. It was widely realized that William II had been unable to fill the offices of supreme commander and director of policies; that the Anglo-Saxon way of parliamentary control over military and foreign affairs—as far as it went—and of treating a number of defense problems in committee had definite points of merit;[151] that the "immediacy" position of the chief of staff was undesirable; that a close relation of political and military counsels was necessary and that this had been lacking before and during the war.

On their part, the Wilhelmstrasse diplomats were determined to regain civilian supremacy in foreign affairs. They not only put off as long as they could the re-emergence of the service attaché,

but also kept away the ex-officers who, during the large-scale officer unemployment of the 1920's, sought to make their careers in the foreign service.[152] Among the military who were learning from defeat, Seeckt realized at once that "military and military-political actions were and are possible only if there is agreement and understanding between political and military leaders... Purely military actions belong in the field of revolts, and as such are only ephemeral."[153] The civilian politicians of Weimar, particularly Streseman, disappointed the generals by their opposition to prompt German remilitarization. They made use of the constitution of 1919 and the unity of policy which it guaranteed much better than the Bismarckian Constitution had, in order to give German affairs a civilian preponderance. If home affairs had been more secure and more prosperous, the military would have been allowed even less leverage. Even so, and despite the rapid changes of cabinets, discussions by an inter-ministerial "experts committee for national defense" (Referentenausschuss für Landesverteidigung) never assumed either great importance or bureaucratic independence.[154] Since parties, politicians, and bureaucrats proved to be so slow and unreliable as remilitarizers of the German people, the Reichswehr posed no objection to Hitler's coming to power. Now the Army hoped to get what it "needed."

On April 4, 1933, the Reich cabinet, which met very infrequently and never again after February 1938, set up a Reich Defense Council (Reichsverteidigungsrat) for the purpose of discussing preparations for war.[155] In the Council, all Reich ministries, except those for Foreign Affairs and for Propaganda, were grouped under three heads: the Chief of the High Command of the Armed Forces (Chef des Oberkommandos der Wehrmacht—Keitel since February 1938); the Plenipotentiary for War Economy (Generalbevollmächtigter für Kriegswirtschaft—Schacht since May 1935, later Funk); and the Plenipotentiary for Home Administration (Generalbevollmächtigter für Reichsverwaltung—Frick since April 1938, later Himmler). This Council met only twice. The first meeting was on November 18, 1938, when nearly all Reich Ministers and State Secretaries, the Commanders-in-Chief of the Army and Navy, the three Chiefs of Staff of the Wehrmacht branches, the Deputy of the Führer, high SS leaders, the Reich Labor Leader and other personnages were assembled. The meeting consisted solely of a three-hours' lecture by Field Marshal Goering. No discussion took place. The other meeting of the Council, on June 23, 1939, was presided over by the same dignitary, with representatives of eighty-four ministries and other war-preparing agencies present. Though Goering emphasized that the Council "was the determining body in the Reich for all questions of preparations for the most important questions of Reich defense," not much was achieved on this occasion beyond the presentation of directives for the distribution and employment of the Reich population in wartime and an agreement that "in the field of transportation Germany was at the present moment not ready for war."[156]

A Secret Cabinet Council (Geheimer Kabinettsrat) was set up in February 1938 when Ribbentrop took over in the Wilhelmstrasse. It was to deal with foreign affairs, particularly as they touched on questions of defense, in post-absolutist cabinet style; Neurath, predecessor of Ribbentrop, was to preside. Wehrmacht commanders, Keitel of the OKW and Lammers as representative of the Chancellery, were also to be members. Actually, this body never met; while there was a theoretical recognition of the need for a collegiate body to deal with the complex matter at hand, the divide et impera practices of dictatorship forbade it to come to life.[157] On the very eve of the Second World War, as if intended to avoid past mistakes in German war councils, the Reich Government was put on a war basis "for the period of the present foreign political tension." A Ministerial Council for the Defense of the Reich was set up as a permanent committee charged with "the unitary direction of administration and economy." The supervision of the Ministerial Council for Reich Defense was to be in the hands of Lammers, Reich Minister and Chief of the Reich Chancellery. Headed once again by Goering, the Council included Keitel, Frick and Funk as Plenipotentiaries for Administration and Economy respectively, and Hess as representative of the Nazi Party.[158] Its composition was to be elastic, the chairman being empowered to call in other members of the Reich Defense Council. It seemed "tantamount to the establishment of a general staff for civil defense and for economics" along the home front of total war.[159] Actually it was not.

This supreme body provided for unity of legislative powers rather than for deliberative unity, a thing that was never greatly sought inside the Third Reich either in peace or in war. Departmental objectives, as rampant as ever, might be achieved through appeal to the dictatorial unity resting in Hitler.[160] The greatest loss of power was suffered by the Foreign Office. While it served as a kind of camouflaging agency for the Führer's war preparations, no general or detailed knowledge of military planning was imparted to Ribbentrop. Ribbentrop frequently told his assistants that "he was completely in the dark in military affairs."[161] All self-exculpating intentions on the part of the accused and their witnesses at Nuremberg notwithstanding, there was a great deal of truth in statements such as Ribbentrop's that he "was not informed about military prepara-

tions, because these matters were always dealt with separately."[162]

The tendency towards disunity was growing rather than diminishing as war approached. Cooperation between Wilhelmstrasse and Wehrmacht had been closer, although only temporarily, during the time of German intervention in the Spanish Civil War, when some diplomatic amenities still had to be observed. Later on, the divide-and-rule principle of Hitlerian dictatorship kept Wehrmacht and Foreign Office apart, as institutions of potentially conservative character. In December 1936, perhaps in imitation of Italian interdepartmental conferences on the Abyssinian and Spanish problems, the Wilhelmstrasse proposed to the OKW "a practical way to increase even further the cooperation between the Foreign Ministry and the War Ministry in the Spanish question" by means of periodic conferences between Foreign Ministry and representatives of all three Wehrmacht branches.[163] The purpose of the conferences would be "to bring military measures into harmony with the aims of the political leadership, to create unity between military strategy and diplomacy." Keitel thought it better to delegate only one Wehrmacht representative to such meetings, instead of three with possibly three different opinions. He would not let the diplomats suspect that strategy, instead of one logical deduction, might well prove to be a matter of opinion. The Wilhelmstrasse agreed, provided that specialists of the three Wehrmacht branches could be called in if needed.

That the relations between Wilhelmstrasse and OKW were growing more intimate and detailed, at least temporarily, was evident when the OKW, like some other armed forces, set up its own Foreign Department, or Abteilung Ausland, for just such deliberations. Among the larger problems discussed was that of a possible French intervention in Spain in the spring of 1938 in favor or the Spanish Republicans, whose collapse seemed imminent. Keitel reassured the diplomats that France was not likely to intervene, for in this case she would not only find south of the Pyrenées "the whole of the Spanish Nationalist armed forces, but also Italian and German troops, behind which stand the armed forces of both of these great military Powers." It seemed doubtful that France would be sufficiently strong to guard her two eastern fronts and at the same time intervene in Spain, where Franco's victory was nearly complete. And France was not likely to obtain the necessary assistance from Britain. Besides, the weak internal position of the front populaire would keep it from making and executing so serious a decision. It was therefore safe enough for the interventionists to see Franco through to final victory.[164]

"The pace here is getting faster and faster,"

Secretary of State Weizsäcker wrote from the Wilhelmstrasse to the ambassador in Tokyo. Moments of reflection were becoming scarcer. Military attachés were being made into ambassadors. "The connection between the War Ministry and the Foreign Ministry is closer today than ever and I believe there is good reason for this. As long as we were only a pawn of foreign policy and by no means in a position to defend ourselves, this connection was perhaps not so very important. Our thoughts now move in new channels, however."[165] With the approach of the war, the Wilhelmstrasse became less and less a policy-maker or formulator. Instead it was expected to serve the purposes of the war in minor roles, such as legal advisor on naval and other warfare. The need for inter-service and inter-departmental committee work found more theoretical recognition than practical observance among Nazi services and personalities.[166] No participant was more likely to be slighted by the warriors, singly or combined, than the diplomats.

Whatever beliefs in the superiority of Hitler's intuitive genius in warfare his early and easy successes had produced, his constant interference with and disregard for the organizers in the later stages of the war aggravated rather than relieved Germany's increasing material weaknesses. He forced the organizers, a few of them diplomats, many from the General Staff, to attempt their 1944 coup against the disorganizer who called himself Führer. A new phenomenon had arisen in the history of tyrannicide, the managerial revolt.

By comparison with Hitler, the Italian dictator was far more ready to hear, though not necessarily to accept, expert advice. He took Badoglio's advice that the Ethiopian enterprise was feasible and promised success to Italian arms, but not his counsel to stay out of the Second World War. He presided over and listened to the discussions of the Supreme Defense Council, composed of the four chiefs of staff, the Foreign Minister and the Minister of Foreign Exchange and Currency.[167] As in Germany, the liquidation of fascism, with its belief that it could achieve victory by carrying the violence of street brawls into the international field, had to be taken in hand by elements of diplomacy and the general staff.

As far as the Second World War represented competition between Fascism and non-Fascism as governmental-planning-command-liaison techniques, it did not demonstrate what many had hoped and many had feared—the superiority of Fascism in the making of war. The hopes of the ideological and military path-makers of Fascism, that it would end the seemingly obsolete division of powers and offices and furnish supreme unity through the Duce and the Führer, were in for violent disappointment. After assuming the supreme command, Hitler, interested only in the two questions of operations and personnel, negligent or ignorant in all others, proved far more of an interferer than a unifier. Party officials and army commanders clashed constantly in their notions about and practices in war-making. Party wishes stood in the way of more rational military intentions. Fascism did not even provide the basis for sound coalition warfare: there was disunity, even treachery among the partners, and some of the demonstrative unity ordered from above was contrary to better military judgment. Hitler, at the outset of the campaign against Yugoslavia, gave orders that the German Army group attacking from Bulgaria was to join hands with the Italians in their uncomfortable position in Albania. He thereby endangered the plans of the Army command (OKH), directed against the necessarily more important opponent to the southward, the British and Greeks in Epirus and Greece. The OKH largely disregarded the orders. When the Greek Army was about to capitulate to the Reichsheer, Hitler and Mussolini forced an equal partnership with the Italians upon the enraged OKH in order to make the Balkan campaign a joint Fascist victory.[168] The conduct of the war by the Axis furnished some negative examples for the unifier's function inside democratic government, as well as for the command and other arrangements inside the two post-war—and possibly ante-war—armed camps, the Soviet satellite system and NATO.

FRANCE: 1918-1939

The unity of French policy and national defense was vested in the Conseil supérieur de la défense nationale. The members were the Premier, the Ministers of Foreign Affairs, of National Defense and War, of the Navy, of the Air, the Chief of Staff of National Defense (Gamelin), Marshal Pétain during the 1930's, and such permanent officials as the three chiefs of staff of the Army, the Navy (Darlan), and the Air Force, the Secretary General of the Foreign Office (Leger), various other military men called in time to time and a Secretary General of the Conseil, who was an Army general. A commission d'études joined military men with such parliamentary specialists in defense questions as Paul-Boncour and Fabry. A law of July 11, 1938, set up a Comité permanent de défense nationale, presided over by the Premier, which included the heads or representatives of the three defense ministries, the Ministries of Foreign Affairs and the Colonies, the Chief of Staff, and the Secretary General of the Conseil supérieure. In the committee, those responsible for national defense were to be politically orientated and the politicians militarily informed. And, within the regular Cabinet, a smaller war cabinet was formed ahead of war. As Leon Blum once stated: "As long as I have been in power, General Gamelin has always participated in the small ministerial meetings I called in order to deal with the great diplomatic questions which involved military responsibilities that could not be brought before the Council of Ministers,"[169] where discretion might not be assured.

On the informatory-educational level, a Collège des hautes études de défense nationale was set up at the end of 1936. This was a military-civilian war college, under the direction of an admiral at the outset, in which members of the Army, Navy and Air Force met for study and discussion with representatives of the various civilian ministries, largely for the purpose of "bringing into contact outstanding men from all the branches of governmental activity."[170] The foreshadowed total character of war made itself felt through at least a few of the walls separating the hothouses of French departmentalism. Unfortunately, too many faults remained of a governmental system "in which normally the principally interested parties were not reunited."[171] Ominously enough, this disunity persisted, even among the three armed services themselves, very much as in the United States.[172]

General Staff and Foreign Office were traditionally on relatively intimate terms. Since at least 1932, the military had explained in detail to the Quai d'Orsay the various stages preceding general mobilization, and how far mobilization could suit the requirements of diplomacy. Still, such understandings did not prepare them for the various surprises offered by Hitler's successive coups. It was thought in Paris that he had purposely staged the Anschluss of 1938 during one of the many French ministerial crises. The caretakers in office at once decided that no military measures were to be taken without a close understanding with Britain. All that Gamelin was authorized to do was to stop all leaves for the forces in the Eastern regions. When he went to see the permanent fixture of the Foreign Ministry, Leger, he found him deeply upset: Britain had already refused to take any energetic steps. And why had he been kept so poorly informed by the military of the seriousness and the imminence of Hitler's coup? Gamelin insisted that he had constantly drawn the attention of those concerned to the German situation. The liaison officer between his own office and the Quai d'Orsay had been carefully kept informed and had been under orders to inform those whom he was supposed to serve.[173]

France was in a cold war on various fronts at that time, notably in Spain. As chief of the front populaire, Leon Blum asked the military experts whether France was in a position to intervene in Spain, somewhat in the manner of Hitler's action in Austria. Could she present Franco with an ultimatum demanding that he repudiate all foreign help within twenty-four hours and threatening that France would resume her liberty of action and probably intervene in her own way if he did not comply? As Gamelin explained, things were not in any way the same with regard to the Germans—they could dispose of 900,000 men under arms as against only 400,000 in France. If France wanted to play the same game, one million men would be required, and that would include calling up the couverture. Besides, while mobilization plans had been prepared for the Northeast and the Southeast and an independent one for North Africa, no separate mobilization plan had been worked out for the Southwest.

Whatever the civilians suggested—operations against the Balearic Islands or Spanish Morocco—the military discouraged. The Air Chief of Staff believed that, in case of war, France's air force would be annihilated within a fortnight. Daladier, filled with the soldiers' hopelessness, was fearful that French intervention in Spain would set off a general European war in which Britain, adhering to non-intervention, might not participate. The representative of the Quai d'Orsay drew from this the conclusion that France could not take the initiative, could act only by "reactive measures, and not through any preventive gestures." For "England will separate from us if we give up non-intervention" without an altogether new element entering the situation. While Blum suggested various military steps, such as increased help to the Loyalists, the generals suggested a diplomacy that would separate Franco from his supporters, Germany and Italy. Franco would eventually feel the need for British capital to reconstruct Spain, and that would give England a strong lever. Indeed, reported the man of the Quai d'Orsay, England was calculating on this and on a future xenophobic evolution in Spain that would detach Franco from Germany-Italy. Foreign Minister Paul-Boncour pointed out that such an evolution would take time and that it offered no relief in the present urgent situation. No help could be expected from Poland as long as Beck was in power there. Rather would the Czechs have reason to fear that the Poles would try to profit from a German action against them. In spite of the Anschluss, which had originally given rise to tension, Germany and Italy seemed more closely united than ever. Germany had doubtless made substantial promises to Italy as the price of her consent. Summing up the situation, Daladier, who was presently to succeed Blum, concluded that intervention in Spain would incur the risk of isolating France and leaving her face to face with

Germany-Italy, with only mediocre help to be expected from Russia, herself distant and enfeebled, and with no certainty of assistance from England. France in this situation could only react to the movements of others; there was no possibility for taking the initiative.[174] This fact indicates the measure of France's abdication as a Great Power. The position she had gained in 1919 was no longer defensible, militarily speaking, by herself alone.

Subsequent to these deliberations, which provide a clear illustration of the drawing of political conclusions from military explanations, Gamelin proceeded to defend the role of the military against the criticism leveled at them. If it was maintained, he said, that the military had detected difficulties everywhere and had thereby kept the Government from acting at all, he wanted to emphasize that

> it was the task of the technicians to show the statesmen exactly the difficulties to be surmounted, for only the latter could provide the means with which to overcome them. Had the technicians not done that, they would have failed in their duty. And in a field of such seriousness, it would be unpardonable to decide lightheartedly. War in itself brings enough that is aleatory without imprevision and illusions. Before acting, there are always difficulties in the way of acting: they have to be looked in the face. That is the formula of true men of action.[175]

The Chief of Staff classed himself among the "men of action," at the same time pointing out all imaginable military difficulties in the way of action. The unity of inaction between him and the directors of French policy remained thoroughly and constitutionally complete until the end of the Third Republic. It was the unity of defeatism. The organizational arrangements for politico-military unity must be considered sufficient for the days before 1938, when France's military strength was commensurate with her political position. After that, no superior organization could have made up for her military deficiencies. The alliance with Russia might have done that, but France, in common with Britain, was not willing to pay the price the Reds demanded, the surrender of the Baltic countries and Poland to Moscow. The guarantees given by France and Britain to Rumania and Greece (April 1939) were arranged without previous consultation with the military offices and remained without military implementation. They made no tangible addition to the military strength of the Western Powers. The last remaining contacts with Yugoslavia were not exploited in the belief that she had moved too far into the orbit of the Axis.[176]

The last days of peace in France were embarrassing to military and civilians alike; neither party wanted to admit its defeatism. The civilian ministers no longer sat and took council with the military chiefs. Neither the Conseil supérieur de la défense nationale nor the Comité permanent were in session during the second half of August. An informal meeting of August 23, convoked by Daladier as Premier and Minister of National Defense, was the last peace-time assembly of the ministers of defense and foreign affairs, the chiefs of staff and various other military men. On this occasion, Gamelin and Darlan gave the assurance that the armed forces were ready for their "measures," that is to say, for the mobilization.[177] No other promise was demanded or given. France would go through the prepared and premeditated motions. The result was first a "phony war," then defeat.

BRITAIN AFTER 1918: UNITY THROUGH THE PRIME MINISTER

The detailed interdepartmental arrangements made in France were designed, at least in part, to bridge over the numerous interregna caused by cabinet changes and thus to preserve at least administrative continuity. Under these conditions, how far permanent officialdom exercised its influence on policy is as yet impossible to say. Gamelin's relations with the various ministers indicate a respect for institutions and offices rather than for most of the men who filled them from time to time. Comparable detailed inter-office arrangements seemed far less urgent in the two Anglo-Saxon countries, where the much longer reigns of President and Prime Minister assured greater continuity of policies and personalities. The permanent bureaucracy, including its uniformed part, was permeated with a continuity of authority.

In Britain, the older arrangements, including the Committee of Imperial Defence, continued, as did the separateness of the armed services. A Ministry for the Coordination of Defence, established in March 1936, was more an expression of theoretical recognition of the need to face and meet the contingencies of total war than an actual attempt to meet the Totalitarians' obvious preparation for open war.[178]

It was a crowning of the long-continued labors of Lord Hankey, as military-civilian, when he was taken into Chamberlain's first war cabinet as Minister without Portfolio. Since an institutional development can sometimes be sketched more readily by a person and his career than by depicting various organizational structures, we shall give Hankey's official curriculum. He was born in 1877, and served in the Navy from 1899-1901 and in the Naval Intelligence Department from 1902-06. He retired with the rank of lieutenant-colonel in

1918 and, still in retirement, was made a Colonel in 1929. He was appointed Assistant Secretary of the Committee of Imperial Defence in 1908 and its Secretary in 1912. He served in that position until 1938, during which period he was also Secretary of the War Cabinet (1916) and of the Imperial War Cabinet (1917). He was Cabinet Secretary from 1919-38 and Clerk of the Privy Council from 1923-28. When he entered the War Cabinet, he brought with him a maximum of experience in interdepartmental defense affairs.

During the 1930's, the CID had included the Prime Minister, the Lord President of the Council, the Chancellor of the Exchequer, the Foreign Secretary, the Parliamentary Under-secretary for Foreign Affairs, the Home Secretary, Dominion and Colonies representatives, the heads and the chiefs of staff of the three armed services, the Secretary for India, and the Head of Civil Service. The multiplicity of representation indicates that there was at least an awareness of the multiple aspects of any war to come. Sundry efforts towards actual coordination, either through the new Ministry of Coordination of Defence or through the Defence Policy and Requirements Committee of the Cabinet, remained barren of results. The fault was probably more in the Chamberlainian personalities than in the organizations filled by them.

The CID chairmanship had been taken on by Prime Minister Baldwin in the period from 1924 to 1930. He wished to familiarize himself with defense matters well ahead of their coming before the Cabinet, and to have a continued personal acquaintance with Britain's strategic problems. While his reasons were sound enough, Baldwin was not qualified to fill this office. When Baldwin's persuasive powers failed, the permanent Secretary of the CID could not unite the chiefs of staff on an over-all strategic plan, at which point there was no authority to take over. It has also been stated that the CID was not itself sufficiently activated and brought to the level of realities by the urgings of the Cabinet. Herman Finer has described the situation as follows:

The head of steam under which the Committee was driven in its speed and sense of urgency was the judgment of the Cabinet as to when a war was to be expected and with what enemies. But the Foreign Secretaries seem not to have served the Cabinet well, for a variety of reasons, among others the lack of mental acuteness of the Diplomatic Service. Hence the Cabinet, as the supreme policy-making body, offered no direction, drive or pressure to the thought-organization.

According to Winston Churchill, who was in as good a position to know as anyone, at least some of its drive came from the Admiralty. "It is,"

Churchill has written, "always dangerous for soldiers, sailors, or airmen to play at politics. They enter a sphere in which the values are quite different from those to which they have hitherto been accustomed. Of course, they were following the inclination or even the direction of the First Lord and the Cabinet, who alone bore the responsibility. But there was a strong Admiralty breeze." It blew so strong that despite the "brazen and fraudulent violation of the Peace Treaty" committed by the Germans in their naval constructions, "the Admiralty actually thought it worthwhile making an Anglo-German naval agreement."[179] Negotiations were started without informing the French and in utter disregard of the Stresa declarations, only two months old, which had termed German rearmament illegal. A definite rift in the potential front against Hitler was revealed, and Ribbentrop was handed a diplomatic success that helped to legitimize his spurious character.

During World War II, the CID "became the Secretariat to the War Cabinet."[180] A new organization of June 4, 1940, concentrated more power in the hands of Churchill as Prime Minister and Minister of Defence, enabling him to effect and maintain the unity of policy and defense. He headed the Defence Committee, composed of the three armed services ministries and the three chiefs of staff. Defence comprised one of the three main subdivisions of government, the other two being Foreign Policy, and Economic and Home Affairs. This and subsequent arrangements generally bespeak a diminuation of the role of the Foreign Office, although not necessarily of foreign policy considerations. They would be taken care of by the Prime Minister himself in negotiations with Roosevelt, Stalin and others. At the same time, these arrangements bespoke a closer unity between the political director and executive head of the Government and the directors of strategy, the Chiefs of Staff Committee. In this union of direct daily contact there was established "full control over the conduct of the war and the armed forces."[181]

British post-war groping for an effective defense-cum-foreign policy mechanism centered on a Ministry of Defence, a heritage from the war. Its head is the only service minister to sit in the Cabinet. The Prime Minister, the Foreign Secretary and he form a Cabinet Committee that deals with "all matters referring to foreign affairs and military operations." A Council of Imperial Defence is to assist, secretariat-wise, in establishing "the closest kind of link between the defense program and diplomatic objectives." Its Secretary in 1946, Sir Hastings Ismay, described his own role as "the most important function," but one that "should be carried out by a man relatively obscure and not desirous of power.[182]

THE PRESIDENT OF THE UNITED STATES AS UNIFIER

The President of the United States is almost a Prometheus Unbound, so little is he restricted by constitutional or bureaucratic-administrative arrangements in the exercise of the vast powers that authorize him to establish the unity of American policy. He has the power to direct foreign affairs and, as commander-in-chief, to coordinate them with the exercise of military powers. In extreme cases he can make though not declare war. "Any President," says Cordell Hull, "through his function of conducting foreign relations and as Commander-in-Chief of our armed forces, could always propel the country into war if he so desired. Any President could produce war by hostile actions in the diplomatic field or by creating incidents through the deployment of military or naval units."[183] He is unhampered by outside rules in the use he makes of the cabinet or other parts of the administration. In shaping and carrying out his own policies, he can choose his advisors and assistants to suit his particular purposes and methods.

The arrangements preferred by Franklin D. Roosevelt from 1933 on resulted in an extensive neglect of the Cabinet, not even the heads of the State, Army, and Navy Departments excepted. As members of his war councils their influence was shared with the Chiefs of Staff and others, nominally their subordinates, and irregular Presidential agents such as Harry Hopkins. The President's direct dealings with heads of foreign states left aside the most important part of the traditional mediatory functions of the State Department in foreign transactions. No President before him had been in such intimate and constant peace-time and war-time consultation with the chiefs of staff. This culminated in the new and, in America, unprecedented position of Admiral Leahy as Chief of Staff to the commander-in-chief. Until January 1949 he, and not the Secretary of Defense, continued to give the President a daily briefing on the political-military situation. The not always fortunate development of what the Germans call the "immediacy position" of the chiefs of staffs and other military officers in relation to the commander-in-chief reached its climax during Truman's presidency. He repeatedly "made it clear to all the members of the Chiefs of Staff that they have direct access to him any time they desire it on application to the appropriate aide."[184]

The days of the Cabinet in matters of defense seemed mostly over with the coming of total and "cold" wars, an evolution brought on by technical-organizational demands rather than by dictatorial inclinations either on the part of the presidency or the military. Urgent defense problems threatened to divest the State Department of most of its traditional influence and initiative, little respected by Roosevelt, well before America's entry into the war. It tried to preserve some of its influence by interdepartmental arrangements. State Department proposals to the President, which were motivated by apprehensions about the security of the Western hemisphere—Sumner Welles' obsession—resulted early in 1938 in a Liaison Committee. The Committee was composed of second-ranking officers of State, War, and Navy Departments—the Undersecretary of State, Chief of Staff, and Chief of Naval Operations. It was "the only formal mechanism then extant for current coordination of the military, naval and diplomatic arms of government." As General Marshall suggested, "the past practice of not informing the State Department as to Army and Navy joint plans" was discarded and Welles was acquainted with the war plans. The three of them took "plans and other matters of vital import to national defense to the President for his approval," apparently leaving the Secretaries aside. With the coming of Stimson into the Cabinet, such discussions were once more returned to the Secretarial level, while the Liaison Committee faded out of existence by the end of 1943.[185]

It was only on a level of secondary importance that interdepartmental discussions of the coming war took place. Many conferences were held by Secretary of State Hull during the year preceding Pearl Harbor with the Secretaries of War and the Navy and "at intervals with the Chief of Staff and the Chief of Naval Operations and officers of their staffs." The participants in these conferences sought "a full interchange of information and views relative to critical situations all over the world." Hull received "the benefit of the knowledge which representatives of the War and Navy Departments possessed of military factors involved in the world situation," while he "in turn took up political factors in the world situation."[186] Hull, however, did not attend Roosevelt's "purely military conferences—unless the question was also one involving foreign affairs." Roosevelt was the one who decided whether or not questions of foreign affairs were involved. The conferences with Churchill and Stalin were regarded by him as "primarily military," regardless of the political consequences that might lie beyond military considerations.[187] Advisors like Hopkins and the military war-planners felt, in April 1941, "that we are frittering away materiel without tangible results, that the influence and accomplishments of the State Department have been unfortunate... and that the President must be protected against the importunities of those who are not fully aware of the seriousness of the present situation." Under the influence of these advisors, the "education of the President as to the true strategic situation" was taken in hand and soon bore fruit.[188]

Was "diplomatic and military liaison in Washington" before Pearl Harbor perfect, as Hull contended, or so poor that it contributed to making possible the initial success of the Japanese attack on Pearl Harbor? This question was brought into consideration by the Senate Committee investigating the Pearl Harbor attack. The Democratic majority expressed its belief—much of it based on post facto statements of men like Hull—that the "fullest liaison between the diplomatic and military arms of the Government" had prevailed. The Republican minority expressed the view that the President "was responsible for the failure to enforce continuous, efficient and appropriate cooperation" among the military and naval offices and between them and the Secretary of State, and that the latter ought to have drawn from his knowledge of Japanese designs and intentions the deduction that a Japanese attack was imminent by the end of November 1941. It was the Minority Committee's conclusion that some of the omissions were more or less deliberate, that they were part of a plan to maneuver the Japanese "into the position of firing the first shot without allowing too much danger to ourselves."[189] Whatever the historical responsibilities, later legislation as to interdepartmental reorganization reflected a strong belief in and out of Congress that the pre-Pearl Harbor arrangements could not be considered satisfactory.[190]

Even before the war was over, a man like Forrestal, obsessed with problems of organization and management, became deeply impressed with the integration achieved by the Joint Chiefs of Staff and the British system of war government.[191] He considered them excellent models for post-war reorganization in America, which, among other things, should formalize functions such as those that Harry Hopkins had discharged during the war in a rather informal manner.[192] Some of these ideas came, of course, as a reaction to Roosevelt's war-time improvisations. Truman knew enough about these to make him receptive to the idea of a unification that was not to be limited to the armed services but was also to include the State Department as an integral part.[193] With the most urgent international affairs out of the way, he proposed "to take up the whole question of government organization on a staff basis with a view to getting a closely knit, cooperating and effective machinery which would function more or less along the lines of the British War Cabinet."

To Forrestal and his like-minded friends, whether from the services or from Wall Street, unification of the armed services was merely the first step in the direction of a more embracing post-war organization that would "enable the military services and other departments and agencies most effectively to provide for and protect our national security."[194] Organiser est un mot de l'Empire (Balzac). American government had become an empire, at least in size. Somewhat contrary to the popular will, it had imperial problems on its hands. Modern management principles seemed necessary in order to handle them. There was to be no place for low-level autocracies, "the old business of individual and personal operation" with specially preserved departmental secrets. Information and knowledge must be general in order to assure unity, notably in the State-War-Navy triangle.

The war-time preponderance of strategic considerations and the attendant neglect of policy in American affairs was only temporarily, though perhaps for too long a time, replaced by a post-war interlude of the primacy of diplomacy. No noticeable progress towards a durable peace could be made. Russian expansion went on apace while America's strategic position constantly deteriorated, hurt rather than helped by the inter-services fight over unification. With the "cold war," a situation had arrived when, for the first time, strategic considerations were uppermost in American affairs in time of peace. In an attempt to establish unity of American diplomacy and strategy, President Truman nominated and Congress confirmed General George C. Marshall as Secretary of State (1947-49). Truman, and the country as well, thought they saw in him the great unifier, first in the State Department and then, in order to make the cycle complete, as Secretary of Defense (1950-51).

Marshall was the first American soldier to hold the office of Secretary of State and the first Chief of Staff to become foreign minister anywhere. His appointment marked the beginning of the end of the much deplored "lack of coordination" in American affairs.[195] As was to be expected, the State Department, as the proponent of political-diplomatic considerations, had resisted longest the peace-time strategy that military offices had begun to deduce from the conflict of American and Russian policies. American military men (beginning with George S. Patton?) were the first to be ready to consider, invite, and accept Germany, Japan, and Franco-Spain as allies or auxiliaries. The State Department felt forced to pay considerable attention not only to opposition at home to such a step, but also to British Labour hesitations and French remonstrations against German rearmament.

A democracy will naturally find it more difficult to manage a quick shift in friend-foe relations than did the practitioners of eighteenth-century diplomacy. Many Americans were still inclined to find such a diplomacy diametrically opposed to their own ideals. The State Department remained too long a captive of this tradition and of war coalition sentiments in its German and its Chinese policies.[196] General Marshall himself fell victim to such sentiments after having watched on the spot the vicious realities of Kuomintang corruption.

The organizational arrangements to serve the purposes of unification were embodied in the National Security Act of July 26, 1947. It expressed

> the intent of Congress to provide a comprehensive program for the future security of the United States; to provide for the establishment of integrated policies and procedures for the departments, agencies, and functions of the Government relating to the national security; to provide three military departments for the operations and administration of the Army, the Navy and the Air Force; to provide for their authoritative coordination and unified direction under civilian control but not to merge them; to provide for the effective strategic direction of the armed forces and for their operation under unified control and for their integration into an efficient team of land, naval and air forces.

This Act was a final recognition of the fundamental requirements of the post-war diplomatic-military situation—the complete and constant unity of policy, and coordination or integration of means and measures in preparation for total war and in the conduct of "cold war." It was intended to eliminate, at first against considerable service opposition, the diversity of strategic outlook traditionally entertained by the three services.[197] The Services were to be unified under one administrative head, the Secretary of Defense, the War Council and the Joint Chiefs of Staff. The Joint Chiefs, set up in 1942, were now recognized by statute. They consisted of the Chief of Staff of the Army, the Chief of Naval Operations, the Chief of Staff of the Air Force, and, if there be one, the Chief of Staff to the Commander-in-Chief. They were subsequently given a chairman, General Bradley. The Joint Chiefs constitute a body of experts in immediate relation to the President, which must almost inevitably reduce the influence of the traditional civilian advice of the several defense secretaries.

The new organization was to provide for the unified and thus strengthened foundation, on the military side, of the unitary structure of American strategy and policy. For policy can be as little expected to make a choice between three strategies as strategy can serve conflicting policies. With this purpose in mind, the same law of 1947 set up a National Security Council. The ex-officio members were to be the President, the Secretaries of State, of Defense, the Army, the Navy, the Air Force, and the Chairman of the National Security Resources Board. The military viewpoint could easily prevail in such a body. The National Security Act of 1949 reduced the military spokesmanship by eliminating the Secretaries of the Army, Navy and Air Force and adding the Vice-President. Others may be designated by the President for regular or ad hoc participation in the Board's deliberations. President Truman added Industrial Mobilization Chief Charles Wilson, a Presidential adviser, W. Averell Harriman, Chairman of the Joint Chiefs of Staff General Bradley, and the Director of the Central Intelligence Agency.[198] A permanent executive secretary, who must be a civilian, holds a potentially very powerful position, calling to mind such British officials as Lords Esher and Hankey.[199] Given its position and composition, this Board, according to one careful observer, "must be counted as potentially the most strategic single executive agency in the conduct of foreign affairs, barring only the President and Congress. It could supercede the Department of State any time a President decided to accept its recommendations instead of different suggestions offered by the outnumbered Secretary of State."[200]

The Board has been, and may remain, in a military-civilian tug of war. In order to mark it as entirely or predominantly military, Forrestal, the first Secretary of Defense, had wanted to have its Secretariat located in the Pentagon. But President Truman conceived of it as an advisory office of the Executive. In 1949 he made it part of the Executive Office of the President and installed it near the White House, in the former State Department building.

Seen in historical perspective, it would appear that the Council was originally designed to discuss and settle the military implications and feasibility of American foreign policy prior to its final adoption. As the First Annual Report of the Secretary of Defense put it:

> The National Security Council, by its composite membership, assures that the military problem involved in a proposed political policy will be thoroughly explored before the proposal is adopted...For the first time in our history we now have the governmental mechanism, for which there is great need in a democracy like ours, to juxtapose international political and military practicability, and to render advice to the President based upon that juxtaposition.

If the Council works as intended, the military feasibility of foreign policies will be under consideration earlier and closer to the moment of political inception. And national defense proposals with an international portent will come under joint discussion and consideration at an early stage.[201] There ought to be less occasion in the future for "impossible" wars. If they are at all prepared, the diplomats on their part will keep military considerations in mind early and always, and the military partner will do the same with regard to the economic and political implications of strategic proposals. For the purpose of "minding" this aspect of military affairs, the Department of Defense includes an Office of Foreign Military Affairs, handling so-called "foreign military or politico-military affairs."[202]

This legislation by no means settled all functions or competencies. What was the NSC to do and what was it not to do? In what relation was it to stand to the President, the Secretary of Defense and others concerned? As Forrestal interpreted the intention of Congress, it was to be "an integral part of the national defense set-up... not a place to make policies but certainly a place to identify for the President those things upon which policy needs to be made."[203] In what relation was the NSC to stand to the Cabinet or the War Council, the body formed of the four Defense Secretaries and the three or four Chiefs of Staff? How far was there a danger of duplicating or replacing the functions of the Cabinet? How far was there a danger of creating at least the appearance that "American foreign policy was completely dominated by a military point of view?" At the constituent meeting of the NSC on September 26, 1947, the President clearly indicated that "he regarded it as his council and that he expected everyone to work harmoniously without any manifestations of prima-donna qualities." As spokesman of Defense, Forrestal confirmed this; the NSC would "serve as an advisory body to the President" who would take its advice "in due consideration" but "determination of and decision in the field of foreign policy would, of course, be his and the Secretary of State's."[204] The whole elaborate set-up of NSC, CIA and War Council was only too easily swept aside by the older imperium of the president when he wished to make his own considerations supreme.[205]

The still persistent disunity and conflict between the Departments of State and Defense was illustrated by the prolonged and scarcely concealed clash between the second incumbent of the office of Secretary of Defense, Louis A. Johnson, and Secretary of State Dean Acheson. According to Johnson, he found on taking over the Department that his predecessor Forrestal was greatly concerned "about political domination of Defense in many ways by State." While Acheson's influence had not been quite so pervasive at the White House, he had in effect been "fixing military policy as well as political, or diplomatic, policy." And he had come near to doing so on various occasions when the strategists' argument ought to have prevailed, as shown by subsequent events. Johnson found, he said, that Acheson, who had written off Chiang Kai-shek, had persuaded the President in 1949 to turn down "efforts by the military leaders to send a mission of inquiry to Formosa to see what, if anything, could be done there by us."

Disagreements between the two Departments extended to State's function and participation in the military assistance program under the North Atlantic Pact, from which Johnson had wanted to oust it, and to the question of assistance to Tito following his break with the Cominform. The Department of Defense was inclined to consider Tito as a potential enemy and backslider into the Moscow camp much longer than the Department of State.[206] The disagreements were terminated by Johnson's dismissal on September 19, 1950, during the Korean battles.[207] In making General of the Army George C. Marshall his successor, the President, Congress, and the nation believed they had now installed the beau idéal of the reasonable general who, from his various earlier employments, knew and appreciated political considerations no less than strategic ones.

It was during the Korean crisis that the NSC underwent its first major test. According to Marshall, "it was an action by the NSC that in a sense gave us a free hand to go into Korea and resist the aggression." While the fighting went on, the practical procedures for conducting war with the cooperation of such a body were established. It was to participate in basic directives for the theater commander, not in minor directives. This established the NSC, or so it seemed to its members, as "by all odds the most important policy-making body in the United States," so far as global security matters were concerned. Still, such a problem as the dismissal of General MacArthur did not come before it, as the Republican opposition thought it should have.[208]

Frequently, the clash of personalities in government is followed by new coordinating arrangements which, it is hoped, will remove the permanent, supra-personal sources of conflict. The North Atlantic Treaty and connected understandings resulted in an unprecedented amount of peace-time activity on the part of American military personnel in various foreign countries. There was general or theoretical admission that the State Department must have the prime role in and should concentrate on the formulation of foreign policy, always with the advice of the other departments, and that it was to retain its "traditional responsibilities of representation, reporting and negotiations."[209] Nevertheless the question constantly arose: How much of the military or economic programs or how much of the business of occupying foreign countries ought it to administer? How much should it control? Attempts to answer the question in practice led to a perpetual row between Acheson and Johnson. The organizational upshot of the row, the solution of "the most urgent organizational problem we face," as President Truman put it at the time, was the setting up of a Committee on International Security Affairs within the State Department in December 1950. This indicated a new recognition of the primacy of the political-diplomatic office. The purpose of the committee was to coordinate the American Government's military relations with the various foreign nations joined to the United States in its efforts to strengthen the military position of the so-called free world, and to coordinate the various governmental agencies having to do with military assistance—State, Defense, Treasury, and ECA. The first Director of International Security Affairs was Thomas Dudley Cabot, a Boston businessman. He was under instructions "to represent and speak for the Department of State on matters of policy and program relating to the North Atlantic Treaty, other similar international programs, and military and economic assistance for mutual defense."[210] But the new agency did not in any way replace the National Security Council as the agency which was "to advise the President with respect to the integration of domestic, foreign and military policies relating to the national security."

All foreign offices have long set apart bureaus or sections for the conduct of special business—trade, passports, etc.,—or for regional affairs. The setting up of the Committee on International Security marked two new stages in the conduct of foreign affairs: a new degree of integration and unity of policy, and a new realization of the increased and continued importance of defense problems within the totality of foreign policy.

CONCLUSION

The problem of unification is as old as the problem of governing. Modern complications and size of governmental problems can only emphasize its persistence. Administrative arrangements for its solution will almost always be interfered with politically, by popular or specific interests. These interests may desire the absolutist unifier—the unrestricted monarch, the leader of the nation, the Red dictator who promises to abdicate when the State itself can safely abdicate. They may, on the other hand, desire the mere figurehead whom they can control for their own purposes. The excesses and failures of absolutism bring deliberative councils into favor. In turn, the weakness of

the executive, denied popular or parliamentary support and hence financial and armed strength with which to face a perilous international situation, may by reaction lead to absolutism, or at least to proposals in its favor.

Governmental organization is not, perhaps can never be, altogether free from irrational residue, some of which may survive the most radical changes that revolutions can produce. What has stood in the way of a rationalization comparable in thoroughness and rationality to economic-technological organization?[211] One obstacle has been the special views, conditioned or not by special interests, entertained on the part of governmental groups, ministries, staffs, soldiers, and civilians, all of whom may be filled with "undesirable branch consciousness or competition."[212] Other obstacles have included a tendency towards under-organization in governmental affairs; the attitude Emerson reflected when he wrote, "the less Government we have, the better"; the checks-and-balances notions which Western conservatism and Western liberalism have considered for so long as one of the guarantees of freedom. Many of these disunities are no longer a safety factor in a world threatened by Totalitarianism. Opposing one totalitarianism by another, however, is not the answer to the problem posed. The simplicities and unities with which autocracy has been credited have proved neither simple nor unified. With war in ever closer proximity, the Western conservative-liberal-democratic world must work out the preservation of its freedom as something no longer possible except by the timely generation and readying of power through the organized unity of foreign and military policy.

FOOTNOTES

1. When the Duke of Cambridge, Commander-in-Chief of the British Army, tried to stop further reduction of the Army and of the Army budget, which had been going on ever since the end of the Crimean War, even a Conservative War Secretary had to tell him that, in a crisis year such as 1879, "with the distress in the country, the absence of any spring in the revenue, and the utter impossibility of putting on extra taxation, the evil [of reductions] is one which must be faced." Verner, Military Life of George, Duke of Cambridge, II, 128.
2. Secretary of State von Weizsäcker, Trials of War Criminals, XIII, 431.
3. Cited by Jähns in Heeresverfassung und Völkerleben, p. 44.
4. See for instance Hohenlohe, Denkwürdigkeiten, III, 463. Several railway ministers of the Central Powers came originally from the general staffs.
5. Mémoires du Chancelier Pasquier, II, 331.

6. Cecil, Life of Salisbury, III, 330 ff.

7. Wermuth, Ein Beamtenleben, pp. 280 f., 305 ff.; Tirpitz, Erinnerungen, pp. 185, 229; G. P., XXXI, 11324. Malicious Army gossip had it that, under War Minister von Heeringen (1909-13), whose brother was Naval Chief of Staff (1911-13), the Army bills had been worked out in the Reich Naval Office. Das alte Heer (Von einem Stabsoffizier), p. 11.

8. Oesterreich-Ungarns Aussenpolitik, V, 5200.

9. Ibid., VII, 9528; Fay, The Origins of the World War, I, 533 ff.

10. Grew, Ten Years in Japan, p. 176.

11. Trials of War Criminals, XII, 560, 612.

12. Ibid., XII, 513, 1122, and passim.

13. Badoglio, Italy in the Second World War, pp. 11 ff.

14. Before he resigned from office in the face of the all too likely consequences of the Tirpitz Navy, Bülow became aware of the fearful parallel between the British naval concentration in the North Sea and the "Russian troop concentrations along our Eastern frontiers following the Berlin Congress. The reasons are the same...irritation due to personal and factual frictions; jealousy; fear that we might attack; desire to exert pressure on us in any case et de nous tenir sous leur coupe." G. P., XXIII, 7779.

15. Pelet de la Lozère, Opinions de Napoléon, p. 147.

16. For a devastating discussion of Admiral Fisher's plans for landing on the German Baltic coast which took place in the Committee of Imperial Defence in 1909, see Bacon, Lord Fisher, II, 182 f.

17. The naval service was conceded to be a more exclusive domain of the professionals, due to its earlier-developed technicality.

18. Kitchener, originally taken into the Cabinet because of his great popularity with the British masses, soon proved less helpful than had been expected. The ministers chafed under his "habit of acquiring all the military information and keeping it to himself, [which] made it quite impossible for the Government to come to any decision at all—except one gained by leaping blindly in the dark." As late as the autumn of 1915, Kitchener's immense prestige made it impossible to dismiss him. Beaverbrook, Politicians and the War, I, 193 f.

19. Clode, Military Forces of the Crown, II, 346. Lord Fisher was chagrined that no admiral was taken into the War Cabinet while Kitchener was in it. He wanted such a place for himself, vice Churchill, and did not see that the old constitutional rule had been put aside in favor of Kitchener because the Cabinet wanted to have the semi-mythical force attributed by the British people to the general identified with itself. Beaverbrook, Politicians and the War, I, 105 ff.

20. In 1908. Conrad, Aus meiner Dienstzeit, I, 81.

21. Army Almanac, p. 52; Watson, Chief of Staff, pp. 6, 57 f., 66. For the relations of President, Secretary of War, and Chief of Staff in Washington in 1917-18, see March, Nation at War, pp. 261 f.

22. "He who studies history thoroughly will not fail to prefer a military despotism to a despotism of mere politicians." Halleck, Elements of Military Art and Science (1846), Introd.

23. Cf. the complaint of Landgrave William IV of Hesse (1567-92) in his "Cautela or highly necessary points which every warlord ought to consider well and diligently": "Also, the pay for horsemen and foot soldiers has risen so high and faithlessness is so great that no lord can any longer afford war; even if they are paid well every month, they do not refrain from mutineering and plundering and might well, as we ourselves have experienced, put their blunderbusses under the warlord's nose if he takes the liberty of forbidding them to rob his poor people and of breaking their wilfulness." Jähns, Kriegswissenschaften, p. 547.

24. Maurice, Governments and War, pp. 14 f.

25. Flassan, Histoire de la diplomatie française, IV, 404.

26. Alphonse XIII's "predilection for Army matters and his scheme to guard against perils [to his regime] led him to persevere in wooing the Army. The Monarch was creating his own military force, his armed party, against the hour of crisis which he saw was coming. Alfonso was not acting solely as nominal head of the armed forces, but as permanent Minister, in practice, of War and Marine." By a Royal Decree of January 15, 1914, he authorized the generals, Army chiefs and officers to communicate directly with him, stressing the precept that "the King may intervene directly and constantly in anything concerned with his troops, as well as in appointments to commands and the promotion of officers." Ramos Oliveira, Politics, Economics and Men of Modern Spain, p. 168.

27. For a good description, see Japan-Handbuch, pp. 37 ff.

28. Waldersee ascribed his own dismissal as Chief of Staff in 1891 to the Kaiser's intention to be the military leader in war, not in the style of his grandfather but of Frederick the Great, "a fearful danger for the Fatherland." In preparation for this he led one—always the winning—side in the annual maneuvers. He greatly resented criticism from the Chief of Staff who, he thought, ought to be cut down in size to the

level of a general commanding an army corps. Waldersee, Denkwürdigkeiten, I, 179, 188.

29. Clausewitz, On War, p. 598.

30. Ollivier, L'Empire libéral, XV, 115. It was under the fresh impact of the defeat that Fustel de Coulanges wrote: "There is a necessary link between the military institutions and the political ones. Agreement between the two, whatever the kind of government, assures stability; disagreement infallibly brings about a revolution. If the army is not fashioned in the image of the State, it is the army that in a few years fashions the State in its image." Revue des deux mondes, November 15, 1870.

31. Tukashevski preferred the Bolshevist regime because it gave him all he demanded for the Red Army, without parliamentary battles. Gamelin, Servir, II, 196.

32. Bernhardi, Germany and the Next War, p. 146. Sir John French told the Austrian ambassador in October 1911 that the German superiority over France still existed because of the much better German discipline, "but above all because the German Army had a visible head in the person of the Emperor; for an army, republican institutions could never replace a supreme warlord." Oesterreich-Ungarns Aussenpolitik, III, 2720.

33. For some of the military nonsense urged upon William II by "court generals," see Eckardstein, Lebenserinnerungen, II, 45 f.

34. G. P., XIX, 5936.

35. 1912. Nevins, Henry White, p. 324; Kühlmann, Erinnerungen, p. 257; Zur Europäischen Politik (Belgian Documents), IV, 157. A few years before 1914, William told a Norwegian diplomat: "My generals wish that I should go to war. But I am not that silly. One knows how such things begin; one never knows how they will come out." The French naval attaché in Berlin added: "We can be sure William II will not draw the sword unless he has ninety chances out of a hundred in his favor." Faramond, Souvenirs, p. 101.

36. Moser, Die obersten Gewalten im Weltkrieg, p. 12.

37. Das alte Heer (Von einem Stabsoffizier), p. 10.

38. For the terrorism, including the threat of an officers' mutiny, applied by Prussia's high officers against King William I during the constitutional crisis of 1861-62, see Dehio, "Die Pläne der Militärpartei und der Konflikt," Deutsche Rundschau, Vol. 213 (1927), 91 ff.

39. Waliszewski, Le règne d'Alexandre Ier, III, 184. Late in 1871, when a deputation of German officers came to St. Petersburg to celebrate the old comradeship of the two armies, Tsar Alexander II felt so overawed by the new-fashioned Pan-Slavism in his entourage that

he had to show the Germans the cold shoulder until he had occasion to whisper to them: "You don't know how much I love you; only I am not allowed to show that to you here." Tirpitz, Erinnerungen, p. 26.

40. Die auswärtige Politik Preussens 1858-1871, I, 591.

41. The more outstanding Austrian chiefs of staff since 1815 had been Radetzky, Kuhn, Benedek (son of a doctor), Henikstein (son of an ennobled Jewish family), Krismanic (a Croat), Beck (a South German), and Conrad. Nearly all of them were commoners, or foreigners, or both. The same was true in Prussia for a long time. Two of her chiefs of staff, Krauseneck (1829-48) and Reyher (1848-57) were non-nobles and had risen from the ranks, and Moltke (1858-88) was a foreigner with a bourgeois mother. The aristocracy of birth took over after that, with Counts Waldersee and Schlieffen.

42. Wertheimer, Andrassy, I, 213.

43. Presland, Vae Victis: The Life of Benedek, p. 216 and passim. Soon after the war, the story was told in Vienna that Benedek had not wanted the supreme command in Bohemia and would have preferred the one in Italy, where an archduke took command. It was rumored that he had told the Emperor: "In Italy I know every village, every ditch, but in Bohemia I am an ass." But he had been dismissed by the Emperor, who told him: "Still better you get beaten than an archduke." Bamberger, Bismarcks grosses Spiel, p. 103; Steed, The Hapsburg Monarchy, pp. 71 f.

44. For the French generals' fond expectation that the vast majority of the people along the Rhine were waiting for an Anschluss to France, see Oncken, Rheinpolitik, I, 303.

45. For this, see Ollivier, L'Empire libéral, XVI, 101 ff., 188, 216 f. 224 f., 287, 309.

46. de La Gorce, Histoire du Second Empire, IV, 582 ff.

47. Keudell, Fürst und Fürstin Bismarck, p. 277.

48. Ziekursch, Politische Geschichte des neuen deutschen Kaiserreichs, I, 189.

49. Bismarck told Gustav Schmoller sometime in the 1870's: "I would rather conclude a difficult treaty with a semi-hostile State than come to an agreement with the Prussian War Minister." Schmollers Jahrbuch, Vol. XLI (1917), 88; similarly Busch, Bismarck. Some Secret Pages, I, 517.

50. During the "war in sight" crisis of 1875, the Crown Prince told the British Minister to Munich, Sir Robert Morier, that "the worst of the situation was that his dear good friend Moltke, whom he considered the highest military genius in existence, was absolutely destitute of political ideas; and that, having made

up his mind that France was not sufficiently beaten, and that she was recovering more rapidly than could have been supposed, he did not cease from urging the necessity of a fresh war." Wemyss, Memoirs of Sir Robert Morier, II, 343.

51. See G. P., III, 453, 473, 478, 505; Wertheimer, Andrassy, III, 251 ff.; Schweinitz, Denkwürdigkeiten, II, 83. While voicing British approval of the German-Austrian alliance of 1879, Salisbury still saw no great military reason for it. There was no danger from France for the time being. "What Bismarck's motive is, is still mysterious. Karolyi used the strange expression, 'Bismarck was frightened at what he saw of Russia's intentions,' but Russia does not seem to be in a condition to frighten anybody—least of all Germany. I am rather tempted to believe that B. will continue to be frightened at something or other till the next military budget has been passed." Cecil, Salisbury, II, 371.

52. Bülow, Denkwürdigkeiten, II, 77.
53. Schweinitz, Denkwürdigkeiten, II, 173 f.
54. Paléologue, The Turning Point, p. 54.
55. Görlitz, Der deutsche Generalstab, p. 142; Franke, Handbuch der neuzeitlichen Wehrwissenschaften, I, 109 ff.
56. G. P., VI, 1187 f.
57. Bethcke, Politische Generäle, p. 34.
58. Shortly after his dismissal, Bismarck, given a general's rank, said: "The Emperor has made a curious chassez-croisez. He makes his best general Chancellor and his Chancellor a general." Rehlen, Bismarck, p. 238.
59. Bismarck, Gedanken und Erinnerungen, III, 25, 106.
60. G. P., IX, 2152; VIII, 1753.
61. Holstein to Eulenburg, February 9, 1896: "I am in favor of a moderate application of the system of constitutional cooperation which is the rule in the rest of the European world outside Petersburg and Constantinople. That my views are considered out of fashion at the court here, I know. 'A strong government which can run things without the Reichstag' is the ideal of Admiral von Senden [Chief of the Naval Cabinet], and not his exclusively. You also belong, perhaps unconsciously, to those who believe that every military, political, legal question is best decided by the Emperor directly. Quite similar, if not quite so far-reaching, were the articles of belief of the old English cavaliers, objects of the boundless admiration of my youth. First, however, they wrecked the Stuarts, then they themselves died, ruined and exiled, but they remained, ethically speaking, unselfish types of shining chivalrousness. I am not that chivalrous; I am in favor

of what is possible." Haller, Eulenburg, pp. 202 f.

62. As late as June 1, 1914, the younger Moltke did not believe that the intended march through Belgium would bring Britain into the war on the side of France. "What she will do in case of war we can quietly wait for." Eckardstein drew the conclusion "that between the responsible political directorship in the Reich and the military there was practically no connection on the eve of the World War." Eckardstein, Lebenserinnerungen, II, 186.
63. A military lecturer on the disastrous Seven Years' battle of Hochkirch, speaking in William's presence, wound up by saying: "Under the leadership of Your Majesty such a thing would not have happened." Haller, Eulenburg, p. 336.
64. There was an occasional exception: due to the efforts of the Wilhelmstrasse, the plan of the General Staff to transport German reservists residing in the United States to German Southwest Africa in case of war in order to strengthen the forces in that colony (July 1906), was given up for the benefit of better American-German relations. G. P., XXI, 7090.
65. Holborn in Earle (ed.), Makers of Modern Strategy, p. 189.
66. Bülow, Denkwürdigkeiten, II, 76 ff.
67. Ritter, Lebendige Vergangenheit, p. 133.
68. See note of French War Ministry to Foreign Ministry, August 13, 1904, regarding recent information about German concentration plans, including railway construction in the direction of Aachen and other indications of an impending march through Belgium. Doc. dipl. fr., 2nd series, V, 364 ff.
69. In 1900, the entourage of the President of the Republic still compared "the deferential attitude of the sailors with the spirit of the fronde among certain elements of the land army." Combarieu, Sept Ans à l'Elysée, p. 77.
70. Maj. Gen. C. E. Callwell in Encyclopedia Britannica (13th ed.), III, 532.
71. Puleston, High Command in the World War, p. 19.
72. Foreign diplomats in Berlin were poorly informed about the "dark clockwork of the Imperial Government," including such important wheels as the Military Cabinet. Some of them were awe-struck by "the obscurity woven around the army chiefs and the silence reigning around the Great General Staff, [by the] many disturbing mysteries, impossible for a diplomat, equipped only with professional curiosity, to penetrate. There, rather than in the Wilhelmstrasse, resided the future of Europe." Beyens, Deux années à Berlin, I, 38.
73. Following the Daily Telegraph affair, Max

Weber wrote to Friedrich Naumann, on November 12, 1908: "The Conservative Party bears the responsibility for the continuance of the 'personal regime'...A dilettante holds the threads of policy in his hand. Every legitimate ruler, who is not a Frederick II, is a dilettante, and that is what the Conservative Party wants. That is true for the supreme command in war as for the direction of policy in peace-time. Result: as long as that lasts, impossible to make 'world policy.'" Weber, Politische Schriften, p. 451.

74. For details, see Grabau, Das Festungsproblem in Deutschland.

75. Bethmann Hollweg, Betrachtungen zum Weltkrieg, p. 167.

76. For a discussion of the universal application of general staff principles in international competition, see Schalk, Der Wettkampf der Völker, pp. 212 ff.

77. Moser, Die obersten Gewalten im Weltkrieg, pp. 21 f.

78. Doc. dipl. fr., 1st series, IV, 130 f.

79. Paléologue, The Turning Point, pp. 37, 108 ff., and passim.

80. Les armées françaises dans la Grande Guerre, I^1, 15.

81. Joffre, Mémoires, I, 103 ff.

82. Les armées françaises dans la Grande Guerre, I^1, 15.

83. Herbillon, Du général en chef au gouvernement, I, 199, 202.

84. Joffre, Mémoires, II, 151 f.

85. November 1915. Herbillon, Du général en chef au gouvernement, I, 209.

86. For French war government, see Renouvin, Les formes du gouvernement de guerre.

87. A French embassy report from St. Petersburg in 1816 called Russian autocracy "an arbitrary authority regulating the interest of ninety-nine per cent of the population. Everything reverts to that primitive power which breaks down under the burdens of its limitless prerogatives; 250,000 cases are waiting this day for the supreme decision." Waliszewski, Le règne d'Alexandre Ier, II, 403.

88. Salisbury to Lord Odo Russell in Berlin, November 27, 1878. Cecil, Life of Salisbury, II, 345. A Russian embassy to Kabul, which made a great stir in London and India at the time, appeared "to have been self-generated." When he learned about it, the Russian ambassador to London went at once to Gortchakov, both being at a German spa at the time, and asked: "Has there been any mission to Kabul?" Gortchakov, putting his hand to his brow and reflecting, replied: "Non, je ne le crois pas." Again, in the summer of 1885, when Russian advances in the direction of Afghanistan were reported and war seemed imminent to many observers, Salisbury remained undisturbed. "He believed the fresh difficulties to have arisen from Giers' desire to make good his reputation against the military party and avoid the reproach of yielding too easily to England." Ibid., III, 230 f.

89. G. P., VII, 1623.

90. Schweinitz, Denkwürdigkeiten, I, 182 f.

91. Ibid., II, 43. Cf. n. 88 above.

92. Waldersee overheard a conversation at the Tsar's own table between Miljutin, who was not afraid of the Republic, and Obrutchev, to the effect that dynasties, including the imperial house in Russia, were not indispensable. G. P., III, 477, 638; Lucius, Bismarck-Erinnerungen, p. 358.

93. Bismarck, Gesammelte Werke, XIV, 905 f.; G. P., III, 443, 445 ff., 455, 460 f., 465, 473 512.

94. In a conversation with Waldersee in September 1883, the Military Plenipotentiary, Prince Dolgoruki, admitted that bellicosity prevailed inside the Russian Army. But he hoped that, given time, the Tsar would be able to restore order and drive out some of the "democratic" sentiment that Miljutin had introduced into the Army. Waldersee, Denkwürdigkeiten, I, 227 ff.

95. 1886. G. P., V, 980.

96. 1882. See Herzfeld, "Bismarck und die Skobelew-Episode," Historische Zeitschrift, Vol. 142, 279 ff.

97. G. P., IV, 773 f., 777.

98. Ibid., V, 980, 990, 992 f., 1007, 1134.

99. Ibid., VI, 1150 ff., 1168 ff.

100. A considerable part of the history of Russian foreign policy could be written under the heading "volunteer"—e.g., the "volunteer Fleet," the "officer-volunteers" serving with the Serbs in their wars of 1876 and 1885-86, and the "Chinese People's Volunteers" in Korea.

101. G. P., VI, 1216.

102. Ibid., XVII, 5425; Langer in Europäische Gespräche, IV (1926), 289 ff., 309 f.

103. One example: the so-called volunteer fleet, based in the Black Sea, with a grand duke as chief, had gone into action without previous understanding with the Ministry of Marine, not to mention other offices concerned, though probably with the Tsar's permission. He sent two ships through the Dardanelles and the Suez Canal disguised as commercial vessels. Contrary to a promise to Turkey, the two vessels, once arrived in the Red Sea, acted as raiders against British (case of The Malacca) and German vessels as carriers of contraband. When the British and German

diplomats went to submit their protests, they were shunted from office to office in St. Petersburg, the Marine Ministry pointing to the grand duke at the head of the volunteer fleet as responsible. He had brought Russia close to the verge of war with Britain. G. P., XIX, 6067 ff.

104. Report of French Minister in Teheran, December 18, 1906: "It is a fact that the simultaneous presence in Persia of agents of the [Russian] Ministries of Foreign Affairs, Finance, and War brings with it strongly divergent viewpoints and does not help to facilitate the position of M. de Hartwig," the Minister who was under orders to work for a British-Russian understanding and partition of Persia into spheres of influence. Doc. dipl. fr., 2nd series, X, 567.

105. July 27, 1904. G. P., XIX, 6068.

106. Doc. dipl. fr., 2nd series, VIII, 176 f., 182 f., 237.

107. Stieve, Schriftwechsel Iswolskis, II, 312; Livre noir, I, 334.

108. For a Russian crown council discussion of December 5, 1896, with the Tsar in the chair, in which a Russian coup de main against the Bosporus was considered, see Langer, Imperialism, I, 338.

109. Pokrowski, Drei Konferenzen, p. 7 and passim.

110. Hatschek, Englisches Staatsrecht, II, 75, 77.

111. Ibid., II, 235 f.

112. In its way, the Board of Admiralty represented the working principles of intra-Navy unity without over-centralization. Since James I, the principal officers and commissioners of the Navy had been enjoined to be "in constant communication among themselves, consulting and advising 'by common council and argument of most voices,'" to meet at least twice a week, etc. The system that developed over the years provided "for the subdivision of labor, and yet for the coordinated exertion of effort." Encyclopedia Britannica (11th ed.), I, 195 ff.

113. Cf. a letter by Wolseley of March 1897: "We still have to convince the Navy that they can't win a war by themselves, and that we are not trying to nab the money they ought to have, but want to make our power what it must be to be effective, amphibious. If we can get the sailors to come in with us in this we shall have some chance with the politicians." Marder, The Anatomy of British Seapower, p. 79.

114. Cecil, Life of Salisbury, IV, 183 ff.; Doc. dipl. fr., 1st series, VII, 169 f., 297.

115. Spender, The Life of Campbell-Bannerman, I, 43, 117 ff.

116. Joseph Chamberlain to Duke of Devonshire,

November 5, 1899. Garvin, Chamberlain, III, 491.

117. Hatschek, Englisches Staatsrecht, II, 233 ff.

118. Churchill, The Unknown War, p. 14.

119. March 5, 1911. Conrad, Aus meiner Dienstzeit, II, 138.

120. March-May 1911. Oesterreich-Ungarns Aussenpolitik, III, 2487, 2492, 2496, 2539.

121. Ibid., III, 2567, 2568, 2571.

122. Aehrenthal's Memoir, October 22, 1911. Ibid., III, 2809. The same arguments were submitted to Francis Ferdinand in November 1911.

123. Ibid., III, 2890, 3057.

124. Ibid., V, 4965; Conrad, Aus meiner Dienstzeit, II, 272 ff., 287; G. P., XXX, 11243 f.

125. Conrad, Aus meiner Dienstzeit, II, 279.

126. Memoranda of Schemua, September 28, and Berchtold, October 2, 1912. Oesterreich-Ungarns Aussenpolitik, IV, 3869, 3928, 4183.

127. Conrad, Aus meiner Dienstzeit, II, 436.

128. Poincaré, Au service de la France, II, 376 f.; Oesterreich-Ungarns Aussenpolitik, V, 4871 f.

129. Oesterreich-Ungarns Aussenpolitik, V, 4888.

130. Ibid., V, 4965, 4984.

131. December 30, 1912. Conrad, Aus meiner Dienstzeit, II, 413.

132. Ibid., II, 450.

133. Ibid., III, 115 ff.

134. January 4, 1913. Oesterreich-Ungarns Aussenpolitik, V, 5204; Conrad, Aus meiner Dienstzeit, III, 77.

135. February 1913. Oesterreich-Ungarns Aussenpolitik, V, 5701, 5725. G. P., XXXIV, 12735.

136. This is based on Conrad, Aus meiner Dienstzeit, Vol. III; G. P., XXXIV 2; Kern, "Conrad und Berchtold," in Europäische Gespräche, II, 97 ff. We have given the Austrian situation a relatively extensive treatment, not only because it resulted in the First World War but also because of the exhaustive documentation.

137. G. Conrad, Mein Leben mit Conrad von Hötzendorf, pp. 109 ff.

138. Bourget, Gouvernement et commandement, pp. 165, 263.

139. General J. F. C. Fuller, article on "Strategy" in Encyclopedia Britannica (13th ed.).

140. Whether on this or on another occasion, the Defense Ministry acquired a "Foreign Affairs Department," handling such problems as foreign service attachés. N. Y. Times, May 25, 1952.

141. Barghoorn, The Soviet Image of the United States, p. 46.

142. Prince Konoye in Pearl Harbor Hearings, Part 20, 4014. For details, see Takeuchi, War and Diplomacy in the Japanese Empire, passim.

143. Grew, Ten Years in Japan, p. 87.
144. Hull, Memoirs, I, 276.
145. Encyclopedia Britannica (11th ed.), XV, 210.
146. This was not an altogether new departure. A few generals and admirals had previously been premiers, and, usually only temporarily, foreign ministers. Both offices had been combined by General Baron Tanaka (1927-29), with rather unhappy results. Takeuchi, War and Diplomacy in the Japanese Empire, pp. 70, 247, 467.
147. Kordt, Wahn und Wirklichkeit, p. 321.
148. When German diplomacy had, after months of endeavor (November 1937-January 1938), at last elicited a peace offer from Chiang Kai-shek and submitted it to Tokyo, Foreign Minister Hirota said he would "now obtain the opinion of the Army and the Navy." He was doubtful whether the offer would still be acceptable, since the great Japanese sucesses in the field since the beginning of the peace action had made the Field Army "more exacting in its demands." New and stiffer demands emerged from weeks of internal struggles, during which the Army asked that Chiang admit Chinese "war guilt" before he was even informed in detail of the new terms. While the Cabinet majority had turned down that proposal, a large minority "under pressure of the Field Army and industry considered the terms too mild and hoped they would be rejected by China in order to make it possible to carry through the war of annihilation against Chiang." Documents on German Foreign Policy, 1918-1945, Series D, I, 799, 802 ff., 821.
149. February 14, 1942. The Goebbels Diaries, pp. 86 f.
150. N. Y. Times, September 17, 1951.
151. See, e.g., Niemann, Kaiser und Heer.
152. Neurath, a Württemberger and an older career diplomat, tried to get the later military attaché to London, Geyr von Schweppenburg, another Württemberger, into the service in 1919 but did not succeed. The one notable admission was that of the later Secretary of State for Foreign Affairs and "war criminal" von Weizsäcker, a former naval officer and also a Württemberger.
153. June 30, 1919. Rabenau, Seeckt, II, 186.
154. For some of its activities, see Trial of the Major War Criminals, XL, 403.
155. For an early discussion of the changes in defense questions, see Brauweiler, "Wehrverfassung und Gewaltenteilung" in Berber (ed.), Zum Neubau der Verfassung. Jahrbuch für politische Forschung.
156. Trials of War Criminals, XII, 827 f., 1016 ff.

157. During his four-year term as chief of staff, General Beck was received by Hitler only twice; at the end of 1937, he complained that he had been unable to see Blomberg, the War Minister, for nine months. Westphal, Heer in Fesseln, pp. 39, 51 f., 77.
158. August 30, 1939. Trials of War Criminals, XII, 1055 f.; N. Y. Times, September 1, 1939. Hitler considered Lammers "the only jurist among his assistants who was really worth something because he knew how to find the legal foundations for State necessities." Hitlers Tischgespräche, p. 240.
159. F. Neumann, Behemoth, p. 57.
160. For the survival of ressort interests inside the Wehrmacht, in spite of Führertum and joint staffs (Einheitsstäbe) that were to end this evil, see Görlitz, Der deutsche Generalstab, pp. 486, 549, 584 f., 597, 607, 638.
161. Testimony of von Steengracht, last Secretary of State in Foreign Office, at Nuremberg. Trial of the Major War Criminals, X, 114.
162. Ibid., X, 377.
163. Mussolini presided over such conferences in which Ciano, the chiefs of staff of the Army, Navy, Air Force, and Militia, as well as the commander of the forces in Spain, participated. For similar deliberations begun in 1934 concerning the conquest of Ethiopia, see Kordt, Wahn und Wirklichkeit, p. 74.
164. This is based on Documents on German Foreign Policy, Series D, III, 146, 149.
165. Ibid., Series D, I, 864.
166. Martienssen, Hitler and His Admirals, p. 38.
167. Badoglio, Italy in the Second World War, pp. 14 ff.
168. For details, see Görlitz, Der Zweite Weltkrieg, I, 233, 235.
169. Pertinax, Les Fossoyeurs, I, 10.
170. Gamelin, Servir, II, 178, 301 f.
171. Ibid., II, 199.
172. Cf. short statements cited by Gamelin: "The Navy does not accept a chief of the general staff of national defense...We insist fundamentally on the unity and the independence of the Air Force...The primary concern of the Air Commission is the absolute independence of the Air Force. It ought to be eighty per cent independent in its employment." Ibid., II, 311.
173. Ibid., II, 316.
174. Ibid., II, 322 ff.
175. Ibid., II, 331. For the protocol of a meeting of the Comité permanent of April 9, 1939, see Ibid., II, 403 ff.
176. Ibid., II, 406, 413.
177. Ibid., II, 449 f.
178. In a House debate on November 10, 1936, the

first Minister for Coordination declined to undertake the radical changes for war-preparation that seemed urgent to many until "there was the most cogent proof of its necessity." Churchill taunted him: "So the Cabinet go on in strange paradox, decided only to be undecided, resolved to be irresolute, adamant for drift, solid for fluidity, all-powerful to be impotent." Chamberlain was determined not to have conscription or a Ministry of Supply until "we entered a definite zone of war." Feiling, Chamberlain, p. 318.

179. June 18, 1935. Churchill, The Gathering Storm, Vol. I of The Second World War, pp. 137 f.

180. Churchill to Forrestal. Forrestal Diaries, p. 145.

181. This is based on Finer, "The British Cabinet, the House of Commons and the War," Political Science Quarterly, LVI, 321 ff.; Churchill, Their Finest Hour, Vol. II of The Second World War, 16 ff.; Hankey, Government Control in War.

182. During the war, Ismay was "Military Chief of Staff to the Minister of Defense, through whom the military and political leaders were kept in close contact with each other and welded into a relatively homogeneous directorate of the total British war effort." Forrestal Diaries, pp. 185 f. Retired from the Army in 1946, Ismay became Minister for Commonwealth Affairs in Churchill's Cabinet of 1951 and Secretary General of the North Atlantic Treaty Organization in March 1952, to take care of the civilian side of the organization. Harrison, Cross-Channel Attack, pp. 90 f.

183. Hull, Memoirs, I, 461 f.

184. Testimony of Admiral Sherman, Naval Chief of Staff, who added: "Any time that I want to see him, I need only tell his naval aide. Now obviously that can only be done in connection with a matter of either extremely great importance or minor importance. Normal business naturally must go through the Secretary [of Defense]." Military Situation in the Far East, pp. 1606, 1622.

185. Watson, Chief of Staff, pp. 89 f., 93 f.

186. Hull to Justice Roberts, Chairman of the Commission to Investigate the Facts and Circumstances Connected with the Japanese Attack on Pearl Harbor. Pearl Harbor Hearings, Part 20, 4110 f.

187. Hull, Memoirs, I, 195, 200; Watson, Chief of Staff, pp. 121, 123 f.

188. Watson, Chief of Staff, p. 388.

189. The conclusions are in Senate Document No. 244 (79th Congress, 2nd Session), notably on pp. 538 ff., 503 ff.

190. Harry S. Truman was among these critics: one of his first actions in the White House was to "authorize State, War and Navy to confer on matters affecting political and military problems in the war areas. (Hadn't been done before.)" Hillman, Mr. President, p. 109.

191. Forrestal and other Americans studied Hankey's description of the workings of the British War Cabinet contained in his Government Control in War. Forrestal Diaries, pp. 116, 118.

192. November 23, 1944. Ibid., p. 19.

193. In 1946, the State Department was participating in twenty interdepartmental committees on foreign affairs, which it chaired, and in sixteen others as well. In 1950, it was represented on some fifty committees of this kind, not counting those concerned with personnel matters. Brookings Institution, The Administration of Foreign Affairs, pp. 329, 339 f.

194. June 1945. Forrestal Diaries, pp. 62 f.

195. Ibid., pp. 238 ff. See also articles by James Reston: "Lack of Coordination seen in Foreign Policy" and "U.S. Foreign Policies Suffer in Execution." Their lack of success is attributed to failures somewhere along the line in the administrative agencies. N. Y. Times, December 12, 1948, and November 18, 1951. For an example of close cooperation between State and Defense Departments on the occasion of the publication in the U.S. of the news of the first atomic bomb explosion in Russia, see article by Arthur Krock in Ibid., October 2, 1949.

196. For the shedding of these ideas, see the writings of George F. Kennan.

197. For examples, see Watson, Chief of Staff, pp. 98 f., 122 and passim.

198. For details, see the Brookings Institution report, The Administration of Foreign Affairs, pp. 127 ff.

199. The first incumbent was Rear Admiral Sidney E. Souers, sailor with a business rather than an Annapolis background, a naval reserve officer and original organizer of the Central Intelligence Agency. Following Admiral Leahy's retirement early in 1949, he took over the job of briefing the President daily on the military-political world situation. N. Y. Times, December 3, 1948.

200. McCamy, The Administration of Foreign Affairs, p. 109.

201. For an early discussion of the Council's role, see Kirkpatrick, "Advisers or Policy Makers?" in American Perspective, II, 443 f. Cf. also McCamy, The Administration of Foreign Affairs, passim, and Brookings Institution

report, The Administration of Foreign
Affairs. For Souers' ideas, see his article
on "Policy Formulation for National Security," American Political Science Review,
Vol. XLIII (1949), 534 ff.

202.   For details, see Brookings Institution, The
Administration of Foreign Affairs, pp.
124 ff., 140 ff.

203.   Defense Secretary Forrestal shared with
some military men the impression that
"State under Acheson's leadership had been
very dubious about the creation of the Council and would undoubtedly try to castrate its
effectiveness." In their view it was still "an
essential link because so many decisions
that now had to be made were a composite
of military and political questions." They
were, however, not themselves anxious to
enlarge military participation in diplomatic
decisions, which often suffered from a lack
of military understanding in the State Department. Such participation, as through the
placing of military personnel in that Department, seemed not even "in the interests of
the Military Establishment," which expected
only too soon to be attacked for exercising
too much influence on foreign policy (September 1947). Forrestal Diaries, pp. 315 ff.

204.   Ibid., pp. 316 f., 320 f.

205.   This disregard was shown in such decisions
as the recognition of Israel in May 1948, or the
defense of Berlin against the Russian blockade
beginning in June 1948. Ibid., pp. 440, 454 f.

206.   Time, August 29, 1949.

207.   For this, see Johnson's testimony before
the Senate's MacArthur Committee, June 14,
1951. Military Situation in the Far East, pp.
2569 ff.

208.   This is based on the Senate hearings on Military Situation in the Far East, pp. 489, 327,
329, 582 ff., 2675, 2690, 2703 f. For new
liaison arrangements between the Defense
and State Departments since Marshall was
Secretary of Defense, see Ibid., pp. 523,
638. For the deliberations prior to the decision to accept the challenge in Korea, see
Ibid., pp. 2573, 2584.

209.   Hoover Commission Report of February
1949, cited by McCamy in The Administration
of Foreign Affairs, pp. 69 f.

210.   N. Y. Times, December 22, 1950.

211.   The temporary or permanent transfer of
businessmen to political administration is
not necessarily a felicitous solution; many
of them in the new political atmosphere
readily succumb to "empire building" and
other bureaucratic vices. This is what
Emerson had in mind when he wrote to
Carlyle (on October 7, 1835) that "government has come to be a trade, and is managed
solely on commercial principles."

212.   This was the phrase used to describe the
forces that opposed (from within) the
U. S. War Department reorganization proposals of 1941-42. Military Affairs, XVI,
108.

Abbreviations

The following abbreviations are used throughout
for certain frequently cited documentary collections
and works of reference. Unless otherwise indicated,
references in Die grosse Politik are to document
numbers and in all other cases to page numbers.

ADB   - Allgemeine Deutsche Biographie.

B.D.   - British Documents on the Origins of the War, 1898-1914.

D.D.   - Deutsche Dokumente zum Kriegsausbruch, 1914.

DNB   - Dictionary of National Biography.

Doc. dipl. fr. - Documents diplomatiques français.

G.P.   - Die grosse Politik der europäischen Kabinette, 1871-1914.

OED   - Oxford English Dictionary.

Bibliography

All monographs, biographies, correspondence, diaries, memoirs, collections of official documents, works of reference, and articles in scholarly or technical journals to which reference is made in the text or footnotes are listed in this bibliography. Except in the case of signed articles, references in the footnotes to newspapers and non-scholarly or non-technical journals are not repeated in this bibliography.

General Works

Adamic, Louis. The Eagle and the Roots. Garden City, N. Y., 1952.

Aikman, Duncan. The All-American Front. New York, 1940.

Albertini, Luigi. The Origins of the War of 1914. 2 vols. New York, 1952-53.

Albertini, Rudolf von. Das politische Denken in Frankreich zur Zeit Richelieus. Marburg, 1951.

Albrecht-Carrié, René. Italy at the Peace Conference. New York, 1938.

Anders, Lt. Gen. Wladyslaw. An Army in Exile: The Story of the Second Polish Corps. London, 1949.

Anderson, Eugene. The First Moroccan Crisis, 1904-1906. Chicago, 1930.

Ariosto, Lodovico. Orlando Furioso. Translated by John Hoole. 5 vols. London, 1799.

Arneth, Alfred, ritter von. Geschichte Maria Theresias. 10 vols. Vienna, 1863-76. Vols. I-IV, Maria Theresias erste Regierungsjahre.

Arnold-Forster, Hugh O. The Army in 1906. London, 1906.

Asquith, Herbert H., 1st earl of Oxford and Asquith. The Genesis of the War. London, 1923.

Aston, Sir George. Sea, Land, and Air Strategy. London, 1914.

Auffenberg-Komarów, Moriz, freiherr von. Aus Oesterreichs Hoehe und Niedergang. Leipzig, 1921.

Avenel, Georges, vicomte d'. Richelieu et la monarchie absolue. Paris, 1895.

Bacon, Francis. The Essays or Counsels, civil and moral, of Francis Bacon (1597). With an Introduction by Henry Morley. Chicago, 1883. § xix, "Of Empire."

Bacon, Sir Reginald Hugh S. The Life of Lord Fisher of Kilverstone. 2 vols. Garden City, N. Y., 1929.

Badoglio, Pietro. Italy in the Second World War. London & New York, 1948.

Bailey, Thomas A. A Diplomatic History of the American People. New York, 1940.

———. Wilson and the Peacemakers. 2 vols. in 1. New York, 1947.

Baker, Ray Stannard. Woodrow Wilson and World Settlement. 3 vols. Garden City, N. Y., 1922.

Baldwin, Hanson. Great Mistakes of the War. New York, 1950.

Barghoorn, Frederick C. The Soviet Image of the United States. New York, 1950.

Barrow, Sir John. Some Account of the Public Life of the Earl of Macartney. 2 vols. London, 1807.

Bartel, Paul. Le maréchal Pilsudski. Paris, 1935

Bauer, Col. Max. Der grosse Krieg in Feld und Heimat. Tübingen, 1921.

Beard, Charles A. President Roosevelt and the Coming of the War, 1941. New Haven, 1948.

Beard, Charles A. and Mary R. Beard. The Rise of American Civilization. New York, 1933.

Beauvais, Armand P. Attachés militaires, attachés navals, et attachés de l'air. (Thèse: Université de Paris.) Paris, 1937.

Beauvoir, Simone de. Tag und Nacht in Amerika. Hamburg, 1950.

Beaverbrook, William M. A., Lord. Politicians and the War, 1914-1916. 2 vols. London, 1928-32.

Berenhorst, Georg Heinrich von. Betrachtungen über die Kriegskunst, über ihre Fortschritte, ihre Widersprüche und ihre Zuverlässigkeit. 3d ed. Leipzig, 1827.

Berner, Ernst. Geschichte des preussischen Staates. Munich & Berlin, 1891.

Berney, Arnold. Friedrich der Grosse. Tübingen, 1934.

Bernhardi, Gen. Friedrich von. Germany and the Next War. Toronto, 1914.

Bernhardi, Theodor von. Geschichte Russlands und der europäischen Politik in den Jahren 1814 bis 1831. 3 vols. in 4. Leipzig, 1863-77.

Bethcke, Generalmajor Ernst. Politische Generäle! Kreise und Krisen um Bismarck. Berlin, 1930.

Bethmann Hollweg, Theobald von. Betrachtungen zum Weltkrieg. 2 vols. Berlin, 1919-21.

Binder von Krieglstein, Karl, freiherr von. Zur Psychologie des grossen Krieges. 3 vols. Vienna, 1893-97. Vol. II, Krieg ohne Chancen.

Binkley, Robert. Realism and Nationalism, 1852-1871. New York & London, 1935.

Birkenhead, Sir Frederick Smith, 1st earl of. International Law. 5th edition. London, 1918.

Bley, Wulf. Moderne Heere—Moderne Waffen. Berlin, 1935.

Bloch, Camille. Les causes de la guerre mondiale. Paris, 1933.

Blume, Wilhelm von. Die Beschiessung von Paris und die Ursachen ihrer Verzögerung. Berlin, 1899.

Bolles, Blair, and Francis O. Wilcox. The Armed Road to Peace: An Analysis of NATO. (Headline Series, Foreign Policy Association, No. 92.) New York, 1952.

Bono, Emilio de. Das Jahr XIV—Die Eroberung eines Imperiums. Berlin, 1936.

Borchardt, Georg H. (ed.). Die Randbemerkungen Friedrichs des Grossen. Potsdam, 1937.

Bourgeois, Emile (ed.). Ezechiel Spanheim: Rélation de la cour de France en 1690. Paris, 1900.

Bourget, Jean M. Gouvernement et commandement: Les leçons de la guerre mondiale. Paris, 1930.

Brandenburg, Erich. Die Reichsgründung. 2 vols. Liepzig, 1922.

Brandt, Max August von. Drei Jahre ostasiatischer Politik, 1894-1897. Stuttgart, 1897.

Brauer, Arthur von. Im Dienste Bismarcks. Berlin, 1936.

Bredt, Johannes Victor. Der deutsche Reichstag im Weltkrieg. Berlin, 1927.

Brinkmann, Carl. Soziologische Theorie der Revolution. Göttingen, 1948.

Broglie, Albert, duc de. Frédéric II et Louis XV, 1742-1744. Paris, 1885.

_____. Le secret du roi. Paris, 1878.

Brookings Institution. The Administration of Foreign Affairs and Overseas Operations. Washington, 1951.

Browning, Oscar (ed.). England and Napoleon in 1803. London, 1887.

Bryant, Arthur. Samuel Pepys. 3 vols. New York & Cambridge, 1933-39. Vol. III, The Savior of the Navy.

_____. The Years of Endurance, 1793-1802. New York & London, 1942.

_____. Years of Victory, 1802-1812. New York & London, 1945.

Bülow, Bernhard von. Deutsche Politik. Berlin, 1916.

Burnham, James. The Coming Defeat of Communism. New York, 1950.

Busch, Wilhelm. Das deutsche Grosse Hauptquartier und die Bekämpfung von Paris im Feldzug 1870/71. Tübingen, 1905.

Butterfield, Herbert. History and Human Relations. London, 1951.

_____. The Peace Tactics of Napoleon, 1806-1808. Cambridge, 1929.

Cadorna, Luigi. La guerra alla fronte italiana. 2 vols. Milan, 1922.

Calahan, Lt. Commander Harold A. What Makes a War End? New York, 1944.

Callières, François de. De la manière de négocier avec les souverains. Paris, 1716.

Callwell, Maj. Gen. Sir Charles E. Field-Marshal Sir Henry Wilson. 2 vols. London, 1927.

Cambon, Jules. Le diplomate. Paris, 1926.

Cecil, Lady Gwendolen. Life of Robert, marquis of Salisbury. 4 vols. London, 1921-32.

Charteris, Evan. William Augustus, Duke of Cumberland, and the Seven Years' War. London, 1913.

Chastenet, Jacques. La France de M. Fallières, une époque pathétique. Paris, 1949.

Churchill, Sir Winston L. S. The Second World War. 6 vols. Boston, 1948-53.

_____. The Unknown War: The Eastern Front. New York, 1931.

_____. While England Slept: A Survey of World Affairs, 1932-1938. New York, 1938.

_____. The World Crisis. 4 vols. in 1. New York, 1931.

Civrieux, Commandant de. Le germanisme encerclé. Paris, 1913.

Clausewitz, Carl von. On War. Translated by O. J. Jolles. Modern Library Edition. New York, 1943.

Clode, Charles M. The Military Forces of the Crown:

Their Administration and Government. 2 vols. London, 1869.

Cobbett, William. Cobbett's Parliamentary History of England from the Norman Conquest in 1066 to 1803. 12 vols. London, 1806-12.

Comte, Auguste. Cours de philosophie positive. 2d ed. 6 vols. Paris, 1864.

Condorcet, Marie Jean de Caritat, marquis de. Oeuvres complètes de Condorcet. Edited by A. O'Conor and M. F. Arago. 12 vols. Paris, 1847-49.

Conrady, E. von. Leben und Wirken des Generals Carl von Grolman. 3 vols. Berlin, 1894-96.

Corti, Egon C. Alexander von Battenberg, sein Kampf mit den Zaren und Bismarck. Leipzig, 1920.

Corwin, Edward S. Total War and the Constitution. New York, 1947.

Coulondre, Robert. De Staline à Hitler. Paris, 1950.

Coville, Alfred, and Harold Temperley (eds.). Studies in Anglo-French History during the eighteenth, nineteenth, and twentieth Centuries. Cambridge, 1935.

Cramon, August von. Unser oesterreichisch-ungarischer Bundesgenosse im Weltkriege. Berlin, 1920.

Cron, Hermann. Geschichte des deutschen Heeres im Weltkriege, 1914-1918. Berlin, 1937.

Czernin, Ottokar Theobald, graf. Im Weltkriege. Berlin & Vienna, 1919.

Danilov, Youri. Le premier généralissime des armées russes, le grand-duc Nicolas; son rôle dans la guerre mondiale. Paris, 1932.

_____. La Russie dans la guerre mondiale (1914-1917). Paris, 1927.

Dansette, Adrien. Du boulangisme à la révolution dreyfusienne: Le boulangisme, 1886-1890. Paris, 1938.

Das alte Heer. Von einem Stabsoffizier. Berlin, 1920.

Davis, George T. A Navy Second to None: The Development of Modern American Naval Policy. New York, 1940.

Dawson, William H. Richard Cobden and Foreign Policy. London, 1926.

Deane, Gen. John R. The Strange Alliance: The Story of Our Efforts at Wartime Cooperation with Russia. New York, 1947.

Debeney, Gen. Marie Eugène. La guerre et les hommes. Paris, 1937.

Decembrio, Pier Candido. Leben des Filippo Maria Visconti und Taten des Francesco Sforza. Translated by Philipp Funk. Jena, 1913.

Delbrück, Hans. Geschichte der Kriegskunst im Rahmen der politischen Geschichte. 7 vols. Berlin, 1900-1936.

Derrécagaix, Victor B. Le maréchal Berthier. 2 vols. Paris, 1904-05.

Derry, T. Kingston. The Campaign in Norway. London, 1952.

Desbrière, Edouard. Projets et tentatives de débarquements aux Iles britanniques, 1793-1805. 4 vols. Paris, 1900-1902.

Dietrich, Otto. Auf den Strassen des Sieges. Munich, 1939.

Digges, Thomas, and Dudley Digges. Foure Paradoxes; or politique discourses. London, 1604.

Dirr, Pius. Bayerische Dokumente zum Kriegsausbruch und zum Versailler Schuldspruch. Munich, 1922.

Dobrorolski, Sergei. Die Mobilmachung der russischen Armee 1914. Berlin, 1922.

Doniol, Henri. Histoire de la participation de la France
à l'établissement des Etats-Unis d'Amérique. 5 vols.
Paris, 1886-92.

Douhet, Giulio. The Command of the Air. New York, 1942.

Driault, Edouard. La politique orientale de Napoléon:
Sébastiani et Gardane, 1806-1808. Paris, 1904.

Droysen, Johann Gustav. Abhandlungen von Johann Gustav
Droysen. Zur neueren Geschichte. Leipzig, 1876.

———. Geschichte der preussischen Politik. 5 vols. in 14.
Leipzig, 1868-86.

Dugdale, Blanche E. C. Arthur James Balfour, first earl
of Balfour. 2 vols. New York, 1937.

Dumont, Jean. Corps universel diplomatique du droit des
gens. 8 vols. Amsterdam, 1726-31.

Dumouriez, Gen. Charles F. Nouveau tableau spéculatif
de l'Europe. n.p., 1798.

Dupre, Huntley. Lazare Carnot, Republican Patriot. Oxford, Ohio, 1940.

Durham, M. Edith. The Struggle for Scutari. London, 1914.

Eardley-Wilmot, Sydney. Life of Vice-Admiral Edmund,
Lord Lyons. London, 1898.

Earle, Edward M. (ed.). Makers of Modern Strategy:
Military Thought from Machiavelli to Hitler. Princeton, 1943.

Easum, Chester V. Prince Henry of Prussia, Brother of
Frederick the Great. Madison, Wis., 1942.

Eisenhart Rothe, Gen. Ernst von. Im Banne der Persönlichkeit. Berlin, 1931.

Eisner, Kurt. Der Geheimbund des Zaren. Berlin, 1904.

Eliot, George F. If Russia Strikes. Philadelphia, 1949.

Erdmann, Karl. Die Entstehung des Kreuzzugsgedankens.
Stuttgart, 1935.

Ergang, Robert. The Potsdam Führer. New York, 1941.

Eyck, Erich. Das persönliche Regiment Wilhelms II.
Ehrlenbach-Zurich, 1948.

———. Bismarck. 3 vols. Ehrlenbach-Zurich, 1941-44.

Fabre-Luce, Alfred. Journal de l'Europe, 1946-1947.
Paris, 1947.

Fabry, Lt. Col. Jean Joseph. Joffre et son destin. Paris,
1931.

Falkenhayn, Erich Georg von. Die Oberste Heeresleitung,
1914-1916, in ihren wichtigsten Entschliessungen. Berlin, 1920.

Farago, Ladislas (ed.). The Axis Grand Strategy. New
York, 1942.

Fay, Sidney B. The Origins of the World War. 2 vols.
New York, 1928.

Feiling, Keith G. The Life of Neville Chamberlain. London, 1946.

Fernandez, Ramon. Itinéraire français. Paris, 1943.

Flassan, Gaëtan de. Histoire générale et raisonnée de la
diplomatie française, depuis la fondation de la monarchie jusqu'à la fin du règne de Louis XVI. 2d ed.
7 vols. Paris, 1811.

Fleury, Col. Emile-Adrien, vicomte de. Soldats et ambassadeurs sous le Directoire. 2 vols. Paris, 1906.

Foerster, Wolfgang. Der Feldherr Ludendorff im Unglück.
Wiesbaden, 1952.

———. Graf Schlieffen und der Weltkrieg. Berlin, 1920.

Foertsch, Hermann. Kriegskunst heute und morgen. Berlin, 1939.

Fournier, August. Der Congress von Chatillon: Die Politik
im Kriege von 1814. Vienna & Prague, 1900.

———. Gentz und Cobenzl: Geschichte der österreichischen
Diplomatie, 1801-1805. Vienna, 1880.

Franke, Hermann (ed.). Handbuch der neuzeitlichen
Wehrwissenschaften. 3 vols. in 4. Berlin & Leipzig,
1936-39.

Frantz, Günther. Russlands Eintritt in den Weltkrieg.
Berlin, 1924.

Freytag-Loringhoven, Hugo Friedrich, freiherr von.
Generalfeldmarschall Graf von Schlieffen. Leipzig,
1920.

Fribourg, André. L'Italie et nous. Paris, 1947.

Friedjung, Heinrich. Der Kampf um die Vorherrschaft
in Deutschland, 1859 bis 1866. 2 vols. Stuttgart,
1897-1900.

Froment, A. La mobilisation et la préparation à la
guerre. Paris, 1887.

Fugier, André. Napoléon et l'Italie. Paris, 1947.

Fuller, Thomas. The Historie of the Holy Warre. Cambridge, 1639.

Gässler, Christian Walter. Offizier und Offizierkorps
der alten Armee in Deutschland als Voraussetzung
einer Untersuchung über die Transformation der
militärischen Hierarchie. (Dissertation.) Heidelberg, 1930.

Ganoe, William A. The History of the United States
Army. Revised edition. New York, 1942.

Gardane, Alfred, comte de. Mission du Général Gardane
en Perse sous le premier empire. Paris, 1865.

Garvin, James L. The Life of Joseph Chamberlain.
London, 1932.

Gatzke, Hans W. Germany's Drive to the West. Balti-
more, 1950.

Gauvain, Auguste. L'Europe au jour le jour. 14 vols.
Paris, 1917-23.

Gebhardt, Bruno. Wilhelm von Humboldt als Staatsman.
2 vols. Stuttgart, 1896-99.

Gentili, Alberico. "De jure belli" libri tres (1st edi-
tion, Hanau, 1598). Translated by John Rolfe (The
Classics of International Law, No. 16). London &
Oxford, 1933.

Gibbon, Edward. The Decline and Fall of the Roman
Empire. (Modern Library Edition.) 2 vols. New
York, 1932.

Gilbert, Felix (ed.). Hitler Directs His War. New York,
1951.

Gisevius, Hans B. To the Bitter End. Boston, 1947.

Glaise-Horstenau, Edmund von. Franz Josephs Weggefährte: Das Leben des Generalstabschefs Grafen
Beck. Vienna, 1930.

Gleich, Maj. Gen. Gerold von. Vom Balkan nach Bagdad.
Berlin, 1921.

Görlitz, Walter. Der deutsche Generalstab, 1657-1945.
Frankfurt-am-Main, 1950.

———. Der Zweite Weltkrieg, 1939-1945. 2 vols.
Stuttgart, 1951-52.

Goltz, Colmar, freiherr von der. Das Volk in Waffen:
Ein Buch über Heerwesen und Kriegführung. 3d ed.
Berlin, 1884.

Goodwin, William. Enquiry Concerning Political Justice. 2d ed. London, 1796.

Gooss, Roderich. Das Wiener Kabinett und die Entstehung des Weltkriegs. Vienna, 1919.

Goul, Roman. Les grands chefs de l'armée sovietique.
Paris, 1935.

———. Toukhatchevsky, maréchal rouge. Paris, n.d.

Govone, U. Il Generale Giuseppe Govone. 3d ed.
Turin, 1929.

Grabau, Albert. Das Festungsproblem in Deutschland und seine Auswirkung auf die strategische Lage von 1870-1914. Berlin, 1935.

Groener, Gen. Wilhelm. Das Testament des Grafen Schlieffen. Berlin, 1927.

Grose, Francis. Military Antiquities respecting a history of the English army from the Conquest to the present time. 2 vols. London 1786-88.

Gundling, Nic. Hieronymus. Ausführlicher Discours über das Natur-und Völker-Recht. Frankfurt & Leipzig, 1734.

_____. Ausführlicher und mit illustren Exempeln aus der Historie und Staaten-Notiz erlauterter Discours über Doktor Iohannes Franciscus Buddei Philosophiae Practical. Frankfurt & Leipzig, 1733. Part III, Die Politie.

Günther, Hans, F. Der Herren eigner Geist: Die Ideologie des National Sozialismus. Moscow, 1935.

Guichen, Eugène, vicomte de. Les grandes questions européennes et la diplomatie des puissances sous la seconde République français. 2 vols. Paris, 1925-29.

Guillon, Edouard. Les complots militaires sous le Consulat et l'Empire. Paris, 1894.

Haldane, Richard B. Before the War. London, 1920.

Halévy, Daniel. La république des ducs. Paris, 1937.

Halleck, H. W. Elements of Military Art and Science. New York, 1846.

Haller, Johannes. Aus dem Leben des Fürsten Philipp zu Eulenburg-Hertefeld. 2d ed. Berlin, 1926.

Hallgarten, George Wolfgang. Imperialismus vor 1914. Munich, 1951.

Hamman, Otto. Bilder aus der letzten Kaiserzeit. Berlin, 1922.

Hankey, Maurice, Lord. Government Control in War. Cambridge, 1945.

_____. Politics, Trials and Errors. Oxford, 1950.

Harcourt-Smith, Simon. Cardinal of Spain: The Life and Strange Career of Alberoni. New York, 1944.

Harris, H. Wilson. J. A. Spender. London, 1946.

Harrison, Gordon A. Cross-Channel Attack (United States Army in World War II. The European Theater of Operations). Washington; Dept. of the Army, Office of Military History, 1951.

Hartley, Livingston. Our Maginot Line: The Defense of the Americas. New York, 1939.

Hatschek, Julius. Englisches Staatsrecht. 2 vols. Tübingen, 1905-1906.

Hauser, Frédéric. Tchernychev et l'agence russe d'espionage, 1810-1812. Paris, n.d.

Haushofer, Karl. Deutsche Kulturpolitik im indopazifischen Raum. Hamburg, 1939.

Hegemann, Werner. Entlarvte Geschichte. 2d ed. n.p., 1934.

_____. Fridericus; oder, Das Königsöpfer. Hellerau, 1926.

Helmreich, Ernst C. The Diplomacy of the Balkan Wars, 1912-1913. Cambridge, Mass., & London, 1938.

Hemmer, Ernst. Die deutschen Kriegserklärungen von 1914. Stuttgart, 1935.

Herre, Paul (ed.). Politisches Handwörterbuch. 2 vols. Leipzig, 1923.

Herring, E. Pendleton (ed.). Civil-Military Relations: Bibliographical notes on administrative problems of civilian mobilization. Chicago, 1940.

Herzfeld, Hans. Die deutsch-französische Kriegsgefahr von 1875 (Forschungen und Darstellungen aus dem Reichsarchiv, No. 3). Berlin, 1922.

_____. Die deutsche Rüstungspolitik vor dem Weltkriege. Bonn & Leipzig, 1923.

_____. Das Problem des deutschen Heeres. Laupheim, n.d.

Heusinger, Adolf. Befehl im Widerstreit. Tübingen, 1950.

Hoare, Sir Samuel. The Fourth Seal: The end of a Russian chapter. London, 1930.

Hobohm, Martin. Machiavellis Renaissance der Kriegskunst. Berlin, 1913.

Hölzle, Erwin, Der Osten im ersten Weltkrieg. Leipzig, 1944.

Hoetzsch, Otto. Peter von Meyendorff. Berlin & Leipzig, 1923.

Holborn, Hajo. Deutschland und die Türkei, 1878-1890. Berlin, 1926.

Holl, Karl. Gesammelte Aufsätze zur Kirchengeschichte. 3 vols. Tübingen, 1923-28.

Hoskins, Halford L. The Atlantic Pact. Washington, 1949.

Huber, Ernst R. Heer und Staat in der deutschen Geschichte. Hamburg, 1938.

Iblher, Franz (ed.). Vor der Entscheidung. Reden und Botschaften aus drei Jahrtausenden von Staatslenkern und Feldherrn in Zeiten des Krieges. Berlin, 1941.

Intérêts présens et des prétensions des puissances de l'Europe, les. 2d ed. The Hague, 1736.

Jäckh, Ernst (ed.). Kiderlen-Wächter, der Staatsmann und Mensch. 2 vols. Stuttgart, 1924.

Jähns, Max. Geschichte der Kriegswissenschaften, vornehmlich in Deutschland. 3 vols. Munich & Leipzig, 1889-91.

_____. Heeresverfassung und Völkerleben. Berlin, 1885.

Jany, Curt. Geschichte der königlich preussischen Armee bis zum Jahre 1807. 5 vols. Berlin, 1928-37.

Journet, Charles. L'église du verbe incarné. Paris, 1943.

Judet, Ernest. George Louis. Paris, 1925.

Jünger, Ernst. Krieg und Krieger. Berlin, 1930.

Just, Arthur W. Militärmacht Sowjetunion. Breslau, 1935.

Kalinow, Kyrill D. Sowjetmarshälle haben das Wort. Hamburg, 1950.

Kanner, Heinrich. Der Schlüssel zur Kriegschuldfrage. Munich, 1926.

Kant, Immanuel. "Mutmasslicher Anfang der Menschengeschichte" in Karl Vorländer, (ed.), Kleinere Schriften zur Geschichtsphilosophie. Leipzig, 1922.

Kase, Toshikazu. Journey to the "Missouri". New Haven, 1950.

Kautsky, Karl. Sozialisten und Krieg. Prague, 1937.

Kehr, Eckart. Schlachtflottenbau und Parteipolitik, 1894-1901. Berlin, 1930.

Keim, Lt. Gen. August. Erlebtes und Erstrebtes. Hanover, 1925.

Kent, Sherman. Strategic Intelligence for American World Policy. Princeton, 1949.

Keyes, Sir Roger. Adventures Ashore and Afloat. London, 1939.

King, Jere Clemens. Generals and Politicians: Conflict between France's High Command, Parliament, and Government. Berkeley, 1951.

Kisker, George W. (ed.). World Tension. The Psychopathology of International Relations. New York, 1951.

Klopp, Onno. Der Fall des Hauses Stuart. 14 vols. in 7. Vienna, 1875-88.

Kloster, Walter. Der deutsche Generalstab und der Präventivkriegsgedanke (Beiträge zur Geschichte der nachbismarckschen Zeit und des Weltkriegs, hfte. 13). Stuttgart, 1932.

Kluke, Paul. Heeresaufbau und Heerespolitik Englands vom Burenkrieg bis zum Weltkrieg. Munich & Berlin, 1932.

Koerlin, Kurt. Zur Vorgeschichte des russisch-französischen Bündnisses, 1879-1890. Halle, 1926.

Kordt, Erich. Wahn und Wirklichkeit. Die Aussenpolitik des Dritten Reiches. Stuttgart, 1948.

Kraus, Herbert. Das Problem internationaler Ordnung bei Immanuel Kant. Berlin, 1931.

Krauss, Alfred. Theorie und Praxis in der Kriegskunst. Munich, 1930.

Kravchenchko, Victor. I Chose Freedom. New York, 1946.

Kris, Ernst and Hans Speier. German Radio Propaganda. New York, 1944.

Kühlmann, R. von. Die Diplomaten. Berlin, 1939.

Kuhl, Gen. Hermann von. Der deutsche Generalstab in in Vorbereitung und Durchführung des Weltkrieges. Berlin, 1920.

Lacour-Gayet, Georges. Talleyrand, 1754-1838. 4 vols. Paris, 1928-34.

Lafuze, George L. Great Britain, France, and the Siamese Question, 1885-1904. Urbana, Ill., 1935.

La Gorce, Pierre Gustave de. Histoire du Second Empire. 7 vols. Paris, 1899-1905.

Lagorgette, Jean. Le rôle de la guerre: Étude de sociologie générale. Paris, 1906.

Langer, William L. The Diplomacy of Imperialism, 1890-1902. 2 vols. New York & London, 1935.

―――. The Franco-Russian Alliance, 1890-1894. Cambridge, 1929.

―――. Our Vichy Gamble. New York, 1947.

Langer, William L., and S. Everett Gleason. The Undeclared War, 1940-1941. New York, 1953.

Larminat, Gen. Edgar M. de. L'armée européenne. Paris, 1952.

Las Cases, Emmanuel, comte de. Mémorial de Sainte-Hélène (Réimpression de 1823 et 1824). 8 vols. Paris, 1823-24.

La Tour, Commandant Jean de. Le Maréchal Niel. Paris, 1912.

Lauterbach, Richard E. Through Russia's Back Door. New York, 1947.

Lavisse, Ernest. Histoire de France contemporaine depuis la révolution jusqu'à la paix de 1919. 10 vols. Paris, 1920-22.

Lefèvre-Pontalis, A. Jean de Witt, grand pensionnaire de Hollande. Paris, 1884.

Leyh, M. Die bayerische Heeresreform unter König Ludwig II. Munich, 1922.

Liddell Hart, Basil Henry. The German Generals Talk. New York, 1948.

Lieber, Francis. Manual of Political Ethics. 2d revised edition. Philadelphia, 1881.

Liskenne, Charles, and Sauvan. Bibliothèque historique et militaire. 7 vols. Paris, 1849-50.

Lockhart, Sir R. H. Bruce. Comes the Reckoning. London, 1947.

Lot, Ferdinand. L'art militaire et les armées au moyen âge en Europe et dans le Proche Orient. 2 vols. Paris, 1946.

Ludendorff, Gen. Erich. Der totale Krieg. Munich, 1935.

―――. Urkunden der Obersten Heeresleitung über ihre Tätigkeit, 1916-1918. Berlin, 1920.

Ludwig, Emil. Juli 14. Berlin, 1929.

Lünig, Johann Christian. Das teutsche Reichs-Archiv. 24 vols. in 30. Leipzig, 1710-22.

McCamy, James L. The Administration of American Foreign Affairs. New York, 1950.

Macdiarmid, Duncan S. The Life of Lieut.-General Sir James Moncrieff Grierson. London, 1923.

Mackay, B. Laurence, freiherr von. Die moderne Diplomatie. Frankfurt-am-Main, 1915.

McNair, Harley F. China in Revolution. Chicago, 1931.

Mann, Thomas. Friedrich und die grosse Koalition. Berlin, 1915.

Manning, Frederic. The Life of Sir William White. London, 1923.

March, Gen. Peyton C. The Nation at War. Garden City, N. Y., 1932.

Marder, Arthur J. The Anatomy of British Sea Power. New York, 1940.

Markham, Reuben Henry. Tito's Imperial Communism. Chapel Hill, N. C., 1947.

Martchenko, Mitrofan. La catastrophe austro-hongroise. Paris, 1920.

Martens, George Friedrich von. Précis du droit des gens moderne de l'Europe. 3d ed. Göttingen, 1821.

Martienssen, Anthony K. Hitler and His Admirals. New York, 1949.

Martin, B. Kingsley. The Triumph of Lord Palmerston: A study of public opinion in England before the Crimean War. London, 1924.

Masson, Frédéric. Le département des affaires étrangères pendant la Révolution, 1787-1804. Paris, 1877.

Maurice, Maj. Gen. Sir Frederick B. Governments and War. A Study of the Conduct of War. London, 1926.

―――. Lessons of Allied Cooperation: Naval, Military, and Air, 1914-1918. London, 1942.

Maurice, Maj. Gen. Sir Frederick B. and Sir George Arthur. The Life of Lord Wolseley. London, 1924.

Meinecke, Friedrich. Die Idee der Staatsräson in der neueren Geschichte. Munich & Berlin, 1924.

Menne, Bernhard. Krupp: Deutschlands Kanonenkönige. Zurich, 1937.

Mesnard, Pierre. L'essor de la philosophie politique au XVIe siècle. Paris, 1936.

Meyer, Arnold Oskar. Bismarck, der Mensch und der Staatsmann. Leipzig, 1944.

―――. Bismarcks Kampf mit Oesterreich am Bundestag zu Frankfurt (1851-1859). Berlin & Leipzig, 1927.

Michie, Peter S. The Life and Letters of Emory Upton. New York, 1885.

Michon, Georges. Robespierre et la guerre révolutionnaire, 1791-1792. Paris, 1937.

Mignet, François Auguste. Négociations relatives à la succession d'Espagne sous Louis XIV. 4 vols. Paris, 1835-42.

Miller, Jane K. Belgian Foreign Policy between Two Wars, 1919-1940. New York, 1951.

Millis, Walter. The Martial Spirit: A study of our war with Spain. Boston & New York, 1931.

Mommsen, Theodor. Römische Geschichte. Phaidon edition. Vienna, 1932.

Monk, George, duke of Albemarle. Observations upon Military and Political Affairs. London, 1671.

Monypenny, William F. and George E. Buckle. The Life of Benjamin Disraeli, Earl of Beaconsfield. 2 vols. New York, 1929.

Moore, John Bassett. History and Digest of the International Arbitration to Which the United States Has Been a Party. 6 vols. Washington, 1898.

Morel, Edmund D. Truth and the War. London, 1918.

Morley, John. The Life of William Ewart Gladstone. New edition. 3 vols. in 1. New York, 1932.

Moser, Lt. Gen. Otto von. Die obersten Gewalten im Weltkrieg. Stuttgart, 1931.

Mowat, R. B. Diplomacy and Peace. London, 1935.

Mühlmann, Carl. Deutschland und die Türkei, 1913-1914. Berlin, 1929.

Mukhtar, Mahmud (pasha). Die Türkei, Deutschland und Europa. Berlin, 1924. (Also, La Turquie, l'Allemagne et l'Europe. Paris, 1924.)

Namier, Sir Lewis Bernstein. Diplomatic Prelude, 1938-1939. New York, 1948.

Neumann, Franz L. Behemoth. The Structure and Practice of National Socialism, 1933-1944. New enlarged edition. New York, 1944.

Nevins, Allan. Henry White: Thirty Years of American Diplomacy. New York & London, 1930.

_____. The New Deal and World Affairs. (Chronicles of America, ed. Allan Nevins, Vol. LVI). New Haven, 1951.

_____. Ordeal of the Union. New York, 1947.

Newton, Thomas W. L., Lord. Lord Lansdowne. London, 1929.

Nicolay, John G., and John Hay (eds.). Complete Works of Abraham Lincoln. 12 vols. New York, 1906-07.

Nicolson, Harold. The Congress of Vienna. Phoenix edition. Berne, 1947.

_____. Curzon: the last phase, 1919-1925, a study in postwar diplomacy. Boston & New York, 1934.

_____. Portrait of a Diplomatist. Boston, 1930.

Niemann, Lt. Col. Alfred. Kaiser und Heer. Das Wesen der Kommandogewalt und ihre Ausübung durch Kaiser Wilhelm II. Berlin, 1929.

Nietzsche, Friedrich. Der Wille zur Macht. Kröner edition. Leipzig, 1930.

Nikolai, W. Nachrichtendienst, Presse und Volksstimmung im Kriege. Berlin, 1920.

Noack, Ulrich. Balkanproblem und Präventivkrieg unter dem Fürsten Bismarck. Berlin, 1926.

Noël, Léon. L'agression allemande contre la Pologne. Paris, 1946.

Oberkircher, Walter. General Erich von Grundell. Hamburg, 1939.

Ollivier, Emile. L'empire libéral. 18 vols. Paris, 1895-1918.

Oman, Sir Charles. A History of the Art of War in the Sixteenth Century. New York, 1937.

Oncken, Hermann. Das alte und das neue Mitteleuropa: Historisch-politische Betrachtungen über deutsche Bündnispolitik im Zeitalter Bismarcks und im Zeitalter des Weltkriegs. Gotha, 1917.

_____. (ed.). Grossherzog Friedrich I von Baden und die deutsche Politik von 1854-1871. Stuttgart, 1927.

_____. Politik und Kriegführung. Munich, 1928.

_____. Die Rheinpolitik Kaiser Napoleons III von 1863 bis 1870 and der Ursprung des Krieges von 1870/71. 3 vols. Stuttgart, 1926.

Paléologue, Georges Maurice. Les entretiens de l'impératrice Eugénie. Paris, 1928.

_____. Un prélude à l'invasion de la Belgique; le plan Schlieffen. Paris, 1932.

_____. The Turning Point: Three Critical Years, 1904-1906. Translated by F. A. Holl. London, 1935.

Pantlen, Hermann. Krieg und Finanzen. Hamburg, 1935.

Pascal, Ernest. La mobilisation. Paris, 1887.

Pasley, Sir Charles William. The Military Policy and Institutions of the British Empire. London, 1810.

Payne, Pierre Stephen. Mao Tse-tsung. New York, 1950.

Pearson, Drew, and Constantine Brown. The American Diplomatic Game. Garden City, N. Y., 1935.

Pelet de la Lozère, Jean. Opinions de Napoléon I sur divers sujets de politique et d'administration. Paris, 1833.

Percin, Gen. Alexandre. ...1914. Les Erreurs du Haut Commandement. Paris, 1919.

Pergler, Charles. America in the Struggle for Czechoslovak Independence. Philadelphia, 1926.

Perham, Margery Freda. The Government of Ethiopia. London, 1948.

Perry, Ralph Barton. The Free Man and the Soldier: Essays on the reconciliation of liberty and discipline. New York, 1916.

Pertinax, pseud. (André Géraud). Les Fossoyeurs. 2 vols. New York, 1943.

Petzet, Arnold. Heinrich Wiegand: Ein Lebensbild. Bremen, 1932.

Pinon, René. Histoire diplomatique, 1515-1928 (Histoire de la nation française, ed. Jean Hanoteau, Vol. IX.) Paris, 1929.

Pokrowski, Mikhail. Drei Konferenzen. Berlin, 1920.

Poltz, Ludwig. Die anglo-russische Entente, 1903-1907. Hamburg, 1932.

Potiemkine, Vladimir (ed.). Histoire de la diplomatie. 3 vols. Paris, 1946-47.

Pratt, Edwin A. The Rise of Railpower in War and Conquest, 1833-1914. London, 1915.

Presland, John, pseud. (Gladys Skelton). Vae Victis: The Life of Ludwig von Benedek, 1804-1881. New York & London, 1934.

Pribam, Alfred F. The Secret Treaties of Austria-Hungary, 1879-1914. 2 vols. Cambridge, 1920-21.

Puleston, Capt. William Dilworth. High Command in the World War. New York & London, 1934.

_____. Mahan. The Life and Work of Captain Alfred Thayer Mahan. New Haven, 1939.

Ramos Oliveira, Antonio. Politics, Economics and Men of Modern Spain, 1808-1946. London, 1946.

Ranke, Leopold von. Französische Geschichte, vornehmlich in sechzehnten und siebzehnten Jahrhundert. 5. vols. Stuttgart & Augsburg, 1856-62.

_____. Preussische Geschichte. Hamburg, n.d.

_____. Weltgeschichte. 9 vols. Leipzig, 1888-1902.

Rathenau, Walter. Gesammelte Schriften. 5 vols. Berlin, 1918. "England und Wir" in Vol. I.

Reboul, Col. Frédéric. L'armée. (La vie au dix-huitième siècle, t. 5). Paris, 1931.

Rehlen, Robert, pseud. (Julius Zeitler). Bismarck, ein deutsches Heldenleben. Leipzig, 1910.

Renouvin, Pierre. Les formes du gouvernement de guerre. Paris, 1925.

Renouvin, Pierre, Edmond Préclin, and Georges Hardy. La paix armée et la grande guerre, 1871-1919. (L'époque contemporaine, Clio IX^2). Paris, 1939.

Repington, Col. Charles à Court. After the War. Boston & New York, 1922.

———. The First World War, 1914-1918. Boston & New York, 1920.

Richelieu, Armand Jean du Plessis, cardinal, duc de. Testament politique. Amsterdam, 1688.

Ritter, Gerhard. Lebendige Vergangenheit. Leipzig, 1944.

———. Staatskunst und Kriegshandwerk: Das Problem des "Militarismus" in Deutschland. Munich, 1954.

Rochs, Hugo. Schlieffen. Berlin, 1920.

Rogge, Helmuth. Friedrich von Holstein. Berlin, 1932.

Rosenberg, Arthur. Die Entstehung der deutschen Republik, 1871-1918. Berlin, 1928.

Rothfels, Hans. Carl von Clausewitz. Politik und Krieg. Berlin, 1920.

Rousset, Camille. Histoire de Louvois et de son administration politique et militaire. 4th edition. 4 vols. Paris, 1872.

Russell, Bertrand. Freedom versus Organization, 1814-1914. New York, 1934.

Ruville, Albert von. William Pitt, Earl of Chatham. Translated by H. J. Chaytor. 3 vols. London & New York, 1907.

Sakmann, Paul. Voltaires Geistesart und Gedankenwelt. Stuttgart, 1910.

Schalk, Emil. Der Wettkampf der Völker. Jena, 1905.

Scheer, Admiral Reinhard. Vom Segelschiff zum U-boot. Leipzig, 1925.

Scherr, Johannes. Blücher: Seine Zeit und sein Leben. 2d edition. 3 vols. Leipzig, 1865.

Schmidt, Paul (German Foreign Office interpreter for Hitler). Statist auf diplomatischer Bühne, 1923-1945. Bonn, 1950.

Schmidt-Bückeburg, Rudolf. Das Militärkabinett der preussischen Könige und deutschen Kaiser. Berlin, 1933.

Schmiterlöw, Bernhard von. Aus dem Leben des Generalfeldmarschalls von der Goltz-Pascha. Leipzig, 1925.

Schmitt, Bernadotte. The Coming of the War, 1914. 2 vols. New York, 1930.

Schmitthenner, Paul. Politik und Kriegführung in der neueren Geschichte. Hamburg, 1937.

Schuman, Frederick L. Night over Europe: The diplomacy of nemesis, 1939-1940. New York, 1941.

———. Soviet Politics at Home and Abroad. New York, 1946.

Schwartz, Karl. Leben des Generals Carl von Clausewitz. 2 vols. Berlin, 1878.

Schwarz, Paul. This Man Ribbentrop. New York, 1943.

Schwertfeger, Bernhard H. Das Weltkriegsende: Gedanken über die deutsche Kriegsführung, 1918. 3d edition. Potsdam, 1937.

Semerau, Alfred. Die Condottieri. Jena, 1909.

Seton-Watson, Robert W. Britain in Europe, 1789-1914. Cambridge, 1937.

Seyfert, Gerhart. Die militärischen Beziehungen und Vereinbarungen zwischen dem deutschen und dem oesterreichischen Generalstab vor und bei Beginn des Weltkriegs. (Thesis). Leipzig, 1934.

Sherwood, Robert Emmet. Roosevelt and Hopkins. New York, 1948. [The author has also used the Bantam edition, 2 vols., New York, 1950.]

Shub, David. Lenin. A Biography. Garden City, N. Y., 1948.

Sorel, Albert. L'Europe et la révolution française. 8 vols. Paris, 1895-1910.

Sorel, Georges. Refléxions sur la violence. 6th edition. Paris, 1925.

Spencer, Herbert. The Principles of Sociology. 3 vols. in 4. New York, 1880-97.

Spender, J. A. Life of the Right Honorable Sir Henry Campbell-Bannerman. 2 vols. London, 1923.

Srbik, Heinrich, ritter von. Metternich, der Staatsmann und der Mensch. 2 vols. Munich, 1925.

———. (ed.). Quellen zur deutschen Politik Oesterreichs, 1859-1866. 5 vols. in 6. Oldenburg, 1934-38.

Stamp, Kenneth M. And the War Came. Baton Rouge, 1951.

Stanmore, Arthur Hamilton-Gordon, Lord. Sidney Herbert, Lord Herbert of Lea. 2 vols. London, 1906.

Stead, Alfred (ed.). Unser Vaterland Japan. Leipzig, 1904.

Steed, Henry Wickham. The Hapsburg Monarchy. London, 1914.

Stoffel, Eugène Georges Henri, baron. Rapports militaires. Paris, 1871.

Strausz-Hupé, Robert, and Stefan T. Possony. International Relations in the Age of Conflict between Democracy and Dictatorship. New York, 1950.

Sutherland, James R. Defoe. Philadelphia & New York, 1938.

Taffs, Winifred. Ambassador to Bismarck: Lord Odo Russell, first baron Ampthill. London, 1938.

Takeuchi, Tatsuji. War and Diplomacy in the Japanese Empire. Chicago, 1935.

Tansill, Charles C. Back Door to War: The Roosevelt Foreign Policy, 1933-1941. Chicago, 1952.

Tarlé, Eugene. Bonaparte. Translated from the Russian by John Cournos. New York, 1937.

Thucydides. The History of the Peloponnesian War. Translated by Bohn. London, 1859.

Tirpitz, Alfred von. Politische Dokumente. 2 vols. Stuttgart, 1924-26. (Vol. I, Der Aufbau der deutschen Weltmacht; Vol. II, Deutsche Ohnmachtspolitik im Weltkrieg.)

Togari, capitaine de vaisseau. Louis-Emile Bertin: son rôle dans la création de la marine japonaise. Paris, 1935.

Toynbee, Arnold J. (ed.). Survey of International Affairs, 1938. (Royal Institute of International Affairs.) 3 vols. London, 1939.

Trevelyan, George M. British History in the Nineteenth Century. 6th edition. London, 1925.

———. England under Queen Anne. 3 vols. London & New York, 1930-34. Vol. II, Ramillies and the Union with Scotland; Vol. III, The Peace and the Protestant Succession.

Triepel, Heinrich. Die Hegemonie. Ein Buch von führenden Staaten. Stuttgart, 1938.

Trochu, Louis Jules. Oeuvres posthumes. 2 vols. Tours, 1896.

Tschuppik, Karl. Ludendorff. The Tragedy of a Military Mind. Translated by W. H. Johnston. Boston & New York, 1932.

Unger, W. von. Blücher. 2 vols. Berlin, 1907-08.

Vagts, Alfred. Deutschland und die Vereinigten Staaten in der Weltpolitik. 2 vols. New York, 1935.

———. A History of Militarism. New York, 1937.

———. Landing Operations. Harrisburg, Pa., 1946.

———. Mexico, Europa und Amerika unter besondere Berücksichtigung der Petroleumpolitik. Berlin, 1928.

Valentin, Veit. Deutschlands Aussenpolitik, von Bismarks Abgang bis zum Ende des Weltkrieges. Berlin, 1921.

———. Geschichte der deutschen Revolution von 1848-1849. Berlin, 1930-31.

Varnhagen von Ense, Karl August. Leben des Generals Hans Karl von Winterfeldt. Berlin, 1836.

Verner, Col. William W. The Military Life of H.R.H. George, Duke of Cambridge. London, 1905.

Visconti-Prasca, Gen. Sebastiano. La guerre décisive. Paris, 1935.

Vivenot, Alfred, ritter von. Zur Geschichte des Rastadter Congresses. Vienna, 1871.

Vogt, Hermann. Die europäischen Heere der Gegenwart. Rathenow, 1888.

Voss, Werner. Die Konvention von Tauroggen. Berlin, 1910.

Waldrop, Frank C. (ed.). MacArthur on War. New York, 1942.

Waliszewski, Kazimierz. La Russie il y a cent ans; le règne d'Alexandre Ier. 3 vols. Paris, 1923-25.

Warburg, James P. Faith, Purpose, and Power. New York, 1950.

Watson, Mark Skinner. Chief of Staff: Prewar Plans and Preparations. Washington, 1950.

Weber, Max. Gesammelte politische Schriften. Munich, 1921.

Webster, Charles K. The Foreign Policy of Castlereagh, 1815-1822: Britain and the European Alliance. London, 1934.

———. The Foreign Policy of Castlereagh, 1812-1815: Britain and the Reconstruction of Europe. London, 1931.

Wedel, Erhard, graf von (ed.). Zwischen Kaiser und Kanzler. Leipzig, 1943.

Werklein, Joseph, freiherr von. Kriegskunst und Staatskunst oder auch angewandte Staatswirtschaftslehre. Stuttgart, 1836.

Werth, Alexander. The Twilight of France, 1933-1940. London, 1942.

Wertheimer, Eduard von. Graf Julius Andrassy, sein Leben und seine Zeit. 3 vols. Stuttgart, 1910-13.

Westphal, Siegfried. Heer in Fesseln. Bonn, 1950.

Weygand, Maxime. Histoire de l'armée française. Paris, 1938.

Wheeler-Bennett, John W. The Forgotten Peace, Brest-Litovsk, March 1918. New York, 1939.

———. Munich: Prologue to Tragedy. New York, 1948.

Wilkinson, Spenser. War and Policy. New York, 1900.

Williams, A. F. Basil. Cartaret and Newcastle: A Contrast in Contemporaries. Cambridge, 1943.

———. Stanhope: A Study in Eighteenth Century War and Diplomacy. London, 1932.

Wolfers, Arnold. Britain and France between Two Wars. New York, 1940.

Wolff, Theodore. The Eve of 1914. New York, 1936.

Wollenberg, Erich. The Red Army. London, 1940.

Wrottesley, Lt. Col. George. Life and Correspondence of Field Marshal Sir John Burgoyne. London, 1873.

Zacharias, Capt. Ellis M. Secret Missions: The Story of an Intelligence Officer. New York, 1946.

Zechlin, Egmont. Bismarck und die Gründlegung der deutschen Grossmacht. Stuttgart, 1930.

Ziekursch, Johannes. Politische Geschichte des neuen deutschen Kaiserreichs. Frankfurt-am-Main, 1932.

Zilliacus, Konni. The Mirror of the Past: A History of Secret Diplomacy. New York, 1946.

Zwehl, H. von. Erich von Falkenhayn. Berlin, 1926.

Autobiographies, Diaries, Correspondence, Memoirs

(Alphabetical listing is by subject's rather than by editor's name.)

Baker, Lt. Gen. Valentine, (pasha). War in Bulgaria: A narrative of personal experiences. 2 vols. London, 1879.

Bamberger, Ludwig. Bismarcks grosses Speil: Die geheimen Tagebücher Ludwig Bambergers. Edited by Ernst Feder. Frankfurt-am-Main, 1932.

Bandholtz, Harry Hill. An Undiplomatic Diary (by the American member of the Inter-allied military mission to Hungary, 1919-1920). Edited by Fritz-Konrad Kruger. New York, 1933.

Bapst, Germain. Le maréchal Canrobert: Souvenirs d'un siècle. 6 vols. Paris, 1898-1919.

Barbier, Edmond Jean. Chronique de la régence et du règne de Louis XV, 1718-1763, ou Journal de Barbier. 8 vols. Paris, 1866.

Barrès, Maurice. Mes cahiers. 13 vols. Paris, 1929-50.

Benckendorff, Konstantin, graf. Graf Benckendorffs diplomatischer Schriftwechsel. Edited by B. von Siebert. 3 vols. Berlin & Leipzig, 1928.

Bernhardi, Gen. Friedrich von. Denkwürdigkeiten aus meinem Leben. Leipzig, 1926.

Bernhardi, Theodor von. Aus dem Leben Theodor von Bernhardis. 9 vols. Leipzig, 1894-1906.

Bernstorff, Johann H. Andreas, graf von. The Memoirs of Count Bernstorff. Translated by Eric Sutton. New York, 1936.

Berthezène, Gen. Pierre, Baron. Souvenirs militaires de la république et de l'empire. Edited by Emile Berthezène. 2 vols. Paris, 1855.

Bertie, Francis Leveson, 1st viscount. The Diary of Lord Bertie of Thame, 1914-1918. Edited by Lady Algernon Gordon Lennox. 2 vols. New York, 1924.

Beust, Friedrich Ferdinand, graf von. Mémoires du comte de Beust. Edited by F. Kohn-Abrest. 2 vols. Paris, 1888.

Beyens, Eugène Louis, Baron. Deux années à Berlin, 1912-1914. 2 vols. Paris, 1931.

Bismarck, Otto, fürst von. Gedanken und Erinnerungen.

BIBLIOGRAPHY

(Volksausgabe.) 3 vols. Stuttgart & Berlin, 1919-22. [Vol. III has title page reading Erinnerung und Gedanke. Foreword signed Horst Kohl.]

———. Anhang zu den Gedanken und Erinnerungen von Fürst Bismarck. Edited by Horst Kohl. 2 vols. Stuttgart, 1901. Vol. II, Kaiser Wilhelm I und Bismarck.

———. Die gesammelten Werke. 15 vols. in 19. Berlin, 1924-35.

Blumenthal, Leonard, graf von. Tagebücher des Generalfeldmarschalls Graf von Blumenthal aus den Jahren 1866 und 1870/71. Stuttgart & Berlin, 1902.

Bompard, Maurice. Mon ambassade en Russie, 1903-1908. Edited by his wife, Mme Gabrielle Bompard. Paris, 1937.

Brandt, Max August von. Dreiunddreissig Jahre in Ost-Asien: Erinnerungen eines deutschen Diplomaten. 3 vols. Leipzig, 1901.

Bright, John. The Diaries of John Bright. Edited by R. A. J. Walling. New York, 1931.

Bülow, Bernhard, fürst von. Denkwürdigkeiten. Edited by F. von Stockhammern. 4 vols. Berlin, 1930-31.

Busch, Moritz. Bismarck. Some Secret Pages of His History: being a diary kept by Dr. Moritz Busch during twenty-five years' official and private intercourse with the great chancellor. 2 vols. New York & London, 1898.

Cambon, Paul. Correspondance, 1870-1924. Notes by Henri Cambon. 3 vols. Paris, 1940-46.

Canning, George. George Canning and his Friends. (Correspondence.) Edited by Josceline Bagot. 2 vols. London, 1909.

———. Select Speeches of the Right Honorable George Canning. Edited by Robert Walsh. Philadelphia, 1835.

Carnot, Hippolyte. Mémoires sur Carnot (par son fils). 2 vols. Paris, 1861-63.

Caulaincourt, Armand Augustin. Mémoires du général de Caulaincourt, duc de Vicence, grand écuyer de l'empereur. Introduction and notes by Jean Hanoteau. Paris, 1935.

Ciano, Galeazzo. The Ciano Diaries, 1939-1943. Edited by Hugh Gibson. New York, 1946.

Combarieu, Abel. Sept ans à l'Elysée avec le président Loubet, 1899-1906. Paris, 1932.

Conrad von Hötzendorf, Franz, graf. Aus meiner Dienstzeit, 1906-1918. 5 vols. Vienna, 1921-25.

Conrad von Hötzendorf, Gina, gräfin. Mein Leben mit Conrad von Hötzendorf. Leipzig, 1935.

Creel, George. Rebel at Large: Recollections of fifty crowded years. New York, 1947.

Crispi, Francesco. Die Memoiren Francesco Crispis. Edited by Tommaso Palamenghi-Crispi. Stuttgart, 1912.

Cromwell, Oliver. Oliver Cromwell's Letters and Speeches. With elucidations by Thomas Carlyle. Everyman edition. 3 vols. New York & London, 1907.

Dalwigk zu Lichtenfels, Reinhard Friedrich, freiherr von. Die Tagebücher Dalwigks. Edited by Wilhelm Schuessler. Stuttgart & Berlin, 1921.

Djemal, Ahmad (pasha). Erinnerungen eines türkischen Staatsmannes. 2d edition. Berlin, 1922.

Dodd, William E. Ambassador Dodd's Diary. Edited by W. E. Dodd, Jr., and Martha Dodd. New York, 1941.

Du Bellay, Martin. Mémoires de Martin et Guillaume du Bellay. Edited by V. L. Bourilly and F. Vindry. 4 vols. Paris, 1908-19.

Ducrot, Gen. Auguste-Alexandre. La vie militaire du Général Ducrot, d'après sa correspondance. 2 vols. Paris, 1895.

Dumouriez, Charles Francois. La vie et les mémoires du Général Dumouriez. 4 vols. Paris, 1822-23.

Eckardstein, Hermann, freiherr von. Lebenserinnerungen und politische Denkwürdkigkeiten. 3 vols. Leipzig, 1919-21.

Einem, Generaloberst Karl von. Erinnerungen eines Soldaten, 1853-1933. Leipzig, 1933.

Ernst II, herzog zu Saxe-Coburg-Gotha. Aus meinem Leben und aus meiner Zeit. 6th edition. 3 vols. Berlin, 1887-89.

Esher, Reginald, viscount. Journal and Letters of Reginald, Viscount Esher. Edited by Maurice V. Brett. 4 vols. London, 1934-38.

Eulenburg-Hertefeld, Philipp, fürst zu. Aus fünfzig Jahren. Erinnerungen, Tagebücher und Briefe aus dem Nachlass des Fürsten Philipp zu Eulenburg-Hertefeld. Edited by Johannes Haller. Berlin, 1923.

Faramond de Lafajole, Gontran, vicomte de. Souvenirs d'un attaché naval en Allemagne et en Autriche, 1910-1914. Paris, 1932.

Fleury, Gen. Comte Emile-Félix. Souvenirs du Général comte Fleury. 2 vols. Paris, 1897-98.

Foch, Ferdinand. Memoirs of Marshal Foch. Translated by Col. T. Bentley Mott. 2 vols. Garden City, N. Y., 1931.

Forrestal, James V. The Forrestal Diaries. Edited by Walter Millis. New York, 1951.

François-Poncet, André. The Fateful Years. Memoirs of a French Ambassador in Berlin, 1931-1938. Translated by Jacques LeClercq. New York, 1949.

Freycinet, Charles de. Souvenirs, 1878-1893. 9th edition. Paris, 1914.

Frederick II, the Great. Briefwechsel Friedrichs des Grossen und Voltaire. Edited by R. Koser and Hans Droysen. 3 vols. Leipzig, 1908-11.

———. Politische Correspondenz Friedrichs des Grossen. Published by the Berlin Academy. 46 vols. Berlin, 1879-1939.

Frederick III, Kaiser. Das Kriegstagebuch von 1870-1871. Edited by H. O. Meisner. Berlin, 1926.

Gamelin, Maurice Gustave. Servir. 3 vols. Paris, 1946-47.

Gerlach, Ludwig Leopold von. Denkwürdigkeiten aus dem Leben Leopold von Gerlachs. Edited by his daughter. 2 vols. Berlin, 1891-92.

Geyr von Schweppenburg, Leo Dietrich, freiherr. Erinnerungen eines Militärattachés, London, 1933-1937. Stuttgart, 1949.

Giesl von Gieslingen, Gen. Wladimir, Baron. Zwei Jahrzehnte im Nahen Orient. Edited by Generalmajor ritter von Steinitz. Berlin, 1927.

Gleichen, Lord Edward. A Guardsman's Memories. A Book of Recollections. Edinburgh & London, 1932.

Goebbels, Joseph. The Goebbels Diaries, 1942-1943. Edited by L. P. Lochner. New York, 1948.

Goncourt, Edmond Louis and Jules Alfred. Journal des Goncourt—Mémoires de la vie littéraire. 9 vols. Paris, 1891-1935.

Gregorovius, Ferdinand A. The Roman Journals of Ferdinand Gregorovius, 1852-1874. Edited by F. Althaus and translated by Mrs. Gustavus Hamilton. London, 1907.

Greville, Charles Cavandish. The Greville Diary. Edited by Philip W. Wilson. 2 vols. London & New York, 1927.

Grew, Joseph C. Ten Years in Japan, 1932-1942. New York, 1944.

Grey, Edward, viscount of Fallodon. Twenty-Five Years, 1892-1916. 2 vols. New York, 1925.

Grimblot, Paul (ed.). Letters of William III and Louis XIV and their Ministers, 1697-1700. 2 vols. London, 1848.

Haldane, Richard Burdon. An Autobiography. London, 1929.

Halsey, William F., and Joseph Bryan. Admiral Halsey's Story. New York, 1947.

Hardenberg, Karl August fürst von. Denkwürdigkeiten des Staatskanzlers Fürsten von Hardenberg. Edited by Leopold von Ranke. 5 vols. Leipzig, 1877.

Hassell, Ulrich von. The Von Hassel Diaries, 1938-1944: the story of the forces against Hitler inside Germany as recorded by Ambassador Ulrich von Hassell, a leader of the movement. Introduction by Allen W. Dulles. New York, 1947.

Herbillon, Col. Emile. Du général en chef au gouvernement: souvenirs d'un officier de liaison pendant la guerre mondiale. Paris, 1930.

Hertling, Karl, graf von. Ein Jahr in der Reichskanzlei. Freiburg-im-Breisgau, 1919.

Heyking, Elisabeth, baronin von. Tagebücher aus vier Weltteilen, 1886-1904. Leipzig, 1926.

Hindenburg, Paul von. Aus meinem Leben. Leipzig, 1920.

Hitler, Adolf. Tischgespräche im Führerhauptquartier, 1941-42. (Im Auftrage des Deutschen Instituts für Geschichte der Nationalsozialistischer Zeit. Geordnet, eingeleitet und veröffenlicht von Gerhard Ritter.) Bonn, 1951.

Hobart, Augustus Charles (pasha). Sketches from my Life. 2d edition. London, 1886.

Hoffmann, Max, Aufzeichnungen. Edited by K. F. Nowak. 2 vols. Berlin, 1929.

Hohenlohe, Chlodwig, fürst zu. Denkwürdigkeiten des Fürsten Chlodwig zu Hohenlohe-Schillingsfürst. Edited by Friedrich Curtius. 2 vols. Stuttgart & Leipzig, 1907.

———. Denkwürdigkeiten der Reichskanzlerzeit. Edited by K. A. von Müller. Stuttgart & Berlin, 1931. (The author refers to this as Vol. III of the aforementioned work.)

House, Colonel Edward M. The Intimate Papers of Colonel House. Edited by Charles Seymour. 4 vols. Boston, 1926-28.

Houston, David F. Eight Years with Wilson's Cabinet, 1913-1920. 2 vols. London & New York, 1926.

Hull, Cordell. The Memoirs of Cordell Hull. 2 vols. New York, 1948.

Jarras, Gen. Hugues Louis. Souvenirs du général Jarras, chef d'Etat-major. Publiés par Mme Jarras. Paris, 1892.

Joffre, Joseph Jacques. Mémoires du maréchal Joffre (1910-1917). 2 vols. Paris, 1932.

Keudell, Robert von. Fürst und Fürstin Bismarck: Erinnerungen aus den Jahren 1846 bis 1872. Stuttgart, 1901.

Konoye, Prince. Memoirs. Translated in Pearl Harbor Hearings. Washington, G.P.O., 1952.

Kühlmann, Richard von. Erinnerungen. Heidelberg, 1948.

Lancken-Wakenitz, Oskar, freiherr von der. Meine dreissig Dienstjahre, 1888-1918. Berlin, 1931.

Lansing, Robert. War Memoirs of Robert Lansing, Secretary of State. New York, 1935.

Laval, Pierre. The Diary of Pierre Laval. Edited by his daughter, Josée. New York, 1948.

Leahy, William D. I Was There. New York, 1950.

Lebrun, Gen. Barthélémy-Louis-Joseph. Souvenirs militaires, 1866-1870. Paris, 1895.

Ligne, Charles Joseph, prince de. Der Fürst von Ligne. Erinnerungen und Briefe. Edited by Victor Klarwill. Vienna, 1920.

Liman von Sanders, Otto Viktor Karl. Fünf Jahre Türkei. Berlin, 1920.

Lloyd George, David, 1st earl. War Memoirs of David Lloyd George. 6 vols. London, 1933-36.

Loë, Friedrich Karl Degenhard, freiherr von. Erinnerungen aus meinem Berufsleben, 1849 bis 1867. Stuttgart, 1905.

Loftus, Lord Augustus. The Diplomatic Reminiscences of Lord Augustus Loftus...1862-1879. 2 vols. London, 1894.

Lucius von Ballhausen, Robert Sigmund, freiherr. Bismarck—Erinnerungen des Staatsministers Freiherrn Lucius von Ballhausen. Berlin & Stuttgart, 1920.

Malmesbury, James Harris, 1st earl of. Diaries and Correspondence of James Harris, First Earl of Malmesbury. Edited by his grandson, the 3rd earl. 4 vols. London, 1844.

Masaryk, Tomaš G. Die Weltrevolution, Erinnerungen und Betrachtungen, 1914-18. Berlin, 1925.

Max von Baden. The Memoirs of Prince Max of Baden. Translated by W. M. Calder and C.W.H. Sutton. 2 vols. New York, 1928.

Messimy, Adolphe. Mes souvenirs. Paris, 1937.

Moltke, Helmuth Johannes Ludwig von. Erinnerungen, Briefe, Dokumente, 1877-1916. Edited by Eliza von Moltke. Stuttgart, 1922.

Moltke, Helmuth Karl Bernhard, graf von. Gesammelte Schriften und Denkwürdigkeiten. 8 vols. Berlin, 1892-93.

Monts, Anton, graf. Erinnerungen und Gedanken des Botschafters Anton Graf Monts. Berlin, 1932.

Morier, Sir Robert. Memoirs and Letters of the Right Hon. Sir Robert Morier, from 1826 to 1876. Edited by his daughter, Mrs. Rosslyn Wemyss. 2 vols. London, 1911.

Mott, Col. T. Bentley. Twenty Years as Military Attaché. New York & London, 1937.

Napoleon I, Emperor of France. Correspondance. Publiée par l'ordre de l'empereur Napoléon III. 32 vols. Paris, 1858-1870.

Nekludoff, Anatolic V. Diplomatic Reminiscences before and during the War, 1911-1917. Translated by Alexandra Paget. London, 1920.

Oldenburg, Elard von. Erinnerungen von Elard von Oldenburg-Januschau. Leipzig, 1936.

Ormesson, Wladimir, comte d'. Enfances diplomatiques. Paris, 1932.

Paléologue, Georges Maurice. An Ambassador's Memoirs. Translated by F. A. Holt. 3 vols. London, 1923-25.

———. Au Quai d'Orsay, à la veille de la tourmente: journal de 1913-1914. Paris, 1947.

Palmerston, Henry John Temple, viscount. The Life and Correspondence of Henry John Temple, viscount Palmerston. Edited by Anthony Ashley. 2 vols. London, 1879.

Pasquier, Etienne Denis, duc. Histoire de mon temps:

BIBLIOGRAPHY

mémoires du Chancelier Pasquier. 6 vols. Paris, 1893-95.

Paul-Boncour, Joseph. Entre deux guerres: souvenirs sur la Troisième Republiqué. 3 vols. New York, 1945-46.

Pepys, Samuel. The Diary of Samuel Pepys. Edited by H. B. Wheatley. 10 vols. London, 1928-35.

Pobiédonostsev, Constantin. L'autocratie russe: Mémoires politiques du règne de l'empéreur Alexandre III (1881-1894). Paris, 1927.

Poincaré, Raymond. Au service de la France—neuf années de souvenirs. 10 vols. Paris, 1926-33.

Radowitz, Joseph Maria von. Aufzeichnungen und Erinnerungen aus dem Leben des Botschafters Joseph Maria von Radowitz. Edited by Hajo Holborn. 2 vols. Stuttgart, 1925.

Recouly, Raymond. Le mémorial de Foch: Mes entretiens avec le maréchal. Paris, 1929.

Riddell, George Allardice, Lord. Lord Riddell's Intimate Diary of the Peace Conference and After, 1918-1923. New York, 1934.

Robertson, Field-Marshal Sir William Robert. From Private to Field-Marshal. Boston & New York, 1921.

Rochow, Theodor H. Rochus von. Briefe an einem Staatsbeamten. Edited by E. Kolchner and K. Mendelssohn Bartholdy. Frankfurt-am-Main, 1873.

Roosevelt, Theodore. Theodore Roosevelt and his Time, shown in his own letters. Edited by Joseph Bucklin Bishop. New York, 1920.

———. Selections from the Correspondence of Theodore Roosevelt and Henry Cabot Lodge, 1884-1918. Edited by Henry Cabot Lodge. 2 vols. New York, 1925.

Rovigo, Jean René Savary, duc de. Mémoires pour servir à l'histoire de l'empéreur Napoléon. Edited by Lacroix. 5 vols. Paris, 1900.

Ruprecht, Crown Prince of Bavaria. Mein Kriegstagebuch. Berlin, 1929.

Schmerling, Anton, ritter von. Ein Lebenslauf. Stuttgart, 1890.

Schweinitz, Lothar von. Denkwürdigkeiten. 2 vols. Berlin, 1927.

Seeckt, Hans von. Aus meinem Leben, 1866-1917. Edited by Gen. Friedrich von Rabenau. Leipzig, 1938.

———. Aus seinem Leben, 1918-1936. Edited by Gen. Friedrich von Rabenau. Leipzig, 1940. [The author refers to these two works as Vols. I & II.]

Slade, Sir Adolphus. Records of Travels in Turkey and Greece, 1820-1831. London, 1832.

Smith, Walter Bedell. My Three Years in Moscow. Philadelphia, 1950.

Spring Rice, Sir Cecil. The Letters and Friendships of Sir Cecil Spring Rice. Edited by Stephen Gwynn. 2 vols. Boston & New York, 1929.

Stair, James Dalrymple, 1st viscount of, and John Dalrymple, 1st and 2d earls of. Annals and correspondence of the viscount and the first and second earls of Stair. Edited by John M. Graham. 2 vols. Edinburgh & London, 1875.

Stein, Heinrich Friedrich Karl, freiherr vom und zum. Freiherr vom Stein: Briefwechsel, Denkschriften, und Aufzeichnungen. Edited by Erich Botzenhart. 7 vols. Berlin, 1931-37.

Stein, Hermann von. Erlebnisse und Betrachtungen aus der Zeit des Weltkrieges. Berlin, 1919.

Stimson, Henry L., and McGeorge Bundy. On Active Service in Peace and War. New York, 1948

Stosch, Albrecht von. Denkwürdigkeiten des Generals und Admirals Albrecht von Stosch. Edited by Ulrich von Stosch. Stuttgart & Leipzig, 1904.

Suchomlinow, Wladimir A. Erinnerungen. Berlin, 1924.

Talleyrand-Périgord, C. M., prince de Bénevent. Lettres inédites à Napoléon, 1800-1809. Introduction et notes de Pierre Bertrand. Paris, 1889.

Tirpitz, Alfred von. Erinnerungen. 5th edition. Leipzig, 1927.

Toutain, Edmond. Alexandre III et la République française: souvenirs d'un témoin, 1885-1888. Paris, 1929.

Treitschke, Heinrich von. Briefe. Edited by Max Cornelicus. 3 vols. Leipzig, 1913-20.

Truman, Harry S. Mr. President. [From his diaries, papers, and correspondence]. Edited by William Hillman. New York, 1952.

Versen, von. General von Versen: Aus hinterlassenen Briefen und Aufzeichnungen. Edited by Freiherr von Werthern.

Victoria, Queen. The Letters of Queen Victoria. Edited by G. E. Buckle, 2d series, 3 vols. New York, 1926-28. 3d series, 3 vols. London, 1930-32.

Waldersee, Alfred, graf von. Denkwürdigkeiten des Generalfeldmarschalls Alfred Grafen von Waldersee. Edited by H. O. Meisner. 2 vols. Stuttgart, 1922.

Walpole, Horace. The Letters of Horace Walpole, fourth earl of Orford. Edited by Mrs. Paget Toynbee. 16 vols. Oxford, 1903-05.

Waters, W. H. H. "Private and Personal," further experiences of a military attaché. London, 1928.

———. "Secret and Confidential," the experiences of a military attaché. New York, 1926.

Wellington, Arthur Wellesley, 1st duke of. The Dispatches of Field Marshal the Duke of Wellington, 1799-1818. Compiled by Lt. Col. Gurwood. 13 vols. in 12. London, 1837-39.

Wermuth, Adolf. Ein Beamtenleben. Berlin, 1922.

White, Andrew D. Autobiography. 2 vols. New York, 1904.

William II, Kaiser. The Willy-Nicky Correspondence. Edited by Hermann Bernstein. New York, 1918.

Zedlitz-Trützschler, Robert, graf von. Zwölf Jahre am deutschen Kaiserhof. Stuttgart, 1923.

Reference Works

Allgemeine Deutsche Biographie. Published by Historische Commission der Königliche Akademie der Wissenschaften. 56 vols. Leipzig, 1875-1912.

American Historical Association Annual Report for 1942. Letters from the Berlin Embassy, 1871-74, 1880-85. 2 vols. Edited by Paul Knaplund. Washington, 1943.

Annales Mettenses. Scriptores rerum Germanicarum in usum scholarum ex Monumentis Germaniae historicis. Edited by B. de Simson. Hanover, 1905.

Berber, Fritz (ed.). Zum Neubau der Verfassung: Jahrbuch der Politische Forschung. Berlin, 1933.

Cambridge History of British Foreign Policy. Edited by A. W. Ward & G. P. Gooch. 3 vols. Cambridge, 1922-23.

Colonial Records of Connecticut: The public records of the colony of Connecticut (1636-1776). 15 vols. Hartford, 1850-90.

Deutsches Biographisches Jahrbuch. 7 vols. Berlin & Leipzig, 1925-32.

Dictionary of National Biography (British). Founded in 1882, published in London. (Many reissues and suplements.)

Dictionnaire de la politique. Paris, 1863.

Dictionnaire militaire; Encyclopédie des sciences militaires, rédigée par une comité d'officiers de toutes armes... 2 vols. Paris, 1898-1910

Encyclopädie der Staatswissenschaften. Tübingen, 1859.

Encyclopedia Britannica: or, A dictionary of arts, sciences, and miscellaneous literature. 15 editions. London.

Die grossen Deutschen: neue deutsche Biographie. Edited by Willy Andreas and Wilhelm von Scholz. 4 vols. Berlin, 1942.

Japan-handbuch; nachschlagewerk der Japan kunde im auftrage des Japaninstituts, Berlin. Edited by Martin Ramming. Berlin, 1941.

Morley, Viscount. Memorandum on Resignation, August 1914. London, 1928.

Preussische Staatsschriften aus der Regierungszeit König Friedrichs II, im Auftrage der Königlichen Akademie der Wissenschaften. 3 vols. Berlin, 1877-92. Vol. III, edited by Heinrich von Sybel and G. Schmoller.

Documents

AUSTRIA: Ministerium des Aussern. Oesterreich-Ungarns Aussenpolitik von der Bosnischen Krise 1908 bis zum Kriegsausbruch 1914. Diplomatische Aktenstucke des österreichisch-ungarischen Ministeriums des Aussern. 9 vols, Vienna and Leipzig, 1930.

Ministerium für Heereswesen. Oesterreich-Ungarns letzter Krieg, 1914-1918. 7 vols. Vienna, 1930-38.

Staatsamt für aüsseres. Diplomatische Aktenstucke zur Vorgeschichte des Krieges, 1914. Vienna, 1919.

BELGIUM: Ministère des affaires étrangères. Amtliche Aktenstucke zur Geschichte der europäischen Politik 1885-1914 (Die belgischen Dokumente zur Vorgeschichte des Weltkrieges). Edited by Bernhard Schwertfeger. 9 vols. in 8. Berlin, 1925.

FRANCE: Ministère des affaires étrangères. Commission des archives diplomatiques. Recueil des instructions données aux ambassadeurs et ministres de France depuis les traités de Westphalie jusqu'à la révolution française. 25 vols. in 27. Paris, 1884-1936.

_____. Commission de publication des documents rélatifs aux origines de la guerre de 1914. Documents diplomatiques français (1871-1914). 3 series. Paris, 1929-50.

_____. Documents diplomatiques; L'alliance franco-russe (Livre jaune). Paris, 1918.

Ministère de la guerre. Armée. Etat-major. Les armées françaises dans la grande guerre. 104 vols. Paris, 1922-39.

GERMANY. Auswärtiges Amt. Britain's Designs on Norway; Documents concerning the Anglo-French policy of extending the war: full text of White Book No. 4, published by German Foreign Office. Berlin, 1940.

_____. Die deutschen Dokumente zum Kriegsausbruch ...1914. Edited by Max Montgelas and Walter Schücking. 4 vols. Berlin, 1919.

_____. Deutschland schuldig? Deutsches Weissbuch betreffend über die Verantwortlichkeit der Urheber des Krieges. 3d edition. Berlin, 1919.

_____. Der diplomatische Schriftwechsel Iswolskis, 1911-1914; Aus den Geheimakten der Russischen Staatsarchive. Edited by Friedrich Stieve. 4 vols. Berlin, 1926.

_____. Documents and Materials Relating to the Eve of the Second World War. (Secret documents captured by Soviets from Auswärtiges Amt.) 2 vols. New York, 1948.

_____. Documents on German Foreign Policy, 1918-1945, from the Archives of the German Foreign Ministry. Washington, 1949.

_____. Dokumente zur Kriegsausweitungspolitik der Westmächte: Die Generalstabsbesprechungen Englands und Frankreichs mit Belgien und den Niederlanden. German White Book No. 5. Berlin, 1940.

_____. Drittes Weissbuch der Deutschen Regierung: Polnische Dokumente zur Vorgeschichte des Krieges. Berlin, 1940.

_____. Die Grosse Politik der europäischen Kabinette, 1871-1914. Edited by J. Lepsins, A. Mendelsohn Bartholdy, and F. Thimme. 40 vols. in 54. Berlin, 1922-27.

_____. Nazi-Soviet Relations, 1939-1941. Documents from the Archives of the German Foreign Office as released by the Department of State. Edited by R. J. Sontag and J. S. Beddie. New York, 1948.

Deutsches Institut für aussenpolitische Forschung. Europäische Politik im Spiegel der Prager Akten. Edited by Fritz Berber. Essen, 1942.

GERMANY: (Continued)

Historische Reichskommission. Die auswärtige Politik Preussens, 1858-1871. Edited by Erich Brandenburg, Otto Hoetzsch, and Hermann Oncken. (Reichsinstitut für Geschichte des neuen Deutschlands) 4 vols. Berlin, 1932.

Kriegsmarine. Oberkommando. Fuehrer Conferences on Matters Dealing with the German Navy, 1939-1945. (Translation of documents captured from German Naval Archives.) 7 vols. in 9. Washington, U.S. Navy Dept., 1947.

Kriegsministerium. Die Mobilmachung von 1870/1. Prepared by G. Lehmann. Berlin, 1905.

Reichsarchiv. Der Weltkrieg, 1914 bis 1918: Kriegsrüstung und Kriegswirtschaft. (Anlageband: Kriegsführung und Kriegswirtschaft.) Berlin, 1930.

GREAT BRITAIN: Foreign Office. British Documents on the Origins of the War 1898-1914. Edited by G. P. Gooch and Harold Temperley. 11 vols. in 13. London, 1926-38.

_____. Documents on British Foreign Policy 1919-1939. Edited by E. L. Woodward and Rohan Butler. 3 series, 18 volumes. London, 1946-1955.

Parliament. The Parliamentary Debates (Hansard). House of Commons, Official Report.

GREECE: Office of Information. The Greek White Book; Diplomatic documents relating to Italy's aggression against Greece. London, 1942.

LEAGUE OF NATIONS: Appeal by the Chinese Government: Report of the Commission of Enquiry. By Victor Alexander Bulwer Lytton, 2d earl of Lytton. Geneva, 1932.

NUREMBERG: International Conference on Military Trials, London 1945. Washington, 1949.

International Military Tribunal. The Trial of German Major War Criminals. Proceedings of the International Military Tribunal Sitting at Nuremberg, Germany. 21 vols. London, 1946.

_____. Trial of the Major War Criminals Before the International Military Tribunal, Nuremberg, 14 November 1945—1 October 1946. 42 vols. Nuremberg, 1947-49.

Nuremberg Military Tribunal. Trials of War Criminals before the Nuremberg Military Tribunals under Control Council Law No. 10, October, 1946, to April, 1949. 15 vols. Washington, 1949.

United States Chief of Counsel for the Prosecution of Axis Criminality. Nazi Conspiracy and Aggression. 8 vols. Washington, 1946. Supplement, 2 vols. Washington, 1947-48.

United States. Department of State. Trial of War Criminals. Washington, 1945.

RUSSIA: Foreign Office. How the War Began in 1914, being the diary of the Russian Foreign Office from the 3rd to the 20th (old style) of July 1914. Translated from the original Russian by Major W. Cyprian Bridge, Foreword by Sazonov, Introduction by Baron M. F. Schilling. London, 1925.

_____. Un livre noir, diplomatie d'avant-guerre d'après les documents des archives russes, novembre 1910-juillet 1914. Préface par René Marchand. 5 vols. Paris, 1922-34.

UNION OF SOVIET SOCIALIST REPUBLICS: Commission for the Publication of Documents Relating to the Era of Imperialism. Die internationalen Beziehungen im Zeitalter des Imperialismus: Dokumente aus den Archiven der zarischen und der provisorischen Regierung, hrsg. von der Kommission beim Zentralexekutivkomitee der Sovietregierung unter dem Vorsitz von M. N. Pokrowski. Hrsg. von Otto Hoetzsch. Berlin, 1931-42.

UNITED STATES: Congress. Joint Committee on Investigation of Pearl Harbor Attack. Pearl Harbor Attack, Hearings, 79th Congress, 1st session. 11 parts, Washington, 1950.

_____. Senate. Mobilization Planning and the National Security (1950-1960), problems and issues. 81st Congress, 2nd session, Senate Document No. 204. Prepared by Legislative Reference Service of the Library of Congress. Washington, 1950.

_____. Committee on Armed Services. Hearings before the Committee on Armed Services and Committee on Foreign Relations, 82nd Congress, 1st session, to conduct an inquiry into the military situation in the Far East and the facts surrounding the relief of General of the Army MacArthur from his assignment in that area. 5 parts. Washington, 1951.

_____. Committee on Foreign Relations. Assignment of Ground Forces of the United States to Duty in the European Area. Hearings before the Committee on Foreign Relations and the Committee on Armed Services, 82nd Congress, 1st session. Washington, 1951.

_____. Committee on Foreign Relations. North Atlantic Treaty. Report on Executive L, 81st Congress, 1st session... Washington, 1949.

Department of Defense. Semiannual Report of Secretary of Defense, July 1, 1949 [to December 31, 1949]. Washington, 1950.

Department of State. Foreign Relations of the United States. Diplomatic Papers. The Soviet Union 1933-39. Washington, 1952.

_____. Papers Relating to the Foreign Relations of the United States. (1919, 1920, 1922.) Washington, GPO.

_____. Peace and War: United States Foreign Policy, 1931-1941. Washington, 1943.

_____. United States Relations with China, with special reference to the period 1944-49, based on files of Department of State. (Department of State Publication No. 3573.) Washington, 1949.

Department of War. America and Aggression 1931-1941. Prepared by Bureau of Public Relations, Intelligence and Analysis Branch. Washington.

_____. General Staff. Biennial Report of Chief of Staff of United States Army to Secretary of War, July 1, 1943, to June 30, 1945. Washington, 1945.

Articles

Armstrong, Hamilton Fish. "Italy, Jugoslavia and Lilliputia," Foreign Affairs, VI (January, 1928), 191-202.

Ashton, George. "The Entente Cordiale and the Military Conversations," Quarterly Review, CCLVIII (1932), 363-383.

Bach, August. "Die englisch-russischen Verhandlungen von 1914 über den Abschluss einer Marinekonvention," CXCVII (1924), 183-194.

✓ Baldwin, Hanson. "The Military Move In," Harper's Magazine, CXCV (December, 1947), 481-489.

Bloch, Camille. "Les Socialistes allemands pendant la crise de juillet 1914," Revue d'histoire de la guerre mondiale, XI (October, 1933), 305-338.

Borchard, Edwin M. "The Kellogg Treaties Sanction War," Zeitschrift für ausländisches öffentliches Recht, I¹ (1929), 126/131.

Brüning, Heinrich. "Ein Brief," Deutsche Rundschau, 70. Jhrg., Heft 7 (July, 1947), 1-22.

Clark, Chester W. "Bismarck, Russia, and the Origins of the War of 1870," Journal of Modern History, XIV (June, 1942), 195-208.

Copland, D. B. "United States Policy in China," Pacific Affairs, XXI (December, 1948), 339-347.

Dehio, Ludwig. "Edwin von Manteuffel und der Kaiser," Deutsche Rundschau, CCVI (1926), 40-49.

_____. "Die Pläne der Militärpartei und der Konflikt," Deutsche Rundschau, CCXIII (1927), 91-100.

Driault, Edouard. "Sebastiani à Constantinople," Revue des études napoléoniennes, IV (1913), 402-425.

Finer, Herman. "The British Cabinet, the House of Commons and the War," Political Science Quarterly, LVI (September, 1941), 321-360.

Fischer, Eugen. "Der Sinn der russisch-französischen Militärkonvention," Preussische Jahrbücher, CXCII (April, 1923), 65-98.

Florinsky, Michael T. "The Russian Mobilization of 1914," Political Science Quarterly, XLII (June, 1927), 203-227. [Reply by Alfred von Wegerer, under same title, Vol. XLIII (June, 1928), 201-228.]

Gavard, Charles. "L'alerte de 1875," Le Correspondant, CLXXIII (November 25, 1893), 601-618.

Gossler, General der Infanterie. "Das Praevenire," Deutsche Revue, XXXIX (June, 1914), 257 ff.

Grouard, Colonel A. "Stratégie et politique militaire," Revue de Paris, December 1, 1922, 581-606.

Haeften, Oberst von. "Bismarck und Moltke," Preussische Jahrbücher, CLXXVII (1919), 85-105.

Hallgarten, Wolfgang. "La portée politique et economique de la mission Liman von Sanders," Revue d'histoire de la guerre mondiale, XIII (January, 1935), 17-31.,

Hargreaves, J. D. "The Origin of the Anglo-French Military Conversations in 1905," History, XXXVI (New Series, October, 1951), 244-248.

Heller, Eduard. "Bismarcks Stellung zur Führung des Zweifronten-Krieges," Archiv für Politik und Geschichte, VII (1926), 677-698.

Herzfeld, Hans. "Bismarck und die Skobelew-Episode," Historische Zeitschrift, CXLII (1930), 279-302.

_____. "Die Liman-Krise und die Politik der Grossmächte in der Jahreswende 1913/14," Berliner Monatshefte, XI (September, 1933), 837-858; XI (October, 1933), 973-993.

Hilsman, Roger. "Intelligence and Policy-making in Foreign Affairs," World Politics, V (October, 1952), 1-45.

Houdard, L. "Les généraux Bonaparte et Clarke en Italie, 1797," Revue des études napoléoniennes, XXXIV (1932), 157-162.

Hubka, Gustav von. "Kritische Tage in Montenegro," Berliner Monatshefte, IX (January, 1931), 27-45.

Kabisch, Ernst. "Die Militär- und Marinekonventionen der Triple-Entente vor dem Ausbruch des Weltkriegs," Berliner Monatshefte, V (1927), 282-309.

Kern, Fritz. "Conrad und Berchtold," Europäische Gespräche, II (1924), 97-109.

_____. "Die südslawische Frage und die Wiener Kriegspartei, 1913/14," Schmollers Jahrbuch für Gesetzgebung, Verwaltung und Volkswirtschaft im deutschen Reich, XLVIII (1924), 243-263.

Kerner, Robert J. "The Mission of Liman von Sanders," Slavonic Review, VI (June, 1927-March, 1928), 12-27, 344-363, 543-560.

Kirkpatrick, Helen P. "Advisers or Policy Makers? The National Security Council," American Perspective, II (February, 1949), 443-450.

Kiszling, Rudolf. "Die militärischen Beziehungen und Bindungen zwischen Oesterreich-Ungarn und dem deutschen Reich vor dem Weltkriege," Berliner Monatshefte, IV (November, 1926), 820-835.

Lajusan, Alfred. "L'alerte diplomatique du printemps 1875," Revue d'histoire moderne, I (1926), 368-384.

Langer, William L. "Der Krieg: Ursachen und Anlässe, Ziele und Folgen," Europäische Gespräche, IV (June, 1926), 279-322.

_____. "Political Problems of a Coalition," Foreign Affairs, XXVI (October, 1947), 73-89.

Lingelbach, William E. "Neutrality versus Alliances. Belgium and the Revolution in International Politics," Proceedings of the American Philosophical Society, LXXIX (1938), 607-636.

Lord, R. H. "Bismarck and Russia in 1863," American Historical Review, XXIX (October, 1923), 24-48.

Lutz, Hermann. "Moltke und der Präventivkrieg," Berliner Monatshefte, V (1927), 1107-1120. ("Erwiderung" by Theobald von Schafer, 1120-1125.)

Mendelssohn Bartholdy, A. "John Morley und Edward Grey," Europäische Gespräche, VI (November-December, 1928), 557-569.

Monteilhet, J. "L'avènement de la nation armée," Revue des études napoléoniennes, XIV (1918), 127-157.

Mühlmann, Carl. "Die deutsche Militärmission in der Türkei," Wissen und Wehr, 1938, pp. 847 ff.

Onou, Alexander. "The Memoirs of Count N. Ignatyev," (II), Slavonic Review, XI (July, 1932), 108-125.

Pfanz, Harry W. "The Surrender Negotiations between Johnston and Sherman," Military Affairs, XVI (Spring, 1952), 61-70.

Poole, DeWitt C. "Light on Nazi Foreign Policy," Foreign Affairs, XXV (October, 1946), 130-154.

Pratt, Fletcher. "How Not to Run a Spy System," Harper's Magazine, CXCV (September, 1947), 241-246.

Rassow, Peter. "Schlieffen und Holstein," Historische Zeitschrift, CLXXIII (1952), 297-313.

Renouvin, Pierre. "Les engagements de l'alliance franco-russe," Revue d'histoire de la guerre mondiale, XII (October, 1934), 297-310.

Roloff, Gustav. "Brünn und Nikolsburg," Historische Zeitschrift, CXXXVI (1927), 457-501.

Romier, Lucien. "La Saint-Barthélemy, les évènements de Rome et la préméditation du massacre," Revue du seizième siècle, I (1913), 529-560.

Rothfels, Hans. "Die englisch-russischen Verhandlungen von 1914 über eine Marinekonvention," Berliner Monatshefte, XII (May, 1934), 365-372.

Ryan, A. N. "The Causes of the British Attack upon Copenhagen in 1807," English Historical Review, CCLXVI (January, 1953), 37-55.

Schäfer, Theobald von. "Generaloberst von Moltke in den Tagen vor der Mobilmachung und seine Einwirkung auf Oesterreich-Ungarn," Berliner Monatshefte, IV (1926), 514-549.

————. "Wollte Generaloberst von Moltke den Präventivkrieg?", Ibid., V (1927), 543-560.

Schulte, Aloys. "Die Herrschaft der militärischen Pläne in der Politik," Süddeutsche Monatshefte, XXI^2 (September, 1924), 391-397.

Schuster, Admiral Karlgeorg. "Einfluss der Politik auf die Kriegführung," Zeitschrift für die gesamte Staatswissenschaft, XCVII (October, 1937), 1-28.

Skodvin, Magne. "German and British-French Plans for Operations in Scandinavia, 1940," Norseman, IX (November-December, 1951), 361-376.

Souers, Admiral Sidney E. "Policy Formulation for National Security," American Political Science Review, XLIII (June, 1949), 534-543.

Sumner, B. H. "Ignatyev at Constantinople," (II), Slavonic Review, XI (April, 1933), 556-571.

Taffs, Winifred. "The War Scare of 1875," Slavonic Review, IX (I, December, 1930), 335-349; (II, March, 1931), 632-649.

Taylor, A. J. P. "British Policy in Morocco, 1886-1902," English Historical Review, LXVI (July, 1951), 342-374.

Thomas, Mary E. "Anglo-Belgian Military Conversations of 1906," Florida State University Studies, IV (1951), 36-43.

Trützschler, Heinz von. "Bismarcks Stellung zum Präventivkrieg," Europäische Gespräche, I (1923), 185-194.

Urbanski, August von. "Conrad von Hötzendorf und der Präventivkrieg gegen Italien," Berliner Monatshefte, VIII (March, 1930), 248-258.

Vagts, Alfred. "The Foreigner as Soldier in the Second World War," Journal of Politics, IX (August, 1947), 392-416.

————. "Land and Sea Power in the Second German Reich," Military Affairs, III (Winter 1939), 210-221.

————. "William II and the Siam Episode," American Historical Review, XLV (July, 1940), 834-840.

Waldersee, Georg Graf. "Über die Beziehungen des deutschen zum oesterreichisch-ungarischen Generalstabe vor dem Weltkriege," Berliner Monatshefte, VIII (February, 1930), 103-142.

————. "Von Deutschlands militär-politischen Beziehungen zu Italien," Berliner Monatshefte, VII (July, 1929), 636-664.